Limpopo
p397

Kruger
National
Park
p379

Mpumalanga
p359

North-West
Province
p421

Gauteng
p309

Swaziland
p483

Free State
p291

KwaZulu-Natal
p221

Northern Cape
p433

Lesotho
p460

Eastern Cape
p162

Western Cape
p93

Cape Town
p42

PAGE
571

SURVIVAL GUIDE

VITAL PRACTICAL INFORMATION TO
HELP YOU HAVE A SMOOTH TRIP

Directory A–Z

Accommodation

South Africa offers a range of good-value accommodation. You'll generally find high standards, often for significantly less than you'd pay in Europe or North America. Their nightly rates are often quoted in this high season.

Rates rise steeply during the summer school break (early December to mid-January) and the Easter break (late March to mid-April). Room prices often double and minimum stays are imposed; advance bookings are essential. The other school holidays (late June to mid-July and late September to early October) are often classified as high- or shoulder-season. You can get excellent value during the winter season.

Lesotho Follow cable to South-Africa you usually get better value for money regulations in towns, especially in Maseru. Self-catering options such as backpackers' in Maletsunyane and Roma are commonly found. The highland guesthouses and homestays offer a better experience of life at high altitude but may be hard to find.

Swaziland

THIS EDITION WRITTEN AND RESEARCHED BY

James Bainbridge

Kate Armstrong, Lucy Corne, Michael Grosberg
Murphy, Helen Ranger, Simon Richmond

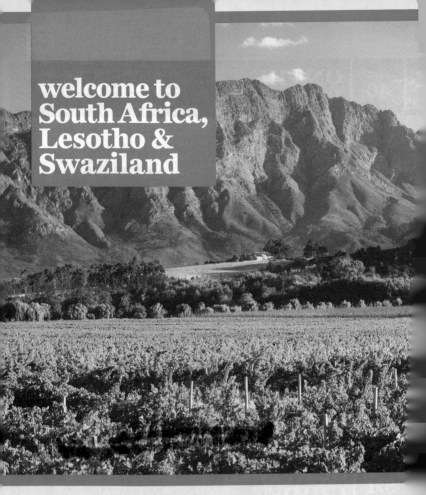

welcome to South Africa, Lesotho & Swaziland

Rainbow Experiences

South Africa, its mountains, deserts and rivers leading to vibrant cities and sprawling townships, is truly a rainbow nation in the experiences it offers. This vast and beautiful, troubled but developing land's diversity is reflected by its world-famous associations: Table Mountain, Soweto, the Big Five, Zulu culture, Robben Island, big skies, broad smiles and the Drakensberg. To get the most out of your time here, ditch any preconceived ideas about South African history and society, pack a pair of binoculars for spotting lions – and get ready for a country that stuns and surprises at every turn, from the Wild Coast's bendy back roads to Cape Town's lanes.

Accessible Africa

South Africa has a reputation as 'Afri[ca] light' – an accessible corner of the con[ti]nent, relatively safe and comfortable. [It] does indeed shine on this front, offeri[ng] superb accommodation and opportunit[ies] to interact with various African peo[ple] and cultures; wildlife watching in terr[ain] from bushveld to the Kalahari, at pri[ces] well below some nearby countries; [and] scenic spots where you can just relax [and] enjoy the *lekker* (tasty) views and hosp[ital]ity, including the Cape Winelands, Ind[ian] Ocean getaways, wilderness lodges an[d re]fined Karoo towns.

Rhinos at waterholes, township art, clouds pouring over Table Mountain, Kalahari dunes, Drakensberg peaks, Swazi and Zulu ceremonies: Southern Africa's famous trio is rich with adventures and experiences, culture and scenery.

(left) Vineyards, Franschhoek (p103)
(below) Xhosa woman, Lesedi Cultural Village (p427)

Cultural Experiences

Groups including the Brits, Boers, Zulu and Xhosa have jostled for position at the tip of Africa, resulting in today's multicultural mash-up. In a country with 11 official languages, you can learn how to cook Cape Malay curries, visit a shebeen and catch some township jazz, see reed dances in Zululand (and over the border in Swaziland), visit craft cooperatives in former homelands, and eat samosas in Indian-dominated Durban. Meeting locals whose lives were directly affected by momentous 20th-century events, you will hear stories laced with the courage and humour that got them through apartheid. Escaping the westernised bubble of the tourist trail rewards with a broader view of this fascinating, fragmented land.

Landscapes & Activities

Nature reflects social diversity in the region's landscapes, ranging from the parched Kalahari and Namakwa to the Drakensberg's towering peaks, overlooking Zulu *rondavels* (round huts with conical roofs) and, across the Lesotho border, Basotho ponies trekking between villages. In just a couple of weeks, you could travel from the predator-stalked Kruger National Park, down the tropical east coast, and across the wide-open Karoo to the Cape's sublime mix of mountains, vineyards and beaches. In such varied terrain, activities range from shark-cage diving to some of Africa's greatest multiday hikes, and from wine tasting to spotting southern rights in the world's best land-based whale-watching spot.

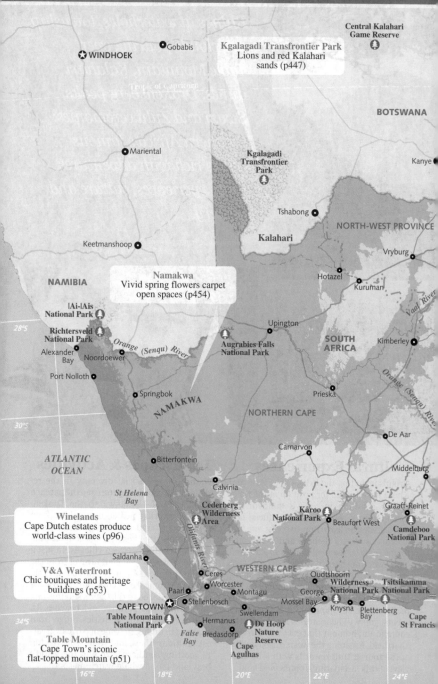

Kgalagadi Transfrontier Park
Lions and red Kalahari sands (p447)

Central Kalahari Game Reserve

Gobabis

❁ WINDHOEK

BOTSWANA

Mariental

Kanye

Kgalagadi Transfrontier Park

Tshabong

Keetmanshoop

Kalahari

NORTH-WEST PROVINCE

Vryburg

NAMIBIA

Namakwa
Vivid spring flowers carpet open spaces (p454)

Hotazel

Kuruman

|Ai-|Ais National Park

Upington

SOUTH AFRICA

Kimberley

Richtersveld National Park

Orange (Senqu) River

Augrabies Falls National Park

28°S

Alexander Bay

Noordoewer

Port Nolloth

Springbok

Prieska

Orange (Senqu) River

NAMAKWA

NORTHERN CAPE

Vaal River

De Aar

30°S

ATLANTIC OCEAN

Bitterfontein

Carnarvon

Middelburg

St Helena Bay

Calvinia

Graaff-Reinet

Cederberg Wilderness Area

Karoo National Park

Winelands
Cape Dutch estates produce world-class wines (p96)

Olifants River

Beaufort West

Camdeboo National Park

Saldanha

V&A Waterfront
Chic boutiques and heritage buildings (p53)

Ceres

WESTERN CAPE

Oudtshoorn

Wilderness National Park

Tsitsikamma National Park

Paarl

Worcester

Montagu

George

Mossel Bay

Knysna

Plettenberg Bay

CAPE TOWN

Stellenbosch

Cape St Francis

Table Mountain National Park

Hermanus

Swellendam

34°S

False Bay

Bredasdorp

De Hoop Nature Reserve

Table Mountain
Cape Town's iconic flat-topped mountain (p51)

Cape Agulhas

16°E   18°E   20°E   22°E   24°E

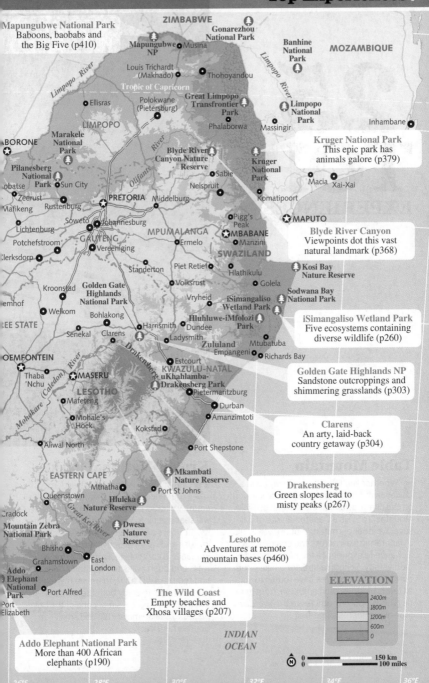

Mapungubwe National Park
Baboons, baobabs and
the Big Five (p410)

ZIMBABWE

Gonarezhou National Park

Mapungubwe NP — Musina

Banhine National Park

MOZAMBIQUE

Louis Trichardt (Makhado) — Thohoyandou

Limpopo River

Ellisras

Tropic of Capricorn

Polokwane (Pietersburg)

Great Limpopo Transfrontier Park

Limpopo National Park

Inhambane

LIMPOPO

Phalaborwa — Massingir

Marakele National Park

Olifants River

Kruger National Park
This epic park has
animals galore (p379)

BORONE

Pilanesberg National Park — Sun City

Blyde River Canyon Nature Reserve

Sabie

Kruger National Park

Macia — Xai-Xai

obatse — Zeerust — Rustenburg

PRETORIA

Nelspruit

Mafikeng

Middelburg

Komatipoort

Lichtenburg

Soweto — Johannesburg

Pigg's Peak

MAPUTO

Potchefstroom

GAUTENG

MPUMALANGA

MBABANE

Klerksdorp

Vereeniging

Ermelo

Manzini

Blyde River Canyon
Viewpoints dot this vast
natural landmark (p368)

SWAZILAND

Standerton

Piet Retief

Hlathikulu

Kosi Bay Nature Reserve

Kroonstad

Golden Gate Highlands National Park

Volksrust — Golela

Sodwana Bay National Park

emhof — Welkom

Bohlakong

Vryheid

iSimangaliso Wetland Park

REE STATE

Senekal — Clarens

Harrismith — Dundee

Hluhluwe-iMfolozi Park

iSimangaliso Wetland Park
Five ecosystems containing
diverse wildlife (p260)

Ladysmith

Zululand

Mtubatuba

OEMFONTEIN

Thaba 'Nchu

MASERU

Drakensberg

Estcourt

Empangeni — Richards Bay

uKhahlamba-Drakensberg Park

Golden Gate Highlands NP
Sandstone outcroppings and
shimmering grasslands (p303)

Mafeteng

LESOTHO

Pietermaritzburg

Mohale's Hoëk

KWAZULU-NATAL

Durban

Aliwal North

Kokstad

Amanzimtoti

Clarens
An arty, laid-back
country getaway (p304)

Mohokare (Caledon) River

Port Shepstone

EASTERN CAPE

Mkambati Nature Reserve

Drakensberg
Green slopes lead to
misty peaks (p267)

Queenstown

Mthatha

Port St Johns

Cradock

Great Kei River

Hluleka Nature Reserve

Mountain Zebra National Park

Dwesa Nature Reserve

Lesotho
Adventures at remote
mountain bases (p460)

Bhisho — Grahamstown

East London

Addo Elephant National Park — Port Alfred

The Wild Coast
Empty beaches and
Xhosa villages (p207)

Port Elizabeth

INDIAN OCEAN

Addo Elephant National Park
More than 400 African
elephants (p190)

ELEVATION

2400m
1800m
1200m
600m
0

0 — 150 km
0 — 100 miles

26°E   28°E   30°E   32°E   34°E   36°E

25 TOP EXPERIENCES

Table Mountain

1 Whether you take the easy way up in a revolving cable car, or put in the leg work on the climb, attaining the summit of Table Mountain (p51) is a Capetonian rite of passage. Weather permitting, your rewards are a panoramic view across the peninsula and a chance to experience the park's incredible biodiversity. Schedule time for a hike – the park's 24,500 hectares have routes to suit all levels of fitness and ambition, from gentle *fynbos*-spotting ambles to the five-day, four-night Hoerikwaggo Trail.

Kruger National Park

2 One of South Africa's great wilderness experiences and the mightiest of all the country's national parks (p379), a trip here will sear itself into your mind. Its accessibility, numbers and variety of wildlife, staggering size and range of activities make Kruger unique and compelling. From wilderness trails and bush walks to mountain biking and remote 4WD trails, there are myriad opportunities to enjoy both the wild and the wildlife. Kruger is simply one of the best places to see animals – big and small – in Southern Africa.

Drakensberg Region

3 Majestic, stunning and mysterious, the mountains and surrounds of the World Heritage–listed uKhahlamba-Drakensberg Park (p267) are among the country's most awe-inspiring landscapes. Drakensberg means 'Dragon Mountains' (in Afrikaans), and the Zulu named the range Quathlamba ('Battlement of Spears'). People have lived here for thousands of years, evidenced by the many San rock-art sites. With Zulu villages, excellent eateries, wilderness areas and wildflowers, the Drakensberg region is the perfect place for photographers, hikers and adventurous travellers. Monk's Cowl (p273), uKhahlamba-Drakensberg Park

Sipping in the Winelands

4 Whitewashed Cape Dutch architecture dots the endlessly photographic landscape of rolling hills and neat rows of vines. This is the quintessential Cape (p96), where the world-class wines are the icing on the picture-perfect cake. Stellenbosch (p96), Franschhoek (p103) and Paarl (p106), the area's holy trinity of wine-tasting towns, boast some of the oldest, largest and prettiest wine estates on the continent. But this is not the province's only wine region; head to Tulbagh (p122) for sparkling wines, Route 62 (p122) for robust reds and port, or the heights of the Cederberg (p158) for crisp sauvignon blancs. Stellenbosch

IAN TROWER/CORBIS ©

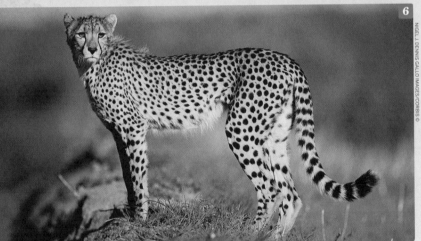

Wild Coast Walks

5 The hauntingly beautiful Wild Coast (p207) is aptly named. With its rugged cliffs plunging into the sea, remote beaches, Xhosa villages, and history of shipwrecks and stranded sailors, it's a region ideally explored on foot. From the Great Kei River near East London to Port St Johns, pathways hug the shoreline, snaking across denuded hillsides and gorges, and overlooking massive southern right whales and dolphins in the turquoise blue seas. Power down in rustic accommodation or overnight with families in traditionally designed *rondavels* (round huts with conical roofs).
Silaka Nature Reserve (p213), Port St Johns

Kgalagadi Transfrontier Park

6 Kgalagadi (p447) covers almost 40,000 sq km of raw Kalahari in the Northern Cape and Botswana, roamed by some 2000 predators. But such statistics, albeit impressive, barely scrape the surface of this immense land of sizzling sunsets, velvety night skies and rolling red dunes. You might spot black-maned lions napping under thorn trees or purring along the road; the park is one of the world's best places to spot big cats, with about 800 lions, cheetahs and leopards. Best of all, you don't need a 4WD to access Kgalagadi.

iSimangaliso Wetland Park

7 Its name, which means 'miracle' or 'wonder', is fitting. The iSimangaliso Wetland Park (p260), a Unesco World Heritage site, stretches for 220 glorious kilometres, from the Mozambique border to Maphelane, at the southern end of Lake St Lucia. The 328,000-hectare park protects five distinct ecosystems, with everything from offshore reefs and beaches, to lakes, wetlands, woodlands and coastal forests. It's nature's playground, offering wildlife drives, hikes, cycling and swimming, plus extraordinary animals: loggerhead and leatherback turtles, whales and dolphins, rhinos, antelopes, zebras and hippos galore.

Clarens

8 The odd international star popping in for a lungful of fresh mountain air gives this well-heeled town (p304) an air of celebrity. Filled with galleries, antiques, classy restaurants and adventure activities in the surrounding countryside, there's something appealing for most visitors. There is money here, sure, but the town is laid-back and perfect for an evening stroll. With pubs to drop into for a drink and bookshops to browse, Clarens is the best place in the Free State to simply wind down.

Mapungubwe National Park

9 A real stand-out among South Africa's national parks (p410), this trans-frontier conservation area in-the-making has cultural links so important that the park has been deemed a Unesco World Heritage Site. The landscape is riveting: mighty intersecting rivers, a harsh climate, and arid, dry, ancient terrain twisted and knotted against rocky bluffs with majestic viewpoints. The Big Five can all be found here, as well as more unusual fauna such as elands and meerkats. Getting around can be tough but the rewards are sublime.

Addo Elephant National Park

10 At Addo (p190), a national park created from farmland only 70km from Port Elizabeth, more than 400 African elephants roam through low bushes, tall grass and distant hills. Hyenas and lions also roam free, brought here from the Kalahari in 2003 to bring the kudu, ostrich and warthog populations down; warthogs, meerkats and white-striped kudu can also be seen. But elephants steal the limelight when bursting from the undergrowth, flapping their ears and dwarfing other creatures.

V&A Waterfront

11 Cape Town's top sight in terms of visitor numbers, the V&A Waterfront (p53) is big, busy and pretty much what you make of it. The location is spectacular, with Table Mountain as a backdrop. There's a pirate's booty of consumer opportunities, from chic boutiques to department stores, plus plenty of cultural and educational experiences, including walking tours of its well-preserved heritage buildings and public sculptures. The excellent Two Oceans Aquarium is a firm family favourite; be sure to take a harbour cruise, too – preferably at sunset.

CAROL POLYCH/LONELY PLANET IMAGES ©

Blyde River Canyon

12 This canyon (p368), the third largest in the world – and possibly the greenest – is one of South Africa's great sights. The absence of foreign visitors to the canyon is both perplexing and a real bonus for those who do make it here. There are viewpoints with names such as 'the Three Rondavels' and 'God's Window', which, on a clear day, will leave you breathless. On foot is the best way to discover this vast natural landmark scarring northern Mpumalanga.

Golden Gate Highlands National Park

13 It may not be blessed with the Big Five, but this park (p303) produces extraordinary sunsets, and its sandstone outcrop and grasslands hide plenty of antelopes, zebras, jackals and birds. It's great walking territory, or if you are pressed for time you can take some short drives. Either way, views of the Drakensberg and Maluti Mountains loom large and there's something almost fairytale about the wind sweeping patterns through the nodding grass. If you don't have the chance to explore Lesotho, there's also a Basotho Cultural Village for tourists.

Lesotho Trading Posts

14 Travel in Lesotho has been arduous ever since King Moshoeshoe told the Boers to bugger off from his mound on Thaba-Bosiu. The ever-pragmatic British established trading posts to maintain commercial (nay, political) links with the isolated Basotho nation. Today's traveller benefits greatly from this spirit of endeavour, as the former trading posts afford some of Southern Africa's most spectacular adventures. At Malealea (p479), Ramabanta (p470), Semonkong (p478) and Roma (p470), hikers, trekkers, pony riders, motor bikers and those seeking village-style solace gather at mealtimes to rejoice in giddy silence. Malealea

Namakwa Wildflowers

15 Namakwa is one of South Africa's forgotten corners, stretching up the west coast towards Namibia. Crossing the remote region, and reaching Port Nolloth's refreshing Atlantic vistas after hundreds of kilometres on empty roads, is wonderful throughout the year. In spring, there's the added bonus of the wildflower bloom, which turns Namakwa's rocky expanses into a technicolour carpet. You could spend days travelling through the multicoloured fields, stopping at spots such as Namaqua National Park and Goegap Nature Reserve – both dedicated to wildflower watching (p455).

Hiking & Stargazing in the Cederberg

16 By day the clear blue skies provide an arresting contrast to the fiery orange peaks of the craggy Cederberg (p158); by night the Milky Way shines so brightly you can almost read by its light. The Cederberg is the promised land for stargazers, for hikers seeking an otherworldly landscape, for rock climbers and for those simply in search of silent nights. Tackle the challenging Wolfberg Arch hike, the shorter walk to the Maltese Cross, or the three-day Wupperthal trail, visiting remote and forgotten mission villages en route. Wolfberg Arch

15

BLICKWINKEL/ALAMY ©

16

IMAGES OF AFRICA PHOTOBANK/ALAMY ©

Venda Region

17 A lush region (p411) steeped in mystique and ancient custom, this African landscape is marked by mist-clad hills, dusty streets and mud huts. Sprinkled with lakes and forests of enormous spiritual significance, and marking the primeval ties between indigenous culture and the land, the former homeland is an area worth discovering, exploring and ultimately embracing. Begin by embarking on the arts and crafts trail – the area is noted for its fine original artwork, with workshops and cooperatives scattered throughout the landscape. Venda weaver

Hluhluwe-iMfolozi Park

18 Sometimes overshadowed by Kruger National Park, Hluhluwe-iMfolozi (p258) is nonetheless one of South Africa's best known, most evocative parks. Stunningly beautiful, it features a variety of landscapes, from mountains with wildflowers to savannah, and, of course, it teems with wildlife – the Big Five and other amazing creatures. Hluhluwe-iMfolozi can be visited at any time – there's always something happening and plenty to see, from elephants munching Marula trees to impala, zebra, wildebeest and baby giraffes. Great wildlife drives, accommodation and scenery ensure a memorable experience.

FRED DE NOYELLE/GODONG/PHOTONONSTOP/CORBIS ©

HOLGER LEUE/LONELY PLANET IMAGES ©

RICHARD I'ANSON/LONELY PLANET IMAGES ©

Madikwe Game Reserve

19 One of the country's most exclusive reserves on this scale, Madikwe (p428) occupies 760 sq km of bushveld, savannah grassland and riverine forest. There's a good chance of spotting some of the Big Five, as guides share radio updates about where they've spotted, say, a pride of lions or a bull elephant. The 20 lodges are experiences in themselves, from an ecolodge to five-star options that blend creature comforts into the wilderness. Visits to Madikwe are on an all-inclusive basis, allowing you to relax once you're through the gates.

Garden Route

20 The enduring popularity of this verdant strip abutting the coast lies not only in its undeniable scenic beauty. The Garden Route (p136) is also a magnet for those in search of a little outdoor adventure. Whether you're hiking the Knysna forests, surfing in Victoria Bay, canoeing on Wilderness's lagoon or getting up close with great whites below the waters of Mossel Bay (p137), the Garden Route guarantees an adventure for every taste and budget.
Humpback whale, Mossel Bay

Sani Pass & Sani Top

21 The highest pub in Africa (p476) is a hell of a place to get to. From the west, it's a gravelly endurance drive over the awesome Central Highlands and huge dams that constitute all of Gauteng's water supply. From southern Lesotho, it's 4WD country through the eerie Maluti Mountains and the grasslands of Sehlabathebe National Park. From Maseru the road skirts dinosaur tracks and snow-capped peaks. From Durban, madmen push pedals. But you're here now, on top of the world. Bottoms up!

ARIADNE VAN ZANDBERGEN/LONELY PLANET IMAGES ©

Mkhaya Game Reserve

22 This top-notch private reserve (p501) was named after the *mkhaya* (knobthorn) trees found here. You're more likely to meet rhinos here than anywhere else in Africa, thanks to Mkhaya's rhino protection program. The reserve might be one of Africa's best-value spots; accommodation rates include wildlife drives, walking safaris, park entry and meals. And as for the accommodation – where else can you sleep in luxurious semi-open stone-and-thatch cottages in a secluded bush zone? All that, plus a loo with a bush view.

Cradle of Humankind

23 As the Chemical Brothers sampled: 'it began in Afrika' (or Western Gauteng to be precise). Today, the Cradle of Humankind (p343) nurses hundreds of square kilometres of beautiful green and brown veld – and an increasing migration of tourists, descended from hominids, who sit with the fossils of their ancestors deep underground, before returning to civilisation at fine restaurants and day spas. There's wilderness to be gawked at, too; only 50km northwest of Jo'burg are free-roaming elands, zebras, giraffes and gazelles. Maropeng (p343)

Pilanesberg National Park

24 Sprawling away from Sun City is this underrated park (p426), where the Big Five and day-tripping Jo'burgers roam an extinct volcano crater. With its tarred roads, Pilanesberg is sometimes dismissed as tame, yet the rhinos lapping at waterholes seem to disagree. To escape the other cars and score an up-close sighting, hit the gravel roads through the bush and stake out a dam. Guided drives and a range of accommodation are available, making this a winner for families and those short on time.

JON HICKS/CORBIS ©

Lessons in History

25 The impact of apartheid on present-day South Africa is impossible to measure as it informs so much of daily life. Yet trying to understand the history of this social project should be requisite for every visitor to the country. The curatorship and design of the Apartheid Museum (p321) in southern Jo'burg does not condone moral tub-thumping, but rather reminds us of the capacity of the human spirit to overcome wretchedness. Also in Gauteng, Pretoria's Freedom Park (p348), Constitution Hill and the township of Soweto reward in similar ways. Freedom Park

25

VIEW PICTURES LTD/ALAMY ©

need to know

Currency
» South African rand (R)
» Lesothan loti (plural maloti, M)
» Swazi lilangeni (plural emalangeni, E)

Languages
» Zulu
» Xhosa
» Afrikaans
» English
» Southern Sotho (Lesotho)
» Swati (Swaziland)

When to Go

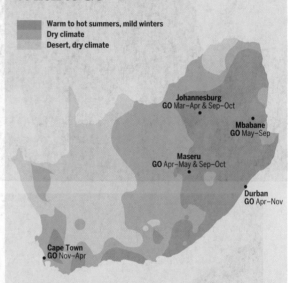

Warm to hot summers, mild winters
Dry climate
Desert, dry climate

Johannesburg GO Mar–Apr & Sep–Oct
Mbabane GO May–Sep
Maseru GO Apr–May & Sep–Oct
Durban GO Apr–Nov
Cape Town GO Nov–Apr

High Season
(Dec–Mar)
» Peak times are around Christmas, New Year and Easter.
» Prices rise steeply.
» Accommodation in national parks and the coast books up months in advance.
» Tourist areas and roads busy.

Shoulder Season (Apr–May)
» Also October to November.
» There is a school holiday from late September to early October.
» Sunny spring and autumn weather in much of the country.
» Optimum wildlife-watching conditions begin in autumn.

Low Season
(Jun–Sep)
» Winter is ideal for wildlife-watching.
» There is a school holiday from late June to mid-July.
» Prices sometimes reflect this holiday; otherwise they are low, with discounts and packages offered.

Your Daily Budget

Budget
R500
» Hostel & dorm bed from R150
» Budget main less than R60
» Four-hour minibus taxi ride R200
» Free entry to many museums
» Don't get stuck in Cape Town

Midrange from
R750
» Double room R400-2500
» Midrange main R60-150
» Jo'burg-Cape Town tourist-class train R430
» Wildlife drive R250
» Single room supplements common

Top end over
R1200
» Double room from R1500
» Top-end main over R150
» Jo'burg-Cape Town flight from R800
» 4WD tour per person per day R1000
» Luxury lodges offer all-inclusive packages

Money

» ATMs widespread and credit cards widely accepted in South Africa. In Lesotho and Swaziland, ATMs and businesses accepting credit cards are scarce outside the capitals.

Visas

» Generally not required for stays of up to 90 days; same applies for up to 14 days in Lesotho and up to 30 in Swaziland.

Mobile Phones

» Most foreign phones can be used on roaming. Local SIM cards can be used in most unlocked foreign phones.

Transport

» Drive on the left; steering wheel is on the right side of the car.

Websites

» **SouthAfrica.info** (www.southafrica.info) News and information.

» **South Africa National Parks Forums** (www.sanparks.co.za/forums) Rangers post.

» **BBC** (www.bbc.co.uk) Country profiles.

» **Fair Trade in Tourism South Africa** (www.fairtourismsa.org.za) Nationwide ideas.

» **Backpacking Africa** (www.backpacking southafrica.co.za) Useful guide.

» **Lonely Planet** (www.lonelyplanet.com/south-africa) Information, bookings and forums.

Exchange Rates

Australia	A$1	R8.20
Botswana	P1	R1.06
Canada	C$1	R8.14
Europe	€1	R10.46
Japan	¥100	R10.45
Mozambique	Mtc10	R3.00
New Zealand	NZ$1	R6.34
UK	UK$1	R13.08
USA	US$1	R8.34

For current exchange rates see www.xe.com.

Important Numbers

Dial the local area code even if you are dialling from the same town or code area.

South Africa country code	☎27
Lesotho country code	☎266
Swaziland country code	☎268
International access code (all three countries)	☎00

Arriving in South Africa

» **OR Tambo International Airport, Jo'burg**

Gautrain – Jo'burg/Pretoria R115/125, 25/35 minutes, every 12-30 minutes

Shuttle and taxi – Jo'burg/Pretoria R350/400, one hour

Car – hire companies at airport, N12/Rte 21 to Jo'burg/Pretoria

» **Cape Town International Airport**

MyCiTi bus – R53.50, 20-60 minutes, every 20 minutes

Shuttle – R160-180

Taxi – R200

Car – hire companies at airport, straight along N2

Safe Travel

South Africa has a bad reputation for crime, but it's easy for travellers to avoid. Most accommodation has security; even some backpackers employ guards.

If you are driving, you will be partly protected from dangers found on the streets. Do not leave valuables on display in your car, or open the boot to reveal bags before leaving the vehicle.

The impression you give is paramount. Walking around cities, do not appear to be loaded with cash and valuables, and consider carrying a dummy wallet or purse. Always be vigilant, particularly when using ATMs and conducting financial transactions.

Seek local advice, as risks vary between provinces. For example, walking down a well-lit, central street in Cape Town at night is safer than walking around Jo'burg after dark, which should be avoided.

if you like...

Dramatic Landscapes

From the Cape's mix of coastline and mountains to expanses like Namakwa, the Kalahari and Karoo, South Africa and mountainous Lesotho feature some of Africa's most impressive landscapes.

Drakensberg Awesome peaks and formations, such as the Ampitheatre make up the Dragon Mountains. The view from the top of the escarpment is reputed to be one of the world's best (p267).

Cape Peninsula A spine of mountains runs down the peninsula from Table Mountain to Cape Point (p55).

Wild Coast The green hills dotted with pastel *rondavels* (round huts with a conical roof), rugged cliffs and empty Indian Ocean beaches are unforgettable (p207).

Augrabies Falls National Park The world's sixth-tallest waterfall, where the Orange River thunders into a ravine, is a raw and elemental focal point in the wild Northern Cape (p451).

Lesotho highlands Peaks climb more than 3000m in the mountain kingdom's raw section of the Drakensberg, riven by verdant valleys and tumbling streams (p474).

Wildlife

Diverse, accessible and swarming with wildlife, the parks and reserves here are some of the world's best destinations to see the Big Five and their prey.

Kruger National Park South Africa's famous park has 5000 rhinos alone, and landscapes from woodland to mopaneveld (p379).

Kgalagadi Transfrontier Park Deep in the Kalahari, Kgalagadi is one of the world's best places to spot big cats, from cheetahs to black-maned lions (p447).

Mkhaya Game Reserve Swaziland's stunning reserve has endangered species plus leopards, buffaloes, elephants and an impressive rhino population (p501).

Addo Elephant Park South Africa's third-largest national park offers some of the world's best elephant viewing, plus black rhinos, Cape buffaloes and lions (p190).

Madikwe Game Reserve The exclusive bushveld reserve hosts the Big Five in diverse environments (p428).

Elephant Coast KwaZulu-Natal's wildlife hub offers sightings in tropical settings; highlights include uMkhuze Game Reserve (p266).

Open Spaces

Whether you head inland or along the coast, the largely rural country offers an invigorating sense of freedom.

Namakwa The rocky hills and plains covering the country's western quarters fill with spring wildflowers (p454).

Free State Golden sunflower and corn fields carpet the interior, between the wide waters of Gariep Dam and Golden Gate Highlands Natural Park (p291).

Kalahari Red dunes ripple as far as the eye can see; the Orange River snakes through the semidesert surrounded by greenery (p443).

Southern Lesotho Between Malealea and the Drakensberg, the mountainous area has musk- and orange-coloured valleys, rivers and off-the-beaten-track villages (p479).

Karoo Stretching across three provinces, the semi-arid plateau is a land of blazing summer and icy winters, stunning sunsets and starscapes (p151).

Beaches Quiet beaches are common on South Africa's 2500km-plus coastline, from the West Coast to less-popular southern sands like Buffalo Bay (p142).

» Cheetah, Kgalagadi Transfrontier Park (p447)

Art

Artworks reflecting South Africa's dramatic landscapes and social issues can be seen from the bushveld to the Cape.

Cape Town The World Design Capital 2014 has private galleries galore. Church St and the surrounding lanes are good for galleries and antique shops; edgier operations cluster in Woodstock (p88).

Eastern Karoo Nieu Bethesda's Owl House swarms with cement owls and sculptures. Architecturally refined Graaff-Reinet has some worthwhile galleries and museum houses (p163).

Art towns A few small towns have added sophistication to their sylvan settings with local art scenes. Clarens has some 20 galleries, and Montagu, Kalk Bay, Paternoster, Parys and Dullstroom are following suit (p304).

Venda region Down red tracks in Limpopo's former homeland, studios produce raw woodcarvings, pottery, and stripy batiks and textiles (p411).

William Humphreys Art Gallery Exhibits in Kimberley's public gallery range from work by South African prison inmates to Dutch and Flemish old masters (p437).

History

Numerous sights remember South Africa's tumultuous history, and a strong sense of the past lingers in rural areas such as the Winelands and Karoo.

Cape Town South Africa's Mother City mixes the likes of the Castle of Good Hope with sights telling less renowned stories, including the Bo-Kaap and District Six Museum (p46).

Kimberley A Victorian mining settlement, historic pubs, ghost tours, Anglo-Boer battlefields and one of South Africa's oldest townships evoke the diamond city's past (p436).

Liberation trail Spots from Robben Island to the Wild Coast's Nelson Mandela Museum celebrate the anti-apartheid struggle (p53).

Apartheid Museum Entered through racial classification gates, Jo'burg's museum evokes the era of segregation (p321).

Oudtshoorn Above the mansions built by ostrich-farming 'feather barons', the 19th-century Swartberg Pass leads to the Great Karoo, with its time-warp quality (p133).

Mapungubwe National Park The Unesco World Heritage Site was home to a significant Iron Age civilisation (p410).

Cultural Experiences

Escaping the comfortable, westernised bubble of South Africa's tourist industry, and having hands-on experiences of the region's diverse traditions and beliefs, is hugely rewarding.

Townships Rather than whizzing through on a bus, stay the night or take an interactive, themed tour (p65).

Umhlanga Dance Swazi debutantes dance with reeds in hand at the annual festival (p485).

Wild Coast With its Xhosa *rondavels*, the former homeland offers numerous opportunities to stay in community-run accommodation and take part in local projects (p207).

!Xaus Lodge The Khomani San share their tracking skills on dawn dune walks at this community-owned Kalahari lodge. Other locations offering culture alongside wildlife include Madikwe Game Reserve and Makuleke Contract Park (p449).

Zululand Head to Eshowe to learn about South Africa's largest ethnic group, on visits to villages and ceremonies (p251).

Venda region Meet the former homeland's artists and explore a sacred forest above Lake Fundudzi (p411).

» Rafting, Senqu (Orange) River (p454)

Food & Drink

From Cape Dutch wine estates to braais smoking away on township corners, sampling South Africa's *lekker* (tasty) produce is the best way to this agricultural country's heart.

Cooking safari Learn how to make Cape Malay curries in Cape Town's Bo-Kaap (p66).

Fresh grapes Think outside the Stellenbosch; explore wine-growing regions like the Swartland, Breede River Valley and Green Kalahari (p154).

Food markets Try farm-fresh goodies from feta to vino at Cape Town's Neighbourhoods Markets and rural events (p88).

Beer cruise On Cape Town's Long St, Durban's Florida Rd and Jo'burg's 7th St, Melville, forget the heat over frosted glasses. Look out for beers from South Africa's numerous microbreweries (p535).

Bush braai Devouring *braaivleis* (barbequed meat) and *braaibroodjies* (barbequed toasted sandwich) in scenic surrounds is a quintessential South African experience (p536).

Bunny chow Regional specialities include this creation from Durbs: a hollow bread loaf filled with curry (p236).

Activities & Adventures

Whether you want to cross vast wildernesses, search for predators in the bushveld, or just lounge on the beach, Africa's southernmost trio has it covered.

Garden Route With old-growth forests stretching to the water's edge, the holiday strip offers surfing, diving, boat trips, shark-cage diving, canoeing, kloofing, horse riding and hiking (p136).

Kalahari From Senqu (Orange) River rafting and canoeing to safaris, 4WD trails and sandboarding, the semi-desert is an explorer's playground (p443).

Walking safaris In wildlife-stalked wildernesses including Kruger National Park, experience the bush on foot with armed rangers (p381).

Pony trekking Explore Lesotho's rugged highlands in the traditional way, on a Basotho pony (p471).

Hands on Harvest Wine on the River Picnic by the Breede River at this wine festival, one of five in Robertson and many across South Africa (p125).

Multiday hikes Carry your equipment, or take the easy option and have your bags transported, on overnight wilderness walks (p576).

Eccentric Corners

Isolated from the outside world under apartheid, South Africa's country towns and villages, by turns quirky and refined, have been preserved in all their idiosyncratic glory.

Matjiesfontein Deep in the Karoo, 'tour' the Victorian village's single street on a vintage London bus (p153).

Wild Coast Beach towns like Port St Johns offer an alluring combo of friendly Xhosa locals, dreadlocked runaways, sandy beaches and hammocks (p213).

Darling Evita Bezuidenhout, co-median Pieter-Dirk Uys' answer to Dame Edna Everage, performs in the old train station (p154).

Hogsback High in the Amathole Mountains, locals will tell you the environmentally conscious village, with its Ecoshrine and fairy walk, inspired JRR Tolkien (p205).

Haenertsburg An incongruous mountain village in Limpopo's subtropical Letaba Valley, with pine plantations and congenial pubs (p413).

Cape Peninsula The self-proclaimed 'republic of Hout Bay' and nearby hippyish seaside villages are nicknamed the 'lentil curtain' (p55).

month by month

January

South Africans descend on tourist areas, including the coast and major parks, during summer school holidays (early December to mid-January). Book accommodation and transport well in advance. High season December to March.

Cape Town Minstrel Carnival (Kaapse Klopse)

The Mother City's most colourful street party runs for a month from 2 January. With satin- and sequin-clad minstrel troupes, ribald song and dance parades, floats and general revelry, it's the Cape's Mardi Gras (p68).

February

Summer continues: smiles on southern beaches, half-price cable cars up Table Mountain for sunset, and rain in the north. Elephants munch Marula trees and baby antelopes, zebras and giraffes cavort in the parks.

Buganu (Marula) Festival

One of Swaziland's most popular 'first fruits' harvest festivals, Buganu celebrates the marvellous Marula. Throughout February and March, women make *buganu* (Marula wine), men drink the results and everyone celebrates. Swazi royals attend the three-day ceremony (p485).

Hands on Harvest

At the first of Robertson's five annual wine festivals, budding vintners can help with the harvest and sample the results. Activities include grape picking, bunch sorting, grape stomping, wine blending and vineyard tractor trips (p125).

March

Summer rolls towards autumn, although days remain sunny, the lowveld steamy and landscapes green. Good for both walking and beach bumming in the Western Cape; festivals happen in Cape Town and Jo'burg.

Cape Argus Cycle Tour

Held in mid-March, this spin around the Cape Peninsula is the world's largest timed cycling event. More than 30,000 contestants, from serious racers to costumed Capetonians, tackle Table Mountain and Champman's Peak Drive (p67).

April

A two-week school holiday around Easter, generally regarded as the beginning of autumn. Temperatures drop; wildlife watching in the bushveld starts to look more attractive than mountain walking. Shoulder season, and rutting season, until May.

AfrikaBurn

Africa's entry in the calendar of festivals inspired by America's Burning Man is a subcultural blowout and a survivalist challenge. Art installations and themed camps turn a corner of the Karoo into a surreal paradise (www.afrikaburn.com; p459).

July

Winter brings rain to the Cape and cloud to Table Mountain. Northern areas experience fresh, sunny days and clear night skies. School holidays are in late June to mid-July. Otherwise, it's low season June to September.

 Oyster Festival
Knysna's 10-day oyster orgy is one of a few seafood-oriented events on the South African coastline. Fixtures include oyster eating and shucking competitions, wine tastings, cycle races and the Kynsna Forest Marathon (www.oysterfestival.co.za; p145).

Lesotho ski season
That's right, skiing in Southern Africa. Lesotho's peaks and passes receive snow in winter – particularly around Oxbow, where a ski slope makes the most of snowfalls. The Afri-Ski resort even has a snow park for snowboarders (p475).

Wildlife watching
Cooler, drier winter weather is perfect for wildlife watching. Thirsty animals congregate at waterholes and foliage is sparser, making spotting easier. The lower temperatures make toasty northern areas like the bushveld and Kalahari more enjoyable (p548).

National Arts Festival
Feel South Africa's creative pulse at the country's premier arts festival, from late June to early July in studenty Grahamstown. Performers from every conceivable discipline descend on the refined city, hijacking spaces from squares to sports fields (p194).

September

Winter starts giving way to spring. Cherry trees bloom in the Free State Eastern Highlands in September and October, also the last dry months for wildlife viewing. School holidays late September to early October.

Namakwa wildflowers
In late August and early September, nature plays a springtime trick and covers this barren area with wildflowers. Namakwa's parched terrain sprouts improbable meadows of flowers in rainbow hues. The spectacle also happens elsewhere in the Northern and Western Capes (p455).

Whale watching
Watch Southern right whales calve in Walker Bay throughout the second half of the year; the best time to spot them is the months around the Hermanus Whale Festival (September/October). During this period, Hermanus is the world's best land-based whale-watching destination (p114).

 Traditional festivals
Swaziland's Umhlanga Dance, in which Swazi women dance with reeds, takes place in late August/ early September. A similar Zulu event happens around the same time, leading up to King Shaka Day, celebrating the Zulu hero. Lesotho's Morija Festival showcases Basotho culture (p256).

Jo'burg festivals
Jozi's festival season between late August and late September starts with Joy of Jazz in Newtown, which also hosts the Arts Alive Festival. The Soweto Festival and Soweto Wine Festival take place at the University of Johannesburg's campus in the township (p321).

November

Spring drifts into summer: wildflowers in the Drakensberg; beach potential before the worst humidity hits KwaZulu-Natal; all of the above in Cape Town and Western Cape. Rain in the lowveld. Shoulder season ends.

Summer music festivals
Music festivals take place in stunning settings nationwide. In the Western Cape alone, the choice includes the Kirstenbosch Summer Sunset Concerts in Cape Town's botanical gardens (November/December to April; p68); Rocking the Daisies (www.rockingthe daisies.com) and Up the Creek (www.upthecreek.co.za).

itineraries

Whether you've got six days or 60, these itineraries provide a starting point for the trip of a lifetime. Want more inspiration? Head online to lonelyplanet. com/thorntree to chat with other travellers.

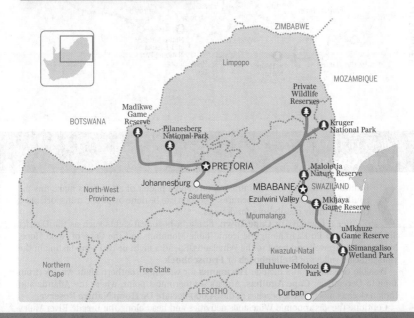

One to Two Weeks
Safari Special

South Africa is one of the continent's best safari destinations; in just a week or two it's possible to do some serious wildlife spotting. From Jo'burg, head east to Mpumalanga and the country's safari showpiece, **Kruger National Park**. The wildlife here and in the adjoining **private wildlife reserves** will hold you captivated for several days. If time is tight, **Madikwe Game Reserve** and **Pilanesberg National Park**, both within four hours' drive of Jo'burg, are worthwhile additions to a bushveld itinerary.

From Kruger, head south to Swaziland's **Malolotja Nature Reserve**, where 200km of hiking trails cross grasslands and forests, and along the **Ezulwini Valley**, stopping to admire the woodlands and pick up local craftwork, to **Mkhaya Game Reserve**. Wildlife-rich Mkhaya is known for its unsurpassed black and white rhino populations. Leaving Swaziland, hit the N2 to KwaZulu-Natal's **uMkhuze Game Reserve**, where animals lap at waterholes in pans surrounded by fever trees. Nearby are the waterways and diverse ecosystems of the 200km-long **iSimangaliso Wetland Park**, and **Hluhluwe-iMfolozi Park**, where hiking the wilderness trails is a once-in-a-lifetime experience. From there, continue south along the Indian Ocean to **Durban's** bars, restaurants and beaches.

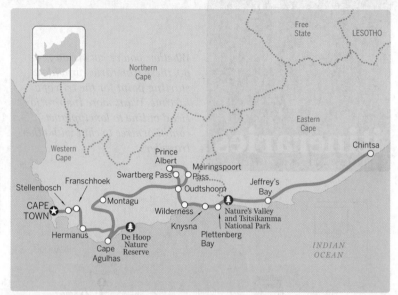

One to Three Weeks
Cape Coast

Beautiful scenery, excellent infrastructure and a platter of attractions make this the South Africa of the glossy brochures. The loop can be done by public transport, but a car offers many possibilities for detours.

After a few days in **Cape Town**, fitting in historical sights such as the District Six Museum and Bo-Kaap alongside iconic Table Mountain and the Cape of Good Hope, bid a tearful farewell and head to the Winelands. Spend a night or two wine-tasting in the vineyard-clad valleys of **Stellenbosch** or **Franschhoek**.

Possible coastal detours include **Hermanus** for watching southern right whales (from June to December); **Cape Agulhas**, Africa's southernmost point, where the Atlantic and Indian Oceans meet; or the beaches of the 34,000-hectare **De Hoop Nature Reserve**.

Continue the gastronomic Winelands activities and head along the Breede River Valley to refined **Montagu**, its thatched cottages and gourmet restaurants reached through a hole in the Cogmanskloof mountains. From here, scenic Route 62, one of the world's longest wine routes, leads through the Little Karoo to **Oudtshoorn**, South Africa's ostrich capital.

With its 19th-century mansions built by 'feather barons', Oudtshoorn is a convenient stopover before tackling the untarred **Swartberg Pass**, an engineering marvel, or **Meiringspoort Pass**, with a waterfall en route. On the far side of the Swartberg (Black Mountain) in the Great Karoo, the 18th-century village of **Prince Albert** is near the N1 back to Cape Town. Alternatively, backtrack south past Oudtshoorn to the Garden Route, where **Wilderness'** beaches and lagoons are less developed than other parts of the coast. Heading east along the Indian Ocean, old-growth forests rise into the mountains above the resort towns of **Knysna** and **Plettenberg Bay**, both offering water sports and activities.

Shortly before entering the Eastern Cape, detour down a windy road to **Nature's Valley**, an aptly named beach village where happy hikers finishing the Otter Trail hang their boots in a tree. Shorter hikes also lead into the rippling valleys of rainforest and fynbos in the surrounding **Tsitsikamma National Park**.

Back on the N2, surf hub **Jeffrey's Bay** is worth a stop if you can tell a supertube from a point break. Otherwise, continue to **Chintsa** for an accessible taste of the Wild Coast area's dreamy coves and Xhosa villages.

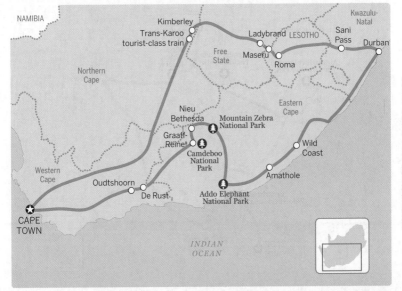

One Month
Grand Circuit

Getting off to a stunning start in **Cape Town**, head east along Route 62 and the Garden Route, as described in our Cape Coast itinerary. Alternatively, if the Great Karoo's open spaces seem more appealing than cruising along the Indian Ocean, head east from sleepy **De Rust**, on the N12 northeast of Oudtshoorn, along Rte 341, the N9 and Rte 329. Kicking up dust on secondary roads is one of South Africa's unsung pleasures, but check road conditions locally.

An inland detour along the N9 leads to **Graaff-Reinet**, South Africa's fourth-oldest European-settled town, with 220-plus national monuments. Also in this quirky corner of the Karoo are **Camdeboo National Park**, with Cape buffaloes and views over the plains, and arty **Nieu Bethesda**, home of the sculpture-adorned Owl House. Stop at **Mountain Zebra National Park** for some final Karoo panoramas, or continue straight to **Addo Elephant National Park**, where great white sharks and southern right whales complete the 'Big Seven'.

Moving east, **Amathole**, formerly the Xhosa homeland of Ciskei, is well worth exploring, before the next batch of stellar highlights on the rugged **Wild Coast** and laidback **Durban's** funky Florida Rd hangouts. From Durbs, head back inland, along the Midlands Meander and into the Drakensberg, where the **Sani Pass** climbs into Lesotho. Hiking and pony trekking in the mountain kingdom, you will meet Basotho people clad in their distinctive conical hats and patterned woollen blankets.

Rather than stay in the capital **Maseru**, spend your last Lesothan night among sandstone cliffs in nearby **Roma**, a 19th-century mission station and now the country's seat of learning. Across the international border in the Free State's Eastern Highlands, **Ladybrand** is another pleasant stopover, its sandstone buildings overlooked by jagged peaks.

Zip through the Free State's shimmering golden fields and cross another border to the Northern Cape capital, **Kimberley**. The city that witnessed the world's greatest diamond rush is a great place to get a feel for South African history, with Anglo-Boer battlefields, ghost tours, 150-year-old pubs and the township of Galeshewe. If time is tight, pick up a postcard of the world's largest hand-dug hole and hop on the **Trans-Karoo tourist-class train**, which will whisk you back to Cape Town (or up to Jo'burg) in 12 hours.

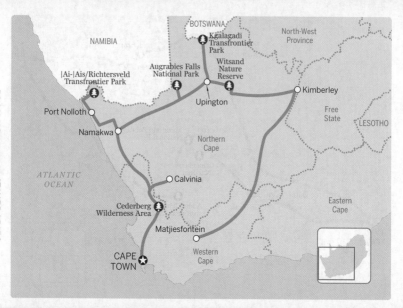

Two to Four Weeks
The Wild Northwest

From **Cape Town**, head north to the **Cederberg Wilderness Area**, with its sandstone formations, lodges and campsites. Citrusdal and Clanwilliam are convenient bases.

Head over Vanrhyns Pass, or the untarred Pakhuis Pass, to the Hantam Karoo outpost of **Calvinia**. Back on the N7, continue north to **Namakwa**, its rocky expanses carpeted with wildflowers in spring. Almost at the end of the region's arrow-straight roads, between the Atlantic and the middle of nowhere, is **Port Nolloth**. If you have a 4WD and an adventurous streak, continue to the surreal mountain desert of **|Ai-|Ais/Richtersveld Transfrontier Park**.

Back on the freeway, head east to the epic **Augrabies Falls National Park**, for hiking, rafting and canoeing. Catch the Orange River in a more mellow mood on a sunset cruise in **Upington**, before heading boldly north, between red Kalahari dunes, to **Kgalagadi Transfrontier Park**, one of the world's best places to see big cats.

Hit the tar back to Upington, or 4WD southeast, and continue through the Kalahari to **Witsand Nature Reserve**, where the wind roars over the dunes. Head east to **Kimberley**, famous for its 19th-century diamond rush, and turn south into the Karoo. Possible stops on the N1 include historic, perfectly preserved **Matjiesfontein**.

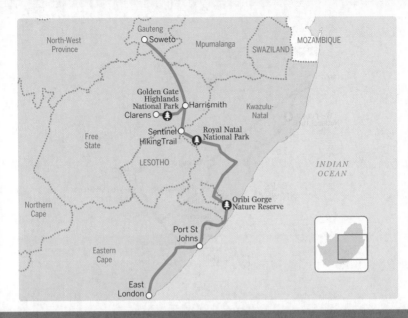

Two to Three Weeks
Eastern Wander

Start your trip with a night in South Africa's most famous township, **Soweto**. Visit a shebeen and see the street where Nobel Peace Prize winners Mandela and Tutu lived.

Cross the Free State and, leaving the N3 at Harrismith, take scenic Rte 712 past Sterkfontein Dam to **Clarens**. The arty town, with its galleries and microbrewery, has surroundings worthy of an impressionist landscape. In the nearby **Golden Gate Highlands National Park**, stay in a riverside chalet and hike between sandstone outcrop; preparation for the mighty Drakensberg. To climb the iconic Ampitheatre to the top of the Drakensberg Escarpment, tackle the day-long **Sentinel Hiking Trail**.

Spend a couple of days enjoying the spectacular day walks, such as Tugela Gorge, in the **Royal Natal National Park**, and continue southeast. Declimatise from the Draks in **Oribi Gorge Nature Reserve**, with its cliffs and forests above the Umzilkulwana River, and hit the Wild Coast. **Port St Johns** is a possible base for exploring the tribal region, where Xhosa *rondavels* (round huts with a conical roof) dot the green hills and sandy beaches meet the Indian Ocean.

Pick up a connection from **East London** to Jo'burg or Cape Town, or continue west and join our Cape Coast or Grand Circuit itinerary.

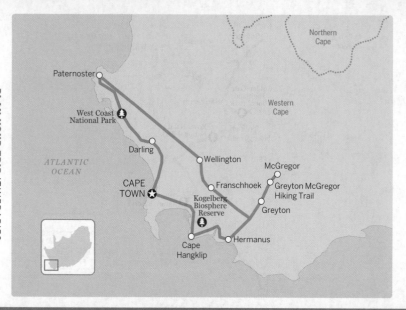

One Week
Alternative Cape

> From Cape Town, head north and stop in **Darling**, where Evita se Perron shows give cross-dressing comedian Pieter-Dirk Uys' distinctive take on South African life. Surrounding the Langebaan Lagoon, the **West Coast National Park** offers an accessible, southern look at the spring wildflower bloom. Overnight in **Paternoster**, with art galleries and restaurants among the whitewashed cottages. Head inland to **Wellington**, where there are some superb wineries in the shadow of Bainskloof Pass. Further into the Winelands, **Franschhoek** distils the area's refined, European charm, with its French Huguenot heritage, vineyards and restaurants. Head southeast over the Franschhoek Pass and hit the N2 through the Overberg to reach the delightful village of **Greyton**. The twee, well-preserved spot has thatched self-catering cottages, good restaurants, mountain views, and a neighbouring 18th-century Moravian mission station. The 14km **Greyton McGregor Hiking Trail** leads through the Riviersonderendberge range to **McGregor**, a new age village in the Breede River Valley.

From Greyton, return to Cape Town via **Hermanus**, the world's best land-based whale-watching destination (June to December). Finish the journey on the stunning, coastal Rte 44, which winds around **Cape Hangklip** and skirts **Kogelberg Biosphere Reserve**.

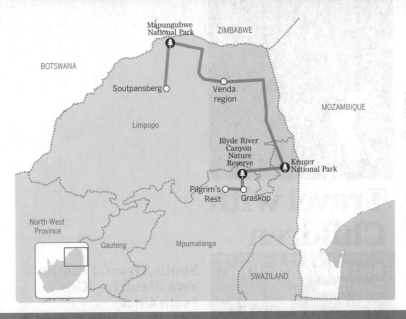

Two Weeks
Bushveld Blast

Head directly north from Jo'burg's OR Tambo International Airport and spend a couple of nights in Limpopo's biodiverse **Soutpansberg** range. West of Louis Trichardt (Makhado) are some wonderfully remote lodges, reached up rocky tracks and decorated with local artworks. Up on the Botswana and Zimbabwe border, one of South Africa's unsung highlights, **Mapungubwe National Park**, sprawls across 28,000 hot hectares in the Limpopo River Valley.

Returning south, even the landscape around the roads is extraordinary, with baboons scuttling between giant baobab trees. Spend a day or two discovering the mystic **Venda region**, where artists produce distinctive work and a python god is believed to live in Lake Fundudzi.

Enter **Kruger National Park** through one of the northern gates and spend a few days ogling the Big Five, heading slowly south. Nip west from Kruger's central section to the spectacular **Blyde River Canyon Nature Reserve**, where the river snakes down from the Drakensberg Escarpment to the lowveld.

Before hitting the N4 back to Jo'burg, relax in **Graskop**, with gently sloping hills beyond its sleepy backstreets and craft shops. The town is a good base for **Pilgrim's Rest**, a perfectly preserved 19th-century gold-rush village, and outdoor activities.

Travel with Children

Best Regions for Kids

Cape Town

Botanical gardens, an aquarium, the Table Mountain cable car, beaches, Greenmarket Square market, harbour cruises, activities, good facilities, and a relaxed atmosphere; the vibrant Mother City is a superb family destination.

Western Cape

Surrounding Cape Town, the Western Cape has good infrastructure as well as stunning scenery. Garden Route spots such as Mossel Bay are particularly well set up for family holidays, with beaches and activities galore.

KwaZulu-Natal

Durban has beaches, one of the world's largest aquariums and hot weather. The sandy fun continues on the surrounding Indian Ocean coastline, with activities from whale watching to kayak safaris in iSimangaliso Wetland Park. Inland are walking and camping opportunities in the stunning Drakensberg.

South Africa, Lesotho & Swaziland for Kids

South Africa

South Africa is an eminently suitable destination for travelling with children. With its abundance of national parks, beaches, swimming pools and hiking trails suitable for a wide range of competencies, plus a good collection of museums and a handful of amusement parks, it offers plenty for children of all ages in hazard-free settings.

Most South Africans are welcoming to children, and you will probably receive many offers of assistance. Get used to passing your child around like a curio; they will induce much interest and attention, particularly in traditional parts of the country.

Lesotho

Lesotho is also a welcoming destination for children. The rugged terrain and conditions are better suited to older children who would enjoy hiking or pony trekking. Most pony trekking centres arrange treks only for people aged over 12 years old.

There's no malaria, but everything is rougher around the edges than in many parts of South Africa. If you (and your children) are of an adventurous bent, however, you'll likely find travel here straightforward and enjoyable.

Swaziland

Swaziland in particular is a good family destination, with a child-friendly attitude and a relaxed pace. The main caveat is that malaria is a real risk in lower-lying areas of the country.

Many hotels in Swaziland offer family-friendly accommodation, and there are amusements such as minigolf to keep children occupied.

Children's Highlights
Wildlife

» Guided drives in large vehicles are excellent, with more chance of sightings and an expert to answer questions and take care of safety.

» Inhabited by the Big Five, Kruger National Park has easy accessibility and family-friendly rest camps.

» Also near Jo'burg, malaria-free Pilanesberg National Park, constructed with weekending families in mind, has tarred roads.

» Activities for children are offered in Kruger, Pilanesberg and other parks.

» There is a good chance of spotting elephants in malaria-free Addo Elephant National Park.

» Oudtshoorn has ostrich farms, a meerkat conservation project and a cheetah ranch.

Walking

» Walking up Table Mountain will give older children a tremendous sense of achievement.

» Hiking and camping in the Drakensberg will also be a memorable experience for older children and teenagers.

Beaches

» Sitting on a Cape Town beach such as Clifton No 4, among multicultural Capetonians, will be an interesting experience for all the family.

» Arniston, near Africa's southernmost point, has a sheltered beach with caves and rock pools.

» South Africa offers lots of water sports for older children to get stuck into, including surfing, diving, canoeing, kayaking and rafting.

» Jeffrey's Bay is one of the world's best surf spots.

Horse riding

» Pony trekking in Lesotho is a wonderful way to see the mountainous country.

» Limpopo's Waterberg range has a number of operators offering horseback safaris and tours.

» Horse riding along Noordhoek beach is a breezy day out from Cape Town.

African culture

» Teenagers will enjoy themed tours geared towards their interests, such as Cape Malay cooking, township jazz and Venda art.

» On the Wild Coast, adventurous teenagers will enjoy glimpses of Xhosa culture at community-run accommodation such as Bulungula Backpackers, which offers activities and cultural experiences.

Planning
Accommodation

» Family-oriented accommodation, such as triple-bed hotel rooms and four- to six-person self-catering cottages, are common throughout South Africa.

» In KwaZulu-Natal, Ezemvelo KZN Wildlife offers good-value accommodation to groups and families in its parks – although animals roam freely in many.

» Many hotels can provide cots.

» Many wildlife lodges have restrictions on children under 12, so in parks and reserves the main accommodation options will sometimes be camping and self-catering.

Activities

» Self-drive safaris are suitable for older children who have the patience to sit for long periods in a vehicle or hide, but less suitable for younger kids.

Childcare

» Many upscale hotels and resorts in tourist areas can arrange childcare, and short-term day care may also be available.

» **Lesotho and Swaziland** Informal childcare arrangements can be made; if you are staying in a good hotel, staff may be able to assist.

Discounts

» Children are usually admitted at discounted rates to national parks, museums and other sights (often free for babies and toddlers, and discounted for teenagers and younger).

» Many hotels offer children's discounts.

» Restaurants often have children's menus with dishes at good prices, or offer smaller portions of regular dishes at discounted prices.

Facilities

» Baby-changing rooms are not common, but clean restrooms abound; in most, you should be able to find a makeshift spot to change a nappy (diaper).

» **Lesotho and Swaziland** Major hotels have western-style toilets, but in rural areas sometimes the only choice is a long-drop.

Health

» See also p608.

» Breastfeeding in public won't raise an eyebrow among many Africans, but in other circles it's best to be discreet.

» Overall, there are few health risks, and should your child become ill, good-quality medical care is available in the cities.

» **Mediclinic** (www.mediclinic.co.za) operates private hospitals from Cape Town to Limpopo.

» Seek medical advice about vaccinations months before your trip; not all are suitable for children.

» Specifically, seek medical advice on malaria prophylactics for children if you'll be in malarial areas (including Kruger National Park and the lowveld).

» Think twice before taking young children to malarial areas and try to visit in the winter, when the risk of mosquito bite is lower.

» Regardless of malaria, insect bites can be painful, so come prepared with nets, repellent and suitable clothing.

» Swimming in streams should generally be avoided, due to the risk of bilharzia (schistosomiasis) infection.

» **Lesotho and Swaziland** There are reasonable medical facilities in Mbabane and Maseru, but for anything serious, you'll need to head to South Africa. Malaria is present in lower-lying regions of Swaziland.

Resources

» The monthly magazine **Child** (www.childmag. co.za) has Jo'burg, Cape Town and Durban editions and a useful website.

» Lonely Planet's *Travel with Children* has tips for keeping children and parents happy on the road.

Supplies

» Nappies, powdered milk and baby food are widely available, except in very rural areas.

» Outside supermarkets in major towns, it's difficult to find processed baby food without added sugar.

» **Merry Pop Ins** (www.merrypopins.co.za) in central Cape Town sells used clothes, furniture and equipment for children from newborns to 10-year-olds. It has a cafe, play area, puppet shows, story readings and children's hairdresser.

» **Lesotho and Swaziland** Nappies, powdered milk and baby food are available in Mbabane, Manzini and Maseru, with only a limited selection in smaller towns.

Transport

» Most car-rental agencies can provide safety seats, but you'll need to book them in advance, and usually pay extra.

» Distances can be vast (the bus from Cape Town to Upington takes 12 hours), so try to stagger journeys where possible.

» Tourist-class trains with private compartments, such as the 24-hour trans-Karoo service from Jo'burg to Cape Town, have ample space and dining cars.

regions at a glance

Cape Town and the Western Cape are refined, developed spots, where you can sip wine and enjoy activities on beaches and mountains. Head north to the Northern Cape and North-West Province for rugged experiences in wildernesses and wildlife parks.

Surfers, hikers and lovers of African culture will enjoy the Eastern Cape, bordering the mountain kingdom of Lesotho and the Free State. The latter's golden fields lead to the Drakensberg, which stretch into KwaZulu-Natal, where beaches, wildlife parks and Zululand spread north from Durban.

Turning northwest, Swaziland has excellent reserves, Mpumulanga offers lowveld, Drakensberg Escarpment and activities, and Gauteng is South Africa's urban heartbeat. The Big Five's hangout, Kruger National Park, crowns the region, alongside Limpopo's diverse landscapes and Venda culture.

Cape Town

Outdoor Activities ✓✓✓
Eating ✓✓✓
Shopping ✓✓✓

Outdoor Activities
Its mountainous national park, beaches and ocean make Cape Town a supremo location for activities, including kitesurfing, rock climbing and paragliding. The beautiful landscapes make hiking and even just strolling along Sea Point promenade a sheer pleasure.

Eating
Cape Town's multi-ethnic peoples have bequeathed it a range of cuisines. Sample Cape Malay cooking or mouth-watering meats and fish from the braai (barbecue). The region's top restaurants are some of the world's best with their quality, price and creativity.

Shopping
The city that will be World Design Capital 2014 is bursting with creativity. Whether you're looking for intricately beaded dolls, contemporary light fixtures made from recycled plastic, or stylish buckskin and leather pillows, Cape Town's emporiums and artisan craft markets will have it.

p42

Western Cape

Food & Wine ✓✓✓
Hiking ✓✓✓
Adventure Sports ✓✓

Food & Wine
The Winelands around Stellenbosch and Franshhoek are justifiably famous for their beautiful wine estates. Intrepid palates should also explore up-and-coming wine areas like Elgin, Wellington and Stanford, and the province's emerging craft breweries. For the main course, choose between feasts such as Karoo lamb, Knysna oysters and West Coast seafood.

Hiking
Hiking opportunities include the Oystercatcher Trail and De Hoop Nature Reserve whale route; shorter strolls near towns such as Swellendam, Greyton and McGregor; and wilderness like the Cederberg and Swartberg Nature Reserve.

Adventure Sports
The Garden Route is renowned for water sports and activities; other opportunities include climbing around Montagu, shark-cage diving in Gansbaai and sky-diving in the Cederberg.

p93

Eastern Cape

Hiking ✓✓✓
Beaches ✓✓✓
Wildlife ✓✓

Hiking
The province's sublime stretch of coastline and misty Amathole Mountains offer possibilities including Tsitsikamma National Park, where the big challenges are the Otter and Dolphin multi-day trails. Wild Coast routes to/from Coffee Bay include Hole in the Wall (hours) and Port St Johns (days). Around Hogsback are forest hikes to stunning waterfalls.

Beaches
Bulungula, Kraal, Mdumbi and Wild Lubanzi backpackers offer a mix of empty beaches and Xhosa culture. Jeffrey's Bay beaches are dedicated to surfing, Cape St Francis is a wind-whipped getaway, and thick forests overlook the sands at Nature's Valley.

Wildlife
Head east for cheetahs in Mountain Zebra National Park; dolphin and whale sightings; Addo Elephant National Park's lions, hyenas and elephants; and Schotia and Amakhala private wildlife reserves.

p162

KwaZulu-Natal

Wildlife ✓✓✓
Culture ✓✓
Activities ✓✓✓

Wildlife
Head to iSimangaliso Wetland Park and St Lucia for whales, turtles, hippos, crocs, plenty of rhinos, leopards, and uMkhuze Game Reserve's excellent bird hides; to Hluhluwe-iMfolozi Park for the Big Five; and to the Drakensberg for birds including the Lammergeier.

Culture
Eshowe and Ulundi are capitals of Zulu culture, while Shakaland offers a Disneyfied look at the ethnic group. Durban galleries exhibit and sell Zulu beaded items, and Durban Tourism offers cultural and township tours. Township Vibe Backpackers is a homestay in a poet's house.

Activities
Umkomaas and Scottburgh are diving centres, with Aliwal Shoal and Protea Banks sites. Oribi Gorge Nature Reserve offers zip lining, and the Drakensberg region has added canopy tours to its hiking trails. Activities around Durban range from surfing to skydiving.

p221

Free State

Landscape ✓✓
Relaxed Travel ✓✓
Walking ✓✓

Gauteng

History ✓✓✓
Archaeology ✓✓✓
Culture ✓✓✓

Mpumalanga

Landscape ✓✓✓
Adventure Sports ✓✓✓
Historic Towns ✓✓

Landscape

This is big sky country, with golden fields leading to the rugged Eastern Highlands. Rte 26 from Ladybrand to Clarens is one of the country's most scenic roads, overlooked by the Drakensberg and Lesotho. Just past Clarens' poplar trees are the Golden Gate Highlands National Park's shimmering grasslands and sandstone bluffs.

Relaxed Travel

Mellow to the province's rural pace and downgrade concerns about crime. Bloemfontein is one of South Africa's safest cities; small towns like Clarens promote their streets as safe to walk throughout the day and night.

Walking

Eastern Highlands trails range from ambles around Clarens to the Golden Gate Highlands National Park, where routes include the two-day Rhebok Hiking Trail. The nearby Sentinel trail climbs the Drakensberg; across the province, Parys's hills and valleys offer numerous opportunities.

p291

History

The Apartheid Museum's emotional pull and historiographical detail are unrivalled. Also in Jo'burg, Constitution Hill unpacks apartheid and provides a blueprint for democracy. Soweto is a hotbed of social history, and Pretoria's Freedom Park sits opposite the Voortrekker Monument.

Archaeology

Our prehistoric beginnings can be traced back to the Cradle of Humankind's caves. Indeed, the entire Maropeng district is an open fossil site; the pretty region also has bluffs and green valleys, restaurants and an artistic project.

Culture

Jozi sparkles in Newtown and Braamfontein bars and clubs. Melville is perhaps the country's most integrated suburb, with new media and literature scenes. Sandton's glitzy malls and 44 Stanley exhibit local fashion labels, and the Maboneng Precinct encompasses a new artistic vision for the city.

p309

Landscape

This province between Jo'burg and Mozambique covers both lowveld and the Drakensberg Escarpment. At the dramatic meeting of the two regions is the Blyde River Canyon, one of South Africa's most outstanding natural sights. Around Sabie, Graskop, Pilgrim's Rest, Barberton and Dullstroom are mountainous landscapes.

Adventure Sports

Graskop has one of the world's highest cable gorge swings. Sabie offers activities, including mountainbike trails, kloofing, caving by candlelight, rafting and swimming holes. Head to Hazyview for hot-air ballooning, rafting, quad biking and zip lining, and to Nelspruit for hiking trails.

Historic Towns

Pilgrim's Rest is a preserved gold-rush town. Also on the Drakensberg Escarpment, historic buildings stand on Lydenburg's wide streets. Barberton, another gold-rush town, was home to South Africa's first stock exchange.

p359

Kruger National Park

Wildlife ✓✓✓
Wilderness ✓✓✓
Walks ✓✓

Wildlife
Kruger's vital statistics say it all: 147 mammal species, including about 200,000 lions, white rhinos, giraffes, elephants, buffaloes, zebras and impalas. That's a larger number than the human population in most of the surrounding towns put together. It's one of Africa's most epic places to see the Big Five acting out the daily drama of life and death.

Wilderness
Kruger is about the size of Belgium or Wales, with landscapes ranging from tropical riverine forest to mopaneveld. Despite its reputation as a busy park, if you visit at a quiet time (such as late January to March) or go on a bush walk, nature will ring in your ears.

Walks
For a whole new take on the phrase 'walk in the park', strike out with gun-toting rangers on a half-day bush walk; or disappear into the wild on a three-day wilderness trail, accessing parts of the bush not glimpsed by vehicles.

p379

Limpopo

Arts & Crafts ✓✓
Culture ✓✓✓
Cool Climates ✓✓

Arts & Crafts
The Venda region's artists from woodcarvers to potters are famous nationwide; tour their studios and pick up some distinctive work. Further south are Kaross, producing Shangaan embroidery, and the Mapusha Weavers Cooperative, where women make excellent carpets and tapestries in Acornhoek township.

Culture
Mapungubwe National Park, declared a World Heritage Site for its cultural importance, contains a significant Iron Age site. There's vivid African culture in the Venda region and the Modjadji area, mystic home of rain-summoning queens.

Cool Climates
Escape the heat by climbing to Haenertsburg and the Magoebaskloof Pass, where the pine plantations and waterfalls make a refreshing change from the steamy surrounds. In the nearby Modjadji Nature Reserve, summer mists wrap around cycads and the Bolobedu Mountains.

p397

North-West Province

Wildlife ✓✓✓
Luxury ✓✓✓
Day Trips ✓✓✓

Wildlife
Madikwe Game Reserve and Pilanesberg National Park collectively offer about 130,000 hectares of prime, Big Five-inhabited bushveld. Both are convenient additions to trips around other northern spots like Kruger National Park.

Luxury
Sun City's hotels, particularly the Palace of the Lost City, are South Africa's last, Vegas-style word in over-the-top glitz. Madikwe's exclusive lodges offer wildlife watching in the lap of luxury, with such features as spas and private decks.

Day Trips
If you're bound for one of Jo'burg's airports and don't want to finish your trip in a city, there are alternatives out in the bushveld. Kitschy Sun City and neighbouring Pilanesberg make a fun combo. En route there from Gauteng is the 120km-long Magaliesberg range, with Hartbeespoort Dam, markets and zip-line canopy tours.

p421

Northern Cape

Wildernesses ✓✓✓
Wildlife ✓✓
Activities ✓✓

Wildernesses

The most epic province covers all of South Africa's cracked, arid wildernesses. Like a tumbleweed along a back road, the Karoo sweeps past attractive towns such as Sutherland. Further north, nature is an untrammelled, awe-inspiring force in rocky Namakwa and the sandy Kalahari.

Wildlife

Kgalagadi Transfrontier Park is one of the world's best places to spot big cats; national parks such as Mokala and Augrabies Falls also offer classic African sightings. Witsand Nature Reserve's dunes support smaller creatures and Namakwa erupts with wildflowers annually. Kimberley's pubs offer wildlife of a different kind.

Activities

Raft, canoe and cruise on the Orange River; 4WD around Riemvasmaak and the transfrontier parks; go on wildlife drives and walks; sandboard, stargaze, sample Green Kalahari wines; and hit Kimberley for ghost tours and the Big Hole.

p433

Lesotho

Adventure ✓✓✓
Culture ✓✓✓
Wilderness ✓✓✓

Adventure

Malealea, Ramabanta and Semonkong, former trading posts, are mountainside way stations that wow adventurers. Hiking is superb, and sturdy Basotho ponies literally take travellers to another level. Four-wheel drives are recommended, abseilers descend Southern Africa's highest waterfall, and summer sees the Roof of Africa Rally.

Culture

The Basotho have maintained cultural autonomy for centuries, and traditional life continues. Lowland craft villages produce woven garments, including Basotho blankets. You can sample dancing, music and Lesotho's literary history at the Morija Festival.

Wilderness

Sehlathebethebe National Park is an eerie green and grey moonscape; Ts'ehlanyane National Park, lush and rugged, is becoming the nation's poster child. The Central Highlands all the way to Sani Pass afford intense 'on-road' driving.

p460

Swaziland

Craft Shopping ✓✓✓
Activities ✓✓✓
Culture ✓✓

Craft Shopping

Outlets abound, from Manzini Market, its handicrafts and textiles supplied by rural vendors and Mozambican traders, to the Ezulwini and Malkerns Valleys. These neighbouring valleys have a well-earned reputation for their craft centres and markets, filled with surprises such as animal-shaped candles and zesty contemporary batiks.

Activities

Choose between Malolotja Nature Reserve's hiking and canopy tours; walks, mountain biking and horse riding in Mlilwane Wildlife Sanctuary; Great Usutu River rafting, caving in Gobholo Cave, the community-run Ngwempisi Hiking Trail and climbing sheer Sibebe Rock.

Culture

Swaziland's ceremonies are famous African festivals, among them the *umhlanga* (reed) dance, essentially a debutante ball for Swazi maidens, and the Buganu (Marula) Festival. Experience everyday Swazi life on Lobamba tours and overnight village stays.

p483

> **Every listing is recommended by our authors, and their favourite places are listed first**

> **Look out for these icons:**

 Our author's top recommendation

 A green or sustainable option

 No payment required

On the Road

Cape Town

Best Places to Eat

» Bizerca Bistro (p73)
» Bombay Brasserie (p73)
» Dear Me (p73)
» Roundhouse (p77)
» Kitchen (p75)
» Pot Luck Club & the Test Kitchen (p75)

Best Places to Stay

» Mannabay (p69)
» Backpack (p69)
» Villa Zest (p71)
» POD (p71)
» Dutch Manor (p68)

Why Go?

Known as the 'Mother City' for its historical role in the development of modern South Africa, Cape Town is dominated by magnificent Table Mountain, its summit draped with cascading clouds, its flanks coated with unique flora and vineyards, its base fringed by golden beaches. Few cities can boast such a wonderful national park at their heart or provide the wide range of adventurous activities that take full advantage of it.

The World Design Capital 2014 is in the process of using design to transform the city and the quality of life of its population. From the brightly painted facades of the Bo-Kaap and the bathing chalets of Muizenberg to striking street art and the Afro-chic decor of countless guesthouses, this is one good-looking metropolis. Above all it's a multicultural city where everyone has a fascinating, sometimes heartbreaking story to tell. When the time comes to leave, you may find your heart breaking, too.

When to Go
Cape Town

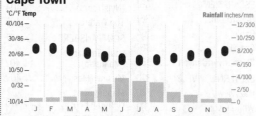

Jan Peak season but also a chance to see the Minstrel Carnival.

Mar Enjoy arts events such as Infecting the City and the International Jazz Festival.

Nov Spring sees beautiful flowers begin to bloom and the start of sunset concerts at Kirstenbosch.

History

Long before the Dutch East India Company (Vereenigde Oost-Indische Compagnie; VOC) established a base here in 1652, the Cape Town area was settled by the San and Khoekhoen nomadic tribes, collectively known as the Khoe-San. The indigenous peoples shunned the Dutch, so the VOC was forced to import slaves from Madagascar, India, Ceylon, Malaya and Indonesia to deal with the colony's chronic labour shortage. Women were in even shorter supply, so the Europeans exploited the female slaves and the local Khoe-San for both labour and sex. In time the slaves also intermixed with the Khoe-San. The offspring of these unions formed the basis of sections of today's coloured population and also helps explain the unique character of the city's Cape Muslim population.

Under the 150-odd years of Dutch rule, Kaapstad, as the Cape settlement became known, thrived and gained a wider reputation as the 'Tavern of the Seas', a riotous port used by every sailor travelling between Europe and the East. Following the British defeat of the Dutch in 1806 at Bloubergstrand, 25km north of Cape Town, the colony was ceded to the Crown on 13 August 1814. Cape Town continued to prosper after the slave trade was abolished in 1808, and all slaves were emancipated in 1833.

The discovery and exploitation of diamonds and gold in the centre of South Africa from the 1870s led to rapid changes. Cape Town was soon no longer the single dominant metropolis in the country, but as a major port it too was a beneficiary of the mineral wealth that laid the foundations for an industrial society. The same wealth led to imperialist dreams of grandeur on the part of Cecil John Rhodes (premier of the Cape Colony in 1890), who had made his millions at the head of De Beers Consolidated Mines.

An outbreak of bubonic plague in 1901 was blamed on the black African workers (although it actually came on boats from Argentina) and gave the government an excuse to introduce racial segregation: blacks were moved to two locations, one near the docks and the other at Ndabeni on the eastern flank of Table Mountain. This was the start of what would later develop into the townships of the Cape Flats.

◉ Sights

☑ 021 / POP 3.1 MILLION

Cape Town's commercial centre, known as the City Bowl, is bounded by Table Mountain and the suburbs of Bo-Kaap to the west, Gardens to the south and the Fringe, District Six and Woodstock to the east. Moving west around the Atlantic Coast you'll first hit the Waterfront and Green Point, then Sea Point, Camps Bay and Hout Bay.

CAPE TOWN IN...

Two Days

Ride the cable car up **Table Mountain**, then return to the city and wander through the **Company's Gardens**, nipping into the **South Africa National Gallery** to view its latest exhibition. Go souvenir shopping at **Greenmarket Square** segueing into drinks on **Long Street**.

On day two explore the southern end of the Cape Peninsula starting at the magnificent **Cape of Good Hope**. Move on to the cute penguin colony at **Boulders**, charming **Simon's Town**, and the shops and picturesque fishing harbour at **Kalk Bay**. A good option for lunch is Kalk Bay's **Olympia Café & Deli** or **Live Bait** beside the harbour. Return to the city via the Atlantic Coast and **Chapman's Peak Drive**.

Four Days

Drop by the **District Six Museum**, then take a half-day **township tour**. Sail out to **Robben Island** in the afternoon, hanging out at the **Waterfront** after for sunset drinks.

On day four head to **Groot Constantia** for a spot of wine tasting and the gorgeous grounds of the **Kirstenbosch Botanical Gardens**. You could have afternoon tea here or at the tearoom beside the **Rhodes Memorial**, with its sweeping view across the Cape Flats. Cap off your trip with a meal to remember at either **Roundhouse** or **Bombay Brasserie**.

Cape Town Highlights

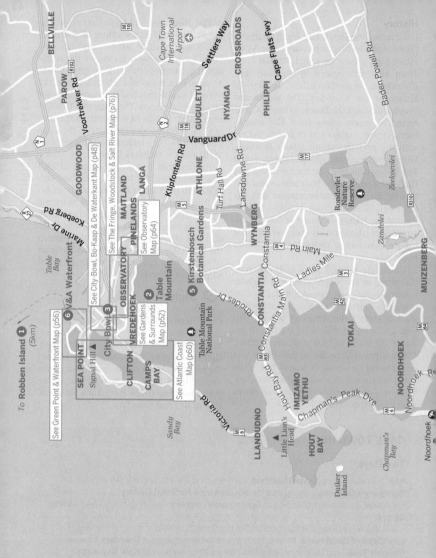

❶ Sailing out to the infamous prison **Robben Island** (p53), and pondering the country's past and present

❷ Taking the cable car to the top of magnificent **Table Mountain** (p51) and looking down on the city

❸ Exploring the **City Bowl** (p46), with its museums, the Company's Gardens and wonderful art-deco and Victorian architecture

❹ Heading to the **Cape of Good Hope** (p58) for wide open spaces, wildlife, empty beaches and the dramatic scenery of the peninsula's rugged tip

5 Wandering through the beautiful **Kirstenbosch Botanical Gardens** (p57) learning about the magnificent Cape Floral Kingdom

6 Enjoying the shops, restaurants, harbour cruises and buzzing carnival atmosphere of the **V&A Waterfront** (p53)

7 Snapping photos of the superstar African penguins paddling along the beach at **Boulders** (p59)

Seal Island

False Bay

KALK BAY

CLOVELLY

FISH HOEK

Kommetjie Rd

Simon's Town Rd

Boulders Beach

7 Boulders

SIMON'S TOWN

BOULDERS

SCARBOROUGH

Red Hill

Smitswinkel Bay

Table Mountain National Park

Paulsberg

Buffels Bay

Cape of Good Hope Nature Reserve

Cape of Good Hope

4 Cape Point

Maclear Beach

Dias Point Lighthouse

Diaz Beach

Platboom Beach

ATLANTIC OCEAN

Long Beach

Kommetjie Beaches

Slangkop Lighthouse

M4 · M6 · M65

N

0 — 5 km
0 — 2.5 miles

The city sprawls quite a distance to the north and east across the Cape Flats. To the south, skirting the eastern flank of the mountains are the leafy, wealthy Southern Suburbs. Apart from the large Cape of Good Hope section of Table Mountain National Park, the southern tip of the peninsula includes the small communities of Muizenberg, Kalk Bay and Simon's Town.

CITY BOWL & SURROUNDS

Castle of Good Hope
MUSEUM

(Map p48; www.castleofgoodhope.co.za; entrance on Buitenkant St; adult/child R28/12, Sun adult/child R20/5; ⊙9am-4pm; P; ⊒St George's) Built by the Dutch between 1666 and 1679 to defend Cape Town, this stone-walled pentagonal castle remains the headquarters for the Western Cape military command. Try timing your visit to coincide with one of the free guided tours (11am, noon and 2pm Monday to Saturday). The Military Museum is interesting, as are the displays of antiques and decorative arts in the William Fehr Collection at the Castle of Good Hope (www.iziko.org.za/static/page/william-fehr-collection). Don't miss climbing up to the bastions for an elevated view of the castle's layout and across to Grand Parade.

Company's Gardens
GARDENS

(Map p48; ⊙7am-7pm; ⊒Dorp) These shady green gardens, which started as the vegetable patch for the Dutch East India Company, are a lovely place to relax. In the 19th century the grounds became a superb pleasure garden, planted with a fine collection of botanical specimens from South Africa and the rest of the world, including frangipani and African flame trees, aloes and roses. The squirrels that scamper here were imported to Cape Town from North America by Cecil Rhodes, whose statue stands in the centre of the gardens.

District Six Museum
MUSEUM

(Map p48; ☑021-466 7200; www.districtsix.co.za; 25A Buitenkant St; adult/child R20/5, with Sacks Futeran Building R25/10; ⊙9am-2pm Mon, 9am-4pm Tue-Sat) This moving museum is as much for the people of the now-vanished District Six as it is about them. Prior to the forced evictions of the 1960s and 1970s some 50,000 people of all races lived in the area. Many township tours stop here first to explain the history of the pass laws.

Displays include a floor map of District Six on which former residents have labelled where their demolished homes and features

of their neighbourhood once stood; reconstructions of home interiors; and faded photographs and recordings. Many of the staff, practically all displaced residents themselves, have heartbreaking stories to tell. The museum's annex in the nearby Sacks Futeran Building (15 Buitenkant St) houses a couple of good permanent exhibitions related to soccer on the Cape from its emergence in the late 1800s to the current day.

Bo-Kaap
NEIGHBOURHOOD

(Map p48; ⊒Dorp) Meaning 'Upper Cape', the Bo-Kaap with its vividly painted low-roofed houses, many of them historic monuments, strung along narrow cobbled streets, is one of the most photographed sections of the city. Initially a garrison for soldiers in the mid-18th century, this area of town was where freed slaves started to settle after emancipation in the 1830s. Find out about the district's history at the small but engaging Bo-Kaap Museum (www.iziko.org.za/museums/bo-kaap-museum; 71 Wale St, Bo-Kaap; adult/child R10/free; ⊙10am-5pm Mon-Sat).

Michaelis Collection at the Old Town House
MUSEUM

(Map p48; http://www.iziko.org.za/museums/michaelis-collection-at-the-old-town-house; Greenmarket Sq; admission R10; ⊙10am-5pm Mon-Sat; ⊒Longmarket) On the south side of cobbled Greenmarket Sq is the beautifully restored Old Town House, a Cape rococo building dating from 1755 that was once City Hall. It now houses the impressive art collection of Sir Max Michaelis. Dutch and Flemish paintings and etchings from the 16th and 17th centuries (including works by Rembrandt, Frans Hals and Anthony van Dyck) hang side by side with contemporary works – the contrasts between old and new are fascinating.

Greenmarket Square, Cape Town's second-oldest public space after the Grand Parade, hosts a lively and colourful daily crafts and souvenir market. Apart from the Old Town House, it's surrounded by some choice examples of art-deco architecture.

Long Street
NEIGHBOURHOOD

(Map p48; ⊒Castle) Whether you come to browse the antique shops, bookstores or fashion boutiques, or to party at the host of bars and clubs that crank up at night, a stroll along Long St is a Cape Town rite of passage. The most attractive section, lined with Victorian-era buildings with wrought-iron balconies, runs from the junction with Buitensingel St north to around the Strand.

MUSLIM CAPE TOWN

Islam first came to the Cape with the slaves brought by the Dutch from the Indian sub-continent and Indonesia (hence the term Cape Malays, although few of them actually hailed from what is today called Malaysia). Among them were educated political dissidents such as the exiled Islamic leader Tuan Guru from Tidore (Indonesia), who arrived in 1780. During his 13 years on Robben Island, Tuan Guru accurately copied the Quran from memory. In 1789 he helped establish the **Auwal Mosque** (43 Dorp St), the city's first mosque, in the Bo-Kaap, thus making this area the heart of the Islamic community in Cape Town.

Tuan Guru is buried in the Bo-Kaap's **Tana Baru cemetery** off the western end of Longmarket St. His grave is one of the 20 or so *karamats* (tombs of Muslim saints) encircling Cape Town and visited by the faithful on a minipilgrimage. Islam is still widely practised in the city, predominantly among the coloured community.

Signal Hill & Noon Gun   VIEWPOINT

There are magnificent views from the 350m-high summit of this hill separating Sea Point from the City Bowl. At noon Monday to Saturday, a cannon known as the **Noon Gun** is fired from the lower slopes of Signal Hill. You can hear it all over town. Traditionally this allowed the burghers in the town below to check their watches. It's a stiff walk up here through the Bo-Kaap. Take Longmarket St and keep going until it ends; the gate at the end of the path leading to where the gun is fired is usually opened around 11.30am. The **Noon Gun Tearoom & Restaurant** (off Map p48) is a good place to catch your breath. To drive up to the summit follow Kloof Nek Rd from the city and take the first turn-off to the right at the top of the hill.

Slave Lodge   MUSEUM

(Map p48; www.iziko.org.za/museums/slave-lodge; 49 Adderley St; adult/child R20/10; ☺10am-5pm Mon-Sat; ☐Dorp) This museum, mainly devoted to the history and experience of slaves and their descendants in the Cape, also has artefacts from ancient Egypt, Greece, Rome and the Far East on the 1st floor.

One of the oldest buildings in South Africa, dating back to 1660, the Slave Lodge has a fascinating history in itself. Until 1811 the building was home, if you could call it that, to as many as 1000 slaves, who lived in damp, insanitary, crowded conditions. Up to 20% died each year. The slaves were bought and sold just around the corner on Spin St. The walls of the original Slave Lodge flank the interior courtyard, where you can find the tombstones of Cape Town's founder, Jan van Riebeeck, and his wife, Maria de la Queillerie. The tombstones were moved here from Jakarta where Van Riebeeck is buried.

FREE Prestwich Memorial & Park   MEMORIAL

(Map p48; cnr Somerset & Buitengracht Sts; ☺8am-6pm Mon-Fri, 8am-2pm Sat & Sun; ☐Prestwich) This memorial building houses an ossuary for the bones of former slaves and other unfortunates uncovered on and around this site in 2003. There are good interpretive displays, including a replica of the remarkable 360-degree panorama of Table Bay painted by Robert Gordon in 1778, and a branch of the coffee shop Truth. In the park outside you can see the outline of tram tracks – horse-drawn trams once used to run past here along Somerset and down through Sea Point to terminate in Camps Bay – as well as a collection of quirky statues by Capetonian artists.

Mutual Heights   ARCHITECTURE

(Map p48; cnr Parliament & Darling Sts; ☐St George's) This impressive art-deco building was once not only the tallest structure in Africa apart from the Pyramids, but also the most expensive. It is clad in rose- and gold-veined black marble and decorated with one of the longest continuous stone friezes in the world. When the former office block was converted to apartments in 2004, it kicked off a frenzy among developers to refashion similarly long-neglected and empty city-centre properties.

South African National Gallery   GALLERY

(Map p48; www.iziko.org.za/museums/south-african-national-gallery; Government Ave, Gardens; adult/child R20/free; ☺10am-5pm Tue-Sun; ☐ Government Avenue) The impressive permanent collection of the nation's premier art space harks back to Dutch times and includes some extraordinary pieces. But it's often

City Bowl, Bo-Kaap & De Waterkant

0 M
0 0.2 miles
400 m

FORESHORE

Salazar Sq

To Artscape (20m)

Civic Centre

Hertzog Blvd

Merriman Sq

Heerengracht

57

Pier Pl

Long Distance Bus Terminus

Table Bay Blvd

Lower Long St

Coen Steytler Ave

Convention Centre

Adderley

32

Jetty Sq

Tulbagh Sq

N2

Lower Long St

Prestwich

Thibault Sq

Dock Rd

Lower Burg St

Hans Strijdom Ave

Long St

Prestwich

Waterkant St

Alfred St

Port Rd

Helen Suzman Blvd

Mechau St

Bree St

Buitengracht

Castle

Hospital St

Jerry St

Chiappini St

Prestwich St

Riebeeck St

Lower Bree St

42

68

Castle

DE WATERKANT

Napier St

Alfred St

Schiebe St

Somerset Rd

Waterkant St

Prestwich Memorial Park

8

Lelie La

Grouse La

Strand St

Castle St

To Trinity (92m)

31

Cohern St

Liddle St

De Smit St

30
55
56
58

65

Dixon St

Hudson St

35

62

Buitengracht St

Rose St

Strand St

Castle St

Hout La

29

15

Heritage Sq

Jarvis St

45

27
44

Vos St

53

36

Chiappini St

Strand St

23

20

Berg St

69

Bo-Kaap

Church St

Loader St

Table Mountain National Park

To Noon Gun Tearoom & Restaurant (230m)

Longmarket St

11

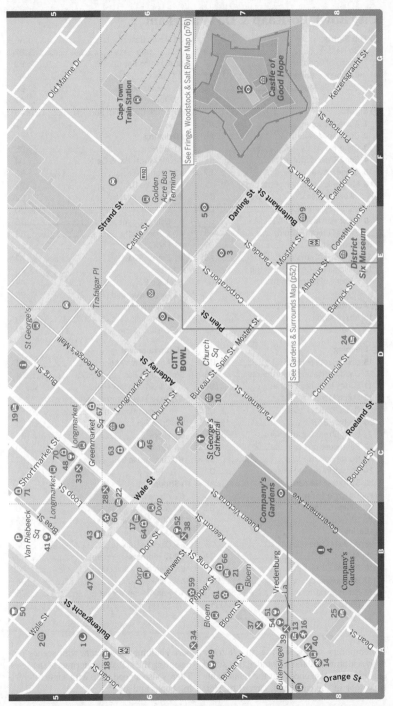

City Bowl, Bo-Kaap & De Waterkant

contemporary works, such as the *Butcher Boys* sculpture by Jane Alexander, that stand out the most. Also check out the remarkable teak door in the courtyard, carved by Her-bert Vladimir Meyerowitz with scenes representing the global wanderings of the Jews. There's also a good shop with some interesting books and gifts.

Grand Parade
ARCHITECTURE

(Map p48; Darling St; ☐St George's) A prime location in Cape Town's history, the Grand Parade is where the Dutch built their first fort in 1652; slaves were sold and punished; crowds gathered to watch Nelson Mandela's first address to the nation as a free man after 27 years in jail; and the official FIFA fan park for the 2010 World Cup was set up. A market is held on part of the square, which is also used for parking. The city has allotted R7 million for the renovation of the grand Edwardian **Cape Town City Hall**, which faces the parade and is now used occasionally for music and cultural events.

GARDENS & SURROUNDS

Table Mountain Cableway
VIEWPOINT

(Map p60; ☎021-424 8181; www.tablemountain .net; Tafelberg Rd; adult 1-way/return R100/195, child R50/95; ☺8.30am-7pm Feb-Nov, 8am-10pm Dec & Jan) For the vast majority of visitors the main attraction of Table Mountain National Park is the 1086m-high mountain itself, the top of which can easily be accessed by the cableway; the views from the revolving car and the summit are phenomenal. At the top there are souvenir shops, a good cafe and some easy walks to follow. Departures are every 10 minutes in high season (December to February) and every 20 minutes in low season (May to September), but the cableway doesn't operate when it's dangerously windy, and there's obviously little point going up if you are simply going to be wrapped in the cloud known as the 'tablecloth'. Call in advance to see if it's operating. The best

visibility and conditions are likely to be first thing in the morning or in the evening.

South African Jewish Museum
MUSEUM

(Map p52; www.sajewishmuseum.co.za; 88 Hatfield St, Gardens; adult/child 40/free; ☺10am-5pm Sun-Thu, 10am-2pm Fri; ℗; ☐ Government Avenue) This imaginatively designed museum incorporates the beautifully restored **Old Synagogue** (1863). The permanent exhibition *Hidden Treasures of Japanese Art* showcases a collection of exquisite *netsuke* (carved pieces of ivory and wood). There are also temporary exhibitions that are usually worth seeing.

Your ticket also covers the fascinating 25min documentary *Nelson Mandela: A Righteous Man* screened in the building across the courtyard from the museum's exit. Upstairs the **Cape Town Holocaust Centre** (www.holocaust.org.za; admission free; ☺10am-5pm Sun-Thu, 10am-2pm Fri) packs a lot in with a considerable emotional punch. The history of anti-Semitism is set in a South African context with parallels drawn to the local struggle for freedom.

Also within the compound is the functioning and beautifully decorated **Great Synagogue** (guided tours free; ☺10am-4pm Sun-Thu), a 1905 building in the neo-Egyptian style; a good gift shop; and the kosher Café Riteve. You need a photo ID to enter the compound.

Lion's Head
VIEWPOINT

(Signal Hill Rd, Tamboerskloof; ℗) The main access for this giant nipplelike outcrop is from the road leading to the top of Signal Hill just

---

WORTH A TRIP

THE FRINGE TO SALT RIVER

East of the City Bowl are a series of working-class and industrial suburbs that are regenerating and partly gentrifying. The process is a patchy, controversial one and has long been so – this is where you'll find the empty lots of District Six, a multicultural area destroyed during apartheid.

Closest to the city, the area newly dubbed the Fringe is set to be a showcase hub of Cape Town's successful bid to become World Design Capital 2014. Check out the dazzling street art on **Substation 13** (Map p76; Canterbury St) and **Land & Liberty** (Map p76; Keizersgracht), an eight-storey tall painting of a mother with a baby strapped to her back by the prolific street artist Faith47 (www.faith47.com).

Moving eastwards, Woodstock and Salt River continue their upward mobility trajectory, with the Woodstock Foundry and Salt Circle Arcade, both along Albert Rd, among the latest big redevelopments following in the wake of the phenomenal Old Biscuit Mill. Also drop by the art galleries **Stevenson** (Map p76; www.stevenson.info; 160 Sir Lowry Rd, Woodstock; ☺9am-5pm Mon-Fri, 10am-1pm Sat; ☒Woodstock) and **What If the World** (Map p76; www.whatiftheworld.com; 1 Argyle St, Woodstock; ☺10am-4.30pm Tue-Fri, 10am-3pm Sat; ☒Woodstock).

Gardens & Surrounds

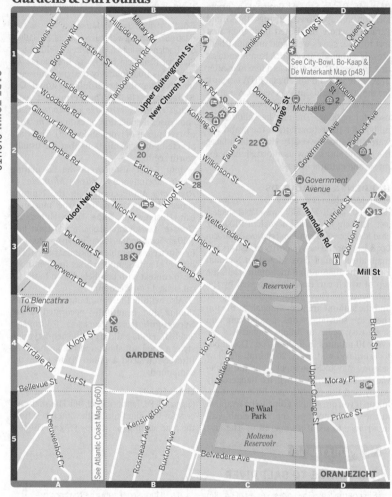

See City-Bowl, Bo-Kaap & De Waterkant Map (p48)

To Blencathra (1km)

See Atlantic Coast Map (p60)

GARDENS

Reservoir

De Waal Park

Molteno Reservoir

Belvedere Ave

ORANJEZICHT

Mill St

Government Avenue

off Kloof Nek Rd, although there are also hiking routes up from the Sea Point side. It takes about 45 minutes to cover the 2.2km hike from Kloof Nek to the 669m summit and it is deservedly popular. A lot of people do it as an early-morning constitutional and it's a ritual to go up and watch the sun go down on a full-moon night. The moonlight aids the walk back down, although you should always bring a torch (flashlight) and go with company.

South African Museum MUSEUM
(Map p52; www.iziko.org.za/museums/south-african
-museum; 25 Queen Victoria St, Gardens; adult/
child R20/10, Sat by donation; ⊙10am-5pm; ☐
Bloem) South Africa's oldest museum may be showing its age but it does contain a wide and often intriguing series of exhibitions, many on the country's natural history. The best galleries are the newest, showcasing the art and culture of the area's first peoples, the Khoekhoen (Khoikhoi) and the San, and including the famous Linton Panel, an amazing example of San rock art. Also worth looking out for are the startlingly lifelike displays in the African Cultures Gallery of African people (cast from living subjects); a 2m-wide nest of the sociable weaver bird

GREEN POINT & WATERFRONT

Robben Island & Nelson Mandela Gateway
MUSEUM

(Map p56; ☎021-413 4220; www.robben-island
.org.za; adult/child R230/120; ☺ferries depart at
9am, 11am, 1pm & 3pm weather permitting; ☒Wa-
terfront) Used as a prison from the early days
of the VOC right up until 1996, this UN
World Heritage Site is preserved as a memorial to those such as Nelson Mandela who
spent many years incarcerated here.

While we heartily recommend going to
Robben Island, a visit here is not without its
drawbacks. The first hurdle is getting a ticket – in peak times these often sell out days
in advance. Reserve well in advance via the
web, or book a ticket in conjunction with a
township tour – many tour operators have
access to blocks of tickets not available to
the public. The packed guided tour allows a
maximum of two hours on the island (plus
a 30-minute boat ride in both directions).
One of the former inmates will lead you
around the prison. It seems a perverse form
of torture to have these guys recount their
harrowing time as prisoners here, but the
best of the guides rise above this to embody
the true spirit of reconciliation.

The standard tours, which have set departure and return times, include a walk
through the old prison (with the obligatory peek into Mandela's cell), as well as a
45-minute bus ride around the island with
commentary on the various places of note,
such as the lime quarry in which Mandela
and many others slaved, and the church
used during the island's stint as a leper
colony. If you're lucky, you'll have about 10
minutes to wander around on your own.

Tours depart from the **Nelson Mandela
Gateway** (admission free; ☺9am-8.30pm) beside
the Clock Tower at the Waterfront. Even
if you don't plan a visit to the island, it's
worth dropping by the museum here, with
its focus on the struggle for equality. Also
preserved as a small museum is the Waterfront's **Jetty 1** (admission free; ☺7am-9pm),
the departure point for Robben Island
when it was a prison.

V&A Waterfront
NEIGHBOURHOOD

(Map p56; www.waterfront.co.za; ℙ; ☒Waterfront)
This historic working harbour has a spectacular setting and many tourist-oriented
attractions including masses of shops, restaurants, bars, cinemas and cruises. The
Alfred and Victoria Basins date from 1860
and are named after Queen Victoria and

in the Wonders of Nature Gallery; and the
atmospheric Whale Well, hung with giant
whale skeletons and models and resounding
with taped recordings of their calls.

Attached to the museum is the **Planetarium** (www.iziko.org.za/museums/planetarium;
25 Queen Victoria St, Gardens; adult/child R25/10;
☺10am-5pm; ☒Bloem); check the website for
times of daily shows using images caught by
the Southern African Large Telescope in the
Karoo (which has the largest aperture of any
telescope in the world); there's a kids' show
at noon daily.

Gardens & Surrounds

her son Alfred. Although these wharves are too small for modern container vessels and tankers, the Victoria Basin is still used by tugs, harbour vessels of various kinds, and fishing boats. In the Alfred Basin you'll see ships under repair, and there are always seals splashing around or lazing on the giant tyres that line the docks.

Apart from the Nelson Mandela Gateway, departure point for Robben Island, the most interesting attractions are as follows.

Two Oceans Aquarium
(Map p56; www.aquarium.co.za; Dock Rd; adult/child R105/50; ◎9.30am-6pm) This excellent aquarium features denizens of the deep from the cold and the warm oceans that border the Cape Peninsula, including ragged-tooth sharks. There are seals, penguins, turtles, an astounding kelp forest open to the sky, and pools in which kids can touch sea creatures. Qualified divers can get into the water for a closer look (R595 including dive gear). Get your hand stamped on entry and you can return any time during the same day for free.

Chavonnes Battery Museum
(Map p56; ☎021-416 6230; www.chavonnes museum.co.za; Clock Tower Precinct; adult/child R25/10; ◎9am-4pm Wed-Sun) Along with the Castle of Good Hope the Dutch built a series of fortifications around Table Bay. The Chavonnes Battery Museum houses the remains of an early 18th-century cannon battery. Although it had been partly demolished and built over during the construction of the docks in 1860, an excavation of the site in 1999 revealed the remains. You can walk around the entire site and get a good feel for what it would have originally been like. **Historical walking tours** (☎021-408 7600; adult/child R50/20) of the Waterfront start from here (minimum of four people).

Nobel Square
Here's your chance to have your photo taken with Desmond Tutu and Nelson Mandela. The larger-than-life statues of both men, designed by Claudette Schreuders, stand beside those of South Africa's two other Nobel Prize winners – Nkosi Albert Luthuli and FW de Klerk. Also here is the *Peace and Democracy* sculpture by Noria Mahasa, which

symbolises the contribution of women and children to the struggle. It's etched with pertinent quotes by each of the great men, translated into all the major languages of the country.

Green Point Urban Park   PARK

(Map p56; Bay Rd, Green Point; ☉7am-7pm; P; ☐Stadium) One of the best things to come out of the 2010 World Cup is this park and biodiversity garden. It has three imaginatively designed areas: People & Plants, Wetlands, and Discovering Biodiversity that, along with educational information boards, act as the best kind of outdoor museum. There's plenty of space for picnics with brilliant views of the stadium, Signal Hill and Lion's Head, and two kids' playgrounds – one for toddlers and one for older kids. Guided tours (adult/child R34.20/17.10) of the park can be arranged through Cape Town Stadium.

Cape Town Stadium   STADIUM

(Map p56; ☑021-417 0101; Granger Bay Blvd, Green Point; tours adult/child R45.60/17.10; ☉tours 10am, noon & 2pm Tue-Sat; P; ☐Stadium) The city's most striking piece of contemporary architecture cost R4.5 billion and regularly seats 55,000. It's the home ground of the soccer team Ajax Cape Town and has been used for concerts by the likes of U2 and the Eagles. Hour-long tours take you behind the scenes into the VIP and press boxes as well as the teams' dressing rooms.

ATLANTIC COAST

Cape Town's Atlantic Coast is all about spectacular scenery and soft-sand beaches. Strong winds can be a downer and while it's possible to shelter from the summer southeasterlies at some beaches, the water at them all, flowing straight from the Antarctic, is freezing. From Sea Point (which has an excellent outdoor swimming pavilion), you can head down to Clifton and Camps Bay. The road then hugs the coast for a thrilling drive to the fishing community of Hout Bay, which has a good beach and harbour with boat trips.

Clifton Beaches   BEACHES

(Map p60) Giant granite boulders split the four linked beaches at Clifton, accessible by steps from Victoria Rd. Almost always sheltered from the wind, these are Cape Town's top sunbathing spots. Local lore has it that No 1 and No 2 beaches are for models and confirmed narcissists, No 3 is the gay beach, and No 4 – the busiest – is for families. Vendors hawk drinks and ice creams along the beach, and you can rent a sun lounger and umbrella for around R80.

Camps Bay Beach   BEACHES

(Map p60) With soft white sand, and the spectacular Twelve Apostles of Table Mountain as a backdrop, Camps Bay is one of the city's most popular beaches despite its being one of the windiest. It can get crowded, particularly on weekends. There are no lifeguards on duty and the surf is strong, so take care if you do decide to swim. The strip of smart bars and restaurants here are very popular places for drinks at sunset or just general all-day lounging.

Sea Point Promenade   PROMENADE

(Map p60; Beach Rd, Sea Point) A stroll or jog along Sea Point's wide paved and grassy promenade is a pleasure shared by Capetonians from all walks of life – it's a great place to come at sunset and see how multicultural the city is.

World of Birds   AVIARY

(www.worldofbirds.org.za; Valley Rd, Hout Bay; adult/child R75/40; ☉9am-5pm; P) Barbets, weavers, flamingos and ostriches are among

---

WORTH A TRIP

RHODES MEMORIAL

High on the eastern slopes of Table Mountain, at a spot where the mining magnate and former prime minister used to admire the view, is the monumental Rhodes Memorial (www.rhodesmemorial.co.za/memorial.aspx; off M3, below Devil's Peak, Groote Schuur Estate, Rondebosch; free; ☉7am-7pm; P). Despite providing sweeping vistas to the Cape Flats and the mountain ranges beyond – and, by implication, right into the heart of Africa – the bust of Cecil Rhodes has the man looking rather grumpy. The exit for the memorial is at the Princess Anne Interchange on the M3. Behind the memorial is a pleasant restaurant and tea garden (☉7am-5pm; P) specialising in Cape Malay dishes such as bredies (pot stews of meat or fish and vegetables) and bobotie (delicately flavoured ostrich-meat curry with a topping of beaten egg baked to a crust).

Green Point & Waterfront

N
0 — 500 m
0 — 0.25 miles

ATLANTIC OCEAN

Three Anchor Bay

Table Bay

Victoria Basin

Duncan Dock

South Arm

Nelson Mandela Gateway

Clock Tower

Clock Tower Centre

Fish Quay

Old Port Captain's Office

Market Sq

Alfred Basin

Small Vessels Marina

East Pier

Waterfront

Breakwater

Granger Bay

Information Centre

Dock Rd

City Sightseeing Cape Town tour bus start/end point

Fort Wynyard Rd

Green Point Track

Postwood Rd

Dock Rd

Helen Suzman Blvd

Beach Rd

Granger St

Granger Bay Blvd

Granger Bay

Fan Walk

Stadium

Main Rd

York Rd

Varney's Rd

Cavalcade Rd

Fritz Sonnenberg Rd

Viel Rd

Bill Peters Dr

Stephan Way

Green Point Urban Park

Kiewiet La

Bay Rd

Beach Rd

Bill Peters Dr

See Atlantic Coast Map (p60)

Wigtown Rd

Pine Rd

Clyde Rd

St Georges Rd

Cheviot Pl

High Level Rd

Helen Suzman Blvd

Antrim Rd

Hill Rd

St Bedes Rd

Glengariff Rd

Green Point & Waterfront

the 3000 different birds and small mammals covering some 400 different species that can be found here. A real effort has been made to make the aviaries, which are South Africa's largest, as natural-looking as possible with the use of lots of tropical landscaping. In the **monkey jungle** (☯11.30am-1pm, 2-3.30pm) you can interact with the cheeky squirrel monkeys.

SOUTHERN SUBURBS
Kirstenbosch Botanical
Gardens   GARDENS
(www.sanbi.org/gardens/kirstenbosch; Rhodes Dr, Newlands; adult/child R40/10; ☯8am-7pm Sep-Mar, 8am-6pm Apr-Aug) Location and unique flora combine to make these 36-hectare botanical gardens among the most beautiful in the world. The main entrance at the Newlands end of the gardens is where you'll find the information centre, an excellent souvenir shop and the **conservatory** (☯9am-5pm). Further along Rhodes Dr is the Rycroft Gate entrance, the first you'll come to if you approach the gardens from Constantia. Call to find out about free guided walks, or hire the My Guide electronic gizmo (R40) to receive

recorded information about the various plants you'll pass on the three signposted circular walks.

About 9000 of Southern Africa's 22,000 plant species are grown here. You'll find a fragrance garden that has been elevated so you can more easily sample the scents of the plants, a Braille trail, a kopje (hill) that has been planted with pelargoniums, a sculpture garden and a section for plants used for *muti* (traditional medicine) by *sangoma* (traditional healers), as well as a section of the wild almond hedge planted in 1660 by Jan van Riebeeck to form the boundary of the Dutch outpost.

The outdoor Sunday afternoon concerts held here between November and March are a Cape Town institution. The gardens are a stop on the City Sightseeing Cape Town bus.

Constantia Valley
Wine Route   WINERIES
South Africa's wine farming industry began here back in 1685 when Governor Simon van der Stel was granted around 763 hectares of land behind Table Mountain. He named his farm Constantia and by 1709 there were

70,000 vines producing 5630L of wine. Four years after Van der Stel's death in 1712 the estate was split up. The area is now home to a **route** (www.constantiavalley.com) covering nine vineyards – the key ones to visit are covered below.

Groot Constantia

(www.grootconstantia.co.za; Groot Constantia Rd, Constantia; tastings R33, museum adult/child R20/free, cellar tours R45; ◎9am-5pm; P) Simon van der Stel's manor house, a superb example of Cape Dutch architecture, is maintained as a museum at Groot Constantia. Set in beautiful grounds, the estate can become busy with tour groups, but is big enough for you to escape the crowds. The large tasting room is first on your right as you enter the estate. Further on is the free orientation centre, which provides an overview of the estate's history, and the beautifully restored homestead. The **Cloete Cellar**, with a beautiful moulded pediment, was the estate's original wine cellar. It now houses old carriages and a display of storage vessels. Hour-long tours of the modern cellar depart at 2pm.

Steenberg Vineyards

(www.steenberg-vineyards.co.za; Steenberg Rd, Steenberg; ◎10am-6pm; P) Enjoy the gorgeous contemporary tasting bar and lounge at Steenberg Vineyards in which you can sample its great merlot, sauvignon blanc reserve, semillon and Méthode Cap Classique sparkler. Picnics (R300 for two) include a bottle of wine. The farm estate is the oldest on the Cape, dating back to 1682 when it was known as Swaane-weide (Feeding Place of the Swans). Tastings are either free for the basic set of wines or R50 to sample a wider range including their premium products. Also here is the five-star Steenberg Hotel (www.steenberghotel.com) in the original manor house, Catharina's Restaurant and an 18-hole golf course.

Buitenverwachting

(http://buitenverwachting.co.za; Klein Constantia Rd, Constantia; tastings free; ◎9am-5pm Mon-Fri, 10am-3pm Sat; P) Meaning 'beyond expectation', Buitenverwachting is known for offering good working and living conditions to its employees. Order ahead to enjoy a blissful **picnic lunch** (☎083 257 6083; lunch R125; ◎noon-4pm Mon-Sat Nov-Apr) in front of the 1796 manor house.

Klein Constantia

(www.kleinconstantia.com; Klein Constantia Rd, Constantia; tastings free; ◎tastings 9am-5pm Mon-Fri, 9am-3pm Sat; P) Part of the original Constantia estate, Klein Constantia is famous for its vin de constance, a deliciously sweet muscat wine. It was Napoleon's solace on St Helena, and Jane Austen had one of her heroines recommend it for having the power to heal 'a disappointed heart'. It's worth visiting for its excellent tasting room and informative displays.

SOUTHERN PENINSULA

The southern end of the peninsula holds a variety of delights apart from the star attraction of Cape Point. A popular holiday resort in the early 20th century, Muizenberg, 25km south of the City Bowl, is on the up again after a period in the economic doldrums. Next along the coast the charming fishing village of Kalk Bay is packed with interesting craft shops and galleries as well as lovely places to eat and drink. A naval town ever since colonial times, Simon's Town remains the main base for South Africa's navy.

Cape of Good Hope NATURE RESERVE
(www.sanparks.org/parks/table_mountain; admission adult/child R85/30; ◎6am-6pm Oct-Mar, 7am-5pm Apr-Sep; P) Commonly called Cape Point, this 7750-hectare section of Table Mountain National Park, includes awesome scenery, fantastic walks and often deserted beaches. Some 250 species of birds live here, including cormorants and a family of ostriches that hang out near the Cape of Good Hope, the southwesternmost point of the continent.

Many people visit on organised bus tours but, if you have the time, exploring the reserve on foot or by bicycle is much more rewarding. Bear in mind, though, that there is minimal shade and that the weather can change quickly. Bookings are required for the two-day **Cape of Good Hope Trail** (not including the park entry fee R200), a spectacular 33.8km circular route with one night spent at the basic Protea and Restio huts. Contact the **Buffelfontein Visitors Centre** (☎021-780 9204) for further details.

It's not a hard walk uphill, but if you're feeling lazy the **Flying Dutchman Funicular** (www.capepoint.co.za; 1 way/return adult R37/47, child R15/20; ◎10am-5.30pm) runs up from beside the restaurant to the souvenir kiosk next to the old lighthouse, dating from 1860. A 1km trail runs from here to its successor. Ignore the signs: it takes less than 30

GETTING AROUND THE SOUTHERN PENINSULA

A car is essential for getting the most out of the scattered sights of the southern peninsula, although the train will also do for many False Bay destinations including Muizenberg, Kalk Bay and Simon's Town; a R30 day ticket allows unlimited travel between Cape Town and Simon's Town and all stations in between from 8am to 4.30pm.

The Mellow Yellow Water Taxi (☏073-473 7684; www.watertaxi.co.za; single/return R100/150) shuttles between Kalk Bay and Simon's Town – it's recommended to take the train to Simon's Town and the water taxi back to Kalk Bay rather than the other way around.

minutes to walk along a spectacular ridgeway path to look down on the new lighthouse and the sheer cliffs plunging into the pounding ocean.

Boulders PENGUIN COLONY
(www.sanparks.org/parks/table_mountain; adult/child R30/10; ⊙7am-7.30pm Dec & Jan, 8am-6.30pm Feb-May & Sep-Nov, 8am-5pm Jun-Aug) This picturesque area with a number of enormous boulders dividing sandy coves is home to a colony of 2800 delightful African penguins. A boardwalk runs from the visitor centre at the Foxy Beach end of the protected area (another part of Table Mountain National Park) to Boulders Beach, where you can get down onto the sand and mingle with the waddling penguins. Don't be tempted to pet them: the penguins have sharp beaks that can cause serious injuries. The sea is calm and shallow in the coves, so Boulders is popular with families and can get extremely crowded, especially on holidays and at weekends.

FREE **Casa Labia Cultural Centre** CULTURAL BUILDING
(☏021-788 6068; www.casalabia.co.za; 192 Main Rd, Muizenberg; ⊙10am-4pm Tue-Sun; ℝMuizenberg) This magnificent seaside villa dating from 1930 was the palatial home of Count Natale Labia and his South African wife. Labia was the Italian Ambassador to South Africa at the time so this grand building, furnished by a Venetian interior designer with antique fixtures and fittings, doubled as the embassy residency and legation.

After a varied history, the rights to oversee the building were handed back to the Labias' son in 2008. It has since undergone a loving restoration to emerge as a beautiful building that hosts a programme of concerts, lectures and events, as well as housing works from the family's art collection and regularly changing contemporary art exhibitions. There's a branch of Africa Nova arts and crafts shop here as well as an excellent cafe.

Muizenberg Beach BEACH
(Beach Rd, Muizenberg; ℝKalk Bay) This surf beach, popular with families, is famous for its row of primary-colour-painted Victorian bathing chalets. Surf boards can be hired and lessons booked at either Roxy Surf Club or Gary's Surf School, and lockers are available in the pavilions on the promenade. The beach shelves gently and the sea is generally safer than elsewhere along the peninsula. At the eastern end of the promenade there's a fun water slide (1hr/day pass R35/65; ⊙9.30am-5.30pm Sat & Sun, daily in school holidays).

Kalk Bay Harbour HARBOUR
(Main Rd, Kalk Bay; ℝKalk Bay) Visit this picturesque harbour in the late morning when the community's few remaining fishing boats pitch up with their daily catch and a lively quayside market ensues. This is also an excellent place to spot whales during the whale-watching season. Nearby, next to Kalk Bay station and the Brass Bell pub, are a couple of tidal swimming pools.

Simon's Town Museum MUSEUM
(www.simonstown.com/museum/stm_main.htm; Court Rd; adult/child R5/2; ⊙10am-4pm Mon-Fri, 10am-1pm Sat; ℝSimon's Town) Housed in the old governor's residence (1777), the exhibits in this rambling museum trace Simon's Town's history. Included is a display on Just Nuisance, the Great Dane that was adopted as a navy mascot in WWII, and whose grave, off Red Hill Rd above the town, makes for a long walk from the harbour. There's also a statue of Just Nuisance in Jubilee Sq, by the harbour.

Heritage Museum MUSEUM
(www.simonstown.com/museum/sthm.htm; Almay House, King George Way, Simon's Town; admission R5; ⊙11am-4pm Tue-Thu & Sun; ℝSimon's Town) Simon's Town's community of Cape Muslims was 7000 strong before apartheid forcibly removed most of them, mainly to the suburb of Ocean's View across on the

Atlantic Coast

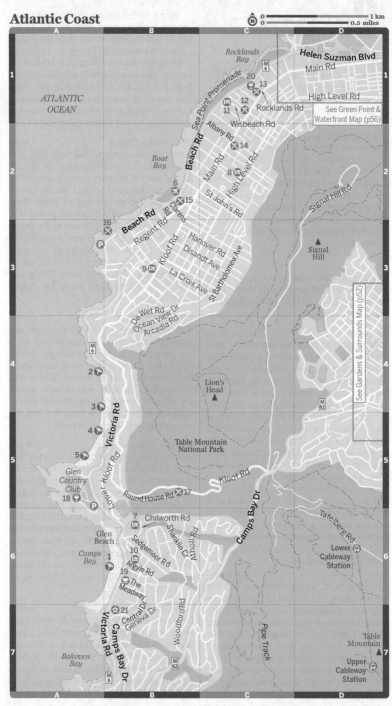

0 — 1 km
0 — 0.5 miles

A **B** **C** **D**

1

Rocklands Bay

20
13
12
11
Rocklands Rd

Helen Suzman Blvd
Main Rd

High Level Rd

See Green Point &
Waterfront Map (p56)

ATLANTIC OCEAN

Sea Point Promenade
Beach Rd

Albany Rd
Wisbeach Rd

14
Main Rd
8
High Level Rd

2

Boat Bay

6
24
15
Clarens

St John's Rd

Signal Hill Rd

Beach Rd

16

Regent Rd
Kloof Rd
Hanover Rd
Disandt Ave
La Croix Ave
St Bartholomew Ave

9

▲ Signal Hill

See Gardens & Surrounds Map (p52)

3

De Wet Rd
Ocean View Dr
Arcadia Rd

4

M6
2
Victoria Rd
3
4
5

Lion's Head ▲

M62

5

Glen Country Club
18

Lower Kloof Rd
Round House Rd
17

Kloof Rd

Table Mountain
National Park

Camps Bay Dr

6

7
Chilworth Rd
Sedgemoor Rd
Shanklin Cr
Atholl Rd

Glen Beach
Camps Bay
1
10
Argyle Rd
19
The Meadway

Tafelberg Rd

Lower Cableway Station

7

21
Central Dr
Geneva Dr

Camps Bay Dr
Victoria Rd

Woodford Rd

M62

Pipe Track

Table Mountain ▲

Upper Cableway Station

Bakoven Bay

M6

Atlantic Coast

Atlantic side of the peninsula. This interesting small museum, with a lovely front garden, is dedicated to the evictees and based in Almay House (dating from 1858).

 Activities

Abseiling & Kloofing

Abseil Africa   ABSEILING
(☏021-424 4760; www.abseilafrica.co.za; abseiling R595) The 112m drop off the top of Table Mountain with this long-established outfit is a guaranteed adrenaline rush. Don't even think of tackling it unless you've got a head (and a stomach) for heights. Tag on a guided hike up Platteklip Gorge for R250.

Abseil Africa also offers kloofing (canyoning) trips around Cape Town. The sport of clambering into and out of kloofs (cliffs or gorges) also entails abseiling, climbing, hiking, swimming and jumping.

Cycling & Mountain Biking

City-tour outfits AWOL and Day-trippers also offer cycling itineraries. See p91 for places where you can rent bikes.

**Downhill
Adventures**   CYCLING, MOUNTAIN BIKING
(Map p52; ☏021-422 0388; www.downhilladventures.com; cnr Orange & Kloof Sts, Gardens; activities from R595; 🚌Buitensingel) This adrenaline-focused company offers a variety of cycling trips as well as sandboarding out at Atlantis and a surf school. Options include a thrilling mountain-bike ride down from the lower cable station on Table Mountain, moun-

tain biking in the Tokai Forest, or a pedal through the Constantia Winelands and the Cape of Good Hope.

Diving

In the Blue (Map p60; ☏021-434 3358; www.diveschoolcapetown.co.za; 88B Main Rd, Sea Point; open-water PADI courses from R3450, shore/boat dives R200/300, gear hire per day R380) and **Table Bay Diving** (Map p56; ☏021-419 8822; www.tablebaydiving.com; Shop 7, Quay 5, Waterfront; 🅿; 🚌Breakwater) offer a number of excellent shore and boat dives.

Flying & Paragliding

There are several legal ways to get high in Cape Town and all are guaranteed to give you a fantastic buzz.

**Cape Town Tandem
Paragliding**   PARAGLIDING
(☏076-892 2283; www.paraglide.co.za) Feel like James Bond as you paraglide off Lion's Head, land near the Glen Country Club and then sink a cocktail at Camps Bay. This is one of several outfits through whom novices can arrange a tandem paraglide with an experienced flyer. Make enquiries on your first day in Cape Town as the weather conditions have to be right.

Hopper   SCENIC FLIGHT
(Map p56; ☏021-419 8951; www.thehopper.co.za; Shop 6, Quay 5; R600; 🅿; 🚌Waterfront) Single bookings are accepted for this helicopter operation with tours starting from a 15-minute flight over either Sandy Bay or out to the Twelve Apostles.

HIKING IN TABLE MOUNTAIN NATIONAL PARK

Covering some three-quarters of the peninsula, **Table Mountain National Park** (www .sanparks.org/parks/table_mountain), stretching from flat-topped Table Mountain to Cape Point, is criss-crossed by a myriad hiking routes, ranging from easy strolls to extreme rock climbing. Entrance fees have to be paid for the Boulders, Cape of Good Hope, Ouderkraal, Silvermine and Tokai sections of the park, but otherwise the routes are free. Signage is far from comprehensive and even with a map it's easy to get lost; follow our safety tips (p63) and consider hiring a guide.

Platteklip Gorge, the most straightforward route up the mountain, takes around two hours and is steep and fully exposed to the sun. Less of a slog is the **Pipe Track** but following it takes roughly double the time. Climbing **Lion's Head** and the walk from the upper cableway station to **Maclear's Beacon**, the highest point of the mountain, are both easily achievable in around an hour.

There are two popular routes up the mountain from Kirstenbosch Botanical Gardens along either **Skeleton Gorge** (which involves negotiating some sections with chains) or **Nursery Ravine**. Both can be done in three hours by someone of moderate fitness. The trails are well marked, and steep in places, but the way to the gardens from the cableway and vice versa is not signposted.

Possibilities for overnight hikes include the two-day/one-night, 33.8km **Cape of Good Hope Trail** and the five-day, four-night, 80km **Hoerikwaggo Trail** running the full length of the peninsula from Cape Point to the upper cableway station. The former has to be booked and includes accommodation; the latter can be done freely. Bookings for the beautifully designed tented camps along the trail can be made online (www .sanparks.org/parks/table_mountain/tourism/accommodation.php#tented) or by phone (☎021-422 2816) between 7.30am and 4pm Monday to Friday.

Huey Helicopter Co SCENIC FLIGHT
(☎021-419 4839; www.thehueyhelicopterco.co.za; East Pier Rd, Waterfront; flights from R2200; P; ⛴Waterfront) To add to the exhilaration, this ex–Vietnam US Marine Corps Huey chopper, which takes off from the Waterfront, flies with open doors for that authentic *Apocalypse Now* experience. Standard tours last 20 minutes and take you down towards Hout Bay and back; the one long tour gets you down to Cape Point.

Golf

There are scores of superb courses on and around the Cape and many welcome visitors (but you should book). Contact the **Western Province Golf Union** (www.wpgu.co.za) for more details of fees etc.

Metropolitan Golf Club GOLF
(Map p56; ☎021-430 6011; metropolitangolfclub. co.za/index.php; Fritz Sonnenberg Rd, Mouille Point; P; ⛴Stadium) The wind-sheltered position between Cape Town Stadium and Green Point Park, with Signal Hill in the background, can't be beat.

Mowbray Golf Club GOLF
(☎021-685 3018; www.mowbraygolfclub.co.za; 1 Raapenberg Rd, Mowbray; P) Considered by some to be the best in-town course for its rural setting and abundant birdlife. It certainly has a lovely view of Devil's Peak.

Logical Golf Academy GOLF
(Map p64; ☎021-448 6358; www.logicalgolf.co.za; River Club, Liesbeek Parkway, ⛴Observatory) Behind the River Club is this driving range and golf school where you can perfect your swing. A 90-minute lesson is R550.

Hiking & Rock Climbing

The mountainous spine of the Cape Peninsula is a hiker's and rock climber's paradise, but it's not without its dangers, chief of which is the capricious weather conditions. Numerous books and maps give details, including Mike Lundy's *Best Walks in the Cape Peninsula* (www.hikecapetown.co.za) but to get the best out of the mountains hire a local guide.

City Rock ROCK CLIMBING
(Map p64; ☎021-447 1326; www.cityrock.co.za; cnr Collingwood & Anson Rds, Observatory; ⊙9am-9pm Mon-Thu, 9am-6pm Fri, 10am-6pm Sat & Sun; ⛴Observatory) This popular indoor climbing gym offers climbing courses (from R190), and hires out and sells climbing gear. A day pass for the climbing wall is R85.

Mountain Club of South Africa
ROCK CLIMBING

(Map p52; ☎021-465 3412; http://mcsacapetown .co.za; 97 Hatfield St; 🚇Government Avenue) This club, which can recommend guides to serious climbers, also has a climbing wall (R5); call to check on opening times for the public.

Venture Forth
HIKING

(☎021-554 3225, 086 110 6548; www.ventureforth .co.za) Excellent guided hikes and rock climbs with enthusiastic, savvy guides. Outings (around R500 per person) are tailored to individual requirements and aim to get you off the beaten track.

Walk in Africa
HIKING

(☎021-785 2264; http://walkinafrica.com) Steve Bolnick, an experienced and passionate safari and mountain guide, runs this company. Its flagship hike is the five-day, four-night Mountain in the Sea trail (R14,000 per person) that runs from Platteklip Gorge to Cape Point, partly following the Hoerikwaggo Trail.

Horse Riding

Sleepy Hollow Horse Riding
HORSE RIDING

(☎021-789 2341, 083 261 0104; www.sleepyhollow horseriding.co.za; Sleepy Hollow Ln, Noordhoek) This reliable operation can arrange horse riding along the wide, sandy Noordhoek beach, as well as in the mountainous hinterland.

Kayaking, Surfing & Sandboarding

For the daily surf report check www.waves cape.co.za. If you don't want to get wet, there's sandboarding, which is like snowboarding except on sand dunes.

Boardroom Adventure Centre
KAYAKING, SURFING

(☎021-790 8132; 072-763 4486; www.theboard roomadventures.co.za; 37 Victoria Rd, Hout Bay; kayaking/surf lessons from R350) Kayaking out to Duiker Island or around Hout Bay and various surfing trips are offered by the guys at this surf gear rental shop. It also has bikes for rent (per hour/day R50/160).

Sea Kayak Simon's Town
KAYAKING

(☎082 501 8930; www.kayakcapetown.co.za; 62 St Georges St, Simon's Town; 🚇Simon's Town) Paddle out to the penguins at Boulders (R250) with this Simon's Town–based operation. It also offers a variety of other tours, including one to Cape Point (R950).

Sunscene Outdoor Adventures
SANDBOARDING, SURFING

(☎021-783 0203, 084 352 4925; http://sunscene.co .za; Cape Farm House, cnr M65 & M66, Redhill) As well as offering sandboarding lessons at Atlantis (R395), with expert guides and refreshments (essential!) included, it also runs traditional surfing courses and a host of other adrenaline-pumping activities for adults and kids.

Gary's Surf School
SANDBOARDING, SURFING

(☎021-788 9839; www.garysurf.co.za; Surfer's Corner, Beach Rd, Muizenberg; ⊙8.30am-5pm; 🚇Muizenberg) If genial surfing coach Gary Kleynhans can't get you to stand on a board

---

SAFE HIKING TIPS

» Hike with long trousers. Much of the *fynbos* ('fine bush', proteas, heaths and ericas) is tough and scratchy. There's also the seriously nasty blister bush (its leaves look like those of continental parsley); if you brush against this plant cover the spot immediately; exposure to sunlight activates the plant's toxins, which can leave blisters on your skin that may refuse to heal for years.

» Tell someone the route you're planning to climb and take a map (or better still, a guide).

» Stick to well-used paths and don't be tempted to take shortcuts.

» Take plenty of water and some food.

» Take weatherproof clothing – the weather can change for the worse with lightning speed.

» Wear proper hiking boots or shoes and a sun hat.

» Take a fully charged mobile phone, if you have one.

» Don't climb alone – the park recommends going in groups of four.

» Don't leave litter on the mountain.

» Don't make a fire on the mountain – they're banned.

Observatory

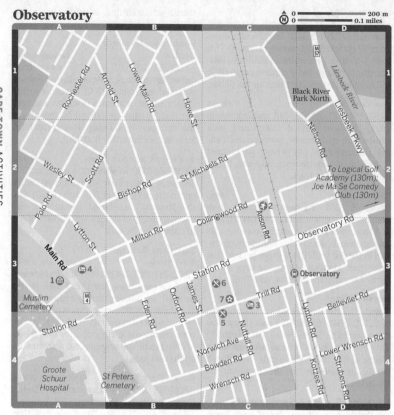

within a day, you don't pay for the two-hour lesson (R500). His shop, the focus of Muizenberg's surf scene, hires out boards and wetsuits (per hour/day R100/300). It also runs sandboarding trips to the dunes at Kommetjie (R300).

Skydiving

Skydive Cape Town   SKYDIVING
(☎082-800 6290; www.skydivecapetown.za.net; R27/West Coast Rd; R1500) Based about 20km north of the city centre in Melkboshstrand, this experienced outfit offers tandem skydives, with spectacular views.

Swimming

If you want to swim safely in the sea, Sea Point has a couple of rock pools, although the water here will be freezing. The sea on the False Bay side of the peninsula is usually a little warmer; try the beaches and rock pools at Muizenberg, St James, Kalk Bay of Buffels Bay at Cape Point.

Sea Point Pavilion   SWIMMING
(Map p60; Beach Rd, Sea Point; adult/child R16/7.50; ☺7am-7pm Oct-Apr, 9am-5pm May-Sep) This huge outdoor pool complex is a Sea Point institution and has some lovely art-deco decoration. It gets very busy on hot summer days, not surprisingly, since the pools are always at least 10°C warmer than the always-frigid ocean.

Long Street Baths   SWIMMING
(Map p48;cnr Long & Buitensingel Sts; adult/child R13/7.50; ☺7am-7pm; ☐Buitensingel) Dating from 1906, these nicely restored baths, featuring painted murals of city-centre life, are heated and very popular with the local community. The separate Turkish steam baths (R42) are a great way to sweat away some time, especially during the cooler months. Women are admitted 9am to 6pm Monday, Thursday and Saturday, and 9am to 1pm Tuesday; men 1pm to 7pm Tuesday, 8am to 7pm Wednesday and Friday, and 8am to noon Sunday.

Observatory

Sights
1 Cape Town Science Centre A3

Activities, Courses & Tours
2 City Rock C2

Sleeping
3 33 South Boutique
    Backpackers.................................... C3
4 Green Elephant A3

Eating
5 Café Ganesh C4
6 Hello Sailor C3

Entertainment
7 Tagore C3

Windsurfing & Kite-Surfing

Windswept   WINDSURFING, KITE-SURFING
(☑082 961 3070; www.windswept.co.za) Philip Baker runs windsurfing and kite-surfing camps out of his base in Bloubergstrand, 25km north of the city. Two-hour group lessons are R495 (R990 for individuals), or if you know the ropes you can hire a kite and board for R395. Packages including accommodation are available.

Driving

Chapman's Peak Drive   DRIVING
(Map p44; www.chapmanspeakdrive.co.za; Chapman's Peak Dr; cars/motorcycles R31/20; P) Whether you choose to drive, pedal or walk along 'Chappies', a 5km toll road linking Hout Bay with Noordhoek, take your time as it's one of the most spectacular stretches of coastal road in the world. There are picnic spots to admire the views. If you don't plan to go all the way to Noordhoek, ask for a free day pass as you enter at the Hout Bay end (where the toll booths are) to allow you to drive out to the viewpoint that overlooks the bay.

Tours

Cape Town Tourism should be your first stop to find out about all the many tours on offer in and around the city. Our top picks include the following:

City Sightseeing Cape Town   BUS TOUR
(☑021-511 6000; www.citysightseeing.co.za; adult/child 1 day R140/70, 2 day R250/150) These hop-on, hop-off buses, running two routes, are perfect for a quick orientation, with commentary available in 16 languages. Also the open-top double-deckers provide elevated platform for photos. Buses run at roughly half-hourly intervals between 9am and 4.30pm with extra services in peak season. City Sightseeing also offers a canal cruise (R20) with five stops between the Waterfront and the Cape Town International Convention Centre.

Coffeebeans Routes   CULTURAL TOUR
(☑021-424 3572; www.coffeebeansroutes.com; tours R650) The concept – hooking up visitors with interesting local personalities, including musicians, artists and gardeners – is fantastic. Among innovative programs is its Friday-night reggae safari trip to Marcus Garvey, a Rastafarian settlement in Philippi, for a night.

Awol Tours   CYCLING TOUR
(☑021 4183803, 083 234 6428; www.awoltours.co.za; Information Centre, Dock Rd, V&A Waterfront) Discover Cape Town's cycle lanes on this superb city bike tour (R300, three hours, daily) from Awol's Waterfront base. Other pedalling itineraries including the winelands, Cape Point and the township of Masiphumelele – a great alternative to traditional township tours. They also offer guided hikes on Table Mountain (R950).

Sex and Slaves in the City   WALKING TOUR
(☑021-785 2264; www.capetownwalks.com; tour R150) Learn about the contribution of slaves to Cape Town's history on this hilarious, actor-led, two-hour tour around the city centre. The same company also arranges literary themed walks on Long St with a local author and hikes on Table Mountain.

Uthando   TOWNSHIP TOUR
(☑021-683 8523; www.uthandosa.org; R650) The extra cost of these township tours is because half the money goes towards the fantastic range of social upliftment projects that the tours visit and are specifically designed to support. Usually four or so projects are visited and could be anything from an organic farm to an old folks' centre.

Good Hope Adventures   WALKING TOUR
(☑021-510 7517; http://goodhopeadventures.com; 3- to 5-hour tours R250-500) Go underground on these fascinating walking tours like no other, as you explore the historic tunnels and canals that run beneath the city. Not for

TOURING THE CAPE FLATS

The down-at-heel coloured communities and informal settlements (ie shacks) of the largely black townships would seem to be unlikely as tourist destinations. However, a visit to the Cape Flats might end up providing your fondest memories of Cape Town, particularly if you choose to spend a night in one of the B&Bs that are found there.

Close to the city, Langa, founded in 1927, is the oldest planned township in South Africa and has areas of affluence as well as poverty – a pattern repeated in the other main townships of Guguletu and Khayelitsha (the largest with an estimated population of over 1.5 million). It's not all one-note misery. The infrastructure in the townships has improved since 1994 (it could hardly have got any worse), with the rows of concrete Reconstruction and Development Programme (RDP) houses being the most visible examples.

In Langa don't miss the brilliantly decorated Guga S'Thebe Arts & Cultural Centre (cnr Washington & Church Sts, Langa; ⊘8am-4.30pm Mon-Fri, 8.30am-2pm Sat & Sun). In Guguletu, on the corner of NY1 and NY111 the Guguletu Seven Memorial commemorates seven young black activists who were killed by the police here in 1986. Nearby is the Amy Biehl Memorial, celebrating the life of the US anti-apartheid activist who died under tragic circumstances in Guguletu in 1993, and a mosaic-covered bench, one in a series around Cape Town installed by Rock Girl (www.rockgirlsa.org) as part of a project to create safe spaces for girls and women.

If you take public transport into the townships, make sure you have a local meet you at the other end. More convenient for most visitors are township tours. The half-day itineraries of most tours are similar, often including a visit to the District Six Museum, then being driven to visit some of the main townships. Tour guides are generally flexible in where they go, and respond to the wishes of the group.

the claustrophobic; you'll need to be wearing old shoes and clothes and have a torch.

Andulela CULTURAL TOUR
(☑021-790 2592; www.andulela.com) Offers a variety of cultural, culinary and wildlife themed tours.

Hout Bay Harbour Tours BOAT TOUR
(Harbour Rd, Hout Bay) Although partly given over to tourism, Hout Bay's harbour still functions, and the southern arm of the bay is an important fishing port and processing centre. The best thing you can do here is board a cruise to Duiker Island (also known as Seal Island because of its large colony of Cape fur seals, but not to be confused with the official Seal Island in False Bay). Circe Launches (☑021-790 1040; www.circelaunches. co.za; adult/child R45/18), Drumbeat Charters (☑021-791 4441; www.drumbeatcharters. co.za; adult/child R65/25) and Nauticat Charters (☑021-790 7278; www.nauticatcharters. co.za; adult/child R60/30) run near-identical cruises, lasting between 40 minutes and an hour, usually with guaranteed sailings in the mornings.

Simon's Town Boat Company BOAT TOUR
(☑021-786 2136; www.boatcompany.co.za; The Town Pier, Simon's Town; harbour cruise adult/child R40/20; ⓡSimon's Town) This company runs the popular *Spirit of Just Nuisance* cruise around Simon's Town harbour, as well as longer boat trips to Cape Point (adult/child R350/200) and Seal Island (adult/child R250/150). During the whale-watching season it also offers cruises that allow you to get up close to these magnificent animals.

✱ Festivals & Events

For a full rundown of festivals and events check Cape Town Tourism (www.capetown .travel/visitors).

January

Cape Town Minstrel Carnival CULTURAL
(www.capetown-minstrels.co.za) *Tweede Nuwe Jaar*, on 2 January, is when the satin- and sequin-clad minstrel troupes traditionally march through the city for the Kaapse Klopse (Cape Minstrel Festival) from Keizergracht St, along Adderley and Wale Sts to the Bo-Kaap. Throughout January into early

February there are Saturday competitions between troupes at Athlone Stadium.

J&B Met   SPORT
(www.jbmet.co.za) At Kenilworth Race Course, South Africa's richest horse race, with a jackpot of R1.5 million, is a time for big bets and even bigger hats. Generally held on the last Saturday in January.

February & March

Design Indaba   DESIGN
(www.designindaba.com) This creative convention, bringing together the varied worlds of fashion, architecture, visual arts, crafts and media, is held at the end of February and early March, usually at the Cape Town International Convention Centre.

Infecting the City   ARTS
(www.infecting-the-city.com) Cape Town's wonderful squares, fountains, museums and theatres are the venues for this innovative end-of-February performing-arts festival featuring artists from across the continent.

Cape Argus Cycle Tour   SPORT
(www.cycletour.co.za) Held on a Saturday in the middle of March, this is the world's largest timed cycling event, attracting more than 30,000 contestants. The route circles Table Mountain, heading down the Atlantic Coast and along Chapman's Peak Dr.

Cape Town International
Jazz Festival   MUSIC
(www.capetownjazzfest.com) Cape Town's biggest jazz event, attracting big names from both South Africa and overseas, is usually held at the Cape Town International Convention Centre at the end of March. It includes a free concert in Greenmarket Sq.

April

Just Nuisance Great Dane
Parade   CULTURAL
(www.simonstown.com/tourism/nuisance/nuisance.htm) On 1 April a dog parade is held through Jubilee Sq in Simon's Town to commemorate Able Seaman Just Nuisance, the Great Dane who was a mascot of the Royal Navy during WWII.

Old Mutual Two Oceans Marathon   SPORTS
(www.twooceansmarathon.org.za) This 56km marathon follows a similar route to the Pick 'n' Pay Cycle Tour around Table Mountain. It generally attracts about 9000 competitors.

July

Cape Town Fashion Week   FASHION
(www.afisa.co.za) Fashionistas line the catwalks to spot the hottest local designers' work and pick up on the latest trends.

September & October

Nando's Comedy Festival   COMEDY
(www.comedyfestival.co.za/main_arena.php) Catch some of South Africa's top comedians at this festival held at a range of venues across the city including the Baxter Theatre.

Outsurance Gun Run   SPORT
(www.outsurance.co.za/gunrun) This popular half-marathon (21km) is the only time that the Noon Gun on Signal Hill gets fired on a Sunday – competitors try to finish the race before the gun goes off.

HARBOUR CRUISES

See Table Mountain as mariners of yore did on a cruise into Table Bay. The Waterfront has a host of operators, among them:

Waterfront Boat Company (Map p56; ☎021-418 5806; www.waterfrontboats.co.za; Shop 5, Quay 5) Its cruises include highly recommended 1½-hour sunset cruises (R220) on the handsome wood-and-brass-fitted schooners *Spirit of Victoria* and *Esperance*. A jet-boat ride is R500 per hour.

Yacoob Tourism (Map p56; ☎021-421 0909; www.ytourism.co.za; Shop 8, Quay 5) Among the several boat trips that this company runs are the *Jolly Roger Pirate Boat* (adult/child from R100/50) and *Tommy the Tugboat* (adult/child R50/25), both perfect for families. Adults may prefer the *Adrenalin* speed-boat jaunts or a cruise on the catamarans *Ameera* and *Tigress*.

Cape Charters (☎021-418 0782; www.capecharters.co.za) This company can arrange fishing trips as well as luxury cruises and small boat trips around the harbour.

November & December

Kirstenbosch Summer Sunset Concerts
MUSIC

(www.oldmutual.co.za/music) The start of the Sunday afternoon outdoor concerts at Kirstenbosch Botanical Gardens, which run through until April. Bring a blanket and a picnic and join the crowds enjoying anything from arias performed by local divas to a funky jazz combo. There's always a special concert for New Year's Eve, too.

Obs Arts Festival
ARTS

(http://obsarts.org.za) South Africa's biggest street festival takes over the suburb of Observatory on the first weekend of December.

Adderely Street Christmas Lights
MUSIC

Join the tens of thousands who turn out for the concert in front of Cape Town Railway station followed by a parade along festively illuminated Adderley St. The same street is pedestrianised each night from around 17 to 30 December for a night market also with live music.

Sleeping

Lively hostels, characterful guesthouses or unfettered luxury: Cape Town's accommodation choices tick all boxes. If beaches are your thing, then choose accommodation along the Atlantic or False Bay Coast. If you have transport, then anywhere is OK, but do enquire about the parking options when making a booking and check whether there's a charge (anything from R30 to R70 per day for city-centre hotels).

Advance booking is recommended, especially from mid-December to the end of January, and at Easter – prices can double and many places are fully booked. We quote high-season rates following, which cover the peak Christmas and New Year period. Hostels typically don't include breakfast; for other properties, unless otherwise mentioned rates also include breakfast. Budget places are ones with a double room for under R650; midrange places charge R650 to R2500; and top-end ones are over R2500.

Apartment & House Rentals

For longer-term stays or self-catering options a serviced apartment or villa can work out as a good deal. Cape Breaks (☏083 383 4888; http://capebreaks.co.za) offers a range of attractively decorated studios and apartments in St Martini Gardens (Map p48) beside the Company's Gardens. Cape Stay (www.capestay.co.za) offers accommodation across the Cape, while Cape Town Budget Accommodation (☏021-447 4398; www.capetownbudgetaccommodation.co.za) has units in Woodstock from R270 per night. In Awe Stays (☏083 658 6975; www.inawestays.co.za) has a lovely collection of stylish studios and cottages in Gardens and Fresnaye from R750 per night for a double. Village & Life (Map p48; ☏021-430 4444; www.villageandlife.com; 1 Loader St, De Waterkant) is focused mainly on properties in De Waterkant and Camp's Bay.

CITY BOWL & BO-KAAP

TOP CHOICE Dutch Manor
BOUTIQUE HOTEL $$

(Map p48; ☏021-422 4767; www.dutchmanor.co.za; 158 Buitengracht St; s/d R1200/1700; ❋☎; ⬚Bloem) Four-poster beds, giant armoires and creaking floorboards lend terrific atmosphere to this six-room property crafted from an 1812 building. Although it overlooks busy

---

JOIN THE MERRY MINSTRELS

The riotous Cape Town Minstrel Carnival, also known in Afrikaans as the Kaapse Klopse, is the Mother City's equivalent of Rio's Mardi Gras parade – a noisy, joyous and disorganised affair with practically every colour of satin, sequin and glitter used in the costumes of the marching troupes, which can number more than 1000 members.

Although the festival dates back to the early colonial times when slaves enjoyed a day of freedom the day after New Year, the look of today's carnival was inspired by visiting American minstrels in the late 19th century, hence the face make-up, colourful costumes and ribald song-and-dance routines. The vast majority of participants come from the coloured community.

Despite the carnival being a permanent fixture on Cape Town's calendar, it has had a controversial history with problems over funding and clashes between rival carnival organisations. It has also always been something of a demonstration of coloured people power: whites who came to watch the parade in apartheid times would risk having their faces blacked up with boot polish.

Buitengracht the noise is largely kept at bay thanks to modern renovations.

Cape Heritage Hotel
BOUTIQUE HOTEL $$

(Map p48; ☑021-424 4646; www.capeheritage.co.za; 90 Bree St; d/ste from R2260/3020, parking R55; P✳@; ☐Longmarket) Each room at this elegant boutique hotel, part of the Heritage Sq redevelopment of 18th-century buildings, has its own character. Some have four-poster beds and all have modern conveniences such as satellite TV and clothes presses.

Taj Cape Town
LUXURY HOTEL $$$

(Map p48; ☑021-819 2000; www.tajhotels.com; Wale St; s/d/ste from R5500/5700/11,000; P✳@🛜☒; ☐Dorp) India's luxury hotel group has breathed brilliant new life into the old Board of Executors building. A new tower houses the chic contemporary-styled rooms, many of which offer spectacular views of Table Mountain. Service and facilities, including the excellent Bombay Brasserie restaurant, are top grade.

Grand Daddy Hotel
DESIGN HOTEL $$

(Map p48; ☑021-424 7247; www.granddaddy.co.za; 38 Long St; r or trailer R1750, parking per day R30; P✳@🛜; ☐Castle) The Grand Daddy's star attraction is its roof-top trailer park of penthouse suites made from seven vintage Airstream trailers decorated by different artists and designers, in wacky themes. The regular rooms are also stylish and incorporate playful references to South African culture.

Daddy Long Legs Hotel
BOUTIQUE HOTEL $$

(Map p48; ☑021-422 3074; www.daddylonglegs.co.za; 134 Long St; r/apt from R735/830; ✳@🛜; ☐Dorp) A stay at this boutique hotel–cum–art installation is anything but boring. Thirteen artists were given free rein to design the boudoirs of their dreams. The results range from a bohemian garret to a hospital ward! It also offers superstylish apartments (263 Long St), an ideal choice if you crave hotel-suite luxury and want to self-cater.

Rouge on Rose
BOUTIQUE HOTEL $$

(Map p48; ☑021-426 0298; www.rougeonrose.co.za; 25 Rose St; s/d R900/1200; ✳🛜; ☐Longmarket) Rustically chic rooms including suites (for no extra charge) with kitchenettes, lounges and lots of workspace. The fun wall paintings are by a resident artist and all rooms have luxurious open bath spaces with stand-alone tubs.

La Rose B&B
B&B $$

(Map p48; ☑021-422 5883; www.larosecapetown.com; 32 Rose St; s/d from R500/650; P✳🛜; ☐Longmarket) Adheena and Yoann are the very welcoming South African–French couple running this charming B&B, which is beautifully decorated and has a rooftop garden with the best views of the area.

Scalabrini Guest House
HOSTEL $

(Map p48; ☑021-465 6433; www.scalabrini.org.za; 47 Commercial St; dm/s/d or tw R180/300/480; 🛜) Above a soup kitchen and social programmers run by a charity, this pleasant guesthouse has 11 immaculately clean en-suite rooms, plus a great kitchen for self-catering in which you can watch satellite TV.

Long Street Backpackers
HOSTEL $

(Map p48; ☑021-423 0615; www.longstreetbackpackers.co.za; 209 Long St; dm/s/d R120/220/330; 🛜; ☐Bloem) Little has changed at this backpackers since it opened in 1993 (making it the longest running of the many that dot Long St). In a block of 14 small flats, with four beds and a bathroom in each, accommodation is arranged around a leafy, courtyard decorated with funky mosaics.

Penthouse on Long
HOSTEL $

(Map p48; ☑021-424 8356; www.penthouseonlong.com; 6th fl, 112 Long St; d R500, dm/d without bathroom from R140/450; ✳@🛜; ☐Dorp) High above Long, this backpackers does amazing things with what was formerly office space. The cheapest dorm has 22 beds. Private rooms have colourful themes such as Hollywood, the Orient or Moroccan nights. In the rafters is a spacious bar and lounge.

GARDENS & SURROUNDS

TOP CHOICE Mannabay
BOUTIQUE HOTEL $$

(Map p52; ☑021-461 1094; www.mannabay.com; 1 Denholm Rd, Oranjezicht; r/ste from R1425/4000; P✳@🛜☒) This gorgeous luxury property offers seven guest rooms, each uniquely decorated with different themes. It's just far enough up the mountain to provide great views, but not so far that it's a slog home should you walk.

Backpack
HOSTEL $$

(Map p52; ☑021-423 4530; www.backpackers.co.za; 74 New Church St, Tamboerskloof; s/d R550/750, dm/s/d without bathroom R160/500/650, parking per day R20; P@🛜☒; ☐Buitensingel) This 'boutique backpackers' offers affordable style, a buzzy vibe and fantastic staff. Its dorms may not be Cape Town's cheapest but they're among its nicest, while the private rooms are charmingly decorated. There's a lovely mosaic-decorated pool and relaxing gardens with Table Mountain views. Rates are room only.

Mount Nelson Hotel
LUXURY HOTEL **$$$**

(Map p52; ☑021-483 1000; www.mountnelson.co.za; 76 Orange St, Gardens; r/ste from R3595/5395; P❀@🛜⛱; ⛟Government Avenue) The sugar-pink painted 'Nellie' recalls Cape Town's colonial era with its chintz decor and doormen dressed in pith helmets. Recently renovated rooms sport elegant silver and mossy green decorations.

Hippo Boutique Hotel
BOUTIQUE HOTEL **$$**

(Map p52; ☑021-423 2500; www.hippotique.co.za; 5-9 Park Rd, Gardens; d/ste R1290/2200; P❀@🛜⛱; ⛟Michaelis) Brilliantly located and appealing boutique property offering spacious, stylish rooms each with a small kitchen for self-catering. Larger suites, with mezzanine-level bedrooms and arty themes such as Red Bull and Mini Cooper, are worth the extra spend.

Ashanti Gardens
HOSTEL **$**

(Map p52; ☑021-423 8721; www.ashanti.co.za; 11 Hof St, Gardens; d R640, dm/s/d without bathroom R150/320/460; P@🛜⛱; ⛟Government Avenue) One of Cape Town's slickest backpackers, with much of the action focused on its lively bar and deck, which overlooks Table Mountain. The beautiful old house, newly decorated with a tasteful collection of local contemporary art, holds the dorms and a lawn on which you can camp (R80 per person). There are excellent self-catering en-suite rooms in two separate heritage-listed houses around the corner. Rates are room only.

Cape Cadogan
BOUTIQUE HOTEL **$$$**

(Map p52; ☑021-480 8080; www.capecadogan.com; 5 Upper Union St, Gardens; s/d/apt from R1330/2660/2670; P@🛜⛱; ⛟Michaelis) This *Gone with the Wind*–style heritage-listed villa presents a very classy boutique operation with some rooms opening on to the secluded courtyard. If you'd prefer more privacy, it also offers appealing one- and two-bed self-catering apartments in the mews of nearby Nicol St.

Cactusberry Lodge
B&B **$$**

(Map p52; ☑021-461 9787; www.cactusberrylodge.com; 30 Breda St, Oranjezicht; s/d from R640/1050; P🛜⛱) There are just six rooms at this red-wine-coloured lodge with a striking con-

---

CAPE TOWN FOR CHILDREN

Cape Town, with its beaches and fun attractions such as the **Two Oceans Aquarium**, is a great place for a family vacation.

Among other animal-spotting opportunities are the seals at the **Waterfront**, which can usually be seen behind the aquarium; those crowd pleasers – the penguins – at **Boulders**; and thousands of birds and monkeys at **World of Birds**. Camel rides are on offer at **Imhoff Farm** (www.imhofffarm.co.za; Kommetjie Rd, Kommetjie; admission free; ⏲10am-5pm Tue-Sun; P) where you'll also find a snake and reptile park.

The **Planetarium** screens a kids' star show daily, and there are plenty of other displays to grab the attention of inquisitive children at the attached **South African Museum**.

North of the city centre you'll find the amusement park **Ratanga Junction** (www.ratanga.co.za; Century Boulevard, Century City; adult/child R152/75; ⏲10am-5pm Sat & Sun Jan-Mar, daily in school holidays; P). A more educational, but no less fun alternative is the **Cape Town Science Centre** (Map p64; ☑021-300 3200; www.ctsc.org.za; 370B Main Rd, Observatory; admission R40; ⏲9am-4.30pm; P; ⛟Observatory).

At the beach, parents should watch out for rough surf (not to mention hypothermia-inducing water temperatures!); **Muizenberg beach** on a warm, calm day is the best bet as is the rock pool at neighbouring **St James**. The **Sea Point Pavilion** has a great family swimming pool that is significantly warmer than the surrounding ocean.

There are two inventively designed playgrounds at **Green Point Park**, plus educational gardens of native plants. Nearby **Moullie Point** has a big play area, toy train, maze and golf putting course.

For other ideas, including kid-friendly cafes, restaurants and shops, check out **Cape Town Kids** (www.capetownkids.co.za).

temporary design, mixing arty photography, African crafts and Euro style. Its sun deck overlooks Table Mountain and there's a tiny splash pool in the courtyard to cool down in.

GREEN POINT & WATERFRONT

Cape Grace
LUXURY HOTEL $$$

(Map p56; ☑021-410 7100; www.capegrace.com; West Quay; s/d or tw from R5290/5450, ste s/d from R10,680/10,840; P✷@☎; ☐Breakwater) An arty combination of antiques and crafts decoration – including hand-painted bed covers and curtains – provides a unique sense of place and Cape Town's history at this lovely luxury hotel. It also has a good spa and a private yacht should you wish to sail out into the bay.

One & Only Cape Town
LUXURY HOTEL $$$

(Map p56; ☑021-431 5888; www.oneandonly capetown.com; Dock Rd, V&A Watefront; r/ste from R5990/11,940; P✷@☎; ☐Breakwater) Take your pick between enormous, plush rooms in the main building (with panoramic views of Table Mountain) or the even more exclusive island, beside the pool and spa. The bar turns out inventive cocktails and is a nice place to plonk yourself before a meal at celeb-chef restaurants Nobu or Reuben's.

Villa Zest
BOUTIQUE HOTEL $$

(Map p56; ☑021-433 1246; www.villazest.co.za; 2 Braemar Rd, Green Point; s/d R1390/1690, ste s/d R2290/2590; P✷@) This Bauhaus-style villa has been converted into a quirkily decorated boutique hotel that wittily avoids the clichés of the genre. The seven guest rooms have bold retro-design furniture and wallpaper-covered walls accented with furry pillows and shagpile rugs.

Cape Standard
BOUTIQUE HOTEL $$

(Map p56; ☑021-430 3060; www.capestandard .co.za; 3 Romney Rd, Green Point; s/d with breakfast R1050/1380; P@☎) This hidden-away gem offers whitewashed beach-house-style rooms downstairs or contemporary-style rooms upstairs. The mosaic-tiled bathrooms have showers big enough to dance in.

Atlantic Point Backpackers
HOSTEL $$

(Map p56; ☑021-433 1663; www.atlanticpoint .co.za; 2 Cavalcade Rd, Green Point; d R660, dm/d without bathroom from R140/495; P@☎) This imaginatively designed, playful and well-run place steps away from Green Point's main drag. Features include a big balcony and bar and the loft lounge covered in astro turf.

Rates include a basic breakfast, wi-fi and parking – all of which make it extra good value.

Ashanti Green Point
HOSTEL $

(Map p56; ☑021-433 1619; www.ashanti.co.za; 23 Antrim Rd, Three Anchor Bay; d R600, dm/s/d without bathroom R130/320/460; P@☎) More chilled than its original Gardens branch, this Ashanti has a breezy hillside position with sea views and is nicely decorated with old Cape Town photos. Rates are room only.

ATLANTIC COAST & HOUT BAY

TOP CHOICE POD
BOUTIQUE HOTEL $$$

(Map p60; ☑021-438 8550; www.pod.co.za; 3 Argyle Rd, Camps Bay; r/ste from R2700/7100; P✷@☎) Lovers of clean contemporary design will adore the slate- and wood-decorated POD which is perfectly angled to catch the Camps Bay action from its bar and spacious pool deck area. The cheapest rooms have mountain rather than sea views; luxury rooms have their own private plunge pools.

Camps Bay Retreat
BOUTIQUE HOTEL $$$

(Map p60; ☑021-437 8300; www.campsbayretreat .com; 7 Chilworth Rd, The Glen; d/ste from R4380/6700; P✷@☎) Set in a secluded nature reserve, there is a choice of 15 rooms in either the 1929 main house or the contemporary Deck House, reached by a rope bridge over a ravine. Take your pick from three pools, including one fed by a stream from Table Mountain.

O on Kloof
HOTEL $$

(Map p60; ☑021-439 2081; www.oonkloof.co.za; 92 Kloof Rd, Sea Point; d/ste from R2130/3950; P✷@☎) Cross the minibridge over the ornamental pool leading to this gorgeous contemporary-styled guesthouse. Not all of the eight spacious rooms have full sea views but the good facilities, including a big indoor pool and gym, are ample compensation.

Glen Boutique Hotel
HOTEL $$

(Map p60; ☑021-439 0086; www.glenhotel.co.za; 3 The Glen, Sea Point; d/ste from R1450/3250; P✷@☎) One of Cape Town's premier gay-friendly boutique hotels occupies an elegant old house and a newer block behind. Spacious rooms are decorated in natural tones of stone and wood. In the middle is a fabulous pool and spa, the playground for the monthly Saturday-afternoon pool parties.

Winchester Mansions Hotel
HOTEL $$

(Map p60; ☑021-434 2351; www.winchester.co.za; 221 Beach Rd, Sea Point; s/d from R1650/2125, ste s/d from R2050/2585; P❄@🛜🏊) The Winchester offers a seaside location (you'll pay extra for rooms with views), old-fashioned style and some corridors lined with putting greens for a spot of golf practice. The pool is a decent size and there's a lovely courtyard, with a central fountain, which is a romantic place to dine.

Hout Bay Manor
HOTEL $$$

(☑021-790 0116; www.houtbaymanor.co.za; Baviaanskloof Rd, Hout Bay; s/d from R2100/3200; P❄@🛜🏊) Your eyes will pop at the fab Afro-chic makeover to which the 1871 Hout Bay Manor has been treated. Tribal artefacts are mixed with brightly coloured contemporary furnishings and handicrafts in rooms that all contain the expected electronic conveniences.

Chapman's Peak Hotel
HOTEL $$$

(☑021-790 1036; www.chapmanspeakhotel.co.za; Chapman's Peak Dr, Hout Bay; s/d from R2070/2810; P❄@🛜🏊) Take your pick between chic, contemporary-designed rooms with balconies and to-die-for views across Hout Bay, or the much cheaper and smaller rooms (R660 for a mountain view, R960 for a partial sea view) in the original building, which also houses a lively bar and restaurant.

OBSERVATORY & SOUTHERN SUBURBS

Vineyard Hotel & Spa
HOTEL $$

(☑021-657 4500; www.vineyard.co.za; Colinton Rd, Newlands; s/d from R1300/1750, s/d ste from R4500/4950; P❄@🏊) The rooms at this delightful hotel have a contemporary look and are decorated in soothing natural tones. It's surrounded by lush gardens with views onto Table Mountain. Friendly staff, the fabulous Angsana Spa, a great gym and pool, and gourmet restaurant Myoga complete the picture.

Green Elephant
HOSTEL $

(Map p64; ☑021-448 6359; www.greenelephant.co.za; 57 Milton Rd, Observatory; s/d R450/550, dm/s/d without bathroom R140/350/440; P@🛜🏊; 🚆Observatory) Under new management, this long-running backpackers, split between three houses, remains a popular alternative to the city-centre hostels. Camping is possible (R80 per tent) and staff can also arrange climbs up Table Mountain with a qualified guide (R250 per person). Rates are room only but include unlimited wi-fi.

33 South Boutique Backpackers
HOSTEL $

(Map p64; ☑021-447 2423; www.33southbackpackers.com; 48 Trill Rd, Observatory; s/d R350/470, dm/s/d without bathroom from R130/300/410; @🛜; 🚆Observatory) Not exactly boutique but certainly imaginative is this cosy backpackers in a Victorian cottage, which has sought inspiration from different Cape Town suburbs as themes for its rooms. There's a delightful shared kitchen and a pretty courtyard. Staff conduct free tours of Obs. Rates are room only.

SOUTHERN PENINSULA

Bella Ev
B&B $$

(☑021-788 1293; www.bellaevguesthouse.co.za; 8 Camp Rd, Muizenberg; s/d R650/1200; @; 🚆Muizenberg) This charming guesthouse with a delightful courtyard garden could be the setting for an Agatha Christie mystery, one in which the home's owner has a penchant for all things Turkish – hence the Ottoman slippers for guests' use and the option of a Turkish-style breakfast.

Chartfield Guest House
B&B $

(☑021-788 3793; www.chartfield.co.za; 30 Gatesville Rd, Kalk Bay; s/d from R480/550; P@🛜🏊; 🚆Kalk Bay) This rambling 1920s wooden-floored guesthouse is decorated with choice pieces of contemporary local arts and crafts. There's a variety of rooms each with crisp linen, and bathrooms with a rain-style shower. It has an internet cafe (open to non-guests) and a lovely cafe-bar with a terrace and garden overlooking the harbour.

Boulders Beach Lodge
B&B $$

(☑021-786 1758; www.bouldersbeach.co.za; 4 Boulders Pl, Simon's Town; s/d/apt from R500/900/1875; P@🛜; 🚆Simon's Town) Penguins waddle right up to the doors of this smart guesthouse with rooms decorated in wicker and wood and a range of self-catering units where the rates also include breakfast. Note: penguins are not the quietest creatures so you may want to bring earplugs.

Simon's Town Backpackers
HOSTEL $

(☑021-786 1964; www.capepax.co.za; 66 St George's St, Simon's Town; dm/d R150/440, en suite d R500; @; 🚆Simon's Town) The ship-shape rooms at this relaxed backpackers are spacious with several overlooking the harbour. There is bike hire for R120 per day and the friendly staff can help you arrange a host of activities in the area. Rates are room only.

CAPE FLATS

Liziwe Guest House   B&B $
(☏021-633 7406; www.sa-venues.com/liziwe; 121 NY111, Guguletu; s/d R300/600; @) Liziwe has made her mansion into a palace with four delightful en-suite rooms all sporting satellite TV and African-themed decor. She was featured on a BBC cooking show, so you can be sure her food is delicious.

Radebe's B&B   B&B $
(☏021-695 0508, 082-393 3117; www.radebes .co.za; 23 Mama Way, Settlers Pl, Langa; s/d without bathroom R280/500; ℗@) The best of Langa's B&Bs offers three smartly decorated guest rooms (one with a private bathroom). There's a nice sitting room with TV and DVD. Enormous meals are served or you can cook for yourself in the fully equipped kitchen.

Kopanong   B&B $
(☏082 476 1278, 021-361 2084; www.kopanong -township.co.za; 329 Velani Cres, Section C, Khayelitsha; s/d R300/600; ℗) 'Mama Africa' Thope Lekau runs this excellent B&B with her equally ebullient daughter, Mpho. Her substantial brick home offers two stylishly decorated guest rooms, each with their own bathrooms. A guide and experienced development worker, Thope will give you an excellent insight into township life, as well as cook a delicious dinner (R110).

✗ Eating

Dining in the Mother City is a pleasure offering everything from fresh seafood to traditional African and Cape Malay cuisine. There are places to suit practically everyone's taste and budget, with a particularly strong selection of cafes and eat-in delis. Most restaurants are licensed but some allow you to bring your own wine for little or no corkage. Call ahead to check the restaurant's policy. Several bars and pubs serve good food, too.

There are many great places in the city to buy provisions for a picnic or to self-cater. Stock up at the major supermarkets Pick 'n' Pay and Woolworths; there are branches located all over the city, usually at the major malls. For specialist products there are excellent delis, such as Giovanni's Deli World and Melissa's.

Cafes and restaurants generally open daily, the former serving food from 7.30am to around 5pm. A few places (more usually in the City Bowl) will be closed on Sunday or occasionally Monday. Restaurant lunch service generally runs from 11.30am to 3pm, with dinner from 7pm and last orders at 10pm. Variations of more than an hour from these times are listed in the reviews.

CITY BOWL

Upper Long St has many inexpensive places to eat, plus interesting street life. Head to the Bo-Kaap to sample authentic Cape Malay dishes in unpretentious surroundings.

⌐TOP⌐ CHOICE⌐ Bizerca Bistro   FRENCH, CONTEMPORARY $$
(Map p48; ☏021-418 0001; www.bizerca.com; 15 Anton Anreith Arcade, Jetty St; mains R110-150; ▣Convention Centre) At this fantastic bistro the atmosphere is contemporary and relaxed, and the expertly prepared food is bursting with flavour. Menu items, chalked up on a blackboard, are explained at the table by the knowledgeable waiters.

Bombay Brasserie   INDIAN $$
(Map p48; ☏021-819 2000; www.tajhotels.com; Wale St; mains R150, 4 course menu R395; ⊙6-10.30pm Mon-Sat; ℗; ▣Dorp) Far from your average curry house, the Taj's darkly luxurious restaurant hung with glittering chandeliers and mirrors is a winner. Chef Harpreet Kaur's cooking is creative and delicious, the presentation spot on, as is the service.

Dear Me   CONTEMPORARY, DELI $$$
(Map p48; ☏021-422 4920; www.dearme.co.za; 165 Longmarket St; mains R100; ⊙7am-4pm Mon-Fri, 7-10pm Thu; ⚲; ▣Longmarket) High-quality ingredients, creatively combined and served by gracious staff in a pleasant playful space where pot plants dangle from the ceiling – what more could you wish for? There is a deli and bakery section, too. Book for the excellent Thursday-night **gourmet dinners** (three/five courses R210/310).

Africa Café   AFRICAN $$
(Map p48; ☏021-422 0221; www.africacafe.co.za; 108 Shortmarket St; set banquet R245; ⊙cafe 8am-4pm Mon-Fri, 10am-2pm Sat, restaurant 6.30-11pm Mon-Sat; ▣Longmarket) Touristy, yes, but still one of the best places to sample African food. Come with a hearty appetite as the set feast comprises some 15 dishes from across the continent, of which you can eat as much as you like. The new daytime cafe specialises in wheat-free baked goodies and a variety of tasty 'raw' foods including salads and cassava.

ℹ️ MORE DINING REVIEWS

For up-to-date online reviews of the Capetonian dining scene check out the following:

Rossou Restaurants (www.rossouws restaurants.com) Independent reviews and sprightly criticism of Cape Town's restaurant scene.

Eat Out (www.eatout.co.za) Online reviews and annual print magazine guide with Cape Town and Western Cape reviews.

Eat Cape Town (http://www.eatcapetown .co.za)

Once Bitten (http://oncebitten.co.za)

Jason Bakery   BAKERY, CAFE $
(Map p48; www.jasonbakery.com; 185 Bree St; mains R50; ⊙7am-3.30pm Mon-Sat; 🚌Bloem) Good luck securing a seat at this super popular street-corner cafe that makes splendid breakfasts and sandwiches as well as serving decent coffee, &Union beers and MCC bubbles by the glass and bottle. Good job that it has a takeaway counter. On Thursday and Friday nights it often stays open later for pizzas and drinks.

Addis in Cape   ETHIOPIAN $$
(Map p48; ☎021-424 5722; www.addisincape.co.za; 41 Church St; mains R75-90; ⊙noon-2.30pm & 6.30-10.30pm Mon-Sat; 🛜; 🚌Longmarket) Sit at a low basket-weave *mesob* table and enjoy tasty Ethiopian cuisine served traditionally on plate-sized *injera* (sourdough pancakes), which you rip and use to eat instead of cutlery. Also try its homemade honey wine *tej* and an authentic Ethiopian coffee.

Royale Eatery   BURGERS $$
(Map p48; www.royaleeatery.com; 279 Long St; mains R60-70; ⊙noon-11.30pm Mon-Sat; 🚌Bloem) Gourmet burgers are grilled to perfection here; downstairs is casual and buzzy while upstairs is a restaurant where you can book a table. For something different try the Big Bird ostrich burger.

Masala Dosa   INDIAN $
(Map p48; ☎021-424 6772; www.masaladosa .co.za; 167 Long St; mains R40-85; ⊙noon-4.30pm, 6-10.30pm Mon-Sat; 🚌Dorp) Bollywood chic rules at this colourful South Indian cuisine outpost serving decent *dosas* (lentil pancakes) and *thalis* (set meals with a variety of curries). Get a group of eight together and the owner will run a cooking class (R350 per person) at the weekend.

Lola's   INTERNATIONAL $
(Map p48; www.lolas.co.za; 228 Long St; mains R30-40; ⊙7am-9pm Mon-Sat, 7.30am-4pm Sun; 🛜; 🚌Bloem) Old Lola has traded her hippy veggie past for a trendier look and meatier menu. The vibe remains relaxed and the breakfasts, including sweet-corn fritters and eggs Benedict, are still good. Linger over a drink and watch Long St's passing parade.

South China Dim Sum Bar   CHINESE $
(Map p48; 289 Long St; mains R30-50; ⊙noon-3pm Tue-Fri, 6-11pm Tue-Sun; 🚌Longmarket) No frills, and service can be very slow, but the food – succulent dumplings, savoury noodles, spring rolls and homemade iced teas – is authentic and worth the wait. The decor – packing-crate stools, tattered Bruce Lee posters – has a rustic, Asian cafe charm.

BO-KAAP & DE WATERKANT

Noon Gun Tearoom & Restaurant   CAPE MALAY $$
(off Map p48; 273 Longmarket St; mains R70-100; ⊙10am-4pm, 7-10pm Mon-Sat; 🅿) High on Signal Hill, this is a fine place to sample Cape Malay dishes such as *bobotie* (curried mince pie topped with egg custard), curries and *dhaltjies* (deep-fried balls of chickpea-flour batter mixed with potato, coriander and spinach).

Anatoli   TURKISH $$
(Map p48; ☎021-419 2501; www.anatoli.co.za; 24 Napier St; meze R35-40, mains R75-120; ⊙7-10.30pm Mon-Sat) You can always rely on this atmospheric Turkish joint that's a little piece of Istanbul in Cape Town. Make a meal out of its delicious meze both hot and cold, or try the kebabs.

Loading Bay   LEBANESE $
(Map p48; ☎021-425 6320; 30 Hudson St; mains R50; ⊙7am-5pm Mon, 7am-9pm Tue-Fri, 8am-4pm Sat) Hang with De Waterkant style set at this low-key 'luxury cafe' serving Lebanese-style nibbles such as *manoushe* (flat bread) sandwiches and *spedini* (kebabs). There's an attached boutique offering menswear fashion lines from overseas labels. Make a booking for the Thursday evening burger nights – the patties, both premium beef and vegetarian, are top grade.

La Petite Tarte CAFE $

(Map p48; Shop A11, Cape Quarter, 72 Waterkant St; mains R30-50; ⊗8.30am-4.30pm Mon-Fri, 8.30am-2.30pm Sat; ℗) Fancy teas and delicious homemade, sweet and savoury French-style tarts are served at this adorable cafe on the Dixon St side of the Cape Quarter.

THE FRINGE, WOODSTOCK & OBSERVATORY

Also mark your calendar with a big red cross for Saturday's brunch fest at the Neighbourgoods Market in the Old Biscuit Mill.

TOP CHOICE **Kitchen** SANDWICHES $

(Map p76; www.karendudley.co.za; 111 Sir Lowry Road, Woodstock; sandwiches & salads R50-60; ⊗8.30am-4pm Mon-Fri; 🚊Woodstock) Over all the swanky restaurants in town, it was this little charmer that Michelle Obama chose for lunch, proving the First Lady has excellent taste. Tuck into plates of divine salads, rustic sandwiches made with love, and sweet treats with tea served from china teapots.

TOP CHOICE **Pot Luck Club & the Test Kitchen** CONTEMPORARY $$

(Map p76; ☎021-447 0804; http://thetestkitchen.co.za/info.html; Shop 104A, Old Biscuit Mill, 375 Albert Rd, Woodstock; mains R55-140, 3/5 courses R375/470; ⊗Pot Luck Club 6-10pm Tue-Sat; Test Kitchen 12.30-2.30pm & 7-10pm Tue-Sat; ℗; 🚊Woodstock) Make reservations well in advance for dinner at either of these side-by-side operations under the stewardship of top chef Luke Dale-Roberts. Pot Luck is the more affordable of the two serving delicious tapas-style plates designed to be shared; we defy you not to order a second plate of the smoked beef with truffle cafe-au-lait sauce.

Hello Sailor BISTRO $

(Map p64; ☎021-448 2420; www.hellosailorbistro.co.za; 86 Lower Main Rd, Observatory; mains R50; ⊗8.30am-11pm Mon-Fri, 9am-11pm Sat & Sun; 🚊Observatory) A slick new bistro serving comfort food – burgers, salads, pastas – all done well and affordably. The opening times refer to food; the bar here can kick on until 2am at weekends.

Charly's Bakery BAKERY, CAFE $

(Map p76; www.charlysbakery.co.za; 38 Canterbury St; baked goods R12.50-20; ⊗8am-5pm Tue-Fri, 8.30am-2pm Sat; ℗; 🚊Golden Acre Bus Terminal) The fabulous female team here make – as they say – 'mucking afazing' cupcakes and other baked goods. In a heritage building

that is as colourfully decorated as one of their cakes, the team have recently added a shop upstairs to sell cup-cake-inspired Ts, cushions, soft toys, aprons and the like.

Café Ganesh AFRO-INDIAN $

(Map p64; 38B Trill Rd, Observatory; mains R40-70; ⊗6-11.30pm Mon-Sat; 🚊Observatory) Sample pap (maize porridge) and veg, grilled springbok or lamb curry at this funky hang-out, squeezed into an alley between two buildings. Junkyard decor and matchbox-label wallpaper create that chic-shack look.

GARDENS & SURROUNDS

Kloof St offers the best dining selection in Gardens. Both the Lifestyles on Kloof and Gardens Centre malls have some pleasant cafes.

Maria's GREEK $$

(Map p52; ☎021-461 3333; Dunkley Sq, Barnet St, Gardens; mains R50-90; ⊗11am-10.30pm Mon-Fri, 5.30-10.30pm Sat; ℗; 🚊Government Avenue) There are few places as romantic or relaxing for a meal than Maria's on a warm night when you can tuck into classic Greek mezze and dishes such as moussaka on rustic tables beneath the trees in the square.

Manna Epicure CONTEMPORARY, BAKERY $$

(Map p52; ☎021-426 2413; 151 Kloof St; mains R40-110; ⊗9am-6pm Tue-Sat, 9am-4pm Sun) Come for a deliciously simple breakfast or lunch or for late-afternoon cocktails and tapas on the veranda of this white-box cafe. The freshly baked breads alone – coconut, or pecan and raisin – are worth dragging yourself up the hill for.

Aubergine CONTEMPORARY $$$

(Map p52; www.aubergine.co.za; 39 Barnet St, Gardens; mains R200, 3/4/5 courses R375/455/565; ⊗noon-2pm Wed-Fri, 5-10pm Mon-Sat; 🚊Government Avenue) Harald Bresselschmidt is one of Cape Town's most consistent chefs, producing creative yet unfussy dishes. Service and ambience are equally impeccable. It's a good pre-theatre option as from 5pm to 7pm it serves drinks and a selection of smaller dishes from the dinner menu.

Dog's Bollocks BURGERS $

(Map p52; 6 Roodehek St, Gardens; burgers R50; ⊗5-10pm Mon-Sat; 🚊Gardens) One-man-band Nigel Wood tosses just 30 premium patties per night in this alleyway operation, so get there early if you want to sample some of the best burgers in Cape Town. They come with a variety of sauces and, if you're lucky,

The Fringe, Woodstock & Salt River

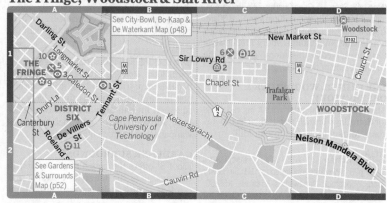

The Fringe, Woodstock & Salt River

a bowl of his nachos, as well as Nige's wine in a tube.

Melissa's INTERNATIONAL, DELI **$**
(Map p52; www.melissas.co.za; 94 Kloof St, Gardens; mains R50-70; ⊙7.30am-7pm Mon-Fri, 8am-7pm Sat & Sun) Pay by weight for the delicious breakfast and lunch buffets (R17.50 per 100g) then browse the grocery shelves for picnic fare or gourmet gifts. Other branches can be found in **Newlands** (cnr Kildare Lane & Main St) and **Victoria Wharf** (Map p56; Waterfront).

Fat Cactus MEXICAN **$$**
(Map p52; ☎021-422 5022; www.fatcactus.co.za; 5 Park Rd, Gardens; mains R70-100; ⊙11am-11pm; 🚌Michaelis) This much-loved operation – its original location in Mowbray is still going strong – brings its fine fajitas and margaritas to town.

GREEN POINT & WATERFRONT
The Waterfront's plethora of restaurants and cafes provide ocean views and open long hours daily, but choose carefully as this is real tourist-trap territory.

Wakame SEAFOOD, ASIAN **$$**
(Map p56; ☎021-433 2377; www.wakame.co.za; cnr Beach Rd & Surrey Pl, Mouille Point; mains R70-120; ⊙noon-11.30pm) Tucking into Wakame's salt and pepper squid or sushi platter while gazing at the glorious coastal view is Capetonian dining bliss. On the second level it specialises in Asian dumplings and sunset cocktails, when its deck can get packed.

Willoughby & Co SEAFOOD, JAPANESE **$$**
(Map p56; ☎021-418 6115; www.willoughbyandco .co.za; Shop 6132, Victoria Wharf, Breakwater Blvd, Waterfront; mains R60-70; ⊙deli 9.30am-8.30pm,

CAPE TOWN EATING

Roundhouse [TOP CHOICE]
CONTEMPORARY $$$

(Map p60; ☎021-438 4347; http://theroundhouse restaurant.com; The Glen, Camps Bay; restaurant 4-/6-course menu R450/595, Rumbullion mains R65-85; ⏱restaurant 6-10pm Tue-Sat year-round, noon-4pm Wed-Sat & noon-3pm Sun May-Sep; Rumbullion 9am-sunset Oct-Apr; [P]) This 18th-century heritage-listed building, in wooded grounds overlooking Camps Bay, is perfect for the elegant restaurant it now houses. If it's full for dinner, then a relaxed lunch or breakfast (weekends only) on the lawns at their Rumbullion operation is a pleasure.

La Boheme
SPANISH $$

(Map p60; ☎021-434 8797; www.labohemebistro .co.za; 341 Main Rd, Sea Point; 2/3 courses R95/120; ⏱8.30am-10.30pm Mon-Sat; ☎) With twinkling candles and fake Picassos on the walls, this superb-value wine bar and bistro is a lovely place to dine at night. At its daytime operation La Bruixa you can stoke up on espresso and the delicious tapas.

Mussel Bar
SEAFOOD $$

(Map p60; http://themusselbar.co.za; 69 Victoria Rd, Camps Bay; Camps Bay mussels R75-150; ⏱1pm-11pm) Keeping it simple pays off at this streetside operation serving fresh and plump Saldanha Bay mussels in a creamy wine sauce, chunky chips with aoli and rosemary salt. Wash them down with the quaffable Darling Slow Brew beer.

La Perla
ITALIAN $$

(Map p60; ☎021-439 9538; www.laperla.co.za; cnr Church & Beach Rds; mains R95-160; ⏱10am-midnight) This eternally stylish restaurant, with its waiters in white jackets, has been a fixture of Sea Point's promenade for decades. Enjoy something from the menu of pasta, fish and meat dishes on the terrace shaded by stout palms, or retreat to the intimate bar.

Cedar
LEBANESE $$

(Map p60; 100 Main Rd, Sea Point; mains R50-80; ⏱11am-1pm & 5-9.30pm Mon-Sat; ☑) It's nothing fancy, but this family-run operation rates highly for its scrumptious range of meze and Middle Eastern dishes, such as falafel, baba ganoush and hummus.

Hesheng
CHINESE $

(Map p60; 70 Main Rd, Sea Point; mains R40-60; ⏱11am-11pm Mon & Wed-Sun, 5-11pm Tue) Sea Point is stacked with Chinese restaurants,

restaurant noon-10.30pm; [P]; ☐Waterfront) Commonly acknowledged as one of the better places to eat at the Waterfront – with long queues to prove it. Huge servings of sushi are the standout from a good-value, fish-based menu at this casual eatery inside the mall.

El Burro
MEXICAN $

(Map p56; ☎021-433 2364; www.elburro.co.za; 81 Main Rd, Green Point; mains R50-70; ⏱noon-10.30pm; [P]; ☐Stadium) On the upper floor of the Exhibition Building, with a balcony overlooking Cape Town Stadium, this is one stylish donkey, the decor a bit more chic than your average Mexican joint, the menu more inventive. Supplementing the usual tacos and enchiladas are trad dishes such as chicken mole pablano.

Café Neo
GREEK, CAFE $

(Map p56; 129 Beach Rd, Mouille Point; mains R50-70; ⏱7am-7pm; ☎) This favourite seaside cafe has a relaxed vibe and pleasingly contemporary design. Check out the big blackboard menu while sitting at the long communal table inside or from a seat on the deck overlooking the red-and-white lighthouse.

Giovanni's Deli World
CAFE, DELI $

(Map p56; 103 Main Rd, Green Point; mains R20-40; ⏱7.30am-8.30pm) Bursting with flavoursome products, Giovanni's can make any sandwich you fancy, which is ideal for a picnic if you're on your way to the beach. The pavement cafe is a popular hang-out.

PETER ADAMS/JAI/CORBIS ©

1. Kirstenbosch Botanical Gardens (p57)

Alienlike king proteas bloom in these stunning gardens, where 9000 of Southern Africa's 22,000 plant species are grown.

2. Clifton Beaches (p55)

A popular sunbathing spot, the four beaches at Clifton are divided by piles of huge granite boulders.

3. Bo-Kaap (p46)

Known for its vibrantly painted historic houses, Bo-Kaap was where freed slaves settled after their emancipation in the 1830s.

4. Cape of Good Hope (p58)

A birdwatchers' and hikers' paradise, the Cape of Good Hope boasts spectacular vistas and tranquil beaches.

SERGIO PITAMITZ/CORBIS ©

but this inauspicious-looking hole in the wall is the real deal, run by a friendly Chinese couple and frequented by Chinese expats. They make their dumplings and noodles by hand.

SOUTHERN SUBURBS

La Colombe
FRENCH $$$

(021-794 2390; www.constantia-uitsig.com; Constantia Uitsig, Spaanschemat River Rd, Constantia; mains R100-215, 6-course menu R600; 12.30-2.30pm & 7.30-9.30pm; P) The shady garden setting makes this wine-estate restaurant one of most pleasant places to dine in Cape Town. British chef Scott Kirkton rustles up skilful dishes such as trout *sou vide*, beetroot cannelloni and smoked tomato risotto.

Bistro Sixteen82
TAPAS, INTERNATIONAL $$

(021-713 2211; www.steenberg-vineyards.co.za; Steenberg Vineyard, Tokai; mains R60-100; 9am-8pm; P) Perfectly complementing the dazzlingly contemporary wine-tasting lounge is Steenberg Vineyard's highly appealing bistro serving everything from breakfast with a glass of bubbly to an early supper of tapas with their quaffable merlot. Seating is both indoor and outdoor, with beguiling views of the gardens and mountain.

River Café
INTERNATIONAL $$

(021-794 3010; www.constantia-uitsig.com; Constantia Uitsig, Spaanschemat River Rd, Constantia; mains R60-100; 8.30am-5pm; P) A back up if La Colombe is full or beyond your budget, this delightful and popular cafe at the entrance to the estate is worthy of a visit in its own right. It can be relied on for big portions of food made with organic and free-range products. Booking is essential, especially for weekend brunch.

Gardener's Cottage
INTERNATIONAL $

(021-689 3158; Montebello Craft Studios, 31 Newlands Ave, Newlands; mains R45-70; 8am-2.30pm Mon-Fri, 8.30am-3pm Sat & Sun) After exploring the Montebello craft studios, relax at this lovely cafe and tea garden in the grounds. It serves simple, hearty meals in the shade of leafy trees.

Jonkershuis
CAPE MALAY $$

(021-794 6255; www.jonkershuisconstantia .co.za; Groot Constantia, Groot Constantia Rd, Constantia; mains R50-80, 2/3 courses R140/160; 9am-10pm Mon-Sat, 9am-5pm Sun; P) This casual brasserie-style restaurant in the grounds of Groot Constantia has a pleasant vine-shaded courtyard and tables looking onto the manor house. Sample Cape Malay dishes, including a tasting plate for R128, cured meats with a glass or two of the local wines, or satisfy your sweet tooth with the desserts.

SOUTHERN PENINSULA

Casa Labia
INTERNATIONAL $

(021-788 6068; www.casalabia.co.za; 192 Main Rd, Muizenberg; mains R45-70; 10am-4pm Tue-Thu, 9am-4pm Fri-Sun; Muizenberg) Some of the ingredients at this exceedingly pleasant cafe in the gorgeous cultural centre come from the adjoining garden. Enjoy home-baked treats and delicious breakfasts and open sandwiches.

Live Bait
SEAFOOD $$

(021-788 5755; www.harbourhouse.co.za; Kalk Bay harbour; mains R70-120; noon-4pm & 6-10pm; Kalk Bay) Sit within arm's reach of the crashing waves and the bustle of the Kalk Bay harbour at this breezy, Greek-island–style fish restaurant. It's one the best options for a relaxed seafood meal.

Olympia Café & Deli
BAKERY, INTERNATIONAL $$

(021-788 6396; 134 Main Rd, Kalk Bay; mains R60-100; 7am-9pm; Kalk Bay) Still setting the standard for relaxed rustic cafes by the sea, Olympia bakes its own breads and pastries on the premises. It's great for breakfast, and its Mediterranean-influenced lunch dishes are delicious, too.

Empire Café
INTERNATIONAL $

(www.empirecafe.co.za; 11 York Rd, Muizenberg; mains R40-50; 7am-4pm Mon-Sat, 8am-4pm Sun; ; Muizenberg) The surfies' favourite hang-out is a great place for a hearty egg-on-toast-type breakfast or lunch.

Knead
BAKERY, INTERNATIONAL $

(Map p52; http://kneadbakery.co.za; Surfer's Corner, Beach Rd, Muizenberg; mains R30-70; 10am-5pm Mon, 7am-5pm Tue-Sun; Muizenberg) Anything involving dough, these guys have it covered. The chandelier and mirror tiles add glamour to this hit seaside venue, but its product can also be relied on at its branches at the Lifestyle Centre and Wembley Sq both in Gardens.

Meeting Place
INTERNATIONAL $$

(021-786 1986; www.themeetingplaceupstairs.co .za; 98 St George's St, Simon's Town; mains R65-120; 9am-9pm Mon-Sat, 9am-3pm Sun; Simon's Town) A foodie's delight, there's a casual deli-cafe on the ground floor and an arty restaurant upstairs with a balcony overlooking Simon Town's main drag. Sample gourmet sandwiches or the homemade ice creams.

Sophea Gallery & Tibetan Teahouse
VEGETARIAN $
(www.sopheagallery.com; 2 Harrington Rd, Seaforth; mains R50-70; ⊙10am-5pm Tue-Sun) Tasty vegetarian and vegan food, based on recipes from Tibet, are served in part of this colourful gallery stocking artefacts and jewellery from the East. From its raised perch there's a nice view out to sea.

CAPE FLATS

Mzoli's
BARBECUE $
(☏021-638 1355; 150 NY111, Guguletu; meals R50; ⊙9am-6pm) Tourists, TV stars and locals gather at this busy butchery serving Cape Town's tastiest grilled meat. It gets super hectic here at weekends so arrive early. Beers and other drinks are available from vendors nearby. Bring plenty of napkins as cutlery is nonexistent.

Lelapa
AFRICAN $$
(☏021-694 2681; 49 Harlem Ave, Langa; buffets R120) Sheila cooks delicious African-style buffets in her extended home-restaurant. Book ahead, as there are no set opening hours at this place.

Nomzamo
BARBECUE $
(☏021-695 4250; 15 Washington St, Langa; meals R50; ⊙9am-7pm) This spotlessly clean butcher is the Langa equivalent of Mzoli's but with a more relaxed, peaceful vibe since they don't sell alcohol. Call ahead if you want to add side dishes such as bread, salads etc to make a full meal.

 Drinking

The 'Tavern of the Seven Seas' is awash with watering holes; its hostelries ranging from well-stocked wine bars to microbrew pubs. Most bars open around 3pm and close after midnight, and much later on Friday and Saturday when the crowds come out to party. Any alternative opening times are listed following.

CITY BOWL

TOP CHOICE French Toast
WINE BAR
(Map p48; ☏021-422 4084; www.frenchtoastwine.com; 199 Bree St; ⊙noon-11pm Mon-Sat; ☐Buitensingel) More than 80 local and international wines are served by the glass, including flights so you can compare samples of particular styles of varietals. It's a nicely designed space with both small and long tables on two levels. The tapas bites are very tasty and include desserts, such as *churros* (Spanish doughnuts) and chocolate.

&Union
BEER HALL, CAFE
(Map p48; www.andunion.com; 110 Bree St; ⊙noon-midnight; ℙ☎; ☐Longmarket) To the rear of St Stephen's Church this cool hang-out specialises in imported craft beers – seven types all bottled – as well as summer outdoor table tennis and the occasional live gig. It also prides itself on its ethically sourced meats used in tasty sandwiches, hot dogs and braais.

Tjing Tjing
BAR
(Map p48; www.tjingtjing.co.za; 165 Longmarket St; ⊙4pm-4am Tue-Fri, 6.30pm-4am Sat; ☎; ☐Longmarket) This slick rooftop bar, perched above the restaurant Dear Me, is a stylish hang-out for cocktails and wine. The interior is like a chic barn with exposed beams, a photo mural of Tokyo and a scarlet lacquered bar.

Waiting Room
BAR
(Map p48; 273 Long St; cover Fri & Sat R20; ⊙6pm-2am Mon-Sat; ☐Bloem) Climb the narrow stairway beside the Royale Eatery to find this totally hip bar decorated in retro furniture with DJs spinning funky tunes. Climb even further and you'll eventually reach the roof deck, the perfect spot from which to admire the city's glittering nightlights.

Fork
WINE BAR $$
(Map p48; ☏021-424 6334; www.fork-restaurants.co.za; 84 Long St; tapas R25-55; ⊙noon-11pm Mon-Sat; ☐Longmarket) Whether you just want to graze on a few tapas-style dishes or cobble together a full meal, this super-relaxed venue is the business, serving inventive if not strictly Spanish nibbles with excellent wines, many by the glass.

Julep Bar
COCKTAIL BAR
(Map p48; Vredenburg Lane; ⊙5pm-2am Tue-Sat; ☐Bloem) Occupying the ground floor of a former brothel, this hidden gem, a favourite with local hipsters, will set you apart from the riff-raff on nearby Long St.

Neigbourhood
BAR
(Map p48; www.goodinthehood.co.za; 163 Long St; ☐Dorp) At this relaxed bar and casual restaurant, styled after British gastropubs, the

colour divide of Cape Town melts away. The long balcony is a good place to cool off or keep tabs on Long St.

Caveau
WINE BAR

(Map p48; ☎021-422 1367; www.caveau.co.za; Heritage Sq, 92 Bree St; ⊙7am-11.30pm Mon-Sat; 🖳Longmarket) Cape Town should have more wine bars like this excellent one at Heritage Sq. It has a decent selection of local drops and very good food from both its restaurant and deli, which you can enjoy alfresco in the courtyard or on a raised terrace on Bree St.

WOODSTOCK

Amadoda
BAR

(Map p76; www.amadoda.co.za; 1-4 Strand St, Woodstock;⊙5pm-midnight Tue-Thu, noon-2am Fri & Sat, 1pm-midnight Sun; 🖳Woodstock) Pulling off a township braai (barbecue) and she-been atmosphere is this slickly decorated venue tucked away down a side road beside the railway tracks that attracts a racially mixed crowd. Worth checking out late on a weekend evening when patrons start to boogie.

Don Pedro
BAR

(Map p76; ☎021-447 6125; http://donpedros.co.za; 113 Roodebloem Rd, Woodstock; ⊙4pm-midnight Tue-Sat) Madame Zingara has sprinkled her magic across this old place and created a romantic boudoir suitable for all the Don's 'beautiful wives'. Torch singers belt out numbers from beside the self-playing piano and the menu is equally retro. Of course, it still does a wide range of Don Pedros – liqueur coffees made with ice cream.

GARDENS & SURROUNDS

Planet
COCKTAIL BAR

(Map p52; ☎021-483 1864; Mount Nelson Hotel, 76 Orange St, Gardens; ℗; 🖳Government Avenue) Enjoy some 250 different bubblies and 50-odd alcoholic concoctions in the old Nellie's cool silver-coated champagne and cocktail bar.

Power & the Glory/Black Ram
CAFE, BAR

(Map p52; 13B Kloof Nek Rd, Tamboerskloof; ⊙Cafe 8am-10pm, bar 5pm-late Mon-Sat) The coffee and food (pretzel hot dogs, crusty pies and other artisan munchies) are good but it's the smoky, cosy bar that packs the hipsters in.

Saints
CRAFT BEER

(Map p52; www.saintsburgerjoint.co.za; 84 Kloof St, Gardens) It serves gourmet burgers (doesn't everywhere in Cape Town these days?) but what we like is its range of Camelthorn craft beers, which you can sample in 100mL tast-ing glasses (R6 or four for R22) before deciding which pint to go for. Also a nice touch: the lyrics of 'Stairway to Heaven' painted on the stairs.

Perseverance Tavern
PUB

(Map p52; www.perseverancetavern.co.za; 83 Buitenkant St; ⊙4pm-2am Mon, noon-2am Tue-Sat, 11am-8pm Sun) This convivial heritage-listed pub, which is affectionately known as Per-sies and has been around since 1808, was once Cecil Rhodes' local. There are beers on tap and you can order decent pub grub, such as fish and chips (R55).

GREEN POINT & WATERFRONT

Bascule
BAR

(Map p56; ☎021-410 7097; www.capegrace.com; Cape Grace, West Quay Rd, Waterfront; ⊙noon-2am) More than 450 varieties of whisky are served at the Grace's sophisticated bar, and there are still a few slugs of the 50-year-old Glenfiddich (just R18,000 a tot) left. Make a booking for one of the whisky tastings (R175 or R220) in which you can try six drams, three of which are paired with food. Outdoor tables facing the marina are a pleasant spot for drinks and tasty tapas.

Harbour House
BAR

(Map p56; ☎021-418 4744; Quay 4, Waterfront ⊙noon-10pm; ℗; 🖳Breakwater) The Kalk Bay institution makes its debut at the Waterfront with a good restaurant on the ground floor and even better sushi and lounge bar on the upper deck – just the spot for a chilled glass of wine at sunset.

Grand Café & Beach
BAR

(Map p56; ☎072 586 2052; www.grandafrica .com; Granger Bay Rd, off Beach Rd, Granger Bay; ⊙noon-11pm; ℗; 🖳Granger Bay) Sand was imported to created the beach for this oh-so-chic bar and restaurant operating out of a former warehouse. Locals love to gather on weekends here to enjoy the laid-back vibe, rather than the so-so food. DJs kick in later at night.

W Tapas Bar
CAFE, WINE BAR

(Map p56; ☎021-415 3411; Woolworths, Victoria Wharf, Breakwater Blvd, Waterfront; ⊙9am-9pm; ℗; 🖳Waterfront) Tucked away on the top floor of Woolworths, with a sweeping view across the harbour, is this modern, uncrowded wine bar where you can sample the best of the department store's selection of local drops along with tapas platters of charcuterie, sea-food or vegetarian dips (R65 to R95).

COFFEE LOVE

Cape Town is in the midst of a coffee crush with digital odes to the roasted bean including **I Love Coffee** (http://ilovecoffee.co.za) and **From Coffee With Love** (http://from coffeewithlove.wordpress.com), a blog written by Lameen Abdul-Malik, the English-Nigerian owner of **Escape Caffe** (Map p48; http://escapecaffe.wordpress.com; Manhattan Pl, 130 Bree St; ☺7am-4pm Mon-Fri; 🚇Dorp). Abdul-Malik serves all his coffees with a double shot; for the truly addicted there's his Sleep Suicide: a double espresso plus a French press coffee.

Coffee lovers should also drop by the following:

Espressolab Microroasters (Map p76; http://espressolabmicroroasters.com; Old Biscuit Mill, 375 Albert Rd, Woodstock; ☺8am-4pm Mon-Fri, 8am-2pm Sat; P; 🚇Woodstock) Its beans, which come from single farms, estates and co-ops from around the world, are packaged with tasting notes such as found for fine wines.

Bean There (Map p48; www.beanthere.co.za; 58 Wale St; 🚇Dorp) An ultrachic cafe serving Fair Trade coffees from across Africa and a few sweet snacks.

Deluxe Coffeeworks (Map p48; 25 Church St; 🚇Longmarket) Get your daily caffeine fix at this hole-in-the-wall with what looks like a giant model kit for parts of a Vespa hanging on the wall.

Haas (Map p48; www.haascollective.com; 67 Rose St; ☺7am-5pm Mon-Fri, 8am-3pm Sat & Sun; 📶; 🚇Longmarket) Both a cafe and a very appealing arty gift and interior decor shop, Haas serves house-roasted single-origin and blended versions of coffee as well as tasty bakes and meals.

Origin & Nigiro (Map p48; www.originroasting.co.za; 28 Hudson St; ☺7am-5pm Mon-Fri, 9am-2pm Sat & Sun; 📶) Holds coffee and tea appreciation courses (R200). At the rear, the caffeinated buzz of Origin gives way to the zen calm of Nigiro's tea salon where you can sample scores of the leaf or have a traditional Taiwanese tea ceremony (R125).

Truth (Map p76; www.truthcoffee.com; 36 Buitenkant, The Fringe; ☺6am-midnight) Occupying a 16,000-sq-metre space is this self-described 'steampunk roastery and coffee bar'.

Mitchell's Scottish Ale House & Brewery
PUB
(Map p56; www.mitchellsbreweries.co.za; East Pier Rd, Waterfront; ☺11am-2am; P; 🚇Breakwater) Check all airs and graces at the door of South Africa's oldest microbrewery (established 1983 in Knysna), serving a variety of freshly brewed ales and good-value meals. Its 'Old Wobbly' packs an alcoholic punch.

ATLANTIC COAST
La Vie
BAR, CAFE
(Map p60; 205 Beach Rd; ☺7.30am-midnight; 📶) One of the very few places you can have anything from breakfast to late-night cocktails within sight of Sea Point promenade. Lounge on the outdoor terrace and enjoy the thin-crust pizza (R40 to R90).

Bungalow
BAR
(Map p60; ☎021-438 2018; www.thebungalow .co.za; Glen Country Club, 1 Victoria Rd, Clifton; ☺noon-2am; P) This Euro-chic restaurant and lounge bar is a great place for beers, cocktails or a boozy meal after which you can crash in the day-bed section under a billowing white awning or dangle your feet in the tiny bar-side splash pool. A DJ creates a more clubby atmosphere by night.

Dunes
BAR
(www.dunesrestaurant.co.za; 1 Beach Rd, Hout Bay; ☺10am-10pm Mon-Fri, 8am-10pm Sat & Sun) You can hardly get closer to the beach than this – in fact, the front courtyard *is* the beach with a safe kids' play area. Up on the terrace or from inside the restaurant-bar there's a great view of Hout Bay to go with the decent pub grub and tapas.

Café Caprice
CAFE, BAR
(Map p60; ☎021-438 8315; www.cafecaprice.co.za; 37 Victoria Rd; ☺9am-2am) The bronzed and beautiful gather at this cafe-bar, which is as popular for breakfast as it is for sundowner drinks. Reserve a pavement table for the best view.

SOUTHERN SUBURBS

Banana Jam
CRAFT BEER

(www.bananajamcafe.co.za; 157 2nd Ave, Harfield Village, Kenilworth; ⊙11am-11pm Mon-Sat, 5pm-11pm Sun; P ？; 🚇 Kenilworth) Real beer-lovers rejoice – this convivial Caribbean restaurant and bar is like manna from heaven with a host of on-tap and bottled ales from local microbrewers including Jack Black, Triggerfish, Darling Brew, Camelthorne and Boston Brewery. Try a taster set of six types for R45.

Forrester's Arms
PUB

(52 Newlands Ave, Newlands; ⊙11am-11pm Mon-Sat, 10am-6pm Sun; P) 'Forries', around for well over a century, offers up a convivial atmosphere, good pub meals, including wood-fired pizza, and a very pleasant beer garden with a play area for the kids.

O'ways Teacafe
TEAHOUSE

(📞021-617 2850; www.oways.co.za; 20 Dreyer St, Claremont; mains R47-150; ⊙7.30am-5pm Mon-Fri, 9am-2pm Sat; 🚇 Claremont) Pronounced 'Always', this stylish, relaxing place has 60-odd loose teas to sample as well as coffee. The menu is fully vegetarian, including tasty dishes, such as dim sum dumplings, and Portobello mushrooms filled with couscous.

Barristers
PUB

(📞021-674 1792; www.barristersgrill.co.za; cnr Kildare Rd & Main St; ⊙9.30am-10.30pm; P ？) A locals' favourite watering hole with a series of cosy rooms hung with an eye-catching assortment of items in ye-olde-country-pub style. It's also an excellent spot for warming pub grub on a chilly night.

SOUTHERN PENINSULA

Brass Bell
BAR

(www.brassbell.co.za; Kalk Bay Train Station, Main Rd, Kalk Bay; ⊙11am-10pm; 🚇 Kalk Bay) Take the tunnel beneath the train tracks to reach this Kalk Bay institution overlooking the fishing harbour. On a sunny day there are few places better to drink and eat (mains R50 to R80) by the sea. Before or after you could take a dip in the adjacent tidal pools.

Polana
BAR

(📞021-788 7162; www.harbourhouse.co.za; Kalk Bay harbour; 🚇 Kalk Bay) Providing an excellent reason to hang out in Kalk Bay rather than rush back to the city is this chic bar, right over the rocks at the edge of the harbour. It serves Portuguese-style seafood – sardines, mussels and delicious *peri peri* prawns.

There's often live music, mainly jazz, Friday to Sunday.

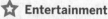 Entertainment

The Mother City dazzles with a diverse and creative range of entertainments, with live music a particular highlight. Tickets for many events can be booked with Webtickets (www.webtickets.co.za) or Computicket (http://online.computicket.com/web), which has outlets in Cape Town Tourism's main office on Burg St, the Gardens Centre and at the Waterfront.

CINEMAS

Multiplexes can be found in Victoria Wharf at the Waterfront, Cavendish Sq and Canal Walk.

Labia
CINEMA

(Map p52; www.labia.co.za; 68 Orange St; tickets R35; 🚇 Michaelis) This lifeline to the nonmainstream movie fan is named after the old Italian ambassador and local philanthropist Count Labia. It is Cape Town's best cinema in terms of price and programming. Also check out what's playing at the two-screen Labia on Kloof, in the Lifestyles on Kloof centre around the corner.

Live Music

Cape Town City Hall
CLASSICAL MUSIC

(Map p48; www.creativecapetown.net/cape-town-city-hall; Darling St; P; 🚇 St George's) One of several venues where the Cape Philharmonic Orchestra (www.cpo.org.za), South Africa's 'orchestra for all seasons', plays concerts. Local choirs also take advantage of the auditorium's very good acoustics.

Cape Town International Convention Centre
CONCERT VENUE

(Map p48; CTICC; 📞021-410 5000; www.cticc.co.za; 1 Lower Long St; P; 🚇 Convention Centre) The Convention Centre hosts a busy program of musical performances, exhibitions, conferences and other events such as the Cape Town International Jazz Festival and Design Indaba. There are plans to extend the CTICC towards Artscape, almost doubling its size.

Zula Sound Bar
LIVE MUSIC, COMEDY

(Map p48; 📞021-424 2442; www.zulabar.co.za; 98 Long St; admission from R30; 🚇 Longmarket) Progress from the cafe and bar fronting the street to performance spaces upstairs and downstairs at the back. The line-up includes a range of hip local bands, DJs and comedy every Monday night.

ONLINE ENTERTAINMENT GUIDES

What's On! (http://www.whatson.co.za/index.php)

Next 48 Hours (www.48hours.co.za)

Mail & Guardian (www.theguide.co.za)

Tonight (www.iol.co.za/tonight)

Cape Town Magazine (www.capetownmagazine.co.za)

Assembly　　　　　　　　　LIVE MUSIC, DJ
(Map p76; www.theassembly.co.za; 61 Harrington St, The Fringe; cover R30-50) In an old furniture assembly factory, this live-music and DJ performance space has made its mark with an exciting, eclectic line-up of both local and international artists.

Mercury Live & Lounge　　　LIVE MUSIC, DJ
(Map p76; www.mercuryl.co.za; 43 De Villiers St, District Six; admission R20-40) Cape Town's premier rock venue plays host to top South African bands and overseas visitors. The sound quality is good and if you don't like the band, there's always the DJ bar **Mercury Lounge**, below, and the **Shack** bar, next door.

Mahogany Lounge　　　　　　　JAZZ
(Map p52; ☎079 679 2697; www.facebook.com/MahoganyRoom; 79 Buitenkant St, Gardens; 1/2 sets R60/100; ⏰7pm-2am Wed-Sat) This tiny jazz club aims to recreate the atmosphere of Ronny Scotts and Village Vanguard. It's run by hard-core jazz cats who have the connections to get top-class talent on the stage. Bookings essential for the two sets starting at 8.30pm and 10.30pm.

Tagore　　　　　　　　　　LIVE MUSIC
(Map p64; ☎021-447 8717; 42 Trill Rd, Observatory; ⏰5pm-midnight; 🚉Observatory) Candles, cosy nooks and crannies, and avant-garde music set the scene at this tiny cafe-bar, a favourite with the Obs alternative set. There's no cover for the sets that usually kick off at 9.30pm Wednesday, Friday and Saturday.

Nightclubs

Trinity　　　　　　　　　　　CLUB
(off Map p48; www.trinitycapetown.co.za; 15 Bennett St; cover R50-150) Occupying an enormous warehouse space, one part decorated with an organ salvaged from an old church, Trinity offers a state-of-the art dance club with one of the most sophisticated sound systems in South Africa, as well as bars and an all-day restaurant serving sushi, pizza and burgers. Naturally, big-name DJs play here but you should also look out for events such as live jazz on Tuesday and, once a month, a jazz orchestra band playing in the main hall.

Vinyl Digz　　　　　　　　DANCE, CLUB
(Map p48; www.facebook.com/VinylDIGZ; 113 Loop St; admission R20; ⏰1pm-1am; 🚉Dorp) This rooftop dance party, which happens every other Saturday, is a more casual bring-and-buy LP record swapmeet during the afternoon, with braai available too. As the sun sets the grooving to classic soul and R&B from the '60s onwards starts and the very chilled, mixed crowd makes it one of the best dance events in Cape Town.

Loop　　　　　　　　　　　CLUB
(Map p48; www.theloopnightclub.co.za; 161 Loop St; cover R50, VIP area R80; 🚉Bloem) Brightly coloured outside and roomy inside, this latest entry to Cape Town's hip club scene is worth checking out depending on the DJ they have playing. Everything and anything is promised music-wise.

St Yves　　　　　　　　　　CLUB
(Map p60; www.styves.co.za; The Promenade, Victoria Rd, Camps Bay) The latest incarnation of this slick Camps Bay nightspot has a groove going on with a class line-up of DJs and live acts, including local sensations Goldfish, on most Sundays during the summer season (tickets available for R110 via webtickets).

Sport

With tickets costing from around R30, attending the footy (soccer) in Cape Town is not only cheap but also a hugely fun and loud night out, with supporters taking every opportunity to blow their *vuvuzelas* (plastic trumpets). The season runs from August to May. **Ajax Cape Town** (www.ajaxct.com) plays at Cape Town Stadium while **Athlone Stadium** (Cross Blvd, Athlone) is home to the team **Santos** (www.santosfc.co.za).

Sahara Park Newlands　　　　CRICKET
(☎021-657 3300, ticket hotline 021-657 2099; www.capecobras.co.za; 146 Campground Rd, Newlands; 🚉Newlands) The official name is part of a sponsorship deal, but everyone still knows the venue as Newlands Cricket Ground. With room for 25,000, it's used for all international matches. The season runs from September to March with the one-day matches drawing the biggest crowds. Tickets cost around R50 for local matches – the

GAY & LESBIAN CAPE TOWN

What the Mother City may lack in terms of breadth and depth of its gay and lesbian scene it makes up for in terms of friendliness and the drop-dead glamour of its location. Start by topping up your tan and checking out the talent on **Clifton No 3 beach** or **Sandy Bay**, the clothing-optional stretch of sand discreetly located near Llandudno Bay.

Come nightfall, the first port of call for savvy sisters is the city's gay village De Waterkant, ground central for gay-friendly guesthouses, bars, clubs and restaurants. The long-running **Cafe Manhattan** (Map p48; ☏021-421 6666; www.manhattan.co.za; 74 Waterkant St, De Waterkant) is a friendly place to kick off your night and grab a bite to eat. A broad balcony allows a wide view of passersby. Also justly popular is **Beefcakes** (Map p48; ☏021-425 9019; www.beefcakes.co.za; 40 Somerset Rd, De Waterkant; burgers R55-85; ⊗11am-10pm Mon-Sat, 6pm-10pm Sun; 🕾), a camp burger bar where you can play bitchy bingo on Tuesday or enjoy the professional drag shows on Wednesday and Thursday. Friday and Saturday nights it's for the boys only.

The **Amsterdam Action Bar** (Map p48; www.amsterdambar.co.za; 10-12 Cobern St, De Waterkant; ⊗5pm-2am) has dark rooms and cubicles on its upper level, a pool table in the nonsmoking area, and a street-side balcony to watch the comings and goings. Move on later around the corner to **Crew Bar** (Map p48; www.crewbar.co.za; 30 Napier St, De Waterkant; Fri & Sat cover R20; ⊗5pm-4am) with its hunky bar dancers dressed only in skimpy shorts and glitter, or the lesbian-friendly **Beaulah Bar** (Map p48; www.beaulahbar.co.za; 30 Somerset Rd; cover R20; ⊗8pm-4am). Pronounced 'byoo-lah', this fun bar and dance venue, up a floor from the street, has a devoted crowd of young boys and girls who are always ready to bop to the DJ's poppy tunes. The divas of Cape Town's flourishing drag scene and their admirers gather at **Bubbles Bar** (Map p48; www.facebook.com/pages/Bubbles-Bar; 125A Waterkant St, De Waterkant; ⊗7pm-2am); depending on the crowd it can be a hoot, but beware the open mic karaoke, which can get aurally ugly.

On the edge of the City Bowl, **Alexander Bar & Café** (Map p48; http://alexanderbar .co.za; 76 Strand St; ⊗ 11am-1am Mon-Sat; 🚇Castle) is a fun, eccentric space in a gorgeous heritage building. Pick up the antique telephones on the tables to chat with fellow patrons, place an order at the bar or send a telegram to someone you might have your eye on.

If you really want to go local, swing by a *gat* party at which you can catch *langarm*-style ballroom dancing favoured by Afrikaner gays and lesbians; a regular one is **Deon Nagel's gat party** (☏082-821 9185; www.facebook.com/groups/117474602037; Theo Marais Park, Koeberg Rd, Milnerton; cover R30; ⊗9pm-2am, 1st, 2nd & last Sat of month).

For the latest openings and events check the annually updated *Pink Map* (www .mapsinfo.co.za); **Gaynet Cape Town** (www.gaynetcapetown.co.za); and the monthly free newspaper *Pink Tongue* (www.pinktongue.co.za). Also mark your travel calendar for the city's two main gay events – **Cape Town Pride** (http://capetownpride.org) in early March and the **Mother City Queer Project** (www.mcqp.co.za), a fabulous fancy-dress dance event every December.

Nashua Mobile Cape Cobras play here – and up to R200 for internationals.

Newlands Rugby Stadium RUGBY
(☏021-659 4600; www.wprugby.com; 8 Boundary Rd, Newlands; 🚇Newlands) This hallowed ground of South African rugby is home to the **Stormers** (www.iamastormer.com). Tickets for Super 12 games cost from R50, and for international matches around R350.

Theatre & Comedy

Artscape THEATRE
(off Map p48; ☏021-410 9800; www.artscape.co.za; 1-10 DF Malan St; 🅿; 🚇Foreshore) Consisting of three different-sized auditoriums (including the studio On the Side), this behemoth is the city's main arts complex. Theatre, classical music, ballet, opera and cabaret shows – Artscape offers it all. The desolate area means walking around here at night is not recommended. There's plenty of secure parking.

Baxter Theatre
THEATRE

(☎021-685 7880; www.baxter.co.za; Main Rd, Rondebosch) The three venues at this landmark theatre in the Southern Suburbs cover everything from kids' shows to Zulu dance spectaculars and co-productions with the Royal Shakespeare Company.

Fugard
THEATRE

(Map p76; ☎021-461 4554; www.thefugard.com; Caledon St, The Fringe) Named in honour of Athol Fugard, South Africa's best known living playwright, this very impressive arts centre contains two stages, the largest theatre also doubling up as a 'bioscope', a fancy word for a digital cinema where top international dance and opera performances are screened (tickets including a glass of bubbly).

Jou Ma Se Comedy Club
COMEDY

(off Map p64; http://www.kurt.co.za/jmscc; River Club, Liesbeek Parkway; tickets R80; ⊗8.30pm Thu; ◙Observatory) The title means 'Your mother's ...*&£!' but you don't need to understand Afrikaans slang to get the jokes of funny-guy Kurt Schoonraad and his pals at this laugh-a-minute comedy club, one of the best of several such shows in the city.

🔒 Shopping

Bring a big empty bag because chances are that you'll be leaving Cape Town laden with local booty.

CITY BOWL

TOP CHOICE **African Music Store**
MUSIC

(Map p48; www.africanmusicstore.co.za; 134 Long St; ◙Dorp) The range of local music here, including all top jazz, kwaito (a form of township music), dance and trance recordings, can't be surpassed. You'll also find DVDs and other souvenirs.

Merchants on Long
FASHION, GIFTS

(Map p48; www.merchantsonlong.com; 34 Long St, City Bowl; ◙Castle) A gallery of top contemporary design from fashion and perfume to stationery sourced from across Africa. There's also a cafe.

African Image
ARTS & CRAFTS

(Map p48; www.african-image.co.za; cnr Church & Burg Sts; ◙Longmarket) There's a fab range of new and old crafts and artefacts at reasonable prices, including the funky colourful designed pillow covers and aprons of Shine Shine.

Pan African Market
ARTS & CRAFTS

(Map p48; www.panafrican.co.za; 76 Long St; ◙Longmarket) A microcosm of the continent with a bewildering range of arts and crafts. There are also a cheap cafe, Timbuktu, with seating on the balcony overlooking Long St, a tailor and a music shop packed into the three floors.

Clarke's Books
BOOKS

(Map p48; www.clarkesbooks.co.za; 199 Long St; ◙Dorp) Stocks the best range of books on South Africa and the continent, and has a great second-hand section.

BO-KAAP & DE WATERKANT

TOP CHOICE **Streetwires**
ARTS & CRAFTS

(Map p48; www.streetwires.co.za; 77 Shortmarket St; ◙Longmarket) The motto is 'anything you can dream up in wire we will build'. And if you visit this social project designed to create sustainable employment and see the wire sculptors at work, you'll see what that means! It stocks an amazing range, including working radios and chandeliers and life-sized animals.

Africa Nova
ARTS & CRAFTS

(Map p48; www.africanova.co.za; Cape Quarter, 72 Waterkant St; ⊗9am-5pm Mon-Fri, 10am-5pm Sat, 10am-2pm Sun) One of the most stylish and desirable collections of contemporary African textiles, arts and crafts. They also have a smaller branch at Casa Labia in Muizenberg.

Monkeybiz
ARTS & CRAFTS

(Map p48; www.monkeybiz.co.za; 43 Rose St; ⊗9am-5pm Mon-Thu, Sat 9am-4pm Fri, 10am-1pm Sat; ◙Longmarket) Colourful beadwork crafts, made by township women, are Monkeybiz' supersuccessful stock in trade. Profits from the project are reinvested in community services, such as soup kitchens and a burial fund for artists and their families.

Cape Quarter
SHOPPING CENTRE

(Map p48; www.capequarter.co.za; 27 Somerset Rd; ⊗9am-6pm Mon-Fri, 9am-4pm Sat, 10am-2pm Sun; ℗) Split over two adjacent locations the Cape Quarter's newer, larger block is anchored by a snazzy branch of the supermarket Spar (⊗7am-9pm Mon-Sat, 8am-9pm Sun), handy if you're self-catering in one of the area's cottages or flats. There's also a lively food and goods market held on the upper floors every Sunday 10am to 3pm.

THE FRINGE, WOODSTOCK & SALT RIVER

TOP CHOICE Old Biscuit Mill SHOPPING CENTRE
(Map p76; www.theoldbiscuitmill.co.za; 373-375 Albert Rd, Salt River; P; Salt River) A one-time biscuit factory is home to a very appealing collection of arts, craft, fashion and design shops as well as places to eat and drink. It's also the venue for the phenomenally successful Neighbourgoods Market every Saturday.

TOP CHOICE Book Lounge BOOKS
(Map p76; 021-462 2425; www.booklounge.co.za; 71 Roeland St, The Fringe; 9.30am-7.30pm Mon-Fri, 8.30am-6pm Sat, 10am-4pm Sun) A heavenly bookshop that has become the hub of Cape Town's literary scene, thanks to its great selection of titles, comfy chairs, simple cafe and program of events. There are up to three talks or book launches a week, generally with free drinks and nibbles, and readings for kids at the weekend.

Ashanti ARTS & CRAFTS
(Map p76; www.ashantidesign.com; 133-135 Sir Lowry Rd, Woodstock; Woodstock) Baskets, mats, lamp shades, pillows, bags and cushions are among the many rainbow-coloured products on sale, gathered from across Africa at this great artisan design shop. Often no two pieces are alike.

South African Print Gallery ART
(Map p76; www.printgallery.co.za; 109 Sir Lowry Rd, Woodstock; 9.30am-4pm Tue-Fri, 10am-1pm Sat; Woodstock) Specialising in prints by local artists – both well established and up-and-coming – this gallery is likely to have something that is both affordable and small enough to fit comfortably in your suitcase for transport home.

GARDENS

Fringe Arts ARTS & CRAFTS
(Map p52; www.thefringearts.co.za; 99B Kloof St, Gardens) You're sure to find some unique gift or item for yourself at this creative boutique representing almost 100 South African artists and designers, ranging from ceramics and jewellery to prints and bags.

Bluecollarwhitecollar FASHION
(Map p52; www.bluecollarwhitecollar.co.za; Lifestyle on Kloof, 50 Kloof St, Gardens; P; Michaelis) A wonderful selection of tailored shirts – formal (white collar) and informal (blue collar). Recently added to the range are T-shirts and

shorts. Also find them at the Old Biscuit Mill Saturday market.

LIM HOMEWARES
(Map p52; www.lim.co.za; 86A Kloof St, Gardens) Wander through the rooms admiring the stylish, pared-back selection of homewares, including fashion accessory items made from buckskin.

GREEN POINT & WATERFRONT

Victoria Wharf SHOPPING CENTRE
(Map p56; Breakwater Blvd, Waterfront; 9am-9pm; P; Waterfront) All the big names of South African retail, including Woolworths, CNA, Pick 'n' Pay, Exclusive Books and Musica, plus international luxury brands are represented at this appealing mall, one of Cape Town's best. Attached to it is the **Red Shed Craft Workshop**, a permanent market focused on local crafts, including ceramics, textiles and jewellery.

Waterfront Craft Market & Wellness Centre ARTS & CRAFTS
(Map p56; Dock Rd, Waterfront; 9.30am-6pm; P; Breakwater) Also known as the Blue Shed, this eclectic arts and crafts market harbours some great buys. In the Wellness Centre section you'll find various holistic products and can have a massage.

Vaughan Johnson's Wine & Cigar Shop WINE
(Map p56; www.vaughanjohnson.co.za; Market Sq, Dock Rd, Waterfront; 9am-6pm Mon-Fri, 9am-5pm Sat, 10am-5pm Sun; P; Breakwater) Selling practically every South African wine of repute you could wish to buy (plus a few more from other countries), it's open, unlike most wine sellers, on Sundays.

Cape Union Mart Adventure Centre OUTDOOR EQUIPMENT
(Map p56; www.capeunionmart.co.za; Quay 4, Waterfront; 9am-9pm; P; Waterfront) This emporium is packed with backpacks, boots, clothing and practically everything else you might need for outdoor adventures, from a hike up Table Mountain to a Cape-to-Cairo safari.

ATLANTIC COAST

Hout Bay Craft Market MARKET
(Baviaanskloof Rd, Hout Bay; 10am-5pm Sun) Browsing the stalls at this market held on the village green is a lovely way to while an hour or so away on Sunday.

WEEKLY ARTISAN FOOD & GOODS MARKETS

The roaring success of the Neighbourgoods Market (www.neighbourgoodsmarket.co.za; 373-375 Albert Rd, Salt River; ☺9am-2pm Sat; P; ®Salt River) at the Old Biscuit Mill has sparked a number of similar ventures across the city. The original is still the best, but it gets very busy so come early. Food and drinks are gathered in the main area where you can pick up groceries and gourmet goodies or just graze, while the separate Designergoods area hosts a must-buy selection of local fashions and accessories.

Other top weekly markets include the following:

City Bowl Market (Map p52; http://citybowlmarket.co.za; 14 Hope St, Gardens; ☺9am-2pm Sat; ®Gardens) Based in a lovely old building with a lofty hall and outside garden areas, this is the Gardens' best Saturday-morning hang-out and has a very chilled vibe. There's a fashion store downstairs and occasionally it has a larger selection of fashion vendors.

Bay Harbour Market (http://bayharbour.co.za/home.html; 31 Harbour Rd, Hout Bay; ☺5-10pm Fri, 9am-5pm Sat, 10am-4pm Sun) At the far western end of the harbour this imaginatively designed indoor market offers a good range of gifts and crafts as well as very tempting food and drink options and live music. Friday nights run only from November to the end of February, but the weekend opening times are year-round.

Blue Bird Garage Food & Goods Market (39 Albertyn Rd, Muizenberg; ☺4-10pm Fri, 10am-3pm Sat; ®Valsbaai) Based in a 1940s hangar, once the location for the first southern hemisphere airmail delivery service, then a garage in the 1950s. It's a fun place to shop and graze, particularly on Friday nights when there's live music.

SOUTHERN SUBURBS

Montebello   ARTS & CRAFTS
(www.montebello.co.za; 31 Newlands Ave; ☺9am-5pm Mon-Fri, 9am-4pm Sat, 9am-3pm Sun; P) This development project has helped several great craftspeople and designers along the way. In the leafy compound, check out the colourful bags made from recycled materials at Mielie (www.mielie.co.za); Sitali Jewellers (www.sitalijewellers.com) hand-making gold and platinum pieces in old stables; and David Krut Projects (www.davidkrutprojectscapetown.com), a gallery specialising in prints and works on paper. There's also an organic deli and the excellent cafe, Gardener's Cottage.

Cavendish Square   SHOPPING CENTRE
(www.cavendish.co.za; Cavendish Square Dreyer St, Claremont; ☺9am-7pm Mon-Sat, 10am-5pm Sun; P; ®Claremont) This top-class shopping mall has outlets of many of Cape Town's premier fashion designers, as well as supermarkets, department stores and two multiplex cinemas.

ℹ Information

Dangers & Annoyances

Cape Town's relaxed vibe can instil a false sense of security. Thefts are most likely to happen when visitors do something foolish such as leaving their gear on a beach while they go swimming.

Paranoia is not required, but common sense is. There is tremendous poverty on the peninsula and the 'informal redistribution of wealth' is reasonably common. The townships on the Cape Flats have an appalling crime rate and unless you have a trustworthy guide or are on a tour they are not places for a casual stroll.

While the city centre is generally safe to walk around, always listen to local advice on where and where not to go. There is safety in numbers.

Swimming at any of the Cape beaches is potentially hazardous, especially for those inexperienced in surf. Check for warning signs about rips and rocks, and only swim in patrolled areas.

Emergency

In any emergency call ☎107, or ☎021-480 7700 if using a mobile phone. Other useful phone numbers include the following:
Police (☎10111)
Sea Rescue (☎021-449 3500)
Table Mountain National Park (☎086-106 417)

Internet Access

Practically all hotels and hostels have internet facilities and/or wi-fi. If not, you'll seldom have to hunt far for an internet cafe. Rates are pretty uniform at R30 per hour. Wi-fi access is available at many hotels and hostels as well as several cafes and restaurants throughout the city; we list places where it is available (☎) – at some it will be free (ask for the password) at others you'll have to pay. General providers include **Red Button** (www.redbutton.co.za) and **Skyrove** (www.skyrove.com).

Media

Cape Town's morning newspaper, the *Cape Times* (www.iol.co.za/capetimes), and the afternoon *Cape Argus* (www.iol.co.za/capeargus), print practically the same news. The weekly *Mail & Guardian* (http://mg.co.za) published on Friday, has a good arts review supplement with details of what's going on in Cape Town. *Cape Etc* (www.capeetc.com) is a decent bimonthly arts and listings magazine dedicated to what's going on around town. The online *Cape Town Magazine* (www.capetownmagazine.com) with editions in English, German and Dutch is also a useful source of information with up-to-date listings of places and events.

Medical Services

Medical services are of a high standard in Cape Town. Hotels and most other accommodation places can arrange a visit from a doctor if required.

Groote Schuur Hospital (☎021-404 9111; www.westerncape.gov.za/your_gov/5972; Main Rd, Observatory)

Netcare Christiaan Barnard Memorial Hospital (☎021-480 6111; www.netcare.co.za/live/content.php?Item_ID=250; 181 Longmarket St, City Bowl)

Netcare Travel Clinic (☎021-419 3172; www.travelclinics.co.za; 11th fl, Picbal Arcade, 58 Strand St, City Bowl; ⊗8am-4pm Mon-Fri)

Money

Money can be changed at the airport and there are ATMs all over town; see p590 for information on ATM scams.

Post

There are post office branches across Cape Town; see www.sapo.co.za to find the nearest. The post is reliable but can be slow. If you're mailing anything of value, consider using the private mail services such as **Postnet** (www.postnet.co.za), which uses DHL for international deliveries.

General post office (Map p48; www.postoffice.co.za; Parliament St, City Bowl; ⊗8am-4.30pm Mon-Fri, 8am-noon Sat).

Telephone

At phone boxes a phonecard is useful; you can buy one at newsagents and general stores.

You can rent mobile phones or get a pay-as-you-go SIM card from the MTM and Vodacom desks at the airport or in town, where you'll also find Cell-C and Virgin Mobile shops. Top-up cards are available all over town.

Tourist Information

At the head office of **Cape Town Tourism** (Map p48; ☎021-426 4260; www.capetown.travel; cnr Castle & Burg Sts; ⊗8am-6pm daily Oct-Mar, 9am-5pm Mon-Fri, 9am-1pm Sat & Sun Apr-Sep) there are advisers who can book accommodation, tours and car hire. You can also get information on national parks and reserves, safaris and overland tours.

Other Cape Town Tourism branches:

Hout Bay (☎021-790 8380; 4 Andrews Rd; ⊗9am-5.30pm Mon-Fri, 9am-1pm Sat & Sun Oct-Apr, 9am-5pm Mon-Fri May-Sep)

Kirstenbosch Visitor Information Centre (☎021-762 0687; Kirstenbosch Botanical Gardens, Main Entrance, Rhodes Dr, Newlands; ⊗9am-6pm)

Muizenberg Visitor Information Centre (☎021-787 9140; The Pavilion, Beach Rd; ⊗9am-5.30pm Mon-Fri, 9am-1pm Sat & Sun)

Simon's Town Visitor Information Centre (☎021-786 8440; 111 St George's St; ⊗8.30am-5.30pm Mon-Fri, 9am-1pm Sat & Sun)

V&A Waterfront Visitor Information Centre (☎021-408 7600; Dock Rd; ⊗9am-6pm)

❶ Getting There & Away

Air

Cape Town International Airport (☎021-937 1200; www.acsa.co.za/home.asp?pid=229), 22km east of the city centre, has a tourist information office.

Airlines with offices in Cape Town:

1time (☎011-086 8000; www.1time.aero)

Air Mauritius (☎087 1507 242; www.airmauritius.com)

Air Namibia (☎021-422 3224; www.airnamibia.com.na)

British Airways (☎021-936 9000; www.ba.com)

Emirates (☎021-403 1100; www.emirates.com)

KLM (☎0860 247 747; www.klm.com)

Kulula.com (☎0861 585 852; www.kulula.com)

Lufthansa (☎0861 842 538; www.lufthansa.com)

Malaysia Airlines (☎021-419 8010; www.malaysiaairlines.com)

Mango (☎021-815 4100, 0861 162 646; www.flymango.com)

Qatar Airways (☎021-936 3080; www.qatarairways.com)

Singapore Airlines (☎021-674 0601; www.singaporeair.com)

South African Airways (☎021-936 1111; www.flysaa.com)

Virgin Atlantic (☎011-340 3400; www.virgin-atlantic.com)

Bus

Interstate buses arrive at the bus terminus next to **Cape Town Train Station** (Map p48; Heerengracht), where you'll find the booking offices for the following bus companies, all open 6am to 6.30pm daily.

Greyhound (📞083 915 9000; www.greyhound .co.za)

Intercape Mainliner (📞021-380 4400; www .intercape.co.za)

SA Roadlink (📞083 918 3999; www.saroadlink .co.za)

Translux (📞021-449 6942; www.translux.co.za)

Baz Bus (📞021-422 5202; www.bazbus.com) offers hop-on, hop-off fares and door-to-door service between Cape Town and Jo'burg/Pretoria via the Northern Drakensberg, Durban and the Garden Route.

Train

Long distance trains arrive at **Cape Town Train Station** (Map p48; Heerengracht). There are services Wednesday, Friday and Sunday to and from Jo'burg via Kimberley on the **Shosholoza Meyl** (📞0860 008 888; www.shosholozameyl .co.za). These sleeper trains offer comfortable accommodation and dining cars, but if you require something more luxurious opt either for the elegant **Blue Train** (📞021-449 2672; www .bluetrain.co.za), which stops at Matjiesfontein on its way to Pretoria and Kimberley on the way back to Cape Town, or **Rovos Rail** (📞012-315 8242; www.rovos.com).

❶ Getting Around

A listing includes details of the nearest Cape Metro Rail Station or MyCiTi bus stop when it is within 100m or so of the station or stop.

To/From the Airport

MyCiTi buses run every 20 minutes between 5am and 10pm to Civic Centre station. The **fare** (adult/child 4-11/under 4 R53.50/26.50/free) can be paid in cash or using a myconnect card.

Backpacker Bus (📞021-439 7600; www .backpackerbus.co.za) picks up from hostels and hotels in the city and offers airport transfers from R160 per person (R180 between 5pm and 8am).

Expect to pay around R200 for a nonshared taxi; the officially authorised airport taxi company is **Touch Down Taxis** (📞021-919 4659).

All the major car-hire companies have desks at the airport. Driving along the N2 into the city centre from the airport usually takes 15 to 20 minutes, although during rush hours (7am to 9am and 4.30pm to 6.30pm) this can extend up to an hour. There is a petrol station just outside the airport, handy for refilling before drop-off.

Bicycle

If you're prepared for the many hills and long distances between sights, the Cape Peninsula is a terrific place to explore by bicycle. Dedicated

WANT MORE?

For in-depth information, reviews and recommendations at your fingertips, head to the Apple App Store to purchase Lonely Planet's Cape Town City Guide iPhone app.

cycle lanes are a legacy of the World Cup: there's a good one north out of the city towards Table View, and another runs along side the Fan Walk from Cape Town Train Station to Green Point. Unfortunately, bicycles are banned from suburban trains.

The following offer bicycle hire:

Bike & Saddle (📞021-813 6433; www.bikeand saddle.com; hourly rental R30-80)

Cape Town Cycle Hire (📞021-434 1270, 084-400 1604; www.capetowncyclehire.co.za; per day from R150)

Downhill Adventures (Map p52; 📞021-422 0388; www.downhilladventures.com; cnr Orange & Kloof Sts; ⏰8am-6pm Mon-Fri, 8am-1pm Sat; 🚇Buitensingel)

Bus

The new **MyCiTi** (📞0800 656 463; www. capetown.gov.za/myciti) network of commuter buses runs daily between 5am and 10pm. The main routes currently are from the airport to the city centre, from Table Bay to the city and around the City Bowl up to Gardens and out to the Waterfront. There are plans to extend routes along the Atlantic seaboard to Camps Bay and Hout Bay and east to Woodstock and Salt River.

For most city-centre routes the fare is R5; to Table View it is R10 and to the airport R53.50. Fares have to be paid with a stored value myconnect card; the exception is for the Airport–Civic Centre route on which tickets can paid for with cash.

At the time of research the myconnect card could be purchased only from the kiosks at Civic Centre and Table View stations. There is an issuing fee of R22: keep your receipt and you should be able to get this back if you return the card to the kiosk. You then need to charge the card with credit. A bank fee of 2.5% of the value loaded (with a minimum of R1.50) will be charged; so if you load the card with R200 you will have R195 in credit. The card, issued by ABSA, can also be used to pay for low-value transactions at shops and businesses displaying the Mastercard sign.

Golden Arrow (📞0800 656 463; www.gabs .co.za) buses run from the **Golden Acre Terminal** (Map p48; Grand Pde; City Bowl) and are most useful for getting along the Atlantic coast from the city centre to Hout Bay. Destinations and off-peak fares (applicable from 8am to 4pm) from the city include the Waterfront

(R4), Sea Point (R4), Kloof Nek (R4), Camps Bay (R5) and Hout Bay (R8). Peak fares are about 30% higher.

Car & Motorcycle

Cape Town has an excellent road and freeway system that, outside the late-afternoon rush hour, carries surprisingly little traffic. The downside is getting used to the erratic, sometimes dangerous driving by fellow drivers.

Car-hire companies:

Around About Cars (☎021-422 4022; www .aroundaboutcars.com; 20 Bloem St; ☺7.30am-5pm Mon-Fri, 7.30am-1pm Sat & Sun)

Avis (☎021-424 1177; www.avis.co.za; 123 Strand St)

Budget (☎021-418-5232; www.budget.co.za; 120 Strand St)

Hertz (☎021-410 6800; www.hertz.co.za; 40 Loop St)

Status Luxury Vehicles (☎021-510 0108; http://slv.co.za)

The following places hire out two-wheeled motors:

Cape Sidecar Adventures (☎021-434 9855; www.sidecars.co.za; 2 Glengariff Rd)

Harley-Davidson Cape Town (☎021-446 2999; www.harley-davidson-capetown.com; 9 Somerset Rd)

Scoot Dr (☎021-418-5995; www.scootdr.co.za; 61 Waterkant St, City Bowl)

Shared Taxi

In Cape Town (and South Africa in general) a shared taxi means a minibus. These private services, which cover most of the city with an informal network of routes, are a cheap and fast way of getting around. On the downside they're usually crowded and some drivers can be reckless. Useful routes are from Adderley St, opposite the Golden Acre Centre, to Sea Point along Main Rd (R5) and up Long St to Kloof Nek (R5).

The main rank is on the upper deck of Cape Town Train Station and is accessible from a walkway in the Golden Acre Centre or from stairways on Strand St. It's well organised, and finding the right rank is easy. Anywhere else, you just hail shared taxis from the side of the road and ask the driver where they're going.

Rikkis

A cross between a taxi and a shared taxi are **Rikkis** (☎0861 745 547; www.rikkis.co.za). They offer shared rides most places around the City Bowl and down the Atlantic coast to Camps Bay, or in and around Hout Bay, for R15 to R30. They also do regular cab trips for R35 to R55 according to distance travelled, and airport transfers from R180 per person. See the website for locations of its free direct phones including one at the Cape Town Tourism office on Burg St. Rikkis are not the quickest way to get around the city and they are notoriously slow to turn up to a booking.

Taxi

Consider taking a nonshared taxi at night or if you're in a group. Rates are about R10 per kilometre. There's a taxi rank on Adderley St, or call:

Excite Taxis (☎021-448 4444; www.excitetaxis .co.za)

Marine Taxi (☎0861-434 0434, 021-913 6813; www.marinetaxis.co.za)

SA Cab (☎0861 172 222; www.sacab.co.za)

Telecab (☎021-788 2717, 082-222 0282) For transfers from Simon's Town to Boulders and Cape Point.

Train

Cape Metro Rail (☎0800 656 463; www.cape metrorail.co.za) trains are a handy way to get around, although there are few (or no) trains after 6pm on weekdays and after noon on Saturday.

The difference between 1st- and economy-class carriages in price and comfort is negligible. The most important line for visitors is the Simon's Town line, which runs through Observatory and around the back of Table Mountain through upper-income suburbs such as Newlands, on to Muizenberg and the False Bay coast. These trains run at least every hour from 5am to 7.30pm Monday to Friday (to 6pm on Saturday), and from 7.30am to 6.30pm on Sunday.

Metro trains also run out to Strand on the eastern side of False Bay, and into the Winelands to Stellenbosch and Paarl. They are the cheapest and easiest means of transport to these areas; security is best at peak times.

Some economy/1st-class fares are Observatory (R5/7), Muizenberg (R6.50/10), Simon's Town (R7.50/15), Paarl (R10/16) and Stellenbosch (R7.50/13). There's also a R30 ticket that allows unlimited travel between Cape Town and Simon's Town and all stations in between from 8am to 4.30pm daily.

Western Cape

Includes »

Best Places to Eat

» Tasting Room (p105)
» Die Strandloper (p156)
» Jessica's (p132)
» Bosman's Restaurant (p109)
» Old Gaol on Church Square (p121)

Best Places to Stay

» Phantom Forest Eco-Reserve (p145)
» Grootbos Private Nature Reserve (p117)
» Nothando Backpackers Hostel (p149)
» Beaverlac (p159)
» Ballinderry Guesthouse (p126)

Why Go?

The splendours of the Western Cape lie not only in its world-class vineyards, its stunning beaches and its mountains, but also in its lesser known regions, such as the wide-open spaces of the Karoo, the nature reserves and wilderness areas. Make sure you get out into these wild, less-visited areas for birdwatching and wildlife adventure as well as pure relaxation under vast skies.

The Western Cape offers a huge range of activities, from sedate endeavours such as wine tasting or scenic drives to more hair-raising encounters such as skydiving or rock climbing.

The melting pot of cultures of the region begs to be explored. Khoe-San rock art is at its best in the Cederberg mountains and there are some fine opportunities to visit black townships and be entranced by the fascinating culture of the Xhosa people.

When to Go
Knysna

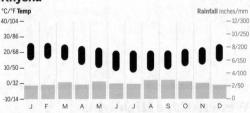

Feb-Mar & Nov Temperatures are perfect, not too hot to hike but still beach weather.

Jun-Aug Whale-watching season begins; flowers bloom on the West Coast.

Dec-Jan Prices rise and visitor numbers increase. Hot days and abundant festivals.

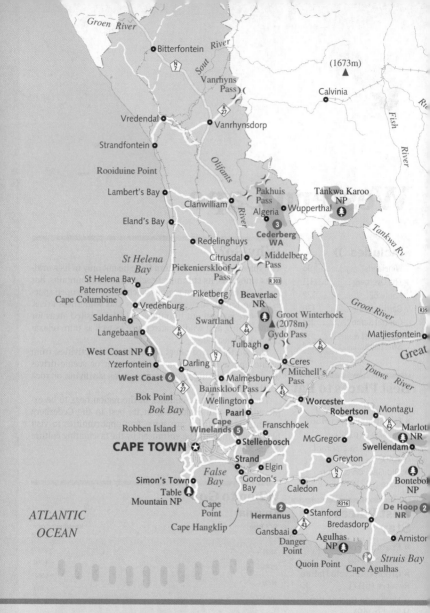

ATLANTIC OCEAN

Western Cape Highlights

① Hiking the **Knysna** (p143) forests or feasting on oysters (p146) along the lagoon

② Watching whales from the cliffs in **Hermanus** (p114) or the dunes of **De Hoop Nature Reserve** (p119)

③ Exploring Khoe-San culture in the **Cederberg Wilderness Area** (p158), where you can hike past bizarre rock formations

④ Following Rte 62 to the ostrich capital, **Oudtshoorn** (p133), then taking the remarkable **Swartberg Pass** (p151) to enjoy Karoo hospitality in **Prince Albert** (p151)

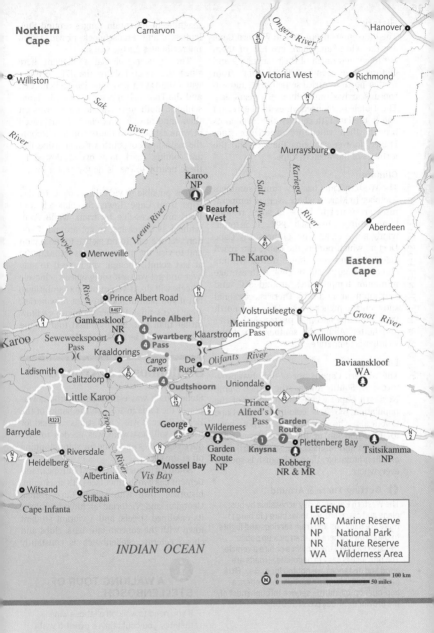

Northern Cape

Carnarvon

Ongers River

Hanover

Williston

Victoria West

Richmond

Murraysburg

Karoo NP

Beaufort West

Merweville

The Karoo

Aberdeen

Eastern Cape

Dwyka River

Prince Albert Road

Karoo

Seweeweekspoort Pass

Gamkaskloof NR

Prince Albert

Swartberg Pass

Klaarstroom

Meiringspoort Pass

Volstruisleegte

Willowmore

Groot River

Baviaanskloof WA

Kraaldorings

Cango Caves

De Rust

Olifants River

Ladismith

Calitzdorp

Little Karoo

Oudtshoorn

Uniondale

Prince Alfred's Pass

Garden Route

Barrydale

Riversdale

George

Wilderness

Garden Route NP

Knysna

Plettenberg Bay

Tsitsikamma NP

Heidelberg

Albertinia

Mossel Bay

Robberg NR & MR

Witsand

Stilbaai

Gouritsmond

Vis Bay

Cape Infanta

INDIAN OCEAN

LEGEND

MR	Marine Reserve
NP	National Park
NR	Nature Reserve
WA	Wilderness Area

0 100 km
0 50 miles

5 Sampling magnificent wines – and food – in the historic towns of the **Cape Winelands** (p96)

6 Learning to kite-surf on the **West Coast** (p156) and rewarding yourself with a beachside seafood extravaganza (p156)

7 Experiencing up-close animal encounters along the **Garden Route** (p136), where you can walk with cheetahs or hang out with elephants

History

The indigenous people of the Western Cape are the Khoe-San. There are few of them left today and much of their languages and cultures have been lost. Bantu tribes from further north in Africa settled here, and Europeans arrived more than 350 years ago. The Dutch introduced vines to the region and in the late 17th century, the Huguenots brought their viticulture experience from France, forever changing the face and the fortunes of the Western Cape.

Climate

The Western Cape has dry, sunny summers (October to March) where average temperatures are warm to hot – in some regions temperatures can reach 38°C. It is often windy, however, and the southeasterly 'Cape Doctor', which buffets the Cape, can reach gale force and cool things down. Winters (June to August) can be cool, with average minimum temperatures around 5°C, and maximums around 17°C. There is occasional snow on the higher peaks. The coast north from the Cape becomes progressively drier and hotter. Along the southern coast the weather is temperate.

Language

The Western Cape is one of only two provinces in South Africa (the other being Northern Cape) where the majority of the population (55%) is coloured. Most Cape Coloureds, who can trace their roots back to the Khoe-San or imported slaves from Indonesia and Madagascar, speak Afrikaans as a first language, though English is spoken everywhere.

ℹ Getting There & Around

The Western Cape is easily accessible by bus, plane and car. From Johannesburg (Jo'burg) there are daily bus and train services and flights to Cape Town, where you can pick up public transport around the province or hire a vehicle. The province is easy to negotiate – roads are good and distances are not too long. Baz Bus (☑0861 229 287; www.bazbus.com) offers a hop-on/hop-off shuttle service through most of the province (14-day pass R1900).

WINELANDS

Venturing inland and upwards from Cape Town you'll find the Boland, meaning 'upland'. It's a superb wine-producing area, and indeed the best known in South Africa. The magnificent mountain ranges around Stellenbosch and Franschhoek provide ideal microclimates for the vines.

There's been colonial settlement here since the latter half of the 17th century when the Dutch first founded Stellenbosch and the French Huguenots settled in Franschhoek. Both towns pride themselves on their innovative young chefs, many based at wine estates, and the region has become the mainspring of South African cuisine. Up-and-coming Paarl, long overshadowed by these nearby towns, is now worth a longer look.

It is possible to visit these towns on day trips from Cape Town. Stellenbosch and Paarl are accessible by train, while Franschhoek is the easiest to get around if you don't have a car. To do justice to the region and to visit the many wineries (around 300 at last count), though, you'll need to stay over and get yourself some wheels – bicycle wheels will do, if you're not too ambitious, but if you plan to pack in a lot of wineries, a car is essential. If you're going to swallow rather than spit, an organised tour of the wineries might be a good idea!

Stellenbosch & Around

☑021 / POP 200,000

Stellenbosch was established by the governor of the Cape in 1679 on the banks of the Eerste River. It was – and still is – famed for its rich soil, just what was needed to produce vegetables and wine for ships stopping off at the Cape.

South Africa's second-oldest European settlement has two distinct faces: it's an elegant, historical town with stately Cape Dutch, Georgian and Victorian architecture along its oak-lined streets, and a vibrant student town with the concomitant bars, clubs and cheap eateries. Stellenbosch is constantly

---

ℹ A WALKING TOUR OF STELLENBOSCH

If you need to walk off all those wine tastings, you could take a guided walk (per person R90; ☐11am & 3pm) from Stellenbosch Tourism (Map p98; ☑021-883 3584; www.stellenbosch tourism.co.za; 36 Market St; ☐8am-5pm Mon-Fri, 9am-2pm Sat & Sun). Bookings are essential for weekend walks.

abuzz as Capetonians, wine-farm workers and tourists descend on its interesting museums, quality hotels and varied eating and nightlife options.

Sights & Activities

IN STELLENBOSCH

TOP CHOICE **Bergkelder**   WINERY

(Map p98; ☎021-809 8025; www.bergkelder.co.za; ⏰8am-5pm Mon-Fri, 9am-2pm Sat, tours 10am, 11am, 2pm & 3pm Mon-Fri, 10am, 11am & noon Sat) For wine lovers without wheels, this cellar a short walk from the town centre is ideal. Hour-long tours (R30) are followed by an atmospheric candle-lit tasting in the cellar. Informal tastings are also available throughout the day.

Village Museum   MUSEUM

(Map p98; 18 Ryneveld St; adult/child R30/5; ⏰9am-5pm Mon-Sat, 10am-4pm Sun) A group of exquisitely restored and period-furnished houses dating from 1709 to 1850 make up this museum, which occupies the entire city block bounded by Ryneveld, Plein, Drostdy and Church Sts and is a must-see. Also included are charming gardens and, on the other side of Drostdy St, stately **Grosvenor House**.

Sasol Art Museum   GALLERY

(Map p98; 52 Ryneveld St; admission by donation; ⏰9am-4.30pm Tue-Sat) Featuring one of the country's best selections of local art, both famous and emerging, this museum also contains an irreplaceable collection of African anthropological treasures.

Toy & Miniature Museum   MUSEUM

(Map p98; Rhenish Parsonage, 42 Market St; adult/child R10/5; ⏰9am-4pm Mon-Fri, 9am-2pm Sat) This delightfully surprising museum features a remarkable collection of amazingly detailed toys ranging from railway sets to dollhouses – ask curator Philip Kleynhans to point out some of the more interesting pieces.

Braak   PARK

(Map p98; Town Sq) At the north end of the Braak, an open stretch of grass, you'll find the neo-Gothic **St Mary's on the Braak Church**, completed in 1852. To the west of the church is the **VOC Kruithuis** (Powder House; adult/child R5/2; ⏰9am-4.30pm Mon-Fri), which was built in 1777 to store the town's weapons and gunpowder and now houses a small military museum. On the northwest

---

DON'T MISS

LYNEDOCH ECOVILLAGE

On Rte 310, some 15km southwest of Stellenbosch and on the railway line from Cape Town, **Lynedoch EcoVillage** (Map p100) is the first ecologically designed, socially mixed community in South Africa. Home of the **Sustainability Institute** (www.sustainability institute.net), there's a preschool and primary school for farm workers' children. Its aim is to promote a sustainable lifestyle based on good governance and alternative energy strategies. Book in advance for a tour (R150 per group).

corner of the square is **Fick House**, also known as the Burgerhuis, a fine example of Cape Dutch style from the late 18th century.

FREE **University of Stellenbosch Art Gallery**   GALLERY

(Map p98; cnr Bird & Dorp Sts; ⏰9am-5pm Mon-Fri, 9am-1pm Sat) In an old Lutheran Church, the university's art gallery focuses on contemporary works by South African artists and art students. It's well worth a visit.

AROUND STELLENBOSCH

There are too many good wineries in the Stellenbosch area to list all of them. Get the free booklet *Stellenbosch and its Wine Routes* from Stellenbosch Tourism for a more complete picture.

TOP CHOICE **Villiera**   WINERY

(Map p100; ☎021-865 2002; www.villiera.com; tastings free; ⏰8.30am-5pm Mon-Fri, 8.30am-3pm Sat) Villiera produces several excellent Méthode Cap Classique wines and a highly rated and very well-priced shiraz. Excellent two-hour wildlife drives (R150 per person) with knowledgeable guides take in the various antelope, zebra and bird species on the farm.

Warwick Estate   WINERY

(Map p100; ☎021-884 4410; www.warwickwine. com; tastings R25; ⏰10am-5pm) Warwick's red wines are legendary, particularly their Bordeaux blends. The winery offers an informative 'Big Five' wine safari through the vineyards (think grape varieties, not large mammals) and picnics to enjoy on the lawns.

Stellenbosch

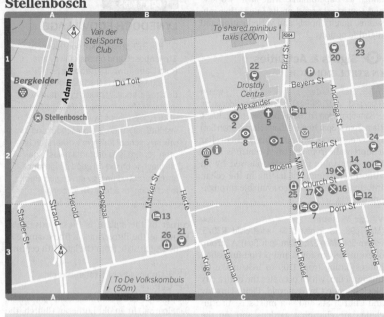

Stellenbosch

Hartenberg Estate WINERY
(Map p100; ☏021-865 2541; www.hartenbergestate.com; tastings free; ⏱9am-5.15pm Mon-Fri, 9am-3pm Sat, 10am-3.30pm Sun) Thanks to a favourable microclimate, Hartenberg produces superlative red wines, particularly cabernet, merlot and shiraz. Lunch is served from noon to 2pm (bookings essential). Picnics

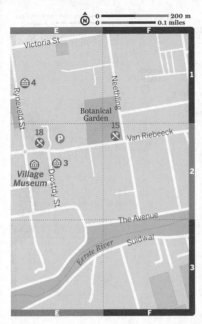

Tours

Bikes 'n Wines WINE
(☎082 492 5429; www.bikesnwines.com; per person R495-690) This innovative company comes highly recommended. Cycling routes range from 9km to 21km and take in three or four Stellenbosch wineries.

Easy Rider Wine Tours WINE
(Map p98; ☎021-886 4651; www.winetour.co.za; 12 Market St) Operates from the Stumble Inn and is a long-established company offering good value for a full-day trip to R400 including lunch and all tastings.

Vine Hopper WINE
(☎021-882 8112; 1-day pass R200) A hop-on/hop-off bus with two routes each covering six estates, the Hopper departs hourly from Stellenbosch Tourism, where you can buy tickets.

Festivals & Events

Spier Festival ARTS
A performing-arts festivals hosted by Spier wine estate and held between January and March.

Rag Week MUSIC
If you're into live music, try to catch early February's Rag Week where local band members vie for the attention of freshmen to celebrate their recent student status.

Wine Festival WINE
(www.wineroute.co.za) This event in early August offers visitors the chance to sample up to 400 different drops in one spot as well as attend talks and tutorials on wine.

Oude Libertas Amphitheatre ARTS
(Map p100; www.oudelibertas.co.za) A performing-arts festival is held here between November and March.

are also available to take on a wetland walk through the estate.

Spier WINERY
(Map p100; ☎021-809 1100; www.spier.co.za; tastings from R35; ◷10am-5pm) Spier has some excellent shiraz, cabernet and red blends, though a visit to this vast winery is less about wine and more about the other activities available. There are bird of prey displays, horse rides through the vines and several restaurants, including Moyo (see p102).

Van Ryn Brandy Cellar WINERY
(Map p100; ☎021-881 3875; www.vanryn.co.za; tastings from R30; ◷8am-5pm Mon-Fri, 9am-2pm Sat) One of 14 stops on the **Western Cape Brandy Route** (www.sabrandy.co.za). It generally runs three tours a day (except for Sunday), including a choice of tastings pairing brandy with coffee, chocolate or cured meats.

Jonkershoek Nature Reserve PARK
(Map p100; adult/child R30/15) This small nature reserve is 8km southeast of town along the WR4 and set within a timber plantation. There are walking and cycling trails ranging from 2.9km to 18km. A hiking map is available at the entrance.

Sleeping

Contact **Stellenbosch Tourism** (☎021-883 3584; www.stellenboschtourism.co.za) if you find the recommendations listed here are booked up.

TOP CHOICE Banghoek Place BACKPACKERS $$
(☎021-887 0048; www.banghoek.co.za; 193 Banghoek Rd; dm/r R150/450; @☎) The owners of this stylish suburban hostel are keen to organise tours of the district. The recreation area has satellite TV and a pool table.

Around Stellenbosch

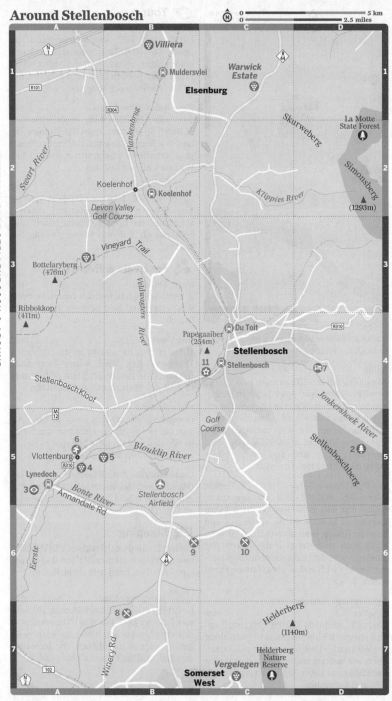

N

0 — 5 km
0 — 2.5 miles

Villiera

Muldersvlei

Warwick Estate

Elsenburg

Skurweberg

La Motte State Forest

R101

R304

Plankenbrug

Koelenhof

Koelenhof

Devon Valley Golf Course

Klippies River

Simonsberg (1293m)

Vineyard Trail

Bottelaryberg (476m)

Ribbokkop (411m)

Veldwagters River

Papegaaiberg (254m)

Du Toit

Stellenbosch

R310

Stellenbosch

7

Stellenbosch Kloof

M12

Golf Course

Jonkershoek River

6

Vlottenburg

5

R310

4

Blouklip River

Stellenboschberg

2

Lynedoch

3

Bonte River

Annandale Rd

Stellenbosch Airfield

Eerste

R44

9

10

8

Winery Rd

R44

Helderberg (1140m)

N2

102

Vergelegen

Somerset West

Helderberg Nature Reserve

N1

Lanzerac Hotel
LUXURY HOTEL $$$

(Map p100; ☎021-887 1132; www.lanzerac.co.za; Jonkershoek Valley; s/d/ste incl breakfast R2560/3410/5780; ✸@☲) This opulent place consists of a 300-year-old manor house and winery. Some suites have private pools and views are stunning.

Ikhaya Backpackers
BACKPACKERS $

(Map p98; ☎021-886 9290; www.stellenbosch backpackers.co.za; 56 Bird St; dm/d R100/360; @) The superb, central location means you're within easy stumbling distance of the bars. Rooms are in converted apartments, so all come with their own kitchen and bathroom.

Stellenbosch Hotel
HOTEL $$

(Map p98; ☎021-887 3644; www.stellenbosch .co.za/hotel; 162 Dorp St; s/d incl breakfast from R835/1040; ✸@) A comfortable country-style hotel with a variety of rooms, including some with self-catering facilities and others with four-poster beds. A section dating from 1743 houses the Jan Cats Brasserie, a good spot for a drink.

D'Ouwe Werf
HISTORIC HOTEL $$$

(Map p98; ☎021-887 4608; www.ouwewerf.co.za; 30 Church St; s/d incl breakfast R1200/1550; ✸☲) This is an appealing, old-style hotel (dating back to 1802). The more expensive luxury

Around Stellenbosch

rooms are furnished with antiques and brass beds.

De Oude Meul
GUESTHOUSE $$

(Map p98; ☎021-887 7085; www.deoudemeul.com; 10A Mill St; s/d incl breakfast R550/790; ✸@) Above an antiques shop in the centre of town, the accommodation here is good and reasonable for the price (which is lower in winter). Some rooms have balconies.

Stumble Inn
BACKPACKERS $

(Map p98; ☎021-887 4049; www.stumbleinnstellen bosch.hostel.com; 12 Market St; campsites per person R50, dm R100, d with shared bathroom R280; @☲) Stellenbosch's undisputed party hostel is split over two old houses. Travellers have expressed concerns over security, so take extra care with your belongings.

✖ Eating

Stellenbosch is a gourmet's delight, with a plethora of restaurants and bars. The surrounding Winelands have the most interesting and innovative options in the country.

TOP CHOICE Apprentice@Institute of Culinary Arts
FUSION $$

(Map p98; Andringa St; mains R45-130; ☺breakfast & lunch Sun & Mon, breakfast, lunch & dinner Tue-Sat) This is a stylish restaurant with a small, inspired menu. The restaurant is operated by students attending the Institute of Culinary Arts and service is excellent.

Rust en Vrede
FUSION $$$

(Map p100; ☎021-881 3757; ☺dinner Tue-Sat) Chef John Shuttleworth prepares a four-course à la carte menu (R480) as well as a six-course tasting menu (with/without wines R880/585) with a contemporary take on the classics. Also a winery, it's at the end of Annandale Rd.

De Oude Bank
DELI $

(Map p98; 7 Church St; platters R45-60; ☺breakfast & lunch Tue-Sun, dinner Wed & Sat) A vibrant bakery and deli priding itself on locally sourced ingredients. The menu changes weekly but always features salads, sandwiches and mezze-style platters. There's live music on Saturday evenings and if you're all wined out it also serves superlative craft beer from a nearby brewery.

96 Winery Road
INTERNATIONAL $$

(Map p100; Zandberg Farm, Winery Rd; mains R105-155; ☺lunch & dinner Mon-Sat, lunch Sun) Off Rte 44 between Stellenbosch and Somerset

West, it's one of the most respected restaurants in the area, known for its dry aged beef.

Brampton Wine Studio MEDITERRANEAN $$
(Map p98; 11 Church St; mains R40-80; ⊙10am-7pm Mon-Sat) Play games and scribble on tables while munching on gourmet pizzas and sipping shiraz at this trendy pavement cafe that also serves as Brampton winery's tasting room.

Overture Restaurant FUSION $$$
(Map p100; ☏021-880 2721; Hidden Valley Wine Estate, off Annandale Rd; 4 courses with/without wines R490/R350; ⊙lunch Tue-Sun, dinner Thu & Fri) A very modern wine estate and restaurant where chef Bertus Basson focuses on local, seasonal produce paired with Hidden Valley wines.

Decameron ITALIAN $$
(Map p98; 50 Plein St; mains R60-140; ⊙lunch & dinner Mon-Sat, lunch Sun) This Italian-food stalwart of Stellenbosch's dining scene has a shady patio next to the botanical gardens.

Botanical Garden Restaurant CAFE $$
(Map p98; Van Riebeeck St; mains R50-90; ⊙9am-5pm) Surrounded by exotic plants, this is a lovely spot for coffee, cake or a light lunch.

Moyo SOUTH AFRICAN $$$
(Map p100; Spier Estate, Lynedoch Rd; buffet R195-250; ⊙lunch & dinner) It seems you have to have your face painted, but this tourist-pleasing place brings a fantasy vision of Africa to the Winelands, and guests love it. It's a lot of fun, with roving musicians and

DON'T MISS

VERGELEGEN

Arguably the most beautiful estate in the Cape. The buildings and elegant grounds have ravishing mountain views and a 'stately home' feel to them. Tasting the flagship **Vergelegen** (Map p100; ☏021-847 1334; www.vergelegen.co.za; Lourensford Rd, Somerset West; adult/child R10/5, tastings R30; ⊙9.30am-4.30pm) wines costs an extra R10. On the dining front you can choose from the casual Rose Terrace, the upmarket Stables at Vergelegen or a picnic hamper (per person R165, November to April) – bookings are essential for the last two options.

dancers, and alfresco dining in tents and up in the trees.

Wijnhuis ITALIAN $$
(Map p98; cnr Church & Andringa Sts; mains R60-185; ⊙breakfast, lunch & dinner) There's an interesting menu here and an extensive wine list stretching to more than 500 labels. Around 20 wines are available by the glass and tastings are available.

De Volkskombuis CAPE MALAY $$
(off Map p98; Aan de Wagenweg; mains R65-130; ⊙lunch & dinner Mon-Sat, lunch Sun) A local favourite that's open year-round, this no-frills, atmospheric place specialises in traditional Cape Malay cuisine.

Drinking

Stellenbosch's nightlife scene is geared largely towards the interests of the university students, but there are classier options. It's safe to walk around the centre at night, so a pub crawl could certainly be on the cards (if you're staying at the Stumble Inn one will probably be organised for you).

Dros, the **Terrace** and **Tollies**, clustered together in the Drostdy Centre complex, just off Bird St and north of the Braak, are among the liveliest bars. Tollies brews its own beer on the premises.

Mystic Boer PUB
(Map p98; 3 Victoria St) Cool kids hang out here in surroundings that can perhaps best described as posttransformation-era retro-Boer chic. Pizzas and steaks are on the menu.

Bohemia BAR
(Map p98; cnr Andringa & Victoria Sts) Offers live music every Tuesday, Thursday and Sunday and hubbly-bubblies (R40) with a range of different tobaccos.

De Akker PUB
(Map p98; 90 Dorp St) Stellenbosch's oldest pub has meals from under R50 and an upstairs cellar for live music.

Nu Bar BAR
(Map p98; 51 Plein St) This place has a nightclub feel, with a small dance floor beyond the long bar where the DJ pumps out hip hop and house.

Shopping

The **craft market** (Map p98; ⊙9am-5pm Mon-Sat) near the Braak is a great place to haggle for African carvings, paintings and costume jewellery.

Oom Samie se Winkel SOUVENIRS
(Uncle Sammy's Shop; Map p98; 84 Dorp St; ⊙8.30am-5.30pm Mon-Fri, 9am-5pm Sat & Sun) This place was on the Stellenbosch map before Stellenbosch was on the map. It's an unashamedly touristy general dealer but still worth visiting for its curious range of goods – from high kitsch to genuine antiques and everything in between.

ℹ Information

Snow Cafe (12 Mill St; per hr R25; ⊙8am-10pm Mon-Fri, 9am-6pm Sat & Sun) Reliable internet access.

Stellenbosch Tourism (Map p98; ☑021-883 3584; www.stellenboschtourism.co.za; 36 Market St; ⊙8am-5pm Mon-Fri, 9am-2pm Sat & Sun) The staff here is extremely helpful. Pick up the excellent brochure *Historical Stellenbosch on Foot* (R5), with a walking-tour map and information on many of the historic buildings (also available in French and German).

ℹ Getting There & Away

Long-distance bus services charge high prices for the short sector to Cape Town and do not take bookings. The **Baz Bus** (☑021-439 2323; www.bazbus.com) runs daily to and from Cape Town (R160, 30 minutes).

Shared taxis to Paarl leave from the stand on Bird St (about R45, 45 minutes).

Metro trains run the 46km between Cape Town and Stellenbosch (1st/economy class R13/7.50, about one hour). For inquiries, call **Metrorail** (☑0800 656 463). To be safe, travel in the middle of the day. If coming from Jo'burg, change to a metro train at Wellington.

ℹ Getting Around

Stellenbosch is navigable on foot and, being largely flat, this is good cycling territory. Bikes can be hired from the **Adventure Centre** (☑021-882 8112; per day R140), next to Stellenbosch Tourism.

For local trips in a private taxi call **Daksi Cab** (☑082 854 1541).

Franschhoek

☑021 / POP 13,000

French Huguenots settled in this spectacular valley more than 300 years ago, bringing their vines with them. Ever since, the town has clung to its French roots; Bastille Day is celebrated with boules matches, berets and brie. Franschhoek bills itself as the country's gastronomic capital, and you'll certainly have a tough time deciding where to eat.

And with a clutch of art galleries, wine farms and stylish guesthouses thrown in, it really is one of the loveliest towns in the Cape.

◉ Sights & Activities

Huguenot Fine Chocolates CHOCOLATIER
(☑021-876 4096; www.huguenotchocolates.com; 62 Huguenot St; ⊙8am-5pm Mon-Fri, 9am-5.30pm Sat & Sun) An empowerment program gave the two local guys who run this chocolatier a leg up and now people are raving about their confections. Call in advance to arrange a tour and chocolate-making demonstration including a tasting (R35).

Huguenot Memorial Museum MUSEUM
(Lambrecht St; adult/child R10/5; ⊙9am-5pm Mon-Sat, 2-5pm Sun) This museum celebrates South Africa's Huguenots and houses the genealogical records of their descendants. Behind the main complex is a pleasant cafe; in front is the **Huguenot Monument** (admission free; ⊙9am-5pm), opened in 1948, and across the road is the **annexe**, which offers displays on the Anglo-Boer War and natural history.

Ceramics Gallery GALLERY
(24 Dirkie Uys St; ⊙10am-5pm) You can watch David Walters, one of South Africa's most distinguished potters, at work in the beautifully restored home of Franschhoek's first teacher. There are also exhibits of work by other artists.

Paradise Stables HORSE RIDING
(www.paradisestables.co.za; per hr R200; ⊙Mon-Sat) As well as hourly rides through Franschhoek's surrounds, there are four-hour trips taking in two vineyards (R600 including tastings).

Manic Cycles CYCLING
(www.maniccycles.co.za; Fabriek St; half/full day R120/200) You can rent bikes or join a guided cycling tour visiting three different wine estates (R315).

Wineries

Many of Franschhoek's wineries are within walking distance of the town centre.

Chamonix WINERY
(www.chamonix.co.za; Uitkyk St; tastings R20; ⊙9.30am-4.30pm) Chamonix has cellar tours at 11am and 3pm by appointment (R10). The tasting room is in a converted blacksmith's; there's also a range of schnapps and grappa to sample. The pretty, bistro-style restaurant, **Mon Plaisir** (mains R135-200; ⊙lunch Tue-Sun,

Franschhoek

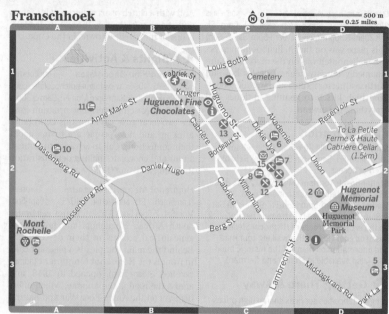

dinner Wed-Sat), has a French menu featuring seasonal produce. Chamonix has self-catering cottages amid the vineyards.

Mont Rochelle   WINERY
(www.montrochelle.co.za; Dassenberg Rd; tastings R20; ⊙tastings 10am-7pm, tours 11am, 12.30pm & 3pm Mon-Fri, 11am & 3pm Sat & Sun) You can combine your wine tasting with a cheese platter (R75) here or enjoy lunch (mains R50 to R90) with a view of the town and the mountains beyond.

Grande Provence   WINERY
(www.grandeprovence.co.za; Main Rd; tastings R20; ⊙10am-6pm) A beautifully revamped, 18th-century manor house that is home to a stylish restaurant and a splendid gallery showcasing contemporary South African art. Tasting the flagship Grande Provence red costs an extra R80.

🛏 Sleeping

TOP CHOICE Reeden Lodge   CHALET $$
(☑021-876 3174; www.reedenlodge.co.za; Anne Marie St; cottage from R600; 🆇) A good-value, terrific option for families, with well-equipped, self-catering cottages sleeping up to eight people, situated on a farm about 10 minutes' walk from town. Parents will love the peace and quiet and their kids will love the sheep, tree house and open space.

Otter's Bend Lodge   BACKPACKERS $
(☑021-876 3200; www.ottersbendlodge.co.za; Dassenberg Rd; campsite R100, s/d R250/450) A delightful budget option in a town lacking in affordable accommodation. Double rooms lead on to a shared deck shaded by poplar trees or there's space for a couple of tents on the lawn. It's a 15-minute walk from town and close to the Mont Rochelle winery.

Chamonix Guest Cottages   CHALET $
(☑021-876 8406; www.chamonix.co.za; Uitkyk St; cottage per person from R300) Pleasant cottages sleeping up to four are set in the middle of the vineyards, a 20-minute walk uphill north of Huguenot St.

Le Quartier Français   BOUTIQUE HOTEL $$$
(☑021-876 2151; www.lequartier.co.za; 16 Huguenot St; d from R3900; 🅰@🆇) This is one of the best places to stay in the Winelands. Set around a leafy courtyard and pool, guest rooms are very large with fireplaces, huge beds and stylish decor. There's a bistro here as well as arguably the country's top restaurant, the Tasting Room (p105).

Franschhoek

Le Ballon Rouge
GUESTHOUSE $$

(☎021-876 2651; www.ballonrouge.co.za; 7 Reservoir St East; s/d incl breakfast R700/850; ❄@☎) A small guesthouse with good-quality rooms and stylish suites (with underfloor heating and stunning bathrooms) all opening onto a patio.

La Cabrière Country House
GUESTHOUSE $$

(☎021-876 4780; www.lacabriere.co.za; Park Lane; d incl breakfast from R1200; ❄@☎) A modern boutique guesthouse that's a refreshing break from all that Cape Dutch architecture. There are six sumptuously decorated rooms with underfloor heating, personal service and sweeping views to the mountains.

Mont Rochelle Hotel
BOUTIQUE HOTEL $$$

(☎021-876 2110; www.montrochelle.co.za; Dassenberg Rd; d incl breakfast from R3500; ❄@☎) A boutique hotel-and-restaurant partly built into the hills, this place offers gilt-edged luxury and magnificent views across the valley.

La Fontaine
GUESTHOUSE $$$

(☎021-876 2112; www.la fontainefranschhoek.co.za; 21 Dirkie Uys St; s/d incl breakfast R1010/1600; ❄☎) A stylishly appointed, very comfortable family home featuring 14 spacious rooms with wooden floors and mountain views.

✕ Eating

Franschhoek's compactness means it's possible to stroll around and let your nose tell you where to eat. The following places are well established, however, and advance booking is best.

TOP CHOICE Common Room
SOUTH AFRICAN $$

(☎021-876 2151; 16 Huguenot St; mains R45-85; ⏰breakfast, lunch & dinner) The recently revamped bistro option at Le Quartier Français still offers South African ingredients such as wildebeest and crayfish in modern, original dishes. Also here is the **Tasting Room** (5-course meal R620; ⏰dinner) consistently rated as one of the world's 50 top restaurants by *Restaurant Magazine* UK. If you're really serious about food, chef Margot Janse will whip up the gourmet, nine-course menu at R770 (R1150 with wine pairings).

Haute Cabrière Cellar
FUSION $$

(☎021-876 3688; Franschhoek Pass Rd; mains R75-145; ⏰lunch Tue-Sun, dinner Wed-Mon) As well as the delectable à la carte option offering imaginative dishes, there is a six-course set menu with accompanying wines (R750). Tastings are also available at the cellar and on Saturdays the proprietor's performs the *sabrage:* slicing open a bottle of bubbly with a sabre.

La Petite Ferme
SOUTH AFRICAN $$

(Franschhoek Pass Rd; mains R90-140; ⏰noon-4pm) In a stupendous setting overlooking the valley, this is a must for foodies. Sample the boutique wines and smoked, deboned salmon trout, its delicately flavoured signature dish. There are some luxurious rooms if you can't bear to leave.

Reuben's
FUSION $$$

(☎021-876 3772; 19 Huguenot St; mains R80-220; ⏰breakfast, lunch & dinner) The flagship restaurant for this local celebrity chef has a deli-style eatery as well as a courtyard for

LOCAL KNOWLEDGE

WINE TASTING OFF THE BEATEN TRACK

The Cape Winelands are glorious but some of the more famous estates can get crowded. We asked Cathy Marston, wine journalist and educator, for her top tip on where to head for wonderful wine without the throngs.

'Once you reach the heights of Sir Lowry's Pass, don't just zoom on through to Hermanus, but stay a while and wander around the most up-and-coming wine region in South Africa – Elgin. Much lauded for its cool-climate whites from sauvignon blanc to chardonnay, the area has also produced some of the country's top pinot noirs from the likes of Catherine Marshall Wines, Paul Cluver Wines, Shannon Vineyards and Oak Valley. Turn off past the Peregrine Farmstall (N2, ⊙7.30am-6pm), meander down scenic lanes through stunning scenery and taste at will. Elgin is part of the world's first biodiversity wine route, the Green Mountain Eco Route, and there are plenty of scenic walks in the area as well as delicious wine. If you're feeling active, get on your bike at Oak Valley (⊘021-859 2510; R321 to Villiersdorp; tastings R20; ⊙9am-5pm Mon-Fri, 10am-2pm Sat) and cycle through one of the well-marked trails or catch your supper at one of the three trout dams in the area. If you're lucky, you might catch top international performers at the Paul Cluver Amphitheatre (⊘021-844 0605; De Rust Estate, off N2; tastings free; picnics R120 per person; ⊙8am-5pm Mon-Fri, 10am-2pm Sat) set in among the trees, which also offers picnic baskets and exquisite wines. There's also great food to be had at South Hill Wines (⊘021 844 0888; The Valley Road, off the N2; tastings R20; ⊙9am-5pm Mon-Fri, 10am-3pm Sat) and black-empowerment wine farm Thandi (⊘021-844 0247; off the N2; tastings R20; ⊙7.30am-5pm Mon-Thu, 7.30am-4.30pm Fri-Sun), and at Highlands Road (⊘071 271 0161; Highlands Road; tastings free; ⊙9.30pm-3pm) pizza night is not to be missed!'

breakfast and lunch. Dinner is served in the restaurant.

Kalfi's   SOUTH AFRICAN $$
(17 Huguenot St; mains R55-190; ⊙breakfast, lunch & dinner) You can watch the world go by from the shady verandah of this family-oriented restaurant. There's a children's menu and a number of vegetarian options.

French Connection   INTERNATIONAL $$
(48 Huguenot St; mains R70-125; ⊙lunch & dinner) No-nonsense bistro-style food using only fresh ingredients is dished up at this deservedly popular place.

ⓘ Information

Franschhoek Photolab (28 Huguenot St; per hr 30) There's internet access on offer here.

Franschhoek Wine Valley Tourism (⊘021-876 2861; www.franschhoek.org.za; 62 Huguenot St; ⊙8am-6pm Mon-Fri, 9am-5pm Sat, 9am-4pm Sun) Staff here can provide you with a map of the area's scenic walks and issue permits (R10) for walks in nearby forestry areas, as well as book accommodation.

ⓘ Getting There & Away

Franschhoek is 32km east of Stellenbosch and 25km south of Paarl. The best way to reach Franschhoek is in your own vehicle. Some

visitors choose to cycle here from Stellenbosch, but roads are winding and can be treacherous, with drivers returning from all-day wine-tasting sessions. Still, it's certainly a scenic ride. Normal out-of-shape souls can take a shared taxi from Stellenbosch (R20) or Paarl station (R22). A private taxi is an option: call **Isak de Wet** (⊘083 951 1733).

Paarl & Around

⊘021 / POP 165,000

The largest town in the Winelands, Paarl lies on the banks of the Berg River and is surrounded by mountains and vineyards. Long overlooked by people heading for Stellenbosch and Franschhoek, its charm is now being rediscovered. The town has interesting Cape Dutch architecture and gracious homesteads, a good range of places to stay and a rash of new restaurants.

It's not a town to tour on foot because the main road is over 11km long, but there is still quite a lot to see and do, including visiting vineyards within the town limits.

◉ Sights & Activities

IN PAARL

For information about wineries in the area, contact **Paarl Vintners** (⊘021-863 4886).

Laborie Cellar
WINERY

(Map p108; Taillefer St; tastings R15; ⏱9am-5pm Mon-Fri, 10am-5pm Sat) Best known for its award-winning shiraz, Laborie also produces good MCC and dessert wines. Tasting options including wine and olives (R22), chocolate (R35) or combining its vintages with an estate tour (R30). There's an excellent artisanal food market held here on Saturday mornings.

KWV Emporium
WINERY

(Map p108; www.kwvwineemporium.co.za; Kohler St; cellar tour with tastings R35; ⏱9am-4pm Mon-Sat, 11am-4pm Sun) This winery is a good first stop when exploring the Paarl region. Its fortified wines, in particular, are among the world's best. **Cellar tours** (⏱10am, 10.30am & 2.15pm) are available and there is a range of tasting options, including chocolate and brandy (R40).

Paarl Mountain Nature Reserve
PARK

(Map p110) The three giant granite domes that dominate this popular reserve and loom over the western side of town glisten like pearls when washed by rain – hence the name 'Paarl'. The reserve has mountain *fynbos* (literally 'fine bush'; primarily proteas, heaths and ericas), a cultivated wildflower garden in the middle that's a delightful picnic spot, and numerous walks with excellent views over the valley. A map showing walking trails is available from Paarl Tourism.

While up this way you could also visit the **Taal Monument** (Map p108; adult/child R15/5; ⏱8am-5pm), a giant needlelike edifice that commemorates the Afrikaans language (*taal* is Afrikaans for 'language'). On a clear day there are stunning views from here as far as Cape Town.

Paarl Museum
MUSEUM

(Map p108; www.museums.org.za/paarlmuseum; 303 Main St; admission by donation of R5; ⏱9am-5pm Mon-Fri, 9am-1pm Sat) Housed in the Oude Pastorie (Old Parsonage), built in 1714, this museum has an interesting collection of Cape Dutch antiques and relics of Huguenot and early Afrikaner culture.

Afrikaans Language Museum
MUSEUM

(Map p108; www.taalmuseum.co.za; 11 Pastorie Ave; adult/child R15/5; ⏱9am-4pm Mon-Fri) Paarl is considered the wellspring of the Afrikaans language, a fact covered by this interesting museum. It also shows, thanks to a multimedia exhibition, how three continents contributed to the formation of what is a fascinating language.

Wineland Ballooning
SCENIC FLIGHTS

(Map p108; ☎021-863 3192; 64 Main St; per person R2580) You'll need to get up very early in the morning, but a hot-air balloon trip over the Winelands will be unforgettable. Trips run between November and May when the weather conditions are right.

AROUND PAARL

TOP CHOICE Boschendal
WINERY

(Map p110; ☎021-870 4210; www.boschendal.com; Rte 310, Groot Drakenstein; tastings R20; ⏱9am-5.30pm) You'll need transport to reach this quintessential Winelands estate, with lovely architecture, food and wine. The vineyard (R35) and cellar tours (R25) are well worth it; booking is essential. For a dose of history with your wine, take the self-guided tour of the **manor house** (R15). Boschendal has three eating options: the huge buffet lunch (R240) in the main restaurant, light lunches in **Le Café** or a 'Le Pique Nique' hamper (adult/child R150/59; bookings essential), served under parasols on the lawn from September to May.

Solms-Delta
WINERY

(Map p110; ☎021-874 3937; www.solms-delta.com; Delta Rd, off R45; tastings R10; ⏱9am-5pm Sun & Mon, 9am-6pm Tue-Sat) In addition to its excellent museum telling the story of the wine farm from the perspective of farm workers throughout the years, there's also an indigenous plants garden, **Fyndraai restaurant** (mains R90-140) serving delicious Cape Malay–inspired food and picnics that can be enjoyed along an enchanting trail beside the Dwars River.

Fairview
WINERY

(Map p110; ☎021-863 2450; www.fairview.co.za; wine & cheese tasting R25; ⏱9am-5pm) This hugely popular estate on the Suid-Agter-Paarl Rd, off Rte 101, 6km south of Paarl is a wonderful winery but not the place to come for a calm tasting. It is great value though, since tasting options cover some 30 wines *and* a wide range of goats'- and cows'-milk cheeses.

Spice Route
WINERY

(Map p110; ☎021-863 5200; www.spiceroutewines.co.za; tastings with/without cellar tour R35/25; ⏱9am-5pm Sun-Thu, 9am-6pm Fri & Sat) Also owned by Charles Back of Fairview, Spice Route, off Suid-Agter-Paarl Rd, is known for its complex red wines, particularly the Flagship syrah. Aside from wine there is a

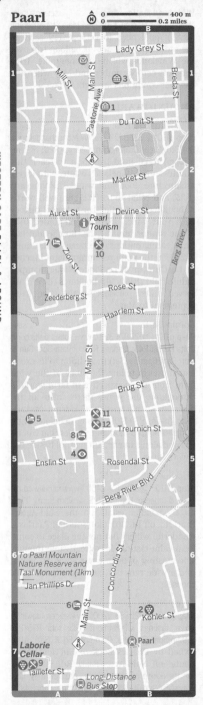

Paarl

◎ Top Sights

◎ Sights

⌂ Sleeping

✕ Eating

lot going on here, including glass-blowing demonstrations, food and wine pairings and a **restaurant** (mains R90-135). Plans to open a chocolate factory, distillery and microbrewery were underway when this guide was being researched.

Backsberg WINERY
(Map p110; ☎021-875 5141; www.backsberg.co.za; tastings R15; ⊙8am-5pm Mon-Fri, 9.30am-4.30pm Sat, 10.30am-4.30pm Sun) Backsberg is an immensely popular estate thanks to its reliable label and lavish outdoor lunches. This was South Africa's first carbon-neutral wine farm and its wines include the easy-drinking Tread Lightly range, packaged in lightweight, environmentally friendly bottles.

Nederburg Wines WINERY
(Map p110; ☎021-862 3104; www.nederburg.co.za; tastings R20-85; ⊙8am-5pm Mon-Fri year-round, plus 10am-4pm Sat, 11am-4pm Sun Nov-Mar) This is one of South Africa's best known labels, a big but professional and welcoming operation featuring a vast range of wines. Inventive tasting options include a brandy, coffee and biscotti experience and the Burgermaster Tasting – pairing reserve wines with a range of mini burgers.

Glen Carlou WINERY
(Map p110; ☎021-875 5528; www.glencarlou.co.za; Simonium Rd, Klapmuts; tastings R25-35;

⊙8.30am-5pm Mon-Fri, 10am-4pm Sat & Sun) Sitting south of the N1, the tasting room here has a panoramic view of Tortoise Hill. Enjoy a glass of the sumptuous chardonnay or renowned Bordeaux blend, Grand Classique, over lunch (mains R85 to R150). There's an art gallery here too.

Drakenstein Prison HISTORIC SITE

(Map p110) On 11 February 1990, when Nelson Mandela walked free from incarceration for the first time in more than 27 years, the jail in question was not Robben Island, but here. There's a superb statue of him, fist raised in *viva* position, at the entrance. Then called the Victor Verster, this prison was where Mandela spent his last two years of captivity in the relative comfort of the warders cottage, negotiating the end of apartheid. It's still a working prison so there are no tours, but there is a grill-style **restaurant** (⊘reservations 021-864 8095).

⎧ Sleeping

TOP CHOICE **Oak Tree Lodge** GUESTHOUSE $$

(Map p108; ⊘021-863 2631; www.oaktreelodge .co.za; 32 Main St; garden s/d incl breakfast R570/790; ✳@✳) Centrally located, this old house has comfortable, well-appointed rooms, some with balconies, as well as modern rooms and suites at the back (which are quieter, being off the main road).

Berg River Resort CAMPGROUND $

(Map p110; ⊘021-863 1650; www.bergriverresort .co.za; campsites from R55, d chalets from R425; ✳) An attractive camping ground beside the Berg River, 5km from Paarl on the N45 towards Franschhoek. Facilities include canoes, trampolines and a cafe. It gets very crowded during school holidays and is best avoided then.

Grande Roche Hotel LUXURY HOTEL $$$

(Map p108; ⊘021-863 2727; www.granderoche .co.za; Plantasie St; d from R3025; ✳@✳) A superluxurious hotel set in a Cape Dutch manor house, offering wonderful mountain views, a heated swimming pool and the award-winning Bosman's Restaurant.

Mooikelder Manor House GUESTHOUSE $$

(Map p110; ⊘021-869 8787; www.mooikelder.co.za; Main St, Noorder Paarl; s/d incl breakfast R470/840; @✳) Around 5km north of the town centre in an elegant homestead once occupied by British empire-builder and former governor of the Cape Colony Cecil John Rhodes, this

is a lovely, quiet spot amid citrus orchardss. There is plenty of antique atmosphere in the rooms.

Rodeberg Lodge GUESTHOUSE $$

(Map p108; ⊘021-863 3202; www.rodeberglodge .co.za; 74 Main St; s/d incl breakfast R450/700; ✳@) Good rooms, some with air-con and TV. There's also a family room (R300 per person) in the attic. The hosts are friendly and travellers love the breakfasts taken in the conservatory.

Pontac Manor BOUTIQUE HOTEL $$

(Map p108; ⊘021-872 0445; www.pontac.com; 16 Zion St; s/d incl breakfast R790/995; ✳@✳) A small, stylish hotel in a delightful Victorian house with good views over the valley. The rooms are comfortable and have underfloor heating. The restaurant here is recommended.

✕ Eating & Drinking

Several local wineries also have excellent restaurants or do picnic lunches.

TOP CHOICE **Bosman's Restaurant**

(Map p108; ⊘021-863 2727; www.granderoche.co .za; Plantasie St; mains from R130) This elegant spot within the Grande Roche Hotel is one of the country's top restaurants. They're best known for the eight-course tasting menu (R660) and the spectacular wine list, which runs to more than 40 pages! Bookings highly recommended.

TOP CHOICE **Harvest at Laborie** SOUTH AFRICAN $$

(Map p108; Taillefer St; mains R70-115; ⊙breakfast Sat, lunch Mon-Sun, dinner Wed-Sat) Eat on a patio overlooking vines at this elegant wine estate a short walk from Main St. Local produce dominates the menu, including West Coast mussels, Karoo lamb and seasonal game steaks.

Noop FUSION $$

(Map p108; 127 Main St; mains R95-135; ⊙lunch & dinner Mon-Fri) Recommended by locals all over the Winelands, this restaurant and wine bar has a small but excellent menu and really fresh salads.

Marc's Mediterranean Cuisine & Garden MEDITERRANEAN $$

(Map p108; 129 Main St; mains R90-140; ⊙lunch & dinner Mon-Sat, lunch Sun) Another favourite, and with good reason. Patron Marc Friedrich has created a light and bright place

Around Paarl

N

0 _____ 5 km
0 _____ 2.5 miles

A | B | C | D

1

R44

11

Wellington

Mbekweni

R45

Leeu River

Hawekwaberge

2

R45

R301

Dal Josefat

Paarl

Huguenot

6

Paarlberge

Du Toits Kloof Pass

3

7

Jan Phillips Dr

N1

Huguenot Toll Tunnel

Wemmershoekberge

Suid-Agter-Paarl Rd

9

Paarl

4

4

R101

10

R303

Drakenstein River

5

Cillie

WR1

5

Klein Drakensteinberge

Berg River

Wemmershoek Dam

Wemmers River

6

1

Simondium

R45

3

Groot Drakenstein

8

Wemmershoek

Lategan

La Motte

12

13

Robertsvlei Rd

7

La Motte State Forest

2

R310

Rhone

Pniel

Kylemore

Banhoek

Hottentotsholland Nature Reserve

Around Paarl

with food to match and a Provence-style garden to dine in.

Kikka   CAFE $
(Map p108; 217 Main St; mains R20-70; ⊘7.30am-5pm Mon-Fri, 7.30am-3pm Sat) Watch florists at work in this delightful deli and cafe with its funky, retro decor. It's a great spot for breakfast and a little people-watching.

**Farm Kitchen at
Goederust**   SOUTH AFRICAN $$
(Map p110; ☏021-876 3687; Main Rd, La Motte; mains R60-105; ⊘breakfast & lunch Tue-Sun) A new take on Cape farm-kitchen food is served in this charming old-fashioned farm-restaurant that's set in a pleasant garden. On Sundays there's a spit-braai (barbecue) lamb buffet (bookings essential).

Bread & Wine   MEDITERRANEAN $$
(Map p110; Môreson Wine Farm, Happy Valley Rd, La Motte; mains R65-105; ⊘lunch) Hidden away down a dirt road as you approach town along Rte 45, this place is worth searching out. It's known for its breads, pizzas, cured meats and tasty Mediterranean-style cuisine.

ⓘ Information

Paarl Tourism (Map p108; ☏021-872 4842; www.paarlonline.com; 216 Main St; ⊘8am-5pm Mon-Fri, 10am-1pm Sat & Sun) This office has an excellent supply of information on the whole region.

ⓘ Getting There & Away
Bus

All the major long-distance bus companies offer services going through Paarl, making it easy to build it into your itinerary. The bus segment between Paarl and Cape Town is R160, so consider taking the cheaper train to Paarl and then linking up with the buses.

The **long-distance bus stop** (Map p108) is opposite the Shell petrol station on Main St as you enter the town from the N1.

Train

Metro trains run roughly every hour between Cape Town and Paarl (1st/economy class R16/10, 1¼ hours). Services are less frequent on weekends. Take care to travel on trains during the busy part of the day, for safety reasons.

You can travel by train from Paarl to Stellenbosch; take a Cape Town–bound train and change at Muldersvlei. If coming from Jo'burg, change to a metro train at Wellington.

ⓘ Getting Around

If you don't have your own transport, your only option for getting around Paarl, apart from walking and cycling, is to call a taxi; try **Paarl Taxis** (☏021-872 5671).

THE OVERBERG

Over the mountain – the literal meaning of Overberg – you'll find a landscape that's quite different from the Cape Flats. Here the rolling wheat fields are bordered by the mountains of the Franschhoekberge, Wemmershoekberge and the Riviersonderendberge, the Breede River and the coast.

There are no unattractive routes leading to the Overberg; the N2 snakes up Sir Lowry's Pass, which has magnificent views from the top, while Rte 44 stays at sea level and winds its way round Cape Hangklip, skirts the Kogelberg Biosphere Reserve and eventually reaches Hermanus. It's a stunning coastal drive, on a par with Chapman's Peak Dr in Cape Town, but without the toll.

Hermanus is a major draw for whales in the calving season (June to December) and for people wanting to watch them from easily accessed points throughout the town. If you're keen to escape the crowds that gather here, head for the less crowded whale-watching spots around Gansbaai, Arniston and the magical De Hoop Nature Reserve. Further inland is the elegant town of Swellendam, which makes a perfect base for exploring the entire region.

The Overberg & Route 62

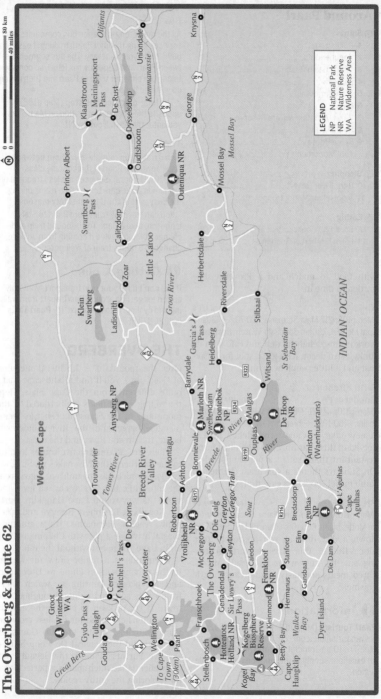

WELLINGTON

This sedate and reasonably pretty town is 10km north of Paarl. Like surrounding towns, the main draw card is the range of wineries, which offer a less touristy experience than those in Paarl. Ask at the **tourism bureau** (☎021-873 4604; www.wellington.co.za; 104 Main St; ⊙8am-5pm Mon-Fri, 10am-1pm Sat & Sun) for a list of local wineries and information on the **Wellington Wine Walk**. While in the area, don't miss the chance to drive the spectacular **Bainskloof Pass**, one of South Africa's finest. It was built between 1848 and 1852 by legendary pass builder Thomas Bain, and other than having its surface tarred, the road has not been altered since.

There are several nearby walks, including the five-hour **Bobbejaans River Walk** to a waterfall. This walk starts at Eerste Tol and you need to buy a **permit** (adult/child R30/15), which is available from Wellington Tourism.

Kogelberg Biosphere Reserve

Proclaimed in 1988 as the first Unesco Biosphere Reserve in South Africa, the **Kogelberg Biosphere Reserve** (☎028-271 4792; www.capenature.co.za; adult/child R30/15) encompasses 1000 sq km.

The reserve has the most complex biodiversity on the planet, including more than 1880 plant species. Birdlife is prolific, wild horses live in the wetlands, and whales can be seen offshore. There are day hikes and overnight trails, and the reserve is used by mountain bikers; permits are required for all activities in the reserve. There are eco-friendly self-catering **cabins** (☎021-483 0190; 4-person cabin R1600) available if you want to stay over.

Kogel Bay Pleasure Resort (☎021-850 4172; Rte 44; campsites R90) has campsites and reasonable facilities on a fantastic surf beach (although it's unsafe for swimming and often windy). Bring all your own food.

You'll need your own vehicle to visit the Kogelberg reserve. Take the N2 from Cape Town to Somerset West, then turn right towards Gordon's Bay and follow Rte 44 that winds its spectacular way around the coastline.

Betty's Bay
☎028

The small, scattered holiday village of Betty's Bay, on Rte 44, is worth a pause. Just before entering Betty's Bay proper as you approach from Cape Town, look out for **Stony Point African Penguin Colony** (admission R10; ⊙8am-5pm). It's a much quieter place

to watch the diminutive penguins than at the infinitely more famous Boulders Beach, across the other side of False Bay. After driving through Betty's Bay, you'll find the **Harold Porter National Botanical Gardens** (adult/child R17/7; ⊙8am-4.30pm Mon-Fri, 8am-5pm Sat & Sun), definitely worth visiting. There are paths exploring the indigenous plant life in the area and, at the entrance, a tearoom and plenty of places to picnic. Try the Leopard Kloof Trail, which leads through fern forests and up to a waterfall – it's a 3km round-trip. You'll need to pay a key deposit (R30) and get your key and permit before 2pm.

Kleinmond
☎028

Close to a wild and beautiful beach, Kleinmond (on Rte 44) has recently become a rather chic destination. It's a great place to spend an afternoon, eat some fresh seafood and browse the shops. It's much less commercialised than Hermanus and has excellent opportunities for whale-watching, consistent waves for surfers and good walking.

🛏 Sleeping & Eating

Most eating options are on Harbour Rd.

Palmiet Caravan Park   CAMPGROUND $
(☎076 371 8938; sea-view campsites from R185) Beside the beach on the western side of town. You can hear the waves breaking from your tent. Follow the signs from Rte 44.

Alive Alive-O   SEAFOOD $$
(☎028-271 3774; 35 Harbour Rd; mains R50-250; ⊙lunch Mon-Sat, dinner Wed-Sat) This outdoor beach-shack shellfish-bar serves a wide

range of fresh fish and sushi and there's a great whale-viewing deck.

ℹ️ Information

Staff at the new **Hangklip-Kleinmond tourism bureau** (☎028-271 5657; www.ecoscape.org .za; 14 Harbour Rd; ☺8.30am-5pm Mon-Fri, 9am-2pm Sat, 10am-2pm Sun) have information on the Kogelberg Biosphere Reserve, Pringle Bay, Rooi Els, Betty's Bay and Kleinmond.

Hermanus

📋028 / POP 45,000

Hermanus might once have been a small fishing village, but today is a large, bustling town with an excellent range of accommodation, restaurants and shops. Only 122km from Cape Town, it's perfect for a day trip as well as being extremely popular with South African holidaymakers. The surge in growth in recent years is due not only to its pretty beaches but also mainly to the presence in Walker Bay, from June to December, of large numbers of southern right whales. Hermanus is considered the best land-based whale-watching destination in the world.

The town stretches over a long main road, but the centre is easily navigable on foot. There's a superb cliff-path walk and plenty of other walks in the *fynbos*-covered hills around the town, good wine tasting, and the **Hermanus Whale Festival** (www.whalefestival .co.za) in September. The town gets very crowded at this time and during the December and January school holidays.

◎ Sights & Activities

TOP CHOICE **Cliff Path Walking Trail** HIKING
The path meanders for 10km from the new harbour, 2km west of town, along the sea to the mouth of the Klein River, though you can join it anywhere along the cliffs.

Along the way you will pass Grotto Beach, the most popular beach with excellent facilities; Kwaaiwater, a good whale-watching lookout; as well as Langbaai and Voelklip Beaches.

Old Harbour HISTORIC SITE
The old harbour clings to the cliffs in front of the town centre; the **museum** (adult/child R15/5; ☺9am-1pm & 2-5pm Mon-Sat, noon-4pm Sun) doesn't really have a lot going for it, but outside there's a display of old fishing boats. The admission fee includes entrance to the more interesting **Whale House Museum**

Hermanus

(☺9am-4pm Mon-Sat, whale shows 10am & 3pm) and the **Photographic Museum** (☺9am-4pm Mon-Fri, 9am-1pm Sat) located on Market Sq. There's a permanent craft market in the square as well.

FREE **Fernkloof Nature Reserve** PARK
(http://fernkloof.com; Fir Ave; ☺9am-5pm) This 14-sq-km reserve is wonderful if you're interested in *fynbos*. Researchers have identified 1474 species so far. There's a 60km network of hiking trails for all fitness levels and views over the sea are spectacular.

Walker Bay Adventures WATER SPORTS
(☑082 739 0159; www.walkerbayadventures.co.za;
kayaking R300, canoeing R450, boat-based whale-
watching R650) A vast range of activities is on
offer, including sea-kayaking tours that give
you the opportunity to see whales up close
and personal. The company also rents kayaks and boats.

🛏 Sleeping

There is a huge amount of accommodation
in Hermanus, but you might still find yourself searching in vain for a bed in the holiday
season, so take care to book ahead.

TOP CHOICE Potting Shed GUESTHOUSE $$
(☑028-312 1712; www.thepottingshedguesthouse
.co.za; 28 Albertyn St; s/d incl breakfast R525/700;
@☀) An excellent-value guesthouse enjoyed
by readers. The neat rooms are comfortable
and have bright, imaginative decor. A self-
catering unit (R950 for four people) is also
available.

Hermanus Backpackers BACKPACKERS $
(☑028-312 4293; www.hermanusbackpackers.co
.za; 26 Flower St; dm R130, d R380, d with shared
bathroom R350; @☀) This is a great place
with upbeat decor, good facilities and clued-
up staff who can help with activities. Free
breakfast is served in the morning, and
evening braais are R90.

Auberge Burgundy GUESTHOUSE $$
(☑028-313 1201; www.auberge.co.za; 16 Harbour
Rd; s/d incl breakfast R840/1120; ☀) This wonderful place, built in the style of a Provençal
villa, has just about the most perfect position overlooking the sea in the centre of
town.

Hermanus Esplanade APARTMENT $
(☑028-312 3610; www.hermanusesplanade.com;
63 Marine Dr; sea-facing apt from R300) Some of
these self-catering apartments overlook the
sea. There are also simpler options catering
to backpackers (R200 for two people).

Marine LUXURY HOTEL $$$
(☑028-313 1000; www.marine-hermanus.co.za;
Marine Dr; s/d incl breakfast from R2500/4000;
❄@☀) Right on the sea with immaculate
grounds and amenities. The hotel has two
restaurants, both sea-facing. The **Pavilion**
(mains R95-175, ☺breakfast & dinner) serves con-
temporary South African cuisine while the
Seafood Restaurant (☺lunch & dinner) of-
fers two-/three-course meals for R195/240.

Zoete Inval Travellers Lodge BACKPACKERS $
(☑028-312 1242; www.zoeteinval.co.za; 23 Main
Rd; dm from R100, d R450, d with shared bathroom
R350; @) A budget option for those want-
ing less of a party atmosphere, this is a qui-
eter place with good amenities (including a
Jacuzzi) and neatly furnished rooms. Fami-
lies are accommodated in four-person rooms
and there is one wheelchair-friendly room.

Baleia de Hermanus GUESTHOUSE $$
(☑021-312 2513; www.hermanusbaleia.com; 57
Main Rd; s/d R420/760; @☀) Rooms here are
very comfortable, have underfloor heating
and are set around a swimming pool with
an anti-allergic water system.

Windsor Hotel HOTEL $$
(☑028-312 3727; www.windsorhotel.co.za; 49 Ma-
rine Dr; sea-facing s/d incl breakfast R960/1360;
@) A sea-facing room at this old stalwart
situated on an oceanside cliff means you'll
be able to whale-watch from your bed. The
worn rooms were getting a revamp at the
time of research.

🍴 Eating & Drinking

TOP CHOICE Fisherman's Cottage SEAFOOD $$
(Lemm's Cnr; mains R55-120; ☺lunch & dinner
Mon-Sat) The emphasis is on excellent seafood at this 1860s thatched cottage draped
with fishing nets, though it also serves
steaks and traditional meals.

Burgundy Restaurant SEAFOOD $$
(☑028-312 2800; Marine Dr; mains R60-140;
☺breakfast, lunch & dinner) Booking is recom-
mended at this eatery, one of the most ac-
claimed and popular in the area. The menu
is mostly seafood with a different vegetarian
dish each day.

Bientang's Cave SEAFOOD $$
(www.bientangscave.com; Marine Dr; mains R80-
150; ☺breakfast & lunch) You can get closer to
the whales here than on any boat trip. This
really is a cave, occupied by the last Strandlopers (coastal indigenous people) at the
turn of the 19th century. Its remarkable setting obscures the fact that the restaurant is
only so-so. Access is only via a steep flight of
cliff-side stairs.

Annie se Kombuis SOUTH AFRICAN $$
(Annie's Kitchen; Warrington Pl; mains R65-130;
☺lunch & dinner Tue-Sun) If you're looking for
traditional food such as oxtail (delicately fla-
voured curry with a topping of beaten egg

LOCAL KNOWLEDGE

BLOWING HIS OWN HORN: ERIC DAVALALA

Eric Davalala has a unique job: he's reputedly the only whale crier in the world. During whale season (June to December) you'll find Eric, dressed in a jaunty hat with whale tail tucked into the band, patrolling the cliff path between 9am and 5pm on the lookout for whales. Out of whale season, seek him out at Hermanus Tourism for a chat about whales, Hermanus or just to say hi.

So what exactly does a whale crier do? Well, some people think I am calling the whales when I blow my horn, but that's not it at all! My main job is to keep an eye on the water to see where the whales are. Once I see something – making sure it's not a bird or a rock, of course – I have to blow a Morse code signal on the kelp horn to let people know where to look for the whales. I wear a board which has Morse code on it so that people will know what the different signals mean.

Do you enjoy the job? Yes! Very much. It makes me very proud to think that I'm the only one in the world. The best thing is that I get to meet people from other countries. Most people want to take photos of me, which is fine, but I really like it when they ask me a few questions and I can also ask them where they are from and learn about their countries.

Why do the whales come to this spot? We have a very important thing in Hermanus – our water. It's a little bit warmer than the Antarctic and it is protected because of the bay. They come here to give birth in comparatively warm water. They stay here for about three months to make sure that the babies are strong enough to survive. They don't stay forever as we don't have the right kind of food for them here so they head back to the Antarctic to get something to eat.

baked to a crust) or game meat, this cosy place off Harbour Rd will fit the bill.

Gecko Bar BAR
(New Harbour; mains R45-75; ☺lunch & dinner) With wood-fired pizzas, beer from Birkenhead brewery in Stanford and a deck hanging over the ocean, this is a top spot for sundowners that turn into late-night drinks. There's live music on weekends.

Zebra Crossing PUB
(121 Main Rd; mains R40-90; ☺breakfast, lunch & dinner) This bar with a funky zebra theme is a great late-night party spot on weekends, and popular with backpackers.

Shimmi BAR
(☑Village Sq, Marine Dr; ☺2pm-2am Wed-Sun) A chilled-out bar with good cocktails and DJs most nights.

ⓘ Information

Hermanus Tourism (☑028-312 2629; www
.hermanus.co.za; Old Station Bldg, Mitchell St; ☺8am-6pm Mon-Fri, 9am-5pm Sat, 11am-3pm Sun) East of the town centre, this helpful office has a large supply of information about the area, including walks and drives in the surrounding hills, and can book accommodation.
Internet City (Waterkant Bldg, Main Rd; per

hr R15; ☺8am-6pm Mon-Fri, 8.30am-3pm Sat, 9am-1pm Sun) Offers reliable and speedy internet connections.

ⓘ Getting There & Away

Trevi's Tours (☑072 608 9213) offers daily shuttles to Gansbaai (R300, 30 minutes) and Cape Town (R800, 1½ hours).

The hostels run a shuttle service (R50 one-way, 30 minutes) to the Baz Bus drop-off point in Botrivier, 50km west of town. There are no regular bus services to Hermanus from Cape Town.

Gansbaai

 028 / POP 20,000

Gansbaai's star has risen in recent years thanks to shark-cage diving, though most people just visit on a day trip from Cape Town. The unspoilt coastline is perfect for those wishing to explore more out-of-the-way Overberg nature spots.

The road from Hermanus leads you past the village of De Kelders – a great spot for secluded whale-watching – straight into Main Rd, which runs parallel to the coastline. Kleinbaai, 7km further east along the coast, is the launch point for shark-cage diving tours.

⊙ Sights & Activities

Danger Point
Lighthouse HISTORIC BUILDING
(adult/child R16/8; ⊙10am-3pm Mon-Fri) Dating from 1895, the lighthouse is worth a visit, as is the **Walker Bay Reserve** (adult/child R30/15; ⊙7am-7pm). There's birdwatching here, some good walks and the Klipgat Caves, site of an archaeological discovery of Khoe-San artefacts.

Shark-Cage Diving DIVING
A number of shark-cage diving operators are clustered around the harbour in Kleinbaai including **Shark Lady** (⊉028-313 2306; www .sharklady.co.za; R1350), which has Scuba equipment available for qualified divers, and **Marine Dynamics** (⊉028-384 1005; www .sharkwatchsa.com; R1400).

⊨ Sleeping & Eating

Grootbos Private Nature
Reserve LODGE $$$
(⊉028-384 8000; www.grootbos.com; Rte 43; s/d full board R6300/8400; ✱◉≋) This superb luxury choice set on 1715 hectares includes all activities in the price. There are two lodges each with 11 cottages. Certified by Fair Trade in Tourism, the Grootbos Foundation runs Green Futures, a horticultural school for locals that produces sought-after graduates, and Spaces for Sports, providing soccer pitches and coaching in Gansbaai.

TOP
CHOICE **Aire del Mar** GUESTHOUSE $$
(⊉028-384 2848; www.airedelmar.co.za; 77 Van Dyk St, Kleinbaai; s/d incl breakfast R430/720; ◉) A friendly place offering a good range of prices, including basic self-catering units (for two R520). The rooms have panoramic sea views out to Dyer Island.

Gansbaai Backpackers BACKPACKERS $
(⊉083-626 4150; www.gansbaybackpackers.com; 6 Strand St; dm/d R130/400) Efficient and friendly, this is a great place for budget accommodation and tour and activity bookings.

TOP
CHOICE **Coffee on the Rocks** CAFE $
(⊉028-384 2017; Cliff St, De Kelders; mains R40-80; ⊙10am-5pm Wed-Sun) All breads here are baked daily on-site and everything is home-made. The ocean-facing deck is a great place for a sandwich, a salad or just a coffee while you look out for whales in season.

Oppideck PIZZERIA $$
(⊉028-384 1666; 2 Old Harbour Rd, Gansbaai; mains R50-120; ⊙lunch & dinner Tue-Sat) This

WESTERN CAPE GANSBAAI

SHARK-CAGE DIVING

There has been much controversy over the last few years regarding shark-cage diving. Detractors believe that operators use bait to attract sharks to the cages in which people dive, thereby teaching these killer-fish that boats and humans are associated with food. Attacks on swimmers and surfers were said to have increased as a direct result. Cage diving with white sharks once again returned to the spotlight as this activity is undertaken at Seal Island in False Bay and, despite the absence of any link, many suggest that cage diving operations are responsible for the increase in attacks.

But the activity has many supporters, including marine scientists and even some environmentalists. Their argument is that shark-cage diving is a positive educative tool that helps to remove fear and alleviate the bad rep these fish have had since the *Jaws* movie back in 1975.

Licensed operators are actually not allowed to use bait. Instead they throw 'chum' into the water – blood and guts from other fish. The sharks are attracted by the smell but there's nothing for them to eat – their diet consists of penguins and seals. Once the sharks come close, participants clad in wetsuits and snorkel masks take a deep breath and submerge into the water for a close encounter with Great Whites – no Scuba experience is necessary. Underwater visibility is best from May to September.

If you want to experience this close encounter with a wild animal, make sure you use a licensed operator who is fully insured.

If you prefer to avoid shark-cage diving, get in touch with an operator such as the **Simon's Town Boat Company** (⊉083 257 7760; www.boatcompany.co.za), which offers boat trips to view sharks feasting at Seal Island.

chilled-out pizzeria has a large deck overlooking the harbour. Downstairs there's an à la carte restaurant and the pub is open until the early hours.

Great White House SEAFOOD $$
(☑028-384 3273; www.thegreatwhitehouse.co.za; 5 Geelbek St, Kleinbaai; mains R50-140; ⊙breakfast, lunch & dinner Mon-Sun) A multifarious place that dishes up fresh seafood, clothing and curios, helps with tour information and offers three-star accommodation (singles/doubles including breakfast R450/700). Out of whale season, there are ecotrips to see penguins, seals, sharks and, sometimes, dolphins.

❶ Information

Follow the signs to **Gansbaai Tourism** (☑028-384 1439; www.gansbaaiinfo.com; Gateway Centre, Main Rd; ⊙9am-5pm Mon-Fri, 9am-4pm Sat, 10am-2pm Sun). Staff can help with activities and accommodation.

❶ Getting There & Away

Entry and exit to the town is largely limited to private vehicles. The Fynbos Rd project that will eventually link Danger Point Peninsula with Cape Agulhas has only got as far as providing a tarred road from Bredasdorp to Elim.

Trevi's Tours (☑072 608 9213, 028-312 1413) has daily shuttles to Hermanus (R300, 30 minutes) and Cape Town (R1000, two hours).

WORTH A TRIP

STANFORD

This picture-perfect village on the banks of the Klein River is a popular spot with Capetonians on weekends and for good reason. The surrounding area boasts a handful of uncrowded wineries – try **Robert Stanford Estate** (☑028-341 0441; tastings free; ⊙9am-4pm Thu-Mon) for its excellent sauvignon blanc as well as a host of family-friendly activities including horse or tractor rides through the vines and picnics to enjoy in the grounds. In Stanford itself you'll find birdwatching trips on the river, kayaks for hire and a picturesque craft **brewery** offering tastings on the lawn in summer or by a log fire in winter.

Cape Agulhas

Cape Agulhas is the southernmost tip of Africa, where the Atlantic and Indian Oceans meet. It's a rugged, windswept coastline and the graveyard for many a ship. Most people head straight for a photo with the signs marking where the oceans meet but it's also worth climbing the 71 steps to the top of the **lighthouse** (adult/child R20/10; ⊙9am-5pm). There's an interesting **museum** and a restaurant inside.

There's also the **Agulhas National Park** (☑028-435 6078; www.sanparks.org.za; adult/child R88/44), which has luxurious self-catering accommodation by the sea (two people R910). The 5.5km Rasperpunt Trail takes in the *Meisho Maru* shipwreck and three other short hikes were in progress at the time of research.

The small town of **L'Agulhas** lies just to the east of Cape Agulhas. The **tourism bureau** (☑028-435 6015; www.discovercapeagulhas.co.za), next to the lighthouse, is manned by friendly, enthusiastic staff. **Cape Agulhas Backpackers** (☑082-372 3354; www.capeagulhasbackpackers.com; cnr Main & Duiker Sts; dm/d R100/370) is a good base for exploring the area. This is a prime **kite-surfing** spot, with the backpacker hostel offering lessons as well as surfboard rentals.

Cape Agulhas can be reached by car, or if you don't have wheels, Fynbus Tours in Swellendam offers day tours (R495). Backpackers hostels in Hermanus also offer tours.

Arniston (Waenhuiskrans)

☑028 / POP 1200

One of the Western Cape's gems, Arniston is a charming village in a dramatic, windswept setting. It has a bit of an identity crisis – it's named after *both* the vessel wrecked off its treacherous coast in 1815 and the sea cave large enough to turn an ox-wagon (Waenhuiskrans means 'ox-wagon crag'); not that a wagon could have got inside the cave as the small entrance is down a cliff.

To visit the **cave**, follow the signs marked 'Grot' (cave) south of Roman Beach, along the sandy road and down the cliffside to the sea. Note the cave is only accessible at low tide.

Colourful boats, warm blue-green waters and the backdrop of **Kassiesbaai**, the 200-year-old hamlet of whitewashed cottages that forms the core of the town, make

WORTH A TRIP

ELIM

Even in a province awash with pretty villages, Elim stands out. This Moravian mission village lies some 30km from anywhere and while one paved road now reaches the sprinkling of delightful, thatched cottages, it's still a remote and largely unvisited part of the Western Cape. Seek out local guide Emile Richter (074 544 7733) for a fascinating tour of the outsized church, slave monument and fully functioning watermill dating back to the mid-19th century. These days the watermill houses a pleasant tearoom, certainly the best place to get a drink and a snack. Adjoining Elim is the Geelkkop (Yellow Hill) Nature Reserve, which takes its name from the masses of yellow plants that bloom in the spring months. There is a half-day hiking trail here. There is also a trio of wineries on the tarred road from Bredasdorp.

a pretty picture. South of Kassiesbaai is Roman Beach with white sand and gentle waves. It's a good place to bring the children as there are caves, coves and rock pools filled with sea urchins and colourful anemones at both ends. Be careful not to touch the sea urchins, though, as they can cause nasty cuts.

🛏 Sleeping & Eating

TOP CHOICE Arniston Spa Hotel   HOTEL $$$
(028-445 9000; www.arnistonhotel.com; Beach Rd; s/d sea-facing incl breakfast R1350/1800; ▨) The Arniston is a light-filled luxury hotel with a nautical theme, and its own spa. Seafacing rooms have floor-to-ceiling windows. The ocean-view restaurant serves lunch (R50 to R120) and dinner (R80 to R265) and has an extensive wine list.

Waenhuiskrans
Caravan Park   CAMPGROUND $
(028-445 9620; Main Rd; campsites/bungalows from R115/400) This decent budget option is a short walk from the beach. Bring your own bedding as well as provisions.

Die Herberg &
South of Africa
Backpackers' Resort   HOTEL, BACKPACKERS $$
(028-445 2500; www.dieherberg.co.za; s/d with shared bathroom R205/405, s/d incl breakfast R665/740; ▨) This soulless backpackers and hotel is in a particularly odd location, next to a military test site signposted off Rte 316, 2km outside Arniston. It's a modern place with tons of amenities. The attached Castaway Restaurant (mains R40-100) has something for everyone, including the kids. Its distance from the beach is a serious drawback.

Wilene's Restaurant   SOUTH AFRICAN
(028-445 9995; House C26, Kassiesbaai; ⊙ lunch & dinner) You can sample true local cooking at this restaurant, based in a local home. Wilene will rustle up a traditional fisherman's meal. You'll need to book in advance, and bring your own wine.

De Hoop Nature Reserve

This nature reserve (www.capenature.org.za; adult/child R30/15; ⊙7am-6pm) covers 340 sq km and extends 5km out to sea. The coastline is magnificent, with long stretches of pristine beach and huge dunes. It's an important breeding and calving area for the southern right whale. In the reserve you'll find exceptional coastal *fynbos* and animals such as endangered Cape mountain zebras and bonteboks. Prolific birdlife can be found, including the only remaining breeding colony of the rare Cape vultures.

Although there are numerous day walks, an overnight mountain-bike trail and good snorkelling along the coast, the reserve's most interesting feature is the five-day whale route (per person R1550). Covering 55km of moderate to strenuous walking, it offers excellent opportunities to see whales between June and December. Accommodation is in modern, fully equipped self-catering cottages. If you don't feel like carrying your own bags, you can pay an extra R380 to have your belongings transported every morning to that night's overnight cottage.

Accommodation at De Hoop is managed by De Hoop Collection (028-542 1253; www.dehoopcollection.co.za; campsites/rondavel for 2 with shared bathroom R295/580, cottage per person from R440, luxury r per person R1380). There are plenty of activities on offer including stargazing, quad biking and guided birdwatching walks.

The reserve is about 260km from Cape Town, and the final 50km to 60km from either Bredasdorp or Swellendam is untarred.

The only access to the reserve is via Wydge-leë on the Bredasdorp–Malgas road. The village of Ouplaas, 15km away from the reserve entrance, is the nearest place to buy fuel and supplies. If you don't have your own car you can reach the reserve by joining a tour from Swellendam.

Swellendam

028 / POP 22,000

Surrounded by the undulating wheat lands of the Overberg and protected by the Langeberge mountain range, Swellendam is perfectly positioned for exploring the Little Karoo and it makes a good stopover on the way further east to the Garden Route. One of the oldest towns in South Africa, it has beautiful Cape Dutch architecture and dates back to 1745.

⊙ Sights & Activities

Drostdy Museum   MUSEUM
(18 Swellengrebel St; adult/child R20/5; ⊙9am-4.45pm Mon-Fri, 10am-3pm Sat & Sun) The centrepiece of this excellent museum is the beautiful *drostdy* (residence of an official) itself, which dates from 1747. The museum ticket also covers entrance to the nearby Old Gaol, where you'll find part of the original administrative buildings and a watermill;

and Mayville (Hermanus Steyn St), another residence dating back to 1853, with a formal Victorian garden. On-site there's a shop selling stylish African curios.

Dutch Reformed Church   RELIGIOUS
(Voortrek St) Swellendam residents swear every visitor takes a photograph of this enormous church in the centre of town. Access is via a door to the right of the church should you want to peek inside.

Marloth Nature Reserve   PARK
For day permits (adult/child R30/15) to walk in the Langeberge, 1.5km north of town, contact the Nature Conservation Department (028-514 1410) at the entrance to the reserve, or Swellendam Backpackers Adventure Lodge. It's particularly pretty in October and November when the ericas are in flower. If the day hikes don't hit the spot, try the demanding five-day Swellendam Hiking Trail (reservations 021-659 3500; www.capenature.co.za; admission R38) regarded as one of South Africa's top 10 hikes. There are two basic overnight huts, and you'll need to be self-sufficient.

Fynbus Tours   GUIDED TOUR
(028-514 3303; www.fynbus.co.za; 23 Swellengrebel St) This local company offers loads of

Swellendam

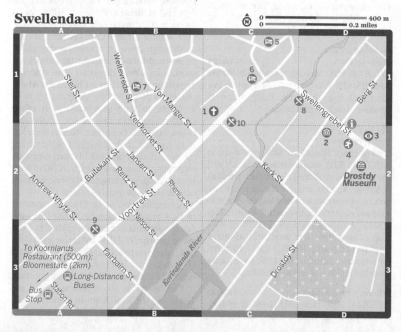

options including trips to Cape Agulhas and De Hoop Nature Reserve (both R495).

Two Feathers Horse Trails HORSE RIDING
(☑082 494 8279; Swellendam Backpackers Adventure Lodge, 5 Lichtenstein St; per hr R200) Both inexperienced and experienced riders are catered for. Advance booking is essential.

🛏 Sleeping

TOP CHOICE Cypress Cottage GUESTHOUSE $$
(☑028-514 3296; www.cypresscottage.info; 3 Voortrek St; s/d R450/700; ❄@☒) There are six rooms that are individually decorated in this 200-year-old house with a gorgeous garden and a refreshing pool.

De Kloof GUESTHOUSE $$$
(☑028-514 1303; www.dekloof.co.za; 8 Weltevrede St; s/d incl breakfast R800/1500; ❄@☒) One of Swellendam's swankiest options, this is a supremely stylish guesthouse with a surprisingly personal touch. Set in a large estate dating back to 1801, it offers a library, cigar room, gym, putting green and wonderful views.

Swellendam Backpackers Adventure Lodge BACKPACKERS $
(☑028-514 2648; www.swellendambackpackers. co.za; 5 Lichtenstein St; campsites per person R80, dm R120, s/d with shared bathroom R200/260, s/d R350/410) Set on a huge plot of land with its own river, lots of horses and Marloth Nature Reserve next door, this is an excellent hostel with enthusiastic management. Horse

Swellendam

◎ **Top Sights**
Drostdy Museum D2

◎ **Sights**
1 Dutch Reformed Church C1
2 Mayville D2
3 Old Gaol D2

◎ **Activities, Courses & Tours**
4 Fynbus Tours D2

◎ **Sleeping**
5 Braeside B&B C1
6 Cypress Cottage C1
7 De Kloof B1

◎ **Eating**
8 La Belle Alliance D1
9 Milestone A3
10 Old Gaol on Church C1

riding, permits to the nature reserve and day trips to Cape Agulhas (R450) can all be arranged. The Baz Bus will drop you right outside.

Bloomestate GUESTHOUSE $$$
(☑028-514 2984; www.bloomestate.com; 276 Voortrek St; s/d incl breakfast R1200/1650; ❄@☎☒) A modern guesthouse set on a beautiful 2.5-hectare property, which offers Zenlike privacy to go with the luxurious, colourful rooms. All have wireless internet access and there's an outside Jacuzzi, heated saltwater pool and treatment room.

Braeside B&B B&B $$
(☑028-514 3325; www.braeside.co.za; 13 Van Oudtshoorn Rd; s/d incl breakfast from R570/840; ❄☒) This quiet, gracious Cape Edwardian home boasts a beautiful garden, fantastic views and knowledgeable, gay-friendly hosts.

🍴 Eating

TOP CHOICE Old Gaol on Church Square SOUTH AFRICAN $
(8a Voortrekker St; light meals R40-65; ⏱breakfast & lunch) It might not be in the Old Gaol any longer but the food at this empowerment venture is still just as good. There's lots of seating outside under the trees where you can enjoy delicious snacks, traditional breads and excellent service.

Koornlands Restaurant SOUTH AFRICAN $$
(☑082 430 8188; 192 Voortrek St; mains R85-155; ⏱dinner) An eclectic menu of mostly African meat is served in an intimate candlelit setting. It's generally considered the top place in town. Try the crocodile sashimi (R55) and kudu fillet.

La Belle Alliance SOUTH AFRICAN $$
(1 Swellengrebel St; mains R35-100; ⏱breakfast & lunch) This appealing tearoom had the honour of serving Nelson Mandela in 1999. In an old Masonic lodge with shaded outdoor tables beside the Koringlands River, it's a good spot for lunch.

Milestone CAFE, BRAAI $$
(cnr Voortrek & Andrew Whyte Sts; mains R65-110; ⏱breakfast, lunch & dinner Mon-Fri, breakfast & lunch Sat) As well as fresh salads, daily specials and decadent cakes to enjoy in the shady garden, there is now a full South African braai available in the evenings. Booking essential for the braai.

WESTERN CAPE SWELLENDAM

❶ Information

Premium Computers (79 Voortrek St; per hr R32; ⊘9am-5pm Mon-Fri, 9am-noon Sat)

Swellendam tourism bureau (☑028-514 2770; www.swellendamtourism.co.za; 22 Swellengrebel St; ⊘9am-5pm Mon-Fri, 10am-3pm Sat, 9am-2pm Sun) An exceptionally helpful office based in the Old Gaoler's Cottage.

❶ Getting There & Away

All three major bus companies pass through Swellendam on their runs between Cape Town and Port Elizabeth, stopping opposite the Swellengrebel Hotel on Voortrek St. The Baz Bus stops at Swellendam Backpackers Adventure Lodge.

Bontebok National Park

Some 6km south of Swellendam is this **national park** (☑028-514 2735; adult/child R54/27; ⊘7am-7pm Oct-Apr, 7am-6pm May-Sep), proclaimed in 1931 to save the remaining 30 bontebok. The project was successful, and bontebok as well as other antelopes and mountain zebras can be found in this smallest of South Africa's national parks. The *fynbos* that flowers in late winter and spring and an abundance of birdlife are features of the park. Swimming is possible in the Breede River.

A lot of thought has gone into the provision of accommodation in the park. Ten **chalets** (for 2 people R840) incorporating 'Touch the Earth Lightly' principles have been built at Lang Elsie's Kraal (named after a Khoe-San chieftain who lived there with her clan). Two of the chalets are adapted for people with special needs. **Campsites** (with/without electricity R205/170) are available. Basic commodities, as well as curios, are available at the entrance shop, but otherwise, stock up in Swellendam.

To reach the park, take the N2 east of Swellendam. The entrance is signposted and is 5km along a gravel road to the south. Alternatively, take a tour organised by Fynbus Tours in Swellendam.

ROUTE 62

Following all, or part, of Rte 62 will take you through varied scenery from Tulbagh in the northwest to Oudtshoorn in the southeast. It's touted as the longest wine route in the world and takes in the Breede River Valley

and the Little Karoo. It's a great alternative to the N2 if you're travelling from Cape Town towards the Garden Route.

Europeans had settled most of the Breede River Valley by the beginning of the 18th century, but the area did not really take off until passes were pushed through the mountains a century later. The Little Karoo is east of the Breede River Valley and bordered in the south by the Outeniqua and Langkloof ranges and by the Swartberg range in the north. It is more fertile and better watered than the harsher Great Karoo to the north.

The towns in this region are presented in the order they would be reached driving the route from Cape Town.

Tulbagh

☑023 / POP 18,000

Beneath the dramatic backdrop of the Witsenberg range, Tulbagh is a pretty town, established in 1699, with historic buildings and delightful places to stay and eat. Church St, lined with trees and flowering shrubs, is a near-perfect example of an 18th- and 19th-century Cape Dutch village street. It was badly damaged in an earthquake in 1969, but the painstaking restoration has paid off.

◉ Sights & Activities

Wandering down Church St is a pleasant way to spend an afternoon. When you finish, take in a few wine tastings.

Oude Kerk Volksmuseum   MUSEUM
(Old Church Folk Museum; 1 Church St; adult/child R15/5; ⊘9am-5pm Mon-Fri, 9am-3pm Sat, 11am-3pm Sun) This museum is worth a pause; it's made up of four buildings. Start at No 4, which has a photographic history of Church St, covering the earthquake and reconstruction; visit the beautiful Oude Kerk itself (1743); move to No 14, featuring Victorian furnishings then end at No 22, a reconstructed town dwelling from the 18th century.

Wineries

The Tulbagh Valley produces a variety of wines and has a number of cellars to visit, all of which are well signposted. There are however, some standouts.

TOP CHOICE **Twee Jonge Gezellen**   WINERY
(tastings free; ⊘9am-4pm Mon-Fri, 10am-2pm Sat, cellar tours 11am & 3pm Mon-Fri, 11am Sat) The second-oldest family-owned wine estate in South Africa was the first to introduce night harvest-

ing. The friendly, informed staff conduct tours of the champagne-making process (they make only Méthode Cap Classique here – sparkling wine made in the same way as champagne). If you buy a bottle, you can try your hand at *sabrage* (opening it with a sword).

Saronsberg Cellar WINERY
(www.saronsberg.com; tastings R25; ⊙8am-5pm Mon-Fri, 10am-2pm Sat) Sip superlative red blends while admiring the contemporary art that lines the walls of this smart cellar close to Twee Jonge Gezellen.

Drostdy Wines WINERY
(Van der Stel St; museum admission R10, tastings R20; ⊙10am-5pm Mon-Fri, 10am-2pm Sat) Built in 1806 and almost destroyed in the earthquake but completely restored, Drostdy is worth a visit. Informal help-yourself tastings take place by candlelight in the atmospheric dungeon.

🛏 Sleeping

TOP CHOICE Vindoux Treehouses LUXURY HOTEL $$
(☑023-230 0635; www.vindoux.com; Vindoux Farm, Waveren Rd; d with breakfast R1200; 🐾) A definite for the romantically inclined, these luxury tree houses each have a spa bath and views of the vineyards. Hire bikes for a self-guided vineyard cycle then revive with a *fynbos* body wrap at the day spa (R400). There are also simpler family cottages on the farm (R550).

Cape Dutch Quarter BACKPACKERS, GUESTHOUSE $$
(☑023-230 1171; www.cdq.co.za; 24 Church St; s/d from R250/450) There is a variety of accommodation on offer here, ranging from basic backpacker-style rooms to self-catering houses and smart doubles with four-poster beds. The owner is a mine of information on the area.

De Oude Herberg HISTORIC HOTEL $$
(☑023-230 0260; www.deoude herberg.co.za; 6 Church St; s/d incl breakfast R500/800; 🖈@🐾) A guesthouse since 1885, this is a very friendly place with traditional country furniture and a lovely patio.

Rijk's Country House BOUTIQUE HOTEL $$$
(☑023-230 1006; www.rijkscountryhouse.co.za; Van der Stel St; s/d incl breakfast R1190/1980; 🖈@🐾) Rijk's provides luxurious accommodation on a beautiful wine estate. There's

a winery here too, as well as a **restaurant** (mains R55-85), serving good food at refreshingly modest prices. The hotel is 2km north of the town centre.

🍴 Eating & Drinking

TOP CHOICE Reader's Restaurant SOUTH AFRICAN $$
(12 Church St; mains R75-110; ⊙lunch & dinner Tue-Sun) As its name suggests, this is a good place for literature (and feline) lovers, with books and cat sculptures everywhere. The menu changes daily, but is based on traditional South African cuisine with an eclectic twist.

Olive Terrace SOUTH AFRICAN $$
(22 Van der Stel St; mains R65-110; ⊙breakfast, lunch & dinner) Based in the Tulbagh Hotel, this restaurant serves traditional favourites, some of which are given an original twist. The shady terrace is a delight in the Tulbagh summer heat.

Paddagang Restaurant BOEREKOS $$
(23 Church St; mains R60-90; ⊙breakfast, lunch & dinner) The town's best-known restaurant, in a beautiful old homestead with a courtyard shaded by vines, also serves snacks and light meals (R45 to R60).

ℹ Information

Tulbagh Tourism (☑023-230 1348; www.tulbaghtourism.org.za; 4 Church St; ⊙9am-5pm Mon-Fri, 9am-3pm Sat & Sun) Helpful staff provide information and maps about the area, including the Tulbagh Wine Route.

ℹ Getting There & Away

Tulbagh is reached either via Rte 44 from Wellington or Rte 43 from Worcester, a more scenic route.

To get to Rte 46 (from where you can head east to Ceres or west towards Piketberg, which is on the N7), head south down Van der Stel St. Halfway up the hill leading away from the town, turn right. There's a small, faded sign to Kaapstad (Cape Town) and Gouda on Rte 46.

Ceres & Around
☑023 / POP 55,500

Named after the Roman goddess of agriculture, the small town of Ceres is nestled in a magnificent valley. It's the most important deciduous fruit- and juice-producing district in South Africa.

The valley is most beautiful in spring and particularly in autumn, when the fruit trees change colour. The town is perhaps best for a lunch stop in between spending the morning and afternoon exploring the region's mountain passes.

◎ Sights

Togryers' Museum
MUSEUM

(Transport Riders' Museum; 8 Oranje St; adult/child R5/0.50; ⊗8am-5pm Mon-Fri) Ceres was once a famous centre for making horse-drawn vehicles. Consequently, the museum has an interesting collection of original wagons and carriages alongside excellent exhibits on local history.

☞ Tours

Mountain Passes
DRIVING TOUR

For some stupendous scenery don't miss a drive through these winding passes. The Gydo Pass rises steeply as you head north from Ceres towards Citrusdal and the Cederberg mountains. On the southern side of town is Mitchell's Pass. Completed in 1848, this became the main route onto the South African plateau to the north, remaining so until the Hex River Pass was opened in 1875. Stop for tea and cake at the cafe situated in the old tollhouse.

Ceres Zipline Adventures
ADVENTURE TOUR

(☎079-245 0354; 1 Voortrekker St; R400) This 1.4km, three-hour tour sees participants dangling from cables stretched across ravines, giving an unusual view of the surrounding Skurweberg mountains.

🛏 Sleeping & Eating

Four Seasons
B&B $$

(☎023-312 1918; 1 Staff St; s/d incl breakfast R460/640; ❈☤) A comfortable B&B with a personal touch: each room is cool and comfortable, and designed to reflect each season. There is a self-catering option, which knocks R65 off the per-person price.

Ceres Inn
HOTEL $$

(☎023-312 2325; www.ceresinn.co.za; 125 Voortrekker St; s/d with shared bathroom R295/530, s/d R415/675; ❈☤) The recently upgraded rooms all have TV and most come with air-con. The adjoining Witherley's Bistro (mains R40-75) dishes up reliable fare covering all tastes, which can be served in the shady garden.

❶ Information

Ceres tourism bureau (☎023-316 1287; www
.ceres.org.za; cnr Owen & Voortrekker Sts; ⊗9am-5pm Mon-Fri, 9am-noon Sat) In the

library. Staff are friendly and have information on accommodation and activities in the area.

❶ Getting There & Away

Ceres is on Rte 46, 53km north of Wellington. As with many destinations, having your own vehicle is best, but there are shared taxis running between Voortrekker St and Worcester (R40, 35 minutes).

Worcester
♩023 / POP 107,000

A market town serving the rich farmland of the Breede River Valley, Worcester is a large and fairly nondescript place that needn't detain you longer than it takes to visit its farm museum and botanic garden. Most of the town lies south of the N1.

◎ Sights & Activities

Kleinplasie Farm Museum
MUSEUM

(adult/child R15/5; ⊗8am-4.30pm Mon-Sat, 10am-3pm Sun) This farm museum is one of South Africa's best museums, and takes you from a Trekboer's hut to a complete, functioning 18th-century farm complex. It's a 'live' museum, meaning there are people wandering around in period clothes and rolling tobacco, milling wheat, spinning wool and so on.

At the museum shop you can sample and buy various flavours of toe-curling *witblitz* (white lightning), a traditional Boer spirit distilled from fruit. The adjoining restaurant (mains R50-120; ⊗breakfast & lunch) offers traditional Cape Malay and Afrikaner dishes such as *bobotie* and chicken pie.

FREE Karoo National Botanic
Garden
GARDENS

(⊗7am-7pm) This outstanding garden takes in 154 hectares of semidesert vegetation – with Karoo and *fynbos* elements – and 11 hectares of landscaped garden, where many of the indigenous plants have been labelled. It's 2km north of town on the other side of the N1.

🛏 Sleeping & Eating

Nuy Valley Guest
Farm
BACKPACKERS, GUESTHOUSE $$

(☎023-342 7025; www.nuyvallei.co.za; s/d with shared bathroom R170/300, s/d R280/520; ☤) Affordable accommodation bordering a wine estate 15km east of Worcester, off Rte 60. As well as comfy doubles with garden views, there are backpacker rooms based in the old wine tanks – cool in both senses of the word.

Wykeham Lodge
B&B $$

(☑023-347 3467; www.theguesthouse.ch; 168 Church St; s/d incl breakfast R520/720; @☎) This fine guesthouse is in a thatched-roof building dating from 1835. Rooms face onto a quiet courtyard and there's also a large garden. Dinner is available if prebooked.

Fowlers
STEAKHOUSE $$

(☑023-347 8761; 48 Church St; mains R60-110; ◷lunch & dinner Mon-Fri, dinner Sat) This popular steakhouse in the town centre is considered Worcester's top place to eat by locals. Fresh fish and lots of farm produce also grace the menu.

ℹ Information

For local information, visit **Breede Valley Tourism** (☑023-348 2795; 23 Baring St; ◷8am-4.30pm Mon-Fri, 9am-noon Sat), on the east side of Church Sq.

ℹ Getting There & Away

All long-distance buses stop at the Shell Ultra City petrol station in town. Fares include Cape Town (R180, two hours, daily) and Jo'burg (R560, 16 hours, daily). The corner of Durban and Grey Sts is a good place to look for shared taxis. Rates include Cape Town (R90, two hours, daily).

Tourist-class trains run by **Shosholoza Meyl** (☑086 000 8888; www.shosholozameyl.co.za) travelling between Johannesburg and Cape Town stop at Worcester.

Robertson

☑023 / POP 60,000

In a valley located between the Langeberge and Riviersonderendberge, Robertson is the prosperous centre of one of the largest wine-growing areas in the country. It offers an excellent wine route encompassing the neighbouring villages of Ashton, Bonnievale and McGregor, as well as a wider range of outdoor activities than other towns on Rte 62. There's hiking in the mountains, gentle rafting on the river and horse riding – the town is famous for its horse studs.

◉ Sights & Activities

The Robertson Wine Valley is worth a visit for its unpretentious wineries, its scenery and the general absence of tourist buses. There were 50 wineries at last count and al-

KAGGA KAMMA PRIVATE GAME RESERVE

Far from towns and paved roads, Kagga Kamma (☑021-872 4343; www.kaggakamma.co.za; full board s/d from R3210/5020, outcrop extra per person R950, day visits R1150) is the perfect place to recharge. Wildlife drives explore the Karoo landscape, there are hikes to see San rock art and in the evenings 'sky safaris' take place in the mini observatory. Rooms are situated in mock-caves that blend seamlessly with the rugged surrounds and for the ultimate in 'glamping' there is the Outcrop Room – an entire luxury suite transported out into the desert. The reserve is 92km northeast of Ceres.

most all offer free tastings! Ask the tourism bureau for a map.

TOP CHOICE Viljoensdrift
WINERY

(www.viljoensdrift.co.za; ◷9am-5pm Mon-Fri, 10am-5pm Sat) One of Robertson's most popular places to sip, especially on weekends. Put together a picnic from the deli, buy a bottle from the cellar door and taste on an hour-long Breede River boat trip (adult/child R40/15). Boats leave on the hour from 11am (noon on weekdays).

Graham Beck
WINERY

(www.grahambeckwines.co.za; ◷9am-5pm Mon-Fri, 10am-4pm Sat & Sun) Tastings of award-winning syrah and the world-class bubblies are in a striking modern building with huge plate-glass windows. The winery comes as a breath of fresh air after all those Cape Dutch estates.

Van Loveren
WINERY

(www.vanloveren.co.za; ◷8.30am-5pm Mon-Fri, 9.30am-3pm Sat, 11am-2pm Sun) Each of the trees in the tropical garden tells a story – grab the information pamphlet from reception or just sip in verdant surrounds. The low-key **bistro** (mains R55-75) serves excellent burgers and pizzas.

Springfield
WINERY

(www.springfieldestate.com; ◷8am-5pm Mon-Fri, 9am-4pm Sat) Some of the wines here are unfiltered – try the uncrushed Whole Berry for something different.

De Wetshof
WINERY

(www.dewetshof.com; ⏱8.30am-4.30pm Mon-Fri, 9.30am-1pm Sat) While it dabbles in other varieties, De Wetshof is best known for its highly awarded chardonnays.

Nerina Guest Farm
HORSE RIDING

(☎082-744 2580; www.nerinaguestfarm.com; Goree Rd) This outfit offers horse trails along the river or through the vineyards with an option to swim with the horses afterwards. Trails last from one hour (R150) to half a day (R600).

⭐ Festivals & Events

There are a number of wine-related events, including the **Hands on Harvest** in February, the **Wacky Wine Weekend** in June and the **Wine on the River Festival** (☎all events 023-626 3167; www.robertsonwinevalley.com) in October. Accommodation in the town is scarce at these times, so book well in advance.

🛏 Sleeping & Eating

TOP CHOICE **Ballinderry**
GUESTHOUSE $$

(☎023-626 5365; www.ballinderryguesthouse.com; 8 Le Roux St; s/d incl breakfast R700/1200; ✻@🐾) This modern, colourful boutique guesthouse is impeccable, thanks to hosts Luc and Hilde. A champagne breakfast is served, as is dinner on request, and Dutch, French and German are spoken. Try to get either the downstairs double with garden views, or the two separate rooms in the garden.

Robertson Backpackers
BACKPACKERS $

(☎023-626 1280; www.robertsonbackpackers. co.za; 4 Dordrecht Ave; campsites per person R60,

dm R110, d with shared bathroom R300, d R390; @) A terrific place to hang your hat, with spacious dorms and doubles and a cosy bohemian vibe. There's a big grassy backyard with a fire pit for chilling out at night, and wine and activity tours can be arranged.

Gubas De Hoek
GUESTHOUSE $$

(☎023-626 6218; www.gubas-dehoek.com; 45 Reitz St; s/d R450/700; @🐾) Highly recommended by readers is this comfortable home with well-appointed rooms. Owner-chef Gunther Huerttlen will cook you dinner (three courses R230) and there's a shared self-catering kitchen for preparing light meals.

Pat Busch Private Nature Reserve
CHALET $$

(☎023-626 2033; www.patbusch.co.za; per person R280; 🐾) Simple but well-equipped cottages based on the edge of a nature reserve 16km northeast of Robertson off Rte 60. Wildlife drives are available. There are discounts midweek and for stays of more than two nights.

Bourbon Street
INTERNATIONAL $$

(☎023-626 5934; 22 Voortrekker St; mains R60-120; ⏱breakfast, lunch & dinner) A firm favourite with both locals and overseas visitors, this New Orleans–feel deli-restaurant impresses with its menu offering a little of everything.

Café Rosa
CAFE $

(☎023-626 5403; 9 Voortrekker St; mains R45-60; ⏱breakfast & lunch Mon-Sat) Situated in a plant nursery, this is the perfect spot for a lunch-time salad or pizza.

ℹ Information

Robertson tourism bureau (☎023-626 4437; www.robertsontourism.co.za; cnr Reitz & Voortrekker Sts; ⏱8am-5pm Mon-Fri, 9am-2pm Sat, 10am-2pm Sun) A friendly office with information about the wine region, Rte 62 and hiking trails in the mountains above the town.

ℹ Getting There & Away

Translux (www.translux.co.za) buses stop opposite the police station on Voortrekker St. Routes include Knysna (R250, five hours), Cape Town (R180, two hours, daily) and Port Elizabeth (R300, nine hours, daily).

Shared taxis running between Cape Town (R65, 1½ hours), Oudtshoorn (R160, three hours) and Montagu (R65, 30 minutes) stop opposite the **Shell petrol station** (cnr Voortrekker & John Sts). These are not necessarily daily services;

FINDING THE BIG FIVE IN THE WESTERN CAPE

Just about the only thing that Western Cape lacks is national parks boasting the Big Five, but there are still opportunities to spot lion, elephant, leopard, buffalo and rhino. They might lack the spontaneity of a national park and the big cats are kept apart from potential food, but at private wildlife reserves you're at least guaranteed sightings – and a little luxury on the side. **Aquila** (☎0861 7373 783; www.aquilasafari.com) and **Fairy Glen** (☎0861 244 348; www.fairyglen.co.za) are both close to Worcester. They offer similar day packages including a wildlife drive, lunch and use of the lodge's pool (R1225 to R1300).

check with the taxi drivers about when they're leaving.

McGregor

 023 / POP 1500

Dreaming away at the end of a road going nowhere, quiet and sleepy McGregor is an increasingly popular retreat with lots of accommodation on offer. The main thoroughfare, Voortrekker St, has pretty white-washed cottages dating from the mid-19th century, and the village is surrounded by farmland. It's a good base for hiking in the nearby Riviersonderendberge and is also one end of the excellent Greyton McGregor Trail (formerly known as the Boesmanskloof Trail).

Activities

Greyton McGregor Trail HIKING
(1-day trail adult/child R30/15, 2-day trail R60/30) One of the best reasons for coming to McGregor is to hike the trail to Greyton, roughly 14km through the spectacular *fynbos*-clad Riviersonderendberge mountains. The trail actually starts at Die Galg, about 15km south of McGregor; you'll need your own transport to get here. The McGregor-to-Greyton direction is easier. You must book in advance at all times at Cape Nature (023-625 1621; www.capenature.org.za; 7.30am-4pm Mon-Fri), but especially for weekends and during the holidays, since only 50 people per day are allowed on the trail. Permits are available from the tourism bureau.

Oakes Falls HIKING
(1-day permit adult/child R30/15) If you don't fancy the full hike, it's feasible to do a six-hour round-trip to these lovely waterfalls, roughly 6km from Die Galg, where you can cool off with a swim in the tannin-stained waters.

Wine Tasting WINERY
There are half a dozen wineries in the McGregor area, which are encompassed in the Robertson Wine Valley route. Try ruby port at McGregor Wines (023-625 1741; www.mcgregorwinery.co.za; 8am-5pm Mon-Fri, 10am-3pm Sat) or sip grappa alongside earthy red wines at Tanagra Winery (023-625 1780; www.tanagra-wines.co.za; by appointment).

Sleeping & Eating

TOP CHOICE Temenos Retreat RETREAT $$
(023-625 1871; www.temenos.org.za; cnr Bree St & Voortrekker Rd; s/d R480/690;) These cottages set in spacious gardens are open to all (except children under 12), not just those on retreat. It's a peaceful place, with a decent lap pool, health treatments and a popular restaurant serving light lunches and daily dinner specials (mains R45 to R120). Accommodation prices drop considerably during the week.

Old Mill GUESTHOUSE $$
(023-625 1626; www.oldmilllodge.co.za; cnr Smith & Mill Sts; s/d incl breakfast R400/760;) Sitting on the southern border of town, this is a family-friendly place with well-kept grounds, friendly hosts and a nice pool. A self-catering cottage with its own splash pool (two people R700) is also available.

Lord's Guest Lodge GUESTHOUSE $$
(023-625 1881; www.lordsguestlodge.co.za; s/d from R750/1000; @) Accommodation is in thatched, stone cottages each with its own clan name and accompanying tartan. The Lady Grey Restaurant (mains R70-115) is open to the public, though booking is essential. Look out for the turn-off 10km before McGregor.

Karoux SOUTH AFRICAN $$
(023-625 1421; Voortrekker Rd; mains R60-110; dinner Fri-Tue) The menu changes regularly at this small restaurant with a bohemian vibe, but always features traditional dishes showcasing local ingredients.

Information

Cape Nature (023-625 1621; www.cape nature.org.za; 7.30am-4pm Mon-Fri) Administers the Greyton McGregor Trail. Its offices are about 15km south of Robertson on the McGregor Rd.

McGregor tourism bureau (023-625 1954; www.tourismmcgregor.co.za; Voortrekker St; 9am-4.30pm Mon-Fri, 9am-2pm Sat & Sun) Based at the museum.

Getting There & Away

Apart from hiking in from Greyton, there's only one road in and out of McGregor (the road to Robertson), so your own transport is essential.

FRANS LEMMENS/GETTY IMAGES ©

1. Swartberg Pass (p152)
This remarkable pass is an engineering marvel and a challenging mountain-biking route.

2. Muizenberg Beach (p59)
Kite-surfers ride the waves at this popular family beach.

3. Knysna Forests (p147)
These ancient forests offer a wide range of excellent hiking trails.

4. Stellenbosch (p96)
The rich soil of this wine region produces superb red wines, such as cabernet, merlot and shiraz.

Greyton

028 / POP 1100

Although officially part of the Overberg region, we've included Greyton and the neighbouring village of Genadendal here because of their link to McGregor along the Greyton McGregor Trail.

Much more twee than McGregor, even locals admit that the whitewashed, thatched-roof cottages of Greyton are a bit artificial. As pleasant as the village is, it needs to be seen in conjunction with the old Moravian Mission of neighbouring Genadendal, with its well-preserved historic buildings that couldn't be more authentic.

◉ Sights & Activities

TOP CHOICE Genadendal Mission Station
HISTORIC SITE

Some 5km west of Greyton is Genadendal, the oldest mission station in South Africa, founded in 1738 and for a brief time the largest settlement in the colony after Cape Town. It now has a population of 3500. Entering the village from Rte 406, head down Main Rd until you arrive at the cluster of national monuments around Church Sq. The Moravian Church is a handsome, simply decorated building. There's a cafe here selling homemade bread and souvenirs. The village's fascinating history is documented in the excellent Mission Museum (028-251 8582; adult/child R8/4; 8.30am-5pm Mon-Thu, 8.30am-3.30pm Fri, 10am-2pm Sat), situated in what was South Africa's first teacher training college. Elsewhere is one of the oldest printing presses in the country and a watermill. In 1995, Nelson Mandela renamed his official residence in Cape Town after this mission station.

Genadendal Trail
HIKING

Greyton is a perfect base for hiking in the Riviersonderendberge mountains, which rise dramatically to the village's north. Apart from the Greyton McGregor Trail there are several shorter walks, as well as the two-day Genadendal Trail for the serious hiker. This is a 25.3km circular route that begins and ends at Genadendal's Moravian Church; for more details ask at the tourist information office in Genadendal.

🛏 Sleeping & Eating

TOP CHOICE Post House
HISTORIC HOTEL $$

(028-254 9995; www.theposthouse.co.za; 22 Main Rd; s/d incl breakfast R960/1440) Based in the town's historic former post house and set around a pretty garden, rooms are named after Beatrix Potter characters (we told you Greyton was a twee place). Its English-style pub is a wonderfully atmospheric spot for a drink or meal.

High Hopes
B&B $$

(028-254 9898; www.highhopes.co.za; 89 Main Rd; s/d incl breakfast from R600/800) This delightful place comes highly recommended, with tastefully furnished rooms, lovely gardens and a well-stocked library. It's close to the start of the Greyton McGregor Trail, and if you've overdone it, you can book a massage at the on-site Healing Energy Centre.

Zebra Moon
BACKPACKERS $

(028-254 9039; www.zebramoon.co.za; dm R100, s/d with shared bathroom R180/280) Once the hostel for Greyton's boarding school, this is now a perfect base for hiking. It's a cavernous place but the views of the Sonderend Mountains are awesome and staff know all there is to know about hiking the region. Some trails start from the property and there's a guide available for trickier hikes.

Oak & Vigne Café
CAFE $

(DS Botha St; mains R45-70; breakfast & lunch) This trendy deli-cafe–art gallery is a pleasant place to grab a meal, relax and watch the world go by. All wines served are local and the ice cream is made on the premises.

Peccadillo's
FUSION $$

(028-254 9066; 23 Main Rd; mains R80-95; lunch & dinner Thu-Mon) Traditional dishes are given a new twist at this popular spot with minimalist decor and a creative menu that changes daily.

ⓘ Information

Tourist information office (028-254 9414; www.greytontourism.com; 29 Main Rd; 9am-5pm Mon-Fri, 10am-1pm Sat & Sun) There's a small tourist office where internet access is available.

ⓘ Getting There & Away

If you're not hiking in from McGregor, the only way to Greyton is by your own transport. Route 406 leads into town from the N2 from east and west, but note that the eastern section of Rte 406 is a gravel road in poor condition.

Montagu

023 / POP 9500

Coming into Montagu along Rte 62 from Robertson, the road passes through a narrow arch in the Cogmanskloof mountains, and suddenly the town appears before you. Its wide streets are bordered by 24 restored national monuments, including some fine art-deco architecture. There's a wide range of activities, including hot springs, easy walks and more serious hikes, as well as excellent accommodation and restaurants.

◎ Sights & Activities

TOP CHOICE Tractor-Trailer Rides   ECOTOUR

(023-614 3012; www.proteafarm.co.za; adult/child R90/45; ☉tours 10am & 2pm Wed & Sat) Niel Burger, owner of Protea Farm 29km from Montagu, takes fun tractor-trailer rides to the farm, from where you can look way down into the Breede River Valley. It's a wonderful three-hour trip. Enjoy a delicious lunch of *potjiekos* (traditional pot stew) with homemade bread for R100/70 per adult/child, and stay on at the farm accommodation (four-person cottage from R650).

Montagu Museum & Joubert House   MUSEUM

Interesting displays and some good examples of antique furniture can be found at the **Montagu Museum** (41 Long St; adult/child R5/2; ☉9am-5pm Mon-Fri, 10.30am-12.30pm Sat & Sun) in the old mission church. **Joubert House** (023-614 1774; 25 Long St; adult/child R5/2; ☉9am-4.30pm Mon-Fri, 10.30am-12.30pm Sat & Sun), a short walk away, is the oldest house in Montagu (built in 1853) and has been restored to its Victorian glory.

Hot Springs   SWIMMING

(adult/child R60/40; ☉8am-11pm) Water from the hot mineral springs finds its way into the swimming pools of the Avalon Springs Hotel, about 3km from town by road. The water gushes from a rock face in an underground cavern at a constant 43°C, and is renowned for its healing properties. Don't expect natural-looking pools – they're commercialised and can get unpleasantly busy on weekends and in school holidays.

A great way to get there is to hike along 2.4km trail from the car park at the end of Tanner St. The route leads past Montagu's top rock-climbing spots. For guidance on climbing, abseiling and hiking in the area contact **De Bos** (023-614 2532; www.debos.co.za).

Hiking

The **Bloupunt Trail** (admission R18) is 15.6km long and can be walked in six to eight hours; it traverses ravines and mountain streams, and climbs to 1000m. The **Cogmanskloof Trail** (admission R18) is 12.1km and can be completed in four to six hours; it's not as steep as the Bloupunt Trail but is still fairly strenuous. Both trails start from the car park at the northern end of Tanner St. You can book the overnight huts near the start of the trails through the tourism bureau. The huts (per person R80) are fairly basic (wood stoves, showers and toilet facilities), but they are cheap.

🛏 Sleeping

TOP CHOICE 7 Church Street   GUESTHOUSE $$

(023-614 1186; www.7churchstreet.co.za; 7 Church St; s/d incl breakfast from R650/1100; @) A friendly, upmarket guesthouse in a charming Karoo building with traditional wrought-iron *broekie* (panty) lace trim. There are also luxury rooms in the manicured garden. The stylish interior doubles as a gallery of the owner's personal art collection.

De Bos   BACKPACKERS, CAMPGROUND $

(023-614 2532; www.debos.co.za; Bath St; campsites per person R50, dm R80, s/d R185/330;) A genuine farmstay for backpackers – there's a river, chickens and pecan-nut trees on this 7-hectare property, where colourful old workers' cottages have been converted into self-catering cottages (from R360). On weekends there is a two-night minimum stay, except for camping. Mountain bikes are available to hire and there are maps of the region's trails.

Mimosa Lodge   HOTEL $$

(023-614 2351; www.mimosa.co.za; Church St; s/d incl breakfast from R675/990; @) A delightful, upmarket lodge in a restored Edwardian landmark building with lovely gardens and a pool with a thatched-roof gazebo for shade. The award-winning restaurant serves four-course dinners (R320) and is open to nonguests.

WORTH A TRIP

BARRYDALE

Often overshadowed by its better-known neighbour, Montagu, Barrydale is one of Rte 62's gems. Venture off the main road and you'll find stylish accommodation, craft shops and quirky restaurants with a bohemian feel. **Hiking** and **birdwatching** are on offer in surrounding nature reserves, there's a luxury **wildlife reserve** (www.sanbona.com; off Rte 62, 18km west of Barrydale; s/d R6750/9000 incl meals and game drives) boasting the Big Five nearby and a **hot springs** (www.warmwaterbergspa.co.za; off Rte 62; day visitors R30) resort that's far less crowded than that of Montagu. This is brandy country and there's a **brandy cellar** (☑028-572 1012; 1 Van Riebeeck St; ☺8am-5pm Mon-Fri, 9am-3pm Sat; cellar tours by appointment) offering tours and tastings. West of town, **Joubert-Tradauw** is a charming spot for some boutique wine tasting and a light lunch from its small but sublime menu. And of course, there's the inimitable **Ronnie's Sex Shop** (☺8.30am-9pm, mains R50-90), on Rte 62 towards Ladismith, whose bra-adorned bar draws in a constant stream of bikers and curious passersby looking for lunch or a beer.

Montagu Caravan Park CAMPGROUND $
(☑023-614 3034; Bath St; campsites per person R70, 4-person chalet from R480) This park is in a pleasant location with apricot trees and lots of shade and grass. The chalets come with cooking equipment and TVs. There are also hikers' cabins (for two R260).

Airlies Guest House GUESTHOUSE $$
(☑023-614 2943; www.airlies.co.za; Bath St; s/d incl breakfast R525/750; @☒) Readers recommend this quaint, thatched guesthouse with spacious wood-floored rooms looking out on the mountains. The hosts are very obliging and the breakfast is excellent.

**Montagu Springs
Holiday Resort** RESORT $$
(☑023-614 1050; www.montagusprings.co.za; Warmbronne Hot Springs; 4-person chalet from R970) These self-catering chalets are the cheaper option at the hot-springs resort. Those interested in waterfowl should check out the 'feathered friends' sanctuary where more than 55 types of exotic birds are on display.

✗ Eating

TOP CHOICE **Jessica's** FUSION $$
(☑023-614 1805; 47 Bath St; mains R80-135; ☺dinner) Named after the family dog, cosy Jessica's serves up inventive bistro dishes, many of them melding South African ingredients with Asian flavours.

Templeton's@Four Oaks FUSION $$
(46 Long St; mains R85-145; ☺lunch & dinner Mon-Sat) Set in a lovely old house, the style is minimalist rather than the usual country decor and the food and service are excellent.

Die Stal INTERNATIONAL $$
(Touwsrivier Rd; mains R60-110; ☺breakfast & lunch Tue-Sun) A countryside dining experience just 7km north of town off Rte 318, on a working citrus farm. The menu here changes daily, but large country breakfasts are always on offer.

ⓘ Information

Printmor (61 Bath St; per hr R30; ☺7.30am-5.30pm Mon-Fri, 8am-1pm Sat) Internet access.

Tourism bureau (☑023-614 2471; www.montagu-ashton.info; 24 Bath St; ☺8.30am-5pm Mon-Fri, 9am-5pm Sat, 9.30am-5pm Sun) This office is extremely efficient and helpful. Opening hours are slightly shorter between May and October.

ⓘ Getting There & Around

Buses stop at Ashton, 9km from Montagu.
Translux (www.translux.co.za) buses stop here on the run between Cape Town (R180, three hours, daily) and Port Elizabeth (R300, eight hours, daily).

Most accommodation establishments in town offer (prebooked) shuttles from Ashton to Montagu, but you can also jump in one of the shared taxis (R15) that ply this route. They stop in Montagu at **Foodzone** (Bath St). If you're arriving after hours, you may need to hire a vehicle from one of the companies at the Ashton bus depot.

Calitzdorp

☑044 / POP 8400

Behind the nondescript main road lies a charming little town with architecture typical of the Little Karoo. Known for its excellent port-style wines, Calitzdorp has a stunning setting on rolling farmland overlooked by the Groot Swartberge range to the north and the Rooiberge to the southwest. Apart from the vineyards, there's a **museum** (cnr Van Riebeeck & Geyser Sts; adult/child R10/5; ⊙9.30am-12.30pm Mon-Sat) housing Calitzdorp memorabilia.

The **tourism bureau** (www.calitzdorp.org.za) can provide details on accommodation and the local wineries. It's in a building at the side of the **Shell petrol station** (☎044-213 3775; 4 Van Riebeeck St; ⊙8am-5pm Mon-Fri, 10am-3pm Sat & Sun Oct-Apr).

Of the eight wineries in the area, five are within walking distance of the town centre. The best set up for visitors is **Boplaas** (www.boplaas.co.za; Zaayman St; tastings R20; ⊙8am-5pm Mon-Fri, 9am-3pm Sat). The farm claims a negative carbon footprint due to its sensitive farming methods and the amount of land left to nature that bears carbon-gobbling *spekboom* (elephant bush). Follow the signs from Voortrekker Rd, and call ahead to book a cellar tour. There's also a **port festival** held each year in May.

Opposite Boplaas is the **Port-Wine Guest House** (☎044-213 3131; www.portwine.net; 7 Queen St; s/d incl breakfast R525/840; ✴✷), in a beautifully appointed, thatched Cape cottage with four-poster beds in the rooms. On the other side of Rte 62, **Spekboom Cottages** (☎044-213 3067; www.spekboomcottages.com; cottage per person R260; ✷) offers an affordable place to stay. Its self-catering cottages are fully equipped and each has a large deck boasting its own plunge pool. Locals recommend **Lorenzo's** (☎044-213 3939; Voortrekker St; mains R50-110; ⊙breakfast, lunch & dinner) for its pies, pizzas and traditional food that can be enjoyed in the garden.

Oudtshoorn

☎044 / POP 79,000

In the late 1860s, no self-respecting society lady in the Western world would be seen dead without an ostrich plume adorning her headgear. The fashion boom in ostrich feathers lasted until the slump of 1914 and during this time, the 'feather barons' of Oudtshoorn made their fortunes.

You can still see their gracious homes today, along with other architectural pointers to Oudtshoorn's former wealth such as the CP Nel Museum. The town remains the ostrich capital of the world and is now the prosperous tourist centre of the Little Karoo. Ostrich leather is much sought after, and expensive; feathers, eggs and biltong are available everywhere and the meat is always on the menu (a healthy option with no cholesterol).

Oudtshoorn, though, has much more to offer than ostriches and makes a great base for exploring the different environments of the Little Karoo, the Garden Route (it's 55km to George along the N12) and the Great Karoo.

Oudtshoorn 0 ——— 200 m / 0 ——— 0.1 miles

Oudtshoorn

◉ Sights & Activities

Many of Oudtshoorn's sights are outside the town limits. Some hostels and B&Bs offer discounts on attractions if you stay the night.

TOP CHOICE Meerkat Adventures   WILDLIFE RESERVE

(☎084 772 9678; www.meerkatadventures.co.za; admission R550; ☺sunrise on sunny days) This unique wildlife encounter comes highly recommended by travellers and could well be the highlight of your trip. Passionate conservationist Devey Glinister operates the sunrise experience on De Zeekoe Farm, 9km west of Oudtshoorn. His passion for the endearing animals comes shining through in his unique meerkat experience. At this pioneering conservation project, you will get to see up close how these curious, highly intelligent creatures communicate and live. Once you're at the meeting point (where Rte 62 and Rte 328 meet), sightings of the animals warming up in the morning sun are guaranteed since Devey seeks them out in their burrows each night. Little extras such as camping chairs, coffee and blankets make this a delightful way to start a day. No children under 10 years.

Cango Caves   CAVE

(☎044-272 7410; www.cangocaves.co.za; adult/child R69/33; ☺9am-4pm) Named after the Khoe-San word for 'a wet place', the Cango Caves are heavily commercialised but impressive. The one-hour tour gives you just a glimpse, while the 90-minute Adventure Tour (adult/child R90/55) lets you explore deeper into the caves. It does involve crawling through tight and damp places though, so is not recommended for the claustrophobic or unfit. Advance booking for both tours is highly recommended. The caves are 30km north of Oudtshoorn.

CP Nel Museum & Le Roux Townhouse   MUSEUM

(3 Baron van Rheede St; adult/child R15/5; ☺8am-5pm Mon-Fri, 9am-1pm Sat) Extensive displays about ostriches, as well as Karoo history, make up this large and interesting museum, housed in a striking sandstone building completed in 1906 at the height of ostrich fever.

Included in the ticket price is admission to Le Roux Townhouse (cnr Loop & High Sts; ☺9am-5pm Mon-Fri). This place is decorated in authentic period furniture and is as good an example of a 'feather palace' as you're likely to see.

Ostrich Farms   FARM

There are three show farms that offer guided tours of 45 minutes to 1½ hours. There's little to choose between them; we found the staff at Highgate Ostrich Show Farm (www.highgate.co.za; adult/child R70/32; ☺8am-5pm) very knowledgeable. It's 10km from Oudtshoorn en route to Mossel Bay. Nearby is Safari Ostrich Show Farm (www.safariostrich.co.za; adult/child R70/37; ☺8am-4pm). Cango Ostrich Show Farm (www.cangoostrich.co.za; Cango Caves Rd; adult/child R70/40; ☺8am-5pm) also receives good reviews.

Two Passes Route   DRIVING TOUR

A wonderful day's excursion is the round-trip from Oudtshoorn to Prince Albert taking in two magnificent passes. Head up the untarred Swartberg Pass and all the way down to Prince Albert, then return via the Meiringspoort Pass. Halfway down the latter is a waterfall and small visitor centre. Both passes are engineering masterpieces, and will take you through the town of De Rust on the way home. Ask at your accommodation or the tourism bureau for a route map.

If driving isn't challenging enough, then hop on a mountain bike and ride from the top of Swartberg Pass down into Oudtshoorn. Backpackers Paradise (☎044-272 3436; 148 Baron van Rheede St; tours R290) runs these trips, which depart daily at 8.30am. You'll be driven up and then cycle back to town. Be warned: it's not all downhill and it's a long ride.

★彡 Festivals & Events

ABSA Klein Karoo Nationale Kunstefees   ARTS

(Little Karoo National Arts Festival; www.kknk.co.za) This enthralling April festival dedicates itself to the 'renaissance of Afrikaans' and showcases indigenous artists, poets, thespians and musicians in a riotous week-long festival of creativity.

🛏 Sleeping

TOP CHOICE Backpackers Paradise   BACKPACKERS $

(☎044-272 3436; www.backpackersparadise.net; 148 Baron van Rheede St; campsites per person R60, dm R110, r R290, d R360; @☎) In a large old house, this lively hostel has a bar, ostrich braais and free ostrich-egg breakfasts (in season, you'll be given an egg – cook it any way you please). It also offers curios at knock-down prices, discounts to attractions in the area, and can set you up with a host of activities.

Karoo Soul Travel Lodge   BACKPACKERS **$**
(☏044-272 0330; www.karoosoul.com; 170 Langenhoven Rd; campsites per person R60, dm R120, d with shared bathroom R320, d R380; @☀) The gracious old house with its luxury linens and comfort are proof that the backpacker has come of age. Try to get one of the west-facing doubles for a romantic sundowner from your bed, or ask about the garden cottages with en suite (R420).

La Pension   GUESTHOUSE **$$**
(☏044-279 2445; www.lapension.co.za; 169 Church St; s/d incl breakfast R650/940; ✳@☀) A reliable choice with spacious, stylish rooms and superb bathrooms, La Pension also has one self-catering cottage, plus a good-sized pool, sauna and large, immaculate garden.

Kleinplaas Resort   CAMPGROUND **$**
(☏044-272 5811; www.kleinplaas.co.za; cnr North & Baron van Rheede Sts; campsites R280, 4-person chalet R660-900; ☀) A terrific caravan park, with a big pool. The restaurant is only open for breakfast.

Bisibee Guesthouse   GUESTHOUSE **$$**
(☏044-272 4784; www.bisibee.co.za; 171 Church St; s/d R275/540; @☀) One of the original guesthouses in town, this is a friendly place offering excellent value and comfort.

Oakdene Guesthouse   GUESTHOUSE **$$**
(☏044-272 3018; www.oakdene.co.za; 99 Baron van Rheede St; s/d R695/990; ✳☀) Elegant cottage furniture, wooden floors, good linens and an earthy-coloured paint job make each room special. The lush gardens and excellent pool add to the charm.

Queen's Hotel   HOTEL **$$**
(☏044-272 2101; www.queenshotel.co.za; 11 Baron van Rheede St; s/d R950/1300; ✳@☀) Bang in the middle of town, this attractive old-style country hotel with spacious, understated rooms is refreshingly cool inside and has an inviting appeal. The attached **Die Kolonie Restaurant** (mains R75-130) serves a range of local and international dishes.

✖ Eating

As you'd expect, most places serve ostrich in one form or another.

TOP CHOICE Jemima's   SOUTH AFRICAN **$$$**
(94 Baron van Rheede St; mains R95-180; ☺lunch & dinner) With a small menu specialising in traditional Cape fare, this restaurant is set in an attractive old house and garden. After your meal try a *swepie* (a mix of brandy and *jerepigo*, a dessert wine).

Kalinka   FUSION **$$**
(☏044-279 2596; 93 Baron van Rheede St; mains R85-170; ☺dinner Mon-Sun) This stylish, up-market restaurant is a long-standing favourite that serves imaginative dishes featuring game meat with an Asian flair. The menu changes regularly, but is always excellent.

Bella Cibo   ITALIAN **$$**
(146 Baron van Rheede St; mains R40-85; ☺dinner Mon-Sat) Popular with locals and widely recommended around town, this Italian restaurant serves very well-priced pizza, pasta and seafood and has a great vibe on weekends.

La Dolce Vita   INTERNATIONAL **$$**
(60 Baron van Rheede St; mains R35-120; ☺breakfast, lunch & dinner Mon-Sat) Recommended by readers, this is a great spot to enjoy a light lunch on the shady patio. Be warned: portions are huge.

Montague House   ITALIAN **$$**
(cnr Baron van Rheede & Olivier Sts; mains R48-115; ☺breakfast & lunch) Breakfast is served here until 2.30pm and there is a huge number of choices on offer. Otherwise enjoy pasta, salads or sandwiches under umbrellas in the large flowery garden.

🛍 Shopping

There's plenty for the shopper in Oudtshoorn, with Baron van Rheede St providing most of the outlets. Ostrich goods are naturally in demand, particularly items made from ostrich leather. The leather is very pricey because of the low hide yield per bird, so it's worth shopping around here, including at show ranches and in hotels.

Lugro Ostrich Leather Products   ACCESSORIES
(133 Langenhoven Rd; ☺9am-5pm Mon-Sat) Considered one of the best-value ostrich-leather purveyors in town, Lugro is independent of

local ranches, so offers a shopping experience that avoids the tacky tourist vibe usually accompanying the search for ostrich goods.

ℹ Information

Cyber Ostrich Internet Café (37 Baron van Rheede St; per hr R35; ⊗8am-9pm Mon-Fri, 9am-6pm Sat & Sun) Yes, even the internet cafe has an ostrich-related name!

Oudtshoorn tourism bureau (☎044-279 2532; www.oudtshoorn.com; cnr Baron van Rheede & Voortrekker Sts; ⊗8.30am-5pm Mon-Fri, 8.30am-1pm Sat) This helpful bureau is behind the CP Nel Museum.

ℹ Getting There & Around

Buses stop in the Riverside Centre off Voortrekker St. **Intercape** (www.intercape.co.za) has services to Johannesburg (R650, 14½ hours, daily), Cape Town (R380, eight hours, daily) and Mossel Bay (R250, two hours, daily).

The Baz Bus stops at George, from where you can arrange a transfer to Oudtshoorn with Backpackers Paradise (R60 one-way).

Shared taxis leave from behind the Spar supermarket on Adderley St en route to George (R35, 30 minutes) or Cape Town (R200, three hours). The area east of Adderley St has a slightly dodgy feel to it, so be careful.

GARDEN ROUTE

High on the must-see list of most visitors to South Africa is the Garden Route, and with good reason: you can't help but be seduced by the glorious natural beauty of the scenery. It's less than 300km from Mossel Bay in the west to just beyond Plettenberg Bay in the east, yet the range of topography, vegetation, wildlife and outdoor activity in this short space is breathtaking.

The coast is dotted with excellent beaches, while inland you'll find picturesque lagoons and lakes, rolling hills and eventually the mountains of the Outeniqua and Tsitsikamma ranges that divide the Garden Route from the arid Little Karoo. The ancient indigenous forests that line the coast from Wilderness to Knysna offer adventure trails and hiking, birdwatching, canoeing on the rivers, sliding through the tree canopy or simply taking an easy walk through the forest to gasp at the size of a yellowwood tree over six hundred years old. Wildlife enthusiasts will enjoy spotting brilliant green and red Knysna louries in the forest or maybe even catching sight of one of the few remaining Knysna elephants.

With such a diverse range of things to do in this internationally renowned region, it's

Garden Route

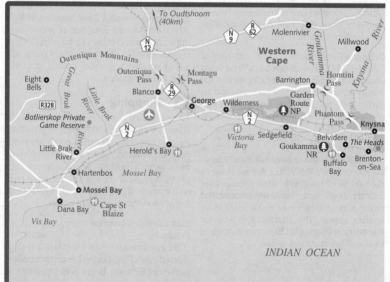

not surprising that the scope of the accommodation comes up trumps. In fact, strong competition in the tourist industry has led to high standards in everything from activities to restaurants. The downside of this is the high volume of people in the most popular towns of Knysna and Plettenberg Bay. While they make good bases for exploring the area, they can get very crowded during December and January, when prices rise significantly. This makes it important to book ahead if you're travelling at these times, or head for less crowded Wilderness.

Mossel Bay

📋 044 / POP 117,000

There's more to Mossel Bay than meets the eye at first glance. It used to be a hugely popular destination until the 1980s, when the building of the world's largest gas-to-oil refinery and concomitant industrial sprawl uglified it, and it fell into a slump. But if you can see beyond the unimpressive approach road, you'll find some fine beaches, gnarly surfing spots (see the boxed text, p150), a wealth of activities and good places to stay. It has a way to go to catch up with its more glamorous neighbours, but it's trying hard to grab back its former glory.

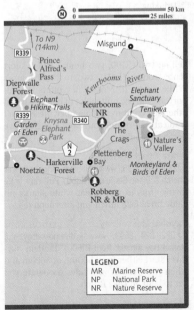

LEGEND
MR	Marine Reserve
NP	National Park
NR	Nature Reserve

The Portuguese explorers Bartholomeu Dias and Vasco da Gama were the first Europeans to visit the bay late in the 15th century. It became a useful place for ships to stop off as there was fresh water available and deals could be struck with the local Khoekhoen people. A large milkwood tree beside the spring was used as a postal collection point – expeditions heading east would leave mail to be picked up by ships returning home. The spring and the tree still exist, and you can post letters (they receive a special postmark) from a letterbox within the museum.

⊙ Sights & Activities

Mossel Bay is chock-full of activities. From the harbour, there are regular boat trips on both the **Romonza** (📋044-690 3101) and the **Seven Seas** (📋082-297 7165) to view the seal colony, birds and dolphins that frequent the waters around Seal Island. One-hour trips cost R125. In late winter and spring the *Romonza* also runs whale-watching trips (R600, 2½ hours).

TOP
CHOICE **Dias Museum Complex**   MUSEUM
(Market St; adult/child R20/5; ⊙9am-4.45pm Mon-Fri, 9am-3.45pm Sat & Sun) This excellent museum includes the **spring** where Dias watered the **postal tree**, the 1786 Dutch East India Company (Vereenigde Oost-Indische Compagnie; VOC) **granary**, a **shell museum** (with some interesting aquarium tanks) and a local **history museum**.

The highlight of the complex is the replica of the caravel that Dias used on his 1488 voyage of discovery. Its small size brings home the extraordinary skill and courage of the early explorers. The replica was built in Portugal and sailed to Mossel Bay in 1988 to commemorate the 500th anniversary of Dias' trip. Boarding the caravel costs an extra R20.

Botlierskop Private
Game Reserve   WILDLIFE RESERVE
(📋044-696 6055; www.botlierskop.co.za; Little Brak River; s/d with dinner, breakfast & wildlife drive R2500/3340) This wildlife reserve offers the chance to stay on a ranch and view a vast range of wildlife, including lions, elephants, rhinos, buffalos and giraffes. Day visitors are welcome for a variety of activities including wildlife drives (adult/child R395/198), horse riding (per hour R200) and elephant rides (adult/child over six years R595/300). The

Mossel Bay

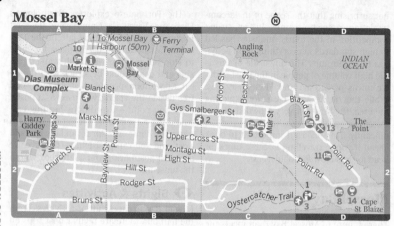

Mossel Bay

reserve is about 20km northeast of Mossel Bay along the N2 (take the Little Brak River turn-off and follow the signs towards Sorgfontein). Booking ahead is essential.

Oystercatcher Trail   HIKING
(www.oystercatchertrail.co.za) Hikers can tackle this four-day (R7690) trail from Mossel Bay to Dana Bay via Cape St Blaize, where you're likely to see the endangered black oystercatcher. Included in the price are excellent accommodation and meals as well as luggage transportation en route. While out here, it's worth a stop at the **Cape St Blaize Lighthouse** (adult/child R16/8; ⊙10am-3pm).

Electrodive   DIVING
(☎082 561 1259; 2 Field St; gear hire per day R200, shore- & boat-based dives R190-230) A family-run operation offering a number of options. In addition to PADI courses, it does a snor-

kelling trip (R190, two hours) and a short scuba course (R550, two to three hours). While diving in Mossel Bay offers the opportunity to see quite a lot of coral, fish and other sea creatures, remember these aren't tropical waters and you're not going to have perfect visibility.

White Shark Africa   WATER SPORTS
(☎044-691 3796; www.whitesharkafrica.com; cnr Church & Bland Sts; dives R1350) Full-day cage diving trips to view great white sharks include breakfast, lunch and afternoon tea.

Skydive Mossel Bay   EXTREME SPORTS
(☎082 824 8599; www.skydivemosselbay.com; Mossel Bay Airfield; from R1600) Tandem skydives start either from 3000m or 3650m and when the weather and tides cooperate you get to land on Diaz Beach.

Back Road Safaris GUIDED TOURS
(☎044-690 8150; www.backroadsafaris.co.za)
A vast range of tours is on offer, including
Meet the People (4hr tour per person R450),
which offers home visits with traditional
meals on request (R30) in nearby Friemersheim and KwaNonqaba townships – preferable to the sometimes voyeuristic township
tours offered in larger cities.

🛏 Sleeping

There are three municipal **caravan parks**
(☎044-690 3501; campsites from R190, chalet
from R430) in town. Bakke and Santos are
next to each other on pretty Santos Beach;
Bakke is the one with chalets. Punt is on the
Point and very close to the surf. Prices rise
steeply in the high season.

TOP CHOICE Park House Lodge &
Travel Centre BACKPACKERS $
(☎044-691 1937; www.park-house.co.za; 121 High
St; dm R150, d with shared bathroom from R400, d
from R520; @) This place, in a gracious old
sandstone house next to the park, is friendly
and smartly decorated and has beautiful
gardens. Breakfast is R40, and staff can organise activities.

Point Village Hotel HOTEL $$
(☎044-690 3156; www.pointvillagehotel.co.za; 5
Point Rd; s/d R420/720; @) The quirky, fake
lighthouse on this well-priced hotel's exterior is a sign of what's inside: a range of
fun, funky, bright rooms and exceptionally
friendly service. Rooms have a kitchenette
and some have balconies.

Mossel Bay Backpackers BACKPACKERS $
(☎044-691 3182; www.gardenrouteadventures.
com; 1 Marsh St; dm R120, d with shared bathroom
R340, d R450; @☎) Close to the beach at the
Point and the bars on Marsh St, this longestablished place is reliable and well run.
It offers comfortable rooms, a pool and bar
and an impressive fully equipped kitchen.
Staff can arrange all sorts of activities.

Point Hotel HOTEL $$
(☎044-691 3512; www.pointhotel.co.za; Point Rd;
s/d R1075/1430; @) This modern hotel boasts
a spectacular location, right above the wavepounded rocks at the Point. There's a decent
restaurant (mains R55-110) and the spacious
rooms have balconies with ocean views.

Santos Express BACKPACKERS $
(☎044-691 1995; www.santosexpress.co.za; Santos
Beach; dm R100, s/d with shared bathroom & breakfast R210/400) The position of this converted
train, right beside the beach, can't be beaten, but the compartments are undeniably
cramped. There's an attached bar-restaurant,
with a very large menu (mains R40 to R125).

Huis te Marquette GUESTHOUSE $$
(☎044-691 3182; www.marquette.co.za; 1 Marsh St;
s/d from R580/680; ☎) This comfortable, longrunning guesthouse, near the Point, has its
more-expensive rooms facing the pool. Some
come with spa baths. The place is attached
to Mossel Bay Backpackers.

Protea Hotel Mossel Bay HOTEL $$
(☎044-691 3738; www.proteahotels.com/mossel
bay; Market St; s/d from R1375/1800; ❄@☎) Part
of the Protea chain, this is a classy hotel set
in the old post-office building. Its restaurant,
Café Gannet (mains R40-170, ⊘breakfast, lunch
& dinner), has a large seafood, meat and pizza
menu.

🍴 Eating & Drinking

Marsh St and the Point are where it all happens in Mossel Bay.

TOP CHOICE Kaai 4 BRAAI $
(Mossel Bay Harbour; mains R25-60; ⊘lunch & dinner) Boasting one of Mossel Bay's best locations,
this low-key seafood spot has picnic tables
on the sand overlooking the ocean. Food is
cooked on massive fire pits and the hungry
can take the all-you-can-eat option (R125).

Café Havana INTERNATIONAL $$
(38 Marsh St; mains R50-110; ⊘lunch & dinner)
About as Cuban as Mossel Bay can get, this
restaurant and cocktail bar has a great vibe.
The stews and steaks are a nice antidote to
all the seafood in town – though of course
there's plenty of that as well.

Kingfisher SEAFOOD $$
(Point Rd; mains R45-120; ⊘lunch & dinner) Locals love the seafood dishes and ocean views
here. It also serves salads and meat, and has
a children's menu.

Pavilion INTERNATIONAL $$
(Santos Beach; mains R50-150; ⊘lunch & dinner)
In a 19th-century bathing pavilion modelled
on the one in Brighton, this is a fine choice
for a beachside meal. The menu offers just
about everything.

Big Blu BAR $$
(Point Rd; mains R40-135) This ramshackle
place right on the rocks at the Point draws a

young crowd. It's great for a sundowner and serves burgers, seafood, steaks and tapas (R15 to R25) of a kind not found in Spain.

ⓘ Information

Tourism bureau (☎044-691 2202; www.mosselbay.net; Market St; ◐8am-6pm Mon-Fri, 9am-4pm Sat, 9am-2pm Sun) Staff are very friendly and can help with accommodation bookings.

ⓘ Getting There & Away

Mossel Bay is off the highway, so the long-distance buses don't come into town; they drop you at the Voorbaai Shell petrol station, 8km away. The hostels can usually collect you if you give notice, but private taxis (R80) are often waiting for bus passengers who need onward travel. If none are there call (☎082 932 5809) or during the day take a shared taxi (R10). The Baz Bus will drop you in town.

Translux (www.translux.co.za), **Greyhound** (www.greyhound.co.za) and **Intercape** (www.intercape.co.za) buses stop here on their Cape Town–Port Elizabeth runs. Intercape fares from Mossel Bay include Knysna (R260, two hours, twice daily), Plettenberg Bay (R260, 2½ hours, twice daily), Cape Town (R280, six hours, twice daily) and Port Elizabeth (R310, 6½ hours, twice daily).

George

☑044 / POP 136,000

George, founded in 1811, is the largest town on the Garden Route yet remains little more than a commercial centre with not much to keep visitors for long. It has some attractive old buildings, including the tiny St Mark's Cathedral and the more imposing Dutch Reformed Mother Church, but it's 8km from the coast and for most people its chief draw is the range of championship golf courses.

⊙ Sights

George was the hub of the indigenous timber industry and thus the **George Museum** (Courtenay St; admission by donation; ◐9am-4pm Mon-Fri, 9am-12.30pm Sat) contains a wealth of related artefacts.

The starting point and terminus for journeys on the Outeniqua Power Van (p141) is the **Outeniqua Transport Museum** (cnr Courtenay & York Sts; adult/child R20/10; ◐8am-4.30pm Mon-Fri, 8am-2pm Sat). It's worth a visit if you're interested in trains. Some 11 locomotives and 15 carriages, as well as many detailed models, have found a retirement home here, including a carriage used by the British royal family in the 1940s.

🛏 Sleeping & Eating

TOP CHOICE French Lodge International GUESTHOUSE $$
(☎044-874 0345; www.frenchlodge.co.za; 29 York St; s/d incl breakfast from R550/800; ❄@☲) You can't miss this place with its mini Eiffel Tower in the garden. Rooms are in luxurious thatched-roof *rondavels* (round hut with a conical roof) or apartments set around the pool, with satellite TV and bathrooms with Jacuzzis. It's possibly the best deal in town.

Fancourt Hotel LUXURY HOTEL $$$
(☎044-804 0000; www.fancourt.co.za; Montagu St, Blanco; d from R3200; ❄@☲) This is the area's most luxurious place, about 10km from the town centre, and has three 18-hole golf courses (two designed by Gary Player). The hotel and country club has a range of top-notch accommodation options, a health spa and five restaurants.

Outeniqua Travel Lodge BACKPACKERS $
(☎082 316 7720; www.outeniqualodge.com; 70 Langenhoven St; dm R120, s/d R300/440; @) It's a way from the centre, but this is a great budget option with en-suite rooms in a quiet, residential area. Staff are friendly and can arrange activities.

Old Townhouse STEAKHOUSE $$
(Market St; mains R50-115; ◐lunch & dinner Mon-Fri, dinner Sat) Situated in the one-time town administration building dating back to 1848, this longstanding restaurant is known for its excellent steaks and ever-changing game-meat options.

ⓘ Information

George Tourism (☎044-801 9295; www.visitgeorge.co.za; 124 York St; ◐7.45am-4.30pm Mon-Fri, 9am-1pm Sat) This office has a wealth of information for George and the surrounding area.

ⓘ Getting There & Away

Kulula (www.kulula.com), **1Time** (www.1time.aero), **Airlink** (www.saairlink.co.za) and **SA Express** (www.saexpressco.za) fly to **George airport** (☎044-876 9310), which is 7km west of town.

Bus services stop in George on their route between Cape Town and Port Elizabeth and on their runs between Jo'burg and the Garden Route. **Greyhound** (www.greyhound.co.za)

services stop in St Mark's Sq behind the Spar supermarket on the main street, while **Translux** (www.translux.co.za) and **Intercape** (www.intercape.co.za) stop at the Sasol petrol station on the N2 just east of town. Intercape fares include Knysna (R260, 1½ hours, twice daily), Plettenberg Bay (R270, two hours), Port Elizabeth (R310, 5½ hours, twice daily), Cape Town (R320, seven hours, twice daily), Bloemfontein (R450, 10 hours, daily) and Jo'burg (R690, 16 hours, daily).

The Baz Bus drops off in town and you can call the hostels in Oudtshoorn for shuttle services there.

Around George

MONTAGU & OUTENIQUA PASSES

Leaving George, the Montagu Pass is a quiet dirt road that winds its way through the mountains; it was opened in 1847 and is now a national monument. Head back on the Outeniqua Pass, where views are even better; but, because it's a main road, it's more difficult to stop when you want to.

Alternatively, you could opt for the **Outeniqua Power Van** (☎082 490 5627; adult/child R110/90; ☺on demand Mon-Sat), a motorised trolley van that will take you from the Outeniqua Transport Museum on a 2½-hour trip into the Outeniqua mountains. You can even take a bike and cycle back down the Montagu Pass.

HEROLD'S BAY
☎044

On a beautiful stretch of beach that provides consistent swells for surfers (see the boxed text, p150) is the tiny village of Herold's Bay. It's generally quiet, although it can become crowded on summer weekends. The town is 16km southwest of George. If you fancy staying the night try **Dutton's Cove** (☎044-851 0155; 21 Rooidraai Rd; r incl breakfast R1300; ☒), which has upmarket accommodation and a restaurant (mains from R60). If you prefer to be closer to the sea, **Makarios** (☎044-872 9019; www.makariosonsea.co.za; 4 Gericke's Cnr; self-catering suite from R850), is a stone's throw from the sand. The luxury suites have full kitchens and sea views or there is a smaller room (from R540) without the view.

VICTORIA BAY

Victoria Bay is tiny and picturesque, and sits at the foot of steep cliffs, around 8km south of George. It's also a popular surf spot (see the boxed text, p150) and has a tidal pool for children. If the waves are too good to leave,

try either the **caravan park** (☎044-889 0081; campsites from R148) or the **Surfari Backpackers** (☎044-874 5672; www.vicbaysurfari.co.za; dm R150, d from R450), which has bright, spotless rooms a short drive from the beach. Surf lessons and day trips for the more advanced are available.

Wilderness

The name says it all: dense old-growth forests and steep hills run down to a beautiful stretch of coastline of rolling breakers, kilometres of white sand, bird-rich estuaries and sheltered lagoons. All this has made Wilderness very popular but thankfully it doesn't show – the town does not come across as hugely touristy. The myriad holiday homes blend into the verdant green hills, and the town centre is compact and unobtrusive. If you're a beach bum, the beach here is beautiful, but be warned: a strong riptide means swimming is not advised. The only drawback is everything is quite widely scattered, making life very difficult if you don't have a vehicle.

◉ Sights & Activities

Eden Adventures   ADVENTURE SPORTS
(☎044-877 0179; www.eden.co.za; Garden Route National Park) Offers canoe rental (R250 per day), abseiling (R375) or kloofing (canyoning, R495). The company also organises tours of the area.

Timberlake Organic Village   VILLAGE
(www.timberlakeorganic.co.za) This complex off the N2 between Wilderness and Sedgefield has small shops selling organically grown fresh produce and crafts. There's live music on Sundays, and activities such as quad biking and zip line tours available.

🛏 Sleeping & Eating

TOP CHOICE **Interlaken**   GUESTHOUSE $
(☎044-877 1374; www.interlaken.co.za; 713 North St; r per person incl breakfast R495; @) Rave reviews from readers, and we can't argue: this is a well-run and very friendly guesthouse offering magnificent lagoon views. Delicious dinners are available on request.

Fairy Knowe Backpackers   BACKPACKERS $
(☎044-877 1285; www.wildernessbackpackers.com; Dumbleton Rd; dm R120, d with shared bathroom R350, d R450; @) Set in spacious, leafy grounds overlooking the Touws River, this

1874 farmhouse was the first in the area. The bar and cafe are in another building some distance away, so boozers won't keep you awake. The Baz Bus comes to the door. If you're driving, head into Wilderness town and follow the main road for 2km to the Fairy Knowe turn-off.

Sea Paradise
GUESTHOUSE $$

(☎044-877 0793; www.seaparadise.co.za; 79a Sands Rd; s/d incl breakfast from R550/880) Nothing is too far from the sea in Wilderness, but this delightful guesthouse has direct access to the beach. All rooms are sea-facing and from July to November you might spot whales from the comfort of your bed.

Palms Wilderness Retreat & Guesthouse
GUESTHOUSE $$

(☎044-877 1420; www.palms-wilderness.com; 1 Owen Grant St; s/d incl breakfast R1350/1750; ✴@☀) This stylish place has African decor and its gallery stocks African art and jewellery. Rooms are luxurious and it's a five-minute walk from the beach.

TOP CHOICE Zucchini
EUROPEAN $$

(Timberlake Organic Village; mains R40-125; ☺lunch & dinner) Stylish decor combines with home-grown organic produce, free-range meats and lots of vegetarian options at this delightful place.

Serendipity
SOUTH AFRICAN $$$

(☎044-877 0433; Freesia Ave; 5-course set menu R300; ☺dinner Mon-Sat) Readers and locals alike recommend this elegant restaurant with a deck overlooking the lagoon. The South African–inspired menu changes monthly but always features original takes on old classics.

Girls Restaurant
INTERNATIONAL $$

(1 George Rd; mains R50-175; ☺dinner Tue-Sun) It doesn't look much from afar – a restaurant tucked down the side of a petrol station – but the Girls gets rave reviews. Try the fresh prawns in a range of divine sauces. There's internet access here too.

Beejuice
CAFE $

(Sands Rd; light meals R40-80; ☺breakfast, lunch & dinner) Although no trains ply the tracks any more, this cafe filling the old station building is still a great spot for freshly made salads and sandwiches. In the evenings, traditional South African fare is served.

ℹ Information

Internet cafe (Brydon Building, George Rd; per hr R40; ☺8.30am-5pm Mon-Fri, 8.30am-noon Sat)

Wilderness tourism bureau (☎044-877 0045; Milkwood Village, George Rd; ☺7.45am-4.30pm Mon-Fri, 9am-1pm Sat) This office is just off the N2 as you pull into the village.

Garden Route National Park

Formerly the Wilderness National Park, this section has now been incorporated into the vast and scattered **Garden Route National Park** (☎044-877 1197; adult/child R88/44; ☺24hr) along with the Knysna Forests and Tsitsikamma. The park covers a unique system of lakes, rivers, wetlands and estuaries that are vital for the survival of many species.

There are several nature trails in the national park for all levels of fitness, taking in the lakes, the beach and the indigenous forest. The **Kingfisher Trail** is a day walk that traverses the region and includes a boardwalk across the intertidal zone of the Touws River. The lakes offer anglers, canoeists, windsurfers and sailors an ideal venue. Canoes can be hired at Eden Adventures in Wilderness.

There are two similar camping grounds in the park with basic but comfortable accommodation: **Ebb & Flow North** (campsites from R150, d rondavel with shared bathroom R280, d rondavel R325), which is the smaller, and **Ebb & Flow South** (campsites from R150, forest cabins R540, 4-person log cottage R1015;).

Buffalo Bay

Blissful Buffalo Bay, 17km west of Knysna, is distinctly un–Garden Route: a long, almost deserted surf beach, only a tiny enclave of holiday homes and a nature reserve. That's about it, and it's all you need. Signposts also read Buffel's Bay or Buffelsbaai.

Buffelsbaai Waterfront (☎044-383 0038; www.buffelsbaai.co.za) is basically a one-stop shop for accommodation (apartments from R350), meals and information on the area. It's a vast building behind the beach – you can't miss it.

You can also explore the **Goukamma Nature Reserve** (www.capenature.co.za; adult/child R30/15; ☺8am-6pm), which is accessible from the Buffalo Bay road, and protects 14km of rocky coastline, sandstone cliffs, dunes covered with coastal *fynbos* and forest, and Groenvlei, a large freshwater lake.

The nature reserve also extends 1.8km out to sea and you can often see dolphins (and whales, in season) along the coast. There are four day trails ranging from the short Lake Walk along Groenvlei's southern shore up to four-hour beach and dune walks. Permits can be obtained on arrival. Canoeing and fishing are great here, and canoes can be hired (R60 per day). Accommodation options are Groenvlei bush camp (4 people R800), Musselcracker house (4 people R800) or the more luxurious Mbuvu bush camp (4 people R960). Prices increase vastly during school holidays.

Knysna

☏ 044 / POP 65,000

Embracing an exquisitely beautiful lagoon and surrounded by ancient forests, Knysna (pronounced ny-znah) is the most important town on the Garden Route. Formerly the centre of the timber industry, supplying yellowwood and stinkwood for railway lines, shipping and house-building, it still has several shops specialising in woodwork and traditional furniture. The lagoon has always been popular for sailing enthusiasts, and there's a thriving oyster industry.

With its serene setting, arty and gay-friendly vibe, excellent places to stay, eat and drink, and wide range of activities, Knysna has plenty going for it. But if you're after something quiet and undeveloped, you might like to look elsewhere, particularly in high season, when the numbers of visitors threaten to overwhelm it.

◉ Sights & Activities

⬛ Township Tours & Homestays
CULTURAL TOUR

Follow Gray St uphill and eventually you'll emerge on the wooded slopes of the hills behind. On top are the sprawling Knysna townships, best visited on an excellent tour (R350) run by Emzini Tours (☏ 044-382 1087; www.emzinitours.co.za). Readers can't get enough of these three-hour trips, with many claiming it to be a highlight of their entire South Africa stay. Township resident Ella leads the way to some of the projects that Emzini has set up in the local community. You might visit the soup kitchen, animal welfare centre or a school – tours can be tailored to suit your interests but generally end at Ella's home for tea, drumming and a group giggle as you try to wrap your tongue around the clicks of the Xhosa language. You can visit the Rastafarian community for an extra R50, and lunch in a township home (R70) is available if you prebook. Plans to start cycling tours, an African restaurant and home stays were underway when this guide was being researched.

If you want to stay overnight in either the Rastafarian community or in the township, contact Knysna Tourism and ask for its brochure, *Living Local*.

Knysna Lagoon
PARK

Although regulated by SAN Parks (Map p146; www.sanparks.org; Long St, Thesen's Island), Knysna Lagoon is not a national park or wilderness area. Much is still privately owned, and the lagoon is used by industry and for recreation. The protected area starts just to the east of Buffalo Bay and follows the coastline to the mouth of the Noetzie River. The lagoon opens

---

KNYSNA FACTS (& FICTION)

» The story goes that George Rex, said to be an illegitimate son of George III of England, and a Quaker named Sarah Lightfoot, settled in Knysna after being banished from England in 1797. His grave in Old Place (Map p146) is a National Monument.

» The Knysna seahorse *(hippocampus capensis),* endemic to this area, is the most endangered seahorse on the planet. It's the only fish species where the *male* bears the offspring!

» Are there any elephants left in the Knysna forests? SAN Parks says there might be one. In 1876 there were 400; by 1969 there were only 10. There are four elephant trails around the Diepwalle Forest Station (Map p136) for you to do your own survey.

» Gold was discovered at Millwood (Map p136) just north of the Homtini Pass in 1876. Within weeks there were shops, hotels and houses. But the mining was not sustainable and Millwood became a ghost town. You can still see old foundations, street signs and a forlorn graveyard. There are good walks in the area.

Knysna

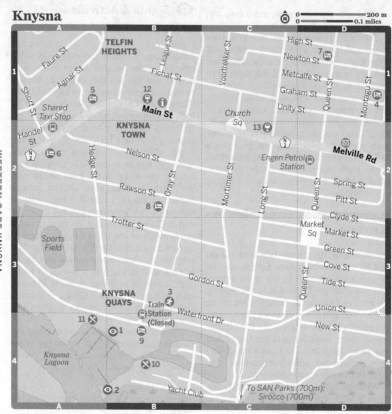

up between two sandstone cliffs, known as the Heads – once proclaimed by the British Royal Navy the most dangerous harbour entrance in the world. There are good views from a lookout on the eastern head, and the privately owned **Featherbed Nature Reserve** on the western head.

The best way to appreciate the lagoon is to take a cruise. The **Featherbed Company** (Map p144; ☎044-382 1697; www.featherbed.co.za; Waterfront) has several vessels, including the **MV John Benn** (Map p144; adult/child R130/60; ☺departures 12.30pm & 5pm winter, 6pm summer), that take you to Featherbed Nature Reserve.

Mitchell's Brewery BREWERY
(Map p146; ☎044-382 4685; Arend St; tastings R30, tours R50; ☺11am-4pm Mon-Fri, tours 11am, 12.30pm & 2.30pm Mon-Fri) South African's oldest microbrewery is in an industrial area to the east of town. The English-style beers and one cider can be found all over Western Cape.

There's also a beer and oyster pairing option (R125 including tour). Bookings essential.

Belvidere & Brenton VILLAGE
Belvidere, 10km from Knysna, is so immaculate it's positively creepy. But it's worth a quick look for the beautiful Norman-style **Belvidere church** (Map p146) built in the 1850s by homesick English expats. Further on is the Featherbed Nature Reserve (see p143), and on the seaward side, Brenton-on-Sea.

Other Activities
There are plenty of other activities on offer in the area, including abseiling, kloofing, horse riding, kayaking and quad biking. Start by contacting the **Adventure Centre** (Map p144; ☎083 260 7198; www.theadventurecentre.co.za), based at Highfield Backpackers. **Go Vertical** (☎082 731 4696; www.govertical.co.za) offers rock climbing, abseiling and canoeing, while **Liquid Grace** (☎044-343

Knysna

◎ Sights

Adventure Centre	(see 4)
1 Featherbed Company	B4
2 MV John Benn	B4

◎ Activities, Courses & Tours

3 Knysna Cycle Works	B3

◎ Sleeping

4 Highfield Backpackers	D1
5 Inyathi Guest Lodge	A1
6 Island Vibe	A2
7 Knysna Backpackers	D1
8 Knysna Log Inn	B2
9 Protea Hotel Knysna Quays	B4

◎ Eating

10 34 South	B4
Caffé Mario	(see 10)
11 Oystercatcher	A4

◎ Drinking

12 Harry B's	B1
13 Zanzibar Lounge	C2

WESTERN CAPE KNYSNA

3245; www.liquidgrace.co.za) based 30km from Knysna in Sedgefield has you covered when it comes to water sports. There are also bike trails around the area; for more information on cycling, and for bike rentals and maps, head to **Knysna Cycle Works** (Map p144; ☑044-382 5152; 20 Waterfront Dr; per day R170).

Festivals & Events

Pink Loerie Festival　　　　　　　GAY
(www.pinkloerie.com) Knysna celebrates its gay-friendliness at the end of April and beginning of May.

Oyster Festival　　　　　　　　　FOOD
There's a homage to the oyster in July, which includes the Knysna Marathon.

Sleeping

Low-season competition between the several backpackers and many guesthouses in town keeps prices down, but in high season expect steep rate hikes (except at the backpackers), and book ahead.

**Phantom Forest
Eco-Reserve**　　　　　　　　LODGE $$$
(off Map p146; ☑044-386 0046; www.phantomforest.com; s/d from R2375/3750; ☒) This 137-hectare private ecoreserve, 6km west of Knysna along the Phantom Pass road comprises 14 cleverly designed and elegantly decorated tree houses built with sustainable materials. Various activities, including conducted nature walks and a spa, are available. If nothing else, visit for the award-winning six-course African dinner (R30) served in the Forest Boma daily; booking is essential.

TOP CHOICE Brenton Cottages　　　CHALET $$
(Map p146; ☑044-381 0082; www.brentononsea.net; 2-person cabin R890, 6-person cottage R1940) On the seaward side of the lagoon, the *fynbos*-covered hills drop to Brenton-on-Sea, overlooking a magnificent 8km beach. The cottages here have a full kitchen while cabins have a kitchenette; some have ocean views. There are plenty of braai areas dotted around the manicured lawns.

Inyathi Guest Lodge　　　　　　LODGE $$
(Map p144; ☑044-382 7768; www.inyathiguestlodge.co.za; 52 Main St; s/d from R500/720) This is an imaginatively designed guesthouse, with a real African flair that avoids the kitsch. Accommodation is in decorated timber lodges – some with Victorian bath tubs, others with stained-glass windows.

Island Vibe　　　　　　　　BACKPACKERS $
(Map p144; ☑044-382 1728; www.islandvibe.co.za; 67 Main St; dm R120, d with shared bathroom R330, d R385; @☒) This funky backpackers has excellent communal areas, cheery staff and nicely decorated rooms. There's a bar, free internet and a great view from the deck.

Knysna Backpackers　　　　　BACKPACKERS $
(Map p144; ☑044-382 2554; www.knysnabackpackers.co.za; 42 Queen St; dm R120, d with shared bathroom R330, d R400) You'll find mainly double rooms at this large, spruce Victorian house on the hill a few blocks up from Main St. It tends to be quieter and more relaxing than other places and there's a free breakfast.

Woodbourne Resort　　　　　CAMPGROUND $
(Map p146; ☑044-384 0316; www.gardenroute.co.za/woodbourne; George Rex Dr; campsites from R330, chalet from R900; ☒) Here you'll find spacious, shaded camping and simple chalets with TVs. It's a quiet place a little way out of town. Follow the signs to the Heads.

Under Milk Wood　　　　　　　CHALET $$$
(Map p146; ☑044-384 0745; www.milkwood.co.za; George Rex Dr; 4-person cabin R3200) This is a series of highly impressive self-catering log cabins on the shores of Knysna Lagoon, with

Around Knysna

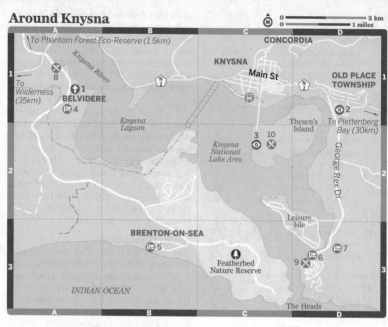

Around Knysna

a small beach. There are B&B tariffs (double from R610) if you don't feel like cooking.

Knysna Log Inn HOTEL $$
(Map p144; ☎044-382 5835; www.log-inn.co.za; 16 Gray St; s/d incl breakfast R995/1440; ❄@☲) The Knysna Log Inn is said to be the largest log structure in the southern hemisphere. The rooms are comfortable and there's a pool, but the wood theme is a bit overwhelming.

Protea Hotel Knysna Quays HOTEL $$
(Map p144; ☎044-382 5005; www.proteahotels. com; Waterfront Dr; s/d R1850/2240; ❄@☲) Rooms are tastefully decorated at this stylish hotel. It has an inviting, heated pool and is moments away from shopping and eating options at the Waterfront. You'll want a lagoon-facing room.

Belvidere Manor HOTEL $$
(Map p146; ☎044-387 1055; www.belvidere.co.za; Duthie Dr; d incl breakfast from R2060) An impressive collection of luxury guest cottages, some with lagoon views, in a garden setting. There is also a **restaurant** (mains R55-120) serving regional and international dishes.

Highfields Backpackers BACKPACKERS $
(Map p144; ☎044-382 6266; www.highfieldsback packers.co.za; 2 Graham St; dm R110, d with shared bathroom from R300; ☲) Now under new management, Highfields was about to get a much-needed facelift when we visited. The pool area is great for sundowners.

✗ Eating

There are plenty of good snack and coffee places along Main St. In the Knysna Quays centre, the best coffee and snack option is **Caffé Mario** (Map p144; ⊗breakfast, lunch & dinner).

East Head Café CAFE $$
(Map p146; The Heads; mains R45-110; ⊗breakfast & lunch) There's an outdoor deck here, over-looking the lagoon and ocean, and a good range of vegetarian dishes, plus wild oysters at R15 each.

Oystercatcher SEAFOOD $
(Map p144; Knysna Quays; ⊗lunch & dinner) The Oystercatcher is a relaxed place serving four sizes of farmed oyster and other light dishes such as fish and chips in a great waterside setting.

Sirocco INTERNATIONAL $$
(Map p146; Thesen's Island; mains R50-130; ⊗lunch & dinner) Inside it's a stylish place to dine on steaks and seafood; outside it's a laidback bar with wood-fired pizzas and the full range of Mitchell's beers.

34 South INTERNATIONAL $$
(Map p144; Waterfront; mains R50-175; ⊗lunch & dinner) With outdoor tables overlooking the water, lavish salads, deli produce and sea-food pâtés, this is a great place for lunch. The wine selection is one of the best in town.

Crab's Creek PUB $$
(Map p146; mains R50-200; ⊗lunch & dinner) This is a favourite local watering hole, in a chilled-out setting right on the lagoon, off the N2. There's a buffet lunch (R65) on Sundays. Children will enjoy the sandpit and climbing frames.

⛾ Drinking & Entertainment

Head along Main St and check out the local bars, many of which are seasonal.

Zanzibar Lounge BAR
(Map p144; Main St; ⊗Tue-Sat) This place offers a relaxed vibe, a balcony area for lounging and a theatre where shows are held occasionally.

Harry B's PUB
(Map p144; 42 Main St; mains R45-220; ⊗noon-late Sun-Fri, 9am-2am Sat) Knysna's first residence (1863) houses a popular restaurant and pub.

ℹ Information

Motion Café (3 Gray St; per hr R30; ⊗8am-6pm Mon-Fri, 8am-3pm Sat & Sun) High-speed internet access. There's a coffee shop downstairs.

Knysna Tourism (Map p144; ☎044-382 5510; www.visitknysna.co.za; 40 Main St; ⊗8am-5pm Mon-Fri, 8.30am-1pm Sat year-round, plus 9am-1pm Sun Dec-Jan & Jul) An excellent information office, with very knowledgeable staff.

ℹ Getting There & Away
Bus

The major bus companies, **Translux** (www.translux.co.za) and **Intercape** (www.intercape.co.za) stop at the Waterfront. **Greyhound** (www.greyhound.co.za) stops at the **Engen petrol station** (Map p144; Main St); Baz Bus drops at all the hostels. For travel between nearby towns on the Garden Route, you're better off looking for a shared taxi than travelling with the major bus lines, which are very expensive on short sectors.

DON'T MISS

HIKING THE KNYSNA FORESTS

Now part of the Garden Route National Park, the Knysna Forests are the perfect place for hikers of all levels. At the easy end of the scale is the **Garden of Eden** (Map p136) where there are lovely forest picnic spots and a wheelchair-friendly walk. The **Millwood Gold Mine Walk** (Map p136) is also a gentle hike and the Elephant Trails at **Diepwalle** (Map p136) offer varying degrees of difficulty.

If you're looking for something more challenging, the **Harkerville Coast Trail** (R165) is a two-day hike that leads on to the popular Outeniqua Trail. The **Outeniqua Trail** is 108km long and takes a week to walk, although you can also do two- or three-day sections. The trail costs R66 per night to stay in a basic hut. You will need your own bedding. For permits, maps and further information, contact **SAN Parks** (Map p146; ☎044-302 5656; www.sanparks.org; Long St, Thesen's Island).

There are also plenty of mountain-biking trails. **Outeniqua Biking Trails** (☎044-532 7644; www.gardenroute.co.za/plett/obt) rents bikes (R100 per day, including helmets) and will give you a map to the surrounding trails.

Intercape destinations include towns such as George (R260, 1½ hours, twice daily), Mossel Bay (R260, two hours, twice daily), Port Elizabeth (R300, 4½ hours, twice daily), Cape Town (R350, eight hours, twice daily) and Jo'burg (R640, 17½ hours, daily).

Shared Taxi

The main **shared taxi stop** (Map p144) is at the Shell petrol station on Main St. Routes include Plettenberg Bay (R20, 30 minutes, daily) and Cape Town (R150, 7½ hours, daily).

Knysna to Plettenberg Bay

The N2 from Knysna to Plettenberg Bay has turn-offs both north and south that offer interesting detours.

The Knysna–Avontour road, Rte 339, climbs through the Outeniqua range via the beautiful **Prince Alfred's Pass**, regarded by some as even better than the Swartberg Pass. Be warned that the road is a bit on the rough side and it's slow going. The road has few really steep sections but the pass reaches a height of over 1000m, and there are great views to the north before the road winds its way into the Langkloof Valley.

Reached by a turn-off along the N2 10km east of Knysna, **Noetzie** is a quirky little place with holiday homes in mock-castle style. There's a lovely surf beach (spacious but dangerous) and a sheltered lagoon running through a forested gorge. The trail between the car park and beach is steep.

While you won't see any wild elephants in Knysna's forests, you are sure to see some if you head to **Knysna Elephant Park** (☏044-532 7732; www.knysnaelephantpark.co.za; 1hr tours adult/child R190/100; ☉8.30am-4.30pm), 22km east of Knysna off the N2. Here, small groups of visitors go on walking tours with the elephants or take a short ride (adult/child R815/390). The tours might not be authentic wildlife encounters, but are guaranteed to bring out the child in any visitor.

Plettenberg Bay

☏044 / POP 34,000

Plettenberg Bay, or 'Plett' as it's more commonly known, is a resort town through and through, with mountains, white sand and crystal-blue water making it one of the country's top local tourist spots. As a result, things can get very busy and somewhat

overpriced, but the town retains a relaxed, friendly atmosphere and does have very good-value hostels. The scenery to the east in particular is superb, with some of the best coast and indigenous forest in South Africa.

 Activities

Apart from lounging on the beaches or hiking on the Robberg Peninsula (see p151) there's a lot to do in Plett; check with Albergo for Backpackers, which can organise most things, often at a discount.

At the **Crags** you'll find the following four wildlife parks in close proximity.

TOP
CHOICE **Tenikwa** WILDLIFE RESERVE
(☏044-534 8170; www.tenikwa.co.za; cheetah walk R500; ☉9am-4.30pm) Considered a trip highlight by many, this is a chance to spend some quality time with cheetahs. Tenikwa is a sanctuary and rehabilitation centre for injured or abandoned animals, though the majority of its inhabitants are cats. The hour-long **Wild Cat Experience** (adult/child R160/80) visits all the lesser cats of South Africa, but it's the two-hour sunrise and sunset cheetah walks that have people sending postcards home. The cheetahs are on leads, but you're pretty much guaranteed personal contact. Bookings recommended.

Monkeyland WILDLIFE RESERVE
(www.monkeyland.co.za; 1hr tours adult/child R135/67.50; ☉8am-5pm) This very popular attraction helps rehabilitate wild monkeys that have been in zoos or private homes. The walking safari through a dense forest and across a 128m-long rope bridge is a brilliant way to find out more about the monkeys.

Birds of Eden WILDLIFE RESERVE
(www.birdsofeden.co.za; adult/child R135/67.50) This is the world's largest free-flight aviary with a 2-hectare dome over the forest. Combo tickets to Monkeyland and Birds of Eden cost R216/108 per adult/child.

Elephant Sanctuary WILDLIFE RESERVE
(www.elephantsanctuary.co.za; tours from adult/child R325/175, rides adult/child over 8yr R435/220; ☉8am-5pm) There are various tour and ride options allowing up-close pachyderm encounters.

Boat Trips WHALE-WATCHING
Ocean Blue Adventures (☏044-533 5083; www.oceanadventures.co.za; Milkwood Centre, Hopewood St) and **Ocean Safaris** (☏044-533 4963; www.oceansafaris.co.za; Milkwood

Plettenberg Bay

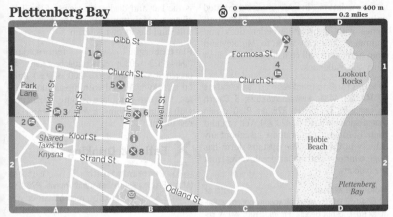

Centre, Hopewood St; 1½hr trip R400) offer boat trips to view dolphins and whales in season. Both operators charge R650 for whale-watching, R400 for dolphin trips.

Adventure Sports
ADVENTURE SPORTS, SURFING

For skydiving try **Sky Dive Plettenberg Bay** (☎044-533 9048; www.skydiveplett.com; Plettenberg Airport; tandem jump R1600). For surf lessons contact **Garden Route Surf Academy** (☎082 436 6410; www.gardenroutesurfacademy.com; 2hr group lesson incl equipment R300).

Old Nick Village
VILLAGE

(www.oldnickvillage.co.za) For a bit of retail therapy after all that action, head for this complex just 3km east of town, with resident artists, a weaving museum, antiques and a restaurant.

🛏 Sleeping

The tourism bureau has a full list of accommodation and can tell you about the many camping options, all in nearby Keurboomstrand. In low season there are bargains to be found.

TOP CHOICE Nothando Backpackers Hostel
BACKPACKERS $

(☎044-533 0220; www.nothando.com; 5 Wilder St; dm R130, d with shared bathroom R350, d R400) This excellent, five-star budget option, YHA-affiliated and award-winning, is owner-run and it shows. There's a great bar area with satellite TV, yet you can still find peace and quiet in the large grounds.

Abalone Beach House
BACKPACKERS $

(☎044-535 9602; www.abalonebeachhouse.co.za; 50 Milkwood Glen, Keurboomstrand; d with shared bathroom R380, d R450; @🞉) This relaxing and extremely friendly backpackers is more like a budget guesthouse. A magnificent beach is two minutes away and surf and body boards are provided free. To reach the house follow the Keurboomstrand signs from the N2 (about 6km east of Plett), then turn into Milkwood Glen.

Periwinkle Guest Lodge
GUESTHOUSE $$

(☎044-533 1345; www.periwinkle.co.za; 75 Beachy Head Dr; d incl breakfast R2230) This bright, colourful beachfront guesthouse offers individually decorated rooms, all with great views – you might even be able to spot whales and dolphins.

Hog Hollow
LODGE $$$

(☎044-534 8879; www.hog-hollow.com; s/d incl breakfast R2190/2900) Hog Hollow, 18km east of Plett along the N2, provides delightful accommodation in African-art-decorated units overlooking the forest. Each unit comes with a private wooden deck and hammock. You can walk to Monkeyland from here; staff will collect you if you don't fancy the walk back.

Albergo for Backpackers BACKPACKERS $
(☎044-533 4434; www.albergo.co.za; 8 Church St; campsites per person R75, dm R130, d with shared bathroom R350, d R420; @) Well run and friendly, Albergo can organise just about any activity in the area. The upstairs dorm has huge windows and stellar ocean views from the balcony.

Milkwood Manor HOTEL $$
(☎044-533 0420; www.milkwoodmanor.co.za; Salmack Rd, Lookout Beach; d from R1100; @) A remarkable location, right on the beach and overlooking the lagoon. Rooms are smart if not spectacular, there's a restaurant on-site and kayaks are free for guests who want to explore the lagoon.

Amakaya Backpackers BACKPACKERS $
(☎044-533 4010; www.amakaya.co.za; 15 Park Lane; dm R110-130, d with shared bathroom R300, d R350) A total overhaul has turned this into a great backpacker hostel whose focal point

is the bar and deck with views of the Tsitsikamma Mountains. One of the dorms is en suite and has its own kitchen.

Plettenberg LUXURY HOTEL $$$
(☎044-533 2030; www.plettenberg.com; 40 Church St; s/d from R2500/4200; ❄@☀) Built on a rocky headland with breathtaking vistas, this five-star place is pure decadence, with fantastic rooms, a spa and a top-class restaurant.

✗ Eating & Drinking

TOP CHOICE Ristorante Enrico SEAFOOD $$
(Main Beach, Keurboomstrand; mains R70-120; ☺lunch & dinner) Highly recommended by readers, this is *the* place to try seafood in Plett. Enrico has his own boat that, weather permitting, heads out each morning. The large deck has awesome views of the beach. If you book ahead you can join the fishing trips.

Table ITALIAN $$
(9 Main St; mains R60-105; ☺lunch & dinner) A funky, minimalist venue with pizzas featuring an array of unusual toppings. At lunch

---

SURFING ALONG THE GARDEN ROUTE

With the water warming up as you round Cape Agulhas where the Indian Ocean takes over, you can be happy surfing in just baggies/boardshorts or a short suit during summer. You'll need a full suit in winter, though.

In Mossel Bay, there's a good right in a big swell called Ding Dangs that's best at a lowish tide, especially in a southwesterly or easterly wind. It might be a bit of a hassle paddling out, but the right is better than the left. To the right of the tidal pool, there's a soft wave called Inner Pool. Outer Pool (left of the tidal pool) is a better bet and is a great reef and point break.

You might find something at Grootbrak and Kleinbrak, but better is Herold's Bay. When it's on, there's a left-hand wedge along the beach, and it's unusual in that it works in a northwesterly wind.

Best of all though is Victoria Bay, which has the most consistent breaks along this coast. It's perfect when the swell is about 1m to 2m and you get a great right-hander.

A little further along is Buffalo Bay (Buffel's Bay) where there's another right-hand point. Buffalo's Bay is at one end of Brenton Beach; at the northern end, you'll find some good peaks, but watch out for sharks.

On to Plettenberg Bay: avoid Robberg Peninsula as that's home to a seal colony. But the swimming area at Robberg Beach (where the lifeguards are stationed) can have some good waves if the swell isn't too big. Central Beach has one of the best known waves, the Wedge, which is perfect for goofy-footers. Lookout Beach can have some sandbanks and the Point can be good, but there's a lot of erosion here and the beach is slowly disappearing. Watch out for rip currents, especially when there are no lifeguards on duty.

Nature's Valley has a long beach that has consistent sandbanks and is fine in a swell. When it's up, there's a left-hand sandbar that is perfect for experienced surfers.

time there's a 'harvest table' with ever-changing local produce.

Europa
ITALIAN $$
(cnr Church & Main Sts; mains R42-120; ⊘breakfast, lunch & dinner) This is a snazzy restaurant-bar with a great deck. There's a good range of salads and plenty of Italian fare.

Lookout
SEAFOOD $$
(☑044-533 1379; Lookout Rocks; mains R60-130; ⊘breakfast, lunch & dinner) With a deck overlooking the beach, this is a great place for a simple meal and perhaps views of dolphins surfing the waves.

LM in Plett Mozambican Restaurant
SEAFOOD $$
(6 Yellowwood Centre, Main St; mains R60-125; ⊘lunch & dinner) A smart restaurant concentrating on the famous 'LM' (Laurenço Marques) prawns. A dozen of the best will cost you R315.

❶ Information

Internet cafe (Melville's Corner Shopping Centre, Main St; per hr R60; ⊘8am-5pm Mon-Fri, 9am-1pm Sat)

Plett Tourism (☑044-533 4065; www.plettenbergbay.co.za; 5 Main St; ⊘8.30am-5pm Mon-Fri year-round, plus 9am-2pm Sat Apr-Oct) This office has a great deal of useful information on accommodation and walks in the surrounding hills and reserves.

❶ Getting There & Away

All the major buses off stop at the Shell Ultra City on the N2; the Baz Bus comes into town.
Intercape (www.intercape.co.za) destinations from Plett include George (R270, two hours, twice daily), Port Elizabeth (R300, 3½ hours, twice daily), Cape Town (R320, nine hours, twice daily), Jo'burg (R770, 18 hours, daily), Graaff-Reinet (R370, 6½ hours, daily) and Bloemfontein (R520, 12 hours, daily).

If you're heading to Knysna (R15, 30 minutes) you're better off taking a shared taxi – services leave from the corner of Kloof and High Sts. Most other shared taxis stop at the Shell Ultra City on the N2.

Robberg Nature & Marine Reserve

This **reserve** (☑044-533 2125; www.capenature.org.za; adult/child R30/15; ⊘7am-5pm Feb-Nov, 7am-8pm Dec-Jan), 9km southeast of Plettenberg Bay, protects a 4km-long peninsula with a rugged coastline of cliffs and rocks.

There are three circular walks of increasing difficulty, with rich intertidal marine life and coastal-dune *fynbos*, but it's very rocky and not for the unfit or anyone with knee problems! The Point and the Fountain are overnight huts (R360). To get to the reserve head along Robberg Rd, off Piesang Valley Rd, until you see the signs.

CENTRAL KAROO

The seemingly endless Karoo has a truly magical feel. It's a vast, semi-arid plateau (its name is a Khoe-San word meaning 'land of thirst') that features stunning sunsets and starscapes. Inhabited for more than half a million years, the region is rich in archaeological sites, fossils, San paintings, wildlife and some 9000 plant species.

The Karoo covers almost one-third of South Africa's total area and is demarcated in the south and west by the coastal mountain ranges, and to the east and north by the mighty Senqu (Orange) River. It's often split into the Great Karoo (north) and the Little Karoo (south), but it doesn't respect provincial boundaries and sprawls into three provinces, so for our purposes it's the Central Karoo here, Eastern Karoo in the Eastern Cape chapter and Upper Karoo in the Northern Cape chapter.

Prince Albert & Around

☑023 / POP 2500

To many urban South African people, Prince Albert – a charming village dating back to 1762 – represents an idyllic life in the Karoo. If you have your own transport, you can easily visit on a day trip from Oudtshoorn or even from the coast. Alternatively, stay in Prince Albert and make a day trip to Oudtshoorn via the spectacular Swartberg and Meiringspoort Passes, or – if the weather isn't too hot – consider going on a hike.

Despite being surrounded by very harsh country, the town is green and fertile (producing peaches, apricots, grapes and olives), thanks to the run-off from the mountain springs. There's an Olive Festival each April.

⊙ Sights & Activities

Swartberg Nature Reserve
PARK
Prince Albert's best attractions are outside the town, including the russet peaks of this reserve. There are over 100km of hik-

ing trails all administered by Cape Nature (☎021-659 3500; www.capenature.org.za). Check with them for updates on which trails are open and to book overnight walks. For guides, contact Prince Albert Tourism.

Two Passes Route DRIVING TOUR

Many people drive along the circular route to Oudtshoorn, taking the Meiringspoort Pass one way and returning by the winding and beautiful gravel road that is the Swartberg Pass. Meiringspoort, although remarkable, is the less spectacular of the two, following a river that cuts right through the Swartberg range. There is a small visitor centre next to the waterfall – worth a stop. Swartberg is suitable for sedan vehicles, but can be slow going. It's also a popular spot for mountain bikers. If you don't fancy cycling up, contact Dennehof Tours (see p152) to arrange a one-way ride.

🛏 Sleeping & Eating

TOP CHOICE Bushman Valley CAMPGROUND $

(☎023-541 1322; www.bushmanvalley.com; Rte 407; campsite per person R60, dorm R100, cottages R250 per person; 🐾) Prince Albert's only real budget option is just south of town and a fantastic base for hiking in the Swartberg mountains. The thatched cottages have decent kitchen facilities or you can camp in the grounds (tents available to hire for R30). Tours delving into San culture are available.

Prince Albert of Saxe-Coburg Lodge GUESTHOUSE $$

(☎023-541 1267; www.saxecoburg.co.za; 60 Church St; s/d incl breakfast from R700/1040; ❋🐾) This place offers quality accommodation in lovely garden rooms. Owners Dick and Regina are a great source of information and offer guided hikes in the area.

Karoo Lodge GUESTHOUSE $$

(☎023-541 1467; www.karoolodge.com; 66 Church St; s/d from R450/790; ❋@🐾) This lodge is an owner-run guesthouse with a large garden and beautiful antique furniture. The restaurant (mains R80-130) promises a fusion of Karoo and Mediterranean fare. It's open to nonguests but bookings are essential.

TOP CHOICE Gallery FUSION $$

(57 Church St; mains R85-135; ⊙dinner) Prince Albert's smartest dining option has an everchanging menu featuring modern takes on local classics such as Karoo lamb and game

steaks. There's also a good range of vegetarian choices.

Karoo Kombuis SOUTH AFRICAN $$

(Karoo Kitchen; ☎023-541 1110; 18 Deurdrift St; mains R80-95; ⊙dinner Mon-Sat) If it ain't broke, don't fix it, they say, and this cosy restaurant has been serving the same three home-cooked dishes for the past 13 years. Bring your own drinks and make sure you book ahead.

Lazy Lizard CAFE $

(9 Church St; ⊙7am-6pm; @) This bright, cosy house offers the best coffee in town and stocks home-baked goodies and crafts. Try its legendary apple pie. There is internet access here (per hour R30).

❶ Information

Prince Albert Tourism (☎023-541 1366; www.patourism.co.za; Church St; ⊙9am-5pm Mon-Fri, 9am-1pm Sat) Can help with guides and accommodation.

❶ Getting There & Away

Most people visit by driving over one of the area's passes from Oudtshoorn, or from the N1 between Cape Town and Jo'burg. However, if you've come for hiking there's no reason not to take a **train** (Shosholoza Meyl, ☎0860 008888; www.shosholozameyl.co.za), which is cheaper than the buses. There is no direct bus or train service to Prince Albert; the closest drop-off point is at Prince Albert Road, 45km northwest of Prince Albert. This is also the long-distance bus stop. Private taxis cost R130, but most places to stay will pick you up from the train station.

Gamkaskloof Nature Reserve (Die Hel)

In a narrow valley in the Swartberg range is Gamkaskloof, better known as Die Hel. The first citizens of Die Hel were early Trekboers, who developed their own dialect. There was no road into Die Hel until the 1960s, and donkeys carried in the few goods the self-sufficient community needed from Prince Albert.

Now the area is part of the Swartberg Nature Reserve where there is self-catering accommodation (☎023-541 1107; www.diehel.com; on-site caravans & campsites R200, cottages per person R250) in restored farm cottages.

There are various trails and overnight huts operated by Cape Nature.

The dirt road to Die Hel turns off the Swartberg Pass road 18km from Prince Albert and extends for another 50km or so before hitting a dead end. Be warned: this short distance takes at least two hours to drive *each way*. The road is in terrible condition so you might want to leave your car in Prince Albert and opt for a guided tour instead. Lindsay Steyn from Dennehof Tours (☎023-5411 227; www.dennehof.co.za) is a mine of information on the region and offers superb full-day tours (R800) taking in the top of the Swartberg Pass before descending the vertiginous road to Hell for lunch.

Beaufort West

☎ 023 / POP 37,000

A transit town if ever there were one, Beaufort West is not a place to linger but nonetheless has a strange faded charm if you know where to look. Established in 1818, it's the oldest and largest town in the Karoo and in summer becomes a sluice gate for the torrent of South Africans heading for the coast – accommodation is booked out and prices rise.

The town museum (☎023-415 2308; cnr Donkin & Church Sts; adult/child R15/8; ☉8.30am-4.45pm Mon-Fri, 9am-noon Sat) is spread over three buildings, and it is largely devoted to its local hero Dr Christiaan Barnard, who performed the world's first human heart transplant.

Given the plethora of accommodation options established to shore up all the through traffic (and the fly-by-night nature of much

of it), any accommodation listing for Beaufort West has become an exercise in futility. Inquire at the tourist office or see its website for more information.

ⓘ Information

Tourist information (☎023-415 1488; www.beaufortwest.net; 57 Donkin St; ☉8am-5pm Mon-Fri, 9am-1pm Sat) On the main street.

ⓘ Getting There & Away

Beaufort West is a junction for many bus services. **Translux** (www.translux.co.za) stops at the **Total petrol station** (Donkin St), located in the centre of town. **Greyhound** (www.greyhound.co.za), **SA Roadlink** (www.saroadlink.co.za) and **Intercape** (www.intercape.co.za) stop at the Engen petrol station north of town. Long-distance shared taxis stop at the **BP petrol station** (Donkin St) en route to Jo'burg, Cape Town and Bloemfontein.

The *Shosholoza Meyl* and the *Blue Train* stop at the station on Church St on their journeys between Cape Town and Jo'burg.

Karoo National Park

Just 5km north of Beaufort West, the **Karoo National Park** (☎023-415 2828/9; www.sanparks.org; adult/child R108/54; ☉7am-7pm) covers 330 sq km of impressive Karoo landscapes and representative flora.

The park has 61 species of mammal, the most common of which are dassies (agile, rodentlike mammals, also called hyraxes) and bat-eared foxes. The antelope population is small but some species have been reintroduced and their numbers are growing. These include springboks, kudus, gemsboks

---

WORTH A TRIP

MATJIESFONTEIN

One of the most curious and fascinating places in the Karoo, Matjiesfontein (pronounced 'mikeys-fontein') is an almost entirely privately owned railway siding around a grand hotel that has remained virtually unchanged for 100 years. It has a slight theme-park feel, but visiting the Victorian buildings, manned by staff in period costume, is a lot of fun. There are two museums (admission R5; ☉8am-1pm & 2pm-5pm), one looking at transport, the other a right old jumble sale, containing everything from trophy heads to a collection of commodes. There's one hotel (☎023-561 3011; www.matjiesfontein.com; s/d from R490/750; ▨) offering evening meals and a cafe (mains R35-75; ☉9am-5pm) serving light lunches.

Matjiesfontein is just off the N1, 240km from Cape Town and 198km from Beaufort West. Trains running between Cape Town and Jo'burg stop here and the *Blue Train* also pauses for an hour, with travellers being given a tour of town on the double-decker London bus that stands outside the station.

and red hartebeests as well as mountain zebras and black rhinos. There are a great many reptiles and birds, including black eagles.

Facilities include a shop and restaurant. Guided walks are available and there's a 400m fossil trail that's accessible by wheelchair.

Accommodation is either at pleasant **campsites** (R190) or in Cape Dutch–style **cottages** (d R945). The cottages are fully equipped with kitchens, towels and bedding. Two of the cottages have wheelchair access.

You cannot get out of your vehicle in the park, except at designated spots, so hiking the 10km from the gate to the rest camp is definitely not an option. You'll need your own transport.

WEST COAST & SWARTLAND

The windswept coastline and desolate mountains on the western side of Western Cape are a peaceful, undeveloped paradise. Head north of Cape Town and you'll find whitewashed fishing villages, unspoilt beaches, a lagoon and wetlands teeming with birds, fascinating country towns and one of the best hiking regions in the country.

The West Coast National Park is a must for birdwatchers and lovers of seascapes, while inland lies the richly fertile Olifants River Valley where citrus orchards and vineyards sit at the foot of the Cederberg mountains – a hiker's heaven. This remote area has spectacular rock formations and a wealth of San rock paintings.

Between the coast and the mountains lies the Swartland, undulating hills of wheat and yet more vineyards. Swartland, meaning Black Land, gets its name from the threat-ened indigenous vegetation, *renosterveld,* that turns a dark grey in summer. This entire area is ablaze with colour in early spring (August and September) when the veld is carpeted with wildflowers. In season, you can check where the flowers are at their best on a daily basis by calling the **Flower Hotline** (☎083 910 1028).

Most public transport through this area travels from Cape Town north along the N7, either going all the way to Springbok and Namibia or leaving the N7 and heading through Calvinia to Upington. Getting to the coastal towns west of the N7 isn't easy if you don't have a car.

Darling

☎022 / 7600

A quiet country town, Darling was famous for its good-quality milk until the actor and satirist Pieter-Dirk Uys, along with his alter ego Evita Bezuidenhout, set up home here.

Most Capetonians who make the 70km trek north do so to catch the uniquely South African cabaret at **Evita se Perron** (☎022-492 2831; www.evita.co.za; 8 Arcadia St, Old Darling Station; tickets R90; ☉performances 2pm & 7pm Sat &Sun). The shows touch on everything from South African politics to history to ecology. Nothing is off limits – including the country's racially charged past and the AIDS epidemic. Although the shows include a smattering of Afrikaans, they're largely in English and always hilarious and thought-provoking.

The splendidly kitsch **restaurant** (mains R40-65; ☉lunch Tue-Sun) serves traditional Afrikaner food including *bobotie.*

Uys set up the **Darling Trust** (☎021-492 2851; www.thedarlingtrust.org) to assist Swartland communities to empower themselves through participation in education, skills development and health. The **A en C Shop** at the Old Darling Station stocks beading, clothes, wire-art and paintings.

Don't forget to ask tourist information or your guesthouse about the underrated **Darling Wine Experience**, the collective name for the five estates in the vicinity.

🛏 Sleeping & Eating

Trinity GUESTHOUSE $$
(☎022-492 3430; 19 Long St; s/d incl breakfast from R450/700; ⛶) A painstakingly renovated Victorian homestead with cosy country-style bedrooms.

GROOTE POST WINERY

Of all the Darling wineries, **Groote Post** (www.grootepost.com; ☉9am-5pm Mon-Fri, 10am-4pm Sat & Sun) has the most to offer the visitor, with wildlife drives, nature walks, a superb restaurant and of course free tastings of its excellent chardonnays and sauvignon blancs.

DON'T MISS

!KHWA TTU

Billed as the San Culture & Education Centre, **!Khwa ttu** (www.khwattu.org; Rte 27, Yzerfontein; ⊘9am-5pm) is a joint venture by the San people and a Swiss philanthropic foundation (Ubuntu) and is the only San-owned and operated culture centre in the Western Cape.

Set within the ancestral lands of the San, !Khwa ttu is based on an 850-hectare nature reserve. There's a good **restaurant** (mains R50-95; ⊘breakfast & lunch) serving traditional South African cuisine and a wonderful craft shop. Excellent **tours** (2hr R250; ⊘10am & 2pm) with a San guide involve a nature walk, a wildlife drive and learning about San culture.

You can stay on the reserve in well-equipped self-catering **accommodation** (4-person bush camp tents R400, 4-person bush cottage R770, 6-person guesthouse R880). !Khwa ttu is off Rte 27 just south of Yzerfontein, 70km from Cape Town.

Darling Guest Lodge GUESTHOUSE $$
(☑022-492 3062; 22 Pastorie St; s/d incl breakfast R550/880; @☒) An elegant and imaginatively decorated place, one of the first in the area. Rooms are named after local artists.

 Marmalade Cat CAFE $
(☑022-492 2515; 19 Main Rd; mains R30-60; ⊘breakfast & lunch daily, dinner Fri & Sat) For an afternoon coffee or all-day breakfast, this is the place. It also serves sandwiches, delicious cheeses and homemade sweet treats and Friday night is pizza night. Bookings advisable.

Drinking

Slow Quarter BAR
(5 Main Rd; light meals R55-85; ⊘Mon-Sat 11am-7pm, closed Tue) The home base of the popular local beer, Darling Brew, is a chic place to munch on ale-inspired tapas and sip one of its four flagship beers.

❶ Information

Tourist information (☑022-492 3361; cnr Hill Rd & Pastorie St; ⊘9am-1pm & 2-4pm Mon-Thu, 9am-3.30pm Fri, 10am-3pm Sat & Sun) Can be found in the museum (adult/child R10/5).

❶ Getting There & Away

Drive up Rte 27 from Cape Town and look out for the signs. An alternative route back to Cape Town, which is much more scenic and not nearly as busy as Rte 27, is to head east out of the town and turn south down Rte 307. Turn right just before the town of Mamre to rejoin Rte 27. Do not follow Rte 304 past Atlantis.

West Coast National Park

Encompassing the clear, blue waters of the Langebaan Lagoon and home to an enormous number of birds is the **West Coast National Park** (www.sanparks.org; adult/child R88/44; ⊘7am-7.30pm). The park covers around 310 sq km and protects wetlands of international significance and important seabird breeding colonies. Wading birds flock here by the thousands in summer. The most numerically dominant species is the curlew sandpiper, which migrates north from the sub-Antarctic in huge flocks. The offshore islands are home to colonies of African penguins.

The park is famous for its wildflower display, which is usually between August and October. The park is only about 120km from Cape Town, 7km south of Langebaan. The return trip from Langebaan to the northern end of the Postberg section is more than 80km; allow plenty of time. The rainy season is between May and August.

The **Geelbek Visitor's Centre & Restaurant** (☑022-772 2134; West Coast National Park; mains R65-105; ⊘breakfast & lunch) has a wide menu specialising in traditional fare. It's also an information centre for the park and can help with accommodation options.

There are various overnight options, including **Duinepos** (☑022-707 9900; www.duinepos.co.za; 2-/4-person chalet R635/850; ☒) and the romantic lagoon **houseboats** (☑021-689 9718; www.houseboating.co.za; 4-person boat R1400) moored at pretty Kraalbaai.

ELAND'S BAY

While much of the peninsula north of Paternoster is marred by smelly fish-processing factories and rampant housing developments wherever there's a beach, past Veldrif the coast is undeveloped and the beaches beautiful. Eland's Bay in particular is a pretty spot oozing rustic charm and with a supreme setting: mountains run to the sea past a large lagoon frequented by waterbirds – this is a bird-lover's mecca.

There is one **hotel** (☎022-972 1640; Hunter St; dm R100, s/d incl breakfast from R250/420) that acts as the tourist information office and also has a restaurant serving average food with awesome views.

Eland's Bay is primarily a surf spot and is known as a goofy-footer's (surfing with the right foot at the front of the board) paradise, with extremely fast left-point waves working at a range of swell sizes. Body boards are available to hire in the town, but surfers will need their own gear.

The gravel road to Lambert's Bay is a toll road and not in great condition. The tarred road via Leipoldtville is recommended.

Langebaan

☎022 / 3500

Its beautiful location overlooking the Langebaan Lagoon has made this seaside resort a favourite holiday destination with locals. If you're looking for untouched you might be happier elsewhere, but the town does support an excellent hotel, seafood restaurants, phenomenal sunset views, windsurfing on the lagoon and a few good beaches, the best of which is **Langebaan Beach**, in town and popular with swimmers. The town is also a good base for exploring the West Coast National Park.

Sights & Activities

TOP CHOICE **West Coast Fossil Park** ARCHAEOLOGICAL SITE

(☎022-766 1606; www.fossilpark.org.za; adult/child R50/15; ⏰8am-4pm Mon-Fri, 10am-1pm Sat & Sun) The first bear discovered south of the Sahara, lion-sized sabre-toothed cats, three-toed horses and short-necked giraffes are all on display at this excellent fossil park on Rte 45 about 16km outside Langebaan. Fascinating tours depart hourly from 10am to 3pm (until 1pm on weekends) and take you to the excavation sites – among the richest fossil sites in the world. There are also mountain-biking and walking trails, and a coffee and gift shop.

Cape Sports Centre WATER SPORTS

(☎022-772 1114; www.capesport.co.za; 98 Main Rd) Langebaan is a water sports mecca, particularly for windsurfing and kite-surfing. This cheery office offers kite-surfing courses (three-day course R2185) and windsurfing lessons (two hours R500), and rents out surfboards and kayaks (R185/295 per day).

Sleeping & Eating

Many of the sleeping options double as restaurants. There is also a cluster of restaurants on Bree St, some with beach views.

TOP CHOICE **Farmhouse** HOTEL $$$

(☎022-772 2062; www.thefarmhousehotel.com; 5 Egret St; d incl breakfast R1850; ✱) Langebaan's only hotel sits on a hill overlooking the bay and has lovely sunset views. Rooms are large, with country decor and their own fireplaces. For such a classy place the **restaurant** (mains R70-195) is reasonably priced with a creative menu, and a rustic, intimate dining room.

Oliphantskop Farm Inn GUESTHOUSE $$

(☎022-772 2326; www.olifantskop.co.za; Main Rd; d R520; ✱) A rustic place around 3km from town, across the road from the Mykonos resort complex, Oliphantskop offers comfy rooms and fully equipped self-catering cottages (for four R820). Horse rides are available (R200 per hour).

Club Mykonos RESORT $$

(☎0800226770; www.clubmykonos.co.za; 2-person unit from R1200; @✱) This is a major resort geared towards families, but its Greek-themed, pseudo-Mediterranean architecture and crowds mean you'll either love it or hate it. There are no fewer than six outdoor swimming pools, a casino, restaurants and an arcade. Prices rise on weekends and there's a minimum stay of seven nights during school holidays.

TOP CHOICE **Die Strandloper** SEAFOOD **$$$**

(☑022-772 2490; buffet R205; ☺lunch Sat & Sun, dinner Fri & Sat, lunch & dinner daily Dec-Jan) The West Coast life exemplified – a *10*-course outdoor fish and seafood braai right on the beach. There's also freshly made bread, bottomless *moerkoffie* (freshly ground coffee) and a local crooner who plays West Coast ballads at your table. You can BYO (corkage free) or get drinks from the rustic bar, whose view is sensational. Bookings essential.

❶ Information

Tourist information centre (☑022-772 1515; www.langebaaninfo.com; Bree St; ☺9am-5pm Mon-Fri, 9am-2pm Sat)

❶ Getting There & Away

Langebaan is an hour's drive north of Cape Town, but no public transport runs here. Shared taxis run from the 7-Eleven car park to Vredenburg (R15, 10 minutes) and daily to Cape Town (R70, 1¼ hours).

Paternoster

☑022 / 1500

Not so many years ago, Paternoster was the West Coast's last traditional fishing village, little more than a clutch of simple whitewashed homes set against the blue sea. Then

---

WORTH A TRIP

OLIFANTS RIVER VALLEY

The lush landscape of the Olifants River Valley – so-named for the elephants that roamed here in the 17th century – comes as quite a surprise after you've spent time in the arid surrounds. This is the location of an up-and-coming wine region, best known for its robust reds. **Teubes Family Wines** (☑027-213 2377) has a brand-new winery near Vredendal, offering olive and cheese platters with its wines. The largest winery in the region, **Namaqua** (☑027-213 1080; www. namaquawines.com), is best known for its easy-drinking boxed wine. There's a restaurant here, open for lunch.

---

wealthy Capetonians and foreigners became captivated by its charms and property is now a hot commodity.

Still, it remains a lovely town to visit, and the surrounding countryside – rolling hills scattered with strange granite outcrops – is attractive. It's busiest during crayfish season, which, to a certain extent, is a moveable feast (sometime from mid-November to mid-April). Be aware that *kreef,* Afrikaans for this delicacy, sold from roadside vendors may have been illegally caught. If you want to try your hand at catching your own (or collect any other shellfish), make sure you get a permit from any post office and that you know the bag limits – rules are stringently applied.

Further north along the coast is the similar village of **St Helena Bay**, with a lovely sheltered stretch of water, but no real beach.

Cape Columbine Nature Reserve PARK

(☑022-752 2718; adult/child R13/9; ☺7am-7pm) Three kilometres south of Paternoster lies the windswept but stunningly beautiful Cape Columbine Nature Reserve. There are **campsites** (R108) with basic facilities at Tieties Bay. The **lighthouse tower** (adult/child R16/8; ☺10am-3pm Mon-Fri May-Sep, 10am-3pm daily Oct-Apr) is worth a climb and you can also stay here in renovated **keepers' cottages** (per 2 people R700).

Just before you reach the lighthouse is **Beach Camp** (☑082 926 2267; www.beach camp.co.za; tent from R250). In a blissful setting right on the beach, this ecofriendly place has A-frame tents and is perfect for kayaking and chilling in the bar in the evenings. There's no electricity, and you'll need your own bedding.

🛌 Sleeping & Eating

Paternoster is rather lacking in street signs; instead look out for individual guesthouse signs. There are many B&Bs, so it may be worth checking out a few places first.

Paternoster Lodge GUESTHOUSE **$$**

(☑022-752 2023; www.paternosterlodge.co.za; s/d R720/990) This is a snazzy place, with seven neat minimalist rooms, all with a sea view, and a breezy **restaurant** (mains R55-200) that's open all day. From the sun deck you can watch the fishermen bringing in their catch.

Paternoster Hotel HOTEL **$$**

(☑022-752 2703; www.paternosterhotel.co.za; Main Rd; d with sea view R900) This comfortable country hotel has the laidback atmosphere of a fisherman's retreat. Its trademark graffiti-covered walls and the underwear-festooned Panty Bar remain, housed in the old town jail.

Voorstrandt Restaurant   SEAFOOD $$
(Strandloperweg; mains R70-140, crayfish R240-295; ⊙breakfast, lunch & dinner) A better location you couldn't wish for – you can hop from your table right onto the sand. Specialising in seafood, this is also an excellent spot to watch the sunset over a beer.

Lambert's Bay
☎027 / 5200

The refreshing sea breezes of Lambert's Bay offer respite from the West Coast sun, but the ubiquitous fish-processing factories mean you'd be advised to stay upwind.

The helpful information centre (☎027-432 1000; Main Rd; ⊙9am-1pm & 2-5pm Mon-Fri, 9am-12.30pm Sat) can tell you about attractions in the area. The Lambert's Bay Hotel (☎027-432 1126; Voortrekker St; s/d incl breakfast from R500/670; ✹) is the largest place to stay, with a restaurant and bar open to all. Rooms were being upgraded when we visited.

Lambert's Bay is also known for its large gannet rookery situated on Bird Island (adult/child R30/15, ⊙7am-6pm).

Lambert's Bay is a little-known whale-watching spot – look out for southern right whales in the spring and humpback whales in winter. The waters are also home to Heaviside's dolphin, an endemic species. For boat trips contact Lambert's Bay Boat Trips (☎072 595 2166). You can also try quad biking and sand boarding (☎083 229 0819; per person R250) at the Dunes, 10km east of town.

In March, the Crayfish Festival means cheap seafood and plenty of entertainment, but if you can't wait till then, try a seafood buffet at one of the two open-air restaurants just outside town. There's not much to choose between Muisbosskerm (☎027-432 1017; meals R195, crayfish extra) and Bosduifklip (☎027-432 2735; meals R185); call ahead as opening times vary and bookings are essential.

Cederberg Wilderness Area

Some of the finest scenery in the Cape is to be found in the desolate Cederberg. The 830-sq-km wilderness area is administered by Cape Nature (www.capenature.org.za) and boasts bizarre-shaped, weathered-sandstone formations, San rock art, craggy and rugged mountains and clear streams. The peaks and valleys extend roughly north-south for 100km, between Vanrhynsdorp and Citrusdal. The highest peaks are Sneeuberg (2027m) and Tafelberg (1969m).

The region is famous for its plant life, which is predominantly mountain *fynbos*. Spring is the best time to see the wildflowers, although there's plenty of interest at other times of the year. The vegetation varies with altitude but includes the Clanwilliam cedar (which gives the region its name) and the rare snowball protea. The cedar survives only in relatively small numbers, growing between 1000m and 1500m, and the snowball protea (now limited to isolated pockets) grows only above the snow line.

There are small populations of baboons, rheboks, klipspringers and grysboks; and predators such as caracals, Cape foxes, honey badgers and the elusive leopard.

DON'T MISS

DWARSRIVIER FARM

Deep in the Cederberg, this is an excellent base for hiking – both the Wolfberg Arch and Maltese Cross hikes leave from this area. At Sanddrif (☎027-482 2825; campsites R120, cottage R650) there are shady campsites by the river or well-equipped cottages with patios gazing out at the mountains. Don't miss the Cederberg Winery, also on the premises. All of its wines are stupendous. There's an excellent astronomical observatory (www.cederbergobs.org.za) nearby, open on Saturday evenings as well as the San art of the Stadsaal Caves.

To get to Dwarsrivier, follow the Algeria turnoff from the N7, 30km north of Citrusdal. From here a gravel road winds into the mountains; it's 46km to Dwarsrivier.

🛏 Sleeping

See also Citrusdal and Clanwilliam for places to stay outside the Cederberg Wilderness Area.

TOP CHOICE Gecko Creek

Wilderness Lodge BACKPACKERS $$
(☏027-482 1300; www.geckocreek.com; campsite/tent/cabin per person R130/200/290; @ 🐾) Highly recommended by readers, and rightly so. There are magnificent views, San rock art and hiking trails over 1000 hectares. Meals are available, and owner Linton Pope can arrange scenic flights. To find it, take the Algeria turn-off on the N7 and look out for the sign on the right.

Algeria CAMPGROUND $$
(☏027-482 2404; 6-person campsites R185, 4-person cottage R730) This is the main camping spot in the area, with exceptional grounds in a beautiful, shaded site alongside the Rondegat River. There is a swimming hole and lovely spots to picnic. Rates do not include the park entry fee. It can get quite noisy at weekends and school holidays. Entrance to the camping ground closes at 4.30pm (9pm on Friday).

ℹ Information

The Cederberg is divided into three excellent hiking areas of around 240 sq km. Each area has a network of trails. Two of the most popular hikes are to the **Maltese Cross** and the **Wolfberg Cracks and Arch**.

There is a buffer zone of conserved land between the wilderness area and the farmland, and here more intrusive activities such as mountain biking are allowed.

There are no eating places in the area so you will need to bring your own food.

ℹ Getting There & Away

The Cederberg range is about 200km from Cape Town, accessible from Citrusdal, Clanwilliam and the N7.

It takes about 45 minutes to get to Algeria from Clanwilliam by car. Algeria is not signposted from Clanwilliam, but you just follow the road above the dam to the south. Algeria *is* signposted from the N7 and it's only 20 minutes from the main road; there's an amazing collection of plants, including proteas, along the side of the road.

There are some dusty but interesting back roads that run southeast through the hamlet of Cederberg on Rte 303, and on to Ceres.

ℹ HIKING PERMITS

At quiet times you can pick up a permit on the spot at Algeria or Dwarsrivier but during school holidays it's best to book ahead (☏021-483 0190) as hiker numbers are limited. The maximum group size is 12 and, for safety, the minimum is two adults.

Unfortunately, public transport into Algeria is nonexistent.

Citrusdal & Around

☏022 / POP 9000

The small town of Citrusdal is a good base for exploring the Cederberg. August to September is wildflower season, and the displays can be spectacular. This is also one of the best times for hiking. Although the town itself is quaint, some of the most interesting and beautiful places to stay are in the surrounding mountains. Be sure to explore beyond the town limits because the scenery is stupendous.

🛏 Sleeping

TOP CHOICE Beaverlac

CAMPGROUND $
(☏022-931 2945; Beaverlac Nature Reserve; admission per car R15, campsites per person R45, hut R200, 4-person cottage R280) A valley hidden beneath pine trees is the base for this wonderful campground. There are rock pools for swimming and fascinating terrain to explore. Head down Rte 44 south of Citrusdal until the signs to Dasklipspas, 5km north of Porterville. Follow the road for 20km up a magnificent pass and down a poor dirt road, until you see the signs to Beaverlac Nature Reserve. No car radios or parties allowed!

Baths RESORT $$
(☏022-921 8026/7; www.thebaths.co.za; campsites per person R100, 2-person chalet from R590; 🐾) In a glorious location thick with trees and right up against the craggy peaks is this hot-water spring resort with two outdoor pools, Jacuzzis and steam baths. There's also a decent restaurant. The place is about 18km from Citrusdal and is well signposted. Booking ahead is essential.

Ukholo Lodge BACKPACKERS $
(☏022-921 3988; www.ukholo-lodge.co.za; campsites per person R70, dm R100, d with shared bathroom

R350) Formerly Gekko Backpackers, this hostel is under new management and it shows. Rooms are stylish, each decorated with a different theme. There's plenty of space to pitch a tent and bathrooms all over the place. Activities include tubing on the adjacent river or hiking through the mountains. It's 21km from Citrusdal on the N7 towards Clanwilliam.

Burton's Farm at Steelwater CHALET $
(☎022-921 3337; www.burtonsfarm.co.za; 2-person cottage R350, d incl breakfast R450) A twisty dirt road leading off Rte 303 to Citrusdal climbs past groves of citrus trees and flowering bushes before ending at the whitewashed farm buildings of Steelwater. The property is large, the hosts exceptionally friendly and there are decent walks on the grounds. It's 12km from town on the way to the Baths.

✗ Eating

Die Sitrus INTERNATIONAL $$
(☎022-921 2228; 41 Voortrekker St; mains R70-100; ☺lunch & dinner Tue-Sun) This is the best place for dinner in town. It's best known for steak but also serves burgers, pizza and fresh fish.

❶ Information

Tourism bureau (☎022-921 3210; www.citrusdal.info; 39 Voortrekker St; ☺8.30am-5pm Mon-Fri, 9am-noon Sat) Can help you find accommodation in the area and provide information on mountain-biking and hiking trails.

❶ Getting There & Around

Intercape (www.intercape.co.za) buses stop at the Sonop petrol station on the N7 outside town. Destinations include Cape Town (R230, three hours) and Springbok (R280, five hours).

There's an excellent scenic road (Rte 303) over Middelberg Pass into the Koue (Cold) Bokkeveld and a beautiful valley on the other side, which is topped by the Gydo Pass and the view over the Ceres Valley. The back road into the wilderness area is also excellent.

Clanwilliam & Around

☎027 / POP 37,000

The adjacent dam and some adventurous dirt roads into the Cederberg make the compact town of Clanwilliam a popular weekend resort. Well-preserved examples of Cape Dutch architecture and trees line the main street. The dam is a favourite with waterskiers.

Clanwilliam is the centre of the **rooibos** (red bush) tea industry. It's made from the leaves of the *Aspalathus linearis* plant, that only grows in the Cederberg region. The drink contains no caffeine and much less tannin than normal tea and is said to be beneficial to health. Tours of the **Elandsberg Rooibos Estate** (☎027-482 2022; www.elandsberg.co.za; R125), 22km west of Clanwilliam, are an excellent way to follow the process from planting to packaging.

🛌 Sleeping & Eating

TOP CHOICE Saint du Barrys Country Lodge GUESTHOUSE $$
(☎027-482 1537; www.saintdubarrys.com; 13 Augsburg Dr; s/d incl breakfast R600/1000; ❉❉) A 150-year-old banyan tree looms over this thatched-roof guesthouse with five en suite, rooms and a charming garden. Dinner is by arrangement.

Bushmans Kloof LUXURY HOTEL $$$
(☎021-481 1860; www.bushmanskloof.co.za; s/d from R4300/6100; ❉❉) This is an upmarket private reserve, 46km east of Clanwilliam along the Pakhuis Pass, known for its excellent San rock-art sites and extensive animal and birdlife. If you've got the cash, staff can also arrange fly-in safaris from Cape Town.

Traveller's Rest CHALET $
(☎027-482 1824; www.travellersrest.co.za; Rte 364; chalet R200 per person; @) The cottages could do with a revamp, but are well equipped and well priced. The real draw is the **Sevilla Rock Art Trail** (R30) that starts from here. There are 10 sites along a relatively easy 4km hike. It's 36km from Clanwilliam on the way to Bushmans Kloof.

WORTH A TRIP

WUPPERTAL

This Moravian **mission station** (☎027-492 3410), 74km southeast of Clanwilliam, dates back to 1830 and is reached along a gravel road just after Bushmans Kloof. Attractions include the original church, the country's oldest shoe producer and a Rooibos factory. For an in-depth look at the mission villages, join a two-night tour with **Cedarberg African Travel** (☎027-482 2444; R2175; www.cedarbergtravel.com), which includes donkey cart rides through the mountains.

SAN ROCK-ART SITES

The nomadic San, South Africa's indigenous people, inhabited the area north of Clanwilliam for millennia. While as a people they have been decimated and/or assimilated, thankfully the area is still home to some of the finest examples of their rock art in the country. Indeed, archaeologists consider some of the sites the best preserved of their kind in the world.

Several tour operators have sprung up, but they can be pricey. If you're interested in learning more or visiting sites, contact the highly reputable **Living Landscape Project** (☑027-482 1911; www.cllp.uct.ac.za; 16 Park St, Clanwilliam; tours from R65), which hosts art-site visits and runs a community development program. If you'd like to use other organised tour operators, contact the Clanwilliam information centre.

An accessible spot with a cluster of rock-art sites is the **Sevilla Rock Art Trail** at the Traveller's Rest.

Clanwilliam Dam Municipal Caravan Park & Chalets
CAMPGROUND $

(☑027-482 8012; campsites with/without electricity R168/128, 4-person chalet R635) This caravan park overlooks the waterskiing action on the other side of the dam from the N7. The water is disappointingly oily from the boat engines. Book ahead for school holidays and weekends.

Olifantshuis
SOUTH AFRICAN $$

(cnr Augsburg Dr & Main St; mains from R65; ☺dinner) This pub and restaurant in a big house is a nice place for a drink and a traditional meal but watch out for biting horseflies at sundown.

Nancy's Tearoom
CAFE $

(Main St; mains R35-65; ☺breakfast & lunch Mon-Sat) Enjoy light meals on the shady patio at this friendly spot. Locals rave about the scones – try one with a Rooibos cappuccino.

ℹ Information

Information centre (☑027-482 2024; ☺8.30am-5pm Mon-Fri, 8.30am-12.30pm Sat & Sun in season) At the top end of the Main St, across from the old *tronk* (jail), dating from 1808, which doubles as the town's museum.

ℹ Getting There & Away

Buses that go through Citrusdal also go through Clanwilliam. It's about 45 minutes between the two. Shared taxis running between Springbok (R300, five hours) and Cape Town (R150, three hours) go through Clanwilliam, stopping at the post office.

Eastern Cape

Best Places to Eat

» Die Walskipper (p179)
» Polka Café (p168)
» Stanley St (p187)
» Tea Thyme (p207)
» Haricot's Deli & Bistro (p195)

Best Places to Stay

» Camp Figtree (p191)
» Bulungula Backpackers (p209)
» Die Tuishuise & Victoria Manor (p171)
» Mdumbi Backpackers (p211)
» Prana Lodge (p204)

Why Go?

From uninhabited desert expanses to lush tropical forests, from seriously easygoing hammock time to adrenalin-pumping adventures, the Eastern Cape offers up a wide range of topography and experiences. Compared to the much wealthier and more developed Western Cape, it can feel like a different country and provides an opportunity to gain familiarity with Xhosa culture. Some of the finest hiking trails wind their way along stunning coastlines and through mountainous, waterfall-filled landscapes.

Private wildlife reserves and national and regional parks abound; see the Big Five (lion, leopard, buffalo, elephant and rhino) or migrating whales and dolphins. The imposing mountains and little-known valleys of the northeastern highlands are relatively unexplored. You'll find stillness and tranquillity in the semiarid Karoo; seriously good surfing up and down the coast; and history (much of it bloody), including the legacy of some of the region's famous sons – Nelson Mandela, Oliver Tambo and Steve Biko.

When to Go
Port Elizabeth

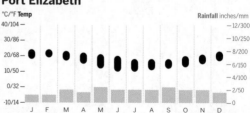

Sep–Nov Visit the Karoo in spring to avoid extreme summer temps, which can exceed 40°C.

Nov–Jan The rainy season along the Wild Coast – temperatures average 28°C.

Jul A huge arts festival in Grahamstown and a world surfing competition in Jeffrey's Bay.

Language

Start practising those tongue clicks – Xhosa is the predominant language in the Eastern Cape. Whites here speak both English and Afrikaans.

ⓘ Getting There & Around

Travelling around the western side of the Eastern Cape isn't too hard. Numerous bus services, including **Greyhound** (☎041-363 4555; www .greyhound.co.za), **Intercape** (☎086 128 7287; www.intercape.co.za), **Translux** (City to City; ☎046-622 3241; www.translux.co.za) and **Baz Bus** (☎086 122 9287; www.bazbus.com), ply the route between Cape Town, Port Elizabeth and East London (both of which also have airports), stopping at major towns on the way and continuing to Durban, Johannesburg (Jo'burg) and Pretoria.

Further off the beaten track, notably on the Wild Coast and in the Eastern Highlands, users of public transport will have to take to minibus taxis to find their way into more-obscure spots. Roads can be impassable after heavy rains. Some places on the Wild Coast are accessible only on foot or horseback. Having your own car is the best way to explore the region.

EASTERN KAROO

The Karoo is a vast semidesert stretching across the great South African plateau inland from the Cape coast. Its beauty and serenity has inspired writers such as Athol Fugard and André Brink and artists such as Pierneef. 'Kuru' means 'dry' or 'barren' in the original Khoikhoi language; dry it certainly is, though the landscape bears a wide variety of grasses, hardy shrubs and succulents, including the trademark red aloe.

Its southeastern extension is in the Eastern Cape and includes the history-steeped towns of Graaff-Reinet and Cradock, the stunning scenery of Camdeboo and Mountain Zebra National Parks and the out-of-the-way bohemian village of Nieu Bethesda. It's one of the region's most intriguing areas, with an overwhelming sense of space and peace that stands in sharp contrast to the overdeveloped areas of the coastline.

Between December and February temperatures in Karoo towns can reach 45°C, and things barely cool down in March and April. June and July see the thermometer plummet to -5°C, with snow in the mountain passes and hard frosts.

See p151 for more information about the central section of the Karoo, and p436 for more about the northern section of the Karoo.

LOOP DRIVE

It's worth approaching this region as a scenic loop drive, approaching Graaff-Reinet from the south on the R75 or N9, moving on to Nieu Bethesda and Cradock and then heading back south to Addo or Port Elizabeth along the N10 (or vice versa).

Graaff-Reinet

POP 44,317

Cradled in a curve of the Sundays River and within walking distance of the Camdeboo National Park, Graaff-Reinet is often referred to as the 'jewel of the Karoo'. 'Camdeboo', the Khoekhoen word for 'green valleys', is used to describe the hills surrounding the town, which is the fourth-oldest European town (established 1786) in South Africa. Graaff-Reinet has a superb architectural heritage with more than 220 buildings designated as national monuments, ranging from Cape Dutch houses, with their distinctive gables, to classic, flat-roofed Karoo cottages and ornate Victorian villas. Add in a small-town ambience, excellent accommodation and a few outstanding restaurants and you'll begin to understand why it aquired its moniker.

History

In the 18th century the interior of the Cape was wild and dangerous, with Boers clashing frequently with the Khoe-San in the Sneeuberg Range and the Xhosa to the east around the Great Fish River. The settlement was named after former provincial governor Van der Graaff and his wife (whose maiden name was Reinet), and became an outpost in a harsh countryside. It was the fourth district in the Cape Colony to be granted a *drostdy* – the residence of a *landdrost* (local official) and seat of local government. This came about through an attempt by the British to establish a bit of law and order. The idea failed and the town's citizens promptly threw out the *landdrost* and established an independent republic. The British regained a semblance of control soon afterwards, but were constantly harried by both disgruntled Boers and a joint force of Khoe-San and Xhosa warriors.

Eastern Cape Highlights

❶ Walk the coastal pathways and secluded beaches of the **Wild Coast** (p210)

❷ Experience traditional Xhosa culture by staying in a rural Wild Coast **rondavel** (a round hut; p209)

❸ Take in a stunning sunset with views of Graaf-Reinet below in **Camdeboo National Park** (p169)

❹ Surf **Jeffrey's Bay** (p179) or simply marvel at Supertubes, one of the world's top-ranked waves

❺ Hike the forested trails to waterfalls around **Hogsback** (p205)

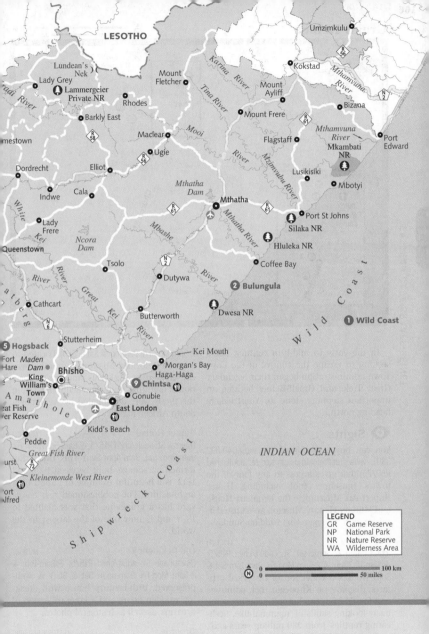

6 Gaze up at star-filled skies in the Karoo hamlet of **Nieu Bethesda** (p169)

7 Observe African elephants up close at **Addo Elephant National Park** (p190) or at one of the surrounding reserves

8 Marvel at the plunging rivers and rocky cliffs of **Tsitsikamma National Park** (p175)

9 Swim in the surf off the picturesque beach of **Chintsa** (p203)

Graaff-Reinet

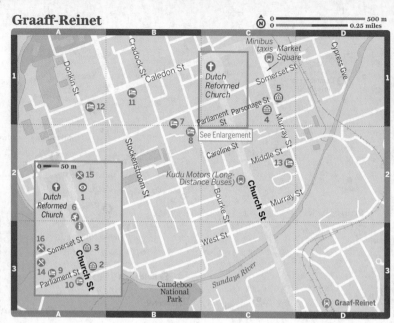

In the early to mid-19th century, Boers seeking to escape the control of the Cape Town administration began their legendary Great Trek, and Graaff-Reinet became an important stepping stone for Voortrekkers heading north.

⊙ Sights

You can buy a combined **pass** (☑049-892 3801; www.graaffreinetmuseums.co.za; adult/child R50/25) that gives access to any four of the town's museums (not including Hester Rupert Art Museum) – the Urquhart House and Military History Museum aren't listed in this section. The pass isn't valid on Sundays.

Old Library MUSEUM
(cnr Church & Somerset Sts; adult/child R15/5; ⊘8am-12.30pm & 2-5pm Mon-Fri, 9am-1pm Sat & Sun) Houses a collection of historical artifacts, displays on Khoe-San rock paintings and fossils from the Karoo (including some nasty-looking skulls of 'mammal-like, flesh-eating reptiles' from 230 million years ago), and an exhibition telling the life story of Robert Mangaliso Sobukwe, the founder of the Pan African Congress (PAC).

Hester Rupert Art Museum MUSEUM
(☑049-892 2121; www.rupertartmuseum.co.za; Church St; adult/child R10/free; ⊘9am-12.30pm &

2-5pm Mon-Fri, 9am-noon Sat & Sun) Located in a Dutch Reformed Mission church that was consecrated in 1821, this museum's collection of paintings (and a few sculptures) from the 1960s were all donated by well-known South African artists.

Reinet House MUSEUM
(Murray St; adult/child R15/5; ⊘8am-5pm Mon-Fri, 9am-3pm Sat, 9am-4pm Sun) This Dutch Reformed parsonage, built between 1806 and 1812, is a beautiful example of Cape Dutch architecture. The cobblestoned rear courtyard has a grapevine that was planted in 1870 and is now one of the largest in the world.

Old Residency MUSEUM
(Parsonage St; adult/child R15/5; ⊘8am-1pm & 2-5pm Mon-Fri, 9am-noon Sat & Sun) A well-preserved, 19th-century house with creaking wooden floors and a large collection of firearms, as well as historical photos.

Drostdy HISTORIC BUILDING
(Church St) A *drostdy* was the *landdrost's* residence and included his office and courtroom as well as his family's living quarters. The Graaff-Reinet *drostdy* was built in 1806. Have a look at the old slave bell, which was restored and then, in an awful piece of irony,

Graaff-Reinet

⊙ Sights

✪ Activities, Courses & Tours

🛏 Sleeping

✪ Eating

🛍 Shopping

unveiled by apartheid-era prime minister BJ Vorster. The *drostdy* is now a hotel (p168).

Graaff-Reinet Club　　　HISTORIC BUILDING
(Church St; ⊙6-9pm) This atmospheric one-time 'men only' club, the second oldest in South Africa still in operation, has walls and halls adorned with numerous hunting trophies and a bar with bullet holes in it. The Coldstream Guards, billeted in Graaff-Reinet during the Anglo-Boer War, showed their exuberance on being recalled to Blighty by firing eight bullets into the counter. Overseas visitors are welcome to have a drink with locals. Stays open later on Friday evenings.

☞ Tours

Camdeboo Adventure Tours　　　GUIDED TOURS
(☎049-892 3410; www.karoopark.co.za; 81 Caledon St) Buks and Chantelle Marais of Camdeboo Cottages and Karoopark Guest House can organise Camdeboo National Park trips, guided town walks and wildlife-viewing drives.

Ingomso Tours　　　CULTURAL TOURS
(☎083 559 1207; mashoengisaac@yahoo.com; 2hr tours per person R100) Isaac Mashoeng leads tours of Umasizakhe township. Umasizakhe is one of the oldest townships in the country and is the birthplace of Robert Mangaliso Sobukwe. The tours provide insight into Xhosa culture and history and modern township life.

Karoo Connections　　　GUIDED TOURS
(☎049-892 3978; www.karooconnections.co.za; 7 Church St) David McNaughton organises tours to the Valley of Desolation at sunset (R370 with sundowners), a half-day trip to Nieu Bethesda and the Owl House (R550), and wildlife-watching drives to Camdeboo National Park (R350). He also arranges township walks, nature walks and city tours.

🛏 Sleeping

TOP CHOICE **Aa 'Qtansisi**　　　GUESTHOUSE **$$**
(☎049-891 0243; www.aaqtansisi.co.za; 69 Somerset St; s/d incl breakfast R650/950; ✸🛜🐾) Translating as 'We welcome you' in Khoe-San (when asking for directions, simply drop the 'Q', or ask for 69 Somerset), this lavishly designed guesthouse's rooms are evocative of an *Arabian Nights'* harem: high ceilings, regal-looking four-poster beds, elaborate woodwork and luxurious bathrooms with claw-footed tubs. A lovely trellis-covered backyard has a plunge pool and hammocks, and the gourmet breakfast includes a fruit platter and shot glass of muesli and nuts.

TOP CHOICE **Camdeboo Cottages**　　　GUESTHOUSE **$$**
(☎049-892 3180; www.camdeboocottages.co.za; 16 Parliament St; 2-/4-bed cottage R400/600; @🛜🐾) Behind the classically restored facades of these Karoo-style cottages are contemporary creature comforts. Spacious rooms in the building across the street from reception feature yellowwood floors and black-and-white-tiled bathrooms with claw-footed baths. There's a lovely pool and patio area – a much-needed refuge from midday heat.

Buiten Verwagten B&B　　　B&B **$$**
(☎049-892 4504; www.buitenverwagten.co.za; 58 Bourke St; s/d incl breakfast R700/900; ✸@🛜🐾) Every aspect of this Victorian-era home is tastefully curated by its friendly and professional owners. Inside are high ceilings, cedar and pine floors, and elegant antiques; outside are a trellis-covered garden, a perfectly

manicured lawn and a courtyard pool. A four-person self-catering cottage is also available (R800).

Drostdy Hotel
HOTEL $$

(☎049-892 2161; www.drostdy.co.za; 30 Church St; s/d R595/845; ❄@≋) Exuding old-world charm and nostalgia, this landmark hotel is in the beautifully restored *drostdy*. Guests stay in renovated mid-19th-century cottages, originally built for freed slaves, along Stretch's Ct; mismatched furniture and dated decor are a bit of a letdown. The courtyard cafe is enchanting, surrounded by fruit trees and the scent of flowers from the stunning gardens. It will be closed for renovations until the end of 2013.

Karoopark Guest House
GUESTHOUSE $$

(☎049-892 2557; www.karoopark.co.za; 81 Caledon St; s/d from 350/450; ❄@≋) This family-owned and -run complex is a good base. There's a restaurant, bar and pool, and a tour company run out of here. Small tiled-floor rooms in the back of the garden are comfortably furnished; some of the rooms in the main building are but larger.

Le Jardin Backpackin'
GUESTHOUSE $

(☎049-892 5890; nitagush@telkom.sa.net; cnr Donkin & Caledon Sts; s/d without bathroom R150/250; ❄) Hosts Terrence and Nita Gush share their time-capsule home – not a backpackers in the conventional sense – and knowledge about the area with enthusiasm. The small and homely rooms are worth considering for those short on rand.

Obesa Lodge
LODGE $

(☎049-892 3143; www.graaffreinet.co.za; 64 Murray St; s/d R260/360; ❄≋) Obesa is a whole street of psychedelically coloured self-catering cottages, with names like 'Moody Blues' and 'Bad Mama', featuring simple carpeted rooms. Opposite the lodge is a Cactus Garden, which features an enormous collection of succulents from around the world.

✖ Eating

TOP CHOICE Polka Café
DESSERTS, SOUTH AFRICAN $$

(52 Somerset St; mains R85; ⊘7am-10pm Mon-Sat) Polka has an ambitious nouvelle cuisine menu that improves upon conventional fare – for example, springbok *bobotie* (delicately flavoured curry with a topping of beaten egg baked to a crust) and kudu schnitzel – with subtle twists, beautiful presentation and upgrades in taste. The candlelit outdoor porch turns romantic at night while the rustic farm-style dining room has a bakery selling homemade crispy cookies, frosting-heavy cupcakes and pastries.

Agave
SOUTH AFRICAN $$

(Somerset St; mains R65; ☎) Not to be outdone by Polka Café directly across the street, Agave's menu features a gourmand's interpretation of the sandwich, elevating the ordinary to mouth-watering levels – try the Malay chicken with mango chutney. Salads, burgers, pasta and meat platters all receive expert makeovers and the trellis-covered backyard garden is perhaps the loveliest spot in town for a meal.

Coldstream
SOUTH AFRICAN, STEAKHOUSE $$

(3 Church St; mains R95; ⊘Mon-Sat; ☎) Though more traditional than Agave and Polka, Coldstream's somewhat more buttoned-down fine-dining aesthetic, especially for dinner, delivers the juiciest and best-prepared steaks in town. The 'trio' platter of beef, ostrich and kudu or springbok will satiate the most ardent meat lover.

🔒 Shopping

Graaff-Reinet has a handful of stores selling antiques, homewares and Karoo crafts, to say nothing of the healthy business done by the town's taxidermy shops.

Africa Adventure Curios & Gifts
HANDICRAFTS

(cnr Parsonage & Church Sts) Carries a selection of quality handicrafts from all over southern Africa.

ℹ Information

Graaff-Reinet Tourism (☎049-892 4248; www.graaffreinet.co.za; 13A Church St; ⊘8am-5pm Mon-Fri, 9am-noon Sat) This helpful office has information about accommodation in the area and an abundance of maps, and books bus tickets.

Karoo Connections (www.karooconnections.co.za; Church St; per hr R30; ⊘8am-5pm Mon-Fri, 9am-noon Sat) Internet access next to the publicity association. The bookshop stocks South African fiction and nonfiction.

ℹ Getting There & Away

Long-distance buses stop at **Kudu Motors** (Church St). **Intercape** and **Translux** service Cape Town (R300, 8½ hours) and Jo'burg (R400, 11 hours); the latter also runs to East London (R260, five hours) and Port Elizabeth (R190, three hours). Tickets and info are available at the tourist office.

Minibus taxis leave from Market Sq. Major destinations are Port Elizabeth (R150) and Cape Town (R350).

Avis ([☏] 049-891 0786) now has a rental-car operation running out of the Karoopark Guest House.

Camdeboo National Park

Covering an area of 19,102 hectares, Camdeboo National Park ([☏]049-892 6128; www .sanparks.org; adult/child R64/32; ☉6am-8pm) has plenty of animals, but the real attraction is the spectacular geological formations and great views overlooking Graaff-Reinet and the plains below. The park is divided into three main sections: the wildlife-viewing area to the north of the Nqweba dam; the western section with the Valley of Desolation; and the eastern section with various hiking trails.

In the wildlife-watching area there are buffaloes, elands, kudus, hartebeests, wildebeests, springboks, rare Cape mountain zebras and a host of smaller mammals. Bird species include black eagles, blue cranes and kori bustards. Visitors must stay in their vehicles except at the picnic sites.

The Valley of Desolation is the park's most popular sight. It's a hauntingly beautiful valley with an outstanding view – the rugged, piled dolerite columns here are set against the backdrop of the endless Karoo plains. Graaff-Reinet is also visible, nestled in a bend of the Sundays River. The valley, 14km from town, can be reached by car on a steep but sealed road, and there's a 1.5km circuit walk. It's the sort of place that makes you wish you were an eagle and, in fact, you can paraglide from here. The best times to visit the valley are at sunrise or sunset.

The Eerstefontein Day Trail is also in the western section and has three trail options with distances of 5km, 11km and 14km. The information office has a map. The Drie Koppie Trail overnight trail costs R40 per person for the use of the hut.

You'll need to have your own vehicle to get around the reserve; otherwise, contact Karoo Connections in Graaff-Reinet for a tour. Newly opened in the spring of 2012 are the highly recommended Lakeview Tented Camp (R500) and the Nqweba Campsite (campsites R175); contact the Graaf-Reinet Tourism office for bookings. Accommodation is also available on the overnight trail.

Nieu Bethesda

POP 1000

Tucked away in the Karoo, the tiny, isolated village of Nieu Bethesda was once one of the most obscure places in South Africa. Interest surged when the extraordinary Owl House was brought to light – the home of 'outsider' artist Helen Martins. These days Nieu Bethesda has become a minor artistic colony – rooms are hard to come by at the end of September during the Athol Fugard festival. With its dirt roads, water furrow system, brewery, fine accommodation, a couple of pretty cafes and endless stars, it's a great place to experience life as it was in a Karoo village and to unwind for a few days.

Nieu Bethesda is about 55km from Graaff-Reinet. The drive here is very scenic, with the Sneeuberg Range dominating the region as you approach. Note that there are no petrol stations or ATMs in Nieu Bethesda, and credit cards are generally not accepted for accommodation.

◉ Sights & Activities

Owl House MUSEUM
([☏]049-841 1603; River St; admission R35; ☉9am-5pm) The idiosyncratic vision that inspired artist Helen Martins (1897–1976) to turn her home and studio into a singular monument to oddity is now nearly synonymous with the quirky bohemian reputation of the village. Martins and her long-time assistant Koos Malgas worked for years designing and constructing the menagerie of concrete animal and human sculptures in the backyard; nearly every inch of the wacky, somewhat disturbing interior is covered with colorful painted glass shards or textiles and tchotchkes, pointing to a tragic, isolated figure who eventually took her own life at the age of 78.

Kitching Fossil Exploration Centre MUSEUM
([☏]049-849 1733; Martin St; admission R20; ☉9am-5pm) Scholars estimate that the casts of fossils of prehistoric animals here (gorgonopsians, dicynodonts and the like) are around 253 million years old – 50 million years before the age of dinosaurs! Whoever is on hand will take you to see the real thing untouched and embedded in rocks in the nearby dry riverbed. This museum, named after renowned palaeontologist James Kitching, is a joint project of the University of the Witwatersrand and the Albany Museum in Grahamstown.

Compassberg HIKING

The biggest peak in the region at 2502m, Compassberg is about four hours each way from the start of the trail at Compassberg farm, 35km out of Nieu Bethesda. There is also the Canyon Hike, a fairly flat 3km walk that includes a visit to sites of some Anglo-Boer War engravings. Ask in the village for directions to the trail.

Ganora Guest Farm, 7km east of Nieu Bethesda, has a guided walking tour takes in rock-art sites and medicinal plants. There's an expertly curated fossil and artifact museum on-site (R25), and a demonstration of sheep shearing (for groups, if arranged in advance). Ganora also rehabilitates meerkats so you might see one or two scurrying around.

🛏 Sleeping

Other than Ganora Guest Farm, listings are located in the centre of the village, close to one another.

Ganora Guest Farm GUESTHOUSE $$

(☑049-841 1302; www.ganora.co.za; per person incl breakfast from R340; 🐾) If you'd rather be out of town under the soaring skies of the Karoo, this 4000-hectare sheep farm is an excellent option. Renovated kraals have been transformed into luxurious boutique-style rooms with stone walls and sisal ceilings. A self-catering cottage that sleeps six goes for R820. Meals are served (breakfast R35, dinner R50) in a rustic-frontier dining room.

Owl House Backpackers BACKPACKERS $

(☑049-841 1642, 072 742 7113; www.owlhouse. info; Martin St; campsites/dm/s/d/cottage R65/115/200/295/390) The simple Karoo-style exterior conceals a home with old-fashioned character, funky nooks and crannies and a lovely and sizeable back garden. For more privacy, try the cottage with kitchenette or the loftlike backyard water tower with circular bed, compost toilet and ground-floor kitchen. The friendly owners can organise donkey cart rides and visits to Khoe-San painting sites. Meals can also be arranged.

Outsiders B&B GUESTHOUSE $

(☑049-841 1642; www.owlhouse.info; Martin St; s/d incl breakfast R260/390) Owned by the same couple who own Owl House Backpackers across the street, Outsiders has two comfy high-ceilinged rooms with a few artistic touches and mohair blankets for cold winter nights; the room facing the street is larger and has a picnic table on the porch.

Water Tower GUESTHOUSE $$

(☑073 028 8887; info@bethesdatower.co.za; Muiller St; s/d without bathroom R250/350) A cross between a church and castle, a night in the wood-floored top room whose round bed fills the space feels like a fairy tale; two brick-walled non-tower rooms are immaculate. The restaurant can provide all meals (mains R55) inside or in the large patio.

House No 1 GUESTHOUSE $$

(☑049-841 1700; cnr Coete & Hudson Sts; s/d incl breakfast R260/390) The two bedrooms in this restored Victorian-era Karoo home have polished-wood floors and a backyard garden with braai (barbecue) area.

🍴 Eating

Karoo Lamb Restaurant SOUTH AFRICAN $$

(mains R80; ⊙7am-9pm; 🐾) This large eatery-cum-deli-cum-gift shop is the most sophisticated restaurant in the village. When all the elements of breakfast (complimentary for guests of Outsiders B&B) are laid out half a picnic table is occupied, and set menus of dishes like lamb chops and *potjiekos* (stews cooked in a cast-iron pot) are served for lunch and dinner. Good selection of wine and beer, crafts, books, paintings and light snacks daily and braais every Friday.

Brewery & Two Goats Deli DELI $$

(Pioneer St; mains R70; ⊙8am-5pm Mon-Sat, to 3pm Sun) Across a bridge from the main part of the village is this charmingly rustic farmhouse – also a working dairy farm – where owner Andre Cilliers prepares handcrafted goat's milk cheeses, meat platters (R50) and his own house beer.

❶ Getting There & Away

There is no public transport to or from Nieu Bethesda. However, Owl House Backpackers will organise a local to do a pick-up/drop-off (one way R100) to Graaff-Reinet. Le Jardin Backpackin' in Graaff-Reinet also organises transport.

Cradock

POP 28,689

Originally established as a military outpost in 1813 to stop the Xhosa from crossing the Great Fish River, Cradock became a bustling agricultural and commercial settlement in later decades. Market St was home to the artisans (harness-makers, carpenters, smithies etc) who served the ox-wagons passing through. They came up against tough economic times with the introduction of trains and cars, and many were forced to abandon their homes. It's still an important farming district and although it may appear rather shabby at first, it's worth taking a closer look at the beautiful old buildings and tree-lined avenues. Stroll down lovely Dundas and Bree Sts, the latter the oldest in Cradock, past fine well-preserved 19th-century gabled homes. Meanwhile, modernist mansions owned mostly by overseas residents line the streets just to the east of the centre.

The town's most famous sons were the Cradock Four, struggle activists Matthew Goniwe, Sparrow Mkhonto, Fort Calata and Sicelo Mhlauli, who were abducted, assaulted and killed by members of the security police in 1985. There's a memorial to them just outside the town.

◉ Sights & Activities

Contact the front desk of Victoria Manor Hotel to organise tours (R250 per person) of the local township.

Olive Schreiner House MUSEUM
(☏048-881 5251; 9 Cross St; small donation suggested; ⊙8am-1pm & 2-4.30pm Mon-Fri) Schreiner is best known for her provocative novel *Story of an African Farm,* published in 1883 but advocating views considered radical even by today's standards. She lived in this typical Karoo house for only three years; however, several of its small rooms are now dedicated to a detailed textual and photographic chronicle of her interesting life and prolific literary career (she published several books under the pseudonym Ralph Iron). She's buried in a sarcophagus, along with her husband and dog, on a hilltop south of town.

Great Fish River Museum MUSEUM
(☏048-881 4509; High St; small donation suggested; ⊙8am-1pm & 2-4pm Mon-Fri) Housed in a building from around 1825 that was originally the parsonage of the Dutch Reformed Church, displays here depict the ordinary household items of 19th-century pioneer life. Find it behind the Municipal Building.

Karoo River Rafting RAFTING
(☏049-842 4543; www.karoo-river-rafting.co.za) Offers rafting, canoeing, kayaking and tubing trips down the Fish River and its tributaries.

🛌 Sleeping

There are loads of B&Bs; check with the tourism office for a list.

TOP CHOICE **Die Tuishuise & Victoria Manor** BUNGALOW, INN **$$**
(☏048-881 1322; www.tuishuise.co.za; cnr Market & Voortrekker Sts; s/d cottage R415/730, hotel per person incl breakfast R470; ✸❋☎) Die Tuishuise are one-of-a-kind accommodation in beautifully restored and handsomely furnished homes on one of Cradock's oldest streets. Some are decorated and furnished in the old Boer manner while others are more Victorian; however, all have at least two bedrooms, self-catering kitchen, a sitting room with fireplace and a garden. There are also smaller, more modest one- and two-bedroom garden cottages. Anchoring the corner of Market St is well-appointed Victoria Manor, an inn with atmospheric, charmingly decorated wood-panelled rooms and claw-footed tubs in the bathrooms. Out the back is a Karoo farm–style plunge pool and garden area. Meals are served at Victoria Manor's restaurant.

Heritage House B&B B&B **$$**
(☏078 538 0555; 45 Bree St; s/d incl breakfast R295/490; ✸) Homely Heritage House offers gay-friendly, old-fashioned hospitality in comfortable rooms, each with its own entrance, TV and fridge. Try to get a room in the pleasant garden, complete with koi (Japanese carp) the pond.

🍴 Eating & Drinking

Victoria Manor Hotel SOUTH AFRICAN **$$**
(cnr Market & Voortrekker Sts; mains R75) Hands down the best place to eat in town: the dining room has dark-wood panelling and richly upholstered furnishings in 19th-century English style. Service is friendly and attentive but, most importantly, the food is tasty and portions are large. The dinner buffet is R140.

Buffalo Dan's STEAKHOUSE **$$**
(R61; mains R65) It's mostly local farmers who come to this restaurant (unappetizingly located in the forecourt of the Engen petrol station), to chow down on delicious steaks. It's on the other side of the bridge on the road out of Cradock towards Mountain Zebra park.

EASTERN CAPE CRADOCK

DESIGN PICS INC./ALAMY ©

1. Hogsback (p205)
JRR Tolkien drew inspiration from this magical place surrounded by verdant valleys.

2. Camdeboo National Park (p169)
Camdeboo's Valley of Desolation sprouts striking geological pillars above the vast expanse of the Karoo.

3. Xhosa Woman
Married Xhosa women often apply white clay to their faces and wear large, turbanlike hats.

4. Jeffrey's Bay (p179)
South Africa's surfing capital attracts international thrillseekers to its legendary Supertubes.

Country Living
SOUTH AFRICAN $$

(Beeren St; mains R60; ⊘noon-9pm) A country restaurant popular with farmers' wives, with a lovely outdoor space and Italian espresso.

Mila's
PIZZERIA $$

(27 Durban St; mains R75; ⊘noon-9pm) Wood-fired pizzas and handmade pasta dishes a few blocks from the centre of town.

ⓘ Information

Cradock Tourism (⌨048-881 2383; www .cradock.co.za; Stockenstroom St) has helpful staff, and is in the town hall building opposite the Spar Centre (which has an ABSA Bank ATM). Other banks and ATMs are found mainly on Adderley St.

ⓘ Getting There & Away

City to City, **Translux** and **Intercape** run daily to Cape Town (R270, 11 hours, twice a week) via Graaff-Reinet (R110, 1½ hours), and to Jo'burg (R360, 11 hours, daily) and East London (R219, 4½ hours).

Most minibus taxis leave from the nearby township; ask at the petrol stations in town.

The **Shosholoza Meyl** (⌨0860 008 888; www.shosholozameyl.co.za) tourist-class train stops here en route between Port Elizabeth (R120, five hours) and Jo'burg (R400, 15½ hours) via Bloemfontein on Friday and Sunday. There are also economy-class trains (seat only) plying the same route six days a week; for all trains, travelling from Port Elizabeth to Cradock gets you into town at a more civilised time.

Mountain Zebra National Park

This **national park** (⌨048-881 2427; www .sanparks.org.com; adult/child R108/54; ⊘7am-7pm Oct-Mar, to 6pm Apr-Sep), 20km west of Cradock on the northern slopes of the Bankberg Range (2000m), covers 28,000 hectares and has superb views over the Karoo. The park protects one of the rarest animals in the world: the mountain zebra *(Equus zebra)*. There are now over 350 mountain zebras in the park; they're distinguished from other zebra species by their small stature, reddish-brown nose and dewlap (a loose fold of skin hanging beneath the throat).

Along with the silence and wide, open spaces, thick patches of sweet thorn and wild olive intersperse with rolling grasslands and succulents. The park also supports many antelope species, buffaloes and black rhinos. The largest predator is the cheetah, and there are several species of small cats, genets, bat-eared foxes and black-backed jackals. In addition, some 200 bird species have been recorded.

The entrance gate is well signposted off the R61. It's easily possible to get a taste of the park in a half-day excursion from Cradock; the road that loops from the main gate across to the rest camp and back can take under two hours, depending on how often you stop. You'll find a shop and restaurant in the main camp. There are three **hiking trails** ranging from 1km to 10km, and a 25km, three-day hike where you stay overnight in mountain huts (R150 per person). A guided **wildlife drive** costs R140 per adult, and a cheetah-tracking guided tour costs R250 per person. Staff at reception can reveal where you're likely to find various animals.

The park has a range of **accommodation** (⌨bookings 0861 114 845; campsites/4-bed family cottage R175/730; ❄). The cottages at the park's rest camp are comfortable and well equipped, with their own bathrooms. The most interesting place to stay is at Doornhoek (sleeps six for R1930), a restored historic farmhouse, built in 1836 and hidden in a secluded valley.

The park headquarters has a **restaurant** (mains R55-120) with lethargic service and a selection of inattentively prepared pasta, salad, steaks (kudu, springbok etc) and burgers.

There's no public transport to the park so the only option is to bring your own car.

WESTERN REGION

This region includes the western edge of the Eastern Cape coast, an extension of the well-travelled Garden Route and, for that reason, probably the most visited part of the province. Tsitsikamma National Park and Jeffrey's Bay are deservedly well known but other lesser-known destinations like Cape St Francis and the Baviaanskloof Wilderness Area are worthy of attention.

Nature's Valley

Even though the small village of Nature's Valley is in the Western Cape, we've included it here because it's so much a part of exploring the Tsitsikamma area. It's nestled in yellowwood forest next to a magnificent beach in the west of Tsitsikamma National Park. This is where the Otter Trail ends and the Tsitsikamma Mountain Trail begins (see p176), but if you don't want to walk for that long, there are plenty of shorter hikes in this area, which is referred to as the De Vasselot Section of the park.

🛏 Sleeping & Eating

Wild Spirit   BACKPACKERS $
(☑044-534 8888; www.wildspiritlodge.co.za; dm/d R100/300; 🛜) This friendly hideaway with a bohemian sensibility is tucked away at the end of a dirt road overlooking Tsitsikamma forest. An ivy-covered building has nice carpeted rooms, including bunk bed–free dorms, while nightly bonfires with drumming sessions are held next door. The turnoff is just past the farm stall, around 8km inland from the beach and village.

Nature's Valley Rest Camp   CAMPGROUND $
(☑in Pretoria 012-428 9111; www.sanparks.org; campsites/forest hut R125/275) The national park campsite is a lovely spot at the edge of the river east of town, and it's a 2km walk from the beach. There are clean ablutions and shared kitchens and laundry. Keep food well stored; there are pesky primates everywhere. **Tsitsikamma Eco Guides** (☑044-531 6700) can be hired here to provide guided interpretive walks.

**Nature's Valley Guesthouse
& Hikers Haven**   GUESTHOUSE $$
(☑044-531 6805; www.hikershaven.co.za; 411 St Patrick's Ave; d without/with bathroom incl breakfast per person R250/340) This comfortable home, near the beach, is popular with Otter Trail groups so bookings are essential. Staff can arrange transport to the start of the trail.

Nature's Valley Shop (Beach Rd) is the hub of the village, featuring an informal **pub-restaurant** (burgers R55); staff can provide info and maps of the surrounding area. Just a few kilometres off the N2, on the R102 on the way to the village, is **Nature's Valley Farm Stall** (sandwiches R25), a charming store selling locally made jams, cheeses and cured meats as well as a small selection of paninis and cakes.

ⓘ Getting There & Away

There's no public transport to Nature's Valley, although **Baz Bus** stops at the village.

Tsitsikamma National Park

Cut through by dark, coffee-coloured churning rivers, deep ravines and dense forests, **Tsitsikamma National Park** (☑042-281 1607; www.sanparks.org; adult/child R108/54; ⏱6am-10pm) encompasses 65,000 hectares between Plettenberg Bay and Humansdorp, as well a Marine Protected Area 5km out to sea. Two suspension bridges cross the Storms River Mouth (not to be confused with the village of Storms River) near the park's main entrance, where several walking trails pass thickets of ferns, lilies, orchids, coastal and mountain *fynbos* (fine bush), and yellowwood and milkwood trees, some hundreds of years old. Millennia-old sandstone and quartz rock formations line the gorges and rocky shoreline and southern right whales and dolphins are visible out in the ocean.

Tsitsikamma, a Khoe-San word meaning 'many waters', gets over 1200mm of rainfall annually – the river waters' striking shade is the result of tannin released from *fynbos* roots, the bitter taste of which discourages foraging hungry animals. Elusive Cape clawless otters, after which the Otter Trail (a multiday hike) is named, inhabit this park; there are also baboons, monkeys, small antelopes and furry little dassie rats. Birdlife is plentiful, including endangered African black oystercatchers.

If you don't have time for one of the longer, overnight trails, shorter walks are plentiful.

🏊 Activities

Otter Trail   HIKING
(☑in Pretoria 012-426 5111; www.sanparks.org; per person R810) The 42km Otter Trail, hugging the coastline from Storms River Mouth to Nature's Valley, is one of the most acclaimed hikes in South Africa. The walk, which lasts five days and four nights, involves fording a number of rivers and gives access to some superb stretches of coast. A good level of fitness is required in order to do the walk, as it goes uphill and downhill quite steeply in many places.

Book the trail as far in advance as possible through SAN Parks. However, there are often cancellations, so it's always worth trying, especially if you are in a group of only two or three people (single hikers are not permitted).

Accommodation is in six-bed rest huts with mattresses but without bedding, cooking utensils or running water. Camping is not allowed.

Tsitsikamma Mountain Trail HIKING
(☏042-281 1712; www.mtoecotourism.co.za; per day R80) This 60km trail begins at Nature's Valley and ends at Storms River, taking you inland through the forests and mountains. It takes up to six days and five nights, but you can opt for two, three, four or five days because each overnight hut has its own access route. Porterage is also available, as are guided day walks and mountain bike trails.

Dolphin Trail HIKING
(☏042-280 3588; www.dolphintrail.co.za; per person R4620) Ideal for hikers who don't want to carry heavy equipment or sleep in huts. Accommodation on this 17km three-day, two-night hike, which runs from Storms River Mouth to Forest Fern, is in comfortable hotels, and luggage is carried on vehicles between overnight stops. The price includes all accommodation and meals, guides and a boat trip into the Storms River Gorge on the way back. Book through the trail's website at least a year in advance.

Untouched Adventures WATER SPORTS
(☏073 130 0689; www.untouchedadventures.com) Offers kayaking up Storms River, scuba diving in the national park Marine Protected Area, and snorkelling (trips are weather dependent). It operates out of the parking area below the Storms River Restaurant.

Bloukrans River Bridge Bungee BUNGEE JUMPING
(☏042-281 1458; www.faceadrenalin.com; per jump R690; ⏰9am-4.30pm) The world's highest bridge bungee jump (216m) is 21km west of Storms River directly under the N2. If you're not sure whether you have the gumption – eardrum-pounding music is played in order to…quiet your fears? – walk out to the jumping-off point under the bridge for R70. Unexpectedly scary is the post-jump upside-down hang while you wait to be reeled back up. Photos and video of your glorious lapse of judgment are available.

🛏 Sleeping & Eating

Storms River Mouth Camp Backpackers BACKPACKERS $$
(☏in Pretoria 012-428 9111; www.sanparks.org; campsites/forest hut/family cottage R250/400/1300) This camp offers forest huts, chalets, cottages and 'oceanettes'; all except the forest huts are equipped with kitchens (including utensils), bedding and bathrooms. During the winter months (May to August) there's a 10% discount on accommodation, and a 30% discount on campsites from May to November.

Bloukrans Backpackers Lodge BACKPACKERS $
(☏042-281 1185; www.tsitsikamma.org.za; dm/d without bathroom R100/200; 🛜) A functional backpackers that has a well-equipped kitchen, located next to the bungee jump site and near the start of some shorter walking trails. You can also stay at the adjoining **Bloukrans Chalets** (four/six people R550/750) or set up **camp** (two people without/with electricity R130/140).

Storms River Restaurant INTERNATIONAL $$
(mains R55-135) At the reception complex to Tsitsikamma National Park, this place this place has a wide selection of meals at reasonable prices and superb views of the coast. There's also a small shop and an outdoor terrace with a boardwalk over the rocks to the river mouth.

❶ Information

The main information centre for the national park is Storms River Mouth Rest Camp (p176). It's 2km from the gate to the main camp, which is open 24 hours and has accommodation, a restaurant and a shop selling supplies, as well as an information and reception centre. You can also pay park entrance fees and get information at Nature's Valley Rest Camp (p175).

❶ Getting There & Away

There is no public transport to either Nature's Valley Rest Camp or Storms River Mouth. Greyhound, Intercape and Translux buses run along the N2 (68km from Plettenberg Bay, 99km from Humansdorp), from where it's 8km from the turn-off to Storms River Mouth. **Baz Bus** stops at Nature's Valley.

Storms River & Around

Tree-lined Storms River is a little hamlet with an excellent selection of accommodation options and a big tourism profile, in large part because of its proximity to Tsitsikamma National Park. Don't confuse Storms River and the turn-off 4km to the west for Storms River Mouth (Stormsriviermond in Afrikaans), located in the park.

Just east of the village on the other side of the N2 is the **Big Tree** (adult/child R12/8), a 36m-high yellowwood that's over 1000 years old, and a forest with many fine examples of candlewood, stinkwood and assegai. The 4.2km **Ratel Trail** begins here, with signs describing the trees in this forest, one of the best preserved in South Africa.

Activities

Several companies run half-day tubing trips on the Storms River. Because the river is susceptible to flooding there are no departures for several days after rains of any significance. It's worth asking how the river is flowing because with lower water levels you'll be doing almost as much walking as floating.

Blackwater Tubing   ADVENTURE TOUR
(☏079 636 8008; www.tubenaxe.co.za) Run out of Tube 'n Axe Backpackers. Tubing and mountain-bike rentals.

Mild 2 Wild   ADVENTURE TOUR
(Storms River Tubing; ☏042-281 1842; www.stormsrivertubing.co.za) In addition to tubing trips (including lunch, R550), runs horse-riding trips (R250), rents out mountain bikes and doubles as a pizzeria (wood-fired) and deli. Opposite Marilyn's Diner in the village, and same owners as Dijembe Backpackers.

Tsitsikamma Falls Adventure Park   ADVENTURE TOUR
(☏042-280 3770; www.tsitsikammaadventure.co.za; Witelsbos; per person R350) Around 12km east of the Storm's River on the N2 and near a beautiful waterfall where you can abseil (R100) and take a *foefie*-slide across the falls (R350).

Tsitsikamma Canopy Tours   ADVENTURE TOUR
(☏042-281 1836; www.stormsriver.com; Darnell St, Storms River) This massive operation (which shuttles in tourists from far afield) runs a series of zip-lines cut through the forest canopy (R450, includes meal); it's more relaxing than thrilling. Departs every half-hour from 8am to 3.30pm.

Sleeping

IN THE VILLAGE
Dijembe Backpackers   BACKPACKERS $
(☏042-281 1842; www.dijembebackpackers.com; cnr Formosa & Assegai Sts; campsites/dm/s/d R75/120/250/350; @🖥) Reflecting the spirit of its owner – a self-described frog, horse and tree whisperer – much of this intimate backpackers is made from recycled wood. The 'nature room', a cottage in the back garden, is a handmade showcase for reusable building. There's a Jacuzzi on the upper deck, and there are bonfires, and dinners (R55) prepared with locally grown vegetables. Down the road is a three-bedroom, self-catering timber annexe (double room R350). See Mild 2 Wild (left), owned by Djembe, for slew of activities.

Tube 'n Axe   BACKPACKERS $
(☏042-281 1757; www.tubenaxe.co.za; cnr Darnell & Saffron Sts; campsites/dm/d R70/130/360; @🖥) The social center of this well-oiled operation is the large bar and restaurant area that opens onto a large fire pit. If it's busy, some dorm rooms in the main building are close enough to this area for noise to be an issue. Private rooms are nicely decorated and the equal of any guesthouse in terms of comfort, and the elevated two-person tents (R200) in a beautifully manicured garden are recommended. Rents out mountain bikes and organizes tubing trips on the Witels River (R550) – see Blackwater Tubing (p177).

Armagh Country Lodge & Spa   LODGE $$
(☏042-281 1512; www.thearmagh.com; s/d R500/700; 🖥🏊) Just off the main access road into the village from the N2, Armagh is practically hidden from view by a lush and leafy garden. The rooms are spacious and warm and most have individual patios; one loft room (sleeps four) in the main building is a homey suite with views of the mountains. There's a full-service spa, and on-site Rafters restaurant is one of the best places to eat in town.

Tsitsikamma Village Inn   INN $$
(☏042-281 1711; www.village-inn.co.za; d from R750; ❄@🖥🏊) Busloads of tour groups occupy this handsome mini-village, occupying a good portion of the town's real estate. The majority of rooms are in a collection of old-fashioned low-slung cottages with four-poster beds and private porches surrounding a manicured lawn. A restaurant, bar, hair stylist and spa are on the premises.

Tsitsikamma Backpackers   BACKPACKERS $
(☏042-281 1868; www.tsitsikammabackpackers.co.za; 54 Formosa St; dm/d R130/320; @🖥) The faux log-cabin facade aside, a stay here feels like bedding down in a new, fairly prosperous suburban home. Spic-and-span rooms have a few colourful flourishes in bedding and artwork on the walls. Watch the tube

from the living room sofa or play foosball in the attached bar area. A good choice is the outdoor tented units with small verandahs.

Village Lodge & Flashpackers
LODGE $$

(☑042-281 1438; www.stormsrivervillagelodge .com; dm/s/d R125/330/440; 🐾) This handsome country home is set back from the road on an immaculately kept lawn, across the street from Tsitsikamma Village Inn. Good for hikers who crave a little modest comfort, the clean, carpeted rooms are complemented by a fully stocked open-air kitchen and lounge area.

OUTSIDE THE VILLAGE

TOP CHOICE Fernery Lodge & Chalets
RESORT $$$

(☑042-280 3588; www.fernery-ferns.co.za; s/d from R770/1550; ❋@🐾🏊) Hugging the edge of a cliff overlooking the Sandrift River gorge with falls and pools, Fernery takes full advantage of its dramatic setting. Luxurious cottages are scattered throughout; a Jacuzzi hovers over the void and the restaurant is a cosy nook with floor-to-ceiling windows. To get here from the N2 look out for the Blue-lilliesbush turn-off on the N2, 8km east of Storms River village; it's 10km down this road.

Misty Mountain Reserve
CHALET $$

(☑042-280 3699; www.misty-sa.co.za; chalet per person R450, 4-person cottage R1200) A string of large, individual A-frame cottages set back from a bluff over the ocean. Each has a large Jacuzzi bath and some have separate living rooms with TVs. This is the perfect second-night stopover for those who wish to walk the Dolphin Trail (p176). There's a restaurant (three-course set menu for R150), and mountain bikes are available for rental. It's the same turn-off from the N2 as for Fernery; follow the signage for another 6.5km.

✗ Eating

Marilyn's 60's Diner
AMERICAN, SOUTH AFRICAN $$

(mains R70; ⊘10am-9pm; 🐾) Although a little like a fish out of water, this pastel-coloured Americana-inspired diner dominates the village streetscape. In addition to the jukebox and three restored Cadillacs is a large menu featuring 'classics' like apple pie and burgers, and less thematically sourced dishes such as springbok carpaccio, lamb curry and calamari.

Rafter's
CAPE MALAY $$

(mains R85) The Armagh Country Lodge's restaurant has a homey dining room and patio seating. There's a nightly buffet (R140) and an à la carte menu with South African specialties like ostrich *bobotie* and inventive fare such as venison lasagne and Malay shrimp and fish cakes.

ℹ Information

Just off the N2 is **Storms River Information Centre** (☑042-281 1098), which has a wall of brochures and flyers and can help with accommodation. There's a liquor store and coffee shop across from Marilyn's 60's Diner, and an ATM in the small supermarket.

ℹ Getting There & Away

Baz Bus stops at Storms River, but there's no other public transport to the village. Main-line bus companies that run between Cape Town and Port Elizabeth (PE) can drop you at Storms River Bridge, 5km east of town on the N2; it's probably possible to arrange a pick-up with your accommodation from here. A private service called **All Areas Shuttle** (☑072 226 4385) runs between Storms River and the start of the Otter Trail, the Tsitsikamma park entrance and Bloukrans River Bridge Bungee (R80); other fares depend on number of passengers.

Cape St Francis & Around

Cape St Francis, 22km south of Humansdorp, is a small and unpretentious town – it's chiefly famous for a beautiful wind-whipped beach and the Seal Point surf break. If you prefer land-based activities, there's a number of walking trails through Irma Boysen Nature Reserve. Or head to the lighthouse, built in 1888 and the tallest masonry tower on the South African coast, marking the second-southernmost tip of Africa. Here you'll find the Penguin Rehabilitation Centre (www.penguin-rescue.org.za), funded entirely by donations. You can adopt a starving penguin (R600) that will be cared for and released when healthy. Southern right and humpback whales can be seen offshore between July and November; dolphins are seen throughout the year.

St Francis Bay, 8km north of Cape St Francis, is an upmarket resort partially constructed around a network of canals. It has a uniform building code that calls for black thatched roofs and white stucco walls. The beach here is nice, though much narrower than Cape St Francis, and the surf is good for

BAVIAANSKLOOF WILDERNESS

Despite being the largest unfenced wilderness area in southern Africa, Baviaanskloof Wilderness Area (sometimes referred to as the Baviaanskloof Mega Reserve) is really only known by Eastern and Western Cape South Africans, who swear that it's one of the most beautiful parts of the country to explore.

It's best discovered by car (one with high ground clearance), at least until you've decided upon a base for hikes. The rugged topography is dotted with campsites, guest-houses and a handful of quaint towns like Willowmore and Steytlerville.

Leopards, zebras, antelopes, Cape buffaloes and mountain zebras can be seen while hiking through the region's forests. One spot worth checking out for campsites, cabins and chalets is **Kouga Wilderness** (☑042-273 9903; www.kougawildernis.co.za; campsites per person R80, d R450) guest farm, at the end of a gravel road 28km north of R331. Patensie, along R331, is the area's eastern gateway. Try www.baviaans.net and www.travelbaviaans.com.za for more information.

beginners. Off season, it's pretty much deserted and has an air of immaculate sterility. It does, however, come to life in the high season, when there are many B&Bs and houses to rent. There's a petrol station, ATM, internet cafe and a few shops and restaurants, not to mention a well-regarded golf course.

A working port surrounded by a high-end condominium development, **Port St Francis** is one of the centers of the calamari fishing industry. At night you can see these ships floating offshore, lit by lamps meant to attract the calamari. A few yachts and motorboats are docked in the marina and the small mall includes several good restaurants.

Sleeping & Eating

TOP CHOICE Cape St Francis Resort RESORT $
(☑042-298 0054; www.capestfrancis.co.za; Da Gama Way, Cape St Francis; campsite per person R100, dm R160, s/d from R225/300, cottages from R605; ☎☀) The various chalets and units at this well-run resort are clean and attractive, each with TV and kitchen. There are 330 beds in total – Cape Dutch houses, beachfront luxury homes (with their own small pools), 'backpackers' with small clean rooms and communal braai area, and other rooms with large dining rooms, small kitchens and tiled floors. There's a restaurant, small shop and bar on site. Also on offer are boat cruises 15km upriver for braais at the resort's farm.

Raggies BACKPACKERS $
(☑042-294 1747; www.raggiesbackpackers.co.za; 167 St Francis Dr, St Francis Bay; dm/d R120/395; ☎) Above a gift shop, cafe and pizza place in what passes for the centre of St Francis Bay

village, Raggies has spotless, carpeted rooms and a communal kitchen and lounge. If groups are around, the fire pit, beer pong table, Big Buck Hunter arcade game, outdoor deck, backyard and braai area get lively. It's only 350m or so to the beach.

Big Time Taverna GREEK $$
(☑042-294 1309; 10 Mayotte Circle; mains R120) Can you say *dolce vita* in Greek? Take a dip in the plunge pool while waiting for dessert to truly appreciate the decadent air of this restaurant, which overlooks a canal in St Francis Bay. The menu includes grilled fish and prawns, several lamb dishes, calamari and a meze platter, plus an extensive wine collection. Reservations recommended.

Chez Patrick FRENCH $$
(Triton Ave; mains R85; ☎) Floor-to-ceiling windows with views of the Port St Francis marina below and a stylish contemporary decor complement the inventively presented light and locally sourced fusion fare. Live jazz every Sunday lunchtime.

ⓘ Getting There & Away

There's no public transport to Cape St Francis, but Raggies will pick up from Humansdorp, where both main-line buses and **Baz Bus** stop.

Jeffrey's Bay

POP 25,000
Once just a sleepy seaside town, 'J-Bay' is now one of the world's top surfing destinations. It's certainly South Africa's foremost centre of surfing and surf culture. Boardies from all over the planet flock here to ride waves such as the famous Supertubes,

once described as 'the most perfect wave in the world'. June to September are the best months for experienced surfers, but novices can learn at any time of year. The biggest surf crowd comes to town every July for the Billabong Pro championship.

 Activities

For nonsurfers, there's **windsurfing** and great **birdwatching** at Kabeljous Beach, **horse riding** (head to Papiesfontein Beach for a Lawrence of Arabia–like experience – 7.5km through the bush and another 7.5km along the beach), **dolphin-** and **whale-watching** from many of the surrounding beaches or **sandboarding** on nearby dunes (like snowboarding, with sand dunes instead of snow).

Wavecrest Surf School SURFING
(☑073 509 0400; www.wavecrestsurfschool.co.za; Drommedaris St; 2hr lesson incl board & wetsuit R200) A highly recommended long-running operation.

Jeffrey's Bay Surf School & Camp SURFING
(☑042-293 4214; www.jbaysurfschool.com; 2hr lesson incl board & wetsuit R200) Run out of Island Vibe.

Play in J Bay Adventure Centre ADVENTURE SPORTS
(☑042-293 3002; www.playinjbay.co.za; 5 Pepper St) Surfing, sandboarding, kite-surfing, fishing etc. Run out of a charming postage stamp–sized cafe across from African Perfection.

Sleeping

Like many places in this part of Eastern Cape, J-Bay is chock-a-block with holidaymakers between mid-December and mid-January, so you'll have to book way ahead for accommodation at this time. Low-season discounts are often offered. Other than Island Vibe, the accommodations listed here are clustered around Supertubes and Pepper St; African Ubuntu is a short walk away. Stay in Jbay (www.stayinjbay.co.za) is a good resource for other accommodation options.

African Perfection B&B $$
(☑042-293 1401; www.africanperfection.co.za; 20 Pepper St; s/d incl breakfast R600/800; ✿@☎) Occupying prime real estate directly in front of Supertubes, this luxury option is perfect for surfing voyeurs. Every room comes with a private balcony offering stunning sea views.

The fabulous four-sleeper self-catering loft (R2400) is ready for a season of *Real World J-Bay*. Helpful staff can arrange a shuttle from Port Elizabeth airport for R400 for two people.

Island Vibe BACKPACKERS $
(☑042-293 1625; 10 Dageraad St; campsites/dm/d R80/120/400; @☎) The most popular backpackers in town, Island Vibe is 500m south of the city centre, but the attendant raft of surfers attests to its prime location. Activities on offer include surf lessons (R180), horse riding and kite-surfing plus, of course, plenty of hanging out and socialising. For more privacy, the tastefully decorated beach house has double rooms with balconies and a large kitchen and lounge area; another building just down the street has five rooms with TVs and one has a Jacuzzi. Breakfast and dinner are on offer in the restaurant and bar; the latter can become raucous at night.

Beach Music GUESTHOUSE $
(☑042-293 2291; www.beachmusic.co.za; 33 Flame Cres; s/d from R200/300; ☎) This burnt-umber-coloured building overlooking Supertubes resembles a Mexican villa. The wonderfully airy 2nd-floor lounge and kitchen has superb ocean views, and each of the well-cared-for rooms has a small porch; some downstairs ones share a kitchenette.

Dreamland GUESTHOUSE $
(☑082 769 4060; www.jbaylocal.com; 29 Flame Cres; d from R350; ☎) Next door to Beach Music and with equally privileged views is this thatch-roofed hand-crafted home. Four individually designed units have Oregon pine wooden floors, white stucco and private decks. Vegan food and breakfast is served upon request, and owners make a point of welcoming kids and dogs.

African Ubuntu BACKPACKERS $
(☑042-296 0376; www.jaybay.co.za; 8 Cherry St; campsites R85, dm/d without bathroom R110/300; @☎) A suburban home transformed into an intimate and friendly backpackers by its passionate, young surfer owner. A handful of private rooms are small but well kept and the small garden, verandah and balcony are good places to chill. There are regular braais, and a simple breakfast is complimentary for all. On a hill a block above Checkers supermarket; a short walk to Supertubes.

SURFING THE EASTERN CAPE

Surfing on the Eastern Cape coast is legendary. While Supertubes at Jeffrey's Bay is world class, and Bruce's Beauties at St Francis Bay inspired the movie *Endless Summer,* you can generally check out breaks anywhere along the coast, from Jeffrey's Bay to Port Edward. And if you find that secret spot, don't let on. When the surf is up everyone is said to be at a 'board meeting'.

The water temperature ranges from 16°C to 22°C, so you can get away with a short wetsuit (or even baggies) in summer, but you'll need a full wetsuit in winter.

Starting in the south, **Jeffrey's Bay** is on the list of 'waves I must surf before I die' and is one of the planet's 10 best spots. In July it hosts the Billabong Pro competition. Consequently, it can become crowded when the surf's up: remember your manners and say 'howzit' to the locals. Supertubes is a perfect right-hand point break, and once you've caught this, you'll be spoilt rotten. If you're a beginner, head for the softer Kitchen Windows at the southern end of town.

Cape St Francis is home to legendary Seal Point, one of the most consistent right-handed breaks. Nearby **St Francis Bay** has Bruce's Beauties and Hullets, the perfect long board wave.

In the rush to J-Bay, many surfers overlook **Port Elizabeth** (PE). While the predominant southwesterly winds can blow everything away, Pipe in Summerstrand is PE's most popular break and on a good day the Fence is a good bet.

Further north in **Port Alfred** there are excellent right-handers at East Pier, while West Pier has a more sheltered left.

East London, home to some well-known surfing pros such as Greg Emslie and Roseanne Hodge, is best known for the consistent Nahoon Reef; Gonubie Point and Gonubie Lefts can also come up with the goodies. Nursery 'grommets' will find what they need at Nahoon Beach and Corner. There can be some dirty water in the area, which encourages shark activity, so keep an eye out and don't surf at dusk.

Further north is **Whacky Point** at Kei Mouth, and then you're on to the **Wild Coast**. Wild, it is: a spectacular though often dangerous coast that hasn't really been explored or exploited. Be careful at polluted river mouths – you're a long way from medical attention. **Mdumbi** has a long, right-hand point break with a nice sandy bottom, and **Whale Rock** is just around the corner. **Coffee Bay** has a couple of waves...and then there are those secret spots that no one's ever going to tell you about...

Aloe Again   BACKPACKERS **$**
(☏042-293 2671; www.africanperfection.co.za; 1 Pepper St; dm R110, d from R300; ☜) Formerly called Surfpackers and run out of African Perfection across the street, Aloe Again has small, clean rooms and a large 2nd-floor lounge and kitchen area with billiard and foosball tables. A huge backyard garden with braai area means there's plenty of space to chill and hang your wetsuit out to dry.

Cristal Cove   GUESTHOUSE **$$**
(☏042-293 2101; www.cristalcove.co.za; 49 Flame Cres; dm/d R100/280, d without bathroom R200; @☜) Only a stone's throw from Supertubes, this two-story brick home has five carpeted and clean units – essentially mini apartments with lounge area, kitchen and several bedrooms. The sea-facing double goes for R350.

 Eating

Two of the most enjoyable restaurants, **Die Walskipper** (mains R95; ⏱11.30am-9pm Tue-Sat, to 3pm Sun) and **Tapas** (mains R70; ⏱5.30-10pm Mon-Fri, 11.30am-3pm & 5.30-10pm Sat & Sun), share a beachfront car park a short drive south of town on Claptons Beach in Marina Martinique. Both serve freshly caught seafood (mussels, crayfish, scallops etc) and South African meat dishes (marrow bones, crocodile steak) and have outdoor seating with sandy floors and oceanfront views. Meals at Die Walskipper come with homemade bread and a variety of pâtés. A taxi from town costs R25 one way.

In Food   INTERNATIONAL **$$**
(cnr Schelde & Jeffrey Sts; mains R65; ⏱7am-5pm Mon-Sat; ☜) The sandwiches, burgers and other fare at this coffee shop–cum-bakery

Jeffrey's Bay

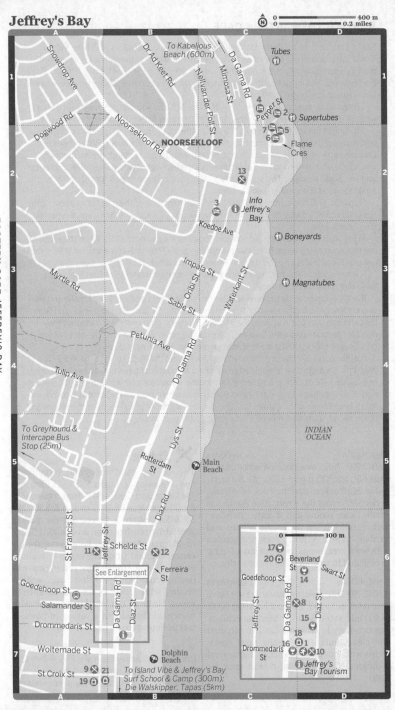

0   400 m
0   0.2 miles

To Kabeljous Beach (600m)

Tubes

Snowdrop Ave

Dr Ad Keet Rd

Nel van der Poll St

Mimosa St

Da Gama Rd

Pepper St

Supertubes

Dogwood Rd

Noorsekloof Rd

NOORSEKLOOF

Flame Cres

13

Info
Jeffrey's Bay

Koedoe Ave

Boneyards

Myrtle Rd

Impala St

Oribi St

Sable St

Waterkant St

Magnatubes

Petunia Ave

Da Gama Rd

Tulip Ave

To Greyhound & Intercape Bus Stop (25m)

Uys St

Rotterdam St

Main Beach

INDIAN OCEAN

Diaz Rd

St Francis St

Jeffrey St

Schelde St

11

12

See Enlargement

Ferreira St

Goedehoop St

Da Gama Rd

Diaz St

Salamander St

Drommedaris St

Woltemade St

St Croix St

9

21

19

Dolphin Beach

To Island Vibe & Jeffrey's Bay Surf School & Camp (300m);
Die Walskipper, Tapas (5km)

Enlargement

0   100 m

17

20

Beverland St

Swart St

Goedehoop St

Da Gama Rd

14

Jeffrey St

8

Diaz St

15

18

Drommedaris St

16

1

10

Jeffrey's Bay Tourism

Jeffrey's Bay

EASTERN CAPE JEFFREY'S BAY

are far from ordinary. This is not surprising, considering the owner-chef's impressive CV – including once having cooked for the Queen of England. An attention to organic, locally sourced ingredients (Karoo *fynbos* honey) and wide-ranging culinary tastes – the menu includes samosas, Greek salads and Thai chicken curry – make In Food a worthy foodie destination.

Kitchen Windows　　　　　SEAFOOD $$
(23 Ferreira St; mains R55-125; ⊙11am-late Mon-St, to 3pm Sun) Sea views and white stucco walls give this airy restaurant a Mediterranean island feel. Less-expensive fare like calamari burgers, Thai fish cakes and salads complement a sophisticated menu of creatively prepared fish, prawns and steaks. Enter on Diaz Rd or at the end of Ferreira St.

Café Kima　　　　　INTERNATIONAL $
(32 Diaz Rd; mains R50; 📶) This cafe on the beachfront road has outdoor patio seating and an open-air dining area with contemporary furnishings, flat-screen TVs and blankets for chilly breezes. The smoked salmon and poached eggs is a good choice for breakfast (R52) and gargantuan slices of cake are recommended; burgers, pastas and sandwiches round out the menu.

3 Fat Fish　　　　　SEAFOOD, ITALIAN $$
(📞042-293 4147; 23A Da Gama Rd; mains R55-100; ⊙closed Sun) Specialising in – you guessed it – fish and more than two dozen pizzas. Live music on Friday from 3pm to 5pm, and cooking lessons (R150) every Thursday from 6pm to 8pm.

Nina's　　　　　INTERNATIONAL $$
(Da Gama Rd; mains R65; ⊙7am-10pm) Nina's is something of a local's secret because of a below-the-radar location in the Spar Centre strip mall. It's a stylish diner with a variety of Thai noodle and curry dishes, nearly three dozen pizzas, grilled meats, pastas, seafood and burgers, and thick and creamy gelato.

Bay Pasta Co　　　　　ITALIAN $$
(34 Jeffrey St; mains R60; 📶) More than a dozen varieties of pizzas and pastas, as well as paninis, are on the menu at this casual eatery. It's next to a cluster of surfer outlet stores and is the closest restaurant for those staying at Island Vibe.

Drinking

Sovereign Sports Café　　　　　BAR
(Da Gama Rd) A cavernous and popular bar with the requisite big-screen TV and gambling slots.

Jolly Dolphin　　　　　PUB
(Diaz Rd) The large 2nd-floor outdoor balcony is a sometimes rowdy drinking spot.

Greek (Beverland St; mains R80) and **Mexican** (Da Gama Rd; mains R65), around the corner from each other, wear their ethnic bona fides like theme park restaurants, though both are more appealing as bars.

Shopping

Check the various factory shops, primarily **Quiksilver** (there's a 'museum' about the history of J-Bay on the second floor) and **Billabong**, at the lower end of Jeffrey St for the best bargains (look out for periodic sales, otherwise prices aren't significantly less than ordinary), as well as the local independent stores like Rebel Surfboards (cnr St Croix St & Jeffrey St; www.jbaysurfboards.co.za), which does custom board shaping.

Information

Most ATMs are on Da Gama Rd, the main thoroughfare.

Cornerstone Laundromat (Da Gama Rd) In a strip mall next to Checkers supermarket. Also a coffee shop and internet cafe.

Internet Café (Da Gama Rd; per hr R22) Next door to 3 Fat Fish.

Jeffrey's Bay Tourism (☑042-293 2923; www.jeffreysbaytourism.org; Da Gama Rd; ☺9am-5pm Mon-Fri, to noon Sat) Friendly and helpful, and can make bookings for accommodation.

ℹ Getting There & Away

Baz Bus stops daily at various backpackers. Journeys include Jeffrey's Bay to Cape Town (R950, 12 hours) and Port Elizabeth to Jeffrey's Bay (R170, one hour).

Minibus taxis depart when full, generally on the hour, from the corner of Goedehoop and St Francis Sts; it's R15 to Humansdorp (30 minutes) and R45 to Port Elizabeth (one hour).

Greyhound and Intercape long-distance buses plying the Cape Town–Port Elizabeth–Durban route arrive at and depart from the Caltex petrol station on St Francis St.

Port Elizabeth

NELSON MANDELA BAY METRO CITY POP 1.5 MILLION

Port Elizabeth (PE for short) lies on the Sunshine Coast and certainly has good bathing beaches and surf spots. It's also a convenient gateway to worthy destinations in either direction along the coast, as well as to the eastern Karoo. However, the downtown area, like many city centres throughout the country, is mostly run-down and full of fast-food chains and cheap stores. The more-upmarket shops, chic bars and restaurants have moved out to the suburban shopping centres. PE, its industrial satellite towns of Uitenhage and Despatch, and the massive surrounding townships, is collectively referred to by the rather clunky 'Nelson Mandela Bay Metro City'.

◉ Sights

FREE South End Museum   MUSEUM

(☑041-582 3325; www.southendmuseum.co.za; cnr Walmer Blvd & Humewood Rd; ☺9am-4pm Mon-Fri,

10am-3pm Sat & Sun) This small museum tells the history of South End, a vibrant multicultural district destroyed by apartheid bulldozers during forced removals between 1965 and 1975 (under the infamous Group Areas Act). The inhabitants were relocated to other parts of the city, designated by race.

FREE Nelson Mandela

Metropolitan Art Museum   MUSEUM

(☑041-506 2000; www.artmuseum.co.za; 1 Park Dr, St George's Park; ☺9am-5pm Mon & Wed-Fri, to 2pm Sat & Sun) The museum housed in two handsome buildings at the entrance to St George's Park has a small gallery of paintings and sculpture by contemporary South African artists, some older British and Eastern Cape works, plus temporary exhibitions and graduate shows.

Bayworld   AQUARIUM, MUSEUM

(☑041-584 0650; www.bayworld.co.za; Beach Rd; adult/child R25/15; ☺9am-4.30pm) This ageing complex includes a small museum, an oceanarium and a snake park. Alongside the many stuffed and pickled marine mammals in the museum is some beautiful Xhosa beadwork incorporating modern materials, and a replica of the Algoasaurus dinosaur. Trained seals perform at the old-fashioned oceanarium at 11am and 3pm daily.

Donkin Reserve   PARK

Located on a hill, immediately behind the town centre, Donkin Reserve is a handy point for getting your bearings. Climb up inside the lighthouse (adult/child R5/3; ☺8.30am-4pm) for good views over the bay. The pyramid on the reserve is a memorial to Elizabeth Donkin, beloved wife of Sir Rufane Donkin, once the governor of Cape Province.

Activities

Port Elizabeth's major attraction as a holiday destination is its wide sandy beaches and the warm waters of the Indian Ocean. Sardinia Bay, 20km south of downtown, is easily the nicest in the area; to reach the 10km-long beach you walk over large sand dunes. However, strong currents mean it's best to play in the shallows and not venture out far from shore. There are broad beaches south of Central; Kings Beach stretches from the harbour to Humewood and there are more beaches at Summerstrand that are all fairly sheltered. But PE is not known as the 'windy city' for nothing; windsurfers and sailors will find what they need at Hobie Beach, 5km south of Central.

Surfers are not left out either, with the best breaks between the harbour wall and Summerstrand, and at Pollok beach. Stop by the **Surf Centre** (☏041-585 6027; Dolphins Leap) for board rentals (R100 for a half-day) or lessons (R200 per two-hour lesson).

Good **diving sites** around Port Elizabeth include some wrecks and the St Croix Islands (a marine reserve). Both **Ocean Divers International** (☏041-581 5121; www.odipe.co.za; 10 Albert Rd, Walmer) and **Pro Dive** (☏041-583 1144; www.prodive.co.za; Shark Rock Pier, Beach Rd, Summerstrand) offer PADI diving courses starting at around R1400, with dives from R280 per dive.

There's **sandboarding** on the Maitlands dunes west of PE.

Two places to cool off in chlorinated water on a hot day are the **MacArthur Leisure Centre** (☏041-582 2285; Kings Beach Promenade; adult/child R30/15; ◷9am-5pm), a complex with a bar, restaurant and direct beach access, and the **public swimming pool** (☏041-585 7751; adult/child R8.50/6; ◷10am-6pm) in St George's Park.

👉 Tours

Afrovibe Adventures   DAY TOURS
(☏082 854 4136; 12 La Roche Dr, Humewood) Based at Lungile Backpackers, it runs various day trips, including sandboarding.

Calabash Tours   CULTURAL TOUR
(☏041-585 6162; www.calabashtours.co.za; 8 Dollery St, Central) Runs local tours, including trips to Addo Elephant National Park (R750) and several cross-cultural township tours (from R350), including stops at squatter camps and shebeens (unlicensed drinking establishments). The guides are locals who are proud of the Port Elizabeth townships' part in the anti-apartheid struggle, and they highlight places of historical and political interest along the way.

Raggy Charters   BOAT TOUR
(☏073 152 2277; www.raggycharters.co.za) Offers cruises led by a qualified marine biologist to St Croix, Jahleel and Benton Islands. You can see penguins, Cape fur seals, dolphins and whales on its half-day tour, which departs at 8.30am daily (R800).

🛏 Sleeping

The tourist offices can help with lists of B&Bs. Most of Port Elizabeth's choicest

hotels and dozens of self-catering flats are lined up along the beachfront.

BEACHFRONT & AROUND

Beach Hotel   HOTEL $$
(☏041-583 2161; www.thebeachhotel.co.za; Marine Dr, Summerstrand; per person incl breakfast R650; ❋@🛜🏊) The friendly four-star Beach Hotel is beautifully positioned opposite Hobie Beach and next to the Boardwalk. Its Ginger restaurant (mains R92 to R110) faces the sea. The exquisite 1920s building is worth a visit if only to take a look at the amazing breakfast room.

Windermere   GUESTHOUSE $$$
(☏041-582 2245; www.thewindermere.co.za; 35 Humewood Rd; d incl breakfast R1500; ❋🛜🏊) Located on a quiet street, only a block from the beach, is this oasis of boutique-style luxury. There are plush and contemporary furnishings throughout and the rooms and bathrooms are large. Expect exceptionally attentive service, an outdoor lounge area and a garden plunge pool.

Algoa Bay B&B   B&B $$
(☏041-582 5134; www.algoabay.co.za; 13 Ferndale Rd; s/d incl breakfast R550/900; ❋🛜🏊) Just around the corner from the Windermere is this modern B&B. Rooms are tastefully furnished and come with flat-screen TVs; you can see King's Beach from the top-floor rooms. There's an outdoor deck and solar-heated swimming pool.

Lungile Backpackers   BACKPACKERS $
(☏041-582 2042; www.lungilebackpackers.co.za; 12 La Roche Dr, Humewood; campsites/dm R60/120, d without/with bathroom R220/270; @🛜🏊) This well-managed operation is in a suburban neighbourhood, up a hill and minutes from the beachfront. The airy, A-frame home's large entertainment area rocks most nights, and the dorms and tiny campsite can get full when the Baz Bus arrives. There are also some handsome stone-flagged en-suite doubles (R300). Pick-ups from the airport and city centre. Afrovibe Adventures is based here.

Chapman Hotel   HOTEL $$
(☏041-584 0678; www.chapman.co.za; 1 Lady Bea Cres, Brookes Hill Dr, Summerstrand; s/d incl breakfast R450/600; ❋@🏊) The friendly, family-run Chapman, overlooking the sea next to Dolphin's Leap Centre, is a good midrange option with a waterfall, rim-flow pool. Modern rooms have private balconies with sea views.

Port Elizabeth

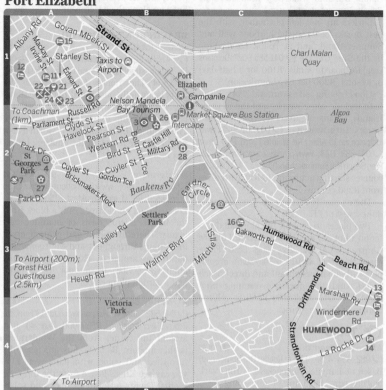

99 Mile Lodge
LODGE $

(☎041-583 1256; www.99miles.co.za; 4 Jenvey Way; dm/s/d R120/270/385; ☎▩) A somewhat non-descript guesthouse in a suburban neighbourhood only a few minutes' walk to Polo and Hobie beaches; the latter has good surf. There's a communal kitchen and the large pool has a big deck area.

Kings Beach Backpackers
BACKPACKERS $

(☎041-585 8113; kingsb@agnet.co.za; 41 Windermere Rd, Humewood; campsites R60, dm/d without bathroom R120/250; @☎) A small, very lived-in home on a quiet street and a short walk to the beach. There are a few makeshift cottages in the backyard. Staff can help organise tours in the area.

Radisson Blu Hotel
HOTEL $$

(☎041-509 5000; www.radissonblu.com; cnr Marine Dr & 9th Ave; d R1200; ❋@☎▩) This shining tower overlooking the beach has some of the most contemporary and stylish rooms in the city, and all the facilities of an international business-class hotel.

Paxton Hotel
HOTEL $$

(☎041-585 9655; www.paxton.co.za; Carnarvon Pl, Humewood; s/d R955/1300; ❋@☎▩) Another option for first-class accommodation. However, it's not beachfront; it's tucked behind a mini-mall and requires a short drive to the beach.

ELSEWHERE

No 1 Sherlock St
GUESTHOUSE $

(☎082 570 1565; rath@iafrica.com; 1 Sherlock St, Richmond Hill; r R250) The two rooms here are a good-value option, and a short walk uphill to the Stanley St restaurants. Each has a kitchenette, TVs and private back deck with million-rand ocean views. Contact the owner, who lives in the attached house, before turning up.

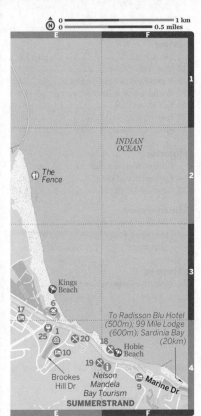

0 _____ **1 km**
0 _____ **0.5 miles**

INDIAN
OCEAN

The Fence

Kings Beach

To Radisson Blu Hotel
(500m); 99 Mile Lodge
(600m); Sardinia Bay
(20km)

Hobie
Beach

Brookes
Hill Dr

Nelson
Mandela
Bay Tourism

Marine Dr

SUMMERSTRAND

EASTERN CAPE PORT ELIZABETH

Guesthouse on Irvine
GUESTHOUSE **$$**

(☎084 650 0056; www.guesthouseonirvine.com.
za; 40 Irvine St, Richmond Hill; s/d R450/580; 🛜)
A refurbished Victorian house in a trendy
neighbourhood only a few doors down from
the Stanley St restaurants. Wood-floored
rooms are small and clean and beds have
nice linens.

Eating

On **Stanley St**, between Glen and Mackay
Sts in the Richmond Hill neighborhood,
are more than half a dozen quality restau-
rants. There's a night market here the first
Wednesday of every month. **Brooke's on
the Bay Pavilion** has Primi Piatti, Ocean
Basket and the Coachman. The **Boardwalk
Casino Complex** in Summerstrand has sev-
eral fast-food eateries, a good Chinese food
restaurant and a couple of cafes with out-
door patio seating. There are a handful of
recommended restaurants on 6th Ave in the
suburb of Walmer, including **Wicker Woods**
(50 6th Ave; mains R95), **Cobblestone Bakery**
(40 6th Ave; mains R45) and **Boccadillos** (42
6th Ave; mains R60).

Deli Street
Café
SANDWICHES, SOUTH AFRICAN **$$**

(Stanley St; mains R60, sandwiches R45; ⊙7.30am-
10pm; 🛜) Looking as though it could have
been airlifted from the trendier precincts
of any up-and-coming gentrified former
warehouse district, this restaurant adheres
to the farm-to-table theme in its menu and
aesthetic. Diners munch on salads, burgers
and 'build-your-own' sandwiches in an airy
space with lofty ceilings, exposed brick walls
and floors, and picnic tables.

Cubata
BARBECUE **$$**

(cnr Arthur & Stebonheath Sts, Sydenham; mains
R65; ⊙Mon-Sat) In a large converted garage
in a gritty neighborhood around the corner
from the stadium, Cubata has a dedicated
following of loyal locals who chow down in
festive groups on Portuguese-style barbe-
cued prawns, ribs and chicken. BYOB.

Vovo Telo Bakery & Café
CAFE **$**

(Irvine St; mains R55; ⊙7.30am-3.30pm) Charm-
ingly rustic, this restaurant is abuzz with lo-
cal regulars sharing strongly brewed coffee
and light meals like frittata tartlets (R35),
thin-crust pizza and salads out on the wrap-
around porch.

Hippo Backpackers
BACKPACKERS **$**

(☎041-585 6350; www.thehippo.co.za; 14 Glen St,
Richmond Hill; dm/s/d without bathroom R100/
150/280; @🛜🏊) Now with the Stanley St
restaurant row nearby, Hippo is a conven-
ient as well as comfortable option. There's a
very nice backyard pool and braai area, two
attractive lounges, two kitchens and nicely
furnished rooms; the room for five (R350) is
a good deal for groups.

Forest Hall Guest House
GUESTHOUSE **$$**

(☎041-581 3356; www.foresthall.co.za.com; 84
River Rd, btwn 9th & 10th Aves, Walmer; s/d incl
breakfast R600/850; ✹🛜🏊) Huge rooms with
lots of natural light overlook the expansive
grounds and beautiful garden at this gracious Walmer home. The hosts will bend
over backwards to accommodate guests
and the three-course home-cooked dinners
(R120) are excellent.

Port Elizabeth

Fushin JAPANESE $$
(15 Stanley St; mains R100) This restaurant's experienced owner and chef creates high-quality sushi and handmade Singapore-inspired noodle dishes as well as creative fare like stuffed giant squid. You can choose to eat inside the small, modern dining room or, like at all Stanley St restaurants, outside on the street.

Blue Waters Café INTERNATIONAL $$
(Marine Dr, Summerstrand; mains R75) Recommended as much for its beachfront location and place for a drink on the 2nd-floor outdoor porch as for its large and varied menu – although, perhaps because of the breadth of choices on offer, the food doesn't rise above the ordinary.

Coachman INTERNATIONAL $$
(103 Cape Rd, Glendinningvale; mains R110) Locals claim this is one of the city's best steakhouses. Choose from a 1kg prime cut, T-bone or chops. Also seafood, chicken and pastas.

Blackbeard's SEAFOOD/SOUTH AFRICAN $$
(Chapman Hotel, 1 Lady Bea Cres, Brookes Hill Dr, Summerstrand; mains R60-100; ◎7-9am & 6pm-late) Specialises in large and tasty seafood platters – you can pick the ingredients to create your own.

Drinking

Stanley St has several bars, and its restaurants are great for after-dinner drinks. Half a dozen bars line nearby **Parliament St**, though it's considered a sketchy area at night.

TOP CHOICE For the Love of Wine WINE BAR
(Stanley St, Richmond Hill; ◎1-8pm Tue-Sat) One of the few wine bars in PE, this owner-run friendly spot is above Yiayias Mediterranean Restaurant. The wrap-around porch gets cool breezes (blankets on offer for the chilly) and is great for sunsets. There's a nice selection of very reasonably priced wines (R25 per glass), and several Stanley St restaurants deliver food here so there's no need to leave when doors close around 8pm (guests are welcome to stay till late).

Gondwana Café (◎9am-late Tue-Sun) and **Coco de Mer Restobar** (◎noon-late) in the Dolphin's Leap centre in Humewood; the former has DJs on Fridays and Saturdays, and live jazz on Sundays from 5.30pm and the latter, a restaurant and cocktail lounge has DJs on Wednesdays and Saturdays.

☆ Entertainment

Port Elizabeth Opera House   OPERA
(☎041-586 3177; www.peoperahouse.co.za; Whites Rd) This opera house, the oldest in South Africa, hosts a wide range of concerts, ballets, plays and jazz recitals – drop into the box office for the latest.

Savoy Club Theatre   THEATRE
(☎083 471 8893; cnr Stirk & Colett Sts, Adcockvale) The Gilbert and Sullivan Society puts on small productions here.

St George's Park Cricket Ground   STADIUM
(☎041-585 1646; www.stgeorgespark.co.za) Home of Eastern Province Cricket and famous for its band-playing supporters who turn one-day internationals into tub-thumping affairs.

Nelson Mandela Stadium   STADIUM
(www.nmbstadium; 70 Prince Alfred Rd, North End) Built for the 2010 soccer World Cup, this futuristic-looking stadium stands out in the otherwise run-down North End section of the city.

🛍 Shopping

Wezandla Gallery & Craft Centre   HANDICRAFTS
(27 Baakens St) This brightly coloured arts and crafts centre has a huge array of artefacts made by local groups and a small coffee shop. Staff can also help with tourist information.

There are also craft shops at the Boardwalk in Summerstrand, and you should head to the King's Beach flea market on Sundays for curios.

ℹ Information

Nelson Mandela Bay Tourism (☎041-585 8884; www.nmbt.co.za; Donkin Reserve; ⊙8am-4.30pm Mon-Fri, 9.30am-3.30pm Sat & Sun) has an excellent supply of information and maps. Also has a cafe with good city views. Other branches are at the Boardwalk (Summerstrand), in front of Brooke's on the Bay Pavilion (Beach Rd, Humewood) and the airport.

ℹ Getting There & Away

Air

South African Airways (SAA; ☎041-507 1111; www.flysaa.com) and **Kulula** (☎0861 585 852; www.kulula.com) have daily flights between Cape Town (R1400, 1¾ hours), Durban (R1400, 1¼ hours) and Jo'burg (R1000, 1½ hours).

Bus

Greyhound and **Translux** (Ernst & Young Bldg, Greenacres Shopping Centre, Ring Rd) buses depart from the Greenacres Shopping Centre, about 3km from Humewood. Reservations can also be made at **Computicket** (☎083 915 8000; www.computicket.com; Greenacres Shopping Centre). **Intercape** (cnr Fleming & North Union Sts) buses depart from behind the old post office.

TO CAPE TOWN

City to City, Intercape and Translux have two daily buses to and from Cape Town (R320, 11 hours) via the Garden Route.

Baz Bus runs daily from Port Elizabeth to Cape Town (R1110 one way – hop-on, hop-off).

TO JOHANNESBURG

Greyhound and Intercape have nightly buses from Port Elizabeth to Jo'burg (R380, 15 hours) via East London. Translux has daily services from Port Elizabeth to Jo'burg (R360, 14½ hours) via Bloemfontein (R240, nine hours) and Graaff-Reinet (140, 3½ hours).

TO DURBAN & EAST LONDON

City to City and Translux run to Durban daily (R380, 13 hours) via Grahamstown (R80, 1½ hours), East London (R140, four hours), Mthatha (R240, seven hours) and Port Shepstone (R310, 11½ hours). Greyhound runs to Durban daily (R375, 12½ hours); Intercape has a direct daily 7am service to East London (R225). **Mini-Lux** (☎043-741 3107; 33 Main Rd, Amalinda) has a regular bus service that goes to East London via Grahamstown.

Baz Bus runs on Monday, Tuesday, Thursday, Friday and Sunday from Port Elizabeth to Durban, and returns on Monday, Wednesday Thursday, Saturday and Sunday; it's R1110 for a one-way hop-on, hop-off ticket.

Car

All the big car-rental operators have offices in Port Elizabeth or at the airport, including **Avis** (☎041-501 7200) and **Hertz** (☎041-581 6600).

Minibus Taxi

Most minibus taxis leave from the large townships surrounding Port Elizabeth and can be difficult to find. The **minibus taxi rank** (Strand St), a few blocks north of the bell tower, services the local area.

Train

Shosholoza Meyl (www.shosholozameyl.co.za) runs to Jo'burg (from R370, 20 hours, Wed, Fri & Sun) via Cradock, Bloemfontein and Kroonstad. There are tourist-class and economy-class services. There's also a weekly **Premier Classe** (☎in Cape Town 011-773 9247; www.premierclasse.co.za) service to Cape Town (R1250, 8½ hours) via Oudtshoorn.

ⓘ Getting Around

The **airport** (Allister Miller Rd, Walmer) is about 5km from the city centre. Taxis and hire cars are available at the airport. For a private taxi (around R65), call **Hurter Cabs** (☏041-585 5500) or **Alpha Cabs** (☏041-484 5554).

Algoa Bus Company runs most routes (R6.50 one way) around the city and to the surrounding suburbs every 25 minutes, leaving from the Market Square bus station on Strand St.

CENTRAL EASTERN CAPE

While this is something of an artificial geographic designation, it makes sense (from a traveller's perspective) to think of the area immediately east of Port Elizabeth as a self-contained region. Addo Elephant National Park, as well as many other private wildlife reserves, are a big attraction; Grahamstown – at the heart of an Anglocentric territory originally home to the 1820 Settlers (see boxed text, p196) – is the largest town; and Port Alfred has dune-backed beaches that go on for kilometres.

Addo Elephant National Park

Located 72km north of Port Elizabeth, near the Zuurberg Range in the Sundays River Valley, this national park (☏042-233 8600; www.sanparks.org; adult/child R150/50; ☺7am-7pm) protects the remnants of the huge elephant herds that once roamed the Eastern Cape. When Addo was proclaimed a national park in 1931, there were only 16 elephants left; today there are more than 450 in the park (their rehabilitation has been so successful that contraceptive measures are being considered), and you'd be unlucky not to see some. Addo, which was once farmland, now encompasses five biomes and over 180,000 hectares, and extends to the coastal area between the point at which the Sundays and Bushman's Rivers flow into the sea. There are plans to add a marine reserve that encompasses islands featuring the second-largest breeding population of African penguins.

A day or two at Addo is a highlight of any visit to this part of the Eastern Cape, not only for the elephants but for the zebras, black rhinos, Cape buffaloes, leopards, lions, myriad birds and even the prehistoric-looking dung beetles, endemic only to Addo. Female beetles bury elephant dung underground to eat, which both fertilises the soil and encourages the growth of the bright-green spekboom plants – the leaves of which are the main source of moisture for elephants and are referred to as 'elephant's food'. Great white sharks and southern right whales (in season) complete the 'Big Seven'.

🏃 Activities

During summer it's best to arrive at the park by midmorning and to stake out one of the waterholes where the elephants tend to gather during the heat of the day. In winter, early mornings are the best time to see animals. Two-hour guided wildlife drives (☏042-233 8657; per person R235) in large 4WDs with good viewing angles should be booked in advance, especially during the high season (October to March); hop-on guides (per vehicle R140; ☺8am-5pm) can ride along in your own vehicle and are arranged at the main gate.

The elephants of Addo were once addicted to – and even fought violently over – the oranges and grapefruits fed to them by the park's first rangers to encourage them to stay within the park's boundaries. A fruit ban has been in place since the late 1970s; however, as the old adage goes, 'elephants have good memories' and the smell alone could provoke an old-timer. And, of course, do *not* get out of your car except at designated climb-out points.

Criss Cross Adventures CANOEING
(☏072 125 9152; www.crisscrossadventures.co.za; Chrislin Lodge) When in flood, the Sundays River is the fastest flowing river in South Africa, but at other times it's perfect for a guided canoe trip. Tunnels of river grass open onto widened vistas, and kingfishers and spotted eagle owls nest in the riverbanks. Tour operator Christopher Pickens grew up on the river and knows it intimately. He also offers four-hour wildlife drives (R600) and a full-day mountain tour (R1100).

Horse trails HORSE RIDING
(☏042-233 8657; addogamedrives@sanparks.org) Morning and afternoon rides are in the Nyathi section of the park. For beautiful scenery but not wildlife, rides are also offered in the Zuurberg mountain section: there are one- (R165), three- (R230) and five-hour (R250) rides as well as an overnight trail to Narina Bush Camp (excluding accommodation R440).

🛏 Sleeping & Eating

Park accommodation can get booked up at busy periods, so always reserve in advance, if possible. There is a lot of B&Bs around the blink-and-you-missed it town of Addo, just a few kilometres from the park gate.

Mediocre meals are available at the **park's restaurant** (mains R65), which is presided over by the stuffed head of the legendary bull, Hapoor. If you've brought your own grub, the rest camp's shady picnic area has a fine view of the waterhole. Most overnight visitors eat at their accommodation.

TOP / **Camp Figtree** RESORT $$$
CHOICE
(☑082 611 3603; www.campfigtree.co.za; cottage per person incl breakfast R890; @🐾) Luxurious in the colonial-chic manner, this property takes full advantage of breathtaking panoramic views from its perch in the Zuurberg mountains above Addo. Tastefully appointed cottages with elephantine bathrooms and private porches share the grounds with a pool, library, lounge area and restaurant, where afternoon tea is served. Pampering aside, there's emphasis on the environmental – electricity is limited and ingenious solar-powered jar lamps are used at night. Figtree is around 11km from the R335 turnoff towards the Zuurberg Pass.

Aardvark Guesthouse GUESTHOUSE $
(☑042-233 1244; www.theaardvarkbackpackers.co.za; dm R120, s/d R300/400; @) This handsome guesthouse is set around a manicured lawn down a tree-shaded country lane only 2.5km north of Addo village. Rooms in the main building have solid wood floors and artistic flourishes, and there are en-suite *rondavels* in the yard. Or choose between a 25-bed safari tent (R100 per person) and the contemporary-design dormitory with a massive Ikea-style kitchen. Lunch and dinner only served for groups.

Chrislin African Lodge LODGE $$
(☑042-233 0022; www.chrislin.co.za; s/d incl breakfast R780/900; 🐾) Within easy driving distance of Addo Park, this family-run lodge has a handful of traditionally designed and very comfortable *rondavels* set out on a wide lawn adjacent to a working citrus farm. A dip in the pool and night-time braai offer a welcome change of pace after a long day of wildlife drives. A three-course dinner, featuring organically grown vegetables, can be provided for R135 per person.

Orange Elephant Backpackers BACKPACKERS $
(☑042-233 0023; www.addobackpackers.com; dm/d without bathroom R120/250; 🛜) Appealing, though somewhat ramshackle, Orange Elephant is on a 500-tree citrus farm not far from Aardvark Guesthouse and Addo village. The so-so, private rooms are carpeted and groups can bunk in a 10-person *rondavel*. The restaurant does pizza and there's plenty of space to lounge around. Provides pick-ups from Port Elizabeth (return R200) and runs half-day Addo tours for R550.

Addo Rest Camp CAMPGROUND $$
(☑in Pretoria 012-428 9111; www.sanparks.org; campsites/safari tent R175/450, forest cabin without bathroom R590, 4-person chalet R690) Addo's main campsite at the main park headquarters is a great value spot with various accommodation options, some of which overlooks a waterhole where elephants come to slake their thirst.

Avoca River Cabins GUESTHOUSE $
(☑042-234 0421; www.gardenroute.co.za/addo/avoca; r from R400) A tranquil haven 15km south of the park entrance on in the direction of Kirkwood. Choose from a tree-house lodge, mud huts made out of cow dung, chalets directly on the Sundays River or a two-bedroom flat in a castlelike annex.

Lenmore SOUTH AFRICAN $$
(cnr Addo & Zuurberg Rds; mains R45-100) Found 6km north of Addo, Lenmore is a pleasant restaurant specialising in steaks and game, to please local farmers. There's also a shop and a reptile and raptor park.

❶ Information

The 'village' of Addo is nothing more than a few shops, a petrol station and a bank with ATMs sharing a dusty car park on R335. The park headquarters is 7km to the north – there's a well-stocked **shop** (⊙8am-7pm) here with food and curios.

The park's dirt roads can become impassable, so the park is closed if there has been heavy rain – if in doubt, call ahead on ☑042-233 8600.

Private Eastern Cape Wildlife Reserves

With over a million hectares of malaria-free wildlife-watching, the Eastern Cape's private reserves are a major attraction. Along with Addo Elephant National Park, they're often the end of the line for people travelling the Garden Route. All reserves organise wildlife-watching, and many have multi-day walking trails available. There's a significant cluster located between Addo and Grahamstown, including Shamwari, Amakhala, Schotia, Kwantu, Lalibela, Pumba and Kariega. Most of the reserves are dedicated to restocking large tracts of reclaimed land with animals that were common in the region before the advent of the farmers and big-wildlife hunters.

There is a handful of private lodges, varying in terms of comforts and price – from over-the-top honeymoon-level luxury to more-modest tent camps – within each of the reserves. Rates are all inclusive and many are discounted May to September.

Most of the reserves can be reached by travelling along the N2 out of Port Elizabeth towards Grahamstown.

Undoubtedly the most high-powered and internationally renowned of the Eastern Cape's wildlife reserves, **Shamwari Game Reserve** (⌘042-203 1111; www.shamwari.com; d all inclusive May-Sep R7000, Oct-Apr R11,000; ❋@✉), 30km east of Addo, has all of the Big Five (elephant, rhino, lion, leopard and buffalo). The **volunteer program** (www .worldwideexperience.com) involves hands-on conservation work.

Four farming families, descendants of the 1820 Settlers, combined their properties to create **Amakhala Game Reserve** (www.amakhala.co.za), 18,000 hectares of stunning rolling hills, bushveld and savannah. Meaning 'place of many aloes', Amakhala, only 70km from PE and southeast of Addo, has the Big Five; the lions are in a separate section of the reserve. As well as wildlife-watching drives, early-morning birdwatching boat cruises along the Bushman's River are offered. There are 11 different accommodation options including the five-star Bukela, Bush and Hlosi lodges. The Gush family runs highly recommended **Woodbury Tented Camp** (per person with full board R2080; ☎) and cliffside **Woodbury Lodge** (⌘046-636 2750; per person with full board R2300; ☎). The reserve also runs a community and conservation foundation.

Schotia Game Reserve (⌘042-235 1436; www.schotiasafaris.co.za), one of the longest-running operations, is a good option for those wanting to go on a wildlife drive but not stay overnight; try a late afternoon tour

that includes a bonfire and dinner in the outdoor *lapa* (South African English for a shelter without walls on all sides).

Grahamstown

POP 120,000

This town wears many hats. It's sometimes referred to as GOG (Good Old Grahamstown) or, more commonly, as the City of Saints because of its 40 or so religious buildings (primarily active and disused churches). Grahamstown is also the historical capital of Settler Country, and it's one of the liveliest university towns and host of more festivals than anywhere else in the country. The town's genteel conservatism and English-style prettiness belie a bloody history. The town centre has some fine examples of Victorian and early Edwardian building styles, with beautiful pastel shop fronts.

The British weren't the only people to settle in the Grahamstown area. Visit the nearby townships for a glimpse into the culture of the Xhosa – once rulers of the region, they were defeated by British and Boer forces after a fierce struggle.

Socially, the students from Rhodes University, who are to be found packing out pubs and bars during term time, dominate the town. But, as established artists settle here and the population ages, a more sophisticated side of Grahamstown is developing.

◉ Sights & Activities

Grahamstown is rightly proud of its museums, four of which are administered by the **Albany Museum Group** (⌘046-622 4450; www.ru.ac.za/albanymuseum).

Observatory Museum   MUSEUM
(Bathurst St; adult/child R10/5; ◷9am-1pm & 2-5pm Mon-Fri, 9am-1pm Sat). In this old house you'll find rare Victorian memorabilia, the refurbished Meridian Room (which shows that Grahamstown is 14 minutes behind South African standard time because the latter is set in Durban!), and the truly wonderful camera obscura. Built in 1882 and the only one of its kind in the world outside the UK, this is a series of lenses that reflect a perfect panoramic image of the town onto a flat, white disc hidden in a tower in the roof. It was built as a communication tool – people climbing up to the roof could see, for example, where the doctor was.

Grahamstown

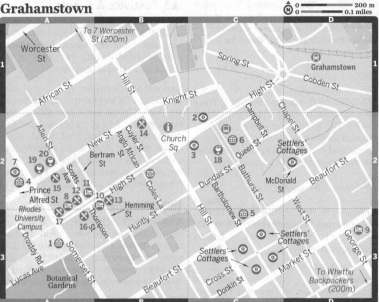

Grahamstown

⊙ Sights

Albany History Museum	(see 1)
1 Albany Natural Science Museum	A3
2 Birch's Gentlemen's Outfitters	C2
3 Grocott's Mail	C2
4 International Library of African Music	A2
5 National English Literary Museum	C3
6 Observatory Museum	C2
7 South African Institute for Aquatic Biodiversity	A2

🛏 Sleeping

8 137 High Street	A2
9 Cock House	D3

10 Evelyn House	B2
11 Graham Hotel	A2

🍴 Eating

12 Bella Vita	A2
13 Cafe Dulce	B2
Calabash	(see 11)
14 Gino's Italian Restaurant	B2
15 Haricot's Deli & Bistro	A2
16 Mad Hatters	A3
17 Maxwell's	A3

☕ Drinking

18 Copper Kettle	C2
19 Olde 65	A2
20 Rat & Parrot	A2

Albany History Museum   MUSEUM
(Somerset St; adult/child R10/5; ⊙9am-1pm & 2-5pm Mon-Fri, 9am-1pm Sat) Dedicated to detailing the history and art of the peoples of the Eastern Cape, including the Xhosa and the 1820 Settlers. The art exhibitions in its gallery change regularly.

Albany Natural Science Museum   MUSEUM
(Somerset St; adult/child R10/5; ⊙9am-1pm & 2-5pm Mon-Fri, 9am-1pm Sat) Exhibits depict

early human history, including some interesting artifacts and a traditional Xhosa hut.

FREE **International Library of African Music**   MUSEUM
(ILAM; ☎046-603 8557; www.ilam.ru.ac.za; Prince Alfred St, Rhodes University; ⊙8.30am-12.45pm & 2-5pm Mon-Fri) There are 200 or so instruments to examine – and you can listen to field recordings and then try to emulate

what you've heard on *nyanga* (pan) pipes from Mozambique, a *kora* (stringed instrument) from West Africa or a Ugandan *kalimba* (thumb piano). Call ahead for an appointment.

FREE **South African Institute for Aquatic Biodiversity** MUSEUM
(☏046-603 5800; www.jlbsmith.ru.ac.za; Prince Alfred St, Rhodes University; ⊙8am-1pm & 2-5pm Mon-Fri) The second coelacanth (a marine fish with limblike pectoral fins) ever caught is exhibited here; until 1938 this primitive fish was thought to have been extinct.

FREE **National English Literary Museum** MUSEUM
(87 Beaufort St; ⊙8.30am-1pm & 2-5pm Mon-Fri) The collection here contains the first editions of just about every work by famous South African writers.

Victorian & Edwardian Storefronts HISTORIC BUILDINGS
The best examples of preserved Victorian and Edwardian storefronts are **Grocott's Mail** (Church Sq), with its working newspaper office at the back of a charity store, and **Birch's Gentlemen's Outfitters** (Church Sq). The latter still has a marvellously old-fashioned 'slider' – a pulley system that sends money and change across the ceiling to and from the central till. Staff will demonstrate, if you ask them nicely.

FREE **1820 Settlers National Monument** MONUMENT
(Gunfire Hill; ⊙8am-4.30pm Mon-Thu, to 6pm Fri) Built to commemorate British settlers, this monument has stupendous views of the surrounding countryside, and contains a large theatre.

For a taste of local student life, head to the **Dam** (Grey St), on the way out of town to the south. It's a place to chill out and have a swim, and on Fridays there are drumming sessions.

The surrounding area offers many outdoor activities including excursions to the Fish River and Addo Elephant National Park or any of the other nearby private wildlife reserves, as well as skydiving with **EP Skydivers** (☏082 800 9263; www.epskydivers.co.za; R1400).

🎉 Festivals & Events

Makana Freedom Festival MUSIC
(☏082 932 1304) This late-April festival of song and dance is growing in popularity, with live bands playing in venues in the townships around Grahamstown.

National Arts Festival ARTS
(☏046-603 1103; www.nafest.co.za) The largest arts festival in the world after Edinburgh's, running for 10 days at the beginning of July. Remember two things: book ahead, as accommodation at this time can be booked out a year in advance; and nights can be freezing, so bring something warm. Its associated Fringe Festival has more than 200 events.

🛏 Sleeping

With more than 100 accommodation options in the area, we recommend checking in with **Makana Tourism** (☏046-622 3241; www.grahamstown.co.za) for a full list. It also organises overnight homestays in rooms of good standard in Grahamstown's townships.

7 Worcester Street GUESTHOUSE $$$
(☏046-622 2843; 7 Worcester St; s/d incl breakfast R1120/1790; ❄❅) This luxurious guesthouse is filled with artworks and sumptuous period furniture. The house was built in 1888 and once served as a student hostel – these days it provides accommodation to parents visiting their children at Grahamstown's private boarding schools. A three-course dinner is available for R160.

Cock House GUESTHOUSE $$
(☏046-636 1287; www.cockhouse.co.za; 10 Market St; s/d incl breakfast R535/950; 🕾) Named after William Cock, an enterprising 1820 Settler, and once home to author André Brink. Today it's a National Monument and a hugely popular guesthouse with old-fashioned furnishings in converted stables and a pretty garden. There are also two luxury, self-catering apartments. The **restaurant** (mains R65-85) is very highly regarded, a favourite of students when parents are treating.

137 High Street GUESTHOUSE $$
(☏046-622 3242; www.137highstreet.co.za; 137 High St; s/d incl breakfast R460/750; 🕾) Well situated within walking distance of museums and shops, this guesthouse in a charming Georgian cottage also has a restaurant that locals claim makes the best cappuccino in town. Rooms are tiny, but well appointed and comfortable.

Whethu Backpackers BACKPACKERS $
(☑083 982 5966; info@smileyfacetours.com; 6 George St; dm/d R120/400; 🛜) The owner of the now-defunct Old Gaol backpackers has relocated to a decidedly less penal-like setting, though this messily decorated and furnished converted suburban home does have small rooms. A tour company is also based here.

Evelyn House GUESTHOUSE $$
(☑046-622 2324; www.afritemba.com; 115A High St; s/d incl breakfast R680/940; ❄) An annexe of the Graham Hotel across the road, this is quieter and more upmarket, with a small pool of its own.

Graham Hotel HOTEL $$
(☑086 128 3737; www.afritemba.com; 123 High St; per person incl breakfast R430; ❄❄) This hotel, in a characterless building in the centre of town, has modern, standard rooms with TV.

Eating

Grahamstown's culinary scene is divided between pubs, cafes, fast-food joints catering to students on tight budgets, and swanky eateries for when the parents come to town.

Haricot's Deli & Bistro DELI, MEDITERRANEAN $$
(32 New St; mains R50-100; ☺9am-late; 🛜) Mingling the best qualities of a casual courtyard cafe with those of a refined bistro, Haricots is sure to please a range of discerning appetites. Fill up a picnic basket with made-to-order sandwiches, enormous scones, muffins and delicious lemon meringue pie or sit down to a lamb and apricot tagine paired with a glass of wine from one of the city's best lists.

Calabash SOUTH AFRICAN $$
(123 High St; mains R75) Traditional South African food, including specialties like Xhosa hotpots and *samp* (maize and beans) are served up in a warm, reed-ceilinged dining room. Vegetarian options and standard burger and pasta fare are on the menu as well.

Maxwell's SOUTH AFRICAN $$
(☑046-622 5119; 38 Somerset St; mains R85; ☺Tue-Sat) This is one of Grahamstown's best-regarded restaurants, taking its inspiration from hearty Eastern Cape food such as venison pie, kudu steak and ostrich carpaccio. Bookings are essential.

Bella Vita INTERNATIONAL $$
(131 High St; mains R65) This stylish cafe, housed in a handsome historical building, serves a huge variety of buffet dishes (R14 per 100g) as well as a small à la carte menu. There's live music on Saturday nights and an outdoor cocktail bar.

Gino's Italian Restaurant ITALIAN/PIZZERIA $
(8 New St; mains R30-60; ☺lunch & dinner) A local institution satisfying the student population's pizza craving for years; pasta and other Italian dishes are on the menu. The quirky entrance is on Hill St.

Mad Hatters SANDWICHES $
(118 High St; mains R45; ☺8am-5pm Mon-Fri, 9am-3pm Sat) Unassuming eatery with indoor and outdoor seating serving up basic burgers, sandwiches and salads.

Cafe Dulce ICE CREAM, INTERNATIONAL $
(High St; mains R45, ice cream R30) The place for ice cream; light meals are also served.

Drinking

Copper Kettle BAR
(7 Bathurst St; ☺7.30am-midnight Mon-Thu, 8am-2am Fri & Sat, 11am-midnight Sun) While many places come and go, Copper Kettle lives on. Largely operating as a bar, it also serves lunch (mains R50), and has live jazz on Sunday afternoons from 2pm.

Rat & Parrot BAR
(59 New St; ☺11am-late) A popular student haunt with decent pub grub (mains R55), loud music, big-screen TV (rugby matches are a staple) and a beer garden. It's closed on Sundays out of term time.

Olde 65 BAR
(65 New St; ☺11am-midnight Mon-Thu, to 2am Fri & Sat, to 10pm Sun) Attracts students interested in football (soccer) – that's what's shown on the TV here.

ℹ Information

Makana Tourism (☑046-622 3241; www.grahamstown.co.za; 63 High St; ☺8.30am-5pm Mon-Fri, 9am-1pm Sat) has lots of accommodation information available and sells Translux bus tickets. Offers free wi-fi and a computer with internet access.

ℹ Getting There & Away

Greyhound and Translux buses depart from the **terminus** (cnr High & Bathurst Sts) on their daily runs daily to Cape Town (R310, 13 hours), Port Elizabeth (R110, two hours) and Durban (R310, 12½ hours). **Mini-Lux** (☑in Amalinda 043-741 3107) runs to East London and Port Elizabeth

A(NOTHER) GREEN & PLEASANT LAND

In 1819, 90,000 applications were received by the British Government in reply to their offer of free land in South Africa. Most applicants were very poor and unemployed. Only 4000 were approved, and the following year the settlers (now referred to as the '1820 Settlers') arrived in Algoa Bay. Duped by their government into believing they were migrating to a peaceful land of plenty, they were, in fact, used as a buffer between the Boers on one side of the Great Fish River and the Xhosa on the other, who battled interminably over the cattle-rich country known as the Zuurveld.

Life on the frontier was harsh. Beset by war, inexperience, crop disease, hostile neighbours, floods and droughts, many of the families retreated to the towns, particularly Port Elizabeth, East London and Grahamstown. There they pursued the trades and businesses they had followed in England. Grahamstown, in particular, developed into a trading and manufacturing centre, where axes, knives and blankets were exchanged for ivory and skins. Tradespeople among the settlers produced metal implements, wagons and clothes. Port Elizabeth and Port Alfred initially developed to service Grahamstown, which had quickly become the second-largest city in the Cape Colony.

The settlers made a significant contribution to South African society. They insisted on a free press, which they'd enjoyed in England, and this was reluctantly granted in 1825. They also played an important part in establishing the Council of Advice in the same year, which advised the governor on matters of importance. Some who remained on the frontier became successful farmers and initiated wool farming, which became very lucrative.

from here. Check with the tourist office for prices and times.

You'll find minibus taxis on Raglan St, but most leave from Rhini township. Destinations include Fort Beaufort (R30, two hours), King William's Town (R42, three hours), Port Elizabeth (R40, 2½ hours) and East London (R60, four hours).

Bathurst

The small, quaint village of Bathurst lies on the road between Port Alfred and Grahamstown. It's a famous Eastern Cape drinking spot, particularly during the annual December Ox Braai, a huge party that takes place around New Year's Eve to raise money for charity. It's also known for Bathurst Agricultural Museum (☑079 987 9507; www.bathurst.co.za; adult/child R15/10; ☺9am-4pm Mon-Sat, 1-4pm Sun), which displays a large collection of tractors and other farm equipment as well as a working beehive.

Watersmeeting Nature Reserve (☑046-425 0876; admission per vehicle R10, plus per person R5; ☺7am-5pm), just outside town, protects the start of the Kowie River, where fresh and tidal waters meet. There's birdwatching in the forests here; canoes can be hired for a 21km paddle down to Port Alfred; and there's wildlife to watch out for – kudus, bushpigs and bushbucks – plus a nice view

of Horseshoe Bend in the river. The road down to the river, 4.5km from the intersection, is steep and shouldn't be attempted after rain.

Local farmers own the 16.7m-tall fibreglass Big Pineapple (Summerhill Farm, off R67; adult/child R10/5; ☺8.30am-4.30pm), a few kilometres south on the way to Port Alfred, where you can climb to the top for great views of the surrounding countryside; inside are displays covering the pineapple industry from A to Z. There are also tractor farm tours (adult/child R25/15) that include a pineapple tasting.

Just behind the Big Pineapple is Summerhill Inn (☑086 128 3737; www.afritemba. com; off R67; per person R275; ☎☎), with large comfortable rooms, lots of peacocks and views over the pineapple fields.

Built in 1832 and occupying the only intersection in the village is the very comfortable Pig 'n Whistle Hotel Restaurant & Pub (☑046-625 0673; www.pigandwhistle.co.za; r R225; ☎). The spacious rooms retain the original exposed timber joists, and bathrooms have porcelain tubs and rain-water showerheads. Grab pub grub inside or on one of the picnic tables outside. Pic-Kwick's Restaurant (mains R44) across the street has two dozen varieties of pizza.

On the R67, about 37km southeast of Grahamstown, Bathurst is best visited in your own vehicle, though minibus taxis ply the 15km from Port Alfred daily (R12).

Port Alfred

POP 32.500

Known as 'the Kowie' for the picturesque canal-like river that flows through its centre, Port Alfred is blessed with beautiful beaches, with some to the north backed by massive sand dunes. Upscale, contemporary vacation homes line the canal (à la Miami) and the hills surrounding town. It's quiet out of season except for Grahamstown students, but from mid-December to January it bustles with holidaymakers from elsewhere in South Africa. Because there's little budget accommodation it's not on the backpacker map.

◉ Sights & Activities

For surfers, there are good right- and left-hand breaks at the river mouth. There's an 8km walking trail through the Kowie Nature Reserve – maps are available from the tourist office – and a stroll along the pristine beaches is always an option.

Outdoor Focus   BOATING, DIVING

(☑046-624 4432; www.outdoorfocus.co.za; Beach Rd) A one-stop shop for diving and other outdoor activities. Diving is between May and August. Visibility is not outstanding (5m to 8m) but there are plenty of big fish, soft corals and raggy sharks. Also rents out canoes (R60 per two hours) and mountain bikes (R150 per day) and organises river and sea cruises. It can book the two-day Kowie Canoe Trail (per person R125), which is a fairly easy 21km canoe trip upriver from Port Alfred, with an overnight stay in a hut at Horseshoe Bend in the Watersmeeting Nature Reserve. Mattresses, water and wood are provided, but you'll need your own food and bedding.

Great Fish Point Lighthouse   HISTORIC BUILDING, VIEWPOINT

(adult/child R16/8; ⊙10am-noon & 12.30-3pm) Views from this lighthouse, 25km east of Port Alfred, encompass magnificent dunes and coastline. You can also stay in the comfortable lighthouse keepers' cottage (☑in Cape Town 021-780 9232; salato@npa.co.za; 3-bedroom, 2-bathroom cottage R800; ✴); reservations are required. The dirt road from the

highway turn-off is somewhat rough and probably shouldn't be attempted in a non-4WD after rain.

3 Sisters Horse Trails & Equestrian Centre   HORSE RIDING

(☑082 645 6345; www.threesistershorsetrail.co.za; R250) Offers horse rides of several hours on the beach, or overnight trips along a river valley. Located 15km from Port Alfred on R72 towards East London.

Let's Go Boat Cruises   CRUISE

(☑072 447 4801; adult/child R70/30) Two-hour cruises up the Kowie River.

Royal Port Alfred Golf Course   GOLF

(☑046-624 4796; www.rpagc.co.za; St Andrews Rd; 18-hole round R220) One of the four 'Royals' in South Africa.

🛏 Sleeping

Most places bump their rates up during the busier times of the year, which are December, January and over Easter.

BEACHFRONT & AROUND

Kelly's   APARTMENT $$

(☑082 657 0345; www.kellys.co.za; 56 West Beach Dr; ste R350) These self-catering apartments, ideally located directly across the street from Kelly's Beach, are one of the best values in town. Each is outfitted with a full kitchen, living room and spacious bedroom, as well as an outdoor deck. There's also a communal braai pit.

4 Carnoustie   GUESTHOUSE $$

(☑046-624 3306; www.4carnoustie.co.za; Carnoustie Av; s/d R500/800; ☎✺) This house, on a rise on a block between the edge of the golf course and the beach, could be featured in a glossy architectural magazine. There are chic and sunny rooms and a beautiful upstairs deck with Jacuzzi and magnificent sea views.

Villa de Mer   B&B $$

(☑046-624 2315; www.villademer.co.za; 22 West Beach Dr; s/d incl breakfast from R450/700; ✴☎✺) A large, bright, ultramodern four-star B&B right on the beachfront road, behind the dunes. Rooms are smart and have their own fridge, and the breakfasts are sumptuous.

Beach House   GUESTHOUSE $$$

(☑046-624 1920; www.thebeachouseportalfred.co.za; 80 West Beach Dr; s/d incl breakfast R880/1500; ✴☎✺) A lovely beachfront

Port Alfred

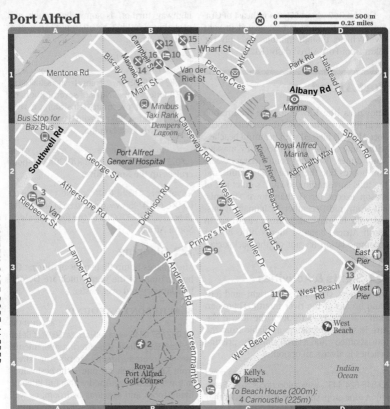

EASTERN CAPE PORT ALFRED

home with sleek and clean decor plus lush bedding.

Medolino Caravan Park   CAMPGROUND $
(☎046-624 1651; www.medolino.co.za; 23 Stewart St; campsites per person R120, 2- or 4-bedroom chalet R800; 🛜🐕) This highly recommended tranquil, shaded park has two-bedroom chalets that are heavily discounted outside the high season.

IN & AROUND TOWN

My Pond Hotel   HOTEL $$
(☎046-624 4626; www.mypondhotel.com; Van der Riet St; s/d incl breakfast R645/855; ❄🛜🐕) On the banks of the Kowie River, this sleek, new boutique-style hotel is operated and staffed by a hotel management school, so service is especially conscientious. **Lily** (mains R80), the hotel restaurant, serves new South African cuisine and has riverfront dining.

Links Coastal Inn   INN $$
(☎046-624 4533; www.linkscoastalinn.co.za; 14 Wesley Hill; s/d R370/585; @) This friendly inn has warm and well-decorated rooms and a self-catering cottage in a garden setting. The inn's highly recommended **restaurant** (mains R85) serves specialities like crayfish thermidor and ostrich filet.

Lookout   INN $$
(☎046-624 4564; www.thelookout.co.za; 24 Park Rd; s/d incl breakfast R445/740; 🛜🐕) Perched on a hill just east of the river and marina, this contemporary whitewashed home has three units with wonderful views.

Halyards Hotel   HOTEL $$
(☎046-604 3379; www.riverhotels.co.za; Royal Alfred Marina, Albany Rd; s/d incl breakfast R830/1200; ❄🛜🐕) This comfy riverfront hotel and spa with attractive Cape Cod–style architecture has large well-equipped rooms overlooking the harbour.

Port Alfred

First Stop Lodge LODGE $
(☑046-624 4917; www.firststop.co.za; Van Riebeck St; s/d R300/400) Dated but clean rooms amid a manicured lawn; on our visit, the hosts were somewhat somnolent.

Kowie Backpackers BACKPACKERS $
(☑046-624 3583; 13 Van Riebeck St; campsites per person R60, dm/d R100/250) Next door to First Stop, this institutional-looking place has the only dorm rooms in town.

✕ Eating & Drinking

TOP CHOICE **Zest Café** MEDITERRANEAN $
(Van der Riet St; mains R55; ☺8am-5pm Mon-Fri, to 3pm Sat) Friendly owners Liefie and Gaz have created a little Mediterranean refuge in their charming trellis-covered garden. Besides good ol' falafel and a variety of pizzas, try one of the more inventively prepared dishes like spicy seafood, red pepper and almond stew or couscous, hot chorizo, fava bean and tomato salad; tapas include pork filet, lentil curry and squid steak.

Wharf Street Brew Pub INTERNATIONAL $$
(☑046-624 5705; 18 Wharf St; mains R70) The handsome dining room of exposed stone and brick, wood floors and poster-sized photos overshadows an uninspiring menu

of dishes like chicken parm; dinner includes fish and a little more variety. The attached brewery offers tours (11am and 2.30pm Monday to Friday, 11am Saturday) – tour reservations required.

Barmuda SOUTH AFRICAN $$
(23 Van der Riet St; mains R70; ☺10am-late) Worth a visit for its lovely setting overlooking the river and for the adjoining beach volleyball court where you can burn off calories from its menu of slightly elevated pub food like schnitzel, steaks and calamari.

Ocean Basket SEAFOOD $$
(Van der Riet St; mains R65; ☺11.30am-10pm Mon-Sat, to 9pm Sun) South African seafood chain restaurant known for its large portions of seafood (line fish, calamari, prawns, crayfish) and sushi and sashimi platters.

Guido's Restaurant ITALIAN $$
(West Beach Dr; mains R42-120; ☺lunch & dinner) Guido's is a pizza-and-pasta restaurant on the beach and is popular with Grahamstown students during the week and families on weekends.

Lifestyle Café CAFE $
(38 Campbell St; mains R35; ☎) A laid-back place with indoor and outdoor seating, good burgers, shakes and coffee.

⊙ Information

Sunshine Coast Tourism Port Alfred (☑046-624 1235; www.sunshinecoasttourism.co.za; Causeway Rd; ☺8am-4.30pm Mon-Fri, 8.30am-noon Sat) On the western bank of the Kowie River. Has brochures detailing accommodation, walks and canoe trails. Shares its building with Avis.

Palms Video (Heritage Mall, Main St; per hr R36; ☺8am-10pm) Internet access.

⊙ Getting There & Away

Baz Bus stops at Beavers Restaurant (Southwell Rd) out near Rosehill Mall on its run from Port Elizabeth (two hours, R175) to Durban (about 13 hours, R1060) on Monday, Tuesday, Thursday, Friday and Sunday.

The **minibus taxi rank** (Biscay Rd) is outside the Heritage Mall. There are daily services to Port Elizabeth (R75), Grahamstown (R25) and East London (R75). Local daily services include Bathurst (R12).

Shipwreck Coast

As the graveyard for many errant ships, the coast between the Great Fish River and East London is deservedly known as the Shipwreck Coast. The 69km, six-day, five-night Shipwreck Hiking & Canoe Trail (per person R700) leads from Port Alfred to the Great Fish River Mouth and includes canoeing. You are rewarded with wild, unspoiled sections of surf beach, rich coastal vegetation and beautiful estuaries. The trail can be booked through Dave Marais (☎082 391 0647; www.shipwreckhiking.co.za). A four-night, five-day trip (R560 per person) excluding canoeing, and an overnight canoe trail on the Kleinemonde West River (R150 per person), are also options.

AMATHOLE REGION

The stretch of coast and hinterland known as Amathole (pronounced 'ama-*tawl*-eh', from the Xhosa for 'calves') extends from the Great Fish River to the Great Kei River on the so-called Shipwreck Coast, and inland as far as Queenstown. It includes the enchanting mountain village of Hogsback, the surf-side city of East London and little-visited and wild nature reserves. A good part of this area was the former Xhosa homeland of Ciskei.

There is much large wildlife – including black rhinos, hippos, kudus and buffaloes – to be seen in Great Fish River Reserve (☎043-742 4450; www.ecparks.co.za; adult/child R20/10; ◷8am-5pm), a park of thick bushveld. Sandwiched between the Great Fish and Keiskamma Rivers near Fort Beaufort, it has rugged terrain and panoramic views and a

good selection of lodges for overnight accommodation (☎043-701 9600; from R385).

East London

POP 980,000

Population-wise, geographically and economically, this industrial and manufacturing centre (and the country's only river port) is an important Eastern Cape city. However, despite East London's bay-front location that curves round to huge sand hills, there's little reason to spend much time here when more appealing destinations nearby beckon. The city, whose Khoe-San name means 'Place of Buffaloes' is a transport hub because of its airport and location central to the Sunshine and Wild Coasts. Much of the downtown is dilapidated, dotted with falling-to-pieces Victorian buildings and downright ugly 1960s and '70s monstrosities. Wealthy neighbourhoods with sizeable homes and neatly clipped lawns and gardens extend north of Eastern Beach.

◉ Sights & Activities

The best surfing is at Nahoon Reef at the southern end of Nahoon Beach.

East London Museum   MUSEUM
(☎043-743 0686; www.elmuseum.za.org; 319 Oxford St; adult/child R12/5; ◷9.30am-4.30pm Mon-Fri) One of the first coelacanths, a type of fish thought to have become extinct over 50 million years ago, was discovered nearby in 1938; the stuffed original is on display here. Other exhibits at the museum include trace-fossil human footprints and a living beehive. Coelacanth Café (light meals R20-50; ◷9.30am-3pm) at the museum doesn't serve fish.

AMATHOLE TRAIL

The 121km six-day Amathole Trail (per person per night R135) begins at the Maden Dam, 23km north of King William's Town, and ends at the Tyumie River near Hogsback. Accommodation is in huts.

It ranks as one of South Africa's top mountain walks, but it's pretty tough and should be attempted only if you are reasonably experienced and fit. Walkers are rewarded with great views, although about a third of the walk goes through dense forest and numerous streams with waterfalls and swimming holes. Shorter sections of the hike are available outside school holidays. Guides can be arranged. The trail can be booked with the Department of Water Affairs & Forestry (☎ in King William's Town 043-642 2571; ama-tolhk@dwaf.gov.za; 2 Hargreaves Ave, King William's Town) or through the Hogsback Information Centre (see p213).

FREE Ann Bryant Art Gallery   MUSEUM
(☏043-722 4044; St Marks Rd; ⊙9am-5pm Mon-Fri, to noon Sat) South of the museum is an old mansion featuring an eclectic collection of paintings and sculptures, mostly by South African artists. There's also a small coffee shop.

👉 Tours

Imonti Tours   CULTURAL TOURS
(☏083 487 8975; www.imontitours.co.za) Owner Velile Ndlumbini runs a variety of tours in the area including to Mdantsane (half-day R250), the second largest township in the country after Soweto; a trip to typical Xhosa villages; and tours to Qunu, an inland town on the Wild Coast, where Nelson Mandela spent his childhood. Importantly, Velile also does transfers from the airport to East London and to accommodation in Chintsa (R180 per person).

🛏 Sleeping

There isn't much reason to overnight in East London when a range of more appealing accommodation is available in nearby Chintsa. If stuck for the night you're probably better off opting for one of B&Bs in the suburbs, only a few kilometres north of Eastern Beach.

CITY CENTRE

Hampton Court Guest Lodge   HOTEL $$
(☏043-722 7924; www.hampton-court.co.za; 2 Marine Terrace; s/d incl breakfast R650/850; ✳🛜) This renovated 1920s landmark building with a waterfront location and contemporary furnishings is a good choice for the centre. Sea-facing rooms, while more expensive, have panoramic views.

Majestic Boutique Hotel   HOTEL $$
(☏043-743 7477; www.majestic-hotel.co.za; 21 Orient Rd; s/d R390/560; 🛜) While the rooms could use a makeover, this is a clean and secure place that is only a short walk to the Esplanade; there is an attached pub and restaurant.

Niki Nana Backpackers   BACKPACKERS $
(☏043-722 8509; www.nikinana.co.za; 4 Hillview Rd; campsites R65, dm/d without bathroom R110/300; @✳) Easily recognisable by its striking zebra-striped frontage, Niki Nana has a garden, swimming pool and braai area; however, beds are old and the mattresses uncomfortably soft.

Sugarshack Backpackers   BACKPACKERS $
(☏043-722 8240; www.sugarshack.co.za; Eastern Esplanade; campsites R50, dm/d without bathroom R80/190; @🛜) The upside is the same as the downside: you're just steps from the beach. Sugarshack is not the place for quiet (or a feeling of security if you have a car, since there's no car park). It's a faux log-cabin complex with small dorms and mini cabins – all have seen better days.

Premier Hotel Regent   HOTEL $$
(☏043-709 5000; www.premierhotels.co.za; 22 Esplanade; d R1100; ✳@🛜) Beachfront behemoth convention centre–style hotel. Ask for a room with a sea view.

NORTHERN SUBURBS

White House   GUESTHOUSE $$
(☏043-740 0344; www.thewhitehousebandb.co.za; 10 Whitthaus St, Gonubie; s/d incl breakfast R495/595; ✳🛜✳) Somewhat grand and slightly institutional-looking, almost like an embassy, the aptly named White House has glass windows for panoramic views of cliffs and sea – you can watch whales and dolphins passing by while having breakfast. A variety of rooms – some have chintzy decor or feel under-furnished.

John Bailie Guest Lodge   GUESTHOUSE $
(☏043-735 1058; www.johnbailieguestlodge.co.za; 9 John Bailie Rd, Bunkers Hill; d from R350; ✳🛜✳) Feel at home at this family-run guesthouse, near the golf course and on the way to Nahoon. There are a half-dozen carpeted rooms with TVs; a few north-facing ones have sliding glass doors and get natural light. Breakfast is an option and there's a nice garden pool area.

Quarry Lake Inn   INN $$
(☏043-707 5400; www.quarrylakeinn.co.za; Quartzite Dr, Selbourne; s/d incl breakfast R860/1200; ✳@🛜✳) Built next to a tranquil artificial lake north of the city centre, Quarry Lake is a comfortable if fairly bland development. The carpeted rooms are clean and spacious and there's a restaurant and outdoor deck and patio that's good for coffee and tea and the sound of birdcalls.

See More Guest House   GUESTHOUSE $$
(☏043-735 1070; 14 Montrose Av, Bunkers Hill; s/d incl breakfast R480/680; ✳🛜✳) A well-appointed home with a tropical garden and pool patio.

East London

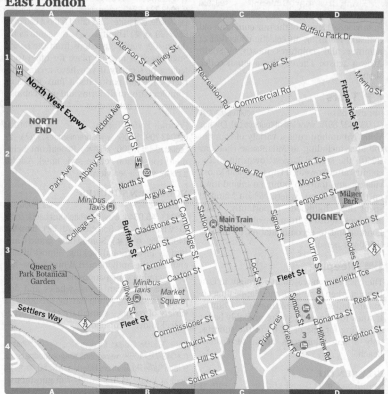

🍴 Eating & Drinking

Conveniently, the small complex with the main-line bus company offices and terminals (at the corner of Moore St and Marine Terrace) includes two informal restaurants – **Windmill Roadhouse** (mains R28), where burgers and sandwiches are delivered to your car or outdoor picnic tables, and **Windmill Pizza** (mains R40), part of a convenience store – as well as Café Neo.

Café Neo　　　　MEDITERRANEAN $$
(Windmill Roadhouse; mains R65; 📶) Views from the outdoor balcony of this stylish eatery on the 2nd floor of the Windmill complex extend from the car park to the ocean. The large menu covers the gamut from healthy light wraps and grilled line fish to steaks and decadent desserts. The bar stays open late.

Grazia Fine Food & Wine　　MEDITERRANEAN $$
(☎043-722 2209; Upper Esplanade; mains R90; ⏰noon-10.30pm) This stylish centrally located restaurant has large windows with sea views as well as an outdoor deck for dining. The Italian-born owner has helped create a sophisticated menu with a variety of European influences and includes pasta, pizza, meat and seafood. Reservations recommended.

Buccaneers Pub & Grill　　　GRILL, BAR $$
(Eastern Esplanade; mains R60-80; ⏰lunch & dinner) Overlooking the action on Eastern Beach and next to Sugarshack Backpackers, this is a lively, sometimes raucous spot; it serves steaks, burgers and pizzas to soak up the alcohol.

Le Petit Restaurant　　FRENCH, SOUTH AFRICAN $$
(54 Beach Rd, Nahoon; mains R89-150; ⏰closed Sun) Head north for fine, albeit old-fashioned, South African dining with Swiss influences; try the crocodile fritters (R59) or buffalo steak (R148).

East London

Sleeping

1 Premier Hotel Regent	E3
2 Hampton Court Guest Lodge	E2
3 Majestic Boutique Hotel	D4
4 Niki Nana Backpackers	D4
5 Sugarshack Backpackers	F1

Eating

6 Buccaneers Pub & Grill	F1
Café Nero	(see 9)
7 Grazia Fine Food & Wine	E2
8 Imbizo Café	D3
Windmill Pizza	(see 9)
9 Windmill Roadhouse	E2

Baz Bus stops at backpackers in East London on its runs between Port Elizabeth and Durban.

Minibus Taxi

On the corner of Buffalo and College Sts are long-distance minibus taxis to destinations north of East London. Nearby, on the corner of Caxton and Gillwell Sts, are minibus taxis for King William's Town, Bhisho and the local area. The following are sample fares: King William's Town (R18, one hour), Butterworth (R40, three hours), Mthatha (R70, five hours), Port Elizabeth (R100, six hours), Jo'burg (R250, 15 hours) and Cape Town (R350, 18 hours).

Train

Shosholoza Meyl runs a tourist-class (with sleepers) train from Jo'burg to East London on Friday, and East London to Jo'burg on Sunday (20 hours) via Bloemfontein. On this route, there is also the only economy-class train (seats R190) in South Africa with sleeping compartments, departing daily except Saturday. An economy-class train runs from Cape Town to East London on Sunday (28 hours) and returns to Cape Town on Tuesday.

Imbizo Café SOUTH AFRICAN $
(22 Currie St; mains R50; ⊙7am-9pm) Mozambican and South African cuisine served up in a building meant to resemble a castle; live jazz Friday and Saturday nights.

❶ Getting There & Away

Air

The airport is 10km from the centre. **SAA** (☑043-706 0247) and **1time** (☑043-706 0345; www.1time.com.za) fly from East London daily to Jo'burg (R1250, 1½ hours) and Cape Town (R1100, 1½ hours); SAA also flies to Durban (R1200, one hour) and Port Elizabeth (R1100, 50 minutes).

Bus

Translux, City to City, Greyhound and Intercape all conveniently stop at the **Windmill Park Roadhouse** (cnr Moore St & Marine Tce). Connections are available to Mthatha (R150, 2½ hours), Port Elizabeth (R140, three to four hours), Durban (R265, nine to 10 hours), Cape Town (R360, 17 to 19 hours) and Jo'burg/Pretoria (R330, 14 hours).

Chintsa

POP 2000

Though only 38km to the north of East London off the N2, Chintsa feels worlds away. It comprises two small villages – Chintsa East and Chintsa West, on either side of the Chintsa River – fronted by a spectacular white-sand beach with good, swimmable surf. It's a great place to hang out for a few days (or weeks) on this part of the coast.

Also in the area is the private, upmarket Inkwenkwezi Game Reserve (☑043-734 3234; www.inkwenkwezi.com; tented bush camp deluxe/luxury per person incl meals & activities

R1800/2300), which features each of the Big Five (although the elephants are, for now, kept in their own separate section). In addition to wildlife-watching drives (R495 per person) and elephant walks (R250 per person), the reserve offers guided mountain biking, quad-biking, horse riding and canoeing. Inkwenkwezi has volunteer programs and is heavily involved in local community projects such as housing and education, as well as environmental conservation. The reserve hosted the wedding of President Jacob Zuma's daughter Duduzile in 2011.

Mama Tofu (☑073 148 7511), reputedly the oldest tour guide in South Africa, explains Xhosa cultures and customs in her home in Ngxingxolo village. Buccaneers Lodge arranges these tours (R195 per person) and also has a surf school (R185 per person). It also offers horse riding (R295 per person), and visits to schools partly supported by Bucks' associated foundation.

🛏 Sleeping

Chintsa offers excellent accommodation for a wide range of budgets; it makes much more sense to travel directly here rather than overnighting in East London.

TOP CHOICE Buccaneers Lodge & Backpackers
BACKPACKERS $

(☑043-734 3012; www.cintsa.com; Chintsa West; campsites/dm/d R55/110/395; @⛵) Something of a rarity, 'Bucks' is a sort of all-inclusive holiday resort for backpackers. Sleeping options include comfortable dorms, contemporary rooms and safari tents with porches, and en-suite cottages (R750 for four people) with private sundecks. There's free use of canoes and surfboards, and daily afternoon offerings include beach volleyball with complimentary wine – and there's a 'spa bungalow' with a range of treatments. Meals are served, family-style, in the charming candlelit dining room and outdoor deck. To get to Bucs, follow the Chintsa West turn-off for about 200m until you reach the entrance; it's a further 2km along the dirt road.

Prana Lodge
RESORT $$$

(☑043-704 5100; www.pranalodge.co.za; Chintsa Dr, Chintsa East; ste incl breakfast from R2400; ✳@🛜⛵) Combining old-world European sophistication and a Southeast Asian resort's mix of decadence and tranquillity, Prana is absolutely ideal for those seeking top-flight pampering. Seven suites, each with its own private plunge pool and enclosed garden courtyard, come with king-sized beds and voluminous outdoor showers. The property is hidden in a dune forest a short walk to the beach and includes an open-air dining area and bar, library and luxurious spa facilities.

Areena Riverside Resort
RESORT $$

(☑043-734 3055; www.areenaresort.com; campsites R135, r from R355, cottages R650; 🛜⛵) Hugging the tree-shaded shore of the Kwelera River, this unique property has everything from thatched-roof *rondavels* and log-cabin chalets to riverside tent and caravan camping – and a wildlife reserve, to say nothing of a wandering semidomesticated giraffe named Abby. Facilities include a tennis court and full-service restaurant, and there are quad-bike wildlife drives, abseiling, ziplines and river cruises.

Crawford's Beach Lodge
RESORT $$

(☑043-738 5000; www.crawfordsbeachlodge.co.za; 42 Steenbras Dr, Chintsa East; s/d incl breakfast & dinner R550/990; ✳@🛜⛵) A sprawling complex of attractively designed Cape Cod–style white clapboard buildings with stylishly appointed rooms. There's an appealing restaurant, pool, tennis courts and easy beach access.

🍴 Eating

All of the accommodation listed in the previous section has recommended restaurants that are open to nonguests. Inkwenkwezi's restaurant has a Wednesday night burger special – the patties are massive.

Michaela's
SOUTH AFRICAN $$

(☑043-738 5139; Steenbras Dr, Chintsa East; meals R75-120; ⏱lunch & dinner) Reached via a steep wooden staircase from the car park of Crawford's (or on an air-conditioned funicular), this restaurant has a formal upstairs and a casual brasserie downstairs. The kitchen does fusion-style food with South African ingredients, steaks and seafood like black mussel pot. Book early for Sunday lunches. Michaela's is under new ownership (it has the same owners as Barefoot Café).

Barefoot Café
BURGERS, SOUTH AFRICAN $$

(Chintsa East; mains R60; 🛜) What nightlife there is in Chintsa centers on this casual bar and restaurant where foreign volunteers, young backpackers and locals mix; food is no afterthought and the menu features creative burger combinations.

❶ Getting There & Away

To reach Chintsa from East London, take Exit 26 (East Coast Resorts) off the N2. Go over the overpass and follow the road for 1km to the Chintsa East turn-off. The Chintsa West turn-off is another 16km further on.

Morgan's Bay & Kei Mouth

POP 2200

North along the coast from Chintsa, and reached by turning off the N2 onto the R349, is the village of Morgan's Bay. It's a good place for some peace and quiet and for beachcombing and surfing. Prices skyrocket and places get booked solid between mid-December and mid-January.

Just after Morgan's Bay is the somewhat ramshackle Kei Mouth (www.keimouth.co.za), the last resort before the beginning of the Wild Coast. It's reached by taking the pont (vehicle ferry; per car R60; ⊙7am-5.30pm) across the Great Kei River.

Light and airy Morgan Bay Hotel (☑043-841 1062; www.morganbay.co.za; Beach Rd, Morgan Bay; r with half board R555; @⊕⊛⊠) is perched directly over the beachfront and has an attached bar and restaurant with a menu of pub grub and seafood and great outside deck seating.

Yellowwood Forest (☑043-841 1598; www .yellowwoodforest.co.za; campsites R165, loft R195; ⊛), about 1km from Morgan's Bay beach, is a tranquil campsite surrounded by indigenous forest and frequented by birds and monkeys. There's a charming tea garden, craft shop and wood-fired pizzas on offer.

Strandloper & Sundowner Trails

The 57km, four-day three-night Strandloper Trail (☑bookings 043-841 1046; www.strandloper trails.org.za; per person R500, conservation fee R60) runs between Kei Mouth and Gonubie, just outside East London. The hiking trail is fairly easy, but good fitness is required. Profits are channelled into environmental education for local children. The Strandlopers (meaning 'Beach Walkers') were a Khoe-San tribe who lived on the coast but disappeared as a distinct group after white settlement. There are three overnight huts and the cost of staying in these is included in the booking fee. Camping on the beach is prohibited, but most of the coastal hotels have campsites.

A newly developed option for those looking to end their vigorous days of hiking with a little luxury is the five-day, four-night Sundowner Trail (☑043-841 1046; www. strandlopertrails.org.za; per person R4000) from Trennery's Hotel to Chintsa East (the first night is spent at Crawford's in Chintsa East before being transferred to Trennery's to begin the hike). All meals and transfers are included.

Hogsback

POP 1500 / ELEV 1238M

There's something about Hogsback that inspires people. An Edenic little village 1300m up in the beautiful Amathole Mountains above Alice, the village's name is derived from the 'bristles' (known geologically as a 'hogsback') that cover peaks of the surrounding hills – but the name doesn't evoke the tranquillity the village is famous for. Locals will tell you that JRR Tolkien, who lived his early years in Bloemfontein and spent childhood holidays here, was influenced by Hogsback. For years now, artists, alternative therapists and other like-minded folk, as well as politicians and celebrities, have helped create an environmentally inclined community, an easy sensibility to adopt with fabulous views of mountains and forested valleys right out your door. The town's climate and history of green-fingered English people who settled here mean it's blessed with gorgeous (though seasonal) market garden estates.

The highest of the three hogs peaks in the distance is 1937m. The steepest slopes around Hogsback are still covered in beautiful rainforest: yellowwood, assegai and tree fuchsia can be found. There are also, sadly, extensive pine plantations on land that was once indigenous forest.

The weather is unpredictable and rainy, and misty days can occur any time of year. Winter (June to August) sees occasional snowfall, though it's generally dry with night-time temperatures dropping as low as -2°C. Spring (September to November) brings stunning sunshine and blooming flowers while summer (December to February) days can be extremely warm and sunny with occasional short but heavy thunderstorms. Trees change colour in autumn (March to May).

◉ Sights & Activities

There are some great walks, bike rides and drives in the area through indigenous forests and pine plantations. The tourist office has a map. A recommended hike leaves from behind the Away with the Fairies backpackers and takes in a massive 800-year-old yellowwood tree, Swallow Tail Falls, Bridal Veil Falls and the Madonna & Child Falls before ending at Wolfbridge Rd, which takes you back to the village.

Ecoshrine
GARDEN

(www.ecologyshrine.co.za; 22 Summerton Dr; adult/child R20/free; ⊙9am-4pm Wed, Fri, Sat & Sun) Well-known mixed-media artist Diana Graham, a passionate environmental advocate, has created a cement sculpture garden dedicated to the forces of nature. The images, about which Graham will explain, reflect both the mysterious and scientific limits of our understanding. The property has beautiful views (when the haze in the valley has cleared off) and is south of the village centre near the Edge.

Garden Club
GARDEN

(☑045-962 1228; admission varies; ⊙by appointment) Flower-lovers should definitely contact this club – its aim is to turn Hogsback into a 'botanical paradise'. More than a dozen gardens with short walks can be visited by prior arrangement. The town hosts a Spring Festival, held in late September.

Starways Art Centre
GALLERY

(☑045-962 1174; www.starways.org; ⊙10am-5pm) Award-winning potter Anton van der Merwe operates from this place out near Terra Khaya, southwest of the village. Performances are held in the theatre periodically.

Fairy Realm
GARDEN

(☑045-962 1098; Camelot, 5 Main Rd; adult/child R20/10; ⊙9.30am-4.30pm) Small children will love seeking out the elves and fairies on this easy garden walk; there's a tea shop, too.

🛏 Sleeping

While there are lots of signposts on the way into the village, there are only a few genuinely worthy, well-established places to stay, as listed below.

TOP CHOICE Away with the Fairies
BACKPACKERS $

(☑045-962 1031; www.awaywiththefairies.co.za; Hydrangea Lane; campsites/dm R70/120, r from R290; @�🠒🠒) Location isn't everything – but it's just one of the distinguishing features of this delightful backpackers. Terrific views abound: take an alfresco bath in the cliff-side tub or climb to the top of the 15m platform that's perched in the forest among parrots, monkeys and baboons. Or simply gaze out of your room window; interiors are painted with fantastical designs featuring nubile fairies. Horse riding (1½-hour trails R175) and a guided 16km mountain biking trip (R250) taking in eight waterfalls are offered. The Wizard's Sleeve Inn (mains R50), which doubles as reception, is the spot to down a few beers in the evenings, order a made-to-order pizza or sandwich and trade travel tales around a log fire. Regular shuttles to East London (R125) and Chintsa (R150) are available, with reservations.

🌿 Terra Khaya
BACKPACKERS $

(☑082 897 7503; www.hogsbackecobackpackers.com; campsites per person incl breakfast R60, dm/d incl breakfast R110/265) Get way off the grid at this one-of-a-kind mountainside farm retreat. The DIY aesthetic and philosophy of the owner (bareback-riding Shane) is suffused throughout: everything is made from recyclable materials; there are no electrical plug-in points; showers are heated by wood fire; and toilets are outside. This is a wonderfully tranquil place that is difficult to leave. A range of horse-riding trails is offered (R250 per person), including overnight trips. Plaatjieskraal Rd, the turn-off for Terra Khaya, is several kilometres northwest of the village on the main road; from here it's another few kilometres south.

Edge Mountain Retreat
LODGE $$

(☑082 603 5246; www.theedge-hogsback.co.za; Bluff End; self-catering cottage from R495; @🠒) This collection of tastefully decorated cottages and garden rooms is strung out along a mountain edge that once marked the border between Ciskei and South Africa proper. The cottages all have one big bedroom (there's one twin and one family unit) with a log fire and TV, plus separate bathroom and kitchen. The vibe here is peace, quiet and relaxation. It's an unbeatable place for a healthy rest – or a romantic weekend. The restaurant is highly recommended.

Arminel Hotel
HOTEL $$

(☑045-962 1005; www.arminelhogsback.co.za; Main Rd; s/d with half board R620/1100; ✱) Possibly Hogsback's largest development, this is a lovely landscaped property with thatched-roof buildings and shady courtyards and outdoor areas. A range of accommodation is offered, including cottages and *rondavels*; rooms in the main building are carpeted and the bathrooms have attractive stone floors. The inclusion of a four-course, country-fare dinner in the room rate makes it a good deal.

Granny Mouse House GUESTHOUSE $$
(☏045-962 1059; www.grannymousehouse.co.za; 1 Nutwoods Dr; r from R450; ☒) This is a charming guesthouse with rooms in an old wattle-and-daub house, plus a self-catering cottage in the garden. Breakfast and dinner, prepared with care and organic ingredients, are recommended. The very friendly owner speaks German.

Maylodge Cottages BUNGALOW $
(☏045-962 1016; www.maylodge.co.za; r from R260) Several thatch-roofed cottages set in a shady lawn and fruit orchard, with a koi pond as centerpiece.

Hogsback Inn INN $
(☏045-962 1006; www.hogsbackinn.co.za; per person incl breakfast R385; ☒) An 1880s country home with updated contemporary rooms and an old-fashioned English tavern.

🍴 Eating

Most of the accommodation have restaurants or can provide meals with advance notice.

Tea Thyme INTERNATIONAL $
(The Edge; mains R55; ⏲7.30am-8pm) A perfectly charming garden restaurant serving hogsback trout for breakfast, ciabatta roll sandwiches, burgers and freshly baked cakes. Throw in homemade bread, fresh, organic local produce and a cosy dining room for cool days and nights, and a meal here is a delight.

Butterfly's Bistro SANDWICHES, VEGETARIAN $
(Main Rd; mains R55; ⏲9am-8pm Mon & Wed-Sun) This popular restaurant and deli, in a quaint, A-frame house next to the tourist office, specialises in vegie dishes as well as more than a dozen types of pizza.

ℹ️ Information

There's an ATM in the small supermarket, just off the main road. Food and other supplies available here.

Hogsback Information Centre (☏082 554 5337; www.hogsbackinfo.co.za; Main Rd; ⏲10am-4pm Mon-Sat, 9am-3pm Sun) can provide accommodation help and maps for walks. Next to Butterfly's Bistro.

ℹ️ Getting There & Away

The way up to Hogsback on the R345 (the turn-off is 4km south of Alice) is tarred, but try to arrive in daylight. Itinerant livestock and a general lack of street lighting in the village make finding accommodation difficult in the dark. Definitely do not take the back road via Seymour; the road to Cathcart, a shortcut to the Eastern Highlands, is gravel and dirt and in good condition except after rains. The easiest way to get to Hogsback without a car is by shuttle bus from East London (two hours, R125 one way, daily) and from Buccaneers Lodge & Backpackers in Chintsa West (2½ hours, R150 one way) to Away with the Fairies.

THE WILD COAST

This shoreline rivals any in the country in terms of beauty, stretching for 350km from just east of Chintsa to Port Edward. Often referred to as the 'Transkei' (the name of the apartheid-era homeland the area once covered), the 'Wild Coast' is increasingly used to include inland areas as well: the pastoral landscapes where clusters of *rondavels* are scattered over rolling hills covered in short grass. Whatever the name for the region, the Xhosa people are some of the friendliest you'll meet anywhere in South Africa, and chances are you'll be invited inside a home or, at the very least, a shebeen. South of the Mbashe River live the Gcaleka tribe; Mpondomise live to the north. There are some absolutely amazing overnight hiking trails, far-flung river estuaries and backpackers that resemble Xhosa settlements. Birdlife, including fish eagles, egrets, cormorants and kingfishers, is abundant, especially in the parks, though, surprisingly, fishing – shad, kob, musselcrackers, crayfish, oysters and sardines – is mostly subsistence level.

👣 Tours

Even if guided tours aren't your usual style, the following outfits can help immeasurably with your understanding of the rich and complex culture of the Xhosa and Mpondo peoples who live on the Wild Coast. Check out www.wildcoastbookings.com to make accommodation bookings all along the coast.

African Heartland Journeys ADVENTURE TOURS, CULTURAL TOURS
(☏in Chintsa 043-738 5523; www.ahj.co.za; Chintsa East) A well-regarded tour company with the same ownership as Buccaneer's Lodge in

The Wild Coast

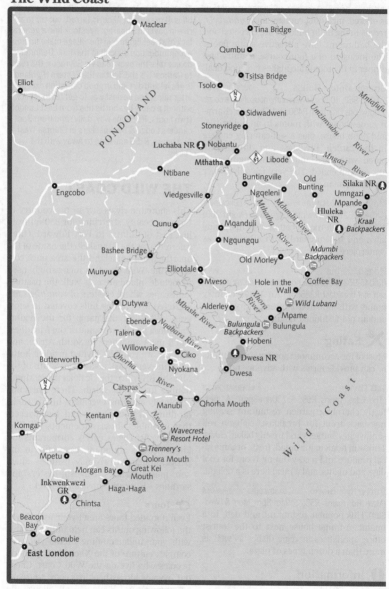

Chintsa West. Small-group adventure tours encompass travel by 4WD, canoe, horse or mountain bike. Tents and camping equipment are provided. It also has a surf school and is affiliated with a volunteer program called Volunteer Africa 32 South (see p587).

Wild Coast Holiday Reservations

WALKING TOURS

(☎in East London 043-743-6181; www.wildcoast holidays.co.za) Organises seven different trails along the length of the coast, some only for the fit, and others more gentle with

Great Kei River to Coffee Bay

One of the most remote and beautiful reserves in South Africa, **Dwesa Nature Reserve** (☑bookings 047-499 7900; www.ecparks.co.za; adult/child R20/10; ⊘6am-6pm) is bounded by the Nqabara River in the south and extending over the Mbashe River in the north. You may see rhinos come down to the beach. Other species present include zebras, leopards and buffaloes, and crocodiles have been reintroduced to the rivers. Some 290 species of birds have been identified. On the Mbashe is a small cluster of white mangroves where crabs and mudskippers live among the roots. On offer is a guided wildlife drive (R45 per person) and there's a number of hiking trails. **Self-catering accommodation** (1-/2-bedroom chalet R300/600) and **camping** (campsites R220) are available.

The only way to get to Dwesa is via Haven Hotel (p210) in your own vehicle; go to Willowvale and turn off at the large blue Emsengeni store towards the Kob Inn. Dwesa is signposted from this road.

🛏 Sleeping

Most places, other than Bulungula and Wild Lubanzi, cater to anglers and South African families; prices rise sharply around Christmas and Easter. The food is homely 'hotel fare'; all resorts offer a seafood special on Saturdays and usually a braai on Sundays.

TOP CHOICE Bulungula

Backpackers   BACKPACKERS $
(☑047-577 8900; www.bulungula.com; campsites per person R70, dm/safari tent R130/300, d without bathroom R330) Bulungula has legendary status on the Wild Coast for its stunning location, community-based activities and ecofriendly ethos. It's 40% owned by the local Xhosa community who run all the tours, including horse riding, hiking and canoeing trips. There's an overall mellow vibe, but it does get raucous when a beach party is organised. (These are well away from the main camp so noise is not a problem for those who want to sleep.) Creatively painted, Xhosa-style *rondavels* serve as guest quarters. Ablution blocks include ecofriendly compost loos and 'rocket showers'. All meals are offered (sandwiches R18, dinner R55).

overnight stays in hotels. Local guides are employed. A number of midrange to up-market hotels can be booked through this outfit.

A WILD RIDE

Access to the coast from the N2 (which connects East London and Port St Johns via Mthatha) is limited by the rugged terrain, and exploring the area inevitably leads travellers down more than one bone-jarring road.

This is the place to forego the bus or your car for a while and make use of the walking paths that connect the coastal villages. There are a number of trails, some making use of hotels along the way and offering porterage, and some where you can stay with locals.

It's likely you'll enjoy yourself more when you're off the road, so pick one of the out-of-the-way lodges, such as Bulungula (p209), Wild Lubanzi (p210), Mdumbi (212) or Kraal (p213), and spend at least several days there. Port St Johns or Coffee Bay are good bases from which to branch out and explore.

Don't drive after dark; remember that many of the roads here don't appear on maps; and expect that signposts will be few and far between. It's also important to watch out for animals and people in the middle of the roads. Unsealed roads can be impassable after rain.

Self-caterers should bring their own supplies because there isn't much available nearby.

Bulungula is 4km north of the Xora River mouth and around two hours' drive from Coffee Bay. If you're coming in your own car, contact Bulungula in advance to get directions. An improved gravel road means it's now possible to drive all the way to the parking area from where it's a 500m walk to the lodge. Pick-ups from the Shell Ultra City station in Mthatha (R70) are also possible, but these must be booked in advance.

Wild Lubanzi
BACKPACKERS $

(078 530 8997; www.lubanzi.co.za; dm/d without bathroom R100/260;) Although somewhat under the radar compared to Bulungula, with which it shares a similar environmental and culturally sensibility, Wild Lubanzi is hardly second fiddle. There are magnificent ocean views, a pristine beach and cosy rooms. To get to here take the Coffee Bay turn-off from the N2, from where it's around 75km (approximately a two-hour drive). Four-wheel drives can make it all the way here; 2WDs will likely need to arrange pick-up from the Zithulele Hospital.

Haven Hotel
HOTEL $$

(047-576 8904; www.havenhotel.co.za; Dwesa Nature Reserve; s/d cottage with full board from R425/890) This is a friendly, rustic resort that's a good base for exploring Dwesa Nature Reserve. You can cross the mouth of the Mbashe River by canoe, and there's good horse riding (R120 per hour). Check with the hotel for driving directions; alternatively, staff can collect you from Mthatha (R200).

Kob Inn
INN $$

(047-499 0011; www.kobinn.co.za; per person with full board from R600;) At the Qhorha River mouth, Kob Inn has enough activities to keep the whole family happy: fishing, mountain biking, hiking, tennis and babysitting if the adults need some time alone. It's 32km via Willowvale from the N2 turn-off at Dutywa. It provides a shuttle from East London or Mthatha (R1300).

Trennery's Hotel
HOTEL $$

(047-498 0095; www.trennerys.co.za; s/d with full board R750/1100;) About 16km north of the Great Kei River pont (ferry), Trennery's has attractive thatched bungalows. It's all a bit run-down but still comfortable. There's a basic restaurant, a lovely beach, gardens and a pool.

Wavecrest Resort Hotel
RESORT $$

(047-498 0022; www.wavecrest.co.za; s/d with full board R795/1060;) The wooden deck at this smart hotel has some amazing views over sand dunes at the mouth of the Nxaxo River. There are plenty of activities to keep you occupied here, including fishing, boat rides and a spa. It's reached from Butterworth via Kentani; turn left at Kentani.

Getting There & Around

Locals take share taxis to get around the area, but the best way to explore is with your own vehicle. Alternatively, contact East Coast Shuttle (083 282 8790; ecshuttle@gmail. com). Trevor's Trails (047-498 0006; per 3hr R50) offers interesting cultural trips to Xhosa villages.

Coffee Bay

POP 600

Because of its beautiful kilometre-long beach and easy access to dramatic surrounding scenery, this once remote village, otherwise a scruffy nondescript place, has been transformed into something of a *de rigueur* stop on many people's Wild Coast itineraries. No one is sure how tiny Coffee Bay got its name, but there is a theory that a ship, wrecked here in 1863, deposited its cargo of coffee beans on the beach. A few hopeful locals hover near the backpackers enclave, trying to sell *dagga* (marijuana), curios and day trips.

⊙ Sights & Activities

Two of the backpackers, Bomvu Paradise and Coffee Shack, run all sorts of day trips, including horse riding (2hr treks R150), cultural visits (from R60), surfing trips (R60) and guided hikes; the most popular of the latter is to Hole in the Wall (3hr one-way R75). Further on from here, Wild Lubanzi (p210) can also be reached in a day. Overnight guided hikes to Bulungula (two days, one night) to the south and Port St Johns (four nights, five days) to the north can be arranged; typically, prices are R250 per person, per day (food and accommodation extra). If you choose, nights on most of the hikes can be spent in the traditional *rondavel* of a Xhosa family.

🍴 Sleeping & Eating

Competition is fierce for backpacker bucks in Coffee Bay. Most visitors eat at one of these or you can buy crayfish (in season), mussels and shad from locals. There's a well-stocked grocery store and the gift shop next to Coffee Shack has good gelato.

Bomvu Paradise
BACKPACKERS $

(☏047-575 2073; www.bomvubackpackers.com; campsites/dm R60/100, d without/with bathroom R240/300) A family-run property founded in 1996, Bomvu's overarching aesthetic and philosophy is summed up by the yoga classes, fire poi performances and mesmerizing in-house band drumming sessions. It's a rambling complex of small buildings – private en-suite rooms are especially comfortable – and gardens and outdoor nooks and crannies. There's an emphasis on organic food (dinner R55), and long-term guests often turn into volunteers or staff drawn to the camaraderie and laid-back lifestyle.

The Earth Dance International Festival held every September in Bomvu's riverside amphitheatre draws massive crowds.

Coffee Shack
BACKPACKERS $

(☏047-575 2048; www.coffeeshack.co.za; campsites/dm R70/120, d without/with bathroom R320/380; @) Just across the road from Bomvu, Coffee Shack is a big operation catering to Baz bus-loads of young travellers looking for a party. The complex is rather labyrinthine and the rooms are fairly institutional (dorms can feel congested); however, there are *rondavels* across the river with more privacy. Camping is out back with river and ocean views. The bar social scene gets lively and the kitchen churns out all meals. Surfing lessons, board rentals and all manner of day and overnight hikes can be arranged.

Sugarloaf Backpackers
BACKPACKERS $

(☏079 183 5274; www.sugarloafbackpackers.com; dm/d without bathroom R120/275; 🐾) On the main road before you come to Bomvu and Coffee Shack, Sugarloaf is more subdued and orderly than its competition. A suburban-style home and a few *rondavels* and safari tents (R250 per person) share a tranquil lawn overlooking an inlet, with the ocean visible in the distance.

Ocean View Hotel
HOTEL $$

(☏047-575 2005; www.oceanview.co.za; s/d with full board R650/1300; ❄@≋) Families looking for typical holiday accommodation would do well to check out this place, enviably located at the far end of the main beach. Chalet-style rooms have private decks and there's a pool and restaurant (set dinner R100), though decor throughout is passé.

❶ Getting There & Away

If you're driving to Coffee Bay, take the sealed but dangerously potholed road (many holes are difficult to see, so it's best to drive cautiously unless you want to lose a hubcap – or worse) that leaves the N2 at Viedgesville. When you reach Coffee Bay, you'll see signs for the Ocean View Hotel to the left. A little further on is the backpackers' enclave. A minibus taxi from Mthatha to Coffee Bay costs R25 and takes one hour. The backpacker shuttles (R60) meet Baz Bus at the Shell Ultra City station, 4km south of Mthatha.

Around Coffee Bay

The walking around Coffee Bay is spectacular – one of the best and easily most popular walks is to the Hole in the Wall, an offshore rock formation featuring a large, photogenic natural gap created by the pounding of the ocean waves. The signposted turn-off to Hole in the Wall village is about 20km before Coffee Bay. There is also a direct, badly rutted dirt road from Coffee Bay (about 9km).

The fenced-in Hole in the Wall Hotel (☎047-575 0009; www.holeinthewall.co.za; d with half board R1470, 3-bedroom cottage R1600; @☎) has plain rooms and good-value, well-decorated self-catering cottages. Prices fall significantly outside the high season. Part of the same complex is a backpackers (campsites R50, dm/d without bathroom R80/220), giving you access to the hotel's facilities, which include a swimming pool and volleyball court. Meals are available at the hotel (breakfast R55, dinner R150).

Adventurous sorts can jump into the ocean from the rocks above the Mapuzi Caves, around 7km north of Coffee Bay. Guides (R100 per person) can be organised from one of the backpackers; the grass-covered cliffs above are an ideal spot for a sundowner.

If Coffee Bay feels too 'big city', head to Mdumbi Backpackers (☎047-575 0437; www .mdumbi.co.za; campsites R60, dm/d without bathroom R100/220), 22km to the north (the dirt road is in relatively good condition). It's a rural retreat set in rolling hills above a wide white-sand beach. A collection of simply furnished *rondavels* shares the grounds with a kindergarten and former chapel used as a dorm for large groups. There are lots of water-based activities (the surf can be phenomenal here) and lots of opportunities to meet the local Xhosa people in a genuine setting. You can also get involved in various community projects undertaken by Mdumbi's affiliated organisation, Transcape (www.trans cape.org). Ask at any backpackers in Coffee Bay for van service here (R50).

Coffee Bay to Port St Johns

Midway between Coffee Bay and Port St Johns is Hluleka Nature Reserve (☎043-705 4400; www.ecparks.co.za; adult/child R20/10; ☺8am-5pm), a spectacular coastline of rocky

THE XHOSA

Travelling along the southwestern Wild Coast is an excellent way to get to know Xhosa culture. You may hear the term 'red people', which refers to the red clay and red clothes worn by many Xhosa adults.

Clothing, colours and beaded jewellery all indicate a Xhosa's subgroup. The Tembu and Bomvana, for example, favour red and orange ochres in the dyeing of their clothing, while the Pondo and Mpondomise use light blue. The *isi-danga* – a long, turquoise necklace that identifies the wearer to their ancestors – is also still seen today.

Belief in witches (male and female) among the Xhosa is strong, and witch burning is not unknown. Most witchcraft is considered evil, with possession by depraved spirits a major fear. The *igqirha* (spiritual healer) is empowered to deal with both the forces of nature and the trouble caused by witches, and so holds an important place in traditional society. The *ixhwele* (herbalist) performs some magic, but is more concerned with health. Both are healers, and are often referred to as *sangomas*, though this is a Zulu word.

Many Xhosa have the top of their left little finger removed during childhood to prevent misfortune. Puberty and marriage rituals also play a central role. Males must not be seen by women during the three-month initiation period following circumcision at the age of 18; during this time the initiates disguise themselves with white clay, or in intricate costumes made of dried palm leaves.

In the female puberty ritual, a girl is confined in a darkened hut while her friends tour the area singing for gifts. Unmarried girls wear short skirts, which are worn longer as marriage approaches. Married women wear long skirts and cover their breasts. They often put white clay on their faces and wear large, turbanlike cloth hats and may smoke long-stemmed pipes. The length of the pipe denotes the woman's status in the clan.

Most villages comprise a series of *rondavels* (round huts), many of them painted a bright turquoise, grouped around the cattle kraal. The roofs are thatched and often sport an old tyre at the apex, filled with earth for stabilisation. The earth can be planted with cacti or shards of glass: sharp objects dissuade bad omens such as owls from alighting. On the death of the owner, the hut is abandoned and left to collapse.

seashores and lagoons, as well as evergreen forests and grassy hilltops. The reserve is a favourite escape for a cross-section of in-the-know residents of Wild Coast towns. Burchell's zebras, blesboks and blue wilde-beests have all been introduced and there's abundant birdlife. Quite beautiful self-catering chalets (☑079 493 3566; d R700), the equal of any privately owned resort, are available overlooking the ocean and a small secluded cove with a sandy beach.

To get to the reserve, take the road from Mthatha to Port St Johns and turn right several kilometres after Libode, about 30km from Mthatha. The reserve is another 90km further on.

If you have the opportunity, the five- or six-day walk between Coffee Bay and Port St Johns is the highlight of any trip in the region. Always arrange a local guide from one of the backpackers in either town or at the Port St Johns tourism office. Local family-run huts, found every four hours or so of walking along the trail (at Mdumbi, the Hluleka Nature Reserve, Mpande, Mngazana and Stambeni in the Silaka Nature Reserve), have mattresses, bedding, a shower and toilet, and breakfast and dinner is available.

🛏 Sleeping

TOP CHOICE **Kraal Backpackers** BUNGALOW $
(☑082 871 4964; www.thekraal-backpackers.co.za; campsites R100, dm/d without bathroom R150/270) Power down and disconnect at this ecologically minded coastal retreat at the end of a bone-jarring road. A rustically cosy lounge, dining area and fully stocked kitchen opens onto a back porch where the ocean view is framed by a V in the hillside. Accommodation is in traditionally designed *rondavels* illuminated by candlelight. Hiking, horse riding, surfing and kayaking are possibilities and you can visit the nearby shebeen or local *sangoma* (medicine practitioner). It's a short walk straight down to a rocky shore with tidal pools or a beach at the mouth of the Sinangwana River. Meals (eg dinners for R75) are available, usually prepared by nearby villagers, but it's best to bring supplies of your own.

The turn-off to the Kraal is 70km from Mthatha and 25km from Port St Johns; look for the Mpande and Isilimela Hospital signs. It is another 20km (around a 50-minute drive) on a sometimes very rough road from the turn-off; do not attempt it after rains in anything other than a 4WD vehicle. It's best to ring or SMS ahead before turning up. The Kraal can also arrange transport from Mthatha, Mpande or Port St Johns.

Umngazi River Bungalows & Spa RESORT $$$
(☑047-564 1115; www.umngazi.co.za; per person with full board from R850; ☒) Overlooking a large estuary and a deserted beach, this popular resort at the mouth of the Umngazi River is good for honeymooners or families. Activities include canoeing through mangroves, fishing, mountain biking and hiking – there's also a nanny service and kids' lounge for when you want to hit the spa. To get here in your own car from Port St Johns (21km to the north), take the Mthatha-bound road for 10km to the signposted turn-off on your left. From here it's another 11km to the hotel.

Port St Johns

POP 2100

Dramatically located at the mouth of the Umzimvubu River and framed by towering cliffs covered with dense tropical vegetation, the laid-back town of Port St Johns is the original Wild Coast journey's end. These days, there's something of a run-down quality to the town, the largest between East London and Port Edward, and it feels less out of the ordinary than more remotely situated spots elsewhere in the area. Bull Zambezi sharks calve upriver and there have been six fatal attacks in the last half-dozen years; therefore, when it comes to the water, it's recommended that you do nothing more than wade off the town's beaches.

◉ Sights & Activities

Mt Thesiger VIEWPOINT
Just north of the town centre on the banks of the Umzimvubu River is this favourite sunset spot, a flat-topped hill with a disused airstrip and one of the more spectacular views on the Wild Coast.

Museum MUSEUM
(Main St; admission free; ⊘8am-4.30pm Mon-Fri) A funky building with exhibits chronicling local history, including stories of close to a dozen nearby shipwrecks (the earliest is from 1847).

Silaka Nature Reserve PARK
(☑in East London 043-705 4400; www.ecparks.co.za; admission R20; ⊘6am-6pm) This small

EASTERN CAPE PORT ST JOHNS

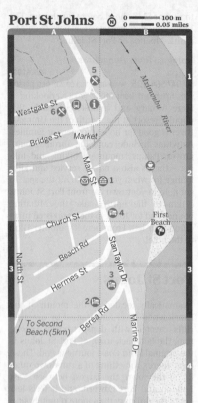

Port St Johns

Port St Johns

reserve, 6km south of Port St Johns, runs from Second Beach to Sugarloaf Rock near the estuary where the Gxwaleni River flows into the sea and aloes grow down almost to the water. Clawless otters are often seen on the beach, and white-breasted cormorants clamber up onto Bird Island. The overgrown pathway (wear long pants), which is in need of maintenance, leaves from near the Lodge at Second Beach. **Accommodation** (☎047-564 1188; d R450) in Silaka is in comfortable thatched chalets with kitchenettes.

For diving, and dolphin- and whale-watching, contact **Offshore Africa Port St Johns** (☎084 951 1325; www.offshoreportstjohns.com). Walk to the **Gap blowhole**, between First and Second Beach, at high tide. Several steep pathways from near Second Beach lead uphill to **Bulolo Waterfall**; there's a small pool at the bottom.

🛏 Sleeping

Accommodation in Port St Johns is scattered, but all of our recommendations (except Outspan Inn) are located on the way to, or near, Second Beach.

Delicious Monster Lodge LODGE $$
(☎083 997 9856; www.deliciousmonsterpsj.co.za; r from R450; ☎) Only steps from the restaurant of the same name you'll find this airy loft-style cottage with ocean views from its front porch. Outfitted with homey comforts and full kitchen and living room, this lodge is ideal for small groups looking to share a holiday space.

Lodge on the Beach LODGE $
(☎047-564 1276; www.wildcoast.co.za/thelodge; r from R350) Perched on a slight rise with unobstructed views of Second Beach, this well-kept thatched-roofed home has three rooms, each with its own small deck and an individual bathroom in the hallway. Breakfast and dinner can be provided.

Amapondo Backpackers BACKPACKERS $
(☎047-564 1344; www.amapondo.co.za; Second Beach Rd; campsites R60, dm/s/d without bathroom R100/250/350; ☎) A mellow place with several low-slung buildings lining a hilltop with excellent views of Second Beach. Simple, almost austere concrete-floored rooms have fans and ragged couches just outside. Activities offered include horse riding (R250 per day), boat trips, canoeing and surfing – plus hanging out at the restaurant (mains R35) and bar, which can get lively with a mix of locals and travellers.

Jungle Monkey BACKPACKERS $
(☎047-564 1517; www.junglemonkey.co.za; 2 Berea Rd; campsites/dm R40/70; ☎) Jungle Monkey and Island Backpackers Lodge – its more modern and generic sister next door – share a pool and garden, and a sometimes loud and raucous bar and restaurant (mains

R45). There's also a big camping area. Hiking, horse riding (R250 per day) and other trips are on offer.

Outspan Inn INN $$

(047-564 1057; www.outspaninn.co.za; Main Rd; s/d incl breakfast R390/590, self-catering per person R195; ☒) The ground floor rooms with kitchenette and small lounge are more appealing than the 2nd-floor rooms. You can hear the sea, but can't see it – a path through the trees leads to First Beach.

Eating & Drinking

Most of the eating options are within the backpackers and hotels themselves. Outside the two large grocery stores on Main St is a small street market where you might be able to buy fresh seafood – mussels, crayfish and fish – to cook your own meal.

Delicious Monster INTERNATIONAL, SEAFOOD $$

(Second Beach; mains R70; ⊙9am-3pm & 6-10pm; ☎) This restaurant has a fabulous view of Second Beach and the sea, and an eclectic menu that includes a meze platter (R54), *shwarma* (R68), line fish and steaks.

Wood 'n Spoon SEAFOOD, SOUTH AFRICAN $

(Second Beach; mains R55; ⊙10.30am-9pm) A ramshackle restaurant just below Delicious Monster, with a chalkboard menu of fresh seafood and steaks.

Fish Eagle
Restaurant INTERNATIONAL, SOUTH AFRICAN $

(mains R55) Slow service means there's time to take in the views of the river and Mt Sullivan from the backyard deck seating. Choose from a large selection of standard chicken and pasta dishes and sandwiches.

ⓘ Information

There are several ATMs in town; be cautious when withdrawing money because locals report several cases of surreptitious fraud (where a wireless device that records pin numbers is attached the machine).

Jesters Coffee Shop Internet Café (Main St; per hr R40; ⊙8.30am-4pm Mon-Fri, to 1pm Sat)

Tourism Port St Johns (☎047-564 1187; www .portstjohns.org.za/tourism.htm) Located at the top of the roundabout when you enter Port St Johns. Very helpful and knowledgeable staff.

ⓘ Getting There & Away

The R61 from Mthatha to Port St Johns is sealed, but it involves switchbacks and sharp curves.

Most backpacker places will pick you up from the Shell Ultra City, 4km south of Mthatha (where Baz Bus stops) for around R70, but it's essential to book ahead (and turn up when you've booked). There are also regular minibus taxis to Port St Johns from here (R40, two hours), East London (R120) and Durban (R160).

If there's enough demand, Amapondo Backpackers offers boat transfers to Mbotyi (R300 per person), Mpande (R300 per person) and Coffee Bay (R350 per person).

Pondoland

On the 110km stretch of coast between Port St Johns and the Mthamvuna River lies some of the most biologically rich landscape of the whole region. Currently unspoiled (although mining and road-building plans are on the cards), there are velvety hills dotted with brightly painted houses, serene tea plantations and waterfalls galore.

MBOTYI

You'll soon realise that the journey to Mbotyi ('Place of Beans') is worth the effort when the road drops down through indigenous subtropical forest to a pristine river mouth and beach.

Mbotyi Campsite (☎039-253 8295; mbotyi@pondoland.co.za; campsites per person R75, d R290, 6-person pondo hut R500) is the place for total relaxation and long walks on the beach. You'll need to be totally self-sufficient with food. **Mbotyi River Lodge** (☎039-253 7200; www.mbotyi.co.za; s/d with full board R892/1190; ✿@☒), an upmarket resort set on a beautiful beach, has all the trimmings. Log cabins are set around the pool and overlook the sea. Various activities such as horse riding, hiking trails and fishing can be arranged. The owners are involved in local community projects.

To get to Mbotyi from Port St Johns, take the R61 to Lusikisiki. Less than 1km before the town, turn onto a concrete road for Mbotyi; if you reach the Total petrol station, you've gone too far. From the turn-off, Mbotyi is 27km through the Magwa Tea plantations.

MKAMBATI NATURE RESERVE

North of Mbotyi, and 30km south of Port Edward, lies the absolutely breathtaking **Mkambati Nature Reserve** (☎043-705 4400; www.ecparks.co.za; adult/child R20/10; ⊙6am-6pm). A waterfall mecca with two rivers that drop directly into the ocean, the park

EASTERN CAPE PONDOLAND

includes the deep Msikaba and Mtentu River gorges, interesting geological formations, wells and springs and 7720 hectares of grassland, dotted with forest and a large array of wildlife.

Mkambati's magnificent coastal scenery is a haven for a spectacular variety of birds, including trumpeter hornbills and African fish eagles. Animal species include eland, zebra and red hartebeest, and dolphins and whales can be seen off the coast. Fishing is permitted in designated areas.

There are canoe and walking trails, or you can hire the park's own open vehicle and guide for a wildlife drive. A shop sells basic food. There are waterfront located self-catering rondavels (R340) near the Gwe Gwe River.

THE BATTLE FOR PONDOLAND

In September 2005, even while mining and road-building plans advanced apace, the government of South Africa approved the creation of a national park in Pondoland. The heart of the proposed 'Wild Coast Park' meant to save rainforest, sensitive animal habitats and important archaeological sites was the Mkambati Nature Reserve. While some environmental groups advocated for the establishment of the park, many alleged that the government was merely trying to throw them a bone while it allowed investors to swarm around the park's boundaries, laying toll roads and mining the coastal sand dunes, which are rich in titanium. However, the park never came to fruition in good part because of resistance from local people who objected that it would deprive them of their ancestral land rights.

In July 2008 the government granted MRC, an Australian company, and its South African partner, TME, the right to mine the dunes in the Xolobeni area (north of Mkambati Nature Reserve). Such large investment in the area, said the government, would be of great benefit locally. Shortly afterwards, the AmaDiba Crisis Committee and residents of Xolobeni lodged an appeal against this decision. They argued that mining in this pristine stretch of the Wild Coast will damage the environment and the community. They questioned whether the investment in the area would benefit those most in need. Eventually, the Minister of Minerals and Energy Affairs revoked the company's license after community leaders challenged the legality of the project on the grounds that they were not consulted adequately and that the environmental review process was insufficient and problematic.

However, the battle over the future of the region continues unabated. Another mining application was resubmitted in June 2012. But it's something of a two-pronged conflict. With or without the mining, the government says it still wants a road built through Pondoland; most would argue though that it certainly seems unlikely that one would move forward without the other. The long-standing highway proposal is part of a major scheme to upgrade and change the course of the N2. The new toll road between Durban and East London would shave 80km off the route, but carries a massive price tag, both financial and environmental. Bridges would cross pristine rivers and gorges, and 90km of new roadway would be built, threatening the biodiversity of the region as well as the natural beauty of the land, which many see as the most valuable asset in terms of sustainable development. While some government officials argue that the roadway would in fact open up the area to tourism and economic development, those opposed point out that it's not the type of tourism that would benefit local communities.

There is now a fledgling eco-tourism industry for adventurous travellers that take them off the beaten track on long hikes through the heart of rural Pondoland. The European Union once pumped money into a handful of these businesses and initiatives; however, this effort was under-planned and under-budgeted. And with the mining situation and road in a state of flux, some communities divided over support, as well as land rights issues, eco-tourism has struggled. Environmental groups, some in the NGO sector and many locals, however, see tourism as the key to conservation and economic opportunity moving forward (check out www.wildcoast.co.za for up-to-date information on environmental issues and tourism). For now, Pondoland sits undisturbed, its rushing waterfalls still flowing towards the sea and its wildlife still roaming without hindrance.

You get here from Flagstaff, which is 70km south of the N2. Take the turn-off just north of Flagstaff to Holy Cross Hospital. There are also buses running from Port St Johns to Msikaba, on the southern edge of the reserve.

On the isolated northern bank of the beautiful Mtentu Estuary, just across from the Mkambati Nature Reserve is the rustic retreat, **Mtentu River Lodge Cabins** (☑084 209 8543; www.mtenturiverlodge.co.za; 4-person cabins R600). Six comfortable wood cabins with ocean views are linked by a boardwalk running through the naturally landscaped property. Toilets are communal and there's a choice of paraffin or solar-powered showers. Three meals a day can be provided for R200 per person. A range of activities, from hiking to kite surfing, are on tap as well as good old-fashioned chilling out at the nearby beach. The closest Baz Bus stop is at Port Shepstone; from here take a mini-bus taxi towards Bizana and ask to be let off at the Umkolora sign 18km past the Wild Coast Sun. From here there are two mini-bus taxis to the lodge in the afternoons. A 4WD vehicle is necessary if you plan to get here on your own – consult Mtentu for directions.

Mthatha

POP 500,000

Busy and bustling and clogged with traffic, Mthatha (formerly Umtata) is chaotic, noisy, dusty and growing. There are some elegant, historic buildings in among the modern blocks. *Muti* (traditional medicine) sellers trade outside western doctors' rooms and rural people mingle with urban dwellers in this cultural melting pot.

The town was originally founded in 1882, when Europeans settled on the Mthatha River at the request of the Thembu tribe, to act as a buffer against Pondo raiders. During the apartheid era it became the capital of the Transkei, the largest of the black homelands.

The village of **Mveso**, around 32km west of Mthatha on the Mbashe River south of the N2, is where Nelson Mandela, the first president of a free South Africa, was born. Nearby is **Qunu** on the other side of the highway; this is where he spent most of his childhood and it's the site of the **Nelson Mandela Museum** (☑047-532 5110; www.mandelamuseum.org.za; admission free; ⊙9am-4pm Mon-Fri, to noon Sat). The complex of modern buildings includes a permanent exhibit charting the history of the ANC and profiling its most important leaders.

🛏 Sleeping & Eating

Most accommodation is aimed at visiting businesspeople and there's little reason to spend the night.

Ekhaya Guesthouse GUESTHOUSE $$
(☑072 432 7244; www.mthathaguesthouse.co.za; 36 Delville Rd; r incl breakfast from R537) This is a smart place on the edge of the golf course, spread over three houses. There's a pretty garden with a braai area and modern rooms with TV.

Country Lodge LODGE $$
(☑047-532 5730; clodge@wildcoast.co.biz; Port St Johns Rd; d R500; @☕) Situated just 2.5km out of town on the Port St Johns road, this lodge is often a great relief after Mthatha's urban hustle, with guinea fowl pecking contentedly in the shady garden. Dinner (mains about R65) is available.

Mthatha Backpackers BACKPACKERS $
(☑047-531 3654; www.mthathabackpackers.co.za; 12 Aloe St, off Sisson Rd; dm R150, d without/with bathroom R200/300; ☕☕) A blandly decorated suburban home offers clean accommodation options, including four-person tents (per person 130) and a pool table in the lapa.

It's a good idea to eat where you stay, because the culinary scene in Mthatha is dominated by South African and international fast-food chains. The **Savoy Shopping Centre** (Nelson Mandela Dr) has a selection of these and a few other restaurants, ATMs and an internet cafe.

ℹ Getting There & Away

The R61 to Port St Johns passes through the centre of town, which is usually a gridlocked mess. It's worth avoiding Sutherland Dr, the most direct route and the slowest, and instead detour south of the centre along Nelson Mandela Dr before turning north on Madeira Rd, where you'll find signs for the R61.

Air

Mthatha's Mantanzima airport is 17km from the city. **SAAirlink** (☑047-536 0024; www.flyairlink.com) has daily services to Jo'burg (R1243).

Bus

Translux offers a twice-daily service from Cape Town (R450, 18 hours) to Mthatha.

Greyhound stops in Mthatha on its daily run between Durban (R255, 6½ hours) and Cape

EASTERN CAPE MTHATHA

Town (R435, 20½ hours). A much speedier option is the Cape Town bus company **DMJ Transport** (☑in Cape Town 021-419 4368; www.dmjtransport.com), which only takes 13 hours from Cape Town to Mthatha (R350).

Translux, Greyhound and Baz Bus (which passes through Mthatha on its Port Elizabeth to Durban run) stop at the Shell Ultra City station.

Minibus Taxi

Minibus taxis in Mthatha depart from both Shell Ultra City and the main bus stop and taxi rank near Bridge St. Destinations of interest include Port St Johns or Kraal Backpackers (R30), Coffee Bay (R40) and East London (R80).

NORTH-EASTERN HIGHLANDS

Leaving the lush valleys of the Wild Coast and travelling north, the area bordered by the sharply ascending peaks of Lesotho in the east, and the Free State, abounds in dramatic mountain scenery. There are tranquil small towns little visited by tourists; rushing streams and rivers where trout and other fish abound; day hikes past bucolic scenery; and even snow-covered mountain passes north of Rhodes in the winter – exercise caution when driving, since weather and road conditions can be harsh.

Queenstown & Around

POP 80,000

Queenstown is a rather nondescript bustling and dusty commercial centre. It was laid out in the shape of a hexagon for defence purposes when it was established in 1847; this pattern enabled defenders to shoot down the streets from a central point.

The rolling plains of the Tsolwana Nature Reserve (☑043-742 4450; www.ecparks .co.za; adult/child R20/10; ⊗8am-6pm), 60km southwest of Queenstown, are interspersed with valleys, cliffs, waterfalls, caves and gullies. The reserve, managed in conjunction with the local Tsolwana people, protects some rugged Karoo landscape south of the spectacular Tafelberg (1965m) and adjoining the Swart Kei River. There's a diverse range of animals including large herds of antelopes and mountain zebras. Wildlife-watching is possible in the park's vehicle (up to four people for R315).

Queenstown is the hub for all transport in and out of the Highlands. Greyhound, City to City and Translux buses stop at the Shell Ultra City petrol station on their way to Jo'burg/Pretoria, Port Elizabeth and Cape Town.

All trains travelling between Jo'burg and East London via Bloemfontein, and between Cape Town and East London, stop at Queenstown; to East London from here takes about four hours. Contact Shosholoza Meyl (☑0860 008 888; www.shosholozameyl .co.za)for details.

Aliwal North

POP 30,000

Just inside the Eastern Cape border from the Free State, Aliwal North was hugely popular in the early 20th century – people flocked here for the thermal spa, now essentially defunct. Today, however, most visitors are here either on local government business or passing through on their way to or from Jo'burg.

The Conville Guest Farm (☑051-633 2203; www.conville-farm.com; s/d incl breakfast R300/400), a splendid 1908 farmhouse, combines Cape Dutch architecture with castle-like flourishes and looks out on a pond and garden with exquisite country views beyond. There are four rooms, all grand with high ceilings and antique furniture, and an old-fashioned and stately breakfast

SELF-DRIVE HIGH

It's worth approaching this region as though it offers a scenic road trip because, in and of themselves, most of the towns wouldn't necessarily rate high on the average traveller's must-visit list. While the towns are certainly appealing as low-key places to spend an afternoon and evening, you'll likely find a journey here more satisfying (and logical) by thinking of it as a self-drive loop either approached from Queenstown in the southwest (the way this section is organised) or via Maclear in the northeast. Of the towns listed, Rhodes (followed by Lady Grey) is the most scenic – although if you don't intend to back-track (which you shouldn't), it does involve a sometimes hair-raising drive over South Africa's highest mountain pass.

TSITSA FALLS BACKPACKERS

The area outside Maclear, an agricultural and commercial centre, is covered by hectare after hectare of alien pine plantations. The massive mill that's fed by the pine is just outside the nearby town of Ugie. But you didn't come all this way for paper products. Marking the driving-time halfway point between Rhodes and Coffee Bay or Port St Johns, remotely located **Tsitsa Falls Backpackers** (✆ 045-932 1138; www.tsitsafalls.com; campsites/dm R65/150, d without bathroom R300) makes a highly recommended stop between the northeastern highlands and the Wild Coast.

A young couple, Addi and Ang Badenhorst, have created a homey refuge out of an old rustic farmhouse that sits just above the picturesque Tsitsa Falls and not far from the confluence of the Tsitsa, Pot and Mooi rivers. Meals of homemade bread and meat cooked in the outdoor fire pit underneath crystal-clear, star-filled night-time skies will surely rank as trip highlights. During the daytime you can hike, fish, abseil, kloof, ride the 150m zip-line that crosses in front of the falls and white-water kayaking for the experienced (Adie is world class).

To reach the site from the centre of Maclear, take the road to Mt Fletcher for 20km and turn right at the signposted road to Tsitsa Falls (don't take the first signposted road to Tsitsa Falls 10km earlier); from here it's another 7km down a rough dirt road. Transport from Mthatha or Maclear can be arranged.

It's only three hours from Maclear to Coffee Bay via Ugie and over the newly built Langeni Pass road.

room completes the picture. Look for signs while heading east from town along Louis Botha Ave – the farm is around 3km from the centre.

Another highly recommended alternative is **Queens Terrace** (✆ 051-634 2291; 25 Queens Tce Rd; nff@xsinet.co.za; s/d incl breakfast R350/500), the smartest guesthouse in town. It mixes a dash of contemporary with a dollop of homey and a backyard garden.

The best place for a sundowner is the **Pub & Grill** (mains R75) of Riverside Lodge, which overlooks the Senqu (Orange) River. The **Stable** (mains R40; ⊙8am-4pm Mon-Fri, to noon Sat), technically in the Free State as it's just across the bridge over the river, serves sandwiches, salads, burgers and cakes in the peaceful trellis-covered yard or in one of several shop rooms crammed with fairly chintzy gifts and furnishings.

Translux, City to City and Greyhound services stop at the Shell petrol station near General Hertzog Bridge in the north of town. There's a daily service to Jo'burg (R310, eight hours).

Lady Grey

Backed by the imposingly steep and sunbaked cliffs of the Witteberge mountain range, Lady Grey is literally at the end of the (one) road. A small group of artists and a music and drama academy lend some vibrancy to this usually sleepy agricultural community. Accommodation is stretched to capacity at Easter time when the entire town gets involved in a three-day **Passion Play**.

For area information, stop off (or check in) at the delightful **Comfrey Cottage** (✆ 051-603 0407; www.comfreycottage.co.za; 51-59 Stephenson St; s/d with half board R500/900, self-catering per person R280), a group of upmarket cottages with alpacas grazing the lawns of a beautiful garden. Geological, botanical and cycling tours of the area can be arranged, as well as visits to the nearby private Cape vulture restaurant, where the eponymous birds are fed.

At least as appealing is the unique and welcoming **Baggers & Packers** (✆ 051-603 0346; johandp@telkomsa.net; 53 Heut St; campsites per person R35, dm R100), housed in a converted chapel; the shady garden is a good spot for campers. The friendly owner can provide advice on walks in the area or show you his collection of restored pedal organs.

If you have the time – and a 4WD vehicle – it is well worth venturing into splendid and remote mountain scenery at the **Lammergeier Private Nature Reserve** (✆ 051-603 1114; www.adventuretrails.co.za; 4-person self-catering cottage R695, 12-person farmhouse R255). Set in a pristine environment, the cattle farm has won awards for its conservation efforts, and it sponsors adventure sports events. It offers hiking trails, birdwatching and trout fishing, as well as 4WD, mountain-bike and quad-bike trails. The reserve, 11km down the untarred Joubert's Pass road, can be approached from the R58 between Lady Grey and Barkly East.

Rhodes

POP 700

Deep in the southern Drakensberg, in a spectacular valley setting alongside the Bell River, the little village of Rhodes is a bucolic escape. The architecture remains as it was when the town was established in 1891 as a base for agriculture and commerce. Trout fishing is extremely popular throughout the whole district, and the Wild Trout Association (045-974 9292; www.wildtrout.co.za) headquarters is here.

The Deli & Art Gallery (045-971 9236; Muller St; 8am-5pm Mon-Fri, 8am-2pm Sat, 9am-noon Sun) sells just about everything, including meat and vegetables. A small shop has an ATM and there's a single stand-alone pump for petrol – it's not unusual for the supply to run out, so fill up before coming to Rhodes.

All four seasons can be experienced in a single day – winter temps have reached as low as -15°C and as hot as 35°C in summer.

Sleeping & Eating

There are several self-catering cottages (045-974 9298; www.highlandsinfo.co.za; per person from R175) in the village. Book early in the high season (there are three brief high seasons: 1 December to 15 January, 15 March to 30 April, and 25 May to 31 August) and bring warm clothes and blankets in winter; heating in some of the cottages is minimal.

TOP CHOICE Walkerbouts Inn — INN $$

(045-974 9290; www.walkerbouts.co.za; per person with half board R525) Oozing character, Walkerbouts has polished wood floors and cosy rooms with interesting furniture and old artefacts. There is a friendly bar as well as good food (build your own pizza for around R30). The lovely garden has magnificent views, and genial host Dave Walker knows just about everything there is to know about Rhodes and fly-fishing.

Rhodes Hotel — HOTEL $$

(045-974 9305; www.rhodeshotel.co.za; Muller St; per person with half board R580; @) Rhodes' only hotel is located in an atmospheric old complex with wood floors and well-appointed, high-ceilinged rooms. There's a convivial bar and a restaurant (mains R65). Horse riding, tennis and volleyball are on offer.

Getting There & Away

The road to Rhodes from Barkly East (60km, 1½ hours) is untarred but fine for 2WD cars. The stunning scenery calls for several photo-stops. The road to Maclear cuts through the imposing Naudesnek Pass (2500m), the highest in the country, and is best undertaken in a 4WD vehicle – 2WDs can make it – though it's best to check local weather conditions. There is no public transport here.

KwaZulu-Natal

Best Places to Eat

» Market (p237)

» Cafe Bloom (p282)

» Spice (p238)

» Joop's Place (p238)

Best Places to Stay

» Mpila Camp (p259)

» Inkosana (p274)

» Thendele (p271)

» Thonga Beach Lodge (p264)

Why Go?

Rough and ready, smart and sophisticated, rural and rustic, there's no doubting that KwaZulu-Natal (KZN) is eclectic. It's a region where glassy malls touch shabby suburbs, and action-packed adventurers ooze adrenaline while laid-back beach bods drip with suntan lotion. Mountainscapes contrast with flat dry savannahs while the towns' downtown streets, teeming with African life, markets and noise, are in stark contrast to the sedate tribal settlements in rural areas. Here, too, is traditional Zululand, whose people are fiercely proud of their culture.

Throw in the wildlife – the Big Five (lion, leopard, buffalo, elephant and rhino) and rare marine species – the historic intrigue of the old Battlefields, fabulous hiking opportunities, and the sand, sea and surf of coastal resort towns, and you get a tantalising taste of local heritage and authentic African highlights that should be on every tourist 'must-do' list.

When to Go

Durban

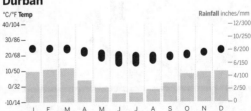

May–Oct Dry season brings cooler days but savannah conditions, perfect for wildlife viewing

Oct & Nov Pleasant beach weather and wildflowers cover the uKhahlamba-Drakensberg

Nov–Feb Brings hot weather, but also the results of mating season – baby animals rule!

KwaZulu-Natal Highlights

1 Wildlife-spotting through the Big Five stomping ground of **Hluhluwe-iMfolozi Park** (p258) or sitting near a pan at dawn at **uMkhuze Game Reserve** (p266)

2 Exploring the beauty of the extraordinary **iSimangaliso Wetland Park** (p260)

3 Walking in the mountainous wonderland of **uKhahlamba-Drakensberg** (p267)

4 Driving through the clouds over **Sani Pass** (p278) to Lesotho

5 Reliving the clashes of the Anglo-Zulu War at **Isandlwana** and **Rorke's Drift** (p289)

6 Sniffing out the funky new cafes and eateries in fast-changing **Durban** (p225)

LEGEND

GR Game Reserve
NP National Park
NR Nature Reserve
WA Wilderness Area

50 miles
100 km

INDIAN OCEAN

Dolphin Coast

Hibiscus Coast

Umhlanga Rocks
Ballito
Umhlanga
Tongaat
Botha's Hill
Durban
Pinetown
Amanzimtoti
Umlazi
Umkomaas
Scottburgh
Kelso
Hibberdene
Port Shepstone
Margate
Trafalgar Marine Reserve
Marina Beach
Port Edward

Pietermaritzburg
Valley of 1000 Hills
Howick
Midmar NR
Edendale
Richmond
Ixopo
Donnybrook
Bulwer
Himeville
Underberg
Sani Pass
Ramatseliso's
Bushman's Nek & Border Post

uKhahlamba-Drakensberg Park

Linakeng River
Mushai River
Tsoelike River

Matatiele
Cedarville
Franklin
Kokstad
Harding
Umzimkulu

Eastern Cape

Umzinto
Umzimkulwana
Lovu River
Mkomazi River
Ntatabor

Oribi Gorge NR
uMtamvuna River
Umtamvuna NR
Mkambati NR

Mount Ayliff
Bizana
Flagstaff
Lusikisiki
Port St Johns
Hluleka NR
Coffee Bay

Mount Frere
Tabankulu
Mount Ayliff
Umzimvubu River
Mtentu River

Eastern Cape

Libode
Umtata

History

Battled over by Boers, Brits and Zulus, Natal was named by Portuguese explorer Vasco da Gama, who sighted the coastline on Christmas Day 1497, and named it for the natal day of Jesus. It took the British Empire more than 300 years to set its sights on the region, proclaiming it a colony in 1843. Briefly linked to the Cape Colony in 1845, Natal again became a separate colony in 1856, when its European population numbered less than 5000.

The introduction of Indian indentured labour in the 1860s – sections of the province still retain a subcontinental feel – and the subsequent development of commercial agriculture (mainly sugar) boosted growth. The colony thrived from 1895, when train lines linked Durban's port (dredged to accommodate big ships) with the booming Witwatersrand.

The recorded history of the province up until the Union of South Africa is full of conflict: the *mfeqane* (the forced migration of South African tribes; Zulu for 'the crushing'), the Boer-Zulu and Anglo-Zulu Wars, which saw the Zulu kingdom subjugated, and the two wars between the British and the Boers. See p510 for more details about the origin and development of the *mfeqane*.

Just after the 1994 elections, Natal Province was renamed KwaZulu-Natal, acknowledging that the Zulu homeland of KwaZulu comprises a large part of the province. From that time, Ulundi (the former KwaZulu capital) and Pietermaritzburg (the former Natal homeland capital) enjoyed joint status as capital of KwaZulu-Natal until 2005, when Pietermaritzburg was named the province's official capital.

Climate

The weather (and the water, thanks to the Agulhas current) stays warm year-round along much of the coast, with Durbanites claiming to lap up a heady 230 sunny days a year. In summer the heat and humidity, combined with the crowds that flood to the coast to enjoy it, can be exhausting, with temperatures regularly in the mid-30s (degrees Celsius). Most of the interior enjoys similarly balmy conditions, but sudden and explosive electrical thunderstorms, especially in the Drakensberg mountains and northern KwaZulu-Natal, often roll in during the afternoon. Winter brings a dusting of snow to the higher peaks.

Language

Eleven official languages are spoken in South Africa, but English, Zulu, Xhosa and Afrikaans are most widely used in KwaZulu-

DON'T MISS

KZN'S PARKS & RESERVES

For those planning to spend time in the province's excellent parks and reserves, Ezemvelo KZN Wildlife (☑033-845 1000; www.kznwildlife.com; Queen Elizabeth Park, Peter Brown Dr, Pietermaritzburg) is an essential first stop. Accommodation within the parks ranges from humble campsites to comfortable safari tents and luxurious lodges; the free *Fees & Charges* booklet lists accommodation options and prices, as well as entrance charges, for all Ezemvelo KZN Wildlife reserves. Maps of the parks are also available here.

All accommodation must be booked in advance by phone, online, or in person through the Pietermaritzburg office. Last-minute bookings (ie those within 48 hours) must be made directly with the camps.

Officially, the gate entry times of all parks are 5am to 7pm (1 October to 31 March) and 6am to 6pm (1 April to 30 September).

While many of the parks are a must-see for animal-lovers and outdoorsy types, their camps – many of which have high-quality bungalows or safari tents – are also excellent for families and those touring South Africa on a budget.

Tip: if you have time to visit only one or two reserves, highlights include Royal Natal National Park (p271) for some uKhahlamba-Drakensberg vistas; Hluhluwe-iMfolozi Park (p258) for the wildlife and wilderness accommodation options; Ithala Game Reserve (p256) and uMkhuze Game Reserve (p266) for its wonderful bird hides and water holes; and iSimangaliso Wetland Park (p260) for its diverse scenery and ecological environments.

FREEDOM TO EXPLORE

To discover the region's true highlights (the uKhahlamba-Drakensberg region, the national parks and wildlife reserves and the Battlefields), you're better off hiring a car. Durban has a reasonable choice of operators. Most roads are good, but a few locations, such as Sani Pass (to which you can easily take a tour from Underberg), Tembe Elephant Park and many parts of iSimangaliso Wetland Park, require a 4WD.

See p599 and the destination sections in this chapter for more details on transport.

Natal. For some key words and phrases, see the Language chapter.

ⓘ Getting There & Around

With flights, buses and trains to destinations across the country, Durban is KwaZulu-Natal's undisputed transport hub and, at least nationally, the city is well connected. However, getting around the province itself is a different story. While long-distance buses run to Port Shepstone, Margate and Kokstad in the south, Richards Bay and Vryheid in the north and a string of towns including Estcourt, Ladysmith and Newcastle in the west, many of the more remote locations are a headache to get to by public transport. Minibus taxis provide a useful back-up, but relying on them as your sole means of getting about will mean many long hours in the back of a cramped van.

Baz Bus (www.bazbus.com) links many of the province's hostels, but no longer runs north via St Lucia and into Swaziland.

DURBAN

031 / POP 3.4 MILLION

Durban, a cosmopolitan Queen, is sometimes unfairly passed over for her 'cooler' Capetonian cousin. But this isn't fair; there's a lot more to fun-loving Durbs (as she's affectionately known) than meets the eye. In preparation for the World Cup in 2010 the city had a major makeover, with a sleek new stadium and a revamped beachfront. With a newfound confidence, the city is still justifiably showing off. It offers stylish cafes, wonderful cultural offerings and excellent shopping opportunities, much of which are clustered in fashionable areas within the suburbs.

South Africa's third-largest city (known as eThekweni in Zulu), Durban also claims to be the country's sporting capital. Thanks to its stadiums and venues, golf courses and a swathe of butter-yellow sand, it's a great city for spectator sports and outdoor enthusiasts.

The downtown area – a buzzing, gritty grid comprising grandiose colonial buildings and fascinating art deco architecture – throbs to a distinctly African beat (but loses its shimmer when the sun goes down). For beach-lovers, the beachfront remains a city trademark for daytime activities.

Home to the largest concentration of people of Indian descent outside India, Durban also boasts a distinctive Asian twang, with the marketplaces and streets of the Indian area teeming with the sights, sounds and scents of the subcontinent.

History

It took some time for Durban to be established. Natal Bay, around which the city is based, provided refuge for seafarers at least as early as 1685, and it's thought that Vasco da Gama anchored here in 1497. Though the Dutch bought a large area of land around the bay from a local chief in 1690, their ships didn't make it across the sand bar at the entrance to the bay until 1705, by which time the chief had died, and his son refused to acknowledge the deal.

Natal Bay attracted little attention from Europeans until 1824, when Henry Fynn and Francis Farewell set up a base here to trade for ivory with the Zulu. Shaka, a powerful Zulu chief (see boxed text, p248), granted land around the bay to the trading company and it was accepted in the name of King George IV.

The settlement was slow to prosper, partly because of the chaos Shaka was causing in the area. By 1835 it had become a small town with a mission station, and that year it took the name D'Urban, after the Cape Colony governor.

In 1837 the Voortrekkers crossed the Drakensberg and founded Pietermaritzburg, 80km northwest of Durban. The next year, after Durban was evacuated during a raid by the Zulu, the Boers claimed control. It was reoccupied by a British force later that year, but the Boers stuck by their claim. The British sent troops to Durban to secure the settlement, but were defeated by the Boers at the Battle of Congella in 1842.

KWAZULU-NATAL DURBAN

Durban

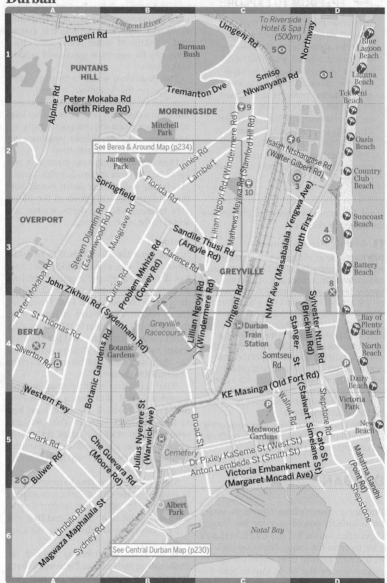

KWAZULU-NATAL DURBAN

The Boers retained control for a month until a British frigate arrived (fetched by teenager Dick King, who rode the 1000km of wild country between Durban and Grahamstown in Eastern Cape in 10 days) and dislodged them. The next year Natal was annexed by the British, and Durban began its growth as an important colonial port city. In 1860 the first indentured Indian labourers arrived to work the cane fields.

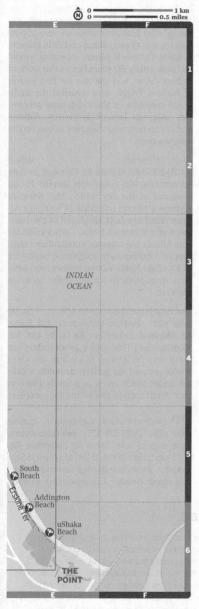

INDIAN OCEAN

South Beach
Addington Beach
uShaka Beach

Erskine Ter

THE POINT

KWAZULU-NATAL DURBAN

◎ Sights

CITY CENTRE

City Hall NOTABLE BUILDING

(Map p230; Anton Lembede St (Smith St)) Dominating the city centre is the opulent 1910 Edwardian neobaroque City Hall. In front of the hall is **Francis Farewell Square**, where Fynn and Farewell made their camp in 1824.

FREE Durban Art Gallery GALLERY

(Map p230; City Hall, Anton Lembede St (Smith St); ☺8.30am-4pm Mon-Sat, 11am-4pm Sun) Houses an excellent collection of contemporary South African works, especially Zulu arts and crafts, and has temporary and rotating exhibitions (look out for the collection of baskets from Hlabisa, finely woven from a variety of grasses and incorporating striking natural colours).

FREE Natural Science Museum MUSEUM

(Map p230; City Hall, Anton Lembede St (Smith St); ☺8.30am-4pm Mon-Sat, 11am-4pm Sun) This museum boasts an impressive, if pleasantly 'retro', display of stuffed birds and insects, plus African animals. Check out the cockroach and dung beetle displays, the reconstructed dodo and the life-sized dinosaur model.

Despite the unjust system – slave labour by another name – many free Indian settlers arrived in 1893, including Mohandas Gandhi (see boxed text, p515).

FREE **Old Courthouse Museum** MUSEUM
(Map p230; 77 Samora Machel St (Aliwal St));
◎8.30am-4pm Mon-Fri, 8.30am-12.30pm Sat)
Found in the beautiful 1866 courthouse located behind City Hall, this museum offers a worthwhile insight into the highs and lows of colonial living and houses an interesting sugar-mill exhibit. Among the wonderful displays of colonial items – from pipes to necklaces – there's a display of corresponding Zulu items; identifying them is especially fun for kids (and some adults, too).

FREE **KwaMuhle Museum** MUSEUM
(Map p230; 130 Ordnance Rd (Bram Fischer Rd);
◎8.30am-4pm Mon-Sat) This was formerly Bantu Administration headquarters, where Durban's colonial authorities formulated the structures of urban racial segregation (the 'Durban System'), which were the blueprints of South Africa's apartheid policy. There are displays on urban Durban as it was, plus another on Cato Manor, Durban's contemporary informal settlement and the site of the new South Africa's ambitious urban-renewal program.

St Paul's Church CHURCH
(Map p230; Dr Pixley KaSeme St (West St)) On the eastern side of the main post office you'll find a square with an old vicarage and the 1909 St Paul's Church.

BEREA & AROUND
Campbell Collections GALLERY
(Map p234; ☑031-207 3432; http://campbell.ukzn.ac.za; 220 Gladys Mazibuko Rd (Marriott Rd); admission R20; ◎by appointment only) These collections are well worth seeing. Muckleneuk, a superb house designed by Sir Herbert Baker, holds the documents and artefacts collected by Dr Killie Campbell and her father Sir Marshall Campbell (KwaMashu township is named after him), and these are very important records of early Natal and Zulu culture.

Killie Campbell began collecting works by black artists 60 years before the Durban Gallery did so, and she was the first patron of Barbara Tyrrell, who recorded the traditional costumes of the indigenous peoples. Her paintings beautifully convey clothing and decoration, and the grace of the people wearing them.

Phansi Museum MUSEUM
(☑031-206 2889; 41 Cedar Rd, Glenwood, cnr Frere Rd; admission R35; ◎8am-4pm Mon-Fri) Found southeast of the city centre, this museum features a private collection of Southern African tribal artefacts, displayed in the basement of a Victorian home. Owner-collector Paul Mikula has amassed outstanding examples of contemporary sculptures, beadwork of KwaZulu-Natal, carved statues, and artefacts from pipes to fertility dolls. Bookings required.

Kwazulu Natal Society of Arts GALLERY
(Map p226; www.kznsagallery.co.za; 166 Bulwer Rd, Glenwood; ◎9am-5pm Tue-Fri, to 4pm Sat, 10am-3pm Sun) This not-for-profit gallery has temporary exhibitions of modern art. Once you've perused the gallery, its outdoor cafe, set under shady trees, is a lovely place to visit. A gift shop is also within the complex.

FREE **Durban Botanic Gardens** GARDENS
(Map p230; ☑031-309 1170; www.durbanbotanicgardens.org.za; John Zikhali Rd (Sydenham Rd); ◎7.30am-5.15pm 16 Apr–15 Sep, to 5.45pm 16 Sep–15 Apr) A 20-hectare garden featuring one of the rarest cycads (*Encephalartos woodii*),

---

STREET SIGNS: IT'S ALL IN A LABEL

During 2007 and 2008 Durban's municipal council took a controversial step when it renamed many of Durban's city and suburban streets to reflect a 'new South Africa'. Debate continues to rage over the changes. Many locals are annoyed about the huge cost involved in altering street signs (saying the money would have been better spent on public services) and about the identities of some of the names – mostly former African National Congress (ANC) members and freedom fighters who, some believe, are inappropriate choices. Not to mention the wider repercussions regarding familiarity and orientation.

Some of the changes were later declared illegal and – at the time of research – efforts were being made to have several changed back to their original names. Confusingly, most locals (including businesses) often refer to the original street names. For the purpose of this edition, we have provided the new street names, plus the former street names (in brackets).

as well as many species of bromeliad. It's a lovely place to wander. On weekends local bridal parties galore pose with their petals for photographers. The gardens play host to an annual concert series featuring the KwaZulu-Natal Philharmonic Orchestra and other concerts.

Moses Mabhida Stadium STADIUM
(Map p226; ☑031-582 8222; www.mmstadium.com; Masabalala Yengwa Ave (NMR Ave)) Durbanites are proud of their state-of-the-art stadium, constructed for the 2010 World Cup. Resembling a giant basket, it seats over 56,000 people, and its arch was inspired by the 'Y' in the country's flag. Visitors can head up to the arch in a SkyCar (per person R55; ☺Sat & Sun), puff up on foot (550 steps) on an Adventure Walk (per person R90; ☺10am, 1pm & 4pm Sat & Sun) or plunge off the 106m arch on the giant Big Swing (per person R595; ☺9am to 5pm). All options offer great views of Durban. Cafes line a section of the stadium base; from here you can hire a bike or walk to the beachfront on a newly constructed pedestrian promenade (see boxed text, p232).

NORTH & WEST DURBAN
Umgeni River Bird Park WILDLIFE RESERVE
(Riverside Rd; adult/child R25/15; ☺9am-4pm) Found on Umgeni River, north of the centre, this bird park makes for a relaxing escape from the throng. You can see many African bird species in lush vegetation and aviaries. Look out for the chicks in the 'baby room'.

Temple of Understanding RELIGIOUS
(Bhaktieedanta Sami Circle; ☺10am-1pm & 4-7.30pm Mon-Sat, 10.30am-7.30pm Sun) Situated in Durban's west, this is the biggest Hare Krishna temple in the southern hemisphere. The unusual building, designed in the shape of a lotus flower, also houses a vegetarian restaurant. Follow the N3 towards Pietermaritzburg and then branch off to the N2 south. Take the Chatsworth turn-off and turn right towards the centre of Chatsworth.

MARGARET MNCADI AVENUE (VICTORIA EMBANKMENT)
Sugar Terminal FACTORY
(Map p226; 51 Maydon Rd; adult/concession R15/7; ☺tours 8.30am, 10am, 11.30am & 2pm Mon-Thu, 8.30am, 10am & 11am Fri) Maydon Wharf, which runs along the southwestern side of the harbour and south of Margaret Mncadi Ave, is home to the Sugar Terminal, which offers an insight into the sugar trade. Three silos are still operating.

Wilson's Wharf WATERFRONT
(Map p230; www.wilsonswharf.co.za) A little further north of the Sugar Terminal, this once-hip waterside development is now a little tired, but it's the best place to get a view of Durban's harbour and its activities. The harbour is the busiest in Southern Africa (and the ninth busiest in the world). The wharf has a clutch of eateries, boat-charter outfits (see boxed text, p232), shops and a theatre. By car, enter opposite Hermitage St.

Port Natal Maritime Museum MUSEUM
(Map p230; Maritime Dr; adult/child R5/3; ☺8.30am-3.30pm Mon-Sat, 11am-3.30pm Sun) On a service road running parallel to Margaret Mncadi Ave you can explore two former steam tugs and see the huge wicker basket once used for hoisting passengers onto ocean liners.

Vasco da Gama Clock MONUMENT
(Map p230) This florid Victorian monument on the Embankment, just east of Stalwart Simelane St (Stanger St), was presented by the Portuguese government in 1897, marking the 400th anniversary of Vasco da Gama's sighting of Natal.

INDIAN AREA
Juma Mosque &
Madrassa Arcade MOSQUE
(Map p230; cnr Denis Hurley St (Queen St) & Dr Yusef Daddo (Grey St); ☺9am-4pm Mon-Fri, to 11am Sat) The largest mosque in the southern hemisphere; call ahead for a guided tour. Madrassa Arcade is next to the mosque between Dr AB Xuma St and Cathedral Rd, near the Catholic Emmanuel Cathedral.

See p239 for information on the nearby Victoria St Market.

BEACHFRONT
The beachfront has experienced a resurgence, thanks to the massive revamp that was completed prior to the World Cup in 2010. The new promenade – a pedestrian super highway – runs behind the beaches, though it offers little shade. Both the beaches and promenade extend from the Blue Lagoon (at the mouth of the Umgeni River) to uShaka Marine World on the Point, an area known as the 'Golden Mile', although it's much longer. The road behind this is OR Tambo Pde (Marine Pde), and it's lined with high-rise hotels and a sprinkling of cafes.

Beaches BEACH
Excellent signage at the beaches provides maps and names of the different beaches,

KWAZULU-NATAL DURBAN

Central Durban

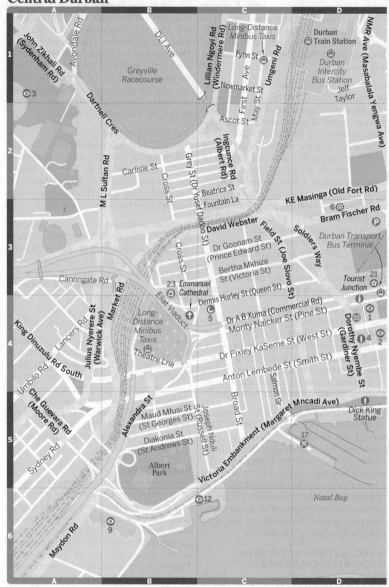

although it's really one stretch of sand with different names. At Suncoast Beach, in front of the casino, brollies and chairs are available on a first come, first served basis. Due to its location at the strip's southern end, uShaka Beach is often slightly more sheltered and

is close to cafes and a small car park. Keep an eye out for the incredible sand sculptures done by locals, depicting anything from mermaids to lions. The uShaka Beach has activities from surfing lessons to kayaking.

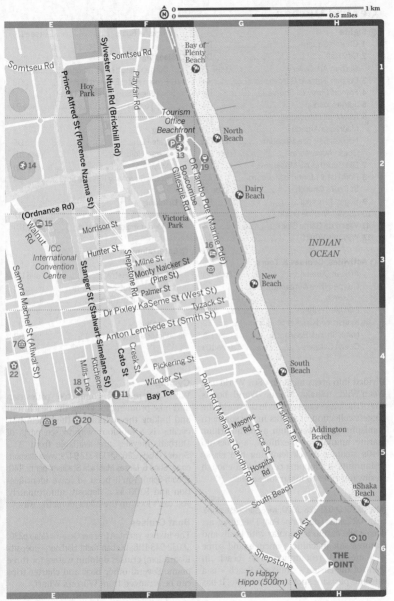

Warning: the surf and currents at Durban's beaches can be dangerous. Always swim in patrolled areas; these are indicated by flags.

uShaka Marine World AMUSEMENT PARK
(Map p230; ☎031-3686675/3288000; www.ushaka marineworld.co.za; uShaka Beach, the Point; Wet'n'Wild adult/child R110/85, Sea World R110/85; ☺9am-5pm high season, 10am-5pm rest of year)

Divided into areas including Sea World and Wet'n'Wild, uShaka Marine World boasts one of the largest aquariums in the world, the biggest collection of sharks in the southern hemisphere, a seal stadium, a dolphinarium, marine animals and exhibits, a mock-up 1940s steamer wreck featuring two classy restaurants, a shopping centre, and enough freshwater rides to make you seasick.

Sun Coast Casino   CASINO
(Map p226; ☎031-328 3000; www.suncoastcasino. co.za; OR Tambo Pde, Marine Pde) The glitzy, art deco–style casino is popular with locals and features slot machines, cinemas and some well-attended restaurants. The beach in front of the casino – Suncoast Beach – is a safe and pleasant spot to lie and bake. It has lawn, deckchairs and brollies.

Activities

With a temperate climate and excellent facilities, Durbanites are passionate about their nature, outdoor and adrenaline-inducing activities.

Cycling
With the recently completed pedestrian and bike promenades along the beachfront and linking the stadium to the beachfront, cycling is a fabulous way to see parts of Durban. Bicycles are available from STS Sport (Map p226; ☎031-312 9479; www.stssport. co.za; Shop 6, Moses Mabhida Stadium; per hr R40; ⊙8am-6pm). You'll need to leave identification and R100 as a deposit; unfortunately, you can't lock up the bikes along the way.

Boat Cruises
The luxury yacht African Queen (Map p230; ☎032-943 1118; Durban Yacht Harbour; ⊙departs 10am & 1pm) cruises dolphin waters for three hours. Several other boat and charter trips can be arranged from Wilson's Wharf.

  Ocean Safaris (Map p230; ☎084 565 5328; www.airandoceansafaris.co.za) is run by a marine scientist and offers one-/two-hour ocean tours (R250/400 per person) in an open, semirigid inflatable superduck. Trips depart from uShaka Marine World.

Diving & Fishing

PADI-qualified operator Calypso Dive & Adventure Centre (Map p230; ☎031-332 0905; www.calypsoushaka.co.za; uShaka Marine World) offers open-water diving courses (from R3000), and advanced courses and dives in nearby wrecks and elsewhere. Beginners' practice dives take place in uShaka's lagoon aquarium. Certified divers can also dive in uShaka's ocean aquarium (R400).

Casea Charters (☎031-561 7381; www .caseacharters.co.za; Grannies Pool, Main Beach, Umhlanga; 3-/4hr trip R400/500) is a family-run fishing charter business operating from Umhlanga (see p246). Rods, tackle and bait are supplied, and you can keep your catch at no additional fee. Whale and dolphin sightings are often an added bonus.

Golf

Durban has an array of decent golf courses. Windsor Park Municipal Golf Course (Map p226; ☎031-312 2245; fax 303 2479; Masabalala Yengwa Ave (NMR Ave); ☺visitors 9am-1pm Sat, 8-11am Sun) is a popular course. On another level is Durban Country Club (Map p226; ☎031-313 1777; Walter Gilbert Rd), considered by some to be the best golf course in South Africa.

Indoor Extreme Activities

Giant Gateway Mall (p240) houses some indoor extreme activities including one of the highest free-standing indoor climbing rocks in the world. Or you could try your surfing prowess at the artificial wave house – the water shots will have you performing tricks left, right and centre (your feet are secured into the board, so nonsurfers can have a go).

Skydiving

Skydive KZN (☎083 793 7055; www.skydivekzn .co.za; tandem jumps R1600) offers a seagull's view of Durban and surrounds.

Spectator Sports

Cricket, football and rugby are played in KwaZulu-Natal. Professional teams such as AmaZulu and Manning Rangers play in town, and international teams also visit.

Durban's proud new addition to its sporting infrastructure, 70,000-seat Moses Mabhida Stadium (p229) was constructed especially to host the 2010 World Cup.

With 60,000 seats, Kings Park Stadium (Map p226; ☎031-312 5022; Jacko Jackson Dr) is currently home to the Natal Sharks (www .sharksrugby.co.za) rugby team.

Cricket fever is cured here at Kingsmead Cricket Stadium (Map p226; ☎031-335 4200; 2 Kingsmead Cl), where the international knockabouts are hosted.

Surfing

For surfers, Durban has a multitude of good surfing beaches. Ocean Adventures (Map p230; ☎086 100 1138; www.surfandadventures. co.za; per lesson R150, board hire per hour/day R100/200; ☺7am-4.30pm) can be found on uShaka Beach, and kayak tours (R200) are also available.

☞ Tours

A good way to experience Durban is in the company of a professional tour guide. As well as those outlined below, many hostels arrange backpacker-oriented tours and activities in the Durban area and around KwaZulu-Natal.

Durban Tourism   CULTURAL TOUR
(Map p230; www.durbanexperience.co.za, www.dur ban.gov.za; 90 Florida Rd and Old Pavilion Site, North Beach, OR Tambo Pde (Marine Pde);) Runs a range of interesting three-hour walking tours of the oriental and historical regions of the city (minimum two people, adult R100), as well as township tours. It can also provide a list of tour guides and operators.

Ricksha Bus   BUS TOUR
(Map p230; Durban Tourism, 90 Florida Rd, Old Pavilion Site, North Beach, OR Tambo Pde (Marine Pde); adult/child R100/50) A three-hour tour in a rickshaw bus is a novel way to see the city. It covers some city highlights and heads to suburbs including Morningside (Florida Road). Buses depart twice daily at 9am and 1pm from the beach branch of Durban Tourism.

Natal Sharks Board   BOAT TOUR
(Map p230; ☎031-566 0400; www.shark.co.za; Wilson's Wharf; 2hr boat trip R250; ☺departs 6.30am) A fascinating trip is to accompany Natal Sharks Board personnel in their boat when they tag and release trapped sharks and other fish from the shark nets that protect Durban's beachfront. Boats depart from Wilson's Wharf, not to be confused with the head office, which is located in Umhlanga Rocks. The Umhlanga Rocks office (1A Herrwood Drive, Umhlanga Rocks; adult/child R35/20; ☺9am & 2pm Tue, Wed & Thu) has one-hour shows in which you can view a dissection.

KWAZULU-NATAL DURBAN

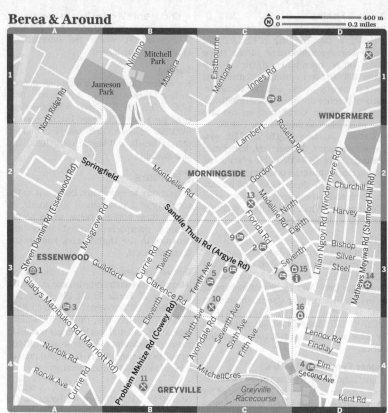

Festivals & Events

Durban International Film Festival FILM
(www.cca.ukzn.ac.za) A cinematic showcase of
200-plus films, held in July.

Awesome Africa Music Festival MUSIC
Highlighting music and theatre from
across the continent; held late September/
early October.

Diwali RELIGIOUS
The three-day Diwali (in December) is also
known as the Festival of Lights.

Sleeping

Despite what you may think when you see
the hotel-lined beachfront promenade,
much of Durban's best accommodation for
all budgets is in the northern, western and
northwestern suburbs, where there are upmarket B&Bs and hostels for the budget
traveller. Unless you are set on sleeping by

the sea, accommodation in the suburbs is
better value than the beachfront options.
Some hostels will collect you from the airport, and many arrange trips to the beach
and other places of interest. Many top-end
options are in the suburbs and towards Umhlanga Rocks, with a few in and around the
city centre.

CITY CENTRE
Note that the city centre shuts down (and is
less safe) at night.

Durban Hilton
International BUSINESS HOTEL $$$
(Map p230; ☎031-336 8100; www.hilton.com; 12
Walnut Rd; r incl breakfast R1550; P※@🛜🏊)
Glitzy and chic, this modern behemoth of-
fers a predictable hotel experience and at-
tracts mainly business travellers. Ask about
the specials.

Berea & Around

Happy Hippo BACKPACKERS **$**

(off Map p230; ☎031-368 7181; www.happy-hippo
.info, www.happy-hippo.co.za; 222 Mahatma Gandhi Rd (Point Rd); dm/d R150/470, dm/s/d without bathroom R140/330/370; 🛜) Close to the
beach, but in the dodgy part of town on Mahatma Gandhi Rd, is this spacious, well-run,
warehouse-style accommodation. The bright
colours, vast spaces and kitchen make for a
laid-back stay, though some travellers report
it's noisy; rooms are off communal areas.

BEREA & AROUND

TOP
CHOICE **Gibela Travellers**

Lodge BACKPACKERS **$$**

(Map p234; ☎031-303 6291; www.gibelaback
packers.co.za; 119 Ninth Ave, Morningside; dm/s/d
without bathroom, incl breakfast R200/390/530;
🅿@🛜) If this hostel (a tastefully converted
1950s Tuscan-style home) were a B&B, it
would be described as 'boutique'. One of
Durban's best hostels, it has sparkling sur-
faces and rooms neat enough to pass an
army major's inspection. It even provides a
continental breakfast – to be enjoyed in an
attractive indoor–outdoor dining area. The
staff is friendly, and helpful owner Elmar is

the man-in-the-know about all things Dur-
ban and beyond.

Rosetta House B&B **$$**

(Map p234; ☎031-303 6180; www.rosettahouse.
com; 126 Rosetta Rd, Morningside; s/d incl breakfast R675/950; 🅿❀🛜) This elegant place has
a country-chic feel – and there's not a thing
out of place. One of the rooms has a pleasant
deck area from where you can glimpse the
stadium and sea. It's perfect for mature travellers who seek comfort in a central location.

Concierge BOUTIQUE HOTEL **$$$**

(Map p234; ☎031-309 4453; www.the-concierge
.co.za; 37-43 St Mary's Ave; s/d incl breakfast
R950/1500; 🅿❀🛜) One of Durbs' most
cutting-edge sleeping options, this cleverly
designed spot – 12 cosy rooms in four pods –
is more about the design (urban, funky,
shape-oriented) than spaces (smallish, but
adequate). For breakfast, roll out of bed and
head to Freedom Cafe (p237), also on the
premises.

Brown's Bed & Breakfast B&B **$$$**

(Map p234; ☎031-208 7630; www.brownsguest
house.co.za; 132 Gladys Mazibuko Rd (Marriott Rd),
Essenwood; s/d incl breakfast R850/1500; 🅿❀)
In short, the chic interior attracts even chic-
er guests who enjoy the 'suites' – a choice
of four spacious rooms, each with a small
kitchen and smart living space.

Benjamin BOUTIQUE HOTEL **$$**

(Map p234; ☎031-303 4233; www.benjamin.co.za;
141 Florida Rd, Morningside; s/d incl breakfast
R850/1075; 🅿❀🛜🏊) This upmarket bou-
tique hotel is filled with smart rooms of the
'heavy drapes and floral furnishing' variety
(although the jute carpet is showing some
wear), around a pretty paved and green
courtyard area.

Quarters BOUTIQUE HOTEL **$$$**

(Map p234; ☎031-303 5246; www.quarters.co.za;
101 Florida Rd; s/d incl breakfast from R1410/1992;
🅿❀) Right in the throbbing heart of Durban's most fashionable eating and drinking
quarter, this attractive boutique hotel – at
two neighbouring locations – balances colonial glamour with small-scale home comforts. A restaurant is on site at both.

Tekweni Backpackers BACKPACKERS **$**

(Map p234; ☎031-303 1433; www.tekweniback
packers.co.za; 169 Ninth Ave, Morningside; dm R125,
s/d/tr without bathroom from R350/400/480;
🅿🛜) This old dog 'keeps on keeping on';
it's a slightly saggy place that nevertheless

KWAZULU-NATAL DURBAN

WORTH A TRIP

DURBAN TOWNSHIP STAY

For the more intrepid traveller, **Township Vibe Backpackers** (☎076 968 3066; www .vibetours.com; dm R120, s/d 220/305) offers an authentic overnight township experience. Situated only 14km from central Durban in the township of Westrich, 'TK' Thami Khuzway Karlijn has opened his home home – basic rooms with bunks and bathrooms – to visitors. He runs a range of cultural activities for his guests and encourages them to mingle with surrounding neighbours. TK is a keen poet, so poetry groups sometimes gather here. To get here, take a minibus taxi from the corner of Joe Slovo and Denis Hurley Sts, direction Newland West (R10); reservations necessary.

attracts the party animals who like raucous, gregarious surrounds.

GLENWOOD

Southeast of the city centre, Glenwood is one of Durban's oldest suburbs and is the most bohemian area. While we're not exactly talking rasta beanies or New York cutting edge, it has nevertheless a genuine sense of creative community, with some great cafes and sleeping options.

Mackaya Bella GUESTHOUSE **$$**
(☎031-205 8790; 137 Penzance Rd; s/d incl breakfast R660/880; P✴🖥🌀) Located near the university, this pretty spot has a lovely indigenous garden (featuring the Mackaya Bella plant) and stylish rooms in a relaxed homestyle environment. Best to reserve ahead as it's popular with university-associated guests. Follows some reasonable environmentally responsible practices.

Roseland Guesthouse GUESTHOUSE **$$**
(☎031-201 3256; www.roseland.co.za; 291 Helen Joseph Rd (Davenport Rd); s/d incl breakfast R700/900; P✴🖥🌀) An established, older-style, nicely appointed place.

NORTH DURBAN

The area north of Umgeni River comprises many suburbs, including Durban North and Umgeni Heights. Leafy, quiet and sedate, Durban North is one of Durban's wealthiest areas and is still easily accessible to the city and the North Coast.

Riverside Hotel & Spa HOTEL **$$$**
(☎031-563 0600; www.riversidehotel.co.za; 10 Northway, Durban North; s/d from R1950/2580; P🖥🌀) It's hard to miss this white behemoth just over Umgeni River on the right-hand side. The corridors have a touch of bling (LA-style neon-lit colonnades) but the rooms offer all the comforts of an upmarket

place. It's readily accessible to the city and Durban's North Coast.

Smith's Cottage BACKPACKERS **$$**
(☎031-564 6313; www.smithscottage.8m.com; 5 Mount Argus Rd, Umgeni Heights; dm R140, d from R400, self-catering cottage R800; P🖥🌀) Travellers praise this comfortable 'home away from home'. Friendly owners Keith and Pat offer accommodation in all shapes and sizes with a laid-back atmosphere. It's a bit further out, though within chirping distance of the Umgeni River Bird Park.

BEACHFRONT
Southern Sun Suncoast Hotel & Towers HOTEL **$$**
(Map p226; ☎031-314 7878; www.southernsun .com; 20 Battery Beach Rd; r from R1400; P✴🖥🌀) This hotel, adjacent to the casino, is a safe, if businesslike, bet. It has over 100 sleek and contemporary rooms with flash trimmings. Be aware that the 'Philadelphia suite' design means that the bathrooms are incorporated into the bedrooms themselves (read: little privacy among friends). Awesome vista from the top floor.

Protea Hotel Edward Durban BUSINESS HOTEL **$$**
(Map p230; ☎031-337 3681; www.proteahotels. com/edwarddurban; 149 OR Tambo Pde (Marine Pde); s R865-1820, d R995-2060; P✴@🌀) King of the seafront hotels, this is classic and comfortable, with fresh-polish smells and full-on decor.

🍴 Eating

Finding a decent bite to eat in Durban is rarely difficult; the ingredients are fresh and the helpings plentiful. Indian and Asian flavours abound, as do healthy meat and salad dishes (although these can become a little repetitive). Look out for the Indian snack (and a thick slice of Durban history), the bunny chow. It's a half or quarter loaf of bread hollowed out and filled with beans or curry stew.

CITY CENTRE

Around Dr Yusuf Dadoo St (Grey St) you'll find Indian takeaways (ask around). Otherwise, there are limited options at which to eat in the centre. The following are worth considering.

Roma Revolving Restaurant
INTERNATIONAL **$$**

(Map p230; ☎031-337 6707; www.roma.co.za; 32nd fl, John Ross House, Margaret Mncadi Ave (Victoria Embankment); mains R70-150; ⊙lunch & dinner; ❋) One of only several revolving restaurants worldwide, and one of the few central restaurants surviving in Durban. It offers stunning views over Durban in its own leaning House of John Ross; offers generous helpings of cuisine, focusing on Italian flavours.

Cafe Fish
SEAFOOD **$$**

(Map p230; ☎031-305 5062; www.cafefish.co.za; 31 Yacht Mole, Margaret Mncadi Ave (Victoria Embankment); mains R45-150; ⊙lunch & dinner) This distinctive green-and-blue construction looks a bit like an upside-down ship. It's a barn-sized spot, whose seafood dishes, while not fine dining, are indeed appealing. So, too, are the city and harbour views, and surrounding moored yachts. The best catch is the good-value set menu (four courses for between R150 and R220). It's not far from Wilson's Wharf.

BEACHFRONT

On the beachfront, you'll be hard-pressed to find much more than eateries serving the usual spread of burgers, pizza and candy floss. You are better off heading to the uShaka Marina or the Casino, both of which have some excellent choices.

Cargo Hold
SEAFOOD **$$**

(Map p230; ☎031-328 8065; uShaka Marina, the Point; mains R75-150; ⊙lunch & dinner) A seafood encounter of the most novel kind. On the *Phantom Ship* in uShaka Marina, your dining companions are fish with very large teeth – the glass tank forms one of the walls to a shark aquarium. Well known for casting some high-quality fish dishes with international flavours.

Cafe Jiran
CAFE **$$**

(Map p226; ☎031-332 4485; 151 Snell Pde; mains R60-150; ⊙6.30am-10pm) Next to Bel-Aire Suites Hotel, this funky space is the spot for a post-dip breakfast, or just for watching the beautiful people walk (run, cycle, skate) by. Evening fine dining options from Tuesday to Saturday.

Moyo
INTERNATIONAL **$$**

(Map p230; ☎031-332 0606; uShaka Marina, the Point; mains R60-110; ⊙lunch & dinner) Housed in the uShaka complex, Moyo is more novelty than quality cuisine, and makes for a fun (if noisy) night out. The concept is great – the decor features sculptures and decorations from recycled materials, and there's face painting, fabulous table-side serenades and bands of a high quality. But the food simply doesn't match the entertainment pizzazz.

BEREA & AROUND

Florida Rd is chock-a-block with lively eateries, cafes and bars, and nearby Lilian Ngoyi Rd (Windermere Rd) has some good options, too. There is a wonderful cafe hub opposite Mitchell Park on Innes Rd.

TOP CHOICE Market
INTERNATIONAL **$$**

(Map p234; www.marketrestaurant.co.za; 40 Gladys Mazibuko Rd (Marriott Rd); mains R60-140; ⊙ Mon-Sat) Both the food and crowd is 'gourmet' here – smart, fashionable and very nice. All meals – breakfasts, casual lunches and more formal dinners – are delectable. Imaginative dishes include the likes of calamari with quinoa and macadamia; produce is locally sourced, free range and organic, where possible. The cafe's tree-lined courtyard and fountain are the perfect antidote to the hot weather.

Freedom Cafe
CAFE **$**

(Map p234; www.tastefreedom.co.za; 37-43 St Mary's Ave; mains R45-75; ⊙7am-6pm Tue-Sun) An upmarket, colourful, funky place in an imaginatively converted space, with pebble garden. Good coffee and cakes, plus salads. It's behind Concierge Boutique Bungalows (p235).

Spiga D'oro
ITALIAN **$$**

(Map p234; ☎031-303 9511; 200 Florida Rd; mains R45-80; ⊙breakfast, lunch & dinner) Locals mention this in the 'of-course-you-already-know-about-Spiga-D'oro' tone. It looks like another typical cafe along this strip, yet it serves up hearty helpings of Italian food and good pasta dishes. A dining section in the rear requires reservations.

Cafe 1999
INTERNATIONAL $$

(Map p226; ☑031-202 3406; www.cafe1999.co.za; Silvervause Centre, Silverton Rd, Berea; mains R65-140; ☉lunch & dinner Sun-Fri, dinner Sat) This buzzing restaurant serves modern Mediterranean fusion food that comes in 'bit-parts' – 'titbit' and 'bigbit'. Reservations are recommended in the evenings. For something more casual but with great atmosphere, the owners also run **Unity Brasserie & Bar** (www.unitybar.co.za; mains R55-115; ☉noon-late Mon-Sat) next door. Think craft beers, including its own eco-friendly brew, Cowbell, and gastro-pub fare.

Spice
FUSION $$

(Map p234; ☑031-303 6375; www.diningout.co.za; 362 Lilian Ngoyi Rd (Windermere Rd), Morningside; mains R130-150; ☉lunch & dinner Tue-Sat, lunch Sun) Those in the cuisine scene rave about this place. Whether it's because the likes of Bill Gates and Bill Clinton have dined here (the latter at the former premises) or because the imaginative menu – South African and Indian fusion dishes – is so good, we'll leave for you to decide.

Joop's Place
STEAKHOUSE $$

(Map p234; ☑031-312 9135; Avonmore Centre, Ninth Ave, Morningside; mains R80-165; ☉dinner Mon-Thu & Sat, lunch & dinner Fri) Durbanites flock to this unpretentious place in a most unlikely location at the rear of a shopping centre for its high-quality steaks – and each steak is cooked by Joop. Rare, indeed.

9th Avenue Bistro
INTERNATIONAL $$

(Map p234; ☑031-312 9134; Avonmore Centre, Ninth Ave, Morningside; mains R120-140; ☉lunch & dinner Tue-Fri, dinner Mon & Sat) The setting, in the car park of the Avonmore Centre, isn't anything to rave about, but the fine dining experience is. This smart, modern spot serves up fabulously reliable international fare. The feature menu changes (often with venison, and the likes of smoked ostrich fillet), while the bistro standards include duck and fish.

GLENWOOD

Corner Cafe
CAFE $

(197 Brand Rd; mains R30-70; ☉6am-5pm Mon-Fri, 8am-3pm Sat) This warehouse-style cafe is one of Durbs' best (note the wonderful blown-up photo of Durbs and its 'burbs). It serves up home-baked pies and breads, great cakes, coffee and fresh juices, and 'green' foods – those with a low carbon footprint.

A breakfast treat are the dippy eggs – boiled eggs with Marmite soldiers!

Hemingway's
INTERNATIONAL $$

(131 Helen Joseph Rd (Davenport Rd); mains R50-130; ☉10am-10pm Mon-Sat, 9am-2.30pm Sun) This reliable, boutique-style spot has a pleasant atmosphere and whips up some good international fare, from beef fillets to curries. At time of research, it was planning to focus more on tapas dishes.

 Drinking & Nightclubs

The best drinking and dancing dens are found in the suburbs along Florida Road; the casino also has some good spots. Nightclubs seem to set up and close down to their own very fast beat; it's best to ask around for the latest offerings. The following have been some reliable stayers. Cover prices start at around R50 at some venues, depending on what's on.

Moyo uShaka Pier Bar
BAR

(Map p230; www.moyo.co.za; uShaka Marine World, the Point; drinks R45-55; ☉11am-late) Perched out on the edge of a pier in front of uShaka Marine World, this is Durban's top spot to head to zfor a South African sundowner (a tipple at sunset) with fabulous views of the harbour on one side, the Indian Ocean on the other, and the stadium and cityscape beyond. This is laid-back, exotic Durban at its chic best.

Bean Green
CAFE $

(147 Helen Joseph Rd (Davenport Rd); ☉8am-5pm Mon-Thu, 9am-1pm Sat; ☏) Calling all coffee snobs and wifi geeks: this is for you. This barely larger than a hole-in-the-wall, award-winning roaster serves single-origin beans (yes, they have finally hit Durbs!). Lounge back on the coffee-sack-covered sofa, listen to a few vinyls (there's a working turntable) and inject that quality caffeine.

Billy the Bum's
CLUB

(Map p226; 504 Lilian Ngoyi Rd (Windermere Rd), Morningside) Attracting a crowd of Durban's upwardly mobile (a sign even says 'elegantly wasted'), this suburban cocktail bar is reliably raucous.

Sasha's
CLUB

(Map p226; 17 Harvey Road; ☉Fri) Beautifully decorated, this relaxed place has seven bars and several dance floors and is currently one of the 'it' places. Mainstream music.

RIDE A 'RICKSHA'

Rickshaws, known locally as 'rickshas', ply their trade along OR Tambo Pde (Marine Pde), many sporting exotic Zulu regalia. In 1904 there were about 2000 registered rickshaw-pullers, and it was an important means of transport. A 15-minute ride costs about R50 (plus R10 for a happy snap).

Joe Kool's   CLUB
(Map p230; Lower OR Tambo Pde (Marine Pde), North Beach) The inevitable finish line for any day on the beach, this venerable nightspot cooks up a cocktail of cold beer, big-screen TV, dance music and feisty crowds.

Lounge   GAY & LESBIAN
(Map p234; ☎031-303 9023; www.thelounge.za.org; 226 Mathews Meyiwa Rd (Stamford Hill Rd)) With a range of different bars, this is a good place to hook up, and it caters to both gay men and women.

Origin   CLUB
(www.330.co.za; 9 Clark Rd, Lower Glenwood; ☺9pm-late Fri & Sat) Covering a range of music from deep house to electro, soul and funk, this stylish spot was the 'in' club at the time of research.

☆ Entertainment

Durban is a lively city with a vibrant cultural scene. Hundreds of events, from Natal Sharks games and cricket matches to film festivals and theatre performances, can be booked through Computicket (Map p230; ☎083 915 8000; www.computicket.co.za). There are outlets at the Playhouse Company, and at MTN shops at Pavilion and Gateway malls.

Live Music

KwaZulu-Natal Philharmonic
Orchestra   CLASSICAL MUSIC
(☎031-369 9438; www.kznpo.co.za) The orchestra has an interesting spring concert program with weekly performances in the City Hall (p227). It also performs in the 'Botanic Gardens Music at the Lake' concert series.

BAT Centre   MUSIC
(Map p230; ☎031-332 0451; www.batcentre.co.za; 45 Maritime Pl, Margaret Mncadi Ave (Victoria Embankment)) One of Durban's more interesting, arty haunts, this venue features jazz performances. Check what's on before heading

down; it can be disorganised and the area is isolated, so don't walk here at night.

Rainbow Restaurant & Jazz Club   JAZZ
(☎031-702 9161; www.therainbow.co.za; 23 Stanfield Lane, Pinetown) In Pinetown, 15km west of the centre, this was the first place in Natal to cater to blacks in a so-called white area in the 1980s. With a reputation as the centre of the jazz scene and still the preferred local haunt, it features concerts and headline acts on the first or last Sunday of the month. See the website for all other gigs.

Centre for Jazz   JAZZ
(Durban Campus University of KZN; South Ridge Rd) University of KwaZulu-Natal has contemporary music and jazz performances every Wednesday afternoon at 5pm during university terms. Performers vary from township jazz players and professional performers (the likes of Jimmy Dludlu and Sipho 'Hotstix' Mabuse) to student performers.

Theatre

Playhouse Company   THEATRE
(Map p230; ☎031-369 9444; www.playhousecompany.com; Anton Lembede St (Smith St)) Opposite City Hall, Durban's central theatre was recently renovated and is a stunning venue. The Zulu mosaics and beadwork in the foyer are alone worth seeing, as are the dance, drama and music performances.

Barnyard Theatre   THEATRE
(☎031-566 3945; www.barnyard theatre.co.za/; Gateway Mall, Umhlanga Ridge) This reconstructed barnyard houses mainstream theatre productions. Audience members can take their own food (and buy drinks at the bar) or buy food at the takeaway outlets.

Catalina Theatre   THEATRE
(Map p230; ☎031-305 6889; www.catalinatheatre.co.za; Wilson's Wharf, Margaret Mncadi Ave (Victoria Embankment)) Showcasing Durban's playwrights, poets and musicians, Catalina offers comedy, drama, musicals and poetry.

🛍 Shopping

Durban is known for its factory outlets. These stock goods at reasonable prices, with everything from surfing items to footwear.

Victoria St Market   MARKET
(Map p230; ☎031-306 4021; www.victoriastreetmarket.co.za; Bertha Mkhize St (Victoria St); ☺6am-6pm Mon-Fri, 8am-2pm Sat & Sun) At the western end of Bertha Mkhize St, this is the hub of the Indian community. It offers

KWAZULU-NATAL DURBAN

WANT MORE?

For in-depth information, reviews and recommendations at your fingertips, head to the Apple App Store to purchase Lonely Planet's *Durban City Guide* iPhone app.

a typically rip-roaring subcontinental shopping experience, with more than 160 stalls selling wares from across Asia. Watch your wallet and don't take valuables. Note: most shops run by Muslims close between noon and 2pm on Friday.

African Art Centre ARTS & CRAFTS
(Map p234; ☑031-312 3804/5; www.afriart.org.za; Florida Rd; ☺8.30am-5pm Mon-Fri, 9am-3pm Sat) This not-for-profit gallery has an excellent selection of high-quality work by rural craftspeople and artists.

Gateway Theatre of Shopping (Gateway Mall) MALL
(☑031-566 2332; www.gatewayworld.co.za; 1 Palm Blvd, Umhlanga Ridge; ☺9am-7pm Mon-Thu, to 9pm Fri & Sat, to 6pm Sun) The mother of all shopping malls is in the north of Durban and is popular with Durbanites.

Ike's Books & Collectables BOOKS
(Map p234; ☑031-303 9214; 48A Florida Rd, Morningside; ☺10am-5pm Mon-Fri, 9am-2pm Sat) More like a museum than a bookshop, this antique-filled delight is chock-a-block with 1st editions and is everything an antiquarian bookshop should be.

For necessities, other major shopping centres include **Musgrave Centre** (Map p226; ☑031-201 5129; Musgrave Rd, Musgrave) and **Pavilion** (☑031-265 0558; ☺9am-6pm Mon-Fri, to 5pm Sat, 10am-5pm Sun) on the city's outskirts in Westville, just an 8km drive from the centre on the N3 towards Pietermaritzburg.

❶ Information

Dangers & Annoyances
As with elsewhere in South Africa, crime against tourists and locals can and does occur in Durban. You should be aware and careful, but not paranoid. Muggings and pickpocketing, once a problem around the beach esplanade, have declined since that area's upgrade, but be careful here at night. Mahatma Gandhi Rd (Point Rd), south of Anton Lembede St (Smith St), should be avoided especially at night (take taxis to and from uShaka Marina).

Extra care should also be taken around the Umgeni Rd side of the train station and the Warwick Triangle markets.

At night, with the exception of the casino and around the Playhouse theatre (if something is on), central Durban becomes a ghost town as people head to the suburbs for entertainment. Always catch a cab to/from nightspots (and with others, if possible).

If you have a car, parking is generally OK outside suburban restaurants, but don't leave your car in the street all night: use off-street parking (note that most accommodation options offer it). Never leave valuables exposed on your car seats, even while driving.

Wherever you are, do not make yourself a target: don't carry or flaunt valuables of any kind and if you are confronted by muggers, never resist – hand over your valuables.

Emergency
Ambulance (☑10177)
General emergency (☑031-361 0000)
Police Main police office (☑10111; Stalwart Simelane St (Stanger St)); OR Tambo Pde (Marine Pde) (☑031-368 3399; OR Tambo Pde (Marine Pde)); Workshop (☑031-325 423; Samora Machel St (Aliwal St)); Prince St (☑031-367 4000; Prince St)

Internet Access
Wi-fi access is available at Europa Cafes (Florida Rd, Morningside, and Broadway, Durban North). Most hostels offer internet access. Charges start at about R40 per hour. Another option:
Citizen (161 Gordon Rd, Morningside; per hr R20; ☺8am-midnight)

Medical Services
Entabeni Hospital (☑031-204 1200, 24hr trauma centre 031-204 1377; 148 South Ridge Rd, Berea)
St Augustines (☑031-268 5000; 107 Chelmsford Rd, Berea) Good emergency department.
Umhlanga Hospital (☑031-560 5500; 323 Umhlanga Rocks Dr, Umhlanga) Handy for the North Coast and north Durban.
Travel Doctor (☑031-360 1122; durban@traveldoctor.co.za; International Convention Centre, 45 Ordinance Rd; ☺8am-4pm Mon-Fri, 8am-noon Sat) For travel-related advice.

Money
There are banks with ATMs and change facilities across the city. These include Standard Bank, FNB, Nedbank and ABSA.
American Express Musgrave Centre (☑031-202 8733; FNB House, 151 Musgrave Rd, Musgrave)

KWAZULU-NATAL DURBAN

Bidvest Bank (☑031-202 7833; Shop 311, Level 3, Musgrave Centre, Musgrave Rd; ◷9am-5pm Mon-Fri, to 1pm Sat)

Post

There are post offices in the major shopping centres, including the Musgrave and Windermere Centres.

Main post office (cnr Dr Pixley KaSeme (West) & Dorothy Nyembe (Gardiner) Sts; ◷8am-4.30pm Mon-Fri, to noon Sat) Near City Hall.

Tourist Information

You can pick up a free copy of the *Events Calendar* or the half-yearly *Destination Durban*. For booking accommodation at Ezemvelo KZN Wildlife parks and reserves, see p283.

Durban Tourism (www.durbanexperience.co .za) uShaka Marine World (☑031-337 8099; ◷9am-6pm); Morningside (☑031-322 4164; 90 Florida Rd; ◷8am-4.30pm Mon-Fri); Beachfront (☑031-322 4205; Old Pavilion Site, OM Tambo Pde (Marine Pde); ◷8am-5pm) A useful information service on Durban and surrounds. It can help with general accommodation and arranges tours of Durban and beyond. Several branches are located around the city.

King Shaka Airport Tourist Information Office (☑032-436 0013; international arrivals hall; ◷7am-9pm) Durban Tourism, KwaZulu-Natal Tourism Authority and Ezemvelo KZN Wildlife all share a desk (the latter open 8am to 4.30pm Monday to Friday only) at the airport.

KwaZulu-Natal Tourism Authority (KZN Tourism; ☑031-366 7500; www.zulu.org.za; ground fl, Tourist Junction) Information office dealing with the whole province and offering a smorgasbord of reference and promotional brochures.

South African Parks Reservations (www .sanparks.org; Green Hub, 31 Steibel Place, Blue Lagoon; ◷8am-4.30pm) Moving at the time of research, possibly to the Green Hub at the eastern end of OR Tambo Pde (Marine Pde). Takes accommodation bookings for national parks across the country.

Getting There & Away

Air

King Shaka International Airport (☑032-436 6585) Opened in 2010, the new airport is at La Mercy, 40km north of the city.

Several airlines link Durban with South Africa's other main centres. Internet fares vary greatly depending on the day of the week, month and even time of day. Prices start at around R400 but can be even cheaper.

1time (www.1time.co.za) A no-frills airline offering some great deals to Johannesburg (Jo'burg) and Cape Town.

Kulula.com (www.kulula.com) A budget competitor to 1time, linking Durban with Jo'burg, Cape Town and Port Elizabeth.

Mango (www.flymango.com) Another no-frills airline with flights to Jo'burg and Cape Town.

South African Airlink (SAAirlink; www.fly airlink.co.za) Flies daily to Port Elizabeth, Bloemfontein and George.

South African Airways (SAA; www.flysaa.com) Flies at least once daily to Jo'burg, Port Elizabeth, East London, Cape Town, George and Nelspruit.

Bus

The **Baz Bus** (www.bazbus.com) is based in Cape Town; see p599 for more information. You can hop on and off as often as you like along the Baz Bus route for a given price, and can be picked up and dropped off at selected hostels. The seven-/14-/21-day pass (R1200/2100/2600) allows you to travel in any direction and as often as you like within the time period. At the time of research, the route to Swaziland and St Lucia was no longer operating.

Long-distance buses leave from the bus stations near the **Durban train station** (Masabalala Yengwa Ave (NMR Ave)). Enter the station from Masabalala Yengwa Ave (NMR Ave), not Umgeni Rd. The following long-distance bus companies have their offices here.

Eldo Coaches (☑031-307 3363) Has three buses daily to Jo'burg (R180 to R270, eight hours).

Greyhound (☑083 915 9000; www.greyhound .co.za) Has daily buses to Jo'burg (R300 to R310, eight hours), Cape Town (R590, 22 to 27 hours), Port Elizabeth (R455, 15 hours) and Port Shepstone (R110, 1¾ hours).

Within KZN, Greyhound buses run daily to Pietermaritzburg (R195 to R265, one hour) and Ladysmith (R275, four hours), among other destinations.

Intercape (☑0861 287 287; www.intercape .co.za) Has several daily buses to Jo'burg (R220 to R300, eight hours). For connections to Mozambique, buses head to Maputo (via Jo'burg; R300, 15 hours).

KWAZULU-NATAL DURBAN

AIRPORT SHUTTLE

The **King Shaka Airport Shuttle Bus** (☑031-465 5573; airportbus@mweb .co.za) runs hourly between hotels and key locations in Durban and the beachfront via Umhlanga Rocks. Costs start from R50 to Umhlanga to R80 and above for Durban suburbs.

MINIBUS TAXI

Some long-distance minibus taxis leave from stops in the streets opposite the Umgeni Rd entrance to the Durban train station. Others running mainly to the South Coast and the Wild Coast region of Eastern Cape leave from around the Berea train station. Check with your cab driver; they usually know the departure points. Be alert in and around the minibus taxi ranks.

Intercity (☎031-305 9090; www.intercity .co.za) Operates daily services from Durban to Margate (R100, 2½ hours), Jo'burg's inter-national airport (R200 to R250, 8½ hours), Jo'burg's Park Station Bus Terminal (R250, 8½ hours) and Pretoria (R200 to R225, nine hours).

Margate Mini Coach (☎039-312 1406) Head to the Greyhound office for this company, which links Durban and Margate three times a day (R110 one way, R220 for a same-day return, 2½ hours).

Translux (☎0861 589 282; www.translux .co.za) Runs daily buses to Jo'burg (R200 to R240, eight hours) and Cape Town (R560, 27 hours). Cheaper City to City buses, operated in partnership with Translux, go to destinations across the country.

Note: tickets for all long-distance buses can be bought from Shoprite/Checkers shops and on-line from **Computicket** (www.computicket.com).

A new service runs between Durban and Mozambique departing from the **Pavilion Hotel** (☎073 427 8220, 072 278 1 921; 15 Old Fort Road; R280) at 6.30am on Wednesday and Sun-days to Maputo. (They depart Maputo for Dur-ban every Tuesday and Saturday.) Tickets can be purchased on the day at the bus; arrive by 6am.

Car

Hiring a car is one of the best options in KZN; car travel is by far the easiest way of getting around.

Aroundabout Cars (☎021-422 4022; www .aroundaboutcars.com) This is a Cape Town–based agent for Sixt/1First in Durban. Its rates are competitive and it has options including unlimited mileage and full insurance.

Most major car-rental companies also have offices at the airport:

Avis (☎0861 021 111, 011-923 3660)

Budget (☎011-398 0123)

Europcar (☎0861 131 000)

Train

Durban train station (Masabalala Yengwa Ave (NMR Ave)) is huge. The local inner-city or suburban trains are not recommended for trav-ellers; these are not commonly used and even hardy travellers report feeling unsafe.

However, mainline passenger long-distance services are another matter – they are efficient and arranged into separate male and female sleeper compartments. These are run by **Shosholoza Meyl** (☎031-361 7167; www .shosholozameyl.co.za) and include the *Trans Natal*, which leaves Durban several times a week for Jo'burg (R220, 12½ hours) via Pietermaritz-burg and Ladysmith.

The fully serviced luxury **Premier Classe** (☎031-361 7167; www.premierclasse.co.za) has Jo'burg to Durban departures on the last Friday of the month, returning Durban to Jo'burg the following Sunday. Tickets should be booked in advance (R1010, about 14 hours).

The **Rovos** (☎012-315 8242; www.rovosrail.co .za) is a luxury steam train on which, from a mere R13,000, you can enjoy old-world luxury on a three-day choof from Durban to Pretoria via the Battlefields and nature reserves.

ℹ Getting Around

To/From the Airport

Some hostels run their own taxi shuttle services for clients at competitive prices. By taxi, the same trip costs around R400. See boxed text, p241, for details on the King Shaka Airport Shuttle Bus.

Bus

The useful **Durban People Mover** (☎031-309 5942; www.durbanpeoplemover.co.za), a shuttle-bus service that operates along several routes within the city, links the beachfront to the city centre and runs the length of the beachfront from uShaka Marine World to Suncoast Casino with designated stops (including the Victoria St Market and City Hall) along the way. Tickets (R15) can be purchased on the bus and allow you to get on and off the route as many times as you like within a day. Single-leg tickets cost R4. The service runs daily between 6.30am and 11pm. Dr A B Xuma St (Commercial Rd) is across from the Workshop.

Durban Transport (☎031-309 5942) runs the bus services Mynah and Aqualine. Mynah covers most of the city and local residential areas. Trips cost around R5 and you get a slight discount if you prepurchase 10 tickets. Stops include North Beach, South Beach, Musgrave Rd/Mitchell Park Circle, the Peter Mokaba Ridge/Vause, Botanic Gardens and Kensington Rd. The larger Aqualine buses run through the outer-lying Durban met-ropolitan area.

Taxi

Always use metered cabs. A taxi between the beach and Florida Rd, Morningside, usually costs about R50. Companies running a reliable 24-hour service include **Mozzie Cabs** (☎0860 669 943), **Zippy Cabs** (☎031-202 7067/8) and **Eagle** (☎0800 330 336).

SOUTH COAST

South of Durban is a 160km-long string of seaside resorts and suburbs running from Amanzimtoti to Port Edward, near the border of Eastern Cape. There's a bit of a groundhog-day feel about this mass of shoulder-to-shoulder getaways that are spread out along two routes – the N2 and the R102. However, the coastal region's sandy beaches are interspersed with some pretty gardens and grassy areas, especially in the southern section. The region is a surfers' and divers' delight (the latter because of Aliwal Shoal dive site; see boxed text, p244), and in summer there ain't much room to swing a brolly. Inland, the sugar cane, bananas and palms provide a pleasant, lush, green contrast to the beach culture. The attractive **Oribi Gorge Nature Reserve**, near Port Shepstone, provides beautiful forest walks, eating and accommodation options.

Pick up the useful brochure *Southern Explorer* (www.southernexplorer.co.za).

WARNER BEACH

Warner Beach is the first place along the strip that offers a bit of breathing space. Further south, Umkomaas and Scottburgh are good diving-off points for Aliwal Shoal (see boxed text, p244).

Information is available from **Tourism Umdoni** (☎039-976 1364; www.scottburgh.co.za; Scott St, Scottburgh; ☉8am-5pm Mon-Fri, to 1pm Sat), next to the Scottburgh Memorial Library.

The best budget accommodation along this strip is **Blue Sky Mining Backpackers & Lodge** (☎031-916 5394; www.blueskymining. co.za; 5 Nelson Palmer Rd, Warner Beach; campsites per person R70, dm R120, d R350, tr R390; P@☎), an ever-expanding designer-recycler's delight with a range of sleeping spaces, including a choice of two main houses and a good outlook over the water below.

UMZUMBE & UMTENTWENI

On the coastal strip north of Port Shepstone, Umzumbe and Umtentweni make for pleasant stopovers.

🛏 Sleeping & Eating

Spot Backpackers BACKPACKERS **$**
(☎039-695 1318; www.spotbackpackers.com; 23 Ambleside Rd, Umtentweni; campsites R80, dm/d without bathroom R120/300, cabin d R400) Close to Port Shepstone, this is spot-on for position (a right-on-the-beach deal for sand, sun and surf) and is a justifiably popular, albeit

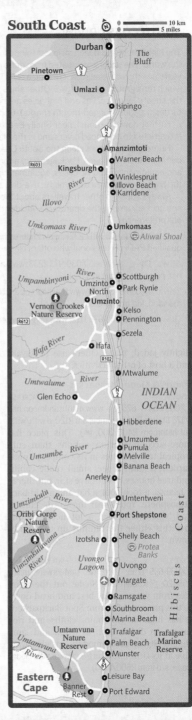

South Coast

KWAZULU-NATAL

SOUTH COAST DIVING

The highlight of this beach strip is **Aliwal Shoal**, touted as one of the best dive sites in the world. The shoal was created from dune rock around 30,000 years ago. A mere 6500 years ago the sea level rose, creating a reef. This reef was named after a ship, the *Aliwal*, which ran aground here in 1849. Other ships have since met a similar fate here. Today, the shoal's ledges, caves and pinnacles are home to everything from wrecks to rays, turtles, 'raggies' (ragged-mouth sharks), tropical fish and soft corals.

Further down the coast, near Shelly Beach, the extraordinary **Protea Banks** dive site is restricted to advanced divers and is the place to see sharks.

Numerous operators along the South Coast offer dive charters, PADI courses and accommodation packages. Packages vary enormously from dive to dive, accommodation and equipment. (In some cases, equipment hire may cost extra.) To give you an idea, at the time of research, a three-night, five-dive package cost around R3000.

Always speak to other travellers about their experiences because safety briefings can, and do, vary among the operators – incidents can, and do, occur. The following reflect our preferences.

2nd Breath (☎039-317 2326; www.2ndbreath.co.za; cnr Bank St & Berea Rd, Margate) Highly qualified PADI professional who offers classes and takes safety issues very seriously.

Aliwal Dive Centre (☎039-973 2233; www.aliwalshoal.co.za; 2 Moodie St, Umkomaas) Also has pleasant rooms available.

Shoal (☎039-973 1777; www.theshoal.co.za; 21 Harvey St, Umkomaas) A newer, but recommended, kid on the block.

Quo Vadis (☎039-978 1112; www.raggiecave.com; Scottburgh) Based at Cutty Sark Hotel.

slightly jaded, place. Offers use of kayaks and a host of other activities.

Mantis & Moon Backpacker Lodge
BACKPACKERS $
(☎039-684 6256; www.mantisandmoon.net; 7/178 Station Rd, Umzumbe; dm R120, d with/without bathroom R400/300; 🐾). This place has more accommodation options than subtropical tree varieties in its compact jungle garden: a giant tepee, small rustic cabins and tree houses. It's not five star, but there's a Jacuzzi, a rock pool, a bar and a laid-back atmosphere. You'll hear the words 'chilled' and 'vibe' mentioned a lot here; visitors give this either the thumbs up or thumbs down.

Zizi's
INTERNATIONAL $$
(☎039-695 1295; Third Ave, Umtentweni; mains R55-120; ⊙8.30am-late) Shake out the wrinkles from your Sunday best and head down to this place, not far from Spot Backpackers. It has high-backed chairs, cloths, and rich sauces on dishes such as oxtail and lamb shanks. Stylish accommodation is also available at its **Umdlalo Lodge** (www.umdlalolodge .co.za; s/d from R600/1100).

❶ Getting There & Away

Greyhound (☎083 915 9000; www.greyhound .co.za) has daily buses between Port Shepstone and Durban (R235, 1¾ hours). If you are staying at one of the backpackers, ask the driver to drop you in Umzumbe or Umtentweni. The **Baz Bus** (www.bazbus.com) also runs here.

ORIBI GORGE NATURE RESERVE & AROUND
☎039

The **Oribi Gorge Nature Reserve** (☎039-679 1644; www.kznwildlife.com; admission R10, campsites R65, 2-bed hut R320; ⊙6am-6pm summer, 7.30am-4.30pm winter) is inland from Port Shepstone, off the N2. The spectacular gorge, on the Umzimkulwana River, is one of the highlights of the South Coast with beautiful scenery, animals and birds, plus walking trails and pretty picnic spots. The reception office is accessed via the N2 on the southern side of the gorge. Here, too, are some delightful wooden chalets, nestled in the forest – the perfect base for those who wish to spend time in this area.

Alternatively, if you come via Oribi Flats Rd, the **Ezinqoleni Information Office** (☎039-687 7561; ⊙8am-4pm) has a useful map of the area.

Organised activities are offered by Wild 5 Extreme Adventures (☑082 566 7424), at Oribi Gorge Hotel. It offers a 100m Wild Swing (free-fall jump and swing) off Lehr's Falls (R380), abseiling (R300), white-water rafting (R495), horse riding (R200 per 1½ hours) and a zip-line across the gorge (R220). It's located 11km off the N2 along Oribi Flats Rd.

Lake Eland Game Reserve (☑039-687 0395; www.lakeeland.co.za; day visitors adult/child R40/30, cottage Mon-Fri per person R100, minimum R400, campsites/dm R80/200, 2-person cabin R450-650; ☺7am-5.30pm) has as over 40 species of animals and 200 bird species. You can head off on a self-drive (R40 per person) or a wildlife drive (R150 per person, minimum four). A 4.7km zip-line is the newest craze (R400 to R500, including gate entry). A short gorge walk crosses a 130m-high suspension bridge, and fishing and canoeing are available. There are well-maintained log cabins overlooking a small lake; fishermen's cottages; camping; and dorm beds in a huge pipe! A restaurant is open from 8am to 4pm. You'll find the reserve 40km from Port Shepstone; drive 26km along Oribi Flats Rd off the N2.

Leopard Rock Lookout Chalets (☑039-687 0303; www.leopardrockc.co.za; Main Oribi Gorge Rd; d incl breakfast R900-1200; ☺9am-4pm Wed-Sun) It's likely you'll find the appetising meals here more tasteful than the sign that reads 'children found unattended in this garden will be sold into slavery'. The dining deck boasts a superb view of the uMzumkulu Gorge, and accommodation is in four pleasant chalets, although it's the vista that's the winner. Thoughtful touches include a sherry bottle and glasses, and two massive chairs in the lounge room for kicking back and letting Africa come to you. Dinner (R40 to R80) is available on request.

RAMSGATE, SOUTHBROOM & AROUND

The tourist hub of Margate is a claustrophobic concrete jungle with a string of loud and lively bars. You're better off heading to nearby Ramsgate, which has a nice little beach, or to the lush green confines of Southbroom, the posh neck of the woods, but delightful for the fact that it's within a bushbuck (a large type of antelope) conservancy.

Information is available from Hibiscus Coast Tourism (☑039-312 2322; www.hibiscus coast.kzn.org.za; Panorama Pde, Main Beach, Margate; ☺8am-5pm Mon-Fri, to 1pm Sat, 9am-1pm Sun).

◉ Sights & Activities

Umtamvuna Nature Reserve (www.kzn wildlife.com; adult/concession R10/5; ☺6am-6pm Apr-Sep, 7am-5pm Oct-Mar) is on a gorge on the Umtamvuna River (which forms part of the border with Eastern Cape). This beautiful dense forest has great nature walks, with wildflowers in spring, plus mammals and many species of birds. To get to the reserve from Port Edward, follow the signs off R61 to Izingolweni and continue for 8km. Pick up a brochure at the reserve's entrance.

🛏 Sleeping

Sunbirds B&B $$

(☑039-316 8202; 643 Outlook Rd, Southbroom; s/d R595/950; P 🅿🛇⛵) Welcoming hosts, wonderful breakfasts on the verandah (with good views), a smart, spacious lounge and homely ambience keep the guests coming here.

Southbroom Backpackers Lodge BACKPACKERS $$

(☑039-316 8448; www.southbroomtravellerslodge. co.za; 11 Cliff Rd, Southbroom; s R220-260, d from 400; P⛵) Joy, oh joy – a good-value place in this upmarket area, a beautiful neck of the (subtropical) woods and a 10-minute walk from the beach. This comfortable, laid-back place resembles a large holiday home with light and airy rooms, a massive lounge, a pool and a lovely garden.

Treetops Lodge B&B $$

(☑039-317 2060; www.treetopslodge.co.za; 3 Poplar Rd, Margate; d from R980, family unit R990; ⛵) This pleasant pebble-dashed place has neat, if dated, double rooms with breakfast, plus a self-catering unit. The rooms overlook green foliage, and there's a massive shared balcony with your own table and chairs. Rates outside the Christmas season are significantly lower.

Vuna Valley Venturers BACKPACKERS $$

(☑039-311 3602; www.vunavalleyventurers.co.za; 9 Mitchell Rd, Banners Rest; d/f R440/560; ❄) By the entrance to the Umtamvuna Nature Reserve – inland from Port Edward – Vuna Valley has stylish double cabins and more budget (but very pleasant) rooms in the main house. Walking, cycling and canoeing opportunities are nearby.

✕ Eating

Waffle House
VEGETARIAN $$

(Marine Dr, Ramsgate; mains R40-100; ☉9am-5pm; 🖋) People flock to this pleasant spot on the edge of a lagoon for fresh Belgian-style waffles with every sweet and savoury filling under the sun. There are queues in the holiday season.

Trattoria La Terrazza
ITALIAN $$

(☎039-316 6162; Southbroom; mains R75-115; ☉lunch Fri-Sun, dinner Tue-Sat) Ask for a restaurant recommendation in the area and the answer is overwhelmingly this Italian option. It has a popular meaty menu such as caramelised pork (R70), and chicken with Parma ham and asparagus cream sauce. The setting, on an estuary, is gorgeous. Reservations recommended.

Burlesque Cafe
INTERNATIONAL $

(Marine Dr, Ramsgate; mains R55-65; ☉9am-4pm) A quirky little retro treat with a chic vintage interior and cheeky menu items featuring organic produce.

❶ Getting There & Away

Margate Mini Coach (☎031-312 1406; www .margate.co.za) links Durban and Margate three times daily (one-way R110). Book through **Hibiscus Coast Tourism** (☎039-312 2322; www .tourismsouthcoast.co.za; Panorama Pde, Main Beach, Margate; ☉8am-5pm Mon-Fri, to 1pm Sat, 9am-1pm Sun).

Intercity Express (☎031-305 9090; www .intercity.co.za) has an office in Hibiscus Coast Tourism, and runs regular buses between Margate and Jo'burg (R330 to R400, 10 hours).

NORTH COAST

The North Coast, the coastal strip from Umhlanga Rocks north to Tugela River, is a profusion of upmarket time-share apartments and retirement villages with some pleasant beaches. The section from Zimbali, slightly north of Umhlanga, to the Tugela is known as the Dolphin Coast. The coast gets its name from the bottlenose dolphins that favour the area, attracted by the continental shelf and warm water conditions.

The North Coast and its surrounds are home to a fascinating mix of peoples: descendants of former colonialists, Indians, French-Mauritian sugar-cane growers and indentured labourers from the Indian subcontinent, plus colourful Zulu cultures.

North Coast

0 ——— 5 km
0 ——— 2.5 miles

Darnall
KwaDukuza (Stanger)
R74
Blythedale
Umvoti River
Groutville
N2
Tinley Manor Beach
Dolphin Coast
Umhlali River
Sheffield Beach
Umhlali
Salt Rock
Shaka's Rock
Ballito
Zimbali
Tongaat
Westbrook Beach
INDIAN OCEAN
R102
La Mercy
uMdloti Beach
Gateway Mall
Umhlanga Lagoon Nature Reserve
Natal Sharks Board
Umhlanga Rocks

King Shaka is said to have established a military camp on the coast; royal handmaidens gathered salt from tidal pools, since immortalised in the name Salt Rock. A memorial to King Shaka can be found at KwaDukuza (Stanger), slightly inland.

Metropolitan buses run between Durban and Umhlanga Rocks, and buses and minibus taxis also run between Durban and KwaDukuza (Stanger) and other inland towns.

Umhlanga Rocks & uMdloti Beach

☐ 031

The buckle of Durban's chichi commuter belt, Umhlanga is a cosmopolitan mix of upmarket beach resort, moneyed suburbia and small malls. Umhlanga means 'Place of Reeds' (the 'h' is pronounced something like 'sh'). Further north, uMdloti Beach has some good restaurants. Both locations are convenient to the airport.

Umhlanga Tourism Information Centre (☏031-561 4257; www.umhlangatourism.co.za; Shop 1A, Chartwell Centre, Chartwell Dr, Umhlanga Rocks; ☺8.30am-5pm Mon-Fri, 9am-1pm Sat) offers advice, and metro buses 716 and 706 run between Umhlanga and Durban.

◉ Sights & Activities

Natal Sharks Board　　　　ECOTOUR
(☏031-566 0400; www.shark.co.za; 1A Herrwood Dr, Umhlanga Rocks; audiovisual & dissection adult/child R35/20; ☺8am-4pm Mon-Fri, noon-6pm Sun) This research institute is dedicated to studying sharks, specifically in relation to their danger to humans. There are audiovisual presentations and shark dissections at 9am and 2pm Tuesday, Wednesday and Thursday. The public can accompany Sharks Board personnel on their boat trips from Durban (see p233).

Natal Sharks Board is signposted; it's about 2km out of town, up steep Umhlanga Rocks Dr (the M12 leading to the N3).

FREE **Umhlanga Lagoon**
Nature Reserve　　　　NATURE RESERVE
(parking R5; ☺6am-9pm) Found on a river mouth just north of town, you'll see many bird species here (despite its small size, at 26 hectares). The trails lead through stunning dune forest, across the lagoon and onto the beach.

🛏 Sleeping

Umhlanga is crowded with holiday apartments and B&Bs, most of which are close to the beach. Hotel prices are seasonal and vary enormously; expect fluctuations between seasons.

Beverley Hills Sun
Intercontinental　　　　HOTEL $$$
(☏031-561 2211; www.southernsun.com; Lighthouse Rd; s/d incl breakfast R3800/4000; P❋🛜🏊) They didn't pull out all stops on the exterior, but this top-notch classic is deliciously stylish on the inside. It's the perfect place for a platinum-card splurge.

On the Beach Backpackers　　BACKPACKERS $$
(☏031-562 1591; www.durbanbackpackers.com; 17 The Promenade, Glenashley; dm R150, d from R500; P🛜🏊) Four kilometres south of Umhlanga is Glenashley, where you'll find this light and airy converted house-cum-backpackers; it's

the best budget beach option in this neck of the woods.

Drifters Dolphin Coast
Lodge　　　　BACKPACKERS $$
(☏011-888 1160; www.drifters.co.za; 76 North Beach Road, uMdloti; s/d R425/690) Part of the Drifters adventure group, this is a reasonably priced beachfront accommodation – it's a freestyle stroke from the beach. Offers basic, clean and airy rooms, all with ocean views. It's sometimes booked with the company's own safari truck groups.

Fairlight Beach House　　GUESTHOUSE $$$
(☏031-568 1835; www.fairlight.co.za; 1 Margaret Bacon Ave, Ballito; with breakfast R1320-1700) A sprawling, smart guesthouse that overlooks the beach, with 10 rooms (not all with views). It's smart, and attracts a business crowd. Prices are lower outside the high season.

🍴 Eating

Ile Maurice　　　　FRENCH $$$
(☏031-561 7609; 9 McCausland Cres, Umhlanga Rocks; mains R90-270; ☺lunch & dinner Tue-Sun) For a special seaside splurge with a Gallic touch, try this chic eatery; it has *bon gout* (good taste), and has a reputation among Durban's connoisseurs as la-place-to-eat-by-la-mer. Reserve in the evenings.

Two excellent side-by-side options, with large terraces overlooking uMdloti Beach, attract the weekend crowds from Durban – and justifiably so. Each serves top-notch international cuisine:

Bel Punto　　　　INTERNATIONAL $$
(☏031-568 2407; www.belpunto.co.za; uMdloti Beach; mains R90-170)

Mundo Vida　　　　INTERNATIONAL $$
(☏031-568 2286; www.mundovida.co.za; uMdloti Beach; mains R100-130)

Ballito
📋032

Ballito – and up to Shaka's Rock and Salt Rock – lacks Zulu flavour; the area is a continuous strip of seaside suburbia, luxury guesthouses and multistorey condos, most with pleasant beaches at their doorstep. The advantage is its proximity to the airport (around 22km).

Sangweni Tourism Centre (☏032-946 1997; www.thedolphincoast.co.za; cnr Ballito Dr &

Link Dr; ⏱7.45am-4.15pm Mon-Fri, 9am-1pm Sat) houses the Dolphin Coast Publicity Association, which lists accommodation in the area. It's located near the BP station, where you leave the N2 to enter Ballito.

🛏 Sleeping & Eating

Guesthouse　　　　　　　　GUESTHOUSE $$
(☎032-525 5683; www.theguesthouse.co.za; Ipahla Lane; s/d with breakfast R600/900; P🅿🛜) Five rooms in a pleasant neat-as-a-pin, slightly dated house (the owner's home). Best is the garden-facing room with private entrance.

Boathouse　　　　　　　　GUESTHOUSE $$$
(☎032-946 0300; www.boathouse.co.za; 33 Compensation Beach Rd; s R1230-1405, d R2090-2460) Upmarket choice for those who'd like treat themselves to a coastal base.

Monkey Bay Backpackers　　BACKPACKERS $
(☎071 348 1278; www.monkeybaybackpackers .co.za; 9C Jack Powell Rd; dm/d R120/250) Calling all surf-rats. This casual place – made from recycled materials, and painted in funky colours inside – has a pleasantly hippie vibe and friendly owner. Bathrooms are slightly limited, but it's handy to the sea and is one of the few budget options in the area.

Waterberry Coffee Shoppe　　DELI/CAFE $$
(☎032-946 2797; www.thewaterberry.co.za; Dolphin Cres; mains R46-80; ⏱8.30am-4pm) The perfect place to eat your way through a hot afternoon, under the canopy of lush coastal forest. Feast on fabulous homemade cakes or a range of healthy salads.

KwaDukuza (Stanger) & Around

📞032 / POP 36,700

In July 1825, Shaka established KwaDukuza as his capital, and royal residence. It was here that he was killed in 1828 by his half-brothers Mhlangane and Dingaan; Dingaan then took power (see boxed text, p248). Each year Zulus don their traditional gear and gather in the Recreational Grounds for the King Shaka Day Celebration (see boxed text, p256).

Also known as Stanger, KwaDukuza is a busy, rough-and-ready town with a large Indian population and an African buzz. The town has no accommodation, but it's an important stop for those undertaking a Shaka pilgrimage or those interested in Zulu culture.

The King Shaka Visitor Centre (☎032-552 7210; 5 King Shaka Rd; admission free; ⏱8am-4pm Mon-Fri, 9am-4pm Sat & Sun) is worth visiting for limited, but clear, historical information about Shaka and his kingdom.

Dukuza Museum (☎032-437 5075; King Shaka Rd; admission by donation; ⏱8.30am-4pm Mon-Fri), opposite the interpretive centre, has related historical exhibits.

Head to King Shaka Rd to visit the Shaka Memorial Gardens, where a memorial stone was erected in 1932 over Shaka's

---

LEGENDARY KING SHAKA

Despite all that is written about him, King Shaka was an enigmatic and controversial figure. Whether fact or mythology, Shaka is frequently portrayed as either a vicious and bloodthirsty tyrant or a military genius.

Shaka was the illegitimate son of Queen Nandi, to whom he was very close. By the 1820s he had created one of the most powerful kingdoms in the subcontinent. Violence was one of his weapons, both against his enemy and his own warriors. (On the death of his mother it is said that he killed many Zulus, whom he believed weren't grieving enough.)

He is probably best known for his fighting tactics: he devised the ingenious 'bull formation' where groups of warriors – the 'head and chest' – penetrated the enemy front on, while the 'horns' encircled the enemy from behind. He shortened the throwing spear to a short-shafted, close-range stabbing spear and lengthened the shield.

In 1828 Shaka's life came to an unpleasant end – he was murdered by his half-brothers Dingaan and Mhlangane (who was later toppled by Dingaan). Contemporary Zulus are incredibly proud of their 'warrior king'. Shaka Day is celebrated annually on 24 September at the Shaka Memorial Gardens in KwaDukuza (see p248). Thousands of Zulus wearing traditional dress and carrying shields, spears and dancing sticks descend upon the gardens. The current king and the chief minister Dr Buthelezi usually lead the celebration.

burial chamber, which was originally a grain pit. There is a rock featuring a well-worn groove where it's believed Shaka sharpened his spears.

Minibus taxis link KwaDukuza, servicing Durban (one hour) and towns along the coast.

In the nearby town of Groutville is **Luthuli Museum** (Nokukhanya Luthuli St; www.luthuli museum.org.za; admission free; ⊙8.30am-4pm Mon-Sat), an interesting tribute to Chief Albert John Mvumbi Luthuli, former president of the African National Congress (ANC) from 1952 and Africa's first recipient of the Nobel Prize for Peace (1960) for his efforts to end apartheid in South Africa. He died in 1967 under suspicious circumstances. The museum is located in Luthuli's original house, where he'd lived all his life, and was his 'site of struggle'. The house interior has changing exhibitions. The house is surrounded by gardens; here, Chief Albert Luthuli met former United States Senator Robert Kennedy when he visited the country in 1966.

ZULULAND

Evoking images of wild landscapes and tribal rhythms, this beautiful swathe of KwaZulu-Natal offers a different face of South Africa, where fine coastline, mist-clad hills and traditional settlements are in contrast to the ordered suburban developments around Durban. Dominated by the Zulu tribal group, the region offers fascinating historical and contemporary insights into one of the country's most enigmatic and best-known cultures. However, while the name Zulu (which means Heaven) aptly describes the rolling expanses that dominate the landscape here, it doesn't tell the whole story. Intense poverty and all the social problems that come with that are still commonplace, and much of the population struggles in a hand-to-mouth existence. Head off the main roads and this becomes glaringly obvious.

Zululand extends roughly from the mouth of the Tugela River up to St Lucia and inland west of the N2 to Vryheid. The region is most visited for the spectacular Hluhluwe-iMfolozi Park and its many traditional Zulu villages. Here you can learn about Zulu history and the legendary King Shaka (see boxed text, p248).

Since 1971, Goodwill Zwelithini kaBhekuzulu has been ruling the Zulu nation.

Mtunzini
☑035

A little oasis of neatly tended lawns surrounded by the wild, rolling hills of Zululand, Mtunzini screams 'Europe' in the heart of Africa. But there is more to this pretty village than herbaceous borders. Sitting above a lush sweep of rare raffia palms, and bordering the Umlalazi Nature Reserve, Mtunzini makes an excellent base for exploring this beautiful slice of Zululand.

The town had a colourful beginning. John Dunn, the first European to settle in the area, was granted land by King Cetshwayo. Dunn became something of a chief himself, taking 49 wives and siring 117 children. He held court here under a tree, hence the town's name (*mtunzini* is Zulu for 'a place in the shade'). After the British defeated Cetshwayo and divided the kingdom, Dunn was one of the chiefs granted power.

The town was declared a conservancy in 1995. Visitors can enjoy its network of nature trails, as well as some antelope and bird species.

👁 Sights & Activities

FREE **Raffia Palm Monument**   NATURE RESERVE
(⊙24hr) Near the mouth of the Mlalazi River, lush tropical forest hides this monument. *Raphia Australis* palms were first planted here in 1916 from seeds. The idea was to use the palm fibres to make brooms for the prison service but, as the fibres were too short, the commercial enterprise soon ended. However, the palms (whose leaves are among the largest in the plant kingdom) flourished and by 1942 had been declared a National Monument. The palms are home to the palmnut vulture (*Gypohierax angolensis*), South Africa's rarest breeding bird of prey.

Umlalazi Nature Reserve   NATURE RESERVE
(☎035-340 1836; www.kznwildlife.com; admission R10; ⊙5am-10pm) Has walking trails through the pretty dune and forested ecosystems and is great for birders. Visit the Indaba Tree, where John Dunn held his court gatherings, and the remains of John Dunn's Pool, which he built so his wives could swim safely, well away from hippos and crocs. The entrance is 1.5km east of town, on the coast.

Zululand & Elephant Coast

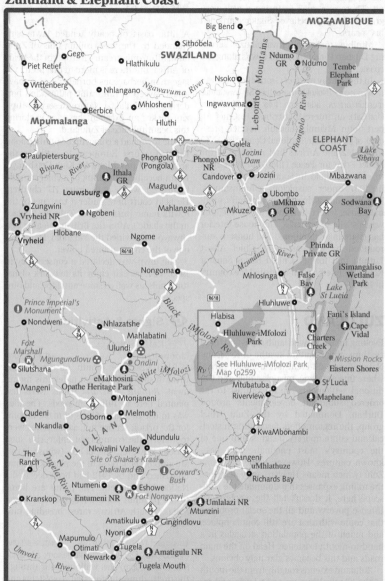

KWAZULU-NATAL MTUNZINI

🛏 Sleeping & Eating

Mtunzini B&B   B&B $$
(📞035-340 1600; 5 Barker St; s/d incl breakfast R400/550; ❄️🛜🏊) A no-nonsense, friendly place with beautiful spaces, set around a beautiful garden. There's a range of rooms from doubles inside the main house to separate cabin, attic and self-catering options. Only some have private bathrooms.

One-on-Hely   BOUTIQUE HOTEL $$
(📞035-340 2498; www.oneonhely.co.za; 1 Hely Hutchinson St; s/d incl breakfast R850/1200; ❄️🏊)

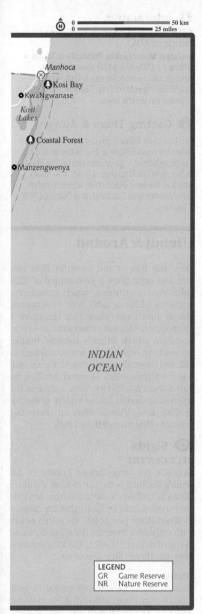

The village's flashest place with enormous decks, forest views and luxury trimmings.

Umlalazi Nature Reserve CAMPGROUND $
(☎035-340 1836; www.kznwildlife.com; campsites R90, 4-person cabin per person R330) Two well-organised camping areas (Inkwazi and Indaba)

are set in gorgeous forest, close to the beach. Minimum charges apply for the cabins.

Fat Cat Coffee Shop CAFE $$
(2 Station Rd; mains R50-100; ☺7.30am-5pm) Casual, friendly Fat Cat is the place for a meal; it's run by a chef.

Zanj INTERNATIONAL $$
(☎035-340 1288; Golden Penny Complex, Hely Hutchinson St; mains R50-100; ☺lunch & dinner Tue-Sun) An upmarket family-run place, headed by qualified (and very good) chefs. The weekly specials board displays a long list of international dishes.

ℹ Information

There is an ATM in the main street.

Eshowe

☎035 / POP 14,700
Situated around a beautiful indigenous forest and surrounded by green rolling hills, Eshowe is idiosyncratic Zululand. The centre has a rural, rough-and-tumble atmosphere, but the suburbs are leafy and quiet. It is well placed for exploring the wider region and there are decent attractions and accommodation options on offer.

Eshowe has been home to four Zulu Kings (Shaka, Mpande, Cetshwayo and Dinuzulu). It was Cetshwayo's stronghold before he moved to Ondini and, like Ondini, it was destroyed during the Anglo-Zulu War. The British occupied the site and built Fort Nongqayi in 1883, establishing Eshowe as the administrative centre of their newly captured territory.

◉ Sights & Activities

Fort Nongqayi Museum Village MUSEUM
(Nongqayi Rd; adult/child R25/5; ☺7.30am-4pm Mon-Fri, 9am-4pm Sat & Sun) Based around three-turreted Fort Nongqayi, the entrance fee includes access to the Zululand Historical Museum, with artefacts and Victoriana; the excellent Vukani Museum; a Zulu basketry collection and a missionary chapel.

At the time of research, a butterfly house was due to open within the village. Here, visitors can enter a large walk-in greenhouse, enjoying indigenous vegetation and hundreds of African butterfly species.

From the museum you can also walk to Mpushini Falls (40 minutes return), but note that bilharzia has been reported here in the past.

KWAZULU-NATAL ESHOWE

FREE **Dlinza Forest Reserve**

NATURE RESERVE

(⊘6am-6pm Sep-Apr, 8am-5pm May-Aug) When war approached, King Shaka is said to have hidden his wives in the thick swathe of forest that now makes up the 200-hectare Dlinza Forest Reserve. There is prolific birdlife – look out for crowned eagles *(Stephanoaetus coronatus)*, as well as a few walking trails, some of which are believed to have been made by British soldiers stationed here after the Anglo-Zulu War. Within the reserve, 125m-long **Dlinza Forest Aerial Boardwalk** (www.zbr.co.za/boardwalk; adult/child R25/5) offers some great views of the canopy and birdlife.

🛏 Sleeping & Eating

Eshowe Guesthouse

B&B $$

(☏082 823 5627; dlinza@telkomsa.net; 3 Oftebro St; s/d incl breakfast R450/600; 🅿✳🐾) This place has a top setting, backing onto the bird-filled Dlinza Forest. The owner is delightful and rooms are spotless, stylish, airy and spacious. Follow the signs to the Dlinza Forest Reserve; the guesthouse is just beyond the entrance. It gets busy; reserve ahead.

Dlinza Forest Accommodation

CABIN $$

(☏035-474 2377; dlinza@zulucom.net; 2 Oftebro St; s/d R400/500) Directly opposite Eshowe Guesthouse, these four self-catering log cabins are neat, modern, clean and spacious. Breakfast costs R50.

George Hotel & Zululand Backpackers

HOTEL, BACKPACKERS $$

(☏035-474 4919; www.eshowe.com; 38 Main St; dm R125, s/d incl breakfast R395/565; 🅿🛜🐾) This attractive, whitewashed building has colonial charm but has seen better days - it's pretty 'faded and jaded'. That said, it's got an excellent, more modern bar. The owner organises a huge range of activities around many activities around Zululand (see boxed text, p256); Groups tend to stay here; the separate backpackers located behind the main hotel offers some doubles for R185 (avoid the claustrophobic dorm).

Adam's Outpost

INTERNATIONAL $$

(mains R60-110; ⊘9am-4pm Mon-Fri, to 3pm Sun) Find refuge in the garden cafe and cosy, corrugated-iron restaurant, complete with real fireplaces and candles – easily the victor in Eshowe's culinary roll call.

ℹ Information

ABSA (Miku Bldg, Osborne Rd) Changes money and has an ATM.

Umlalazi Municipality Publicity & Tourism Office (☏035-473 3474; www.visitzuluand.co.za; cnr Hutchinson & Osborne Rds; ⊘7.30am-4pm Mon-Thu, 7.30am-3pm Fri) For information on the area.

ℹ Getting There & Away

Minibus taxis leave from the bus and taxi rank (downhill from KFC near the Osborne and Main Sts roundabout – go across the bridge and to the right) to Empangeni (R45, one hour), which is the best place from which to catch taxis deeper into Zululand, and Durban (R80, 1½ hours).

Ulundi & Around

☏035 / POP 15,200

Once the hub of the powerful Zulu empire and until 2004 a joint capital of KZN (with Pietermaritzburg, which gained pre-eminence), Ulundi today is an unattractive, merely functional, place that resembles a temporary settlement rather than an important Zulu centre. Brightly coloured boxlike houses have replaced the traditional huts of old, and its small centre-cum-shopping mall has a temporary feel. However, for Zulu fanatics there are historic sites, including the interesting Ondini site, to explore in the immediate area. Ulundi offers an alternative access to Hluhluwe-iMfolozi Park.

◉ Sights

CITY CENTRE

Opposite the large former Legislative Assembly building is the site of King Mpande's iKhanda (palace), **kwaNodwengu**. Mpande won control from Dingaan after the disaster at Blood River (see p290). He seized power with assistance from the Boers but Zululand declined during his reign. The king's grave is here, but there's little else to see.

ONDINI

Established as Cetshwayo's capital in 1873, **Ondini** (High Place; ☏035-870 2050; adult/child R20/10; ⊘8am-4pm Mon-Fri, 9am-4pm Sat & Sun) was razed by British troops after the Battle of Ulundi (July 1879), the final engagement of the 1879 Anglo-Zulu War.

It took the British nearly six months to defeat the Zulu army, but the Battle of Ulundi went the same way as most of the campaign, with 10 to 15 times more Zulus

NKWALINI VALLEY & SHAKALAND

Shaka's kraal (fortified village), KwaBulawayo, once loomed over this beautiful valley but today **Nkwalini Valley** is regimented with citrus orchards and cane fields rather than Zulu warriors. From Eshowe head north for 6km on R66, and turn right onto R230 (a dirt road that will eventually get you to R34).

Across the road from the KwaBulawayo marker is Coward's Bush, now just another marker, where warriors who returned from battle without their spears, or who had received wounds in the back, were executed.

Further west, a few kilometres before R230 meets R66, the Mandawe Cross was erected in the 1930s, against the wishes of the Zulu. There are excellent views from the hill.

Created as a set for the telemovie *Shaka Zulu*, the Disney-fied **Shakaland** (☎035-460 0912; www.shakaland.com; Nandi Experience R275; ⊘display 11am & noon) beats up a touristy blend of perma-grin performance and informative authenticity. The Nandi Experience (Queen Nandi was Shaka's mother) is a display of Zulu culture and customs (including lunch); the Zulu dance performance is said to be the best in the country. You can also stay overnight in luxury beehives at the four-star **hotel** (Shaka Experience cultural programme & s/d with full board R1125/1688), part of the Shaka Programme.

Shakaland is at Norman Hurst Farm, Nkwalini, 3km off R66 and 14km north of Eshowe.

killed than British. Part of the reason for the British victory at Ulundi was the adoption of the Boer *laager* (defence of a camp by a circle of wagons) tactic, with troops forming a hollow square to protect the cavalry, which attacked only after the Zulu army had exhausted itself trying to penetrate the walls.

The royal kraal section of the Ondini site has been rebuilt and you can see where archaeological digs have uncovered the floors of identifiable buildings. The floors, made of mud and cow dung, were preserved by the heat of the fires, which destroyed the huts above. The huge area is enclosed in a defensive perimeter of gnarled branches.

KwaZulu Cultural-Historical Museum (included in Ondini admission; ⊘8am-4pm Mon-Fri, 9am-4pm Sat & Sun), part of the Ondini complex, has excellent exhibits on Zulu history and culture, and displays one of the country's best collections of beadwork. A good collection of books is for sale.

En route to Ondini from Ulundi you'll pass **Ulundi Battlefield Memorial**, a stone structure commemorating the Battle of Ulundi and the final defeat of the Zulus.

To get to Ondini, take the 'Cultural Museum' turn-off from the highway just south of Ulundi centre and keep going for about 5km. Minibus taxis occasionally pass Ondini. This road continues on to Hluhluwe-iMfolozi Park (tarred for 30km).

EMAKHOSINI OPHATHE HERITAGE PARK

Ulundi lies within the Valley of the Kings, the name of which is officially promoted as Emakhosini Ophathe Heritage Park. The area is of great significance to the Zulu. The great *makhosi* (chiefs) Nkhosinkulu, Senzangakhona (father of Shaka, Dingaan and Mpande) and Dinizulu are buried here. Signage for the park can be confusing (some sites are advertised but aren't fully functioning).

A couple of the area's sites are open to the public. Southwest of Ulundi on R34 (the road linking Vryheid and Melmoth) is the military settlement of **Mgungundlovu** (Ungungundhlovu), Dingaan's capital from 1829 to 1838. It was here, too, that Pieter Retief and the other Voortrekkers were killed by their host in 1838, the event that precipitated the Boer-Zulu War. Signs point to the Piet Retief memorial marking the spot. In 1990 excavations revealed the site of Dingaan's *indlu* (great hut) nearby. A new **multimedia information centre** (☎035-450 0916; www.heritagekzn.co.za; adult/child R20/10; ⊘8am-4pm Mon-Fri, 9am-4pm Sat & Sun) has hi-tech displays and information.

From Ulundi head southwest along R66 to R34, turn right and continue on R34 for several kilometres. Mgungundlovu is signed off R34 to the west; it's another 5km to the site.

ARIADNE VAN ZANDBERGEN / ALAMY ©

ROBERT HARDING WORLD IMAGERY / ALAMY ©

onk's Cowl (p273)

 central uKhahlamba-
ensberg Park, Monk's Cowl is
 ground filled with hiking and
climbing options.

2. Hluhluwe-iMfolozi Park (p258)

Nyalas are just one of many animal species you may spot on a wildlife drive through this park.

3. Isandlwana (p289)

White stone cairns mark the spots where British soldiers fell during their annihilation by Zulus in the 1879 Anglo-Zulu war.

Back on R34 and 2km further north of **Mgungundlovu**, signs point west to **Spirit of eMakhosini monument** (⊙8am-4pm Mon-Fri, 9am-4pm Sat & Sun), which is perched on a hill. It comprises a massive bronze Zulu beer pot, surrounded by 18 bronze reliefs depicting Zulu life, and seven large horns symbolising the seven kings buried in the valley. Guides will explain the site's significance.

🛏 Sleeping

There's not much reason to hang around here – if you do get stuck you can try the following places.

Southern Sun Garden Court BUSINESS HOTEL **$$**
(☎035-870 1012; www.southernsun.com; Princess Magogo St,Ulundi; r incl breakfast R1400; ❋🐾❄) Predictably safe comforts of a chain hotel.

uMuzi Bushcamp BEEHIVE HUTS **$$**
(☎035-870 2500, 082 825 6896; www.umuzibush camp.co.za; s/d R580/840, s/d with half board R575/830) Inside the Ondini complex are these traditional beehive huts in pleasant surrounds, near Marula trees. Includes entry to the museum.

❶ Getting There & Away

The minibus taxi park is opposite Southern Sun Garden Court, with services to destinations including Vryheid (R70, 1½ hours) and Eshowe (R65, 1½ hours).

Ithala Game Reserve

Ezemvelo KZN Wildlife's **Ithala Game Reserve** (☎033-845 1000, 034-983 2540; www.kzn wildlife.com; adult/child/vehicle R40/20/30; ⊙5am-7pm Nov-Feb, 6am-6pm Mar-Oct) is severely underrated. It has all the assets of a private wildlife reserve but at much lower prices. It also doesn't get the crowds that flock into Hluhluwe-iMfolozi, as it's slightly off the main routes, but it's captivating in its own way.

Most of the 30,000 hectares are taken up by the steep valleys of six rivers (tributaries of the Phongolo), with some open grassland on the heights, rugged outcrops and bushveld. Some of the world's oldest rock formations are found here, as are Stone Age spear and axe heads.

Animals include black and white rhinos, elephants, tsessebis, buffalos and giraffes (the park's emblem, as they are believed to be indigenous to Ithala Game Reserve) and rare bird species.

ZULU FESTIVALS

Throughout the year there are a few major festivals that celebrate the rich culture of the Zulu people. These peaceful and joyous occasions involve colourful displays of traditional singing and dancing. See www.kzn.org.za for a sneak preview. Zululand Eco-Adventures at **George Hotel & Zululand Backpackers** (☎035-474 4919; www.eshowe. com) in Eshowe offers a large range of genuine Zulu adventure activities, from weddings and coming-of-age ceremonies to visits to witch doctors.

King Shaka Day Celebration In September (to changing dates), thousands of Zulus converge on KwaDukuza (Stanger) for the King Shaka Day Celebration. The annual event, attended by the current Zulu king, pays homage to the Zulu hero.

Reed Dance Every year thousands of young bare-breasted Zulu 'maidens' gather before their king, honouring the ancient tradition of the Reed Dance. In days long gone, the king would select a new bride from the mass of beautiful young maidens before him. The dance takes place at King Enyokeni's Palace (which lies between Nongoma and Ulundi) around the second weekend of September, before the King Shaka Day Celebration.

Shembe Festival During the month of October more than 30,000 Zulus gather at Judea, 15km east of Eshowe, for the annual Shembe Festival. This eye-opening festival celebrates the Shembe, the Church of the Holy Nazareth Baptists – an unofficial religion that somehow manages to combine Zulu traditions with Christianity. Presiding over the festivities is the church's saviour, Prophet Mbusi Vimbeni Shembe. Throughout the festival the emphasis is on celebration, with much dancing and singing and the blowing of the horns of Jericho.

Guided walks (R170 per person) and wild-life and night drives (R190 per person) are available.

🛏 Sleeping

Ntshondwe   CABIN **$$**

(☎033-8451000;www.kznwildlife.com;self-catering 2-bed chalet per person R735, 2-bed nonself-catering unit per person R675; ☳) This is the park's main resort, located at the foot of Ngotshe Mountain, with superb views of the reserve below. It's warthog heaven and home to the red flower, Pride of De Kaap, and redbilled oxpeckers. Facilities include a restaurant, shop and swimming pool. There's a full-board option for the units, on request.

Doornkraal   CAMPGROUND **$**

(☎033-845 1000; www.kznwildlife.com; campsites per person R120) This is one of a range of fabulous bush camps; the others have heftier minimum charges. Note, this is your camping experience – it's cold-water showers only here.

❶ Getting There & Away

Ithala is reached from Louwsburg, about 55km northeast of Vryheid on R69, and about the same distance southwest of Phongolo via R66 and R69. Louwsburg is much smaller than many maps indicate.

THE ELEPHANT COAST

Up there on the podium with the world's great ecotourist destinations, and not far from the top of the scribbled list marked 'Places I Must See in South Africa', the Elephant Coast (formerly 'Maputaland') is a phenomenal stretch of natural beauty, with a fabulously diverse mix of environments and wildlife. The Elephant Coast is bounded in the south by the iMfolozi River just below the St Lucia Estuary, and to the northwest by the Lebombo Mountains.

This large stretch of coastline includes some of the country's true highlights, including the wonderfully diverse and perennially photogenic iSimangaliso Wetland Park that runs from Lake St Lucia in the south to Kosi Bay in the north. Uncompromisingly untamed, this region, away from the scattered resort towns, offers a glimpse of an unaffected heart of Africa. Slightly further inland, the incredible Hluhluwe-iMfolozi Park is KZN's answer to Kruger National

Park. Indeed, it rivals its northern neighbour in beauty, and many prefer it for its accessibility (it's less than a 20th of Kruger's size).

The climate becomes steadily hotter as you go north and, thanks to the warm Indian Ocean, summers are steamy and tropical. The humid coastal air causes frequent dense mists on the inland hills, reducing visibility to a few metres. If driving, be careful of pedestrians and animals that may suddenly appear around a corner.

There is a good network of roads connecting the regions. Minibus taxis and local-bus companies cover the coast. Self-drivers have a world open to them; while a 2WD will get you many places, a 4WD is required for the spectacular sandy road along the coast from Kosi Bay to Sodwana Bay.

Hluhluwe & Around

🖉 035 / POP 3200

Hluhluwe village (roughly pronounced shloo-*shloo*-wee) is northeast of Hluhluwe-iMfolozi Park. There's not much to the village – it spans a wide main road that joins the N2 – but it's the main gateway to the beautiful park itself.

About 20km south of Hluhluwe on the N2 is the great-value Zamimpilo market, a local women's cooperative that sells a variety of local crafts.

👁 Sights & Activities

Ilala Weavers   MUSEUM, HANDICRAFTS

(www.ilala.co.za; ◷8am-5pm Mon-Fri, 9am-4pm Sat & Sat) Sells a large range of Zulu handicrafts, plus there's a museum and a local, slightly contrived 'village' where several craftspeople live on show and create their items.

Endomeni Rehabilitation Project   WILDLIFE RESERVE

(☎035-562 7000; www.emdonenilodge.com/rehabilitation-centre.htm; adult/child R150/80; ◷tours 10.30am winter, 10.30am & 4.30pm summer) The 'purr-fect' experience to get up close and personal with a variety of South African cats, including the caracal, serval, cheetah and African wildcat. This centre feeds and cares for Africa's threatened cats. As well as educational tours, visitors can interact with the cats and watch feeding sessions (note: feeding takes place in afternoons only). Lovely accommodation is also on site (R921 with half board and the cat programme).

ℹ HLUHLUWE SIGNS

Signs to Hluhluwe and surrounds often confuse travellers. Useful to know when exiting the N2 is that Hluhluwe, the village, is on the eastern side of the N2, while the Hluhluwe-iMfolozi Park is 12 km west of the N2 (14km west of town).

🛏 Sleeping

TOP CHOICE **Hluhluwe River Lodge** LODGE $$$
(☎035-562 0246; www.hluhluwe.co.za; d with half board R4100) About 11km from Hluhluwe, on the D540 (off the R22; and near False Bay), is this superb option, a luxurious base from which to explore the park (the lodge offers tours). Set in its own piece of bush, each chalet is stylish, airy and spacious. The communal area features a stunning indoor-outdoor living room with terrace, and the lodge's chef serves up top-notch fare. The indigenous forest has a delightful 'duiker walk', and a range of other activities are on offer.

Bushwillow GUESTHOUSE $$$
(☎035-652 0473; www.bushwillow.com; Kuleni Game Park; d incl breakfast/half board R1570/2000) Within the privately owned Kuleni Game Park and surrounded by superb forest – flat crown, albizia and, of course, bush willows – is this stunning romantic, relaxing hideaway. Two units are linked by a common area with a kitchen for private use. Watch birds from the plunge pool, or laze in the bathroom's claw-foot bath – it, too, has a great outlook. Soft wildlife (the likes of zebra, giraffe and duikers) surround the property and there's a network of working trails. It's located 20km from Hluhluwe village on the Sodwana Bay road; look for the Kuleni sign.

Zululand Tree Lodge LODGE $$$
(☎035-562 1020; s/d R2980/3440; ✳🏊) Seven kilometres outside Hluhluwe, and set in the Ubizane reserve amid fever trees, this romantic spot offers thatched tree houses. There are excellent specials that include half board and safari drives; prices are flexible, depending on the package.

Isinkwe Backpackers Lodge BACKPACKERS $$
(☎035-562 2258; www.isinkwe.co.za; Bushlands; campsites per person R100, dm/d without bathroom R155/210, s/d/tr R430/570/690; @🏊) Located in a sweep of virgin bush 14km south of Hluhluwe, this backpackers has a variety of accommodation options, from tired huts to rooms with bathrooms, a plethora of bush-focused (and other) activities, and a poolside bar where you can exchange tall-as-a-giraffe stories. The owners take safaris into Hluhluwe-iMfolozi and have half-board and accommodation-activity packages (see the website). Ring for directions.

Hluhluwe-iMfolozi Park

☑035

Rivalling Kruger National Park in its beauty and variety of landscapes, **Hluhluwe-iMfolozi Park** (☎035-550 8476; www.kznwildlife.com; adult/child R110/55; ⊙5am-7pm Nov-Feb, 6am-6pm Mar-Oct) is one of South Africa's best-known, most evocative parks. Indeed, some say it's better than Kruger for its accessibility – it covers 96,000 hectares (around one-20th the size of Kruger) and there's plenty of wildlife including lions, elephants, rhinos (black and white), leopards, giraffes, buffalos and African wild dogs.

Hluhluwe-iMfolozi can be visited at any time; there's always something happening and plenty to see. In summer (wet season) it's beautifully lush and animals range widely. Winter (dry season) visits can also be very rewarding, especially in the open savannah country areas and animals often congregate at water sources (the White iMfolozi and Black iMfolozi Rivers flow here). Specific months bring their own rewards – from November to January it's baby time for impala, zebra, wildebeest and giraffe, plus plenty of migratory birds. In February the elephants take to the Marula trees, and October to March sees beautiful grasses and flowers.

The **Centenary Centre** (⊙8am-4pm), a wildlife-holding centre with an attached museum, information centre and excellent craft market, is in the eastern section of iMfolozi. It incorporates rhino enclosures and antelope pens, and was established to allow visitors to view animals in transit to their new homes. To see the animals, ask at the Centenary Centre kiosk; you must be accompanied by a guide (around R35 per person).

Wildlife drives here are very popular. **Hilltop Camp** (☎035-562 0848) offers morning and evening drives, while Mpila Camp does evening drives only. The drives are open to resort residents only and cost R270 per person.

Hluhluwe-iMfolozi Park

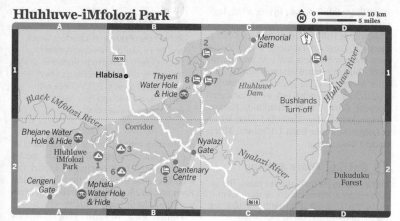

One of iMfolozi's main attractions is its extraordinary trail system, in a special 24,000-hectare wilderness area (note: these trails are seasonal). The **Base Trail** (3 nights & 4 days R3592) is, as the name suggests, at a base camp. These walking trips are truly once-in-a-lifetime experiences. Trailists carry daypacks on the daily outings.

The **Short Wilderness Trail** (2 nights & 3 days R2180) is at satellite camps with no amenities (bucket shower), yet are fully catered. Similar is the **Extended Wilderness Trail** (3 nights & 4 days R3200), but guests must carry their own gear for 7km into camp. On the **Primitive Trail** (3 nights & 4 days R2220, 4 nights & 5 days R2685) you carry equipment, help prepare the food (provided) and sleep under the stars. Some consider this trail to be more fun than the others because you are able to participate more (for example, hikers must sit up in 1½-hour watches during the night).

Bushveld Trail (2 nights & 3 days R2050) is a softer experience; the base camp has amenities (including fridge) and guests have walks and summer siestas.

🛌 Sleeping & Eating

You must book accommodation in advance through **Ezemvelo KZN Wildlife** (☎033-845 1000; www.kznwildlife.com) in Pietermaritzburg. Last-minute bookings – those made up to 48 hours ahead – should be made direct with the camps. Note: all accommodation options are billed per person but are subject to a minimum charge. Additionally, if you are self-catering, remember to bring your own food!

Hluhluwe-iMfolozi Park

🛌 Sleeping

1 Gqoyeni Bush Camp	A2
2 Hilltop Camp	C1
3 Hlatikulu	B2
4 Isinkwe Backpacker's Lodge	D1
5 Masinda Lodge	B2
6 Mpila Camp	B2
Mtwazi Lodge	(see 2)
7 Muntulu Bush Lodge	C1
8 Munywaneni Bush Lodge	B1

Hilltop Camp
CABIN **$$**

(☎035-562 0848; rest hut/chalet per person R276/550, 2-bed unit with full board per person R466) The signature resort on the Hluhluwe side, with stupendous views, a restaurant and a much-needed bar (it gets very hot here). The drawback is that it's the most popular destination for tour buses and is generally quite busy.

If you want peace and quiet, try one of the private and sedate accommodation options. However, although described as 'bush lodges', they are out of this world: fully equipped and reasonably upmarket options. Some come with their own chef – although you supply the food.

⭐ TOP CHOICE Mpila Camp
SAFARI TENT, CABIN **$$**

(2-bed safari camp d R750, d chalet R750) The main accommodation centre on the iMfolozi side – a spectacular and peaceful camp in the centre of the reserve and perched on top of a hill. The safari tents are the most fun, but self-contained cabins (called 'chalets') are available, too. Note: there's an electric

KWAZULU-NATAL HLUHLUWE-IMFOLOZI PARK

fence but wildlife (lions, hyena, wild dogs) can still wander through.

As well as Hilltop Camp and Mpila Camp, there's a range of fabulous lodges (some even come with chefs but you provide the food), but minimum charges apply; they cater for six to eight guests. See www.kzn wildlife.com for more, but we recommend Gooyeni Bush Camp; Hlatikulu; Isinkwe Backpacker's Lodge; Masinda Lodge; Mtwazi Lodge; Muntulu Bush Lodge and Munywaneni Bush Lodge.

🛈 Getting There & Away

You can access the park via three gates. The main entrance, Memorial Gate, is about 15km west of the N2, about 50km north of Mtubatuba. The second entrance, the Nyalazi Gate, is accessed by turning left off the N2 onto R618 just after Mtubatuba on the way to Nongoma. The third, Cengeni Gate, on iMfolozi's western side, is accessible by road (tarred for 30km) from Ulundi.

Petrol is available at Mpila Camp in iMfolozi and at Hilltop Camp in Hluhluwe, where you can also get diesel.

iSimangaliso Wetland Park

📷 035

The iSimangaliso Wetland Park, a Unesco World Heritage Site, stretches for 220 glorious kilometres from the Mozambique border to Maphelane, at the southern end of Lake St Lucia. With the Indian Ocean on one side, and a series of lakes on the other (including Lake St Lucia), the 328,000-hectare park protects five distinct ecosystems, offering everything from offshore reefs and beaches to lakes, wetlands, woodlands and coastal forests. Loggerhead and leatherback turtles nest along the park's shores; whales and dolphins appear offshore and the park is occupied by numerous animals, including antelopes, hippos and zebras. The ocean beaches pull big crowds during the holiday season for their beach and water activities, from diving to fishing.

Within the park, Lake St Lucia is Africa's largest estuary. Despite its past healthy water levels, it is currently at its lowest level for around 55 years, due to former environmental management policy (which is currently under review). The estuary mouth is currently closed; controversy surrounds

CLOSED

At the time of research, Charters Creek and Fani's Island (known as Western Shores) were closed to visitors due to ongoing drought conditions; they were due to open in 2013. Check with iSimangaliso Wetland Park Authority (www.isimangaliso.com).

a long-term solution to the management of the lake, with both animal and plant species being affected by changing ecological factors. The latest thinking is that the iMfolozi River will be allowed to naturally link again with the Lake St Lucia Estuary.

iSimangaliso Wetland Park (formerly Greater St Lucia Wetland Park) relaunched its eco-destination image in 2007, including the park's renaming; iSimangaliso means 'Miracle' or 'Wonder' and, indeed, given its extraordinary beauty, it's an appropriate title.

There's a wonderful range of accommodation, from camping to private lodges and excellent options managed by Ezemvelo KZN Wildlife. Unless otherwise specified, all the latter must be booked at Ezemvelo KZN Wildlife (📞 033-845 1000) with 48 hours' notice. Less than 48 hours before, try your luck directly with the lodges and campsites.

ST LUCIA

Although not officially within the iSimangaliso Wetland Park, the pleasant village of St Lucia is a useful base from which to explore the park's southern sections. In high season, St Lucia is a hotbed of activity as the population swells from 600 to the thousands. The main drag, McKenzie St (a former hippo pathway), is packed with restaurants, lively hostels and bars, but the quieter avenues behind it offer a touch more hush and a good selection of B&Bs. Hippos sometimes amble down the town's quieter streets (beware: these are not cute, just dangerous).

About 1km north of St Lucia, on the road to Cape Vidal, is St Lucia Crocodile Centre (📞 035-590 1386; croc-centre@kznwildlife.com; adult/child Mon-Fri R35/20, Sat & Sun R45/30; ⏰ 8.30am-4.30pm Mon-Fri, to 5pm Sat, 9am-4pm Sun), where a fine array of crocs can be seen in their not-so-natural habitat.

🏃 Activities

As part of the iSimangaliso Wetland Park Authority's responsible tourism practices, every few years, an ecotour operator must officially reapply for a permit – known as a concession – to operate activity tours. Go to www.iSimangaliso.com for a list of current companies and organisations; tour operators listed may have changed by the time you read this.

The following is a selection of operators based in and around iSimangaliso Wetland Park.

Birdwatching

Birdwatching is a delight in St Lucia and beyond. Recommended guides include Themba of **Themba's Birding & Eco Tours** (☎071 413 3243; www.zulubirding.com; St Lucia; per person from R200, minimum 2 people) and **Jabulani** (☎079-868 1111; info@mseni.co.za; Sodwana Bay; birding per person from R150, nature walk per person from R100). Other guides can be found on the **Zululand Birding Route** (www.zbr.co.za) website.

Boat Tours & Whale-Watching

Whatever you do, keep aside some money in the kitty for a whale-watching experience. In season, there's a high chance of spotting whales here, as well as dolphins and other sea creatures. Trips cost around R170 per person. **Advantage Tours** (☎035-590 1250; www.advantagetours.co.za) and **Ocean Experience** (☎035-590 1555; www.stlucia.co.za) run daily tours between June and September, weather permitting. You can also head upriver on boat tours to view hippos and crocodiles. Sodwana Bay also offers whale-watching through **Sodwana Bay Lodge** (☎035-571 6000; www.sodwanabaylodge.com).

Horse Riding

Hluhluwe Horse Safaris (☎035-562 0246; www.hluhluwehorsesafaris.co.za; 2-hour ride per person R450) Horse riding is a wonderful way to see wildlife; these rides are in the False Bay region. You may spot antelope species, as well as other animals. A second option heads to Falaza Game reserve where you can see rhino, buffalo and giraffe (a two-hour ride per person is R450) It operates out of Hluhluwe River Lodge (p257).

Kayak Safaris

St Lucia Kayak Safaris (☎035-590 1047; www.kayaksafaris.co.za; per person R290) offer a novel way to enjoy the wetland. This outfit also offers snorkelling at Cape Vidal and wildlife drives in Hluhluwe-iMfolozi Park.

Turtle-Watching

Fascinating night turtle tours operate from Cape Vidal with **Euro Zulu Safaris** (☎035-590 1635; www.eurozulu.com; per person incl dinner & drinks R900) and **Thompson's Africa** (☎035-590 1584; www.thompsonsafrica.com; per person R795). Sodwana Bay Lodge (p263) runs trips at Sodwana Bay, as does Kosi Bay Lodge (p265) at Kosi Bay.

Wildlife-Watching

There are a number of operators offering excellent day and night trips on the Eastern and Western Shores. Operators are listed on www.iSimangaliso.com. Highly recommended **Shakabarker Tours** (☎035-590 1162; 43 Hornbill St) operates out of St Lucia and conducts a range of fascinating wildlife tours (and at the time of research, had just launched its boat tours on the estuary).

MARINE TURTLES

Five species of turtle live off the South African coast but only two actually nest on the coast: the leatherback turtle *(Dermochelys coriacea)* and the loggerhead turtle *(Caretta caretta)*. The nesting areas of both species extend from the St Lucia mouth, north into Mozambique.

Both species nest at night in summer. The female moves above the high-tide mark, finds a suitable site and lays her eggs. The loggerheads' breeding area is more varied, as they clamber over rocks in the intertidal zone; leatherbacks will only nest on sandy beaches.

About 70 days later, the hatchlings scramble out of the nest at night and make a dash for the sea. Only one or two of each 1000 hatchlings will survive until maturity. The females return 12 to 15 years later to the very same beach to nest.

🛏 Sleeping

There's rarely a shortage of places to stay, but it is worth booking ahead during the summer months.

Hornbill House
B&B $$

(☎035-590 1162; 43 Hornbill St; s/d incl breakfast R475/750; ❄@🐾) A very pleasant place to nest, with homey B&B comforts, friendly dogs and a small pool for a dip. That is, if you're not flitting about on one of the many eco-friendly trips or activities offered by the knowledgeable owner, Kian, who runs a tour company.

Sunset Lodge
CABIN $$

(☎035-590 1197; www.sunsetstlucia.co.za; 154 McKenzie St; d R650-1250; P❄🐾) Seven well-maintained, self-catering log cabins, lined in dark wood and with a safari theme. Affords a lovely view overlooking the estuary – you can watch the hippos, mongooses and monkeys wander onto the lawn. Rates significantly lower outside high season.

Serene Estate Guesthouse
GUESTHOUSE $$$

(☎035-590 1016; www.serene-estate.co.za; 119 Hornbill St; s R875-975, d R1450-1550; ❄🐾🐾) A world away from St Lucia, minimalist Dutch meets lush African forest and creates a stylish experience in its six rooms and beyond. The breakfasts, served with one of Olga's daily surprises, are memorable.

Umlilo Lodge
LODGE $$

(☎035-590 1717; www.umlilolodge.co.za; 9 Dolphin Ave; d R1100; 🐾🐾) Centrally located with a lovely lush garden, 10 separate rooms and a lovely indoor-outdoor lounge in which to kick back after a day's activities. Delightful owner.

Lodge Afrique
LODGE $$

(☎071 592 0366; www.lodgeafrique.com; 71 Hornbill St; d R1300; 🐾) Smart 'African chic' chalets crammed into a suburban block but with lush surrounds. It's a safe bet, if it's not already booked out by groups; reservations required.

St Lucia Wilds
APARTMENT $

(☎035-590 1033; www.stluciawilds.co.za; 174 McKenzie St; budget flat s/d R265/350, chalet s/d from R325/430) An excellent budget alternative for those allergic to backpackers; there's a minimum charge.

Sugarloaf Campsite
CAMPGROUND $

(☎033-845 1000; kznwildlife.com; Pelican St; campsites per person R85) This pretty campground on the estuary is within snorting distance of hippos, monkeys and crocodiles.

Two backpackers are within a hippo's breath of each other along McKenzie Street: **Budget Backpackers** (☎035-590 1047; www.budgetbackpackers.co.za; 81 McKenzie St; dm/d R110/250) and **BiB's International Backpackers** (☎035-590 1056; www.bibs.co.za; 310 McKenzie St; campsites R75, dm without bathroom R115, d R245, self-catering d R315; P@🐾). Neither is luxurious, but hosts organise activities and tours.

🍴 Eating

Gourmet isn't a word that has yet hit St Lucia; the following are the best of a bad lot. Nearly all eating options are along McKenzie St.

St Lucia Deep Sea Angling Club
INTERNATIONAL $$

(Ski Club; mains R40-90; ⏱lunch & dinner) This friendly, casual spot, a popular with locals (it's a 'club'), whips up hearty servings of pasta, meats and fish. And it's not often that you can watch hippos and birds from an outdoor bench table. A pub lunch is R35 (inside only). Head 2km east from the second roundabout on McKenzie St.

Braza
FUSION $$

(McKenzie St; mains R35-100; ⏱lunch & dinner) Cuisine with a touch of Portugal, Brazil, Mozambique and Angola – at least that's what this lively place promotes. It translates as good meaty dishes and grills, although a decent vegetarian platter is on offer (but not on the menu).

ℹ **'DOING' SIMANGALISO WETLAND PARK**

Be aware: you can't enter and 'do' the whole wetland park; it's a huge area spreading for over 220km, much of it sand dunes and forested. There are four main regions of the park: the south (easily accessed via St Lucia, from where you can enter the eastern and western shores); the centre (Sodwana Bay, accessed from the R22) and the least accessible but very beautiful north (Kosi Bay, located at the end of the R22; a 4WD is necessary to enter Banga Nek). A new road into uMkuze Game Reserve allows for easy access west from Sodwana Bay.

❶ Information

The main banks (Standard Chartered Bank, Nedbank and FNB) have an ATM in the main street.

Avis (☏035-590 1634; www.avis.co.za; McKenzie St; ☺8am-4pm Mon-Fri, to noon Sat)

Internet cafe (☏035-590 1056; 310 McKenzie St; per hr R4; ☺7am-10pm) By far the best service; at BiB's International Backpackers.

iSimangaliso Wetland Park Information office (☏035-590 1633; www.isimangaliso.co.za) At the time of research, there were plans to open this office – the building is by the bridge at the approach to town.

❶ Getting There & Away

Minibus taxis connect Durban and Mtubatuba (R110); the latter is 25km from St Lucia, and it's from where you must catch a connecting minibus taxi to St Lucia. Alternatively, buses run between St Lucia, Richards Bay and Mtubatuba; you must change at each point. If you're not doing tours out of St Lucia Estuary, the only way of getting around is to have your own wheels.

A private transfer shuttle, **Mthuyi's** (☏079 026 3660; mthuyis@gmail.com; per person from R250), runs between St Lucia and Durban (airport and accommodation). The price depends on distance and the number of people.

EASTERN & WESTERN SHORES
☏035

From St Lucia Estuary the most southern and accessible areas to the iSimangaliso Wetland Park are the Eastern and Western shores. Both afford opportunities to do self-guided drives through the wonderful network of wildlife-viewing roads (there's excellent wildlife, from hippos to antelopes and prolific birdlife). These areas are part of a rehabilitation scheme, where thousands of hectares of land, formerly plantations, have been returned to their former state (yes, that's why there are all those tree stumps).

The Eastern Shores (☏035-590 1633; www .isimangaliso.com; adult/child/vehicle R30/20/40; ☺5am-7pm Nov-Mar, 6am-6pm Apr-Oct) have four scenic routes – pan, *vlei* (marshland), coastal dune and grassland – that reflect their different features and ecosystems. Hides, decks and viewpoints provide vistas and wildlife-viewing opportunities. About 14km north of the entrance is Mission Rocks, a rugged and rock-covered shoreline where, at low tide, you can view a fabulous array of sea life in the rock pools (note: you cannot swim here). At low tide, you can walk 5km north to Bats Cave, a bat-filled cave. About 4km before Mission Rocks is the Mount Tabor lookout (signed), which pro-

vides a wonderful view of Lake St Lucia and the Indian Ocean.

Twenty kilometres north of Mission Rocks (30km from St Lucia Estuary), taking in the land between Lake Bhangazi and the ocean, is Cape Vidal. Some of the forested sand dunes are 150m high and the beaches are excellent for swimming.

The Eastern Shores have an excellent accommodation option. Ezemvelo KZN Wildlife manages pretty Cape Vidal Camp (☏033-845 1000; www.kznwildlife.com; campsites R400, 5-bed log cabin minimum R930), near the shores of Lake Bhangazi. Minimum charges apply.

Mfazana Bird Hide wins the prize for the quirkiest and chirpiest birdwatching option in Southern Africa. Constructed, we guess, to look like a giant nest in its own right and perched out over the Mafazana Pan, the innovative hide gives you a unique and intimate opportunity to spot birds.

The Eastern Shores' gate lies 2km north of the town of St Lucia, adjacent to the St Lucia Crocodile Centre.

The region northwest of St Lucia Estuary is called the Western Shores, and comprises two stunning lakeside spots, known as Fani's Island (at the time of research this was closed to visitors due to the drought) and Charters Creek (entrance is off the N2, 18km north of Mtubatuba and 32km south of Hluhluwe), an area of dense coastal forest and grasslands. A newly constructed road provides direct access between St Lucia and Charter's Creek, and will offer excellent leisurely wildlife-drive opportunities up the western side of Lake St Lucia (check status on arrival; it had yet to open at the time of research).

To access the Western Shores from the town of St Lucia, leave town on the road to Mtubatuba, and after 2km turn right at the Dukuduku Gate.

SODWANA BAY
☏035

Get past the approach to the park – a mishmash of lodges, signs and temporary-looking constructions – and you're in for a surprise. Spectacular Sodwana Bay (adult/child R25/20; ☺24hr) is bordered by lush forest on one side and glittering sands on another. The area is best known for its scuba diving – the diversity of underwater seascapes and marine flora and fauna makes it one of South Africa's diving capitals. Serious deep-sea fishing occurs here, too; you can be inundated with huntin', shootin', fishin' types who head out in their water machines. On that note: avoid the silly season (summer holidays) when thousands throng here to take the plunge – literally. At all other times it's a beautifully peaceful place.

Many services, including accommodation options, dive operators, a couple of cafes and tour operators, sprawl along the road leading to the park entrance. Facilities inside the park include a campsite plus a couple of lodge-cum-diving operators.

There is an ATM in the general store (8.30am-4.30pm Mon-Fri, to 11.30am Sat) at the park's entrance. Otherwise you'll need to head to Mbazwana, 14km west.

Sleeping & Eating

Ezemvelo KZN Wildlife CAMPGROUND $$
(033-845 1000; www.kznwildlife.com; campsites from R400, 4-bed cabin R1155) Has hundreds of well-organised campsites and cabins set within the park's coastal forest. Minimum charges apply.

The following offer accommodation and dive packages (note: equipment hire is often extra).

Sodwana Bay Lodge LODGE $$
(035-571 6010; www.sodwanabaylodge.co.za, www.sodwanadiving.co.za; s/d with half board R825/1650) This resort has neat boardwalks, banana palms and pine-filled, slightly dated rooms. It caters to high-life divers and offers various dive packages. It's on the main road on the approach to the park. **Sodwana Bay Lodge Scuba Centre** (035-571 0117; www.sodwanadiving.co.za) is on the premises; dive and accommodation packages are available.

Coral Divers LODGE $$
(033-345 6531; www.coraldivers.co.za; Sodwana Bay; d tent R350, d cabin without/with bathroom from R580/700; @) Inside the park proper, this factory-style operation continues to 'net the shoals' with its diving packages and other activities. There's a large dining area-cum-bar, and a tadpole-sized pool. There's something for all budgets, from tents and small dollhouse-style cabins to nicer, upmarket cabins with their own patch of lawn and bathrooms. It can look a bit over-used depending on whether or not maintenance has been done after the hordes have gone.

Natural Moments Bush Lodge & Diving (035-571 0167; www.divesodwana.com; bungalow per person from R185) and **Da Blu Juice** (082 924 7757, 082 681 5459; www.dabluejuice.co.za; dm

per person R150, 6-person cabin from R500) are budget accommodation options of the hippie, laid-back variety. Both can arrange activities.

Getting There & Away
Turn off the N2 at Hluhluwe village heading to Mbazwana, and continue about 20km to the park. Minibus taxis ply this route.

Lake Sibaya & Coastal Forest

Remote grassland plains, lush forests and pristine beaches are the main features of the magical Coastal Forest. Its beauty can, in part, be explained by its location – this area is one of the most remote sections of iSimangaliso – and it is accessed either along the coastal sandy track between Kosi Bay and Sodwana Bay or from KwaNgwanase, in both instances by 4WD. Highlights include Black Rock (a rugged rocky peninsula easily reached by climbing over sand dunes) and Lala Nek, a beautiful and seemingly never-ending stretch of sand.

Further south sits Lake Sibaya, the largest freshwater lake in South Africa. It covers between 60 and 70 sq km, depending on the water level. Hippos, crocs and a large range of birdlife (more than 280 species) occupy the lake. Canoeing trips on the lake can be arranged through Thonga Beach Lodge.

But beauty doesn't always come cheap. Accommodation in this region is made up mainly (but not entirely) of luxury lodges. All offer excellent snorkelling, diving and other activities. The lodges transfer guests from the main road; you leave your cars in secure parking areas.

Day-visitor permits are required for this section of the park – go to the Manzengwenya and Kosi Bay offices of Ezemvelo KZN Wildlife.

Popular with European visitors, **Thonga Beach Lodge** (035-474 1473; www.isibindiafrica.co.za; s with full board R3588-4147, d with full board R5520-6380;) is an isolated and luxurious beach resort offering spacious huts scattered through coastal forest. Spectacular ocean views – whales sometimes pass by – and activities (some included in the price) provide the entertainment, while the wide, white beach and spa treatments (at extra cost) are a welcome relief after the rigours of a safari experience. The cuisine is excellent, especially the buffet lunches.

HEALTH WARNING

In 2004, the World Health Organization declared KZN – as far northeast as St Lucia – malaria free. Note: a low risk area extends from Sodwana Bay (iSimangaliso Wetland Park) northwards. The risk may be higher north and northeast near the borders of Swaziland and Mozambique. There is the risk of bilharzia in some waterways and dams, especially those less than 1200m above sea level. Also beware of crocs and hippos: both can be deadly. Be careful at night (including in the town of St Lucia), as this is when hippos roam. In more remote areas hippos might be encountered on shore during the day – maintain your distance and retreat quietly. Do not enter any inland water (St Lucia Estuary) – there are crocodiles, sharks, hippos and bilharzia. Swimming is possible (in good conditions and at low tide) at Cape Vidal beach. See p610 for more information on malaria.

If you can get to **Mabibi Camp** (☎035-474 1473; www.isibindiafrica.co.za; entry/vehicle/campsite per person R20/15/85), you will have heaven all to yourself – well, almost. This community-owned camp is right next to upmarket Thonga Beach Lodge, but this is luxury of a different kind – it's nestled in a swathe of lush forest and is only a hop, skip and 137 steps (via a stairway) away from the beach. It's rustic and good, old-fashioned camping; bring your own tent, food and gear.

New York Soho meets Durban chic at **Rocktail Beach Camp** (☎in Jo'burg 011-807 1800; www.safariadventurecompany.com; s/d with full board R2700/5200; ☒). Twelve safari tents (with pine floors and tasteful wood-sided bathrooms) and three family units are nestled in the dune forest in a tropical environment, with a choice of forest canopy or sea views. The light and breezy, spacious open communal area is an enjoyable place to relax. Offers seasonal specials.

Kosi Bay

☎035

The jewel of iSimangaliso Wetland Park, **Kosi Bay** (☎035-845 1000; ☺6am-6pm Apr-Oct, 5am-7pm Nov-Mar) features a string of four lakes, starting with an estuary lined with some of the most beautiful and quiet beaches in South Africa. Fig, mangrove and raffia-palm forests provide the greenery (it's the only place in South Africa with five mangrove species in one place). Within the estuary mouth is excellent snorkelling. Note: stonefish are present here, so protect your feet if walking in the estuary.

Hippos, Zambezi sharks and some crocs live within the lake system. More than 250 bird species have been identified here, including rare palmnut vultures.

You'll need a 4WD and permit to visit – see p266 for details. KwaNgwanase is the nearest service centre, some 10km west of the reserve, and you will find shops and an ATM here.

🛏 Sleeping & Eating

Most lodge accommodation is dispersed around the region's sandy dunes, several kilometres from KwaNgwanase. In many cases 4WDs are needed to negotiate the sandy tracks.

Utshwayelo Campsite   CAMPGROUND, CHALET $$
(☎082 909 3113; www.kosimouth.co.za; campsites per person R125, chalets R720) This community-run camp offers basic but neat bamboo-lined chalets with communal kitchen. It's right by the entrance to the park at the Kosi Bay Mouth access road. From here, you can walk to one of the country's best beaches in 30 minutes. Issues car-entry permits to Kosi Bay Mouth.

**Ezemvelo KZN
Wildlife**   CAMPGROUND, CABIN $$
(☎033-845 1000; www.kznwildlife.com; campsites R385, 2-/5-/6-bed cabin R500/1320/1320) Offers camping and fully equipped, pleasant cabin accommodation within lush forest surrounds on the western shore of Lake Nhlange – minimum charges apply. Popular with fishermen.

Maputaland Lodge   CHALET $$
(☎035-592 0654; www.maputalandlodge.co.za; KwaNgwanase; s/d R500/700; ❉☒) These 23 simple, yet pleasant, self-catering chalets in KwaNgwanase have all mod cons including DSTV, a bar and a restaurant. A good option in a creature-free zone.

Kosi Forest Lodge   LODGE $$$
(☎035-474 1473; www.isibindi.co.za; s/d with full board R2200/3380; ☀) The only private lodge in iSimangaliso's Kosi Bay region, and surrounded by the sand forest's Umdoni trees, this intimate 16-bed lodge offers a dreamy, luxurious – given the remote circumstances and lack of electricity – experience. Accommodation is in romantic safari tents. They are a blend of *Out of Africa* (wooden decor and muted furnishings) and natural (the ultimate in ingenious outdoor bathrooms). There are activities on tap, and guest transfers are available.

ⓘ Getting There & Away

A 4WD and permit are required to access Kosi Bay, but don't let this deter you. There are two entrances to the park: at Kosi Bay Camp (7km north of KwaNgwanase) and Kosi Bay Mouth (19km north of KwaNgwanase). Only 4WDs can enter the access roads, and numbers are limited; permits are required to enter **Kosi Bay Mouth** (adult/child/vehicle R20/10/15). These must be arranged one day in advance by calling ☎035-592 0236, or through some lodgings.

Kosi Forest Lodge organises pick-ups from KwaNgwanase, and some lodges in other areas organise trips to Kosi Bay. There is no public transport to the area.

If you are driving – approaching from any direction – the best access is via N2; at Hluhluwe turn onto R22. If heading from Sodwana Bay, continue north up the R22. If you have a 4WD, the sandy coastal route is not to be missed.

uMkhuze Game Reserve & Around

☎035

The **uMkhuze Game Reserve** (☎031-845 1000, 573 9001; www.kznwildlife.com; adult/child/vehicle R35/18/35; ⏰5am-7pm Nov-Mar, 6am-6pm Apr-Oct) is, in a phrase, a trip highlight. Established in 1912, and now part of iSimangaliso Wetland Park, this reserve of dense scrub and open acacia plains covers some 36,000 spectacular hectares. It may lack lions, but just about every other sought-after animal is represented, as well as more than 400 species of birds, including the rare Pel's fishing owl (*Scotopelia peli*). The reserve has fabulous hides, some at waterholes; the pans, surrounded by fever trees, offer some of the best wildlife viewing in the country. It's 15km from Mkuze town (18km from Bayla if heading north). Excellent evening drives (R200) are available. Don't miss the wonderful **Fig Forest Walk** (per person R180), an escorted walk across multilevel walkways.

Ezemvelo KZN Wildlife (☎033-845 1000; www.kznwildlife.com) runs two excellent sleeping choices.

Nhlonhlela bush lodge (8-bed lodge R2280) features a communal area overlooking a pan, and four comfortable units linked by boardwalks. You have your own ranger and chef (but you bring your own food).

Mantuma (2-bed safari camp per person R680, d chalets R560) is another fabulous choice for smaller huts, chalets and safari tents. The latter are equipped with baboon-proofed (bolted!) fridges, alfresco kitchens, mozzie nets, fans and bathroom.

Access from the north is via Mkuze town (from the south, you turn off the N2 around 35km north of Hluhluwe village but it's on a dirt road). A new road from Sodwana Bay (Ophansi Gate) provides easy access on the park's eastern side.

The town of **Mkuze** is southwest of the Lebombo Range on the N2. **Ghost Mountain**, south of the town, was an important burial place for the Ndwandwe tribe and has a reputation for eerie occurrences, usually confined to strange lights and noises. Occasionally human bones, which date from a big battle between rival Zulu factions in 1884, are found near Ghost Mountain.

Ghost Mountain Inn (☎035-573 1025; www.ghostmountaininn.co.za; s/d incl breakfast R975/1725; ❄🐾🛜☀) is an old-school colonial 'country inn' with a modern (and luxurious) touch, indoor-outdoor lounge areas and blooming gardens. It's an excellent base for exploring the reserves. Jean, the guide-in-the-know, takes fascinating cultural tours in the scenic surrounds; recommended tours include trips to uMkhuze Game Reserve and Dingaan's Grave.

Tembe Elephant Park

☎035

Heading westwards along a dirt road to the N2 from Kosi Bay, South Africa's last free-ranging elephants are protected in the sandveld (dry, sandy coastal belt) forests of **Tembe Elephant Park** (☎035-592 0001; www.tembe.co.za; adult/child/vehicle R30/15/35; ⏰6am-6pm). This Transfrontier Park on the Mozambique border is owned by the Tembe tribe and managed by Ezemvelo KZN Wildlife. Around 230 elephants live in its 30,000 hectares; these are the only indigenous elephants in

KZN, and the largest elephants in the world, weighing up to 7000kg. The park boasts the Big Five (lion, leopard, buffalo, elephant and rhino), plus more than 300 bird species.

Tembe Lodge (☎031-267 0144; www.tembe .co.za; with full board & activities per person R800-1250; ☎) offers accommodation in delightful, secluded, upmarket safari tents built on wooden platforms and with bathrooms.

There's a sealed road all the way to the park entrance, but only 4WD vehicles are allowed to drive through the park itself; secure parking is available and visitors are collected in open safari vehicles.

Ndumo Game Reserve

☑035

A little further west of Tembe Elephant Park, **Ndumo Game Reserve** (☎035-845 1000, 591 0004; www.kznwildlife.com; adult/child/vehicle R40/20/35; ☺5am-7pm Oct-Mar, 6am-6pm Apr-Sep) is beside the Mozambique border and close to the Swaziland border, about 100km north of Mkuze. On some 10,000 hectares, there are black and white rhinos, hippos, crocodiles and antelope species but it's the birdlife on the Phongolo and Usutu Rivers, and their flood plains and pans, that attracts visitors. The reserve is known locally as a 'mini Okavango'.

Wildlife-viewing and birdwatching guided walks (R85) and vehicle tours (R180) are available. This is the southernmost limit of the range of many bird species and the reserve is a favourite with birwatchers, with more than 400 species recorded.

Fuel and limited supplies are usually available 2km outside the park gate. Camping and rest huts are offered by **Ezemvelo KZN Wildlife Accommodation** (☎033-845 1000; www .kznwildlife.com; campsites per person R110, 2-bed rest hut R660); minimum charges apply.

DRAKENSBERG & UKHAHLAMBA-DRAKENSBERG PARK

If any landscape lives up to its airbrushed, publicity-shot alter ego, it is the jagged, green sweep of the Drakensberg Range's tabletop peaks. This forms the boundary between South Africa and the mountain kingdom of Lesotho, and offers some of South Africa's most awe-inspiring landscapes. It provided the backdrop for the films *Zulu* (1964) and

'DOING' THE BERG

Be aware that the area is deceptive – it's not easy to cover the whole of Drakensberg (the Berg) – whether outside or inside the park. There is no single road linking all the main areas of interest – you have to enter and exit and re-enter each region of the park from the N3, R103 and R74 or, if road conditions permit, from secondary roads. You are better off basing yourself in one spot and travelling out from there to enjoy each area's offerings – from hiking to birdwatching – rather than spending most of your time behind a wheel in search of sites and sights.

Yesterday (2004) and the setting for Alan Paton's novel *Cry, the Beloved Country,* and is the inspiration for a million picture postcards.

Within the area is a vast 243,000-hectare sweep of basalt summits and buttresses; this section was formally granted World Heritage status in November 2000, and was renamed uKhahlamba-Drakensberg Park. The park is part of the wider Drakensberg region, extending from Royal Natal National Park in the north to Kokstad in the south, the region and battlefields around Estcourt and Ladysmith, and the southern Midlands. Today, some of the vistas are recognisably South African, particularly the unforgettable curve of the Amphitheatre in Royal Natal National Park. Prominent peaks include Mont-aux-Sources, the Sentinel, Eastern Buttress and Devil's Tooth.

Drakensberg means 'Dragon's Mountains'; the Zulu named it Quathlamba, meaning 'Battlement of Spears'. The Zulu word is a more accurate description of the sheer escarpment but the Afrikaans name captures the Drakensberg's otherworldly atmosphere. People have lived here for thousands of years – this is evidenced by the many San rock-art sites (visit Didima, Cathedral Peak, Kamberg and Injisuthi).

The San, already under pressure from the tribes that had moved into the Drakensberg foothills, were finally destroyed with the coming of white settlers. Some moved to Lesotho, where they were absorbed into the Basotho population, but many were killed or simply starved when their hunting grounds were occupied by others. Khoe-San cattle raids annoyed the white settlers to the

Drakensberg

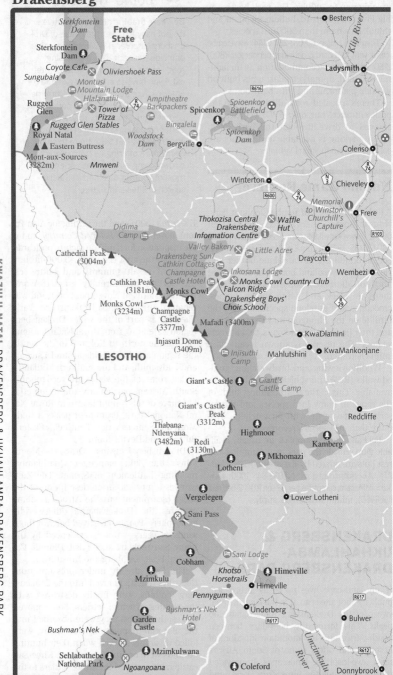

Sterkfontein Dam

Free State

Besters

Klip River

Sterkfontein Dam

Coyote Cafe

Sungubala

Oliviershoek Pass

Ladysmith

Montusi Mountain Lodge

Hlalanathi

Ampitheatre Backpackers

R74

Spioenkop

Spioenkop Battlefield

Rugged Glen

Tower of Pizza

Rugged Glen Stables

Bingalela

Spioenkop

Colenso

Royal Natal

Eastern Buttress

Woodstock Dam

Bergville

Spioenkop Dam

Mont-aux-Sources (3282m)

Mnweni

Winterton

R616

R74

R3

Chieveley

R74

Memorial to Winston Churchill's Capture

Frere

R600

R74

R103

Thokozisa Central Drakensberg Information Centre

Waffle Hut

Didima Camp

Cathedral Peak (3004m)

Valley Bakery

Little Acres

Draycott

Drakensberg Sun/ Cathkin Cottages

Champagne Castle Hotel

Inkosana Lodge

Wembezi

Cathkin Peak (3181m)

Monks Cowl

Monks Cowl Country Club

Falcon Ridge

Monks Cowl (3234m)

Champagne Castle (3377m)

Drakensberg Boys' Choir School

Mafadi (3400m)

R29

Injasuti Dome (3409m)

LESOTHO

Injisuthi Camp

KwaDlamini

Mahlutshini

KwaMankonjane

Giant's Castle

Giant's Castle Camp

Giant's Castle Peak (3312m)

Redcliffe

Thabana-Ntlenyana (3482m)

Redi (3130m)

Highmoor

Kamberg

Lotheni

Mkhomazi

Vergelegen

Lower Lotheni

Sani Pass

Sani Lodge

Cobham

Khotso Horsetrails

Himeville

Mzimkulu

Himeville

Pennygum

Underberg

R617

Bulwer

Garden Castle

Bushman's Nek Hotel

R617

Bushman's Nek

Sehlabathebe National Park

Mzimkulwana

Ngoangoana

Coleford

Umzimkulu River

R612

Donnybrook

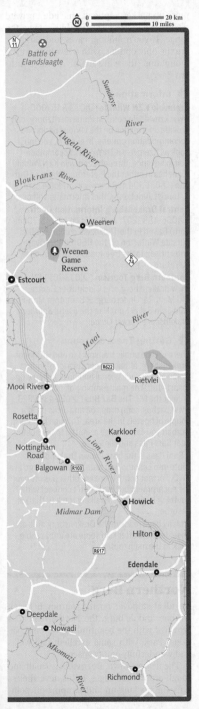

extent that the settlers forced several black tribes to relocate into the Drakensberg foothills to act as a buffer between the whites and the Khoe-San. These early 'Bantu locations' meant there was little development in the area, which later allowed the creation of a chain of parks and reserves.

Climate

The frosts come in winter, but the rain falls in summer, and snow has been recorded on the summit every month of the year. While the summer weather forecasts, posted in each of the Ezemvelo KZN Wildlife park offices, often make bleak reading for those hoping for blue skies and sunshine, you can often bet on clear, dry mornings, with the thunderheads rolling in only during the afternoon. Whenever you visit, always carry wet-weather gear, and be prepared for icy conditions and snowfalls.

Hiking

The Drakensberg range is one of the best hiking destinations in Africa. Valleys, waterfalls, rivers, caves and the escarpment, which rises to an impressive 3000m, provide spectacular wilderness experiences for walkers of all levels. Climbing is popular throughout the Drakensberg; only experienced climbers should attempt peaks in this region.

Broadly speaking, there are three main degrees of difficulty: gentle day walks, moderate half-day hikes and strenuous 10- to 12-hour hikes. Overnight treks and multiday hikes are for more serious and experienced hikers.

The trails are accessed through any of the park's entrances – Royal Natal National Park (renowned for its excellent day walks), Cathedral Peak, Monk's Cowl, Injisuthi and Giant's Castle, and the remote wilderness areas in the Southern Drakensberg.

This being said, there are many overnight trails that may be done following expert advice.

To plan any walk, hike or trek, make sure you obtain the relevant 1:50,000 scale maps that show trails and have essential information for hikers. You should always seek advice on the current status of any trail – consult with experienced hikers, accommodation owners and Ezemvelo KZN Wildlife officers. You must always fill in a register, and permits are needed on all hikes within the Park – organise them with Ezemvelo KZN Wildlife offices at the various trailheads. The only trail accommodation is at

Giant's Castle; in some areas hikers can use caves, but always carry a tent.

Registered guides can be organised for short walks (R100 per person) or longer hikes (R200 per person). Guides for overnight hikes are around R500 per person per night. This depends on numbers and should be established at each point. Hikers are not allowed to light fires, so you'll need to bring a stove.

April to July are good months for hiking. Summer hiking can be made frustrating, and even dangerous, by rain and flooding rivers; in winter, frost is the main hazard, and snow occurs occasionally. Snakes inhabit the area.

Wildlife

With plentiful water, a range of up to 3000m in altitude and distinct areas such as plateaus, cliffs and valleys, it isn't surprising that the flora of the uKhahlamba-Drakensberg is extremely varied. The park is mainly grassland, wooded gorges and high basalt cliffs with small forests in the valleys. There's also some protea savannah and, during spring, swathes of wildflowers. At higher altitudes grass yields to heath and scrub. At lower levels, but confined to valleys (especially around Royal Natal National Park), are small yellowwood forests.

The park is home to numerous and varied animals and hundreds of bird species. Altogether there are thought to be about 60 mammal species. There are several species of antelope, with relatively large numbers of elands (more in the Southern Berg). The rarest antelope is the klipspringer, which is sometimes spotted on the higher slopes. There are otter, African wildcats, porcupine and even the odd leopard. Baboons forage for food on some of the steepest mountains. The rarest species is a small, short-tailed rodent called the ice rat, which lives in the boulders near the mountain summits. The bearded vulture (a rare bird of prey), black eagles and vultures are found around the cliffs, capitalising on the peaks' thermals. Various hides throughout the park allow for closer viewing.

🛏 Sleeping

The perfect way to see the uKhahlamba-Drakensberg Park is to stay at one of Ezemvelo KZN Wildlife's excellent accommodation options – campgrounds, upmarket safari tents, equipped cabins and chalets. Note that a minimum charge may apply. Other more-upmarket options include private resorts, which dot the foothills along the range. If you're hiking, caves and camping are the only options, with a few huts on the mountains (these are mainly in the Southern Berg).

ℹ Information

Ezemvelo KZN Wildlife (☎033-845 1000; www.kznwildlife.com), in Pietermaritzburg, can provide information on the various parks and accommodation options. In general, you must book all Ezemvelo KZN Wildlife accommodation in advance, through Ezemvelo KZN Wildlife branches in either the Pietermaritzburg or **Durban** (☎031-304 4934; www.kznwildlife.com; 1st fl, Tourist Junction). Other information offices:

Central Drakensberg Information Centre (☎036-488 1207; www.cdic.co.za; ⊗8.30am-5pm) Based in the Thokozisa complex, 13km outside Winterton on the R600, this private enterprise stocks tree-loads of promotional literature.

Southern Berg Tourism (☎033-701 1471; www.drakensberg.org; Clocktower Centre, Old Main Rd, Underberg; ⊗8am-4pm Mon-Fri, 9am-1pm Sat & Sun) Has the useful *Southern Drakensberg Pocket Guide*.

ℹ Getting There & Around

There is little public transport to and within the Drakensberg, although there is a lot of tourist traffic and the occasional minibus taxi ferrying resort staff. The main jumping-off points are on or near the N3. The **Baz Bus** (☎021-439 2323; www.bazbus.com) drops off and picks up at a couple of hostels in the area. Through hostels in Durban you can arrange a shuttle to the hostels near Sani Pass and Himeville.

Sani Pass is the best-known Drakensberg route into Lesotho, but note, you can only go in a 4WD. Further south there are other passes over the escarpment but most don't connect with anything larger than a walking track (if that) in Lesotho.

Many back roads in the Drakensberg area are unsealed, and after rain some are impassable – stick to the main routes.

Northern Berg

An ideal stopover on the journey between Durban and Jo'burg, the Northern Berg is crowned with the beautiful Royal Natal National Park, with some excellent day walks and wonderfully empty spaces.

The nearest town, Bergville, is small and rough around the edges, but is nevertheless a useful stocking-up and jumping-off point

ℹ BUSES

None of the long-distance bus lines run very close to Bergville. You'll have to get to Ladysmith and take a minibus taxi from there (45 minutes). A daily Greyhound bus stops at Estcourt and Ladysmith. Taxis run into the Royal Natal National Park area for about R15 but few run all the way to the park entrance.

for the Northern Drakensberg. The minibus taxi park is behind the tourist office.

ABSA (Tatham Rd) has an ATM. The privately owned **Okhahlamba Drakensberg Tourism** (☏036-448 1244; www.drakensberg.org.za; Tugela Sq; ⏰7.30am-4pm Mon-Fri) has plenty of brochures, but the help stops there.

If you've left your run a bit late to reach the Northern Berg, **Bingalela** (☏036-448 1336; s/d incl breakfast R370/560) is one of the few places worth considering to lay down your head and/or grab a meal. It's located 3km from Bergville on R74. Attractive double and family-sized *rondavels* (round huts) are set in dusty, slightly car park–like surrounds, under lovely eucalypts. Locals flock here for the lively restaurant whose massive menu features a lot of grilled meats, woodfired pizza and pasta, and a bar.

ROYAL NATAL NATIONAL PARK
✎036

Spanning out from some of the range's loftiest summits, the 8000-hectare **Royal Natal National Park** (☏036-438 6310; www.kznwildlife.com; adult/child R30/20; ⏰5am-7pm summer, 6am-6pm winter) has a presence that far outstrips its relatively meagre size, with many of the surrounding peaks rising as high into the air as the park stretches across. With some of the Drakensberg's most dramatic and accessible scenery, the park is crowned by the sublime Amphitheatre, an 8km wall of cliff and canyon that's spectacular from below and even more so from up on high. Here, the Tugela Falls drop 850m in five stages (the top one often freezes in winter). Looming up behind is Mont-aux-Sources (3282m), so called because the Tugela, Elands and Western Khubedu Rivers rise here; the latter eventually becomes the Senqu (Orange) River and flows all the way to the Atlantic. The park is renowned for its excellent day walks and hiking opportunities.

Other notable peaks in the area are Devil's Tooth, the Eastern Buttress and the Sentinel. Rugged Glen Nature Reserve adjoins the park on the northeastern side.

The park's **visitors centre** (⏰8am-4.30pm) is 3km in from the main gate. It doubles as a shop selling basic provisions. Day walks are explained in a basic map provided by the centre.

⊙ Sights & Activities

Rock Art   GUIDED WALK

There are several San rock-art sites within the park, but only one is open to tourists. You can organise a **guided walk** (adult/child R20/10; ⏰9am-3pm) with community guides. The return trip takes about one hour, including time to rest and chat. Look for the 'San Rock Art' sign near the first bridge after entry.

Horse Riding   HORSE RIDING

Just outside the park gates, **Rugged Glen Stables** (☏036-438 6422; 1-/2-hr rides R120/160) organises a wide range of horse-riding activities.

🛏 Sleeping & Eating

INSIDE THE PARK

TOP CHOICE **Thendele**   CHALET $$

(☏033-845 1000; www.kznwildlife.com; 2-person chalet R655-745, 4-person chalet R1308-1485) The park's fabulous main camp has two- and four-bed chalets as well as cottages and a lodge for larger groups. The chalets are set around lawns and driveways; all have in-your-face views of the peaks opposite. Those at the top are slightly more expensive for their wondrous views, but all are good. It's a great walking base.

Rustic camping is also available at **Mahai** (campsites per person R90), which is a beautiful campground approximately 1km from the visitors centre, and at **Rugged Glen Nature Reserve** (campsites per person R90), a more basic experience.

OUTSIDE THE PARK

TOP CHOICE **Montusi Mountain Lodge**   LODGE $$$

(☏036-438 6243; www.montusi.co.za; s/d with half board R1500/2000; ☎☀) With oodles of bush-lodge exclusivity, this opulent place blends a thatch-and-fireplace homeliness with plenty of luxury comforts in very swish chalets. There's guided hiking, including a daily morning walk on the property, and horse

PROTECTING THE SAN PAINTINGS

There are thousands of San paintings in caves and rockscapes around KwaZulu-Natal. Sadly, many of these have suffered through the actions of ignorant visitors, and many have been defaced with graffiti, or completely destroyed. Travellers should be aware of taking appropriate measures to ensure the ongoing preservation of these precious cultural treasures. For example, never splash paintings with water.

KwaZulu-Natal currently has an agreement with Amafa (the provincial cultural and heritage conservation body) to have preservation practices in its management plans. This includes ensuring that guides accompany visitors to sites, and educating visitors not to touch or harm the sites.

riding can be arranged. The turn-off is just after the Tower of Pizza; follow the signs.

Sungubala Mountain
Camp
SAFARI TENT, CHALET $$

(☑036-438 6000; www.sungubala.com; dm/d R250/R700) 'Glamping' (glamorous camping) might be an appropriate description of this fabulous option – six safari tents (with thatched gazebos and beds) or three A-frame units with shared bathrooms. Bring your own food (or half-board rates are available for R550 per person). Prices include guided hiking and the 2km transfer to camp from the office in a 4WD. Budget accommodation is available; rates for it are even cheaper if you walk in on your own. The camp office is next to the Cavern Berg Resort on the D119.

Hlalanathi
RESORT $$

(☑036-438 6308; www.hlalanathi.co.za; campsites per person R140, 2-/4-bed chalet R700/1350; ⊛) With a location lifted straight from an African chocolate-box lid and next to the local golf course, this pretty, unpretentious resort offers camping and excellent accommodation in thatched chalets on a finger of land overlooking the Tugela River. Go for a site facing the river and mountains. Prices are substantially cheaper outside high seasons.

Amphitheatre Backpackers
BACKPACKERS $

(☑036-438 6675; www.amphibackpackers.co.za; campsites per person R75; dm R125, d R280-520; ℙ⌘⊛) Facing the Amphitheatre, this is an in-your-face experience with a selection of sleeping options from dorms to the comfortable four-person 'luxury' rooms. There's a busy bar, a pool, and activities galore. Some travellers report feeling pressured to do the backpackers' organised trips (when there are other options around), while others enjoy the rolled-out convenience. Found 21km north of Bergville on R74.

Coyote Cafe
CAFE $$

(mains R60-100; ⊛8.30am-5.30pm Tue-Sat, to 3.30pm Sun & Mon) Catering to the visiting interstaters, this modern and sleek place serves up some almost-gourmet snacks and excellent cakes. It's on the R74 at the entrance to Little Switzerland; on a clear day the views are lovely.

Tower of Pizza
ITALIAN $

(www.towerofpizza.co.za; mains R30-70; ⊛lunch & dinner Tue-Sun) Yep, there really is a tower, where very good oven-fired pizza is prepared. It also offers quaint *rondavels* and cottages (doubles per person, including breakfast, are R350 to R375; weekday rates are slightly lower).

ⓘ Getting There & Away
The road into Royal Natal runs off R74, about 30km northwest of Bergville and about 5km from Oliviershoek Pass.

Central Berg

Crowned with some of the Drakensberg's most formidable peaks, including Giant's Castle Peak (3312m), Monk's Cowl (3234m) and Champagne Castle (3377m), the Central Berg is a big hit with hikers and climbers. But with dramatic scenery aplenty, this beautiful region is just as popular with those who prefer to admire their mountains from a safe distance. Champagne Valley, leading into Monk's Cowl, is full of cafes and accommodation options for all budgets.

The sedate little town of Winterton is the gateway to the Central Drakensberg and makes a short stop en route to the Drakensberg. The tiny, parochial Winterton Museum (☑036-488 1885; Kerk St; minimum donation R10; ⊛9am-4pm Mon-Thu, to 3pm Fri, to noon Sat) offers an insight into San rock art (there are some excellent photos with notes) and the history of local peoples, and there are photos relating to the Spioenkop battle (see boxed text, p284). Winterton's best eatery is the fabulous **Pig & Plough** (www.amblesidefarm .co.za; ⏱7.15am-4.30pm Tue-Fri, 9am-4.30pm Sat & Sun; 🛜), a cafe serving some decent gourmet fare, and it even has free wi-fi. It's located on the main road, just beyond the turn-off to the Champagne Valley.

There are ATMs in the main street. As a last resort, there are accommodation options in the main street, but you're better off driving the 20km to 30km into the Champagne Valley.

Minibus taxis head to Cathedral Peak (30 minutes), Bergville (15 minutes) and Estcourt (45 minutes).

CATHEDRAL PEAK NATURE RESERVE
📍036

In the shadow of the ramparts of Cathedral Peak, **Cathedral Peak Nature Reserve** (📞036-488 8000; www.kznwildlife.com; adult/ child R30/15; ⏱6am-6pm) backs up against a colossal escarpment of peaks between Royal Natal National Park and Giant's Castle, west of Winterton. With the Bell (2930m), the Horns (3005m) and Cleft Peak (3281m) on the horizon, this is a beautifully photogenic park.

The **Didima San Art Centre** (📞036-488 1332; adult/child R55/25; ⏱8am-4pm), at Didima Camp 1km into the park, offers an excellent multimedia insight into San rock art. The entrance price includes entry to the park; you must tell the gate that you intend to visit the centre.

The **park office** (📞036-488 8000; www.kzn wildlife.com), in Didima Camp, sells permits for the scenic drive (4WD only) up Mike's Pass and arranges guides. At the time of research the pass was closed due to the poor conditions; check on its status.

🛏 Sleeping & Eating

Didima Camp CAMPGROUND, CHALET $$
(📞033-845 1000; www.kznwildlife.com; campsites R90, 2-person chalet per person R750-790; 🏊) One of Ezemvelo KZN Wildlife's swankiest offerings, this upmarket thatched lodge, constructed to resemble San rock shelters, boasts huge views, a restaurant, tennis courts and a range of two- and four-bed self-catering chalets (full-board options are also available, on request). Minimum charges apply.

Camping is available near the main gate.

MONK'S COWL & CHAMPAGNE VALLEY
📍036

Within uKhahlamba-Drakensberg Park, **Monk's Cowl** (📞036-468 1103; www.kznwildlife .com; adult/child R35/18; ⏱6am-6pm), another stunning slice of the Drakensberg range, offers superb hiking and rock climbing. Within the reserve are the three peaks Monk's Cowl, Champagne Castle and Cathkin Peak.

The **park office** (📞036-468 1103; campsites 2-person minimum R190) is 3km beyond Champagne Castle Hotel, which is at the end of the R600 running southwest from Winterton. **Overnight hiking** (adult/child R45/22) is also possible but the shelter caves must be booked in advance.

The area en route to the park is known as **Champagne Valley**. This is full of cafes, pleasant accommodation options, bakeries, and enough (nonhiking) tourist activities to keep you busy for days.

The **Thokozisa** complex, 13km out of Winterton on R600 and at the crossroads to Cathedral Peak, Monk's Cowl and Giant's Castle (via Estcourt), is a useful spot to orient yourself. It houses the privately owned **Central Drakensberg Information Centre** (📞036-488 1207; www.cdic.co.za; ⏱8.30am-5pm), a clutch of craft shops and an excellent **restaurant** (mains R70-150; ⏱9am-8.30pm).

Just off Dragon Peaks road are South Africa's singing ambassadors, the **Drakensberg Boys' Choir School** (📞036-468 1012; www .dbchoir.co.za). There are public performances at 3.30pm on Wednesday during school terms. Seven kilometres from the Drakensberg Sun turn-off is **Falcon Ridge** (📞082 774 6398; adult/child R50/20; ⏱displays 10.30am, closed Fri & Mon), with awesome raptor-flying demonstrations and talks.

One-hour to full-day horse trails are available through **Ushaka Horse Trails** (📞072 664 2993; www.monkscowl.com; 4 Bell Park Dam Rd; one hour R100, full day R500).

Drakensberg Canopy Tour (📞036-468 1981; www.drakensbergcanopytour.co.za; per person R450; ⏱7.30am-2.30pm) is the Berg's latest adrenaline-filled activity. The canopy tour boasts superlatives – 12 slides, of which seven are over 100m; the highest point is 65m and the longest is 179m. You 'fly' above a beautiful canopy of an ancient indigenous forest, with a stream and waterfalls. It's an extreme sport – don't attempt it if you have vertigo. Book ahead.

KWAZULU-NATAL CENTRAL BERG

TAKING CARE IN THE MOUNTAINS

Ezemvelo KZN Wildlife warns that walkers should not go alone – even on day walks. Usually, guides are available for hire. For any walk, including short walks, you must always sign the rescue register. Be sure to obtain instructions and times regarding the hikes. For overnight treks, Ezemvelo KZN Wildlife recommends a minimum of four people. Note: attempting peaks in a day – as opposed to the more leisurely 'day walks' – is only for the very fit and experienced.

🛏 Sleeping & Eating

As well as camping in Monk's Cowl, there are some other accommodation options in Champagne Valley.

TOP CHOICE **Inkosana Lodge** BACKPACKERS $$
(☏036-468 1202; www.inkosana.co.za; campsites R100, dm/d without bathroom R150/450, 2-person thatched rondavel without/with bathroom R450/600; P☀) When a sign on a bunk says, 'This bed is ready', you know it's one hell of an organised place. This Drakensberg delight's indigenous garden, eco-friendly swimming pool, clean rooms and lovely *rondavels* make it one of the best spots around. Although promoted as a 'backpacker lodge', it's more than this; its range of rooms would suit any discerning traveller. Excellent cuisine and heaps of activities and walks are on offer. Former mountaineer and welcoming owner Ed can give expert advice on hikes. It's centrally located for activities in and around the area; you'll find it on the R600, en route to Champagne Castle.

Little Acres B&B $$
(☏082 456 1185; www.littleacres.co.za; s R450-530, d R730-790) A neat, tidy and secure B&B on the main road, and conveniently located to the Champagne Valley sights and activities. The two separate bungalows have their own entrance (and kitchenettes), while others are within the main house. It would particularly suit mature travellers.

Cathkin Cottage B&B $$
(☏036-468 1513; www.cathkincottage.co.za; 1 Yellowwood Dr; s/d R600/980; P☀) This neat and perky four-room English-style guesthouse is a lovely surprise. While activities abound in the surrounds, you'll be hard-pressed to leave the lovely garden, lawns and indoor-outdoor lounge area. All rooms have separate entries. It's located on the road to the Drakensberg Sun. Continue 500m past the security boom gate.

Champagne Castle Hotel RESORT $$$
(☏036-468 1063; www.champagnecastle.co.za; d with full board from R2230) The ever-reliable and predictably 'nice' Champagne Castle is one of the best-known resorts, conveniently in the mountains at the end of the road to Monk's Cowl (R600).

Valley Bakery BAKERY $
(snacks R25-40; ⊗8am-5pm Mon-Fri, 7am-2pm Sat) When a visiting 'Durbanite' declares she comes to this place for the 'best quiches in the country', you know it's got a loyal following. Baguettes, croissants and a range of delicious items are baked on the premises (the owners even grow and grind their wheat). A quaint verandah wrought with wrought iron is the place for coffees, snacks and brunches. The bakery is happy to make salad rolls to order – useful for hiking trips.

Waffle Hut CAFE $
(www.kwazuluweavers.com; snacks R22-85; ⊗8am-4.30pm) Located at KwaZulu Weavers, get your fill of handmade rugs (some locally made, others imported) after you've stuffed yourself with savoury and sweet waffles. KwaZulu Weavers is on the R600 en route, south of Winterton.

Monks Cowl Country Club RESTAURANT $
(☏036-468 1300; www.monkscowl.co.za; mains R45-115; ⊗7.30am-10pm Mon-Sat, 7.30am-4pm Sun) The local golf and country club, this homely and quaint spot serves up generous helpings of reasonable fare. Accommodation is also available in its unpretentious A-frame chalets (R600 per person for dinner, bed and breakfast).

INJISUTHI

Injisuthi, on the northern side of Giant's Castle, is another 'wow' spot of the Berg. It's a secluded and extraordinarily beautiful place with a terrific view of the Monk's Cowl peak. This reserve, originally a private farm ('Farm Solitude') was purchased by KZN Wildlife in the late 1970s. Injisuthi features the Drakensberg's highest points, Mafadi (3400m) and Injisuthi (3300m). Please note: these peaks cannot be done in a day. The many day walks include Marble Baths (four to five hours), where you can swim.

Injisuthi is the departure point for the guided hike to the extraordinary **Battle Cave**, a massive rock overhang featuring remarkable San bushmen's paintings. The extraordinary scenes – depicting figures and animals – were believed to represent a battle, but this has been disproven, with experts now proposing that they represent hallucinatory dreams or a spiritual trance. This is a six-hour round-trip hike, both exposed and shady (at times it passes under leafy canopies); the guides will point out medicinal plants and other interesting snippets. Walks must be reserved in advance (☎036 431 9000; around R100 per person, minimum two people – rates can depend on numbers).

Injisuthi Camp   CAMPGROUND, CHALET **$**
(☎033-845 1000, 036-431 7849; campsites R65; safari camp R120, chalet R240) There are self-contained cabins and campsites here; prices quoted are per person. The area has caves for overnight hikers (however, check on their state before departing).

GIANT'S CASTLE
☎036
Established in 1904, mainly to protect the eland, **Giant's Castle** (☎033-845 1000, 036-353 3718; www.kznwildlife.com; adult/child R30/15; ⏰5am-10pm Oct-Mar, 6am-10pm Apr-Sep, reception 8am-4.30pm) is a rugged, remote and popular destination, with varying dramatic landscapes. The Giant's Castle ridge itself is one of the most prominent features of the Berg. (If coming from the south on the N3, use the new off-ramp exit 175, not marked on all maps.)

As is the case elsewhere, there are many excellent day walks and longer trails here. The office at Giant's Castle Camp gives out a basic map of the trails (distances not stated). Here, too, is a shop selling basic provisions, and fuel is available.

The rare lammergeier, also known as the bearded vulture (*Gypaetus barbatus*), which is found only in the Drakensberg, nests in the reserve. Reserve staff sometimes give guests bones to put out to encourage the birds to feed here. The **Lammergeyer Hide** (☎036-353 3718; giants@kznwildlife.com; per person R215, minimum R645) is nearby, and is the best place to see these raptors. The hide is extremely popular so it's necessary to book in advance.

The Giant's Castle area is rich in San rock art, with many sites. It is thought that the last San lived here at the beginning of the 20th century.

To see some of these paintings, you can visit **Main Cave** (adult/child R30/15; ⏰9am-3pm), 2.3km south of Giant's Camp (a 45-minute walk), plus a shorter return of 1.5km. A guide waits at the cave's entrance where, every hour, he conducts an explanatory tour.

🛌 Sleeping
There are several excellent accommodation options inside the reserve, as well as caves and trail huts for hikers (note: at the time of research some of these had been vandalised – check on their status).

Giant's Castle Camp   CHALET **$$**
(☎033-845 1000; www.kznwildlife.com; trail hut per person R45, chalet per person R360-400) The very pretty main camp has two-, four- and six-bed chalets with fireplace, kitchenette, door-to-ceiling windows, TV and thatched verandahs, and eight-bed mountain huts.

ℹ️ Getting There & Away
If coming from the north or south along the N3, take the R29 to Giant's Castle (it links with Estcourt, to the east). From Winterton or Champagne Valley you can get here on the R10 and then south via Draycott. Infrequent minibus taxis do the run from Estcourt to villages near the main entrance (KwaDlamini, Mahlutshini and KwaMankonjane), but these are still several kilometres from Giant's Camp.

Southern Berg
Best accessed from the pleasant towns of Himeville and Underberg, the Southern Berg boasts one of the region's highlights: the journey up to Lesotho over Sani Pass. It is also renowned as a serious hiking area. As well as some great walks (including the fabulous Giant's Cup Trail), the region also offers a smorgasbord of wilderness areas.

SOUTHERN DRAKENSBERG WILDERNESS AREAS
The areas of Highmoor, Kamberg, Lotheni, and Cobham are south of Giant's Castle and are administered by Ezemvelo KZN Wildlife. These areas are more isolated, although they're accessible for those with time. The

GIANT'S CUP TRAIL

If you are planning to stretch your legs anywhere in South Africa, this is the place to do it. Without doubt, the **Giant's Cup Trail** (68km, five days and five nights), running from Sani Pass to Bushman's Nek, is one of the nation's great walks. Any reasonably fit person can walk it, so it's very popular. Early booking, through **Ezemvelo KZN Wildlife** (☑in Pietermaritzburg 033-845 1000) is advisable in local holiday seasons. Weather-wise, the usual precautions for the Drakensberg apply – expect severe cold snaps at any time of the year. Fees are based on the composition of the hiking party.

The stages are: day one, 14km; day two, 9km; day three, 12km; day four, 13km; and day five, 12km (note, it's not a circuit walk). An unofficial sixth day can take you from Bushman's Nek up into Lesotho to Sehlabathebe National Park (passports required). Highlights include the Bathplug Cave with San rock paintings and the breathtaking mountain scenery on day four. You can make the trail more challenging by doing two days in one, and you can do side trips from the huts if the weather is fine. Maps are sold at Sani Lodge for R45.

Camping is not permitted on this trail, so accommodation is in limited shared **huts** (adult/child per trail R65/50), hence the need to book ahead. No firewood is available so you'll need a stove and fuel. Sani Lodge (p279) is almost at the head of the trail; arrange for the lodge to pick you up from Himeville or Underberg.

region is good for hiking (the rates for overnight-hiking permits depend on what you do.)

Highmoor Nature Reserve   NATURE RESERVE

(☑033-845 1000; www.kznwildlife.com; adult/child R50/25, campsites per person R110, cave camping R45; ☺6am-6pm) Although more exposed and less dramatic than some of the Drakensberg region, the undulating hills of Highmoor Nature Reserve make for pleasant walks. It's also one of the few places where you're driving 'on top of' the foothills. There are two caves – Aasvoel Cave and Caracal Cave – both 2.5km from the main office, and Fultons Rock, which has rock paintings (a 4km easy walk), plus caves for overnight hikers. Access is via the towns of Nottingham Road or Rosetta (it's well signed). There are no chalets here, but campsites are available.

Kamberg Nature Reserve &
Rock Art Centre   NATURE RESERVE

(☑033-267 7251; www.kznwildlife.com; adult/child R30/15; ☺5am-7pm Oct-Mar, 6am-6pm Apr-Sep) Southeast of Giant's Castle, Kamberg Nature Reserve has a number of antelope species and guided **rock-art walks** (adult/child R30/15) with community guides. The reserve's **rock-art centre** is well worth visiting, if only to support the local community (the Tandela), who run it. Tours depart at 9am, 11am and 12.30pm. Tours depart from a purpose-built multimedia centre. Allow three hours for the round trip (3.5km). It's an easy walk, if a little steep at the end.

Two **documentaries** (R20) are shown in a purpose-built multimedia centre: the first is about the San people, and the other is a visual tour of the actual walk, aimed at those who are unable to walk to the site (those with disability). You can get here from Nottingham Road or Rosetta, off the N3 south of Mooi River.

For accommodation within the park, **Ezemvelo KZN Wildlife** (☑033-267 7251; www.kznwildlife.com; 2-bed chalet R570) has well-equipped chalets that are in a quaint garden setting and tastefully decorated with small kitchens and floor-to-ceiling glass overlooking lawns and mountains. Bring your own supplies. There are other sleeping options *outside* the park.

Perfect for families or longer stays, **Glengarry Park** (☑033-267 7225; www.glengarry.co.za; campsites per person R90, self-catering chalet per person R260) has pleasant, unpretentious cottages set in a beautiful garden, facing a small lake. There's even a bowling green, a small golf course on site and great walks, and the owner is happy to lead the way on a mountain bike trail. It's near the Glengarry–Highmoor road, just off the Kamberg Rd, 31km from Rosetta.

If God were to top off the beauty of the Drakensberg with an artificial gourmet treat, **Cleopatra Mountain Farmhouse** (☑033-267 7243; www.cleomountain.com; Balgowan; per person R1595-1995) would be it. This luxury retreat is owned by renowned South African chef Richard Poynton. Guests (a maximum of 22) enjoy a nightly six-course menu of quality produce prepared innovatively and accompanied by rich, creamy sauces. Each of the 11 rooms here is decked out in a theme – from Tuscan to garden – and features quirky touches, such as a picket fence bedhead and Boer memorabilia. The experience comes at a price, though, but this is the one place where it's worth forgetting the budget...and the calorie count.

UNDERBERG, HIMEVILLE & AROUND
✆ 033 / POP 1500

Clustered in the foothills of the southern Drakensberg, the small farming town of Underberg fills up in summer, when Durbanites head to the peaks for a breath of the fresh stuff. It has good infrastructure, and is the place to go for money and shopping and to organise activities in the region. Only a few kilometres from Underberg, Himeville is a pretty, if sedate, jumping-off point for the southern Drakensberg. Except for an excellent museum, a characteristic old pub and a cluster of reasonable B&Bs, there's not much else here. Minibus taxis run between Himeville and Underberg (R6, 10 minutes).

◉ Sights & Activities

Himeville Museum   MUSEUM
(admission by donation; ◔9am-3pm Tue-Sat, to 12.30pm Sun) One of the best rural museums in the country. Housed in the last *laager* built in South Africa (c 1896), the museum now contains an incredible array of bric-a-brac, from the Union Jack flown at the siege of Ladysmith to a map of El Alamein signed by Montgomery. Mike, the man at the desk, is the man in the know.

Khotso Horsetrails   HORSE RIDING
(✆033-701 1502; www.khotso trails.co.za) Offers rides and treks (plus tubing and fishing) in the area and into Lesotho – owner Steve is described by readers as 'South Africa's Crocodile Dundee'. It's about 7km northwest of Underberg on the Drakensberg Gardens Rd.

⟴ Tours

Several companies offer day tours up Sani Pass (from around R550, excluding lunch), as well as tailored special-interest packages. These include **Drakensberg Adventures** (✆033-702 0330; www.drakensbergadventures.co .za; Sani Lodge, Sani Pass); **Major Adventures** (✆033-701 1628; www.majoradventures.com; Old Main Rd, Underberg); **Sani Pass Tours** (✆033-701 1064; www.sanipasstours.com; Shop 22, Trout Walk Centre, Underberg), which also takes bookings for Sani Pass Lodge; and **Thaba Tours** (✆033-701 2333; www.thabatours.co.za; Clocktower Centre, Underberg).

🛏 Sleeping

There are several good accommodation options in and near Underberg and Himeville.

Yellowwood Cottage B&B   B&B $$
(✆033-702 1065; www.sa-venues.com/visit/yellow woodcottage; 8 Mackenzie St, Himeville; s/d incl breakfast R290/660; P🖭) An enjoyable homely experience: four cosy, frilly rooms in a pretty house with lovely garden outlook, views of Hodgson's Peaks, and delightful owners. (Rates given are for winter, when heating costs more; rates are cheaper at other times.)

Tumble In   B&B $
(✆033-7011 556; www.tumble-in-bnb.co.za; Underberg; r incl breakfast per person R300) This unpretentious place offers spacious, homely rooms. The rooms overlook a delightful garden of pear and apple blossoms, with birds galore. It's 2.5km from Underberg on the Himeville Rd.

Albizia House B&B   B&B $$
(✆033-702 1837; www.africaalbizia.co.za/bnb; 62 Arbuckle St, Himeville; s/d R410/650; P🖭) Neat, clean and carpeted, with trimmed-lawn views. The owner is a guide.

Khotso Backpackers   BACKPACKERS $
(✆033-701 1502; www.khotsotrails.co.za; Treetower Farm, Underberg; dm from R120; 🖭) A good budget accommodation, located in a rural environment. The owners lead horse rides into Lesotho and surrounds and you can get your adrenaline fix by rafting and tubing. It's about 7km northwest of Underberg on Drakensberg Gardens Rd.

✗ Eating

TOP CHOICE Pucketty Farm   DELI $
(✆033-701 1035; www.pucketty.com; ◔8am-5pm) Beatrix Potter meets Jamie Oliver: there's more to this extraordinary cute gourmet mix than meets the eye. There's a huge selection of great-value gourmet products, plus an art gallery and small cafe. (Surprisingly, there's no Mrs Tiggywinkle here, but other named animals enjoy the attention.) The enterprise started 18 years ago, and it's been organic in every sense. The epicurean corner has a range of gourmet delights (try the sweet berry relish and soused prunes), and the carrot cake is legendary. Perfect for

KWAZULU-NATAL SOUTHERN BERG

CAUGHT MIDWAY IN KZN – KOKSTAD AND VRYHEID

Kokstad, 182km southwest of Pietermaritzburg, serves as a stopover point for many people who underestimate the trip from Mpumalanga Province to KwaZulu-Natal's South Coast, or who are taking public transport to/from Underberg. A convenient place to drop your head is **Mount Currie Inn** (☎039-727 2178; www.mountcurries.co.za; s R330, d R500-950), 2.5km from the town centre on the main road leading to the N2. It has pleasant rooms – budget, standard, executive and deluxe – a good bar and Cassandra's restaurant (mains R30 to R70, open for lunch and dinner Monday to Friday).

Another useful overnight pitstop is **Vryheid**, 62km south of Piet Retief (Mpumalanga Province), especially if you're making a late run from Swaziland or Kruger National Park. Here, you can't go past the ultrafriendly, clean and well-signed **Siesta B&B** (☎034-980 8023; siesta@nkunzi.com; s/d R350/440).

self-caterers. The farm is 1.5km east from the Himeville turn-off.

Lemon Tree Bistro
INTERNATIONAL **$$**

(☎033-701 1589; Clocktower Centre, Main Rd, Underberg; mains R55-130; ☺breakfast, lunch & dinner Tue-Sat, breakfast & lunch Sun & Mon) This friendly place serves up zesty pastas, burgers, wraps and pancakes. If it's on the menu, here's your chance to try a 250g kudu medallion (R130).

Himeville Arms
PUB **$$**

(☎033-702 1305; www.himevillehotel.co.za; Main Rd, Himeville; mains R60-85; ☺breakfast, lunch & dinner) Quaint Middle England comes to Himeville at this old-fashioned inn. Offers a choice of eating options: the bar, an atmospheric old-fashioned dining room and a weekend grill room.

Grind Cafe
CAFE **$**

(Underberg Village Mall, Underberg; mains R20-100; ☺breakfast, lunch & dinner) One of the most popular places in Underberg, this contemporary place in the Village Mall has great coffee, good cakes and a wide selection of salads and pizzas. There's also wi-fi internet access.

❶ Information

First National Bank (Old Main Rd, Underberg) Has an ATM.

Southern Berg Escape (☎033-701 1471; www.drakensberg.org; Clocktower Centre, Old Main Rd, Underberg; ☺8am-4pm Mon-Fri, 9am-1pm Sat & Sun) Has the useful *Southern Drakensberg Pocket Guide.*

Standard Chartered Bank (Underberg Village Mall, Underberg) Has an ATM.

❶ Getting There & Away

NUD Express (☎033-701 2750, 079 696 7018; www.underbergexpress.co.za) operates shuttlebus services between Underberg (and Sani Lodge) and central Durban (R200), Durban's King Shaka International Airport (R290) and Pietermaritzburg (R210). You must book these services; they are not known for their reliability for sticking to times.

If you're arriving at Kokstad from the KZN south coast, or are heading to the Wild Coast/Port Elizabeth, one daily minibus taxi runs between central Kokstad and Underberg, departing Underberg (Spa carpark) at 9am and from Kokstad at 2pm (Baz Bus and bus arrivals are at Mount Currie Inn, 2.5km from the centre; you will have to ask the minibus to take you there, for an extra cost).

Underberg Metered Taxi Association (☎072 016 5809, 076 199 5823 or 076 719 2451) can take up to four passengers to Durban (R1200), Pietermaritzburg (R700), and Kokstad (R550).

Minibus taxis run between Himeville and Underberg (R8, 10 minutes) and from Underberg to Good Hope store ruins (R30, 30 minutes) and Pietermaritzburg (R55, 1½ hours).

See the Sani Pass section (p278) for details on transport into Lesotho.

SANI PASS
☎033

The drive up Sani Pass is a trip to the roof of South Africa: a spectacular ride around hairpin bends into the clouds to the kingdom of Lesotho. At 2865m, this is the highest pass in the country and the vistas (on a clear day!) are magical, offering stunning views out across the Umkhomazana River to the north and looming cliffs, almost directly above, to the south. There are hikes in almost every direction, and inexpensive horse rides are available. Amazingly, this is also the only road link between Lesotho and KwaZulu-Natal.

At the top of the pass, just beyond the Lesotho border crossing, is Sani Top Chalet – various operators run 4WD trips up to the chalet.

Daily minibus taxis bring people from Mokhotlong (Lesotho) to South Africa for shopping; if there's a spare seat going back, this is the cheapest option of heading over the pass to Lesotho, and you are taken to a town, not just the isolated lodge at the top of the pass. Ask at the tourist office. You need a passport to cross into Lesotho. The border is open from 6am to 6pm daily, but check beforehand; times alter. Make sure you allow sufficient time to arrive at either end. Also be aware that coming back into South Africa will require another visa.

🛏 Sleeping

Sani Lodge   BACKPACKERS **$**
(☎033-702 0330; www.sanilodge.co.za; campsites R70, dm/d without bathroom R110/320, 2-bed rondavel R400, self-catering cottage per person R250, minimum R750) At the bottom of the pass and on a recently tarred road, Sani Lodge tops the pops in the local-knowledge stakes, offering a range of fabulous tours and activities and insider tips about the region through its company, Drakensberg Adventures. Some of the rooms are basic (*rondavels* are nicer) but it makes up for this with its communal, ski-lodge-style atmosphere. A kitchen is available for general use, or pre-arranged dinners cost R70. It's about 10km from Himeville on the Sani Pass road.

BUSHMAN'S NEK
☎033

This is a South Africa–Lesotho border post (although with no vehicles!). From here there are hiking trails up into the escarpment, including to Lesotho's Sehlabathebe National Park. You can trot through the border and into Lesotho on horseback with Khotso Horsetrails (see p277).

Accommodation options include **Bushman's Nek Hotel** (☎033-701 1460; www .bushmansnek.co.za; r R902; ☎), a full-on resort about 2km east of the border post, and **Silverstreams Caravan Park** (☎033-701 1249; www.silverstreams.co.za; campsites per person R180-400, cottage from R600), which has campsites and cottages right next to the border.

THE MIDLANDS

The Midlands run northwest from Pietermaritzburg (KwaZulu-Natal's capital) to Estcourt, skirting the Battlefields to the northeast. West of Pietermaritzburg is picturesque, hilly country, with horse studs and plenty of European trees. It was originally settled by English farmers.

Today, the region appeals more to art and craft lovers; it promotes itself heavily as the Midlands Meander, a slightly contrived concoction of craft shops, artistic endeavours, tea shops and B&Bs, winding along and around the R103 west of the N3, northwest of Pietermaritzburg (p279).

Pietermaritzburg
☑036 / POP 457,000

Billed as the heritage city, and KZN's administrative and legislative capital, Pietermaritzburg and its grand historic buildings hark back to an age of pith helmets and midday martinis. While many buildings have been converted into museums, much of the CBD has, sadly, lost its gloss, especially in the past few years. This is partly due to the dire state of the local government coffers (at the time of research, the city had been placed under administration). Elsewhere, the inner suburbs – plus Hilton, a suburb 9km northwest of the city centre – are green, leafy and pretty.

Pietermaritzburg comprises a very contemporary mix: the city's numerous private schools are home to many students; a large Zulu community sets a colourful tone; and the Indian community brings echoes of the subcontinent to the city's busy streets. Pietermaritzburg is a reasonable base from which you can tackle the Midlands Meander (see boxed text, p282).

History

After defeating the Zulu at the decisive Battle of Blood River (see p290), the Voortrekkers began to establish their republic of Natal. Pietermaritzburg (usually known as PMB) was named in honour of leader Pieter Mauritz Retief, and was founded in 1838 as the capital (later the 'u' was dropped and, in 1938, it was decreed that Voortrekker leader Gert Maritz be remembered in the title). In 1841 the Boers built their Church of the Vow here to honour the Blood River promise. The British annexed Natal in 1843 but they

Pietermaritzburg

retained Pietermaritzburg – well positioned and less humid than Durban, and already a neat little town – as the capital. In 2004 it became the provincial capital, and in 2005, street names were altered to reflect a more local flavour.

Alan Paton, the well-known author of *Cry, the Beloved Country,* was born in Pietermaritzburg in 1903.

◉ Sights & Activities

Buildings   NOTABLE BUILDING

Notable buildings are dotted around the city centre's grid. Colonial-era City Hall (cnr Langalibalele St & Chief Albert Luthuli St) is the largest load-bearing red-brick building in the southern hemisphere. The Standard Chartered Bank (Church St Mall) was designed by architect Phillip Dudgeon and modelled on the Bank of Ireland in Belfast. Elsewhere are Hindu temples (Langalibalele St) and a mosque (East St). A statue of Gandhi (Church St), who was famously ejected from a 1st-class carriage at Pietermaritzburg station, also stands defiant opposite old colonial buildings.

FREE Tatham Art Gallery   GALLERY

(www.tatham.org.za; Chief Albert Luthuli St; ⊙10am-6pm Tue-Sun) In keeping with Pietermaritz-burg's self-styled role as the 'heritage city', one of its finest sights, the art gallery, was started in 1903 by Mrs Ada Tatham. Housed in the beautiful Old Supreme Court, it contains a fine collection of French and English 19th- and early 20th-century works. Every 15 minutes, little figurines appear out of the building's treasured ormolu clock to chime the bells.

KwaZulu-Natal National Botanical Garden   GARDENS

(www.sanbi.org; Mayors Walk; adult/child R16/10; ⊙8am-6pm summer, to 5.30pm winter) Located 2km west of the train station on the continuation of Hoosen Haffejee St and spread over 42 hectares, these gardens have exotic species and indigenous mist-belt flora.

Natal Museum   MUSEUM

(237 Jabu Ndlovu St; adult/child R10/3; ⊙8.15am-4.30pm Mon-Fri, 9am-4pm Sat, 10am-3pm Sun) Has a range of displays reflecting a diversity of cultures, including settler history, war records, stuffed birds, marine life and African mammals.

Macrorie House Museum   MUSEUM

(11 Jabu Ndlovu St; adult/child R10/5; ⊙10am-3pm Mon, 9am-1pm Tue-Fri) Here you'll find furni-

Pietermaritzburg

ture and items of the early British settlers, and plenty of documented ghosts!

Msunduzi Museum   MUSEUM
(www.voortrekkermuseum.co.za; 351 Langalibalele St; adult/student R8/5; ⊙9am-4pm Mon-Fri, to 1pm Sat) Formerly known as Voortrekker Museum, Msunduzi Museum comprises a complex that incorporates the Church of the Vow, the home of Andries Pretorius, a Voortrekker house and a girls' school (the museum's administrative building). The **Church of the Vow** was built in 1841 to fulfil the Voortrekkers' promise to God at the Battle of Blood River. The words of the Vow are in the **Modern Memorial Church**, located next door. More recently, history has had been re-written: the museum has had a name change and heralds itself as a multicultural institution, incorporating Zulu and Indian displays.

👉 Tours

Msunduzi Pietermaritzburg Tourism
(☎033-345 1348; www.pmbtourism.co.za; Publicity House; 117 Chief Albert Luthuli St; ⊙8am-5pm Mon-Fri, to 1pm Sat) Organises city walking (R100 per person) and driving (R150 per person) tours. Your own transport is required for the driving tours.

Sleeping

Most B&Bs cater to the business crowds who stay in town tending to council and other matters of commerce. Pietermaritzburg Tour-

ism can help with bookings or you could try the **Pietermaritzburg B&B Network** (☎073-154 4444), a group of B&Bs that help promote each other.

Heritage Guest House   GUESTHOUSE **$$**
(☎033-394 4364; 45 Miller St; s/d incl breakfast R475/650, family ste R1200) It's a good sign when you see the owner in chef's garb cooking a full English breakfast. This place has six small units of varying shapes and sizes surrounding a small pretty garden and pool. It's handy to the city centre and opposite the cemetery, and with comfortable beds, you'll sleep like the dead. It can get booked out by long-term business travellers.

Elbow's Rest   CHALET **$$**
(☎033-343 1594; www.pietermaritzburg.co.za, 15 Azalea Dr, Hilton; s/d R400/580) These three self-catering units have a pretty, cottagelike feel in a secure environment. The decor is slightly old-world with lots of pine trimmings, and a delightful English cottage-style courtyard and garden borders each one. It's only 10km away in Hilton.

Smith Grove   B&B **$$**
(☎033-345 3963; www.smithgrove.co.za; 37 Howick Rd; s/d R400/600) This pleasant, renovated Victorian home offers English-style B&B comforts with spacious, individually styled rooms, each in a different colour.

Redlands Hotel & Lodge   HOTEL **$$**
(☎033-394 3333; www.guestnet.co.za; cnr Howick Rd & George MacFarlane Lane; s R875-1170, d R1080-1280; ❉ ☀) Swish and stately, this elegant place offers contrived but tasteful colonial-style surrounds. It's a favourite among government dignitaries. The spacious grounds add to the escape-from-it-all ambience. It's north of the centre off Howick Rd, past the Royal Agricultural Showgrounds.

**Prince Alfred Street
Backpackers**   BACKPACKERS **$**
(☎033-345 7045; www.chauncey.co.za; 312 Prince Alfred St; per person R180, without bathroom R160; P ⓢ) A bright if ever-so-slightly faded place, with multicoloured mosquito-net extravaganzas and ethnic adornments. It's handy to the centre and, if you're lucky, owner Andre might whip up gourmet cuisine by prior arrangement (breakfast costs R50 and dinner around R90). Singles don't pay extra, even if they have their own room. It's gay friendly but all are welcome.

KWAZULU-NATAL PIETERMARITZBURG

TACKLING THE MIDLANDS MEANDER

For the uninitiated, the Midlands region can be a bit overwhelming. It's full of twee venue names such as 'Piggly Wiggly' and 'Ugly Duckling', with little explanation as to whether they're tasteful galleries or kitsch gift shops. The meander – stretched out over a valley and its offshoots – is relaxing and enjoyable and well worth a detour off the N3. The *Midlands Meander* brochure is available from tourist offices and contains a detailed colour-coded map of the area. Our highlights (of both official and 'non-Meander' entries):

Ardmore Ceramic Studio (☏033-234 4869; www.ardmoreceramics.co.za; Caversham Rd, Lidgetton; ⏰8am-4.30pm) This extraordinary gallery was started by artist Fée Halset-Berning in 1985. She trained Bonnie Ntshalintsahli, the daughter of a farm employee. Sadly, Bonnie has since died, but the studio flourished, first in the Drakensberg with a group of highly gifted artists. In 2009, the studio moved to its current site, set among greenery and stunning trees. The studio's artists create the most extraordinary pieces of ceramic art, some functional, others ornamental. So renowned are the pieces that Christie's holds an annual auction of selected items. You can see the artists at work in the studio and visit the stunning gallery; works are for sale, too.

Dargle Valley Pottery (☏033-234 4377; D66) Started by famous South African potter Ian Glenny, this old-school, '70s-style pottery place is at the other extreme of Ardmore – earthy and rural – and is equally captivating. You can wander through the barnlike gallery and watch the current local potter, Richard, as turns the pots. The pieces are renowned for their stunning glazing; the tagines are popular.

Cafe Bloom (Country Courtyard, Nottingham Road; mains R30-65; ⏰ breakfast & lunch Wed-Mon) One of the nicest cafes in the area. Located in a small complex with a garden, this homely, funky cafe is decked out in a melange of retro decor. You'll find great coffee, snacks and all-day breakfasts, and all products are made on the premises, from breads and cakes to the daily special (the likes of vegie curries and quiches). Ceramics and artworks are for sale.

Granny Mouse Country House (☏033-234 4071; www.grannymouse.co.za; Old Main Rd, Balgowan; d with breakfast from R1840) This deceptively named place near the village of Balgowan, south of Mooi River, is not one abode but more a resort-style range of neat, thatched luxurious cottages, complete with a chapel and spa. Specials are often available.

Sycamore Avenue Tree Houses (☏033-263 2875; www.treehouse-acc.co.za; Hidcote, d R1590) These extraordinary tree houses are functional art at its best. The constructions comprise recycled materials, unique carvings, wooden hinges and ingenious artistic touches incorporated into comfortable surroundings. One even has a 'Jacuzzi in the sky', connected by a walkway. Near Hidcote, Sycamore is located 50km from Giant's Castle, Drakensberg; see the website for directions.

Sleepy Hollow Adventure Backpackers BACKPACKERS $
(☏082 455 8325; www.sleepyhollowbackpackers. com; 80 Leinster Rd; campsite R85, dm/d/family R135/330/495) This rambling 1940s abode in the heart of the student precinct has a preloved feel with well-worn carpets and furniture, and a communal kitchen.

Eating

Rosehurst INTERNATIONAL $$
(239 Boom St; mains R58-70; ⏰8.30am-4.30pm Mon-Fri, to 2pm Sat) This delightful oasis, in a lovely Victorian house behind a rather chintzy gift shop, is a quintessential English garden in the middle of 'Maritzburg – complete with topiary trees, quaint chairs and tables. Relax under blossoms and pink bougainvillea while supping on fresh and very tasty salads, sandwiches and pastries. There are excellent breakfasts, too.

Traffords INTERNATIONAL $$
(43 Miller St; lunch mains R40-70, dinner mains R75-120; ⏰lunch Wed-Fri, dinner Wed-Sat) This place sits snugly next to Heritage Guest House and is run by the same owner, a chef. Not surprisingly, it serves up some quality international cuisine in appealingly quaint surrounds – the

rooms of a converted heritage home. Munch on oxtail, slow roasted lamb shanks and homemade gnocchi. Lunches include more salad-based offerings. Vegetarians are well catered for. Decor is of the pre-loved linen tablecloth variety...it's like having an elegant meal in the home you'd love to have.

Butcher Boys   STEAKHOUSE $$
(9 Armitage Rd, Bird Sanctuary; mains R95-125; ⊙lunch & dinner Sun-Fri, dinner Sat; ❖) This stylish 'meat market's' catchphrase is 'grill by design'. The choice cuts (and we mean the velvety, melt-in-your-mouth variety) are popular with businesspeople, the 'it' market and anyone who enjoys a meaty meal (warning: not surprisingly, the nonmeat dishes are less appealing – stick with what they do best).

Drinking & Entertainment

Dross   PUB
(Chatterton Rd; mains R40-100; ⊙lunch & dinner; ❖) Numerous drinkable draughts, a massive deck and an enormous sports screen are here for those who want a big 'pubby' night out. There's also a grill to appease hearty appetites.

Franki Bananas   BAR
(9 Armitage Rd, Bird Sanctuary; ⊙11am to late) This upmarket cocktail bar is the current place to be seen. It's popular with students and young professionals, especially Friday nights. Good nightly specials are on offer – Monday is beer and burger night (R45), Tuesday is girls' night, and so on. Note: only ever take a taxi to and fro.

❶ Information

Emergency
Police station (☏033-845 2400, 10111; Jabu Ndlovu St)

Internet Access
Orange Ring (☏033-342 9254; 31 Chief Albert Luthuli St; ⊙7am-9pm)
Wireless 4 U (Shop 73, Liberty Midlands Mall, 50 Sanctuary Rd; ⊙9am-6pm Mon-Sat, to 5pm Sun)

Medical Services
Medi-Clinic (☏033-845 3700, 24hr emergency 033-845 3911; www.mediclinic.co.za; 90 Payn St)

Money
There are several banks located across town and in major shopping malls.

ABSA (cnr Langalibalele & Buchanan Sts) Has an ATM and change facilities.
First National Bank (Church St) It's in a handy location in the city centre.

Post
Main post office (Langalibalele St)

Tourist Information
Ezemvelo KZN Wildlife Headquarters (☏033-845 1000; www.kznwildlife.com; Queen Elizabeth Park, Peter Brown Dr; ⊙reception 8am-4.30pm Mon-Fri, reservations 8am-5.30pm Mon-Thu, to 4.30pm Fri, to 12.30pm Sat) Provides information and accommodation bookings for all Ezemvelo KZN Wildlife parks and reserves – at least 48 hours' notice is required for bookings. To get to the office, head out to Howick Rd (an extension of Chief Albert Luthuli St) and after several kilometres you'll come to a roundabout. Veer right and head over the N3 freeway. This road has a very small sign directing you to 'Country Club', which is 2km further on. It's hard to get to without your own transport, although some minibus taxis pass the roundabout on their way to Hilton.

Msunduzi Pietermaritzburg Tourism (☏033-345 1348; www.pmbtourism.co.za; Publicity House, 117 Chief Albert Luthuli St; ⊙8am-5pm Mon-Fri, to 1pm Sat) Has information on the city and surrounds. A tourist office is being built behind the current office.

❶ Getting There & Away

Bus
The head offices of most bus companies are in Berger St, or directly opposite in McDonalds Plaza. **Translux** (☏033-345 0165; www.translux.co.za) and its no-frills affiliate, City to City, are based at the train station.

Greyhound (☏083 915 9000; www.greyhound.co.za), **Luxliner** (☏011-914 4321; www.luxliner.co.za) and **Intercape** (☏086 128 7287; www.intercape.co.za) offer similar prices depending on the level of onboard services.

Destinations offered by the listed companies from Pietermaritzburg include Jo'burg (R300 to R375, six to seven hours), Pretoria (R300 to R350, seven to eight hours) and Durban (R185 to R255, 1½ hours). Offices are generally open 7am or 8am until 11pm. Tickets for all major services can be purchased at Checkers/Shoprite or online at www.computicket.com.

NUD Express (☏033-701 2750, 079 696 7108; www.underbergexpress.co.za) offers a daily service to Durban's King Shaka International Airport (R290) and Durban Central (R200). You must book these services; they are not known for their reliability for sticking to times. The **Baz**

Bus (021-439 2323; www.bazbus.com) travels between Durban and Pietermaritzburg three times a week.

African Link Travel (033-345 3175; www .africanlink.co.za; 267 Burger St) has transfers from King Shaka International Airport to Pietermaritzburg (R750).

Minibus Taxi

Minibus taxis to Durban leave from behind City Hall (R60, one hour), while those to Underberg depart from the corner of West St and Pietermaritz St. Destinations from this stop also include Ladysmith (R80, 2½ hours), Underberg (R65, 2½ hours) and Jo'burg (R160 to R200, eight hours). Those for Estcourt (R55, 1¾ hours) depart from the rank on the corner of Retief and Hoosen Haffejee Sts; this is not a safe part of town.

Train

Pietermaritzburg is serviced by the **Shosholoza Meyl** (0860 008 888, 011-774 4555; www .shosholozameyl.co.za). See p242 for more information.

❶ Getting Around

Most bus companies' head offices are in Berger St, or directly opposite in McDonalds Plaza. To order a taxi, phone **Metro Cabs** (033-397 1912).

BATTLEFIELDS

Big wildlife, big mountains and big waves may top the agenda for many visitors to the province, but the history of KwaZulu-Natal is intrinsically linked to its Battlefields, the stage on which many of the country's bloodiest chapters were played out. The province's northwestern region is where fewer than 600 Voortrekkers avenged the murder of their leader, Piet Retief, by defeating a force of 12,000 Zulu at Blood River, and where the British Empire was crushed by a Zulu army at Isandlwana. Here they subsequently staged the heroic defence of Rorke's Drift, where the Boers and the Brits slogged it out at Ladysmith and Spioenkop. These days, the region offers some luxurious accommodation options, and for keen punters the region can be most rewarding (see boxed text, p287).

Many surrounding towns look as though they've been in more recent wars and, in a way, they have. With the construction (in the 1980s and '90s) of the N3, which bypassed many towns, and the subsequent closure of their factories, many local people left for the cities. See www.battlefields.kzn.org.za or pick up KZN Tourism's *Battlefields Route* brochure from KZN Tourism (see p241).

THE BATTLE OF SPIOENKOP

On 23 January 1900 the British, led by General Buller, made a second attempt to relieve Ladysmith, which had been under siege by the Boers since late October 1899. At Trichardt's Drift, 500 Boers prevented 15,000 of General Buller's men from crossing the Tugela River, and he decided that he needed to take Spioenkop – the flat-topped hill would make a good gun emplacement from which to clear the annoying Boers from their trenches.

During the night, 1700 British troops climbed the hill and chased off the few Boers guarding it. They dug a trench and waited for morning. Meanwhile the Boer commander, Louis Botha, heard of the raid. He ordered his field guns to be pointed towards Spioenkop, and positioned some of his men on nearby hills. A further 400 soldiers began to climb Spioenkop as the misty dawn broke.

The British might have beaten off the 400, but the mist finally lifted, and was immediately replaced by a hail of bullets and shells. The British retreated to their trench and, by midafternoon, continuous shellfire caused many to surrender. By now, reinforcements were on hand and the Boers could not overrun the trench. A bloody stalemate was developing.

After sunset, the British evacuated the hill; so did the Boers. Both retreats were accomplished so smoothly that neither side was aware that the other had left. That night Spioenkop was held by the dead.

It was not until the next morning that the Boers again climbed up Spioenkop and found that it was theirs. The Boers had killed or wounded 1340 British – Gandhi's stretcher-bearer unit performed with distinction at this battle. Buller relieved Ladysmith a month later on 28 February.

Battlefields

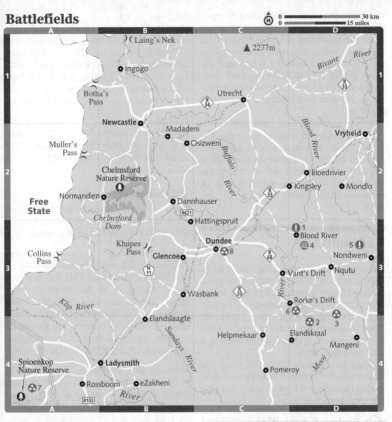

Battlefields

Sights

Spioenkop Nature Reserve

☑036

The 6000-hectare **Spioenkop Nature Reserve** (☑036-488 1578; www.kznwildlife.com; admission R20; ☺5am-7pm Oct-Mar, 6am-6pm Apr-Sep) is based on the Spioenkop Dam, on the Tugela River. The reserve is handy for most of the area's battlefield sites and not too far from the Drakensberg for day trips into the range. Animals include zebras, white rhinos, giraffes, various antelope species and over 270 bird species. You can even head out among the wildlife at a vulture hide, or on horse-riding trips and guided walks. There's a lovely stroll through aloe plants and woodlands.

The Spioenkop Nature Reserve is northeast of Bergville but the entrance is on the eastern side, 13km from Winterton off the R600. If you're coming from the south on the N3, take Exit 194 for R74 towards Winterton. The Spioenkop battlefield is accessed from R616 (not R600; follow the signs). You will need a car to access both places.

Three Trees at Spioenkop (☑036-448 1171; www.threetreehill.co.za; d inc all meals R3900), an upmarket eco-friendly house with plush contemporary-meets-colonial creature comforts, is a treat for those who want to explore the Spioenkop area. Beautiful setting and views, a delightful open-plan living area and an eco focus make for a fabulous stay. Horse riding and battlefield tours are made to order. It's conveniently located near Spioenkop, between Ladysmith and Bergville off the R616.

iPika (campsites/bush camp per person R60/190), inside the reserve in a valley, offers campsites and one four-bed tented bush camp in very pretty surrounds, overlooking a reservoir. It's peaceful, and offers plentiful birdlife plus the odd hoofed wildlife. Book accommodation directly through the reserve.

Ladysmith

036 / POP 41,000

Ladysmith was named after the wife of Cape governor Sir Harry Smith. The town achieved fame during the 1899–1902 Anglo-Boer War when it was besieged by Boer forces for 118 days. Musical group Ladysmith Black Mambazo has its roots here, but the town's pretty colonial vestiges are looking a little tired these days.

Apart from visiting Ladysmith for its historical aspect – several buildings were here during the siege – it's a reasonable base for the area's battlefield tours.

◎ Sights & Activities

Siege Museum   MUSEUM
(Murchison St; adult/child R11/5; ◎9am-4pm Mon-Fri, to 1pm Sat) The excellent museum, next to the town hall in the old Market House (built in 1884), was used to store rations during the siege. It has displays about the Anglo-Boer War, it stocks information about the town and surrounds and it can provide a list of battlefield tour guides.

Emnambithi Cultural Centre   MUSEUM
(316 Murchison St; ◎9am-4pm Mon-Fri) Comprises the **Cultural Museum**, which features a township shack and cultural displays, including traditional attire and beading. A tribute to Ladysmith Black Mambazo is also on display. The centre offers the **Black Mambazo Beat Tour**, showing the important sites and significance of the musical group.

Cannons   MONUMENT
Outside the town hall are two guns, **Castor** and **Pollux**, used by the British in defence of Ladysmith. Nearby is a replica of **Long Tom**, a Boer gun capable of heaving a shell 10km. Long Tom was put out of action by a British raiding party during the siege, but not before it had caused a great deal of damage.

Zulu Fort   NOTABLE BUILDING
On King St (opposite Settlers Dr) is a wall with loopholes from the original fort, built as a refuge from Zulu attack, and now part of the police station.

⫞ Sleeping

There are plenty of B&Bs out of town off Short St. They are often booked out by business travellers – it's best to book ahead.

Buller's Rest Lodge   B&B $$
(☎036-637 6154; www.bullersrestlodge.co.za; 61 Cove Cres; s/d incl breakfast R540/735; ☎⌨) It's worth digging in at this smart thatched abode. There's the snug 'Boer War' pub, scrumptious home cooking (R140 for three courses),and views from the attractive barsundeck area. Turn right at Francis Rd off Harrismith (Poort) Rd, and follow the signs.

Budleigh Guesthouse   B&B $$
(☎036-635 7700; 12 Berea Rd; s/d incl breakfast R450/650; ❄☎⌨) Just like a scene out of a BBC TV production, this mansion, with its verandahs and stunning garden, has a range of neat and smart rooms with wooden bedsteads and faux antiques, set around trimmed lawns and flower beds.

✕ Eating

Guinea Fowl   INTERNATIONAL $$
(☎036-637 8163; San Marco Centre; mains R50-120; ◎lunch & dinner Mon-Sat) One of only a few reasonable restaurants in Ladysmith, this eatery warrants another battlefield analogy: 'you win some, you lose some'. The staff is friendly, but travellers report varying standards of steaks and meat dishes.

Sonia's Pizza & Coffee Shop   ITALIAN $$
(☎036-631 2895; San Marco Centre; mains R20-130; ◎7am-7pm Mon-Sat, 8am-1.30pm Sun) The troops would have killed for this authentic Italian grub; this little place has a reputation around town for its delectable pizzas.

Information

ABSA (cnr Queen & Murchison Sts) Has two branches on the same crossroads, one with an ATM.

Emnambithi Cultural Centre (316 Murchison St; ⏱9am-4pm Mon-Fri) Ask here about guided tours of the Battlefields or to nearby townships.

Police station (☎036-638 3309; King St) By the NG Church.

ⓘ Getting There & Away

Bus

Bus tickets can be purchased from Shoprite/Checkers in the Oval Shopping Centre. Buses depart from the Guinea Fowl petrol station (not to

---

BATTLING IT OUT

Roughly following the N11 and R33 roads and occupying an area that stretches north from Estcourt to the Free State and Mpumalanga borders, the Battlefields are a crusade to get to without a car. Even with a car, they are isolated and can be a challenge to find.

Guides

The best way to tackle the Battlefields is with a guide – that way, you won't feel as though you're traipsing through a string of empty fields peppered with memorials. With a knowledgeable person at hand, and with a bit of swotting up beforehand, the so-called Battlefields Route can be extremely rewarding. Lists of battlefield guides are available from Talana Heritage Park & Battlefield, plus tourism offices in Dundee and Ladysmith. Be sure to pick up a Battlefields brochure or to consult www.battlefields.kzn.org.au.

Guides generally charge between R800 and R1500 for a one-day tour of sites including Rorke's Drift and Isandlwana. Note: some guides quote these rates per person, others per group; rates are cheaper in your own vehicle.

For those on a budget and happy to share the tour with others, **BushBaby Safaris** (☎082 415 4359; www.bushbaby.co.za) is a welcome addition to the battlefield scene. It offers a daily shuttle bus with a guide to Isandlwana and Rorke's Drift for R490 per person (minimum two people; rates exclude lunches and refreshments). Pick-ups are from anywhere in Dundee or from Talana Heritage Park & Battlefield at 8.30 am, returning at around 4.30pm. Staff will also cover other battlefields, on request.

Other (but by no means all) recommended guides:

Paul Garner (☎082 472 3912; garner@xsinet.co.za) Dundee.

Bethuel Manyathi (☎083 531 0061) Nqutu, near Dundee.

Thulani Khuzwayo (☎072 872 9782; thulani.khuzwayo@gmail.com; group tours R540, minimum 2 people) Rorke's Drift.

Ken Gillings (☎083 654 5880; ken.gillings@mweb.co.za) Durban.

Elisabeth Durham (☎072 779 5949; cheznous@dundeeekzn.co.za) Dundee.

Mike Nel (☎082 366 2639; mike@dundeeekzn.co.za) Dundee.

Liz Spiret (☎072 262 9669) Ladysmith.

Battles

These are the main battles:

Battle of Blood River (p511) Voortrekker-Zulu conflict (1838).

Battle of Isandlwana, Battle of Rorke's Drift (p289) Anglo-Zulu War (1879).

Battles of Laing's Nek, Schuinshoogte and Majuba First Anglo-Boer War (Transvaal War of Independence; 1880–81).

Battle of Talana, Battle of Elandlaagte (p286) Second Anglo-Boer War (1899–1902), which led to the Siege of Ladysmith.

Battle of Spioenkop (see boxed text, p284) Occurred on 23 and 24 January 1900, when the British fought to relieve the besieged town of Ladysmith from the surrounding Boer forces.

Battle of Colenso One of the largest battles (15 December 1899) in the southern hemisphere, between Boer and Brits.

be confused with the restaurant) on Murchison Rd, and they connect Ladysmith with Durban (R275 to R315, four hours), Pretoria (R320, seven hours) and Cape Town (R555, 19 hours).

Minibus Taxi

The main taxi rank is east of the town centre near the corner of Queen and Lyell Sts. Taxis bound for Jo'burg are nearby on Alexandra St. Destinations include Pietermaritzburg (1½ hours), Durban (2½ hours) and Jo'burg (five hours).

Dundee

☑034 / POP 29,000

If you can look past the gritty main street (Victoria Street), Dundee is a leafy and quite pretty spot. The reason to come here is to explore the Battlefields and regional history sites.

Tourism Dundee (☑034-212 2121; www.tourdundee.co.za; Victoria St; ☺9am-4.30pm Mon-Fri), by the gardens in the centre, can put you in touch with Battlefields guides (see boxed text, p287) and accommodation options.

Allow time for **Talana Heritage Park & Battlefield** (☑034-212 2654; www.talana.co.za; adult/child R25/2; ☺8am-4.30pm Mon-Fri, 9am-4.30pm Sat & Sun) on the Vryheid road, 1.5km out of town. Talana means 'the shelf where precious items are stored', which is strangely appropriate for this excellent battlefield site–cum–heritage park. There are memorials, cairns and 27 historic buildings relating to the 1899 Anglo-Boer Battle of Talana (the first Anglo-Boer battle was fought on the site). Spread around these buildings are comprehensive displays on the Anglo-Zulu and Anglo-Boer Wars, including a photograph of Mahatma Gandhi during his stretcher-bearing days; local history; exquisite Zulu beading; and a glassworks display. Curator Pam McFadden is Talana's knowledge guru.

East of Dundee, 52km away via the R33 and R66, is the regional centre of **Nqutu**, an important trading hub for the surrounding Zulu community. A further 30km north of Nqutu, near Nondweni, is the **Prince Imperial cenotaph**. Prince Imperial Louis Napoleon, the last of the Bonaparte dynasty, was killed here on 1 June 1879.

🛏 Sleeping & Eating

Some accommodation charges extra during winter months to cover the cost of heating.

Eating choices are ridiculously limited in Dundee, unless you run the gauntlet of fast-food outlets.

TOP CHOICE Sneezewood   B&B $$

(☑034-212 1260; www.sneezewood.co.za; s R660, d R995-1045) Located 5km from the tourist information centre on the Wasbank Rd (south of town), this delightful spot, on a working farm, oozes city-meets-country style: chic designer fabrics and lots of trimmings, plus a delightful lounge and outdoor area. The hospitable, knowledgeable owners ensure a relaxing stay.

Chez Nous   B&B $$

(☑034-212 1014; www.cheznousbb.com; 39 Tatham St; s/d incl breakfast R480/880, self-catering units R1800) This centrally located, comfortable place, run by Elisabeth Durham, efficient French *madame* and tour guide (with a special interest in the Prince Imperial), comes recommended. Half-board options are also available.

Royal Country Inn   HOTEL $$

(☑034-212 2147; www.royalcountryinn.com; 61 Victoria St; backpacker s/d R310/440, s/d incl breakfast R570/790) This old dame exudes a slightly faded, late-19th-century charm, and its English-style flavour is perfect for a spot of post–Rorke's Drift R&R. Rooms are decent (though backpackers' are less than appealing) and the hotel's restaurant serves up a good feed (mains R65 to R85).

Penny Farthing Country House   GUESTHOUSE $$

(☑034-642 1925; www.pennyf.co.za; s/d with half board R810/1350; ✳✳) Located 30km south of Dundee on the R33 towards Greytown, this is well placed for visits to Rorke's Drift and Isandlwana. Owner Foy Vermaak is a renowned tour guide.

Battlefields Backpackers International   BACKPACKERS $

(☑034-212 4040; www.bbibackpackers.co.za; dm/s/d R140/160/300) Run by registered Battlefields guide Evan Jones and his wife, this is the town's simple budget option.

❶ Getting There & Away

There is very little transport to Dundee; this is a location where your own vehicle is ideal. Minibus taxis head to and from Ladysmith to the southwest and Vryheid to the northeast.

Isandlwana & Rorke's Drift

✏ 034

If you've seen *Zulu* (1964), the film that made Michael Caine a star, you will doubtless have heard of Rorke's Drift, a victory of the misty-eyed variety, where on 22 and 23 January 1879, 139 British soldiers successfully defended a small mission station from around 4000 Zulu warriors. A propaganda-minded Queen Victoria lavished 11 Victoria Crosses on the survivors and the battle was assured its dramatic place in British military history.

However, for the full picture you must travel 15km across the plain to Isandlwana, the precursor to Rorke's Drift. It's here that, only hours earlier, the Zulus dealt the Empire one of its great Battlefields disasters by annihilating the main body of the British force in devastating style. Tellingly, *Zulu Dawn* (1979), the film made about Isandlwana, never became the cult classic *Zulu* is now. Victories sell better than defeats.

Ideally, the two battlefields should be visited together. Start at Isandlwana Visitors Centre (adult/child R20/10; ⊗8am-4pm Mon-Fri, 9am-4pm Sat & Sun), where there's a small museum; the entrance fee includes the battlefield. The battlefield itself is extremely evocative. White cairns and memorials mark the spots where British soldiers fell.

If you've seen *Zulu*, which was filmed in the Drakensberg, the scenery around Rorke's Drift may come as a bit of a disappointment. The landscape is still beautifully rugged, however, and Rorke's Drift Orientation Centre (✏034-642 1687; adult/child R20/10; ⊗8am-4pm Mon-Fri, 9am-4pm Sat & Sun), on the site of the original mission station, is excellent. The Zulu know this site as Shiyane, their name for the hill at the back of the village. The *Rorke's Drift–Shiyane Self-Guided Trail* brochure (R3) is a helpful reference. A delightful local Zulu guide, Thulani Khuzwayo (✏072 872 9782; thulani.khuzwayo@gmail.com; group tours R540, minimum 2 people) gives an in-depth tour of the area, providing details of battles from a Zulu perspective.

Near the museum, behind the orientation centre, there's the Evangelical Lutheran Church Art & Craft Centre (✏034-642 1627; www.centre-rorkesdrift.com), one of the few places to offer artistic training to black artists during apartheid. As well as the beautiful craft shop (⊗10am-4pm Mon-Fri, 11am-4pm Sat), several workshops – weaving, print-making and pottery – are in separate buildings in the vicinity; you are welcome to visit these, with the artists' permission.

About 10km from Rorke's Drift is Fugitive's Drift. Two British soldiers were killed here while attempting to rescue the Queen's Colours.

🛏 Sleeping

Several lodges – of varying degrees of luxury – are in the surrounding area; all organise tours of the Battlefields.

Isandalwana Lodge   LODGE $$$
(✏034-271 8301; www.isandlwana.co.za; d with full board R3990-4390; 🛜⊠) Top marks for location – the lodge's stunning rooms have expansive

---

THE BATTLE OF ISANDLWANA

It hardly bears thinking about. When a soldier from one of the five British armies sent to invade Zululand peered over a ridge on 22 January 1879, he was confronted not with an empty stretch of savannah, but with 25,000 Zulu warriors crouching to attack. They had intended to delay their attack until the following day, the day after the full moon, but once discovered they moved into battle formation – two enclosing horns on the flanks and the main force in the centre – and fell on the British, catching them off guard and unprepared. (General Chelmsford had made a fatal decision to divide the column, taking half of it away from the camp after they were lured in another direction by the Zulus.) By the end of the day, the remaining British column had been annihilated and the Anglo-Zulu War, for the invaders at least, had got off to a very bad start.

Meanwhile, the small British contingent that had remained at Rorke's Drift (where the army had crossed into Zululand) to guard supplies heard of the disaster and fortified their camp. They were attacked by about 4000 Zulus but the defenders, numbering fewer than 100 fit soldiers, held on through the night until a relief column arrived. Victoria Crosses were lavished on the defenders – 11 in all – and another couple went to the two officers who died defending the Queen's Colours at Fugitive's Drift, about 10km south of Rorke's Drift.

views over Mt Isandlwana, the Anglo-Zulu battle site. For such a modern construction, the lodge ingeniously blends into the landscape. Specials are offered throughout the year.

Rorke's Drift Lodge
LODGE $$$

(☎034-642 1805; www.rorkesdriftlodge.com; Rorke's Drift; per person with half board R1120-1305; @⛺) This place is an interesting mix of old-world hospitality and contemporary design. It's 5km up a rough track near the Rorke's Drift Orientation Centre. Call ahead to check on road conditions and for pick-ups from Ladysmith and Dundee.

Rorke's Drift Hotel
LODGE $$$

(☎034-642 1760; www.rorkesdrifthotel.com; per person with half board s R645-1185, d R1760) An Isandlwana Lodge wannabe, the common areas and restaurant of this giant rotunda promise big things – a wide expanse with massive sofas and an enormous central fire place. The rooms are less appealing, with a not-quite-there, but pleasant enough, decor. The nearest place to Rorke's Drift, the restaurant is a popular snack spot for day troopers.

ⓘ Getting There & Away

The battle sites are southeast of Dundee. Isandlwana is about 70km from Dundee, off R68; Rorke's Drift is 42km from Dundee, accessible from R68 or R33 (the R33 turn-off is 13km south of Dundee). The roads to both battlefields can be dusty and rough. A dirt road connects Isandlwana and Rorke's Drift. See boxed text, p287 for information about tours from Dundee.

Blood River & Ncome Monuments

☎034

On 16 December 1838 a small force of Voortrekkers avenged the massacre of Piet Retief's diplomatic party by crushing an army of 12,000 Zulu. More than 3000 Zulu died –

the river ran red with their blood – while the Voortrekkers sustained barely a few casualties. The battle became a seminal event in Afrikaner history. The victory came to be seen as the fulfilment of God's side of the bargain and seemed to prove that the Boers had a divine mandate to conquer and 'civilise' southern Africa, and that they were, in fact, a chosen people.

However, Afrikaner nationalism and the significance attached to Blood River grew in strength simultaneously and it has been argued (by Graham Leach in *The Afrikaners – Their Last Great Trek* and others) that the importance of Blood River was deliberately heightened and manipulated for political ends. The standard interpretation of the victory meshed with the former apartheid regime's world view: hordes of untrustworthy black savages were beaten by Boers who were on an Old Testament–style mission from God. Afrikaners still visit the site on 16 December, but the former 'Day of the Vow' is now the 'Day of Reconciliation'.

The battle site is marked by a full-scale bronze re-creation of the 64-wagon *laager*. The cairn of stones was built by the Boers after the battle to mark the centre of their *laager*. The monument and the nearby Blood River Museum (☎034-632 1695; adult/child R20/10; ⊙8am-4.30pm) are 20km southeast of the site; the turn-off is 27km from Dundee and 45km from Vryheid.

The interesting Ncome Museum (☎034-271 8121; www.ncomemuseum.co.za; admission by donation; ⊙8am-4.30pm), on the other side of the river, is accessible by a dirt road that links the two. It offers the Zulu perspective of events. The museum takes the shape of buffalo horns, the traditional method of attack. A symbolic display of Zulu shields (in metal) represents the Zulu regiments that fought in the battle.

Free State

Includes »

Best Places to Eat

» Avanti (p298)

» O's Restaurant (p300)

» Clementine Restaurant (p305)

» Fish Cafe (p307)

Best Places to Stay

» Hobbit Boutique Hotel (p295)

» Protea Hotel Willow Lake (p297)

» Patcham Place (p305)

» Cranberry Cottage (p307)

» Old Jail (p308)

Why Go?

The Free State is one of South Africa's most relaxed provinces, where the country's notorious crime rate seems to dissolve into friendly smiles. It's a place where big skies, unbroken horizons, pistachio hills and craggy sandstone massifs are interrupted only briefly by a smattering of towns and villages.

Lying between the Vaal and Senqu (Orange) Rivers, with Lesotho nestled into the crook of its beanlike shape, the Free State is South Africa's heartland – her breadbasket. Here, farmers in floppy hats drive ancient sheep-packed *bakkies* (pick-up trucks) down dusty roads, and brightly painted Sotho houses languish by giant yellow sunflowers and rows of green corn.

The colour divide here remains stark and dreams of an Afrikaner Arcadia live on. Progress, however, is happening – in the buzzing university town of Bloemfontein, you'll find blacks and whites dining together with increased frequency. And even in the smallest rural enclaves the colour barrier is slowly starting to dissolve.

When to Go
Bloemfontein

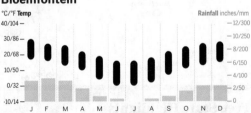

Jun–Aug Dry and sunny weather makes a road trip under big blue skies perfect

Sep–Dec Best time to view the cherry trees in full bloom and go wild at Ficksburg's cherry festival

Jan–Mar To escape the heat head for the snow at the foothills of the Maluti Mountains

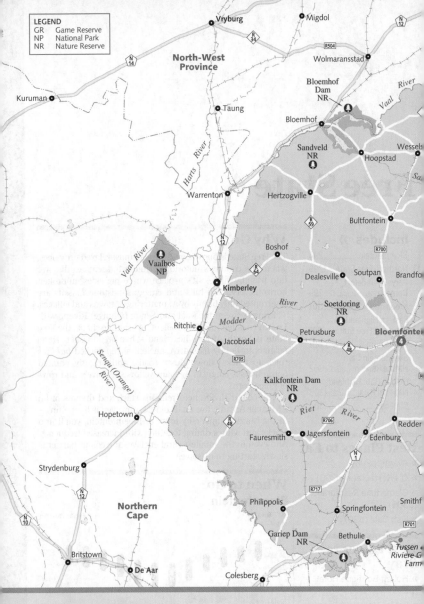

Free State Highlights

1 Unearthing little gems among the small towns and big skies of the Free State such as **Clarens** (p304), a little nugget of sophistication, perfect for people-watching

2 Exploring **Golden Gate Highlands National Park** (p303) and spotting the wildlife that inhabits the grasslands and spectacular sandstone formations

3 Following the **Sentinel Hiking Trail** (p304) up over the dizzying heights of the Drakensberg plateau

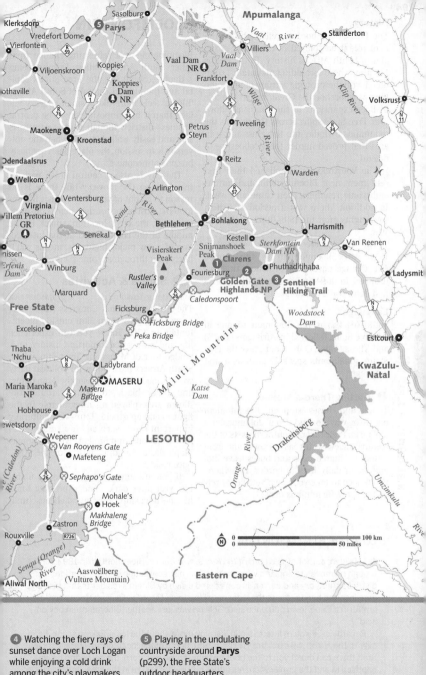

4 Watching the fiery rays of sunset dance over Loch Logan while enjoying a cold drink among the city's playmakers at **Bloemfontein's** (p294) Waterfront area

5 Playing in the undulating countryside around **Parys** (p299), the Free State's outdoor headquarters

History

The Free State's borders reflect the prominent role it has played in the power struggles of South Africa's history. To the east is Lesotho, where forbidding mountains, combined with the strategic warfare of the Sotho king Moshoeshoe the Great, halted the tide of Boer expansion. To the southeast, however, Free State spills across the river as the mountains dwindle into flat grassland – an area that proved harder for Moshoeshoe to defend.

The Voortrekkers established their first settlement near Bloemfontein, and various embryonic republics then came and went. In addition, there was a period of British sovereignty after the 1899–1902 Anglo-Boer War.

The 'Orange Free State' was created in 1854, with Bloemfontein as the capital. The 'Orange' part of the province's title was dropped in 1994, following South Africa's first democratic elections.

Language

Sotho (64.4%) is the dominant tongue in the Free State, followed by Afrikaans (11.9%) and Xhosa (9.1%). Only about 2% of the Free State's inhabitants speak English as a first language.

❶ Getting There & Around

Trains and buses stop in Bloemfontein on their way to and from Johannesburg (Jo'burg), Pretoria and southern parts of the country. Likewise, it's easy to get to and from Lesotho – shared taxis and buses leave Bloemfontein daily for the border. Elsewhere, you'll need to take your own vehicle, or rely on the sporadic minibus taxis.

BLOEMFONTEIN

🔊 051 / POP 645,000

Bloemfontein is a refreshing change from other South African cities. Despite being a double capital (it's the Free State's capital and the judicial capital of South Africa) 'Bloem' feels more like a small country village than a big, imposing city. The central business district, though a little scruffy, is safe and easily walkable, and when the university is in session, the place has a seriously buzzing atmosphere.

The city is also a central crash pad for travellers on the move. While there is no reason to go out of your way to visit Bloemfontein (most of the tourism here is business oriented), the city's location, smack in the middle of the country and at the intersection of a few major highways, means you'll likely pass through at some point.

◉ Sights & Activities

Manguang Township   TOWNSHIP TOUR

The African National Congress (ANC) was born in a shanty town 5km outside Bloemfontein in 1912. Today, you can experience life, and learn some important history, on a guided tour of Manguang Township, where South Africa's most powerful political party was formed. Not surprisingly, Manguang, and other black townships around the Bloem area, played an integral role in the fight to end apartheid. Tours visit culturally important sights such as Mapikela House, now a national monument, where Thomas Mapikela, a founding father of the ANC, once resided.

If you are interested in township nightlife, visit after dark. Guided evening tours hit the township's buzzing shebeens (unli-

---

LORD OF BLOEMFONTEIN

JRR Tolkien, author of *The Lord of the Rings*, was born in Bloemfontein in 1892. Although he moved to England when he was five, his recollection of the Bloemfontein district as 'hot, dry and barren' is considered a sign by Bloem's residents that his years here inspired him to create the legendary kingdom of Mordor. Or perhaps, as some graffiti in a Cape Town pub once said, 'Tolkien was just another Bloemfontein boy on acid'...

Regardless, if you're interested in learning more about the local Tolkien scene, head over to the Hobbit Boutique Hotel (p295), home of the local Tolkien literary society. Staff there can direct you to the house where Tolkien was born, the cathedral he was baptised in and the grave where his father is buried. If you're in the area, and fascinated with all things Tolkien, it is definitely worth strolling over to the Hobbit for a cosy fireside chat.

censed bars), where you can sample home brews and dance to the notes of an enthusiastic jazz quartet. Both day and night tours are informal, and cost about R400. Obtain a list of tour operators from the tourist information centre.

FREE **Oliewenhuis Art Museum** MUSEUM
(16 Harry Smith St; ⏰8am-5pm Mon-Fri, 10am-5pm Sat, 1-5pm Sun) One of South Africa's most striking art galleries, the Oliewenhuis Art Museum is housed in an exquisite 1935 mansion and set in beautiful gardens. An imaginative and poignant contemporary photographic exhibition gives a good insight into modern South Africa. The museum also holds a collection of works by South African artists, including Thomas Baines.

National Women's Memorial MEMORIAL
(Monument Rd) Commemorating the 26,000 women and children who died in British concentration camps during the 1899–1902 Anglo-Boer War, the National Women's Memorial depicts a bearded Afrikaner, setting off on his pony to fight the British, bidding a last farewell to his wife and baby, who are to perish in one of the camps. It's a powerful image and one still buried in the psyche of many Afrikaners.

Anglo-Boer War Museum MUSEUM
(Monument Rd; admission R10; ⏰8am-4.30pm Mon-Fri, 10am-5pm Sat, 11am-5pm Sun) Behind the National Women's Memorial, the Anglo-Boer War Museum has some interesting displays, including photos from concentration camps set up not only in South Africa but also in Bermuda, India and Portugal. Apart from a few modern touches, this museum has remained untouched from its inception. The large paintings depicting battle scenes are striking. If you're interested in this chapter of SA history you could easily spend a couple of hours here.

Naval Hill GAME RESERVE
This was the site of the British naval-gun emplacements during the Anglo-Boer War. On the eastern side of the hill is a large white house that served as a landmark for British cavalry during the war.

There are good views from the top of the hill, which is also home to the Franklin Game Reserve (admission free; ⏰8am-5pm). Walking is permitted, but there was a fair bit of damage from bushfires when we swung through, although you may see ostriches wandering about. Highlights include the big skies and great cityscape views.

FREE **Orchid House** GLASSHOUSE
(Union Ave; ⏰10am-4pm Mon-Fri, 10am-5pm Sat & Sun) Also in the neighbourhood, this glasshouse has a beautiful collection of flowers and some dazzling orchids. The park outside is an ideal place to take the kids for a picnic.

National Museum MUSEUM
(36 Aliwal St; admission R5; ⏰8am-5pm Mon-Fri, 10am-5pm Sat, noon-5.30pm Sun) A great recreation of a 19th-century street, complete with sound effects, is the most interesting display at this museum. There is also a shop and a cafe here.

🛏 Sleeping

Bloem doesn't have the best selection when it comes to shoestring options, but is chock-full of small guesthouses, and has a few luxurious choices.

TOP CHOICE **Hobbit Boutique Hotel** BOUTIQUE HOTEL $$
(☎051-447 0663; www.hobbit.co.za; 19 President Steyn Ave; r with breakfast R1100-1500; ❉@≋) This charming Victorian guesthouse, comprising two 1921 houses, is popular with visiting dignitaries, but also perfect for literati and romantic types. The cottage-style bedrooms have painted bathtubs, plus a couple of teddy bears apiece. At night there's a turn-down service with sherry and chocolate. The reading room has a chess table and the local Tolkien society meets here to talk about all things JRR. Check out the pub and lovely outdoor patio.

Odessa Guesthouse GUESTHOUSE $
(☎081 966 0200; 4 Gannie Viljoen St; s/d from R320/440; @≋) For Ukrainian hospitality in the Free State, check out Odessa. The multilingual (Russian and Ukrainian are spoken along with English) guesthouse has a good rep for its home-away-from-home vibe and friendly hosts. Set in a quiet suburb, just off the N1 (take the Nelson Mandela turn-off, towards the city), its rooms are simple but spotless and homely. Breakfast in bed can be arranged.

Urban Hotel HOTEL $$
(☎051-444 2065; www.urbanhotel.co.za; cnr Parfitt Ave & Henry St; r R750; ❉☎) The rather pitiful attempt at stylish furnishings here is forgiven due to the excellent bathrooms, comfort

Bloemfontein

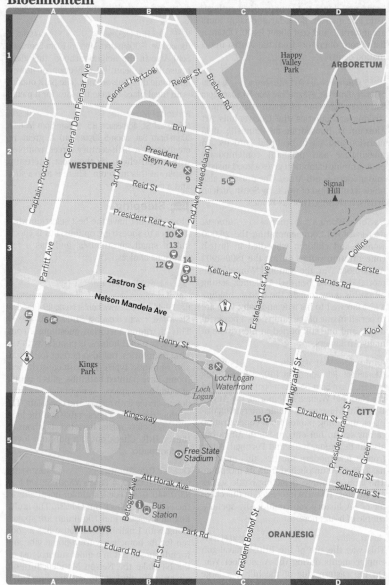

in the rooms and its being slightly better value than competitors in this category. The location is also excellent as you can walk to restaurants, bars and Loch Logan.

Ansu Guesthouse   GUESTHOUSE **$$**
(☎051-436 4654; www.ansuguesthouse.co.za; 80 Waverley Rd; r R450; @☒) The three bungalow-style rooms here give a sense of space, au-

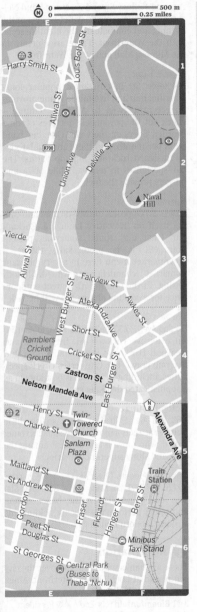

Bloemfontein

Deakker Guest House　　GUESTHOUSE $$
(☏051-444 2010; 25 Parfitt Ave; r R500-600; ☎)
This stylish offering with central location
has eight rooms, including some with sink-
in-and-smile king beds, and both bath and
shower in attached ensuites. It's very friend-
ly and is popular with visiting cricket teams,
so book ahead in summer.

Protea Hotel Willow Lake　　HOTEL $$
(☏051-412 5400; www.proteahotels.com/willow
lake; 101 Henry St; r from R1200; ✱@☎☎) Very
stylish rooms and a big move up from other
mid-range choices in the city. Plump bedding and a shower cubicle that looks like it
belongs at NASA complete the experience. A
genuine touch of luxury close to the Waterfront, and overlooking the zoo.

Reyneke Caravan Park　　CARAVAN PARK $
(☏051-523 3888; www.reynekepark.co.za; Brendar
Rd; campsite R200, r & chalets R350-750; ☎) Two
kilometres out of town (take the N8 towards
Kimberley), this well-organised park has a
swimming pool, a trampoline and a basket-
ball court. It's a good place to bring the kids.
Basic rooms and modern-brick chalets sleep
up to four.

thenticity and Africa, and open onto a leafy
garden area with clipped lawn and wandering waterbirds. There's a gazebo by the pool.
Call for directions as one-way streets make it
difficult to find.

✗ Eating

On a small lake is the Loch Logan Waterfront. Modelled after Cape Town's waterfront, Loch Logan isn't quite as impressive, but it's a good, safe spot for dinner, drinks or a movie on a rainy day. You'll find the usual South African chains in the Waterfront and Mimosa Mall shopping centres. 2nd Ave is the main eating street.

Avanti INTERNATIONAL $$

(☑447 4198; Loch Logan Waterfront; mains R60-130) Possibly the best restaurant at the Waterfront to dine in, with its old leather comfy chairs, and upstairs/outside eating area overlooking the water (dazzling at sunset). Extensive SA wine list and the usual Bloem offerings include pizza, pasta, steaks and seafood.

Cubana LATIN AMERICAN $$

(cnr 2nd Ave & President Reitz St; mains R40-90) This is a self-described 'Latino social cafe' that is a popular and sophisticated spot in the heart of the 2nd Ave scene. The lengthy food menu offers lots of chicken and beef dishes with Cuban sauces; although, if you've spent time in Latin America, you'll know right away the taste is not quite authentic. Still, for the Free State, it's pretty decent. In a semi-open-air, thatched-roof building, the vibe is Caribbean meets Victorian safari – think old school chandeliers, ornate, gold-threaded couches and hookahs.

Picnic CAFE $

(Loch Logan Waterfront; dishes R40-65, tapas R12-24) A cool place with a great outlook over the water, perfect for a long lazy chill. The food is excellent (and so is the service), especially the salads and sandwiches. Try the chicken, haloumi, avocado and sun-dried tomato salad with homemade mayo – divine. Opening hours can be erratic.

Bella Casa Trattoria ITALIAN $$

(☑051-448 9573; 31 President Steyn Ave; mains R60-130; 🖶) This efficient Italian trattoria serves lots of pasta choices, along with pizzas and salads. It's a cheerful, family-friendly place with a cosy indoors and also has ample courtyard seating at blue-chequered-cloth-covered tables. The thin crust Naples-style pizzas are recommended.

🍷 Drinking & Entertainment

As a university town, Bloem has a good range of places to drink, party and, increasingly, listen to live music. The corners of 2nd Ave and Kellner St, and Zastron St and Nelson Mandela Ave bustle with revellers in the evening and compete for the nightlife scene with the Waterfront. There are cinemas in the Mimosa Mall and at the Waterfront.

Mystic Boer PUB

(84 Kellner St) Bloem's most popular long-standing pub and live-music venue provides an eccentric twist to Afrikaner culture – check out the psychedelic pictures of long-bearded Boers on the walls. One 'big' band plays per month, and there are regular gigs by unsigned rock and hip-hop outfits. The bar specialises in tequila, while pizza and burgers provide the fuel.

Karma BAR

(Kellner St) Opposite the Mystic Boer and calling itself an 'Executive Lounge & Cocktail Bar' (that may sound somewhat pretentious...OK it is pretentious) there's a downmarket menu here in a very pleasant upmarket chandelier-and-white-tablecloth setting. In the evening it's a great outdoors place for a cocktail among the well-heeled.

Barba's Café BAR-CAFE

(16 2nd Ave; ⏰7.30am-2am Mon-Thu, to 4am Fri) An extensive cocktail list, live music and weekend DJs make this a staple on a 2nd Ave pub crawl. The cafe serves Greek specialities, including meze, but is best known as a sophisticated drinking spot.

Oolong Lounge LOUNGE

(16B 2nd Ave; ⏰Tue-Sat) This stylish little number attracts a movers-and-shakers young crowd, who move it and shake it among the slick and shiny super-mod interior.

Sand du Plessis Theatre THEATRE

(☑051-447 7771; cnr Markgraaff & St Andrew Sts) The local paper lists music, ballet, drama and opera performances being held at this striking modern building.

ℹ Information

There are banks with ATMs all over the city centre and at Loch Logan Waterfront. Amex is at Mimosa Mall.

3@1 Bloemfontein (cnr 2nd Ave & President Reitz Ave; per hr R30) Fast internet connections and wi-fi.

Free State Department of Economic Development, Tourism & Environmental Affairs (☑086 1102 185; Private Bag X20801, Bloemfontein 9300) For information about national parks and reserves in the area, phone or write.

Tourist Information Centre (☑051-405 8489; www.bloemfontein.co.za; 60 Park Rd; ☺8am-4.15pm Mon-Fri; 8am-noon Sat) Pick up a walking-tour map here or a free tourist guide to Bloem's gallery and handicraft art scene. Also a branch at the airport.

ⓘ Getting There & Around

Air

Bloemfontein airport is 10km from the city centre. A number of international airlines fly into Bloemfontein via Cape Town or Jo'burg. Check with **STA Travel** (☑051-444 6062; bloemfontein @statravel.co.za; Mimosa Mall) to organise flights to other parts of South Africa.

A taxi from the airport (there's often only one available) to the city centre is a standard R180.

Bus & Minibus Taxi

Long-distance buses leave from the tourist centre on Park Rd. Translux (Greyhound and Interstate have similar services) runs daily buses to:

Cape Town (R475, 10 hours).
Durban (R270, nine hours)
East London (R320, seven hours)
Jo'burg/Pretoria (R230, five hours)
Port Elizabeth (R320, nine hours)

Most minibus taxis leave from opposite the train station and head to Maseru, Lesotho (R80, three hours), Kimberley (R90, four hours) and Jo'burg (R150, six hours). There's usually at least one bus daily, but times vary. Note that a new multi-million rand minibus taxi stand in the city was due to come online in early 2012 but protests from taxi drivers about its accessibility meant that it wasn't in use at the time of research.

Train

The *Algoa* runs three times weekly via Bloemfontein between Jo'burg (tourist/economy R130/90, about seven hours) and Port Elizabeth (R200/130). The *Amatola* runs three times weekly via Bloemfontein on the run between Jo'burg (economy R90) and East London (R110). See **Shosholoza Meyl** (☑0860 008 888, 011-774 4555; www.shosholozameyl.co.za) for more details.

NORTHERN FREE STATE

The area around Parys in the far north is the most interesting part of this region. Here you'll find the largest visible meteor crater in the world at Vredefort Dome, one of South Africa's seven Unesco World Heritage Sites. The pretty area of rolling hills offers a growing number of hiking, mountain-biking and fishing opportunities.

Further south is a golden country of maize farms and sunflowers. The small towns around here are decidedly un-touristy, rural enclaves where people live and work rather than visit.

Parys & Vredefort Dome Area

☑056 / POP 44,000

On the banks of the Vaal River, Parys is a small, vibrant town just 120km south of Jo'burg that is a growing adventure-sport hub. It is home to a few impressive buildings, including the 1915 Anglican Church, built from blue granite blocks.

SADDLE UP: MOUNTAIN BIKING THE FREE STATE

There's a lot of activity around Parys these days, but cycling wild veld single-track is our pick for an adrenalin-pumping adventure. Otter's Haunt (the hub of all things outdoors in Parys) maintains 11 mountain-bike trails, catering to all skill levels, that depart from its property 2km outside town. Some trails are open to day visitors (R70), but many require an Otter's guide (R250 for about three hours) to ride – not all are well marked and it's easy to get lost. Bike rental costs an extra R195. Experienced cyclists can challenge themselves on steep and stony single-track, boasting wicked fast descents and lung-busting climbs, while beginners can chill with an easy, gravel-road pedal along the Vaal River.

Tweezer Rocks (about 18km, two hours) is one of the most popular rides, and can be done alone or on a guided trip – locals call it the 'breakfast run' because it's a fast, wake-up ride. Beginners should be OK on this trail (take a guide), but note that the ride includes a few steep climbs and one gnarly, rocky descent into a dry riverbed, which can be walked if necessary. Tweezer Rocks, which takes you in a giant loop past scenic kopjes and features stunning mountain vistas, gets its name from the two giant boulders holding a third between them (like a tweezer) visible from the first hill climb.

For much more trail detail, as well as rules and restrictions, visit www.otters.co.za.

Parys is handy for visiting **Vredefort Dome**, an area of hills created by the impact of a gigantic meteorite two billion years ago. Vredefort, measuring about 200km in diameter, is the oldest and largest meteorite impact site on earth. In 2005 the dome was named a Unesco World Heritage Site, South Africa's sixth. There are a number of good hikes around here – check with the helpful **Parys Info Centre** (☎056-811 4000; www.parys .info; 62B Bree St; ☻8am-5pm Mon-Fri, 9am-4pm Sat & Sun) for details.

☉ Sights

The Parys area is quite beautiful, consisting of valleys, ravines and cliffs, covered in lush flora and home to a variety of different plants, animals and birds. And it's fast becoming a favourite playground for outdoorsy types. Otter's Haunt (see p300) runs **white-water rafting** (half/full day R350/495) excursions down the Vaal River below Parys. The Class I to III rapids are not wild by world standards but, especially in high water, can be quite exciting. The Gatsien Rapid is the best paddle on the 6km stretch – it can be walked up to and ridden down numerous times. Otter's Haunt also runs guided **mountain-bike trails** (see p299) and **fly-fishing float trips** (from R450) on the Vaal, using inflatable, stand-up rafts.

⌂ Sleeping & Eating

Tourism around Parys is growing fast, with hotels and holiday resorts opening each year.

Waterfront Guesthouse   GUESTHOUSE **$$**
(☎056-811 3149; www.waterfrontguesthouseparys .co.za; 22 Grewar Ave; s/d with breakfast from R350/550; ✱@⊛☎) The hospitality is warm at this rambling riverside mansion in downtown Parys. Rooms come with shiny bedspreads and mosquito netting; ask to see a few rooms if they're not busy, but the Yellow Room is a winner any day of the week. All sorts of activities can be arranged, including fishing and rafting trips. Lunch and dinner are prepared upon request.

TOP CHOICE **Otter's Haunt**   GUESTHOUSE **$**
(☎056-818 1814; www.otters.co.za; s/d from R350/550; @☎) A rare dog-friendly accommodation in Free State (you must advise them in advance, and certain breeds are restricted), this secluded gateway right on the Vaal River offers a long list of outdoor activities for humans and their pets (such as grab-

bing one of their canoes and going for a paddle downstream). Accommodation options include rustic bush cabins set around a rock swimming pool and the spacious, three-bedroom River House with its own pool and big jacuzzi. Otter's is hard to spot; turn left after you cross the bridge out of town and go for 2km along the river.

Suikerbos   CHALETS **$**
(☎018-294 3867; www.suikerbos.co.za; campsite R110, huts & chalets R300-650) At this very popular farm-reserve herds of impala graze peacefully between the buildings. Chalets are airy and modern, with giant bubble bathtubs and loads of light. There are also basic hikers' huts and even an onsite caravan. From Parys head to Potch, take the gravel road to Venterskroon and after 20km it's a left to Suikerbos.

O's Restaurant   INTERNATIONAL **$$**
(☎056-811 3683; cnr Kruis & President Sts; mains R60-120; ☻11am-10pm Wed-Sat, 11am-3pm Sun) In a gorgeous garden locale right by the river, O's has been popular since it opened. Using fresh, locally sourced ingredients, the menu here is long and offers something for everyone – from vegie pastas to pork neck steaks, mussel fettuccine and a fine selection of tender beef steaks.

☕ Drinking

Old Ferry House   LOUNGE
(cnr Kruis & President Sts) Sip fine scotch and puff on a cigar by the banks of the Vaal at this alfresco cocktail lounge on the same property as O's and run by the same humorous folks: 'Unfortunately we do not display any sport as our cocktails are wonderful to look at and they would be extremely offended if they are not the centre of attention', the menu brags. The mixed drinks taste as delicious as they look.

ⓘ Getting There & Away

The Rte 59 leads into Parys, which is just west of the N1 heading north from Jo'burg. You will need a vehicle to get here.

Kroonstad & Around

☎056 / POP 111,000
The province's third-largest town, Kroonstad, on the N1, is typical of rural Free State and makes a good base for exploring nearby Koppies Dam Nature Reserve.

WILLEM PRETORIUS GAME RESERVE

Off the N1, about 70km south of Kroonstad, is the Willem Pretorius Game Reserve (admission R50; ⊗7am-6.30pm), one of the Free State's biggest recreation areas. Split in two by the Sand River and Allemanskraal Dam, the reserve encompasses two different ecosystems: grassy plains with large herds of elands, blesboks, springboks, black wildebeests and zebras; and, further north, the bushy mountain region with baboons, mountain reedbucks and duikers. White rhinos and buffalos are equally at home on either side of the reserve.

Adjacent to the reserve, Aldam Resort (☎057-652 2200; www.aldamestate.co.za; campsites from R180, chalets from R510) offers upmarket country chalets, many of which have magnificent views over Allemanskraal Dam (sunsets from your private deck are superb). Chalets are well appointed and quite rustic but with some nice traditional touches. The resort is well signposted in the reserve. Fishing is popular here and there are hiking trails. Meals can be arranged.

The 4000-hectare Koppies Dam Nature Reserve (☎056-777 2034; ⊗7am-9pm), about 70km northeast of Kroonstad on the Rhenoster River, is popular with anglers. Yellowfish, barbell, mudfish and carp are all abundantly available. Windsurfing, sailing and water-skiing are also very popular here.

Accommodation options include Arcadia Guesthouse (☎056-212 8280; www.arcadia kroonstad.co.za; r per person with breakfast R550), a smart, four-star guesthouse with classically elegant rooms in the middle of a large garden scattered with faux-Greek statues. It's in a peaceful spot, on the edge of town, and you'll need a car to get here (it's near the entrance to the N1 – follow the signs in town). Alfredo's (☎056-215 2886; 58 Orange St; cafe mains R20-30, restaurant R40-60) is an Italian restaurant and cafe in Plumbago Garden Centre, with a lovely outdoorsy ambience.

Translux is one of three bus companies doing daily runs to Jo'burg/Pretoria (R250, four hours) from the Shell Ultra petrol station.

EASTERN HIGHLANDS & SOUTHERN FREE STATE

With the Kingdom of Lesotho tucked into its crook, the Eastern Highlands are the Free State's star attraction. Follow the serpentine road along the wild, rugged border, past snow-shrouded mountains in winter and amber foliage in fall, to quaint country villages where the air is fresh, the stars are bright and the people friendly.

Encompassing an area roughly from Rte 26 and Rte 49 east of Bethlehem to Harrismith, the region boasts sandstone monoliths towering above undulating golden fields, fantastic Golden Gate Highlands National Park and South Africa's coolest country village art destination, trendy Clarens.

Harrismith

☎058 / POP 96,000

Although looking a bit scrappy these days, Harrismith is still a jumping-off point for exploring the Drakensberg range. It's a quiet country town with picturesque old buildings around a grassy square, distant Dragon Mountain views and lots of trees.

The very helpful N3 Gateway Tourism Information Centre (☎0800 634357; Bergview complex; ⊗8am-4.30pm Mon-Fri) is in the cluster of restaurants and retail near the entrance to the N3.

🛏 Sleeping & Eating

The Bergview complex is your best bet for eating, where you'll find the usual chains (Debonairs, Nando's and Ocean Basket) along with a couple of classier cafes.

Lala Nathi   RONDAVELS $$
(☎058-623 0282; www.lalanathi.co.za; s/d from R400/600; 豫🖥) Just off the N3, 3km from Harrismith (towards Durban) and offering convenience, great value and traditional rondavels, this is a sure bet – especially if you intend on hitting the highway in the morning. Traditional meets rustic in the

Eastern Highlands

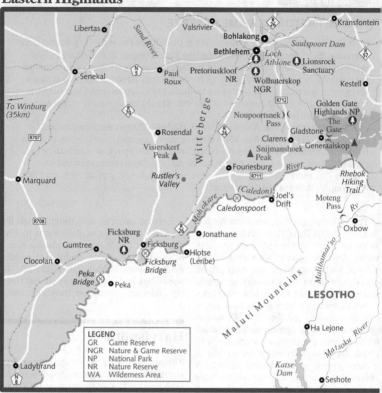

LEGEND
GR — Game Reserve
NGR — Nature & Game Reserve
NP — National Park
NR — Nature Reserve
WA — Wilderness Area

spacious rondavel interiors, which have extra comfy beds.

The Book House Cottage
SELF-CATERING $$

(☎082 411 8838; bookhouse@mweb.co.za; 24 Milner St; unit R600; ❄) Lovely, spacious units in a peaceful suburb good for families and couples. The kitchens are well kitted out and the place is signposted from town.

Platberg Harrismith Backpackers
BACKPACKERS $

(☎058-622 3443; www.platbergbackpackers.co.za; 55 Bidulph St; dm/d 120/300; @) This well-run place has three dorm rooms and a double, all in good shape. You can use the braai outside and there is safe parking along with great views of Platberg mountain. If you want to explore your spectacular surrounds you can also hire a mountain bike (R80 per day) or grab a hiking map.

❶ Getting There & Away

Intercape runs daily bus services to Durban (R270, four hours), Bloemfontein (R300, five hours) and Jo'burg (R200, four hours). The bus station is on McKechnie St.

Sterkfontein Dam Nature Reserve

The small **Sterkfontein Dam Nature Reserve** (☎058-622 3520; admission R40; ☻6am-10pm) is in a beautiful area of the Drakensberg foothills, 23km south of Harrismith on the Oliviershoek Pass road into KwaZulu-Natal. Looking out over this expansive dam with its backdrop of rugged peaks feels like gazing across an inland sea. At one of the many viewpoints there's a vulture 'restaurant', but there's no set day or time for feeding. Sunset cruises on the dam's lake are available.

Free State

Aberfeldy

Mt Everest GR

Harrismith Botanic Gardens

Harrismith

Van Reenen

Swinburne

Platberg

Basotho Cultural Village

Sterkfontein Dam

Sterkfontein Dam NR

Geluksburg

Phuthaditjhaba

Oliviershoek Pass

Sentinel Hiking Trail

Babangiboni (2329m)

Rugged Glen NR

To Estcourt (65km)

Royal Natal NP

Woodstock Dam

Bergville

Mont-aux-Sources (3282m)

M'Weni Rv

Drakensberg

KwaZulu-Natal

Emmaus

Senqu (Orange) River

Mlambonja WA

Cathedral Peak State Forest

0 30 km
0 15 miles

Camping (from R60) and rustic four-bed chalets (R300) are available.

Golden Gate Highlands National Park

Right before the darkness erases the remaining flecks of colour from the sky, something magical happens in Golden Gate Highlands National Park (☎058-255 0000; www.sanparks.org/parks/golden_gate; adult/child R108/54). The jagged sandstone outcroppings fronting the foothills of the wild, maroon-hued Maluti Mountains glow golden in the dying light; lemon yellow rays silhouette a lone kudu standing still in a sea of mint-green grasses before the sky explodes in a fiery collision of purple and red. The park might not boast any of the Big Five, but it does feature fantastic nightly sunsets.

There are quite a few animals in the park though, including grey rheboks, blesboks, elands, oribis, Burchell's zebras, jackals, baboons and numerous bird species, including the rare bearded and Cape vultures as well as the endangered bald ibis. The park is popular with hikers on long treks, but there are also shorter walking trails. You buy entry permits at the park reception.

◉ Sights & Activities

Rhebok Hiking Trail   HIKING
This well-maintained, circular, 33km trail (R80 per person) is a two-day trek and offers a great way to see the park. The trail starts at the Glen Reenen Rest Camp, located next to the park reception, and on the second day the track climbs up to a viewpoint on the side of Generaalskop (2732m), the highest point in the park, from where Mont-aux-Sources and the Maluti Mountains can be seen. The return trail to Glen Reenen passes Langtoon Dam. The trail has some steep sections so hikers need to be reasonably fit. The trail is limited to 18 people and must be booked through the park board in advance – check the park's website.

Blesbok Loop & Oribi Loop   DRIVES
There are two easy drives close to park headquarters. Blesbok Loop (6.7km) is a scenic route of low-cut stony grasslands. The mountain views and sense of isolation alone make it worth the drive. Oribi Loop (4.2km) is similar and has magnificent scenery. You may spot its namesake antelope wandering about, but the highlight is the view of the Drakensberg.

Basotho Cultural Village   CULTURAL VILLAGE
Within the park you'll find the small Basotho Cultural Village (tours R30; ⊙8am-4.30pm Mon-Fri, 8am-5pm Sat & Sun). It's essentially an open-air museum, peopled by actors depicting various aspects of traditional Sotho life. A two-hour guided hiking trail (R60 per person) explores medicinal and other plants, and a rock-art site. You can stay in two-person, self-catering *rondavels* (round huts; R650), but bring your own food. Although this is a friendly place, with a lot of good information on traditional customs and culture, it is also essentially artificial and idealised. To see how most Sotho live, cross the border into Lesotho.

🛏 Sleeping

There are a number of sleeping choices in the park. Clarens (p304), just 17km away, is another sleeping option.

Glen Reenen Rest Camp   REST CAMP **$$**
(🖉058-255 1000; 2-person campsites R165, chalets R635-730) This place is conveniently located on the main road, buried amongst the craggy limestone, and has well-maintained chalets and campsites by the river. A shop sells basic supplies.

Golden Gate Hotel   HOTEL **$$**
(🖉058-255 0000; r & chalets R840-1100) In the heart of the park, this stately old lodge with great mountain views offers self-catering chalets and upmarket rooms. It recently underwent an extensive renovation adding more rooms (decorated as African seasons) and modern interiors. There is a restaurant, bar and coffee shop.

ⓘ Getting There & Away

Rte 712 is a sealed road that runs into the park from Clarens, south of Bethlehem. Minibus taxis run between Bethlehem and Harrismith, via Clarens and Phuthaditjhaba, and go right through the park. Alternatively, with your own vehicle you can approach from Harrismith on Rte 74 and then Rte 712.

Phuthaditjhaba & Around

🖉058 / POP 85,000

Phuthaditjhaba, about 50km southwest of Harrismith, was the capital of the apartheid homeland of QwaQwa (master the 'click' pronunciation and you'll win friends). QwaQwa (meaning 'Whiter than White') was named after the sandstone hill that dominates the area. It was created in the early 1980s as a homeland for southern Sotho people. The dumping of 200,000 people on a tiny patch of agriculturally unviable land, remote from employment centres, was one of the more obscene acts of apartheid. Today, the highlands around Phuthaditjhaba are great hiking country.

The most famous of the hiking trails in the area is the 10km **Sentinel Hiking Trail** (🖉 bookings 083 956 0325; admission R25), which commences in Free State and ends in KwaZulu-Natal. The trail starts at the Sentinel car park, at an altitude of 2540m, and runs for 4km to the top of the Drakensberg plateau, where the average height is 3000m.

QWAQWA TOURS

A local company runs insightful township tours in QwaQwa that are both diverse and sensitively conducted. Included is a visit to a shepherd's village, the oldest Dutch church in the area, Jerusalem – a Rastafarian village – and a shebeen. **Masupatsela Adventure Tourism** (🖉079-551 8356; www.masupatsela-adventures.co.za) run their tour with a minimum of only one person and charge R410 for around five hours.

It's about a two-hour ascent for those of medium fitness. At one point you have to use a chain ladder that runs up over a set of sheer rocks. Those who find the ladder frightening can take the route up The Gully, which emerges at Beacon Buttress (although some hikers argue this route is even more hairraising!). The reward for the steep ascent is majestic mountain scenery and the opportunity to climb Mont-aux-Sources (3282m).

The best accommodation is in Kestell, a small, maize-farming village on Rte 57 about 22km north of Phuthaditjhaba. **Karma Backpackers** (🖉058-653 1433; www.karmalodge.co.za; 2 Piet Retief St; campsites/dm/d R60/130/300; @) is a peaceful, cosy place. The friendly hosts have lots of first-hand knowledge of regional hikes, and there are views of Sentinel Peak and the Maluti Mountains from the gorgeous garden. They also organise bicycle tours (per person R150) of the local Tholong township, which includes a visit to a shebeen, a great way to meet local folk.

Clarens

🖉058 / POP 4500

The jewel of the Free State, Clarens is one of those places you stumble upon expecting little, then find yourself talking about it long after you depart. With a backdrop of craggy limestone rocks, verdant green hills, spun-gold fields and the magnificent Maluti Mountains, Clarens is a picture-perfect village of whitewashed buildings and quiet shady streets. It makes a bucolic country retreat.

Surprisingly sophisticated, it's a bit of an art destination – with many galleries focusing on quality works by well-known

South African artists. It's also home to charming guesthouses (ranging from very simple to extraordinarily posh), gourmet restaurants, eclectic cafes and myriad adventure activities.

Activities

Clarens Xtreme
EXTREME SPORTS

(☎082 56 36 242; www.clarensxtreme.co.za; Sias Oosthuizen St) Head over to this one-stop shop for all things outdoors. Popular activities include quad-biking, white-water rafting (R450/650 half/full day) on the dam-fed Ash River (some rapids rate as high as Class IV), mountain-biking (trails R50 to R100) in the mountains behind Clarens with views over the town and valley, and zip-lining through an adventure park.

Sleeping

TOP CHOICE Patcham Place
B&B $$

(☎058-256 1017; patcham@netactive.co.za; 262 Church St; s/d with breakfast from R375/600) A good central option offering better value in this range than competitors around town, this B&B has airy rooms with giant windows and fab views from the balconies. The bathrooms are spotless, the beds firm and there is even a small kitchen.

Eddie's
SELF-CATERING $

(☎058-256 1059; www.clarenseddies.co.za; Main St; per person R250) This place offers very affordable self-catering accommodation. Set upstairs with awesome views of the Maluti Mountains in Lesotho, it's best to stay in these modern units when the weather is fine so you can take advantage of the outdoor living areas.

Clarens Inn & Backpackers
BACKPACKERS $

(☎058-256 1119; 93 Van Reenan St; campsites R70, tepee R100, dm/s/d R100/150/300) The town's best budget option offers single-sex dorms and basic doubles built around a central courtyard with a big open fire pit and outdoor bar. The locale is rustic and tranquil, pushed up against the mountain at the bottom of Van Reenen St (look for it after the Le Roux turn-off).

Lake Clarens Guesthouse
GUESTHOUSE $$

(☎058-256 1436; r per person with breakfast from R450) This impeccably maintained, four-star guesthouse offers buckets of intimate country charm. Fresh flowers, giant bathtubs, heated floors and silky-soft linens are all highlights of luxuriously appointed bed-rooms. Slightly more expensive rooms in the main house with enormous king beds are worth the extra.

Eating

Clarens has great places to indulge your stomach.

Valley Cats
CAFE $

(Market St; mains R35-50) If you fancy breakfast or lunch under a shady tree in a large outdoor area slightly removed from the village hubbub, this is the place for you. Overlooking the main grassy square, wraps, rolls and ploughman's lunch are simply and delicately prepared. The desserts have been recommended and there's a kids' play area.

Clementines Restaurant
INTERNATIONAL $$

(☎058-256 1616; 733 Van Zyl St; mains R60-100; ⏱Tue-Sun) The food at this souped-up country kitchen tastes just as good as it looks on the gourmet international menu (with the exception of the seafood – steer clear), featuring everything from creamy pastas to tender ostrich fillets. Professional service, intimate ambience, a lengthy wine list and vegie options are more perks. Be sure to check out the daily specials on the wall.

Shopping

With tidy, tree-lined streets and myriad boutiques and galleries to peruse, Clarens is made for aimless wandering. In the galleries, keep an eye out for pieces by Pieter van der Westhuizen or Hannetjie de Clercq, two well-respected South African artists.

Art & Wine Gallery on Main
GALLERY

(☎058-256 1298; 279 Main St; ⏱9am-5pm) Offering a fantastic selection of regional wines and paintings.

Bibliophile
BOOKSHOP

(313 Church St; ⏱9am-4.30pm) A quaint bookshop with a huge range of titles and jazz CDs.

ⓘ Information

Clarens Tourism Centre (☎058-256 1542, 082 963 3398; www.clarenstourism.co.za; Market St; ⏱8am-5pm Mon-Thu, 8am-6pm Fri, 8am-4pm Sat & Sun) Has info on the area.

ⓘ Getting There & Away

Clarens is best reached by private transport. There are a few minibus taxis to Bethlehem and Harrismith from Clarens but there is no set departure point. Head towards the suburbs on the outskirts of town and ask around.

Bethlehem

☑058 / POP 75,000

The main commercial centre of the eastern Free State, Bethlehem has a nice, wide-open feel and, although it's of little interest to travellers beyond a night's rest, the buzzing township makes a good spot to lay your head.

Eighteen kilometres from town, Lionsrock (☑058-304 1691; www.lionsrock.org) is a 12-hectare sanctuary and wildlife park for big cats rescued from all over the world, including lions, cheetah and leopard. There are also many species of antelope and wild dogs, and guided game drives are offered. Accommodation is available from R350 per person.

The best accommodation option is Hoephoep Guest House (☑058-303 7144; 8-10 Thoi Oosthuyse St; s/d with breakfast from R450/500; @) with friendly owners and tastefully furnished rooms in two guesthouses and five luxurious, self-catering chalets. Dinner can be arranged.

The owners love of the Mediterranean is obvious at classy La Croché (☑058-303 9229; www.lacroche.co.za; cnr Kerk & Theron Sts; s/d with breakfast from R450/600), which marries African architecture, including a soaring thatched roof, with Italian and French themes beautifully. Rooms are a good size and the architect's fine touches are everywhere.

You can linger over a few pints and pub faves such as bangers and mash at Nix Pub (Kerk St; mains from R35), an old-fashioned joint with a dive-meets-country vibe.

Translux buses run to Durban (R250, five hours) and Cape Town (R510, 16 hours) and stop at Top Grill in Church St. The minibus-taxi ranks are on the corner of Cambridge and Gholf Sts, north of the town centre on the way to the train station.

Fouriesburg

☑058

Entirely surrounded by wild, craggy mountains, Fouriesburg occupies a magnificent spot just 12km north of the Caledonspoort border post to Lesotho. Two nearby peaks, Snijmanshoek and Visierskerf, are the highest in Free State. You'll also find the largest sandstone overhang in the southern hemisphere, Salpeterkrans, around here – look for the signs off Rte 26; it's just northwest of

town. An eerie example of wind erosion, the area is considered sacred and used by local tribes for ancestral worship.

About 11km outside Fouriesburg, and just 800m from the Lesotho border, Camelroc Guest Farm (☑058-223 0368; www.camelroc.co.za; campsites R150, s/d with breakfast R400/600, chalets from R600) sits in a spectacular location against a camel-shaped sandstone outcropping, with fine views over the Maluti Mountains. It's a great rustic retreat, offering a variety of sleeping options. Good hiking and 4WD trails are nearby.

If your thirst needs quenching or if steak is on your wishlist try Windmill Pub & Grill (Robertson St) in town, which has bench seating in a lush shady setting.

Rustler's Valley

☑051

Dream about a journey into the wildly beautiful heart of nowhere? Ditch the pavement and let your subconscious guide you down rich brown, dusty byways in this remote valley, to random oases scattered amid the rough-and-ready countryside.

Off Rte 26 between Fouriesburg and Ficksburg, Rustler's Valley is home to the enchanting Franshoek Mountain Lodge (☑051-933 2828; www.franshoek.co.za; r per person with half board R580; @☎). A working farm with comfortable sandstone cottages in its garden, a Zulu steam room and great views of the valley, it emits a lovely country charm. If you'd rather not take dinner at the lodge, the B&B rate drops to R440 per person.

The main turn-off for Rustler's Valley is about 25km south of Fouriesburg on Rte 26 to Ficksburg – follow the signposts down a dirt road that crosses a train line. From the turn-off it is 13km to Franshoek.

Ficksburg

☑051

Ficksburg is a lovely little mountain village on the banks of the Caledon River that's home to some fine sandstone buildings; keep an eye out for the town hall and the post office. Nestled into the purple-hued Maluti Mountain range, Ficksburg is particularly fetching in winter when dollops of snow cover the craggy peaks.

Mild summers and cold winters make this area perfect for growing stone fruits, and Ficksburg is the centre of the Free State's cherry industry. There's a Cherry Festival (www.cherryfestival.co.za) in November, but September and October are the best times to see the trees in full bloom.

The African-themed rooms at the **Highlands Hotel Hoogland** (☑051-933 2214; highlandshotel@isat.co.za; 37 Voortrekker St; r from R180) are the best budget option – backpacker rooms share bathrooms, while those with en suites are still rudimentary but spacious, and have more creature comforts. A genuine old-style hotel with loads of character and that great lived-in feel – you'll find it next to the town hall.

In a quiet spot, the **Imperani Guest House & Coffee Shop** (☑051-933 3606; www.imperaniguesthouse.co.za; 53 McCabe Rd; s/d with breakfast from R360/540; ☒) has an African-flavoured, country-cottage vibe. The 11 spotless, modern rooms have wood floors and big windows and are in thatched-roof buildings. In a big airy *boma* (large open-air, thatched-roof hut) nearby, the onsite **restaurant** (mains R40-70) is a good lunch stop if you're passing through Ficksburg. Along with strong coffee, this place is known for its pancakes. It also does salads and other light meals at breakfast and lunch. Very good kids' menu too.

Ladybrand

☑051 / POP 18,000

In a valley surrounded by jagged peaks, just 16km from Lesotho's capital Maseru, Ladybrand is an attractive, small town loaded with sandstone buildings, dramatic scenery and ancient history. It's also a handy place to overnight on your way to and from South Africa's mountain kingdom.

◉ Sights

Archaeologists and anthropologists will dig Ladybrand. There are local rock paintings nearby, and instruments and tools dating back to the Stone Age on display at the town museum.

FREE **Catharina Brand Museum** MUSEUM
(17 Church St; ◔8am-5pm Mon-Fri) The museum's most impressive exhibit explains how ashes taken from an ancient hearth in the **Rose Cottage Cave**, not far from Ladybrand, prove humans first inhabited the area more than 55,000 years ago.

To really delve into the history of the region, ask here about visiting the Khoe-San

rock-art sites (more than 300 in caves around Ladybrand) – guides can be arranged.

Modderpoort Cave Church CHURCH
While at Catharina Brand Museum, pick up a permit to visit this church (c 1869). Nestled under a huge boulder in scenic surroundings about 12km from Ladybrand, it is one of the quaintest churches around.

🛏 Sleeping & Eating

TOP
CHOICE **Cranberry Cottage** GUESTHOUSE $$
(☑051-924 2290; www.cranberry.co.za; 37 Beeton St; s/d with breakfast from R550/920; @☒) The best place to sleep in Ladybrand (and one of the best in Free State) is a charming guesthouse with luxury rooms, each different and unique, in the rambling, stone guesthouse, and cheaper self-catering options down the road also run by Cranberry. Rooms have space, a sense of the rustic, a touch of luxury and the feel of nature. Foliage-decked gardens, a grapevine-covered patio and lovely swimming pool, a cosy, log-fire-crackling dining room and fantastic, old-time, polished dark-wood bar all await.

Fish Cafe SEAFOOD $$
(20 Piet Retief St; mains R60-90) Different days see different fish specials at this popular seafood cafe, including hake fillet in a creamy cheese mushroom sauce (a house specialty). Seafood platters filled with peri-peri prawns, mussels in Portuguese sauce, and crumbly calamari are also delicious. Take-away is available.

❶ Getting There & Away

Ladybrand is 4km off the N8 on Rte 26 – the road to Ficksburg – and about 130km south of Bloemfontein. Minibus taxis can be found near the church on Piet Retief St and run to Ficksburg (R40, one hour). For a wider choice of destinations, take a minibus taxi to Maseru Bridge (R10), at the Lesotho border, and find a long-distance taxi in the big minibus-taxi rank there.

Gariep Dam Nature Reserve

☑051

The Free State's largest **nature reserve** (☑051-754 0026; admission per vehicle R30) is a combination of the 36,487-hectare Gariep Dam (which holds back a vast 6 billion cubic litres of water) on the Senqu (Orange) River and an 11,237-hectare wildlife sanctuary on its northern shore.

During February each year the world's longest inland rubber-duck race takes place on the Gariep Dam.

In the reserve you can choose from chalets (from R350) or campsites (from R70). And there are more accommodation options in the town of Gariep Dam, at the reserve's western edge. **Forever Resorts Gariep** (☏051-754 0045; www.forevergariep.co.za; campsites/chalets from R115/870) is well laid out and has loads of water-sport activities on offer.

Philippolis

☏051

Founded in 1823 as a mission station, Philippolis, on Rte 717, is a beautiful place, and the oldest town in the Free State. Seventy-five of its buildings have been declared national monuments, including the library, and many places are built in Karoo style (made with thick walls to keep the heat at bay).

If you've ever fancied spending a night behind bars, the **Old Jail** (☏082 550 4421; r from R300) is your big chance. The town's former jail has been converted into basic, but comfortable, self-catering accommodation – well, if you consider a 2m x 3m cell with 60cm-thick outer walls and 45cm-thick, inner walls comfortable (the place does stay cool in summer and warm in winter with those wide walls, and cells are virtually soundproof). Rooms come with two authentic, single prison beds, and a mat on the floor accommodates a third person.

Gauteng

Includes »

Best Places to Eat

» Narina Trogon (p325)

» Cradle Restaurant (p344)

» Lucky Bean (p328)

» Gramadoela's (p325)

» Attic (p330)

Best Places to Stay

» 12 Decades Hotel (p322)

» Forum Homini (p344)

» Motel Mipichi (p323)

» Satyagraha Guesthouse (p325)

» Oasis Luxury Guesthouse (p324)

Why Go?

Gauteng, formerly the Boer Republic of Transvaal, remains the pulse of the South African nation.

Johannesburg (Jo'burg) is the country's largest and most happening city, where gold was discovered in the late 19th century and where fortunes are still made and lost. Gauteng's provincial capital is still riding on the back of the World Cup in 2010, and the creative and inventive spirit is alive in the cafes, galleries and clubs popping up across the rejuvenated city streets. The wealth divide is stark, though, and it can be difficult to reconcile the glistening wealth with the sprawling townships.

The political centre of Pretoria, a short drive north, is decidedly less urbane but is somewhat grander with its stately buildings and jacaranda-lined streets.

In the World Heritage–listed Cradle of Humankind, in a vast valley is full of caves and fossils, you can ponder three million years of your own existence.

When to Go
Johannesburg

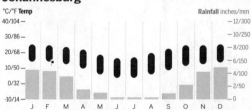

Mar School's back, so Jo'burg's Melville and Braamfontein hop. High fashion is out in Sandton.

Aug Festival season led by Joy of Jazz, the Dance Umbrella and a hectic calendar of theatre.

Late Nov–Mar Spectacular near-daily lightning strikes. Enjoy less traffic and a great NYE carnival.

Gauteng Highlights

1 Hooking up with Southern Africa's cultural hub in the revamped Johannesburg (p312) suburbs of **Newtown** (p317), **Braamfontein** (p317) and **Doornfontein**.

2 Revisiting South Africa's chilling history at Jo'burg's **Apartheid Museum** (p321) and **Constitution Hill** (p319).

3 Leaping off the Orlando Towers in **Soweto** (p337) and spending the night on the township's shebeen trail.

4 Cruising in the bookshops, cafes, guesthouses and bars in the leafy streets of **Melville** (p323) in Jo'burg.

5 Going deep underground in the caves and fossil sites at the **Cradle of Humankind** (p343).

6 Paying respects to the fallen at **Freedom Park** (p348) in Pretoria.

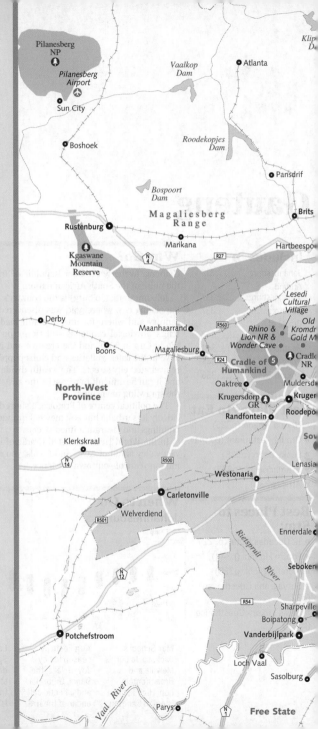

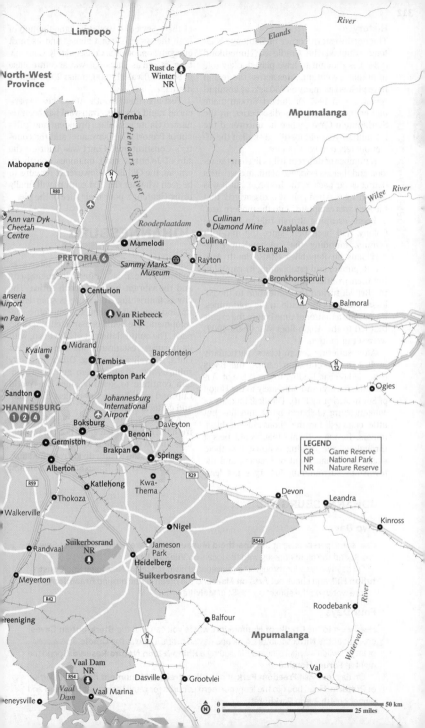

History

The northwestern corner of Gauteng (*how-teng*), dubbed the Cradle of Humankind (p343), is thought to have played a key role in human evolution. Sites across the region have yielded as many as 850 sets of hominid remains – in 1947 Dr Robert Broom made one of the most famous discoveries, in the Sterkfontein Caves, when he uncovered the 2.5-million-year-old fossilised skull of the affectionately named Mrs Ples.

A number of different tribes lived in the region and there is evidence of mining activities dating as far back as the Iron Age, but it was only in 1886, when gold was discovered, that the area was catapulted into the modern age.

Boers, escaping British rule in the Cape Colony, had been here since the mid-19th century, founding the independent Zuid-Afrikaansche Republiek (ZAR; South African Republic) and establishing its capital in the then frontier village of Pretoria. But as the British turned their attention to the colossal profits being made in the gold mines, it was only a matter of time before the events that led to the Anglo-Boer War (1899–1902) were set in motion.

After suffering severe losses, particularly in British concentration camps, the Boers conceded defeat, leading to the Peace of Vereeniging (treaty) and ultimately to the Union of South Africa in 1910. The fledgling city of Johannesburg (Jo'burg) burst into life, but little changed for the thousands of black miners. It was a theme that would persist throughout the coming century. Apartheid would be managed out of Pretoria, and the townships surrounding Jo'burg – not least of them Soweto – would become the hub of both the system's worst abuses and its most energetic opponents. Consequently, Gauteng, then known as Transvaal, was at centre stage in South Africa's all-too-familiar 20th-century drama.

Post-apartheid South Africa has experienced rapid changes. Transvaal has been renamed Gauteng, a black president now rules out of Pretoria (or Tshwaane) and the country's Constitutional Court was built on the site of Jo'burg's most infamous apartheid-era jail, the Old Fort. However, it remains to be seen whether the 21st century will finally bring Gauteng's poor their slice of the pie.

JOHANNESBURG

♪ 011 / POP 5.7 MILLION

Johannesburg, more commonly known as Jo'burg or Jozi, is a rapidly changing city and the vibrant heart of South Africa. The city is flourishing. Its centre is smartening up and new loft apartments and office developments are being constructed at a rapid pace. The cultural district of Newtown, with its theatres, restaurants, museums and jazz clubs, is livelier than ever. Other inner-city suburbs like Braamfontein and Doornfontein continue to gentrify since the World Cup and now house the coolest club, bars and cultural spaces.

A thriving black middle class has risen from the ashes of apartheid, both in the suburbs and in the famous township of Soweto.

However, the wealth divide remains stark. The affluenza of Rosebank and Sandton

JOHANNESBURG IN...

Two Days

Gain some perspective at the **Apartheid Museum**, then take a half-day tour of **Soweto** and spend the night hanging with the locals on **Vilakazi St**.

On day two wander through the rejuvenated civic spaces of **Newtown** and **Constitution Hill**, and check out **Arts on Main** and the creative hub around **Braamfontein** before watching the sunset on 7th St in **Melville**.

Four Days

Head west to the **Cradle of Humankind**, where you can visit the **Sterkfontein Caves**, chill out at the **Nirox** sculpture park and have a divine lunch at the **Cradle**. There are plenty of wildlife options nearby, including a **Rhino & Lion Nature Reserve**. Spend the night at **Forum Homini**.

On day four visit **Freedom Park** and the **Voortrekker Monument** on the outskirts of **Pretoria**. Head back to the leafy northern suburbs for retail therapy at **Sandton** and dinner on 4th Ave in **Parkhurst**.

breeds discontent in desperately poor, neighbouring townships such as Alexandra and Diepskloot. Politicians stagnate while crime continues to disrupt daily life.

Still, Jo'burg is an incredibly friendly, unstuffy city and there's a lot to see here, from sobering reminders of the country's recent past at the Apartheid Museum to the progressive streets of Melville.

History
It all started in 1886 when George Harrison, an Australian prospector, found traces of gold on the Witwatersrand. Mining quickly became the preserve of wealthy magnates, or Randlords who had made their fortunes at the Kimberley diamond fields.

Within three years Jo'burg had become Southern Africa's metropolis. It was a boisterous city where fortune-seekers of all colours lived it up in the city's bars and brothels. The Boers, the Transvaal government and the president, Paul Kruger, regarded these multicultural fortune-seekers with deep distrust. Laws were passed to effectively ensure that only Boers had the right to vote, and laws were also passed to control the movement of blacks. The tensions between the Randlords and uitlanders (foreigners) on one side, and the Transvaal government on the other, were crucial factors in the events that led to the 1899–1902 Anglo-Boer War.

Under increasing pressure in the countryside, thousands of blacks moved to the city in search of jobs. Racial segregation had become entrenched during the interwar years, and from the 1930s onwards, vast squatter camps had developed around the outskirts of Jo'burg. Under black leadership these camps became well-organised cities.

Apartheid officially took hold during the 1960s, but this didn't prevent the arrival of black squatters in their thousands, and the city expanded further. Large-scale violence finally broke out in 1976, when the Soweto Students' Representative Council organised protests against the use of Afrikaans in black schools.

The most important change in the city's history came with the removal of apartheid and the country's first democratic elections in 1994. Since then, the black townships have been integrated into the municipal government system, the city centre is alive with hawkers and street stalls, and the suburbs are becoming increasingly multiracial.

◎ Sights & Activities
Since the mass exodus of white-owned businesses in the 1990s, a steady recovery has been led by both the creative sector and far-sighted property developers. Public art is prettying up the streets and old warehouses, and art deco buildings have been snapped up by those who consider themselves to have good taste.

The most-visited areas are Newtown to the south, and university-oriented Braamfontein to the north. While the city centre is OK during the day, it pays to keep your wits about you when out and about.

CITY CENTRE
Walk around Jo'burg's concrete downtown streets and you'd hardly guess that the city was once an art deco showpiece, because so few good examples remain. Sights aside, the energy generated by the thousands of hawkers, hair-braiders and pungent street food give the centre an urban atmosphere that you won't find in the northern suburbs, and that alone makes it worth a visit.

Colonial-era Buildings   HISTORIC BUILDINGS
There are plenty of colonial-era buildings that are worth a look: the defunct **Rissik St Post Office** (Map p318; Rissik St) and **City Hall** (Map p318; cnr Rissik & Market Sts), now a sometime concert venue, are among the finest.

Mandela & Tambo Law Offices   NOTABLE BUILDING
(Map p318; Chancellor House, 25 Fox St) It was this building where, in the 1950s, these two famous men set up this pioneering law firm.

FREE **Johannesburg Art Gallery**   GALLERY
(Map p318; ☎011-725 3130; Joubert Park; ☉10am-5pm Tue-Sun). This place regularly rotates its large collection of 17th- and 18th-century European landscape and figurative paintings; works by the leading South African painters; and traditional African objects and retrospectives by black artists. It's on the Noord St side of Joubert Park (the park itself a no-go area).

FREE **Standard Bank Art Gallery**   GALLERY
(Map p318; ☎011-631 1889; www.standardbankarts.com/gallery; cnr Simmonds & Frederick Sts; ☉8am-4.30pm Mon-Fri, 9am-1pm Sat) A wonderfully light-filled building featuring regularly changing exhibitions by important South African artists. It also contains a permanent

Johannesburg

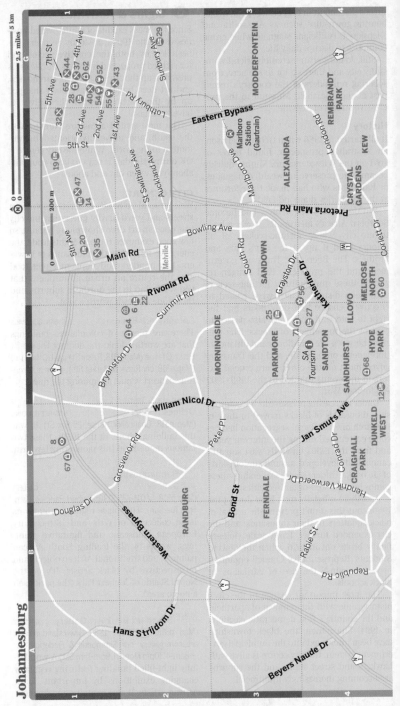

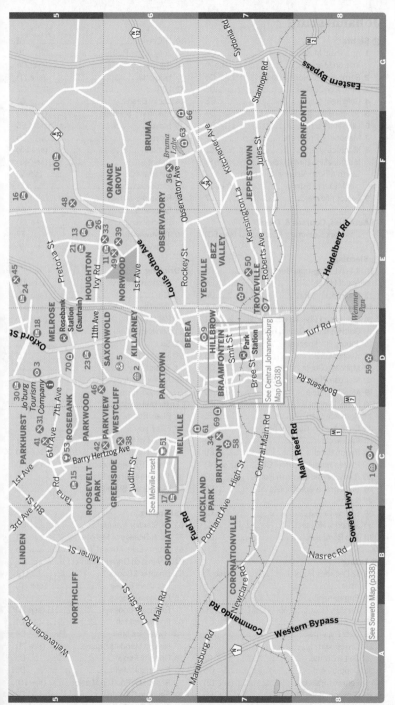

Johannesburg

African art collection, some of which is on display at Wits University.

Top of Africa
VIEWPOINT

(Map p318; ☎011-308 1331; 50th fl, Carlton Centre, 152 Commissioner St; adult/child R20/8; ☺9am-7pm). The entrance is via a special lift one floor below street level. Pick a clear day to enjoy awesome city vistas.

BRAAMFONTEIN

University of the Witwatersrand
UNIVERSITY

(Map p318; ☎011-717 1000; Jan Smuts Ave) More commonly known as Wits (pronounced 'vits') University, this place dominates the quiet suburb of Braamfontein. With more than 20,000 students, it's the largest English-language university in the country. Worth a visit here is the Gertrude Posel Gallery (Map p318; ☎011-717 1365; gallery@atlas. wits.ac.za; ground fl, Senate House; ☺10am-4pm Tue-Fri), and Jan Smuts House (Map p318) to see the eponymous Boer general's study.

Planetarium
MUSEUM

(Map p318; ☎011-717 1390; Yale Rd; shows adult/concession R34/21; ☺8.30am-4pm) You can look around for free, or attend shows on Friday (8pm), Saturday (3pm) and Sunday (4pm). There's an extra 'space travel' show on Saturday mornings at 10.30am.

Origins Centre
MUSEUM

(Map p318; ☎011-717 4700; cnr Yale Rd & Enoch Sontonga; incl audio guide adult/concession/child R75/45/35; ☺9am-5pm Mon-Sat) This excellent centre explores the African origins of humankind through interactive exhibits. The centre is brilliant for school-aged children and holds the most formidable collection of rock art in the world, led by the work of the San tribe. An extra-cool offering is a DNA test that traces your ancestral heritage.

NEWTOWN

Mary Fitzgerald Square
SQUARE

(Map p318; Jeppe St) Named after South Africa's first female trade unionist, this square is the best place to start a visit to central Jo'burg. As well as being the staging ground for a number of annual events – check Jo'burg city's website (www.joburg.org.za) for details – it's also a good place to people-watch at one of the area's cafes. The square is lined with an array of heads, carved from old railway sleepers by Newtown artists, and is bordered by the Jazz Walk of Fame, a Hollywood Boulevard–style walkway that

pays tribute to South Africa's most influential jazz musicians. There's also a bronze sculpture honouring Brenda Fassie, one of the country's most popular musicians, who died in 2004.

FREE Museum Africa
MUSEUM

(Map p318; ☎011-833 5624; museumafrica@joburg. org.za; 121 Bree St; ☺9am-5pm Tue-Sun) This museum is housed in the impressive old Bree St fruit market, next to the Market Theatre complex. The thoughtful curatorship features exhibitions on the Treason Trials of 1956–61, the development of South African music and the history of housing in this city. The satirical 'Cartoons in Context' are worth a look, as is the Sophiatown display, which contains a mock-up of a shebeen (unlicensed bar).

Market Theatre
LANDMARK

This lively complex (p333) puts on regular shows and has a couple of restaurants and some craft stalls.

Nelson Mandela Bridge
BRIDGE

(Map p318) Built two days after Mandela's 85th birthday in 2003, this cable-stayed bridge (295m) is the longest of its kind in Southern Africa and an icon of the rejuvenated city centre.

SAB World of Beer
MUSEUM

(Map p318; ☎011-836 4900; www.worldofbeer.co.za; 15 President St; admission & tour R35; ☺10am-6pm Tue-Sat) Take a 1½-hour jaunt through the history of beer. Taste *chibuku* in a mock African village, sample a cheeky half-pint at a re-created Victorian pub, then nail two free pints in the bar afterwards. You even get a World of Beer glass keepsake.

Turbine Hall
NOTABLE BUILDING

(Map p318; cnr Jeppe & Miriam Makeba Sts) Next to SAB World of Beer, this is one of the city's more impressive buildings. The north boiler house was imploded in 2005 and now houses the impressive new headquarters of AngloGold Ashanti.

Sci-Bono Discovery Centre
MUSEUM

(Map p318; ☎011-639 8400; www.sci-bono.co.za; Miriam Makeba St; adult/child R20/10; ☺9am-4.30pm Mon-Fri, to 4pm Sat & Sun) In the Electric Workshop building, you'll find this museum full of nerdy genius for kids and adults alike.

Central Johannesburg

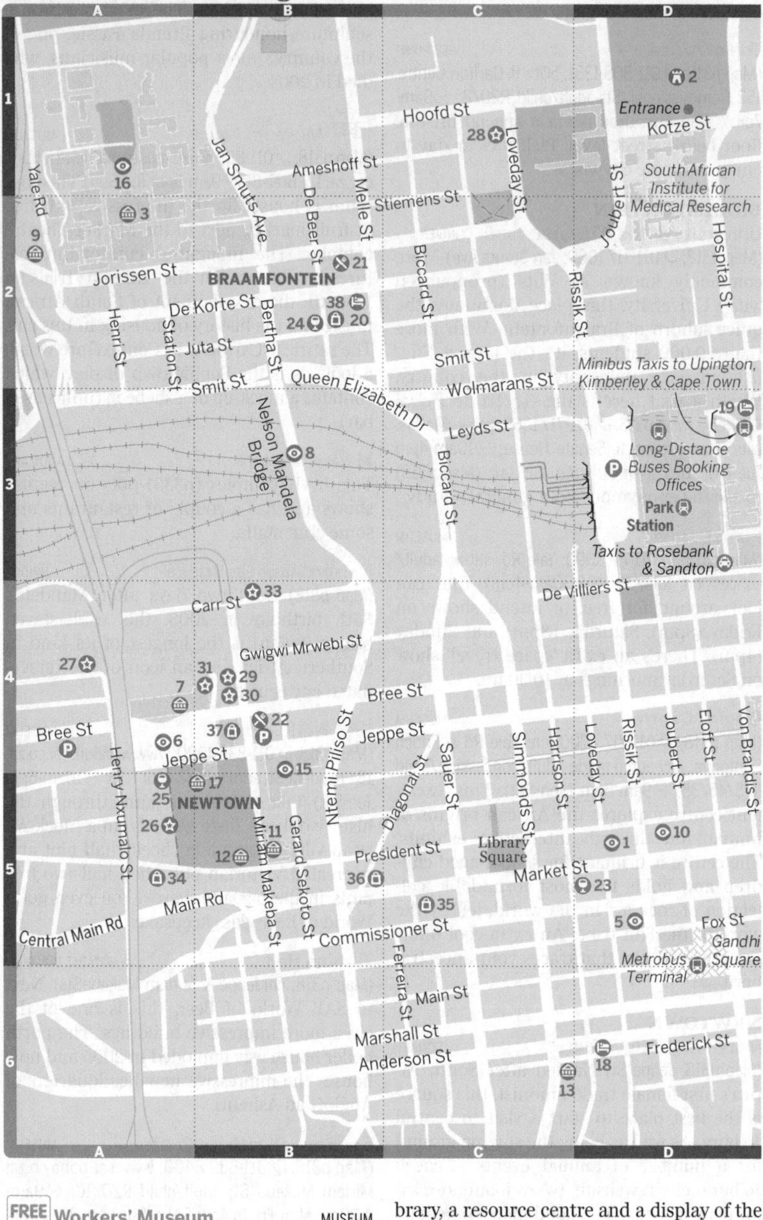

Map labels (grid A–D, rows 1–6):

Row 1
- 2
- Entrance
- Kotze St
- Hoofd St
- 28
- Loveday St
- South African Institute for Medical Research
- 16
- 3
- 9

Row 2
- Jan Smuts Ave
- Ameshoff St
- De Beer St
- Melle St
- Stiemens St
- Biccard St
- Rissik St
- Joubert St
- Hospital St
- Jorissen St
- BRAAMFONTEIN
- 21
- De Korte St
- Bertha St
- 38
- 24
- 20
- Henri St
- Station St
- Juta St
- Smit St
- Smit St
- Queen Elizabeth Dr
- Wolmarans St
- Leyds St
- Minibus Taxis to Upington, Kimberley & Cape Town
- 19

Row 3
- Nelson Mandela Bridge
- 8
- Biccard St
- Long-Distance Buses Booking Offices
- Park Station
- Taxis to Rosebank & Sandton
- De Villiers St

Row 4
- Carr St
- 33
- Gwigwi Mrwebi St
- 27
- 31
- 29
- 7
- 30
- Bree St
- Bree St
- Jeppe St
- 37
- 22
- 6
- Jeppe St
- 15
- Ntemi Piliso St
- Sauer St
- Diagonal St
- Simmonds St
- Harrison St
- Loveday St
- Rissik St
- Joubert St
- Eloff St
- Von Brandis St

Row 5
- 17
- 25
- NEWTOWN
- 11
- 26
- 12
- Gerard Sekoto St
- Miriam Makeba St
- President St
- 36
- Library Square
- Market St
- 1
- 10
- 23
- 34
- Main Rd
- Henry Nxumalo St
- Commissioner St
- 35
- 5
- Fox St
- Gandhi Square
- Metrobus Terminal
- Central Main Rd
- Ferreira St
- Main St

Row 6
- Marshall St
- Anderson St
- 18
- 13
- Frederick St

FREE **Workers' Museum** MUSEUM

(Map p318; 011-832 2447; 52 Jeppe St; 9am-5pm Mon-Sat) This important museum is in the restored Electricity Department's compound, which was built in 1910 for 300-plus municipal workers and has been declared a national monument. There is a workers' library, a resource centre and a display of the living conditions of migrant workers.

FREE **Bus Factory** ARTS & CRAFTS

(Map p318; 2 President St) Includes several outlets selling arts and crafts from around Southern Africa as well as homewares, jewellery

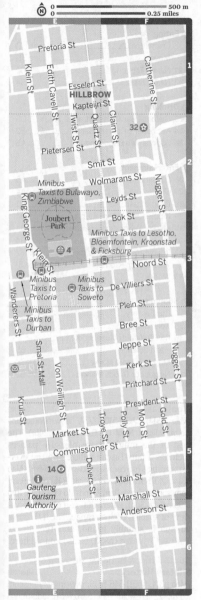

KwaZulu Muti Museum of Man and Science TRADITIONAL MEDICINE
(Map p318; ☎011-836 4470; 14 Diagonal St; ⊙7.30am-5pm). The most accessible of the downtown *muti* (traditional medicine) stores, you can usually find an *asangoma* (traditional medicine practitioner) or *inyanga* (herbalist) here, smiling in the shadows, should you wish to know more about homeopathy and ancestral health.

HILLBROW & CONSTITUTION HILL

Dominated by the 269m Telkom Tower (Map p314; Goldreich St), Hillbrow was once one of the liveliest and most interesting suburbs in the city and was the nation's first 'Grey Area' – a zone where blacks and whites could live side by side. These days, however, it also has a reputation for very real lawlessness, and a trip into its guts, without an extremely savvy guide (see p321), is not recommended.

Constitution Hill (Map p318; ☎011-381 3100; www.constitutionhill.org.za; Kotze St; tours adult/child R42/20, Tue free; ⊙9am-5pm Mon-Fri, to 3pm Sat) is one of the city's most feted attractions. It offers travellers interested in the modern South African story an integral understanding of the legal and historical ramifications of the struggle.

The development focuses on South Africa's new Constitutional Court, built within the ramparts of the Old Fort, which dates from 1892 and was once a notorious prison, where many of the country's high-profile political activists, including Nelson Mandela and Mahatma Gandhi, were held. Ruling on constitutional and human-rights matters, the court itself is a very real symbol of the changing South Africa: a *lekgotla* (place of gathering) rising from the ashes of one of the city's most poignant apartheid-system monuments, with cases heard in all 11 official languages. The modern structure incorporates sections of the old prison walls, plus large windows that allow visitors to watch the proceedings.

Located in the east of the city, Maboneng Precinct (Map p314; ☎011-007 0080; www.mabonengprecinct.com; Fox St) is the darling of the many architectural and creative hubs springing up across the city. It's worth a visit primarily for Arts on Main (Map p314; www.marketonmain.co.za; admission free; ⊙10am-4pm Tue, Wed & Fri-Sun, to 8pm Thu), a retail, studio and gallery space with Johannesburg's finest at work, including William Kentridge and Michael Subotksy. There's a fabulous cafe and a market on Sunday.

and other products by young designers. The on-site Drum Café (Map p318; ☎011-834 4464; www.drumcafe.com; ⊙9am-4pm) has a free drum museum and stages regular drumming events. It's south of the cultural precinct.

Central Johannesburg

NORTHERN SUBURBS

TOP CHOICE CIRCA on Jellicoe   GALLERY

(Map p314; ☎011-788 4805; www.circaonjellicoe .co.za; 2 Jellicoe Ave, Rosebank; ◎9am-6pm Tue-Fri, to 1pm Sat) This remarkable addition to the Jo'burg cultural landscape will soon be its artistic centrepiece. Overlooking the northern suburbs, the spiral structure houses unusual sculptures, sketches and contemporary work from across South Africa. The public space on the rooftop is superb.

Liliesleaf Farm   MUSEUM

(Map p314; ☎011-803 7882/3/4; www.lilies leaf.co.za; 7 George St, Rivonia; admission R95; ◎8.30am-5pm Mon-Fri, 9am-4pm Sat-Sun) The secret headquarters of the ANC (African National Congress) during the 1960s, which reopened as a museum in June 2008. It tells the story of South Africa's liberation struggle through a series of high-tech, interactive exhibits.

Montecasino   CASINO

(Map p314; ☎011-510 7777; www.montecasino .co.za; William Nicol Dr, Fourways; ◎24hr) The best of the multipurpose pleasure palaces includes a faux-Tuscan village and the ever-expanding Montecasino Bird Gardens (Map p314; ☎011-511 1864; adult/child R45/25; ◎9am-5pm, special shows 11am & 3pm Mon-Fri, 11am, 1pm & 3pm Sat & Sun), where you can observe a variety of species at close range. The Il Grande cinema is suitably grand, and the Pieter Toerien Theatre (p333) is also housed here.

South African National Museum of Military History   MUSEUM

(Map p314; ☎011-646 5513; www.militarymuseum .co.za; 22 Erlswold Way, Saxonwold; adult/child R20/10; ◎9am-4.30pm) If you're fascinated by guns, tanks and aircraft, you can see artefacts and implements of destruction from the 1899–1902 Anglo-Boer War through to WWII at one of Jo'burg's most popular museums. It's at the eastern end of the zoo's grounds.

Johannesburg Zoo ZOO
(Map p314; ☑011-646 2000; www.jhbzoo.org.za;
Jan Smuts Ave, Westcliff; adult/child R55/34;
☺8.30am-5.30pm) A worthwhile outing for
the beautiful old trees.

SOUTHERN SUBURBS

TOP
CHOICE **Apartheid Museum** MUSEUM
(Map p314; ☑011-309 4700; www.apartheidmuseum
.org; cnr Gold Reef Rd & Northern Parkway, Ormonde; adult/child R55/40; ☺10am-5pm Tue-Sun)
Illustrates the rise and fall of South Africa's
era of segregation and oppression, and is an
absolute must-see. When they arrive, visitors
are handed a card stating their race and are
required to enter the exhibit through their
allotted gate. The museum uses film, text,
audio and live accounts to provide a chilling
insight into the architecture and implemen-
tation of the apartheid system, as well as
inspiring accounts of the struggle towards
democracy. It's invaluable in understanding
the inequalities and tensions that still exist today. It's an overwhelming experience;
particularly distressing is a small chamber
in which hang 131 nooses, representative of
the 131 government opponents who were executed under antiterrorism laws. If you are
on your way to Soweto, the excellent Hector Pieterson Museum (p339) pads out the
story. It is 8km south of the city centre, just
off the M1 freeway.

Gold Reef City THEME PARK
(Map p314; ☑011-248 6800; www.goldreef
city.co.za; Gold Reef Rd; admission R160, child under 130cm R100; ☺9.30am-5pm Tue-Sun) Offers
a vaudevillian ride through Johannesburg's
gold rush period. Ninety per cent Disney-
land clone, this theme park offers only a
token nod to historical authenticity, but provides ample means for filling a spare afternoon, especially if you have kids in tow.

If you want to stay over, there's the rock-
solid Protea Hotel Gold Reef City and a casino (☑011-248 5000; ☺24hr), whose attached
Gold Reef City Casino Hotel also has rooms.

☞ Tours

All of Jo'burg's guesthouses and hostels
should have information on tours around
the city and further afield. A day trip will
cost roughly R500 to R800 per person, depending on the itinerary.

Cashan Tours CULTURAL TOURS
(☑082 491 9370; www.cashantours.weebly.com)
Run by Jo'burg native and wildlife guide
Chris Green, these tailor-made tours are recommended for their passion, deep knowledge and informality. Accommodation is
also available.

Imbizo Tours TOWNSHIP TOURS
(☑011-838 2667; www.imbizotours.co.za) Specialises in tours to Jo'burg's gritty townships,
including shebeen tours and overnight
township stays, and it also offers a one-day
Mandela's Struggle Trail tour through Gauteng.

Jozi Experience CITY TOURS
(☑011-440 0109; www.joziexperience.co.za) Offers a one-on-one, personalised way to see
the city. Tours include an afternoon walk

JO'BURG FESTIVAL CALENDAR

Chinese New Year At Wemmer Pan, south of the centre. Celebrated in January or
February.

Dance Umbrella (☑011-5492315; www.danceumbrella.co.za) The premier showcase of
South African dance performance takes places in February and March.

Rand Easter Show Held during April at the National Exhibition Centre.

Joy of Jazz Festival (☑011-832 1641; www.joyofjazz.co.za) Staged in venues across
Newtown in late August.

Arts Alive Festival (☑011-549 2315; www.artsalive.co.za) Held in September. The festival
provides a particularly good opportunity to hear excellent music, on or off the official
program. Most events are staged in Newtown.

Gay Pride March (☑082 547 2486; www.sapride.org) Held on the last Saturday every
September.

Johannesburg Carnival (☑011-673 4995) Held on New Year's Eve. This event, which
started on the last night of 2010, sees a parade of choirs, troupes, floats and bands,
from Hillbrow to Newtown, finishing with a party in Mary Fitzgerald Sq.

through downtown Jo'burg, or a night out at the city's coolest bars and most obscure shopping spots.

Queer Johannesburg Tour
GAY & LESBIAN TOUR

(☎011-717 4239; www.gala.co.za/tours; per person R300) This tour offers a fascinating insight into the role of homosexuality in the city's history, taking you deep into Hillbrow and Soweto.

Melville Koppies
WALKING TOUR

(☎011-482 4797; www.mk.org.za; per person R50) This specialist walk through lush forest takes place on the third Saturday morning of each month. A two-hour group amble of the Central Koppies sets off at either 8.30am or 3pm on Sundays, alternating weekly.

Parktown and Westcliff Heritage Trust
WALKING TOURS

(☎011-482 3349; per person from R75) Leads several historical walking tours through the established cliff-side suburbs that house generations of mining magnates.

Walk & Talk Tours
WALKING TOURS

(☎011-444 1639; www.walktours.co.za; per person R300) Offers regular weekend walking tours around parts of Jo'burg as diverse as the city centre, Sandton, Troyeville and Alexandra township. The walks go for between three and six hours and are led by well-informed guides. There's an eight-person minimum, but you can join any group.

🛏 Sleeping

There are tons of sleeping options in Jo'burg, with most of the tourist accommodation concentrated in the northern suburbs.

Melville and Norwood provide the best options if you like to walk to bars and restaurants. Places in the northern suburbs tend to be quite spread out, with no entertainment or shopping options on their doorstep.

The city centre is slowly improving its tourist infrastructure, but there is still only a handful of decent options.

Most hostels offer free pick-up from the airport or the Gautrain stations at Sandton and Rosebank. Nearly all hostels are on the route of the Baz Bus (p335). Guesthouses and hotels will also arrange for an airport pick-up but you'll be charged around R350. Most hotels organise tours to Soweto, Kruger National Park and elsewhere.

CITY CENTRE & NEWTOWN

If you plan to spend most of your time around Newtown and the Market Theatre complex, it's worth staying in the city centre. Be mindful, though, that it's not particularly safe to walk around alone at night.

TOP CHOICE 12 Decades Hotel
BOUTIQUE HOTEL $$

(Map p314 ☎011-026 5601; www.12decadeshotel. co.za; 286 Fox St, Doornfontein; s/d incl breakfast R890/990 Mon-Fri, R650/750 Sat & Sun; P❄@) This terrific concept hotel in the heart of the Maboneng Precinct has a dozen 7th-floor rooms (the rest are residential), each one designed by a different international pairing and inspired by a particular era in the city's history. The Sir Abe Bailey Suite takes on a late-19th-century Chinese gold-rush aesthetic, while 'Perpetual Liberty' is decidedly more contemporary. It's a lot of fun and very comfortable. Don't miss the cranking free neighbourhood parties on the rooftop every Sunday night.

Hotel Lamunu
BOUTIQUE HOTEL $$

(Map p318; ☎011-242 8600; www.lamunu.co.za; 90 De Korte St, Braamfontein; s/d incl breakfast; P❄@) The 'orange' hotel is a new boutique business hotel with 60 citrus-coloured en-suite rooms. Staff are as playful as the interior design, and the location is spot on – across the road from Narina Trogon. The lobby bar is a good place to mix drinks with the inner-city creative set.

Faircity Mapungubwe Apartments
APARTMENT $$

(Map p318; ☎011-429 2600; www.mapungubwe hotel.co.za; 54 Anderson St, Marshalltown; s/d from R1090/1290) Popular with the nearby mining and banking businesses, this renovated office building is a welcome touch of class in downtown Jo'burg. Staff can be a little aloof, but the facilities include a pool deck, excellent restaurant, gymnasium and converted vault bar. The open-plan apartments are spacious and well equipped. Ask about special rates.

Formule 1 Hotel Park Station
HOTEL $

(Map p318; ☎011-720 2111; Park Station, Berea; r R380) You stumble off the bus all bleary-eyed and desperate to lie down. Your mates refuse to yield. There's a hotel across the road, for God's sake. Put that guidebook away. Check-in is fast and efficient and you pay by the room (each room sleeps up to three people).

MELVILLE

TOP CHOICE **Motel Mipichi** BOUTIQUE HOTEL $$
(Map p314; ☑011-726 8844; www.motelmipichi.co.za; 35 3rd Ave; s/d incl breakfast from R520/780; P@) The design duo behind Motel Mipichi turned two semidetached 1930s abodes into a genuine alternative to the traditional Melville guesthouse experience. Mipichi is a minimalist delight, with four calming rooms speckled with pastel splotches, and walk-through showers adjoining private courtyards. The open-plan kitchen and living area, with original Portuguese tiles, is an ideal place for a pre-meeting/post-safari brief/debrief.

Melville House GUESTHOUSE $$
(Map p314; ☑011-726 3503; www.themelvillehouse.com; 59 4th Ave; s/d incl breakfast from R650/980; P@≋) This charming residence is a hit with return travellers, academics, lonesome adventurers and media types, all befriended by owner Heidi Holland, a prominent journalist with a knack for eliciting conversation. The rooms in the main house are functional with bright African-inspired decor. Beware the bathrooms in the cheaper rooms – they're doorless! For long-termers there's a larger granny flat out the back, by the very cute pool (with lifelike crocodiles) and garden.

Ginnegaap Guest House GUESTHOUSE $$
(Map p314; ☑011-482 3507; www.ginnegaap.co.za; 54 4th Ave; s/d incl breakfast from R450/650; P@) Ginnegaap is a contemporary inner-city townhouse attached to an old-world Melville beauty. Guests come for the established garden that runs right up to the front gate, or to slump blissfully on the wraparound verandah. Service is prompt, yet discreet, while the rooms are excellent value for the quality of bedding, the warmth of design and the overall size.

Sunbury House GUESTHOUSE $
(Map p314; ☑011-726 1114; 24 Sunbury Ave; s/d incl breakfast from R250/315; P@≋) This is still the best-value budget accommodation in Melville. Tucked away from the 7th St hoo-ha, this rambling home has a variety of rooms, all with quirky furniture, wooden floorboards and bright colour schemes. The hallway opens into a large communal eating area and, further along, a series of day beds on a covered verandah staring straight into a sizeable pool and grassy garden. The owners also have a cheap backpacker place (singles/doubles R150/250) in nearby Westdene.

Sleepy Gecko GUESTHOUSE $$
(Map p314; ☑011-482 5224; www.sleepygecko.co.za; 84 3rd Ave; s/d incl breakfast from R450/600; P@≋) The laid-back Gecko is an attractive and very popular guesthouse right at the heart of the 7th St mischief. The rooms outside the house, in a semidetached annexe, are preferable, with less noise and more natural light. The communal areas include a spacious, homely dining area and a pleasant front-yard swimming pool. There's a genuine indie travel vibe here that's hard to manufacture.

Makhaya Guest House GUESTHOUSE $$
(Map p314; ☑011-482 6036; 1 2nd Ave; r incl breakfast from R590; ✳@≋) Owned by a friendly Czech fellow, Makhaya is located in the daggier part of Melville, just north of Auckland Park. The rooms here are unpretentious and spacious, with wooden floorboards, huge beds and homely bathrooms. The European breakfast is the best on the block.

NORWOOD

Ascot Hotel BOUTIQUE HOTEL $$
(Map p314; ☑011-483 3371; www.ascothotel.co.za; 59 Grant Ave; r incl breakfast R735-935; P@) The Ascot has successfully filled Norwood's 'High Street' hotel vacuum. It's a stylish boutique business hotel with a red-roped lobby entrance and adjacent day spa – with generous discounts for guests. The sense of affordable prestige suits the suburb's easy-going attitude. Rooms are smallish, but well presented. Features include bouncy beds, flat-screen TVs and old-world fittings and taps. Service is prompt and friendly.

Garden Place GUESTHOUSE $$
(Map p314; ☑011-485 3800; www.gardenplace.co.za; 53 Garden Rd, Orchards; s/d incl breakfast R899/999, studios R1099, 3–4-bed cottages R1199; P✳@≋) The Garden is a versatile establishment with a mix of long-termers, business folk and holidaying families enjoying the cottages and standard rooms surrounded by lush plant-life. Wi-fi is the latest in a series of refurbishments. It's located on a pleasant street, though a decent walk to Grant Ave. Luckily there's a free shuttle service and a couple of pools worth lounging around.

Namaste Mazi GUESTHOUSE $$
(Map p314; ☑011-459 2234; loriancon@gmail.com; 40 Garden Road; s/d incl breakfast R280/560; P) This calm, uncomplicated family home is a very short walk from Grant Ave and provides a personable and affordable stay in

one of two self-contained granny flats. Private reflexology and yoga sessions are available on request in the on-site studio.

NORTHERN SUBURBS

Portfolio (☎011-8803414; www.portfoliocollection .com) agency lists a number of top B&Bs, mainly in the northern suburbs; they're upmarket, with singles from R450, and doubles from R700 to anything approaching R1500.

TOP CHOICE **Oasis Luxury Guesthouse** GUESTHOUSE $$

(Map p314; ☎011-807 4315; www.oasisguesthouse .co.za; 29 Homestead Rd, Rivonia; s/d incl breakfast from R845/1090; P✷@❀)This is a delightful suburban hideaway, presided over by an astute couple who cater for businesspeople and honeymooners with equal aplomb. The lush garden surrounds feature a good-sized pool and a spacious, shared *lapa* (South African thatched gazebo). Rooms vary in size and price, but all are stylish and furnished with art from different periods. The DVD library and breakfast smorgasbord are worthy of special mention.

Peech Hotel BOUTIQUE HOTEL $$$

(Map p314; ☎011-537 9797; www.thepeech.co.za; 61 North St, Melrose; r incl breakfast from R2050; P✷@❀) This converted duplex apartment block is an exercise in African minimalism. The 16 large rooms are affordable for the design quality, one-off sculptures and furnishings. The pool is long enough in which to cut serious laps and there's a decent gym next door. The restaurant boasts one of the best international menus in town.

Melrose Place Guest Lodge GUESTHOUSE $$$

(Map p314; ☎011-442 4231; 12A North St, Melrose; s/d incl breakfast R1100/2200; P✷@❀) This very quiet and secluded country-style home is perfect for those who crave space – the rooms open onto expansive gardens and a large swimming pool. It's well located between Rosebank and Sandton.

Parkwood BOUTIQUE HOTEL $$$

(Map p314; ☎011-880 1748; www.theparkwood .com; 72 Worcester Rd, Parkwood; s/d incl breakfast from R1550/1700; P✷@❀) The Parkwood is a series of separate, narrow, self-contained buildings that ensure discretion during your stay. The rooms are all class, thanks to the interior designer owner, with contemporary art facing stone walls, day beds facing fountains, a lap pool, a library and a gym.

Backpackers Ritz BACKPACKERS $

(Map p314; ☎011-325 7125; www.backpackers-ritz .co.za; 1A North Rd, Dunkeld West; dm/s/d without bathroom R125/250/375; P@❀) Still the most authoritative of the city's hostels, the Ritz is owned by three brothers who ensure that a family atmosphere is maintained on its sprawling, leafy grounds. The rooms are decent enough, aside from the pokey dorms and the odd dampish 'cave' room, but the excellent shared facilities, vibrant social scene, prime location and beautiful views more than make up for boring old sleep.

Joburg Backpackers BACKPACKERS $

(Map p314; ☎011-888 4742; www.joburgbackpackers .com; 14 Umgwezi Rd, Emmerentia; dm R110, r without/with bathroom R330/440, family room R660; P@) This new hostel in the leafy streets of Emmerentia has a range of well-appointed rooms and a relaxed country feel. The ensuite rooms are terrific value and open onto big grassy lawns, while the dorm rooms are spacious and spotless. Greenside's eateries and bars are a 10-minute stroll away.

Radisson Blu Gautrain Hotel HOTEL $$$

(Map p314; ☎011-286 1000; www.radissonblu.com; cnr West St & Rivonia Rd, Sandton; s/d incl breakfast R1500/2400; P✷@❀) A brisk jaywalk from Sandton's Gautrain station exit, this slick hotel is a great place to stay if you have a plane to catch in the morning. The rooms are cleverly designed with showers facing into the bedroom. The restaurant is excellent and the splash pool outside the lobby is a real scene.

Ten Bompas BOUTIQUE HOTEL $$$

(Map p314; ☎011-341 0282; www.tenbompas. com; 10 Bompas Rd, Dunkeld West; r incl breakfast R3000; P✷@❀) More centrally located than some other top Johannesburg hotels, 'Ten Rooms' is also a pioneer of the boutique tag. Dark wood and savannah hues colour an exquisite private collection of African art. The restaurant is a destination in its own right.

Saxon HOTEL $$$

(Map p314; ☎011-292 6000; www.thesaxon.com; 36 Saxon Rd, Sandhurst; r incl breakfast from R7350; P✷@❀) The pride of Sandhurst is a palatial suite hotel where Mandela completed his famed memoir. Private elevators, personal attendants, the finest day spa in the country, and rooms of 80 sq metres make the Saxon an otherworldly experience for the 99%.

EASTERN SUBURBS

TOP CHOICE Satyagraha House GUESTHOUSE $$$
(Map p314; ☎011-485 5928; www.satyagrahahouse
.com; 15 Pine Road, Orchards; s/d incl breakfast
from R1500/2560; P@) The former home of
Mahatma Gandhi, who lived here between
1907 and 1908 with its German architect
Hermann Kallenbach, has been restored as a
serene, innovative guesthouse and museum.
The seven rooms are organised into a kraal,
and the intimate history of the great paci-
fist's time here is on display to reward guests
in unexpected ways. Meals are vegetarian.

44 on Livingstone
Guesthouse GUESTHOUSE $$
(Map p314; ☎011-485 1156; www.44onlivingston
.com; 5 Sandler Rd, Linksfield; s/d incl breakfast
from R410/820; P✲@☂) This lovely, small
guesthouse near the Johannesburg Golf
Course is a good option – it has a beautiful
pool, while the seven tasteful, immaculate
rooms feature swish bathrooms and luxurious linens, though only some have wooden
floorboards. In-house massage is available.

Mbizi Backpackers HOSTEL $
(☎011-892 0421; www.mbizi.com; 288 Trichardt Rd;
campsites R70, dm/d without bathroom R130/300;
P@☂) Mbizi is a totally self-contained
backpacker joint that's handy for the airport. Simple, colourful dorms and Spartan
double rooms are on offer to help stave off
deep vein thrombosis. Excursions to national parks can be arranged around the outdoor
lapa bar, which is a lively place to indulge
your wanderlust.

Africa Footprints GUESTHOUSE $$
(☎011-3918448;www.airportaccommodation.co.za;
1 Crestwood Way, Kempton Park; s/d incl breakfast
from R480/640; P✲@☂) For airport refugees
who don't do dorms, Africa Footprints offers
a good combination of business facilities
and home comforts. The 14 tasteful rooms
are well priced and the breakfast is quite
substantial.

SOUTHERN SUBURBS
Protea Hotel Gold Reef City HOTEL $$
(Map p314; ☎011-248 5700; www.proteahotels.com;
14 Shaft St, Ormonde; s/d incl breakfast R900/1010;
P✲) This gold rush–themed joint is a pleasant break from the Protea's modern-day
chain hotel iterations. It's best enjoyed in
a swagger around the spacious rooms with
your pockets full of easy-earned pennies. The
Protea is inside the theme-park gates.

Gold Reef City Casino Hotel HOTEL $$$
(Map p314; ☎011-248 5152; www.goldreefcity.co.za;
cnr Northern Parkway & Data Cres, Ormonde; s/d
R1695/2240; P✲) If you're sleepless in the
southern suburbs, these colourful and plush
rooms are great-value four-star affairs. They
contain faux-riche furniture and reassuring
beds that partly ease chronic financial pain.
Guests receive free entry to the Gold Reef
City Theme Park.

🍴 Eating

Jo'burg is a fabulous city for foodies (especially at the top end), with restaurants to suit
all persuasions. The northern suburbs have
the most options, but you'll need wheels to
get around. The malls are predictable, while
Melville and Newtown have some fun, lively
places to feast. All of Jo'burg's shopping centres have big supermarkets for self-caterers.

NEWTOWN & CITY CENTRE
There are some excellent restaurants in
Newtown, as well as stalls selling braaied
(barbecued) meat all around the city centre.

TOP CHOICE Narina Trogon MODERN AFRICAN $$
(Map p318; ☎011-339 6645; www.narinatrogon
.com; 81 De Korte St, Braamfontein; mains R70-140;
☻lunch & dinner) As rare a sight as the bird
that gave the restaurant its name, Narina
Trogon is an inner-city eatery that sources
both local produce and local designers to
sustain its fine sense of taste. The menu is
constantly changing, but the simple philoso-
phy remains the same. Expect dishes along
the lines of grilled steak with camembert
and polenta (R110), butternut and sweet po-
tato curry (R70) and pan-fried tiger prawns
(R65).

Gramadoela's MODERN AFRICAN $$
(Map p318; ☎011-838 6960; Bree St, Newtown;
mains R70-130; ☻lunch & dinner; ✲) Grama's is
a hit with the glitterati and visiting dignitaries, and makes a perfect all-in-one night
out in Jo'burg. The cuisine features some
strong Cape Malay flavours, in a slightly
fancy, curiosity-cabinet setting. The creamy
mussels (R90) are a hit and, of course, pears
taste better swimming in red wine (R65). It's
alongside the Market Theatre so it feels the
flow-on of creative clientele.

Niki's Oasis SOUTH AFRICAN $$
(Map p318; ☎011-836 5999; 138 Bree St, Newtown;
mains R50-100; ☻noon-10pm Mon & Tue, noon-
midnight Wed-Sat) This informal jazz diner is

DAVE STAMBOULIS/ALAMY ©

CREDIT/LONELY PLANET IMAGES ©

1. Apartheid Museum (p321)

A lifelike display at the museum, where a sobering portrait of apartheid is painted with personal accounts.

2. Cradle of Humankind (p343)

Caves at the Cradle of Humankind, one of the world's most important archaeological sites.

3. Freedom Park (p348)

The memorial at this park honours all fallen South Africans in major conflicts.

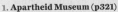

popular with the local arts crowd (it's across from the Market Theatre) and beret-clad hipster cats who dig the jazzy vibe. The food includes wholesome South African favourites like maize porridge, mopane worms and the ubiquitous grilled chicken.

Bismillah INDIAN $

(Map p314; ☎011-838 6429; 78 Mint Rd, Brixton; mains R30-60; ☺lunch & dinner) Over in Brixton you'll find the best Indian food in Jo'burg, and Bismillah is, we reckon, the pick of the lot. The menu is classic North Indian – think *bhindi masala* (spicy okra), *aloo gobi* (potato and cauliflower) and spicy, nut-filled biriani – while the service is refreshingly earnest. Best of all, it's dirt cheap.

Moyo's AFRICAN $$

(www.moyo.co.za; mains R70-140; ✻) Melrose Arch (Map p314; ☎011-684 1477; 5 Melrose Sq; ☺lunch & dinner); Newtown (Map p318; ☎011-838 1715; Bree St; ☺lunch & dinner); Parkview (Map p314; ☎011-646 0058; Zoo Lake; ☺breakfast & lunch) South Africa's 'chic-est' chain restaurant is feeling a little tired, but still draws the family crowd. The Newtown venue is the most reliable.

MELVILLE

The most reliable place to eat well in Jo'burg is on Melville's 7th St, with its wide selection of restaurants and cafes, almost all of which have outdoor seating.

TOP CHOICE Lucky Bean MODERN AFRICAN $$

(Map p314; ☎011-482 5572; www.luckybeantree.co.za; 129 1st Ave; mains R60-130; ☺breakfast, lunch & dinner) The restaurant formerly known as Soulsa may have a different name (copyright, apparently) but the recipe is unchanged. Low lighting, slick tunes, a decked-out cocktail bar and waiters who happily skip down a flight of stairs to serve. The food is spot on, too – light any-time meals, loads of vegetarian options, gamey stews, creative starters and scrumptious steaks.

Catz Pyjamas SOUTH AFRICAN, FAST FOOD $$

(Map p314; ☎011-726 8596; www.catzpyjamas.co.za; 12 Main Rd; mains R40-130; ☺24hr) The nocturnal, the inebriated, the shady and the strange all eat together in Jo'burg's most infamous all-hours restaurant. The balcony overlooking Main Road is a prime people-watching spot where it's hard to nab a table after dark. Indoors, punters wait for the food and cocktails to settle – A MuthaPhukkin-Gud Drink (R40) is pretty gud – before spacing out to murals of the seven chakra points.

Pizza, pasta and steak dishes all get the thumbs up. Booze is switched off between 4am and 10am – an outrage!

Bambanani TAPAS $

(Map p314; ☎011-482 2900; www.bambanini.biz; 85 4th Ave; tapas R25-30; ☺breakfast, lunch & dinner) The leather booths and black chandeliers make Bambanani's seem like a place for trendy young things, but look closely at the bold modern art and you'll see that the target market is happy families. At the back is a huge deck and garden area with a massive, multilevelled children's play den, and the menu features small tapas plates including mini-gourmet burgers for the kids and pumpkin purée for the babies.

Service Station CAFE $

(Map p314; ☎011-726 1701; cnr 9th St & Rustenburg Rd; light meals R45-65; ☺7.30am-6pm Mon-Fri, 8am-4.30pm Sat, 8.30am-3pm Sun) Join the queues of local office workers and drive-by hipsters who swear by the pay-by-weight policy of this darling of the famed Bamboo retail centre. There's award-winning coffee and a good wine store on site. Next door is one of South Africa's most interesting fashion labels (Black Coffee) and the excellent Love Books.

De La Creme CAFE $$

(Map p314; ☎011-726 7716; cnr 7th St & 4th Ave; mains R60-70; ☺breakfast, lunch & dinner) This bakery-cafe does a roaring lunchtime trade in sandwiches, burgers and *bobotie* (delicately flavoured curry with a topping of beaten egg baked to a crust), but it's the morning bread run that really gets up your nose, in a good way. Grab a coffee and a magazine and watch the world go by the huge open windows.

Picobella ITALIAN $$

(Map p314; ☎011-482 4309; 66 4th Ave; mains R55-115; ☺breakfast, lunch & dinner) A favourite with the Afrikaans community, Picobella is the best Italian in the neighbourhood. Nothing too fancy here, just good, honest wood-fired pizza, delicious pasta – try the oglio with cherry tomatoes (R75) – and reliable salads and starters on a faux-Roman terrace. Breakfast is also highly recommended and very popular with coupled-up travellers.

Loft FUSION $$

(Map p314; ☎011-482 8986; 6 7th St; mains R50-90; ☺12.30-4.30pm & 6.30-10.30pm Wed-Sun, 6.30-10.30pm Tue) This 7th St stalwart is

LOCAL KNOWLEDGE

HEIDI HOLLAND: JOURNALIST

Heidi Holland writes a syndicated column for the *Johannesburg Star*. Her latest book is *100 Years of Struggle: Mandela's ANC*.

Describe your relationship with Jo'burg. Though born in Jo'burg, I grew up in Zimbabwe. My four siblings and I were treated by our penniless farming parents to an annual seaside holiday in South Africa. We'd pile joyfully into our jalopy, sleeping, or singing, 'Oh, Jo'burg's the place for me, Jo'burg/Where the liquor and the lights always shine...'.

What should everyone know about South African politics? Don't panic if you encounter street protests featuring toyi-toyi-ing – a blend of political song and dance, which is worth seeing as it's what we do best.

48 hours in Joburg... Although guaranteed to hurt your heart, the Apartheid Museum is a big Jo'burg experience. The Constitutional Court, a wonderful building, incorporates an infamous women's prison. Visit Arts on Main in the city centre, hoping for a glimpse of South Africa's most revered painter, William Kentridge, who has his studio there. At night, seek and find live music, preferably African jazz.

Best books on South Africa? *The Washing of the Spears* by Donald Morris; *Home and Exile* by Lewis Nkosi; *My Traitor's Heart* by Rian Malan; *Long Walk to Freedom* by Nelson Mandela; *Anatomy of a Miracle* by Patti Waldmeier; *Disgrace* by JM Coetzee.

---

friendly, chaotic and cool, thanks to striking artwork, a mezzanine hideaway, a light techno soundtrack and a hand-scrawled specials' board of Asian, African and Modern European flavours.

Nuno's PUB $$
(Map p314; ☏011-482 6990; 4 7th St; mains R50-100; ☺ lunch & dinner) Less about the food – including decent-enough steak and chips (R60) and grilled fish (R70) – and more about the beer-sodden carpet, fiery banter, surly staff and kick-arse location at the left-leaning ventricle of 7th St. It also serves later than most.

GRANT AVENUE
A large section of Grant Ave is lined with cafes and restaurants, most of which are open every day, and provide a cross-section of street life.

Barrio KOSHER $$
(Map p314; ☏011-728 2577; 80 Grant Ave; mains R90-170; ☺lunch & dinner Sun-Thu, lunch Fri, dinner Sat; ✴) Rub shoulders with rabbis and Jewish families in this welcoming kosher restaurant, which fills up quickly most evenings. Well-lit wall-length mirrors add a touch of glam, while the large menu covers the globe. Sushi and steak are well done. Next door is its cheap pizza joint, Next Door, which is free from the tyranny of meat.

ShahiKhana NDIAN $$
(Map p314; ☏011-728 8157; 80 Grant Ave; mains R55-70; ☺lunch & dinner; ✴) Super tasty and fiery North Indian cuisine, with plenty of vegetarian and fish dishes on offer.

Zahava's MIDDLE EASTERN $
(Map p314; ☏011-728 6511; 47A Grant Ave; snacks R15-30; ☺breakfast & lunch; ✴) Good live 'world' music on weekends, strong coffee and fragrant hookahs at this Middle Eastern hangout serving the ethnic staples, plus snack-size *zivas* (flatbread) and *latkes* (potato fritters).

Schwarma Co MIDDLE EASTERN $$
(Map p314; ☏011-483 1776; 71 Grant Ave; mains R30-110; ☺11am-11pm) The smell of future franchise wafts through this high-class kebab joint on a raised terrace overlooking the street. Come for delicious platters of *shwarma* (meat sliced off a spit, served in pitas with chopped tomatoes) and kebabs, with bowls of pickles, olives, tahini and (particularly good) hummus.

Giovanni Pane Vino ITALIAN $$
(Map p314; ☏011-483 1515; 66 Grant Ave; mains R55-100; ☺lunch & dinner Tue-Sun) This classic Italian joint has the requisite red-and-white tablecloths and bowlsful of pasta big enough to feed a small soccer team. There's another premises in Sandton.

NORTHERN SUBURBS

The many eating options in these affluent suburbs are centred on the huge shopping malls that form the core of northern-suburb society.

Not far from Melville, the suburbs of Greenside and Parkhurst have a couple of excellent restaurants and trendy bars, although the crowd isn't as young as in Melville. The restaurants are in a little cluster on Gleneagles Rd and Greenway, just off Barry Hertzog Ave, and along adjacent 4th Avenue.

Attic
MODERN $$

(Map p314; 011-880 6102; 24 4th Ave, Parkhurst; mains R70-130; ☉lunch & dinner) Patrons at this quality corner restaurant happily spill from the homely interiors onto the street seats. Try dishes like crab fettuccini (R98) and sparkling wine and pea risotto (R78). There's an attached tapas and cocktail bar, while the same crew also runs the Office, a cool speakeasy around the corner in Greenside.

Karma
INDIAN $$

(Map p314; 011-646 8555; cnr Barry Hertzog Ave & Gleneagles Rd, Greenside; mains R60-90; ☉lunch & dinner) Regularly voted best this and top that, Karma's interior feels like New Age Indian with a Hollywood makeover. The mostly North Indian offerings are flavoursome and generously proportioned, with loads of interesting vegie options. Karma has recently come around again in Fourways.

Lekgotla
AFRICAN $$

(Map p314; 011-884 9555; www.lekgotla.com; Nelson Mandela Sq, Sandton; mains R90-160; ☉lunch & dinner; ☀) Set beneath traditional huts on the edge of Nelson Mandela Sq, the 'Meeting Place' is the city's most reputed African restaurant and provides a good sample of the diversity of the continent's cuisine. The Ethiopian coffee steak (R110) and Nile crocodile curry (R130) are worth a shot. Closer to home, this is a great place to sample South African staples like mealie pap (cornmeal porridge) and sweet *chakalaka* (fry-up of onions, tomatoes, peppers, garlic, ginger, sweet chilli sauce and curry powder).

Mamma's Shebeen
AFRICAN $$

(Map p314; 011-646 7453; 18 Gleneagles Rd, Greenside; mains R45-110; ☉lunch & dinner) In the heart of white establishment, Mama's has reinvented itself from a faux-township bar to a purveyor of authentic local cuisine. The decor is 'African funky' – all the prints and sculptures are for sale – and the menu includes local delicacies like mopane worms, chicken feet, and marrow bones in red wine.

Orient
ASIAN $$

(Map p314; 011-684 1616; 4 High St, Melrose Arch; mains R60-170; ☉lunch & dinner; ☀) Orient is the best of a number of Asian-themed restaurants imagined into existence by the same clever company. The A-list crowd laps it up, partly for the fusion food and fresh sushi, and partly for the future-metro decor.

Doppio Zero
ITALIAN $$

(Map p314; 011-646 8740; cnr Barry Hertzog Dr & Gleneagles Rd, Greenside; mains R40-90; ☉breakfast & lunch; ☀) Gauteng's edition of this lowscale Italian cafe franchise is hugely popular, with good reason. The corner terrace is packed on weekends with the breakfast crowd who linger for goodies baked on-site or the excellent pasta and pizza.

EASTERN SUBURBS

Near Bruma Lake is Derrick Ave, Cyrildene, off Observatory Rd, and there's an established Chinatown with a number of cheap restaurants. Most close at about 9.30pm.

Troyeville Hotel
PORTUGUESE $$

(Map p314; 011-402 7709; www.troyevillehotel. co.za; 25 Bezuidenhout St; mains R70-130 ☉lunch & dinner) Located in a tough old part of town, the Troyeville is a memorable place for a long lunch. This character-filled hotel has been frequented by the Portuguese community since well before the paint began to peel. The Iberian influence is found in the deliciously spiced fish, the whitewashed walls and the chilled red wine. It's close to Ellis Park.

🍷 Drinking

Jo'burg has an ever-revolving bar scene and you'll find everything from crusty bohemian haunts to chic cocktail lounges to conservative wine bars here. Newtown and Braamfontein have a few lively places, but much of the nightlife is in the northern suburbs, particularly around Melville, Greenside and Rosebank.

For a listing of live-music venues and nightclubs, see p332.

NEWTOWN & CITY CENTRE

Guildhall Bar & Restaurant
PUB

(Map p318; 011-833 1770; 88 Market St, Marshalltown; mains R45-70; ☉lunch & dinner) Established c 1888, City of Gold fortunes have been squandered in Jo'burg's oldest bar. This is one of the CBD's best meeting places and it's completely unpretentious. DJs perform most weekends; if not, you can often bust out the karaoke. Good Portuguese-style pub food is also available.

Sophiatown Bar Lounge
BAR

(Map p318; ☑011-836 5999; 1 Central Pl, cnr Jeppe & Henry Nxumalo Sts, Newtown; ☺10.30am-10pm Mon-Thu, to 1am Fri & Sat, to 8pm Sun) Sophiatown was once the heart of African cultural resistance, and the township's spirit is celebrated in one of Newtown's most enjoyable venues. Grainy photographs add a touch of whimsy to the jazzy sounds – there's live music on Friday and Saturday nights – while the food is hearty and gamey. A second site recently opened on 7th St, Melville.

Radium Beerhall
PUB

(Map p314; ☑011-728 3866; 282 Louis Botha Ave, Orange Grove; mains R60-100; ☺lunch & dinner) The shining light of Louis Botha's faded nightlife, the Radium has been a favourite of all strata of Jo'burg society for decades. The memorabilia gives the feel of boozing in a museum, and the live music is world class. Steaks and Portuguese flavours dominate the dependable pub menu.

PataPata
BAR

(Map p314; ☑011-676 9603; 282 Fox St, Doornfontein; mains R60-90; ☺lunch & dinner) Next to the 12 Decades Hotel, and named after a classic Miriam Makeba track, this open-plan bar lounge has a small menu of gourmet burgers and wood-fired pizzas.

MELVILLE

Six
COCKTAIL BAR

(Map p314; ☑011-482 8306; 7th St) Six has single-handedly shifted the 7th St dress code, thanks to its so-far-above-average cocktails and so-better-looking-than-you clientele. This is a wonderful place for a drink. Fabulous artwork, soft orange and red colour scheme, iconic reggae, and soul and house music at a level conducive to hearing key questions: want another one?

XaiXai Lounge
PUB

(Map p314; ☑011-482 6990; Shop 7 Melville Gardens, 7th St) Air your grievances loudly and proudly in this left-leaning Mozambican pub that has the busiest tables on the street, all day and night long. A half-kilo of prawns is R120.

Ratz Bar
COCKTAIL BAR

(Map p314; ☑011-726 2019; 9B 7th St) Ratz is a tiny cocktail bar that cranks the '80s rock and cheesy pop. There's always a crowd for cheap cocktails.

Trance Sky
BAR

(Map p314; ☑011-726 2241; 7 7th St) A Durban-style open-front music bar that plays deep, dark coastal breaks and grimy, oily techno. Wash down good bar snacks with cheap cocktails.

NORTHERN SUBURBS

Gin
COCKTAIL BAR

(Map p314; ☑011-486 2404; 12 Gleneagles Rd, Greenside) A very young crowd inhabits this bar, which is part shabby Caribbean shack, part gallery, with ramshackle whitewashed furniture and pop art plastered on the walls. There's a tiny upstairs balcony overlooking the street, tables out on the pavement, and a psychotic-looking wooden moose-head watching the action from above the bar. Cocktails are the pièce de résistance here, and house and hip hop keep the crowd happy.

Tokyo Star
BAR

(Map p314; ☑011-486 7709; www.tokyostar.co.za; 26 Gleneagles Rd, Greenside; ☺lunch & dinner) The new venture for the Carfax (p332) crew sees the same urban attitude reimagined in a sophisticated Greenside setting. This bar and eatery is like a manga comic on ice, serving cookbook cocktails like Dragon Fire (R38) and Yoshi Matsu (R42). Platters feed four steady drinkers, and the balance between decadence and restraint continues in the furniture and the nightly Class-A synthetic beats.

Jolly Roger Pub
PUB

(Map p314; ☑011-442 3954; 104th Ave, Parkhurst; pizza R50-80; ☺11am-midnight) This two-storey English-style pub on the edge of burgeoning 4th Ave is very good. Upstairs is our favourite pizza in the city and a fabulous view of the busy street below. Downstairs is a more traditional sports pub with tap beer aplenty. Across the road is its newer sports bar.

Fashion Society Cafe
CAFE

(Map p314; ☑011-728 2713; 88 Frances Rd, Norwood; ☺noon-late Tue-Sun) Handy if you're staying in the hood. DJs spin house and hip hop on weekends; the rest of the time friends settle in for an afternoon of beer,

GAY & LESBIAN GAUTENG

Gauteng has a thriving gay scene and, since the liberalisation of the constitution in 1994, the twin metropolises of Jo'burg and Pretoria have become centres for gays and lesbians from across Africa. Gays are well organised and increasingly accepted – a far cry from the puritanical attitudes of the past.

The annual Gay Pride March, held in Johannesburg on the last weekend of September, is the focal point, but by no means the only organised activity. In fact, one of the highlights is taking a Queer Johannesburg Tour (p322).

A number of websites provide information on the province's gay scene: www.gay southafrica.net, www.mask.org.za and out.org.za are packed with useful material. Also check out the monthly *Gay Times* magazine.

coffee and a spot of gossip on white leather couches and chrome cocktail tables.

☆ Entertainment

The best entertainment guide appears in Friday's *Mail & Guardian*. 'Tonight' in the daily *Star* is also good. For entertainment bookings by credit card, contact **Computicket** (☎011-915 8000; www.computicket. com). For parties and get-togethers, check out www.jhblive.co.za or www.joburg.org.za.

Cinemas

Huge cinema centres can be found across Jo'burg, with almost every shopping centre boasting one. **Ster-Kinekor** (☎central bookings 082 16789; www.sterkinekor.co.za) has the widest distribution of multiplexes, with screens in the Fourways, Westgate, Eastgate, Sandton and Rosebank malls.

Imax Theatre   CINEMA
(Map p314; ☎011-325 6182; Hyde Park Mall, Jan Smuts Ave, Hyde Park) An extra-large cinema screen in an extra-large mall.

Live Music & Nightclubs

Jo'burg is an excellent place to see live music, especially across the jazz-tipped and electronic spectrum. See p532 for more on kwaito (a form of township music) and other local sounds.

Newtown and Braamfontein are the best places to kick off an evening.

Johannesburg

Philharmonic Orchestra   CLASSICAL
(☎011-789 2733; www.jpo.co.za) The city's orchestra stages a regular circuit of concerts at venues such as Wits University and City Hall. Call, or check its website, for the latest program.

Kitchener's Carvery Bar   CLUB
(Map p318; ☎011-403 3646; cnr Juta & De Beer Sts; admission Fri & Sat R20-60; ☺5pm-late) The old Milner Park Hotel is now hipster central and epitomises the new swagger of Braamfontein. Dark and driving underground club sounds rule the weekends, while more-experimental rock and live dub outfits entertain jaw-grinding waifs and their nu-ethnic man-bags midweek.

Kippies Jazz International   JAZZ
(Map p318; ☎011-833 3316; Margaret Mcingana St, Newtown; admission from R80, ☺Thu-Sat) Once known as the 'sad man of jazz', Kippies Moeketsi would have a smile on his face if he could see what the city authorities have done to his classic jazz haunt. The club is jumping and all the best players blow, man, blow here throughout the year. Look for Kippies' bronze statue out the front.

Bassline   LIVE MUSIC
(Map p318; ☎011-838 9145; 10 Henry Nxumalo St, Newtown; admission R60-170; ☺6pm-late) This is still the most respected live-music venue in Jo'burg, gaining prominence as a Melville jazz haunt in the late '90s before getting on the world music tip and relocating to Newtown in 2004. Today it covers the full range of international musicianship and more popular reggae, rock and hip hop styles.

Carfax   CLUB
(Map p318; ☎011-834 9187; 39 Pim St, Newtown; admission R70; ☺9pm-late) They still roll up to this Newtown beat factory for progressive/ deep house and hip-hop parties, and the more interesting international acts.

Blues Room   LIVE MUSIC
(Map p314; ☎011-784 5527; Village Walk, cnr Rivonia Rd & Maud St, Sandton; ☺8pm-late) This northern suburbs' nightclub features rock, blues

and jazz acts playing to a more conservative crowd than you might expect.

Woods CLUB

(Map p318; ☑011-332 5772; 66 Carr St; ☺7pm-late Thu-Sun) Woods draws a diverse clientele who gobble up the downbeat vibe and are chattier than most on the lash. It's close enough to the Market Theatre complex to bookend a ripping night out.

Sport

Jo'burg is a great place to catch a cricket, rugby or football (soccer) match, with world-class facilities and dedicated fans.

Wanderers Stadium CRICKET

(Map p314; ☑011-340 1500; Corlett Dr, Illovo) This impressive stadium, just off the M1 freeway to Pretoria, is the city's most important cricketing venue. Either watch from the stands or head to the grassy banks near the Western Pavilion and braai yourself a steak while you watch a local limited-overs match or see South Africa's best take on an international team.

Ellis Park RUGBY

(Map p314; www.ellispark.co.za; Doornfontein) The spiritual home of Jo'burg rugby, just east of the city centre, was the scene of one of the new nation's proudest moments – victory in the 1995 World Cup. Rugby supporters are fanatical: a Saturday afternoon at the rugby can be an almost religious experience.

Ellis Park Swimming Pool SWIMMING

(Map p314; ☑011-4025565; cnr North Park Lane & Erin St, Doornfontein; adult/child R8/5; ☺7am-7pm Mon-Fri, 8am-5pm Sat & Sun) This Olympic-sized public pool is a godsend on a hot, smoggy afternoon. On weekends there's often a braai on.

Turffontein Race Course HORSE RACING

(Map p314; ☑011-681 1500) There are several horse-racing tracks, but this is the best known. It's 3km south of the city. There are race meetings most weeks.

Theatre

Market Theatre THEATRE

(Map p318; ☑011-832 1641; www.markettheatre.co.za; Margaret Mcingana St, Newtown) The city's most important venue for live theatre has three live-theatre spaces (Main, Laager and Barney Simon Theatres) as well as galleries and a cafe. There is always some interesting theatre, from sharply critical contemporary plays to musicals and stand-up comedy – check the program in the *Mail & Guardian* entertainment section.

Johannesburg Theatre THEATRE

(Map p318; ☑011-877 6800; www.showbusiness.co.za; Loveday St, Braamfontein) This leading theatre hosts mainstream local and international acts.

Pieter Toerien Theatre THEATRE

(Map p314; ☑011-511 1818; Montecasino, William Nicol Dr, Fourways) Anyone who used to be someone performs here, alongside some excellent international and local plays and musicals.

Windybrow Centre for the Arts THEATRE

(Map p318; ☑011-720 7009; www.windybrowarts.co.za; cnr Nugget & Pietersen Sts, Hillbrow) A good testing ground for emerging black playwrights.

Market Laboratory Theatre THEATRE

(Map p318; ☑011-836 0516; 50 Margaret Mcingana St, Newtown) An offshoot of the Market Theatre, acting as a showcase for community talent, with free local-theatre shows at 1pm Saturday.

🛍 Shopping

Bookshops

Chapter 1 Books BOOKS

(Map p314; ☑011-726 8506; cnr 7th St & 4th Ave, Melville; ☺9.15am-10pm) A good secondhand bookshop on 7th St.

Book Dealers of Melville BOOKS

(Map p314; ☑011-726 4054; 7th St, Melville; ☺9am-9pm Mon, to 10pm Tue-Sat, 10am-9pm Sun) Another secondhand bookshop.

Boekehuis BOOKS

(Map p314; ☑011-482 3609; cnr Lothbury Rd & Fawley Ave, Melville; ☺8am-6pm Mon-Sat) A fantastic independent bookshop in an old house with polished wood floors and a garden coffee shop. It holds regular readings, book launches and discussions.

Exclusive Books BOOKS

Eastgate Mall (Map p314; ☑011-622 4870; Upper fl; ☺9am-10pm); Rosebank Mall (Map p314; ☑011-447 3028; level 3, the Zone; ☺9am-9pm); Sandton City Mall (Map p314; ☑011-883 1010; lower level; ☺9am-9pm Mon-Sat, to 7pm Sun) This chain is the best in town, with the widest range of local press, travel guides and international newspapers.

Arts & Crafts

For decent-quality African curios, head just over the border into North-West Province for the Welwitischia Country Market (see boxed text, p431) at Hartbeespoort Dam.

TOP CHOICE **Neighbour Goods Market**   MARKET

(Map p318; www.neighbourgoodsmarket.co.za; cnr Juta & de Beer Sts, Braamfontein; ⊘9am-3pm 1st Sat of month) Cape Town's wondrous community market has come to Braamfontein to continually 'reinvent the public market as civic institution'. The two-storey brick warehouse fills with artisan purveyors and their foodie fans, who scoff on healthy brunches, 'slow' beer and stiff coffee. Upstairs you can grab a bench and watch the sun shine off city buildings. The market slogan is 'Lettuce, Turnip, the Beet'.

Rosebank Rooftop Market   CRAFTS

(Map p314; ☑011-442 4488; Cradock Ave, Rosebank; ⊘9am-5pm Sun) This is one of the most convenient places to shop for traditional carvings, beadwork, jewellery, books and fertility dolls. It's held in Rosebank Mall's multilevel car park.

Bryanston Organic Market   MARKET

(Map p314; ☑011-492 3696; Culross Rd, Bryanston; ⊘9am-3pm Thu & Sat) Arts and crafts are on offer here but the main attraction is the splendid organic produce.

Bruma Lake Market World   CRAFTS

(Map p314; ☑011-622 9648; Observatory Rd, Bruma) By Bruma Lake, this place sells a wide range of crafts and cheap electronics, and loads of kitsch.

Market Square Market   CRAFTS

(Map p318; Bree St, Newtown) Held on Saturday mornings in the car park opposite the Market Theatre, there's a lively, cheerful atmosphere (with buskers) and, although many stalls sell flea-market rubbish, there are also some reasonable crafts amid the dross.

Malls

Mall culture is alive and well in Johannesburg.

44 Stanley Avenue   MALL

(Map p314; ☑011-482 1082; Stanley Ave, Milpark) 44 Stanley is the antithesis of consumer tack and is a blueprint for future mall development. It's in a previously disused building and features only local designers and interesting restaurants.

WANT MORE?

For in-depth information, reviews and recommendations at your fingertips, head to the Apple App Store to purchase Lonely Planet's *Johannesburg* City Guide iPhone app.

Oriental Plaza   MALL

(Map p314; ☑011-838 6752; Bree St, Fordsburg; ⊘9am-5pm Mon-Fri, 8.30am-3pm Sat) A bustling collection of mostly Indian-owned stores selling everything from spices to cheap watches to cookware. If you need your mobile phone fixed, this is the place to come, and if you get peckish, there are plenty of stalls selling samosas, sweets and other goodies.

Rosebank Mall   MALL

(Map p314; ☑011-788 5530; www.themallofrosebank.co.za; Cradock Ave, Rosebank) If you're after serious retail therapy, head to this interlocking series of malls, with central parking on the corner of Cradock Ave and Baker St.

Nelson Mandela Square   MALL

(Map p314; ☑011-784 2750; Rivonia Rd, Sandton) Adjoining, and similar to, Sandton City Mall, there's an Italian-style piazza full of restaurants as well as an indoor mall section.

Other malls include: **Hyde Park Mall** (Map p314; William Nicol Dr, Hyde Park); **Fourways Mall** (Map p314; ☑011-465 6095; William Nicol Dr); and **Sandton City Mall** (Map p314; ☑011-883 2011; Rivonia Rd, Sandton).

Music

Kohinoor

(Map p318; ☑011-834 1361; 54 Market St, Newtown) In a basement underneath a furniture store, Kohinoor is one of the best sources of ethnic/African music, and sells everything from kwaito to jazz.

ℹ Information

Emergency

AIDS line (☑0800 012 322)

Fire (☑10111)

Lifeline (☑011-728 1347)

Metro Emergency Rescue Service (☑10177)

Mobile (cell) phone emergency (☑MTN 112, Vodacom 147)

Police (☑10111; Headquarters: Main Rd)

Rape Crisis Line (☑011-806 1888)

Internet Access

Chroma Copy (☑011-483 2320; per hr R30; ⊙8.30am-6pm Mon-Thu, to 5pm Fri, to 1pm Sat) Also has fax and printing facilities.

Medical Services

Jo'burg's medical services are good but they can be pricey, so make sure you get insurance before you leave home.

Charlotte Maxeke Johannesburg Hospital (☑011-488 4911; M1/Jubilee Rd, Parktown) Jo'burg's main public hospital.

Rosebank Clinic (☑011-328 0500; 14 Sturdee Ave, Rosebank; ⊙7am-10pm) A private hospital in the northern suburbs, with casualty, GP and specialist services.

Money

There are banks with ATMs and exchange facilities at every commercial centre. American Express and Rennies Travel (an agent for Thomas Cook) have branches at the airport and in major malls.

Post

Main post office (☑0800 110 226; Jeppe St; ⊙8.30am-4.30pm Mon-Fri, to noon Sat) Has a poste restante service.

Tourist Information

Guesthouses or hostels are your best sources of tourist information, but the following can fill the gaps.

Gauteng Tourism Authority (☑011-085 2500; www.gauteng.net; 124 Main Street; ⊙8am-5pm Mon-Fri) You can pick up a copy of the monthly *Go Gauteng* magazine here.

Johannesburg Tourism Company (☑011-214 0700; info@joburgtourism.com; ground fl, Grosvenor Cnr, 195 Jan Smuts Ave, Parktown North; ⊙8am-5pm Mon-Fri) A private endeavour; covers the city of Jo'burg.

❶ Getting There & Away

Air

South Africa's major international and domestic airport is **OR Tambo International Airport** (Ortia; ☑011-921 6262; www.airports.co.za). For more information, including international flight connections, see p591.

Make sure you deal only with official Airports Company employees. A friendly 'No, thanks' should dissuade any potential crooks. You might consider wrapping your luggage in plastic before a flight, because items have been pilfered from bags at the airport.

If you're in a hurry, some domestic flights are definitely worth considering. Smaller budget airlines **Kulula** (☑0861 444 144; www.kulula .com), **1time** (☑0861 345 345; www.1time.co.za)

and **Mango** (☑0861 162 646; ww5.flymango. com) link Jo'burg with major destinations.

For regular flights to national and regional destinations try **South African Airways** (SAA; ☑0861 359 722; www.flysaa.com), **South African Airlink** (SAAirlink; ☑011-961 1700; www .saairlink.co.za) and **South African Express** (☑011-978 5577; www.saexpress.co.za). All flights can be booked through SAA, which also has offices in the domestic and international terminals of Ortia.

Some more common legs are Cape Town (R850), Durban (R550) and Nelspruit (R850).

Bus

There are a number of international bus services that leave Jo'burg from the Park Station complex and head for Mozambique, Lesotho, Botswana, Namibia, Swaziland and Zimbabwe.

The main long-distance bus lines (national and international) also depart from and arrive at the Park Station transit centre, in the northwest corner of the site, where you'll also find their booking offices.

Baz Bus (☑in Cape Town 021-439 2323; www .bazbus.com) connects Jo'burg with the most popular parts of the region (including Durban, Garden Route and Cape Town) and picks up at hostels in Jo'burg and Pretoria, saving you the hassle of going into the city to arrange transport. Note that Baz Bus no longer services Swaziland. All hostels have current timetables and prices. A seven-day travel pass costs R1200.

The most comprehensive range of services to/ from Jo'burg is provided by government-owned lines **Translux** (☑0861 589 282; www.translux .co.za) and **City to City** (☑0861 589 282).

Other major bus lines:

Greyhound (☑012-323 1154; www.greyhound .co.za)

Intercape (☑0861 287 287; www.intercape.co .za)

SA Roadlink (☑011-333 2223; www.saroadlink .co.za)

(For more information on all bus lines, see p598.)

With the exception of City to City buses, which start at Jo'burg, all services that are not heading north commence in Pretoria, at the Pretoria station.

TO CAPE TOWN Most companies travel to the same destinations. SA Roadlink offers the most competitive rates to Cape Town (R400, 19 hours). Buses depart daily. Translux runs two daily services to Cape Town (R480, 19 hours) via Bloemfontein (R200, five hours). There are also less-frequent services via Kimberley (R270, seven hours). Greyhound also heads to Harare, Zimbabwe (R460, 16½ hours), while Intercape has a bus to Windhoek, Namibia (R400, 12 hours).

TO DURBAN & KWAZULU-NATAL SA Roadlink runs to Durban (R175, seven hours) eight times daily. Greyhound has six daily buses to Durban via Estcourt (R205, eight hours) via Newcastle (R300, nine hours), and then to Richard's Bay (R310, 10 hours). Translux has at least one bus a day to Durban (R240, nine hours), as does Intercape (R195, eight hours).

TO THE SOUTH Translux operates a daily service to East London (R380, 15 hours) via Bloemfontein (R220, seven hours). Translux also has five services a week (not on Sunday and Tuesday) to Port Elizabeth (R360, 14 hours) and Graaff-Reinet (R350, 15½ hours). SA Roadlink has one bus daily to Port Elizabeth (R300, 15 hours). Intercape has daily services to Port Elizabeth via Cradock (R380, 15 hours) and on to Plettenberg Bay (R576, 18 hours). Greyhound has daily buses that travel overnight from Jo'burg to Port Elizabeth (R385, 16 hours) and East London (R375, 13 hours). Translux runs to Knysna (R576, 17 hours) via Kimberley three times weekly or Bloemfontein four times weekly, then to Oudtshoorn, Mossel Bay and George (all R380 from Jo'burg).

TO MPUMALANGA & KRUGER NATIONAL PARK The nearest large town to Kruger National Park is Nelspruit. Greyhound runs to Nelspruit daily (R260, five hours) on the way to Maputo, Mozambique (R300, nine hours). Translux runs to Maputo daily (R280, nine hours) via Nelspruit (R230, five hours). Translux also has daily buses running to Phalaborwa (R220, eight hours), which is a good option if you're staying at a more northerly Kruger National Park camp such as Olifants. **Citybug** (☑011-753 3392; www .citybug.co.za) runs a shuttle service between Jo'burg and Nelspruit (R350, 3½ hours), stopping in Pretoria and a few smaller towns along the way. **Lowveld Link** (☑in White River 013-750 1174; www.lowveldlink.com) also runs a shuttle between Jo'burg and Nelspruit (R330, 3½ to 4½ hours), via Pretoria.

TO THE NORTH Several bus services run north up the N1, although some don't make it as far as Harare and only go as far as Polokwane (Pietersburg). From there you will have to catch a local bus or minibus taxi to get to the border. Intercape also heads north to Gaborone, Botswana (R150, seven hours). Translux has a daily service as far as Louis Trichardt (Makhado; R190, 6½ hours). It goes via Mokopane (Potgietersrus; R130, four hours) and Polokwane (Pietersburg; R150, 4½ hours). It also has services that head east through Limpopo, stopping in Tzaneen (R190, 6½ hours) and Phalaborwa (R200, eight hours). There are daily City to City services to Sibasa, in Limpopo's Venda region (R150, eight hours). These services, which wind north through townships and ex-homelands, also stop in major towns on the N1.

Car

All the major car-rental operators have counters at OR Tambo, Ortia and at various locations around the city, and many offer deals with unlimited mileage.

Hitching

We say don't hitch. If you're strapped for cash, you could ask about share-drives. These are often advertised in the weekly newspaper *Junk Mail* (junkmail.co.za), and most hostels have noticeboards with details of free or shared-cost lifts.

Train

Long-distance train services link Jo'burg with a number of destinations including Pretoria, Cape Town, Bloemfontein, Kimberley, Port Elizabeth, Durban, Komatipoort and Nelspruit. A number of these services have sleeper compartments. Tickets can be booked through **Shosholoza Meyl** (☑0860 008 888; www.shosholozameyl. co.za, www.premierclasse.co.za) or at Jo'burg's Park Station. For details on train classes and routes, see p605.

ⓘ Getting Around

To/From the Airport

OR Tambo International Airport (Ortia) is about 25km east of central Johannesburg in Kempton Park.

Airport Shuttle (☑0861 748 8853; www .airportshuttle.co.za) charges R350 for most destinations in Jo'burg and will pick up 24 hours day, although it should be booked a day

---

GAUTRAIN

The rapid transit Gautrain (☑0800 4288 7246; www.gautrain.co.za) offers a direct service between the airport, Sandton, Rosebank and Pretoria. Trains depart every 15 minutes at peak times (7am to 7pm Monday to Sunday), and every 30 minutes thereafter. A one-way ticket to Sandton costs R115 (including the rechargeable card). If you're travelling in peak periods, or staying near a station, it's a fast, state-of-the-art and cost-effective way to enter/exit the city. The final section of the line – to Park Station in the Jo'burg CBD – should be completed in 2013.

USEFUL BUS ROUTES

ROUTE	DESTINATIONS
5	Parktown, Houghton, Rosebank & Illovo
22	Yeoville & Bruma Lake
75	Braamfontein, Auckland Park & Melville
80	Rosebank & Dunkeld via Jan Smuts Ave

in advance if possible. **Magic Bus** (☏0861 748 8853; www.airportshuttle.co.za) offers a similar service and charges R300 for most destinations.

By car, the airport is easily accessible (via the R24 and the N12), but if you need to get there during the weekday rush-hour (5pm to 7pm) allow up to an extra hour's travelling time. Regular buses connect the airport with the main train station, Park Station. Taxis cost around R350 one way to the northern suburbs. Most hostels will collect you from the airport for free. Guesthouses and hotels will also arrange pick-ups but usually for about the same charge as a taxi.

Bus

Metropolitan Bus Services (Metrobus; ☏011-375 5555; www.mbus.co.za; Gandhi Sq) runs services throughout greater Jo'burg, though waiting for a bus in the car-dominated northern suburbs can be a bit like waiting for Godot. The main bus terminal is at Gandhi Sq, two blocks west of the Carlton Centre, and fares work on a zonal system ranging from Zone 1 (R6.50) to Zone 8 (R16). Travellers buy tags from the bus terminal or **Computicket** (www.computicket. com), and the cost of the journey is automatically deducted each time you travel. You can still pay for journeys with cash, but Metrobus does its best to discourage this.

Rea Vaya Network

Rea Vaya buses were introduced in the build-up to the 2010 World Cup as a way of addressing the lack of safe, reliable public transport between Soweto (and other townships) and the Johannesburg CBD. The fleet is colourful and comfortable, and timetables are more strictly adhered to than metro lines. An inner-city circular route costs R4 (green line), while a full trip from the feeder routes to the CBD (blue line) costs R11.

Minibus Taxi

R5 will get you around the inner suburbs and the city centre and R9 will get you almost anywhere.

If you take a minibus taxi into central Jo'burg, be sure to get off before it reaches the end of the route, and avoid the taxi rank – it's a mugging zone. Getting a minibus taxi home from the city is a more difficult proposition.

There's a complex system of hand/finger signals to tell a passing taxi where you want to go, so it's best to look as though you know where you're going and raise a confident index finger (drivers will stop if they're going the same way).

Taxi

Taxis are a relatively expensive but necessary evil in this city. They all operate meters, but it's wise to ask a local the likely price and agree on a fare from the outset. From Park Station to Rosebank should cost around R90, and it's significantly more to Sandton.

Maxi Taxi Cabs (☏011-648 1212) and **Rose's Radio Taxis** (☏011-403 9625) are two reputable firms.

Train

For enquiries about local train services run by **Metro** (☏011-773 5878), call or visit the helpful information office in the Park Station concourse. There have been serious problems with violent crime on the Metro system, mostly on those lines connecting with townships. The Jo'burg–Pretoria Metro line should also be avoided.

AROUND JOHANNESBURG

The biggest attraction in the Jo'burg surrounds is the pulsating township of Soweto. Dig a little deeper and you'll also discover a World Heritage Site spanning three million years of human history, countryside hiking trails, and several nature reserves where you can discover wildlife on foot or by a safari vehicle.

Soweto

☏011 / POP 2.3 MILLION

The 'South West Townships' have evolved from an area of forced habitation to an address of pride and social prestige. Travellers come to witness the welcoming township life and to visit the former home of Desmond Tutu and Nelson Mandela, and the Hector Pieterson Museum. A stroll down laid-back Vilakazi St offers an insight into modern African sensibilities, while the addition of Soccer City and the Soweto Bungee provide quality, concrete experiences in a place of great political abstraction.

Soweto

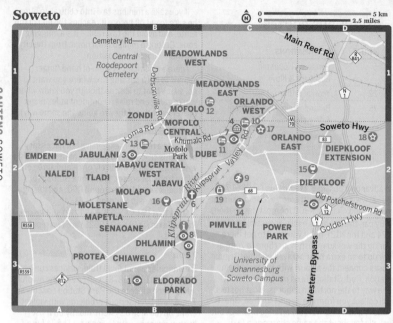

Mirroring much of South Africa, the rising middle class lives here alongside shack dwellers and the mass unemployed, yet all are equally buoyed by the history of Soweto as an icon of the struggle. Crime, HIV/AIDS and a widening wealth gap are evident in daily life here, but the mood is essentially optimistic. Many who break the cycle decide to stay and reinvest, and most laud their Sowetan upbringing. The townships are the heart of the nation and none beats louder than Soweto.

History

As ANC stalwart and long-time Soweto resident Walter Sisulu once said, the history of South Africa cannot be understood outside the history of Soweto.

Using the outbreak of bubonic plague in 1904 as an excuse, the Jo'burg City Council (JCC) moved 1358 Indians and 600 Africans from a Jo'burg slum to Klipspruit, 18km by road from the city centre. It wasn't until the late 1930s, after the suburb of Orlando had been built and cynically marketed by the JCC as 'somewhat of a paradise', that the population began its astonishing growth.

By the end of WWII, Jo'burg's black population had risen by more than 400,000, and by 1958 more than 20 new suburbs had ap-

peared around Orlando, each filled with row upon row of identical houses.

During the 1950s, organisations such as the ANC took a bigger role in opposing apartheid, and before long Soweto (as it was officially named in 1961) would be recognised as the centre of resistance. Confirmation of this came in 1955 when 3000 delegates from around the country gathered in Kliptown Sq (known today as Freedom Sq) at the Congress of the People. The result was the Freedom Charter, which is the pillar of ANC philosophy and integral to the new constitution.

The movement was forced underground in 1960 after the Sharpeville Massacre. While the struggle continued at a slower pace, it was not the only change taking place here. The demographics of the townships were changing, and as second-generation Sowetans matured, so did Soweto style. New forms of music (see p528) emerged and the youth led development of a unique urban culture. Football also offered an escape, and massive support for teams such as Moroka Swallows, Orlando Pirates and (after they split from Pirates) Kaizer Chiefs reflected the development of an urban black identity.

The development of this new identity only served to strengthen the desire to be treated

Soweto

as equals. Resistance eventually spilled over on 16 June 1976, when a student protest became the precursor to the Soweto uprising (see Hector Pieterson Museum, p339).

Within days of the fighting, world opinion had turned irreversibly against the apartheid regime and Soweto became the most potent symbol of resistance to a racist South Africa.

Scenes of burning cars, 'necklaced' people and mass funerals flowed out of Soweto throughout the 1980s, while the death throes of apartheid could be felt. Mandela was released in 1990 and returned to live in his tiny home in Vilakazi St, just 200m from Archbishop Desmond Tutu.

However, Mandela's release was no panacea. Encouraged by the government, supporters of rival political parties murdered each other by the hundreds in the run-up to the 1994 free elections.

More recently life has been stable, and since 1994 Sowetans have had ownership rights over their properties. The relative calm has been further compounded by a number of redevelopment projects. The 2010 World Cup also brought great positive press for the township and the glittering Soccer City as its prime legacy, as well as improved street lighting, parks and paved roads.

Indeed, many parts of Soweto are safer and more laid-back than Johannesburg's wealthy, high-security northern suburbs.

◎ Sights & Activities

Mandela House Museum   MUSEUM
(☏011-936 7754; 8115 Orlando West; admission R60; ◷10am-5pm) Nelson Mandela lived with his first wife, Evelyn, and later with his second wife, Winnie, in this house, just off **Vilakazi St**. The museum, which was renovated in 2009, includes interactive exhibits on the history of the house and some interesting family photos. Just down Vilakazi St, by Sakhumzi Restaurant, is the **home of Archbishop Desmond Tutu**.

Hector Pieterson Memorial   MEMORIAL
North of Vilakazi St is Hector Pieterson Sq. It's named after the 13-year-old who was shot dead in the run-up to the Soweto uprising, and it features this poignant memorial.

Hector Pieterson Museum   MUSEUM
(☏011-536 0611; cnr Khumalo & Pela Sts; adult/child R25/15; ◷10am-5pm) This powerful museum illuminates the role of Sowetan life in the history of the independence struggle. It follows the tragic incidents of 16 June 1976, when a peaceful student protest against the introduction of Afrikaans as a language of instruction was violently quelled by police.

In the resulting chaos police opened fire and a 13-year-old boy, Hector Pieterson, was shot dead. The ensuing hours and days saw students fight running battles with the security forces in what would become known as the Soweto uprising. On the first day alone, close to 200 teenage protesters were killed.

Regina Mundi Church   CHURCH
(Mkhize St; admission by donation) South of Hector Pieterson Museum, down Klipspruit Valley Rd, this church was an important meeting point during the apartheid years and was central to the struggle. Bullet holes and gun butt cracks are testament to its past. Several hearings of the Truth & Reconciliation Commission were heard here.

FREE Credo Mutwa Cultural Village   CULTURAL VILLAGE
(cnr Ntsane & Majoeng Sts, Central Western Jabavu; ⊙6am-6pm) This series of clay sculptures and buildings is inspired by African folklore, and was created in 1974 by Credo Mutwa, a controversial artist and healer.

Avalon Cemetery   CEMETERY
(Tshabuse St; ⊙8am-4pm) Here you'll find the graves of Joe Slovo (Plot B35311; the former leader of the South African Communist Party) and Hector Pieterson (Plot EC462).

Chris Hani Baragwanath Hospital   LANDMARK
(Old Potch Road, Moreleta Park) Southeast of Orlando, this hospital, the largest in the world with some 3000 beds, is a famous Soweto landmark.

DON'T MISS

SOCCER CITY

The headquarters of the 2010 FIFA World Cup, Soccer City stadium is shaped like a calabash and dominates the abandoned mining tracts on the outskirts of Soweto. It's an architectural treat, courtesy of Bobby van Bebber, that reminds hazy locals that they did indeed host the famous sporting event. Some say it looks like the ship from District 9. If you want to walk through the players' race and imagine forgotten glory, take an excellent guided tour (☎011-247 5300; per person R80; ⊙9am, 10.30am, noon & 3pm).

Kliptown   NEIGHBOURHOOD
Established in 1904 and found southwest of Orlando West, Kliptown is the oldest settlement in Jo'burg to accommodate all races. It is also where the Freedom Charter was adopted on 26 June 1955. The site of the adoption, once a football field, has become the Walter Sisulu Square of Dedication (cnr Union Ave & Main Rd), which includes an information centre, a hotel, banks, curio shops, the conical brick Freedom Charter Monument and the Kliptown Open Air Museum (☎10am-5pm Mon-Sat, to 4.30pm Sun), which tells the story of how the Freedom Charter came to be drafted through photos, newspaper clippings, art and song.

TOP CHOICE Orlando Towers   BUNGEE JUMPING
(☎011-536 0611; cnr Khumalo & Pela Sts; viewing platform/bungee jumping R60/360; ⊙10am-5pm Wed, Fri, Sat & Sun) Built originally for Orlando's Power Station, the towers host one of the world's more incongruous bungee jumps. Once painted a drab white, one tower is now decorated with a colourful mural, the largest in South Africa, depicting, among others, Nelson Mandela, singer Yvonne Chaka Chaka, and a football stadium. The other tower displays the FNB logo (the bank commissioned the murals in 2002). There's a bar and hang-out area with good-looking staff and 'Xtreme'-ly loud music.

👉 Tours

Dozens of companies offer tours of Soweto; your accommodation should be able to put you in touch with them or offer an in-house service.

Soweto Bicycle Tours   BICYCLE TOUR
(☎011-936 3444; www.sowetobicycletours.com; 2hr/full-day tour R350/500) Soweto's clay paths and grassy nooks make for fabulous cycling terrain. The company also owns Soweto Backpackers, which offers R50 tour discounts for guests.

Jimmy's Face to Face Tours   NIGHT TOUR
(☎011-331 6109; www.face2face.co.za) Jimmy's signature tour is 'Soweto by Night' (R890 per person), which includes dinner and a tour around some shebeens.

Taste of Africa   GUIDED TOUR
(☎011-482 8114, 082 565 2520; www.tasteofafrica.co.za) Offers an excellent 24-hour tour (R380 per person) where you can explore Soweto with locals, far off the beaten track.

SOWETO FESTIVAL CALENDAR

Soweto Wine Festival University of Johannesburg Soweto campus, early September.

Soweto Festival Music, poetry, food stalls and lifestyle expo on the last weekend of September at the University of Johannesburg Soweto campus.

Tour de Soweto Bike race taking place in October.

Soweto Beer Festival Last weekend of October, SHAP stadium, Mofolo Park.

Soweto Marathon Takes place in early November.

Soweto Arts Festival (www.joburg.org.za) A week-long festival to promote arts, unity and culture. Held annually in mid- to late-December at various locales in Soweto.

Vhupo Tours   SOWETO TOUR
(☑011-936 0411; www.vhupo-tours.com) Run by Soweto resident David Luthanga, this place offers a range of tours around Soweto, including an evening out at a shebeen.

🛏 Sleeping

There are many B&Bs in the township, most in the immediate vicinity of Vilakazi St.

Soweto Backpackers   BACKPACKERS $
(☑011-326 1700; www.sowetobackpackers.co.za; 10823A Power St, Meadowlands East; dm/s/d without bathroom R70/85/170) Lebo is the host of the best hostel in Soweto, set by lovely parklands. It's a healthy walk from the Vilakazi St action, but guests love the shaded beer garden, restaurant and pool table. Dorms are neat and clean and the double rooms are excellent value. The friendly staff encourage interactivity, while all kinds of tours are available.

Ngwenya's B&B   GUESTHOUSE $$
(☑011-936 2604; 7862 Pitsonyane St, Orlando West; s/d incl breakfast R450/600) This white-walled Sowetan mansion, run by bustling California Ngwenya, is a flashy alternative to the more staid home-stay options. The four rooms on the rooftop are deservedly popular, partly for their stylish township decor, mostly for their superb township views.

Nthateng's B&B   GUESTHOUSE $$
(☑011-936 2676; 6991 Inhlwathi St, Orlando West; s/d incl breakfast R400/600) Dark woods, tan linens and sandy-coloured walls give this spacious guesthouse an air of early '80s post-disco chill. However, Nthateng is an animated host who insists on top-shelf personal tours, delicious breakfasts and a *mi casa su casa* state of mind. It's in an ideal location near the museum.

Thuto's B&B   GUESTHOUSE $$
(☑011-936 8123, 072 376 9205; 8123 Ngakane St, Orlando West; s/d incl breakfast R450/700) Thuto's is an icon of Soweto for its pioneering hospitality, close historical links to the struggle and warm, dowdy rooms. There's a calming mood in the huge lounge room, while the rooms have nanna-chic furniture, large TVs and huge bathrooms. This is the most reliable guesthouse for up-to-date information on the town's happenings.

Soweto Hotel   HOTEL $$$
(☑011-527 7300; www.sowetohotel.co.za; Walter Sisulu Sq of Dedication, cnr Union Ave & Main Rd, Kliptown; s/d incl breakfast from R1125/1257; P@🖙) Formerly a Holiday Inn franchise, the Soweto is a sign of the township's changing sensibilities. Mostly an above-average business hotel, with a smattering of celebrity guests, the rooms are modern and hip, with a jazz design that continues in the restaurant and bar.

Wandie's Place   GUESTHOUSE $$
(☑011-982 2796; www.wandiesplace.co.za; 618 Makhalemele St, Dube; s/d R450/700; @) This seven-room boutique hotel has a restaurant next door. Wandie's is firmly on the tourist trail and bus parties regularly pass through for the tasty daily buffets (R95 buffet, open lunch and dinner). The restaurant also has an alfresco area for sunny days.

🍴 Eating & Drinking

There are tons of places to go out for a drink in Soweto, from informal shebeens to more upmarket bars and restaurants. Soweto's answer to the burger is the 'Russian', a bread roll stuffed with chips, processed meat, processed cheese and mango chutney.

INNOCENT TUMI: DJ

How would you describe the Jo'burg music scene at the moment? The Jo'burg music scene has grown, matured. It's moving, vibey, professional and versatile. It has really improved, attracting a lot of music-lovers outside SA.

What are your own favourite musical styles? I'm a very versatile DJ. I try a lot of new things. At a gig I play a lot of soulful, jazzy Afro-house and a bit of commercial vibey tunes. When I'm relaxed I prefer a lot of soul, R'n'B and a bit of hip hop and rock.

Where could we find you playing on a weekend? If I'm not doing tours around the country in different cities then I'll be doing my gigs around Jo'burg at places like Blacklife in Sefateng, Newscafe in Northriding and Cappello on Gandhi Sq, or maybe hosting my own events.

Who are your favourite South African DJs? Black Coffee, Sai and Ribatone, DJ Mbuso and Vinnie da Vinci.

What's the craziest thing that ever happened at a party you played at? Craziest thing ever happened to me at a gig must have been when a crowd pushed me back to the decks after doing a 4am slot. They wanted more of me. Memories!

Sakhumzi Restaurant SOUTH AFRICAN $$
(☎011-939 4427; www.sakhumzi.co.za; 6980 Vilakazi St, Orlando West; buffet R90; ☺lunch & dinner) This is a great place to hang out if you only have a night in Soweto. Patrons spill onto the street tables and mingle joyfully with passers-by. It serves local favourites such as mutton stew and mealie pap as well as more conventional burgers and breakfasts.

Nambitha SOUTH AFRICAN $$
(☎082 785 7190; 6877 Vilakazi St, Orlando West; mains R50-95; ☺breakfast, lunch & dinner) This stylish, open-fronted bar and restaurant is popular with Soweto's bright young 20-somethings, and serves a whole range of food from toasted sandwiches to steaks to *mogodu* (tripe).

Restaurant Vilakazi SOUTH AFRICAN $
(☎082 108 4088; Vilakazi St, Orlando West; mains R40-65; ☺breakfast, lunch & dinner) Next to Nambitha is the latest restaurant on the block, owned by a popular TV actress and frequented by her lookalikes and their boyfriends. The simple menu features fish and grilled meats served with generous vegie sides.

Rock BAR
(☎011-986 8182; 1897 Vundla St, Rockville; ☺10am-11pm Mon-Thu, to 2am Fri & Sat) Located in Rockville, and surrounded by rocky stretches of road, the Rock, er, rocks. The night slides on seamlessly between house music and live jazz, all while a sassy crowd of local scenesters and out-of-town artist types sip fruity cocktails and tall beers on the roof deck.

Backroom BAR
(☎011-938 9388; Shop 20, Pimville; ☺10am-2am Thu-Sun) New money and old-fashioned sounds are on show at Soweto's most uppity joint. The courtyard garden is a good place for a sundowner with friends and friendly strangers.

Danish Pub CLUB
(☎011-982 2796; Immink Dve, Diepkloof; ☺3pm-late) This sure-fire late-night venue features the best local DJs who entertain a young, relaxed crowd lounging on leather and cheap drinks.

☆ Entertainment

Soccer City (Baragwanath Rd, Diepkloof), also known as FNB Stadium, is the new headquarters of South African football (see boxed text, p342). It's a destination in its own right, due to its architectural brilliance. **Orlando Stadium** (Mooki St & Valley Rd, Orlando East) is also worth a visit, especially when the Orlando Pirates meet their sworn enemy, the Kaizer Chiefs.

🛍 Shopping

There are informal shops and stalls all over Soweto. A number of craft sellers set up outside the Hector Pieterson Museum and there's also Kliptown Plaza, which is a market next to Walter Sisulu Sq of Dedication.

Maponya Mall MALL
(☑011-938 4448; 2127 Chris Hani Road, Klipsruit; ⊙9am-7pm Mon-Thu, 9am-8pm Fri & Sat, 9am-5pm Sun) This mall caused some tension when it first opened, but locals seem ambivalent now about the eight cinemas, chain stores and fast-food joints.

ℹ Information

Soweto Tourism and Information Centre
(☑011-945 3111; Walter Sisulu Sq of Dedication, Kliptown; ⊙8am-5pm Mon-Fri) is the first tourist centre to be opened in a township. There are ABSA and FNB banks with ATMs in Walter Sisulu Sq of Dedication. Foreign exchange is available at the Soweto Hotel, also in the square.

ℹ Getting There & Away

Most transport in and out of Soweto is by motor vehicle, usually by one of the minibus taxis (R15 one way) that arrive in Diepkloof or Orlando from the taxi rank near Joubert Park in the Jo'burg city centre. Make sure the driver knows exactly where to stop, and it would be best to do so in the more touristy area of Orlando West.

Cradle of Humankind

The area to the west of Jo'burg is one of the world's most important palaeontological zones, focused around the Sterkfontein hominid fossil fields. The area is part of the 47,000-hectare Cradle of Humankind (www. cradleofhumankind.co.za), which is listed for preservation by Unesco. Most Jo'burg-based tour operators (p321) offer full- and half-day tours of the area.

MAROPENG

Off the R563 and on the way to Hekpoort, Maropeng (☑014-577 9000; www.maropeng. co.za; adult/child R120/70, with Sterkfontein Caves entry R200/120; ⊙9am-5pm) is an impressive complex housed in a building that looks like a giant grassy mound on one side and shiny modern steel on the other (representing humanity's journey through the ages). There are visitor attractions, an entertainment complex, an information centre and the excellent Maropeng Hotel (s/d incl breakfast R1000/1700; ⓟ❀@☀☎). Its name is Tswana for 'returning to your origin', and the exhibits here show how the human race has progressed since its very beginnings. There's a pretty cool boat ride back in time that takes visitors through the ice age and even to a simulated black hole.

STERKFONTEIN CAVES & AROUND

The Sterkfontein Caves (☑011-577 9000; Sterkfontein Caves Rd; adult/child R125/75; ⊙9am-5pm) include a permanent hominid exhibit and a walkway past the excavation site. Tours down into the caves, one of the most significant archaeological sites in the world, leave every 30 minutes. The last tour is at 4pm. A discount ticket that covers the caves and Maropeng (R200) must be purchased by 1pm.

It's worth a creepy, bat-infested afternoon descent at nearby Old Kromdraai Gold Mine (☑011-957 0211; Ibis Ridge Farm, Kromdraai Rd; adult/child R60/40; ⊙Tue-Fri by appointment, 9am-5pm Sat & Sun, last tour 4pm), the first gold mine on the Witwatersrand. Guided tours leave the converted shed every hour.

Near the Swartkop Mountains is the Rhino & Lion Nature Reserve (☑011-957 0106; www.rhinolion.co.za; Kromdraai Rd; adult/child R120/80; ⊙8am-5pm Mon-Fri, to 6pm Sat & Sun). This is an easy way to get up close to three of the Big Five (lion, buffalo and rhino). Lovers of fluffy cuteness can hug cubs at the animal crèche. There are also three four-person chalets (R1025), and wildlife drives (R180) are offered. Within the reserve is Wonder Cave (☑011-957 0106; www.wondercave.net; adult/child R50/30), where you can gaze up at stalactites in an eerily beautiful interior. If you're planning to do both the reserve and the cave, ask

Side margin: GAUTENG CRADLE OF HUMANKIND

WORTH A TRIP

MULDERSDRIFT

North of Krugersdorp, alongside the N14, is the pretty hamlet of Muldersdrift. It's part of a section of restaurants and country lifestyle stores known as Crocodile Ramble, and is particularly popular for weddings and with weekenders. **Kloofzicht Lodge & Spa** (0861 148 866; buffet R120) is on a small nature reserve featuring elands, blue wildebeests, red hartebeests, gemsbok and zebras. There's also a fly-fishing academy where visitors can rent a rod and cast off. On Sunday it hosts a stupendous buffet lunch with 'cliff views', which is open to the public and books out every week. The day spa is equally impressive. You'll feel a long way from downtown Johannesburg.

at the gate about the combined ticket that gives a 20% discount.

Near Lanseria airport is a **Lion Park** (011-460 1814; www.lion-park.com; cnr Malibongwe Dr & R114, Lanseria; adult/child R150/75, guided wildlife drives R225/140; 8.30am-9pm) where you can see rare white lions as well as the boring regular kind. The main attraction is the opportunity to feed giraffes or to play with baby lions at Cub World. You can spend the night here in a **tented camp** (s/d R600/900).

CRADLE NATURE RESERVE

About halfway between Pretoria and Johannesburg is the **Cradle Nature Reserve** (011-659 1622; www.thecradle.co.za; Kromdraai Rd; admission free; 8am-10pm), a more up-market take on the wildlife experience, with wildlife walks and drives, and palaeontological tours. Home base here is superlative **Cradle Restaurant** (mains R70-120; breakfast, lunch & dinner), offering international cuisine, a cocktail bar, a log fire in winter and one of the best restaurant views in the country. Dishes include Trout Almondine and Veal Saltimbocca and other mod-posh favourites. Accommodation is offered in self-catering thatched cottages at **Forest Camp** (cottages per person R320) or you can head 16km to the outstanding **Forum Homini** (011-668 7000; www.forumhomini.com; d R3500), which has another well-regarded restaurant featuring local produce. Rooms here are large yet intimate with rain showers, massage chairs and contemporary African decor.

Southern Gauteng

Bisected by the Vaal River, this area is home to the cities of Vereeniging, Sebokeng and Vanderbijlpark, and has an eventful past. The Vaal River – the *gij!garib* (tawny) to the San, *lekoa* (erratic) to the Sotho and *vaal*

(dirty) to the Afrikaners – played an important role in Southern African history, serving as a natural dividing line between the 'Transvaal' and the south.

It was near the Vaal that the Treaty of Vereeniging, which led to the end of the 1899–1902 Anglo-Boer War, was negotiated. And more recently, at Sharpeville and Evaton, on 21 March 1960, black civilians protested against the pass laws by publicly burning their passbooks. Police opened fire on the protestors at Sharpeville, killing 69 and wounding about 180; most were shot in the back. Today, 21 March is commemorated in South Africa as Human Rights Day (a public holiday).

In 1984 in Sebokeng, security forces violently reacted to a black boycott of rent and service tariffs. About 95 people were killed. Such slaughters galvanised the black population into a more unified force, and ultimately hastened the fall of apartheid.

Named after the sugar bush *Protea caffra*, the **Suikerbosrand Nature Reserve** (011-904 3930; Klip River Rd; adult/child R30/15, vehicle R10; 7.15am-6pm Mon-Fri, 7am-6pm Sat & Sun) is between the N3 freeway and the R59, and can be reached by either. There are 66km of walking trails, several drives and the historic **Diepkloof Farm Museum** (011-904 3964; admission R10), originally built in 1850 by Voortrekker Gabriel Marais and renovated in the 1970s after being burnt during the 1899–1902 Anglo-Boer War. Its opening hours are the same as for the reserve.

PRETORIA

012 / POP 1.65 MILLION

South Africa's administrative centre is a handsome city, with a number of number of gracious old houses in the city centre, large, leafy green suburbs, and wide streets that are lined with a purple haze of jacarandas in October and November.

It's more of an Afrikaner city than Jo'burg, and its bars and restaurants are less cosmopolitan – sedate Pretoria was once at the heart of the apartheid regime, and its very name a symbol of oppression. Today it's home to a growing number of black civil servants and foreign embassy workers, who are infusing the city with a new sense of multiculturalism.

Pretoria's most impressive sights include the vast Herbert Baker–designed Union Buildings; Burgers Park, greenery in the city centre; the Transvaal Museum, South Africa's premier natural history exhibition; the vast Voortrekker Monument; and Freedom Park, offering a more holistic approach to history.

History

The fertile Apies River, on which the city of Pretoria sits today, was the support system for a large population of Nguni-speaking cattle farmers for hundreds of years.

However, the Zulu wars caused massive destruction and dislocation. Much of the black population was slaughtered and most of the remaining people fled north into present-day Zimbabwe. In 1841 the first Boers trekked into a temporary vacuum. With no one around, they laid claim to the land that would become their capital.

By the time the British granted independence to the Zuid-Afrikaansche Republiek (ZAR) in the early 1850s, there were estimated to be 15,000 whites and 100,000 blacks living between the Vaal and Limpopo Rivers. The whites were widely scattered, and in 1853 two farms on the Apies River were bought as the site for the republic's capital.

Pretoria, which was named after Andries Pretorius, was nothing more than a tiny frontier village with a grandiose title, but the servants of the British Empire were watching it with growing misgivings. They acted

in 1877, annexing the republic; the Boers went to war (Pretoria came under siege at the beginning of 1881) and won back their independence.

The discovery of gold on the Witwatersrand in the late 1880s changed everything and within 20 years the Boers would again be at war with the British.

With the British making efforts towards reconciliation, self-government was again granted to the Transvaal in 1906, and through an unwieldy compromise Pretoria was made the administrative capital. The Union of South Africa came into being in 1910, but Pretoria was not to regain its status until 1961, when the Republic of South Africa came into existence under the leadership of Hendrik Verwoerd.

◎ Sights & Activities

Voortrekker Monument & Nature Reserve

MONUMENT

The imposing **Voortrekker Monument** (Map p356; ☑012-323 0682; Eeufees Rd; adult/child R40/20, vehicle R20; ◷8am-6pm Sep-Apr, to 5pm May-Aug) is a place of pilgrimage for many Afrikaners. It was constructed between 1938 and 1949 – a time of great Afrikaner nationalism – to honour the journey of the Voortrekkers, who trekked north over the coastal mountains of the Cape into the heart of the African veld.

The edifice is surrounded by a stone wall carved with 64 wagons in a traditional defensive *laager* (circle). The building itself is a huge stone cube and each corner bears the face of a great Afrikaner hero. A staircase and elevator lead to the roof and a great panoramic view of Pretoria and the highveld.

The monument is 3km south of the city and is clearly signposted from the N1 freeway. It is surrounded by a 340-hectare nature reserve full of zebras, wildebeests, bucks and other small mammals.

WORTH A TRIP

VAAL DAM

With over 600km of coastline and a 5km-long island, South Africa's largest dam is hugely popular with the boating fraternity. There are nine yacht clubs and seven marinas hosting a number of nautical events that are worth checking out, including the 'Round the Island' **yacht race** in April, the Keelboat Week Regatta in September and the Bayshore Marina Treasure Hunt in spring.

It's about a two-hour drive from Johannesburg and there are plenty of places to stay and eat in towns like **VaalMarina** in Gauteng, and Deneysville, Villiers and Franfort across the border in Free State.

Central Pretoria

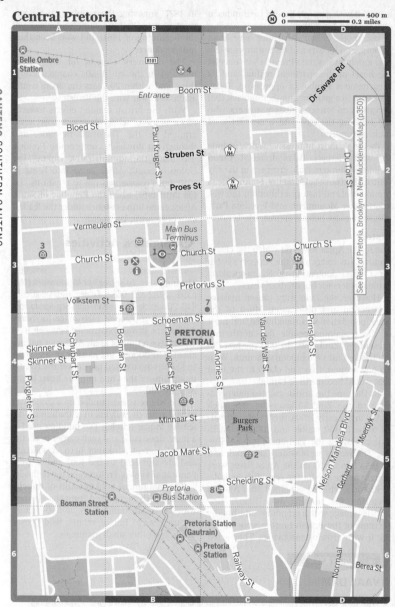

Church Square   SQUARE

At the heart of Pretoria, imposing public buildings surround **Church Square** (Map p346). These include the **Palace of Justice**, where the Rivonia Trial that sentenced Nelson Mandela to life imprisonment was held, on the northern side; the **OuRaadsaal (Old Government) building** on the southern side; the **Old Capitol Theatre** in the north-western corner; **First National Bank** in the northeast; the **Old Nederlandsche Bank building**, which adjoins Café Riche and

Central Pretoria

houses the tourist information centre; and the **main post office** on the western side. Look for the **clock**, surrounded by nude figures by Anton van Wouw, above the Church Sq entrance to the post office.

Old Lion (Paul Kruger) takes pride of place in the centre, surveying his miniature kingdom.

Melrose House   HISTORIC BUILDING
In 1886 a splendid mansion was built for George Heys opposite Burgers Park. Today **Melrose House** (Map p346; ☑012-322 2805; 275 Jacob Maré St; adult/child R9/6, guided tour R90; ☺10am-5pm Tue-Sun) is a national monument, and an interesting blend of English Victorian and Cape Dutch styles.

During the 1899–1902 Anglo-Boer War, Lords Roberts and Kitchener (both British commanders) lived here. On 31 May 1902 the Treaty of Vereeniging, which marked the end of the war, was signed in the dining room. Highlights of the house include a grand billiard room with a vibrant stained-glass smoking nook and a conservatory containing a collection of political cartoons from the Anglo-Boer War.

Pretoria National Zoological Gardens   ZOO
(Map p346; ☑012-328 3265; cnr Paul Kruger & Boom Sts; adult/child R45/30; ☺8.30am-5.30pm) There's a reptile park and an aquarium here, as well as a vast collection of exotic trees and

plenty of picnic spots. The highlight, though, is the **cable car** (adult/child R7/5), which runs up to the top of a hill that overlooks the city. It's about 1km out of the city centre.

Heroes' Acre Cemetery   CEMETERY
Around 1.5km west of Church Sq you'll find this **cemetery** (Map p356; Church St; ☺8am-6pm), the burial place of a number of historical figures including Andries Pretorius, Paul Kruger and Hendrik Verwoerd. Henry H 'Breaker' Morant, the Australian Boer War antihero executed by the British for war crimes, is also buried here – look for the low sign pointing to the gravestone from one of the north–south avenues. If you miss the sign, you'll never find it.

To get here by bus, take the West Park 2 or Danville service from Church Sq.

Union Buildings   NOTABLE BUILDINGS
(Map p350) These sweeping sandstone buildings are the headquarters of government and home to the presidential offices. The gardens are often used for public celebrations, and Mandela's inauguration took place here back in 1994. Statues of a few former prime ministers inhabit the grounds, including an impressive General Louis Botha on horseback. There's also a WWI memorial here, and a memorial to the South African police.

The buildings, designed by Sir Herbert Baker, are about a 2km walk from the city centre. There are no tours here, and the buildings themselves aren't open to the public but the grounds are open seven days a week.

☞ Tours

Footprints in Africa   ADVENTURE TOURS
(Map p350; ☑083 302 1976; www.footprintsinafrica.com) Located at Pretoria Backpackers, offering day tours of Jo'burg and Pretoria, Sun City, Lion Park and other local attractions as well as tours further afield such as Kruger, Botswana and Mozambique.

Siyazakha Travel & Tours   PRETORIA & GAUTENG TOURS
(Map p346; ☑012-322 5491; www.siyazakha.net; office ste 2014, 20th fl, SaluBldg, 316 Andries St) Takes tours around Pretoria and Gauteng, including the Cullinan Diamond Mine and the De Wildt Cheetah Research Centre. It also offers a day tour into Mamelodi township.

Mo Africa   ADVENTURE TOURS
(Map p356; ☑012-322 5491; www.moafricatours.com) A fun and enthusiastic Jo'burg-based

FREEDOM PARK

The remarkable memorial at **Freedom Park** (Map p356; ☎012-470 7400, 361 0021; www.freedompark.co.za; Koch St, Salvokop; guided tours per person R45; ☺8am-4.30pm, tours 9am, noon & 3pm) adopts an integrated approach to South Africa's war history and is a place of architectural imagination and collective healing. Located across the *kopjie* (rocky hill) from the austere Voortrekker Monument, Freedom Park is a legacy of the Mandela regime and honours all fallen South Africans in all major conflicts. Highlights include the Isivivane Garden of Remembrance; Sikhimbuto, the wall of inscribed names of fallen heroes; and Mveledzo, a spiral path that cuts into the natural landscape and encourages a contemplative stroll. There's also a politically charged public gallery, a state-of-the-art convention centre and an academic archive.

outfit with a creative array of tour options. It uses 1322 Backpackers as an agent and comes highly recommended.

✖ Festivals & Events

Oppikoppi Music Festival　　　　MUSIC
(www.oppikoppi.co.za) A Woodstock-type bash where local and international rock bands congregate in a celebration of peace, love and music. It's staged once or twice a year – visit the website for the latest.

Pretoria Show　　　　　　　　　SHOW
This immensely popular event is held during the third week of August, at the showgrounds.

🛏 Sleeping

CITY CENTRE

TOP CHOICE / Manhattan Hotel　　　HOTEL $$
(Map p346; ☎012-392 0000; www.manhattanhotel.co.za; 247 Scheiding St, City Centre; s/d R920/1070; P✳🏊🛜) A thorough renovation has lifted this mid-level city hotel into a whole new category. Five-star service, complimentary wi-fi and shuttles to the Pretoria and Hatfield Gautrain stations, extensive dining options and well-appointed rooms. The area is not ideal for an evening amble, but the in-room amenities more than compensate.

That's It　　　　　　　GUESTHOUSE $$
(Map p350; ☎012-344 3404; www.thatsit.co.za; 5 Brecher St, Clydesdale; s/d incl breakfast R420/600; P✳@🏊) Professionally run and competitively priced, That's It makes good use of the lush garden and wraparound verandah. The plain-ish rooms face out towards a sofa-filled *lapa* and the owners are quick to attend to guest needs. There's also a family unit in the garden that sleeps four.

ARCADIA, HATFIELD & BROOKLYN

TOP CHOICE / Crane's Nest Guesthouse　　　GUESTHOUSE $$
(Map p350; ☎012-460 7223; www.cranesnest.co.za; 212 Boshoff St, New Muckleneuk; s/d R630/1000; P✳@🏊) The Crane (and her two nearby sister properties) is our favourite place to stay in Pretoria, with easy access to the bird sanctuary across the road. The large white house is modern and stylish, with a full-time reception area and hotelier touches like minibars and wine lists. An afternoon on your room's small terrace overlooking the gorgeous garden is an afternoon well spent.

1322 Backpackers International　　　BACKPACKERS $
(Map p356; ☎012-362 3905; www.1322backpackers.com; 1322 Arcadia St, Hatfield; dm/s/d without bathroom from R110/215/295, d R385; P@🏊) This is our favourite hostel for miles around, where young and old adventurous travellers congregate around a huge backyard pool and a buzzing little anteroom bar. You can stay in neat, clean dorms, or cosy, converted wood and brick sheds at the bottom of the garden (very warm in winter!). Tours are run by Mo Africa.

Hotel 224　　　　　　　　　HOTEL $$
(Map p350; ☎012-440 5281; www.hotel224.com; cnr Schoeman & Leyds Sts, Arcadia; s/d R345/420; P✳) A smart, serviceable option if you need to be close to the city, and a good choice if you tire of the guesthouse banter.

Brooklyn Guesthouses　　　GUESTHOUSE $$
(Map p350; ☎012-362 1728; www.brooklynguesthouses.co.za; 128 Murray St, Brooklyn; s R495-790, d R700-990; P✳@🏊) This is a magical place to stay thanks to the dedication of proprietor Yolande Nel. Now expanded to six resi-

dences, the 'urban village' of 30-odd en-suite rooms draws savvy conference-goers and travellers in search of respite. The gardens and swimming pool are immaculately presented.

Village in Hatfield
GUESTHOUSE $$

(Map p356; ☎012-362 5370; www.hatfieldvillage.com; 324 Glyn St, Hatfield; s/d from R350/650; [P][@][≋]) On the corner of Arcadia St is this delightful blue and orange house that offers good-value and well-presented private rooms and helpful service. The small kitchen area is more farmhouse than inner-city pad. There's a swimming pool and a shaded courtyard.

B' Guest House
GUESTHOUSE $$

(Map p350; ☎012-344 0524; www.bguesthouse.co.za; 751 Park St, Arcadia; s/d incl breakfast R675/850; [P][@][❋]) The pick of the mid-rangers has a smashing pool and surrounding gardens that can be viewed from private patios or through the foyer's exquisite glass doors. The cuisine comes highly recommended, and there's a wine cellar and whisky lounge that add a certain old-world charm.

Courtyard Arcadia Hotel
HOTEL $$

(Map p350; ☎012-342 4940; www.citylodge.co.za; cnr Park & Hill Sts, Arcadia; s/d R920/1030; [P][❋][@]) At the upper end of the City Lodge chain spectrum is this Cape Dutch manor house in the heart of the embassy district. The rooms are a little pedestrian for the grandeur of the setting, but the service is assured and the evening happy hours are a nice touch.

Court Classique
LUXURY HOTEL $$$

(Map p350; ☎012-344 4420; www.courtclassique.co.za; cnr Schoeman & Beckett Sts, Arcadia; r from 1870; [P][❋][@][☏]) The CC is a mainstay of the regional tourism awards, and rightly so. All rooms are, in fact, suites, which are suitable for families and business folk alike. The kitchenettes – hidden behind double doors – open up the living area. The pool is long enough to cut morning laps or float away a hot afternoon. Your evening is settled, as the chef prepares world-class cuisine.

Protea Hotel Hatfield
HOTEL $$

(Map p350; ☎012-364 0300; www.citylodge.co.za; 1141 Burnett St, Hatfield; s/d R675/800; [❋][@]) If you're after stumbling access to Hatfield's shops and bars, then this is the only place to consider. Luckily it's pretty good, too. The tall, modern building has sparkling three-star hotel rooms, a busy reception and decent-sized bathrooms.

Khayalethu Guest House
GUESTHOUSE $$

(Map p356; ☎012-362 5403; www.ghk.co.za; 1322 Arcadia St, Hatfield; s/d R400/600; [P][@][❋]) Colourful and quirky, Khayalethu is a fine addition to the quality Hatfield budget scene. The bedrooms are small but immaculate. Local curios and kitsch adorn the kitchen walls, while the swimming pool is a little beauty.

Eating

There are plenty of good places to eat in Pretoria and prices are a little lower than Jo'burg's. You'll find the best places in Hatfield, Brooklyn and New Muckleneuk.

PRETORIA'S MANY MUSEUMS

Pretoria has a number of museums that can be visited in a day:

Paul Kruger House Museum (Map p346; ☎012-326 9172; 60 Church St; adult/child R18/10; ◷8am-4.30pm Mon-Fri) Interesting re-creation of the former President of the Boer Republic's residence.

Transvaal Museum (Map p346; ☎012-322 7632; Paul Kruger St; admission R20; ◷8am-4pm Mon-Sun) Essentially a natural history museum.

South African Police Museum (Map p346; ☎021-353 6770; cnr Pretorius & Volkstem Sts; adult/child R10/6; ◷9am-5pm Mon-Sat, 11am-5pm Sun) Fascinating, sometimes gory, criminal history.

National Cultural History Museum (Map p346; ☎012-324 6082; cnr Visagie & Schubert Sts; adult/child R20/12; ◷8am-4pm)

Pretoria Art Museum (Map p350; ☎021-353 6770; cnr Pretorius & Volkstem Sts; adult/child R10/6; ◷9am-5pm Mon-Sat, 11am-5pm Sun) Small collection of mostly South African art.

Rest of Pretoria, Brooklyn & New Muckleneuk

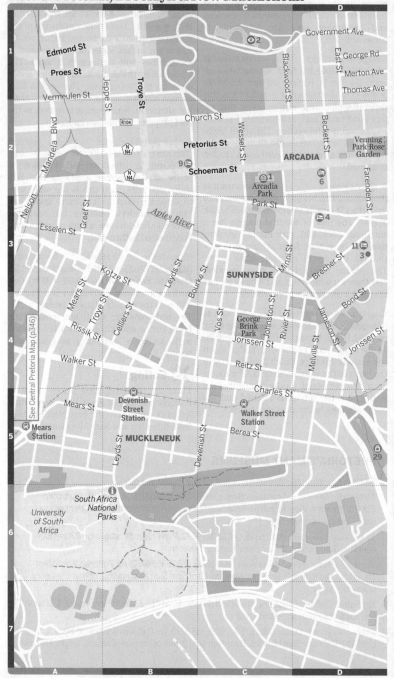

Edmond St

Proes St

Vermeulen St

Jeppe St

Troye St

R104

Church St

N4

Pretorius St

N4

9

Schoeman St

Wessels St

ARCADIA

Beckett St

Government Ave

East St

George Rd

Merton Ave

Thomas Ave

Blackwood St

Venning
Park Rose
Garden

6

1
Arcadia
Park

Park St

Mandela Blvd

Nelson

Esselen St

Greef St

Apies River

4

Farenden St

Minni St

Brecher St

11
3

SUNNYSIDE

See Central Pretoria Map (p346)

Mears St

Troye St

Kotze St

Leyds St

Bourke St

Vos St

Johnston St

Rivier St

Bond St

Rissik St

Celliers St

George
Brink
Park

Jorissen St

Melville St

Jameson St

Jorissen St

Walker St

Reitz St

Charles St

Mears St

Devenish
Street
Station

Walker Street
Station

Berea St

Mears
Station

Leyds St

MUCKLENEUK

Devenish St

29

South Africa
National
Parks

University
of South
Africa

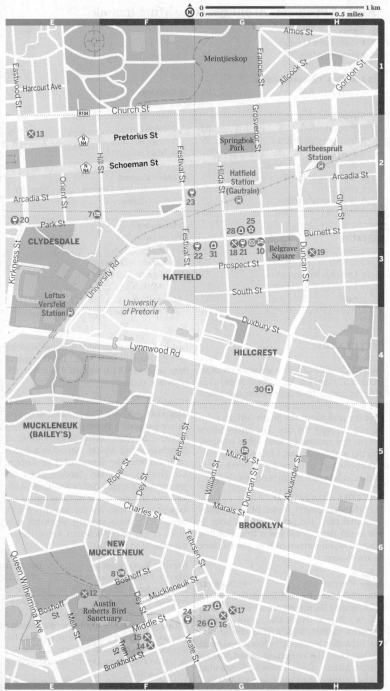

Rest of Pretoria, Brooklyn New Muckleneuk

CITY CENTRE

Café Riche   PUB $

(Map p346; ☎012-328 3173; www.caferiche.co.za; 2 Church St; mains R35-70; ⊙6am-midnight) This historic, early 20th-century European bistro in the heart of Church Sq is the ideal place to sip beer and watch the South African capital roll through the day. The street tables are quickly nabbed by local office workers, tourists and politicians, while inside the atmospheric bar, unhurried staff serve sandwiches, salads and cheap bistro meals.

ARCADIA & HATFIELD

Hatfield and Arcadia are full of restaurants, cafes and bars, and are safe at any hour. If you're out for a drink and a feed, bustling Hatfield Sq on Burnett St is as good a place as any to start.

TOP CHOICE **Pappas**   RESTAURANT $$

(Map p350; ☎012-362 2224; Duncan Yard, cnr Duncan & Prospect Sts, Hatfield; mains R60-95; ⊙8am-late; ❄) Pappas is located inside a mini antiques market, with a cool on-site pub and bookshop providing welcome post-meal distractions. The restaurant serves various South African faves, including steaming *potjiekos* (meat and vegetables cooked in a cast-iron pot over an open fire), and doubles as a low-key brunch joint. Try the parma ham omelette (R49) washed down with the city's best coffee.

Hombaz   AFRICAN $$

(Map p350; ☎012-342 7753; Eastwood Village Centre, cnr Eastwood & Pretorius Sts, Arcadia; mains R45-90; ⊙breakfast, lunch & dinner) This small franchise serves African staples in a family environment. The slogan of 'Live Longer, Eat Healthy' is a tad dubious given the prevalence of meaty dishes and fried sides; however, the vegetarian menu is one of the longest in the city. Try the boiled rice with beans (R70), the dodo with vegetable stew (R60) or any of the delicious soups, including oxtail and fish (R45).

Harrie's Pannekoek Huis   PANCAKES $

(Harry's Pancake House; Map p350; ☎012-342 3613; Eastwood Village Centre, cnr Eastwood & Pretorius Sts, Arcadia; mains R30-75; ⊙breakfast, lunch & dinner) Harry's is equally adept at curing hangovers or feeding a fussy family's hunger. The breakfast is decent, too, and the service is friendly and efficient. It's located in Eastwood Village Centre, next to a popular curios store.

Café 41
MEDITERRANEAN **$$**

(Map p350; ✒012-342 8914; Eastwood Village, cnr Eastwood & Pretoria Sts, Arcadia; mains R50-110; ☺breakfast, lunch & dinner) A huge menu and a plethora of seating options – go for the outdoor deck – make this one of Pretoria's more enjoyable lunch spots. The pasta dishes and sandwiches are good deals, as are the meze platters.

News Café
CAFE **$$**

(Map p350; ✒012-362 7190; Hatfield Sq, Burnett St, Hatfield; mains R50-100; ☺8am-late; ▣) The pick of the Burnett St coffee houses is this popular chain cafe, which does dependable breakfast and burgers. The TV screens, fast wi-fi and laissez-faire feel make this a hit with the student population.

BROOKLYN & NEW MUCKLENEUK
The area around Middle and Fehrsen Sts has some good restaurants, amid the shopping mall staples.

TOP CHOICE Kream
CONTEMPORARY **$$**

(Map p350; ✒012-346 4642; 570 Fehrsen St, Brooklyn Bridge; mains R80-160; ☺noon-late Mon-Sat, lunch Sun; ▣) A bold concept in a conservative city, Kream, in many ways, *is* the crop. The uber-trendy menu features exotic starters and the usual grilled suspects for main course. Finish the night with the brown pudding with a dash of the long whisky list.

Blue Crane
SOUTH AFRICAN **$**

(Map p350; ✒012-460 7615; Melk St, New Muckleneuk; mains R40-80; ☺lunch & dinner; ▣) As part of the Austin Roberts Bird Sanctuary, Blue Crane is famed among ornithologists worldwide (and anyone else who enjoys a Castle at sunset). The pretty blue bird is not the only national emblem on display; the menu is a bastion of Afrikaner favourites. The entrance to the restaurant is off Melk St, which is a right turn off Middle St as you head west.

Geet
INDIAN **$$**

(Map p350; ✒012-460 3199; 541 Fehrsen St, Brooklyn; mains R90; ☺11.30am-10.30pm; ▣) Gita Jivan has created a superlative subcontinental restaurant from scratch, fusing Indian flavours with European presentation. The huge menu emphasises North Indian delights, and vegetarians can feast. The whisky lounge is a treat.

Lotus Thai
THAI **$$**

(Map p350; ✒012-991 5406; 46-47 Glen Village North, cnr Hans Strydom & Olympus Drs, Brooklyn; mains R60-90; ☺11am-10pm Mon-Sun; ▣) All the pads and the tom yums are well handled, but it's the nourishing curries that steal the show (oh, and there's sushi if you feel like travelling 'northeast'). Bamboo uprights, rainbow umbrellas, hung silks and a caged bird help to heighten the exotic flavour.

Cynthia's Indigo Moon
BISTRO **$$**

(Map p350; ✒012-346 8926; 283 Dey St, Brooklyn; mains R70-155; ☺lunch & dinner; ▣) An effortless familiarity is achieved at Cynthia's, with nods to Paris and New York. Witty repartee bubbles over copious bottles of fine wine. Steaks are consumed en masse in dimly lit corner tables. Plans are hatched and foiled. The chicken couscous salad (R50) is a hit.

Cassidy's Restaurant
PORTUGUESE, SEAFOOD **$$**

(Map p350; cnr Dey & Bronkhorst Sts, Brooklyn; mains R80-130; ☺breakfast, lunch & dinner; ▣) Formerly an Adega franchise, the same owners have gone solo with this venture. The menu is mostly Portuguese-flavoured, with special attention paid to prawns.

🍷 Drinking

Hatfield is the best place for a night out with bars, restaurants and clubs catering for all types. Hatfield Sq is a university student stronghold after dark.

Stone Lion
BAR

(Map p350; ✒012-362 0100; 1075 Burnett St, Hatfield) The former Cool Runnings crew may be hard on the lamb, but the Rasta legacy lives on at Stone Lion. Stiff rum cocktails in a faux-Jamaican beach bar are good fun any day of the week. Keep your eye on the sparrow, man!

Herr Gunther's
GERMAN BAR

(Map p350; ✒012-362 6975; Hatfield Sq, Burnett St, Hatfield) The recipe is simple: slosh a gigantic mug of beer into your reddening face, choke on a sweaty sausage fest, sledge the cheesy DJ. Repeat nightly.

Tings an' Times
BAR

(Map p350; ✒012-430 3176; 1065 Arcadia St) This bohemian bar attracts an eclectic crowd to chill out to a reggae soundtrack, punctuated by regular live performances. Late on weekend nights it pulls in a crowd of up-for-it students and dancing goes on till the small hours. If you get the munchies, the speciality is pitas (R28 to R50), which come toasted with toppings or stuffed with all kinds of tasty treats.

TriBeCa Lounge
COCKTAIL BAR

(Map p350; ☎012-460 3068; Brooklyn Sq, Veale St, Brooklyn) Laid-back and stylish, this trendy cafe is the perfect place to chill out with a latte and browse the magazines for a few hours, or join the beautiful people in sipping exquisite cocktails on weekend nights.

Eastwood's
PUB

(Map p350; ☎012-344 0243; cnr Eastwood & Park Sts, Arcadia; ◷10am-late) This hugely popular pub is often packed, especially at lunchtime and after work hours. There's a large outdoor deck, and banquette seating and a big bar inside. It has won the 'best pub in Pretoria' award several times and has good-value steak-and-beer deals, such as a 500g T-bone and a Castle beer for R49.

☆ Entertainment

Cinemas

There are several large cinema complexes in Pretoria. Call Ster-Kinekor (☎central bookings 082 16789; www.sterkinekor.com) for listings and bookings. The *Pretoria News* lists screenings daily.

Head to Brooklyn Mall Cinemas (Map p350; ☎0860 300 222; tickets R38; Brooklyn Mall, Fehrson St, Brooklyn); Menlyn Park Drive-In (Map p356; ☎012-348 8766; Menlyn Park Shopping Centre); and Imax Theatre (Map p356; ☎012-368 1168; Menlyn Park Shopping Centre).

Live Music & Nightclubs

Pretoria is home to a large student population that's more into hard drinking than quality live music. Check the *Pretoria News* for listings. If there's nothing you fancy, ask at your accommodation, or head to Burnett St in Hatfield and join the nearest queue.

The surrounding townships, especially Mamelodi and Atteridgeville, have plenty of shebeens; these are best visited with a local resident or as part of a tour. Siyazakha Tours & Travel (p347) organises tours of Mamelodi.

Theatre

Most shows can be booked through Computicket (Map p350; ☎in Johannesburg 011-915 8000; www.computicket.com; Hatfield Plaza, Burnett St; ◷8.30am-4.30pm Mon-Sat).

State Theatre
THEATRE

(Map p346; ☎012-392 4027; www.statetheatre .co.za; cnr Prinsloo & Church Sts) Designed by Hans and Roelf Botha, this theatre complex hosts productions (including opera, music, ballet and theatre) in its five theatres: the Arena, Studio, Opera, Drama and Momentum.

Barnyard Theatre
THEATRE

(Map p356; ☎012-368 1555; top fl, Menlyn Park Shopping Centre) Pretoria's Barnyard branch is out at Menlyn Park Shopping Centre; it stages plays, musicals and live-music acts.

🛍 Shopping

Apart from the Brooklyn Mall (Map p350), Design Square (Map p350) and Menlyn Park (Map p356) centres, where you'll find all the usual air-conditioned chain stores, Pretoria is best known for its markets.

Boeremark
FARMERS MARKET

(Map p356; Pioneer Park; ◷6-9am Sat) Held by the Pioneer Park Museum in Silverton, this market is full of stalls selling all kinds of organic food, from cheeses to cakes to preserves. Come early because it's all sold out by 9am.

Hatfield Flea Market
FLEA MARKET

(Map p350; ☎012-362 5941; Hatfield Plaza car park, Burnett St, Hatfield; ◷9.30am-5.30pm Sun) It peddles the usual flea-market paraphernalia, and has some cheap African curios.

Magnolia Dell Moonlight Market
CRAFT

(Map p350; ☎012-308 8820; Magnolia Dell, Queen Wilhelmina Ave, New Muckleneuk; ◷5.30-9.30pm last Fri of month) This is an excellent event and is the place to pick up local crafts.

For decent-quality African curios, you can head just over the border into North-West Province for the Welwitischia Country Market at Hartbeespoort Dam. See the boxed text, p431, for details.

Bookshops

Most of the malls have branches of Exclusive Books and CNA. Also check out Owl Books (Map p350; ☎012-362 4481; 529 Duncan St, Hatfield; ◷9am-5pm Mon-Sat) and Protea Book House (Map p350; ☎012-362 5683; 1067 Burnett St, Hatfield; ◷9am-4.30pm Mon-Fri, to noon Sat).

❶ Information

Emergency
Fire (☎10111)

Metro Emergency Rescue Service (☎10177)

Police (☎10111) There are police stations on Railway St and on the corner of Leyds and Esselen Sts.

Internet Access

Most hostels and hotels offer internet facilities, but cheaper alternatives are also available.

4 in love Internet Café (◷9am-7pm Mon-Fri, to 6pm Sat, 10am-5pm Sun)

Videorama (☑012-342 5878; The Fields, Burnett St; per 30min R20)

Medical Services

Hatfield Clinic (☑012-362 7180; 454 Hilda St) A well-known suburban clinic.

Pretoria Academic Hospital (☑011-354 1000; Dr Savage Rd) The place to head in a medical emergency.

Money

There are banks with ATMs and change facilities across town.

ABSA (Hilda St)

American Express (☑012-346 2599; Brooklyn Mall; ☺9am-5pm)

Nedbank (cnr Burnett & Festival Sts) Next to Hatfield Galleries.

Photography

Kodak Express (☑012-362 0678; cnr Burnett & Festival Sts; ☺8am-6pm Mon-Fri, to 1pm Sat) Offers a one-hour developing service and full digital studio.

Post

Hatfield post office (Hatfield Sq; ☺8am-4.30pm Mon-Fri, to noon Sat) The most commonly used post office.

Main post office (cnr Church St & Church Sq; ☺8am-4.30pm Mon-Fri, to noon Sat) In a historic building on the main square.

Tourist Information

South African National Parks (☑012-428 9111; www.sanparks.org; 643 Leyds St, New Muckleneuk; ☺offices 7.45am-3.45pm Mon-Fri, 8am-12.15pm Sat, call centre 7.30am-5pm Mon-Fri, 8am-2pm Sat) Your best bet for all wildlife-reserve bookings and enquiries. You can also purchase a Wild Card (see p391) here.

Tourist Information Centre (☑012-358 1430; www.tshwane.gov.za; Old Nederlandsche Bank Bldg, Church Sq; ☺7.30am-4pm Mon-Fri) Fairly unhelpful for the common traveller; better off asking your hotel or locals for advice.

Travel Agencies

STA Travel (☑012-342 5292; 1102 Hilda St, Hatfield; ☺9am-5pm Mon-Fri, to noon Sat)

Student Flights (☑012-460 9889; Brooklyn Mall; ☺9am-5pm Mon-Fri, to noon Sat)

ⓘ Getting There & Away

Air

OR Tambo International Airport (Ortia) is South Africa's international hub, accepting flights from across the globe. See p591 for details of airlines and flight options, and p356 for information on getting into town from Ortia.

Bus

Most national and international bus services commence in Pretoria before picking up in Jo'burg, unless the general direction is north. The **Pretoria Bus Station** (Railway St) is next to Pretoria's train station. You will also find the major companies' booking and information offices here, as well as a good cafe and an ATM.

Most **Translux** (☑0861 589 282; www.trans lux.co.za), **City to City** (☑0861 589 282; www .translux.co.za), **Intercape** (☑0861 287 287; www.intercape.co.za), **Greyhound** (☑012-323 1154; www.greyhound.co.za) and **SA Roadlink** (☑012-323 5105; www.saroadlink.co.za) services running from Jo'burg to Durban, the South Coast and Cape Town originate in Pretoria. Services running north up the N1 also stop here; see p335 for full details of these services.

Translux, Greyhound and Intercape fares from Pretoria are identical to those from Jo'burg, regardless of the one-hour difference in time. If you only want to go between the two cities, it will cost about R60.

Baz Bus (☑in Cape Town 021-439 2323; www .bazbus.com) will pick up and drop off at Pretoria hostels.

Car

Local car-rental agencies can offer good deals. Many larger local and international companies are represented in Pretoria; see p600 for details.

If you're staying for a long time, it might be worth your while to check out the weekly *Junk Mail* newspaper or monthly *Auto Trader* magazine for secondhand car sales.

Minibus Taxis

Minibus taxis go from the main terminal by the train station and travel to a host of destinations including Jo'burg (R45, one hour), but this is not the place to be wandering around with lots of luggage or after dark. See p604 for more information regarding minibus taxi travel.

Train

The historic Pretoria train station is an attractive location to commence or complete a journey. The new **Gautrain** (☑0800 4288 7246 www.gautrain. co.za) service offers regular high-speed connections with Hatfield, Johannesburg and the airport.

For longer distances, **Shosholoza Meyl** (☑0860 008 888; www.shoholoza meyl.co.za) trains running through Pretoria are the *Trans Karoo* (daily from Pretoria to Cape Town) and the *Komati* (daily from Jo'burg to Komatipoort via Nelspruit). The *Bosvelder* runs north via Polokwane (Pietersburg) to Musina, near the Zimbabwe border. The luxury *Blue Train*, which links Pretoria, Jo'burg and Cape Town originates here (see boxed text, p606, for details of named train services).

Pretoria train station is about a 20-minute walk from the city centre. Buses run along Paul Kruger St to Church Sq, where you'll find the main local bus terminal.

Metro

Because of a high incidence of crime, we don't recommend travelling between Pretoria and Jo'burg by Metro. For more info about the Gautrain, see boxed text, p355.

Getting Around

To/From the Airport

If you call ahead, most hostels, and many hotels, offer free pick-up.

Get You There Transfers (012-346 3175; www.getyoutheretransfers.co.za) operates shuttle buses between Ortia and Pretoria. They can pick you up from the airport and deposit you in Pretoria for about R400 (the same price as a taxi).

Bus & Minibus Taxi

There's an extensive network of local buses. A booklet of timetables and route maps is available from the enquiry office in the **main bus terminus** (012-308 0839; Church Sq) or from pharmacies. Fares range from R5 to R10, depending on the distance. Handy services include buses 5 and 8, which run between Church Sq and Brooklyn via Burnett St in Hatfield.

Minibus taxis run pretty much everywhere and the standard fare is about R5.

Taxi

There are taxi ranks on the corner of Church and Van der Walt Sts, and on the corner of Pretorius and Paul Kruger Sts. Or you can get a metered taxi from **Rixi Taxis** (012-362 6262; per km around R10).

AROUND PRETORIA

Think of Gauteng and you think of big cities, but there is some beautiful countryside out there, as well as a few interesting museums and other attractions.

Around Pretoria

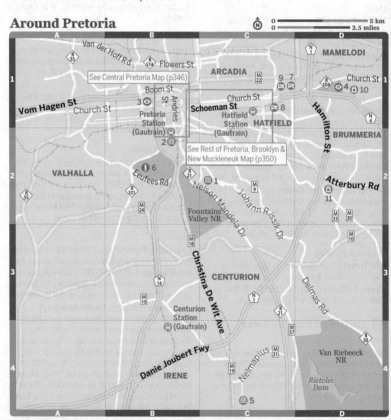

Smuts' House Museum

Scholar, Boer general, politician and international statesman, JC Smuts was instrumental in creating the Union of South Africa, and served as prime minister from 1919 to 1924 and from 1939 to 1948.

Once known as Doornkloof, Smut's home for over 40 years has been turned into an interesting museum (☎012-667 1941; www .smutshouse.co.za; Nelmapius Rd, Irene; adult/child R10/5, picnic garden per car R5; ☼9.30am-4.30pm Mon-Fri, to 5pm Sat & Sun). If you're travelling to/from Pretoria by car, it's worth dropping in for a look. The wood-and-iron building was a British officers' mess at Middelburg, but Smuts bought it and re-erected it on his 1600-hectare property at Irene, 16km south of Pretoria. Surrounded by a wide verandah and shaded by trees, it has a family atmosphere and gives a vivid insight into Smuts' life.

There's no access by public transport. The house is signposted from both the N14 freeway (the R28) and the R21. The most direct route from Pretoria is along Louis Botha Ave to Irene.

Around Pretoria

Fort Klapperkop Military Museum

This fort (☎082 807 5278; Johann Rissik Dr; adult/child R10/5; ☼10am-3.30pm) was one of four built to defend Pretoria, although in the end it was never used for that purpose. Located 6km south of the city, it's one of the best-preserved forts in South Africa, and its museum tells the story of the country's military history from 1852 to the end of the 1899–1902 Anglo-Boer War. There are panoramic views across the city and the region.

National Botanical Garden

Around 9km east of the city centre, these gardens (☎012-843 5104; Cussonia Ave, Brummeria; adult/child R15/5; ☼6am-6pm) cover 77 hectares and are planted with indigenous flora from around the country. The 20,000-odd plant species are labelled and grouped according to their region of origin, so a visit is a must for keen botanists. Garden picnic concerts are held from May to September.

By car, head east along Church St (the R104) for about 8km, then turn right into Cussonia Rd; the gardens are on the left-hand side. Take the Meyerspark or Murrayfield bus from Church Sq.

Sammy Marks' Museum

This handsome Victorian mansion was built in 1884 for English industrial, mining and agricultural magnate Sammy Marks. Now it's a museum (☎012-803 6158; R104, Old Bronkhorstspruit Rd; adult/child R20/10; ☼9am-4pm Tue-Fri, 10am-4pm Sat & Sun). There are regular tours of the mansion, its green surrounds, outbuildings and a Victorian tea garden. To get to the museum, follow signposting off the R104, 20km east of Pretoria.

Cullinan Diamond Mine

After visiting Sammy Marks' Museum, head north to historic Cullinan, a pretty 100-year-old village full of quaint Herbert Baker architecture. The village is home to Cullinan Diamond Mine, one of the biggest and most productive diamond-bearing kimberlite pipes in the world. It has produced three of the largest diamonds ever found. You can don a tin hat and take a tour with **Premier Diamond Tours** (☑012-734 0081; www .diamondtourscullinan.co.za).

To get here, take the N4 east and the Hans Strijdom off-ramp, then turn left and follow the signs.

The aviation-themed **Cockpit Brewhouse** (☑012-734 0656; www.cockpitbrewhouse .co.za; 80 Oak Ave; mains R60-120; ☉noon-9pm Thu, 11am-9pm Fri & Sat, 11am-4pm Sun) serves deliciously hoppy pale ales and decent beer food, including a massive Ploughman's Platter (R85). It's in the middle of town.

Ann van Dyk Cheetah Centre

Just past Hartbeespoort, about 50km northwest of Pretoria, is the highly impressive **Ann van Dyk Cheetah Centre** (☑012-504 1921; www.dewildt.co.za; Farm 22, R513 Pretoria North Rd; tour only R220, cheetah run & guided tour R310; ☉tours 8.30am & 1.30pm Tue, Thu, Sat & Sun, cheetah runs Tue & Thu summer/winter 7/8am),

famous for its success in breeding rare and endangered animals.

Work began at the centre (formerly called De Wildt) in the 1960s, when the cheetah was regarded as highly endangered. The king cheetah, with its distinctive black pelt pattern, was successfully bred here in 1981; it was previously thought to be extinct.

As well as cheetahs, visitors can see animals such as wild dogs, brown hyenas, servals, caracals, honey badgers, meerkats, a few different antelope species and vultures.

You can tour in an open truck to see cheetahs of different age groups being fed. You can also go on a thrilling cheetah run, but only if you're fit! Bookings for all activities are essential and you should call at least a week in advance. Should you want to stay the night there's a simple nine-room **lodge** (s/d R1150/1600).

To get to the centre from Pretoria (via Hartbeespoort), take the R5131 northwest for 34km – the centre is on the left, about 500m off the main road.

Mpumalanga

Best Places to Eat

» Wild Fig Tree (p365)
» Mayfly Restaurant (p363)
» Summerfields (p370)
» Jock & Java (p374)
» Orange Restaurant (p374)

Best Places to Stay

» Artists' Café & Guest House (p364)
» Graskop Valley View Backpackers (p367)
» Idle & Wild (p370)
» Utopia (p373)
» River House Lodge (p375)

Why Go?

Mpumalanga is one of South Africa's smallest provinces and one of its most exciting. Visually it is a simply beautiful region with vistas of mountains, lush green valleys and a collection of cool climate towns. Its natural assets make it a prime target for outdoor enthusiasts, who head here to abseil down waterfalls, throw themselves off cliffs, negotiate rivers by raft, inner tube or canoe, and hike or bike numerous wilderness trails.

Mpumalanga's major draw though is the massive Blyde River Canyon, which carves its way spectacularly through the Drakensberg Escarpment. It is one of South Africa's iconic sights and on a clear day one of the many vantage points can leave you breathless.

And, of course, the province is tantalisingly close to Kruger's park gates, with an excellent selection of lodges and wilderness activities right on the mighty park's doorstep.

When to Go
Nelspruit

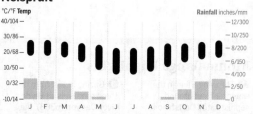

Jun–Aug The capital goes off during InniBos with artists and theatre groups packing venues

Sep–Dec Worth heading to the alpine town of Dullstroom to catch its Arts & Cultural Festival

Jan–Mar Head onto the escarpment to escape the steamy lowveld during summer

Mpumalanga Highlights

1 Throwing a line in the water for trout around sophisticated **Dullstroom** (p361) and enjoying the cool alpine climate.

2 Picking up fine African arts and crafts in **Graskop** (p367) before hurling yourself into a gorge on the Big Swing outside town.

3 Gazing in awe from the 'three rondavels' at **Blyde River Canyon** (p368), the world's third largest canyon.

4 Hitting the mountain bike trails around **Sabie** (p364), or simply taking in the misty mountain views.

5 Discovering the heritage of **Barberton** (p376), with a stroll around the province's most enjoyable town.

History

During the *difaqane* (forced migration) of the early 19th century, groups of Shangaan, Swazi and Ndebele entered the area, escaping turbulent times in Zululand.

Voortrekkers first arrived on the scene in the late 1830s and had established the Transvaal (the province's previous name) as a republic within 10 years. The Transvaal was the scene for the first Anglo-Boer War; the Boers were victorious, claiming back their territory and making Paul Kruger their first president. This independence lasted only a few years, until the end of the war, when the Transvaal (and the Orange Free State) was returned to British hands.

National Parks & Reserves

The southern part of Kruger National Park (p379) lies in Mpumalanga, and is by far the province's biggest name. Other conservation areas include the many private wildlife reserves on Kruger's southwestern edge (p392) and the Blyde River Canyon Nature Reserve (p368).

Language

Swati, Zulu and Ndebele are the main languages spoken in Mpumalanga, but it's easy to get by with English. In and around Nelspruit, you'll also hear a lot of Afrikaans.

❶ Getting There & Around

Mpumalanga Kruger International Airport (MKIA), about 28km northeast of Nelspruit, off Rte 40, has regular connections to major South African cities as well as a couple of regional services.

The Mpumalanga roads are good-quality tarmac (although ongoing roadworks mean long delays on some routes) and there are excellent connections between towns. Around the transport hub of Nelspruit, there are good bus and minibus services, but away from the main routes public transport is virtually nonexistent and to get around easily you'll certainly need a hire car.

A passenger train line cuts through the middle of the province, connecting Johannesburg (Jo'burg) with Komatipoort via Nelspruit.

For details on air, road and train connections to/from Jo'burg, see p375. For details on connections between Nelspruit and Kruger National Park, see p392. For information on crossing between Nelspruit and Swaziland and Mozambique, see p593 and p593, respectively.

DRAKENSBERG ESCARPMENT

Home to some of South Africa's most striking landscapes, the Drakensberg Escarpment was, until a couple of centuries ago, untamed rainforest roamed by elephants, buffalo and even lions. Today it's holidaying South Africans who wander the highlands, enjoying the beautiful landscape in their droves. The escarpment marks the point where the highveld plateau plunges down over 1000m, before spilling out onto the eastern lowveld, forming a dramatic knot of soaring cliffs, canyons, sweeping hillsides and cool valleys thick with pine trees – an apt backdrop for the myriad adventure activities that are on offer here.

Dullstroom

♪ 013 / POP 6000 / ELEVATION 2053M

This little oasis is all about good food, old-fashioned English pubs, piles of accommodation, fresh country air and fishing in the surrounding cool waters. When you arrive you would be forgiven for thinking you had taken a wrong turn and ended up in Canada. Encased with pine trees and lined with pretty clapboard buildings, Dullstroom is one of the coldest towns in the country. It's famous for one thing: trout, but there's lots more to do here, including hiking and horse riding outside town.

◉ Sights & Activities

Dullstroom Bird of Prey & Rehabilitation Centre   BIRDS OF PREY
(🖉072 378 8562; www.birdsofprey.co.za; adult/child R40/15; ⊙9am-4pm, flying displays at 10.30am & 2.30pm) Just outside the town, off the Rte 540, is this centre where you can learn all about the raptor species and the dangers that are facing them and even learn the art of falconry for a day. There are regular flying displays that involve peregrine falcons, kestrels, buzzards and black eagles among other birds.

Dullstroom Riding Centre   HORSE RIDING
(🖉082 442 9766; www.dullstroomhorseriding.co.za; 2hr countryside ride adult & child R200, town ride R450) This place offers horseback tours through the surrounding countryside or, for more experienced riders, through the town itself (including a tour of the local pubs!). It

Drakensberg Escarpment & Eastern Lowveld

is at the Owl & Oak Trading Post, 9km from Dullstroom on Rte 540 to Lydenburg.

Festivals & Events

Dullstroom Arts & Cultural Festival ARTS
Try catching this platform for showcasing local talent in mid-December. Expect photography, art, sculpture, music and food.

Sleeping & Eating

TOP CHOICE **Cherry Grove** VILLAS **$$**
(☎013-254 0421; www.cherry-grove.co.za; Cherry Grove Centre, Main Rd; s/d R500/970;❋) Next to the Duck & Trout, these luxury Mediterranean villas are stylishly constructed in stone and wood and have upstairs 'piazza-view' balconies. They've been intelligently built to capture the light and working fireplaces keep the suites warm and cosy on cold evenings.

Old Transvaal Inn INN **$**
(☎013-254 0222; Naledi St; r R175-300) Set in a beautiful old building, this inn is a decent cheapie option with basic rooms out the back. Rooms have low-slung roofs and tiny bathrooms, and are very rudimentary but clean and would do at a pinch. It's also home

to the town's best sweet shop, which sells homemade fudge, truffles and other treats.

Critchley Hackle   COTTAGES $$$
(☎0861 226 787; www.critchleyhackle.co.za; Teding van Berkhout St; s/d incl breakfast from R1250/1900; @☎) This is the best place to stay in town. Accommodation is in stone cottages dotted around grassy, flower-filled lawns. Rooms have vaulted ceilings, a sitting area, an open fireplace and a terrace overlooking a small lake. The great restaurant is glass-fronted and has views over the gardens. It's at the northeastern edge of town, signposted from the main road.

Duck & Trout   INN $
(☎013-254 0047; light meals from R25; ☺11am-10pm Sun-Thu, 10am-10pm Fri & Sat) A good place for a wood-fired pizza and a beer or two with the locals while the kids whoop it up in the playground. It also has accommodation out the back. Rooms (singles/doubles R230/360) have decent furnishings, space and, best of all, a front deck with country views.

Mayfly Restaurant   INTERNATIONAL $$
(Naledi St; mains R60-90) This classy setup specialises in pizzas, pastas and steak dishes (the plump, succulent mussels in a garlic and white-wine sauce are excellent) and has an extensive wine list. The cavernous interior with wood-burning heater and simple stylish furniture creates an intimate dining atmosphere.

Legendz Cafe   CAFE $
(Cherry Grove Shopping Centre; mains R35-45) A courtyard cafe serving decent coffee along with a range of beautifully presented breakfasts, and open sandwiches and salads for lunch. You're not exactly in Italy but they have made a effort to bring the Mediterranean to the 'piazza' here.

ⓘ Information

First National Bank At the main junction, with an ATM.

Video shop & internet cafe (Dullstroom Centre; internet access per min R1; ☺11am-6.30pm)

ⓘ Getting There & Away

Minibus taxis pass through Dullstroom on the Belfast and Lydenburg route, stopping along the main road, but the best way to get here is by car.

Waterval Boven
☎013 / POP 2500

Rock climbers, mountain bikers and other adrenalin junkies flock to this minute town, just off the N4, for serious adventure-sport action. The main facilitator in the area is **Roc 'n Rope Adventures** (☎013-257 0363; www.rocrope.com), which organises a range of climbing excursions around the area. In the past there have been incidents of muggings on the cliffs and trails surrounding the town, so enquire about this before you head off. Tell the tourist office or Roc 'n Rope if you plan to camp around here and try not to take too many valuables with you out on the trails.

Tourist information (☎013-257 0444; www.linx.co.za/waterval-boven; ☺8.30am-4pm Mon-Fri, 8.30am-1pm Sat) is on the left as you enter the town from the N4.

Horse riding is available at **Blaaubosch Kraal Horse Trails** (☎013-256 9081; www.bbktrails.co.za), which offers two-hour horse trips for R150. It's 8km from town on the road to Lydenburg.

The home-style **Shamrock Arms** (☎013 257 0888; www.shamrockarms.co.za; 68 Third Ave; s/d incl breakfast R560/890; ☺ dinner) serves large portions of country English food in a cosy old pub-restaurant and the hosts are the friendliest around. The Shamrock also has seven lovely rooms in four-star lodgings.

If you want to eat, sleep and breathe climbing, **Climbers' Lodge** (☎013-257 0363; www.rocrope.com; dm/d/chalet R80/170/550) is the place to do it. There are a couple of dorm rooms, four doubles, a self-catering kitchen, a sun deck and fully-equipped chalets. Half a day of climbing (with equipment and instruction included) costs R400 per person.

Minibus taxis to Nelspruit cost R40 (about two hours); you can pick one up on Third Ave.

Lydenburg
☎013 / POP 25,000

Lydenburg has wide streets, open spaces and the feel of history in its worn streets and landmark buildings. It makes a pleasant stopover on the way to Jo'burg or Kruger.

On a rainy day, **Lydenburg Museum** (Long Tom Pass Rd; admission free; ☺8am-4pm) is worth poking your nose into. It's located at the entrance to **Gustav Klingbiel Nature**

Reserve (admission R10; ◷8am-4pm Mon-Fri, 8am-5pm Sat & Sun), about 3km east of town along Rte 37. The reserve itself is prime bird-watching territory and also has zebras, impala and kudus.

It's worth paying the extra for a deluxe room at De Ark Guest House (☑013-235 1125; www.dearkguesthouse.co.za; 37 Kantoor St; luxury/deluxe r R770/945; ⌨), a four-star B&B housed in one of the town's oldest buildings. Each room drips with 19th-century touches. Backpacker rooms are available at Lodge Laske Nakke (☑013-235 2886; www.laskenakke. co.za; R540; r per person R90), along with self-catering units.

The minibus taxi stop is in the town centre on the corner of Voortrekker and Clerq Sts, with daily vehicles to Sabie (R35, one hour) and Belfast (R45, 1½ hours).

Sabie

☑013 / POP 12,000 / ELEVATION 1100M

Sabie's surroundings are lovely – the roads are lined with pine plantations, and green mountains hide waterfalls, streams and walking trails – and it makes an excellent base for a couple of days. Outdoorsy types can enjoy the heart-pumping opportunities – including rafting, canyoning (known as kloofing around these parts) and hiking – that abound in the area. The 2012 UCI World Mountain Bike Marathon Series kicked off in Sabie in early 2012.

◉ Sights & Activities

Waterfalls WATERFALLS
Waterfall fanatics will be in their element here – the area around Sabie positively gushes with falls (admission to each R5-10). They include Sabie Falls, just north of town on Rte 532 to Graskop; the 70m Bridal Veil Falls, northwest of Sabie, off Old Lydenburg Rd; the 68m Lone Creek Falls, also off Old Lydenburg Rd, and with wheelchair access

---

ALL THE SMALL TREES YOU SEE...

The plantation forest around Sabie is pine and eucalyptus – one of the largest artificial forests in the world. Decimated by fires five or six years ago, it will be around 25 years before the forests are fully recovered.

---

on the right-hand path; and the nearby Horseshoe Falls, about 5km southwest of Lone Creek Falls. The popular Mac-Mac Falls, about 12km north of Sabie, off Rte 532 to Graskop, take their name from the many Scots on the local mining register. About 3km southeast of the falls are the Mac-Mac Pools, where you can swim.

Cycle Junkies BICYCLE RENTAL
(☑013-764 1149; www.cyclejunkies.co.za) There are several excellent mountain-bike trails, ranging from 13km to 45km. This is the place to hire mountain bikes (three hours R60, full day R300) and ask about permits (R30).

Sabie Xtreme Adventures ADVENTURE
(☑013-764 2118; www.sabiextreme.co.za) If you're into adventure activities this outfit, based in the Sabie Backpackers Lodge, can organise kloofing, candlelight caving, rafting, tours of Blyde River Canyon, and more.

Komatiland Forestry Museum MUSEUM
(cnr Ford St & Tenth Ave; adult/child R5/2; ◷8am-4.30pm Mon-Fri, 8am-noon Sat) This museum has displays on local forests and the history of the South African timber industry. The museum has wheelchair access.

🛏 Sleeping

Artists' Café & Guest House TRAIN STATION ROOMS $
[TOP CHOICE] (☑078 876 9293; r per person R250) Wonderfully quirky place in Hendriksdal, about 15km south of Sabie along Rte 37. Accommodation is in old train station buildings that have been converted into rooms, retaining lots of the old signs and quirks. Our fave is the 'first class waiting room', which has a ginormous bathroom and comfy couch.

Sabie Townhouse B&B $$
(☑013-764 2292; www.sabietownhouse.co.za; Power St; s/d R425/800; ⌨) This is a pretty stone house, with a pool and terrace, and fabulous views over the hills. You will receive old-fashioned hospitality from an ageing Zimbabwe couple who fled the tragedy of their homeland many years ago. You'll get no wi-fi or fancy gadgets here but you will get space, simplicity and birdsong.

Country Kitchen PUB $$
(☑013-764 2091; Main St; s/d R400/600) At the back of this pub-restaurant are some pretty schmick rooms in a slightly soulless setting

Sabie

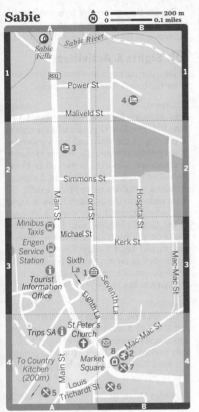

definite party atmosphere with nights full of drinking, bongo drumming and bonfires. It's about 1km down the old Lydenburg Rd, off Main St.

Lone Creek River Lodge   LODGE $$$
(☎013-764 2611; www.lonecreek.co.za; Old Lydenburg Rd; s/d R1075/1650, ste s/d R1325/2150; @❄☲) Luxurious rooms in the main house as well as individual suites right by the river, self-catering timber lodges and two freshwater pools. Rooms overlooking the river are recommended.

✕ Eating & Drinking

TOP CHOICE Wild Fig Tree   SOUTH AFRICAN $$
(☎013-764 2239; cnr Main & Louis Trichardt Sts; light meals R35-60, mains R90-120; ⊗breakfast, lunch & dinner) There's a meat-driven menu and a warm atmosphere here, with candles and African-print wall hangings. Try the SA meze for dinner, which includes ostrich medallions and crocodile kebabs. The ploughman's or trout platter makes a terrific lunch. With seating out on a breezy balcony, it's a very pleasant place to while away a Sabie afternoon.

Woodsman   GREEK $$
(☎013-764 2204; Main St; mains R60-100) Half pub, half restaurant, the Woodsman's fine offerings have a Greek twist with souvlaki, grilled calamari, mezedhes and other offerings mixed with the practicalities of its location: pan-fried trout and ostrich in red wine and oregon also feature. Most folk will find

around a conference room. Rooms are tastefully furnished and excellent value, and you can easily walk to The Wild Fig or Woodsman for meals. It's located a few doors up from Petena's Pancakes.

Sabie Backpackers Lodge   BACKPACKERS $
(☎013-764 2118; www.sabiextreme.co.za; Main St; campsites per person R70, dm R120, d without bathroom R260, d R300; @☲) It's a pretty rustic backpackers with a decent location in the town. Dorms are small and the double with ensuite is pokey but well furnished and clean. There are regular barbecues and parties, but there's plenty of space to chill out as well. Sabie Xtreme Adventures is based here. The lodge owners will pick you up from Nelspruit.

Billy Bongo Backpackers   BACKPACKERS $
(☎072 370 7219; www.billybongobackpackers.co.za; Old Lydenburg Rd; campsites per person R60, dm/s/d R90/100/200) This place has a

their spot, be it raucous beer drinking at the bar or fine dining by candlelight table on the balcony.

Petena's Pancakes PANCAKES $
(Main St; pancakes R40-55; ⊘9am-5pm) With a delicious selection of savoury and sweet pancakes we can't go past the icecream, choc sauce and nuts (scrummy). There are great views to drink in while you waffle it down. It's a few hundred metres down Main St heading south out of town

🛍 Shopping

Mphozeni Crafts ARTS & CRAFTS
(☎013-764 2074; thewoodsman.co.za; 94 Main St; ⊘8.30am-5.30pm) Lots of African arts and crafts and some quality textiles.

ℹ Information

Bookman's Corner (cnr Main & Mac-Mac Sts; ⊘9am-4.30pm Mon-Fri, 8.30am-4pm Sat, 8am-4.30pm Sun) Next to the Woodsman, sells second-hand books; the chat is free.

First National Bank (Market Sq) Has an ATM.

Tourist information office (☎082 736 8253; Main St; ⊘8am-5pm Mon-Fri, 8am-1pm Sat) Next to Engen petrol station. Very helpful; hours can be erratic.

Trips SA (☎013-764 1177; www.sabie.co.za; Main St) Information centre and booking agent for tours and accommodation.

Vodacom (Market Square, Main St; internet 15/60 mins R15/45; ⊘ 9am-5pm Mon-Fri, 9am-noon Sat) Internet access.

ℹ Getting There & Away

There are daily buses from Jo'burg to Nelspruit, from where you can get minibus taxis to Sabie (R30, one hour between Nelspruit and Sabie). Minibus taxis also run frequently to and from Hazyview (R30, one hour). Minibus taxis stop next to the Engen petrol station.

Pilgrim's Rest

☎013 / POP 600

Tiny little Pilgrim's Rest appears frozen in time – a perfectly preserved gold-rush town with wood and corrugated-iron houses lining a pretty, manicured main street. Tourists come here by the coachload and the town can feel swamped and a little Disney-fied during the height of the day. Best to come early in the morning, or even stay the night – when you'll be better able to soak up the ghosts of the past.

Beware the competitive ferociousness between the informal carpark attendants waving cars into parks on the side of the road.

👁 Sights & Activities

At the information centre you can buy a ticket for the town's four main museums.

Museums MUSEUM
(total admission R12; ⊘all 9am-12.45pm & 1.45-4pm). The **Printing Museum** tells the history of printing in the town and has a collection of old printing presses; the **House Museum** is a restored Victorian home full of black-and-white photos, old dolls and furniture, including a wooden carved commode in the main bedroom; the **Dresden Store** is a general store recreated as it would have been in the 1930s, complete with flying ceramic ducks on the wall; and classic-car enthusiasts should head for the **Central Garage Transport Museum**, which illustrates the development of transport in the town from the 1870s to the 1950s.

Alanglade MUSEUM
(☎013-768 1060; admission R20; ⊘tours 11am & 2pm Mon-Sun) A former mine-manager's residence at the northern edge of town, beautifully decked out in 1920s style with original artefacts. Tours need to be booked 30 minutes in advance.

Diggings Museum MUSEUM
(guided tours adult/child R12/6; tours 10am, 11am, 12pm, 2pm, 3pm) Just east of town along the Graskop road is the open-air Diggings Museum, where you can see how gold was panned. You need to visit on a tour, arranged through the information centre.

🛏 Sleeping & Eating

Royal Hotel HOTEL $$
(☎013-768 1100; www.royal-hotel.co.za; s/d incl breakfast from R550/800; ❄) An elegant, historical building at the centre of Uptown, it's definitely worth spending the night here if you can. Rooms have Victorian baths, brass beds and other period features. Most are not in the main building but scattered about in houses on the main street, many with porches and great views. The Church Bar, adjoining, is a good spot for a drink.

Pilgrim's Rest Caravan Park CARAVAN PARK $
(☎072 820 4033; tents R120, campsite adult child R60/35, guesthouse r per person R300; ❄) This

is a beautiful camping spot right alongside the Blyde River, with large grounds and barbecue facilities. There is also guesthouse accommodation here.

Stables Deli & Cafe　　　　CAFE **$**
(Uptown; meals R15-35; ⊘8.30am-5pm) Cute little place in Uptown with a corrugated tin roof and wooden tables and benches outside. It serves light meals, sandwiches, salads, savoury/sweet pancakes and good-value wines by the glass. Limited menu but food is well prepared.

ℹ Information

There's a helpful **Visitor information centre** (☑013-768 1060; Main St, Uptown; ⊘9am-12.45pm & 1.15-4.30pm) in town.

ℹ Getting There & Away

Sporadic minibus taxis run between Pilgrim's Rest and Graskop, but most traffic along this treacherous road is in private vehicles.

Graskop

☑013 / POP 2000 / ELEVATION 1450M

While it's a popular stop with the tour buses, little Graskop somehow seems to swallow them quite well, leaving plenty of room around town for everyone else. The compact town is one of the most appealing in the area, with a sunny disposition, sleepy backstreets and gently sloping hills in every direction you look. There are good guesthouses, restaurants and craft shops to keep visitors happy. On summer afternoons, res-

taurant terraces are full and there's a friendly buzz. It's also a useful base for exploring the Blyde River Canyon, and the nearby views over the edge of the Drakensberg Escarpment are magnificent.

◉ Sights & Activities

There's good hiking and mountain biking in the area. Trips SA or the tourist office can point you in the right direction, or you can hire bikes from Graskop Valley View Backpackers (R280 per day).

Big Swing　　　　CABLE GORGE SWING
(☑013-737 8191; single/tandem jump R320/R480, foefie slide only R70) One of the highest cable gorge swings in the world, it has a freefall of 68m (that's like falling 19 storeys in less than three seconds) into Graskop Gorge. You then swing like a pendulum across the width of the gorge from where you get an outstanding view. There's also a 135m highwire 'foefie slide' (zip line). It's 1km out of town on the Hazyview road. You can work up the courage with a drink at the lodge next door.

🛏 Sleeping

TOP CHOICE **Graskop Valley View Backpackers**　　　　BACKPACKERS **$**
(☑013-767 1112; www.yebo-afrika.nl; 47 de Lange St; campsites per person R70, dm R100, tw R240-290; ✴✴) This friendly Dutch-run backpackers has a variety of rooms in excellent condition, plus *rondavels* (round huts) and a self-catering flat. The owners can organise adventure tours and rent out mountain bikes for private use (R200 per day). Take the road to Sabie, turn left at the first four-way stop and take another left on de Lange St. Highly recommended.

MPUMALANGA GRASKOP

Graskop

Graskop

◎ 0 ▬▬ 100 m
Ⓝ 0 ▬▬ 0.05 miles

Graskop Hotel
HOTEL $$

(☑013-767 1244; www.graskophotel.co.za; cnr Hoof & Louis Trichardt Sts; s/d incl breakfast R550/800; ☎🗑) Rooms here are slick, stylish and individual, several featuring art and design by contemporary South African artists. Rooms out the back are little country cottages with doll-house-like furniture (but are extremely comfortable), an impression exemplified by the glass doors opening onto the lush garden at the rear.

Autumn Breath
B&B $$

(☑082 877 2811; www.autumnbreath.co.za; Louis Trichardt St; r per person incl breakfast R275 to R365) This quaint B&B has three modern rooms. Room no 1 is big, blue, huge and the best. Room no 2 with a balcony is also good. There's a restaurant downstairs, set in a lawn under cheerful yellow awnings, serving sandwiches, homemade pies and home-brewed ginger beer.

Le Gallerie
GUESTHOUSE $$

(☑013-767 1093; www.legallerie.co.za; cnr Louis Trichardt & Oorwinning Sts; s/d R630/1160; @) A luxury guesthouse and art gallery with three rooms, each with sumptuous furnishings and private access, this place gets good feedback from readers.

Blyde Chalets
COTTAGES $$

(☑013-767 1316; www.blydechalets.co.za; Louis Trichardt St; 2-/3-/4-person chalets R495/565/655; ❄☎) Simple self-catering cottages, each with a kitchen, lounge and braai (barbecue), in a central location.

✕ Eating

Canimambo
PORTUGUESE $$

(☑013-767 1868; cnr Hoof & Louis Trichardt Sts; dishes R70-120; ☺breakfast, lunch, dinner; 🗑) A Portuguese and Mozambican joint serving up spicy stews and grills as well as some excellent seafood dishes. Try the bean stew with chorizo or smoked chicken. Alternatively, Canimambo does some wonderful things with prawns.

God's Window Rest
SOUTH AFRICAN $$

(Pilgrim St; mains R60-110, light lunches R40-50; ☺9.15am-8.30pm) Serving light lunches and dinners that include pizzas, curries, grills and the odd vegie dish, the outside bench seating at GWR is a pleasant place to catch the breeze. If you're feeling brave try the biltong and blue cheese soup. Inside, the restaurant has an old-fashioned, country vibe.

Harrie's Pancakes
PANCAKES $

(Louis Trichardt St; pancakes R45-65; ☺8am-7pm) The chic white minimalist interior, full of modern art and quirky touches, is somewhat at odds with the cuisine. You won't find breakfast-style pancakes here, but mostly savoury and exotic fillings, as well as some sweet offerings. Its reputation perhaps outdoes what it delivers, but Harrie's Pancakes is a nice spot for a breakfast croissant and fresh brewed coffee in the morning.

🛍 Shopping

There are several good craft shops in town, concentrated around Louis Trichardt St. Although the craft shops include a lot of dross, there is quality to be found too.

Delagoa
ARTS & CRAFTS

(☑013-767 1081; Louis Trichardt St; ☺ 8am-6pm) This perpetually busy shop has crafts from all over the continent, and the weavings from the Congo are particularly impressive. Their line in kids clothing isn't cheap but it's high quality and quite unique.

❶ Information

Daan's Internet Cafe (cnr Monument & Bloedrivier Sts; per 30 mins R15; ☺8am-6pm).

First National Bank (Kerk St) There's an ATM just north of Louis Trichardt St.

Tourist information office (☑013-767 1833; Pilgrim St; ☺8.30am-5pm Mon-Sat) Inside Spar supermarket.

Trips SA (☑013-767 1886; www.tripsza.com; Louis Trichardt St; ☺8am-4.30pm Mon-Sat).

❶ Getting There & Away

The **minibus taxi stand** (Hoof St) is at the south end of town, with daily morning departures to Pilgrim's Rest (R10, 30 minutes), Sabie (R20, 40 minutes) and Hazyview (R22, one hour).

Blyde River Canyon

☑013

Blyde River Canyon is the third largest canyon in the world, and one of South Africa's most outstanding natural sights. Oddly, it's not on many international visitors' itinerary, but on a fine day the scale and beauty of the canyon will sear itself in your mind.

Much of it is bordered by the Blyde River Canyon Nature Reserve (admission per person/car R25/5), a 26,000-hectare reserve that winds its way north from Graskop, following the Drakensberg Escarpment and meet-

WORTH A TRIP

TOURING AROUND BLYDE RIVER CANYON

Heading north from Graskop, look first for the **Pinnacle**, a striking skyscraperlike rock formation. (Lock up your vehicle here as there have been break-ins.) Just to the north along Rte 534 (a loop off Rte 532) are **God's Window** and **Wonder View** – two viewpoints with amazing vistas and an even more amazing amount of craft stalls. At God's Window take the trail up to the rainforest (300 steps) where you might spot rare birds, including the elusive loerie.

When you return to Rte 532, take a short detour 2km south to the impressive **Lisbon Falls** (or if you are coming back to Graskop, catch it in the afternoon).

The Blyde River Canyon starts north of here, near **Bourke's Luck Potholes**. These bizarre cylindrical holes were carved into the rock by whirlpools near the confluence of the Blyde and Treuer Rivers. There's a **visitors centre** where you can pay the reserve entry fee and get information on the canyon's geology, flora and fauna.

Continuing north past Bourke's Luck Potholes and into the heart of the nature reserve, you'll reach a viewpoint overlooking the **Three Rondavels** – enormous rounds of rock with pointed, grassy tops that look like giant huts carved into the side of the canyon. There are a number of short walks in the surrounding area to points where you can look down to the Blydepoort Dam at the reserve's far north.

West of here, outside the reserve and off Rte 36, are the **Echo Caves** (admission & guided tour adult/child R50/20) where Stone Age relics have been found. The caves get their name from dripstone formations that echo when tapped.

---

ing the Blyde River as it snakes down to the lowveld. The majority of visitors drive along the canyon's edge, and there are plenty of viewpoints along the way where you can stop and gaze in awe. If you have enough time, however, it's even better explored on foot.

🏃 Activities

Belvedere Day Walk — WALKING

(R5; five hours) The short but reasonably strenuous Belvedere walk takes you in a circular route to the Belvedere hydroelectric power station at Bourke's Luck Potholes. The station was built in 1911 and was once the largest of its kind in the southern hemisphere. Bookings should be made at Potholes. When walking here, don't go to the river; instead turn left at the guesthouse, down a path to some beautiful waterfalls and rock pools.

For more walks in the area, visit the Forever Blyde Canyon resort, where you can mix and match a series of six hiking routes.

🛏 Sleeping

It's easy to explore the canyon by vehicle as a day jaunt from Graskop, Sabie or Pilgrim's Rest. If you're continuing further north, a good alternative is to stay in or around the nature reserve, or in Hoedspruit.

Forever Blyde Canyon — RESORT $$

(☎0861 226 966; www.foreverblydecanyon.co.za; campsites per person R120, 2-/4-person self-catering chalets R725/1040, 2-/4-person deluxe chalets from R820/1550; 🅿🛜) This rambling resort has a wide choice of accommodation. For jaw-dropping views of the three *rondavels* ask for chalet Nos 89 to 96. The solid brick chalets are very well set up, and the pricier ones are worth it for the views and extra space. Watch out for the cheeky baboons - this author had one jump in the window and pinch a loaf of bread from the kitchen!

Thaba Tsweni Lodge — CHALETS $$

(☎013-767 1380; www.blyderivercanyonaccommo dation.com; d from R600, breakfast R75) Beautifully located just a short walk from Berlin Falls in the heart of the panorama route, are several self-catering chalets, with stone walls, African-print bedspreads, kitchens, private garden areas with braai facilities, wood-burning fireplaces and beautiful views. It's just off Rte 352 in the direction of Berlin Falls.

Forever Resort Swadini — RESORT $$

(☎015-795 5141; www.foreverswadini.co.za; campsites R105, plus per person R53, 6-person self-catering chalet R1200; 🅿🅿) These basic chalets are improved greatly by the good location and impressive views. In addition to hiking, the resort can organise white-water rafting, abseiling and more. It's at the northern end of the reserve along the Blyde River, and about 5km from Blydepoort Dam. There's a supermarket, liquor store and laundry.

EASTERN LOWVELD

The hot and dry Eastern Lowveld is mostly used as a staging post on the way into and out of Kruger National Park. You can learn about the history of the gold rush in the feel-good town of Barberton or get your big-city fix in Nelspruit, and there are plenty of country lodges to whet your appetite for mighty Kruger National Park.

Hazyview

013 / POP 20,000

Spread out along Rte 40 and with no real centre, Hazyview has developed purely because of its proximity to Kruger National Park. There are good facilities, a couple of decent restaurants and even some activities to keep you busy if you feel the need to stop here for a day or two. It is close to the Phabeni (12km), Numbi (15km) and Paul Kruger (47km) Gates.

Sights & Activities

Shangana Cultural Village CULTURAL VILLAGE
(013-737 5804; www.shangana.co.za; 9am-4pm) About 5km north of town, along Rte 535, is a very touristy recreation of a traditional Shangaan community. At various times of the day it features a market, farming activity, house building, displays of uniforms and weaponry of the *masocho* (warriors), the relating of customs and history by a *sangoma* (traditional healer), cooking, dancing and the imbibing of *byala* (traditional beer). Day tours cost R120, midday visits with a traditional meal cost from R260, and the evening program with a good dinner costs R300. The Marula Crafts Market is also located here.

Elephant Sanctuary ELEPHANTS
(013-737 6609; www.elephantsanctuary.co.za; tours adult/child from R450/225; tours from 7.15am) Located next to Caso Do Sol, on Rte 536, this elephant sanctuary has a range of interactive tours with these majestic creatures, including walking with the elephants, elephant-back riding and a sundowner elephant experience.

Sleeping & Eating

TOP CHOICE Idle & Wild GUESTHOUSE $
(013-737 8173; rondavel from R340; P) In a wonderful, tropical garden that will make your heart sing (no, really!) are these excellent *rondavels*. Standard *rondavels* are just fine – very roomy and include kitchenette. The honeymoon *rondavel* (add R100) has slightly nicer linen and a large spa bath. All have beautiful garden outlooks and outdoor table and chairs to enjoy them. Breakfast is an extra R80. It's 5km from Hazyview on the R536 to Sabie.

Bushpackers BACKPACKERS $
(013-737 8140; www.bushpackers.co.za; campsite R60, dm R100, d R300-400;) This basic setup has clean, roomy dorms and a choice of en-suite or shared-facility twin rooms. There's a great bar, home-cooked meals are offered and lots of outdoor activities can be organised, including rafting, hiking and kloofing, along with trips into Kruger. It's located 3km from Hazyview, just off the R536 (the Sabie Rd).

Summerfields FUSION $$
(013-737 6500; mains R105; lunch & dinner) For something romantic, head to Summerfields, some 5km out of town on Rte 536. The food is generally on the rich side, including meats with creamy sauces, buttery trout and sinful desserts. Everything is beautifully presented, though, and the sweeping deck is something special on a hot afternoon when you can enjoy the cooling breeze from a corner table. Recommended is the Carpaccio salad: springbok, parmesan, tomato and rocket with a passionfruit reduction.

Pioneer Restaurant STEAKHOUSE $$
(013-737 7397; Rendezvous Tourism Centre; mains R70-120; lunch, dinner Mon-Sat) Denee Fick is a well-known South African chef who brings her considerable talents to this modern restaurant. She specialises in fine cuts of beef cooked to perfection: try the sirloin with mushroom sauce. There's also seafood on offer as well as local game such as ostrich.

Information

Simunye Shopping Centre has an ATM and a Checkers supermarket. The Perry's Bridge and Rendezvous centres also have ATMs.
Big 5 Country Tourist Office (013-737 8191; www.big5country.co.za; 8am-5pm Mon-Fri, 8am-2pm Sat) This helpful office is in the

FOR THE ADVENTUROUS

Balloons Over Africa (☎013-737 6950; www.balloonsoverafrica.co.za; flights per person R2600) Offers balloon flights over the Sabie River Valley. Flights leave early in the morning and last about an hour. They include a glass or two of Cape sparkling and breakfast.

Induna Adventures (☎013-737 8308; www.indunaadventures.com) Organises a number of adventure activities in the Hazyview area, including rafting on the Blyde River (R1260 for a full day) and quad biking (R370 per hour). It's at Idle & Wild, 10km from Hazyview on the Sabie Rd.

Skyway Trails (☎013-737 8374; www.skywaytrails.com; per person R450) This is 'Africa's longest Aerial Cable Trail' – a fun three hours flying through the forest while clipped to a wire. It's right next to Bushpackers.

Rendezvous Tourism Centre, as you are coming into Hazyview from the south.

Paper Chain (☎013-737 6537; Perry's Bridge; R15 for 15 mins; ⊙8am-5pm Mon-Fri, 9am-1pm Sat) Fast, expensive internet connections.

❶ Getting There & Around

City to City has a daily Jo'burg–Acornhoek bus that stops at the Shell petrol station in Hazyview (R150 from Jo'burg). Minibus taxis go daily to Nelspruit (R30, one hour) and Sabie (R30, one hour).

White River

☎013 / POP 10,000 / ELEVATION 950M

White River (Witrivier) is a nondescript town dating back to the days of the Anglo-Boer War. Less humid than Nelspruit, it makes a convenient base for a trip into Kruger. There are also two good shopping centres here: the countrified Casterbridge Farm has good restaurants and shops, art galleries and a cinema; and the Bagdad Centre has faux Cape Dutch, Moroccan and Zanzibar architecture and good restaurants. The centres are opposite each other, just 2km north of town on Rte 40 to Hazyview.

🛏 Sleeping & Eating

Karula Hotel HOTEL $$
(☎013-751 2277; www.karulahotel.co.za; Old Plaston Rd; r from R430; ❀❆☎) Situated in a little green oasis just outside town (on the R538, 2km south of White River) this peaceful midrange retreat makes for a relaxing night's kip among the jacaranda and bougainvillea. Rooms are a little dated, but the luxury rooms are well worth the R20 extra being larger and coming with couch and bushy outlooks.

TOP CHOICE Oliver's Restaurant & Lodge LODGE $$
(☎013-7500479;www.olivers.co.za;s/dfromR1250/ 1800; ❀@❆) A gorgeous country lodge with an attached golf course. Rooms are country chic: think huge wooden sleigh beds, pastel armchairs and Laura Ashley–style curtains. Drop-dead gorgeous bathrooms have showers big enough for two (and enough shower heads for three). There's also an excellent restaurant here, open to non-guests. It's north of White River, signposted along Rte 40, just after Casterbridge Farm on the way to Hazyview.

Schneider's Guest House GUESTHOUSE $$$
(☎013-751 2338; www.schneidersguesthouse.com; r R1900-2200, ste 2700; ❀❆☎) This is one swanky outfit and perfect for a bit of indulgence. All the rooms drip with decadence, but the room with the garden patio is our fave. All feature outdoor showers, balconies, fireplaces, views and very contemporary furnishings. It's in a gated community off the R40, on the way to Hazyview 8km from town – look for the signpost.

Courtyard Cafe CAFE $
(Casterbridge Farm; dishes R25-40) Sample excellent, organic local produce at this cool cafe and deli. Why not pull up a chair in the lovely, shady courtyard (complete with raised gazebo area and large outdoor chessboard) or in the snug and welcoming interior? There's also an attached deli selling freshly baked bread, farm cheese and other goodies.

Fez at Baghdad MIDDLE EASTERN $$
(☎013-750 1250; Bagdad Centre; mains from R80; ⊙closed Mon, Sun evening) White-robed and

fez-clad waiters serve up a mix of North African and Middle Eastern favourites, including large sharing plates of meze, *tajines* and grills. The restaurant also houses, somewhat incongruously, a sushi bar.

ℹ Information

First National Bank (Tom Lawrence St) Has an ATM.

Lowveld Tourism (✆0861 102 102; lowveldtourism.com; ⊙9am-4.30pm Mon-Fri, 9am-4pm Sat, 10am-2pm Sun) At the Casterbridge Centre.

ℹ Getting There & Around

Minibus taxis go throughout the day to/from Nelspruit (R15, 20 minutes) and Hazyview (R25, one hour).

Nelspruit

✆013 / POP 235,000

Nelspruit is Mpumalanga's largest town and provincial capital, and while not unpleasant, it's more of a place to get things done than a worthwhile destination for tourists. There are, however, good accommodation options and a couple of excellent restaurants so it makes a good-enough breathing point on the way elsewhere.

◎ Sights & Activities

Lowveld National Botanical Garden
BOTANICAL GARDEN

(adult/child R20/10; ⊙8am-6pm) Out of town, the 150-hectare Botanical Garden is home to tropical African rainforest, and is a nice place for a stroll among the flowers and trees. It's on Rte 40 about 2km north of the junction with the N4.

FREE Sonheuwel Nature Reserve
NATURE RESERVE

The small nature reserve features antelope species, vervet monkeys and rock paintings. It's on the southern edge of Nelspruit, off Van Wijk St.

Chimpanzee Eden
CHIMP SANCTUARY

(✆013-737 8191; www.janegoodall.co.za; adult/child R120/60) This chimp centre, 12km south of Nelspruit on Rte 40, acts as a sanctuary for rescued chimpanzees. Here you can see chimps in a semi-wild environment and learn about primate behaviour and their plight. The entry fee includes a guided tour (10am, noon and 2pm).

Hiking
HIKING

There are also some good (and strenuous) hikes, particularly along the **Kaapsche-hoop Trail** (per night R105; 2, 3 or 4 days) and

Nelspruit

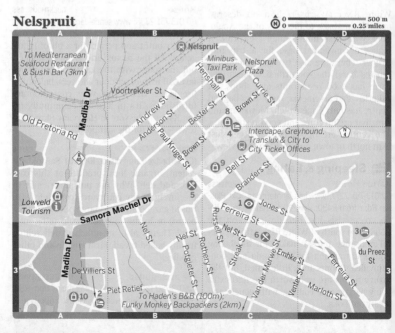

the **Uitsoek Trail** (per night R105; 1 or 2 days). For information and bookings, contact **Komatiland Forests Eco-Tourism** (☎013-754 2724; www.komatiecotourism.co.za; 10 Streak St).

🞊 Tours

Funky Safaris WILDLIFE SAFARI
(☎013-744 1310; www.funkymonkeys.co.za) Based at Funky Monkey Backpackers, it does one-to three-night safaris to Kruger where it has its own tented camp, as well as day trips to Blyde River Canyon.

Kruger and More WILDLIFE SAFARI
(☎013-744 0993; www.krugerandmore.co.za) A well-organised company that leads tours to Kruger National Park, Blyde River Canyon and Mozambique.

🎉 Festivals & Events

InniBos ARTS/MUSIC
(www.innibos.co.za) Held every June or July, this is Nelspruit's biggest festival, bringing together artists, musicians and theatre groups for five days of fun. Entry is around R40 per day.

Nelspruit Jazz Festival JAZZ
If you are around in August, try to catch the Jazz Festival, held at the Rugby Stadium behind Crossing Mall.

Nelspruit

🛏 Sleeping

 Utopia in Africa GUESTHOUSE $$
(☎013-745 7714; www.utopiainafrica.co.za; 6 Daleen St; s/d incl breakfast R650/900; ❄☀) Simplicity, elegance and a masterful design that keeps the premises cool from the afternoon breeze mark this exceptional accommodation. Rooms are beautifully furnished and come with balconies overlooking the nearby nature reserve. It's very much like staying with friends – their friendliness and inclusivity is really appealing. Highly recommended. Head south on Madiba Dr, turn left onto Dr Enos Mabuza Dr, left onto Halssnoer St (which becomes Augusta) and then keep following it – Utopia is well signposted off this road, on Daleen St.

Funky Monkey Backpackers BACKPACKERS $
(☎083 310 4755; www.funkymonkeys.co.za; 102 Van Wijk St; campsites per person R50, dm R120, s/d without bathroom R200/380; @☀) While a little out of town, this is an excellent backpackers, with clean dorms and doubles in a rambling house and a spacious garden. The pool and braai area sees some great parties, and meals are available. To get here take Ferreira St east, then turn right onto Van der Merwe St, which turns into Van Wijk St.

Haden's B&B GUESTHOUSE $$
(☎013-752 3259; www.hadensrest.com; cnr Van Wijk St & Mostert Rd; s/d with breakfast R500/675) This friendly B&B is just up from Jock & Java, one of Nelspruit's best spots for quality food. Rooms are lent a dash of colour from the bright African art on the walls. Some rooms are better (ie larger) than others so ask to see a few: No 4 is a good one. Well located for access to the city. To get here take Ferreira St east, turn right onto Van der Merwe St, which turns into Van Wijk St.

Francolin Lodge GUESTHOUSE $$
(☎013-744 1251; www.francolinlodge.co.za; 4 du Preez St; d incl breakfast from R1000-1300; @☀) This is a top Nelspruit guesthouse. The rooms have double-height ceilings, private patios and corner bathrooms with views. It also owns the equally lovely Loerie's Call next door, with plush rooms set apart from the main house, along decked walkways, each with their own entrance. The easiest way to approach it is off the N4 coming into town from the east – it's well signposted.

MPUMALANGA NELSPRUIT

Old Vic Travellers Inn
BACKPACKERS $

(Crazy Kangaroo Backpackers; ☎013-744 0993; www.krugerandmore.co.za/oldvic.aspx; 12 Impala St; dm R100, d R400, without bathroom R300, 4-person self-catering house R700; @≋) A friendly, somewhat upscale backpackers, with self-catering facilities, and lots of information on the area. Double rooms are a bit dark but clean and well kept; shared bathrooms are in good order. A big, rambling garden leads down to the river. It's about 3km south of the centre, near an extension of Sonheuwel Nature Reserve and a Baz Bus stop.

Auberge Guest Lodge
B&B $$

(☎013-741 2866; www.aubergeguestlodge.com; 3 De Villiers St; s/d incl breakfast R450/650; @≋🤶) A quiet, well-maintained and sunny guesthouse with a plant-filled courtyard and pool. Motel-like rooms are straight-up-and-down, some with ceiling fans. It's a good location behind Sonpark Centre with cafes and restaurants just across the road.

Orion Promenade Hotel
HOTEL $$

(☎011-718 6452; www.oriongroup.co.za; cnr Samora Machel Dr & Henshall Sts; r per person sharing R740; ❄@≋) Right in the town centre, across from the bus offices, this big old bastion has a warren of hallways. Some rooms, like No 204, have been renovated with funky fixtures and a fuss made of the bed and linen. Other rooms, like No 235, have not had the magic wand applied but have acres of space: all are the same price.

✖ Eating

For self-caterers, there's a huge **Superspar** (cnr Madiba & Samora Machel Drs) supermarket at Nelspruit Crossings Mall. There's also a **Shoprite** at Sanlam Sentrum.

TOP CHOICE Jock & Java
PUB $$

(Ferreira St; mains R60-110, breakfast R30; ⊙breakfast, lunch & dinner Mon-Sat; ✎) This rambling 'outback style' pub and separate tearoom set in large grassy lawns is very pleasant and the food is up a notch in quality from many other Nelspruit offerings. Try the Jock Carpetbagger – fillet steak stuffed with smoked mussels and topped with white-wine shrimp sauce. Great salads, wood-fired pizzas, prawns and decent vegetarian selection, too. The only drawback is the at-times terrible service, and staff do look harried. Very popular spot for locals.

Orange Restaurant
FUSION $$

(☎013-744 9507; 4 Du Preez St; lunch mains R50-90, dinner R70-160) Put on your finest and treat your nearest-and-dearest to some beautifully prepared cuisine, such as artful servings of escargot or guinea fowl, at this classy restaurant at the Francolin Lodge. The terrific views are the icing on the cake.

Costa do Sol
PORTUGUESE/ITALIAN $$

(☎013-752 6382; ABSA Sq, Paul Kruger St; meals R50-85; ⊙ closed Sun) An old-fashioned favourite, where the darkish dining room serves Italian or Portuguese food including fish, pasta dishes and prawns. Chef's specials include baby chicken grilled in peri-peri sauce. A good city-centre option – the cool, dark interior is a nice break from the frenetic streets outside.

Mediterranean Seafood Restaurant
MEDITERRANEAN $$$

(The Hub, Riverside Mall, R40; mains R90-130) Cane chairs, a large outdoor seating area, floor to ceiling wine-rack and pretty sundrenched pastels adorn this seafood restaurant. It makes a pretty good fist of all things fishy and we recommend the meze – a tasting platter – as a starter. Mains are prawns, fish, calamari and mussels any way you like 'em.

News Cafe
CAFE-BAR $$

(Nelspruit Crossings Mall; mains R50-70; ⊙ breakfast, lunch, dinner) A suave interior and cool outdoors dining patio greet patrons to this Nelspruit stalwart. It's a good bet for breakfast or lunch in particular, serving cooked breakfasts and even muesli and fresh fruit salads, burgers and wraps. A full bar is on hand if you want lunch to extend into the afternoon.

The Puzzle
CAFE $

(Sonpark Shopping Centre, R40; mains R35; ⊙ breakfast, lunch Mon-Fri) With friendly service and well-prepared meals, this small, simple cafe, a convivial meeting point for locals, is good for breakfast or lunch.

❶ Information

Emergency
Police station (☎013-759 1000; 15 Bester St) Opposite Nelspruit Plaza.

Internet access
Alpha Internet (Nelspruit Crossing Mall; per hr R30; ⊙8am-8pm Mon-Sat, 9am-4pm Sun)
News Cafe (Nelspruit Crossing Mall) Free wi-fi.

Medical Services

Nelmed Forum (☑013-755 1541; www.nelmed.co.za; cnr Nel & Rothery Sts) Offers 24-hour emergency medical care.

Nelspruit Mediclinic (☑013-759 0500; 1 Louise St) Private hospital offering 24-hour emergency medical care.

Money

First National Bank (Bester St) Does foreign exchange.

Nelspruit Crossing Mall (cnr Samora Machel & Madiba Drs) With an ATM.

Standard Bank (Brown St) With an ATM.

Tourist Information

Dana Agency (☑013-753 3571; www.dana agency.co.za; shop 12, Nelspruit Crossing Mall; ⊙8am-4.30pm Mon-Fri, 9am-noon Sat) This long-standing agent can help with air tickets and other travel arrangements.

Lowveld Tourism (☑013-755 1988/9; www.lowveldtourism.com; cnr Madiba & Samora Machel Drs; ⊙7am-6pm Mon-Fri, 8am-1.30pm Sat) This helpful office at Nelspruit Crossing Mall (behind News Cafe) takes bookings for all national parks, including Kruger, and can help arrange accommodation and tours.

Mozambique consulate (☑013-752 7396; 32 Bell St; ⊙8am-3pm Mon-Fri) Does same-day, single-entry visa processing for R600 to R750. Drop visa applications in before noon and pick up visa from 2pm.

❶ Getting There & Around

Air

Mpumalanga Kruger International Airport (MKIA; ☑013-753 7500; www.mceglobal.net) is the closest commercial airport. There are daily flights with **SAAirlink** (☑013-750 2531; www.saairlink.co.za) to Jo'burg (R900-1300, one hour), Cape Town (R2800, two hours 40 minutes) and Durban (R1900, 1½ hours).

Bus

Baz Bus (☑0861 229 287; www.bazbus.com) connects Nelspruit with Jo'burg/Pretoria and Manzini (Swaziland) and stops at all the backpackers in town.

Intercape (☑0861 287 287; www.intercape.co.za), **Greyhound** (☑083 915 9000; www.greyhound.co.za) and **Translux** (☑013-755 1453; www.translux.co.za) all go daily between Jo'burg (and Pretoria) and Maputo (Mozambique) via Nelspruit.

Car Rental

Avis Airport (☑013-750 1015); Downtown (☑013-757 0911; Riverside Auto Centre, Mystic River Crescent)

Europcar (☑013-750 2871) At the airport.

First (☑013-750 2538) At the airport.

Minibus Taxi

The local bus and minibus taxi park is behind Nelspruit Plaza near the corner of Bester and Henshall Sts. Minibus taxi destinations and fares include White River (R15, 20 minutes), Barberton (R25, 40 minutes), Hazyview (R30, one hour), Graskop (30, 1½ hours) and Jo'burg (R120, five hours).

City Bug (☑013-753 3392; www.citybug.co.za) operates a weekly shuttle to Durban (R550 per person one-way, nine hours), a daily shuttle to Pretoria (R350, 3½ to five hours), and several per day to OR Tambo International Airport (R350 per person one-way, four to 5½ hours, four or five daily). Monday to Friday the 10am and 4pm OR Tambo International Airport services also stop at University Rd in Melville, Jo'burg. All services depart from the Sonpark BP petrol station.

Lowveld Link (☑013-750 1174; www.lowveldlink.com) operates a convenient daily shuttle service from Nelspruit to Pretoria (R330 one-way, 3½ hours), OR Tambo International Airport (R330 one-way, 4¼ hours) and Sandton (R330 one-way, 4¾ hours). It leaves from the Lowveld Tourism office.

Train

The seat-only *Komati* run by **Shosholoza Meyl** (☑0860 008 888; www.shosholozameyl.co.za) travels daily except Saturday between Jo'burg (eight hours) and Komatipoort (2½ hours) via Nelspruit.

Malelane

☑013 / POP 6500

Malelane is a small, unexciting town that's no more than a stopover point and service centre for Kruger National Park. There are some good lodges here, however, most with views of Crocodile River and close enough to the wildlife to whet your appetite for the main event.

Malelane is on the N4 and Malelane Gate, 3km northeast of town, will take you into Kruger's southern regions.

🛏 Sleeping & Eating

TOP CHOICE **River House Lodge** GUESTHOUSE **$$**
(☑013-790 1333; www.riverhouse.co.za; 27 Visarend St; s/d R600/1200) This cracking lodge pulls out a lot of yesteryear in its eclectic design and is perched right on the boundary of the park. All rooms have their own balconies from which you can spy all the way into Kruger. The service is very friendly and it would make a great place to relax and

unwind pre or post Kruger. It's west of town and signposted from the main road.

Serenity Lodge
LODGE **$$$**

(☏013-790 2000; www.serenitylodge.co.za; s/d with breakfast R1000/2000, dinner R150; ❄❄) Gorgeous thatched suites tucked away in the forest linked via elevated walkways, all with terraces. It's a perfect place to get away from it all and the grounds have walking trails, small waterfalls, and trees full of birds, butterflies and monkeys.

Masungulo River Camp
BUSH CAMP **$$**

(☏013-744 1310; half-board per person R350; ❄) Run by the good folk at Funky Monkey in Nelspruit, this new bush camp is in a wildlife reserve that overlooks Crocodile River, and is a great base for safaris into Kruger, which can be booked on site. Accommodation is in safari tents. Between the Malelane and Crocodile Bridge Kruger entrance gates, it's also only 25km from the Mozambique border gate. Transfers to Maputo or Mozambique border available.

Komatipoort

☏013 / POP 4700

Cradled by the Lebombo Mountains, Komatipoort sits near the confluence of the Komati and Crocodile Rivers, only 10km from Kruger National Park's Crocodile Bridge Gate. If you're travelling to/from Mozambique or Swaziland it makes for a good stopover. There's a Spar supermarket, a petrol station and an ABSA bank with exchange facilities.

If you happen to be in Komatipoort in late June, ask around for the **Prawn Festival**, which celebrates the modest crayfish in all its glory.

🛏 Sleeping & Eating

TOP CHOICE **Trees Too**
GUESTHOUSE **$$**

(☏013-793 8262; www.treestoo.com; s/d incl breakfast R460/720; ❄❄) This place is a standout accommodation with great thatch and brick rooms, an honesty bar, pool and very friendly service. Staff have heaps of info about Kruger and serve breakfast and dinner. Wildlife artworks decorate rooms along with quality furniture. It's on a leafy side street about 500m in from Rissik St and signposted.

Kruger View Backpackers
BACKPACKERS **$**

(☏013-793 7373; www.krugerview.com; 61 Bosbok St; dm/d R125/425; @❄) With gorgeous views into Kruger, there are spacious dorms and doubles sleeping two to five people here. We receive good feedback about this place from readers.

Stoep Café
B&B **$$**

(☏013-793 7850; 74 Rissik St; r per person with breakfast R300; ❄) Very pretty, green and white colonial-style house with a small garden and pool in the heart of things on Rissik St. There are three tidy rooms with small kitchenettes and an on-site coffee shop, with a large shady verandah, serving tasty meals, snacks and pancakes.

ℹ Getting There & Away

Minibus taxis leave from just off Rissik St near the Score supermarket, and regularly do the run between Komatipoort and Maputo (Mozambique; R80, 1½ to two hours). If you're driving, there are two tolls along the N4 on the Mozambique side. Exit procedures are fairly swift.

The *Komati* train travels daily except Saturday between Jo'burg and Komatipoort (R100, 11 hours) via Malelane and Nelspruit. For more details on onward travel in Mozambique, see p591.

Barberton

☏013 / POP 29,500

Barberton is a friendly, walkable, safe town, full of quiet, leafy streets and beautifully preserved old buildings, against a striking backdrop of green and purple mountains. This little town has a great feel to it, no doubt enhanced by its historical buildings, the laidback nonchalance of its inhabitants and its compact centre. It makes an excellent alternative base to Nelspruit with its heritage giving it a unique flavour and interest.

Dating back to the gold-rush days, the town boomed in the late 19th century and was home to South Africa's first stock exchange.

◉ Sights & Activities

You can pick up a **Heritage Walk** map and leaflet at the tourist information centre. It's a self-guided tour that takes in the restored houses as well as other sights.

Barberton boasts several restored houses dating back to the late 19th and early 20th

Barberton

Barberton

◎ Sights

1 Belhaven House	B2
2 Blockhouse	B1
3 Fernlea House	B2
4 Stopforth House	A2
5 Umjindi Gallery	B1

⬛ Sleeping

6 Kloof House	B2

✕ Eating

7 Pappa's	B2
8 Victorian Tea Garden &	
Restaurant	B1

centuries. All are open for touring (contact the Barberton Museum for more details) and give a glimpse into the town's early history. They include **Belhaven House** (Lee St; adult/child R12/6; ⊙tours on the hour 10am-3pm Mon-Fri); **Stopforth House** (Bowness St; adult/child R12/6; ⊙tours on the hour 10am-3pm Mon-Fri) at the top of the town, with incredible views, and wonderful front deck; and **Fernlea House** (Lee St; admission free; ⊙9am-4pm Mon-Fri), which is in a beautiful wooded location.

FREE **Umjindi Gallery**   GALLERY
(☎013-712 5807; Pilgrim St; ⊙8am-5pm Mon-Fri) This outfit sells a range of craftworks and has a jewellery workshop where you can watch the artists at work. The jewellery is stunning, especially the silverwork. You can pick up a set of silver earrings with pendant for R575 and the animal carvings decorating them are delightful.

🛏 Sleeping

Kloof House   GUESTHOUSE $$
(☎013-712 4268; www.kloofhuis.co.za; 1 Kloof St; s/d incl breakfast R400/600; @⊛) A lovely old hillside Victorian house with grand views from the wraparound verandah onto which the comfortable guest rooms open out. Rooms are a simple affair but appealingly large and with homespun comforts. There is also a self-catering chalet.

Fountain Baths Holiday Guest Cottages   COTTAGES $$
(☎013-712 2707; 48 Pilgrim St; cottages per person R275) These cottages, in a beautiful and historical location just on the north-eastern edge of town, are looking a bit worse for wear – ie they could do with a refit. They are, however, a good size, perfectly comfortable and well priced. The lovely quiet garden also goes a long way to making up for the drawbacks.

Barberton Chalets & Caravan Park   CARAVAN PARK $
(☎013-712 3323; www.barbertonchalets.co.za; General St; campsites per person R50, caravan sites R70, s/d/tr cottages R300/400/500; ⊛) This caravan park, in large grassy, shady grounds, is conveniently close to the town centre. Nineteen seventies-style chalets sleep four, but two would be more comfortable in the pokey but clean and tidy interiors.

✕ Eating & Drinking

Victorian Tea Garden & Restaurant   TEA GARDEN $
(Market Sq, Crown St; light meals R25-40; ⊙ closed Sun) Here you can munch on sandwiches, cakes and more substantial offerings while sitting in a gazebo and watching the world go by. It's between Pilgrim and Crown Sts, next to the tourist information office, and it's also a wi-fi hot spot.

Papa's   MEDITERRANEAN $
(18 Judge St; mains R30-50; ⊙breakfast, lunch, dinner; 🌢) Family-friendly and with a nice, large garden courtyard this pseudo-Mediterranean establishment is the best show in town for dinner or a hot lunch. Throwing pizzas, pastas, the odd burger and even shwarmas at patrons, it's also an exceedingly pleasant place for a beer and afternoon read of the newspaper.

❶ Information

Shoprite (Crown St) Has an ATM.

Standard Bank (Crown St) Has an ATM.

Tourist information centre (✆013-712 2880; www.barberton.co.za; Market Sq, Crown St; ⏲7.30am-4.30pm Mon-Fri, 9am-2pm Sat) This helpful office in the town centre can assist with accommodation, tours of historic sites and day hikes in the area.

Umjindi Resource Centre (Barberton Library, Pilgrim St; internet per hour R15)

❶ Getting There & Away

A few minibus taxis stop in town near Shoprite, but you'll be waiting forever unless you go to the minibus taxi park near Emjindini (3km from town on the Nelspruit road). The fare to Nelspruit is R25 (40 minutes). Most departures are in the early morning.

Around Barberton

◉ Sights & Activities

Songimvelo Game Reserve   RESERVE
(✆017-883 0964; adult/child R25/15; wildlife drive R125) This beautiful 56,000-hectare reserve sits in lowveld country south of Barberton, with high-altitude grassland areas on its eastern edge along the mountainous Swaziland border. There are no lions, but there are numerous other introduced species, including elephants, zebras, giraffes and various antelopes, and both walking and horse riding are popular. (Note that walking is limited to certain areas, and walkers must be accompanied by a guide.) Songimvelo is also home to some of the earth's oldest rocks – perhaps dating to four billion years ago – and some interesting archaeological sites. You can stay overnight at **Kromdraai Camp**

(cabins R425), with simple, self-catering, six-person wooden cabins. There are also **campsites** (R30) in the reserve.

Lone Tree Hill   PARAGLIDING
(admission R20, plus key deposit R50) Just southwest of town past the prison is an excellent paragliding location, at Lone Tree Hill. To get here, follow De Villiers St west from town, and turn left about 500m past the prison. **Hi Tech Security** (✆013-712 3256; McPherson St), just off Kruger St, can assist with keys and access.

Piet Retief

✆017 / POP 32,000

This dull farming backwater is not the kind of place you'd make a special visit to, but it's the largest town in southern Mpumalanga and a good spot to break your journey if you're headed for Swaziland or KwaZulu-Natal. The area south of Piet Retief is famous for its many Anglo-Boer War battlefields.

Greendoor (✆017-826 3208; www.thegreen door.co.za; 1 Mark St; s/d R330/440, breakfast per person R50) has simple, good-value en-suite rooms, some with African decor, in the centre of town. **Holme Lea Manor** (✆017-826 2767; 10 Hansen St; s/d R490/650, 5-person self-catering unit R1300) has a handful of comfortable (but snug) rooms, some with private entrances, set in a palm-filled garden around a pool.

Greyhound buses stop in town on their daily Pretoria–Durban run. The fare from Piet Retief to Pretoria is R260; to Durban it's R300.

The minibus taxi stand is at the back of **SuperMac** (cnr Kerk & Brand Sts). From here to the Swaziland border post at Mahamba costs R25 (30 minutes).

Kruger National Park

Best Places to See Wildlife

» For lions: Satara (p386), Sabi Sands (p393)

» For elephants: Olifants (p386), Letaba (p387)

» For birds: northen Kruger (p381)

» For wild dogs: Skukuza (p386)

» For impala: parkwide

Best Rest Camps

» Olifants (p386)

» Shingwedzi (p384)

» Pretoriuskop (p384)

» Letaba (p384)

» Crocodile Bridge (p384)

Why Go?

If you enjoy watching wildlife, this is arguably one of the greatest places on earth to do it. If you're new to watching wildlife then you've chosen well. Kruger is one of the world's most famed protected areas – known for its size, conservation history, wildlife diversity and ease of access. It's a place where the drama of life and death plays out daily, with up-close, action-packed sightings of wildlife almost guaranteed. One morning you may spot lions feasting on a kill, and the next, a newborn impala struggling to take its first steps.

Perhaps one of Kruger's most underrated features is its landscape. Wilderness – be it bushveld, woodland or grassland – surrounds you, with numerous places, such as Olifants Rest Camp, providing the perfect opportunity to really drink it in. Appreciating the landscape is vital to successful wildlife spotting; the animals might not always be around but the views never change.

When to Go

Skukuza

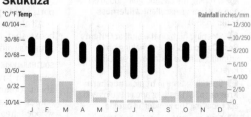

Jun–Sep Wildlife viewing is best in winter when the park is driest and animals meet at waterholes.

Jan–Mar Great quiet time to visit as holidays are over; accommodation easy to find.

Mar–May Rutting season spectacle sees impala, wildebeest and other species go head to head.

History

The area that is now Kruger National Park first came under government protection in 1898, when Paul Kruger (president of the Transvaal Republic and an avid hunter) established the Sabie Game Reserve, between the Sabie and Crocodile Rivers, as a controlled hunting area. In 1902, following the second Anglo-Boer War, James Stevenson Hamilton became the reserve's first warden. Hamilton was also the first to see the tourism potential of wildlife-watching, and to bring a conservation vision to the area. In 1926, Sabie Game Reserve was joined with neighbouring Shingwedzi Game Reserve and various private farms to become Kruger National Park; in 1927, the park was opened to the public.

Significant portions of the park (25% to 50%) remain subject to land claims that are still pending; it is unlikely that these will be settled in the short term.

In 2002, together with Zimbabwe's Gonarezhou National Park and Limpopo National Park in Mozambique, Kruger became part of the Great Limpopo Transfrontier Park.

Plant & Animal Distribution

Kruger encompasses a variety of ecosystems, with each favoured by particular species. Most mammals are distributed throughout the park, but some show a distinct preference for certain regions. Elephants, for example, are especially plentiful around Olifants and Letaba camps and other points north of the Olifants River, where their preferred mopane vegetation predominates. Lions, by contrast, favour the grasslands around Satara, with the large herds of buffalo, impala and other grazers. Impalas, buffaloes, Burchell's zebras, blue wildebeests, kudus, waterbucks, baboons, vervet monkeys, cheetahs, leopards and other smaller predators are all widespread, while birdlife is especially prolific along the rivers and north of the Luvuvhu River. All of Kruger's rivers have riverine forest along their banks (often with enormous fig trees), which supports populations of bushbucks and nyalas.

All the park shops sell maps and guidebooks that help in locating and spotting Kruger's wildlife.

SOUTHERN KRUGER

Southern Kruger is well watered, receiving about 700mm of rainfall annually. Its landscapes range from grasslands to thickly wooded areas with a variety of trees. These include acacias, bushwillows and sycamore figs, as well as flowering species such as the red-and-orange coral tree. The terrain is particularly favoured by white rhinos, buffaloes and zebras, but less so by antelope and, therefore, by predators.

Kruger National Park Highlights

❶ Ditching the car and going bush on one of Kruger's excellent **wilderness trails** (p383)

❷ Sleeping high on the bluff at **Olifants Rest Camp** (p384) and waking up to stunning sunrise vistas over the Olifants River

❸ Spending time in tropical **northern Kruger** (p381) visiting ancient ruins and appreciating the wonderful birdlife

❹ Exploring **Kruger from south to north** (p379), taking in the changing topography and nature's rhythms

❺ Pampering yourself with a few nights at a luxurious **private wildlife reserve** (p392)

KRUGER ESSENTIALS

Internet access Berg-en-Dal, Lower Sabie and Skukuza (all three also have wireless).

ATMs taking international cards Skukuza and Letaba; 'mini-ATMs' at Satara and Punda Maria dispense up to R300 maximum, during shop hours only, and depending on cash availability.

Petrol stations At all 12 main rest camps (petrol and diesel), but nowhere else; all are *cash only*.

Mobile phones You can buy air-time at all park shops; there's reception at all rest camps and many other areas as well, but not on the Olifants River Backpack Trail.

24-hour emergency (☎013-735 4325)

CENTRAL & EASTERN KRUGER

The central and eastern sections of the park, to the south of the Olifants River on the plains around Satara Rest Camp and south to the Crocodile River, experience reasonable rainfall (600mm) and have fertile soils. There are expanses of good grazing, with buffalo grass and red grass interspersed with acacia thorn trees (especially knobthorn), leadwood and marula trees. The area hosts large populations of impalas, zebras, wildebeests, giraffes and black rhinos. Joining them are predators, especially lions, who prey on impalas, zebras and blue wildebeests. Satara in particular is known for its frequent lion sightings, and is one of the most likely places in Kruger to spot cheetahs.

NORTHERN KRUGER

North of the Olifants River, annual rainfall drops below 500mm and the dominant tree is mopane. This grows widely in the west, among red bushwillow, but has a tougher time on the basalt plains of the northeast, where it tends to be more stunted. The mopane is a favoured food of elephants, which are common north of Olifants River around Olifants and Letaba Rest Camps. The mopaneveld also attracts tsessebes, elands, roans and sables.

FAR NORTHERN KRUGER

Kruger's far north, around Punda Maria and Pafuri, lies completely in the tropics and has a higher rainfall (close to 700mm at Punda Maria) than the nearby mopaneveld. This enables it to support a wider variety of plants (baobabs are particularly noticeable), good wildlife concentrations and an exceptional array of birds, including many species not found further south. There is woodland, bushveld and grass plains, and

between the Luvuvhu and Limpopo Rivers, a tropical riverine forest with figs, fever trees and jackalberries. The far north is a winter grazing ground for elephants, and lions and leopards are also regularly encountered.

 ## Activities

Kruger is exceptionally well organised, with a plethora of activities to enhance your wildlife-watching. Guided walks or other bush-based activities are highly recommended to get away from the camps and into the surrounding nature.

All activities need to be booked in advance except short bush walks and day or night wildlife drives, which can be booked from the gates and camps, usually on the day you wish to do them.

Kruger has several 4WD trails, the longest of which is the **Lebombo Motorised Eco Trail** (per vehicle R7500, maximum 4 people), a rugged 500km, five-day route along the park's eastern boundary, departing from Crocodile Bridge and ending at Pafuri. You'll need to provide your own vehicle, food and drink (it's completely self-catering). Only five vehicles are permitted at a time on the trail (plus the accompanying ranger's vehicle). Book a place well in advance through **central reservations** (☎012-428 9111). There are also four shorter 'adventure trails' (R460 per vehicle plus a R100 refundable deposit, about four hours, 50km).

Kruger offers excellent birdwatching, with the far north (from Punda Maria Gate up past Pafuri Gate) arguably one of the best birding areas on the continent. See **SANParks birding pages** (www.sanparks. org/groups/birders) for hide locations and an overview of birding areas.

Guided morning and afternoon **bush walks** (morning/afternoon per person R340/270)

Kruger National Park

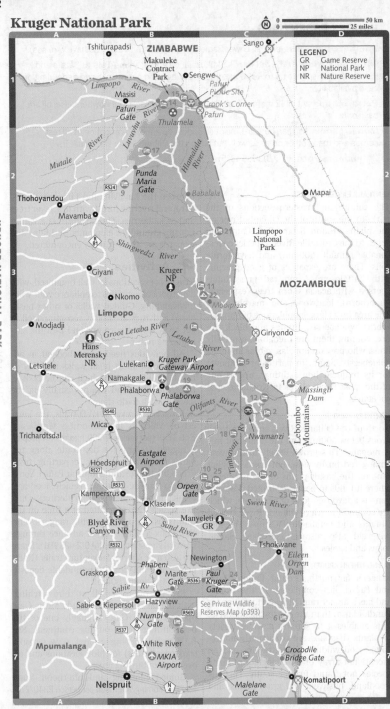

Kruger National Park

Sleeping

are possible at most camps and are highly recommended.

There are currently three **mountainbike trails** (www.sanparks.org/parks/kruger/tourism/activities; morning/afternoon R300/150), ranging from 12km to 24km. All are based out of the Olifants Rest Camp. You need to book at least several days in advance directly through the camp, or through **central reservations** (☎012-428 9111).

Wilderness Trails

Kruger's three-day wilderness **walking trails** (www.sanparks.org/parks/kruger/tourism/activities/wilderness; per person R3675) are one of the park's highlights. The seven wilderness trails are done in small groups (maximum eight people), guided by knowledgeable armed guides, and offer a superb opportunity for a more intimate experience of the bush than is possible in a vehicle. The walks are not overly strenuous, covering about 20km per day at a modest pace, and are appropriate for anyone who is reasonably fit. The itinerary is determined by the interests of the group, the time of year and the disposition of the wildlife.

The price of the trail includes accommodation in rustic huts, plus food and equipment, and they depart on Wednesday and Sunday afternoon. All are extremely popular, and should be booked well in advance through **central reservations** (☎012-428 9111). No children under 12 are allowed. Bring your own beer and wine if you'd like a drink.

There's also the considerably more strenuous four-day, three-night 42km **Olifants River Backpack Trail** (maximum 8 hikers; per person R1930), which departs from Olifants Rest Camp on Wednesdays and Sundays from April through October. There are no huts, and hikers must bring and carry their own tent, gas cookers and all provisions, and are responsible for their own cooking, tent set-up etc. The trail needs to be booked in its entirety.

Wildlife Drives

Dawn (three hours), midmorning (two hours), sunset (three hours) and night (two hours) wildlife drives are available at most rest camps, and offer good chances to maximise your safari experience, especially as you'll have a ranger to point out interesting features. The drives are scheduled to take advantage of the natural rhythms of the wildlife, as many animals – including lions, leopards and rhinos – are at their most active from first light to around 10am, and then again later in the day. The drives are done in 10- or 20-seat vehicles and cost between R180 and R230 per person, depending on time of day and vehicle size.

Tours

At the budget level, the best places to contact for tours into Kruger are the backpacker lodges in Hazyview (p370), Nelspruit (p372) and Graskop (p367), most of which organise tours from about R1000 per day, plus entry fees and meals. Many of the tour operators listed in the Transport chapter (see p605) also organise Kruger itineraries.

At the upper end of the price spectrum, or if you're on a tight schedule and want to connect directly from Johannesburg (Jo'burg) or Cape Town, try:

eHolidaysTours (www.airlinktours.com) Runs flight and accommodation packages between Jo'burg and central Kruger.

Wildlife Safaris (☎011-791 4238; www.wildlifesaf.co.za) Has four-day panorama tours taking in the Blyde River and Kruger for R7900 per person, including half board.

FLOODS

In early 2012, after some exceptionally heavy rains, floods swept through Kruger National Park with devastating results. The waters decimated gravel roads, picnic areas, bridges and washed away pieces of tarmac road, while stranded tourists had to be air-lifted out of the park. At the time of writing, the park was slowly returning to normal – roads were being reopened and all major gates were open for business again. You may still see the damage from the floodwaters, especially visible around watercourses. Closures for the foreseeable future due to flood damage include Balule Camp and Tamboti Hide. Check www.sanparks.org/parks/kruger for updates on road closures and other facilities compromised due to weather damage.

Eco-Ist (☑021-559 2420; www.eco-tourism investments.co.za) Offers 14-day combined Cape–Kruger tours.

🛏 Sleeping & Eating

Kruger has various types of accommodation, all of a high standard. Bookings for all should be made through **central reservations** (☑012-428 9111); see p391 for more information). The numbers listed in this section are for specific rest camp information and emergencies only.

It's also possible to stay outside the park. For budget and midrange travellers, the best places for this are Hazyview (p370), Nelspruit (p372) and Phalaborwa (p418). At the opposite end of the spectrum, there's luxurious accommodation in many of the private reserves bordering Kruger to the west (p392).

Rest Camps

Most visitors stay in one of the park's 12 main rest camps. These are fenced, attractively laid out, and offer campsites, plus a range of huts, bungalows and cottages. The cottages and many bungalows are self-catering, while others share communal cooking facilities consisting of sinks, hotplates and braais (barbecues). Both options come equipped with cutlery, pans, plates etc. All also have electricity, hot-water showers, bedding and towels, and most have fans and/or air-con. All camps have restaurants (meals average R90) and reasonably well-stocked shops, which sell a range of foodstuffs (though supplies of fruit and vegetables are quite limited).

The larger rest camps are like small towns in the middle of the bush, though they're remarkably unobtrusive considering the facilities they offer and the volume of visitors they host. Many have laundromats and some

have swimming pools. Skukuza, the largest, has basic medical services and a post office.

Several of the rest camps have satellite camps. These are delightful options – usually set at least 2km or 3km away from the main rest camp; quiet and rustic, they are without any facilities other than a communal kitchen and ablutions block, and braai areas. Accommodation is in either simple bungalows or permanent safari-style tents, and both options have refrigerators.

The various accommodation types are as follows:

Camping (per campsite for 1 to 2 people R200, per additional adult/child up to 6 maximum R62/31) For those with tents or caravans, camping is available at many rest camps; exceptions are noted in the reviews. As with other types of accommodation, campsites should be booked in advance during the high season. Many tent sites are not equipped with power points.

Huts (2 people from around R410) These are rustic and offer the cheapest noncamping option, with shared ablutions and communal cooking facilities. They sleep between two and six people, depending on the camp, and some have fridges.

Safari Tents (around R420, with bathroom & kitchen around R870) Some camps have safari tents, all of which are furnished, accommodate from two to four people, and have a refrigerator and fan. Most have shared kitchen and ablutions facilities, though several are considerably more luxurious, with private bathrooms and cooking facilities.

Bungalows (2 people from around R805) Bungalows are almost always en suite, and range from simple units with communal cooking facilities to more luxurious versions with kitchenettes.

Cottages (up to 4 people around R1590) These are the next step up in comfort. They usually have a living room area, as well as a kitchen and bathroom, and come in several sizes, including multibedroom 'family cottages'.

The following are the rest camps, where most visitors to Kruger stay. Each has its own character and unique setting.

Berg-en-dal (☎013-735 6106; @☒), a well-equipped medium-sized camp, 12km from Malelane Gate, is one of the most modern, with bungalows and six-person family cottages. It's laid out in an attractive bush landscape by the Matjulu River in the shadow of the Malelane Mountains. There's a visitors centre and nature trails, including a wheel-chair-accessible walk and a Braille walking trail.

Crocodile Bridge (☎013-735 6012), a small camp near the Crocodile River, just in from Crocodile Bridge Gate, is a good choice if you've arrived in Kruger too late to drive further into the park. There are crocodile and hippo pools a few kilometres away, and zebras, buffaloes and wildebeests frequent the surrounding acacia. Accommodation is in bungalows or a safari tent. There is no restaurant, but there's a cafeteria that's open

WILDLIFE WATCHING

Kruger National Park's population is made up of 34 amphibian species, 49 fish species, 116 reptile species, 147 mammal species, 336 tree species, 507 bird species and 1.3 million human visitors per year. Of the animal species, Kruger registered the following in recent censuses: 2000 lions, 31,000 wildebeests, 4000 warthogs, 3500 white rhinos, 7000 giraffes, 15,000 elephants, 16,000 buffaloes, 23,000 zebras and 130,000 impalas.

It's a game of chance, but thanks to the variety and sheer number of animals in Kruger, you have a better probability of spotting wildlife here than anywhere else in the region. Whatever time of year you visit, patience and perseverance are vital for rewarding wildlife-watching. Drive slowly, stop frequently and disengage the motor. It's amazing how often you first notice one animal, only to realise that there are many others in the vicinity after stopping the car. Even elephants can be well camouflaged when not in motion. Sitting still and staking out a waterhole is always rewarding.

Thanks to Kruger's excellent road system, you can get off the main roads quite easily and won't need a 4WD for most secondary gravel roads. (If it has been raining heavily, check with rangers at your rest camp for routes that should be avoided.) Sunglasses and binoculars are essential. See p548 for info on staying safe while watching wildlife.

The more you know about the animals (especially their distribution and behaviour) the better your chance of finding them, so it's worth buying one of the detailed books available at the rest camp shops. Some tips:

» Watch for big cats enjoying the breezes from rocky knolls; leopards will often rest high off the ground in tree branches.

» Warthogs, baboons, zebras, giraffes and many antelope species will happily graze together, so if you see one species, there will often be more close by.

» The presence of feeding herbivores does not preclude the possibility of a predator in the vicinity. Look carefully, as predators are expert stalkers and may not be obvious. Many animals do, however, seem to know whether a predator is actually hunting; if it isn't, they will be quite relaxed in its presence.

» Antelopes will be nervous and alert if they are aware of a predator on the hunt, but may not immediately flee. They know they can nearly always outrun a predator if they have a sufficient head start, so they maintain a 'flight distance' between themselves and the threat.

» Avoid driving too close to the animals, so as not to disturb their natural behaviour. If you do approach, be slow and steady, without sudden movements.

» Avoid frequent stopping and starting of the car engine – if you stop, it's best to stay put for a while. However, bear in mind that engine vibrations may create a problem with camera shake. There are a few designated spots in Kruger where you are permitted to get out of your car.

till 6.30pm serving basic meals (toasted sandwiches, burgers, *boerewors* (farmer's sausage) roll, breakfasts, coffee); diesel fuel is not available.

Pretoriuskop (☑013-735 5128/32; ☎), Kruger's oldest camp, is also one of its largest. It's located near Numbi Gate, in higher country than other places in the park, and thus a bit cooler in summer. Accommodation is in huts, bungalows and several large cottages sleeping between six and nine people. The camp includes a natural rock swimming pool that is popular with children. The surrounding countryside is attractive, with granite outcrops, and is frequented by white rhinos.

Lower Sabie (☑013-735 6056; @☎), about one hour (35km) from Crocodile Bridge Gate, overlooks a dam on the Sabie River that attracts many animals, and is one of the best situated of the southern Kruger camps for overall wildlife-watching. For sleeping, there's a good selection of huts, safari tents, bungalows and cottages. Campsites here have individual water taps. It also has one of the best restaurant viewing areas in the park, with wide sweeping outlooks over the Sabie River and surrounding landscape. Hippos are easily spotted.

Skukuza (☑013-735 4152; @☎), also on the Sabie River, is the main camp in Kruger and the park's administrative headquarters. There's a bank with an ATM, an Automobile Association (AA) workshop, petrol station, a doctor, a library, the police, a post office, a small museum and a helpful information centre. There's also an extensive range of accommodation, including luxury bungalows and various cottages. Skukuza has a fantastic view from its restaurant outdoor area over the river, with lovely shady trees to take advantage of in summer. There's also a choice of food here not found at other camps.

Orpen (☑013-735 6355), near Orpen Gate and convenient for late arrivals, is a small camp. There's no restaurant, cooking facilities are shared and no utensils are provided. Some accommodation doesn't have electricity, so bring a torch (flashlight). There are two satellite camps near Orpen. Maroela, 4km northeast, has basic campsites with power points. The appealing Tamboti, 4km east, has nice safari tents on a ridge above the Timbavati River, complete with wildlife wandering around outside. Two of the tents have wheelchair-access ramps. For both Maroela and Tamboti, you'll need to check in at Orpen.

Satara (☑013-735 6306; ☎), the second largest after Skukuza, is optimally situated in an area of flat and fertile plains that attracts large numbers of grazing animals and is known for its lion sightings (the population here is the largest in Kruger). About 45km north of Satara near the Olifants River is the atmospheric Balule Satellite Camp, with camping and several rustic three-person huts. There's no electricity (kerosene lanterns are available at the camp, but bring a torch). There's a large freezer and a stove, but otherwise, you'll need to bring everything in with you, including cooking utensils.

Olifants (☑013-735 6606; ☎) has a prime position on the bluff high above the Olifants River, making the most of the wide views. From the camp, you can see elephants, hippos and many other animals as they come down to the river 100m below. There are no campsites, but it is possible to camp at nearby Balule satellite camp. Olifants is particularly notable for its many activities, including mountain-bike trails, the Olifants River Backpack Trail and 'astronomy wildlife drives' each evening (per person R320, three hours), including telescope viewing and a presentation about the Southern African night skies.

Letaba (☑013-735 6636; ☎), about 20km to the north of Olifants, has excellent views over a wide bend of the Letaba River. It's an attractive, peaceful camp with lots of shade

OLI-FABULOUS

We'll come clean...we have a favourite – and this is it. Olifants is the most spectacular of the rest camps and, if you stay here, it is worth shelling out a few hundred more rand for a fully equipped chalet that teeters on the edge of the bluff. You'll enjoy the most spectacular of sunrises and sunsets over the sweeping Olifants River and shimmering plains, unfurling a carpet of greenery that blankets the landscape into the distance. But if you don't feel like splashing out, or are just dropping in, wildlife watching doesn't come much better than the nearby viewing area at the restaurant, also built on the edge of the bluff.

RHINO POACHING & STRIKING RANGERS

In February 2012, about half of Kruger's park rangers went on strike, with major demonstrations at key locations in the park, including a particularly energetic and impassioned call for recognition of their grievances at Phalaborwa Gate. Their demands included better pay and better resourcing to fight the tragic and barbaric poaching that is once again on rise in South Africa and especially in Kruger National Park. In 2011, 448 rhinos were lost to poaching (including 19 critically endangered black rhinos), 252 from Kruger, a figure that is significantly higher than in previous years. Sadly, early 2012 saw the arrest of four Kruger park employees, all based at Pretoriuskop, in connection with rhino poaching, including a ranger and a member of the Protection Services unit, a traffic cop.

One of the main issues for the rangers is that they are paid virtually no 'danger money' for the work they do, putting their life on the line when it comes to the protection of the park and its animals. They are often engaged in ferocious fire-fights with poachers in remote areas of the park, frequently sustaining bad injuries. Guides in the park are similarly underpaid and may also go down the path of striking. The most heartbroken over the brutal deaths of these magnificent creatures are the rangers who come across their bloodied and dehorned bodies in the wild, and their frustration at a lack of resources (and working conditions) to fight poaching has culminated in these strikes. At March 2012, amid the strikes, the annual death toll stood at 75 rhinos in Kruger, and counting…

and grassy areas and a restaurant fronting a promenade from where you can often observe elephants on the river banks below. Bungalows are looking a little worse for wear these days and the cheaper ones are cramped. Try to nab numbers D32 or 33: with their sensational views over the river and into the park, they are the best by far. If you're lucky enough to be here during a full moon, there are fewer places lovelier in the evening than the footpath overlooking the Letaba River – with the moon in the background, you're likely to have bushbucks behind you and elephants on the riverbanks below.

Mopani (☏013-735 6536; ⌗) is a modern rest camp on the edge of the Pioneer Dam, 45km north of Letaba. The buildings are all made of natural materials and thatch, although the overall impression is rather bare, and it lacks the atmosphere of many of the older camps. As compensation, it's quite serene, and there are lovely views over the dam. No campsites.

Shingwedzi (☏013-735 6806; ⌗) is an old-style place in the northern section of the park, with huts and cottages arranged in circles and shaded by tall mopane trees and palms. Shingwedzi has a relaxed, old-fashioned feel and the smiling staff at reception helped the camp win the 'rest camp of the year 2011'. Birdlife is prolific in the camp and bundles of feathers will probably be hopping around your feet should you appear with anything resembling food.

Punda Maria (☏013-735 6873), Kruger's northernmost rest camp, is in sandveld country by Dimbo Mountain. The camp is one of the park's oldest, with many of the buildings dating to the 1930s. Although rooms in the original blocks are cramped, the camp has a lovely, lightly wooded setting and its own charm – especially in the evenings when the small terrace in front of the rooms is lit by lanterns. There are also seven much newer, spacious and beautifully appointed 'luxury' safari tents set just above the main camp area.

Bushveld Camps

Bushveld camps are a recommended option if you want more of a wilderness experience than is possible at the rest camps, and are equipped for self-catering. There are five in the park. All are much smaller than the main rest camps – with between six and 15 self-catering cottages or chalets – and more remote. There are no shops, restaurants or any other of the supporting infrastructure found at the rest camps, although most are reasonably close to a rest camp where supplies can be bought.

Access to the camps is limited to guests with confirmed bookings, so they remain quiet throughout the day. Most have electricity, and some sell firewood, and all of the sleeping options have private bathrooms. Prices range from R1320 to R1910 for four people, plus R314/157 per additional adult/

1. Sabie River (p386)
This river is a great spot for wildlife-watching; it attracts a broad range of animals.

2. Meerkat
A curious meerkat stands to attention.

3. Striped Kingfisher
A striped kingfisher perched at Letaba.

MARTIN CREASSER/ALAMY ©

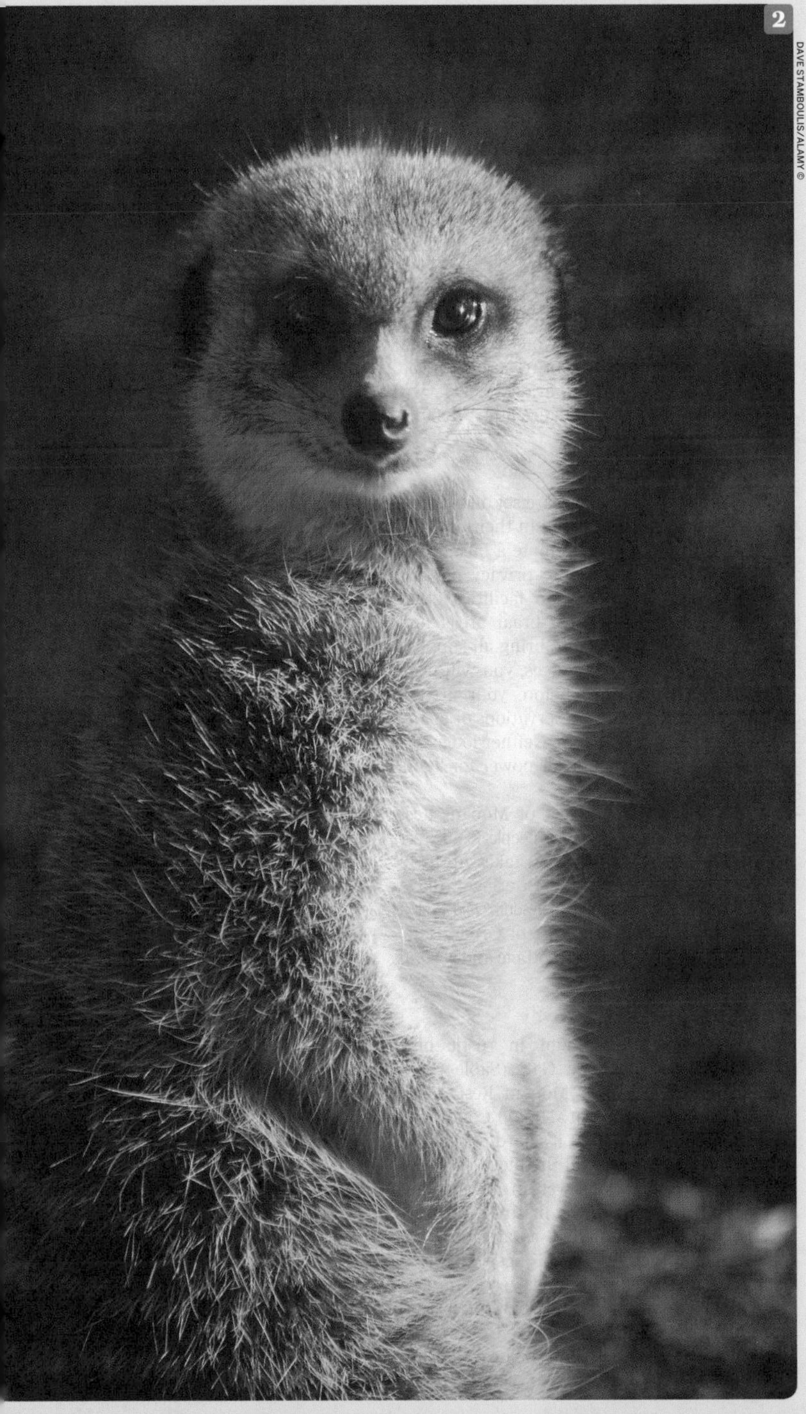

2

DAVE STAMBOULIS/ALAMY ©

KRUGER FOR CHILDREN

Kruger is very family-friendly, and is ideally set up for taking children with you on safari. The rest camps are all fenced, many of the main ones have swimming pools and restaurants offering special children's meals, and several have children's play areas. Letaba, Skukuza, Satara and Shingwedzi also have regular evening wildlife movies shortly after dusk that are good for viewers of all ages, and Letaba has an elephant museum where children (and adults) can see former giant tuskers up close, plus various other attractions. Camp shops, however, generally don't stock children's nappies, processed baby food or baby milk mixtures, so bring these items with you.

child. If you are just one person staying at the accommodation, you will still pay the unit price for the entire cottage. Read up on the five camps available at www .sanparks.org/parks/kruger/camps/default. php£bushveld.

Bush Lodges

Kruger's two bush lodges are set off on their own and must be reserved in their entirety. The idea is to have as remote a bush experience as possible, in the privacy of your own group. There are no facilities other than equipped kitchens, braai areas and bedding; you will need to bring all supplies in with you. For both lodges, you will need to make reservations before your arrival, either through central reservations or at any Kruger gate or rest camp. Neither lodge has electricity, other than solar power for lights and fans.

About 23km southwest of Mopani Rest Camp, **Boulders** (up to 4 people R2465, per additional adult/child R504/252) takes up to 12 people in six rooms; and **Roodewal** (up to 8 people R5100, per additional adult/child R546/273), about 28km northeast of Orpen Gate, takes up to 19 people in a cottage and several bungalows.

Overnight Hides

It's possible to overnight in rustic bird hides near Phalaborwa Gate (Sable Overnight Hide) and near Mopani Rest Camp (Shipandani Overnight Hide). Conditions are extremely basic, but it's hard to beat the proximity to nature and the hides book out quickly – reservations well in advance are essential. Basic bedding – mattresses, sheets and duvets – is supplied, as are mosquito nets, but otherwise you'll need to bring everything, including food, water and a torch. There's a braai area, but you'll need to bring wood/fuel. The hides can only be occupied from half an hour before park gate

closing time to half an hour after the gate opening time, and each can be booked by a minimum of two people and maximum of six people. Prices are R445 for two people, plus an additional R214 charged for each extra person.

Located about 10km from Phalaborwa Gate (where bookings should be made), **Sable Overnight Hide** (☏013-735 6509) overlooks Sable Dam; and **Shipandani Overnight Hide** (☏013-735 6535/6) is about 3km south of Mopani Rest Camp (where bookings are made), overlooking the Tsendze River.

Private Concessions

There are several private concessions within Kruger National Park. All are located in wildlife-rich areas of the park and offer the chance to go on safari while enjoying all the amenities, in an experience similar to those offered in the private wildlife reserves (p392). Although these concessions are within the park proper, access is restricted to lodge guests only, and advance bookings are essential. Book directly with the relevant concession operator or through the links from the SANParks website, on which all are previewed.

Lukimbi Safari Lodge (☏011-431 1120; www .lukimbi.com; s/d all-inclusive R6540/9700) is an attractive 16-suite lodge that is overlooking the Lwakhale River. The lodge is located near the southern border of the park, just southwest of the Biyamiti Bushveld Camp. It endeavours to forge ties with local communities and supports several small-scale community-oriented projects.

Singita Lebombo Lodge (☏021-683 3424; www.singita.com; per person all-inclusive R12,250) This is the flagship lodge of the Singita group; it is another lovely accommodation option.

ⓘ Information

Kruger is a long, narrow wedge bordered by Mozambique to the east, Zimbabwe on its northern tip, Limpopo province to the west and Mpumalanga to the west and south. It averages about 65km across, and is about 350km long. Rimming the park to the west, and sharing the same unfenced terrain, is a chain of private wildlife reserves.

Much of Kruger's topography ranges from flat to gently undulating, with the Lebombo Mountains rising up to the east along the Mozambique border. Major rivers flowing across Kruger from west to east include the Limpopo, Luvuvhu, Shingwedzi, Letaba, Olifants, Timbavati and Sabie. Kruger's northern third – from about 12km north of Mopani Rest Camp upwards – lies north of the Tropic of Capricorn, although tropical vegetation only really becomes evident in the far north.

There are nine South African entry gates (*heks* in Afrikaans). Entry gate (and camp) opening times vary slightly with the season, and are currently as shown in the Entry Gates table:

It's also possible to enter Kruger from Mozambique at the **Giriyondo Gate** (⊘8am-4pm Oct-Mar, to 3pm Apr-Sep) and the **Pafuri Gate** (⊘8am-4pm), both of which double as international border crossings (see p394). It is 95km from Kruger's Phalaborwa Gate (and 65km from Letaba Rest Camp) to Giriyondo and 75km further from Giriyondo to Massingir (Mozambique), the first major town on the Mozambique side. It's easily possible to do the stretch in less than a day. The Pafuri border post is 11km east of Kruger's Pafuri Rest Camp (and 29km from Pafuri Gate).

On the Mozambique side, there is an unbridged crossing of the Limpopo River near Mapai that's only possible during the dry season, and a rough bush track thereafter via Mabote and Mapinhane to Vilankulo, on the Mozambican coast. Allow two full days from Pafuri to Vilankulo; there's a **campsite** (per person R45) with hot-water showers near Mapai.

Once inside the park, Kruger is laced with a network of sealed roads, one of which runs along its entire spine. These, together with more lightly travelled but generally well-maintained gravel side roads, form a road network of about 1900km.

Bookings

Kruger accommodation can be booked through the **South African National (SAN) Parks central reservations office** (☎012-428 9111; fax 012-426 5500; www.sanparks.org; 643 Leyds St, Muckleneuk, Pretoria), online, in person, via telephone or email. It's also possible to book through **Lowveld Tourism** (www.lowveldtourism.com) offices in Nelspruit (p374) and Cape Town.

Bookings for park accommodation and wilderness trails can be made up to 11 months in advance. Except in the high season (school holidays, Christmas and Easter) and weekends, bookings are advisable but not essential. For high-season travel, book as far in advance as possible. The exception to all this is park accommodation with disabled facilities, which can only be booked one month in advance via regular post, fax or telephone.

Entry

Park entry costs R192/96 per adult/child per day or for an overnight stay, with discounts for South African citizens and residents, and for South African Development Community (SADC) nationals. The SANParks Wild Card (see www.sanparks.org/wild), which allows unlimited entry to South African national parks (and some in Swaziland) for an annual fee, also applies to Kruger.

Bicycles and motorcycles are not permitted to enter the park. During school holidays, you can stay in the park for a maximum of 10 days, and at any one rest camp for five days (10 days if you're camping). Throughout the year, park authorities restrict the total number of visitors within the park on any given day, so in the high season it pays to arrive early if you don't have a booking.

It's an offence to arrive late at a camp and you can be fined for doing so (the camps are fenced). With strictly enforced speed limits of 50km/h on sealed roads and 40km/h on dirt roads (monitored by rangers with radars), it can take a while to travel from camp to camp, especially if you encounter a traffic jam near an interesting animal.

ENTRY GATES

MONTH	GATES/ CAMPS OPEN (AM)	GATES/ CAMPS CLOSE (PM)
Jan	5.30/4.30	6.30
Feb	5.30/5.30	6.30
Mar	5.30/5.30	6
Apr	6/6	6
May-Jul	6/6	5.30
Aug & Sep	6/6	6
Oct	5.30/5.30	6
Nov & Dec	5.30/4.30	6.30

KRUGER FOR DISABLED TRAVELLERS

Facilities for disabled persons are available at Berg-en-dal, Crocodile Bridge, Pretoriuskop, Lower Sabie, Skukuza, Satara, Olifants, Letaba, Mopani, Shingwedzi and Tamboti. The website for SANParks (www.sanparks.org) has an excellent overview of conditions at each camp for disabled travellers, and is well worth browsing when planning your travels.

❶ Getting There & Around

Air

SAAirlink (0861 606 606; www.flyairlink.com) has daily flights linking both Jo'burg and Cape Town with Mpumalanga Kruger International Airport (MKIA) near Nelspruit (for Numbi, Malelane and Crocodile Bridge Gates), and with Kruger Park Gateway Airport in Phalaborwa (2km from Phalaborwa Gate). Sample one-way fares and flight times: Jo'burg to Phalaborwa, R1655, one hour; Jo'burg to MKIA, from about R900 to R1500, one hour; Cape Town to MKIA, R2500 to R3500, 2¼ hours. SAAirlink also has daily flights (three weekly direct) connecting Cape Town with Hoedspruit (for Orpen Gate) via Jo'burg (from R2600, 3¼ hours).

South African Airways (0861 359 722; www.flysaa.com) flies daily between Durban and MKIA (from about R1300 to R1800, 1½ hours); while **South African Express** (011-978 9905; www.flyexpress.aero) flies daily between Jo'burg and Hoedspruit Eastgate Airport (from about R1100, 1½ hours), with connections to Cape Town.

Bus & Minibus Taxi

Nelspruit is the most convenient large town near Kruger, and is well served by buses and minibus taxis to and from Jo'burg (see p335). Numbi Gate is about 50km away, and Malelane Gate about 65km away. Phalaborwa, in the north on the edge of Kruger, is being increasingly promoted as a gateway for northern Kruger. It is served by regular bus services to/from Jo'burg and elsewhere in South Africa. Hoedspruit is another possible hub, with reasonable bus connections to elsewhere in South Africa. It's also the most convenient gateway for many of the private reserves bordering Kruger, and an easy 70km drive from the park's Orpen Gate. All of these towns have car rental agencies, or you can book a Kruger tour through local hotels; see the individual listings for more. From the Venda region in Limpopo province, minibus taxis run close to

the Punda Maria Gate, but you'll need your own vehicle to get around inside the park.

Car

Most visitors drive themselves around the park, and this is the best and most economical way to experience Kruger. If you're running low on funds, hiring a car between three or four people for a few days is relatively cheap (see p599).

Skukuza is 500km from Jo'burg (six hours). **Avis** (in Johannesburg 011-923 3600, in Skukuza 013-735 5651; www.avis.co.za) has a branch at Skukuza, and there is car rental at the Nelspruit, Hoedspruit and Phalaborwa airports.

Driving on the paved roads in Kruger is easy. There is little traffic and speed limits are controlled. However, keep an eye out for sudden stops and distracted drivers. There are petrol stations at most of the larger camps, but you'll save a little money by filling up before entering the park.

Train

The *Komati* train runs from Jo'burg via Nelspruit to Komatipoort (economy class only), which is about 12km from Kruger's Crocodile Bridge Gate. Once there, you'll need to arrange vehicle rental or a tour to visit the park.

PRIVATE WILDLIFE RESERVES

Spreading over a vast lowveld area just west of Kruger is a string of private reserves that offer comparable wildlife-watching to what you'll experience in the park. The main reserves – Sabi Sand, Manyeleti and Timbavati – directly border Kruger (with no fences), and the same Big Five (lion, leopard, buffalo, elephant and rhino) populations that roam the park are also at home here.

There are around 200 lodges and camps in the private reserves and most are expensive. Together with the handful of private concessions operating within the park's boundaries, the private reserves offer some of Africa's best opportunities for safari connoisseurs, and are the place to go for those who want to experience the bush in the lap of luxury. Prices tend to be seasonal so it's best to have a look at the websites for the most accurate costs. Note that many of these places like to call themselves 'game reserves'. They're not. They are simply lodges inside a designated wildlife reserve.

If your budget permits, it's also worth considering the private reserves as a complement to spending a few nights in the park. The rangers have a wealth of knowledge and, because of the personalised safari attention,

Private Wildlife Reserves

N 0 ———— 30 km
0 ———— 15 miles

Private Wildlife Reserves

🛏 Sleeping

KRUGER NATIONAL PARK SABI SAND GAME RESERVE

can train you in the art of wildlife-watching before you head to Kruger for a self-guided trip. The major reserves and a few of their camps are described here. There are many more lodges and dozens of operators handling tours in this area. Hoedspruit has emerged as the gateway to the private lodges.

Note that even if you arrive with your own vehicle, self-drive safaris aren't permitted in any of the private reserves, and most can only be visited with advance booking. In addition to the reserves described here, there are numerous other smaller ones further north and west, including Klaserie, Makalali (which doesn't share any borders with Kruger) and Balule (which also has no borders with Kruger).

Sabi Sand Game Reserve

Within the borders of the large Sabi Sand Game Reserve (www.sabisand.co.za) are some of Southern Africa's most luxurious safari lodges and the best wildlife-watching on the continent. The area is routinely selected by safari connoisseurs as their destination of choice. As there's no fencing between the various private lodges within the greater Sabi Sand area, all share the same wealth of birds and animals. There's a R160 vehicle fee and R40 passenger fee to enter Sabi Sand.

In the northern part of Sabi Sand, Nkorho Bush Lodge (☎013-735 5367; www.nkorho .com; s/d all-inclusive R3250/4600; 🏊) is one of the more moderately priced lodges, with comfortable thatched chalets set around grassy grounds, and a low-key ambience.

Djuma Game Reserve (☎013-735 5118; www.djuma.co.za; Vuyatela Camp R13,500; 🏊) is notable for its straightforward, good-value accommodation (the rate includes five chalets sleeping 10 persons). The most intriguing option here is Vuyatela Lodge, where the local culture has been incorporated into every aspect of the building. It's an ideal choice if you're interested in learning about local people as well as the local wildlife. There's also the slightly less expensive Bush Lodge, and the self-catering Galago Camp (R9500 for the entire 10-person camp, including wildlife drives and bush walks).

The exclusive Londolozi Private Game Reserve (☎011-280 6655; www.londolozi.com; all-inclusive per person r R6000-10,000; ❄🏊) is renowned for its luxury, its leopards and its location. You have your choice of accommodation here in one of several intimate camps – all are within walking distance of each other and are in excellent settings along the Sand River. This is the place to go if you want a

GREAT LIMPOPO TRANSFRONTIER PARK

Together with Mozambique's **Limpopo National Park** (entry per visit per adult/child/vehicle US$8/4/8) and Zimbabwe's Gonarezhou National Park, Kruger forms part of the **Great Limpopo Transfrontier Park** (www.greatlimpopopark.com) – a vast area that will ultimately encompass 35,000 sq km. Gonarezhou links are still a work in progress, but Kruger and Limpopo are linked via two fully functioning border posts.

While wildlife in Limpopo can't compare with that in Kruger, the Mozambican side of the border makes a satisfyingly adventurous bush experience. Cultural activities can be arranged through several of the Limpopo lodges, and Machampane Wilderness Camp has a full array of bush activities.

The most straightforward access is via Giriyondo border post (see p593), which is reached via a well-maintained gravel road branching off the tarmac road about 12km north of Letaba. There's also a crossing at Pafuri (see p593), though this puts you well away from the core of Limpopo National Park, and is mainly of interest as a transit point for travellers with their own 4WDs who are heading to/from the Mozambican coast. Officially, you're required to have a 4WD to cross both borders; 4WD is essential for the Pafuri crossing. If you're in a rental vehicle, you'll need to arrange the necessary paperwork in advance (easier done on the Mozambique side, as most South African rental agencies don't permit their vehicles to cross). Once at the border, you'll need to fill out the necessary paperwork for your vehicle (temporary import permit and third-party insurance – both are available at the borders) and pass through immigration. Mozambique visas are readily available at both Giriyondo and Pafuri for R590. You'll also need to pay Limpopo park fees (payable in US dollars, South African rand or Mozambican meticais).

Note that proof of overnight accommodation in the Kruger National Park or Limpopo National Park is an official requirement of crossing the border. SANParks should still allow you through, but will charge a R150 'cross border' fee if you're not sleeping in the park.

five-star-plus experience in the bush, combined with excellent wildlife-watching.

Singita (☎021-683 3424; www.singita.com; all-inclusive per person r R12,250; ✻@✻) has been distinguished by the top-end travel industry as having among the best lodges in Africa. Its South African properties – three lodges in the Singita Private Game Reserve, and two operated as a private concession on Kruger's eastern edge, southeast of Satara Rest Camp – are outstanding in the upper price bracket. Its Singita Lebombo Lodge draws most of the attention, with a superb riverine location, an excess of amenities and impeccable service. Singita also has top-end camps in Tanzania and can arrange combination top-end itineraries.

Other places in the area that come with recommendations are:

Exeter Private Game Lodges (☎011-809 4300; www.andbeyondafrica.com; all-inclusive per person from R5500; ✻✻) is an upmarket entity under the &Beyond Africa (formerly CC Africa) flag, with three exclusive lodges – Leadwood, Dulini and River.

Idube Private Game Reserve (☎011-431 1120; www.idube.com; s/d all-inclusive R5630/8360;

✻) is nice and comfortable, without the finesse of some of the other places, but with a more manageable price tag.

Sabi Sabi Private Game Reserve (☎011-447 7172; www.sabisabi.com; all-inclusive per person from R5750; ✻✻) is known especially for its lions and for its subterranean and ultra-luxurious Earth Lodge.

Manyeleti Game Reserve

During the apartheid era, the 23,000-hectare Manyeleti was the only wildlife reserve that blacks were permitted to visit. Today, it's the least crowded of the private wildlife reserves, with only a few camps. It is possible to see all the Big Five here, although it will take somewhat more effort than in Sabi Sand, its neighbour to the south. As compensation, accommodation here is significantly less expensive than in Sabi Sand.

Entry to Manyeleti is R50 per car and R20 per person (payable at the gate). There is also a community levy of R75 per person. Access is via Orpen Gate Road.

Approaching Limpopo and Kruger from the Mozambique side, the main route is from Mozambique's EN1 coastal road to Macia junction, and then northwestwards via Chokwé to Massingir town and Limpopo National Park's Massingir entry gate.

Machampane Wilderness Camp (www.dolimpopo.com; s or d tent with full board per person R2300) is Limpopo's only upmarket camp, with five spacious safari tents directly overlooking the Machampane River, about 20km from the Giriyondo border post. Machampane is also the best camp to contact for arranging bush activities in and around the park. These include guided walks from camp; a four-day hiking trail from Massingir Dam west along the Machampane River (fully portered, catered version per person R4250); and a four-day canoe expedition along the Olifants River (per person R4900). There's also the six-day Shingwedzi 4WD trail (per vehicle R6700), starting at Kruger's Punda Maria camp and continuing south through Limpopo National Park to the Lebombo/Ressano Garcia border post.

Further accommodation options in Limpopo National Park include the following: **Aguia Pesqueira Campsite** (campsite per person US$4, tents US$5), a basic but good park-run camping ground with cold-water ablutions, which overlooks Massingir Dam about 50km from the Giriyondo border post; **Campismo Albufeira** (campsite per person US$8, s or d chalets US$40), just inside Massingir Gate, near the dam wall, with four simple, clean en-suite self-catering chalets and camping; and **Covane Community Lodge** (www.covanelodge.com; campsite per person US$10, d in traditional unit US$65, 5-person houseboat US$200), a community-run place about 15km outside Limpopo's Massingir Gate, with local-style or self-catering accommodation and cultural activities.

Coming from Kruger, you can leave your vehicle in the fenced Letaba ranger post compound (about 2km from Letaba Rest Camp), and Machampane Wilderness Camp staff will provide return transport between Letaba and Machampane for R500 per person (minimum two people; return between Letaba camp and Phalaborwa per person R550, return between Machampane and Massingir per person R500).

Honeyguide (Khoka Moya; ☎011-341 0282; www.honeyguidecamp.com; all-inclusive per person R4100; ✹) is one of the better-value private reserves – a small place, with just 12 simple but quite adequately furnished tents. It also has a special children's educational program focusing on nature and wildlife.

Timbavati Private Game Reserve

Timbavati (timbavati.co.za) was originally known for its white lion population, although none remain – just their yellow cousins. It's less crowded than Sabi Sand, and its accommodation – while lacking the sumptuous settings of the lodges in Sabi Sand – tends to be more reasonably priced, without forgoing too many amenities. There's a R160 per person conservation fee and R120 vehicle fee to pay when entering the reserve.

Gomo Gomo (☎015-793 2346; www.gomogomo.co.za; s/d R2500/3800) is a moderately priced place, with rustic stone-and-thatch chalets and tents.

Umlani Bushcamp (☎021-785 5547; www.umlani.co.za; s/d R4000/6000; ✹) is a good place if you want to immerse yourself in the bush, with no electricity; accommodation is in straightforward but comfortable reed and thatch bungalows.

Ngala Tented Camp (☎011-809 4300; www.andbeyondafrica.com; all-inclusive shared tent per person R6600, shared lodge per person R4400; ✹✹) is a subdued but luxurious place in a superb location on the border of Kruger, managed by &Beyond Africa. Accommodation is in your choice of a safari tent or lodge, and it comes with all the amenities; a portion of profits are channelled back into conservation through the South Africa National Parks Trust and World Wildlife Fund.

Tanda Tula (☎015-793 3191; www.tandatula.co.za; all-inclusive per person R4700; ✹), Timbavati's most luxurious option, offers cosy safari tents and a waterhole practically at your doorstep. Children under 12 aren't permitted.

Motswari (☎011-463 1990; www.motswari.co.za; all-inclusive s/d R5250/7000) is a lovely, unfussed place with 15 well-appointed chalets and a small art gallery.

THE MAKULEKE CONTRACT

The heart of Kruger's far north is Makuleke concession – a beautiful and geologically ancient area consisting of a 24,000-hectare wedge of land rimmed by the Limpopo and Luvuvhu Rivers. In 1969, South Africa's apartheid government forcibly removed the local Makuleke people from the area in order to incorporate their traditional lands into Kruger National Park.

In the late 1990s, the land was returned to the Makuleke, who in turn agreed not to resettle it but to use it for ecotourism purposes. A 'contract park' was created in which the land is administered and managed environmentally as part of Kruger, with tourism developments owned by the Makuleke, who have since granted concessions to three companies, including two lodges.

Thornybush Private Game Reserve

When Thornybush opened in 1977, it was on a small property. It has since expanded more than five-fold to 10,000 hectares and is one of the few reserves in the area that is still enclosed by fences. There are close to a dozen lodges on the reserve. It has no gate entrance fees.

The electricity-free Tangala (☏015-7930488; www.tangala.co.za; per person all-inclusive from R1850; ✸) is a well-designed, well-maintained, disabled-accessible and good-value camp.

Makuleke Contract Park

Although enjoying a different legal status than the other private game reserves covered in this section, Makuleke is still very much a secluded, upmarket experience, well apart from Kruger's network of parkrun camps. Elephants favour the area during the winter months, buffaloes, hippos, lions, leopards and nyalas are plentiful year-round, and birding is excellent. The local community is an active tourism partner, and cultural activities can be arranged.

In addition to the two lodges within the concession, Makuleke is also home to EcoTraining (www.ecotraining.co.za), which offers month-long field-guide training courses, as well as courses in birding, wildlife photography and other nature-related topics.

Makuleke Community Centre & Homestay (☏079-151 7127; www.makuleke.com; s/d R250/350), a reconstructed cultural village outside Kruger National Park, about 45km southwest of Punda Maria Gate near Thohoyandou, is run by the local Makuleke people. It offers a handful of simple but modernised local-style huts, traditional meals (breakfast/lunch/dinner R30/45/60) and village tours, and is recommended for anyone wanting to gain an introduction to local life. Transfers can be arranged with either of the upmarket camps in Makuleke concession (see the following two listings). If you're driving, follow Rte 524 from Louis Trichardt (Makhado) past Thohoyandou. Continue until the Mhinga village junction, from where Makuleke is signposted via Maphophe and Boxahuku villages. Bookings can be made directly, or through www.responsibletravel.com.

Pafuri Camp (☏011-257 5111; www.wilderness -adventures.com/countries/south-africa/pafuri-camp; s/d all-inclusive R2500/3600; ✸), a 20-tent camp (including six four-person 'family' tents), has a lovely setting overlooking the Luvuvhu River, with rewarding wildlife-watching and birding directly from camp. A portion of revenues goes directly to the local Makuleke community.

The Outpost (☏011-327 3910; www.theout post.co.za; s/d all-inclusive from R4450/8300; ✸) consists of 12 very open and super-contemporary 'living spaces' overlooking the Luvuvhu River. The lodge – which employs mostly local staff – operates under a community-partnership arrangement where a portion of profits is paid to the Makuleke community. Then, after expiry of its initial 30-year lease, the lodge will be turned over in its entirety to the community.

Limpopo

Best Places to Eat

» Cafe Pavilion (p402)
» Pebbles (p402)
» Casa C+afé (p407)
» Red Plate (p414)
» Cala la Pasta (p420)

Best Places to Stay

» Plumtree Lodge (p401)
» Ultimate Guest House (p407)
» Game Breeding Centre (p403)
» Ilala Country Lodge (p409)
» Kaia Tani (p418)

Why Go?

Limpopo is a rambling province characterised by traditional culture, wildlife and vast open spaces. With icons ranging from Mapungubwe's gold-plated rhino figurine to 'Breaker' Morant, the second Anglo-Boer War folk hero, Limpopo is an extraordinarily diverse province.

The subtropical area includes mysterious Modjadji, home of rain-summoning queens; and the Venda region, a traditional area where a python god is believed to live in Lake Fundudzi, and artists produce highly original work. The province also contains national parks featuring the Big Five, ancient and striking landscapes and the remains of a millennium-old civilisation. And if you feel the need to get away from it all, the Waterberg Biosphere Reserve offers endless skies and a distinctly South African beauty.

When to Go
Polokwane (Pietersburg)

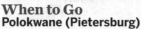

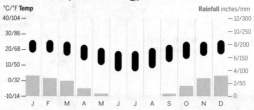

°C/°F **Temp**   **Rainfall** inches/mm

Jun–Aug Steamy conditions cool down making this a great time to visit Mapungubwe National Park

Sep–Dec The Rain Queen near Modjadjiskloof presides over a festival heralding the coming of the rains

Jan–Mar Summer is hot and dry so head for the cooler hills and the berry festival in Haenertsburg

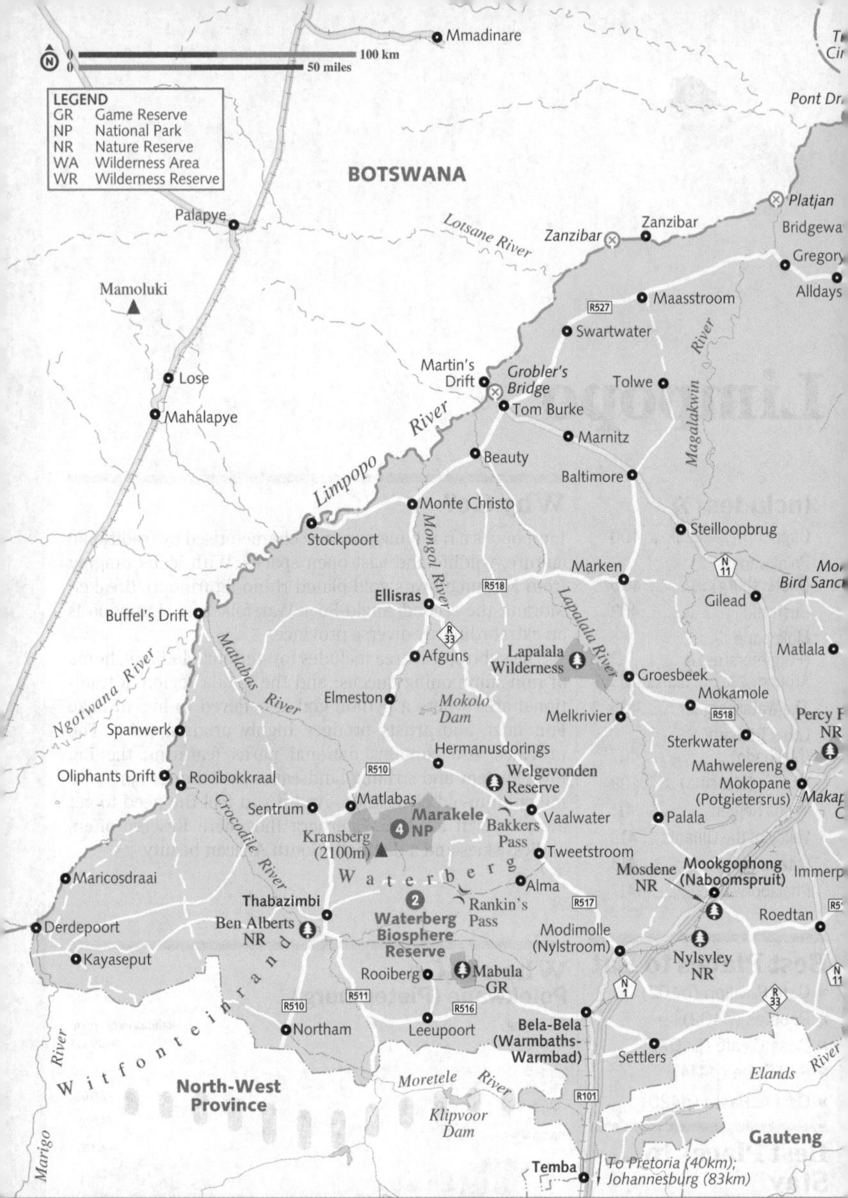

LEGEND
GR Game Reserve
NP National Park
NR Nature Reserve
WA Wilderness Area
WR Wilderness Reserve

BOTSWANA

NORTH-WEST PROVINCE

Gauteng

Limpopo Highlights

❶ Exploring ancient and stunning landscapes in **Mapungubwe National Park** (p410) via the confluence of three countries

❷ Discovering solitude and space amongst the reserves of the vast and wild **Waterberg Biosphere Reserve** (p405)

❸ Searching out traditional crafts in the **Venda region** (p411) or the intricate and colourful weavings at **Kaross** (p417)

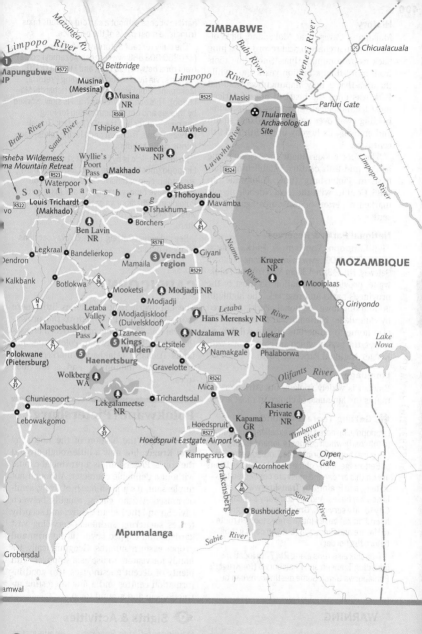

ZIMBABWE

MOZAMBIQUE

Mpumalanga

4 Watching the sun slide behind blue bluffs from vulture-viewing point at **Marakele National Park** (p406)

5 Revelling in the cool climate, misty forests and relaxed living in **Haenertsburg** (p413) and **Kings Walden** (p415)

History

Makapan's Caves, near Mokopane, have offered up an archaeological record stretching back to protohuman times (including tools from more than a million years ago), while the area that is now Mapungubwe National Park was once the heart of one of Africa's most technologically advanced civilisations, holding sway over an area of 30,000 sq km and enjoying its heyday in the 8th and 9th centuries.

The Voortrekkers made this region home in the mid-19th century, establishing their base in Pietersburg (now Polokwane) in 1886. Conflict with the local Ndebele people marked a period of resistance against the settlers.

National Parks & Reserves

The Limpopo Tourism & Parks Board (015-293 3600; www.golimpopo.com; Southern Gateway, N1; 8am-4.30pm Mon-Fri), in Polokwane, provides information on most of the province's parks and reserves. The highlight is Mapungubwe National Park, followed by Marakele National Park. Limpopo is also home to numerous private wildlife reserves, the best of which are contiguous with Kruger National Park (see p379).

Language

English is widely spoken, but Afrikaans remains the language of choice in most areas.

ⓘ Getting There & Around

Limpopo is bisected by the excellent N1 highway (a toll road), which connects Johannesburg (Jo'burg) and Pretoria to the Zimbabwe border at Beitbridge. Many of the province's large towns are on this artery and most are connected to Jo'burg and Pretoria by **Translux** (www.translux.co.za) buses, and the company's cheaper City to City services. **Greyhound** (www.greyhound.co.za) buses make a few stops en route to Harare and Bulawayo (but you can't get off before the border).

Translux also runs along Rte 71 to locations including Tzaneen and Phalaborwa (for Kruger's Phalaborwa Gate). Some destinations can be

hard to access without a car, but minibus taxis trundle to most parts of the province.

The daily (except Saturday) **Bosvelder** (0860 008 888; www.shosholozameyl.co.za) train runs between Jo'burg and Musina (R110, 17 hours) via five locations including Pretoria, Mokopane, Polokwane and Louis Trichardt (Makhado). This economy-class train is slow, worked by thieves and not recommended for long journeys – or for any travel after dark. Travel between Louis Trichardt and Musina takes place during daylight hours.

Hiring a vehicle is by far the best way to see Limpopo (most roads are good, although many are undergoing extensive repair work); if you want to save time, you can fly from Jo'burg to Polokwane, Phalaborwa or Hoedspruit (northwest of Kruger's Orpen Gate) and hire a car there.

See individual Getting There & Away sections for more details.

CAPRICORN

The Capricorn region includes little more than Polokwane (Pietersburg), the provincial capital. The Tropic of Capricorn crosses the N1 halfway between Polokwane and Louis Trichardt (Makhado), marked by an anticlimactic monument and a few aloe trees.

Polokwane (Pietersburg)

015 / POP 140,000

Once called 'the bastion of the north' by Paul Kruger, but now a little rough around the edges, Pietersburg is a provincial capital without a definable character. Although not unpleasant, it's a mish-mash of lively, semi-organised African chaos, roughly between Civic Sq and the Indian Centre; and security fences sheltering sprinklers servicing vast gardens and clipped lawns in the prim and proper eastern suburbs. Geographically, it's handy for visitors to use as a stopover, with plenty of decent guesthouses, two good information centres and a few interesting attractions in and around town.

◉ Sights & Activities

Polokwane Game Reserve　WILDLIFE RESERVE
(015-290 2331; adult/child/vehicle R17/13/25; 7am-5.30pm, last entry 3.30pm May-Sep, to 6.30pm, last entry 4.30pm Oct-Apr) You can go on safari at this 3250-hectare reserve less than 5km south of Polokwane. It's one of the

---

WARNING

Malaria and bilharzia are prevalent in Limpopo, mainly in the northeast near Kruger National Park and the Zimbabwe border. For more information on malaria, see p610.

Polokwane (Pietersburg)

alism, many depictions of Nelson Mandela and interesting display on women and art in South Africa. It features artists from Limpopo and across the country.

👉 Tours

Vuwa Safari & Tours CULTURAL, WILDLIFE
(☑015-291 1384; www.vuwasafaritours.co.za) For cultural, heritage and wildlife tours around Limpopo.

🛏 Sleeping

As is the case throughout Limpopo, accommodation options are concentrated in the midrange bracket, and budget travellers will struggle.

TOP CHOICE Plumtree Lodge GUESTHOUSE $$
(☑015-295 6153; www.plumtree.co.za; 138 Marshall St; r incl breakfast R620; 🅿️🛜🏊) This German-run guesthouse's bungalow rooms are some of the most spacious and appealing in town. Standard features are high ceilings, lounge areas, minibars, DSTV and desks where you can tap into the free wi-fi. A poolside *lapa* (circular building with low walls and a thatched roof) bar and generous breakfasts complete the package.

Rustic Rest GUESTHOUSE $$
(☑015-295 7402; www.rusticrest.co.za; 36 Rabe St; s/d incl breakfast R630/840; 🅿️) Occupying a 1940s house and a purpose-built building, the family-run Rustic Rest is one of the best deals in Polokwane, offering DSTV, minibars and friendly service. Decorative items such as wheelbarrows and LP records create some rustic ambience in the eight rooms.

Victoria Place GUESTHOUSE $$
(☑015-295 7599; www.victoriaplace.co.za; 32 Burger St; s/d incl breakfast R600/800; 🅿️) Victoria

country's largest municipal nature reserves, with 21 wildlife species including zebras, giraffes and white rhinos, plus a good network of roads and hiking trails.

Bakone Malapa Open-Air Museum MUSEUM
(☑015-295 2432; adult/child R7.50/5; ⊙9am-3.30pm Mon-Sat) Located 9km south of Polokwane on Rte 37 to Chuniespoort, this museum evokes the customs of the Northern Sotho people who lived here 300 years ago. The tour of the re-created village shows pots being made and demonstrations of tools such as the antelope horn trumpet and marula root matches.

FREE Hugh Exton Photographic Museum MUSEUM
(☑015-290 2186; Civic Sq; ⊙9am-3.30pm Mon-Fri) Set in a restored 19th-century church, Hugh Exton covers Polokwane's first half-century and the second Anglo-Boer War through the work of the prolific photographer, who left 3,000 glass negatives.

FREE Polokwane Art Museum MUSEUM
(☑015-290 2177; Library Gardens; ⊙9am-4pm Mon-Fri, to noon Sat) This museum is worth tucking into for its modern take on coloni-

Place is graced with elegance and plenty of smiles. It has spacious rooms with beautiful linen and basic bathrooms. You can eat breakfast among pot plants on the verandah. Self-catering units, incorporating a kitchenette, are also available. It's a block south from the corner of Burger and Thabo Mbeki streets.

Cycad Guest House
GUESTHOUSE $$

(☎015-291 2123; www.cycadguesthouse.co.za; cnr Schoeman & Suid Sts; s/d R750/920; ✳@) An arboreal option to file under 'motel-style', Cycad makes the most of its brutal brick shell with modern, glossy rooms and slick service. There's an all-weather balcony good for lounging in the evening and a laundry service.

Protea Hotel – Ranch Resort
HOTEL $$$

(☎015-290 5000; www.theranch.co.za; Farm Hollandrift; r R1000-3000; ✳@☎) If it's a touch of luxury you're after and don't mind being out of town, the Ranch offers four-star rooms. They feature varnished wooden furniture and large bathrooms with marble sinks. It's 25km southwest of Polokwane (on the N1).

✗ Eating

You can find the usual takeaways in and around Library Gardens, but the Savannah Centre (Rte 71) offers the widest selection of sit-down meals.

 Cafe Pavilion
CAFE $$

(Sterkloop Garden Pavilion, Kerk St; mains R55-90; ⊙8am-10pm Mon-Sat, to 2pm Sun) Overlooking a garden centre, and boasting its own water feature in the covered outdoor area, the Pavilion is Polokwane's venue of choice for long, leisurely meals. Food has the usual focus on meat feasts (think biltong and avo T-bone) prepared in a variety of styles, with a couple of salads thrown in for good measure.

Pebbles
INTERNATIONAL $$

(☎015-295 6999; cnr Grobler & Burger Sts; mains R80-120) Polokwane's only eating option with historic surroundings, Pebbles occupies a former parliamentarian's residence, parts of which date to 1918. The menu includes a good meat and fish selection and the building offers patio dining and also a pub.

Cofi
INTERNATIONAL $$

(☎015-296 2538; Savannah Centre; mains R50-100; ⊙8am-late) With an enormous round bar

and a postmodern dining room, this place is as trendy as fine dining gets in the city. Meat-driven mains dominate the menu with the Afro Fusion platter featuring Russian flowers and pap (maize porridge), the most interesting dish on the menu.

❶ Information

Emergency

Police station (☎015-290 6000; cnr Schoeman & Bodenstein Sts)

Internet Access

There are cafes with wi-fi in the Savannah Centre (Rte 71).

PostNet (Shop 8A, Library Gardens; per hr R45; ⊙8am-4.30pm Mon-Fri, to 1pm Sat) Next to Chicken Licken.

Medical Services

Medi-Clinic (☎015-290 3600, 24hr emergency 015-290 3747; cnr Thabo Mbeki & Burger Sts) Private hospital.

Polokwane Hospital (☎015-287 5000; cnr Hospital & Dorp Sts)

Money

There are plenty of banks throughout the centre.
ABSA (70 Hans van Rensburg St) Has an ATM and exchange facilities.

Post

Main post office (Landdros Mare St; ⊙8am-5.30pm Mon-Fri, to 1pm Sat)

Tourist information

Limpopo Tourism & Parks Board (☎015-293 3600; www.golimpopo.com; N1; ⊙8am-4.30pm Mon-Fri) Covers the whole province and offers the useful *Limpopo Explorer* map and the *Know Limpopo* guide. On the N1, approaching town from the south.

Polokwane Municipality Local Development Office (☏015-290 2010; www.polokwane.gov za; Civic Sq, Landdros Mare St; ☺7.45am-5pm Mon-Fri, 9am-1pm Sat) A better source of Polokwane information; has brochures and a list of accommodation.

ⓘ Getting There & Away

Air

SAAirlink (☏015-288 0166; www.saairlink .co.za) Offices at the airport; flies daily to/from Jo'burg (around R1080 one way). Polokwane airport is 5km north of town.

Bus

Greyhound (☏083 915 9000; www.grey hound.co.za) Has daily departures for Harare, Zimbabwe (R350, 16 hours). Buses stop at Civic Sq.

Translux (☏015-295 5548; www.translux .co.za; cnr Joubert & Thabo Mbeki Sts) Runs services to Jo'burg (R160, four hours) via Pretoria (R160, 3½ hours) at 10.30am, 11.15am and 2.45pm. Two cheaper City to City buses (R130) leave in the mornings.

Car

Located at the airport:

Avis (☏015-288 0171)

Budget (☏015-288 0169)

First (☏015-288 1510)

Minibus Taxi

Minibus taxis run to destinations including Louis Trichardt (R50, 1½ hours) and Thohoyandou (R60, 2½ hours) from the rank at the Indian Centre, on the corner of Kerk and Excelsior Sts. For Jo'burg and Pretoria, head to the main rank, on the corner of Kerk and Devenish Sts (prices are similar to the bus, which is faster and safer).

Train

The *Bosvelder* train (see p400) stops in Polokwane.

BUSHVELD

The main reason to head southwest of Polokwane is to visit the Waterberg, a Unesco biosphere reserve the size of the Okavango Delta. The source of four of Limpopo's perennial rivers, its biodiversity is reflected in the San rock paintings of large mammals on the area's sandstone cliffs. Elsewhere, the Bushveld region is typical African savannah. If you want to break your journey up the N1, there is a string of roadside towns with some pit-stop potential.

Mokopane (Potgietersrus) & Around

☏015 / POP 120,000

Mokopane is a tough Bushveld town. The main attraction for visitors are Makapan's Caves – a fossil trove of world significance and the site of the Ndebele people's resistance to the advancing Voortrekkers. The area forms part of a mineral-rich region the size of Ireland. Over the weekend, accommodation empties as mine workers flood home.

⊙ Sights

Makapan's Caves CAVE
(☏079 515 6491; adult/student R25/15) Declared a World Heritage Site for its palaeontological significance, these caves yielded the famous Taung skull, which belonged to a 3.3-million-year-old humanoid known as *Australopithecus africanus*. The fossilised remains of long-extinct animals such as the sivatherium, an offshoot of the giraffe clan, have been discovered in the caves, which are littered with fossils and bones. In the Historic Cave, chief Makapan and 1000-plus followers were besieged for a month in 1854 by Paul Kruger and the Voortrekkers. You must prebook visits to the site, 23km northeast of town, via the phone number above; the guide also speaks French.

Game Breeding Centre WILDLIFE RESERVE
(☏015-491 4314; Thabo Mbeki Dr; adult/child R18/10, feeding tours R35; ☺8am-4pm Mon-Fri, to 6pm Sat & Sun) This 1300-hectare reserve on Rte 101 is a breeding centre for the National Zoo in Pretoria and has a wide variety of native and exotic animals, including gibbons, wild dogs, giraffes and lions. You can drive through the reserve; go in the morning when its inhabitants are animated.

Arend Dieperink Museum MUSEUM
(97 Thabo Mbeki Dr; adult/child R3/1; ☺7.30am-4pm Mon-Fri) At the back of the tourism association, this museum recounts local history, with a focus on the town's development after Voortrekkers founded it in 1852.

🛏 Sleeping & Eating

Game Breeding Centre GUESTHOUSE **$**
(☏015-491 4314; Thabo Mbeki Dr; campsites per person R30, s/d R200/260; ❄) Certainly the most novel choice, this centre has a guesthouse. The rooms are all a bit different here – some with interior or exterior kitchens and bathrooms. But all are a good size with a

lovely outlook onto the reserve. Room No 1 is our fave – you can see the gibbons at play from your window.

Thabaphaswa HUTS $
(☎015-491 4882; www.thabaphaswa; campsites per person R85, hut per person R125-180; ☀) If you don't mind roughing it a little, this unique property offers accommodation in climbers' huts beneath rocky escarpments. The glass-walled huts have bunk beds and patios with braai (barbecue) pits and open-air showers. Biking and walking trails are also on the property. Follow the Percy Fyfe Rd (signposted from Rte 101 after it crosses the bridge just north of Mokopane) for 13km, then turn at the brown 'Thabaphaswa Hiking and Mountain Bike Trail' sign. It's 2km to the gate, then straight on for another 1.3km to the homestead.

The Platinum GUESTHOUSE $$
(☎015-491 3510; theplatinum@connectit.co.za; 4 Totius St; s/d R400/675; ☀) This suburban house belies the luxury accommodation on offer here. Rooms are beautifully presented with touches of elegance and comfort everywhere. The friendly owner is happy to show her rooms so have a look at a few as layout and size differ – all are first class. It's signposted off the R101 as you enter town from Modimolle.

Jenets CAFETERIA $
(Rt 101; mains R35-60; ☺breakfast, lunch & dinner; ⚐) This family restaurant does the usual meat-driven dishes, however it also has some local Limpopo specialities such as pap and *boerewors* (sausages) with onion and tomato relish. Inside is a diner-style eating area and there's outdoor seating for cooler evenings, along with a kids' playground. It's opposite the museum.

ⓘ Information

Mokopane Tourism Association (☎015-491 8458; www.mogalakwena.gov.za; 97 Thabo Mbeki Dr; ☺8am-4.30pm Mon-Fri, 9am-noon Sat) On Rte 101; has plenty of local information.
PostNet (Crossing Mall, Thabo Mbeki Dr; per hr R40; ☺8am-5pm Mon-Fri, to 1pm Sat) For internet access.

ⓘ Getting There & Away

Translux and City to City have daily buses to Jo'burg (R160/120 for Translux/City to City, 3¾ hours) via Pretoria; to Phalaborwa (R160, 3¾ hours) via Tzaneen; and to Sibasa (R160/130, four hours) via Polokwane and Louis Trichardt.

Minibus taxis leave from outside Shoprite on Nelson Mandela Dr; from Mokopane to Polokwane costs about R30.

Modimolle (Nylstroom)
☎014 / POP 20,000

Some towns just have that feel-good factor - Modimolle (Place of the Spirits) is one of them. It's hard to put your finger on, perhaps the heat just makes the place languid and easygoing. It's a good stopover on your way to/from Vaalwater in the Waterberg, or on your way up north.

Boshoffstraat Gastehuis (☎014-717 4432; 15 Boshoff St; r per person incl breakfast R295), signposted from Rte 101 on the southern side of town, has good-size, simple rooms on a large suburban property which are basic but clean, well located and come with genial owner. The largest room, with three single beds, is the pick if you can forgive the bathroom decor.

Lekkerbly (☎014-717 3702; lekkerblygh@telkomsa.net; 10 Rupert St; s/d R400/600; ☀) provides cramped self-catering chalets or B&B rooms (add R70 for breakfast). There's also a bar here on-site. It's signposted on the way to/from Vaalwater.

For a coffee, tea or light snack you can sit among the antiques at **Oudewerf** (R101 snacks R15-18; ☺ 9am-4pm Mon-Fri, to 1pm Sat).

WORTH A TRIP

NATURE A STONE'S THROW FROM THE N1

The 4000-hectare **Nylsvley Nature Reserve** (☎014-743 1074; adult/child/vehicle R10/5/20; ☺6am-6pm), on the Nyl River floodplain, is one of the country's best places to see birds (380 species are listed). The **Nylsvley Wildlife Resort** (☎015-293 3611; campsite R50, r per person R550) is birding central and offers well-organised accommodation in the reserve. Nylsvley is 20km south of Mookgophong, signposted from Rte 101 to Modimolle.

Bundox Bush Camp (☎072 523 2796; www.bundox.co.za; tent/chalet per person R400/450), 3km north of Mookgophong off Rte 101, has gorgeous open-plan chalets and East African tents in a reserve with attractions including a cheetah camp, 129 bird species and a thatched library.

Bela-Bela (Warmbaths)

014 / POP 37,200

Bela-Bela is a hot, chaotic, seemingly perpetually busy place, but works as a spot to break a journey, especially if you like to indulge in 'warm baths'. Bela-Bela takes its name from the town's hot springs (which bubble out of the earth at a rate of 22,000L per hour), discovered by the Tswana in the early 19th century. Bathing in the soporific pools is a popular treatment for rheumatic ailments.

Sights & Activities

The Hydro Spa SPA
(014-736 8500; www.aventura.co.za; Chris Hani Dr; day/evening R90/80; 7am-4pm & 5-10pm) At the Forever resort (the town's main spa resort), the hyrdro spa has a series of interlinked indoor and outdoor pools. Children head to the cold pools with twisty slides, while those who prefer a relaxing experience can wallow in 52°C water. There are many other enhancers and therapies involving the cleansing waters available.

Thaba Kwena Crocodile Farm CROC FARM
(014-736 5059; adult/child R30/15; 9am-4pm, feeding 2.30pm Sat) This farm is home to more than 10,000 crocodiles, reaching up to 5.5m in length. The beasts are bred for their skin and meat, which is exported worldwide. It's just north of De Draai Gastehuis, 4km from Rte 101.

Sleeping & Eating

Elephant Springs Hotel HOTEL $$
(014-736 2101; www.elephantsprings.co.za; 31 Sutter Rd; s/d R450/550; ❀ 🛜 ❀) Primarily (but not exclusively!) used for conferences, this old-fashioned little beauty provides spacious lodging. Although underneath its smiling veneer there's some rough edges, it's very friendly, the beds are comfy and it makes a good change from staying at guesthouses.

Flamboyant Guesthouse B&B $$
(014-736 3433; www.flamboyantguesthouse.com; 5 Flamboyant St; r per person incl breakfast R250; ❀) Among the jacaranda trees on the northern edge of town, the Flamboyant has flowery patios aplenty, decor that may take you back a few years and a personable owner. Rooms and flats sleeping up to five are available and it's wheelchair friendly.

Greenfields CAFE $
(The Waterfront, Old Pretoria Rd; mains R30-60; lunch & breakfast) A '70s wood-cabana feel makes this place homely, and importantly it gets the food right. There are croissants, muffins and pancakes from the bakery for breakfast. Lunch is a mix of dishes including burgers, salads and steaks.

Information

Bela-Bela Community Tourism Association
(014-736 3694; www.belabelatourism.co.za; Waterfront, Old Pretoria Rd; 8am-5pm Mon-Fri, 9am-3pm Sat) Located in the Waterfront development, over the bridge from the town centre.

Getting There & Away

Minibus taxis run from Ritchie St, between the Forever Resort and Elephant Springs Hotel, to destinations including Polokwane (R65, 2½ hours) and Jo'burg (R80, two hours). The *Bosvelder* train (see p403) stops in Bela-Bela.

The Waterberg

Paul Kruger used to damn troublesome politicos with the phrase, 'Give him a farm in the Waterberg', but that fate may not strike you as such a hardship. The 150km-long range, which stretches northeast from Thabazimbi past Vaalwater, is protected by the 15,000-sq-km Waterberg Biosphere Reserve, one of Africa's two savannah biospheres. Rising to 2100m, it has a mild climate and some wild terrain for spotting the Big Five (lion, leopard, buffalo, elephant and rhino), with rivers and distinctive mountains scything through bushveld and *sourveld* (a type of grassland).

VAALWATER & AROUND

014 / POP 1100

Strung out along the highway, Vaalwater ('faalvater') is a jumble of tourist and local facilities. It makes a top base for exploring the many attractions the Waterberg has to offer and is by far the pleasantest town between Polokwane and Limpopo's southwestern border.

Sights & Activities

St John's Church CHURCH
Some 10km from town on the Melkrivier road, turn right onto the Vierentwintigriviere road and, after 8.7km, turn left towards Naauwpoort and St John's is on your left. The 'church of thatch and stone...

whose quiet charm doth strike a lovely note' (in the words of the poem by the door) dates to 1914. It is said to have been designed by Sir Herbert Baker but is often overlooked in studies of the great colonial architect.

Horizon Horseback Adventures
HORSE RIDING

(☏083 419 1929; www.ridinginafrica.com) Inspiring fervent loyalty in returning riders, this operation near Waterberg Cottages offers adventurous options including cattle mustering and a four-day horse safari in the Dinaka Wildlife Reserve.

🛏 Sleeping & Eating

Zeederberg Cottage & Backpackers
BACKPACKERS $

(☏082 332 7088; www.zeederbergs.co.za; campsites R60, dm R150, cottages R350-500; ☀) Behind the centre of the same name, Zeederberg has a thatched cottage and a Zulu-style *rondavel* as well as backpacker dorms and doubles. The only drawback is that some beds aren't the greatest. The lawn is dotted with jacaranda and tipuana trees and the main building is well set up for backpackers' lounging needs.

Waterberg Cottages
COTTAGES $$

(☏014-755 4425; www.waterbergcottages.co.za; r per person R260-380; ☀) These cottages, 33km north of town off Melkrivier road, range from 'Butterfly' and the dual-level 'Bushwillow', with its free-standing bath and modern kitchen, to simpler offerings; it's all lent some charm by furniture belonging to the family's ancestors. Activities include astrology with the resident star buff, wildlife-watching and farm tours.

WATERBERG WELFARE SOCIETY

Founded to assist individuals and their families affected by HIV/AIDS, the Waterberg Welfare Society (☏014-755 3633; Timothy House, 208-209 Waterberg St; ☉8.30am-5pm) operates a visitor centre, Timothy House, giving the public an opportunity to interact with the orphans and to learn about its programs and work with HIV/AIDS sufferers. Please call before visiting.

TOP CHOICE Bush Stop Café
CAFE $

(mains R35; ☉lunch & dinner) A popular meeting point, with a secondhand bookshop and shaded outside seating, this funky cafe serves goodies such as panini, croissants that are freshly baked, salads (recommended), fresh fruit juices and a mixed-berry milkshake that is to die for.

La Fleur
ITALIAN $$

(Voortrekker St; mains R35-90; ☉ breakfast, lunch & dinner Mon-Sat) With a pretty classy set-up inside and an outdoor terrace where you can keep an eye on the comings and goings in town, this is Vaalwater's only restaurant. It dabbles in pizza, pasta, salads, pancakes and steaks and the chatty kitchen staff do it well.

🛍 Shopping

There are two craft shops in Zeederberg's Centre. Kamotsogo sells handmade products by local Sotho women living with HIV/AIDS and Black Mamba sells craftwork from across the continent.

Beadle
ARTS & CRAFTS

(☏014-755 4002; Sterkstroom Rd; ☉8am-4.30pm Wed-Sat, 9am-2pm Sun) Next to an essential-oils factory in the Waterberg Cottages area, Beadle is a community project that sells attractive leather and beaded crafts, handmade in the workshop by local villagers.

ℹ Information

Bush Stop Café (Zeederburg Centre; ☉8am-5pm Mon-Fri, to 1.30pm Sat) Offers internet access (R15 per 15 minutes) as well as tourist information.

ℹ Getting There & Away

Heavy roadworks along the R33 from Modimolle to Vaalwater were increasing journey time considerably at the time of writing. Parts of the road were being completely rebuilt. This is likely to continue for some time so seriously consider whether a minibus taxi is worth it. Private transport is your best bet.

MARAKELE NATIONAL PARK

This mountainous national park (☏014-777 6928; www.sanparks.org/parks/marakele; adult/child R108/54; ☉7.30am-5pm May-Aug, to 4pm Sep-Apr) is at the southwest end of the Waterberg biosphere. The animals grazing beneath the red cliffs include elephants, black-and-white rhinos, giraffes, zebras, leopards and cheetahs. A great place to eyeball the landscape is the vulture-viewing point (be warned, the road up there is precipitous), where you can

WATERBERG MEANDER

The **Waterberg Meander** (www.water bergmeander.co.za), a 350km signposted tourist route around the Waterberg, links 13 community projects, and sites of interest such as those significant in the Anglo-Boer War, along with viewpoints of some stunning landscapes, and arts-and-crafts outlets. Look out for the excellent *Waterberg Meander* booklet in tourist offices.

also see one of the world's largest colonies of the endangered Cape vulture (800-plus breeding pairs).

The park is divided into two sections; the second section (you press a buzzer to open the gate) is wilder and richer in wildlife with all the Big Five present. The gravel roads are in much better shape in the first section of the park – if it's been raining in particular this is as far as you may want to go. The park entrance booking office is on the Thabazimbi–Alma road, 3km northeast of the intersection with the Matlabas–Rooiberg road.

There is two-bed tented accommodation in the **Tlopi Tent Camp** (tents R990), 15km from reception. The furnished tents, overlooking a dam where antelope and wildebeest come to drink, have a bathroom and open-air kitchen, with refrigerator, and braai. Note you'll have to bring your own food.

The park also offers **tent sites** (2-person site R185, extra adult/child R62/31) at Bontle camping area.

The easiest route to the park from Vaalwater is on Rte 510 to Thabazimbi. However, the hard-dirt Bakkerspas Rd runs alongside the mountains, with spectacular views. Turn left 6km west of town and, after 60km, right at the T-junction; the park entrance is 45km further on, a few kilometres after the tar begins.

SOUTPANSBERG

The Soutpansberg region incorporates the most northern part of South Africa, scraping southern Zimbabwe. The forested slopes of the Soutpansberg mountains are strikingly lush compared with the lowveld to the north, where baobab trees rise from the dry plains. The highlights here are the

mountains, the Venda region and Mapungubwe National Park, which is well worth the 260km drive from Polokwane.

Louis Trichardt (Makhado)

📵 015 / POP 90,000

Spunky Louis Trichardt has a very busy centre with streets of booming retail chain outlets and hordes of shoppers. The outlying streets, however, reveal verdant parkland, wide roads and shady jacarandas giving the place a very pleasant feel. There's not much to do here but it's a great base, especially if you have wheels – 10km north and south of town are some superb places to stay.

The nearby spectacular Soutpansberg mountains boast an extraordinary diversity of flora and fauna, with one of the continent's highest concentrations of the African leopard and more tree species than you'll spot in the whole of Canada.

🛏 Sleeping & Eating

There are several options in Louis Trichardt, but the best way to soak up the Soutpansberg is to stay in the hills just outside of town.

TOP
CHOICE **Ultimate Guest House** GUESTHOUSE $$
(📵015-517 7005; www.ultimategh.co.za; s/d incl breakfast R430/530; 🖫) After a long day on the N1, this quirky, colourful, mist-shrouded guesthouse's name seems a fair description. It has a bar-restaurant (mains R90) with a verandah (ideal for a g&t in the evening) overlooking a lush valley. It's 10km from the centre; turn left 100m after Mountain Inn, head 1.6km along the dirt track and it'll be on your right.

Madi a Thavha LODGE $$
(📵015-516 0220; www.madiathavha.com; campsite per person R60, s/d incl breakfast R615/1010; 🖫) A cleansing Soutpansberg hideaway, this is a Fair Trade–accredited farm lodge. Accommodation is in colourful little cottages with Venda bedspreads and cushions, tea-light candles aplenty and kitchenettes. The Dutch owners organise tours of local craft studios, and dinner (R165) is available. It's some 10km west of Louis Trichardt, off Rte 522.

Casa Café INTERNATIONAL $
(129 Krogh St; mains R50-60; ☺breakfast, lunch & dinner Mon-Sat, lunch Sun) Presenting seafood dishes, grills, loads of burger variations salads

and pastas, this place is a great stop any time of day. A formal atmosphere pervades but it gets more casual at the outside seating area which opens onto a garden.

Makhado Municipal Caravan Park CAMPGROUND $
(☎015-519 3025; www.makhado.caravanparks. co.za; Grobler St; campsites per person R63) In good nick with clipped lawns ideal for a tent, there's also plenty of shade at this well-cared-for caravan park. Central location.

Louis Trichardt Lodge MOTEL $
(☎015-516 2222; www.lttlodge.co.za; Hlanganani St; s/d R350/420) You'll receive curt service at this red-brick motel on the main road. It has basic, serviceable rooms with kitchenettes and braai areas. Breakfast is R40.

ⓘ Information

ABSA (cnr Songozwi Rd & Krogh Sts) Has ATMs and exchange facilities.

PC Worx (Shop 34, Makhado Crossing, cnr N1 & Sebasa St; per 30 min R10; ◷9am-5pm Mon-Fri, to 1pm Sat) Internet access.

Police station (☎015-519 4300; Krogh St)

Soutpansberg Tourist Office (☎015-516 3415; www.soutpansberg-tourism.co.za; Songozwi Rd; ◷8am-4.30pm Mon-Sat)

ⓘ Getting There & Away

Louis Trichardt Travel Agency (☎015-516 5042; ◷8am-1pm & 2-4.30pm Mon-Fri, 9-11am Sat) is down an alley off Krogh St (opposite Louis Trichardt Stationers); the local agent for Greyhound and Translux buses.

Most buses to Jo'burg (R220, six hours) and Harare, Zimbabwe (R330, 11 hours) stop by the Caltex petrol station on the corner of the N1 and Baobab St.

The minibus taxi rank is in the Shoprite supermarket car park off Burger St. Destinations from Louis Trichardt include Musina (R40, 1½ hours) and Polokwane (R50, 1½ hours).

The train station, at the southwestern end of Kruger St, is served by the *Bosvelder* train (see p400).

Around Louis Trichardt

SOUTPANSBERG MOUNTAINS

Beginning at the Soutpansberg Hut on the outskirts of Louis Trichardt, the two-day, 20.5km **Hanglip Trail** climbs through indigenous forest to a 1719m peak with views across the Bushveld. Take precautions against malaria, bilharzia and ticks. Over-

night accommodation is in huts (per person R105) with bunk beds, showers and braais. A 2½-hour walk begins in the same location. Contact **Komatiland Forests Eco-Tourism** (☎013-754 2724; www.komatiecotourism.co.za; 10 Streak St) in Nelspruit for more information and details of how to make reservations.

Perched in the clouds, **Leshiba Wilderness** (☎015-593 0076; www.leshiba.co.za; s/d from R700/850, s/d with full board & an activity from R1925/3200; @☎) is a Fair Trade–accredited resort based on a Venda village. Surrounded by wildlife, including rare brown hyenas and leopards, and with greenery supplied by 350-plus tree species, the hideaway offers self-catering and full-board accommodation in *rondavels,* with features such as private plunge pools and views of Botswana. It's signposted 36km west of Louis Trichardt on Rte 522.

The first thing you see at **Lajuma Mountain Retreat** (☎083 308 7027; www.lajuma. com; camp units/chalets per person R140/200), soon after crossing a leopard causeway, is Letjuma (1730m), the Soutpansberg's highest peak. Run by a biologist and a medical sociologist who revel in local wildlife including 120 bird species, Sykes monkeys and habituated baboons, the Lajuma retreat hosts biological researchers from all over the world. Accommodation is in the waterfall lodge, teetering on a cliffside next to plunge pools; the forest chalet, built in 1946 as a doctor's surgery; and the more-basic wilderness camp. It takes 30 minutes to drive the 7km to the lodge (which is 46km west of Louis Trichardt) from Rte 522, so there's a minimum two-night stay if you need a lift.

BEN LAVIN NATURE RESERVE

This **reserve** (☎015-516 4534; adult/child R30/10; ◷6am-9.30pm) is worth visiting for its walking and mountain-bike trails. It contains 200-plus bird species, as well as giraffes, zebras and jackals.

A range of excellent renovated **accommodation** (campsites per person R60, d chalet/ safari units R350/500) is available, including chalets with huge outdoor areas and lovely vistas. No kitchens but there are hotplates and a braai. Safari units are innovative, being half chalet and half safari tent. There are even family cottages with separate areas for the kids.

Take the N1 south from Louis Trichardt for about 10km, then follow the signpost on

SAVING LAKE FUNDUDZI

The importance of Lake Fundudzi, located 35km northwest of Thohoyandou, cannot be underestimated. The traditional custodians of the lake, the Netshiavha (People of the Pool), consider it a holy place for the burial of their dead.

For scientists, the lake is also special as it's one of South Africa's few natural freshwater lakes. It is believed to have been created 20,000 years ago when a rock slide blocked the path of a river, causing the lake to rise behind it.

Recent decades, however, have seen severe degradation of the lake including loss of surrounding forest and grassland to plantations. Access has long been a privilege granted by the Netshiavha. This was undermined in the mid-1990s when a road was constructed to the lake's edge, giving open access to the site.

In recent years the chief launched a campaign to protect the lake. The Netshiavha, as well as neighbouring tribes, implemented laws to limit land use around the lake and mitigate the effects of tourism. Long-term management strategies are being developed by the Mondi Wetlands Project, a joint project of the World Wide Fund for Nature (WWF) and a fellow NGO, the Wildlife & Environmental Society of South Africa.

the left. After about 3km, you'll see the entrance gate on your left.

Musina (Messina)

015 / POP 20,000

Some 18km south of the Beitbridge border crossing, Musina hums with typical border-town tension. Many people on the move are visiting from Zimbabwe, to take provisions back to a country where the shops lie empty. Groups of economic refugees from the defunct state trudge along the N1, trekking south in search of work.

You will probably pass through the town en route to the spectacular Mapungubwe National Park; the drive there passes through starkly beautiful landscape on empty, baobab-lined roads.

Sights

Giant baobab trees *(Adansonia digitata)*, which look like they have been planted upside down with their roots in the air, characterise this region. You don't have to drive far from Musina to spot some impressive examples of this distinctive tree. Whoppers such as the largest in the country, known as 'the Big Tree' (located near Sagole in northeast Limpopo) are more than 3000 years old.

Musina Nature Reserve   NATURE RESERVE
(015-534 3235; admission free; 7.30am-6.30pm) With South Africa's highest concentration of baobabs, the reserve is 5km south of the town off the N1, and has animals such as impalas and blue wildebeests.

Sleeping & Eating

TOP
CHOICE **Ilala Country Lodge**   LODGE $$
(076 138 0699; ilala@vodamail.co.za; Rte 572; s/d incl breakfast R500/700;) The sweeping views of the Limpopo River Valley into Zimbabwe are something special at this old country lodge. There are few better places in Limpopo for a cold drink in the evening. The accommodation is outstanding with rooms sleeping four in the main homestead, or huge chalets with lounge area, braai facilities and separate kitchen. It's 8km northwest of town, on the way to Mapungubwe.

Backpackers Lodge   BACKPACKERS $
(082 401 2939; 23 Bachman Ave; r R200) This excellent budget option set up in a suburban home is great value. Beds are firm, the place is clean, rooms have TV and the cooking facilities are well equipped. The four rooms sleep two or three each. Located off the R508 next to the police station.

Old Mine Guest House   GUESTHOUSE $$
(015-534 2250; www.oldmineguesthouse.co.za; 1 Woodburn Ave; r R300-600;) In a residence built in 1919 by the first manager of Musina's copper mine, this guesthouse reeks of class and olde-world charm (and is seemingly out of place in Messina!). A verandah overlooks the leafy grounds, and there are stylish rooms or self-catering units with private outdoor patio areas.

Tikva Coffee Shop   CAFE $
(14 Paul Mills Ave; light meals R50) With an outdoor terrace overlooking a quiet suburban street, Tikva is a great local spot to chow

LIMPOPO MUSINA (MESSINA)

down on freshly prepared wraps, panini and pancakes. Delicious desserts too.

ℹ Information

ABSA (6 National Rd) Has change facilities and an ATM. It is on the N1 as it passes through the centre of town.

Musina Tourism (☎015-534 3500; www.golimpopo.com; National Rd) In a thatched hut on the way into town on the N1 from Polokwane. Erratic hours, always shut when we passed by.

PostNet (National Rd; per hr R60; ⏰8.30am-4.30pm Mon-Fri, 8-11am Sat) Internet access.

ℹ Getting There & Away

The Zimbabwe border at Beitbridge, 15km north of Musina, is open 24 hours. If you are coming from Zimbabwe, there is a large taxi rank on the South African side of the border. If you want to take a minibus taxi further south than Musina, catch one here as there are many more there than in Musina. For detailed information on crossing the border into Zimbabwe, see p594.

Daily buses run by Greyhound go from Beitbridge to Harare (eight hours) and Bulawayo (4½ hours), picking up at the Beitbridge Hotel.

Car rental is available at **Avis** (☎015-534 2220; Lifestyle Corner, 10 Hans van der Merwe Ave; ⏰8am-5pm Mon-Fri).

Taxis between the border and Musina cost R35 (20 minutes).

The *Bosvelder* (see p400) connects Musina with Jo'burg via Louis Trichardt.

Mapungubwe National Park

Stunningly stark, arid, rocky landscapes reverberate with cultural intrigue and wandering wildlife at Mapungubwe National Park (☎015-534 7923; www.sanparks.org/parks/mapungubwe; adult/child R108/54; ⏰6am-6.30pm). A Unesco World Heritage Site, Mapungubwe contains South Africa's most significant Iron Age site, as well as animals ranging from white and black rhinos to the rare Pel's fishing owl to meerkats.

The park will realise its full potential when plans to incorporate it into an 800,000-hectare transfrontier conservation area, which will stretch into Botswana and Zimbabwe, are implemented by respective governments.

The park is as much about history as wildlife. In 1933 archaeologists unearthed a 13th-century grave site on Mapungubwe Hill, containing ornaments, jewellery, bowls and amulets, much of it covered in gold foil. The most spectacular of these pieces was a small gold-covered rhinoceros. Apartheid kept this discovery under wraps, as the regime attempted to suppress any historical information that proved black cultural sophistication.

The impressive Interpretative Centre (adult/child R40/20) pulls back this veil and was built in sympathetic resemblance to the landscape. It's one of the country's finest modern buildings. Inside it is contemporary, air-conditioned and the exhibits are tastefully curated. There's plenty of information on the Mapungubwe cultural landscape, including finds from archaeological digs. Keep an eye out for the exquisite beadwork and the replica of the famous gold rhino. Guided tours are obligatory.

The park itself is divided into an eastern and western section (with private land in between). The main gate is on the eastern side along with the interpretative centre, Mapungubwe Hill, a Treetop Walk, Leokwe (the main camp) and a magnificent viewpoint of the confluence of South Africa, Botswana and Zimbabwe. The four viewing decks on a bluff at the confluence come complete with scurrying rock dassies (little guinea-pig-like creatures) and are well positioned for sweeping views of the landscape, and the Limpopo and Shashe Rivers.

A 2WD will get you around but the tracks are pretty rough and you'll see more with a 4WD. The western side is rougher again and you'll need a 4WD to really see this side of the park.

Self-catering accommodation ranges from camping (per campsite from R170) to forest tents at Limpopo Forest Camp (luxury tents R820) and the chalets at Leokwe Camp (per chalet from R870; ❄✳). The chalets are the best we've seen in South African national parks. They include a huge living space, fully equipped kitchen, outside braai area and a traditional *rondavel*-thatch-roof design. There are also outdoor showers.

Be aware that there is no shop or restaurant here. The closest petrol and food supplies are 30km back towards Musina at the truck stop.

The park is a 60km drive from Musina on Rte 572 to Pont Drift.

Venda Region

With perhaps the most enigmatic ambience of the Soutpansberg region, this is the traditional homeland of the Venda people, who moved to the area from modern-day Zimbabwe in the early 18th century (see the boxed text, p412). Even a short diversion from the freeway takes you through an Africa of mist-clad hilltops, dusty streets and mud huts. A land where myth and legend continue to play a major role in everyday life, Venda is peppered with lakes and forests that are of great spiritual significance, and its distinctive artwork is famous nationwide.

THOHOYANDOU & SIBASA

📋 015 / POP 50,000

Created as the capital of the apartheid-era Venda homeland, Thohoyandou (Elephant Head) is a scrappy and chaotic town in a lush region of beautiful Venda scenery; the adjacent town of Sibasa is 2km north. It's useful as a base for exploring the Venda region or to overnight on the way to/from Kruger's Punda Maria Gate, a 60km drive.

◎ Sights

Dozens of **art and craft studios** dotted around the lush countryside are open to the public. The region is best known for its raw woodcarvings (exemplified by the Venda doyenne Noria Mabasa, whose work adorns Pretoria's Union Buildings); its pottery (often painted silver and maroon using graphite and ochre); and bright, stripy batiks and textiles. It's best to hire a guide, as the studios and other sites are generally lost along red tracks, and there is some important local etiquette to follow. A full-day trip costs approximately R800. Thohoyandou/Sibasa-based guides include **Avhashoni Mainganye** (📞084 725 9613; a.mainganye@yahoo.com). Contact **Ribolla Tourism Association** (📞015-556 4262; ribollata@mweb.co.za; Old Khoja Bldg, Elim) for

Venda Region

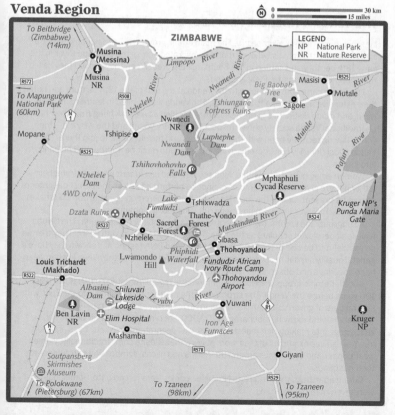

LEGEND	
NP	National Park
NR	Nature Reserve

assistance in locating guides and also look out for its *Ribolla Open Africa Route* brochure at tourist offices.

Thohoyandou Arts & Culture Centre   ARTS & CRAFTS

(Punda Maria Rd, Thohoyandou; ⊙8am-4pm) One starting point for cultural explorations is this haphazard centre which displays craftwork of varying quality by 350-plus local artists.

🛏 Sleeping

Accommodation includes **Muofhe Graceland Lodge** (☑015-962 4926; www.muofhegraceland.co.za; Mphephu St; d incl breakfast R860), overlooking the main drag; or try **Bougainvilla Lodge** (☑015-962 4064; www.bougainvillalodge.com; Mphephu St; r incl breakfast from R460), where rooms are large, sparse and comfy.

❶ Getting There & Away

Translux (R210, eight hours) and City to City (R150) services to Jo'burg are available, all leaving from the Shell petrol station in Thohoyandou and the Caltex petrol station in Sibasa.

The minibus taxi rank next to the Venda Plaza in Thohoyandou serves destinations including Sibasa (R8) and Louis Trichardt (R30, 1½ hours).

LAKE FUNDUDZI & AROUND

Lake Fundudzi is a sacred site that emerges spectacularly from forested hills, a turquoise gem on a bed of green velvet. The python god, who holds an important place in the rites of the Venda's matriarchal culture, is believed to live in the lake and stops it from evaporating in the heat. The water is thought to have healing qualities and ancestor worship takes place on its shores.

You can't visit the lake, 35km northwest of Thohoyandou, without permission from its custodians, the Netshiavha tribe. The easiest way to get permission is to hire a guide in Thohoyandou, Elim or Louis Trichardt. Remember that when you approach the lake you must do so with proper respect;

THE VENDA & NDEBELE PEOPLES

Limpopo has a rich ethnic tapestry. The main ethnic group, the Venda people have obscure origins although it's believed that they migrated across the Limpopo River in the early 18th century and settled in the Soutpansberg area. When they arrived they called their new home 'Venda' or 'Pleasant Land'.

The Boers came into contact with the Venda at the end of the 18th century and noted their extensive use of stone to build walls. The Venda were skilled in leather and beadwork, and made distinctive grain vessels that doubled as artwork hung from their huts.

Traditional Venda society shows respect for the very young and the very old – the young having recently been with their ancestors and the old about to join them. The Venda *kgosi* (king) is considered a living ancestor and must be approached on hands and knees.

Women enjoy high status within Venda society and can inherit property from their father if there is no male heir. Rituals cannot be performed unless the oldest daughter of a family is present. One of the most important Venda ceremonies is the *domba* (snake) dance, which serves as a coming-of-age ritual for young women.

A subgroup, the Lemba, regard themselves as the nobility of the Venda. The Lemba have long perplexed scholars as they seem to have had contact with Islam. They themselves claim to be one of the lost tribes of Israel, and DNA testing has shown they have a genetic quality similar to Jewish people elsewhere. Traditionally, they keep kosher, wear head coverings and observe the Sabbath.

Another ethnic group, the Ndebele, entered the region from KwaZulu-Natal at least 100 years before the Venda. The structure of their authority was similar to the Zulu, with several tiers of governance. An *ikozi* (headman) oversaw each community.

Ndebele, who today number around 700,000, are renowned for their beadwork, which goes into making rich tapestries, toys, wall decorations, baskets, bags and clothing. You can see examples of their work at www.thebeadsite.com. Traditionally, women wear copper and brass rings around their arms and necks, symbolising faithfulness to their husbands.

During apartheid, the Venda and Ndebele peoples were forced onto 'homelands' that were given nominal self-rule.

turn your back to it, bend over and view it from between your legs.

You need 4WD transport to reach the lake, but a car can manage the dirt tracks in the surrounding hills, where there are panoramic viewpoints and the Thathe-Vondo Forest. A sacred section of the forest is home to primeval tangles of creepers and strangler fig trees.

Fundudzi African Ivory Route Camp, located 25km northwest of Thohoyandou and gazing across two tea plantations from its 1400m-high perch, is a branch of the community-run network (see the boxed text, p402) and offers basic accommodation in *rondavels*. You need a 4WD vehicle or a car with good clearance to get there. Manager Nelson offers local tours.

ELIM & AROUND

The tiny township of Elim, some 25km southeast of Louis Trichardt, can be used as a base for touring the Venda and Tsonga-Shangaan art and craft studios. You could equally come across a zebra-dung notebook or a ceremony taking place at a studio. There are also some worthwhile cooperatives including the Twananani weavers and the Mukhondeni Pottery Factory. **Ribolla Tourism Association** (☑015-556 4262; www.openafrica.org; Old Khoja Bldg, Elim) produces a useful brochure and can help to source local guides.

Set among verdant greenery on the shores of Albasini Dam, **Shiluvari Lakeside Lodge** (☑015-556 3406; www.shiluvari.com; r/chalets per person R375/415; ☒) is immersed in the local culture and countryside. Thatched chalets, standard rooms and a family suite, reached on walkways lined with sculptures, are adorned with local craftwork which can be purchased in the on-site shop. A country restaurant and pub are also here.

Translux buses serve Jo'burg (R200, seven hours) and Sibasa (R90, one hour).

VALLEY OF THE OLIFANTS

These days, the Valley of the Olifants may be largely devoid of pachyderms, but the subtropical area feels exotic in places. The region is culturally rich, being the traditional home of the Tsonga-Shangaan and Lobedu peoples. Phalaborwa, a popular entry point to the Kruger National Park, is the start of the 'Kruger to Beach' trail to the Mozambican coast. The main town of Tzaneen and the pretty village of Haenertsburg make pleasant bases for trips to the scenic Modjadji and Magoebaskloof areas.

Letaba Valley

The Letaba Valley, east of Polokwane, is subtropical and lush, with tea plantations and fruit farms overlooked by forested hills. At Haenertsburg, known locally as 'The Mountain', Rte 71 climbs northeast over the steep Magoebaskloof Pass. There are plenty of places where you can stop for short hikes signposted from the road. A less scenic route to Tzaneen is via Rte 528, which runs along the gentler George's Valley.

HAENERTSBURG
POP 300

A small mountain hideaway with a great pub and a couple of upmarket restaurants, Haenertsburg is well worth a stop to breathe in the fresh, crisp mountain air. When the mist rolls in over the surrounding pine plantations, it's easy to imagine yourself far away from Africa – in the Pacific Northwest or the Scottish Highlands, perhaps. It makes an excellent alternative base to Tzaneen, so pull on some outdoor adventure shoes or just prepare for some good old-fashioned lazing around.

⊙ Sights & Activities

War Memorial & Long Tom Monument   MEMORIAL
(Mare St) The last Long Tom gun was destroyed here during the second Anglo-Boer War, which became symbolic of the Boer defeat.

Magoebaskloof Adventures   ADVENTURE SPORTS
(☑083 866 1546; www.thabametsi.com) Off Rte 71, Magoebaskloof Adventures runs adventure trips in the area, including kloofing (canyoning), tubing, fly-fishing, mountain biking, horse riding and canopy tours.

There are good hiking trails near Haenertsburg, including the 11km **Louis Changuion Trail**, which has spectacular views.

With 10-plus dams and four rivers teeming with trout, Haenertsburg is a good place for a spot of fly-fishing. Ask around town – at Pennefather or **The Elms** (Rissik St).

Alternatively, get in touch with Mountain Flyfishing (☏083 255 7817; pirie@mweb.co.za).

🛌 Sleeping

Pennefather   COTTAGES $$

(☏015-276 4885; www.thepennefather.co.za; Rissik St; s/d R400/600) Part of a complex containing antiques, junk, a museum and secondhand books, this olde-worlde place run by appropriately charming older women is hot property, especially at weekends. One of its major assets is its short walking distance to the Iron Crown and Red Plate. The red-roofed cottages have comfortable interiors featuring fireplaces and kitchenettes.

Black Forest Mountain Lodge   LODGE $

(☏082 572 9781; www.wheretostay.co.za/black forestlodge; Black Forest; tents per person R100, cabins R450) You want privacy – you can have privacy. Set among a gorgeous forested landscape, this lodge is 4km from town along a dirt road of varying quality, and is well signposted.

Lamei Lodge   LODGE $

(☏082 266 5724; e.delange@mweb.co.za; s/d R300/450; ✿) Five self-catering chalets in good shape, each sleeping a family or small group, off Rte 71. Kids play area.

🍴 Eating & Drinking

Red Plate   INTERNATIONAL $

(161 Rissik Street; mains R40-80;✐) A classy set-up in the middle of the village, the Red Plate offers dishes using fresh ingredients including crisp salads, a selection of wraps, home-made burgers, and deboned whole trout. Try its signature dish: pork neck steak, topped with fried onions, and stir-fried vegetables. Vegetarians also catered for.

Iron Crown   PUB $$

(Rissik St; mains R60-80; ⊙lunch & dinner) The village pub is a congenial place to get stuck into grub such as steaks and burgers. The pub came under new ownership in 2011 and although the signs were good it can get pretty raucous with young drunken Africaaners on weekend nights.

Pot 'n Plow   PUB $

(☏082 691 5790; pizzas R50-60; ⊙lunch & dinner) Another mountain pub well worth ducking into, and attracting every expat and eccentric in the mountains. The Pot 'n Plow is an essential stop for pizza, pool and plenty of chat. There's also a beer garden and its

Sunday roast is R55 a plate. It's some 10km northeast of Haenertsburg on Rte 71.

ℹ️ Getting There & Away

A car is definitely your best option for accessing the town and for getting around as the attractions and accommodation are quite spread out.

MAGOEBASKLOOF PASS

Magoebaskloof is the escarpment on the edge of the highveld, and the road here careers down to Tzaneen and the lowveld winding through plantations and tracts of thick indigenous forest.

There are a number of waterfalls in the area, including the glorious Debengeni Falls (De Hoek State Forest; adult R10; ⊙8am-5pm), where a suspension bridge leads between pools. To get here, turn left off Rte 71 just after the sign saying 'Tzaneen 15km'.

There are 10 walking trails in the area, taking between two and five days, and six huts including some above Debengeni Falls. A recommended option is the three-night, 40km Dokolewa Waterfall Trail. To book huts, contact Komatiland Eco-Tourism (☏013-754 2724; www.komatiecotourism.co.za; 10 Streak St) in Nelspruit.

Off Rte 71, near the junction of Rte 36, Pekoe View Tea Garden (⊙10am-5pm) is on the estate where Magoebaskloof tea is grown.

Tzaneen & Around

☏015 / POP 81,000

An affluent town with a chaotic street layout, Tzaneen makes a very pleasant place to base yourself for a few days on your way to Kruger, down to the Blyde River Canyon or deeper into Limpopo's arts and crafts territory further north. The Letaba Valley's largest town has personality, not a description we'd bestow on many other Limpopo towns. There's a few attractions and the cool mountainous retreat of Haenerstsburg nearby is well worth a visit if not an overnight stop. It's often hot around here, although while we were in town in the middle of summer there was a misty landscape and fine sheets of drizzle.

👁️ Sights & Activities

Tzaneen Museum   MUSEUM

(Agatha St; donation welcome; ⊙9am-4pm Mon-Fri, to noon Sat) The town museum has an impressive collection of artefacts, ranging

415

Tzaneen

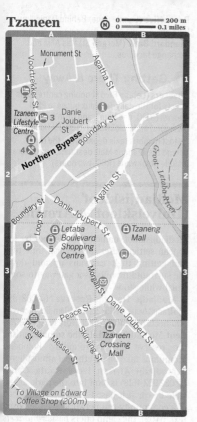

Tzaneen

⊙ Sights
1 Tzaneen Museum A3

🛏 Sleeping
2 Lavenir Manor Guesthouse A1
3 Silver Palms Lodge............................ A1

✕ Eating
4 Market Cafe A2

🛍 Shopping
5 Checkers A3

day **Rooikat Nature Walk** in the Agatha area.

🛏 Sleeping

TOP CHOICE **Kings Walden** HOTEL $$
(☎015-307 3262; www.kingswalden.co.za; Old Coach Rd, Agatha; d incl breakfast R1350; ✸🔊) The sizeable rooms are as dreamy as the gardens and mountains they overlook, with fireplaces, antiquated prints everywhere, and bathrooms you could get lost in. Picnic hampers can be provided.

Silver Palms Lodge HOTEL $$
(☎015-307 3092; Monument St; r economy/luxury incl breakfast R550/800; ✸✸) This good-value hotel has some pleasant touches such as marula-based shower gel in the smart rooms. Cheaper on the weekends but with no breakfast included, the luxury rooms here are newer and in better shape. The big plus to staying here is the gorgeous sunken swimming pool, which backs onto a bar...

Lavenir Manor Guesthouse GUESTHOUSE $
(☎015-307 5460; laveneur@mweb.co.za; 2 Aqua Ave; s/d with breakfast R400/450; ✸) This large, well-run and friendly property with a grand name near the R71 is in a good spot, opposite a Spar supermarket and pub. Standard rooms are a decent size and tidily kept.

Satvik Backpackers Village BACKPACKERS $
(☎015-307 3920; satvik@pixie.co.za; George's Valley Rd; campsites per person R60, dm/d/cottage R100/280/540) These cottages, on a slope above a dam, have a kitchen and a braai along with views of wooded hills. Activities such as fishing are offered, but watch out for the crocs and hippos. Head out of town south on Agatha St – the backpackers is about 4km away.

from a 'house guard' totem used by the Rain Queens to some pretty spine-chilling Congolese masks. It's particularly interesting if you're visiting Modjadji or the Venda region.

Kings Walden GARDENS
(Agatha; admission R10; ☉daylight) If steamy Tzaneen is making you droop, climb to a 3-hectare formal English garden at 1050m. The Drakensberg views from the sweeping lawn are interrupted only by a lightning-struck tree, and leafy walkways wind away from the refreshing swimming pool. Take Joubert St south, turn right onto Claude Wheatley St and follow the signs.

There are plenty of chances to cycle, go climbing or hiking in the nearby mountains. For adventure trips, call Magoebaskloof Adventures (p413); and contact **Komatiland Eco-Tourism** (☎013-754 2724; www komatiecotourism.co.za; 10 Streak St) in Nelspruit for more information about the one-

LIMPOPO TZANEEN & AROUND

✕ Eating

The dining scene around town is painfully ordinary.

 Market Cafe   CAFE $
(Tzaneen Lifestyle Centre; mains R30-40) The new 'lifestyle' centre is sanitised (yes – you overlook a carpark!) but the Market Cafe – a small operation that's part of a larger food market here – delivers quality breakfasts, light lunches (salads and wraps) and even more substantial meals such as steaks and pizzas. Food is beautifully presented and tastes as good as it looks.

Village on Edward Coffee Shop   CAFE $
(King Edward St; snacks R30) In a lovely garden setting, this makes a great place for coffee and a muffin or even a full breakfast. There's off-street parking, a relaxed vibe and also an art gallery next door.

Highgrove Restaurant   INTERNATIONAL $$
(☎015-307 7242; Agatha St; mains R80-90; ☺7am-8.30pm) One of Tzaneen's classiest restaurants, Highgrove serves dishes including steaks with a choice of eight sauces, a seafood pot featuring six types of ocean-dweller, pasta and hearty breakfasts. With a lovely poolside setting, it's the best spot in town for dinner.

❶ Information

ABSA (Danie Joubert St) Has an ATM and exchange facilities.

Copy-it (Morgan St; per 30min R15; ☺8am-5pm Mon-Thu, to 4pm Fri, to noon Sat) Internet access.

Limpopo Parks & Tourism Board (☎015-307 3582; www.tzaneeninfo.co.za; ☺7.30am-4.30pm Mon-Fri) On Rte 71 towards Phalaborwa, one of the better information centres in Limpopo.

DON'T MISS

A POTTERY STOP

For a coffee stop and a browse through some wonderful locally made pottery, stop at **Afrikania** (☎015-781 1139; www.afrikania.co.za; R36), on your way to/from Tzaneen. A little landscaped, grassroots initiative, the pottery reflects traditional patterns found amongst the Tsonga and Pedi people. It's about 90km south of Tzaneen.

Post office (Lannie Lane) Behind Danie Joubert St.

Standard Bank (Morgan St) Has ATM and exchange facilities.

❶ Getting There & Away

Checkers (Letaba Blvd shopping centre) sells tickets for the daily Translux buses to Phalaborwa (R110, one hour), and to Jo'burg (R210, 5½ hours) and Polokwane (R120, 1¾ hours).

Most minibus taxis depart from the rank behind the Tzaneng Mall; destinations and fares include Polokwane (R60, two hours).

Modjadjiskloof (Duivelskloof) & Around

☎015 / POP 25,000

Modjadjiskloof, named Duivelskloof by European settlers after the devilish time they had getting their caravans up and down the surrounding hills, is a gateway to some worthwhile stops.

Modjadji Nature Reserve (☎082 393 5551; adult/vehicle R15/25; ☺7.30am-6pm) covers 305 hectares and protects forests of the ancient Modjadji cycad. In the summer mists, the reserve and surrounding Bolobedu Mountains take on an ethereal atmosphere.

Modjadji African Ivory Route Camp (☎082 902 4618) is 5km into the park, accessible by car if it hasn't rained recently. Part of a community-run network (see the boxed text, p402), the camp offers basic *rondavels* and hiking trails among the 800-year-old cycads.

Take the Modjadji turn-off from Rte 36 about 10km north of Modjadjiskloof (Duivelskloof); after 10km, turn left at the signpost to the reserve, then right at the signpost 12km further on, and continue for 5km.

Sunland Nursery (www.bigbaobab.co.za; adult/child R15/free; ☺9am-5pm) On the road to Modjadji, look out for signs to the 22m-high Sunland Boabab. It takes 40 tree-huggers with outstretched arms to encircle its 47m circumference and, according to carbon dating, it's 6000 years old. The bar no longer occupies the two cavities inside the tree, which 60 drinkers have squeezed into, but you can still take a peek.

Accommodation is available in five thatched **chalets** (per person R300, full board R450; ✺) with fans, mosquito nets and outside bathrooms.

MODJADJI, THE RAIN QUEEN

In Africa it is unusual for a woman to be sovereign of a tribe, but the Rain Queen is an exception. The queen resides in the town of GaModjadji in the Bolobedu district near Modjadjiskloof (Duivelskloof). Every year, around November, the queen traditionally presides over a festival held to celebrate the coming of the rains. The *indunas* (tribal headmen) select people to dance, to call for rain and to perform traditional rituals, including male and female initiation ceremonies. After the ceremony, the rain falls. The absence of rain is usually attributed to some event such as the destruction of a sacred place – a situation resolved only with further ritual.

Henry Rider Haggard's novel *She* is based on the story of the original Modjadji, a 16th-century refugee princess. Successive queens have lived a secluded lifestyle, confined to the royal kraal, and following the custom of never marrying, but bearing children by members of the royal family. However, this millennium has been a time of crisis for the matrilineal line.

In June 2001, Rain Queen Modjadji V died in Polokwane (Pietersburg). However, in an unfortunate turn of events, her immediate heir, Princess Makheala, had died three days earlier, and it wasn't until April 2003 that the 25-year-old Princess Mmakobo Modjadji was crowned Modjadji VI. It was raining on the day of the ceremony, which was taken to be a good omen. Sadly, she passed away two years later, leaving a baby daughter, Princess Masalanabo. The princess may accede when she reaches the age of 16, but traditionalists point out that her father is not a member of the royal family, and the clan has lost a lot of respect.

Route 71 to Phalaborwa

Some 30km east of Tzaneen, turn left onto Rte 529 to Giyani and, after 9km, the 20-year-old **Kaross** (☎086 276 2964; www.kaross.co.za; ⏱7am-4.30pm Mon-Thu, to 3.30pm Fri) embroidery cooperative is on your right. Next to the busy workshop, a shop sells vivid wall hangings, cushion covers, tunics and table mats, designed here and embroidered by 1200 local Shangaan women. The quality of the products is very high and the designs are skilful and colourful. A minibus taxi from Tzaneen costs R15 and there's an excellent courtyard **cafe** (mains R50) with decadent desserts.

With animals including four of the Big Five (everything but buffalo is represented) and klipspringer antelopes roaming its 8000-plus hectares, **Ndzalama Wildlife Reserve** (☎015-307 3065; www.ndzalama.com; Letsitele) is named after a locally revered rock formation, which couldn't be more phallic. No day visitors are allowed into the reserve (you have to stay at least one night); book ahead to stay in a self-catering stone **chalet** (chalets R600; ❄🐾). Meals are available on request.

To get to Ndzalama from Tzaneen, follow Rte 71 for 35km and turn left onto the tarred road to Eiland. After 16km, turn right onto the dirt road and you'll see the reserve entrance after 4km, near the green Rubbervale sign.

Phalaborwa

☎015 / POP 109,000

Phalaborwa makes an ideal starting point if you are intending to explore central and northern Kruger National Park. For people with limited time in South Africa, it is possible to visit Kruger by flying from Jo'burg to Phalaborwa and hiring a car at the airport (with its thatched terminal building). Phalaborwa rocks between suburban tidiness and the bush, with a green belt in the centre and the occasional warthog grazing on a lawn.

Phalaborwa is also a town that acts as a gateway into Mozambique, as it is possible to drive across Kruger National Park and into Mozambique via the Giriyondo Gate (see p394) if you are travelling in a vehicle that has a good clearance.

◉ Sights & Activities

Leka Gape   TOUR
(☎015-783 0467, 082 476 0249; www.lekagape.de; tours R390) A two-hour township tour with

the NGO in Lulekani, 13km northwest of Phalaborwa, includes a visit to a handicrafts workshop. Call to book and ask to speak with Ben.

Hans Merensky Estate
GOLF

(☏015-781 3931; 3 Copper Rd; 9-/18-hole round R240/435) Just south of Phalaborwa is an 18-hole championship golf course with a difference: here you have to hold your shot while wildlife, elephants included, crosses the fairways. Be careful – the wildlife is 'wild'.

Africa Unlimited
ADVENTURE SPORTS

(☏015-781 7825; www.africaunltd.co.za) Offers activities including astronomy safaris, river cruises, bush walks, night drives, mine tours and trips through Kruger to Mozambique.

🛌 Sleeping

There are scores of places to stay in Phalaborwa, many of them just out of town in the bush.

Elephant Walk
BACKPACKERS $

(☏015-781 5860; elephant.walk@nix.co.za; 30 Anna Scheepers Ave; campsites R75, dm/s/tw without bathroom R100/200/300, B&B s/d R300/500; ☀) Close enough to Kruger National Park to hear the lions roar, this is a great spot to plan your foray into the park. The owners offer lifts from the town centre and an excellent range of reasonably priced tours and activities. The rooms with en suite are more like a guesthouse.

Kaia Tani
GUESTHOUSE $$

(☏015-781 1358; www.kaiatani.com; 29 Boekenhout St; r per person incl breakfast R490; ☀☎🏠) This 'exclusive guesthouse', rated by readers and locals, delivers a lot of style for your money. The six rooms have flourishes such as rope-lined wooden walls, and a thatch restaurant-bar overlooks the rock swimming pool.

Basambilu Lodge
BACKPACKERS $

(☏015-783 0467; www.basambilu.com; 348 Akanani St, Lulekani; dm/d R90/275; ☀☎) This basic backpackers in the township of Lulekani has a swimming pool between its five *rondavels*. It's not the best accommodation option, but it offers a township experience if you can't make it to, say, Soweto (Jo'burg). Meals and free lifts from Phalaborwa are available.

Daan & Zena's
BACKPACKERS $

(☏015-781 6049; www.daanzena.co.za; 15 Birkenhead St; s/d from R280/350; ☀@☎) We like this place, with its colourful, happy, rustic spaces brightened up with a splash of paint. Bridging the gap between backpackers and a B&B, Daan & Zena's is brought to life by lashings of colour and a friendly atmosphere. A good spot if you're looking for a comfy bed and a youthful vibe.

Sefapane
LODGE $$

(☏015-780 6700; www.sefapane.co.za; Copper Rd; s/d standard rondavel from R875/1300; ☀☎) With a whiff of exclusivity, this 10-hectare resort has a restaurant and sunken bar, a long list of safaris for guests and mushroom-shaped *rondavels*. There are spacious self-catering 'safari houses' overlooking a dam,

---

THE MIGHTY MARULA

The silhouette of a marula tree at dusk is one of the more evocative images of the African bush, but the real value of this mighty tree is what comes out of it.

In summer, the female marula sags under the weight of its pale yellow fruit. Chacna baboons love the stuff and you can see them by the road chomping on the golden delicacy, which has four times as much vitamin C as an orange. Elephants, also big marula fans, spend their days ramming into tree trunks to knock the fruit to the ground. Their somewhat obsessive behaviour has led to the marula being dubbed the 'Elephant Tree'.

Local people have long valued the marula fruit's medicinal qualities, particularly those of an aphrodisiac nature, and it is now used in a popular cream liqueur. Limpopo's answer to Baileys, Amarula debuted in 1989 and is now available in more than 70 countries.

The best way to enjoy a glass of creamy Amarula is to visit the **Amarula Lapa** (☏015-781 7766; Rte 40; admission free; ⏰8am-5pm Mon-Fri, 9am-4pm Sat), located next to the production plant, 10km west of Phalaborwa. Groups of at least five can visit the plant during harvest season; at other times, exhibits and a seven-minute DVD explain all.

and donations are made to projects for local children. Lots of packages from two to seven nights.

Eating

Eden Square, on Nelson Mandela St, has the usual food chains. Kaia Tani's small Italian restaurant is recommended (book ahead).

Buffalo Pub & Grill   PUB $$
(1 Lekkerbreek St; mains R70-90; ❄) If you've emerged from Kruger feeling like a hungry lion, stop here for some pub grub. There's a terrace for alfresco dining and African trimmings aplenty. Best of all, locals recommend the place.

Villa Luso   MEDITERRANEAN $$
(Molengraaf St; pizza & light meals R50, mains R80-100; ☺breakfast, lunch & dinner Mon-Fri; 🛜) With a Portuguese owner, the Villa's menu displays influences from the Mediterranean. Seafood, buffalo wings, surf and turf and Portuguese steaks are a few of the feeds on offer. With a garden bar (and long cocktail list), it's a reasonable place to dine. Also has a kids playground.

ℹ Information

Bollanoto Tourism Centre (☎015-769 5090; www.phalaborwa.co.za; cnr Hendrick van Eck & Pres Steyn Sts) The centre kept very unpredictable opening hours when we dropped by – try your luck.

Cyber World (Tambotie Park, Tambotie St; wi-fi per hr R30, internet per hr R45) Good, reliable internet connections.

ℹ Getting There & Away

Air

SAAirlink (☎015-781 5823; www.flyairlink. com) has an office at the airport; it flies daily to Jo'burg (from R1630). The airport is 2km north of town.

Bus

Sure Turn Key Travel (☎015-781 7760; Sealene St) is the local agent for Translux and City to City buses; it's right behind the Shoprite supermarket. Sure Turn Key also has an **office** (☎015-781 2498) at the airport.

Translux connects Phalaborwa with Jo'burg (R230, seven hours) via Tzaneen (R120, one hour), Polokwane (R150, 2½ hours) and Pretoria (R230, six hours); City to City buses travel to Jo'burg (R190, 9½ hours) via Middelburg.

Car

Hiring a car is often the cheapest way of seeing Kruger National Park, starting at about R250 per day. The following have offices at the airport, generally open 8am to 5pm Monday to Friday and to meet flights or by appointment at weekends:

Avis (☎015-781 3169)
Budget (☎015-781 5404)
First Car Rental (☎015-781 1500)
Hertz (☎015-781 3565)
Imperial (☎015-781 0376)

Minibus Taxi

There aren't many minibus taxis in this area, and most run from the township of Namakgale (R7, 20 minutes).

Hoedspruit

☎015 / POP 11,000

Located just 70km northwest of Kruger's Orpen Gate, Hoedspruit makes a convenient launch pad for exploring the park's central and southern sections.

🏃 Activities

Hoedspruit Endangered Species Centre   WILDLIFE RESERVE
(☎015-793 1633; www.hesc.co.za; adult/child R130/60) Before heading into Kruger, duck into the Hoedspruit Endangered Species Centre to see some wildlife rarely seen (although not impossible!) in Kruger, including cheetah, wild dog, African wild cats and sable antelope. Head out of town on the R40 south and follow the signs.

1 Africa Safaris   ADVENTURE SPORTS
(☎015-793 1110; www.1africasafaris.com; Kamogelo Centre, Main Rd; ☺9am-4.30pm Mon-Fri) Running a range of activities from white-water rafting to microflights.

🛏 Sleeping & Eating

Loerie Guesthouse   GUESTHOUSE $$
(☎015-793 3990; www.loerieguesthouse.com; 85 Jakkals St; r R530; @☀) Specialising in warm welcomes, the best rooms here are upstairs (nos 14 and 15) in the separate accommodation wing out the back. All rooms are a decent size and well set up.

Maruleng Lodge   HOTEL $$
(☎015-793 0910; www.marulenglodge.co.za; s/d R300/650; 🛜) This lodge has enormous rooms. So big in fact that they're kinda spartan – if you like your space you'll love this

LIMPOPO HOEDSPRUIT

place. Although it lacks character, its convenience can't be questioned – right next to all the services and eating options at the Kamagelo Centre.

Sleepers Railway Station Restaurant
INTERNATIONAL $$

(☑015-793 1014; Train Station, Hoedspruit Crossings, Rte 40; ☺breakfast, lunch & dinner Mon-Sat) This old station house, with sculptures and potted aloes in the garden, is a pleasant venue for devouring quality dishes from French toast to ostrich fillet with Italian black cherry and port sauce. Dine outside under the branches of two enormous trees.

Cala la Pasta
ITALIAN $$

(☑ 015-793 0452; Kamagelo Centre; mains R60-70; ☺ closed Sun) How a slice of Italiana found its way to Hoedspruit we're not sure, but this place serves up authentic and quality dishes from the motherland. Lunch is a good bet – the parma ham and fresh (yes fresh!) mozzarella on ciabatta bread is divine. Or try haloumi, chicken, avo and pear in a sandwich. Food takes a while to prepare but it's well worth the wait.

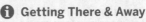 Getting There & Away

SA Express (☑015-793 3681; www.flysax.com) flies daily out of **Hoedspruit Eastgate airport** (Rte 40), 7km south of town, to Jo'burg (R1000 to R1400).

City to City runs a daily bus to Jo'burg (R180, 8½ hours). There is a minibus taxi rank by the Total petrol station, with services to Phalaborwa (R45, 1½ hours).

Acornhoek

Located on the outskirts of Acornhoek township, the **Mapusha Weavers Cooperative** (☑072 469 7060; ☺10am-4pm Mon-Fri) was established in 1973 to give unemployed women a craft and an income.

You can visit the loom-filled workshop next to the Catholic Mission, and take home some of the excellent-quality carpets and tapestries.

To get there, continue south on Rte 40 for 5km after the turning for Mafunyani Cultural Village and the Orpen Gate, then turn left towards Acornhoek. After 4.3km, turn right onto a dirt road marked 'Dingleydale' and, after 1.8km, you will see the Catholic Mission on your right.

North-West Province

Includes »

Best Places to Eat

» Upper Deck (p431)

» Berliner Bistro (p431)

» Deck (p424)

Best Places to Stay

» Palace of the Lost City (p426)

» Mosetlha Bush Camp (p429)

» Tau Game Lodge (p429)

» Bakubung (p428)

» Kwa Maritane (p428)

» Masibambane (p423)

» Sparkling Waters Hotel & Spa (p431)

Why Go?

This stretch of bushveld between Pretoria and the Kalahari is famous for Sun City, the southern hemisphere's answer to Las Vegas. The slot machines and kitsch edifices are grotesquely fascinating, but you may prefer a different kind of gambling in nearby Pilanesberg National Park. Wager that lions and rhinos will wander to the waterhole you have staked out; sightings on self-drive safaris come with a serendipitous thrill.

Alternatively, improve your odds of spotting elusive predators, in Pilanesberg and Madikwe Game Reserve, by joining a guided drive or walk. For that once-in-a-lifetime, romantic *Out of Africa*-style experience, a night in the bush at Madikwe's exclusive lodges can't be beat.

Conveniently, these opportunities to encounter big cats and one-armed bandits are all within four hours' drive of Jo'burg. En route, the Magaliesberg area offers detours from the N4, ranging from zip lining to rural accommodation near Rustenburg.

When to Go
Rustenburg

Apr Autumn temperatures drop; optimum wildlife-watching conditions, through to the winter.

May–Jul Dry, sunny winter days and, bar mid-June to early July, school terms thin crowds.

Dec–Jan Refreshing thunderstorms; South Africans head to the coast for their summer holidays.

History

The North-West Province takes in much of the area once covered by the fragmented apartheid homeland of Bophuthatswana ('Bop'), a dumping ground for thousands of 'relocated' Tswana people. The nominally independent homeland became famous for the excesses of the white South African men, who visited its casinos and pleasure resorts for interracial encounters with prostitutes – illegal elsewhere in South Africa.

The province was the site of a complex and sophisticated Iron Age civilisation, centred on the 'lost city' of Kaditshwene,

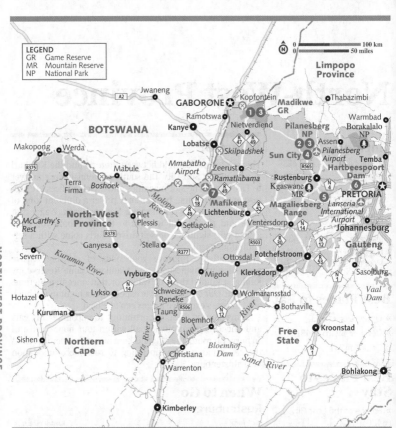

North-West Province Highlights

❶ Stopping within metres of a pride of lions resting under a thorn tree, on a safari in **Madikwe Game Reserve** (p428)

❷ Shacking up with a cooler and binoculars at a waterhole in **Pilanesberg National Park** (p426) and waiting for the animals to come to you

❸ Chilling on the deck at Madikwe and Pilanesberg's **lodges** (p429 and p428), keeping an eye on the bush for Big Five sightings

❹ Surfing the Valley of the Waves and soaking up the deliciously gaudy ambience of **Sun City** (p424)

❺ Zipping past treetops on the **Magaliesberg Canopy Tour** (p431)

❻ Circling **Hartbeespoort Dam** (p431) and shopping at **Welwitischia Country Market** (p431)

❼ Touring the **Mafikeng Museum** (p430) exhibits, such as a shredded corrugated-iron roof, struck by the Boers' Long Tom artillery gun about 30km north of modern-day Zeerust. The people who lived here had an economy so developed they traded copper and iron jewellery with China. By 1820, when European missionaries first visited the city, they found it to be bigger than Cape Town. In the end, Kaditshwene's peace-loving inhabitants proved no match for the Sotho, displaced by Zulu incursions into the Free State. The city was sacked by a horde of 40,000 people and fell into ruins.

Diamonds were discovered in the province in the 1870s, resulting in an enormous rush to the fields around Lichtenburg. Mining is still important here and there are extensive platinum mines near Rustenburg.

Language

Tswana is the principal language; Afrikaans is the first language of most white people, but English is widely spoken.

❶ Getting There & Around

Convenient for Rustenburg and the Magaliesberg area, **Lanseria International Airport** (www.lanseria.co.za; off Rte 512) is 30km south of Hartbeespoort Dam en route to Jo'burg. **Kulula.com** (www.kulula.com) has daily flights from Lanseria to Cape Town, Durban and Maputo (Mozambique); **Mango** (www.flymango.com) flies daily to Cape Town. Car-hire companies operate at the airport.

Hiring a car is the easiest way to travel around the province. Secure parking is readily available at accommodation, restaurants and sights.

Rustenburg

📞 014 / POP 130,000

Sitting on the edge of the Magaliesberg mountains, Rustenburg is a big country town with an urban grittiness to its crowded central business district. Pedestrians weave between honking cars on Nelson Mandela Dr, the main drag through the long downtown area; and the footpaths are bursting with vendors selling rubber mobile-phone cases and the like in front of takeaway chicken shops and undertakers. The Waterfall Mall (Augrabies Ave), off Rte 24 around 3km south of the centre, is safer and more relaxing for shopping and eating.

Rustenburg's location, just 40km southeast of Sun City and Pilanesberg National Park, and two budget accommodation options south of town make it an option for travellers wishing to visit these major attractions without paying high accommodation rates.

Royal Bafokeng Stadium (off Rte 565), 15km northwest of town en route to Sun City, hosted first- and second-round 2010 FIFA World Cup football (soccer) matches. Built in 1999, the stadium seats over 40,000 and its major shareholders are members of the Bafokeng tribe.

🛌 Sleeping

The following are in the countryside south of the Waterfront Mall, reached on Rte 24.

TOP CHOICE **Masibambane** GUESTHOUSE **$$**
(📞083 310 0583; www.masibambaneguesthouse.co.za; Kroondal; s/d incl breakfast R510/780; 🕸🐾) This thatched property exudes colonial charm, its pint-sized bar opening onto a terrace with a lawn and flowerbeds beyond. There's a poolside *lapa* (a circular building with low walls and a thatched roof, used for cooking, partying etc) for braais and the rooms have hot drinks and TV. The welcoming South African–Zimbabwean owners Tony and Gwen offer a three-course dinner (R125) between Monday and Thursday. It's signposted about 5km south of the Waterfall Mall.

Bushwillows B&B B&B **$**
(📞014-537 2333; wjmcgill@lantic.net; r per person incl breakfast R250; 🐾) This quaint country retreat is owned by local wildlife artist Bill McGill, whose paintings decorate the breakfast room. Rescued dogs slope around and the terrace overlooks indigenous trees planted by McGill, with the Magaliesberg beyond. Rooms are basic but the lounge has DSTV and a bar fridge, and birdwatching tours to areas such as Pilanesberg are offered. Coming from the Waterfall Mall, look for the white sign on the right after about 5km. From there, it's 2km up the hill.

Hodge Podge Lodge HOSTEL **$**
(📞084 698 0417; Plot 66, Kommiesdrift; www.hodgepodgebackpackers.co.za; campsites R50, dm R150, r per person R250; 🐾) Right below the cliff tops, Hodge Podge gives a taste of slow-paced country life up a rocky red track. Managed by the formidable Antoinette, the outdoor pool is refreshing in the heat and the verandah bar is ideal for sundowners. Colourful bedspreads and bushveld scenes brighten the dinky en suite cabins; airport shuttles and activities including Sun City and Pilanesberg tours are offered. It's signposted about 10km south of the Waterfall Mall.

✕ Eating

Most restaurants in Rustenburg are found in the Waterfall Mall, which is inevitably sterile, but safe and reliable. Options range from stand-alone restaurants to chains – Woolworths for self-catering, Spur, Wimpy, Steers, Mugg & Bean, Debonairs Pizza and Chicken Licken. The mall is surprisingly atmospheric on weekend evenings, when local couples and families eat out.

TOP CHOICE **Deck** STEAKHOUSE **$$**
(☑014-537 2042; Rte 24; mains R70; ⊙10am-10pm Mon-Sat, 9am-3pm Sun) With gardens and a climbing frame for children, this Bulgarian-owned local favourite's menu is hearty even by South African standards. Your eyes will bulge at the combos, baskets, platters, sauces, sides, and specials including beef Espetada and double-decker chicken breast. Steaks come in a range of cuts and weights, and lasagne and burgers are classed as light meals. There's a smart dining room, a bar and a covered terrace – all located a few kilometres south of the Waterfall Mall.

Cape Town Fish Market SEAFOOD, ASIAN **$$**
(www.ctfm.co.za; Waterfall Mall; mains R85) Put a fish tank between yourself and the rest of the mall in the complex's most stylish restaurant, decorated with B&W photos of Cape fishermen. Order a glass of chardonnay and grab a seat at the Teppanyaki bar, where your rice or noodle dish is stir-fried in front of you. The Japanese-influenced chain also offers bento boxes, platters, a sushi bar and dishes from salads to curries.

Steakout Grill STEAKHOUSE **$$**
(Waterfall Mall; mains R70; ⊙11am-10pm Mon-Sat, to 9pm Sun) Steakout Grill is reputed to be the mall's best restaurant for meat dishes. Options include hunter's steak (with chicken livers in piri piri sauce) and the waiter's tip, medium-rare rump steak. The gaudy menu, splashed with specials such as two-for-one lunches (Monday to Thursday), also features grills, burgers, pasta and shellfish.

❶ Information

The well-stocked **tourist information centre** (☑014-597 0904; Main Rd; ⊙7.30am-4.30pm Mon-Fri, 8am-noon Sat), off Rte 24, has brochures and a local map.

❶ Getting There & Away

Rustenburg is just off the N4, about 120km northwest of Jo'burg and 110km west of Pretoria. It's not well connected; hiring a car is the best option for getting here and travelling around the region.

City to City (www.citytocity.co.za) has daily buses to/from Mthatha (R270, 18½ hours) via Bloemfontein, leaving at 5pm/midday.

Sun City

Welcome to Sin City, South African style. At **Sun City** (☑014-557 1544; www.suncity.co.za; admission R50; ⊙24hr), the legendary creation of entrepreneur Sol Kerzer, Disneyland collides with ancient Egypt in Africa's version of Vegas. Filled with gilded statues of lions and monkeys, acres of artificial beaches, 1200 hotel rooms and line upon line of clinking slot machines, it serves no other purpose than to entertain. Yet even though there's no question this gambling-centric resort is almost grotesquely gaudy, a visit here can also be pretty damn fun.

The complex is dominated by the spectacular Lost City, an extraordinary piece of kitsch claiming to symbolise African heritage. In fact, it has less to do with African heritage than Disneyland Paris has to do with French culture, but it's still entertaining.

Opened in 1979, as an apartheid-era exclusive haven for wealthy whites, these days one of Sun City's best features is the mix of black, white and Asian people who flock here at weekends. Losers at the tables can console themselves with the thought that they are helping to pay more than 7000 salaries.

If you're travelling with children or on a budget, Sun City is a pretty good bargain. The admission fee covers the main attractions, and there are countless activities on offer for an extra outlay. The complex also boasts one of the world's most luxurious hotels – a shrine to all things glittery and golden.

Should the gambling weigh on your conscience, you can rest easy in at least one area – the resort is green. Yes, despite the show of lavishness, Sun City has received awards and recognition for practising sustainable, environmentally friendly tourism.

◉ Sights & Activities

Visit the Welcome Centre for the low-down on the mind-boggling range of activities

LOST CITY

The resort's kitsch heart, Lost City is a sort of mega amusement park in high-glitz style, teeming with attractions from botanic gardens to simulated volcanic eruptions. It's reached from the Entertainment Centre via the **Bridge of Time**, flanked by life-sized fake elephants. Most of the fun takes place in the **Valley of the Waves** (admission adult/pensioner & child 4-12yr/child under 3yr & Sun City hotel guests R110/60/free; ⊙9am-6pm Sep-Apr, 10am-5pm May-Aug) water park, overlooked by the towers of the **Palace of the Lost City** hotel. The water park is gaudy and outlandish even by Sun City's exacting standards – and children love it. Its centrepiece is the **Roaring Lagoon**, a 6500-sq-metre wave pool with a palm-fringed beach. Slides, flumes and chutes such as the 70m-long **Temple of Courage** get the adrenaline flowing; tubing on the **Lazy River** and swimming in the **Royal Bath** pool are two of the slower activities on offer.

available. These include two golf courses, jet skiing, parasailing, horse rides, a crocodile park, zip lining and getting married.

Entertainment Centre
CASINO

As well as smoking and nonsmoking **casinos**, the two-storey centre houses food courts, shops, cinemas and the **Superbowl** venue. It's decorated in a jungle theme with animal murals on the domed ceiling.

Gametrackers
GUIDED TOUR, OUTDOORS

(☑014-552 5020; www.gametrac.co.za; Welcome Centre, Entertainment Complex; ⊙7.30am-6pm) The outdoor-adventure company runs four daily **wildlife drives** in Pilanesberg National Park, departing (depending on the time of year) between 5.30am and 8am, between 8.30am and 11am, between 2.30pm and 4.30pm, and between 6pm and 7.30pm. See p427 for prices and more information. Also on offer at Sun City are **elephant-back safaris** in Pilanesberg (R1600), **elephant interactions** in the nearby Letsatsing Game Reserve (R580) and an **outdoor centre** with quad biking, clay-pigeon shooting, archery, paintballing and *djembe* drumming.

Mankwe Heritage
CULTURAL TOUR, OUTDOORS

(☑014-555 1684; www.mankwesafaris.co.za) The cultural-tour company also runs four daily Pilanesberg drives, some focused on wildlife and others incorporating lessons in local Tswana culture. See p427 for prices and more information.

🛏 Sleeping & Eating

If you have your own transport, consider staying in Pilanesberg and visiting Sun City on a day trip. Rustenburg (p423) is also close enough to use as a base.

Sun International has four hotels at the resort – bookings can be made through the chain's **central reservations** (☑011-780 7810; www.suninternational.com). You can usually find a better rate, however, using an online booking engine. Tariffs fluctuate according to demand – the following give an idea of prices.

All the hotels have a selection of restaurants. There are plenty of fast-food joints in the Entertainment Centre.

Cascades
LUXURY HOTEL $$$

(s/tw/d incl breakfast R4097/4347/5392; ❈❈) In this azure, Mediterranean-inspired environment, waterfalls cascade into a lake and cocktails go down nicely in the beach bar. There are multiple pools, alfresco island dining at Santorini restaurant, and luxuries such as dressing rooms in the palatial bedrooms.

Sun City Hotel
CASINO HOTEL $$$

(s/tw/d incl breakfast R2434/2599/3231; ❈❈) The liveliest hotel packs in casinos, slot machines and an entertainment centre, as well as multiple restaurants and bars. With foliage hanging in the jungle-themed foyer, and oversized roulette chips stacked outside the Raj Indian restaurant, it's a good choice for couples, singles and anyone looking for a little hedonism with their gambling.

Sun City Cabanas
RESORT $$$

(s/tw/d incl breakfast R1533/1678/1926; ❈❈♠) Sun City's most informal and affordable option is the best option for families, with facilities and activities for children. The modern rooms have retro stylings and upmarket conveniences, and the atmosphere is laid-back from the balconied foyer onwards. Family rooms with a fold-out sofa and up to eight beds are available.

REGAL LUXURY

Its turquoise domes surveying Valley of the Waves, the **Palace of the Lost City** (s/tw/d incl breakfast R4097/4347/5392; ※※) is a hallucinatory dazzle of glamour in the bushveld. Frequently rated one of the world's top hotels by travel media, it does a good job of exceeding guests' fantasies of luxury.

The 330-plus rooms and suites have flourishes such as butler service and marble bathrooms, but it's the awesome public spaces that hog the limelight. Beneath the frescos, mosaics and painted ceilings in the grand atriums and halls, restaurants and bars, you almost begin to believe this is the kingly residence of an ancient ruler. In the surrounding pleasure garden, fountains, pools and waterfalls sparkle among the thick foliage.

The Welcome Centre organises tours of the hotel.

ℹ Information

The **Welcome Centre** (☎014-557 1544; ⏰8am-7pm Mon-Thu, to 10pm Sat & Sun) at the entrance to the Entertainment Centre has maps and just about any information you could possibly need. Also here are lockers and branches of Avis and Computicket.

ℹ Getting There & Away

The car park for nonguests is at the entrance, about 2km from the Entertainment Centre. The elevated monorail Sky Train, offering good views of the complex and Pilanesberg, and buses shuttle from the car park to the Entertainment Centre and Cascades, passing Sun City Cabanas and Sun City Hotel.

CAR Sun City is less than three hours' drive northwest of Jo'burg, signposted from the N4. Coming from Gauteng on the N4, the most straightforward route is to stay on the freeway past Rustenburg and take Rte 565 via Phokeng and Boshoek.

SHUTTLE & TOURS Ingelosi Shuttles (☎014-552 3260; www.ingelositours.co.za; Welcome Centre, Entertainment Complex) runs daily air-conditioned shuttles to/from Jo'burg, Pretoria and OR Tambo International Airport (adult R400, pensioner and child under 12 years R300). Tours from Gauteng combine Sun City and Pilanesberg.

Pilanesberg National Park

Occupying an eroded alkaline crater north of Sun City, the 550-sq-km **Pilanesberg National Park** (☎014-555 1600; www.park snorthwest.co.za/pilanesberg; adult/pensioner & child R65/20, vehicle R20, map R20; ⏰5.30am-7pm Nov-Feb, 6am-6.30pm Mar, Apr Sep & Oct, 6.30am-6pm May-Aug, last entry an hour before gates close) is South Africa's most accessible big-game reserve. The malaria-free park is less than a three-hour drive from Jo'burg, and its two southern gates are both within about 10km of Sun City. Conceptualised as a back-to-nature weekend escape for nearby city dwellers at the end of the 1970s, Pilanesberg remains a haven where lions, buffalos and day trippers still roam today. And although the park may appear developed in comparison with some South African wildernesses, don't mistake it for a zoo. The animals roaming the extinct volcano crater are 100% wild.

Pilanesberg started with Operation Genesis in 1979, a mission that reclaimed the land from agriculture and released 6000 animals into the area. Today, all the Big Five (lions, leopards, buffaloes, elephants and rhinos) are here; as are cheetahs, caracals, African wild dogs, hyenas, giraffes, hippos, zebras, a variety of antelopes (including sables, elands and kudus) and 300-plus bird species.

🏃 Activities

Most lodges in the park offer sunrise and sunset wildlife drives.

Self-Drive Safaris   DRIVING TOUR
With nearly 200km of excellent tarred and gravel roads, Pilanesberg was designed with self-drive safaris in mind. Although you have a better chance of spotting big cats on a ranger-led wildlife drive, steering yourself is cheaper, and when you do see an animal, more rewarding. You'll never forget the first time you brake to let a lumbering elephant cross your path – or stop at a waterhole, just as a lion family has the same idea.

A major advantage of self-drive safaris is the ability to move at your own pace, without being encumbered a group. Drive slowly, and devote a few hours to camping out with a cooler of Castles and a pair of binoculars in one of the many hides. The camouflaged

Pilanesberg National Park

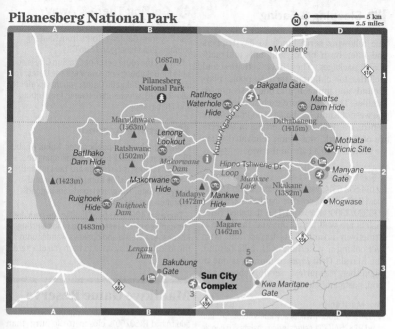

Pilanesberg National Park

hides, basically raised, covered decks with benches, overlook water sources that naturally attract thirsty animals.

Back on the road, it's hard to forget that Pilanesberg is an urban reserve. The park is very popular, and there's often a lot of traffic, particularly over weekends and public holidays. Off-road driving is forbidden, so if you do spot a lion, it may be far away. A good way to get round these disadvantages is to hit the gravel roads winding through the bush, which are quieter and tend to offer closer sightings.

Gametrackers　　　　GUIDED TOUR, OUTDOORS
(☎014-552 5020; www.gametrac.co.za; Manyane, Bakgatla & Sun City) The outdoor-adventure company runs a dizzying variety of organised activities within the park. The 2½-hour sunrise and sunset wildlife drives (adult/child under 16yr/child under 10yr R395/230/145) provide

a good introduction to wildlife watching, and you have a better chance of spotting animals when driven by a knowledgeable ranger. Also on offer are night drives, stargazing trips, bush braais and breakfasts, and safaris on foot (R450, three hours) or up high in a hot-air balloon (R3500 including one-hour flight, breakfast, sparkling wine and transfers; four hours).

Mankwe Heritage　　CULTURAL TOUR, OUTDOORS
(☎014-555 7056; www.mankwesafaris.co.za; Manyane & Sun City) Mankwe's three-hour Heritage Game Drive (adult/child under 16yr/child under 10yr R395/230/145) combines looking for Pilanesberg's wildlife with Tswana cultural lessons. The company also runs cultural tours such as a visit to the Lesedi Cultural Village (R1650), plus many of the activities offered by Gametrackers.

Sleeping & Eating

There are half-a-dozen lodges in the park. The following serve lunch to day trippers and offer bush braais and full- and half-board packages. They have activities and facilities for children, such as pools, playgrounds and minigolf, and offer discounts to families. There are more exclusive lodges to the west of Kudu/Kgabo Dr. The Pilanesberg Centre, overlooking a waterhole in the centre of the park, was being renovated when we visited, with a cafe on the way.

TOP CHOICE Bakubung LODGE $$$

(☎014-552 6314; www.legacyhotels.co.za; s/d half board R3025/4280, self-catering chalets 2/6 sleeper R1320/2300; ❄☎✉📶) The thatched brick chalets are well kitted out and the lodge is attractively arranged, its terrace and lawn overlooking a waterhole with hills beyond. The Marula Grill *lapa* restaurant is one of Pilanesberg's smartest, serving chops, seafood, pasta and chicken dishes.

Kwa Maritane LODGE $$$

(☎014-552 5100; www.legacyhotels.co.za; s/d half board R2825/4000, self-catering chalets 2-5 people from R2000, 6-8 people from R3000; ❄☎✉📶) Kwa Maritane's smart thatched rooms encircle its pool, and the restaurant verandah has a bird's-eye view of bush-covered hills and rocky cliffs. You can check out the watering hole on the TV in your room, then head to the underground viewing hide if there's any activity.

Manyane CAMPGROUND, RESORT $$

(☎014-555 1000; www.goldenleopardresorts.co.za; campsites R250, safari tents s/d incl breakfast R950/1050, chalets s/d/tr/q incl breakfast R1530/1630/2410/2510; ❄✉📶) Facilities here include a shop with a reasonable range of food, a poolside restaurant, full kitchen, lounge and grassy braai areas. The thatched African chalets are comfortable and the safari tents feature a fridge and tea-making facilities.

Bakgatla CAMPGROUND, RESORT $$

(☎014-555 1000; www.goldenleopardresorts.co.za; campsites R250, safari tents s/d/tr/q incl breakfast R1680/1780/1880/1980, chalets s/d/tr/q incl breakfast R1950/2050/2150/2250; ❄✉📶) A similar set-up to the affiliated Manyane, Bakgatla has a campsite feel, with a superette and tents between the pool and bar-restaurant. The colonial-style chalets and 'executive' safari tents have private patios.

ⓘ Getting There & Away

See p426 for information on shuttles to nearby Sun City from Gauteng. Tours from Gauteng combine Pilanesberg and Sun City.

Driving, the route described to Sun City is sensible for Bakubung and Kwa Maritane Gates. For Manyane and Bakgatla Gates, you may prefer to take Rte 510, which runs between Rustenburg and Thabazimbi.

ⓘ Getting Around

Pilanesberg has four public gates. Kubu/Kgabo Dr, crossing the park between Bakubung and Bakgatla Gates, is tarred; as are Tau Link and Tshwene Dr, which link Kubu/Kgabo Dr and Manyane Gate. The gravel roads are in good condition and passable in cars.

There is a 40km/h speed limit in the park and you can't go much faster on the roads skirting Pilanesberg. Cattle and donkeys wander onto the road; locals may wave to warn you of a herd ahead.

Madikwe Game Reserve

Madikwe (www.madikwe-game-reserve.co.za; adult/child R150/60), closer to Jo'burg than Kruger, offers Big Five wildlife-watching and dreamy lodging among striking (and malaria-free) red sand and clay thorn bushveld. There are so many lions that the provincial parks department is in the process of removing some.

While rangers working in the country's fourth-largest reserve are combing its 760 sq km of bushveld, savannah grassland and riverine forest on the edge of the Kalahari for big cats to relocate, we'd suggest scooting up north to check out the action at South Africa's best-kept secret safari destination. Madikwe does not allow self-drive safaris or day visitors, which means you must stay at one of its 20 lodges to play. Experiencing Madikwe isn't cheap, but you get what you pay for at these exclusive bush hideaways. With only the lodge's trained rangers allowed to run tours in the reserve, your chance of seeing wildlife is better here than at Pilanesberg or even Kruger. The animals have become used to the sturdy open-sided jeeps and don't view them as a threat. So when your guide pulls up to a herd of buffalo and cuts the engine, you usually have time to snap some good shots without your subjects tearing off. Rangers also carry radios, allowing them to communicate with the other drivers in the reserve. If a family of lions napping in the shade of a thorn tree or a bull elephant in musk, pursuing a female, is spotted nearby, your driver will hear about it. Restrictions on driving off road are minimal here, and the jeeps are tough enough to tackle most terrain, getting you close to the animals.

Madikwe was formed in 1991 with a dual mandate to protect endangered wildlife and to use sustainable tourism initiatives to create jobs for the poor, remotely located local people. A massive translocation operation reintroduced more than 10,000 once-indigenous animals, whose numbers had been depleted by hunting and farming. The operation took more than seven years to complete, with animals (including entire herds of elephants) being flown in or driven in from other Southern African reserves. Two decades later, Madikwe, run as a joint venture between the North West Parks and Tourism Board, the private sector and local communities, has provided the promised jobs, as well as a home for healthy numbers of all the Big Five, a flourishing population of endangered African wild dogs and 350-plus bird species.

Visit from March to September for the best chance of seeing wildlife.

🛏 Sleeping & Eating

The rates following are per person, based on double occupancy, with full board and two wildlife drives – most lodges charge on this basis. The name of the closest gate is also included.

Advance booking is mandatory: you will not be allowed through the gates without a reservation (the guard will telephone your lodge to check you have a booking). Visits to Madikwe normally run from lunchtime until late the following morning.

TOP CHOICE Mosetlha Bush Camp ECOLODGE $$$
(☏011-444 9345; www.thebushcamp.com; Abjaterskop Gate; including park entrance R1795) Madikwe's second-oldest lodge is also the reserve's only non-five-star option, but Mosetlha's relatively low rates are not its only attraction. The ecolodge features in Hitesh Mehta's authoritative book on the subject, *Authentic Ecolodges*. It made it into Mehta's 'innovative technology' category for its donkey boilers, bucket shower and VIP toilet (ventilation-improved pit). With nine open-fronted cabins around the campfire, Mosetlha is truly off the grid – it has no electricity or running water. Staying in the unfenced camp, which animals wander

ⓘ MADIKWE SAVINGS

The best time to look for discounts is the off season – this varies between lodges, but May to August is generally quiet. Staying for a few nights also reduces rates. Check the following websites for discounts and reviews of lodges not listed here.

» www.madikwegamereserve.net
» www.safarinow.com
» www.uyaphi.com
» madikwe.safari.co.za

into at night, is romantic rather than rough. Paraffin lamps stand in for bedside lamps, conversation for TV, and the meals are as delicious as the bushveld air.

Tau Game Lodge LODGE $$$
(☏011-314 4350; www.taugamelodge.com; Tau Gate; R3300; ❋❄♨) When it comes to value for money, Tau is one of the park's best bets. The 30 cosy thatched chalets have giant bathtubs, massive outdoor bush showers, huge beds, and private decks for watching the waterhole action – improved, in 2012, by the introduction of a croc family of five. Also onsite are a spa and curio shop. The Tau Foundation seeks to benefit the local people, and guests can visit schools and community schemes.

Buffalo Ridge Safari Lodge LODGE $$$
(☏011-234 6500; www.buffaloridgesafari.com; Wonderboom Gate; R3450; ❋❄) This swish lodge exemplifies the sustainable community-based tourism envisioned by Madikwe's founders; owned by the Balete people from the local village of Lekgophung, it is the first of its kind in South Africa. Designed by a well-known local architect, Buffalo Ridge has eight ultraprivate thatched chalet suites that blend seamlessly into the bushveld. Done up in neutral colours, the rooms have huge sliding glass doors onto a private deck and offer lots of natural light. The ravine bridge connects the chalets to the main lodge, which is an impressive place to eat dinner.

Jaci's Lodges LODGE $$$
(☏083 700 2071; www.madikwe.com; Molatedi Gate; from R2995; ❋❄♨) For panache and design flair, Jaci's contiguous lodges – Safari Lodge and Tree Lodge – are excellent places to indulge. Safari Lodge's eight

rooms are constructed to feel like tents, with canvas siding and outdoor showers made from natural stone. Handmade ceramic fireplaces and private decks with waterhole views complete the elegantly natural picture. Even more exclusive, Tree Lodge brushes the canopy, with elevated rooms built around trees and connected by walkways. Constructed from rosewood and thatch, the eight abodes are luxurious, but also built to let nature flow in – while mostly pleasant, this can mean unwanted visitors such as (in rare cases) snakes. There are discounts for children under 12, child minders and wildlife drives geared towards kids and families.

ⓘ Getting There & Away

Madikwe is next to the Kopfontein Gate/Tlokweng Gate border crossing with Botswana, about 400km northwest of J'burg and Pretoria via the N4 and Rte 47/49 (the road is referred to by both numbers).

GATES Madikwe's main gates are Abjaterskop and Wonderboom, adjoining Rte 47/49 on the reserve's western side; Tau and Deerdepoort on the northern side; and Molatedi on the eastern side. All the lodges can be reached from Rte 47/49; when you make a reservation, your lodge will give you directions.

AIR There is one charter flight per day between OR Tambo International Airport in Jo'burg and the landing strip in Madikwe. Tickets cost around R4000 return, and are arranged through your lodge at the time of booking.

CAR Heading from Madikwe to Sun City and Pilanesberg, ask your lodge for directions and take the back roads. This route is quicker and bypasses the R67 charge at the Swartruggens toll gate on the N4. It's not recommended en route to Madikwe as it's trickier in this direction and getting lost is more likely.

TRANSFERS AND BUSES Without your own transport, the best option is to organise a transfer through your lodge. Alternatively, take a Gaborone (Botswana) bus (see p595) and arrange for your lodge to pick you up from the Kopfontein border crossing, where the bus will stop.

Mafikeng

☏ 018 / POP 70,000

'Maftown', as locals call the capital of the North-West Province, is a friendly place with a sizeable middle-class black population. It's quite rundown and not worth a special visit, but if you are passing, Mafikeng Museum makes an interesting pit stop.

The main roads are Shippard St, which leads northeast and turns into Rte 49 to Zeerust; and parallel Main St, which turns into Vryburg Rd at its southwestern end and becomes the N18 to Vryburg. Nelson Mandela Dr intersects them, running northwest towards the Ramatlabama border crossing with Botswana.

History

Mafeking (as the Europeans called it) was the administrative capital of the British Protectorate of Bechuanaland (present-day Botswana). The small frontier town, led by British colonel Lord Baden-Powell, was besieged by Boer forces from October 1899 to May 1900. The siege was in some ways a civilised affair, with the besieging Boers coming into town on Sundays to attend church. The Baralong and Mfengu people, however, sustained casualties in the service of the colonialists and saw their herds of cattle raided by the Boers for food. During the siege Baden-Powell created a cadet corps for the town's boys, which was the forerunner to his Boy Scout movement.

Mafikeng and Mmabatho were previously twin towns about 3km apart, before being combined under one name. Mmabatho, built as the capital of the 'independent' homeland of Bophuthatswana, became famous for the monumental and absurd buildings erected by controversial Bophuthatswana president Lucas Mangope.

⊙ Sights

Mafikeng Museum   MUSEUM
(☏018-381 0773; cnr Carrington & Martin Sts; admission by donation; ⊙8am-4pm Mon-Fri, 10am-12.30pm Sat) Among the many displays in this excellent regional museum is an exhibit charting the rise of the Boy Scout movement, and a room dedicated to the famous 217-day siege, with original photographs and documents, and information about the role played by the town's black population. It occupies the former town hall (built 1904).

🛏 Sleeping & Eating

There are numerous guesthouses on the suburban streets east of the centre, signposted from Shippard St. The Crossing mall (cnr Nelson Mandela Dr & Sekame Rd) has chain restaurants including News Cafe, Ocean Basket and Spur.

Ferns Country House　　GUESTHOUSE $$
(☑018-381 5971; 12 Cooke St; s R500-985, d R540-1085; @☒) Set in the residential area east of the centre, Ferns is a quiet country haven in the city. There are two pools, secure parking and a variety of rooms, occupying thatched bungalows with sliding glass doors. Staff are helpful and the restful **bar-restaurant** (mains R75), with a photo recording Nelson Mandela's stay here, serves good food, although service can be slow.

Protea Hotel Mafikeng　　HOTEL $$
(☑018-381 0400; www.proteahotels.com/protea-hotel-mafikeng.html; 80 Nelson Mandela Dr; s R720-1595, d R875-1750; ✳@☎☒) The Protea is the most stylish option, and one of the pleasantest places in town to loiter, with pillars and vintage photos of old Mafikeng decorating reception. Rooms feature white fluffy duvets with lots of pillows, heavy curtains, mood lighting and international TV channels. Facilities include a car-hire desk, bar and **restaurant** (breakfast R145, dinner mains/buffet R80/150).

Lewoni's　　CAFE $
(58 Proctor Ave; mains R50) In a small suburban complex surrounded by curio shops and nail salons, Lewoni's is a cool retreat from Mafikeng's hectic streets. Dishes such as chicken risotto and tuna pasta bake appear on the specials board; omelettes, salads and toasted sandwiches are also offered, along with drinks from smoothies to fruit teas, and cakes including a commendable milk tart. It's open until 9pm on Wednesday and Friday.

❶ Information

There are shops, banks and a post office on and around Main St, a short walk from Mafikeng Museum.

　There's a **tourist information desk** (☑018-381 0773; www.tourismnorthwest.co.za/mafikeng, www.mafikeng.gov.za; cnr Carrington & Martin Sts) in Mafikeng Museum.

❶ Getting There & Around

Mafikeng is 25km southeast of the Ramatlabama border crossing with Botswana.

　Translux (www.translux.co.za) has daily buses to/from Jo'burg (R130, five hours), leaving at 12.45pm/7am.

Magaliesberg Mountains

Wrap up your South African sojourn with a peaceful night in the mountains. An hour's drive from Pretoria and less than two from Jo'burg, but worlds apart in looks and attitude, the ancient 120km-long Magaliesberg range forms a half moon arc from Hartbeespoort Dam in the east to Rustenburg in the west. Hit the back roads leading off Rtes 104 and 24 to appreciate this region of scrub-covered hills, streams, forests and lots of fresh, clean air – a favourite weekend escape for Gautengers.

　Hartbeespoort Dam, less than an hour's drive from both Jo'burg and Pretoria, has been marked by commercialisation seeping out of the cities. Billboards and building projects line the 55km shoreline and cars zip along en route to the nearby N4. Nonetheless, with the area's rolling hills, winding country roads and green-blue dam waters, it makes a pleasant and convenient stop for lunch and shopping en route to Gauteng.

◉ Sights & Activities

Skim treetops and whizz between cliffs on steel zip lines up to 140m long, suspended 30m above the stream below. **Magaliesberg Canopy Tour** (☑014-535 0150; www.magaliescanopytour.co.za; Sparkling Waters Hotel & Spa, Rietfontein Farm; tours incl lunch R450; ☺6.30am-4.30pm) is a brilliant eco-adventure, taking you on an exhilarating 2½-hour descent through Ysterhout Kloof. Along the way you stop at 11 platforms, built into the cliff's face, for a view of the surroundings and the scoop on local ecology from a guide. There's a minimum of two participants, advance booking is recommended and Sparkling Waters guests receive a R100 discount.

　Stock up on 'Boks tops and biltong, leather goods and wirework at **Welwitischia Country Market** (www.countrymarket.co.za; Damdoryn; admission free; ☺9am-5pm Tue-Sun). Just west of the four-way stop in Damdoryn, near the northwest corner of Hartbeespoort Dam, the market is more authentic than the nearby Chameleon Village tourist complex, with 40 stalls housed in wooden cabins. There's a playground and aviary to keep children occupied, plus three restaurants, and craftwork and classic South African gifts for sale.

　East of the four-way stop in Damdoryn, the road leads through an Arc de Triomphe-style gate, across **Hartbeespoort Dam** and through a tunnel. Art galleries and eateries then line the road as it passes through Schoemansville on the dam's northeastern shore, before meeting the N4 to Pretoria.

🛏 Sleeping & Eating

The tarmac road ends at the gates to **Sparkling Waters Hotel & Spa** (📞014-535 00006; www.sparklingwaters.co.za; Reitfontein Farm; s/d incl breakfast R595/1040, half board R780/1390; ❄️🛜🏊), and the Magaliesberg bush begins beyond its sweeping lawns. Also on the 45-hectare grounds are pools, mini golf, tennis, a health spa and Jacuzzi, a games room, cricket net and playground – all of which leave families sparkling. The bungalows are worn but spacious, with bunks in the family suites, and the buffets in the medieval-themed dining room are veritable banquets. It's 32km southeast of Rustenburg, accessible from Rte 104 near Buffelspoort or Rte 24 via the Oorsaak turn-off in Rex.

The **Upper Deck** (www.theupperdeck.co.za; Welwitischia Country Market, Damdoryn; mains R80) is popular for a beer in the courtyard, between the thatched bar and the double-decker bus adjoining the restaurant. The menu straddles the pub-grub spectrum: the house special is lamb curry, the platters and baskets include a calamari and fillet combo, and the bikers' breakfast stretches to mince and a cheese griller. Specials are offered on Wednesday and Friday, and bands play at weekends.

Park at the 'art bistro' sign to dine on the verandah at the arty **Berliner Bistro** (Main Rd, Schoemansville; mains R60), where tiled rooms display local creations. The meat-oriented blackboard menu, featuring German breakfasts, schnitzel, bratwurst and currywurst, reveals the friendly owners' provenance. Brochures and local information are on hand.

Northern Cape

Places to Eat

» Tauren Steak Ranch (p456)

» Halfway House Hotel (p440)

» Occidental Grill Bar (p440)

» Transkaroo Country Lodge (p442)

Best Places to Stay

» Kimberley Club (p439)

» Le Must River Residence (p445)

» Bitterpan Wilderness Camp (p449)

» Hantam Huis (p459)

» Bedrock Lodge (p456)

» Edgerton House (p439)

Why Go?

With just a million people inhabiting its 373,000 sq km, the Northern Cape is South Africa's last great frontier. The scattered towns are hundreds of kilometres apart, connected by empty roads across the wildernesses of Namakwa, the Kalahari and Upper Karoo. In these sublime, surreal expanses, reality disappears faster than a meerkat into its burrow. Under the remorseless sun, vehicles share park roads with lions, dune boards swish down roaring sands, and Kimberley's pubs serve as they have done since the 19th-century diamond rush.

It's a raw, elemental land, where gnarly camel-thorn, quiver and Halfmens trees break the boundless horizons. Yet some of nature's greatest tricks here are the instances of rejuvenating beauty. The Senqu (Orange) River waters the dry region, creating the Green Kalahari with its vineyards and epic Augrabies Falls. Following the rains, red Kalahari sands shimmer with grasses, and Namakwa's spring bloom carpets rocky hills and plains with wildflowers.

When to Go
Kimberley

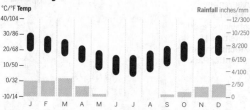

Jan–Mar Harvest at the Senqu (Orange) River wineries, with vineyard tours and events.

May–Jul Winter is cooler, night skies are brighter and dry conditions bring animals to waterholes.

Aug–Sep Namakwa's barren expanses explode with colour during the spring wildflower bloom.

Northern Cape Highlights

1 Watching a black-maned lion nap under a thorn tree in the wild crimson Kalahari wonderland of **Kgalagadi Transfrontier Park** (p447)

2 Taking a spring hike through a sea of brilliant blue, purple and golden wildflowers in **Namakwa** (p455)

3 Stepping into the diamond-dealing past of the **Kimberley** (p436) on a ghost tour or historic pub crawl

4 Gasping at the water surging between vertiginous cliffs in **Augrabies Falls National Park** (p451)

5 Meeting eccentric locals and poking around the museum in **Calvinia** (p458)

6 Finding the Atlantic at the end of Namakwa's straight roads and wandering along the seafront in **Port Nolloth** (p456)

7 Embarking on an adventure across surreal mountainous desert in ultraremote **|Ai-|Ais/Richtersveld Transfrontier Park** (p457)

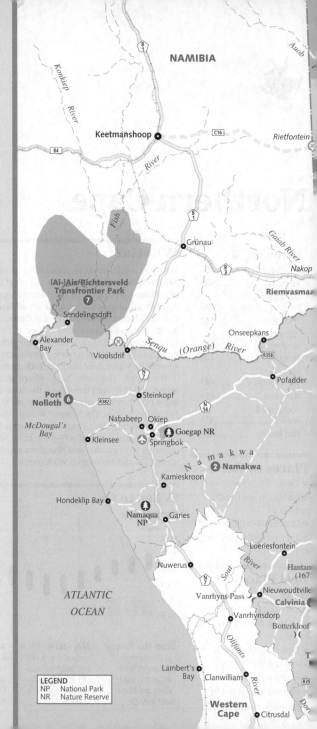

LEGEND
NP National Park
NR Nature Reserve

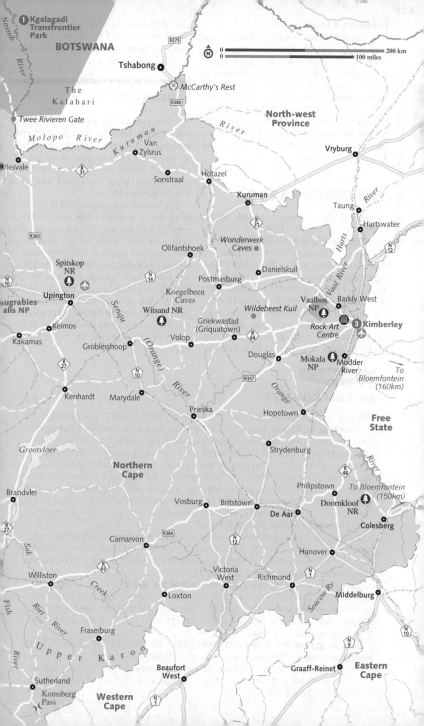

Language & People

The Northern and Western Capes are the only South African provinces where coloured, rather than black, people comprise the majority of the population. English is widely spoken, but Afrikaans is the dominant language, with about 68% of the province speaking it. Tswana (21%) and Xhosa (6%) are the other main languages. The population includes Afrikaners, the Khoe-San (Bushmen), who can still be seen around the Kalahari, and Tswana.

THE UPPER KAROO

Kimberley, the provincial capital, is the centre of the region known as the Diamond Fields. The city that gave birth to De Beers and 'a diamond is forever' remains a captivating place, with a 'Wild West' vibe. Heading southwest, you'll find the sparsely populated plains of the Upper Karoo. Part of the Great Karoo, which extends into the Eastern and Western Capes, this is a desolate land of big skies and empty spaces. Its inhabitants are predominantly Afrikaans sheep farmers, who live as they have for generations on giant tracts of barren land. Towns are few and far between, and are mostly of interest as stopovers offering a taste of Karoo lamb.

Kimberley

053 / POP 170,500

Whether you are drinking in raucous saloons dating back to the diamond rush, surveying the world's largest hand-dug hole, or on a ghost tour, learning about the folk who lived, mined and died here, Kimberley is an excellent place to get stuck into South Africa's eventful history.

The last earth was shovelled at the landmark Big Hole back in 1914, but the Northern Cape's capital remains synonymous with diamonds. Step inside an atmospheric old pub, with dark interiors, scarred wooden tables and last century's liquor ads, and you'll feel you've been transported back to Kimberley's rough-and-ready mining heyday. Wander the period-perfect Victorian mining settlement at the Big Hole Complex, and you'll leave imagining Cecil Rhodes is alive and well and pointing his horse towards Rhodesia.

DON'T MISS

BIG HOLE COMPLEX

Although the R50 million that turned the **Big Hole** (☏053-830 4417; www.thebighole. co.za; West Circular Rd; adult/child R75/45; ☉8am-5pm, tours on the hour Mon-Fri, weekends 9am, 11am, 1pm & 3pm) into a world-class tourist destination came from De Beers Consolidated Mines, touring the world's largest hand-dug hole gives an honest impression of the mining industry's chequered past in Kimberley. You can join a free guided tour or wander round by yourself. Either way, visits generally start with an entertaining 17-minute **film** about mining conditions and characters in late-19th-century Kimberley, and a walk along the Big Hole **viewing platform**. The open-air steel contraption, jutting out over the 1.6km-round, 215m-deep chasm, enhances the vertigo-inducing view of the turquoise water filling all but the last 175m of the hole.

A lift takes you down a shaft for the simulated **mine experience**. Deep in the earth, audio and visual effects give an idea of how bad life was for the black diamond miners. Sounds of tumbling rubble and clamorous workers add claustrophobia, and explosions in the tunnels evoke the dangers faced by diggers.

Exiting the mine, spend some time in the **exhibition centre**, which covers South African history and diamonds in general, as well as Kimberley's story. Also here is the guarded **diamond vault**, holding over 3500 diamonds and replicas of the Eureka and 616 (the world's largest uncut eight-sided diamond, weighing 616 carats), which were unearthed here but are on loan.

Outside, and entered for free, is a perfect partial reconstruction of Kimberley's 1880s **mining settlement**. Using original relocated buildings, this is a surreal place for a stroll. On the village streets are buildings including a corrugated iron church, reading room, funeral parlour, bank and bandstand. Try your luck panning for diamonds and hitting skittles in the bowling alley.

The Northern Cape's only real city is also home to fantastic museums, some wonderful accommodation and Galashewe, a township with plenty of its own history.

Sights

William Humphreys Art Gallery GALLERY
(☎053-831 1724; www.whag.co.za; Civic Centre, 1 Cullinan Cres; adult/child R5/2; ☺8am-4.45pm Mon-Fri, 10am-4.45pm Sat, 9am-noon Sun) One of the country's best public galleries, with changing exhibitions of contemporary South African work, as well as a surprisingly good collection of European masters. There's a cafe and an auditorium where films are shown.

FREE **Northern Cape Legislature Building** ARCHITECTURE
(☎053-839 8024; www.ncpleg.gov.za; off Green St, Galashewe; ☺8am-4pm Mon-Thu, to noon Fri) This striking building reflects Kimberley and the Northern Cape's culture, nature and history. The cone-shaped brown tower, studded with tiles and the faces of South African icons, resembles the outlandish plants and trees found in the province's open spaces. The main buildings recall the rock facades and corrugated iron that dominated early Kimberley, and walkways flow between them like the province's long roads. The building is signposted from central Kimberley and it should be possible to look around, but it is best visited on a guided Galashewe tour (see p437).

McGregor Museum MUSEUM
(☎053-839 2725; Atlas St; adult/child R18/12; ☺8am-4.30pm Mon-Sat, 2-4.30pm Sun) De Beers constructed this building in 1897 as a sanatorium and Rhodes sat out the Siege of Kimberley here. The museum covers the Second Anglo-Boer War and the Kimberley Regiment's service in subsequent conflicts.

Duggan-Cronin Gallery GALLERY
(Edgerton Rd; admission by donation; ☺9am-5pm Mon-Fri) South Africa's first ethnographic gallery holds a collection of photographs of Southern African tribes taken in the 1920s and 1930s, before many aspects of traditional life were lost. Duggan-Cronin lived in this 19th-century house before his death in 1954.

Honoured Dead Memorial MONUMENT
(Memorial & Dalham Rds) This sandstone memorial remembers the soldiers who died defending the British-held city in the 124-day Siege of Kimberley, which took place during the Second Anglo-Boer War (1899–1902). The large gun is Long Cecil, built to repel the Boers' Long Toms.

Sol Plaatje Educational Trust MUSEUM
(32 Angel St; admission by donation; ☺8am-4pm Mon-Fri) The museum dedicated to the activist and writer Sol Plaatje occupies the house where he lived until his death in 1932. He was known for writing the first novel in English by a black South African and translating Shakespeare into Tswana.

Wildebeest Kuil Rock Art Centre ROCK ART
(☎053-833 7069; www.museumsnc.co.za/other/museums.html; Rte 31; adult/child R24/12; ☺9am-4pm Mon-Fri, 10am-4pm Sat & Sun) On a site owned by the !Xun and Khwe San people, who were relocated here from Angola and Namibia in 1990, this small sacred hill has 400-plus rock engravings dating back millennia. The guided tour leads to the mound along an 800m walkway with information boards covering the site and its Khoe-San heritage.

The centre is 16km northwest of town, en route to Barkly West. A shared minibus taxi costs R25; a private taxi costs R300 return, including waiting time.

The Rudd House ARCHITECTURE
(☎053-839 2725; 5-7 Loch Rd; admission R20; ☺by appointment) This townhouse is a fine example of the residences constructed for rich Kimberlites in the 19th century. Named after Rhodes' partner, who built the house in 1888, it has a fernery and a gorgeous rooftop summerhouse.

FREE **Clyde Terry Hall of Militaria** MUSEUM
(☎076 117 4679; 33 Memorial Rd; admission free; ☺10am-noon Sat-Sun) South Africa's largest private collection of militaria.

Tours

 Ghost Tours GUIDED TOUR
(☎083 732 3189; per person R140; ☺tours 6.30pm) Given its history of diamond digging and Anglo-Boer conflict, Kimberley is fertile ground for ghosts and spirits, with 168 haunted houses. Local historian and raconteur Steve Lunderstedt, leader of South Africa's first ghost tour, has been exploring the city for 20 years. As much a historical tour as a paranormal hunt, the four-hour jaunt has six stops, usually including the Clyde Terry

Kimberley

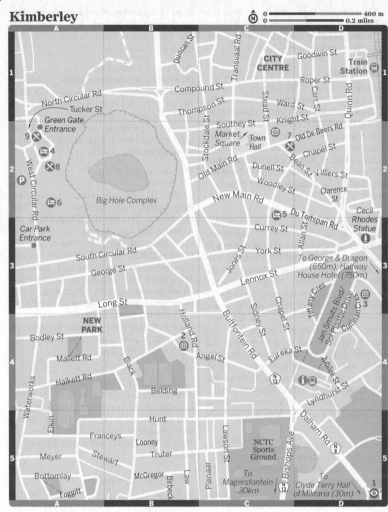

Hall of Militaria, Rudd House and Kimberley Club. It starts at the Honoured Dead Memorial; book ahead. **Jaco Powell** (082 572 0065) offers a three-hour tour with four stops (R120) and Steve also offers a three-hour **Big Hole ghost walk**.

Kimberley Meander   TOUR
(www.kimberleymeander.co.za) Pick up the brochure at the Diamond Visitors Centre (see p441) or visit the website for suggested self-guided walking and driving tours. Themes include ghosts, Anglo-Boer battlefields and historic pubs. Local guides are also listed.

Galeshewe   GUIDED TOUR
(078 069 5104; bphirisi@yahoo.com; half-day R250) One of South Africa's oldest townships, Galeshewe was an integral player in the fight against apartheid. Joy Phirisi leads variously themed tours of this friendly, laid-back township. Stops include the **Mayibuye Uprising Memorial**, where the anti-apartheid protest took place in 1952; adjoining **Robert Sobukwe's practice**, where the Pan African Congress (PAC) founder worked while under house arrest in Kimberley; and the **Northern Cape Legislature Building**. To visit a home or artist's studio, ask in advance.

Kimberley

Second Anglo-Boer War Battlefields DRIVING TOUR

Several battles were fought in the area, including **Magersfontein**, **Modder River**, **Graspan** and **Belmont**, all southwest of Kimberley off the N12. The most important was Magersfontein, where entrenched Boers decimated the famous Highland Brigade. Steve Lunderstedt from Ghost Tours (p437), **Frank Higgo** (☎082 591 5327) and **Veronica Bruce** (☎083 611 6497) offer battlefield tours; Steve also offers a ghost-themed evening at Magersfontein.

Sleeping

Southwest of the Diamond Visitors Centre, Bishops Ave and the adjoining streets are a good area to hunt for budget and midrange accommodation.

TOP CHOICE Kimberley Club BOUTIQUE HOTEL **$$**

(☎053-832 4224; www.kimberleyclub.co.za; Du Toitspan Rd; s/d from R860/1060; ❀🛜) Founded by Rhodes and his diamond cronies as a private club in 1881, and rebuilt following a fire in 1896, the reputedly haunted hotel entertained colonial Kimberley's elite. Renovated 10 years ago, the national monument exudes history in rooms such as the library, billiards room and bar. The 21 bedrooms are period elegant, and offer the chance to pad in the slipper-steps of luminaries from Rhodes onwards. Breakfast is R85.

Edgerton House GUESTHOUSE **$$**

(☎053-831 1150; edgerton@mweb.co.za; 5 Edgerton Rd; s/d incl breakfast R595/750; ❀✹) Combining modern comforts, original fittings and a warm welcome, Edgerton is on a side street near Halfway House Hotel. The bedrooms at the front can pick up noise from the pub; rooms at the rear, entered from a pleasant courtyard, are quieter and more modern. The Madiba Room has hosted dignitaries including Nelson Mandela.

Protea Hotel Kimberley HOTEL **$$**

(☎053-802 8200; www.proteahotels.com/kimberley; West Circular Rd; s/d R690/816; ❀🛜✹) The swanky four-star Protea is the only hotel with Big Hole views – enjoyed from the private viewing deck outside the grand lobby, with its magnificent crystal chandelier. The 94 compact rooms are scattered with antiques, but the Victorian-style elegance really shines in the bar-restaurant and sumptuous public spaces. Weekend specials are normally offered. Breakfast is R75 to R155.

Australian Arms Guest House HOTEL **$$**

(☎053-832 1526; www.australianarms.co.za; Big Hole Complex; s/d incl breakfast R580/700; ❀) The 12 rooms in this property, dating back to 1873, have black-and-white photos of Kimberley, a free-standing bath and shower, DSTV and a fridge. The plain decor doesn't give much of a sense of history, but guests can walk around the mining village at night. The bar-restaurant (mains R55) is more impressive, with an old piano, vintage Castle posters and yellowed newspaper cuttings, though the plasma-screen TV somewhat ruins the effect. Dishes include steaks, ribs and salads. You do not have to pay the Big Hole admission to access the Australian Arms.

Ekhaya Guest House GUESTHOUSE **$**

(☎053-874 3795; ekhayag@telkomsa.net; cnr Hulana & Montshiwa Sts, Galeshewe; r R360-480; ❀✹) Next to Galeshewe municipal centre, Ekhaya has been running seven years and improvements are ongoing. Reception is in a corrugated shack painted with African designs; woodcarvings add character to the site, which also has a restaurant and lapa bar. The thatched cottages are comfortable and stylish, and rooms are a notch above backpacker standards, with tea, coffee and a large TV. Breakfast is R50.

Halfway House Hotel GUESTHOUSE **$$**

(seep440; r R550, breakfast R60; ❀🛜) Above the historic pub, the 11 rooms here are surprisingly modern, with free-standing baths, sofas and occasional antiques.

CECIL RHODES

The sickly son of an English parson, Cecil John Rhodes (1853–1902) was sent to South Africa in 1870 to improve his health. Shortly after arriving he jumped on the diamond-prospecting bandwagon, and in 1888, after working feverishly, he bought Barney Barnato's Kimberley mines for UK£5 million and founded De Beers Consolidated Mines. By 1891, De Beers owned 90% of the world's diamonds and a stake in the fabulous Witwatersrand gold reef near Johannesburg.

But personal wealth and power alone did not satisfy Rhodes. He believed in the concept of the Empire, and dreamed of 'painting the map red' and building a railway from Cape to Cairo, running entirely through British territory. Rhodes established British control in the area that was to become Rhodesia (later Zimbabwe) and his influence was felt across Southern Africa.

In 1890, Rhodes was elected prime minister of the Cape Colony, but was forced to resign five years later, after supporting the disastrous Jameson Raid on Paul Kruger's Transvaal Republic. The British government was publicly embarrassed by the raid, which triggered the Second Anglo-Boer War.

Rhodes' health deteriorated after these disasters. Following his death near Cape Town, his reputation as the poster boy of colonial wrongdoings has steadily grown. More positively, his will left most of his fortune to establishing the Rhodes Scholarship, which sends winners from the Commonwealth and beyond to study at the University of Oxford.

Gum Tree Lodge   HOSTEL **$**
(☑053-832 8577; www.gumtreelodge.com; Hull St; dm R150, r without bathroom R220, s/d/f R350/500/600; ✵❄) As close as Kimberley gets to a backpackers, this former convict station occupies leafy grounds off Rte 64. Rooms are uninspiring, but it's a pleasant environment with greenery overhanging the corrugated roofs and lace trim.

**Heerengracht
Guest House**   GUESTHOUSE, HOSTEL **$$**
(☑053-831 1531; www.heerengracht.co.za; 42 Heerengracht Ave, Royldene; r from R450; ✵❄) This bare brick set-up on a leafy suburban street has rooms and spacious self-catering units. Breakfast is R65. It's walking distance from two malls with fast-food eateries.

Eating & Drinking

The most atmospheric places to eat and drink are the historic pubs, many of which have been around since the diamond rush.

TOP CHOICE Halfway House Hotel   PUB **$$**
(☑053-831 6324; www.halfwayhousehotel.co.za; 229 Du Toitspan Rd; mains R70) Soak up Kimberley's diamonds-and-drink history, quite literally, in this watering hole dating to 1872. It might be the world's only horseback bar; copying Rhodes' habit, locals occasionally saddle up and ride over for a beer. The interiors are beautifully historic, with spittoons

along the base of the scarred, wood-backed bar, marble tables, old liquor ads and frosted windows with Rhodes quotes. Locals flock in to shoot pool, watch bands in the courtyard, and chomp pub grub such as burgers, steaks, crumbed pork chops (recommended), pizzas and pasta. Monday to Saturday, dinner is served in more refined surrounds in adjoining Annabell's.

Occidental Grill Bar   PUB **$$**
(☑053-830 4418; Big Hole Complex; mains R60; ☺9am-7pm Mon-Thu, to 9pm Fri, to 6pm Sat, to 5pm Sun) With a long bar, marble soda fountain and black-and-white photos of old-time prospectors and quaffers, this Victorian-era saloon is a fun place to pause on a Big Hole tour. Dishes include myriad chops, pizzas and salads. You do not have to pay the Big Hole admission to access the Occidental.

Kimberley Club   INTERNATIONAL **$$**
(☑053-802 8200; www.proteahotels.com/kimberley; West Circular Rd; mains R40-100) Wear closed shoes and smart casuals to eat among Rhodes memorabilia in the gentlemen's club he founded, now a boutique hotel. The terrace with wicker chairs is refreshing for a light lunch on a hot day; dishes range from crumbed calamari to Karoo lamb chops.

George & Dragon   PUB **$$**
(☑053-833 2075; 187 Du Toitspan Rd; mains R60; ☺food 9.30am-10pm) With a wood-panelled

bar, the George & Dragon's mix of old English charm, sports and rock music attracts a respectable crowd. Two-for-one burger and pizza deals are offered on Monday and Tuesday respectively, and Sunday lunch (R49) is available if you book ahead.

Gugulethu Kitchen SOUTH AFRICAN $
(6A Bean St; mains R40; ⊘7am-7pm Mon-Sat) Decked out to resemble a shebeen (unlicensed drinking establishment), with corrugated iron screens, Gugulethu is a popular lunch spot for office workers. Various street foods and classic fillers are offered; the easiest option is to ask what's going and opt for that – it will likely be chicken curry with rice, dumplings or pap (maize porridge).

Star of the West PUB $
(North Circular Rd; mains R50) The vintage Castle ads, worn floorboards and wooden tables at this 'old time' hostelry, established in 1870, tell of many raucous nights. Food is pub grub with an emphasis on the Afrikaner clientele's beloved meat, and Day-Glo shooters are de rigueur.

ℹ Information

Diamond (Diamantveld) Visitors Centre
(☏053-832 7298; www.northerncape.co.za; 121 Bultfontein Rd; ⊘8am-5pm Mon-Fri, to noon Sat) Gives out useful brochures.
Small World Net Café (☏053-831 3484; 42 Sidney St; per hr R30; ⊘8am-5pm Mon-Fri) Slow internet access.

NORTHERN CAPE KIMBERLEY

WORTH A TRIP

SUTHERLAND

Surrounded by the Roggeveld Mountains, Sutherland (population 4000) is an attractive Karoo *dorpie* (town) with sandstone houses, a 19th-century church and gravel side streets. Perched at about 1500m above sea level, it's the coldest place in South Africa – snow carpets the ground every year. The resultant clear skies, combined with the minimal light pollution found in Sutherland's remote position, make the area perfect for stargazing. The boffins agree: SALT (Southern African Large Telescope), the southern hemisphere's largest telescope, is 18km east of town. In 2012, the Carnarvon area, about 250km northeast of Sutherland, was also chosen to host 70% of the Square Kilometre Array. Set to be the world's largest radio telescope, consisting of thousands of radio dishes, the SKA will be built over the next decade.

Jurg Wagener (☏023-571 1405; www.sutherlandinfo.co.za; 19 Piet Retief St) offers tours of SALT Monday to Saturday. More interesting for amateur astronomers are the nightly stargazing safaris (R60), on which Jurg reveals the secrets of the Milky Way and beyond with the help of a laser pointer and two powerful telescopes. Once a month on a Saturday night, Stars to Midnight (R100) begins with dinner, with the stargazing continuing until midnight.

Other activities include donkey-cart rides and a 145km self-drive botanical tour, covering both the Roggeveld and lower Tankwa Karoo. The area enjoys an annual wildflower bloom similar to the one that carpets nearby Namakwa (see p455).

With a car with good clearance, you can access the 143,600-hectare Tankwa Karoo National Park (☏027-341 1927; www.sanparks.org/parks/tankwa; adult/child R88/44; ⊘6.30am-6pm), where Tankwa desert moonscapes meet sheer Roggeveld cliffs.

Jurg has a caravan park (campsites per person R60) and four guesthouses (s/d incl breakfast R490/780), including a cute 'honeymoon suite' in a cottage on the edge of town, and a farm cottage 2km from Sutherland with no electricity and an open fire.

On Piet Retief St, Perlman House (☏023-571 1445) and Cluster d'Hote (☏023-571 1436) restaurants serve dinner from 6pm. Go for the Karoo lamb chops. The Roggeveld vegetation chomped by the sheep gives the meat a distinctive taste.

The tourist office (☏023-571 1265; www.karoohoogland.co.za; ⊘8am-5pm Mon-Fri, 9am-noon Sat) has lists of accommodation and restaurants.

There is no public transport to Sutherland; enquire with your accommodation about the shuttle service.

If you've got your own wheels, the only tarred road to Sutherland is Rte 354 from Matjiesfontein, 110km south. There are gravel roads from Calvinia, and Loxton via Fraserburg. Contact your accommodation for an update on the state of the gravel roads, which deteriorate in the rain.

ⓘ Getting There & Around

Air

Taxis connect the airport with the city centre.

SA Express (☏053-838 3337; www.flyex press.aero) Flies to/from Jo'burg and Cape Town.

Hamba Nathi (☏053-831 3982; www.ham-banathi.co.za; Diamond Visitors Centre) The travel agent sells tickets.

Bus

Tickets 4 Africa (☏053-832 6040; tickets4a-frica@hotmail.com; Diamond Visitors Centre) Sells tickets for Greyhound, Translux, Intercape and City to City. Journey times to/from Cape Town and Jo'burg are roughly 12 and seven hours respectively.

City to City (www.citytocity.co.za) Daily services to/from Cape Town (R400) and Jo'burg (R190).

Greyhound (www.greyhound.co.za) Daily services to/from Cape Town (R500) and Jo'burg (R335-370).

Intercape (www.intercape.co.za) Runs to Blo-emfontein (R340, two hours) on Thursday and Saturday, returning on Friday and Sunday.

SA Roadlink (☏053-832 9975; www.saroad-link.co.za; Diamond Visitors Centre) Daily services to/from Cape Town (R500) and Jo'burg (R300).

Translux (www.translux.co.za) Daily services to/from Cape Town (R450) and Jo'burg (R250).

Car

Avis, Budget, Europcar, First, Hertz, Sixt and Tempest have desks at Kimberley airport.

Taxi

Alpha Taxi (073 925 8695)
Ricky's Taxis (053-842 1764)

Train

See p605 for more on the following.

Shosholoza Meyl (www.shosholozameyl.co.za) Trans-Karoo trains stop here en route between Jo'burg and Cape Town.

Blue Train (www.bluetrain.co.za) Stops for a tour of the Big Hole Complex en route from Pretoria to Cape Town.

Mokala National Park

Named after the Tswana for camel thorn, the dominant tree found in South Africa's newest national park, Mokala National Park (☏053-204 8000; www.sanparks.org/parks/mokala; adult/child R88/44; ⊙6.30am-6.30pm Apr, May &Sep–mid-Oct, 7am-6pm Jun & Aug, 6am-7pm mid-Oct–Mar) encompasses grassy plains studded with rocky hills and the trademark trees. Indigenous to Southern Africa, camel thorns can range from small, spiny shrubs standing barely 2m high to 16m-tall trees with wide, spreading crowns. The species is an important resource to both the people and wildlife living in this harsh region, with the local tribes using the gum and bark to treat coughs, colds and nosebleeds. Some even roast the seeds as a coffee substitute.

The 20,000-hectare park is home to animals including black and white rhinos, roan antelopes, Cape buffalos, giraffes, zebras and kudus.

Organised activities include wildlife drives, rock-engraving and bush braais (barbecues).

Mosu Lodge (r from R540; ✳🅿) offers Mokala's most upmarket accommodation, with facilities such as electric blankets, fireplaces and DSTV in the self-catering luxury executive suites. The smart poolside **bar-restaurant** (lunch/dinner mains R40/80; ⊙7-10am, noon-2pm & 6-9.30pm Mon-Fri, from 8am Sat & Sun) serves dishes from vegetable stir-fry to venison pie.

Nearby, **Haak-en-Steek Camp** (1-4 people R875) consists of a rustic self-catering cottage, tucked away in the bush with no electricity and views over a watering hole.

Lilydale Rest Camp (r from R575; ✳) is on the banks of the Riet River, which has good fly-fishing. Its self-catering units are perfect for getting back to nature, especially the thatched chalets. Expect breathtaking sunsets and gorgeous star-studded nights.

Near Mosu, **Motswedi Campsite** (campsites from R290) has six protected sites around a watering hole, each with its own kitchen and ablutions block.

To enter the park, head about 60km southwest of Kimberley on the N12, then turn right at the 'Mokala Mosu' sign and follow the dirt road for 21km. It's possible to cross the park and exit by the Lilydale Gate, then follow a dirt road for 16km and meet the N12 about 40km southwest of Kimberley.

Britstown

☏053

At the centre of a sheep-farming area, tiny Britstown is a pleasant village on the old 'diamond way' to Jo'burg via Kimberley.

Transkaroo Country Lodge (☏053-672 0027; www.transkaroocountrylodge.co.za; dm per person R170, s/d/tr/q R500/600/760/890; ✳🅿) is a welcome oasis on a cross-Karoo journey. The **restaurant** (mains R70; 7am-9pm) has a provincial French feel, with chequered placemats, courtyard seating and wholesome dishes from quiche to casserole. The comfortable rooms have floral bedspreads, DSTV and baths with hand-held showers; the backpacker rooms (dorms) generally share bathrooms, although two have private showers.

Britstown is at the crossroads of the N10 and N12.

Victoria West

053 / POP 11,000

Located roughly halfway between Jo'burg and Cape Town, Victoria West is a gracefully fading old railway town. The place is little more than an overnight stop on the way across the Karoo, but if you want to sleep in farm-fresh country air and get a feel for small-town life, Victoria West has a certain stuck-in-time allure.

On Church St are the **Victoria West Regional Museum** (admission free; 7.45am-1pm & 2-4.45pm Mon-Fri), covering local natural and social history; the quaint whitewashed **St John's Church** (1869); **Apollo Theatre** (079 397 3876; by appointment), an art deco cinema with its original interior intact; and the late-19th-century **Victoria West Hotel**, dominating the street like a colonial dinosaur. The white-balconied throwback of the hotel served as the sleeping quarters for railway barons and, legend has it, Queen Victoria; there are plans to renovate.

There are four guesthouses on Church St. The following are behind the Victoria West Hotel.

De Oude Scholen (053-621 1043; deoudescholen@telkomsa.net; 1 Auret St; s/d/f from R350/400/450;) has restful units with tiled floor, attractive bedspreads, fridges, microwaves and large bathrooms. Breakfast (R60), light lunch (R50) and, on Thursday evenings, a braai (R90) are offered.

Kingwill's B&B (053-621 0453; 5 Victoria St; r R400;) has spacious garden units with a safe, microwave and fridge. Dinner is available by order.

Adjoining Kingwill's, **Karoo Deli** (mains R50; 7am-5pm Mon-Fri, to 1pm Sat) has a light menu including cooked breakfasts, buffet lunches and mains such as lasagna.

Victoria West has ATMs and a garage. The town is at the junction of the N12 and Rte 63, which leads west to Calvinia via the towns of Loxton, Carnarvon and Williston.

THE KALAHARI

A voyage to the Kalahari is akin to being catapulted into a parallel universe. It's a surreal *Alice in Wonderland* experience, where everything looms larger than life in the scorching desert heat. A collage of fiery sunsets and shifting crimson sands, lush green fields and gushing waterfalls, magnificent parks and tidy vineyards, this region will enchant long after you depart. If you want to get a feel for it before you leave home, Laurens Van der Post brought the Kalahari alive in his books, including *The Lost World of the Kalahari* and *A Far-Off Place*.

As well as South Africa, the Kalahari covers much of Botswana and extends as far as Namibia and Angola. In South Africa, it's divided into two distinct areas: arid, semi-desert and desert regions; and the 'Green Kalahari', an irrigated, fertile belt along the banks of the Senqu (Orange) River. In this agricultural area, dunes give way to fruit and wine farms producing goodies such as delicious sultana grapes and some excellent tipples. Nonetheless, the Green Kalahari retains a frontier feel, with dazzling night skies and plenty of wide-open spaces.

Kuruman

053 / POP 9093

A mining town set deep in wild country, rough little Kuruman is not a place to linger, but its remote location makes it a natural staging post on trans-Kalahari trips.

The helpful **tourist office** (078 296 3046; Main Rd; 7.30am-4.30pm Mon-Fri) has Kalahari brochures and maps.

> ### GET OFF THE ROAD: 4WD TRAILS
>
> To truly experience the Northern Cape's wild soul and spectacular scenery, leave the tarmac behind and follow a dusty 4WD trail to some of South Africa's remotest corners. The province is home to 20-plus established 4WD trails, particularly in Namakwa, the Kalahari and the two transfrontier parks. Permits and advance booking are generally necessary, and some trails have rudimentary accommodation. Ring local tourist offices for rates and requirements.

The Eye of Kuruman (053-712 1479; Main Rd; adult/child R11/5.50; 7am-6pm), the town's famed natural spring, is in the park between the tourist office and Palmgate Centre. Discovered in 1801, the prolific spring produces about 20 million litres of water a day – without fail. The park is a pleasant spot with trees ringing the clear pond, where some sizeable fish dart beneath the lily pads.

The local mining activity fills accommodation between Monday and Thursday, so book ahead.

Riverfield Guesthouse (053-712 0003; www.riverfield.co.za; 12 Seodin Rd; s/d R400/600;), 2km north of town, has comfortable, spacious rooms in old bungalows on leafy grounds. The breakfasts (R25) are mighty, and staff will open the bar and braai area on request.

In a small mall on the western side of town, Caffe Palermo (053-712 3951; 7 Main Rd; mains from R65), makes a reviving pit stop, with shaded outside seating. The long menu includes burgers, quiches, pastas, salads and heavier options.

For dinner, Palmgate Centre (22 Main Rd) has a supermarket and restaurant.

Intercape (0861 287 287; www.intercape.co.za) stops here daily en route between Jo'burg (R432 to R510, 7½ hours) and Upington (R351 to R420, 3½ hours).

Moffat Mission

The London Missionary Society established the Moffat Mission (053-732 1352; adult/child R10/2; 8am-5pm) in 1816 to work with the local Batlhaping people. The 14-hectare site is named after the Scottish missionary Robert Moffat and his wife Mary, who lived here from 1826 to 1870. They converted the Batlhaping to Christianity, started a school and translated the Bible into Tswana. The mission became a famous staging point for explorers and missionaries heading further into Africa. The Moffats' daughter, Mary, married David Livingstone in the mission church, a stone-and-thatch building with 800 seats. Other buildings include the Moffats' house, Livingstone's room and a textile workshop.

The mission is a quiet and atmospheric spot shaded by large trees that provide a perfect escape from the desert heat. It is 5km north of Kuruman on Rte 31 to Hotazel, signposted from town.

Witsand Nature Reserve

As if a reserve (053-313 1062; www.witsandkalahari.co.za; adult/child R40/20; 8am-6pm) based on a 9km-by-5km and 70m-high white-sand dune system, standing out in stark contrast with the surrounding red Kalahari sands, wasn't enough, Witsand also comes with a soundtrack. When conditions are hot and dry, the sand sings. The 'roaring sands' effect is created by air escaping from the tightly packed grains; the bass, organlike sound is sometimes audible in the reserve office, 5km away. Walking down the side of a dune produces a muted groan.

Activities include hiking, sandboarding (boards R110), mountain biking (bicycles R100) and a 40km 4WD route through the dunes. The guided walks (free) at sunrise and after dark are a fascinating way to learn about the dunes' formation and meet their inhabitants, from antelopes to the dancing white lady spider.

The bush camp has a swimming pool and thatch-roofed, four-star chalets (from R870;). With sliding doors and dark wood, the self-catering chalets sleep up to six in three comfortable, compact rooms with shared bathroom. The Kalahari Experience package (per person R1450) offers full-board chalet accommodation with a guided dune walk. Two- and four-person bungalows (adult/child R160/80) – more accurately huts with bedding provided, shared ablutions and field kitchen – and camping (campsites per adult/child R100/60) are also available. The bar-restaurant (mains R60; 7-9am, noon-2pm & 6-8pm) is not particularly good, but offers an alternative to self-catering.

From the N14, the turn-off to the reserve is about 5km southwest of Olifantshoek, about 400m southwest of the Postmasburg turning and 105km from Kuruman. From there, the gravel road leads 75km southwest to the reserve. From Rte 62, the turn-off is about 60km east of Groblershoop and 5km east of Volop; the reserve is then 45km north on the gravel road. If it hasn't rained recently, the gravel road should be passable in a 2WD with good clearance. Phone the reserve to check. Witsand does not have a petrol station.

Upington

📞054 / POP 53,000

Home to lush gardens and hundreds of date-palm trees, Upington is a prosperous, orderly town on the banks of the Senqu (Orange) River. The central hub for the Green Kalahari, it's a good place to recoup after a long desert slog – although it gets blazing hot in summer. If you yearn to see the Northern Cape's most remote parts, but don't have the means to do so on your own, this is also where you can organise a guided tour. Wide boulevards, slightly cluttered with supermarkets and chain stores, fill the town centre. Step onto a side street near the river, however, and you'll enter a peaceful world where refreshing, watery views and rows of palms hold quiet court.

⊙ Sights & Activities

FREE **Kalahari-Orange Museum** MUSEUM
(4 Schröder St; admission free; ⊙8.30am-5pm Mon-Fri) Occupying the mission station established by Reverend Schröder in 1875, the museum focuses on local social history, with domestic and agricultural artefacts. Displays cover the Upington 26, who were wrongly jailed under apartheid.

Sakkie se Arkie CRUISE
(📞082 564 5447; www.arkie.co.za; Park St; cruise R80; ⊙6pm Fri-Sun, daily during holidays) Soak up the last rays of the Kalahari sun cruising along the Senqu (Orange) River on the top deck of Sakkie's barge. Dire Straits, Afrikaans pop and other classics keep everyone entertained on the two-hour sunset cruise as the water turns silvery and the barmaid lines up cold beers.

☞ Tours

Upington is the best place to organise a Kalahari adventure.

Kalahari Safaris ADVENTURE TOUR
(📞054-332 5653; www.kalaharisafaris.co.za; 3 Orange St) Runs two- to five-people trips to locations including the Kgalagadi and Augrabies Falls parks, Witsand Nature Reserve and Namakwa. The owner, Pieter, grew up in the Kalahari and knows the bush well. Tours last from one to seven days and cater to all budgets and objectives.

Kalahari Tours & Travel ADVENTURE TOUR
(📞054-338 0375; www.kalahari-tours.co.za; 12 Mazurkadraai) Offers itineraries around the province, including six- to nine-day Kgalagadi 4WD adventures.

Sakkie's Adventures ADVENTURE TOUR
(📞082 564 5447; www.arkie.co.za; Park St) Organises rafting on the Senqu (Orange) River, Kgalagadi tours by 4WD and bus, and quadbike and camping safaris to Riemvasmaak, |Ai-|Ais/Richtersveld Transfrontier Park and Namakwa.

🛏 Sleeping

Guesthouses on Budler St and Murray Ave, including the following, overlook the Senqu (Orange) River, their lawns leading to the water. If your accommodation search yields no results, try the Upington booking agency Sociable Weaver (📞054-332 7993).

TOP CHOICE **Le Must River Residence** BOUTIQUE HOTEL $$
(📞054-332 3971; www.lemustupington.com; 14 Budler St; s/d incl breakfast from R890/1180; ✳❄) Owned by Neil Stemmet, author of the cookbook *Salt and Pepper*, this elegant riverside getaway has 11 sumptuous, African-themed rooms with antique furnishings and crisp white linen. Sitting rooms and terraces open onto the artful garden with its Italianate pool.

Le Must River Manor GUESTHOUSE $$
(📞054-332 3971; www.lemustupington.com; 12 Murray Ave; s/d incl breakfast from R680/900; ✳❄) This restful guesthouse's breakfast room and lounge are decorated with antiques and modern items. Rooms five and seven have showers (the rest have a bath with hand-held shower). Room four features a balcony overlooking the river.

Affinity Guesthouse GUESTHOUSE $$
(📞054-331 2101; www.affinityguesthouse.co.za; 4 Budler St; s/d/f incl breakfast from R550/650/750; ✳❄) The corridors and stairs are in need of renovation and a waft of polish lingers, but the staff are helpful and the rooms pleasant. Facilities include fridges, hot drinks, flat-screen TVs, new showers and shared balcony. Ask for a river-view room.

Protea Hotel Oasis HOTEL $$
(📞054-337 8400; www.proteahotels.com; 26 Schröder St; r from R1035; ✳❄🛜) From the air-conditioned reception with ostrich eggs and objets d'art onwards, the Oasis offers some of Upington's most stylish accommodation. It faces another Protea hotel and a Spur restaurant.

Upington

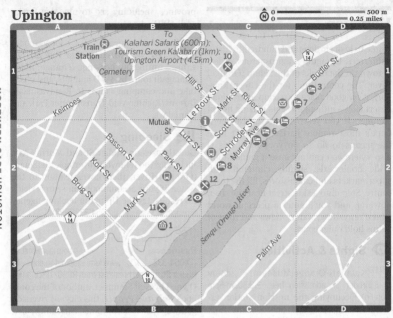

Upington

Die Eiland Holiday Resort   CAMPGROUND **$$**
(☎054-334 0287; www.kharahais.gov.za; campsites
from R93, chalets from R440; ❄🐕) A palm-lined
avenue leads to 'The Island', in a wonderful
natural setting on the river's southeastern
bank. The basic self-catering chalets, good
options for couples and families, have kitch-
enettes with hob and microwave, and tiny
bathrooms with shower. Facilities include
braais and tennis courts.

The Island View House   B&B **$$**
(☎054-331 1328; www.islandviewhouse.co.za; 10
Murray Ave; s/d R420/520, breakfast R60; ❄❄)
The Mocké family offers modern rooms with
showers and a shared lounge, kitchen and
balcony.

✗ Eating & Drinking

**Le Must Country
Restaurant**   SOUTH AFRICAN **$$**
(☎054-332 6700; 11 Schröder St; mains R105;
⊙noon-2pm & 6-10pm) Upington's best res-
taurant does a lively trade in South African
specialities: think Kalahari biltong soup and
Kalahari oysters (grilled lamb-liver parcels)
for starters and *bobotie* (delicately flavoured
curry with a topping of beaten egg baked
to a crust), springbok shank and lamb with
feta for your main course. Towards the end
of the week, book ahead.

O'Hagan's   INTERNATIONAL, PUB **$$**
(☎054-331 2005; 20 Schröder St; mains R85) For
sundowners or an early-evening meal, you
can't beat this chain Irish bar's patio overlooking the river. The menu features pizzas, a few salads, plenty of meat and nary
a shamrock; the funghi pasta is a good vegetarian option.

Dros PUB, SOUTH AFRICAN $$
(☎054-331 3331; Pick 'n Pay Centre; mains R80)
This chain bar-restaurant focuses on meat,
with a few salads, seafood dishes and sa-
voury pancakes. Its wine-cellar pretensions,
with bottles stacked up the walls, make it a
pleasantly cool spot after a hot drive.

ℹ Information

@lantic Internet Cafe (☎054-331 2689; 58 Le
Roux St; one hour R30)
Upington tourist office (☎053-338 7151;
www.northerncape.org.za; Town Library Bldg,
Mutual St; ⏱7.30am-4.30pm Mon-Fri, 9am-
noon Sat) Also visit www.upington.co.za for
tourist info.
Tourism Green Kalahari (☎054-337 2800;
www.greenkalahari.co.za; off Rte 360;
⏱7.30am-4.30pm Mon-Fri) After CTM.

ℹ Getting There & Away

Air
South African Airways (www.flysaa.com) flies
to/from Jo'burg and Cape Town.

Bus
Intercape (Lutz St) goes to Bloemfontein (R340
to R390, 8 hours, Thursday and Saturday); Cape
Town (R440 to R520, 12 hours, Sunday to Friday
nights); Jo'burg (R610 to R30, 11 hours, daily);
and Windhoek, Namibia (R460 to R540, 12
hours, Tuesday, Thursday, Friday and Sundays).

Car
Agencies such as Avis, Budget and Europcar
have offices at Upington airport and in town.

Minibus Taxi
Destinations include Springbok (R190, four
hours).

Kgalagadi Transfrontier Park

A long, hot road leads between crimson dunes
from Upington to the magical **Kgalagadi
Transfrontier Park** (☎054-561 2000; www.san
parks.org/parks/kgalagadi; adult/child R192/96),
one of the world's last great, unspoilt ecosys-
tems. Once you step foot inside Africa's first
transfrontier park, tucked away alongside
Namibia in the Northern Cape and south-
west Botswana, you'll soon see why the jour-
ney was well worth the effort.

The Kgalagadi is a wild land of harsh ex-
tremes and frequent droughts, where shift-
ing red and white sands meet thorn trees
and dry riverbeds. Yet despite the desolate
landscape, it's teeming with wildlife. From
prides of black-maned lion to packs of howl-
ing spotted hyenas, there are some 1775
predators here, including around 200 chee-
tahs, 450 lions and 150 leopards. It's one
of the best places in the world to spot big
cats, especially cheetahs. Add in those gi-
ant, orange-ball sunsets and the black-velvet
night skies studded with twinkling stars,
and you'll feel like you've entered the Africa
of storybooks.

Covering 37,991 sq km (of which 9591 sq
km lie in South Africa), Kgalagadi is one of
Africa's largest protected wilderness areas.
Antelopes, forced to travel great distances in
times of drought to reach water and food,
migrate across the unfenced expanses.

The semiarid countryside (with around
250mm of rainfall a year) is richer than it
appears, and supports large populations of
birds, reptiles, rodents, small mammals and
antelopes. These in turn support the large
population of predators. Most of the animals
are remarkably tolerant of vehicles, allowing
you to get extraordinarily close.

The landscape is hauntingly beautiful. Be-
tween the Nossob and Auob Rivers (usually
dry), the Kalahari dunes are characteristi-
cally red due to iron oxide. Elsewhere, the
sand varies from pink and yellowish to grey;
following the rains, shimmering pioneer
grasses give the land a green tint.

The best time to visit is winter (May to
August), when the weather is coolest (be-
low freezing at night) and the animals are
drawn to the bores along the dry river beds.
Temperatures climb in September and Octo-
ber, but conditions remain dry. November to
April is the wet season; if it does rain, many
animals scatter to fresh pastures across
the plains, making them harder to spot.
However, the extreme heat at the height of
summer, with temperatures passing 40°C
in the shade early in the year, forces many
animals to spend the days wallowing in the
waterholes, making spotting easier. Despite
the high summer temperatures, accommo-
dation in the park fills up during the early-
December-to-mid-January school holidays.

☞ Tours
Sunrise, sunset, night and full-morning
wildlife drives (adult/child from R170/85) and
three-hour **morning walks** (adult from R290)
depart from the rest camps. We recommend
trying a drive; you have a better chance of
spotting predators when accompanied by a

trained ranger. At least two people are needed for tours to depart.

Kgalagadi tours can be organised in Upington (see p445).

🛏 Sleeping & Eating

INSIDE THE PARK

Apart from !Xaus Lodge, accommodation can be booked through the South African National (SAN) Parks reception at Twee Rivieren Gate. Advanced bookings are recommended.

The rest camps have shops selling basic groceries, soft drinks and alcohol, and are open from 7.30am until 15 minutes after the gates close (Nossob and Mata Mata's close between 12.30pm and 1.30pm).

Twee Rivieren Rest Camp has the park's only **restaurant** (mains R85; ⊙7.30-10am & 6-9pm).

Rest Camps

The camps have a range of chalets, bungalows and cottages, with bedding, towels, fully equipped kitchens, braais and bathrooms. Twee Rivieren has 24-hour electricity; at the others, power is cut overnight.

The rest camps all have **campsites** (1-2 people R180, extra adult/child R58/29); Twee Rivieren also has cheaper **sites** (1-2 people R155, extra adult/child R58/29) without power.

Twee Rivieren   REST CAMP $$
(cottages/chalets from R715/1040; ❄ 🛏🛏) The largest camp is also the most convenient, located next to the park entrance, and has the most facilities. The cottages have between two and four single beds; the chalet has six.

Mata-Mata   REST CAMP $$
(chalets R615-1710; 3½ hours from Twee Rivieren Gate; 🛏🛏) Surrounded by thorny Kalahari dune bushveld, Mata-Mata is a good place to spot giraffe. The chalets, which have between two and six single beds, were upgraded as part of a facelift in 2010.

Nossob   REST CAMP $$
(chalets/cottages/guesthouses from R630/1040/1275; 4½ hours from Twee Rivieren Gate; 🛏) Situated within the dry Nossob riverbed and surrounded by tree savannah, this camp is a good place to spot predators. The chalets have between two and six single beds; the guesthouses have four and the cottage has six.

Kgalagadi Transfrontier Park

TASTING GRAPES ON THE ORANGE *LUCY CORNE*

Although not as well known as its Western Cape counterparts, the wine region along the banks of the Senqu (Orange) River has officially taken off – this area is now producing 10% of the country's wines. Tastings here are a much less pretentious affair, wines are generally cheaper than in the Western Cape, and meandering between the vineyards of Kakamas and Upington is a fine way to spend a day.

Wine here used to be limited to the **Orange River Wine Cellars Cooperative** (☑054-337 8800; www.owk.co.za) but while their Upington cellar is a worthy stop, it isn't the region's only producer. In fact, there is far more on offer for the visitor at the following smaller, family-owned wineries.

Bezalel (☑054-491 1325; www.bezalel.co.za), 25km west of Upington on the N14, offers what is probably the most varied tasting of any estate in the country. Work your way through samples of wine, port, brandy, various cream-based liqueurs and the challenge of swigging *mampoer* (moonshine) without grimacing. There's a restaurant here and a charming courtyard where you can enjoy your chosen tipple.

Die Mas van Kakamas (☑054-431 0245; www.diemasvankakamas.co.za) experiments with a wider range of grape varieties than other vineyards in the region, though the *jerepigo* and *hanepoot* wines that the Senqu (Orange) River is known for are still the best bottles available. Farm tours and tastings take place daily (bookings essential) and there's accommodation in case you have one sip too many.

Wilderness Camps

These remote sleeping options offer the opportunity to really immerse yourself in nature. The camps are unfenced, which means animals can wander in, and a ranger is on duty at all times. Stock up on petrol/diesel, drinking water and wood/charcoal for the braai before visiting, and book ahead as the camps are popular.

Bitterpan WILDERNESS CAMP $$
(2-person cabins R945; 3½ hours from Nossob) The stilted cabins perch in a very remote section of the park, with excellent sunset vistas across a pan. Access is via a rough, one-way, 4WD-only route from Nossob.

Gharagab WILDERNESS CAMP $$
(2-person cabins R965; 3½ hours from Nossob) Among the camel-thorn trees and grassy savannah, Gharagab's elevated log cabins survey the red dunes. Perks at the remote spot, accessed on a one-way, 4WD-only trail from Union's End, include wooden decks that overlook a waterhole popular with brown hyenas.

Kalahari Tented Camp WILDERNESS CAMP $$
(2- to 4-person tents from R1070; 3½ hours from Twee Rivieren Gate; 🐾) Kgalagadi's most luxurious wilderness camp is worlds apart from nearby Mata-Mata. The 14 stilted desert tents, created from wooden beams, sand-bags and canvas, have rustic furnishings and views of a waterhole in the Auob riverbed.

It's also the only wilderness camp where children aged under 12 are allowed.

Grootkolk WILDERNESS CAMP $$
(2-person cabins R1050; 3 hours from Nossob) Nestled amid red sand dunes, Grootkolk's desert cabins are made from sand bags and canvas – definitely a different sleeping experience. As if the stars and silence weren't enough, predators are often spotted at the waterhole.

Kieliekrankie WILDERNESS CAMP $$
(2-person cabins R1050; 1½ hours from Twee Rivieren Gate) Kieliekrankie's four cabins are sunk into one of Kgalagadi's highest dunes, with wraparound views of the red sands and a waterhole. The closest wilderness camp to Twee Rivieren.

Urikaruus WILDERNESS CAMP $$
(2-person cabins R1050; 2½ hours from Twee Rivieren Gate) Perched on the banks of the Auob River, the four stilted cabins are connected by raised walkways between the camel-thorn trees. Overlooking a waterhole in the riverbed, Urikaruus is the second-closest wilderness camp to Twee Rivieren.

!Xaus Lodge INDIGENOUS CULTURE $$$
(☑021-701 7860; www.xauslodge.co.za; full board s/d R4030/6200; 3 hours from Twee Rivieren Gate; 🐾) Owned by the Khomani San (Bushmen) and Mier people, !Xaus opened in 2007 after a historic agreement that returned tribal land, incorporated into the park in 1931,

to its original inhabitants. Blending into the red-sand environs and overlooking an enormous salt pan, accommodation is in creatively decorated chalets with decks facing a waterhole. The spacious main building features giant windows, unique wooden architecture and a plunge pool. From desert walks at dawn with the world's best trackers, the Khomani San, to meeting local craftspeople, the focus at !Xaus is on interactive experiences. Rates include activities and 4WD transfers through the dunes from the Auob riverbed road. Children receive discounts of up to 70%.

OUTSIDE THE PARK

There are dozens of places to stay on Rte 360 from Upington to Twee Rivieren Gate. In addition to Molopo, Northern Cape Famous Lodges runs Vischgat Game Lodge and Elandspoor Bush Camp, both about 120km south of Twee Rivieren.

If you arrive late in the afternoon, you may want to spend the night outside the park to avoid paying that day's fees.

Molopo Kalahari Lodge   LODGE **$$**
(✆054-511 0008; www.ncfamouslodges.co.za; Rte 360; campsites R300, s/d/f from R465/640/800, breakfast R65; ✳@☎) About 60km south of Twee Rivieren, Molopo is an attractive place in traditional African safari-lodge style. The *rondavels* (round huts with conical roofs), featuring a fridge and bath with hand-held shower, are a reasonable way to visit Kgalagadi on a budget. The brick chalets are pleasanter, with showers and Khomani San artwork. The thatched main building has a lounge and restaurant (mains R90) – a good stop before or after a park visit – serving meaty dishes, Kalahari baskets and toasted sandwiches. There is a petrol station here and school-going children stay for half-price.

Kalahari Trails   LODGE **$$**
(✆054-511 0900; www.kalahari-trails.co.za; Rte 360; campsites R50, s/d R300/500) This private reserve, 35km south of Twee Rivieren, is home to mammals from hyenas to honey badgers, and offers a Kalahari experience on foot. Guests can walk the dunes by themselves, while guided walks and drives explore the surrounds by day and night. Cheaper rooms with shared bathrooms, safari tents and a self-catering chalet are also available.

ℹ Information

Gates open between 5.30am and 7.30am and shut between 6pm and 7.30pm. Times change between seasons, but generally follow the rising and setting sun.

At Twee Rivieren Gate are the South Africa National (SAN) Parks reception and South African immigration (open 7.30am to 4pm), police and border police; Botswana Wildlife and the Botswana immigration and police are also found there.

Twee Rivieren has public telephones and mobile-phone access.

All the rest camps have displays covering Kgalagadi's wildlife. Twee Rivieren also has an information board near the shop, giving details of recent animal sightings.

If you want to venture into the Botswana side of the park, this is only possible on 4WD trails. Accommodation is in unfenced camps, and campsites at the two Botswana gates, Mabuasehube and Kaa. Book in advance through **Botswana Wildlife** (✆267 653 0226; dwnp@gov.bw; Gaborone). If you want to exit the park via Mabuasehube or Kaa, you must carry out border-crossing formalities at Twee Rivieren and spend at least two nights in the park.

If you want to enter Namibia through Kgalagadi's Mata-Mata Gate, you must spend at least two nights in the park. Present your passport to South African immigration at Twee Rivieren, and to Namibian immigration at Mata-Mata.

ℹ Getting There & Around

Twee Rivieren Gate is 270km northwest of Upington on the tarred Rte 360.

In the park, visitors are restricted to four gravel/sand roads: two leading up the dried beds of the Nossob and Auob Rivers, and two linking these. Try to take one of the roads linking the riverbeds for unobstructed views of the empty expanses of the Kalahari.

The roads are passable in a car, but be careful. If you stop, don't pull too far off the road or you might slip or become bogged in the sand. Beware of patches of deep sand and loose gravel, which make corners treacherous.

For an extra fee, there are 4WD trails to tackle.

Petrol and diesel are available at the rest camps. It's important to carry water, as you will likely have to wait a while for help if you break down.

The speed limit is 50km/h. Allow plenty of time to get to the camps as no driving is permitted after dark.

Visitors must remain in their cars, except at the six designated picnic sites and accommodation.

Keimos & Kakamas

✑ 054

If you've got a hankering to taste Northern Cape grapes, the quaint and quiet agricultural towns of Keimos and Kakamas are gateways to the Senqu (Orange) River Wine Route (see the boxed text, p449).

The **Kalahari Gateway Hotel** (☎054-431 0838; www.kalaharigateway.co.za; Kakamas; s/r from R520/760; ❄❄) has slightly worn but spacious rooms, with comforts such as fridges and TVs. The **bar-restaurant** (mains R75, ☺7am-10pm) has the Northern Cape's first sushi bar and a typically meat-orientated menu with children's offerings. Activities including river rafting, boat tours and abseiling can be organised.

Augrabies Falls National Park

✑ 054

When the waterfall for which this **park** (☎054-452 9200; www.sanparks.org/parks/augrabies; adult/child R108/54; ☺7am-6.30pm) is named is fat with rainy-season run-off, its thunderous roar is nothing short of spectacular. It's the world's sixth-tallest waterfall, formed when the Senqu (Orange) River thunders into an 18km-long ravine with 200m-high cliffs. The main falls drop 56m, while the adjoining Bridal Veil Falls plunge 75m. It's a short walk from the visitor centre to the six viewing platforms, three of which had been destroyed by floods when we visited.

The park has a harsh climate, with an average rainfall of only 107mm and daytime summer temperatures reaching 46°C. There are fascinating desert/riverine ecosystems on both sides of the river, featuring quiver trees (kokerboom aloes), Namakwa figs, thorn trees and succulents. The 50,000-hectare park's 52 mammal species include giraffes, several types of antelope, African clawless otters and endangered Hartmann's mountain zebras; predators are caracals, black-backed jackals, African wild cats, and rarely glimpsed leopards.

Activities

Hiking Trails   HIKING
The three-hour, 5km **Dassie Trail** leads to viewpoints and takes in some of the longer Klipspringer Trail. Another circular route, the three-day, 40km **Klipspringer Trail** (per person R190; ☺Apr–mid-Oct) leads along the southern banks of the Senqu (Orange) River. You'll spend two nights in rustic huts with bunk beds, toilets, drinking water, firewood and rudimentary cooking utensils, but no electricity or showers. There's a minimum of two hikers and advance booking is essential.

WORTH A TRIP

RIEMVASMAAK

From Kakamas, a tarred road leads 55km northwest to Riemvasmaak. The remote village is located on 74,000 hectares of harsh lunar landscape, where the light is otherworldly and intense. In this mountain desert wilderness, donkey carts remain the main mode of transport across the cracked expanse of frosted orange rock and sand. Semi-nomadic locals herd sheep and goats as they have for centuries.

In 1973, the apartheid government removed the local Xhosa and Nama communities, relocating them to the Eastern Cape and Namibia respectively, in order to turn the land into a military training camp. Following South Africa's transition to democracy in 1994, the government began a massive effort to return the local population to Riemvasmaak. In 2002, the formerly displaced residents were given plots of land, and a community-driven tourist initiative started.

Riemvasmaak remains a poor village, relying on self-sustaining farming. Even so, it has much to offer off-the-grid explorers: three challenging **4WD trails** (41km, 49km and 79km) and activities including hiking and mountain-bike trails, abseiling, birdwatching, donkey-cart rides and hot springs. Just beyond the village is the rough and rocky Molopo River gorge.

There are designated **campsites** (from R50) on the trails, and **chalets** (from R375) in the canyon. Contact Clarissa Damara at the **Riemvasmaak Community Centre** (☎054-431 0945, 083 873 7715) to book activities, accommodation and guides.

1. Namakwa Wildflowers (p455)
A vivid blanket of wildflowers dots the landscape at Namakwa, where 4000 species of plant grow.

2. Augrabies Falls (p451)
The world's sixth-tallest waterfall plunges 56m into the Senqu (Orange) River.

3. Kgalagadi Transfrontie Park (p447)
A young Cape fox surveys the landscape of one of Africa's larg protected wilderness areas.

Kalahari
Outventures   RAFTING, KAYAKING
([✆]082 476 8213; www.kalahari-adventures.co.za;
Augrabies) Offers trips on the Senqu (Orange)
River. Its flagship rafting trip, Augrabies
Rush (per person R315, four hours), takes in
grade two and three rapids on a 9km section of the river in the park, finishing 300m
above the main falls. Overnight and multiday
river expeditions are also offered, as is a five-
day tour also incorporating Riemvasmaak
and Kgalagadi Transfrontier Park.

Driving Trails   DRIVING TOUR
In a car, you can drive about 10km along the
gorge from the visitor centre to the viewpoints at **Ararat** and **Oranjekom**. After that
you need a 4WD to carry on.

Night Drive   DRIVING TOUR
(per person R20; [☉]7pm) The two-hour tour ob-
serves animal activities under the stars.

🛏 Sleeping & Eating

Augrabies Falls Lodge & Camp   HOTEL **$$**
([✆]054-451 7203; www.augfallslodge.co.za; Rte
359; s/d R365/530, breakfast R35; [❄]) One of a
number of options on the road to the park,
this 1950s building is 8.5km from the gate.
The spacious rooms have pleasant furnish-
ings and balconies with views across the
countryside. The interior, although slightly
gloomy in places, has been modernised and
adorned with African art. There's a **restau-
rant** (mains R70), bar and a four-person self-
catering room (R650).

SAN Parks   CHALET, CAMPGROUND **$$**
(campsites from R165, tw/d chalets from R700/805,
cottages from R1365; [❄][⊞]) In the park near the
falls, the self-catering chalets and family
cottages have fold-out sofas, allowing extra
children to be squeezed in. The cottages
have two bedrooms, each with two singles
or a double. Solo travellers must pay double
or twin rates. There is also a campsite with
ablutions. The **restaurant** (mains lunch/dinner
R55/100; [☉]7am-8pm) is impressive compared with many in the parks and reserves,
offering a good selection of dishes. The
well-stocked shop sells groceries, alcoholic
drinks, firewood and charcoal.

❶ Getting There & Away
The park is 39km northwest of Kakamas; head
west on the N14 for 8km, then northwest on Rte
359. You need your own transport; alternatively,
tours visit the park from Upington and Kakamas.

NAMAKWA

A land of immense skies and stark countryside, Namakwa, in the Northern Cape's
rugged northwest, is truly South Africa's
Wild West. The roads seemingly stretch on
forever through vast, empty spaces, and
scorching days lead to dramatically quiet
and still nights, when the stars appear bigger and brighter than anywhere else. From
exploring the misty shipwrecked diamond
coastline on the country's far western edge
to four-wheeling through the otherworldly
mountain desert in remote |Ai-|Ais/Rich-
tersveld Transfrontier Park, experiences pile
up fast here.

Namakwa is also a proficient magician,
who performs her favourite trick each
spring. She shakes off winter's bite with an
explosion of colour, covering the sunbaked
desert in a spectacular multihued wildflower blanket.

The region takes its name from the Nama
(also known as Namkwa or Namaqua,
which means 'Nama people'), a Khoekhoen
tribe from northwest Namakwa (previously
known as Namaqualand), who are famous
for their copper metalworking skills.

Springbok & Around
[✐]027
Springbok sits in a valley surrounded by
harsh rocky hills that turn into a rainbow tapestry during the spring wildflower
season. When the flowers aren't blooming, there's little to see or do, although the
town's remoteness, desolate landscape and
300-plus days of sunshine make it a pleasant stopover. Springbok is roughly 550km
north of Cape Town and 115km south of the
Vioolsdrif crossing to Namibia, from where
it is about 550km to Windhoek (Namibia).

From an edgy frontier town, Springbok
has grown into a busy service centre for
Namakwa's copper and diamond mines.
Boers farming in remote areas also point
their *bakkies* (pick-up trucks) to the main
drag, Voortrekker St, for their weekly shopping trips; Springbok is a good place to rest
up and do jobs before continuing into the
wilderness.

◉ Sights & Activities
Goegap Nature Reserve   NATURE RESERVE
([✆]027-718 9906; admission R15; [☉]7am-4pm)
This 15,000-hectare semidesert reserve,

WILDFLOWERS OF NAMAKWA

For most of the year Namakwa appears an inhospitable desert, where nothing but the hardiest shrubs can survive. But the winter rains transform the dry landscape into a kaleidoscope of colours, as daisies, perennial herbs, aloes, lilies and numerous other indigenous flower species blanket the ground. About 4000 species of plant grow in the region, drawing visitors from around the world to this often-forgotten corner of South Africa.

The quality of the bloom and the optimum time to visit are dependent on the rains and vary from year to year. Generally, you have the best chance of catching the flowers at their peak between mid-August and mid-September (sometimes the season can begin early in August and extend to mid-October). The best flower areas also change from year to year, so it is essential to get local advice on where to go.

Bear in mind that most varieties of wildflower are protected by law, and you can incur heavy fines if you pick them.

---

located 15km east of Springbok past the airport, supports some 600 indigenous plant species, 45 mammal species and 94 types of bird. It is one of the best places in the region to take a walk during flower season, with circular 4km and 7km hiking trails. Also check out the Hester Malan Wildflower Garden, home to a rock garden and indigenous succulents including quiver and Halfmens trees. There is a 13km circuit for cars and trails for 4WD vehicles and mountain bikes. Accommodation is available in basic four-bed huts (R100) and campsites (R30).

Driving routes
DRIVING, NATURE

The rocky hills around the village of Nababeep, in the local copper-mining belt, often resemble a sea of flowers during the spring bloom. The route to Nababeep, 16km northwest of Springbok via the N7, passes through prime flower-viewing territory. To head further into the wilds pick up a leaflet covering the multiday Namakwa 4x4 Trail from Springbok tourist office. There are campsites, and permits are required for the two packages, one of which leads west from Vioolsdrif. Richtersveld Challenge, based at Cat Nap Accommodation (see right), hires out 4WD vehicles.

FREE Namakwaland Museum
MUSEUM

(☏027-718 8100; Monument St; ⊘8am-1pm & 2-5pm Mon-Thu, to 4pm Fri) In the 1920s, Springbok had a large population of Jews who traded in the region. Most have moved away and their synagogue (built in 1929) has been converted into the town's small museum.

🛏 Sleeping

During the flower season, accommodation in Springbok fills up and rates rise.

Annie's Cottage
GUESTHOUSE $$

(☏027-712 1451; www.springbokinfo.com; 4 King St; s/d incl breakfast R1000/1200; 🅿❄🌐) With a verandah overlooking a fountain, ferns and fronds in the leafy garden, Annie's is one of Springbok's few options that feels like a place to linger. The 11 ornate, individual bedrooms are cutesy in places, but the attic and Afro-themed rooms are fun choices. Afternoon tea and cake are served and there is a self-catering room.

Mountain View
GUESTHOUSE $$

(☏027-712 1438; www.mountview.co.za; 2 Overberg Ave; r incl breakfast R900; 🅿🛜🌐) Perching in a tranquil location up against the hills, some of the four-star rooms open onto a garden leading to the pool, which has wonderful views. Inside the main building there are more bedrooms, a lounge area and breakfast room; the feel is comfortable and elegant throughout.

Cat Nap Accommodation
HOSTEL $

(☏027-718 1905; richtersveld.challen@kingsley.co.za; Voortrekker St; dm R150, s R180-280, d R360-420; 🅿) The walls of this spacious old house are adorned with nature photos and original art, and rooms are cosy African-themed affairs. There's a self-catering kitchen and dorm beds in the barn, although it gets hot in summer.

Old Mill Lodge
GUESTHOUSE $$

(☏027-718 1705; www.oldmilllodge.com; 69 Van Riebeeck St; s R500, d & tw R600, breakfast R50;

❄@☂) Pleasantly situated in a peaceful garden up against the rocks on a quiet side street, the 11 pleasant rooms are decorated with modern art. Bathrooms are larger than average, mostly with both shower and bath, and flower-season tours can be arranged.

Springbok Lodge
GUESTHOUSE $

(✆027-712 1321; sbklodge@intekom.co.za; 37 Voortrekker St; s R250-300, d R375-425, mains R60; ❄) Springbok's minivillage of whitewashed 1920s houses leads uphill towards the church. Each house has half a dozen quiet, sparse rooms, with TV, fan and hot drinks. The pricier options have air-conditioning and a bar fridge. The main building, decorated with items from number plates to antelope heads, packs in a newsagent, bookshop and cafe-restaurant.

 Eating

TOP CHOICE **Tauren Steak Ranch**
STEAKHOUSE $$

(✆027-712 2717; 2 Hospital St; mains R100; ⊙11.30am-late Mon-Fri, 6pm-late Sat) Meat lovers rejoice, Tauren serves steaks weighing up to a kilogram with delectable toppings such as blue cheese and biltong. All the classics are here: burgers, surf & turf, pizzas with toppings such as biltong and *boerewors* (farm sausage). There are a few vegetarian choices and the pizza schnitzel is a local tip. The ambience is country-relaxed, with *boeremusiek* on the stereo and photos of quiver trees on the walls.

Melkboschkuil Plaaskombuis
BOEREKOS $$

(✆083 255 7689; Voortrekker St; mains R75; ⊙7.30am-9pm Mon-Fri, to 2pm Sat) This *plaaskombuis* (farm kitchen) serves hearty food, such as *braaivleis* (barbequed meat), *potjiekos* (slow-cooked stew), steaks, burgers and salads, in traditional surrounds with bare floorboards, dressers and a terrace.

Titbits Restaurant
CAFE $$

(✆027-718 1455; cnr Namaqua & Voortrekker Sts; mains R90; ⊙8am-10pm Mon-Sat, noon-10pm Sun) A simple setup with flowery local scenes on the walls, and an outside terrace. Sandwiches, steak, pasta, pizzas and breakfasts feature on the menu, along with a few options for children and vegetarians.

ⓘ Information

Something Online (✆027-712 2561; 57 Voortrekker St; 1hr R60; ⊙8am-5pm Mon-Thu, 8am-4pm Fri) Internet access.

Tourist office (✆027-712 8035; www.northerncape.org.za; Voortrekker St; ⊙7.30am-4.15pm Mon-Fri, 9am-noon Sat & Sun)

ⓘ Getting There & Away

Intercape (www.intercape.co.za) Buses serve Cape Town (R330 to R370, 8½ hours) and Windhoek, Namibia (R468 to R520, 13 hours).

Namakwaland Taxi Association (✆027-718 2840; cnr Namaqua and Van der Stel Sts) Minibus taxis serve Upington (R190, four hours), Port Nolloth (R80, two hours) and Cape Town (R270, 8½ hours,).

Port Nolloth

⊘027 / POP 6000

The drive to Port Nolloth alone justifies a visit to the remote seaside town. One minute you're engulfed in nothingness, covered in a layer of red Kalahari sand; the next, you're cresting a hill, watching the icy blue vastness of the Atlantic appear on the horizon. Way off the beaten path near South Africa's northwest corner, the place exudes raw, final-frontier vitality. An exposed and sandy little nowhere town, where the bracing air smells of fish and salt, it's home to a motley, multicultural group of runaways, holiday makers and fortune seekers.

Established as the shipping point for the region's copper, Port Nolloth is now dependent on the diamond dredgers and crayfish trawlers at its small commercial pier. The dredgers are fitted with pumps, which vacuum up the diamond-bearing gravel from the ocean floor. Despite the De Beers complex standing guard, glittery catches do sometimes go astray. However, buying a diamond on the black market is not recommended – pitfalls include *slenters* (fake diamonds cut from lead crystal) and undercover policemen.

Richtersveld Tours (✆082 335 1399; www.richtersveldtours.com) offers 4WD tours of the area, including |Ai-|Ais/Richtersveld Transfrontier Park.

Bedrock Lodge (✆027-851 8865; www.bedrocklodge.co.za; Beach Rd; s/d incl breakfast from R350/500, cottages R500-900; ⊛@☂) is an extremely funky place crammed with all sorts of eccentric knick-knacks and antique collectables. It's right on the seafront, with ocean views through the windows in the corrugated-iron facade, and six nautical-chic self-catering cottages nearby.

The **Scotia Inn Hotel & Restaurant** (✆027-851 8353; scotiainn@mweb.co.za; Beach Rd; s/d from R350/600; ☂) has standard rooms on the ground floor, and deluxe rooms upstairs with sea-facing balconies and DSTV. There's a bar-restaurant.

In the McDougalls Bay holiday resort, 5km south of Port Nolloth, **Port Indigo** (027-851 8012; www.portindigo.co.za; 1245 Kamp St; apartments/houses from R600/780) has four-person apartments and houses accommodating four to six.

During the day, there are five cafes on the seafront. At night, the choice is more limited and the best option is **Vespetti** (027-851 7843; 2099 Beach Rd; mains R60). The Italian restaurant, its awning twined with fishing rope, serves seafood as well as pizzas and pasta.

Port Nolloth has ATMs and a tourist office.

Namakwaland Taxi Association (027-718 2840) runs minibus taxis to/from Springbok (R80, two hours, Monday to Saturday).

|Ai-|Ais/Richtersveld Transfrontier Park

Sculpted by millions of years of harsh elemental exposure, South Africa's remotest **transfrontier park** (027-831 1506; www.sanparks.org/parks/richtersveld; adult/child R130/65; 6am-8pm, office 8am-4pm) is a seemingly barren wilderness of lava rocks, humanlike trees and sandy moonscapes studded with semiprecious stones. The 6000 sq km of surreal mountain desert joins South Africa's Richtersveld National Park with Namibia's |Ai-|Ais Hot Springs Game Park.

Accessible only by 4WD, the Richtersveld is South Africa's final wild frontier. The South African section of the park covers 163,000 hectares, and is most beautiful during the spring wildflower season, when, like elsewhere in Namaqua, it turns into a technicolour wonderland. Hiking here anytime is demanding but spectacular – trails traverse jagged peaks, grotesque rock formations, deep ravines and gorges.

A **petrol station** (7.30am-4pm), small **general store** (weekdays) and public phone at Sendelingsdrift Gate are among the park's few facilities.

 Activities

Hiking Trails   HIKING, OUTDOORS

There are three guided hiking trails on the South African side of the park, open from April to September. Book in advance. Ventersval (four days, three nights) encompasses the southwestern wilderness; Lelieshoek-Oemsberg (three days, two nights) takes in a huge amphitheatre and waterfall; and Kodaspiek (two days, one night) allows the average walker to view mountain desert scenery.

Tours

The easiest way to visit the park is on a tour, which should be booked in advance. Because the park is so remote and slow to travel around, a trip of at least a few days is recommended. Accommodation is normally camping, with equipment provided. Tours can also be organised in Upington.

Richtersveld Tours (082 335 1399; www.richtersveldtours.com) offers 4WD tours of the area, including |Ai-|Ais/Richtersveld Transfrontier Park.

Richtersveld Challenge Based at Cat Nap Accommodation in Springbok (p455), it offers group 4WD tours (about R1000 per person per day) and hiking tours.

Sleeping

Accommodation should be booked in advance. There are four **campsites** (1-2 people R180) on the South African side of the park; Potjiespram is near Sendelingsdrift Gate.

Sendelingsdrift   REST CAMP **$$**

(1-2 people R665; ❄☎) The two- to four-bed self-catering chalets at the entrance are surprisingly comfortable, with porches overlooking the Senqu (Orange) River.

HALF MAN, HALF TREE

Endemic to the Richtersveld and southwest Namibia, the Halfmens tree, also called the Noordpool (North Pole), is a strange plant with a crop of deciduous leaves that always faces north. According to legend, the trees are the frozen souls of Hottentot (a local tribe) ancestors, who were driven south by war-mongering tribes in the north. During the retreat, some people turned back to look pensively across the Senqu (Orange) River, and when they did, they were turned into 'halfmens' – and sentenced to an eternity of northward gazing. The tree, really a stem succulent, is found in clusters around the park, and grows up to 3m in height.

Tatasberg   WILDERNESS CAMP **$$**

(1-2 people R660) Four two-bed, self-catering reed and canvas cabins overlooking the Senqu (Orange) River. There are lights, a fridge, gas stove and shower, but guests should bring drinking water.

Gannakouriep   WILDERNESS CAMP **$$**

(1-2 people R660) Four two-bed, self-catering stone and canvas cabins in a rocky valley, with similar facilities to Tatasberg.

❶ Getting There & Around

A tar road leads 82km from Port Nolloth to Alexander Bay, from where a 90km gravel road leads to Sendelingsdrift Gate. This section is passable in a car, but you need a 4WD vehicle in the park. Richtersveld Challenge (p457) hires out 4WD vehicles and sells maps.

You can cross the Senqu (Orange) River into Namibia on a pontoon boat at Sendelingsdrift. The ferry operates from 8am to 4.15pm weather permitting.

Kamieskroon & Around

📞 027

Out amid the tumbleweed and scrub brush, forgotten-looking Kamieskroon sits in the heart of wild country. Craggy mountains and boulder-strewn hills surround the little place. The feel here is desolate and remote, and many of the roads in town are still not paved.

Namaqua National Park (📞027-672 1948; www.sanparks.org/parks/namaqua; admission R44; ⏰8am-5pm) is 21km west of Kamieskroon on a gravel road. The park's coastal hills catch rain from the Atlantic, making its 103,000 hectares a dependable place to see the wildflower bloom at its best and to photograph the spectacle. There are short nature trails and drives with viewpoints.

In terms of accommodation, there are coastal **campsites** (from R75) and the **Skilpad Rest Camp** (self-catering chalets from R650) in the park. Options in Kamieskroon include **Kuiervreugde** (📞027-672 1904; kuiervreugde @yahoo.com; cottages per person R220), offering well-equipped self-catering cottages and a cafe serving toasted sandwiches and light meals.

Intercape bus services stop in Kamieskroon en route to/from Springbok, 67km north on the N7.

Calvinia

📞 027 / POP 1500

At the base of the dolerite-covered Hantam Mountains, Calvinia is a remote outback town with laid-back charm, located hundreds of miles from anywhere. As locals will happily tell you, Cape Town, Springbok, Upington and Victoria West are all roughly 400km away – reached over empty stretches of Namakwa, the Upper Karoo and the Kalahari. Home to blazing bright light, clear night skies, quaint white-stone buildings and tree-lined streets, Calvinia is the principal town in this sheep-farming region, and is quiet for most of the year. But when the rocky countryside blooms in spring, nearly all of the year's tourists arrive in one frenetic burst.

Type 'Klipwerf Orkes' into YouTube to see some beautiful footage of Calvinia on the video for the *boeremusiek* (country music) song 'Wie se Kind is Jy'.

Calvinia has ATMs, a post office, petrol station and helpful **tourist office** (📞027-341 8100; 19 Parsonage St; ⏰7.30am-4.15pm Mon-Fri).

◉ Sights

4WD routes   DRIVING, NATURE

Especially during the spring wildflower bloom, there are some fantastic drives around the surrounding countryside. One of the prettiest is the unpaved **Rte 364**, which leads southwest to Clanwilliam and the Cederberg via several stunning passes, including the Pakhuis Pass, and endless fields of flowers. Ask in the tourist office for access to the **Hantam Flower 4x4 Route**, which traverses an escarpment north of town. The wildflower viewing is excellent, and the trail follows a dry riverbed where huge fig trees cling to rocky cliffs.

Calvinia Museum   MUSEUM

(📞027-341 1944; 44 Church St; adult/child R5/2; ⏰8am-1pm & 2-5pm Mon-Fri, 8am-noon Sat) In a former synagogue, the museum is surprisingly large and interesting for a small town. It concentrates on the white settlement of the region, with a section devoted to sheepfarming, and has exhibits ranging from Victorian garb to the local telephone-exchange switchboard, used until 1991.

Flower Post Box   MONUMENT

(Hoop St) A water tower has been converted into this giant post box. Letters and postcards posted here receive a special flower postmark.

Junkyard Blues ART
(027-341 1423; 37 Stigling St) Stop at this 'rustic art' emporium to marvel at owner Dirk's collection of found objects, vintage gear, artefacts and general junk. Road signs, sheep skulls, tin cups, watering cans, bed pans, old shoes, bicycles, pottery faces and farm implements decorate the exterior. Dirk plans to offer accommodation here.

Nieuwoudtville ARCHITECTURE, VILLAGE LIFE
(www.nieuwoudtville.com; Rte 27) Halfway between Calvinia and the N7, detour along Nieuwoudtville's main street, which turns into red dirt at the far end of the village. There are some grand sandstone buildings, including the neo-Gothic church (1907). When Calvinia fills up during the flower season, Nieuwoudtville is an alternative base with a few guesthouses.

Akkerendam Nature Reserve WALKING, OUTDOORS
(027-341 8500; off Voortrekker St) North of town, the 2750-hectare reserve has one- and two-day hiking trails. The spring wildflower bloom carpets the mountainous terrain. Contact Calvinia tourist office for advice; the reserve had a vandalism problem, but rangers have been installed.

Festivals & Events

AfrikaBurn FESTIVAL
The subcultural survivalist blowout takes place about 100km south of Calvinia, off Rte 355 (untarred) to Ceres, near Tweefontein and the Tankwa Karoo National Park (see p441).

Sleeping & Eating

During the wildflower season, hotels and restaurants are often fully booked.

TOP CHOICE Hantam Huis GUESTHOUSE $$
(027-341 1606; www.calvinia.co.za/lodge.php; 42 Hope St; s incl breakfast R425-695, d incl breakfast R650-1100, self-catering r per person R260-485;

) Occupying a series of beautifully restored townhouses, Hantam is the perfect place to soak up Calvinia's country quiet and old-world charm. Die Dorphuis, a Victorian national monument, has luxury rooms packed with antiques and original features. At the rear, the cosy standard options occupy former servants' quarters and *nagmaal* rooms, once used by visiting church congregation members; Knegtekamer is particularly cute. Lunch and three-course dinners (R210) are offered in the 19th-century Hantam Huis itself – Calvinia's oldest house.

Die Blou Nartjie GUESTHOUSE $$
(027-341 1263; www.nartjie.co.za; 35 Water St; s/d incl breakfast R375/490;) The Blue Orange's double, twin and family garden bungalow rooms are relaxing after a long drive, with sofa, shower and hot drinks. The restaurant (mains R65-120; from 6.30pm Mon-Sat), occupying a former synagogue, serves traditional tucker such as *bobotie* and Karoo lamb chops.

African Dawn B&B $$
(027-341 1482; www.calviniaretreat.co.za; 17 Strauss Ave; s/d incl breakfast R325/570;) In the leafy surrounds of a nursery, with a weaving cooperative nearby, the three tasteful, modern rooms have DSTV, showers and flower paintings on the grey walls. One has two double beds; another one has a double and a single. Breakfast is served in a *lapa* and the coffee shop (mains R45; 9am-5pm Mon-Fri, to 2pm Sat) serves toasted sandwiches, burgers and light meals.

Getting There & Away

The fastest and easiest route from Cape Town is via the N7 and Rte 27, which climbs the scenic Vanrhyns Pass to Calvinia, then runs northeast to Keimos and Upington. Rte 63 leads east from Calvinia to Victoria West via the quirky Karoo towns of Williston, Carnarvon and Loxton.

Intercape (0861 287 287; www.intercape.co.za) Buses serve Cape Town (R315 to R350, 8 hours) and Upington (R243 to R270, 4½ hours).

Lesotho

Best Places to Eat

» Regal (p467)

» Orion Katse (p477)

» Lesotho Sun (p467)

Best Places to Stay

» Malealea Lodge (p479)

» Maliba Mountain Lodge (p474)

» Semonkong Lodge (p478)

Why Go?

Lesotho (le-*soo*-too) is a vastly underrated travel destination. It's beautiful, culturally rich, safe, cheap and easily accessible from Durban and Johannesburg.

The contrast with South Africa could not be more striking, in both postapartheid attitude and topographical extremes. Even a few days spent in Lesotho's mountain air will give you a fresh perspective on the continent.

This is essentially an alpine country where villagers on horseback in multicoloured balaclavas and blankets greet you round precipitous bends. The hiking and trekking – often on a famed Basotho pony – is world-class and the infrastructure of the four national parks continues to improve.

The 1000m-high 'lowlands' are the scene of low-key Lesotho life, with good craft shopping around Teyateyaneng and the capital, Maseru. But be sure to head inland into the valleys and mountains, where streams traverse an ancient dinosaur playground. This is genuine adventure travel.

When to Go
Maseru

°C/°F Temp — Rainfall inches/mm

[bar chart showing temperature and rainfall for months J F M A M J J A S O N D, with temperature scale 40/104, 30/86, 20/68, 10/50, 0/32, -10/14 and rainfall scale 12/300, 10/250, 8/200, 6/150, 4/100, 2/50, 0]

Jun–Aug Hit the slopes in Southern Africa and catch quality international ski competitions.

Sep Celebrate Lesotho culture at the renowned Morija Arts Festival.

Dec & Jan Feel the full force of Maletsunyane, the region's highest waterfall.

History
THE EARLY DAYS

Lesotho is the homeland of the Basotho – Sotho-Tswana peoples who originally lived in small chiefdoms scattered around the highveld in present-day Free State.

During the 19th century, the Voortrekkers and various other white entrepreneurs began to encroach on Basotho grazing lands. On top of this came the *difaqane* (forced migration; see p510).

Yet the Basotho emerged from this period more united. This was largely due to the leadership of the brilliant Moshoeshoe the Great, a village chief who rallied his people and forged a powerful kingdom. Moshoeshoe first led his own villagers to the mountain stronghold of Butha-Buthe, from which he was able to resist the early incursions of the *difaqane*. He moved his headquarters to the more easily defended hilltop perch of Thaba-Bosiu, from where he repulsed wave after wave of invaders.

By 1840 Moshoeshoe's rule was firmly entrenched. Ultimately, he was able to bring various peoples together as part of the loosely federated Basotho state, which, by the time of his death in 1870, had a population exceeding 150,000.

Moshoeshoe had also welcomed Christian missionaries into his territory. In return for some Christianisation of Basotho customs, the missionaries were disposed to defend the rights of 'their' Basotho against a rising new threat: Boer and British expansion.

DEFENDING THE TERRITORY

In 1843 – in response to continuing Boer incursions – Moshoeshoe allied himself with the British Cape Colony government. While the resulting treaties defined his borders, they did little to stop squabbles with the Boers, who had established themselves in the fertile lowveld west of the Mohokare (Caledon) River. In 1858 tensions peaked with the outbreak of the Orange Free State–Basotho War. Moshoeshoe was ultimately forced to sign away much of his western lowlands.

In 1868 Moshoeshoe again called on the British, this time bypassing the Cape Colony administration and heading straight to the imperial government in London. The British viewed continual war between the Orange Free State and Basotholand as bad for their own interests. To resolve the situation, the British annexed Basotholand.

The decade after Moshoeshoe's death was marked by ongoing squabbles over succession. After briefly changing hands between the British imperial government and the Cape Colony, Basotholand again came under direct British control in 1884. When the Union of South Africa was created in 1910, Basotholand was a British protectorate and was not included; had Cape Colony retained control, Lesotho would have become part of South Africa, and later a homeland under the apartheid regime.

INDEPENDENCE AT LAST

During the early 20th century, migrant labour to South Africa increased, and the Basotho gained greater autonomy under the British administration. In the mid-1950s the council requested internal self-government, with elections to determine its members. Meanwhile, political parties were being formed, led by the Basotholand Congress Party (BCP; similar to South Africa's African National Congress) and the Basotholand National Party (BNP), a conservative group headed by Chief Leabua Jonathan.

Lesotho's first elections in 1960 were won by the BCP, which made full independence from Britain the first item on its agenda. Chief Jonathan became the first prime minister of the newly independent Kingdom of Lesotho, with King Moshoeshoe II as nominal head of state.

Chief Jonathan's rule was unpopular, and in the 1970 election, the BCP regained power. Chief Jonathan suspended the constitution, arrested and expelled the king, and banned opposition parties. Lesotho effectively became a one-party state.

Chief Jonathan was deposed in a military coup in 1986, and Moshoeshoe II restored as head of state. Yet, following ongoing power disputes between the king and the coup leader, Moshoeshoe II was deposed in favour of his son, Prince Mohato Bereng Seeiso (Letsie III).

The BCP split and Mokhehle formed the breakaway Lesotho Congress for Democracy

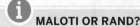

MALOTI OR RAND?

The South African Rand is most welcome in Lesotho, but even though it's tied to its neighbour's currency, the Maloti is not accepted in South Africa. So use it or, effectively, lose it before you leave the country. Most ATMs will dispense Maloti, so don't get caught with a pocketful.

LESOTHO

Lesotho Highlights

1 Visiting a trading post at **Malealea** (p479) and **Semonkong** (p478) to find waterfalls, pony treks and authentic village life.

2 Covering Sani Pass to **Sani Top** (p476) for a dose of African altitude

3 Finding rugged isolation in **Sehlabathebe National Park** (p481)

4 Admiring feats of aquatic engineering at **Katse Dam** (p477)

5 Stomping for dinosaur prints in **Leribe** (p472) and **Quthing** (p480)

6 Experiencing the raw beauty of **Ts'ehlanyane National Park** (p474)

7 Climbing **Thaba-Bosiu** (p469), a place of pilgrimage outside Maseru

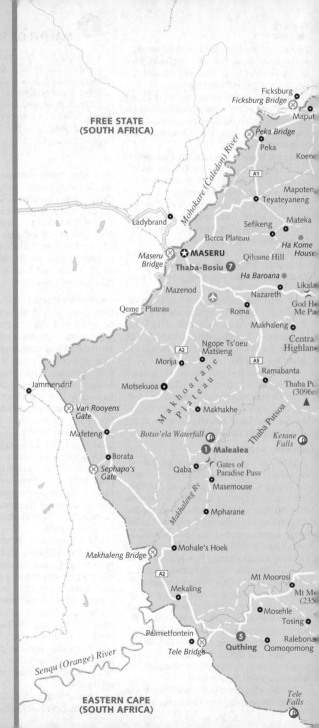

ROAD TRIPS

It's very difficult to circumnavigate Lesotho due to some fairly inaccessible sections, so a degree of backtracking is inevitable. Here are some recommended routes:

» Enter Lesotho at Tele Bridge by Quthing, and make your way east via Mt Moorosi, Mphaki and Qacha's Nek to Sehlabathebe National Park.

» Get a taste of the mountainous 'lowlands' by entering at Qacha's Nek and heading west via Quthing and Mohale's Hoek to Malealea, then to Morija, Roma and up to Semonkong.

» Take in some of Southern Africa's most impressive scenery on a circuit from Butha-Buthe to Oxbow and Mokhotlong (with a detour to Sani Top), then back either via Thaba-Tseka and the Katse Dam, or to Maseru via Likalaneng and Mohale Dam.

» Travel in a loop from Maseru via Morija to Malealea, continue on pony to Semonkong and then make your way back to Maseru via Roma.

(LCD) and continued to govern, with the BCP now in the opposition. Mokhehle died in 1998, and Pakalitha Mosisili took over the leadership of the LCD. Later that year, the LCD won a landslide victory in elections that were declared reasonably fair by international observers, but were widely protested within Lesotho.

In September 1998 the government called on its Southern African Development Community (SADC) treaty partners – Botswana, South Africa and Zimbabwe – to help it restore order in the country. Rebel elements of the Lesotho army resisted, which resulted in heavy fighting and widespread looting in Maseru. Elections – initially scheduled for 2000 – were finally held in May 2002.

CURRENT EVENTS

In 2006 Tom Thabane, along with 17 LCD members had formed the All Basotho Convention (ABC) party. The 2007 elections were highly controversial. National strikes against the government ensued. A two-week curfew was imposed, there was an assassination attempt on Thabane, and many people were detained and tortured. In 2009, there was an assassination attempt on Mosisili.

Lesotho's literacy rate is comparatively high (about 85%), but, nonetheless, it ranks among the poorer countries in the region and it has few natural resources other than water and diamonds. For most of the 20th century, Lesotho's main export was labour, with approximately 60% of males working in South Africa, primarily in the mining industry; since the early 1990s, these numbers have halved. While male migrant workers were being retrenched in large numbers, the Lesotho economy was being transformed through the rapid growth of the textile industry, which has since suffered globally. Unemployment is now estimated at about 45%. Yet, it is hoped that the creation of free trade zones, and the re-emergence of the Letseng Diamond Mine, will help revive the local business sector.

Overshadowing the political and economic issues is the spectre of HIV/AIDS. The infection rate (adult prevalence) is estimated at 24% – one of the highest in the region and the world.

Climate

Clear, cold winters, with frosts and snow in the highlands, await you in Lesotho, so pack warm clothing. In summer (late November to March), dramatic thunderstorms are common, as are all-enveloping clouds of thick mist. Temperatures at this time can rise to over 30°C in the valleys, though it's usually much cooler in the mountains, even dropping below freezing. Nearly all Lesotho's rain falls between October and April. The weather is notoriously changeable throughout the year.

Visits are possible at any time, with spring and autumn optimal. For more information about when to go, see p18.

National Parks & Reserves

Sehlabathebe is Lesotho's most famous national park. While you won't encounter the Big Five (lion, leopard, buffalo, elephant and rhino), its grasslands, lakes and rock formations offer a wonderful wilderness experience. Sehlabathebe is under the jurisdiction of Lesotho National Parks (☎2231 1767).

The country's other main conservation areas – Ts'ehlanyane National Park (p474), Bokong Nature Reserve (p478) and the Liphofung Cave Cultural Historical Site (p474) – are under the jurisdiction of **Lesotho Northern Parks** (☑2246 0723), which handles all accommodation bookings. All have simple accommodation (except for Ts'ehlanyane, which has a luxury resort), established trails and helpful staff; they are relatively easy to access and are a visitor's highlight.

Language

The official languages are South Sotho (Sesotho) and English. For some useful words and phrases in South Sotho, see the Language chapter. For more on Sotho language and culture, see www.sesot ho.web.za.

Dangers & Annoyances

Travellers should not flaunt valuables anywhere. Be especially vigilant in Maseru and Manzini; do not walk around these cities at night – violent muggings have occurred.

If you're hiking without a guide, you might be hassled for money or 'gifts' by shepherds in remote areas, and there's a very slight risk of robbery.

Several lives are lost each year from lightning strikes; keep off high ground during an electrical storm and avoid camping in the open. Waterproof clothing is essential for hiking and pony trekking.

❶ Getting There & Around

It's possible to fly to Lesotho from South Africa, but most travellers enter by bus or private vehicle. For details, see p591. Once in Lesotho, there are good bus and minibus taxi networks that cover the country. See p599 for bus information and minibus taxi information. Note that minibus taxis do not normally operate to a schedule; they wait until the bus is full before departing.

Maseru

POP 430,000 / ELEV 1600M

Maseru is one of the world's more low-key capital cities. It sprawls across Lesotho's lower-lying western edge, rimmed by the Berea and Qeme Plateaus. Occupied by the British in 1869 as an administrative post, over the past few decades Maseru has rapidly expanded, and today there's a modicum of traffic congestion. A major city-rebuilding programme has hidden many of the once-visible scars of the 1998 political unrest.

The city boasts a temperate climate, well-stocked shops and a decent selection of restaurants and accommodation. While the city has few sights, Maseru is where you can get your bearings, sort out logistics and stock up on supplies before heading into the highlands and beyond.

Dangers & Annoyances

Maseru is reasonably safe, but walking around at night is not recommended. As in other cities, bag-snatching and pickpocketing are the main risks during the day.

🛏 Sleeping

The B&B scene is fairly modest in Maseru, but there is certainly no shortage of options. Many people kick on to stay at Roma or Thaba-Bosiu, both of which are easy drives from the capital and have a few good sleeping options.

Black Swan B&B GUESTHOUSE **$$**
(☑22317700; www.blackswan.co.ls; 770 Manong Rd, New Europa; s/d M450/650) The Black Swan makes a smart little refuge from the city centre. The well-kept rooms have satellite TVs and ensuite bathrooms. The lap pool and small gym are a nice touch, as is the outdoor entertaining area. It's located in a very quiet suburb next to a small lake. At dawn and dusk, birdsong fills the air.

Lancer's Inn HOTEL **$$**
(☑2231 2114; lancers-inn@ilesotho.com; cnr Kingsway & Pioneer Rd; s/d/tr incl breakfast M795/995/1040; ❈ ❈) The most popular central business hotel retains a 70s colonial pastel panache, but is a tad expensive and management can be aloof. The warren of garden paths encourages accidental mingling with fellow guests, while the restaurant is more orchestrated and pretty good too. It's behind the French consulate.

Maseru Backpackers & Conference Centre BACKPACKERS **$**
(☑2232 5166; www.maserubackpackers.com; dm/2- to 4-person r M150/400) The best budget choice, which is run by a British NGO, has sparse, clean backpackers' dorms, twins and doubles. The main reason to stay here is for outdoor activities, including canoeing trips on the Caledon River (R200). It's 3km from the city centre and popular with large groups.

Foothills Guesthouse GUESTHOUSE **$**
(☑5870 6566; melvin@xsi net.co.za; 121 Maluti Rd; s/d incl breakfast M380/550) This converted sandstone house offers something different

Maseru

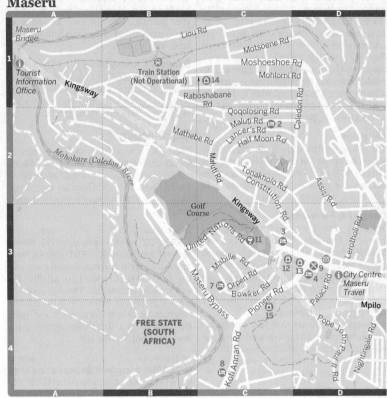

LESOTHO MASERU

Maseru

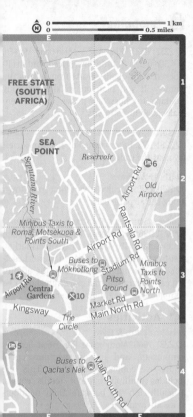

Mohokare Guest House GUESTHOUSE **$**

(☑2231 2224; 260 Kofi Annan Road; s/d incl breakfast M450/600) Closer to town, Mohokare is another good-value option about 3km from the Maseru Bridge on the edge of the centre.

Maseru Sun GUESTHOUSE **$$**

(☑2231 2434; www.suninternational.com; 12 Orpen Rd; r M1285; ❀❄) Part of the Sun International chain.

🍴 Eating

Maseru is a bit limited in the restaurant scene although most of the following offer reasonable cuisine.

Regal INDIAN **$$**

(☑2231 3930; Level 1, Basotho Hat; mains M45-85; ⏱lunch & dinner; ▨) Regal serves surprisingly delicious British-style Indian food (think 'butter chicken' and 'spicy kormas') at the smartest restaurant in town. Located in the Basotho Hat, it's a boon for vegetarians and the go-to place for business meetings and special occasions.

Good Times Cafe DINER **$**

(Level 1, LNDC Centre; M25-60; ⏱breakfast, lunch & dinner) Lesotho's rich, famous, young and beautiful gather here with a small expat community for delicious, deep house music (like local boy Thoroghbred!) and a diner-style menu including burgers, sandwiches, pizza and cocktails. The huge bar is an exercise in chrome and mood lighting, while the 1st-floor terrace sports plush sofas and big-screen TVs.

Ouh La La FRENCH, CAFE **$**

(☑2832 3330; cnr Kingsway & Pioneer Rd; M25-50; ⏱breakfast, lunch & dinner) Locals and expats mix easily in this streetside garden cafe on the doorstep of Alliance Francais. The menu is mostly sandwiches, crepes and pastries, but the coffee is decent and the service is very friendly.

Mediterranée's Restaurant Pizzeriaé PIZZERIA **$**

(☑2231 2960; LNDC Centre; mains M45-75; ⏱lunch & dinner) The Med cooks up yummy wood-fired pizzas and grilled meats and smoking jazz soundtracks. Ethiopian fare is often featured and bohemian crowds gather around the outdoor tables for strong coffee, cigarettes and beret trading. Located in the LNDC Centre.

to the fairly bland capital-city standard. The small, kitschy rooms have garden aspects and guests mingle on the verandah each morning over breakfast. You'll need a taxi to get here.

Lesotho Sun HOTEL **$$**

(☑2224 3000; www.suninternational.com; r M1505; ❀@❄) The radiant Sun is a punter's paradise perched on a hill. A thorough spruce-up has lifted the premier hotel in Lesotho up a notch. It boasts the ubiquitous casino, two restaurants and offers a typical modern hotel experience. Sundowners by the pool are a Maseru must for nonguests.

Phomolo B&B B&B **$**

(☑2231 0755; Matala Phase 2; s M300-380, d M450-500, all incl breakfast) Phomolo B&B is a friendly guesthouse along Main South 1 Road on the way to the airport. It's in Matala Village, 9km from Maseru.

Rendezvous
SOUTH AFRICAN **$**

(2231 2114; Lancer's Inn, Kingsway; mains M47-90; ⊘breakfast, lunch & dinner) The chandeliers and cloth napkins are the only signs of pretence in this wholly down-to-earth restaurant that has a huge menu peppered with South African staples. Return visitors will recognise the clientele as mostly aid workers and local business folk. It's located in Lancer's Inn.

Lehaha Grill
SOUTH AFRICAN **$$**

(2231 3111; Lesotho Sun; meals from M70; ⊘dinner) A busy stalwart that rolls out the fancy linen for the well-dressed dinner crowd, Lehaha is a little overpriced, but service is good for Maseru, and the grills are lean and tasty. If nothing suits, Chinese food is usually served during the evening in the Sun's second restaurant right next door, and its all-you-can-eat luncheon buffet costs M95.

A number of Chinese restaurants are popping up around the city and the new Pioneer Mall can satisfy a fast-food craving.

Self-caterers should head to the well-stocked Shoprite supermarkets in the LNDC Centre or Sefika Mall.

🍷 Drinking & Entertainment

Meloding Club
CLUB

(2231 3687; Victoria Hotel, Kingsway) Local dance-hall, hip-hop and reggae stars are making their presence felt on Thursday, Friday and Saturday nights in this indoor/outdoor club at Hotel Victoria.

Lancer's Inn
BAR

(2231 2114; lancers-inn@ilesotho.com; cnr Kingsway & Pioneer Rd) This atmospheric hotel bar is popular with foreign development workers.

Maseru Club
BAR

(2232 6008; United Nations Rd) The embassy set frequent this low-key collar and frock bar.

Lesotho Sun
BAR

(2231 3111; www.suninternational.com) A definite on Friday nights in summer for city views around the pool.

Times Caffe
BAR, CLUB

(Level 1, LNDC Centre) Great coffee.

🛍 Shopping

Basotho Hat
CRAFT

(2232 2523; Kingsway; ⊘8am-5pm Mon-Fri, to 4.30pm Sat) A little overpriced, but well-stocked, with quality crafts from across the country. If you plan on walking or pony trekking, the horsehair fly whisks sold here make good investments.

Maseru Tapestries & Mats
CRAFT

(2231 1773; Raboshabane Rd) For tapestries, try near the train station.

Seithati Weavers
CRAFT

(2231 3975) Located about 7km from town along the airport road.

Pioneer Shopping Centre
MALL

(2231 1126; cnr Pioneer & Mpilo Rd; ⊘8am-6pm) A new mall with a Pick n Pay supermarket, fast-food outlets, a travel agency and Lesotho's first cinema. Plans to make the adjoining car park into a transport hub should be completed by the time you read this.

🏃 Activities

Lehakoe Club & Gym
SPORTS

(2231 7640; Moshoeshoe Rd; ⊘6am-8pm) A gymnasium and indoor swimming pool impressive enough for any city. This one includes multiple outdoor tennis courts, a health club and bar-cafe. Daily memberships are available.

ℹ Information

Emergency
Ambulance (2231 2501)
Fire Department (115)
Police (2231 9900)

Internet Access
999 Internet (Kingsway; per hr M10; ⊘8am-8pm Mon-Fri, 8am-6pm Sat, 9am-5pm Sun) Opposite post office.
Leo's Internet (Taona Centre, Orpen Rd; per hr M10; 8am-5pm Mon-Fri, to 4pm Sat & Sun) Behind the Basotho Hat.

Medical Services
For anything serious, you'll need to go to South Africa. In an emergency, also try contacting your embassy (p578), as most keep lists of recommended practitioners.
Maseru Private Hospital (2231 3260) Is in Ha Thetsane, about 7km south of Maseru.

Money

The top-end hotels will do foreign-exchange transactions (at poor rates). Otherwise try the following:

International Business Centre (Ground fl, Lesotho Bank Tower, Kingsway; ⏰8.30am-3.30pm Mon-Fri, to noon Sat)

Nedbank (Kingsway) Does foreign-exchange transactions Monday to Friday.

Standard Bank (Kingsway) Has an ATM.

Post

Post office (cnr Kingsway & Palace Rd)

Telephone

International phone calls are expensive; if possible, wait until you are in South Africa. In the highlands, mobile-phone signals should not be relied upon.

Tourist Information

Tourist information office (☎2231 2427; Maseru Bridge Border Post; ⏰8am-5pm Mon-Fri, 8.30am-1pm Sat) Has lists of tour guides, information on public transport and, when in stock, free Maseru city maps. It recently moved here after fire destroyed the old building in Kingsway.

Travel Agencies

City Centre Maseru Travel (☎2231 4536; Maseru Book Centre, Kingsway) Next to Nedbank, does regional and international flight bookings. It can also arrange tickets for Intercape buses. Shoprite's 'Money Market' kiosk in LNDC Centre is the easiest place to buy Greyhound, Intercape, Cityliner, Translux and SA Roadlink bus tickets.

Leloli Travel Agency (☎5885 1513; Pioneer Shopping Centre; ⏰8am-5pm Mon-Fri, 9am-noon Sat) Another helpful tourist agency inside Pioneer Shopping Centre.

ⓘ Getting There & Away

To get to Maseru from South Africa, see p593.

There are three main transport stands to the northeast of the main roundabout: behind Sefika Mall (also called new taxi rank) for minibus taxis to Roma (M12), and points south including Motsekuoa (M13, for Malealea); just off Main North Rd near Pitso Ground for minibus taxis to points north; and, about a block away from here, reached via the same turn-off, for large Lesotho Freight Service buses to points south and north. Lesotho Freight Service buses to Mokhotlong (M80) depart from Stadium Rd behind Pitso Ground, while those to Qacha's Nek (M100) depart from next to St James Primary and High Schools on Main Rd South.

For car-rental agencies, **Avis** (☎2235 0328) is at Lesotho Sun and the airport. **Basotho**

PETROL

Note that while unleaded petrol is readily available in lowland towns, it is *scarce* at petrol stations in the highlands. Here, supplies of any fuel type, including diesel, can be unreliable. Highlanders tend to mix their leaded and unleaded fuels. Keep this in mind if you are driving a 2WD or diesel vehicle; check before departure and take provisions.

Car Rental (☎2232 4123; Camara de Decobos Bldg), opposite the Maseru Bridge border post, offers very competitive deals.

ⓘ Getting Around

Moshoeshoe 1 International Airport is 21km from town, off Main South Rd. Minibus taxis to the airport depart from the transport stand at Sefika Mall/new taxi rank. A private taxi company charges around M100.

The standard minibus taxi fare around town is M4. Taxi companies include **Planet** (☎2231 7777), **Luxury** (☎2232 6211) and **Executive Car Hire & Travel** (☎2231 4460). These can also be chartered for long-distance transport elsewhere in the country.

Around Maseru

Maseru's surrounding areas hold several attractions, all of which make easy day or overnight excursions from the capital. They're covered here clockwise, from north to south.

THABA-BOSIU

About 25km east of Maseru is the famed and flat-topped Thaba-Bosiu (Mountain at Night), where King Moshoeshoe the Great established his mountain stronghold in 1824. It's regarded as the birthplace of the Basotho nation, and, although quite an unassuming spot, is Lesotho's most important historical site.

The origins of its name are unclear and numerous versions exist. The most interesting explanation is that to intimidate the enemies, magic herbs were placed on a rope, which was wrapped around the mountain. When the enemies crossed the rope at night they were overcome with a drugged-like sensation that made it seem that Thaba-Bosiu was 'growing' and thus an unconquerable mountain.

At the mountain's base is a **visitors information centre** (☎2835 7207; admission M10; ⊙8am-5pm Mon-Fri, 9am-1pm Sat) where you can organise an official guide to accompany you on the short walk to the top of the mountain. Gentle pony treks are available with Edgar for M70.

From the summit, there are good views over the surrounding area, including to **Qiloane Hill**, which allegedly provided the inspiration for the Basotho hat. Also fascinating to see are the remains of fortifications, Moshoeshoe's grave and parts of his original settlement.

A new **tourist complex** was long behind schedule when we visited but *should* be open by the time you read this. It features a traditional Basotho village, amphitheatre, restaurant and a hotel.

Mmelesi Lodge (☎5250 0006; www.mmelesilodge.co.ls; r M400), a few hundred metres away, is a lovely place to stay. It has 20-odd sandstone buildings in the style of thatched *mokhoro* (traditional Basotho hut). Each has a private bathroom and can sleep four people very comfortably. The on-site restaurant and bar can get jumping when live musicians are in town.

Nonakeng Backpackers (☎5896 2461; dm M80), situated across the highway, is an admirable community project that offers neat and rustic *rondavels* (round huts with conical roofs) with kitchen. It is well located for explorations of Thaba-Bosiu.

Minibuses to Thaba-Bosiu (M10, 30 minutes) depart from Maseru at the transport stand at Shoprite/Sefika Mall. If you're driving, take the Mafeteng Rd for about 13km and turn left at the Roma turn-off; after about 6km take the signposted road left. Thaba-Bosiu is 10km further along.

HA BAROANA

Ha Baroana is one of Lesotho's more important and publicised rock-art sites. It's worth a visit if you have extra time, although neglect and vandalism have taken their toll.

To get here, take the Roma turn-off from the Mafeteng road; continue for about 8km to the Thaba-Tseka junction. Follow the northern fork (to Thaba-Tseka) about 12km to Nazareth village. Just before Nazareth, there's a signposted gravel track to the paintings. Follow this 3km to Ha Khotso village, turn right at a football field and continue 2.5km to a hilltop overlooking a gorge. A footpath zigzags down the hillside to the rock shelter with the paintings. Minibus taxis go as far as Nazareth.

ROMA

Nestled amid sandstone cliffs about 35km southeast of Maseru, Roma was established as a mission town in the 1860s. Today it's Lesotho's centre of learning, with the country's only university, as well as several seminaries and secondary schools. The southern entry/exit to Roma takes you through a striking gorge landscape, and is best travelled during the morning or late afternoon when the lower sun lights the cliffs to full advantage.

Roma Trading Post Guest House (☎2234 0202, 082 773 2180; www.tradingpost.co.za; campsites per person M75, dm M125, r per person M175, s with half board R375; ◙) is a charming fifth-generation trading post operated since 1903 by the Thorn family. The attached guesthouse includes garden rooms, *rondavels* and the original sandstone homestead, with shared kitchen, set in a lush garden. Meals cost extra. Pony trekking, hiking, 4WD trails and other action adventures can be arranged. There are even *minwane* (dinosaur footprints) nearby. Coming from Maseru on the Semonkong road, turn right about 1km before Roma, or follow an old sign for 'Roma Tourist Information'.

About 40km further along a vastly improved road is **Ramabanta Guest House** (☎2234 0267; tradingpost@leo.co.ls; campsites per person M100, dm per person M150; rondavel half board per person M455). Owned by the same mob who run the Roma Guesthouse, the views from the beautifully presented *rondavels here* are to-drive for. Staying here provides the chance to link up Roma, Ramabanta, Semonkong and other places in the area on overnight hikes and pony treks.

Kaycees (dishes M20-70), off Roma's main drag, is a popular place that serves fast food to mostly students.

Minibus taxis run throughout the day to/from Maseru (M18, 30 minutes). They depart Maseru from the stand next to Sefika Mall/Shoprite.

MORIJA

Tiny Morija is the site of the first European mission in Lesotho. It's an important and attractive town with a rich cultural heritage that makes a pleasant day trip from Maseru or a stopover on route further south. The Morija Museum is the unofficial national

LORATO NKESI: DAUGHTER OF THE CHIEF

Life in Ramabanta village tinkers along to the sounds of cowbells and cock crows. Lorato Nkesi, the eldest daughter of the village chief, is a striking woman, fluent in English and mischievous. She is a guide for Ramabanta Trading Post Guest House (p470).

It appears you've spent some time outside the village. Tell us a bit about yourself. I went to boarding school in Roma then moved to Maseru. In 2007 I lived in Johannesburg and gained a Diploma in Tourism. I was a supervisor at Phillips lighting back in Maseru, but then I decided to come and work for the lodge and help my community.

What does a chief actually do these days? They act like regional administrators. A weekly meeting is held to discuss local concerns, such as roads, water quality, farming and preparations for weddings and funerals. They also help resolve personal disputes.

What's your advice for travellers to a Lesotho village? Everyone greets everyone. So wave, smile, say *dumela* (hello). It's also courtesy to introduce yourself to the chief, especially if you plan to spend the night.

How do the villagers earn their livelihood? I'd say about 90% work in agriculture – mostly maize and sorghum – and those who don't own land can make about M25 per day in the fields. Those flags you see on houses? White means they sell cheap beer [potato liquor], yellow is for regular beer, green is for vegetables, red is for meat, but we rarely have any meat!

What kinds of social issues affect village life? Like everywhere in Lesotho, there is a big problem with HIV/AIDS, so the government is building a new hospital here. *Dagga* (marijuana) is cheap (M5 per matchbox) and alcohol is too popular sometimes. Unemployment is also very high.

What's your plan for the future? I want to promote community tourism here with a Basotho cultural centre and invite travellers to spend a night in the village rather than in their fancy *rondavel!*

How much does it cost for your hand in marriage? Forty cows. But I never want to get married. What's the point, eh?

But what if your village (and the chief) demanded it? No need to worry. I am one of four girls, so he is the last chief!

one and if you're here in late September, don't miss the Morija Festival.

Sights & Activities

Morija Museum & Archives MUSEUM $
(☎2236 0308; www.morijafestival.wordpress.com; admission M10; ☺8am-5pm Mon-Sat, noon-5pm Sun) This small, considered museum contains ethnographical exhibits, archives from the early mission and scientific artefacts. There's an excellent collection of books for sale, including those by Stephen Gill, the curator himself. The museum staff will guide you to nearby dinosaur footprints (for a small fee) and direct you to accommodation. There's even a small courtyard tearoom that comes to life on weekends and during the Morija Festival.

Maeder House Crafts Centre CRAFTS
(☎2236 0487; ☺by appointment) This is a good crafts centre near the museum, and Lesotho's first printing press is on the same grounds.

Mabeoana Quilters CRAFTS
(☎2700 5133; ☺by appointment) A co-op that is well regarded in the neighbouring village of Matsieng. Follow signs from Morija main drag.

Pony Trekking HORSE RIDING, HIKING
(per hr/day M80/250) Pony trekking and overnight hikes and village sleepovers can be organised through the Morija Guest House – you must reserve one day in advance.

MORIJA ARTS FESTIVAL

This highlight of the Lesotho cultural calendar continues to grow in prestige – an increasing number of attendees are making the trip from South Africa each year. The five-day event, held around late September each year, showcases the diversity of Sotho culture through dance, electronic and jazz music, poetry and theatre. Other past highlights have included horse racing and *moraba-raba* (the African equivalent of chess) competitions. For more information, check out the new website at www.morijafest.wordpress.com.

🛏 Sleeping & Eating

Morija Guest House   GUESTHOUSE **$**
(✆6306 5093; www.morijaguesthouses; r per person without bathroom M210-245) Reason enough to linger in Morija is this sterling stone-and-thatch house perched high above the village. Guests can choose between the three cosy main bedrooms and a self-catering cottage out back. Meals and activities can be arranged.

Lindy's B&B   GUESTHOUSE **$**
(✆5885 5309; www.lindysbnb.co.ls; modern house per person M180, historic home per person M220) Lindy lets you stay in either a large, modern stone duplex or a re-created historic home. Both are surrounded by the Makhoarane Mountains and are beautiful bases for exploring the region. Lindy's food is exceptional too.

ℹ Getting There & Away

Minibus taxis run throughout the day between Maseru and Morija (M13, 45 minutes, 40km).

Northern Lesotho

The lowlands of Northern Lesotho are comprised of a number of busy little commercial towns. Only Teyateyaneng and Leribe (also known as Hlotse) draw travellers, mostly for their good craft shopping, but these towns give way to the majestic northeastern highlands and serve as important border crossings to/from South Africa.

TEYATEYANENG

Teyateyaneng (Place of Quick Sands; usually known simply as 'TY') is the craft centre of Lesotho, and is worth a stop to buy tapestries or watch them being made.

Some of the best come from Helang Basali Crafts (⊗8am-5pm), at St Agnes Mission, about 2km before Teyateyaneng and signposted to the east of the Maseru road. Other good places (both open similar hours) include Setsoto Design, near Blue Mountain Inn, and Hatooa Mose Mosali, diagonally opposite Elelloang Basali Weavers, which is 100m before Agnes Mission. At most places you can watch the weavers at work.

Blue Mountain Inn (✆2250 0362; www.skymountainhotels.com; s/d M610/725; ⊛) is a smart corporate hotel set in a pretty and shady compound. The owners run two other hotels and offer similarly forward service and cookie-cutter motel rooms. The pool is a winner.

Another option on the main road before TY is Ka-Pitseng Guest House (✆2250 1638; s/d M380/680) with lots of everything: plastic flowers, digital satellite TV (DSTV), rooms and conference charisma.

Minibus taxis run throughout the day between Teyateyaneng and Maseru (M14, 45 minutes, 35km). Chartering a taxi from Maseru costs about M150 one way (rates can change depending on fuel prices).

HA KOME CAVE HOUSES

The Ha Kome cave houses (⊗8am-4.30pm Mon-Fri, to noon Sat) are an anomaly in this area, 21km from TY and several kilometres from the village of Mateka. These extraordinary inhabited mud dwellings are nestled under a rock overhang, hidden within the pink-and-orange cliffs. There's a small information centre with clean toilets and a few basic maps. The road is unpassable without a 4WD. Camping is possible.

MAPUTSOE

There's no need to enter this chaotic border town, 86km north of Maseru, across the Mohokare (Caledon) River from the Free State town of Ficksburg. For northbound transport from Maseru, you'll usually need to change vehicles here. Minibus taxis to Maseru (M17, one hour), Butha-Buthe (M13, 45 minutes) and Leribe (M7, 30 minutes) run throughout the day from the Total petrol station.

LERIBE (HLOTSE)

Leribe is a busy regional market hub. It served as an administrative centre under the

British, as witnessed by a few old buildings slowly decaying in the leafy streets.

Sights

The main sight is the crumbling Major Bell's Tower near the market. It was built in 1879, and spent most of its career as a storehouse for government records.

Leribe Craft Centre (☑2240 0323; ⊙8am-4.30pm Mon-Fri, 9.30am-1pm Sat), just off the main road at the northern end of town, sells a range of high-quality mohair goods (and excellent books on Lesotho) at reasonable prices.

Dinosaur footprints abound around Leribe. The most accessible set is a few kilometres south of town at Tsikoane village. Immediately after the Tsikoane Primary School, take the small dirt road to the right towards some rocky outcrops. Follow it up to the church. Many children will vie to lead you the 1km slog up the mountainside to the *minwane,* in a series of caves. The prints are clearly visible on the rock ceiling.

About 7km north of Leribe are the Subeng River dinosaur footprints. At the signpost indicating the river, walk down about 250m to a concrete causeway. The worn footprints of at least three species of dinosaur are about 15m downstream on the right bank.

If you're heading into the highlands, Leribe is the last good place to stock up – there's a Shoprite in town and the Total gas station does a mean batch of fat cakes.

🛏 Sleeping & Eating

Mountain View Hotel
HOTEL $

(☑2240 0559; Main St; www.skymountainhotels. com; s/d M530/680; ✳) This is a reliable hotel on the road adjacent to both the highway and the main street. Rooms are fairly bland, but functional. It certainly outdoes anywhere else in town. The GPS coordinates are S 29° 8' 53" E 27° 44' 2".

Kingdom of Fried & Grilled Chicken
FAST FOOD $

(Main St; mains M15-30; ⊙breakfast, lunch & dinner) Get your hot chicken injection with the local bird-eaters. Yummy salads and grilled sandwiches make this a date place for the young and a friendly postwork chow down for everyone else.

ℹ Getting There & Away

Minibus taxis run throughout the day between Leribe and Maseru (M25, 1½ hours), usually with a change of vehicles at Maputsoe. There are also several vehicles daily between Leribe and Katse (M66, three hours), and between Leribe and Butha-Buthe (M11, 35 minutes), many originating further south.

BUTHA-BUTHE

Lesotho's second-largest town, Butha-Buthe (Place of Lying Down) was named by King Moshoeshoe the Great because it was here that his people first retreated during the chaos of the *difaqane.* Its frontier-town scrappiness is redeemed by an attractive

BLANKET COVERAGE

The Basotho blanket is an important part of public, social and private life, not only as a practical article of clothing, but also as a symbol of status. As recently as 1860 European traders presented King Moshoeshoe I with a blanket. The Basotho people were so taken with it that they chose to disregard their animal hides in its favour and by the 1880s traders were overwhelmed with demand. The original blankets were manufactured from high-quality woven cloth in England and sold in Fraser's Stores (few stores survive today).

Today, however, the woollen blanket is an important practical and symbolic item for the Basotho. A blanket provides insulation in the heat and the cold, is fireproof and a status symbol – each costs a hefty M500. Look out for maize cob (a symbol of fertility), a crown or military markings (a legacy of British imperialism) and a cabbage leaf (meaning prosperity). Young married women wear a blanket around their hips until their first child is conceived and young boys are presented with a blanket upon circumcision, symbolising their emergence from boyhood to manhood.

The solid lines on a blanket's edges are worn vertically – the Basotho believe that worn horizontally the blanket can stunt growth, wealth and development.

Less common, but still used in rural areas, is the Basotho hat (*mokorotlo* or *molianyeo*), with its distinctive conical shape and curious top adornment. The style of the hat is supposedly modelled on the shape of Qiloane Hill, near Thaba-Bosiu.

setting alongside the Hlotse River, with the beautiful Maluti Mountains as a backdrop.

🛏 Sleeping & Eating

Ha Thabo Ramakatane Hostel HOMESTAY $
(dm M120) This is a memorable 'village experience' in a small building astride a family home: cool, fresh water from a well, gas cooking and candlelight (bring your own supplies) and graceful, friendly people. It's in Ha Sechele village, 4km from Butha-Buthe. Turn off the main road at the sign for St Paul's High School in central Butha-Buthe, go left up the lane immediately after the school, then take the next right. Ask for directions once you're on this road.

Crocodile Inn HOTEL $
(✆2246 0223; Reserve Rd; s/d/tr from M280/380/490, s/d rondavels M380/708) The rooms and *rondavels* here are simple and clean, though it's overpriced and often booked with noisy government officials. The restaurant here is Butha-Buthe's main dining establishment and makes a good, greasy pizza (R55). The white hotel is about 500m off the main road (signposted to Butha-Buthe Hospital), at the southern end of town.

❶ Getting There & Away

Many minibus taxis travel between Maseru and Butha-Buthe via Maputsoe (1½ hours), where you'll usually need to change vehicles. From Maputsoe to Butha-Buthe costs M18 and takes about 20 minutes. Both minibus taxis and a bus go to Mokhotlong. The minibus taxis cost M73, and the bus costs M50. Butha-Buthe is the last reliable place to buy petrol – including unleaded – if you're heading north.

TS'EHLANYANE NATIONAL PARK

This Lesotho Northern Parks–administered **national park** (✆2246 0723; admission per person/vehicle M30/10) protects a beautiful, high-altitude, 5600-hectare patch of rugged wilderness, including one of Lesotho's only stands of indigenous forest. This underrated and underused place is about as far away from it all as you can get and is perfect for hiking.

In addition to day walks, there is a challenging 39km hiking trail that goes from Ts'ehlanyane southwest to Bokong Nature Reserve through some of Lesotho's most dramatic terrain. Guides to Bokong Nature Reserve can be arranged at the park entrance for M410. **Pony trekking** (per half/full day M150/180) can be arranged through Lesotho

Northern Parks with advance notice or through Maliba Mountain Lodge.

Maliba Mountain Lodge (✆in Durban 031-266 1344; www.maliba-lodge.com; s/d/t full board per person R2239/2999/3910) is the finest accommodation in Lesotho. Five high-end cottages feature lavish beds, antique furniture and jacuzzis facing the dark green mountain range. Heated towel racks and port by the door are a few of the signature touches. The main lodge has a bar, cellar and restaurant with a large terrace to soak up the sun, ambience and splendid vistas. There are all kinds of walks and activities on offer. Down by the water is the charming three-star **River Lodge** (s/d/t/q M1385/1470/1555/1640), which provides value access to the lodge facilities.

The park has various **campsites** (per person from M40) and a **guesthouse** (6 persons M450). Bookings can be made through **Lesotho Northern Parks** (✆2246 0723). Bring your own food and cooking equipment.

If you're driving, take the signposted turn-off from the main road about 6km southwest of Butha-Buthe, from where it's 33km further on a gravel access road (easily negotiable in a 2WD). Occasional taxis run from Butha-Buthe to the park entrance, but mainly towards Khabo, on the access road, from where you'll need to walk or hitch.

Northeastern & Central Highlands

Northeast of Butha-Buthe, the road weaves up dramatically through spectacular mountains – part of the Drakensberg range – with rocky cliffs and rolling hills. South Africa does a good job of marketing its portion of the Drakensberg escarpment, but for raw beauty, it can't compare with the section in Lesotho, where the combination of snow (in winter), low population density and stunning highland panoramas is hard to beat.

All the areas covered in this section are excellent for hiking, but you'll need to be fully equipped with a four-season sleeping bag, waterproof gear, topographical maps and a compass. Trout fishing is reputed to be top notch.

LIPHOFUNG CAVE CULTURAL HISTORICAL SITE

Just beyond the village of Muela is the signposted turn-off for this small Lesotho Northern Parks–administered site, which includes a cave with some San paintings and Stone

CULTURE BASOTHO-STYLE

Traditional Basotho culture is flourishing, and colourful celebrations marking milestones, such as birth, puberty, marriage and death, are a central part of village life. While hiking you may see the *lekolulo*, a flutelike instrument played by herd boys; the *thomo*, a stringed instrument played by women; and the *setolo-tolo*, a stringed instrument played with the mouth by men. Cattle hold an important position in daily life, both as sacrificial animals and symbols of wealth. Crop cultivation and weather are also central, and form the heart of many traditions.

The Basotho believe in a Supreme Being and place a great deal of emphasis on *balimo* (ancestors), who act as intermediaries between people and the capricious forces of nature and the spirit world. Evil is a constant danger, caused by *boloi* (witchcraft; witches can be either male or female) and *thkolosi* (small, maliciously playful beings, similar to the Xhosa's *tokoloshe*). If you're being bothered by these forces, head to the nearest *ngaka* – a learned man, part sorcerer and part doctor – who can combat them. Basotho are traditionally buried in a sitting position, facing the rising sun and ready to leap up when called.

Age artefacts. King Moshoeshoe the Great is rumoured to have stopped here on his travels around Lesotho.

There is a **cultural centre** (adult/child M25/10; ⊙8am-5pm Mon-Fri) and a small shop selling local crafts. Day hikes are possible and you can arrange **pony trekking** (per hr M50) with advance notice. Accommodation is in four simple, but comfortable, stone, four-person **rondavels** (per person M250, minimum 2) with kitchen facilities.

The most novel and atmospheric form of **camping** (M40) is here – in the cave itself. You'll need to bring your own food.

Twenty-seven kilometres from Butha-Buthe, and before Liphofung, is a sign to **Mamohase B&B** (☑580 45597; www.mamohaseruralstay.com; full board per person M200), a wonderful family stay and authentic cultural experience. Dinner consists of a traditional meal with the family and the accommodation is in a brightly decorated *rondavel* or hut. Bathing facilities are basic, but warm water is provided. The family will organise village tours, pony rides or a hike to Liphofung. A 4WD is required to drive the 2km or so, but you can walk 1km cross country on a footpath; ring and they will meet you.

To get here using public transport, take a minibus taxi heading from Butha-Buthe towards Moteng, and get off at the turn-offs to Mamohase or Liphofung (M10, 25 minutes). The buses to Mokhotlong and Maseru pass in the morning (ask around for times). Liphofung is then an easy 1.5km walk down from the main road along a tarmac access ramp.

OXBOW

Reached after crossing the dramatic Moteng Pass (2820m), Oxbow consists of a few huts and a couple of lodges nestled amid some wonderful mountain scenery, and is an ideal place to get away from the bustle while still enjoying amenities. The area regularly receives snow in winter, and boasts a 1.5km ski slope. It's also popular with South African trout anglers and birdwatchers. Except for a small supply of basics at the shop at New Oxbow Lodge, there's nowhere to stock up.

Skiing is available through **Afri-Ski** (☑086 123 747 54; www.afriski.co.za; 1-/3-day pass M350/750), about 10km past Oxbow, which could one day produce the first Basotho winter Olympian. The 1.5km-long slope has a snowboard park and an area for the curious to at least say they went skiing in Southern Africa. Accommodation is available.

On the banks of the Malibamat'so River, **New Oxbow Lodge** (☑in South Africa 051-933 2247; www.oxbow.co.za; s/d incl breakfast M462/759) is a popular, eerily isolated winter retreat. There's a cosy bar and good restaurant, while the rooms are in six-person thatched cottages. Half-board arrangements and triples and quads are all available.

The bus between Maseru and Mokhotlong will drop you at Oxbow (M70, 4½ hours). Several minibus taxis run daily between Butha-Buthe and Oxbow (M35, 1½ hours). The route follows a series of hairpin turns up the pass, and can be treacherous in snow and ice.

MOKHOTLONG

From Oxbow, a tarmac road winds its way over a series of 3200m-plus passes and through some superb, high-altitude scenery before dropping down to Mokhotlong (Place of the Bald Ibis). The route was the original Roof of Africa Rally (www.roofofafrica.org.ls) course. This is still one of the worst stretches of main road in the country – the asphalt has actually made it *more* pot-holey – and makes for a wild and slow road in a regular vehicle.

Near the Letseng Diamond Mine are the Chalets in the Sky (2832 6982/6286 3676; www.chaletsinthesky.co.ls; per person incl breakfast R450), located in Maloraneng village. The six *rondavels* are modern and comfortable and sit on the edge of real wilderness.

Mokhotlong is the main town in eastern Lesotho, albeit an outpost; it has a Wild West feel to it. There's not much to do other than watch life go by, with the locals on their horses, sporting Basotho blankets. However, the Senqu (Orange) River – Lesotho's main waterway – has its source near Mokhotlong, and the town makes a good base for walks. There are a number of reasonably well-stocked shops; petrol and diesel are sometimes available.

🛏 Sleeping & Eating

Grow   DORMITORY $
(2292 0205; dm R90) This development program registered in Lesotho has an office just off the main road into Mokhotlong. It offers clean and basic dorms and a simple kitchen. It's happy to accept travellers if training groups aren't staying.

Molumong Guesthouse & Backpackers   LODGE $
(in South Africa 033-394 3072; www.molumonglodge.com; campsites per person M80, s/d M150/300) About 15km southwest of Mokhotlong, off the road to Thaba-Tseka, is this former colonial trading post that offers a basic (electricity-free), self-catering experience. New owners have begun renovating a number of rooms outside the main house (and built a useful website). Bring whatever food you'll need from Mokhotlong. Pony trekking is a feature.

St James Lodge   LODGE $
(in South Africa 033-326 1601/071-672 6801; www.stjameslodgeco.za; r per person M100-200) This working mission is a humble yet somehow stylish place to stay. It's also an electricity-free, self-catering experience, so

bring your own food. Pony trekking and scenic walks are available. The lodge also runs a number of service projects in the area that guests can witness. It's 12km south of Mokhotlong on the road to Thaba-Tseka.

Senqu Hotel   HOTEL $
(2292 0330; s M260-320, d M320-380) A fairly new wing gives this motel the edge over the limited competition. There's a restaurant too. It's 2.5km from the taxi rank along the main road at the western end of town.

A basic shop in town is Thia-Lala Butchery & Cafe, with takeaway sandwiches and a range of staples, including chilled juices.

ℹ Getting There & Away

There are a few minibus taxis daily to/from Butha-Buthe (M55, six hours). A bus goes daily to/from Maseru, departing in each direction by about 8am (M90, eight hours) except on Sunday (one way, Mokhotlong to Maseru only) and Saturday (one way, Maseru to Mokhotlong only). There's also a daily minibus taxi from Mokhotlong to Sani Top (M75), which continues on to Underberg (South Africa) via the Sani Pass. It departs from Mokhotlong daily at 6am (M65, five hours to Underberg).

Minibus taxis to Linakaneng (on the Thaba-Tseka road; M35) will drop you by Molumong Guesthouse & Backpackers.

SANI TOP

Sani Top sits atop the steep Sani Pass, the only dependable road into Lesotho through the Drakensberg range in KwaZulu-Natal. It offers stupendous views on clear days and unlimited hiking possibilities.

Thabana-Ntlenyana (3482m), Africa's highest peak south of Mt Kilimanjaro, is a popular but long and arduous hike. There's a path but a guide would be handy. It's also possible to do the ascent on horseback.

Hodgson's Peaks (3257m) is a much easier hike 6km south, from where you can see into Sehlabathebe National Park and also KwaZulu-Natal.

Sehlabathebe National Park (266-2231 1767) offers a rugged three- to four-day hike from Sani Top Chalet south along the remote escarpment edge to Sehlabathebe National Park; only try this if you're well prepared, experienced and in a group of at least four people.

Sani Top Chalet (in South Africa 033-702 1158; www.sanitopchalet.co.za; campsites per person M80, dm M150, rondavels s/d R650/1000), at 2874m, Sani Top Chalet stakes a peculiar claim to the highest drinking hole in Southern Africa. Booze trivia aside, cosy *rondavels* and excellent meals reward those who make the steep ascent. Backpackers doss down the road in modern rooms that hold between two and six people. In winter, the snow is sometimes deep enough for skiing; pony trekking can be arranged with advance notice.

There are also several good hostels on the KwaZulu-Natal side of the pass.

A minibus taxi service runs daily from Mokhotlong via Sani Top down to Underberg (South Africa) and back (five hours). Coming from the north, taxis from Butha-Buthe cost M53.

If you're driving, you'll need a 4WD to go up the pass. The border crossings are open 6am to 6pm daily. Note: allow enough time at either end plus always check the times – they do change. Check details with border staff. Hitching is best on weekends to coincide with the exodus from Durban.

THABA-TSEKA

Thaba-Tseka is a remote town on the western edge of the Central Range, over Mokhoabong Pass, which is passable in a 2WD as bulldozers gradually improve the surface. The town was established in 1980 as a centre for the mountain district, and is a scrappy place serving mostly as a convenient transport junction for travel north to Katse or west to Maseru.

Motherland Guest House (☎2700 7664; s/d M350/450) is an excellent new guesthouse in the heart of the town that overlooks the mountainous road to Katse and bubbles with village life. There are plenty of signs to guide you.

Buffalo Hotel (☎2700 7339; s/d M350/450) is 4km past the centre, towards Mokhotlong, down a tough stretch of road. The faux-*rondavels* are a little cramped, but they are perfectly functional. There's a popular restaurant and bar.

Lilala Butchery has a selection of sandwiches, drinks and frozen foods.

Three buses run daily (each way) between Maseru and Thaba-Tseka (M60, seven hours), departing from Maseru between about 8am and 9.30am and from Thaba-Tseka between 7am and 8.30am. Minibuses and buses also go as far as Sehonghong (M28/M45, 2½/four hours); from there you'll need to try your luck for a lift. From Thaba-Tseka to Mokhotlong, get a minibus taxi to Linakaneng (M28, three hours), and

from there another to Mokhotlong (M30, two hours). Several minibus taxis travel daily along the unsealed, but good, road from Thaba-Tseka via Katse (M25), and on to Leribe (M60). One minibus runs to Maseru (via Mohale; M55).

MOHALE DAM

Built across the Senqunyane River, the impressive 145m-high, rock-filled Mohale Dam is the second phase of the Lesotho Highlands Water Project. There are commanding views of the lake and massive mountains beyond. You can drive as far as the Mohale Tunnel, through which water can flow for 32km between the Mohale and Katse Dams.

About 10km east of Mohale, on the banks of the Senqunyane River is **Marakabei Lodge** (☎266-2231 2653; d M330). It recently changed owners, but retains an idyllic natural setting. The en-suite *rondavels* are good value and the lodge is ideal for breaking up the trip to/from the capital. Kayaks are available.

KATSE

Katse is the site of Africa's highest dam (185m). Katse Dam's lake is serene, ringed by steep, green hillsides; even if you're not impressed by engineering feats, the area makes for a relaxing pause. Fishing is allowed from the sides; permits (M10) are on sale at the Bokong Nature Reserve or the information office.

There's a **visitors centre** (☺8am-5pm Mon-Fri, 9am-2pm Sat & Sun), just east of the Katse village junction, along the main road. Look for the bright blue roof. Guided tours depart at 9am and 2pm (weekdays) and 9am and 11am (weekends). Exposed and windy camping is on offer nearby (M20).

The **Katse Botanical Garden** (☎2291 0311; admission M5; ☺8am-5pm Mon-Fri, 9am-6pm Sat & Sun) was originally established to protect the spiral aloes displaced from the dam's construction. It has rapidly flourished to include paved, hillside trails passing via a rock garden, indigenous flowers and a medicinal section. A plant-propagation project takes place in the greenhouse.

Orion Katse Lodge (☎2291 0202, 2291 0813; www.oriongroup.co.za; s/d incl breakfast M590/1000, guesthouse M690-1060), at the far end of the gated Katse village, offers unremarkable hotel accommodation, but the balcony restaurant overlooks the dam and serves delicious trout burgers (M50). To get here, follow the signs to Katse village.

LESOTHO NORTHEASTERN & CENTRAL HIGHLANDS

PONY TREKKING

Pony trekking is one of Lesotho's top drawcards. It's done on sure-footed Basotho ponies, the result of crossbreeding between short Javanese horses and European full mounts.

Advance booking is recommended, and no prior riding experience is necessary. Whatever your experience level, expect to be sore after a day in the saddle. For overnight treks, you'll need to bring food (stock up in Maseru), a sleeping bag and warm, waterproof clothing.

The following places organise treks:

» Malealea Lodge (p479)

» Semonkong Lodge (p478)

» Lesotho Northern Parks conservation areas: Ts'ehlanyane National Park (p474), Bokong Nature Reserve (below) and the Liphofung Cave Cultural Historical Site (p474).

Signposted off the main road in Pitseng village, **Aloes Guest House** (☎2700 5626; s/d M250/730) provides a local 'cushy' base for exploring around Katse or Bokong Nature Reserve. Situated in front of an old sandstone trading post, the rooms and *rondavels* have a stylish African touch. The grounds are the nearest thing to an English cottage garden, and it's a pleasant place to catch up on writing postcards.

The 122km road between Leribe and Katse is excellent, although steep and winding, and slick in the rain. Allow at least two hours for driving, longer if going by public transport.

The Lesotho Freight Services bus leaves Maseru for Katse at 11am and 1pm daily. Minibus taxis go daily from Leribe to Katse (M72, three to five hours), with some continuing on to Thaba-Tseka (M101). In Katse, public transport stops near the Katse village junction.

BOKONG NATURE RESERVE

Bokong has perhaps the most dramatic setting of the three Lesotho Northern Parks reserves, with stunning vistas over the Lepaqoa Valley from the **visitors centre** (adult/child M10/5; ☺8am-5pm), various short walks and a good, rugged two- to three-day hike to Ts'ehlanyane National Park (p474). Bearded vultures, rock shelters and valleyhead fens (wetland areas) are features here.

You can gush about the impressive waterfall at the nearby **camp** (per person M40). You can also stay overnight in a very basic, four-person **hut** (per person M250) – bring your own food, sleeping bag, mattress and stove. **Guides** (per person M30) are available,

and **pony trekking** (per day M180) can be arranged with some prior notice. The reserve sits at just over 3000m and gets cold at night, so come prepared. Bookings must be made through **Lesotho Northern Parks** (☎2246 0813/4).

Bokong lies roughly midway between Katse and Leribe at the top of Mafika-Lisiu Pass (3090m). Minibus taxis from Leribe will drop you at the visitors centre (M32, 1½ hours); when leaving, you may need to wait a while before one with space passes by.

SEMONKONG

Semonkong (Place of Smoke) is a dead-end village in the rugged Thaba Putsoa range. It's beside the beautiful **Maletsunyane Falls** (204m) – at their loudest in summer – and is the starting point for many fine trails. **Ketane Falls** (122m) are a day's ride (30km) from Semonkongalong, a massive gorge.

Semonkong Lodge (☎266 2700 6037, 6202 1021; www.placeofsmoke.co.ls; campsites per person M60, dm/s/d M100/395/660, rondavels s/d M465/720), near the Maletsunyane River, is a model of community tourism and a great place to bring kids. Gourmands make the bumpy, minimum two-hour trip from Ramabanta for the renowned a la carte restaurant (mains M50 to M50), while self-caterers are content with excellent kitchen facilities. Staff can arrange all kinds of tours and hikes (even a pub crawl on a donkey) – often employing locals to navigate the villages and steep trails. Then there's the world's longest commercially operated, single-drop abseil (204m) down the Maletsunyane Falls. The lodge is signposted from the town centre.

Semonkong is about 130km southeast of Maseru, past Roma. The final 70km are on gravel roads and can be a bit rocky. A high-clearance 2WD should make it. Allow three to four hours from Maseru. Buses between Maseru and Semonkong (M110) leave from either town in the morning, arriving in late afternoon; there are two guaranteed departures. The road dead-ends at Semonkong; an excellent alternative to retracing your steps is to hike south to Christ the King Mission, on the Quthing-Qacha's Nek road.

Southern Lesotho

The region from Mafeteng and Malealea southwards, across to Sehlabathebe National Park in the southeast, is less developed than the northwest, but lingers in the image files of all who pass through. The mountain ranges eat up the sky out here, where a velvety orange-pink light pours over putting-green valleys.

Despite what maps show, the road is tarred east to Qacha's Nek, but not between here and Sehlabathebe. If you like hiking and pony trekking in rugged isolation, you'll find company here.

MALEALEA

Malealea is the name of a small village in the west of Lesotho characterised by its breathtaking mountainous surrounds and reputation for successful community-based tourism. Many visitors to Lesotho head straight here to sample Lesotho life or, as the sign outside town says, to just 'pause and look upon a gateway of Paradise'.

The area has been occupied for centuries, as shown by the many San rock paintings in the vicinity. Today, the heart of the village is Malealea Lodge, which offers a smorgasbord of cultural and outdoor activities.

Sights & Activities

Pony Treks   HORSE RIDING
(☑ in South Africa 082 552 4215; per person per day trek M175-280, overnight M380, min 2 persons) Pony Treks will take you to Ribaneng Waterfall (two days, one night); Ribaneng and Ketane Waterfalls (four days, three nights); and Semonkong (five to six days). Bring food, a sleeping bag, rainwear, sunscreen, warm clothing, a torch (flashlight) and water-purification tablets. Accommodation is in Basotho village huts (per person M75).

Hiking   HIKING
Malealea Lodge has maps for hikes in the area and can arrange pack ponies for your gear. Stunning destinations include: Botso'ela Waterfall (about four hours return); Pitseng Gorge (six hours return, bring swimwear); Pitseng Plateau (two hours return); and along the Makhaleng River. The walks include visits to surrounding villages and San art sites. Overnight and longer jaunts are also possible.

Village visits provide a stimulating insight into the local people and their customs. The tiny museum, housed in a traditional Basotho hut, is as interesting for its owner/guide as it is for its traditional exhibits. You can visit a sangoma (traditional medicine practitioner; only for the genuinely interested) and visit the late Mr Musi's reclaimed donga (eroded ravine used for small-scale agriculture). Malealea Lodge can also point you to some good scenic drives suitable for both 2WD and 4WD vehicles.

Sleeping & Eating

TOP CHOICE Malealea Lodge   LODGE **$**
(☑ in South Africa 082 552 4215; www.malealea .co.ls, campsites M75, backpackers huts M135-155, r M220-275) Malealea Lodge is the rightful poster child for the 'Kingdom in the Sky'. The lodge began life in 1905 as a trading post, established by teacher, diamond miner and soldier Mervyn Smith. From 1986 the Jones family ran the store, before transforming it into accommodation and integrating it with the surrounding community. Almost every night the local choir performs at the lodge and a proportion of tourist revenue and donations goes directly to supporting projects in the area. The views, meanwhile, are stupendous.

The accommodation options range from campsites and two-person 'forest', or backpacker, huts in a pretty wooded setting away from the lodge, to simple, cosy rooms and rondavels with en suites.

The lodge also offers a bar, hearty meals (breakfast/lunch/dinner M60/70/95) and self-catering facilities. A village shop stocks basic goods.

There's now intermittent mobile-phone connection at the lodge. September to November are the busy months.

❶ Getting There & Away

Regular minibus taxis connect Maseru and Malealea (M36, 2½ hours, 83km). Otherwise, from Maseru (east) or Mafeteng (west), you catch a minibus taxi to the junction town of Motsekuoa (M13, two hours), from where there are frequent connections to Malealea (M22, 30 minutes).

If you're driving, head south from Maseru on Mafeteng Rd (Main Rd South) for 52km to Motsekuoa. Here, look for the Malealea Lodge sign and the collection of minibus taxis. Turn left (east) onto a tarmac road. Ten kilometres further on take the right fork and continue another 15km. When you reach the signposted turn-off to Malealea, head about 7km along an unsealed road to get to the lodge.

It's also possible to approach Malealea from the south, via Mpharane and Masemouse, but the road is rough and most drivers travel via Motsekuoa.

MAFETENG

Mafeteng (Place of Lefeta's People) is named after an early magistrate, Emile Rolland, who was known to the local Basotho as Lefeta (One Who Passes By). Naturally, the town is an important bus and minibus taxi interchange and a border junction (it's 22km to Wepener in Free State). It's also a busy commercial town and your best stocking-up point before heading south.

The town centre has a small statue commemorating soldiers of the Cape Mounted Rifles who fell in the Gun War of 1880.

The polygon-shaped Mafeteng Hotel (☑2270 0236; s/d/tr from M220/280/360; ☀) is one of the better hotels outside Maseru. It may look like an air traffic control tower, but the rooms' peach interiors are bright and airy, and there's a series of pleasant thatched rooms by the pool in the garden. A restaurant on site serves meals and it even has a disco called Las Vegas. Turn down the road opposite the bright red post office (follow the signs to the hospital).

Frequent minibus taxis connect Mafeteng with Maseru (M25, 1½ hours) and Mohale's Hoek (M16, 30 minutes). For Quthing, change at Mohale's Hoek.

MOHALE'S HOEK

Mohale's Hoek takes its name from the younger brother of King Moshoeshoe the Great, Mohale, who in 1884 gave this land to the British for administrative purposes. The town's brush with royalty continued more recently when Britain's Prince Harry

spent time helping in an orphanage in a nearby village. The town centre is agreeable enough, and a better spot to overnight than Mafeteng.

The best place to stay is Hotel Mount Maluti (☑2278 5224; mmh@leo.co.ls; s/d incl breakfast M257/380), recently expanded, with established gardens and lawns, pleasant rooms (those facing the garden are the nicest) and a restaurant. It's signposted off the main road.

Regular minibus taxis depart for Quthing (M18, 45 minutes) and throughout the day for Mafeteng (M17, 30 minutes). There are also several minibus taxis daily to Maseru (M40, 2½ hours) and a bus (M30).

QUTHING

Quthing, the southernmost major town in Lesotho, is also known as Moyeni (Place of the Wind). It was established in 1877, abandoned during the Gun War of 1880 and then rebuilt at the present site.

Activity centres around Lower Quthing spread out along the main road. Up on the hill, overlooking the Senqu (Orange) River gorge, is Upper Quthing, the former colonial administrative centre, with a post office, hospital, police station, hotel and some good views. There are minibus taxis between Lower and Upper Quthing.

❂ Sights & Activities

Masitise Cave House Museum   MUSEUM
(☑5879 4167; admission by donation) Five kilometres west of Quthing is the intriguing part of an old mission that was built directly into a San rock shelter in 1866 by Reverend David-Frédéric Ellenberger, a Swiss who was among the first missionaries to Lesotho. There's a small museum, with interesting displays on local culture and history. There's a cast of a dinosaur footprint in the ceiling and San paintings nearby.

To get here, take the signposted turn-off near the Masitise Primary School and follow the road about 1.5km back past the small church. At the neighbouring house you can ask for the key from the caretaker, the local church pastor. From here, the museum is five minutes further on foot. It's a great local experience to sleep here; accommodation is available on a B&B basis at the caretaker's house or the basic *rondavels*. Ring in advance to arrange local meals.

Dinosaur Footprints ARCHAEOLOGICAL SITE

Quthing's other claim to fame is a proliferation of dinosaur footprints in the surrounding area. The most easily accessible are just off the main road to Mt Moorosi; watch for the small, pink building to your left. The footprints are believed to be about 180 million years old.

Villa Maria Mission CHURCH

Between Quthing and Masitise, and visible from the main road, is Villa Maria Mission, with a striking, twin-spired sandstone church.

San Paintings ROCK ART

About 10km southeast of town near Qomoqomong is a collection of San paintings. Several minibus taxis ply this route daily; once in Qomoqomong, ask at the General Dealer's store to arrange a guide for the 20-minute walk to the paintings.

Scenic Drives DRIVING TOUR

The road from Quthing to Qacha's Nek is one of Lesotho's most stunning drives, taking you along the winding Senqu (Orange) River gorge and through some striking canyon scenery before climbing up onto the escarpment. If you're equipped, the whole area is ideal for hiking.

On the route are: the village of **Mt Moorosi**, named after a Basotho chieftain who, in 1879, stuck it out for eight months against the British on his fortified mountain until he was killed; the pretty **Mphaki** village, a possible base for hiking; and **Christ the King Mission**, which has wide views over the Senqu (Orange) River valley. From the mission, it's a good two- to three-day hike north to Semonkong.

🛏 Sleeping & Eating

Moorosi Chalets CHALETS $

(🖉 in South Africa 082 552 4215; www.moorosichalets.com; campsites M60, hut without bathroom per person M150, self-catering house per person M150, rondavel per person M175-225) Go fishing or ride ponies with local villagers courtesy of this partnership between Malealea and the Quthing Wildlife Development Trust. The fees go directly to the villages for equipment and supplies. Basic *rondavel* accommodation is also offered in the main camp area.The chalets are located 6km from Mt Moorosi village; take the turn-off to Ha Moqalo 2km out of the village in the direction of Qacha's Nek.

Fuleng Guest House GUESTHOUSE $

(🖉2275 0260; r per person M280-350) Perched on a hill, this is the place for rooms and *rondavels*-with-a-view plus a friendly local experience. It's signposted from the main road just before the bend that goes to Upper Quthing.

Mafikeng Restaurant LOCAL FOOD $

(🕗8am-8pm) For an inexpensive meal you could try this simple place near the minibus taxi rank below Lower Quthing.

🛈 Getting There & Away

Minibuses ply the route between Quthing and Qacha's Nek (M75, three hours) or a bus does the same trip, leaving Quthing at about 9am (M58, five hours). Several minibus and taxis go to Maseru (M65, 3½ hours) as do sprinters (M47, four hours). The transport stand is in Lower Quthing. The Quthing–Qacha's Nek road is tarmac the entire way despite what many maps indicate.

QACHA'S NEK

Originally a mission station, Qacha's Nek was founded in 1888 near the pass (1980m) of the same name. Its more recent claim to fame was as host of King Letsie III's 42nd birthday in 2005. This pleasant place has an attractive church and a variety of colonial-era sandstone buildings. Nearby are stands of California redwood trees, some over 25m high.

Hotel Nthatuoa (🖉2295 0260; s M320-460, d M400-550, all incl breakfast) has a plush, red-carpeted 'dining' room. Rooms are categorised into 'blocks', from the simple to the more luxurious (although once you're past the most basic, other than size there's not a huge difference in value). It's signposted along the main road at the northern edge of town.

Central Hotel (🖉2295 0612; mains M15-50) is a roguish establishment that provides good live African music and greasy fried food.

Regular minibus taxi services go from Qacha's Nek and Maseru via Quthing (M110, six hours). There is also a daily bus service taht runs between Maseru and Qacha's Nek departing from Maseru between 5am and 6am (M110, nine hours), and a bus from Qacha's Nek to Sehlabathebe National Park departing from Qacha's Nek around noon (M35, five hours).

SEHLABATHEBE NATIONAL PARK

Lesotho's most under-visited national park is remote, rugged and beautiful. The rolling grasslands, wildflowers and silence provide a sense of complete isolation, which is the case, apart from the prolific birdlife (including the bearded vulture) and the odd rhebok. Hiking (and horse riding from Sani Top or the Drakensbergs) is the main way to explore the waterfalls and surrounds, and angling is possible in the park's dams and rivers.

You'll need to bring all your food to the park, and be well prepared for the changing elements. This is a summer-rainfall area, and thick mist, potentially hazardous to hikers, is common. The winters are clear but it gets cold at night, with occasional light snowfalls.

Sehlabathebe is currently run under the jurisdiction of the Ministry of Tourism, Environment and Culture (2231 1767, 2232 6075; New Postal Office Bldg, 6th fl, Kingsway, Maseru).

🛏 Sleeping & Eating

Camping is permitted throughout the park, though there are no facilities besides plenty of water.

If you're looking for dramatic isolation, then you've come to the right national park. And with a bit of scouting, you can find a pretty unusual place to sleep too.

Sehlabathebe Park Lodge　　LODGE $

(2231 1767/2232 6075; campsites per person M30, r per person M80) This is the only accommodation option in the park with facilities. Built in the 1970s for a trout-loving prime minister, this time-warped lodge makes for a groovy stay. It's set on flat grasslands, and looks onto hills and ponds. Bring all your own food, plus extra petrol or diesel – there's none available at the park. The lodge takes up to 12 people, and has bedding and a fully equipped kitchen. It is 12km into the park, and 4WD vehicles are required if driving. It's a good idea to book ahead.

Thamathu Rural Homestay　　HOME STAY $

(2231 1767/2232 6075; homestay per person incl breakfast M85) Supported by the Ministry of Tourism, this is the most successful of the home-stay options that has seen a number of homestead owners officially trained to guide and host travellers to Sehlabathebe National Park.

If you're travelling by public transport, the buses reach Sehlabathebe in the evening, which means you'll need to overnight in Mavuka village near the park gate. The clean and modern Range Management Education Centre, 2km down the road to the left after the Mavuka Primary School, has dorm beds available. Alternatively, a novel resort (but by no means a luxury one) is the Mabotle Hotel in Mavuka itself. Despite the dusty and shabby setting, the *rondavels* have clean linoleum floors and bathrooms. There is a reason: there is no water (but staff will bring you a bucket).

❶ Getting There & Away

There's an airstrip at Paolosi, about 3km south of Mavuka, for those coming in on charter flights.

A daily bus connects Qacha's Nek and Sehlabathebe, departing from Qacha's Nek at around noon and Sehlabathebe at 5.30am (M40, five hours). The bus terminates in Mavuka village, near the park gate. From there, it's about 12km further on foot to the lodge.

If you're driving, the main route into the park is via Quthing and Qacha's Nek. The road from Qacha's Nek is unsealed but in reasonable condition, and negotiable at most times of the year in a 2WD. You can arrange to leave your vehicle at the police station in Paolosi village while you're in the park.

Probably the simplest way to get into Sehlabathebe National Park is to hike the 10km up the escarpment from Bushman's Nek in neighbouring KwaZulu-Natal. From Bushman's Nek to the Nkonkoana Gate border crossing takes about six hours.

If you prefer a more leisurely way to get to the park, horses can also be arranged through Khotso Trails (in South Africa 033-701 1502; www.khotsotrails.co.za) in Underberg.

The road between Sehlabathebe and Sehonghong is for 4WDs only. Even then, these roads can be affected by storms and landslides. Always ask locals if the roads are passable – signs are seldom erected; they rely on the 'bush telegraph'.

Swaziland

Best Places to Eat

» Gil Vincente (p496)

» Malandela's Restaurant (p495)

» Lihawu Restaurant (p492)

Best Places to Stay

» Stone Camp (p501)

» Reilly's Rock Hilltop Lodge (p494)

» Malandela's B&B (p494)

» Phophonyane Ecolodge & Nature Reserve (p499)

Why Go?

In short: big things come in small packages. The intriguing kingdom of Swaziland is diminutive, but boasts a huge checklist for any visitor. Rewarding wildlife watching? Tick. Adrenalin-boosting activities such as rafting and mountain biking? Tick. Lively and colourful local culture, with celebrations and ceremonies still common practice? Tick. Plus there are superb walking trails, stunning mountain and flatland scenery, and excellent, high-quality handicrafts.

Presiding over this is King Mswati III, the last remaining absolute monarch in Africa, who, despite his critics, is the source of great national pride. Swaziland is remarkably relaxed, with friendly people and a lack of racial animosities.

The excellent road system makes Swaziland a pleasure to navigate. Accommodation ranges from hostels to family-friendly hotels, wilderness lodges and upmarket retreats. Many travellers make a flying visit here on their way to Kruger National Park but it's worth staying at least a week.

When to Go
Mbabane

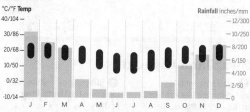

Jan–Apr Full rivers and lush vegetation are the backdrops for photography and adventuring.

Feb–Mar *Buganu* season – enjoy home-brew marula wine in rural Swaziland.

May–Sep Cooler days and winter foliage make for wonderful wildlife viewing in the lowveld.

Swaziland Highlights

❶ Watching wildlife, including rare black rhinos in the wild, at the excellent **Mkhaya Game Reserve** (p501)

❷ Hiking in **Malolotja Nature Reserve** (p497), an enchanting wilderness area

❸ Shooting over white-water rapids on the **Usutu River** (see p501)

❹ Browsing the craft shops and royal heartland of the **Ezulwini Valley** (p490) and the **Malkerns Valley** (p494)

❺ Cycling or meandering around **Mlilwane Wildlife Sanctuary** (p493) and relaxing in its comfortable, lovely lodges

History
BEGINNINGS OF A NATION

The area that is now Swaziland has been inhabited for millennia, and humanlike remains possibly dating back as far as 100,000 years have been discovered around the Lebombo Mountains in eastern Swaziland. However, today's Swazis trace their ancestors to much more recent arrivals. By around AD 500, various Nguni groups had made their way to the region as part of the great Bantu migrations. One of these groups settled in the area around present-day Maputo (Mozambique), eventually founding the Dlamini dynasty. In the mid-18th century, in response to increasing pressure from other clans in the area, the Dlamini king, Ngwane III, led his people southwest to the Pongola River, in present-day southern Swaziland and northern KwaZulu-Natal. This became the first Swazi heartland, and today, Swazis consider Ngwane III to have been their first king.

Ngwane's successor, Sobhuza I, established a base in the Ezulwini Valley, which still remains the centre of Swazi royalty and ritual. Next came King Mswazi (or Mswati), after whom the Swazi take their name. Despite pressure from the neighbouring Zulu, Mswazi succeeded in unifying the whole kingdom. He extended Swazi territory northwards as far as Hhohho, in what is now northwestern Swaziland, largely in response to continued Zulu incursions on Swazi territory to the south. By the time he died in 1868, the foundations of the young Swazi nation were secure.

From the mid-19th century, Swaziland attracted increasing numbers of European farmers in search of land for cattle, as well as hunters, traders and missionaries. Mswazi's successor, Mbandzeni, inherited a kingdom rife with European carpetbaggers, and proved much weaker at reining them in than Mswazi. Under Mbandzeni, increasing amounts of the kingdom's land were alienated through leases granted to Europeans, with bribes for the king featuring heavily in some of the deals.

Over the next decades, the Swazis saw their territory whittled away as the British and Boers jostled for power in the area. In 1902, following the second Anglo-Boer War, the Boers withdrew and the British took control of Swaziland as a protectorate.

STRUGGLE FOR INDEPENDENCE

Swazi history in the early 20th century centred on the ongoing struggle for independence. Under the leadership of King Sobhuza II (guided by the capable hands of his mother acting as regent while Sobhuza was a child), the Swazis succeeded in regaining much of their original territory. This was done in part by direct purchase and in part by British government decree. By the time of independence in 1968, about two-thirds of the kingdom was again under

SWAZI CEREMONIES

Incwala

Incwala (also known as Ncwala) is the most sacred ceremony of the Swazi people. It is a 'first fruits' ceremony, where the king gives permission for his people to eat the first crops of the new year. Preparation for the weeklong Incwala begins some weeks in advance, according to the cycle of the moon.

Umhlanga Dance

Though not as sacred as the Incwala, the *umhlanga* (reed) dance serves a similar function in drawing the nation together and reminding the people of their relationship to the king. It is something like a weeklong debutante ball for marriageable young Swazi women, who journey from all over the kingdom to help repair the queen mother's home at Lobamba. The reed dance is also a showcase of potential wives for the king.

Buganu Festival

Another 'first fruits' festival, this takes place in February and celebrates the Marula fruit. The women gather the fruit and ferment a brew (known as *buganu*; it packs a punch). Locals – mainly males – gather to drink and celebrate. The festival is becoming one of the country's most popular traditional ceremonies, and is attended by King Mswati III and other royalty.

SWAZI SNIPPETS

At the centre of Swazi culture is the monarchy, the power of which rests with both the king (*ngwenyama*, the lion) and his mother (*ndlovukazi*, the she-elephant). In addition to loyalty to the monarchy, Swazi identity is supported by a long-standing tradition of age-related royal military regiments.

Traditionally, the Swazi deity was known as Mkhulumnchanti, and respect for both the aged and ancestors played an important role. You will occasionally see a man wearing a *lihhiya* (traditional Swazi robe), with a *sagila* (knob stick) in one hand and a briefcase in the other. Depending on the manner the *lihhiya* is arranged or worn, this is regarded as formal wear, usually used for important occasions, be it work or cultural.

Swazi control. This was a major development, as Swazi kings are considered to hold the kingdom in trust for their subjects, and land ownership is thus more than just a political and economic issue. During this time, many Swazis began seeking work as migrant labourers in the Witwatersrand mines of South Africa to raise money to buy back their lands.

In 1960 King Sobhuza II proposed the creation of a Legislative Council, to be composed of Europeans elected along European lines, and a National Council formed in accordance with Swazi culture. One of the Swazi political parties formed at this time was the Mbokodvo (Grindstone) National Movement, which pledged to maintain traditional Swazi culture while eschewing racial discrimination. When the British finally agreed to elections in 1964, Mbokodvo won a majority. At the next elections, in 1967, it won all the seats. Independence was finally achieved – the culmination of a long and remarkably nonviolent path – on 6 September 1968, 66 years after the start of the British protectorate.

The first Swazi constitution was largely a British creation, and in 1973 the king suspended it on the grounds that it did not accord with Swazi culture. Four years later parliament reconvened under a new constitution vesting all power in the king.

Sobhuza II died in 1982, at that time the world's longest-reigning monarch. Most significant among his accomplishments was his success in ensuring the continued existence of his country and culture, under threat since his father's reign. In 1986 the young Mswati III ascended the throne, where he continues today to represent and maintain the traditional Swazi way of life, and to assert his pre-eminence, for better and often worse, as absolute monarch.

CURRENT EVENTS

Swaziland still maintains its dual system of governance, with both a government led by cabinet ministers, who report to a partially elected, partially appointed parliament, and various appointed committees such as the Swazi National Council, which deliberate mainly on matters pertaining to the feudal state of chieftaincies. Real political power remains in the hands of the traditional conservatives, often referred to as *labazdala* (the elders). Most Swazis seem happy with (or perhaps apathetic to) their political system, which although delivering an enviable run of stability in an African context, has been blamed also for the country's slow pace of development. Nonetheless, there is an undercurrent of political dissent, and the movement for democratic change has gained momentum. In 1996 the king appointed a constitutional review commission, and in 2003 and 2004 redrafted constitutions were unveiled, though they were promptly dismissed by reform-minded Swazis. In 2005 a constitution was finally passed; it introduced a Bill of Rights, although this, too, was criticised by NGOs as doing little more than preserving the status quo. Under the new constitution, political parties are still unable to participate in elections.

Swaziland has suffered in recent times due to the severe drop in the amount of import customs tax received as a member of SACU (South African Customs Union). A significant reduction in import customs tax receipts in 2011 saw the country's revenue falling from €6 billion to €2.6 billion. This tax revenue makes up a massive 60% of the country's revenue.

King Mswati III comes under attack, especially in the foreign press, for his autocratic status, lax spending habits and polygamous practices. Critics say this hinders economic progress and the fight against HIV/AIDS, with which around 26% of the population is believed to be affected. But even his staunchest Swazi critics don't seem to want to do away with him altogether, calling for a constitutional, not absolute monarch.

Climate

Most of Swaziland enjoys a climate similar to that of South Africa's eastern lowveld, with rainy, steamy summers and agreeably cooler winters. Between December and February, temperatures occasionally exceed 40°C and torrential thunderstorms are common. May to August are the coolest months. In the higher-lying areas of the west, winters bring cool, crisp nights and sometimes even frost.

National Parks & Reserves

Swaziland has five main reserves, reflecting the tiny country's impressively diverse topography. Easiest to get to is Mlilwane Wildlife Sanctuary (p493), which is in the Ezulwini Valley, and privately run by Big Game Parks (☑528 3943/4; www.biggameparks.org), based at Mlilwane. Also under the same jurisdiction, and both well worth visiting, are the excellent Mkhaya Game Reserve (p501), with black rhinos and many other animals, and Hlane Royal National Park (p499).

In the northwestern highlands is the beautiful Malolotja Nature Reserve (p497), known for its hiking trails. Hospitality, including accommodation and the restaurant, are run by the management of Hawane Resort (p497). Meanwhile, Mlawula Nature Reserve (p500), in the eastern lowveld, and tiny Mantenga Nature Reserve (p500), in the Ezulwini Valley, are run by the National Trust Commission (☑2416 1151/78; www.sntc.org.sz), with its head office at the National Museum in Lobamba (Ezulwini Valley). You book all accommodation direct through the reserves or through Swazi Trails (☑2416 2180; www.swazitrails.co.sz).

Language

The official languages are Swati and English, and English is the official written language. For information on Swati, see the Language chapter.

Dangers & Annoyances

Petty crime such as pickpocketing, phone- and bag-snatching can happen in urban areas. Always take common-sense precautions and be vigilant at all times. Never walk around unescorted at night, nor flaunt valu-

ables. Schistosomiasis (bilharzia) and malaria are both present in Swaziland although Swaziland is taking serious steps to be the first country in sub-Saharan Africa to move to malaria-free status; see p610 for information on avoiding these diseases.

ℹ Getting There & Around

There are flights into Swaziland (Matsapha International Airport) from Johannesburg (Jo'burg).

Most travellers enter Swaziland overland. For border-post info, see p594. For bus info, see p595. Car hire is offered by Avis (☑2518 6222; www.avis.co.za; Matsapha Airport) and Europcar (www.europcar.com/airport-swaziland-car-rental.html; ☑Matsapha Airport 2518 4393, Mbabane 2404 1384; Engen Auto Plaza, Mbabane).

Once in Swaziland, there is a good network of minibus taxis covering the country. There are private taxis in Mbabane, the Ezulwini Valley and Manzini. See the Getting Around sections of these destinations.

Mbabane

Swaziland's capital and second-largest city, Mbabane (mm-bah-*bahn*-ee), may sound grand, but it's not. Nevertheless, it's a relaxed and functional place in a pretty setting in the Dlangeni Hills, and is a good place to get things done. There's a handful of OK restaurants, but for the traveller, the nearby Ezulwini and Malkerns Valleys have most of the attractions and on the whole, a better choice of accommodation.

During the colonial era, the British originally had their base in Manzini, but moved it in 1902 to Mbabane to take advantage of the cooler climate in the hills.

🛏 Sights & Activities

About 8km northeast of Mbabane is Sibebe Rock (admission E30), a massive granite dome hulking over the surrounding countryside; the area is managed by the local community, through Sibebe Trails (☑2404 6070). Much of the rock is completely sheer, and dangerous if you should fall, but it's a good adrenalin charge if you're reasonably fit and relish looking down steep rock-faces. Swazi Trails (☑2416 2180; www.swazitrails.co.sz), in Ezulwini Valley, takes half-day nontechnical climbs up the rock (E580 per person, including transport, entry and refreshments; guide only minimum two people, per person E295).

Mbabane

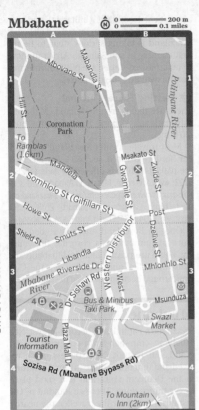

Mbabane

⊗ Eating
1 Indingilizi Gallery & Restaurant B2
   Plaza Tandoori Restaurant .... (see 3)
   Shoprite .... (see 3)
2 Spar A3

⊕ Shopping
3 Swazi Plaza A4
4 The Mall A3

☞ Tours

Many of the overseas-based tour operators listed include short detours into Swaziland in their itineraries.

Swazi Trails   ADVENTURE TOUR
(☎2416 2180; www.swazitrails.co.sz) Based in the Mantenga Craft Centre in Ezulwini Valley, this is one of the country's major activity companies, and the place to go to for cav-

ing, rafting, hikes and general cultural and highlights tours.

All Out Africa   GUIDED TOUR
(☎2550 4951; www.alloutafrica.com) Runs a range of adventure trips and activities throughout Swaziland, plus to Kruger National Park and Mozambique. Highly recommended is the half-day cultural tour through Lobamba, including an unscripted 'what-you-see-is-what-you-get' wander through the local village (per person R250; no minimum numbers).

Mandla Masuku   GUIDED TOUR
(☎7644 3257; www.ekhayatours.com; company vehicle/own car from R650/R500, minimum 2 people) For a taste of rural Swazi life – including a visit to Lobamba, a school and family – or game park visits, a good contact is local, French-speaking Mandla Masuku of Ekhaya Cultural Tours.

⎙ Sleeping

Mbabane is a bit short on decent budget accommodation; Ezulwini or Malkerns Valleys (only 14km and 18km away) have a good selection.

Brackenhill Lodge   GUESTHOUSE $$
(☎2404 2887; www.brackenhillswazi.com; Mountain Dr; s/d incl breakfast from E640/840; ❄ 🕸) Located 4.5km north of Mbabane, this attractive place has a range of comfortable and airy, if dated (but not unpleasantly so) rooms. It's set in tranquil gardens and its 162 hectares have several walking trails. From Pine Valley Rd, turn right into Fonteyn Rd and after 1km left into Mountain Dr, from where it's well signed. Lovely staff; evening meals on request.

Foresters Arms   LODGE $$
(☎2467 4177; www.forestersarms.co.za; s/d incl breakfast E620/960; 🅿 🕸 ❄) Penelope Keith, star of *To the Manor Born*, would be right at home here. But it's not just the cream teas and slightly dated British-style interiors that make this a 'Country Estate'. Situated 27km southwest of Mbabane in picturesque hills, it's a good alternative to city sleeping: cosy rooms, attractive gardens and a smorgasbord of activities (trout fishing, horse riding and water sports on the nearby Luphohlo Dam). Follow the MR19 from Mbabane. If you're leaving Swaziland from here, you can continue southwest along the MR19 and exit via the Nerston border post.

Mountain Inn
INN $$

(☎2404 2781; www.mountaininn.sz; s/d incl breakfast from E795/696; ❋🛜🏊) It's not five-star luxury, but this sprawling inn is friendly, unpretentious and a safe bet. There's a pool, library, lawns and panoramas looking over the valley from the inviting Friar Tuck's restaurant, which is open for breakfast, lunch and dinner.

Kapola Boutique Hotel
BOUTIQUE HOTEL $$

(☎2404 0906; kapola_eden@swazi.net; s/d incl breakfast E800/1100) About 5km from Mbabane, this recently built hotel boasts plush, stylish decor in its eight rooms. A major downside is that it's on, and exposed to, the busy and noisy MR3 (on the downhill route, or the Mbabane–Ezulwini Valley direction). Note: you'll need to do a loop on the MR3 if you miss it.

 Eating

There are supermarkets at Swazi Plaza and the Mall.

Ramblas
INTERNATIONAL $$

(mains E40-100; ⊙8am-late Mon-Sat) Mbabane's top choice for good cuisine and a buzzing audience; located within the Serendipity Health complex; you'll need to drive there. It's worth the trip for a massive menu including great salads and meat dishes; breakfasts are served until 6pm, such is its popularity.

Plaza Tandoori Restaurant
INDIAN $$

(Swazi Plaza; mains E45-80; ⊙lunch & dinner) It's not the size of the Taj Mahal, but it's certainly got the atmosphere. As well as great-value curries, the usual grills and burgers add a touch of the international.

eDladleni
FUSION $$

(Manzini/Mbabane Hwy; mains E45-120; ⊙lunch & dinner; 🌱) This self-proclaimed 'Queen of Swazi food fit for a King' almost lives up to its name; it's got the best vegetarian options around. It's about 6km from Mbabane, off the main highway. Opening hours are unreliable, however.

Indingilizi Gallery & Restaurant
CAFE $$

(112 Dzeliwe St; light meals E40-60; ⊙8am-5pm Mon-Fri, 8.30am-1pm Sat) This long-standing place – a gallery with a small outdoor cafe – offers snacks and light lunches. At the time of writing it was being renovated; it's worth heading here in any case to see the gallery's range of quirky items.

ℹ Information

Emergency

Fire (☎2404 3333, 933)

Police (☎2404 2221, 999)

Internet Access

There are internet centres at **Swazi.net Internet Cafe** (⊙8am-6pm Mon-Fri, to 2pm Sat), located upstairs at Swazi Plaza, and in the Mall, near Pick 'n Pay. Internet access starts from around E30 per hour.

Medical Services

Mbabane Clinic (☎2404 2423; St Michael's Rd) For emergencies try this clinic located in the southwest corner of town just off the bypass road.

Medi-Sun Clinic (☎2416 2800; Ezulwini Valley) Sitauted just behind Gables Shopping Complex.

Money

Banks with ATMs include First National Bank, Nedbank and Standard Bank; these are located in Swazi Plaza.

Post & Telephone

The post office is on Msunduza St; you can also make international (though not reverse-charge) calls here.

Tourist Information

Tourist information office (☎2404 2531; www.welcometoswaziland.com; ⊙8am-4.45pm Mon-Thu, 8am-4pm Fri, 9am-1pm Sat; Cooper Centre access road, Sozisa Rd) Situated in the Cooper Centre on Sozisa Road. It offers a free map of Mbabane, Manzini and Swaziland on one side, and information on the reverse. Be sure to pick up copies of *What's Happening in Swaziland* and the smaller *What's on in Swaziland*, with the latest on hotels, restaurants and entertainment.

ℹ Getting There & Around

The main bus and minibus taxi park is just behind Swazi Plaza. Minibus taxis leave for Jo'burg (E190, four hours) throughout the day; another option is to catch one from Manzini. See p594 for more information on connections to/from South Africa and Mozambique.

There are several minibus taxis daily to Piggs Peak (E25, one hour), Ngwenya and the Oshoek border post (E10, 50 minutes), and Malkerns Valley (E10.50, 45 minutes). All vehicles heading towards Manzini (E15, 35 minutes) and points east pass through the Ezulwini Valley, although most take the highways, bypassing the valley itself.

Nonshared taxis congregate just outside the transport park that is located behind Swazi Plaza. At night, you can also usually find a taxi near the City Inn. Nonshared taxis to the Ezulwini Valley cost from E70, more to the far end of the valley (from E100), and still more if hired at night. Expect to pay from E150 to get to Matsapha International Airport.

Trans Magnifique (☎2404 9977; www.go swaziland.co.sz) is a company that offers a daily luxury shuttle service that runs between Johannesburg (or Tambo International Airport and Sandton) and Mbabane. The cost is R500.

Ezulwini Valley

The Ezulwini Valley (or 'Valley of Heaven' as the region is called) is Swaziland's royal heartland and tourism centre. It begins just outside Mbabane and extends down past Lobamba, 18km away. For most of Swazi history, it has been home to the Swazi royal family. It's possible to whiz through on the MR3, but to see the sights and lush countryside, you'll need to take the old MR103. Don't let the tacky hotel-strip atmosphere along some sections deter you: just in from the road is some beautiful woodland scenery,

with brilliant orange flame trees, flowering jacarandas and views over the surrounding mountains. The area boasts an excellent selection of accommodation options as well as some wonderful opportuntities for craft shopping.

ℹ Information

There are ATMs at the Gables Shopping Centre.

Big Game Parks (☎2528 3943/4; www .biggameparks.org) The central reservations office is accessed through the Mlilwane Wildlife Sanctuary. Contact it for accommodation in Mlilwane Wildlife Sanctuary, Mkhaya Game Reserve and Hlane Royal National Park. It also runs Chubeka Trails, its activities arm at Mlilwane.

National Trust Commission (☎2416 1151/78; www.sntc.org.sz; National Museum in Lobamba) Although this is the headquarters of Mlawula and Mantenga Nature Reserves, reservations are made directly with the reserves or through Swazi Trails.

Swazi Trails (☎2416 2180; www.swazitrails .co.sz; Mantenga Craft Centre) Organises a plethora of activities, trails and tours all over the kingdom. Also houses the Ezulwini Tourist Office with information and bookings services for all the reserves, community tourism facilities, tour operators, activities and general accommodation.

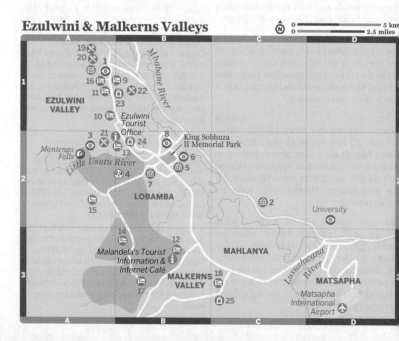

Ezulwini & Malkerns Valleys

Sights & Activities

Mantenga Nature Reserve   NATURE RESERVE
(admission E150; ☉8am-6pm) The entrance fee
to this tranquil, leafy reserve covers a guided
tour of the reserve's Swazi Cultural Village,
a 'living' cultural village with authentic beehive huts and cultural displays, plus a sibhaca dance and a visit to the Mantenga
Falls. (For those who are not in a group: the
sibhaca dance is performed daily at 11.15am
and 3.15pm.) A pleasant restaurant is nearby, set in a lush rainforest (watch out for
thieving monkeys). Day hikers pay only E50
to enter the reserve. It's located 1km from
Mantenga Lodge.

Cuddle Puddle   SPA
(☎2416 1164; adult/child E30/15; ☉8am-11pm)
For personal pampering, head to the Royal
Valley's own hot mineral springs.

Sleeping

Legends Backpackers Lodge   BACKPACKERS $
(☎2416 1870; www.legends.co.sz; campsites per
person E50, dm E100, d without E300; ☎P) This
mellow place isn't five-star luxury, but offers
a straightforward stay in one of the most
central locations, in Ezulwini Valley's bushland, behind the Gables Shopping Centre.

Beds have mosquito nets. In any case, you'll
probably sleep well if you've just spun out
on an activity organised by Swazi Trails, the
lodge's sister company. Free wi-fi.

Lidwala Backpacker Lodge   BACKPACKERS $
(☎2550 4951; www.lidwala.co.sz; campsites R80,
dm & safari tents per person E120, d E330; ☎@☎)
This comfortable spot is set in a lovely garden with a pool. Rooms are a typical dorm-
style, backpacker set-up, with a laid-back,
friendly feel. The separate safari tents are
popular. It's located on the MR103 between
Gables Shopping Centre and the Royal Swazi
Hotel and is run by All Out Africa (p488),
which organises trips and activities.

Mantenga Nature Reserve   HUTS $
(☎2416 1151/78; www.sntc.com; beehives E100,
cottages incl breakfast per person E700) Soft 'safari' adventure in lovely new cottages: these
appealing rooms are set in lush bushland
and offer all the creature comforts and stylish decor. Visitors don't pay entry to the nature reserve.

Mantenga Lodge   HOTEL $$
(☎2416 1049; www.mantengalodge.com; s/d incl
breakfast from E585/720; ☎☎) A safe and peace-
ful option, the rooms of varying standards

SWAZILAND EZULWINI VALLEY

Ezulwini & Malkerns Valleys

LOBAMBA

Lobamba is the heart of Swaziland's Royal Valley – a position it has held since the early days of the Swazi monarchy. The royal Embo State Palace was built by the British in grand proportions, as it had to house the entire royal clan (Sobhuza II had about 600 children). It isn't open to visitors, and photos aren't allowed. Swazi kings now live in Lozitha State House, approximately 10km from Lobamba.

To see the monarchy in action, head to the Royal Kraal (Eludzidzini Royal Residence) during the Incwala ceremony or the *umhlanga* (reed) dance (see the boxed text, p485). It's next to Lozitha State House. Just north of here, towards the main road, is Somhlolo National Stadium, which hosts important state occasions, such as coronations, and soccer matches – try to catch one while you are here.

The nearby National Museum (adult/child E25/15; ☻8am-4.30pm Mon-Fri, 10am-4pm Sat & Sun) has some interesting displays of Swazi culture, as well as a traditional beehive village and cattle enclosure and several of King Sobhuza I's 1940s cars. The ticket price also allows you to enter the King Sobhuza II Memorial Park (King Sobhuza II was the most revered of Swazi kings). It's located across the road from, and has the same hours as, the museum. Near the museum is the parliament, which is sometimes open to visitors; if you want to visit, wear neat clothes and use the side entrance.

(and different prices) are set in a lush wooded area that is located about 1.5km off the main road. The restaurant overlooks the hills and jacaranda trees. Take the signposted turn-off for the Mantenga Craft Centre; the hotel is situated 500m further along this road.

Top-end lodging is dominated by the Sun chain, which has three massive properties here, all clustered along the MR103 about 6km northwest of Lobamba and about 3km from Mbabane. Rates are always changing, and specials are frequent, so inquire in advance. All include breakfast.

Lugogo Sun Hotel HOTEL $$$
(☎2416 4500; www.suninternational.com; s/d E1885/2010; ✳☎☒) The largest and slightly more low-key of the Swazi Suns.

Ezulwini Sun Hotel HOTEL $$$
(☎2416 6500; www.suninternational.com; s/d E2065/2190; ✳☎☒) A two-storey pink palace with a slightly apartment-like feel and less ostentatious than the its sister hotels.

Royal Swazi Spa HOTEL $$$
(☎2416 5000; www.suninternational.com; s/d E2945/3100; ✳☎☒) The most luxurious of the three, with golf course and casino.

✗ Eating

Guava Café CAFE $$
(light meals E40-100; ☻9am-5pm Tue-Sat, 10am-5pm Sun) A pleasant eatery at Guava Gallery, just before Swazi Cultural Village, with salads, soups and lunch fare.

Lihawu Restaurant FUSION $$$
(Royal Villas; www.lihawu.co.sz; mains E78-120; ☻breakfast, lunch & dinner) Within the swish Royal Villa resort nestles Swaziland's most elegant restaurant. It's name is taken from a *lihawu,* the traditional shield made from cow hide. This establishment attracts beautiful people – local politicians and business people – and beautiful cuisine. The menu is Afro-fusion, with meaty signature dishes, such as lamb tajine and pork belly representing 'Africa on a plate'. The outdoor eating area overlooks a swimming pool.

Khazimula's Restaurant ITALIAN $$
(mains E50-80; ☻10am-10pm Tue-Sun) This modest little place has a lovely outlook over the trees and is said to serve the best pizza in Swaziland. It's located in the Mantenga Craft Centre.

Calabash GERMAN $$$
(mains E110-180; ☻lunch & dinner) German and Austrian-Swiss cuisine are the incongruous highlights at this long-standing and dated, but smart, place. It has an impressive wine cellar. It's situated at the upper end of Ezulwini Valley.

Boma Restaurant INTERNATIONAL $$$
(mains E50-150; ☻breakfast, lunch & dinner) This pleasant restaurant in the style of a *boma* (large, open-air thatched-roof hut) has a massive menu with all the favourites – grills to pastas – and is within the grounds of Timbali Lodge. It also serves light meals and has a children's menu.

☆ Entertainment

House on Fire (p495) in the Malkerns Valley is the undisputed place to go but you'll need to check if anything is happening.

🔒 Shopping

The Ezulwini Valley, together with the nearby Malkerns Valley, offers some of the best craft shopping in the region, with a wide selection available of high quality products at reasonable prices.

Ezulwini Craft Market   ARTS & CRAFTS
Don't miss this huge and well-stocked market, recently relocated from the roadside of the M103 to a less obvious location opposite the Zeemans Filling Station on the corner of MR103 and Mpumalanga Loop Rd. Look for the blue tin roofs. The stalls sell a vast array of local carvings, weavings and handicrafts. The vendors are particularly welcoming and prices are extremely competitive.

Mantenga Craft Centre   ARTS & CRAFTS
(☎2416 1136) This colourful, compact craft centre is situated on the access road leading to Mantenga Lodge, with numerous shops featuring everything from weaving and tapestries to candles, woodcarvings and T-shirts.

ℹ Getting There & Away

Nonshared taxis from Mbabane cost E80 to E130, depending on how far down the valley you go. For a pick-up from the Ezulwini Valley, you'll have to call a Mbabane-based taxi service.

During the day you could get on a minibus bound for Manzini, but make sure the driver knows that you want to alight in the valley, as many aren't keen on stopping.

If you are driving from either Mbabane or Manzini, take the Ezulwini Valley/Lobamba exit off the highway. This puts you on the MR103, from where everything is very well signposted.

MLILWANE WILDLIFE SANCTUARY

This beautiful and tranquil *private reserve* (☎2528 3943; www.biggameparks.org; admission E35; ☺6.30am-5.30pm summer, 6am-6pm winter) near Lobamba was Swaziland's first protected area, created by conservationist Ted Reilly on his family farm in the 1950s. Reilly later opened Mkhaya Game Reserve and supervised the establishment of Hlane Royal National Park. Mlilwane means 'Little Fire',

and the wildlife sanctuary was named after the many fires started by lightning strikes in the region.

While it doesn't have the drama or vastness of some of the bigger South African parks, it is well worth a visit: it's both beautiful and easily accessible. Its terrain is dominated by the precipitous Nyonyane (Little Bird) peak, with several fine walks in the area. Animals to be seen include zebras, warthogs, many small antelope species (including the rare blue duiker), crocs, hippos and rare bird species. In summer, you may also spot black eagles near Nyonyane.

Activities on offer in the reserve include *guided walks* (per hr from E75), two-hour *vehicle safaris* (E240), *mountain-bike trips* (per hr from E105) and also *horse-riding trips* (1-3hr E135, fully catered overnight trips from E1190). A wonderful *cultural tour* (per person E70) takes you to a village where you interact with the locals; it's an uncontrived experience. (You might even meet the chief, a female at the time of research).

The entrance is 2km southeast of the Happy Valley Motel on the old Mbabane–Manzini road, and signposted from the turn-off. Night access is via an alternative gate (follow the signs from the gate).

🛏 Sleeping & Eating

All accommodation in the sanctuary can be booked in advance via telephone or email at *Big Game Parks* (☎2528 3943/4; www.biggameparks.org). Bookings need to be paid for in advance.

Sondzela Backpackers (IYHF) Lodge   BACKPACKERS $$
(☎2528 3117; www.biggameparks.org; campsites per person E75, dm E100, s/d without bathroom E190/260, rondavels s/d E190/290; ☒) Sondzela is in the southern part of the reserve, around 1.5km beyond the main camp, and about 2km from both Malandela's B&B in Malkerns Valley. Recently renovated, it boasts fine, breezy dorms and private rooms. And it doesn't end there. The delightful gardens, kitchen, swimming pool and a hilltop perch provide one of the best backpackers' settings in Southern Africa. Breakfast and evening meals are available for a song (cooked on the outside barbecue; the vegetables are from the orchard garden) after which you can prop up the bar at the Hog & Wart Bar. If you're driving, you'll need to use the main Mlilwane Wildlife Sanctuary entrance, pay the entry fee and drive through the park

THE PILLAR OF POLYGAMY

When King Sobhuza II died, at age 83, he left about 69 official wives (and three girl-friends). In line with a polygamous tradition, the current king, King Mswati III, has 13 wives. From an anthropologist's perspective, large families were needed to tend to their fields and thus, survive. These days, formal polygamy is declining in Swaziland. In the past, one of the main reasons for this was that it had become too expensive: each time a man married, he had to pay *lobolo* (a bride price – usually cattle) to the family of his fiancé. Nowadays, the decline is increasingly more to do with changing lifestyles (fewer people live off the land), as well as an increased following in Christian religions and an greater awareness of women's rights.

to reach Sondzela. Alternatively, Sondzela's own shuttle bus departs the lodge at 8am and 5pm, and from Malandela's B&B in Malkerns Valley 30 minutes later.

Mlilwane Wildlife Sanctuary

Main Camp CAMPGROUND, HUTS **$$**
(campsites per person E84, huts s/d E400/570; ☀) This homely camp is set in a scenic wooded location about 3.5km from the entry gate, complete with simple huts – including two-person traditional beehive huts – and the occasional warthog snuffling around. A small shop, the Hippo Haunt restaurant, and an area for *braais* (barbecues) service the groups of people who flock here. There are often dance performances put on in the evenings. The swimming pool is in a wonderful setting.

TOP CHOICE **Reilly's Rock Hilltop Lodge** LODGE **$$**
(s/d with half board E1190/850) Promoted as 'quaintly colonial', this is an oh-so delightfully tranquil, old-world, nonfussy luxury experience at its best. The lodge, formerly the Reilly's home, was built in exchange for a UK£80 ox wagon. Set among an incredible garden – a Royal Botanic Garden with aloes and cycads and an huge jacaranda tree – 'the Rock' has striking views of the valley and Mdzimba Mountains. The massive wood-trimmed lounge area has a fireplace for winter. Staff are delightful; generous dinners are served in a dining room and full breakfasts are enjoyed on the verandah in sight of beautiful birds and even small antelope, including the rare blue duiker. If you are lucky, you might be able to feed the bush babies that visit at night. Entry to the reserve and meals are all included – excellent value, not to mention a pleasurable experience.

Malkerns Valley

About 7km south of Lobamba/Ezulwini Valley on the MR103 is the turn-off to the fertile Malkerns Valley, known for its arts and crafts outlets, and, together with the Ezulwini Valley, offering a scenic and fun, if touristy, drive.

Sleeping & Eating

For budget accommodation, also check out Sondzela Backpackers (IYHF) Lodge (p493), which is readily accessible from Malkerns Valley.

TOP CHOICE **Malandela's B&B** B&B **$$**
(☎2528 3448, 2528 3339; www.malandelas.com; s/d incl breakfast E400/550; ☀☂) Offers fabulously creative and stylish rooms with a touch of ethnic Africa, a pool and a sculpture garden. It serves one of the best breakfasts in Swaziland. Malandela's is along the MR27, about 1km from the junction with the MR103. Reservations are advised; it's understandably popular.

Umdoni B&B **$$**
(☎2528 3009; www.umdoni.com; s/d incl breakfast E460/800; ✱☀) An upmarket experience situated in the heart of the Malkerns Valley. The manicured garden – there's not a leaf out of place – gives a good sense of this place: chic and stylish rooms in two cottages. There are crisp white sheets, digital satellite TV (DSTV) and a breakfast on the patio overlooking flower beds. Wonderful staff is a bonus.

Rainbird Chalets B&B CHALET **$$**
(☎7603 7273; rainbird@swazi.net; s/d incl breakfast E510/880; ✱@☀) Six chalets – three log, and three brick A-frames – are set in a manicured, rose-filled private garden near the

owners' house. All are fully equipped and feature smart bathrooms.

Malandela's Restaurant INTERNATIONAL $$
(mains E50-90; ⊘lunch & dinner Mon-Sun; ☎) Part of the Malandela complex, this is one of the best restaurants in the region, with good old-fashioned meals including an array of meat and seafood dishes. The lunchtime wraps are very popular. There's pleasant outdoor seating; indoors there's a fire for when it's chilly. A bar serves pub grub as well.

☆ **Entertainment**

House on Fire THEATRE, MUSIC
(☎2528 2001; www.house-on-fire.com) People visit this especially for the ever-mutating cultural-site-cum-living-gallery as well as its space for experimental performances. This mosaic- and sculpture-filled site is the hot place for cool locals and it is popular among travellers as well. Part of the Malandela's complex, the well-known venue hosts everything from African theatre, music and films to raves and other forms of entertainment. Since 2007, it has also hosted the annual Bush Fire Festival. Held annually for three days over the last weekend of May, it features music, poetry and theatre among other performances.

🛍 **Shopping**

There's some excellent shopping on the Malkerns Valley loop, well marked on tourist maps and well signed.

Gone Rural ARTS & CRAFTS
(www.goneruralswazi.com; ⊘8am-5pm Mon-Sat, 9am-5pm Sun) This is the place to go for good-quality produce – baskets, mats and traditional clay pots – that is made by groups of local women. It is based at the Malandela's B&B.

Swazi Candles Craft Centre HANDICRAFTS
(☎528 3219; www.swazicandles.com; ⊘7am-5pm) This craft centre, situated 7km south of the MR103 turn-off for Malkerns, houses several interesting sites. At **Swazi Candles** itself, you can wax lyrical about these creative pigment-coloured candles – in every African-animal shape and hue; it's fun to watch the workers hand-mould the designs. **Baobab Batik** (www.baobab-batik.com; ⊘8am-5pm) is the place to head if you're dye-ing for a wall hanging. You can also pop into their onsite workshop that is located west of Malandela's.

ℹ **Information**

You will find internet access as well as tourist information at **Malandela's Tourist Information & Internet Cafe** (per hr E45; ⊘8am-5pm Mon-Sat, 9am-5pm Sun), which is situated at Malandela's complex.

ℹ **Getting There & Away**

Minibus taxis run between here and the Ezulwini Valley for around E5. As the craft shops and sleeping places are spread out, you'll really need a car to get around.

Manzini

Manzini started out as the combined administrative centre for the squabbling British and Boers between 1890 and 1902. So adversarial was their relationship that during the Anglo-Boer War, a renegade Boer *kommando* (militia unit) burned the town down. Today Manzini, Swaziland's largest town, is a chaotic commercial and industrial hub, the small centre of which is dominated by large office blocks and a couple of shopping malls that run down the two main streets. With the exception of the handicrafts market, Manzini itself has limited appeal for the tourist. That said, it functions as a main transport hub, so you are likely to pass through here if you are getting around on public transport.

Accommodation is limited – with the exception of a village stay, you're best heading to the Malkerns or Ezulwini Valley only 12km away.

OVERNIGHT CULTURAL EXPERIENCE

Woza Nawe Tours (☎7642 6780; www.swaziculturaltours.com), headed by local Swazi Myxo Mdluli, runs highly recommended village visits (day tour R1150) and overnight stays (adult/child E1250/625) to Kaphunga, 55km southeast of Manzini. The fee includes transport, meals and a guide. Guests join in on whatever activities are going on in the village – including cooking, planting, and harvesting.

Manzini

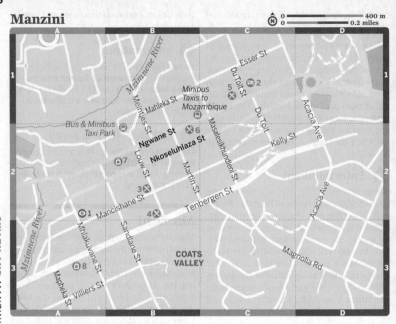

$\hat{N}$ 0   400 m
0   0.2 miles

◉ Sights

Market   MARKET
(cnr Mhlakuvane & Mancishane Sts; ⊙closed Sun)
Manzini's main drawcard is its colourful
market. The upper section of the market is
packed with handicrafts that are made in
Swaziland and elsewhere in Africa. Thursday morning is a good time to see the rural

vendors and Mozambican traders bringing
in their handicrafts and textiles to sell to the
retailers.

🛏 Sleeping

Besides the village stay at Kaphunga (see
the boxed text, p495), good accommodation
is extremely limited in Manzini.

George Hotel   HOTEL $$
(☎205 8991; www.tgh.sz; cnr Ngwane & du Toit Sts;
s/d incl breakfast from E575/810; ❋❋🛜) Manzi-
ni's fanciest hotel attempts an international
atmosphere, and caters for the conference
crowd. It has a pool bar and stylish restau-
rants. The Egg Yolk Coffee Shop/Sports Bar
is within the same complex and serves a se-
lection of snacks.

🍽 Eating

TOP CHOICE **Gil Vincente
Restaurant**   INTERNATIONAL $$
(Mkhaya Centre, Ngwane St; mains R70-100;
⊙lunch & dinner Tue-Sun) Gil Vincente is an
elegant choice, with smart decor and high-
quality Italian and international cuisine. It's
in the Makhaya Centre, down from Tum's
George Hotel.

Bakers Corner
BAKERY $

(cnr Tenbergen & Louw Sts; snacks E8-25; ☻7.30am-5.30pm Mon-Fri, 7am-1pm Sat) This great bakery is the place to head to if you want coffee, sandwiches, fresh doughnuts and chocolate eclairs.

Al-Medina
BURGERS $

(cnr Mancishane & Louw Sts; mains E25-55; ☻7.30am-8pm Mon-Sat, to 8pm Sun) This establishment is the local 'cheap and cheerful' option if you are looking for good curries and burgers.

🛈 Information

Internet cafe (1st fl, Bhunu Mall) Internet outlets can be found in Bhunu Mall.

Standard Bank (cnr Nkoseluhlaza & Louw Sts)

🛈 Getting There & Away

The main bus and minibus taxi park is at the northern end of Louw St, where you can also find some nonshared taxis. A minibus taxi trip up the Ezulwini Valley to Mbabane costs E15 (35 minutes). A nonshared taxi to Matsapha International Airport costs around E80. Minibus taxis to Mozambique leave from the car park that's next to KFC up the hill.

Northern Swaziland

Lush hills, plantations and woodlands, streams and waterfalls, and plunging ravines are the main features of Swaziland's beautiful north. As well as boasting the best scenery in Swaziland, the northern region offers some excellent hiking opportunities and accommodation options. Although it is not reflected on most maps, the MR6 is now paved from Jeppe's Reef to the east (Tshaneni), making the north easily accessible. Especially in the summer months, heavy mists roll in that can limit your visibility to almost zero.

NGWENYA

Tiny Ngwenya (the Crocodile), 5km east of the border with Mpumalanga, is the first town you'll reach if you're arriving in Swaziland via Oshoek. If you can't wait until you reach the Ezulwini Valley to do your shopping, there are several craft outlets here, including Ngwenya Glass (☎2442 4142; www.ngwenyaglass.co.sz; ☻8am-4.30pm Mon-Fri, 8am-4pm Sat & Sun), which creates African animals and items from recycled glass (more recently catering to contemporary tastes). Also here is the very funky Quazi Design Process (www.quazidesign.com). This is an outfit that is run by a group of local women and it sells modern accessories in a range of cutting-edge designs, that are made from recycled paper.

Also here, and part of Malolotja Nature Reserve (see below), is the Ngwenya iron ore mine (admission E28; ☻8am-4pm), within which is the Lion's Cavern. The cavern dates from around 40,000 BC and is one of the world's oldest known mines. The Ngwenya Mines and Visitors Centre has an interesting display of photographs and information about the mine, including the original excavation tools. There is also a picnic area that overlooks the mine. The entrance is signposted near the Ngwenya Glass Factory, although you cannot continue on into the rest of Malolotja from here. In order to visit the mine, you will need to be accompanied by a guide, who will explain the mine's history. This arrangement also applies even if you are travelling by vehicle

Hawane Resort (☎2444 1744; www.hawane.co.sz; dm E115, chalet s/d incl breakfast E550/840; ✲@) has a touch of country luxury, and is framed by the Malolotja peaks. These stylish chalets are a blend of traditional Swazi materials (wattle and grass) and glass, with ethnic African interiors. Backpackers are stabled in a converted barn (heating provided!), one of the most novel dormitory accommodations around. It's a great base for visiting Malolotja Nature Reserve and horse riding is on the premises, after which you can devour delicious African fusion cuisine in the resort restaurant. It is located about 5km up the Piggs Peak road from the junction of the MR1 and MR3, and 1.5km off the main road.

MALOLOTJA NATURE RESERVE

This beautiful middleveld and highveld nature reserve (☎2444 1744, 7613 3990; adult/child E28/14; ☻6am-6pm) is a true wilderness area that's rugged and, in the most part, unspoiled. Malolotja is an excellent walking destination, with a good network of hiking trails, and an ornithologist's paradise, with more than 280 species of birds, including several rare species. Wildflowers and rare plants are added attractions, with several (including the Woolly, Barberton and Kaapschehoop cycads) found only in this region of Africa.

Various antelope species make Malolotja their home, as do herds of zebras, elands and wildebeests. The terrain ranges from mountainous and high-altitude grassland to forest and lower-lying bushveld. The reserve is laced by streams and cut by three rivers, including the Komati River, which flows east through a gorge in a series of falls and rapids until it meets the lowveld.

Printouts of hiking trails are available for free at the restaurant/reception inside the park.

These days, many visit the park for the Malolotja Canopy Tour (7613 3990; www.malolotjacanopytour.com; per person R450; 7am-4pm summer, 8am-3pm winter). You can 'slide' your way across Malolotja's stunning, lush tree canopy on 11 slides (12 platforms). A new restaurant – about 1km beyond the main gates by the cottage accommodation – is the departure point for the canopy tours. From here, you are driven to a base point from where it's a 15-minute walk to the canopy starting point. Snacks are included in the price. Reservations are advised.

Cross-country bikes are available for hire from the reception at the restaurant (per day R95).

Accommodation consists of camping (per person at main camp/on trails E70/50), either at the well-equipped (but infrequently used) main site, with ablutions and braai area, or along the overnight trails (no facilities). There are also cosy, fully equipped, self-catering wooden cabins (per person E250, minimum E400, children half-price), each of which sleeps a maximum of five. All have a fireplace.

The reserve's hospitality (a lovely large restaurant that is open daily 8am to 4pm) and accommodation, including campsites and cabins, is managed by Hawane Resort (see p497).

The entrance gate for Malolotja is about 35km northwest of Mbabane, along the Piggs Peak road (MR1); minibus taxis will drop you here (E15, 45 minutes).

BULEMBU

A fascinating detour from Piggs Peak is to wind your way 20km through scenic plantation country to the historic town of Bulembu. The town has an interesting history. It was built in 1936 for the Havelock Mine, an asbestos mine (note: the mine dumps have not been rehabilitated). At its peak it supported 10,000 mine workers, but it eventually closed; by 2003 Bulembu was a ghost town. Several years ago, the town's new investors started a community tourism project (based on Christian principles) to rehabilitate the village. Meanwhile hundreds of corrugated-iron houses still nestle on a pretty hilly landscape, along with art deco buildings. There are churches, an art deco cinema, a hospital (complete with equipment from the 1930s), and the longest (now unused) cableway in the world, extending from the old mine to Barberton, 20km away. These days, timber production, honey and tourism are the main source of employment.

Stunning hikes include the highest mountain in Swaziland, Emlembe Peak (1863m), plus there's excellent off-road cycling around streams, and waterfalls in the natural riverine forest amid the plantations. The region's mountains contain some of the oldest life forms on Earth.

SWAZI'S SAN ART

If you have time, take a detour to the community-run Nsangwini Rock Art Shelter (per person R25); the community relies on visitors. The paintings are under a small, but impressive rock shelter, which is perched over the Komati River and affords lovely views across the mountains. The cave was believed to be that of the Nsangwini Bushmen and features the only known paintings of winged humans. Nsangwini is signed from the main Piggs Peak road and the Maguga Dam loop road. Follow a dirt road for 7.5km (conditions can get a bit rough after rain); parking is available at the small reception hut. Beep the horn if nobody is there; a local guide will take you on the slightly steep and rocky walk (15 minutes down; 20 minutes up) and will give a brief explanation.

To get there, you'll pass by, or cross over, Maguga Dam, which is on the Komati River, and was constructed to provide irrigation and energy to local communities. The valley views are pleasant enough, but it isn't worth lingering over unless you are an interested engineer, or are turned on by dam walls.

HIDEAWAY

Phophonyane Falls Ecolodge & Nature Reserve (☎2431 3429; www.phophonyane .co.sz; safari tents d from 1360, d beehive from R2040, cottages d from E1780, all incl breakfast; ☒) is a stunning hideaway, run by keen conservationists, northeast of Piggs Peak on a river in its own nature reserve of lush indigenous forest. There's a network of walking trails around the river and waterfall. Accommodation is in comfortable cottages (with a self-catering option), stylish beehives or luxury safari tents overlooking cascades; guests often comment on the feng shui here. Excellent meals are available in the stylish dining area (mains from E50; open for breakfast, lunch and dinner). Day visitors to the reserve are charged E30/20 per adult/child, lodge residents E20/10. The lodge is about 14km north of Piggs Peak. Follow the signposts off the main road; you will cross a bridge over the waterfall and turn right 500m on.

Accommodation is in the main **Bulembu Lodge** (☎7602 1593; www.bulembu.org; per person from E456) in the former general manager's residence or stylish directors' cottages, all renovated. Alternatively, you can choose a spacious and delightfully converted house, known as 'village stays' (E342). Basic meals are served in the lodge's **dining room** (breakfast E75-95, lunch/dinner E75/125).

The stretch of dirt road running west from Piggs Peak to Bulembu can be boggy and rocky in wet conditions. The road to Barberton (Mpumalanga) has been recently paved.

The minibus taxi stand is next to the market at the top end of the main street, with several vehicles daily to Bulembu (E15, 30 minutes) Several buses depart daily to Mbabane (E30, one hour).

Eastern Swaziland

The eastern Swaziland lowveld nestles in the shadow of the Lebombo Mountains, within an easy drive to the Mozambique border. The area is known for its sugar-cane plantations, as well as for the Lubombo Conservancy, a conservation area comprising Hlane Royal National Park, IYSIS, Shewula, Mlawula Nature Reserve and Mbuluzi Game Reserve. Together these provide excellent wildlife-viewing and cultural experiences.

Several minibus taxi services run daily to Simunye (and further north to the junction for Mlawula and Mbuluzi) from Manzini (one hour). There is also at least one minibus taxi daily to/from Piggs Peak (2½ hours).

HLANE ROYAL NATIONAL PARK

This **park** (☎2528 3943; www.biggameparks. org; admission E35; ☉6am-6pm) is located near the former royal hunting grounds. Hlane (the name means 'wilderness') is Swaziland's largest protected area, and home to elephants, lions, cheetahs, leopards, white rhinos and many antelope species, and offers wonderfully low-key wildlife watching opportunities.

There are **guided walking trails** and **birding trips** (per person E155), which afford the opportunity to see elephants and rhinos, as well as two-hour **wildlife drives** (per person E235, minimum 2) at sunrise, sunset and during the day, a **cultural village tour** (per person E70, minimum 4) and **mountain-bike rentals** (per 2hr E175).

Hlane has two good camps. Both can be booked through **Big Game Parks** (☎2528 3943/4; www.biggameparks.org) over at Mlilwane Wildlife Sanctuary.

Ndlovu Camp (campsites per person E40, rondavels s/d from E295/410, 8-person cottages per person E220) is pleasant and rustic, with a gas-cooking area and a smart new restaurant. Accommodation is in *rondavels* (round huts with a conical roof) and self-catering cottages with no electricity. It's just inside the main gate, and near a waterhole (fenced off, although hippos and rhinos often mill around).

Bhubesi Camp (s/d cottages E350/460) is the pick of the spots: it overlooks a river about 14km from Ndlovu Camp. Accommodation is in tasteful, stone, four-person, self-catering cottages (with electricity). They overlook a river and green lawns and are surrounded by lush growth.

WORTH A TRIP

COMMUNITY CONCERNS

Three community-owned and run operations provide fabulous electricity-free experiences with great views, basic facilities and a real rural experience in wonderful regions.

Mahamba Gorge Lodge (☑7617 9880, 2237 0100; Mahamba; s/d E285/400) The Mahamba Gorge Lodge perches, as its name suggests, high on the edge of the gorge. Three lovely stone chalets (each with two bedrooms) provide basic but clean and comfortable rooms; all have decks from which you can look over the Mkhondvo River. Hiking opportunities abound within the gorge; you can hire local guides for around E60 per day. The lodge is located in Mahamba, west of Nhlangano, southwestern Swaziland. From the Mahamba border post, turn left immediately after the post; head for around 2.5km on dirt road to Mahamba Church. The lodge is another 3km.

Shewula Mountain Camp (☑7603 1931, 7605 1160; www.shewulacamp.com; dm/r E100/260) Thirty-seven kilometres northeast of Simunye in the Lebombo Mountains (21km on tarred road and 16km on dirt road; turn at signs indicating Shewula). The camp is situated on a mountain top with amazing views. There are guided cultural walks (per person E30) to nearby villages, plus nature and birdwatching walks. Accommodation is pretty basic – you can camp or there are basic, rustic rondavels with shared ablutions (two have bathrooms) and self-catering facilities. Local meals (breakfast/lunch/dinner E35/50/65) can also be arranged but must be booked in advance. Several minibus taxis run between Simunye and the camp (E15, one hour).

Ngwempisi Hiking Trail (☑7625 6004) Among beautiful natural forests and near the Ngwempisi River, the Ngwempisi Hiking Trail is a community-run 33km trail with the atmospheric double-storey Khopho Hut (also known as Rock Lodge because it's built around massive boulders). For those who don't want to do the complete trail, you can base yourself at Khopho Hut (dm E100), and explore the area from here.

It is located 30km south of the Malkerns Valley in the Ntfungula Hills that are on the Mankayane–Vlelzizweni road.

For those who do undertake the trail, it's recommended you take a local guide (per day E100); you can park your transport in a secure location near reception. You must also take your own food and bedding. Swazi Trails (☑2416 2180; www.swazitrails.co.sz) and All Out Africa (☑2550 4951; www.alloutafrica.com) also take bookings as a community service on their behalf and can provide maps and information.

Minibus taxis to Simunye will drop you at the entrance to Hlane (E5); the gate is about 7km south of Simunye. Once at the park, you can explore most of it with a 2WD, with the notable exception of the special lion compound, which can be visited on the wildlife drives only.

MLAWULA NATURE RESERVE
This tranquil reserve (☑2383 8885; www.sntc.org.sz; adult/child E25/12; ☉6am-6pm), where the lowveld plains meet the Lebombo Mountains, boasts antelope species and hyenas, among others. It also offers rewarding birdwatching opportunities. Walking (from two- to nine-hour treks) along the plateaus, or to caves and a waterfall, is a highlight here.

At the basic Siphiso camping ground (campsites per person E60), you can pitch your own tent. The self-catering Mapelepele Cottage (up to 7 people, per person E150, minimum E500) is equipped with a gas stove and fridge.

The accommodation highlight is Magadzavane (s/d incl breakfast E450/700, s/d without breakfast E399/600), a great option that offers 20 new chalets situated in the southern part of the reserve, set up high with magnificent vistas.

The turn-off for the entrance gates to the reserve is located about 10km north of Simunye, from where it is another 4km from the main road. Minibus taxis will drop you at the junction (E35, 1¼ hours from Manzini). There is no transport from the junction to the reserve but if you call in advance a lift may be possible if there's a reserve vehicle available. Ask for the Trails and Day Walks flier.

MBULUZI GAME RESERVE

The small and privately owned **Mbuluzi Game Reserve** (✆23838861; www.mbuluzigamereserve.co.sz; adult/vehicle E25/25) boasts a range of animals, including giraffes, zebras, hippos, antelope species and wildebeests. There have also been more than 300 bird species recorded here. Several walking trails dot the reserve and make for a fun activity.

Accommodation here, in a choice of lovely five- or eight-person fully equipped, self-catering **lodges** (s E650, d E800-2000; ❄), is more luxurious than at neighbouring Mlawula Nature Reserve, and popular with families. Some lodges have spacious verandahs and wooden viewing decks and are set on the Mlawula River. **Campsites** (per person E60) are also available near the Mbuluzi River on the reserve's northern side.

The turn-off for Mbuluzi is the same as for Mlawula; the reserve entrance is about 300m from the turn-off and on the left.

SITEKI

Siteki (Marrying Place) is a trading town in the foothills of the Lebombo Mountains about 8km from Lonhlupheko off the MR16. It got its name when Mbandzeni (great-grandfather of the present king) gave his frontier troops permission to marry. Siteki is the fastest route to Mozambique from Manzini through the Mhlumeni–Goba border. It lies above the surrounding lowveld, with wide views, cooler temperatures and a bustling market. There's an ATM on the main street.

Mabuda Farm (✆2343 4124; camping E50, dm E130-200, s E300-330, d E560-620), a working farm just outside Siteki town, offers a range of delightful choices in self-contained cottage-style *rondavels* (decorated with colonial relics) or newer self-contained four-person chalets. There's a pleasant backpackers building with kitchen and living area, and a camping area. The green outlook and views provide a tranquil experience, and country walks are great after long hours in the car.

R&B Restaurant (mains E40-110; ◷breakfast, lunch & dinner) is one of the biggest surprises in Swaziland; don't be put off by the plainness of this tiny place. Massive portions of well-prepared and hearty seafood dishes come highly recommended – including the kingklip with mushroom sauce. Don't come here if you're rushing to cross the border – the times it takes to prepare the meals are included on the menu. African time, indeed, but well worth the wait.

Minibus taxis run from Manzini (E25, one hour, six daily). Regular minibus taxis connect Siteki with Big Bend (E20, one hour) and Simunye (E15, 30 minutes).

MKHAYA GAME RESERVE

This top-notch and stunning **private reserve** (✆528 3943; www.biggameparks.org) was established in 1979 to save the pure Nguni breed of cattle from extinction. It's known, however, for its black and white rhino population (it boasts that you're more likely to meet rhinos here than anywhere else in Africa and, judging from our experience, this is true). Its other animals include roan and sable antelopes, tsessebis and elephants. A recently constructed bird hide gives you an opportunity to get up close and personal

WHITE-WATER RAFTING & CAVING

One of the highlights of Swaziland is rafting the Great Usutu River (Lusutfu River). The river varies radically from steep creeks to sluggish flats, but in the vicinity of Mkhaya Game Reserve it passes through the Bulungu Gorge, where a perfect mix of rapids can be encountered all year round.

Swazi Trails (✆2416 2180; www.swazitrails.co.sz) is the best contact to organise a rafting trip – it offers full- and half-day trips (E900/750 per person, including lunch and transport, minimum two people). Abseiling and cliff jumps are added for extra adrenalin in the winter months, that is, if the occasional glimpse of a 'flat dog' (crocodile) isn't enough. The crocs haven't devoured anyone recently, hence the claim that rafting here is '...safer than driving through Jo'burg'. In sections, you'll encounter Grade IV rapids, which aren't for the faint-hearted, although even first-timers with a sense of adventure should handle the day easily.

For an off-the-scale challenge rating, the company's adventure caving trips offer a rare window into the elite world of cave exploration. The vast Gobholo Cave is 98% unexplored. You can choose between the 8.30am departure (E595) or 4.30pm dinner trip (E695; it includes a hot-spring soak, pizza and beer).

SWAZILAND SOUTHERN SWAZILAND

with the likes of vultures, marabou storks and pink throated twinspots. If you're lucky, you might spot the elusive narina trogon and other rare species. It's near the hamlet of Phuzumoya, off the Manzini–Big Bend road. The reserve takes its name from the *mkhaya* (knobthorn) tree, which abounds here.

You can't visit the reserve without booking in advance, and even then you can't drive in alone; you'll be met at Phuzumoya at a specified pick-up time – either 10am or 4pm. While day tours can be arranged, it's ideal to stay for at least one night, and the drive in makes you feel as though you are in a wilderness paradise.

Stone Camp (s/d full board E2210/3320) has a smart, slightly colonial feel; it's well worth the layover. Accommodation is in rustic and luxurious semi-open stone and thatch cottages (a proper loo with a view!), located in secluded bush zones. The price includes the lot: wildlife drives, walking safaris, park entry and meals, making it excellent value compared to many of the private reserves near Kruger National Park in South Africa.

Southern Swaziland

In former years, because of its easy access to KwaZulu-Natal, southern Swaziland was frequently visited for its roulette tables, rather than its surroundings. Nowadays you can bet on the region's peace and tranquillity – it's a good place to set off on a bicycle or on foot to discover the 'real' Swaziland, especially around the Ngwempisi Gorge, and is the base for some good horse-riding (near Nsoko).

NSOKO

Nsoko, halfway between Big Bend and the border post of Lavumisa, lies in the heart of sugar-cane country, with the Lebombo Mountains as a backdrop.

Nisela Safaris (☎2303 0318; www.nisela safaris.com; campsites per person E100, beehive huts E130, rondavels per person incl breakfast s/d E525/860) is a small touristy private reserve, and is convenient if you're coming from the south. Its accommodation includes *rondavels*. The guesthouse is not within the reserve, but a few kilometres away on the main road. Also on offer are wildlife drives (per person from E150, minimum 2) and guided walks (per person E100, minimum 2). There's also a restaurant and curio shop.

NHLANGANO

Nhlangano is the closest town to the border post at Mahamba, useful if you get stuck here; but otherwise, there's no reason to stop.

If you need accommodation, the pleasant **Phumula Guest House** (☎2207 9099; www.phumulaguesthouse.co.za; s/d per person E340/630) is 3km from town (around 10km from the border) and 1km off the main road. Pleasant rooms are around manicured lawns and gardens with a pool and braai area. Breakfast costs R50 to R90 and dinner can also be arranged.

Several minibus taxis run daily between Nhlangano and Manzini (E50, 1½ hours), from where you can get another vehicle on to Mbabane. There are also frequent connections to the Mahamba border post (E10), where you must change for Piet Retief in South Africa (E25, one hour). Large minibus taxis go direct to Jo'burg (E250, 4½ hours).

Understand South Africa, Lesotho & Swaziland

population per sq km

South Africa   Lesotho   Swaziland

≈ 1 person

South Africa, Lesotho & Swaziland Today

Two decades after the end of apartheid, life in South Africa remains dominated by social inequality. Central Cape Town's mountain and beach communities, for example, contrast with the townships sprawling across the Cape Flats, lining the N2 with shacks and portaloos. Seeing first-world wealth alongside African poverty is confronting for first-time visitors.

Yet what makes South Africa an uplifting and intriguing place to visit is the dissolution of divisions. Every day, millions of South Africans try to understand and respect the vastly different outlooks of people from other economic and racial groups. Projects aim to empower inhabitants of the townships and former homelands; to provide work in a country with one of the world's worst unemployment rates (about 25%). Finding common ground can be challenging in this Afro-Euro melting pot with 11 official languages, but race relations are informed by the miracle that Mandela et al performed.

Indeed, the infamous white supremacist Eugene Terre'Blanche is dead – killed by labourers in an argument over money. If anyone has come close to Terre'Blanche's outspoken public persona, it is Julius 'Juju' Malema, former president of the African National Congress (ANC) Youth League. Despite the problem of farm attacks, Malema led supporters in singing the apartheid-era struggle song 'Shoot the Boer' (*boer* means farmer, but can refer to Afrikaners in general). He was found guilty of hate speech, and after subsequent embarrassments, such as corruption allegations and criticising President Jacob Zuma, he was expelled from the ANC. Another episode touching on race relations was the furore over Brett Murray's satirical painting *The Spear*, which depicted Zuma with his genitals exposed and unleashed anger and outrage among many black South Africans.

Zuma came to power in 2009, having famously ousted struggle comrade Thabo Mbeki at the ANC's Polokwane conference. His rein has seen

HIV/AIDS

South Africa 5.6 million people with HIV/AIDS (17.8% of adults). **Lesotho** 290,000 people with HIV/AIDS (23.6% of adults). **Swaziland** 180,000 people with HIV/AIDS (25.9% of adults).

Books

Karoo Plainsong (Barbara Mutch) Apartheid-era drama. **My Traitor's Heart** (Rian Malan) Journalist's hard-hitting memoirs. **50 People Who Stuffed Up South Africa** (Alexander Parker) History's great villains.

Reports Before Daybreak (Brent Meersman) Novel about the '80s. **Zoo City** (Lauren Beukes) Jo'burg crime thriller. **Khayelitsha** (Steven Otter) White journalist lives in the township.

belief systems
(% of population)

80 — Christian
2 — Muslim
1 — Hindu
17 — Other

if South Africa were 100 people

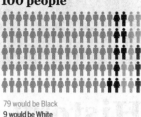

79 would be Black
9 would be White
9 would be Coloured
3 would be Indian/Asian

regular service-delivery protests, with township residents demonstrating against dire housing. South Africa is grappling with both apartheid's legacy – Archbishop Tutu has blamed violent crime and aggressive driving on psychological scars left by the regime – and pan-African problems. Economic refugees continue arriving from neighbouring countries, intensifying pressure on infrastructure and competition for jobs. Foreign-owned shops have been looted during service-delivery protests, echoing the xenophobic violence that swept the country in 2008.

Also reflecting pan-African issues, South Africa has the world's largest population of people with HIV/AIDS. Swaziland has the world's highest HIV/AIDS rate, and Lesotho is not far behind. Educational efforts face numerous taboos; *sangomas* (traditional healers) preach superstitious lore and, every day, funerals commemorate supposed tuberculosis victims.

South Africa's record on gender issues exemplifies the country's contradictions. Its constitution, adopted in 1996, is the world's most progressive, promoting the rights of women and gay people (same-sex marriage is legal) among others. Yet street-level reality is far harsher, with one of the world's highest reported incidences of rape, including 'corrective' rape of lesbians.

Crime and corruption will be hot topics at the 2014 elections, when Helen Zille is likely to shrink the gap between her opposition Democratic Alliance party, which already governs the Western Cape, and the ANC. Two of the ANC's most controversial proposals have been the Protection of State Information (or Secrecy) Bill and Media Appeals Tribunal – intended to tighten control of the press and the flow of state information. Democratic freedom is also an issue in Swaziland, where King Mswati III, one of the world's last absolute monarchs, has been accused of silencing opponents.

South Africa's official languages (in order of prevalence):
» Zulu
» Xhosa
» Afrikaans
» Northern Sotho
» Tswana
» English
» Southern Sotho (also Lesotho)
» Xitsonga
» Swati (also Swaziland)
» Tshivenda
» Ndebele

Film & Music

Hollywood does SA Clint Eastwood's *Invictus* covers the 1995 Rugby World Cup; in Peter Jackson's *District 9*, giant alien 'prawns' overrun Jo'burg.
Emerging bands Die Antwoord, Freshlyground, Goldfish and the Van Coke Kartel.

Rhinos

» South Africa lost 448 rhinos to poaching in 2011, compared with 333 in 2010.
» Less than 5000 black rhinos remain in the wild.
» Rhinos could become extinct in the wild within a decade.
» See also p387.

Comedians

» Leaping between languages and lambasting ethnic groups from Afrikaners to Zulus, comedians are a fun route to understanding South Africa.
» Recommended funny men include Trevor Noah, Marc Lottering and Nik Rabinowitz.

History

Visit South Africa and reminders of its past greet you at every turn. The country's human drama is reflected in the faces and in the body language of millions of its citizens. It's seen in where they live and how they live. It's on display in centuries-old rock paintings and modern-day urban graffiti, in isolated battlefields and sober apartheid-era memorials. It permeates every corner with its pain and injustice, but also with its hope. As South Africa continues the struggle to remake itself into a truly rainbow nation, its history plays out daily in all corners of the country – from dusty, isolated *dorps* (villages) to crowded township shebeens (unlicensed bars); from staid and fortified middle-class neighbourhoods to the carpeted chambers of parliament. Jump in, read as much as you can before you arrive, talk to people of all persuasions and perspectives, and immerse yourself in one of the most tormented yet most inspiring stories to be found anywhere.

For more on the history of Lesotho, see p461; for Swaziland, see p485.

For an overview of rock art in Southern Africa and other parts of the continent, see University of the Witwatersrand's Rock Art Research Institute page at www.wits.ac.za/academic/science/geography/research/5616/rock_art_research_institute.html.

Inauspicious Beginnings

Life at the southern tip of Africa began inauspiciously enough. A scattered collection of striking rock-art paintings provides evidence that as early as 25,000 years ago, and possibly as early as 40,000 years ago, nomadic San hunter-gatherers were living in the area that is now South Africa. Small numbers of San still live in South Africa today, making theirs one of the world's oldest continuous cultures.

Before this, the picture is murkier. But a wealth of fossil finds at Sterkfontein near Johannesburg (Jo'burg) show that the Gauteng area may have been almost as much of a population centre in prehistoric times as it is today, with humanlike creatures (hominids) roaming across the highveld at least three million years ago. By about one million years ago, these creatures had come to closely resemble modern humans, and ranged well beyond Africa, including in Europe and Asia. Somewhere

TIMELINE	40,000–25,000 BC	AD 500	1200–1270
	The San – southern Africa's first residents and one of the world's oldest traditional cultures – leave a series of rock paintings documenting their nomadic lifestyle and hunter-gatherer traditions.	A centuries-long series of migrations from West Africa's Niger Delta culminates when Bantu-speakers reach what is now KwaZulu-Natal. These Bantu-speakers are the ancestors of most modern-day South Africans.	The thriving trade centre of Mapungubwe, in today's Limpopo province, rises to become centre of the largest kingdom in sub-Saharan Africa, with trade links as far afield as Egypt, India and China.

around 100,000 years ago, *Homo sapiens* (modern man) came onto the scene. Although it's still a topic of debate, fossils found near the mouth of the Klasies River in the Eastern Cape indicate that our *Homo sapiens* ancestors may have been travelling around South Africa 90,000 years ago.

Around 2500 years ago the shaping of modern-day South Africa took a dramatic turn with descendants of the early San hunter-gatherer groups acquiring livestock and becoming pastoralists. This introduced concepts of personal wealth and property ownership.

New Arrivals

Around AD 500, a new group of peoples – Bantu-speakers originally from the Niger Delta area in West Africa – began settling in what is now South Africa. Their arrival marked the end of a long migration that had begun about 1000 BC, culminating when the first groups reached present-day KwaZulu-Natal.

A Short History of Lesotho from the Late Stone Age to the 1993 Elections, by Stephen J Gill, is a concise and readable history of the mountain kingdom.

The contrasts between the Bantu-speakers and the early San hunter-gatherers couldn't have been greater. The Bantu-speakers lived in settled villages where they tended their livestock. They were also skilled iron workers and farmers, growing maize and other crops.

While it's certain that Bantu-speakers mixed with the Khoe-San, the type of contact isn't known. Rock paintings show the groups interacting, several Bantu languages (notably Xhosa and Zulu) have incorporated Khoe-San clicks, and Khoe-San artefacts have been found at early Bantu settlements.

Before long, the Bantu-speakers – from whom most modern-day South Africans are descended – had entrenched themselves. Some groups – the ancestors of today's Nguni peoples (Zulu, Xhosa, Swazi and Ndebele) – settled near the coast. Others, now known as the Sotho-Tswana peoples (Tswana, Pedi, Basotho), settled in the highveld, while the Venda, Lemba and Shangaan-Tsonga peoples made their home in what is now northeastern South Africa.

Early Kingdoms

The hills and savannahs in South Africa's northeastern corner are dotted with ruins and artefacts left by a series of highly organised and stratified Iron Age kingdoms that flourished between about AD 1200 and the mid-17th century.

The first major one, Mapungubwe, was in present-day Limpopo province at the confluence of the Limpopo and Shashe Rivers, where Botswana, Zimbabwe and South Africa meet. Although its residents – ancestors of today's Shona people – were farmers, it was trade in gold and other goods that was the source of the kingdom's power. Pottery pieces, beads, seashells and other artefacts have been found at the site, showing that

1487	1497	1647	1652
Portuguese explorer Bartholomeu Dias successfully navigates the Cape of Good Hope. Although he doesn't linger, his journey marks the start of a long history of European involvement in Southern Africa.	Natal is named by Vasco da Gama, who, sighting its coast on Christmas Day 1497, names it for the natal day of Christ.	The marooned crew of a Dutch vessel build a fort in current-day Cape Town; a year passes before they are rescued.	The Dutch East India Company, seeking a secure way-station for its ships en route eastwards, establishes the first permanent European settlement at Table Bay, Cape Town, under Jan van Riebeeck's leadership.

Mapungubwe was one of the major inland trading hubs in the Southern Africa region from about 1220 until 1300. Its trading network extended eastwards to the coast, and from there to places as far afield as Egypt, India and China. Mapungubwe is also notable for the kingdom's inhabitants believing in a mystical relationship between their ruler and the land, similar to that which is part of Shona and Venda traditions today. In the 14th century, Mapungubwe declined. The reason is uncertain, with theories ranging from climate change to shifting trade routes.

Mapungubwe's decline coincided with the rise of a similarly structured but larger early Shona kingdom nearby in what was known as Great Zimbabwe (now Zimbabwe), suggesting that the focus of trade shifted northwards.

With the abandonment of Great Zimbabwe in the mid-15th century, several of the early Shona groups made their way back to the area just south of the Limpopo River that is now part of northern Kruger National Park. There, they established numerous settlements in the Pafuri region. These included the walled kingdom of Thulamela, the last of the great Iron Age kingdoms, which flourished from about the mid-16th to mid-17th centuries. Like Mapungubwe and Great Zimbabwe, Thulamela – which means 'place of giving birth' in the local Venda language – owed its prominence to far-flung trading networks for gold and other goods. Shells, glass beads and Chinese porcelain fragments found at the site show that Thulamela was linked by these trade networks with the coast and beyond.

Thulamela is also significant because several of its artefacts, most notably an iron gong of the type also found in Ghana, show that its trading links stretched as far as West Africa.

First Europeans

Apart from Portuguese explorer Bartholomeu Dias naming the Cabo da Boa Esperança (Cape of Good Hope) in 1487, the Portuguese showed little interest in South Africa – the Mozambique coast, further northeast, was more to their taste.

By the late 16th century, the Portuguese were being significantly challenged along their trade routes by the English and the Dutch.

In 1647 a Dutch vessel was wrecked in what is now Cape Town's Table Bay. The marooned crew built a fort and stayed for a year until they were rescued, becoming the first Europeans to attempt settlement in the area. Shortly thereafter, the Dutch East India Company (Vereenigde Oost-Indische Compagnie; VOC) – one of the major European trading houses sailing the spice route to the East – decided to establish a permanent settlement. A small VOC expedition, under the command of Jan van Riebeeck, was launched, reaching Table Bay in April 1652.

As the pastoralist Khoekhoen mixed with the hunter-gatherer San, it soon became impossible to distinguish between the two groups – hence the oft-used term 'Khoe-San'.

1657	1658	1660	1786
The Dutch East India Company releases employees to establish their own farms and supply the settlement with produce. These farmers – known as free burghers – soon expand into the lands of the Khoekhoen.	Slaves from Madagascar and Indonesia – the first to be imported into South Africa – are brought into the country by the Dutch.	Jan van Riebeeck plants a bitter-almond hedge separating the Dutch from the neighbouring Khoekhoen – in retrospect, an early step towards apartheid.	Moshoeshoe, founder of the Basotho nation, later to become Lesotho, is born; Shaka, future king of the Zulu, is born the following year.

No sooner were they off their boats, than the Dutch expedition found itself in the midst of the, by then, well-established Khoekhoen peoples (who were the pastoralist San – 'men of men'). Yet, while the new settlers traded with the neighbouring Khoekhoen out of necessity, there were deliberate attempts on the part of the Dutch to restrict contact. To alleviate a labour shortage, the VOC released a small group of Dutch employees to establish their own farms, from which they would supply the VOC settlement. The arrangement proved highly successful.

While the majority of these free burghers (as these farmers were called) were of Dutch descent, and members of the Calvinist Reformed Church of the Netherlands, there were also numerous Germans. In 1688 they were joined by French Huguenots, also Calvinists, who were fleeing religious persecution under Louis XIV.

Europeans Leave Their Mark

The VOC also began to import large numbers of slaves, primarily from Madagascar and Indonesia. With this additional labour, not only was South Africa's population mix further stirred up, but the areas occupied by the VOC were expanded further north and east where clashes with the Khoekhoen were inevitable. The beleaguered Khoekhoen were driven from their traditional lands, decimated by introduced diseases and destroyed by superior weapons when they fought back – which they did in a number of major 'wars' and with guerrilla resistance that continued into the 19th century. Most survivors were left with no option but to work for the Europeans in an arrangement that hardly differed from slavery. Over time, the Khoe-San, their European overseers and the imported slaves mixed, with the offspring of these unions forming the basis for modern South Africa's coloured population.

As the burghers continued to expand into the rugged hinterlands of the north and east, many began to take up a seminomadic pastoralist lifestyle, in some ways not so far removed from that of the Khoekhoen who they were displacing. In addition to their herds, a family might have had a wagon, a tent, a Bible and a couple of guns. As they became more settled, a mud-walled cottage would be built – frequently located, by choice, days of hard travel away from the nearest European. These were the first of the Trekboers (Wandering Farmers; later shortened to Boers) – completely independent of official control, extraordinarily self-sufficient and isolated. Their harsh lifestyle produced courageous individualists, but also a people with a narrow view of the world, whose only source of written knowledge was often the Bible.

Some scholars say that it was Calvinism, and especially its doctrine of predestination, that spawned the Afrikaner idea of racial superiority: the separation of the races had been divinely ordained, and thus justified all efforts to preserve the purity of the white race in its promised land.

1814	1816	1820	1828
The British, keen to outmanoeuvre the French, gain sovereignty over the Cape as Dutch mercantile power fades.	Shaka becomes chief of the Zulu, triggering the rise of a militaristic state and setting off the *difaqane* – a wave of disruption and terror that sweeps through Southern Africa.	The British try to mediate between the Boers and the Xhosa in Cape Colony by encouraging British immigration. The plan fails, but the new settlers solidify Britain's presence.	Shaka is killed by his half-brothers, Dingaan and Umhlanga; as the *difaqane* continues for another decade, Dingaan seeks to establish relations with British traders.

Arrival of the British

As the 18th century drew to a close, Dutch power began to fade, and the British moved in to fill the vacuum. They seized the Cape to prevent it from falling into rival French hands, then briefly relinquished it to the Dutch, before finally garnering recognition of their sovereignty of the area in 1814.

Awaiting the British at the Cape was a colony with 25,000 slaves, 20,000 white colonists, 15,000 Khoe-San and 1000 freed black slaves. Power was restricted to a white elite in Cape Town, and differentiation on the basis of race was already deeply entrenched. Outside Cape Town and the immediate hinterland, the country was populated by isolated black and white pastoralists.

One of their first tasks was trying to resolve a troublesome border dispute between the Boers and the Xhosa on the colony's eastern frontier. In 1820 about 5000 middle-class British immigrants – mostly traders and business people – were persuaded to leave England and settle on tracts of land between the feuding groups with the idea, at least officially, of providing a buffer zone. The plan was singularly unsuccessful. By 1823 almost half of the settlers had retreated to the towns – notably Grahamstown and Port Elizabeth – to pursue the jobs they had held in Britain.

While doing nothing to resolve the border dispute, this influx of settlers solidified the British presence in the area, igniting another flame under the now-simmering cauldron. Where the Boers and their ideas had once been largely unchallenged, there were now two language groups and two cultures. A pattern soon emerged whereby English-speakers were highly urbanised and dominated politics, trade, finance, mining and manufacturing, while the largely uneducated Boers were relegated to their farms.

The *difaqane* caused huge suffering and accelerated the formation of several states, notably those of the Sotho (present-day Lesotho) and Swazi (now Swaziland).

The gap between the British settlers and the Boers further widened with the abolition of slavery in 1833 – a move that was generally regarded by Boers as being against the God-given ordering of the races. Meanwhile, British numbers rapidly increased in Cape Town, in the area east of the Cape Colony (present-day Eastern Cape), in Natal (present-day KwaZulu-Natal) and, after the discovery of gold and diamonds, in parts of the Transvaal (mainly around present-day Gauteng).

Difaqane

It was against this backdrop that a time of immense upheaval and suffering among the African peoples of the region began to unfurl. This period is known as the *difaqane* (forced migration) in Sotho and as *mfeqane* (the crushing) in Zulu.

While the roots of the *difaqane* are disputed, certain events stand out. One of the most significant was the rise of the powerful Zulu kingdom.

1838	1843	1852	1860
Several thousand Zulus are killed in the Battle for Blood River. Until 1994, the anniversary was celebrated by whites as the Day of the Vow, before being renamed the Day of Reconciliation.	Boer hopes for a Natal republic are dashed when the British annex the area and set up a colony in modern-day Durban.	The Boer Republic of Transvaal is created. The first president, elected in 1857, is Marthinus Wessel Pretorius, son of Andries Pretorius – the famous Voortrekker leader.	MS *Truro* arrives in Durban with over 300 Indians for indentured service, signalling the beginning of an influx of Indians into South Africa.

In the early 19th century, Nguni tribes in what is now KwaZulu-Natal began to shift from loosely organised collections of kingdoms into a centralised, militaristic state under Shaka, son of the chief of the small Zulu clan. After building large armies, Shaka sent his armies out on a massive program of conquest and terror. Those who stood in his way were either enslaved or decimated.

Tribes in the path of Shaka's armies turned on their heels and fled, in turn becoming aggressors against their neighbours. This wave of disruption and terror spread throughout Southern Africa and beyond, leaving death and destruction in its wake.

In 1828 Shaka met his untimely end when he was killed by his half-brothers Dingaan and Umhlanga. The weaker and less-skilled Dingaan became king and attempted to establish relations with British traders on the Natal coast, but events were unfolding that were to see the demise of Zulu independence.

For an overview of the famous figures who have shaped South African history, check out www.sahistory.org.za for a well-presented list of biographies.

Great Trek & Battle of Blood River

Meanwhile, the Boers were growing increasingly dissatisfied with British rule in the Cape Colony. The British proclamation of equality of the races was a particularly sharp thorn in their side. Beginning in 1836, several groups of Boers, together with large numbers of Khoekhoen and black servants, decided to trek off into the interior in search of greater independence. North and east of the Senqu (Orange) River (which formed the Cape Colony's frontier) these Boers, or Voortrekkers (Pioneers), found vast tracts of apparently uninhabited grazing lands. They had entered, so it seemed, their promised land, with space enough for their cattle to graze, and for their culture of anti-urban independence to flourish. Little did they know that what they found – deserted pasture lands, disorganised bands of refugees and tales of brutality – were the result of the *difaqane*.

With the exception of the relatively powerful Ndebele, the Voortrekkers encountered little resistance among the scattered peoples of the plains. Dispersed by the *difaqane* and lacking horses and firearms, the locals' weakened condition also solidified the Boers' belief that European occupation heralded the coming of civilisation to a savage land.

However, the mountains (where King Moshoeshoe I was forging the Basotho nation later to become Lesotho) and the wooded valleys of Zululand were a more difficult proposition. Resistance here was strong, and the Boer incursions set off a series of skirmishes, squabbles and flimsy treaties that were to litter the next 50 years of increasing white domination.

The Great Trek's first halt was at Thaba 'Nchu, near present-day Bloemfontein, where a republic was established. Following disagreements among their leadership, the various Voortrekker groups split, with

1869	1879	1881
The first diamond is found near Kimberley in the walls of a house. This spells trouble for the Boers as the British quickly move to annex the area.	The Zulus inflict one of the most humiliating defeats on the British army at the Battle of Isandlwana in 1879, but Zululand eventually comes under British control.	First Anglo-Boer War ends with a decisive victory for the Boers at the Battle of Majuba Hill; Transvaal becomes the South African Republic.

GREATSTOCK PHOTOGRAPHIC LIBRARY/ALAMY ©

» Anglo-Boer War Museum (p295)

most crossing the Drakensberg into Natal to try and establish a republic there. As this was Zulu territory, the Voortrekker leader Piet Retief paid a visit to King Dingaan, and was promptly massacred by the suspicious Zulu. This massacre triggered others, as well as a revenge attack by the Boers. The culmination came on 16 December 1838 at the Ncome River in Natal. Several Boers were injured, while several thousand Zulus were killed, reportedly causing the Ncome's waters to run red.

After this victory (the result of superior weapons) in what came to be known as the Battle of Blood River, the Boers felt that their expansion really did have that long-suspected stamp of divine approval. Yet their hopes for establishing a Natal republic were short-lived. The British annexed the area in 1843, and founded their new Natal colony at present-day Durban. Most of the Boers headed north, with yet another grievance against the British.

The British set about establishing large sugar plantations in Natal, and looked to India to resolve their labour shortage. From 1860 into the early 20th century, a stream of over 150,000 indentured Indians arrived, as well as numerous free 'passenger Indians'.

Diamonds & Anglo-Boer Wars

The Boers meanwhile pressed on with their search for land and freedom, ultimately establishing themselves at Transvaal (encompassing parts of present-day Gauteng, Limpopo, North-West and Mpumalanga provinces) and the Orange Free State. Then the Boers' world was turned on its head in 1869 with the discovery of diamonds near Kimberley. The diamonds were found on land belonging to the Griqua, but to which both the Transvaal and Orange Free State laid claim. Among the best-known Khoekhoen groups, the Griqua had originally lived on the western coast between St Helena Bay and the Cederberg Range. In the late 18th century, they managed to acquire guns and horses and began trekking northeastwards. En route, they were joined by other groups of Khoe-San, coloureds and even white adventurers, and rapidly gained a reputation as a formidable military force.

Britain quickly stepped in and resolved the issue of who had rights to the diamonds by annexing the area for itself.

The establishment of the Kimberley diamond mines unleashed a flood of European and black labourers to the area. Towns sprang up in which the 'proper' separation of whites and blacks was ignored, and the Boers were angry that their impoverished republics were missing out on the economic benefits of the mines.

Long-standing Boer resentment became a full-blown rebellion in the Transvaal, and in 1880, the first Anglo-Boer War broke out. (Afrikaners – as the descendants of the early Boers became known – called it the War

Check out www
.southafrica.info/
about/history/
history.htm for a
comprehensive
but easily read-
able overview of
South African
history.

1886	1893	1897	1902
Gold is discovered on the Witwatersrand, setting off rapid population growth and development in Johannesburg. The Witwatersrand contains the world's largest gold deposit.	Mahatma Gandhi sets sail for South Africa. His early days in the country mark the beginning of his doctrine of nonviolent protest and influence his entire life's work.	Enoch Mankayi Sontonga, a choir leader from the Eastern Cape, composes 'Nkosi Sikelel' i Afrika'. It is first recorded in 1923, and made the national anthem in 1994.	Treaty of Vereeniging ends the second Anglo-Boer War, although the peace it brings is fragile and is challenged by all sides.

of Independence.) The war was over almost as soon as it began, with a crushing Boer victory at the Battle of Majuba Hill in early 1881. The republic regained its independence as the Zuid-Afrikaansche Republiek (ZAR; South African Republic). Paul Kruger, one of the leaders of the uprising, became president in 1883. Despite the setbacks, the British forged ahead with their desire to federate the Southern African colonies and republics.

In 1879 Zululand came under British control. Then in 1886, gold was discovered on the Witwatersrand (the area around Johannesburg). This accelerated the federation process and dealt the Boers yet another blow. Johannesburg's population exploded to about 100,000 by the mid-1890s, and the ZAR suddenly found itself hosting thousands of *uitlanders* (foreigners), both black and white, with the Boers squeezed to the sidelines. The influx of black labour was particularly disturbing for the Boers, many of whom were going through hard times and resented the black wage-earners.

The situation peaked in 1899, when the British demanded voting rights for the 60,000 foreign whites on the Witwatersrand. (Until this point, Kruger's government had excluded all foreigners from the franchise.) Kruger refused, calling for British troops to be withdrawn from the ZAR's borders. When the British resisted, Kruger declared war. This second Anglo-Boer War was more protracted and the British were better prepared than at Majuba Hill. By mid-1900, Pretoria, the last of the major Boer towns, had surrendered. Yet resistance by Boer *bittereinders* (bitter enders) continued for two more years with guerrilla-style battles, which in turn were met by scorched-earth tactics by the British. In May 1902, the Treaty of Vereeniging brought a superficial peace. Under its terms, the Boer republics acknowledged British sovereignty.

A Fragile Peace

During the immediate postwar years, the British focused their attention on rebuilding the country, in particular the mining industry. By 1907 the mines of the Witwatersrand were producing almost one-third of the world's gold. But the peace brought by the treaty was fragile, and challenged on all sides. The Afrikaners found themselves in the position of being poor farmers in a country where big mining ventures and foreign capital rendered them irrelevant. They were particularly incensed by Britain's unsuccessful attempts to Anglicise them, and to impose English as the official language in schools and the workplace. Partly as a backlash to this, Afrikaans came to be seen as the *volkstaal* (people's language) and a symbol of Afrikaner nationhood, and several nationalistic organisations sprang up.

All the building blocks for the modern South African pariah state of the mid-20th century were now in place. Blacks and coloureds were completely marginalised. Harsh taxes were imposed, wages were reduced

1902	**1910**	**1912**	**1913**
The brutality of the second Anglo-Boer War is shocking and causes the death of 26,000 people from disease and neglect.	The Union of South Africa is created. English and Dutch are made the official languages, and there are no voting rights for blacks. Lesotho and Swaziland remain British protectorates.	Pixley ka Isaka Seme, a Columbia University–educated lawyer, calls a conference of chiefs. A union of all tribes is proposed, resulting in the formation of what will become the ANC.	The 1913 Immigration Law prohibits further immigration of Indians to South Africa. Any marriage not performed according to Christian rites is also illegal – invalidating Indian and Muslim marriages.

and the British caretaker administrator encouraged the immigration of thousands of Chinese to undercut any resistance. Resentment was given full vent in the Bambatha Rebellion of 1906, in which 4000 Zulu lost their lives after protesting onerous tax legislation.

The British, meanwhile, moved ahead with their plans for union. After several years of negotiation, the 1910 Act of Union was signed, bringing the republics of Cape Colony, Natal, Transvaal and Orange Free State together as the Union of South Africa. Under the provisions of the act, the Union was still a British territory, with home-rule for Afrikaners. The British High Commission Territories of Basotholand (now Lesotho), Bechuanaland (now Botswana), Swaziland and Rhodesia (now Zimbabwe) continued to be ruled directly by Britain.

English and Dutch were made the official languages. Despite a major campaign by blacks and coloureds, only whites could be elected to parliament.

Across Boundaries: The Journey of a South African Woman Leader, by Mamphela Ramphele, traces the life of an extraordinary woman who was internally 'exiled' to the town of Tzaneen for seven years but later rose to become the University of Cape Town's vice-chancellor.

The first government of the new Union was headed by General Louis Botha, with General Jan Smuts as his deputy. Their South African National Party (later known as the South African Party or SAP) followed a generally pro-British, white-unity line. More radical Boers split away under the leadership of General Barry Hertzog, forming the National Party (NP) in 1914. The NP championed Afrikaner interests, advocating separate development for the two white groups and independence from Britain.

Racism Entrenched & Birth of the ANC

There was no place in the new Union for blacks, even though they constituted over 75% of the population. Under the Act of Union, they were denied voting rights in the Transvaal and Orange Free State areas, and in the Cape Colony they were granted the vote only if they met a property ownership qualification. Coming on the heels of British wartime propaganda promising freedom from 'Boer slavery', the failure to grant the franchise was regarded by blacks as a blatant betrayal. It wasn't long before a barrage of oppressive legislation was passed, making it illegal for black workers to strike, reserving skilled jobs for whites, barring blacks from military service and instituting restrictive pass laws. In 1913 the Natives Land Act was enacted, setting aside 8% of South Africa's land for black occupancy. Whites, who made up 20% of the population, were given over 90% of the land. Black Africans were not allowed to buy, rent or even be sharecroppers outside their designated area. Thousands of squatters were evicted from farms and forced into increasingly overcrowded and impoverished reserves or into the cities. Those who remained were reduced to the status of landless labourers.

Against this turbulent background, black and coloured opposition began to coalesce, and leading figures such as John Jabavu, Walter Rubu-

1914	1925	1927
Following demonstrations and strikes, the Indian Relief Bill is passed, restoring recognition of Hindu and Muslim marriages and convincing Gandhi of the power of non-violent resistance.	Afrikaans is made an official language, with the rise of Afrikaner nationalism. Its proposed introduction into township schools is one of the triggers of the 1976 Soweto uprising.	Kruger National Park opens to the public, although its proud history is soured during apartheid when the government kicks people off their traditional lands to allow for the park's expansion.

» Kruger National Park (p37

HISTORY RACISM ENTRENCHED & BIRTH OF THE ANC

MAHATMA GANDHI

In 1893 a young and then completely unknown Indian solicitor named Mohandas Gandhi set sail for Durban, South Africa, to take on a one-year legal contract. Little did he know it, but his experiences in the country were to shape the course of his entire life.

At the time Gandhi arrived, anti-Indian sentiment in Natal was running high, and upon his arrival he was thrown out of a 1st-class train wagon at Pietermaritzburg because of his race. The incident, together with other discrimination that he experienced in the early months after his arrival, had a profound effect on Gandhi. He began schooling himself in methods of nonviolent resistance, and became increasingly involved with the local Indian community, working with them to safeguard their political rights. Within a short period, Gandhi had not only established himself as a successful attorney, but also as the leading spokesperson for Indian interests in South Africa.

In 1896, and again in 1901, Gandhi returned briefly to India where he lobbied extensively to bring attention to the plight of Indians in South Africa. Back in South Africa, Gandhi gave up the trappings of a successful attorney, began washing his own clothes, committed himself to a life of celibacy and nonpossession, and devoted himself fully to service. He also developed his defining philosophy of *satyagraha* (meaning, very loosely, truth through nonviolence).

In 1907 the Transvaal government passed the Asiatic Registration Act, requiring all Indians to register with the Registrar of Asiatics and to carry a certificate of registration. Gandhi called on the Indian community to defy the act, and to offer no resistance if they should be arrested. Over the next seven years, numerous similar discriminatory incidents followed, including a court decision nullifying all Hindu and Muslim marriages, which Gandhi and his followers also peacefully defied. In response, Gandhi – along with thousands of other Indians who had joined him in his *satyagraha* struggle – was repeatedly arrested. He garnered various victories, and became convinced of the importance and effectiveness of nonviolent resistance.

Gandhi finally returned to India in 1914 to begin another chapter of his life.

---

sana and Abdullah Abdurahman laid the foundations for new nontribal black political groups. Most significantly, a Columbia University–educated attorney, Pixley ka Isaka Seme, called together representatives of the various African tribes to form a unified national organisation to represent the interests of blacks and ensure that they had an effective voice in the new Union. Thus was born the South African Native National Congress, known from 1923 onwards as the African National Congress (ANC).

Almost parallel to this, Mohandas (Mahatma) Gandhi had been working with the Indian populations of Natal and the Transvaal to fight against the ever-increasing encroachments on their rights.

1932	1948	1955	1960
World-famous singer Miriam Makeba ('Mama Africa') is born in Johannesburg – she spends 30 years outside South Africa in exile for criticism of the apartheid government.	The darkness descends – the National Party under the leadership of DF Malan gains control of the government after campaigning on a policy of segregation, and apartheid is institutionalised.	At a congress held at Kliptown near Johannesburg, a number of organisations, including the Indian Congress and the ANC, adopt a Freedom Charter, still central to the ANC's vision of South Africa.	Sharpeville massacre; ANC and Pan African Congress (PAC) banned; Miriam Makeba is denied entry to South Africa after trying to return for her mother's funeral.

Rise of Afrikaner Nationalism

In 1924 the NP, under Hertzog, came to power in a coalition government, and Afrikaner nationalism gained a greater hold. Dutch was replaced by Afrikaans (previously only regarded as a low-class dialect of Dutch) as an official language of the Union, and the so-called *swart gevaar* (black threat) was made the dominant issue of the 1929 election. Hertzog joined briefly in a coalition with the more moderate Jan Smuts in the mid-1930s, after which Smuts took the reins. However, any hopes of turning the tide of Afrikaner nationalism were dashed when Daniel François (DF) Malan led a radical breakaway movement, the Purified National Party, to the central position in Afrikaner political life. The Afrikaner Broederbond, a secret Afrikaner brotherhood that had been formed in 1918 to protect Afrikaner culture, soon became an extraordinarily influential force behind both the NP and other organisations designed to promote the *volk* ('people', the Afrikaners).

Due to the booming wartime economy, black labour became increasingly important to the mining and manufacturing industries, and the black urban population nearly doubled. Enormous squatter camps grew up on the outskirts of Johannesburg and, to a lesser extent, outside the other major cities. Conditions in the townships were appalling, but poverty was not only the province of blacks; wartime surveys found that 40% of white school children were malnourished.

Walls of Apartheid Go Up

In the months leading up to the 1948 elections, the NP campaigned on its policy of segregation, or 'apartheid' (an Afrikaans term for the state of being apart). It was voted in, in coalition with the Afrikaner Party (AP), and under the leadership of DF Malan.

Thus it was that apartheid, long a reality of life, became institutionalised under Malan. Within short order, legislation was passed prohibiting mixed marriages, making interracial sex illegal, classifying every individual by race and establishing a classification board to rule in questionable cases. The noxious Group Areas Act of 1950 set aside desirable city properties for whites, while banishing nonwhites into the townships. The Separate Amenities Act created, among other things, separate beaches, buses, hospitals, schools and even park benches.

The existing pass laws were further strengthened: blacks and coloureds were compelled to carry identity documents at all times and were prohibited from remaining in towns, or even visiting them, without specific permission.

In 1960 tensions came to a head in the Sharpeville massacre. Soon thereafter, Prime Minister Hendrik Verwoerd, credited with the unoffi-

1961	1961	1963	1964
Soon after the Sharpeville massacre Prime Minister Hendrik Verwoerd, the 'architect of apartheid' announces a referendum; in May South Africa leaves the Commonwealth and becomes a republic.	On 16 December, Umkhonto we Sizwe, the military wing of the ANC, carries out its first attacks, marking the start of the armed struggle against apartheid.	Miriam Makeba's citizenship is revoked after speaking out against apartheid before the UN.	Nelson Mandela is sentenced to life imprisonment – a sentence that will span 27 years and include 18 years at the notorious Robben Island prison.

cial title of 'architect of apartheid', announced a referendum on whether the country should become a republic. The change was passed by a slim majority of voters. Verwoerd withdrew South Africa from the Commonwealth, and in May 1961 the Republic of South Africa came into existence.

ANC Begins the Long Walk

These developments pushed the hitherto relatively conservative ANC into action. In 1949 it developed an agenda that for the first time advocated open resistance in the form of strikes, acts of public disobedience and protest marches. Resistance continued throughout the 1950s and resulted in occasional violent clashes.

In 1959 a group of disenchanted ANC members, seeking to sever all links with the white government, broke away to form the more militant Pan African Congress (PAC). First on the PAC's agenda was a series of nationwide demonstrations against the hated pass laws. On 21 March 1960, police opened fire on demonstrators surrounding a police station in Sharpeville, a township near Vereeniging. At least 67 people were killed, and 186 wounded; most of those were shot in the back.

To many domestic and international onlookers, the struggle had crossed a crucial line at Sharpeville, and there could no longer be any lingering doubts about the nature of the white regime. In the wake of

After the Party, by former ANC MP Andrew Feinstein, is a detailed and highly critical look at the ANC behind the scenes during the post-Mandela years.

'HOMELANDS'

In 1962 the Transkei was born. It was the first of 10 so-called 'Bantustans' or 'homelands' that were intended to provide a home for all black South Africans. On these lands – so went the white South African propaganda – blacks would be self-governing self-sufficient, citizens, living together with others of their own ethnic group.

The realities were much different. The homeland areas had no infrastructure or industry, and were incapable of producing sufficient food for the burgeoning black population. All the homelands together constituted only 14% of South Africa's land, while blacks made up close to 80% of the country's population. Tribal divisions were made arbitrarily, and once a person had been assigned to a homeland, they could not leave without a pass and permission. The resulting suffering was intense and widespread.

Following creation of the homelands, blacks flooded to the cities seeking work: while life in urban squatter camps was bad, life in the homelands was worse. The government responded by banning blacks from being employed as shop assistants, receptionists, typists and clerks. The construction of housing in the black 'locations' (dormitory suburbs for black workers) was halted, and enormous single-sex hostels were built instead.

Although the homelands concept came to an end with the demise of apartheid, its legacy – including completely insufficient infrastructure and distorted population concentrations in the homeland areas – continues to scar South Africa today.

1966

As a part of the post-WWII independence wind blowing through Africa, Lesotho gains independence from Britain; Swaziland achieves this two years later.

1966

Verwoerd is stabbed to death by Dimitri Tsafendas, a parliamentary messenger suffering from schizophrenia and is resentful of being shunned for being dark-skinned, though he is classified as 'white'.

VERONICA GARBUTT/LONELY PLANET IMAGES ©

» Robben Island (p53)

the shooting, a massive stay-away from work was organised, and demonstrations continued. Prime Minister Verwoerd declared a state of emergency, giving security forces the right to detain people without trial. Over 18,000 demonstrators were arrested, including much of the ANC and PAC leadership, and both organisations were banned.

In response, the ANC and PAC began a campaign of sabotage through the armed wings of their organisations, Umkhonto we Sizwe (Spear of the Nation, MK) and Poqo ('Pure' or 'Alone'), respectively. In July 1963, 17 members of the ANC underground movement were arrested and tried for treason at the widely publicised Rivonia Trial. Among them was Nelson Mandela, an ANC leader and founder of Umkhonto we Sizwe, who had already been arrested on other charges. In June 1964, Mandela and seven others were sentenced to life imprisonment. Oliver Tambo, another member of the ANC leadership, managed to escape South Africa and lead the ANC in exile.

Nelson Mandela's autobiographical *Long Walk to Freedom* is essential reading and the ultimate recounting of the early days of resistance and the years that followed.

I have fought against White domination and I have fought against Black domination. I have cherished the ideal of a democratic and free society in which all persons live together in harmony and with equal opportunities. It is an ideal which I hope to live for and to achieve. But if needs be, it is an ideal for which I am prepared to die.
Nelson Mandela, 20 April 1964, Rivonia Trial

Decades of Darkness

With the ANC banned, and Mandela and most of its leadership in jail or exile, South Africa moved into some of its darkest times. Apartheid legislation was enforced with increasing gusto, and the walls between the races were built ever higher. Most odious was the creation of separate 'homelands' for blacks.

During the 1970s, resistance again gained momentum, first channelled through trade unions and strikes, and then spearheaded by the South African Students' Organisation under the leadership of the charismatic Steve Biko. Biko, a medical student, was the main force behind the growth of South Africa's Black Consciousness Movement, which stressed the need for psychological liberation, black pride and nonviolent opposition to apartheid.

Things culminated in 1976, when the Soweto Students' Representative Council organised protests against the use of Afrikaans (regarded as the language of the oppressor) in black schools. On 16 June, police opened fire on a student march led by Tsietsi Mashinini – a central figure in the book *A Burning Hunger: One Family's Struggle Against Apartheid* and now immortalised by a large monument in Soweto. This began a round

1976	1977		1978–88
On 16 June, the Soweto uprisings begin, setting off a chain of violence around the country, and marking the first major internal challenge to the apartheid government.	Steve Biko is murdered. News of his death draws increased international attention to the brutality of the apartheid regime.		The South African Defence Force (SADF; now the South African National Defence Force, or SANDF) launches a number of major attacks inside Angola, Mozambique, Zimbabwe, Botswana and Lesotho.

MARK PETERS/GETTY IMAGES ©

» Steve Biko

STEVE BIKO

Steve Biko, born in 1946 in the Eastern Cape, was one of the most prominent and influential anti-apartheid activists. His Black Consciousness Movement mobilised urban youth and was a major force behind the 1976 Soweto uprisings. As a result of his activities, Biko was high on the list of those targeted by the apartheid regime. In 1973 he was restricted to his birthplace of King William's Town and prohibited from speaking in public. Despite these restrictions, he continued his activism, as well as community work, including establishing literacy programs and a health clinic.

On 18 August 1977, Biko was detained under the Terrorism Act. Less than a month later, he was dead – from a hunger strike, according to the police. In 1997 the Truth & Reconciliation Commission reported that five former members of the South African security forces had admitted to killing Biko, although they were never prosecuted. Biko had been beaten until he fell into a coma, he went without medical treatment for three days and finally died in Pretoria. At the subsequent inquest, the magistrate found that no one was to blame, although the South African Medical Association eventually took action against the doctors who failed to treat him.

Biko's death prompted a huge public outcry and mobilised international attention on the brutality of the apartheid system. Biko's funeral service, celebrated by the Reverend Desmond Tutu, was attended by thousands, including representatives from various Western countries. Thousands more were barred from attending by security forces. Biko's story was the centrepiece of the 1987 film *Cry Freedom*.

of nationwide demonstrations, strikes, mass arrests, riots and violence that, over the next 12 months, took more than 1000 lives.

In September 1977, Steve Biko was killed by security police. South Africa would never be the same. A generation of young blacks committed themselves to a revolutionary struggle against apartheid ('Liberation before Education' was the catch-cry) and black communities were politicised.

South Africa Under Siege

As international opinion turned decisively against the white regime, the government (and most of the white population) increasingly saw the country as a bastion besieged by communism, atheism and black anarchy. Considerable effort was put into circumventing international sanctions, and the government even developed nuclear weapons (since destroyed).

Negotiating majority rule with the ANC was not considered an option (publicly, at least), which left the government reverting to use of sheer military might. A siege mentality developed among whites, and although many realised that a civil war against the black majority could not be

1982	Late 1980s	1990	1993
The first HIV/AIDS death is recorded in South Africa, marking the start of a horrific, ongoing scourge spreading to, and devastating, communities across the country.	The South African Chamber of Mines begins an ultimately unsuccessful education campaign to try and stem the rise of HIV/AIDs cases.	In what becomes a historic moment in South African history, Nelson Mandela is freed after 27 years in prison, preaching not hatred but forgiveness and reconciliation.	Nelson Mandela and FW de Klerk, the two men shaping the future of South Africa through tough negotiation, are awarded the Nobel Peace Prize.

DESMOND TUTU

Few figures in South Africa's anti-apartheid struggle are as recognisable as Desmond Mpilo Tutu, the retired Anglican Archbishop of Cape Town. Tutu, born in 1931 in Klerksdorp, Transvaal (now in North-West Province), rose from humble beginnings to become an internationally recognised activist. During the apartheid era, Tutu was a vigorous proponent of economic boycotts and international sanctions against South Africa. Following the fall of the apartheid government, Tutu headed South Africa's Truth & Reconciliation Commission, an experience that he chronicles in his book *No Future Without Forgiveness*.

Today, Tutu continues to be a tireless moral advocate. He has been a particularly outspoken critic of the ANC government, lashing out against corruption and HIV/AIDS, and taking the government to task for failing to adequately tackle poverty. Tutu has been awarded the Nobel Peace Prize, the Gandhi Peace Prize and numerous other distinctions. It is Tutu who is generally credited with coining the phrase 'rainbow nation' as a description for postapartheid South Africa.

won, they preferred this to 'giving in' to political reform. To them, brutal police and military actions seemed entirely justifiable. Paradoxically, the international sanctions that cut whites off from the rest of the world enabled black leaders to develop sophisticated political skills, as those in exile forged ties with regional and world leaders.

Winds of Change

In the early 1980s, a fresh wind began to blow across South Africa. Whites constituted only 16% of the total population, in comparison with 20% 50 years earlier, and the percentage was continuing to fall. Recognising the inevitability of change, President PW Botha told white South Africans to 'adapt or die'. Numerous reforms were instituted, including repeal of the pass laws. But Botha stopped well short of full reform, and many blacks (as well as the international community) felt the changes were only cosmetic. Protests and resistance continued at full force, as South Africa became increasingly polarised and fragmented, and unrest was widespread. A white backlash also arose, giving rise to a number of neo-Nazi paramilitary groups, notably the Afrikaner Weerstandsbeweging (AWB), led by Eugène Terre'Blanche. The opposition United Democratic Front (UDF) was also formed at this time. With a broad coalition of members, led by Archbishop Desmond Tutu and the Reverend Allan Boesak, it called for the government to abolish apartheid and eliminate the homelands.

Rabble-Rouser for Peace: The Authorised Biography of Desmond Tutu, by John Allen, is a fascinating and inspirational look into the life of one of South Africa's most influential figures.

1994	1995	1996	1997
In a triumph for democracy and Mandela's path of reconciliation and freedom for all, the first democratic elections are held; Nelson Mandela is elected president.	A vital tool in the country's healing process, the Truth & Reconciliation Commission is established, chaired by Archbishop Desmond Tutu.	After much negotiation and debate, South Africa's parliament approves a revised version of the 1993 constitution that establishes the structure of the country's new, democratic government.	In a move almost unheard of by an African head of state, Nelson Mandela retires as ANC president, and is succeeded by Thabo Mbeki.

International pressures also increased, as economic sanctions began to dig in harder, and the value of the rand collapsed. In 1985 the government declared a state of emergency, which was to stay in effect for five years. The media was censored and by 1988, according to estimates of the ANC, backed up by human-rights groups, 30,000 people had been detained without trial, with thousands tortured.

Mandela is Freed

In 1986 President Botha announced to parliament that South Africa had 'outgrown' apartheid. The government started making a series of minor reforms in the direction of racial equality, while maintaining an iron grip on the media and on all anti-apartheid demonstrations.

In late 1989, a physically ailing Botha was succeeded by FW de Klerk. At his opening address to the parliament in February 1990, de Klerk announced that he would repeal discriminatory laws and legalise the ANC, the PAC and the Communist Party. Media restrictions were lifted, and de Klerk released political prisoners not guilty of common-law crimes. On 11 February 1990, 27 years after he had first been incarcerated, Nelson Mandela walked out of the grounds of Victor Verster prison a free man.

From 1990 to 1991 the legal apparatus of apartheid was abolished. A referendum – the last of the whites-only vote held in South Africa – overwhelmingly gave the government authority to negotiate a new constitution with the ANC and other groups.

'We...shall build the society in which all South Africans, both black and white, will be able to walk tall, without any fear in their hearts, assured of their inalienable right to human dignity – a rainbow nation at peace with itself and the world.'
Nelson Mandela, 1994, Inauguration Speech

MAX DU PREEZ & VRYE WEEKBLAD

In 1988 renegade Afrikaner journalist Max du Preez, together with a handful of other white anti-apartheid activists, founded *Vrye Weekblad,* South Africa's first Afrikaans-language anti-apartheid newspaper. From the start, the newspaper drew the wrath of the state. Its offices were bombed, du Preez received numerous threats and the newspaper was sued for defamation by then-president PW Botha. Yet, during its short life, it was ground-breaking for its commitment to free speech, its tireless campaigning against oppression and its exposés of corruption and brutality on all sides of the political spectrum. After just over five years of cutting-edge investigative reporting, *Vrye Weekblad* was forced to close down shortly before the 1994 elections. Du Preez later went on to work as producer for the South African Broadcasting Corporation's (SABC) TV coverage of the Truth & Reconciliation hearings, and today continues to work as a journalist.

For an account of the paper's history, look for a copy of du Preez' book, *Oranje Blanje Blues*.

1999	2003	2004	2004
The ANC wins a landslide victory in the second democratic elections held in South Africa, falling just short of the 66.7% required to change the constitution.	Walter Sisulu, Mandela's mentor, and a major figure in the anti-apartheid struggle who spent 26 years in prison, dies on 5 May.	In November, Anglican Archbishop Desmond Tutu warns that South Africa is sitting on a powder keg because millions are still living in poverty a decade after the dismantling of apartheid.	Mbeki guides the ANC to a decisive victory in the 2004 national elections. In accordance with his vision of an 'African renaissance', South Africa increases regional engagement.

NELSON MANDELA

Nelson Rolihlahla Mandela, one of the millennium's greatest leaders, was once vilified by South Africa's ruling whites and sentenced to life imprisonment. Twenty-seven years later, he emerged from incarceration calling for reconciliation and forgiveness.

Mandela, son of a Xhosa chief, was born on 18 July 1918 in the village of Mveso on the Mbashe River. After attending the University of Fort Hare, Mandela headed to Johannesburg, where he soon became immersed in politics. He finished his law degree and, together with Oliver Tambo, opened South Africa's first black law firm. Meanwhile, in 1944, together with Tambo and Walter Sisulu, Mandela formed the Youth League of the African National Congress (ANC). During the 1950s, Mandela was at the forefront of the ANC's civil disobedience campaigns, for which he was arrested in 1952, tried and acquitted. After the ANC was banned in the wake of the Sharpeville massacre, Mandela led the establishment of its underground military wing, Umkhonto we Sizwe. In 1964 Mandela was brought to stand trial for sabotage and fomenting revolution in the widely publicised Rivonia Trial. After brilliantly arguing his own defence, he was sentenced to life imprisonment, and spent the next 18 years in the infamous Robben Island prison, before being moved onto the mainland.

Throughout his incarceration, Mandela repeatedly refused to compromise his political beliefs in exchange for freedom, saying that only free men can negotiate.

In February 1990, Mandela was released and in 1991 he was elected president of the ANC. In 1993 Mandela shared the Nobel Peace Prize with FW de Klerk and, in the first free elections the following year, was elected president of South Africa. In his much-quoted speech 'Free at Last!', made after winning the 1994 elections, he focused the nation's attention firmly on the future, declaring, 'This is the time to heal the old wounds and build a new South Africa'.

In 1997 Mandela – or Madiba, his traditional Xhosa name – stepped down as ANC president, although he continues to be revered as an elder statesman.

Elections

In December 1991, the Convention for a Democratic South Africa (Codesa) began negotiations on the formation of a multiracial transitional government and a new constitution extending political rights to all groups.

In 1993 a draft constitution was published guaranteeing freedom of speech and religion, access to adequate housing and numerous other benefits, and explicitly prohibiting discrimination on almost any grounds. Finally, at midnight on 26/27 April 1994, the old national anthem 'Die Stem' (The Call) was sung and the old flag was lowered, followed by the raising of the new rainbow flag and singing of the new anthem 'Nkosi Sikelel i Afrika' (God Bless Africa). The election

2006	2007	2007
Over five million South Africans are living with HIV/AIDS; the devastation wrought by the disease is a reflection on many years of neglect by the government.	The HIV/AIDS tragedy affects the country's most vulnerable. According to Unaids, there are approximately 280,000 South African children living with HIV/AIDS and 1.4 million orphaned by HIV/AIDS.	In December, Thabo Mbeki is defeated by Jacob Zuma as chairman of the ANC. New corruption charges – following the dropping of earlier charges in 2006 – are brought against Zuma.

» ANC flag

went off peacefully, amid a palpable feeling of goodwill throughout the country.

The ANC won 62.7% of the vote, less than the 66.7% that would have enabled it to rewrite the constitution. As well as deciding the national government, the election decided the provincial governments, and the ANC won in all but two provinces. The NP captured most of the white and coloured vote and became the official opposition party.

See www.anc.org. za for the official view of everything past and present on the ANC.

Truth & Reconciliation

Following the elections, focus turned to the Truth & Reconciliation Commission (1994–99), which worked to expose crimes of the apartheid era. The dictum of its chairman Archbishop Desmond Tutu: 'Without forgiveness there is no future, but without confession there can be no forgiveness'. Many stories of horrific brutality and injustice were heard by the commission, offering some catharsis to people and communities shattered by their past.

The commission operated by allowing victims to tell their stories and perpetrators to confess their guilt, with amnesty on offer to those who made a clean breast of it. Those who chose not to appear before the commission would face criminal prosecution if their guilt could be proven. Yet, while some soldiers, police and 'ordinary' citizens confessed their crimes, many of the human-rights criminals who gave the orders and dictated the policies failed to present themselves (PW Botha is one famous no-show).

South Africa Recently

In 1999 South Africa held its second democratic elections. Two years previously Mandela had handed over ANC leadership to his deputy, Thabo Mbeki, and the ANC's share of the vote increased to put the party within one seat of the two-thirds majority that would allow it to alter the constitution.

The Democratic Party (DP) – traditionally a stronghold of liberal whites, with new support from conservatives disenchanted with the NP, and from some middle-class blacks – won official opposition status.

By any account, Mbeki had huge shoes to fill as president, although how close he came is the subject of sharply divided debate, and his years in office can only be characterised as a roller-coaster ride. In the early days of his presidency, Mbeki's effective denial of the HIV/AIDS crisis invited global criticism, and his conspicuous failure to condemn the forced reclamation of white-owned farms in neighbouring Zimbabwe and to speak out publicly against his long-time comrade, Zimbabwean

More people have HIV/AIDs in South Africa than any other country – for more on the history of HIV/ AIDS in South Africa and on what's being done today, see www.avert.org/ aidssouthafrica. htm.

2008	2008	2008	2009
Long-simmering social discontent boils over and xenophobic rioting wrecks townships around the country, causing over 60 deaths and forcing many workers from neighbouring countries to return home.	The Shikota movement, headed by former Gauteng premier Mbhazima Shilowa and Mosiuoa Lekota, form a new ANC-breakaway political party called the Congress of the People (COPE).	Singer Miriam Makeba ('Mama Africa'), dies at the age of 76.	Corruption charges against Jacob Zuma are dropped in April after irregularities by prosecutors are cited; national elections are held later in the month and Zuma becomes president.

president Robert Mugabe, unnerved both South African landowners and foreign investors.

In 2005 Mbeki dismissed his deputy president Jacob Zuma in the wake of corruption charges against Zuma, setting off a ruthless internal ANC power struggle which Zuma won. In September 2008, Mbeki was asked to step down as president in an unprecedented move by the party.

Corruption charges against Zuma were dropped and as widely expected, the ANC won the 2009 election, with Jacob Zuma declared president. Since assuming leadership, Zuma has managed to balance out considerable domestic and international criticism with his approachable personality and strong grassroots popularity. There is a wide-held view, however, that well into his term as president, he has demonstrated weak leadership and failed to fulfil promises to create jobs and alleviate poverty.

The ability of the opposition parties to pressure the government to tackle South Africa's problems will be an important test of South Africa's political maturity in the coming years. Corruption, crime, economic inequality and HIV/AIDS all loom as major challenges.

Reading newspaper headlines presents a mixed picture, but it's likely that most South Africans would agree that the country today is an immeasurably more optimistic and relaxed place than it was in 1990, despite the massive problems that it still confronts.

Thabo Mbeki: The Dream Deferred, by Mark Gevisser, is an intriguing examination of both the man who stood at the forefront of South African politics for over a decade, and of South Africa itself.

2010	2011	2012	2012
The FIFA World Cup of football is held in South Africa and, despite fears of visitors becoming victims of crime, goes without a hitch.	With 2 billion rand 'lost' from its national accounts, Limpopo province is declared bankrupt by the national treasury and the federal ANC government seizes direct control of the province.	The ANC celebrates its 100-year anniversary with major celebrations in Bloemfontein where it was founded; and events commemorating its centennial continue throughout the year all over the country.	Three years after charges of corruption, racketeering, tax evasion and money-laundering against president Jacob Zuma are dropped, the country's supreme court rules to allow a review of the decision.

Music

The curious beauty of African music is that it uplifts even as it tells a sad tale. You may be poor, you may have only a ramshackle house, you may have lost your job, but that song gives you hope.

Nelson Mandela

Just as music fuelled the resistance to apartheid, it continues to sing out for freedom and justice, providing a soundtrack to everyday lives. Music is everywhere in South Africa, coming through every available medium, communicating in every imaginable style. Want a 'typical' South African sound? Forget it: South Africa has the greatest range of musical styles on the African continent, and more than any country of similar size anywhere in the world. A nation of record collectors, the people of South Africa love their music. Rock, jazz, classical, gospel, rap, reggae, Afro-house, *maskanda, mbaqanga,* kwaito and much more. Here centuries-old traditions jostle with new genres sprung from old ones. Western styles are given an idiosyncratic stamp. The country's gargantuan recording industry (with its small-but-determined crop of independent black-owned labels) watches, ready to pounce.

The sounds of South Africa have an inevitable influence on its smaller neighbours Lesotho and Swaziland. Choirs are popular in Lesotho, as are reggae and *famo* (singing, often with ululations, accompanied by an accordion, drum and sometimes a bass), followed by Afropop, jazz and kwaito. Traditional musical instruments such as the *lekolulo* flute and the *setolo-tolo* mouth bow continue to be played by the Sotho. Swaziland, too, has its traditional music, which is used as accompaniment for harvests, weddings, births and other events. It also has local choral music, jazz, Afropop, rock, a hip-hop scene and, above all else, gospel.

In South Africa, almost 20 years' worth of freedom has proved that a recovering country can still produce sophisticated talent to the highest international standards. The rainbow nation continues to address social concerns, express sadness and bring joy. No one sound will ever identify South Africa, which can only be a good thing – the annual **South African Music Awards** (SAMA; www.samusicawards.co.za) is a multicategory, multitextured and very long ceremony as a result. Part of what makes South Africa so astonishing is its range. What follows is a by no means definitive look at the major genres, with their major players. So get humming, swing your hips and dive in.

The first musicians in South Africa were the San people, some 4000 years ago. They sang in a uniquely African click language, played rattles, drums and simple flutes and even their hunting bows.

A Potted History of South African Music

The Zulu, Xhosa and Sotho people have been singing and dancing for thousands of years – this is the music that attracted Paul Simon before he recorded his 1988 album *Graceland* – just as the Venda (and in Lesotho, the Basotho) have been playing their *mbiras* (thumb pianos) and reed pipes. There are eight distinct 'tribal' traditions in South Africa, and democracy has seen a resurgence in traditional musicians making very traditional music. But from the earliest colonial times to the present day, South Africa's music has created and reinvented itself from a mixture of older local and imported styles. Most of the popular ones use either Zulu a-capella singing or harmonic *mbaqanga* as a vocal base, ensuring that whatever the instrument – and the banjo, violin, concertina and electric guitar have all had a profound influence – the sound stays proudly, resolutely African.

Ever wondered why the chord sequences of many South African songs seem familiar? Blame the church: the Protestant missionaries of the 19th century developed a choral tradition that, in tandem with the country's first formal music education, South African composers would blend with traditional harmonic patterns. Enoch Sontonga's 1897 hymn 'Nkosi Sikelel, i Afrika' (God Bless Africa), originally written in Xhosa, is now the country's national anthem. Today the gospel movement is the major industry player. Gloria Bosman, Sibongile Khumalo, Pinise Saul and other top black South African artists now working across a range of genres – classical, jazz, gospel, opera – started singing in mission-school choirs or in church. Others, such as redoubtable gospel superstar Rebecca Malope, crossed over from the shiny world of pop. One of Swaziland's biggest gospel acts is the Ncandweni Christ Ambassadors, fronted by parliamentarian Timothy Myeni.

Zulu music's veteran exponents Ladysmith Black Mambazo – wrongly considered 'typical' South African music by many Westerners, thanks to their rapid-fire album releases and relentless international touring schedule – exemplify the way indigenous harmonies were neatly mixed with the sounds of European and African church choirs (a vocal style known as mbube). In the same way that much contemporary South African art was born from oppression, Ladysmith's 'tiptoe' *isicathamiya* music, with its high-kicking, soft-stepping dance, has its origins in all-male miner's hostels in Natal province in the 1930s, with workers at pains not to wake their bosses. *Isicathamiya* choirs still appear in weekly competitions in Johannesburg (Jo'burg) and Durban; such choirs, or versions thereof, often busk South African city streets.

Kwela music, like most modern South African styles, came out of the townships. Kwela, meaning 'jump up', was the instruction given to those about to be thrown into police vans during raids. Once-infamous areas like Soweto, Sharpeville, District Six and Sophiatown gave rise to urban, pan-tribal genres, mostly inspired by music coming in (or back) from America, such as jazz, swing, jive and soul. Black South Africans added an urban spin: kwela, with its penny whistles (an instrument evolved

MAKING MUSICAL HISTORY

Featuring music and interviews by Abdullah Ibrahim, Hugh Masekela and Miriam Makeba among others, Lee Hirsch's *Amandla! A Revolution in Four-Part Harmony* (2003) explores the role of music in the fight against apartheid. Made over nine years, this is a deeply affecting film.

Pascale Lamche's *Sophiatown* (2003) looks at Jo'burg's bustling Sophiatown, the Harlem of South Africa. Home to many artists and musicians, it was flattened for redevelopment in the 1950s. Its archival footage and interviews make for compulsive viewing.

The 2006 Oscar-winning township drama *Tsotsi* features a soundtrack composed by kwaito star Zola (who also plays local gang boss Fela), as well as haunting tracks by singer-songwriter Vusi Mahlasela (*Music From the Motion Picture Tsotsi*, Milan Records).

In the Time of Cannibals: The Word Music of South Africa's Basotho Migrants (1994) is a legendary tome by ethnomusicologist David B Coplan, who focuses on the sung oral poetry of the workers who migrate from Lesotho to the mines and cities of South Africa.

from the reed flutes of indigenous cattle herders) and one-string bass became sax-jive, also known as *mbaqanga*. *Marabi* soul took off in the 1970s. 'Bubblegum' pop dominated the 1980s. Kwaito, South Africa's very own hip hop, exploded in the 1990s and remains, apart from gospel, rap and a burgeoning R&B scene, the country's most popular genre. Kwaito superstar and TV presenter Zola even has his own media company, Zola 7, and clothing range.

America and Europe were the inspiration for white South African artists. Sixties phenomenon Four Jacks and a Jill were pure Western pop. British punk inspired 1970s working-class outfits á la Wild Youth. The 1980s saw a crossover of black and white musicians: Johnny Clegg and his former bands Juluka and Savuka used a fusion of white rock and pop with traditional Zulu music to challenge racist restrictions and set a precedent for others. Grunge helped shape the likes of Scooters Union, the Springbok Nude Girls and other 1990s guitar bands. The likes of Seether, Prime Circle and former Springbok frontman Arno Carstens means that rock continues to, well, rock the country today. Afrikaans music – through Buckfever Underground, Chris Chameleon, Steve Hofmeyr and Valiant Swart – continues its renaissance. And then there's the huge cutting-edge dance scene: house, techno, acid jazz, R&B, dancehall and all grooves in between, often with live elements thrown in.

The effects of apartheid on lives and culture are still sorely felt; musicians such as jazz legend and former exile Hugh Masekela stress the need for continued vigilance. Award-winning protest singer Vusi 'The Voice' Mahlasela was asked to perform at Mandela's inauguration in 1994 and continues to spread Mandela's message as an official ambassador to Mandela's HIV/AIDS initiative, 46664. The creation of a black-owned, black-run music industry and distribution network is still being fought for (resistance by moguls from the old-school white biz has been fierce), but is vital nonetheless. South African music still needs to be Africanised. In the meantime, the music of the resistance has maintained its fire by changing its focus: other scourges – such as HIV/AIDS, poverty, the abuse of women and children – are being written about, talked about and sung about. Opportunities abound in the current climate of cultural and artistic expression.

In Swaziland, where enthusiastically polygamous absolute monarch King Mswati regularly enjoys watching thousands of bare-breasted virgins dance about in the ancient but controversial reed-dance ceremony, things aren't quite so liberal. Mswati has long hosted fundraising concerts that feature both international stars (such as Eric Clapton and Erykah Badu) and local acts. Music, he has said, 'is a healing weapon for a depressed soul as well as an expression of joy'. And indeed, music pulses strongly in Swaziland, courtesy of everyone from African house DJ Simza and female rapper Pashu – aka Princess Sikhanyiso, King Mswati's eldest daughter – to Franco-Swazi jazzers Lilanga and sweet-voiced soul singer Bholoja.

Up in Lesotho, the hills and valleys are alive with the sound of music. The Basotho people love their songs and instruments: children in villages harmonise their hearts out in choirs; shepherd boys play their *lekolulo* flutes and sing in pure, pitch-perfect voices; women play the stringed *thomo;* and men the *setolo-tolo,* a sort of extended Jew's harp that's played using the mouth. *Famo* is a contemporary Sesotho style featuring accordion and oil-can drum.

In South Africa, however, boundaries are down. Styles are cross-pollinating; many genres, especially jazz and Afro-house, are booming and venues are following suit. Democracy, so bitterly won, has never sounded so sweet.

MUSIC A POTTED HISTORY OF SOUTH AFRICAN MUSIC

MINSTREL CARNIVAL

The Cape Town Minstrel Carnival, or Kaapse Klopse, takes place in the city on 2 January. Some 13,000 coloured minstrels take part, dressed in bright satin outfits, sporting boaters and painted faces. They compete for singing, dancing and costume prizes in a tradition that dates back to the late 19th century.

South African Musical Styles

Marabi

In the early 20th century, travelling African American minstrel shows, vaudeville acts, ragtime piano players and gospel groups impressed local audiences in the growing cities of Cape Town and Jo'burg. Urbanisation had a domino effect on musical styles: visiting American jazz artists and records by the likes of Louis Armstrong and Duke Ellington kick-started what would later become the South African jazz scene. By the 1920s and '30s the urban ghettos were singing and swinging to a defining, dangerous (in Sotho it means 'gangster') small-band sound: *marabi*.

Played on cheap pedal organs and keyboards with accompaniment from pebble-filled cans, *marabi* flooded illegal township shebeens (unlicensed bars) and dancehalls. Its siren call got people in and drinking, but it also offered some dignity and consolation to the oppressed working-class areas where it was played. *Marabi's* trancelike rhythms and cyclical harmonies had links to American Dixieland and ragtime; subsequent decades saw the addition of penny whistle, drums, banjo and a big-band swing, even bebop aesthetic.

Marabi made its way into the jazz-dance bands that produced the first generation of professional black musicians: the Jazz Maniacs, Merry Blackbirds and Jazz Revellers. Often referred to simply (and not always correctly) as 'African jazz' or 'jive', *marabi* went on to spawn other styles. One of these was kwela.

Paul Simon's *Graceland* album has sold more than seven million copies worldwide and, despite the controversy over the breaking of sanctions, was vital in alerting the rest of the world to the music of South Africa.

Kwela

Kwela was the first popular South African style to make the world sit up and take notice. Initially played on acoustic guitar, banjo, one-string bass and, most importantly, the penny whistle, kwela was taken up by kids with no access to horns and pianos but keen to put their own spin on American swing. Groups of tin-flautists would gather to play on street corners in white areas, with the danger of arrest (for creating a 'public disturbance') upping the music's appeal and attracting rebellious white kids known as 'ducktails'. Many such groups were also lookouts for the shebeens.

Kwela combos gained a live following but little recording took place until 1954, when Spokes Mashinyane's 'Ace Blues' became the smash African hit of the year and sent white producers scurrying into the black market. Artists such as Sparks Nyembe and Jerry Mlotshwa became popular; the hit 'Tom Lark' by Elias Lerole and His Zig-Zag Flutes even

TOP 10 SOUTH AFRICAN ALBUMS

» *The Indestructible Beat of Soweto, Volumes 1–6* – various artists
» *Jazz in Africa, Volume 1* – Jazz Epistles
» *Her Essential Recordings* – Miriam Makeba
» *Hope* – Hugh Masekela
» *The Best of Mahlathini and the Mahotella Queens*
» *Shaka Zulu* – Ladysmith Black Mambazo
» *Ibokwe* – Thandiswa Mazwai
» *Acceptance Speech* – Hip Hop Pantsula
» *Naledi Yca Tsela (Guiding Star)* – Vusi Mahlasela
» *The One Love Movement on Banto Biko Street* – Simphiwe Dana

crossed over to Britain, where – probably because of its similarity to skiffle – it stayed in the charts for 14 weeks.

In the early 1960s Mashinyane introduced the saxophone to kwela with his song 'Big Joe Special', ending the penny-whistle boom and creating sax-jive. Sax-jive quickly became *mbaqanga*.

Mbaqanga

The saxophone became vital to jazz music, which, much to the dismay of white kwela fans, was now limited to performances in the townships. *Mbaqanga* ('easy money') had its innovators: Joseph Makwela and Marks Mankwane of celebrated session players the Makhona Tshole Band added electric guitars to the cascading rhythms – notably a funky, muscular bass – while sax player and producer West Nkosi set the pace. This hugely popular electric sound backed singers whose vocal style was later christened '*mqashiyo*' (after a dance style), even though it was really no different from *mbaqanga*.

Mbaqanga's idiosyncratic vocals echoed 1950s groups such as the Manhattan Brothers and Miriam Makeba's Skylarks, groups who copied African American doo-wop outfits but used Africanised five-part harmonies instead of four. In the 1960s Aaron Lerole of Black Mambazo added his groaning vocals to the mix, but it was the growling bass of Simon 'Mahlathini' Nkabinde and his sweet-voiced Mahotella Queens (backed by the Makhona Tshole Band) who would inspire a generation, including Izintombi Zeze Manje Manje and the Boyoyo Boys who would be sampled by British producer/chancer Malcolm McLaren on the 1981 British number one, 'Double Dutch'. The Mahotella Queens – sans Mahlathini – are still going strong.

Mbaqanga remains an important force in South African music, its influence apparent in everything from soul and reggae to R&B, kwaito and, of course, jazz.

Jazz

Structurally, harmonically and melodically distinctive, the force that is South African jazz started as an underground movement and became a statement of protest and identity. In the hands of such talented exiled stars as singer Miriam 'Mama Africa' Makeba, pianist Abdullah Ibrahim (formerly Dollar Brand) and trumpeter Hugh Masekela, it was famously an expatriate music that represented the suffering of a people. Legendary outfit the Blue Notes – led by Chris McGregor and featuring saxophonist Dudu Pukwana – helped change the face of European jazz after relocating to the UK. Jazzers who stayed behind kept a low profile while developing new sounds and followings with, variously, jazz-rock fusion, Latin and even Malay crossovers.

World-renowned exiles who returned home after the end of the anti-apartheid cultural boycott had to work hard to win back local audiences. Most now enjoy healthy followings – with Makeba having passed away in 2008 aged 76, Masekela remains his country's most enduring musical

Trumpeter and vocalist Hugh Masekela remains South Africa's most successful jazz export and most prolific recording artist. Although exiled for many years, he returned in 1990 and is still making music.

MAJOR MUSIC FESTIVALS

March Cape Town International Jazz Festival (p67; www.capetownjazzfest.com)

April Morija Arts & Cultural Festival, near Maseru, Lesotho (p472; www.morijafest.com)

May Bush Fire Festival, Malkerns Valley, Swaziland (p495; www.bush-fire.com)

June National Arts Festival, Grahamstown, Eastern Cape (p194; www.nafest.co.za)

August Joy of Jazz Festival, Johannesburg (p321; www.joyofjazz.co.za)

September Arts Alive, Johannesburg (p321; www.artsalive.co.za)

ambassador – in what is a thriving mainstream scene. Frequent festivals, often featuring top overseas acts, are providing platforms (among the best is the Cape Town International Jazz Festival each April) and the South African media is lending its support.

Well-known locals are moving jazz forward, working with DJs, artists, poets and dance companies. Coltrane-esque saxophonist Zim Ngqawana (who led a group of 100 drummers, singers and dancers at Nelson Mandela's inauguration in 1994) is drawing on folk and rural traditions as well as Indian, avant garde and classical music. His former sideman, pianist Andile Yenana, combines the traditional and experimental with Monk-ish flair. Renowned guitarist Jimmy Dludlu, a sort of African George Benson, takes time out to work with music-school graduates. Lesotho-born Tsopo 'The Village Pope' Tshola has made an astounding comeback. The likes of female vocalists Sibongile Khumalo, Judith Sephumo and jazz fusionist Simphiwe Dana (proclaimed the 'new Miriam Makeba'), are making their mark. Many are enjoying success in another genre with common roots: gospel.

Gospel

The music industry's biggest market (bolstered by the country's 80% Christian black population), South Africa's gospel is an amalgam of European choral music, American influences, Zulu a-cappella singing and other African traditions incorporated within the church (Zionist, Ethiopian, Pentecostal and Apostolic). All joy, colour and exuberance, rhythm, passion and soul, gospel choirs perform throughout South Africa, lifting the roofs off big, formal venues and community halls alike. The 24-piece ensemble and overseas success story Soweto Gospel Choir (which won a Grammy award in 2008 for their album *African Spirit*), like many big choirs, features a band with drummers and dancers.

This vast genre is divided into both traditional gospel – as personified by the heavyweight International Pentecostal Church Choir (IPCC) and others such as Solly Moholo, Hlengiwe Mhlaba and Jabu Hlongwane – and contemporary gospel. Beacons of the latter include tiny diva Rebecca (who also sings in the traditional style), multiplatinum KwaMashu Deborah 'Debs' Fraser, Reverend Benjamin Dube ('the Gospel Maestro') and pastor and former street kid Andile Ka Majola. Popular Swazi gospel groups include France Dlamini, Shongwe & Khuphuka and the aforementioned Ncandweni Christ Ambassadors.

Gospel also comprises much of the oeuvre of Ladysmith Black Mambazo (whose album *Ilembe: Honoring Shaka Zulu* scooped them the 2009 Grammy Award for Best Traditional World Music Album). Their Zulu *isicathamiya* music is a prime example of the way traditional South African music has appropriated Western sounds to produce unique musical styles.

SOWETO GOSPEL CHOIR

The Soweto Gospel Choir (www.sowetogospelchoir. com) is hugely successful. They tour the world, performed at the 2010 FIFA World Cup and Desmond Tutu's 80th birthday in 2011, and have appeared with Diana Ross, Celine Dion, Baaba Maal, Peter Gabriel, Bono and U2.

Neotraditional Music

Away from the urban life of the townships and the cities' recording studios, traditional musicians from the Sotho, Zulu, Pedi and Shangaan regions were creating dynamic social music. By the 1930s many were mixing call-and-response singing with the dreamy 10-button concertina, an instrument that has made a comeback in Zulu pop. The Sotho took up the accordion (accordion players and groups still abound in Lesotho); the Pedi the German autoharp; and the Zulu embraced the guitar.

Maskanda (or *maskandi*) is a form of rhythmic and repetitive guitar picking born through the Zulu experience of labour migration. Many made do with an *igogogo,* an instrument fashioned from an oil can; *maskanda* stalwart Shiyani Ngcobo still uses the *igogogo* in his live sets. Today's top-selling *maskanda* acts include the poetic Bhekumuzi, massively popular duo Shwi No Mtkehala and virtuoso guitarist Phuzekhemisi, whose shows often include dozens of singers, dancers and instrumentalists.

The upbeat and vaguely Latin-sounding Tsonga (formerly Shangaan) music tends to feature a male leader backed by, variously, a female chorus, guitars, synths, percussion and an unabashed disco beat. Best-known acts include Doctor Sithole, George Maluleke, Conny Chauke and Fanie Rhingani.

Young Xhosa artist Lungiswa is one of the few female South African musicians to play the *mbira* in her traditional/urban crossovers. Veteran singer Busi Mhlongo (like Tsepo Tsola, now addiction-free after support from Hugh Masekela's Maapsa drug-rehabilitation program) fuses the traditional Zulu sound with hip hop and kwaito.

In Lesotho, a group of shepherds known as Sotho Sounds play instruments made from rubbish: *qwadinyana* (one-string fiddle), *katara* (guitars) and drums fashioned out of disused oil cans, car tyres, twigs and a kitchen sink. A triumph at Britain's Womad Festival, they are based in Malealea, where they continue to compose and rehearse (and still perform for guests of Malealea Lodge).

But again, it's in South Africa that roots are being mixed with every sound imaginable, from country, blues, rap (check out Hip Hop Pantsula, Molemi, Pro-Kid) and house (see DJs Innocentia, Black Coffee, Mbuso and Vinni da Vinci) to rock, Afro-house, reggae and soul.

Maskanda acts and *maskanda* DJs are a regular feature of Durban's harbourside BAT Centre (www.batcentre.co.za).

Soul & Reggae

The American-led soul music of the 1960s had a huge impact on township teenagers. The local industry tried various cheap imitations; the few South African 'soul' groups that made it did so on the back of a blend of soul and *marabi,* such as the Movers, or soul and electric bass *mbaqanga,* such as the Soul Brothers, a band who spawned dozens of

---

ESSENTIAL LISTENING

» marabi – From Marabi to Disco, Various Artists (Gallo, South Africa)

» kwela – Spokes Mashiyane, King Kwela (Gallo, South Africa)

» mbaqanga – Soul Brothers, Kuze Kuse (Gallo, South Africa)

» jazz – Sheer Jazz, Various Artists (Sheer Sound, South Africa)

» gospel – Tales of Gospel SA (Sheer Sound, South Africa)

» neotraditional music – Sthandwa, Phuzekhemisi (Gallo, South Africa)

» soul and reggae – Respect, Lucky Dube (Gallo, South Africa)

» bubblegum, kwaito and current trends – New Construction, Bongo Maffin (Gallo, South Africa)

imitators and are still going strong today. Contemporary South African soul is often filed under *mbaqanga:* the genre from which evergreen reggae star Lucky Dube – shot dead in a car-jacking in Johannesburg in 2007 – sprang into another style of music entirely. Dube's legacy aside, in South Africa reggae is often subsumed into other genres such as ragga and kwaito: the redoubtable Bongo Maffin throws kwaito, house, reggae, ragga, gospel and hip hop into the pot.

Homegrown R&B has also surged ahead: former choir boys Tumi (hailed as the 'South African Usher') and Loyiso Bala are huge stars. The wonderful Thandiswa Mazwai (Bongo Maffin's erstwhile frontwoman) nods in the R&B direction in her album *Ibokhwe*. The soulful sounds of DJ, singer and media player Unathi Nkayi seem to be everywhere – as does the Afro-fusion of upbeat outfit Freshlyground.

Bubblegum, Kwaito & Current Trends

The disco that surfaced during the 1970s came back – slick, poppy and Africanised – in the 1980s as 'bubblegum'. Vocally led and aimed squarely at the young, this electronic dance style owed a debt to *mbaqanga* as well as America. What the Soul Brothers started, superstars such as the late Brenda Fassie, Sello 'Cicco' Twala and Yvonne Chaka Chaka refined. Bubblegum's popularity waned in the 1990s, and in its place exploded kwaito (kwi-to, meaning 'hot').

The music of young, black, urban South Africa, kwaito is a rowdy mix of everything from bubblegum, hip hop, R&B and ragga to *mbaqanga*, traditional, jazz, and British and American house music. It is also a fashion statement, a state of mind and a lifestyle. Chanted or sung in a mixture of English, Zulu, Sesotho and the street slang *Isicamtho* (usually over programmed beats and backing tapes), kwaito's lyrics range from the anodyne to the fiercely political. A unique fusion, kwaito has caught the imagination of post-apartheid South Africa and is evolving even as the 'Is kwaito dead?' debate rages on. Acts such as Zola, Boom Shaka and Mapaputsi remain major players, while the current crop includes Mandoza, Brickz, Spikiri, and Durban Kwaito Music (DKM) artist Thokozani 'L'vovo Derrango' Ndlovu.

Freedom of expression for black youth is no longer the luxury it was under apartheid. The first place this freedom became visible was the music scene – a scene that is still thriving, creating and reinventing itself in ever-increasing and exciting ways.

Regional Festivals

» February: Up The Creek (www. upthecreek. co.za; on the Breede River near Swellendam, Western Cape)

» April: Splashy Fen (www. splashyfen.co.za; near Underberg, Kwazulu-Natal)

» August: Oppikoppi (www. oppikoppi.co.za; Northam, North West Province)

Food & Drink

Take a bit of black magic, a dash of Dutch heartiness, a pinch of Indian spice and a smidgin of Malay mystery and what you get is an amazing array of cultures all simmering away in the *potjie* (pot) of culinary influences that is South African cuisine.

The earliest inhabitants survived on animals hunted for the pot, seafood gathered from the beaches and sea, and myriad vegetables and tubers. When it became necessary to have fresh vegetables and fruit available for passing ships, the Dutch arrived and planted their famous garden. Their rich cuisine was infused with nutmeg, cinnamon and cassia, as well as rice from their colonies in the east. Malay slaves from Madagascar, Java and Indonesia added to the mix, providing spicier accompaniments to the bland fare on offer.

The Cape was the birthplace of South African cuisine, but KwaZulu-Natal is important too: there were blacks who migrated from other African countries, British settlers, and Mauritians who planted exotic fruits and introduced their spicy tomato sauces. And when the Indian indentured labourers arrived in the mid-19th century, they brought their spices with them. What's exciting is to be aware of the cultural influences that abound in South African cuisine and explore all the options.

While chefs are looking to their inherited culinary roots with renewed energy, there's a back-to-basics move, too: the most innovative chefs, like Shaun Schoeman at Fyndraai Restaurant on the Solms-Delta wine estate (p107) in Franschhoek, are becoming market gardeners. They're planting gardens to have instant access to perfect vegetables and herbs to enhance the flavours of their creations. And it's not just the chefs: the public, too, are seeking out artisanal foods and drinks at neighbourhood markets, craft breweries and boutique cheese makers, all the while conscious of green ethics and sustainability.

There's a happy marriage here: today's chefs and their public are respectful of the intoxicating flavours South Africa is famous for, and enthusiastic about making those flavours surprising, colourful and mouth-wateringly modern.

Need some *padkos* for a long journey? The classic South African choice would be a box or two of natural fruit juices along with biltong, dried sausage, redskin peanuts and dried guava.

COOKING COURSES

Cape Town, a gourmet's paradise, is the best place for cooking courses. A couple to try:

Andulela (☎021-790 2592; www.andulela.com) This company offers a half-day Cape Malay course in the Bo-Kaap (R520) and an African cooking safari (R695) in the township of Kayamandi where you can learn to prepare traditional Xhosa foods.

Kopanong (☎021-361 2084; www.kopanong-township.co.za) Thope Lekau offers a half-day cook-up (R350) at this Khayelitsha-based B&B where groups of four or more can learn to cook African style.

Cultural Staples & Specialities

Trout in Mpumalanga, mealies (or mielies) in Gauteng, *umngqusho* in the Eastern Cape, Free State venison and cherries, maize or sorghum porridge in Swaziland and Lesotho, Durban curries, crayfish on the West Coast and succulent Karoo lamb – the variety is boundless.

The Afrikaner history of trekking led to their developing portable food: hence the traditional biltong (dried strips of salted meat, called *umncweba* in Swaziland), rusks (hard biscuits) for dunking, dried fruit and *boerewors* (sausages) where meat is preserved with spices and vinegar, also found dried.

Cape cuisine is a fusion of Malay influence on Dutch staples, and so you'll find dishes such as *bobotie*, chicken pie and *bredies*. Desserts can be the rich *malva* pudding or *melktert*, usually brightened up with a sprinkling of cinnamon (all described, p537).

Black cuisine is founded on the staples of maize, sorghum and beans, enhanced with *morogo* or *imfino* leaves, cooked with onions, peanuts and chilli.

South African Indian cooking brings delicious curries and *breyanis* (similar to biryanis) and also fuses with Malay cooking, so that you'll get hotter curries in Durban and milder ones in Cape Town.

What brings everyone together is the cross-cultural South African institution of 'braaing' (barbecuing). A social occasion, the braai usually features meat and vegetables – lamb chops or *sosaties* (lamb skewers), *boerewors,* corn cobs and sweet potatoes – and can be found everywhere from the townships to the farmlands to the cities.

Staples

Mealie pap (maize porridge) is the most widely eaten food in South Africa, as well as in Swaziland and Lesotho. It's thinner or stiffer depending on where you eat it, and is completely bland. However, it's ideal if you want something filling and economical, and can be quite satisfying served with a good sauce or stew. *Samp* (dried and crushed maize

MOTOHO

In Lesotho, look for *motoho* – a fermented sorghum porridge. Swazi variants include *sishwala* (maize and bean porridge, usually eaten with meat or vegetables) and *incwancwa* (slightly fermented maize porridge).

SASSI

With more and more people turning to fish as a healthy alternative source of protein, there are fears that stocks around South Africa's coastlines (and beyond) are not sustainable. Overfishing and the use of inappropriate fishing methods are taking their toll on the populations of many fish.

With innovative foresight, South Africa's branch of the World Wide Fund for Nature (WWF) set up the Southern Africa Sustainable Seafood Initiative (Sassi) in 2004 to educate people about which fish are sustainable (Green List), which should be eaten with caution (Orange List) and which are so endangered that catching them is against the law (Red List).

You'll be pleased to know that most of the fish that you're likely to find on a South African restaurant menu is on the Green List: snoek, yellowtail, tuna, dorado, angelfish, hake and West Coast crayfish. Unlikely to be able to sustain heavy fishing are Orange List candidates perlemoen (abalone), haarders, prawns, red roman, white stumpnose, geelbek, kingklip and swordfish. While restaurateurs are allowed to sell them, you might want to consider your actions. Absolute no-nos are galjoen, white musselcracker, steenbras, stumpnose and blue-fin tuna.

Fortunately, you don't need to remember every fish on the lists to make an informed, pro-environment choice. Simply send an SMS with the name of the fish to ☎079-499 8795 and you'll be told right away whether it's a good choice or not.

For more information, see www.wwfsassi.co.za.

kernels) and beans fulfil the same role, making an ideal base for vegetable or meat stews.

Rice and potatoes are widely available and you'll often be served both on the same plate. From *roosterkoek* (bread traditionally cooked on the braai) to panini, bread in South Africa is good and comes in infinite varieties.

Meat

In certain areas of South Africa meat is considered a 'staple'. Afrikaners will eat lamb chops or beef mince for breakfast. Alongside the more traditional beef and lamb, you'll find game meats such as ostrich, warthog and kudu. Steaks in particular are excellent.

Seafood

Considering the fact that South Africa is surrounded by two oceans, it has a remarkably modest reputation as a seafood-lover's destination. Yet Cape Town, the West Coast and the Garden Route have some delicious fish dishes. Among the highlights: lightly spiced fish stews, *snoekbraai* (grilled snoek), mussels, oysters and seawater crayfish. Pickled fish is popular in Cape cuisine, while in Swaziland prawns are a common feature on restaurant menus, courtesy of nearby Mozambique.

Drinks

Water

Tap water is generally safe in South Africa's cities. However, in rural areas (or anywhere that local conditions indicate that water sources may be contaminated), as well as throughout Swaziland and Lesotho, stick to bottled water and purify any stream water.

Beer

Beer is the national beverage. The world's largest brewer, SAB Miller, is based in Johannesburg, so there's no shortage of brands, with Castle and Black Label the best sellers and Peroni a favourite. Boutique brewers are in vogue: look for Darling Brewery and Jack Black. Ciders are also popular, as are cocktails and shooters. Beer comes in bottles (or cans) from around R20, and bars serve draught from around R25.

Wine

South African wine debuted in 1659. Since then, it's had time to age to perfection, and is both of a high standard and reasonably priced. Dry whites are particularly good – try sauvignon blanc, riesling, colombard and chenin blanc – while popular reds include cabernet sauvignon, pinotage (a local cross of pinot and cinsaut, which was known as hermitage), shiraz and pinot noir. Wines are all certified and labels reflect their estate, vintage and origin. In addition, although South African sparkling wine may not be called champagne, a number of producers use chardonnay and pinot noir blends and the méthode champenoise.

Wine prices average from around R50 in a bottle store, twice that in a restaurant. Wine by the glass is often available from around R35.

Where to Eat & Drink

If you're after fine dining in magnificent surroundings, head to the Winelands. Along the Western Cape coast, open-air beachside eateries serve fish braais under the stars. A highlight of visiting a township is experiencing some family-style cooking in a B&B. In addition to speciality restaurants, every larger town has several places offering homogenised Western fare at homogenised prices (from about R55). Almost all restaurants are licensed.

In Lesotho, watch for white or yellow flags hung in villages to advertise home brew – yellow is usually for maize beer and white for *joala* (sorghum beer).

Best Craft Breweries

» Porcupine Quill
» Eversons Cider
» Birkenhead
» Darling Brewery
» Jack Black

Published annually, the *John Platter Wine Guide* is the quintessential guide to South African wines. See also www.platter-wineguide.co.za where there's a host of information on Cape wine routes.

FOOD & DRINK VEGETARIANS & VEGANS

The national pastime and the main food-centred social event is the braai (barbecue). Even the public holiday officially known as Heritage Day (24 September) has been re-branded National Braai Day.

If you're invited to a braai, it's customary to take along a bottle of your favourite tipple. Dress is casual and the atmosphere relaxed. If you're female, do *not* poke the fire or pick up the tongs – men do the cooking, beer in hand, while women make the salads.

All towns have cafes, where you can enjoy a cappuccino and sandwich or other light fare. In rural areas, 'cafe' (*kaffie*) usually refers to a small corner shop selling soft drinks, chips, basic groceries and braai wood. Most places are open from about 8am to 5pm.

Large towns have a good selection of pubs and more-upmarket cocktail lounges. Franchised bars proliferate in urban areas, and most smaller towns have at least one hotel with a bar. In townships, things centre on shebeens – informal drinking establishments that were once illegal but are now merely unlicensed. Throughout South Africa, and in major towns in Lesotho and Swaziland, you can also buy alcoholic drinks at bottle stores and supermarkets (but not on Sundays).

Vegetarians & Vegans

South Africa is a meat-loving society, but most restaurants have at least one vegetarian option on the menu. In larger towns you might find a vegetarian restaurant. Cafes are good bets, as many will make vegetarian food to order. Indian and Italian restaurants are also useful, although many pasta sauces contain animal fat. Larger towns have health-food stores selling tofu, soy milk and other staples, and can point you towards vegetarian-friendly venues.

Eating vegan is more difficult: most nonmeat dishes contain cheese, and eggs and milk are common ingredients. Health-food shops are your best bet, though most are closed in the evenings and on Sundays. Larger supermarkets also stock soy products, and nuts and fruit are widely available. Look out for the bags of avocados sold along the roadside in KwaZulu-Natal.

In Lesotho and Swaziland, you'll find plenty of bean, peanut and other legume dishes, usually offered with vegetables.

Eat Your Words

Want to know *potjie* from *phutu*? Know your *skilpadjies* from your *sosaties*? Get behind the cuisine scene by getting to know the language.

Menu Decoder

It's unlikely that you'll see all of these items on the same menu, but they provide an insight into the diversity of South African cuisine.

Meat Dishes

bobotie – curried-mince pie topped with savoury egg custard, served on a bed of yellow rice with chutney
boerewors – spicy sausage, traditionally made of beef and pork plus seasonings and plenty of fat; an essential ingredient at any braai and often sold like hot dogs by street vendors
bredie – hearty Afrikaner pot stew, traditionally made with lamb and vegetables
breyani – fusion of Hindu and Cape Malay influences, this is a spicy, layered rice-and-lentil dish with meat, similar to the Indian biryani
eisbein – pork knuckles

Ukutya Kwasekhaya (home cooking) – Tastes from Nelson Mandela's Kitchen, by Xoliswa Ndoyiya, includes the traditional recipes enjoyed by Madiba. Xoliswa includes African recipes such as *umqusho* (maize and beans) and *umsila wenkomo* (oxtail stew).

frikkadel – fried meatball

mashonzha – name for mopane worms (see next entry) in Venda, where they're served with *dhofi* (peanut sauce)

mopane worms – caterpillars found on mopane trees; legs are removed, and the caterpillar is dried and served as a crunchy snack; see also '*mashonzha*'

potjiekos – meat and vegetables layered in a three-legged pot, slowly simmered over a fire, often served with *potjiebrood* (bread cooked in another pot)

skilpadjies – (literally 'little tortoises') lamb's liver wrapped in caul fat and braaied

smilies – slang term for boiled and roasted sheep heads; often sold in rural areas

sosatie – lamb cubes, marinated with garlic, tamarind juice and curry powder, then skewered with onions and apricots, and grilled; originally Malay; also made with chicken

venison – often springbok, but could be kudu, warthog, blesbok or any other game meat

vienna – hot dog sausage, usually pork

waterblommetjie bredie – Cape Malay stew of lamb with Cape pondweed (*Aponogeton distachyos*) flowers, lemon juice and sorrel

Capture the flavours of South Africa with Franschhoek chef Reuben Riffel's latest cookbook *Reuben Cooks Local*. Food stories are woven through the recipes, all celebrating superb local produce.

Curries, Condiments & Spices

atchar – Cape Malay pickle of fruits and vegetables, flavoured with garlic, onion and curry

chakalaka sauce – spicy tomato-based sauce seasoned with onions, *peri peri*, green peppers and curry, and used to liven up pap and other dishes

curry – just as good as in India; head to Durban if you like your curry spicy, and to Cape Town (Bo-Kaap) for a milder, Malay version

peri peri/piri piri – hot chilli

samoosa – spicy Indian pastry filled with potatoes and peas; sometimes with mince or chicken

Breads & Sweets

koeksuster – plaited doughnut dripping in honey, which are very gooey and figure-enhancing

konfyt – fruit preserve

malva – delicious sponge dessert; sometimes called vinegar pudding, since it's traditionally made with apricot jam and vinegar

melktert – rich, custardlike tart made with milk, eggs, flour and cinnamon

roosterkoek – bread traditionally cooked on the braai

rusk – twice-cooked biscuit to be dipped in coffee or as a snack and much better than those given to teething babies

vetkoek – deep-fried dough ball sometimes stuffed with mince; called *amagwinya* in Xhosa

Grains, Legumes & Vegetables

amadumbe – yamlike potato; a favourite staple in KwaZulu-Natal

imbasha – Swazi fried delicacy of roasted maize and nuts

imfino – Xhosa dish of mealie meal and vegetables

mealie – cob of corn, popular when braaied

mealie meal – finely ground maize

mealie pap – maize porridge; a Southern African staple, best eaten with sauce or stew

morogo – leafy greens, usually wild spinach, boiled, seasoned and served with pap

pap & sous – maize porridge with a tomato and onion sauce or meat gravy

phutu – Zulu dish of crumbly maize porridge, often eaten with soured milk; called *umphokoqo* in Xhosa

samp – mix of maize and beans; see *umngqusho*

tincheki – boiled pumpkin cubes with sugar, common in Swaziland

ting – sorghum porridge, popular among the Tswana

umngqusho – samp (dried and crushed maize kernels) boiled, then mixed with beans, salt and oil, and simmered; a Xhosa delicacy (called *nyekoe* in Sotho)

umvubo – sour milk and mealie meal

Fish

kingklip – excellent firm-fleshed fish, usually pan-fried; South Africa's favourite fish

line fish – fresh fish caught on a line

snoek – firm-fleshed migratory fish that appears off the Cape in June and July; served smoked, salted or curried, and good braaied

Drinks

mampoer – home-distilled brandy made from peaches and prickly pear

rooibos – literally 'red bush' (Afrikaans); caffeine-free herbal tea that has therapeutic qualities

springbok – cocktail featuring crème de menthe topped with Amarula cream liqueur

steen – chenin blanc; most common variety of white wine

sundowner – any drink, but typically alcohol, drunk at sunset

umnqombothi – Xhosa for rough-and-ready, home-brewed beer; called *umqombotsi* or *tjwala* in Swaziland

witblitz – 60-proof 'white lightning'; a traditional Boer spirit distilled from fruit

Hungry for a quick bite? Try a roasted mealie (cob of corn) or Durban's filling *bunny chow* (curry-to-go: half a loaf of bread, scooped out and filled with curry).

People & Culture

The National Psyche

Dubbed the rainbow nation by Archbishop Desmond Tutu in 1991, South African society has become more homogeneous in the almost 20 years since the country's first democratic elections. There's still a long way to go, perhaps even a generation or two, and there are flare-ups that increase racial tension, such as the hate-speech perpetrated by the likes of Julius Malema, the controversial Black Economic Empowerment and affirmative action, government corruption and the disparity between rich and poor. However, people tend to live and work much more harmoniously these days; the nation is divided less by colour than by class.

While crime continues to undermine South Africa's reputation as a tourism destination, it's important to keep it in perspective. South Africa is one of the most inspiring and hope-filled places on the continent. Visiting provides a rare chance to experience a nation that is rebuilding itself after profound change. As a backdrop to all this is the magnificent natural scenery, and the remarkably deep bond – perhaps best expressed in the country's literature – that most South Africans feel for their land.

Lesotho and Swaziland have both experienced political problems in recent years, but the countries' biggest concern is that they have some of the world's highest HIV/AIDS infection rates.

> **Unemployment in Southern Africa**
>
> » Lesotho: 45%
> » Swaziland: 40%
> » South Africa: 48%

Population & People

South Africa, Lesotho and Swaziland together form a beautiful and rich tapestry of cultures and ethnic groups.

In addition to their cultural roots, the three countries also have fascinatingly complex and interlocking socio-economic compositions. South Africa's Gauteng province, which includes Johannesburg and Pretoria, is the economic engine of the country, generating more than half of South Africa's wealth. It's also the most densely populated and urbanised province. At the other end of the scale is the rural and underdeveloped Limpopo, where more than 30% of adults are illiterate.

Millions of immigrants from across the continent make their way to South Africa to take advantage of the country's powerhouse economy. While some arrive legally, many illegal immigrants live in Jo'burg's impoverished inner city, causing resentment among some South Africans who accuse the outsiders of taking jobs and creating crime.

Swaziland's socio-economic scene is almost completely wrapped up in that of its larger neighbour. Almost two-thirds of Swazi exports go to South Africa and more than 90% of goods and services are imported. Some 70% of Swazis live in rural areas and rely on subsistence farming for survival. Swazi culture is very strong and quite distinct from that of South Africa. The monarchy influences many aspects of life, from cultural ceremonies to politics. While some Swazis are proud of the royal traditions and suspicious of those who call for greater democracy, a growing

> *Sangomas* are the traditional healers of the South African people. These men and women are responsible for the physiological, psychological, emotional and spiritual well-being of their community.

number of human-rights and opposition activists believe power should be transferred from the king to the people.

Lesotho's main link with South Africa has been the mining industry. For most of the 20th century, Lesotho's main export was labour, with about 60% of males working in South Africa, primarily in mining. In the early 1990s, at least 120,000 Basotho men were employed by South African mines, and up to one-third of Lesotho's household incomes were from wages earned by the miners. When the mining industry was restructured from this period, the number of Lesotho miners was halved and many former miners returned home to Lesotho to join the ranks of the unemployed.

Beyond economics, different racial groups have complicated relationships. While much of the focus in South Africa has been on black and white relations, there is also friction and distrust between blacks, coloureds and South Africans of Indian descent. Yet, sometimes locals are surprisingly open when they talk about the stereotypes and prejudices that exist across various groups. Relations within the racial groups are also complex; ask a Zulu what he or she thinks about Xhosas or quiz English-speaking whites about their views on Afrikaners.

South Africans are not shy about referring to themselves as black, coloured or white. This can come as a bit of a shock for those from countries where such referrals to race are considered politically incorrect.

Population Groups

Black

The vast majority of South Africans – about 80% – are black Africans. Although subdivided into dozens of smaller groups, all ultimately trace their ancestry to the Bantu-speakers who migrated to Southern Africa in the early part of the 1st millennium AD. Due to the destruction and dispersal caused by the *difaqane* (forced migration) in the 19th century, and to the forced dislocations and distortions of the apartheid era, tribal affiliation tends to be much weaker in South Africa than in other areas of the continent.

Today, discussions generally focus on ethnolinguistic groupings. With the constitution's elevation of 11 languages to the status of 'official' lan-

SOUTHERN AFRICA'S MELTING POPULATION POT

There are few countries where racial and ethnic conflicts have been as turbulent and high profile as in South Africa. The country's heart pulses with the blood of diverse groups including the ancient San, 17th-century Dutch settlers, 19th-century British traders, Bantu-speaking African peoples, Indians, Indonesians, Chinese, Jews and Portuguese. Yet it is only since 1994 that there has been any significant degree of collaboration and peace between the various groups.

During the apartheid era, the government attempted to categorise everyone into one of four major groups. The classifications – black (at various times also called African, 'native' and 'Bantu'), coloured, Asian or white – were often arbitrary and highly contentious. They were used to regulate where and how people could live and work, and became the basis for institutionalised inequality and intolerance.

Today, discrimination based on wealth is threatening to replace racial discrimination. While the apartheid-era classification terms continue to be used, and we've used them throughout this book, they work only to a certain extent, and within each of the four major categories are dozens of subgroups that are even more subjective and less clearly defined.

Lesotho and Swaziland were never subject to racial categorisation. This, plus the fact that both countries were for the most part formed around a single tribal group (the Basotho in Lesotho and the Swazi in Swaziland), means that the constant awareness of racism that you'll encounter while travelling in South Africa is largely absent from these societies.

guage, the concept of ethnicity is also gaining a second wind. The largest ethnolinguistic group is the Nguni, which includes Zulu, Swazi, Xhosa and Ndebele peoples. Other major groups are the Sotho-Tswana, the Tsonga-Shangaan and the Venda.

The Zulu maintain the highest-profile ethnic identity, and 24% of South Africans speak Zulu as a first language. The second-largest group after the Zulu are the Xhosa, who have been extremely influential in politics. Nelson Mandela is Xhosa, as were many figures in the apartheid struggle, and Xhosa have traditionally formed the heart of the black professional class. About 18% of South Africa's population uses Xhosa as a first language.

Other major groups include the Basotho (found primarily in and around Lesotho and South Africa's Free State), the Swazi (most of whom are in Swaziland) and the Tswana (who live primarily in the provinces bordering Botswana and Namibia, and in Botswana itself). The Ndebele and Venda peoples are fewer in number, but have maintained very distinct cultures.

Coloured

During apartheid, 'coloured' was generally used as a catch-all term for anyone who didn't fit into one of the other racial categories. Despite this, a distinct coloured cultural identity has developed over the years – forged, at least in part, by whites' refusal to accept coloureds as equals, and coloureds' own refusal to be grouped socially with blacks.

Among the diverse ancestors of today's coloured population are Afrikaners and others of European descent, West African slaves, political prisoners and exiles from the Dutch East Indies, and some of South Africa's original Khoe-San peoples. One of the largest subgroups of coloureds is the Griqua.

Another major subgroup is the Cape Malays, with roots in places as widely dispersed as India, Indonesia and parts of East Africa. Most Cape Malays are Muslims and have managed to preserve their culture.

Today, most coloureds live in the Northern Cape and Western Cape, with significant populations also in KwaZulu-Natal. About 20% speak English as their first language. The vast majority – about 80% – are Afrikaans-speakers, and one of the oldest documents in Afrikaans is a Quran transcribed using Arabic script.

White

Most of South Africa's approximately 4.3 million whites (about 9% of South Africans) are either Afrikaans-speaking descendents of the early Dutch settlers or English-speakers. The Afrikaners, who mix German, French, British and other blood with their Dutch ancestry, constitute only about 13% of the country's total population. Yet they have had a disproportionate influence on South Africa's history. Rural areas of the country, with the exception of the Eastern Cape, KwaZulu-Natal and the former homelands, continue to be dominated by Afrikaners, who are united by language and by membership in the Dutch Reformed Church – the focal point of life in country towns.

While a few Afrikaners still dream of a *volkstaat* (an independent, racially pure Boer state), the urbanised middle class has become considerably more moderate. Interestingly, the further the distance between the horrors of the apartheid era and the 'new South Africa', the more room there is for Afrikaners to be proud of their heritage. One expression of this is the growing popularity of the Absa Klein Karoo National Arts Festival.

About two-thirds of South Africa's white English-speakers trace their roots to the English immigrants who began arriving in South Africa in the 1820s. Other white South Africans include about 70,000 Jews, a

Age of Iron, by JM Coetzee, is the tale of a lone elderly woman who is confronted by unexpected bloodshed. Coetzee's writing is exquisite and gives a sense of the violence and isolation of apartheid South Africa.

Greek community numbering 50,000-plus people and a similar amount of Portuguese.

Asian

About 98% of South Africa's almost 1.2 million Asians are Indians. Many are descended from the indentured labourers brought to KwaZulu-Natal in the 19th century, while others trace their ancestry to the free 'passenger Indians' who came to South Africa during the same period as merchants and business people. During apartheid, Indians were both discriminated against by whites and seen as white collaborators by some blacks.

Today's South African Indian population is primarily Hindu, with about 20% Muslims and small numbers of Christians. Close to 90% live in Durban and other urban areas of KwaZulu-Natal. Most speak English as a first language; Tamil or Hindi and Afrikaans are also spoken.

In addition to the Indians, there are more than 200,000 Chinese, concentrated primarily in Johannesburg, and small numbers of other East Asians.

> The Zulu word for grandmother is *gogo*. The *gogo* plays a vital role in many families and her monthly pension is often the only regular source of income for the extended family.

Women

South African women have enjoyed a uniquely high profile during the country's turbulent history. Women were at the centre of the anti-pass law demonstrations and bus boycotts of the 1950s, protesting under the slogan 'You strike the woman and you strike the rock', and women are also strongly represented in South Africa's current parliament. Almost half of government ministers are female. Women's rights are also guaranteed in the constitution, and the African National Congress (ANC) has a quota system for the party.

However, the daily reality for many South African women is very different, with poverty, sexual violence and HIV/AIDS overshadowing other gains. Sexual-violence statistics are particularly sobering. South Africa has the highest incidence of reported rape in the world, with approximately 55,000 cases of rape reported to the police annually.

Women are statistically more likely than men to be infected with HIV/AIDS, and many women become infected at an early age. Worsening the situation is the threat of sexual violence, which often undermines the ability of young women to ensure their partner is wearing a condom.

In Swaziland, women's rights have improved dramatically recently. The 2006 constitution guarantees women equal political, economic and social rights and reserves one-third of parliamentary seats for women. Traditional social systems, however, still discriminate against women, and one survey conducted by Unicef found that one-third of Swazi females had experienced sexual violence before they turned 18. Against this backdrop, it is estimated that more than 70% of small businesses in Swaziland are operated by women.

In Lesotho, women shouldered a big share of economic, social and family responsibilities while their husbands and male relatives went to work in the mines in South Africa. As mining jobs disappeared, the textile industry became an important part of Lesotho's economy, with about 90% of the new jobs going to women. Contrary to the trend elsewhere in the region, Basotho women are often better educated than their male counterparts, as many boys in rural areas are forced to tend cattle (or head off to South Africa to work), instead of spending time in the classroom.

> *Basali: Stories by and about Women in Lesotho*, edited by K Limakatso Kendall, provides good insights into Lesotho's rural life as seen through the eyes of local women.

RADIO

With 10 million radio sets and many more listeners, and 100 community radio stations broadcasting in all 11 official languages, radio is hugely popular. Try these stations:

» Y-FM 99.2 in Gauteng for a taste of the local version of hip hop, known as kwaito (township) music.

» 567 Cape Talk in Cape Town or Radio 702 in Gauteng for talk radio.

» 5FM for Top 40 hits.

Media

Having experienced decades of repression before apartheid ended in 1994, South Africa's media is coming into its own. The national broadcaster, SABC, is an important source of news for millions of South Africans, and is adjusting to its role as an independent voice. SABC currently has 18 radio stations and four TV channels.

Privately owned e-TV has a younger, funkier style as well as a smooth presentation.

South Africa's best-selling dailies are the *Daily Sun,* which has a circulation of about 302,000 and a readership of more than two million, followed by the *Star* and the *Sowetan.* They primarily sell to English-literate black readers; more than 50% of readers of the *Star* are black. The *Sowetan* in particular has a more sophisticated political and social outlook than most of the major white papers.

Swaziland's media, mostly government-controlled, includes the dailies the *Swazi Observer* (www.observer.org.sz) and the *Times of Swaziland* (www.times.co.sz). The Swaziland Broadcasting and Information Services delivers 18 hours daily of English radio programming.

Lesotho's media is in a healthier state, although the government still exercises considerable power. The *Mirror* and *Public Eye* are English-language weeklies; the only national radio station is state-owned Radio Lesotho, but private stations available in Maseru include MoAfrika FM. In both countries, TV is state-run.

South Africa ranks 4th in the world for representation of women in government (44.5%). The country is topped only by Rwanda, Andorra and Sweden.

Religion

Religion plays a central role in the lives of most people in South Africa, Lesotho and Swaziland and church attendance is generally high. Christianity is dominant in all three countries, with almost 80% of South Africans, a similar amount of Lesotho's population, and more than 60% of Swazis identifying themselves as Christians. Major South African denominations include the Dutch Reformed Churches, which have a national congregation of more than 3.5 million people and more than 1200 churches across the country, and the considerably more flamboyant Zion Christian Church (ZCC), with more than four million followers in South Africa, plus more in neighbouring countries including Swaziland.

About 15% of South Africans are atheist and agnostic, while Muslims, Hindus and Jews combined make up less than 6% of the population. Up to two-thirds of South Africa's Indians have retained their Hindu faith. Islam has a small but growing following, particularly in the Cape. There is a declining Jewish community of about 70,000 people, mostly in Jo'burg and the Cape.

African traditional believers make up about 2% of South Africa's population, compared with 20% in Lesotho. However, their traditions and practices have a significant influence on the cultural fabric and life of the region. The use of *muti* (traditional medicine) is widespread, even among those who practise Christianity.

South Africa's ranking according to Reporters Without Borders has dropped to 42nd in the world in terms of press freedoms (the US is 47th); Swaziland is 144th (out of 179); Lesotho is not listed.

Arts

Cinema

South African cinema has seen a turnaround since 1994 and the film industry is bursting with new talent. The first major feature film directed by a black South African was *Fools* (1998) by Ramadan Suleman, who later directed *Zulu Love Letter* (2004). Among today's major players are Zola Maseko *(Drum)*, Zulfah Otto-Sallies *(Raya)*, Teboho Mahlatsi, Simon Wood *(Forerunners)*, Timothy Green *(Skeem)*, Khalo Matabane *(State of Violence)* and Oliver Hermanus *(Skoonheid)*.

Literature

South Africa has an extraordinarily rich literary history, and there's no better way to get a sense of the country than by delving into local literature.

Many of the first black South African writers were missionary-educated, including Solomon Tshekisho Plaatje. In 1930 his epic romance, *Mhudi,* became one of the first books published in English by a black South African.

In 1948 South Africa moved onto the world literary stage with Alan Paton's international bestseller, *Cry, the Beloved Country.* Today, this beautifully crafted tale is still one of the country's most widely recognised titles.

Nadine Gordimer's acclaimed *A Guest of Honour* was published in 1970. The country's first Nobel laureate in literature (1991), her most famous novel, *July's People* (1981), depicts the collapse of white rule.

In the 1960s and '70s Afrikaner writers gained prominence as powerful voices for the opposition. Poet and novelist Breyten Breytenbach was jailed for becoming involved with the liberation movement, while André Brink was the first Afrikaner writer to be banned by the apartheid government. His autobiography, *A Fork in the Road* (2009), gives a fascinating account of anti-apartheid activities by Afrikaaners in South Africa.

The 1970s also gave rise to several influential black poets, including Mongane Wally Serote, a veteran of the liberation struggle. His work gives insights into the lives of black South Africans during the worst years of oppression.

JM Coetzee gained international acclaim with his novel *Disgrace* (1999), which won him his second Booker Prize. Coetzee was awarded the Nobel Prize for Literature in 2003.

One of the most prominent contemporary authors is Zakes Mda. With the publication of *Ways of Dying* in 1995, Mda became an acclaimed novelist. His most recent book, *Sometimes There is a Void: Memoirs of an Outsider* (2011), is a transfixing memoir of his early life in exile in Lesotho and eventual return to South Africa.

Most of the books available about Swaziland were written during the colonial era by Brits. Noted indigenous writers include James Shadrack Mkhulunyelwa Matsebula, who pioneered the use of Swati as a written language. Stanley Musa N Matsebula's novels, including *Siyisike Yinye Nje* (We Are in the Same Boat; 1989), opened up the debate about gender inequality in Swaziland.

Likewise, little Lesothan literature is available in English. However, Thomas Mofolo's *Chaka* (1925), considered to be one of the greatest 20th-century African novels, and *Traveller to the East* (1907) have been translated into English. Other authors to look out for include Mpho 'M'atsepo Nthunya, who writes about female experiences in the autobiographical *Singing Away the Hunger* (1996).

SKOONHEID

Winner of the Queer Palm at the 2011 Cannes Festival, Oliver Hermanus' *Skoonheid* (Beauty) tells the searing tale of the effects of beauty and obsession on a repressed man.

Architecture

Among the highlights of Southern African indigenous architecture are the 'beehive huts' that you'll see dotted throughout the region, including in Swaziland and rural parts of KwaZulu-Natal. A typical homestead or *umuzi,* as it's known in Zulu, consists of a group of these dwellings arranged in a circle around a cattle kraal (enclosure), and surrounded by a fence made of stones or bush. Traditionally the huts were set on an eastward-facing slope, with the chief's residence at the highest point.

In the Xhosa areas of the rural Eastern Cape, you'll see thatched, round, straight-walled huts scattered over the hillsides, often painted turquoise or green.

Elaborately painted Ndebele houses – a relatively recent tradition – are another highlight. Their exteriors sport brightly coloured geometric motifs or more elaborate artwork that may depict anything from airplanes to double-storey dwellings and street lamps.

Basotho homes often feature geometric and sometimes highly symbolic mural art known as *litema.* Beginning during the anti-apartheid struggles, some Basotho women also used *litema* as a political statement, painting their houses in the gold, black and green colours of the ANC. Today, *litema* is used for special celebrations and holidays, such as births, weddings and religious feasts.

The colonial era left a rich architectural legacy. One of its most attractive building styles is the graceful, gabled Cape Dutch house so typical of the Western Cape. Pretoria also showcases colonial-era architecture, with an impressive collection of conservative and stately creations including the famous Union Buildings (p347), designed by English architect Sir Herbert Baker.

Jo'burg grew quickly after the discovery of gold in 1886, and mining magnates were eager to display their wealth with palatial homes and grand offices. In Durban, the designs show more art deco influences, giving the city its own style. Cape Town's building boom in the 1930s also left a wealth of impressive art deco designs, especially around Greenmarket Sq. A highlight is the colourful houses in the Bo-Kaap area (p46).

One of the most noteworthy examples of new South African architecture is the Constitutional Court (p319) in Jo'burg. Another is the new Northern Cape Legislature Building (p437) in Kimberley, notable for its lack of columns and the minimisation of angles and straight lines. In Pretoria, Freedom Park (p348), an inspiring monument to people who died in the name of freedom, faces the modernist celebration of Afrikaner nationalism, the Voortrekker Monument (p345).

South Africa's national football (soccer) team is called Bafana Bafana (Boys Boys in Zulu). The women's team is called Banyana Banyana (Girls Girls).

SPORT: ALMOST A RELIGION

South Africans are sports fanatics, with club sports generating passionate loyalties. Football (soccer) is the most popular spectator sport, followed by rugby and cricket. The majority of football fans are black; while cricket and rugby attracted predominately white crowds, this is now changing.

Hosting the 2010 World Cup was a historic event for South Africa. The action took place at 10 venues from Cape Town to Polokwane (Pietersburg), and the country spent more than US$1 billion on building new stadiums and renovating existing ones.

The second most popular sport, South African rugby has benefited from development programs across the colour divides. South African fans adore their beloved 'Boks', ranked third in the world after New Zealand and Australia after the Rugby World Cup in 2011.

The South African cricket team, known as the Proteas, is up there with the top cricket-playing nations around the world, and fans enjoy friendly rivalry with England, India, Australia, New Zealand and Pakistan.

Visual Arts

South African art had its beginnings with the San, who left their distinctive designs on rock faces and cave walls throughout the region. When European painters arrived, many of their early works centred on depictions of Africa for colonial enthusiasts back home, although with time, a more South Africa–centred focus developed.

Black artists were sidelined for many decades. Gerard Sekoto was one of the first to break through the barriers of racism, and is one of the major figures in the development of South African contemporary art.

Throughout the apartheid era, racism, oppression and violence were common themes. Many black artists who were unable to afford materials adopted cheaper alternatives, such as lino prints.

A more recent lack of public funds for the arts sector has meant that it has become more reliant on corporate collectors and the tourism industry. Contemporary art ranges from the vibrant crafts sold in the Venda region, or on the side of the road in cities and tourist areas, to high-priced paintings that hang in trendy galleries. Innovative artists are using 'found' materials such as telephone wire, safety pins, beads, plastic bags and tin cans to create their works.

Local sculpture is also diverse. Artists working in various media include the Venda-based Jackson Hlungwane (woodcarving) and Dylan Lewis (bronze).

Lesotho is more renowned for its craftwork than its fine art. The colourful Basotho blankets and conical hats are national trademarks and, in addition to the country's textile industry, craft centres in Maseru sell work from tapestries to horsehair fly whisks.

Swaziland has, similarly, realised the value of local crafts as a tourist drawcard, and sophisticated galleries throughout the country sell work from carvings and artefacts to handmade candles and glass.

Theatre & Dance

After the colonial era, home-grown playwrights, performers and directors gradually emerged. Writer and director Athol Fugard was a major influence in the 1950s in developing black talent. He is still active today, with his Fugard Theatre in Cape Town.

Actor and playwright John Kani is another major name in South African theatre.

The **First National Bank Dance Umbrella** (www.at.artslink.co.za/~arts) festival of dance and choreography, held in February and March, brings together local and international artists and provides a stage for new work.

Lesotho and Swaziland both have a strong tradition of dance, famously seen at Swaziland's *umhlanga* (reed) dance, performed by dancing maidens. The country's altogether-more-manly *sibhaca* dance, a vigorous display of foot-stomping, is performed by men and sometimes takes the form of a competition.

See www.artthrob.co.za for the latest on South Africa's contemporary visual-arts scene.

The first all-race theatre venue was the Market Theatre, which opened in 1974. The rundown buildings at Jo'burg's old 'Indian' fruit market were converted and patrons and performers defied the apartheid government's notorious Group Areas Act.

Environment

The Land

A windswept and beautiful coast is the face that South Africa turns to the rest of the world – tempestuous and tamed, stormy and sublime. It spans two oceans as it winds its way down the Atlantic seaboard in the west up into the warmer Indian Ocean waters to the east. However, this is just the start of the region's topographical wealth. Head further inland, and you'll find yourself climbing up from the eastern lowlands (lowveld) to the cool heights of the Drakensberg escarpment and onto the vast plateau (highveld) that forms the heart of the country. This plateau, which averages about 1500m in height, drops off again in the northwestern part of the country to the low-lying Kalahari basin.

The Drakensberg range is at its most rugged in tiny Lesotho – a 30,350-sq-km patch of mountain peaks and highland plateau that is completely surrounded by South Africa. The entire country is above 1000m, and it has the highest lowest point of any country in the world – 1380m, in southern Lesotho's Senqu (Orange) River valley.

Swaziland is the smallest of the Southern Africa trio at only 17,363 sq km in area, but with a remarkable diversity of landscapes, climates and ecological zones for its size. These range from low-lying savannah to the east, rolling hills towards the centre, and rainforest and perpetually fog-draped peaks in the northwest.

> South Africa measures around 1,233,404 sq km, or five times the size of the UK. It's Africa's ninth-largest and fifth-most populous country.

Wildlife

South Africa's four-legged residents are as famous as its two-legged dwellers. With good reason, South Africa can boast some of the most accessible wildlife-viewing on the entire continent.

Animals

South Africa

The best chance of seeing the Big Five – rhino, buffalo, elephant, leopard and lion – is in South Africa. The country is home to the world's three largest land mammals (the African elephant, white rhino and hippopotamus), its tallest (giraffe), fastest (cheetah) and smallest (pygmy shrew).

South Africa's 800-plus bird species include the world's largest bird (ostrich), the heaviest flying bird (Kori bustard) and the smallest raptor (pygmy falcon). For information on birdwatching, see p575.

Endangered species include the black rhino (sometimes spotted in uMkhuze Game Reserve and Hluhluwe-iMfolozi Park); the riverine rabbit (found only near rivers in the central Karoo); the wild dog (Hluhluwe-iMfolozi Park and Kruger National Park); and the roan antelope.

Endangered bird species include the wattled crane and the blue swallow. The African penguin and the Cape vulture are threatened.

> Rhinos aren't named for their colour, but for their lip shape: 'white' comes from *wijde* (wide) – the Boers' term for the fatter-lipped white rhino.

WILD WILDLIFE

One of South Africa's major attractions is the chance to go on safari and get 'up close and personal' with the wildlife. Remember, however, that the animals aren't tame and their actions are often unpredictable. Some tips for staying safe:

» Never get between a mother and her young,

» Never get between a hippo and the water,

» Watch out for black rhinos (although they are rare), which will charge just about anything,

» Be careful around buffalo herds – they charge without warning and the whole herd willl charge together,

» Although elephants often appear docile never take it for granted – be especially careful around females with young and agitated young males,

» Remember that a fake charge from an elephant is probably a precursor to the real thing,

When to Watch Wildlife

Wildlife-watching is rewarding at any time of year, although spotting tends to be easier in the cooler, dry winter months (June to September) when foliage is less dense and animals congregate at waterholes. The summer (late November to March) is rainy, warmer and scenic, with greener landscapes, although animals are more widely dispersed and may be difficult to see. Birding is good year-round, with spring (September to November) and summer generally the best.

Lesotho

Due primarily to its altitude, Lesotho is home to fewer animals than much of the rest of the region. Those you may encounter include rheboks, jackals, mongooses, meerkats, elands and rock hyraxes. However, Lesotho's montane areas are of particular interest for their rare smaller species. Many are found only in the Drakensberg, including the highly threatened Maloti minnow, the African ice rat, several species of lizards and geckos and the Lesotho river frog.

The country's almost 300 recorded bird species include the lammergeier (bearded vulture) and the southern bald ibis.

Among Lesotho's earliest wild inhabitants were dinosaurs: the small, fast-running Lesothosaurus was named after the country.

Birding Guides

» *Birds of Southern Africa*, by Ber Van Perlo

» *Newman's Birds of Southern Africa*, by Kenneth Newman

» *Birds of Southern Africa*, by Ian Sinclair et al

Swaziland

Swaziland has about 120 mammal species, representing one-third of Southern Africa's nonmarine mammal species. Many (including elephants, rhinos and lions) have been introduced, and larger animals are restricted to nature reserves and private wildlife farms. Mongooses and large-spotted genets are common, and hyenas and jackals are found in the reserves. Leopards are rarely seen.

Swaziland's varied terrain supports abundant birdlife, including the blue crane, ground woodpecker and lappet-faced vulture, and more species have been spotted in the country than in the larger Kruger National Park.

Plants

South Africa's more than 20,000 plant species represent 10% of the world's total, although the country constitutes only 1% of the earth's land surface. Dozens of flowers that are domesticated elsewhere grow wild here, including gladioli, proteas, birds of paradise and African lilies. South Africa is also the only country with one of the world's six floral kingdoms within its borders (see the boxed text, p550). In the drier northwest are succulents (dominated by euphorbias and aloes) and annuals, which flower brilliantly after the spring rains.

South Africa has few natural forests, though. They were never extensive, and today there are only remnants. Temperate forests occur on the southern coastal strip between George and Humansdorp, in the KwaZulu-Natal Drakensberg and in Mpumalanga. Subtropical forests are found northeast of Port Elizabeth in areas just inland from the Wild Coast, and in KwaZulu-Natal.

In the north are savannah areas, dotted with acacias and thorn trees.

Lesotho is notable for its high-altitude flora, including Cape alpine flowers and the spiral aloe *(Aloe polyphylla)*, the national flower, which is found on the slopes of the Maluti mountains and occurs naturally only in Lesotho.

Swaziland's grasslands, forests, savannahs and wetlands host about 3500 plant species, or about 14% of Southern Africa's recorded plant life.

National Parks & Reserves

South Africa

South Africa has close to 600 national parks and reserves, many featuring wildlife, while others are primarily wilderness sanctuaries or hiking areas. The table on p552 lists some of the major ones.

Oversight bodies include the following:

CapeNature (☑021-483 0190; www.capenature.org.za) Promotes nature conservation in the Western Cape, and is responsible for permits and bookings for Western Cape reserves.

Ezemvelo KZN Wildlife (☑033-845 1000; www.kznwildlife.com) Responsible for wildlife parks in KwaZulu-Natal.

Komatiland Forests Eco-Tourism (☑013-754 2724; www.komatiecotourism. co.za) Oversees forest areas, promotes ecotourism and manages hiking trails around Mpumalanga.

Sasol eBirds of Southern Africa features images, distribution maps and descriptions of birds. This great app is essentially a digital version of the Sasol Birds of Southern Africa field guidebook. Compare birds, store a list of sightings and verify an identity by matching it to one of 630 recorded birdcalls.

THE GREAT IVORY DEBATE

In 1990, following a massive campaign by various conservation organisations, the UN Convention on International Trade in Endangered Species (Cites) banned ivory trading in an effort to protect Africa's then-declining elephant populations. This promoted recovery of elephant populations in areas where they had previously been ravaged. Yet in South Africa – where elephants had long been protected – the elephant populations continued to grow, leading to widespread habitat destruction.

Solutions to the problem of elephant overpopulation have included creating transfrontier parks to allow animals to migrate over larger areas, relocating animals, small-scale elephant contraception efforts, and – most controversially – culling.

In 2002, after much pressure, Cites relaxed its worldwide ivory trading ban to allow ivory from legally culled elephants to be sold. The idea was that earnings would go to benefit elephant conservation efforts and communities living around elephant areas, and that Cites would monitor whether poaching does indeed increase after such as ban is relaxed.

The decision has been strongly disputed by several other governments on the grounds that resuming trade will increase demand for ivory, and thus encourage poaching. The most recently approved major one-off ivory sale was in mid-2008, when 108 tonnes of ivory from South Africa (51 tonnes), Namibia, Botswana and Zimbabwe was imported to China in a Cites-authorised transaction. Following such a sale, Cites mandates a nine-year resting period during which no additional ivory sales from these countries are permitted. In China – long one of the main markets for the illegal ivory trade – ivory is used for everything from jewellery and artwork to mobile-phone ornamentation.

South African National (SAN) Parks Board (☎012-428 9111; www.sanparks.org) Oversees most larger wildlife parks, except for those in KwaZulu-Natal.

All national parks charge a daily conservation fee, discounted for South African residents and nationals of Southern African Development Community (SADC) countries; see park listings for amounts.

In addition to its national parks, South Africa is party to several transfrontier conservation areas. These include the still-in-process Greater Mapungubwe Transfrontier Conservation Area linking South Africa, Zimbabwe and Botswana; Kgalagadi Transfrontier Park, combining the Northern Cape's former Kalahari Gemsbok National Park with Botswana's Gemsbok National Park; the Maloti-Drakensberg Peace Park, which links Sehlabathebe National Park and other areas of the Lesotho Drakensberg with their South African counterparts in uKhahlamba-Drakensberg; and the Great Limpopo Transfrontier Park, which spans the borders of South Africa, Mozambique and Zimbabwe. Private wildlife reserves also abound.

In total, just under 3% of South African land has national park status, with an estimated 4% to 5% more enjoying other types of protective status. The government has started teaming up with private landowners to bring private conservation land under government protection, with the goal of increasing the total amount of conservation land to over 10%.

Safari Guides

» *Field Guide to Mammals of Southern Africa*, by Chris and Tilde Stuart

» *A Field Guide to the Tracks and Signs of Southern and East African Wildlife*, by Chris and Tilde Stuart

» *The Safari Companion: A Guide to Watching African Mammals*, by Richard Estes.

Lesotho

In part because land tenure allows communal access to natural resources, less than 1% of Lesotho's area is protected – the lowest protected-area coverage of any nation in Africa. Sehlabathebe National Park is the main conservation area, known for its isolated wilderness. Others include Ts'ehlanyane National Park and Bokong Nature Reserve.

Swaziland

About 4% of Swaziland's area is protected. Its conservation areas tend to be low-key, with fewer visitors than their South African counterparts, and good value for money. They include Mlilwane Wildlife Sanctuary, Mkhaya Game Reserve, Malolotja Nature Reserve, which is mainly for hiking, and Hlane Royal National Park. Mlilwane, Mkhaya and Hlane are included in the Wild Card program.

Safaris

The most straightforward and cheapest way to visit the parks (especially if you're in a group) is usually with a hired car. A 2WD is adequate in most parks, but during winter when the grass is high, you'll be able to see more with a 4WD or other high-clearance vehicle. Organised safaris

---

THE CAPE FLORAL KINGDOM

The Cape Floral Kingdom – parts of which are now a Unesco World Heritage Site – is the smallest of the world's six floral kingdoms, but the most diverse, with 1300 species per 10,000 sq km. This is some 900 more species than are found in the South American rainforests. The main vegetation type is *fynbos* (fine bush), characterised by small, narrow leaves and stems. The *fynbos* environment hosts nearly 8500 plant species, most of which are unique to the area. Some members of the main *fynbos* families – heaths, proteas and reeds – have been domesticated elsewhere and are relatively widespread, but many species have a remarkably small range.

The Cape Floral Kingdom extends roughly from Cape Point east almost to Grahamstown and north to the Olifants River, and includes the Kogelberg and parts of several biosphere reserves. However, most of the remaining indigenous vegetation is found only in protected areas, such as Table Mountain and the Cape Peninsula.

UNESCO WORLD HERITAGE SITES

All of the region's World Heritage Sites are in South Africa:

» iSimangaliso Wetland Park (p260)
» Robben Island (p53)
» Hominid fossil sites of Sterkfontein and Kromdraai (p343)
» uKhahlamba-Drakensberg Park (p267)
» Mapungubwe Cultural Landscape (p410)
» Cape Floral Region Protected Areas (p550)
» Vredefort Dome (p299)

Unesco has also designated several areas in South Africa as biosphere reserves – places where local communities and governments pledge to collaborate to promote ecologically sustainable development and conservation. Some are in areas covered in this book:

» Cape Winelands (p96)
» Kogelberg (p113)
» The Waterberg (p405)

are readily arranged with major tour operators and with backpacker-oriented outfits.

Several major parks (including Kruger, Hluhluwe-iMfolozi and Pilanesberg) offer guided wilderness walks accompanied by armed rangers. These are highly recommended, as the subtleties of the bush can be much better experienced on foot than in a vehicle. Book well in advance with the relevant park authority. Shorter morning and afternoon walks are also possible at many wildlife parks, and can generally be booked the same day.

Throughout South Africa, park infrastructure is of high quality. You can often get by without a guide, although you'll almost certainly see and learn more with one. All national parks have rest camps offering good-value accommodation, ranging from campsites to self-catering cottages. Many have restaurants, shops and petrol pumps. Advance bookings for accommodation are essential during holiday periods; otherwise, they are available at short notice.

Environmental Issues

South Africa

South Africa is the world's third most biologically diverse country. It's also one of Africa's most urbanised, with more than 50% of the population living in towns and cities. Major challenges for the government include managing increasing urbanisation while protecting the environment. The picture is complicated by a distorted rural-urban settlement pattern, a legacy of the apartheid era, with huge populations in townships that generally lack adequate utilities and infrastructure.

Land degradation is one of the most serious problems, with about one-quarter of South Africa's land considered to be severely degraded. In former homeland areas (see the boxed text, p517), years of overgrazing and overcropping have resulted in massive soil depletion. This, plus poor overall conditions, is pushing people to the cities, further increasing urban pressures.

South Africa receives an average of only 500mm of rainfall annually, and droughts are common. To meet demand, all major South African rivers have been dammed or modified. While this has improved water supplies to many areas, it has also disrupted local ecosystems and caused increased silting.

The Wildlife & Environmental Society of South Africa (www.wessa.org.za) is a leading environmental advocacy organisation that runs an annual 'Living Green' expo, among many other activities.

LIVING GREEN

TOP PARKS & RESERVES

LOCATION	PARK/RESERVE	FEATURES
Cape Peninsula	Table Mountain National Park	rocky headlands, seascapes, African penguins, elands, water birds, bonteboks
Western Cape	Cederberg Wilderness Area	mountainous and rugged; San rock paintings, sandstone formations, plant life
Mpumalanga/ Limpopo	Kruger National Park	savannah, woodlands, thornveld; the Big Five
	Blyde River Canyon Nature Reserve	canyon, caves, river; stunning vistas
Northern Cape	Augrabies Falls National Park	desert, river, waterfalls; klipspringers, rock dassies; striking scenery
	|Ai-|Ais/Richtersveld Transfrontier Park	mountainous desert; haunting beauty; klipspringers, jackals, zebras, plants, birds
Eastern Cape	Addo Elephant National Park	dense bush, grasslands, forested kloofs; elephants, black rhinos, buffaloes
	Tsitsikamma National Park	coast, cliffs, rivers, ravines, forests; Cape clawless otters, baboons, monkeys, birdlife
KwaZulu-Natal	Hluhluwe-iMfolozi Park	lush, subtropical vegetation, savannah; rhinos, giraffes, lions, elephants, birds
	iSimangaliso Wetland Park	wetlands, coastal grasslands; elephants, birds, hippos
	uMkhuze Game Reserve	savannah, woodlands, swamp; rhinos and almost everything else; hundreds of bird species
	uKhahlamba-Drakensberg Park	awe-inspiring Drakensberg escarpment; fantastic scenery and wilderness areas
Free State	Golden Gate Highlands National Park	spectacular sandstone cliffs and outcrops; zebras, jackals, rheboks, elands, birds
Lesotho	Sehlabathebe National Park	mountain wilderness; wonderful isolation; rheboks, baboons, bearded vultures
Swaziland	Malolotja Nature Reserve	mountains, streams, waterfalls, grasslands, forests; rich bird and plant life, impalas, klipspringers

South Africa has long been at the forefront among African countries in conservation of its fauna. However, funding is tight (and SAN Parks ability to counter an increase in rhino poaching is very worrying), and will likely remain so as long as many South Africans still lack access to basic amenities. Potential solutions include public-private sector conservation partnerships, and increased contributions from private donors and international conservation bodies such as World Wide Fund for Nature (WWF).

Estimates have put South Africa's potential shale gas deposits at 485 trillion cubic feet of gas. That's gained a lot of interest from oil companies, and according to Econometrix (in a report commissioned by Shell) the shale gas industry could be worth R200 billion annually to GDP and lead to the creation of 700,000 jobs.

However hydraulic fracturing, or fracking, to extract the gas, is either banned or under a moratorium in many countries including South Africa. There are serious environmental concerns about the safety of the technology used in fracking, which uses large amounts of clean water mixed with sand and a 'chemical cocktail' to crack underground rocks and release the shale gas. The debate over fracking in South Africa's Northern Cape (in the Karoo) continues to rage with these serious environmental concerns pitted against vested economic interests – in particular large oil companies.

ACTIVITIES	BEST TIME TO VISIT	PAGE
hiking, mountain biking	year-round	p89
hiking	year-round	p158
vehicle safaris, wildlife walks	year-round	p379
hiking, kloofing (canyoning)	year-round	p368
hiking, canoeing, rafting	Apr-Sep	p451
hiking	Apr-Sep	p457
vehicle safaris, walking trails, horse riding	year-round	p190
hiking	year-round	p175
wilderness walks, wildlife-watching	May-Oct	p258
wilderness walks, vehicle/boat safaris	Mar-Nov	p260
guided walks, bird walks, vehicle safaris	year-round	p266
hiking	year-round	p267
hiking	year-round	p303
hiking	Mar-Nov	p481
hiking	year-round	p497

Going Green

There's still a long way to go. More than 90% of South Africa's electricity is coal-generated – more than double the international average. Yet on a local level, there are many commendable projects showcasing the country's slow but sure progress towards going green.

Lynedoch EcoVillage South Africa's first ecologically designed and socially mixed community is slowly taking form, with the design of energy-efficient houses and community buildings, and a focus on the establishment of a self-sufficient community. For more, see p97.

Kuyasa Project 2300 low-income houses in Cape Town's Khayelitsha township have been retrofitted with renewable-energy technologies such as solar water heaters, energy-efficient lighting and insulated ceilings. In addition to promoting energy savings (averaging about 40% per household), the project also created jobs and offered other sustainable development benefits.

Monwabisi Park Eco-Cottages Project Under the auspices of the **Shaster Foundation** (www.shaster.org.za), the Monwabisi Park squatters' settlement of Khayelitsha is gradually being transformed into an ecovillage, as informal shacks are being replaced by community-built eco-cottages.

SAN Parks Facilities at parks in the SAN Parks network are being upgraded with installation of solar water heaters and other energy-saving devices to be more energy efficient.

RESPONSIBLE TRAVEL

Tourism is big in Southern Africa, and making environmentally and culturally sensitive choices can have a significant impact. Following are a few guidelines for visitors:

» Always ask permission before photographing people.

» Avoid indiscriminate gift giving. Donations to recognised projects are more sustainable and less destructive to local cultural values and have a better chance of reaching those who need them most.

» Support local enterprise, buy locally whenever possible, and buy souvenirs directly from those who make them.

» Seek out entities that promote sustainable, community-oriented tourism. The list on the website of **Fair Trade in Tourism South Africa** (www.fairtourismsa.org.za) is a good place to start. See also the boxed text, p117, for some tips on what to look for when selecting a shark-cage diving operator.

» Avoid buying items made from ivory, skin, shells etc.

» Carry a Sassi wallet card (downloadable from www.wwfsassi.co.za) if you enjoy dining at seafood restaurants.

» For cultural attractions, try to pay fees directly to the locals involved, rather than to tour-company guides or other middlemen.

» Respect local culture and customs.

» Don't litter. On treks, in parks or when camping, carry out all your litter (most parks give you a bag for this purpose), and leave trails, parks and campsites cleaner than you found them.

» Maximise your 'real' time with locals, choosing itineraries that are well integrated with the communities in the areas where you will be travelling.

Tree planting More than 200,000 indigenous trees were planted in Soweto as part of the Greening Soweto Project, which sought to beautify the massive township as a legacy of the 2010 FIFA World Cup. It incorporates ongoing environmental awareness programs.

Wind farms Two wind-farm projects are under way near Cape Town, with the Darling Wind Farm – a national demonstration project – already linked to the national power grid.

Scorched: South Africa's Changing Climate, by Leonie Joubert, is a thought-provoking journey through South Africa. It transforms climate change and other environmental issues from dry discourse into sobering, near-at-hand realities.

Lesotho

Environmental discussion in Lesotho centres on the controversial Highlands Water Project. Among the concerns are disruption of traditional communities, flooding of agricultural lands and possible adverse ecological impact on the Senqu (Orange) River.

Other issues include animal population pressure (resulting in overgrazing) and soil erosion. About 40 million tonnes of topsoil are lost annually, with sobering predictions that there may well be no cultivatable land left by 2040.

On a brighter note, Lesotho and South Africa are working together within the framework of the Maluti-Drakensberg Transfrontier Conservation and Development Project to protect these two alpine areas.

Swaziland

Three of Swaziland's major waterways (the Komati, Lomati and Usutu Rivers) arise in South Africa, and Swaziland has been closely involved in South Africa's river-control efforts. Drought is a recurring problem in eastern lowveld areas. Other concerns include lack of community participation in conservation efforts, low levels of environmental awareness and lack of government support.

Wildlife & Habitat

South Africa encompasses one of the most diverse landscapes on the entire continent. There are habitats ranging from verdant forests, stony deserts and soaring mountains to lush grasslands and classic African savannahs. It is home to penguins and flamingos, caracals and sables, wild dogs, dwarf mongooses and hulking African elephants. The number and variation of species is astounding and a deep immersion into wildlife-watching is a pure joy of travel here. Showcasing this diversity are more than 700 publicly owned reserves (including 19 national parks) and about 200 private reserves, with world-renowned Kruger National Park and Kgalagadi Transfrontier Park being the largest.

A male lion basks in the sunset glow at Hluhluwe-iMfolozi Park (p258)

TIM ROCK/LONELY PLANET IMAGES ©

Cats

In terms of behaviour, the cats found in South Africa are little more than souped-up house cats; it's just that they may weigh half as much as a horse, or jet along as fast as a speeding car. With their excellent vision and keen hearing, cats are superb hunters.

Leopard

1 Weight 30kg to 60kg (female), 40kg to 90kg (male); length 170cm to 300cm. The leopard relies on expert camouflage to stay hidden. At night there is no mistaking the bone-chilling groans that sound like wood being sawn at high volume.

Lion

2 Weight 120kg to 150kg (female), 150kg to 225kg (male); length 210cm to 275cm (female), 240cm to 350cm (male). Those lions sprawled out in the shade are actually Africa's most feared predators. Equipped with teeth that tear effortlessly through bone and tendon, they can take down an animal as large as a bull giraffe. Females do all the hunting; swaggering males fight among themselves and eat what the females catch.

Caracal

3 Weight 8kg to 19kg; length 80cm to 120cm. The caracal is a tawny cat with extremely long, pointy ears. It is able to make vertical leaps of 3m and swat birds out of the air.

Wildcat

4 Weight 3kg to 6.5kg; length 65cm to 100cm. If you see what looks like a tabby wandering along fields and forest edges, you may be seeing a wildcat, the direct ancestor of our domesticated house cats.

Cheetah

5 Weight 40kg to 60kg; length 200cm to 220cm. Less cat than greyhound, the cheetah is a world-class sprinter. Although it reaches 112km/h, the cheetah runs out of steam after 300m and must cool down for 30 minutes before hunting again.

Primates

While East Africa is the evolutionary cradle of primate diversity, South Africa is a relative newcomer on the scene and home to just five species of monkeys, apes and prosimians (the primitive ancestors of modern primates). Some of these, however, are common and widespread, meaning that you are likely to see a lot of fascinating primate behaviour.

Vervet Monkey

1 Weight 4kg to 8kg; length 90cm to 140cm. If any monkey epitomises South Africa it is the adaptable vervet monkey. If you think its appearance too drab, check out the bright blue and scarlet colours of the male sexual organs when it gets excited.

Greater Bushbaby

2 Weight up to 1.5kg; length 80cm, including 45cm tail. Named for their plaintive call, bushbabies are actually primitive primates. They have small heads, large rounded ears, thick bushy tails, dark-brown fur and enormous eyes.

Chacma Baboon

3 Weight 12kg to 30kg (female), 25kg to 45kg (male); length 100cm to 200cm. Chacma baboons are worth watching for their complex social dynamics. Look for signs of friendship, deception or deal-making.

Samango Monkey

4 Weight 3.5kg to 5.5kg (female), 5.5kg to 12kg (male); length 100cm to 160cm. Samango monkeys are part of a vast group of African primates called gentle, or blue, monkeys. They are found exclusively in forests.

Greater Galago

5 Weight 550g to 2kg; length 55cm to 100cm. A cat-sized, nocturnal creature with a doglike face, the greater galago belongs to a group of prosimians that have changed little in 60 million years.

JON HICKS/CORBIS ©

ARIADNE VAN ZANDBERGEN/LONELY PLANET IMAGES ©

Cud-Chewing Mammals

Africa is most famous for its astounding variety of ungulates – hoofed mammals that include everything from buffaloes and rhinos to giraffes. The subgroup of ungulates that ruminate (chew their cud) and have horns are bovines. Among this family, antelopes are particularly numerous, with more than 20 species in South Africa.

Wildebeest

1 Weight 140kg to 290kg; length 230cm to 340cm. Look for the black-shouldered blue wildebeest and the white-tailed black wildebeest (a South African speciality).

Impala

2 Weight 40kg to 80kg; length 150cm to 200cm. Gregarious and having a prodigious capacity to reproduce, impalas can reach great numbers.

Springbok

3 Weight 20kg to 40kg (female), 30kg to 60kg (male); length 135cm to 175cm. Lacking the vast grasslands of East Africa, South Africa is home to only one gazellelike antelope – the lithe, little springbok.

Gemsbok

4 Weight 180kg to 240kg; length 230cm. With straight, towering, 1m-long horns and a boldly patterned face, this elegant desert antelope can survive for months on the scant water it derives from the plants it eats.

Sable

5 Weight 200kg to 270kg; length 230cm to 330cm. Looking like a colourful horse with huge soaring horns, the sable ranks as one of Africa's most visually stunning mammals.

Hoofed Mammals

A full stable of Africa's mega-charismatic animals can be found in this group of ungulates. Other than the giraffe, these ungulates are not ruminants. They have been at home in Africa for millions of years and are among the most successful mammals to have ever wandered the continent.

Mountain Zebra

1 Weight 230kg to 380kg; length 260cm to 300cm. South Africa's endemic mountain zebra differs from its savannah relative in having an unstriped belly and rusty muzzle.

Giraffe

2 Weight 450kg to 1200kg (female), 1800kg to 2000kg (male); height 3.5m to 5.2m. Though they stroll along casually, giraffes can outrun any predator.

African Elephant

3 Weight 2200kg to 3500kg (female), 4000kg to 6300kg (male); height 2.4m to 3.4m (female), 3m to 4m (male). Commonly referred to as 'the king of beasts', elephant society is actually ruled by a lineage of elder females.

Hippopotamus

4 Weight 510kg to 3200kg; length 320cm to 400cm. Designed like a floating bean-bag with tiny legs, the 3000kg hippo spends its time in or very near water chowing down on aquatic plants.

White Rhinoceros

5 Weight 1400kg to 2000kg (female), 2000kg to 3600kg (male); length 440cm to 520cm. Brought to the brink of extinction in the early 1990s, this majestic creature was largely saved by the efforts of South African wildlife managers. Poaching has once again become a major problem though, particularly in Kruger.

Other Carnivores

In addition to seven types of cats, South Africa is home to 25 other carnivores ranging from slinky mongooses to highly social hunting dogs. All are linked in having 'carnassial' (slicing) teeth. A highlight for visitors is witnessing the prowess of these highly efficient hunters.

Ratel

1 Weight 7kg to 16kg; length 75cm to 100cm. The ratel or 'honey badger' may be the fiercest of all African animals. It finds its honey by following honey guide birds to beehives.

Aardwolf

2 Weight 8kg to 12kg; length 75cm to 110cm. This animal is actually the smallest hyena, but its carnivorous tendencies are limited to lapping up soft-bodied termites.

Spotted Hyena

3 Weight 40kg to 90kg; length 125cm to 215cm. Living in packs ruled by females that grow penis-like sexual organs, these savage fighters use their bone-crushing jaws to disembowel prey or to do battle with lions.

Hunting (Wild) Dog

4 Weight 20kg to 35kg; length 100cm to 150cm. Uniquely patterned hunting dogs run in packs of 20 to 60 that ruthlessly chase down antelopes and other animals. Organised in complex hierarchies maintained by rules of conduct, these highly social canids are incredibly efficient hunters.

Meerkat

5 Weight 0.5kg to 1kg; length 50cm. South Africa's nine species of mongoose may be best represented by the delightfully named meerkat. Energetic and highly social meerkats spend much of their time standing up with looks of perpetual surprise.

ADRIAN BAILEY/LONELY PLANET IMAGES ©

Birds of Prey

South Africa is home to about 60 species of hawks, eagles, vultures and owls. Look for them perching on trees, soaring high overhead or gathered around a carcass. Your first clue to their presence, however, may be the scolding cries of small birds harassing one of these feared hunters.

African Fish Eagle

1 Length 75cm. Given its name, it's not surprising that you'll see the African fish eagle hunting for fish around water. It is most familiar for the loud ringing vocalisations that have become known as 'the voice of Africa'.

Bateleur

2 Length 60cm. The bateleur is an attractive serpent-eagle. In flight, look for this eagle's white wings and odd tail-less appearance; close up, look for the bold colour pattern and scarlet face.

Bearded Vulture

3 Length 110cm. Around the soaring cliffs of the Drakensberg you may be lucky enough to spot one of the world's most eagerly sought-after birds of prey – the massive bearded vulture, also known as the lammergeyer.

Secretary Bird

4 Length 100cm. In a country full of unique birds, the secretary bird stands head and shoulders above the masses. With the body of an eagle and the legs of a crane, this idiosyncratic, grey-bodied raptor is commonly seen striding across the savannah.

Lappet-Faced Vulture

5 Length 115cm. Seven of South Africa's eight vultures can be seen mingling with lions, hyenas and jackals around carcasses. Here, through sheer numbers, they often compete successfully for scraps of flesh and bone. The monstrous lappet-faced vulture, a giant among vultures, gets its fill before other vultures move in.

VINCENT GRAFHORST/FOTO NATURA/MINDEN PICTURES/CORBIS ©

NIGEL DENNIS / ALAMY ©

MITCH REARDON / LONELY PLANET IMAGES ©

2

Other Birds

Come to South Africa prepared to see an astounding number of birds in every shape and colour imaginable. If you're not already paying attention to every bird you see, you may find them an energising and pleasant diversion after a couple of days staring at impalas and snoring lions.

Lesser Flamingo

1 Length 100cm. Coloured deep rose-pink and gathering by the thousands on salt lakes, the lesser flamingo creates some of the most dramatic wildlife spectacles in Africa, especially when they all fly at once or perform synchronised courtship displays.

Ground Hornbill

2 Length 90cm. Looking somewhat like a turkey, the ground hornbill spends its time on the ground stalking insects, frogs, reptiles and small mammals, which it kills with fierce stabs of its large powerful bill.

Lilac-Breasted Roller

3 Length 40cm. Nearly everyone on safari gets to know the gorgeously coloured lilac-breasted roller. Related to kingfishers, rollers get their name from the tendency to 'roll' from side to side in flight to show off their iridescent blues, purples and greens.

Ostrich

4 Length 200cm to 270cm. If you think the ostrich looks prehistoric, you aren't far off. Standing 2.7m tall and weighing upwards of 130kg, these ancient flightless birds escape predators by running away at 70km/h or lying flat on the ground.

Jackass Penguin

5 Length 60cm. Yes, they are silly looking, but jackass penguins are actually named for their donkeylike calls, part of the ecstatic courtship displays given by the males. Found along the coast and on offshore islands, some penguin colonies are ridiculously tame.

Habitats

Nearly all of South Africa's wildlife occupies a specific type of habitat, and you will hear rangers and fellow travellers refer to these habitats repeatedly. Your wildlife-viewing experience will be greatly enhanced if you learn how to recognise these habitats, and the animals you might expect in each one.

Semiarid Desert

1 Much of western South Africa sees so little rain that shrubs and hardy grasses are the dominant vegetation. Known locally as the Karoo, this area merges with true desert in Namibia. Lack of water keeps larger animals such as zebras and antelopes close to waterholes, but when it rains this habitat explodes with plant and animal life. During the dry season many plants shed their leaves to conserve water.

Fynbos

2 The dense, low shrub cover that can be found around Cape Town is so utterly unique that it is considered one of the six major plant biomes in the world. Of the 8578 plant species found here, 68% occur nowhere else in the world. Many of the plants are unsuitable for grazing animals, but this is a region of remarkable insect and bird diversity.

Savannah & Grassland

3 Savannah is *the* classic African landscape, with broad, rolling grasslands dotted with acacia trees, and best known in East Africa. Known as bushveld in South Africa, this open landscape is home to large herds of zebra and antelope, in addition to fast-sprinting predators such as cheetahs. Grasslands lack woody plants, and on the central plateau they are known as highveld.

Right
1. Little Karoo (p133) 2. Fynbos, Cape of Good Hope (p58)

Survival Guide

Directory
A–Z

Accommodation

South Africa offers a range of good-value accommodation. You'll generally find high standards, often for significantly less than you would pay in Europe or North America.

The rates quoted in this book are for high season, with a private bathroom. Exceptions are noted in listings. Reviews are ordered by preference, and price ranges are based on the cost of a double room:

$ Less than R400
$$ R400–R1500
$$$ More than R1500

In Cape Town, Jo'burg and the Garden Route, price ranges are higher:

$ Less than R650
$$ R650–R2500
$$$ More than R2500

Rates rise steeply during the summer school break (early December to mid-January) and the Easter break (late March to mid-April). Room prices often double and minimum stays are imposed; advance bookings are essential. The other school holidays (late June to mid-July and late September to early October) are either classified as high or shoulder season. You can get excellent deals during the winter low season, which is also the best time for wildlife-watching.

Discounts Discounted midweek rates are common, so always ask. Occasionally, in towns geared towards business travellers rather than tourists, such as mining centres, weekly rates can be more expensive.

Budget accommodation The main budget options are campsites, backpacker hostels, self-catering cottages and community-run offerings including homestays. Campsites are fairly ubiquitous, but other budget options are often scarce outside tourist areas.

Midrange This category is particularly good value, and includes guesthouses, B&Bs and many self-catering options in national parks.

Top end South Africa boasts some of Africa's best wildlife lodges, as well as superb guesthouses and hotels. Prices at this level are similar to, or slightly less than, those in Europe or North America. There are also some not-so-superb hotels and guesthouses, which can be expensive disappointments, so be selective.

Lesotho Rates are comparable to South Africa's, and you usually get excellent value for money. Top end accommodation is scarce – exceptions include the lodges in Malealea, Semonkong and Roma. Camping opportunities abound away from major towns.

Swaziland Rates are similar to those in South Africa. There is a handful of backpacker hostels, and camping is possible on the grounds of many accommodation options.

Townships In Soweto, Khayelitsha and several other areas, you can sleep in township B&Bs, backpackers and homestays, excellent ways to get insights into township life. Many owners offer township tours, and unparalleled African hospitality.

ONLINE BOOKING

A few of the centralised online booking services that cover South Africa are listed below. Because most booking services charge listing fees, the cheapest places aren't always included. Many regions also have B&B and tourist offices or associations that take bookings.

Book a Bed South Africa (www.bookabedsouthafrica.co.za) B&B, self-catering and lodges in all provinces.

BOOK YOUR STAY ONLINE

For more accommodation reviews by Lonely Planet authors, check out http://hotels.lonelyplanet.com. You'll find independent reviews, as well as recommendations on the best places to stay. Best of all, you can book online.

Farmstay (www.farmstay.co.za) Farmstays and rural activities.

Hostel Africa (www.hostelafrica.com) Hostels across Africa, tours and travel.

Portfolio Collection (www.portfoliocollection.com) Upscale B&B, guesthouses, boutique hotels, lodges and self-catering from Cape Town to Kruger National Park and Swaziland.

Safari Now (www.safarinow.com) Thousands of properties nationwide, from tented camps to Cape Dutch villas.

Seastay (www.seastay.co.za) Coastal accommodation.

Where to Stay (www.wheretostay.co.za) Covers South Africa and its neighbouring countries, with wheelchair- and gay-friendly options.

Backpackers

South Africa is backpacker-friendly, with a profusion of hostels in popular areas such as Cape Town and the Garden Route. Visit **Backpacking South Africa** (www.backpackingsouthafrica.co.za) for more ideas.

Accommodation In addition to dorm beds (from about R120 per night), hostels often offer private single/double rooms from about R200/400. Some will also allow you to pitch a tent on their grounds.

Facilities Hostels are often of a high standard, with internet access, self-catering facilities and a travellers' bulletin board. Some offer meals. Staff can provide information on the area and local transport, and organise pick-ups if the hostel is not on the Baz Bus route.

Hostelling International About 25 South African hostels are affiliated with **HI** (www.hihostels.com), so it's worth taking an HI card.

Lesotho and Swaziland Backpacker accommodation is found in areas including Malealea, Semonkong, Mokhotlong and Sani Pass in Lesotho; and Mbabane

---

---

and the Ezulwini Valley in Swaziland. Prices and facilities are similar to those in South Africa. Many towns in Lesotho have agricultural training centres that accommodate travellers is space is available. Accommodation (about R90 per person) is simple but adequate, typically in dorms with shared bathrooms and kitchen.

B&Bs & Guesthouses

B&Bs and guesthouses are two of South Africa's accommodation treats. They're found throughout the country, from cities to villages, while in rural areas you can stay on farms. Some of the cheapest places are unexciting, but in general standards are high and rooms are good value.

Facilities Unlike B&Bs in some other countries, most South African establishments offer much more than someone's spare room; unlike motels, their bedrooms are individual and often luxurious. Antique furniture, a private bathroom and veranda, big gardens and a pool are common. In scenic areas such as the Cape Winelands, wonderful settings are part of the deal. Breakfasts are usually large and delectable.

Rates Prices start around R400 per double, including breakfast and private bathroom. With the odd exception, starting prices are

---

higher in Cape Town, Jo'burg and the Garden Route.

Camping

Camping grounds and caravan parks have long been the accommodation of choice for many South African families. Grounds in popular areas are often booked out during school holidays. Free-camping isn't recommended in South Africa.

Municipal Most towns have an inexpensive municipal campsite and caravan park, ranging from pleasant to unappealing. Those near larger towns are often unsafe.

Private Altogether better are privately run campsites, and those in national parks. These are invariably well equipped and appealing, with ablution blocks, power points, cooking areas and water supply. Tourist areas often have fancy resorts, complete with swimming pool, restaurant and mini-market.

Prices Rates are either per person (averaging R90) or per site (more than R100 for two people).

Rules Some caravan parks ban nonporous groundsheets (which are sewn in to most small tents) to protect the grass. If you're only staying a night or two, you can usually convince the manager that your tent won't do any harm. Some parks may not allow tents at all, though if you explain that you're a foreigner without a caravan, it's usually possible to get a site.

Lesotho and Swaziland

Apart from in national parks and nature reserves, there are few official campsites. It's usually possible to free-camp, but get permission from elders in the nearest village before setting up, both out of respect for the local community and to minimise security risks. You may be offered a hut for the night; expect to pay about R5 for this.

Hotels

These cover the spectrum, from spartan set-ups to exclusive boutique properties.

Budget Most budget hotels are rundown and inadequate. There are a few reasonable old-style country hotels, where you can get a double from R350, have a meal and catch up on gossip in the pub.

Midrange These options are more dependable than their budget counterparts, offering good value and atmospheric surroundings.

CHAIN HOTELS

These are most common, found in major cities and tourist areas. The main chains:

City Lodge (☑0861 563 437, 011-557 2600; www.citylodge.co.za) Decent value, with Road Lodges (slightly superior standards to Formule 1, for about R490 per double); Town Lodges (around R845 per double); City Lodges (about R900 per double); and Courtyard Hotels (around R1100 per double).

Formule 1 (☑0861 367 685; www.hotelformule1.com) The cheapest, with functional but cramped single/double/triple rooms from about R350/360/370.

InterContinental Hotels Group (☑0800 999 136; www.ichotelsgroup.com) Offers a range of accommodation across its Holiday Inn, Holiday Inn Express, Crowne Plaza and InterContinental hotels in the major cities.

Protea (☑0861 119 000, 021-430 5300; www.protea hotels.com) A nationwide network of three- to five-star hotels. Protea's Pro-kard Club offers discounts of up to 20%.

Southern Sun (☑0861 447 744, 011-461 9744; www.southernsun.com) Operates various more-expensive hotels nationwide.

Sun International (☑011-780 7810; www.suninter national.com) Runs top-end, resort-style hotels in the former homelands, plus Lesotho and Swaziland, usually with casinos attached. Standards are generally high and package deals are available.

Lodges

In and around the national parks, you can relax comfortably in bush settings.

Facilities Accommodation is usually in a luxurious lodge

PRACTICALITIES

» All three countries use the metric system for weights and measures.

» Mail & Guardian (mg.co.za) is a national weekly newspaper.

» The Sowetan (www.sowetanlive.co.za) is a national daily.

» Other nationals include the Sunday Independent (www.iol.co.za/sundayindepend-ent), the Sunday Times (www.timeslive.co.za) and Business Day (www.businessday.co.za).

» News24 (www.news24.com) is publisher Media 24's portal, with news and features.

» NewsNow (nn.co.za) is a weekly news-digest magazine covering local and international stories.

» Times of Swaziland (www.times.co.sz) and Swazi Observer (www.observer.org.sz) carry Swazi news.

» The Public Eye (www.publiceye.co.ls) and Lesotho Times (www.lestimes.com) carry Lesothan news.

» Getaway (www.getaway.co.za) and Go! (www.gomag.co.za) are South African travel magazines.

» SABC (www.sabc.co.za) broadcasts local TV programs from soap operas to news.

» M-Net (mnet.dstv.com) offers US films and series.

» e.tv (www.etv.co.za) offers local programs and international favourites.

» SAFM (www.sabc.co.za) broadcasts news and chat online and on 104FM–107FM.

» BBC World Service is available throughout the region, on various radio wavelengths (listed at www.bbc.co.uk/worldservice/programmeguide/waystolisten.shtml) and online.

or a safari-style tent. Expect many of the amenities that you would find in a top-end hotel – including en suites with running hot and cold water, comfortable bedding and delicious cuisine – although many lodges don't have landlines and TVs. Most luxury lodges charge all-inclusive rates, which include wildlife drives and meals.

Reservations It's important to phone ahead if you plan to stay at a lodge or self-catering option in the wilderness. Not only can they be tricky to find without directions, and the staff may need to pick you up if your vehicle doesn't have good clearance, but if you turn up unannounced you might find there's no one home.

Self-Catering Accommodation

This can be excellent value, from around R350 per two-person cottage, also called chalets, cabins and *rondavels* (round huts with a conical roof). Options range from farm cottages to community-run camps.

Facilities Apart from the occasional rundown place, most self-catering accommodation comes with bedding, towels and a fully equipped kitchen, though confirm what is included in advance. In some farm cottages you'll have to do without lights and electricity.

Locations Small-town tourist information centres and their websites are the best places to find out about self-catering accommodation. Self-catering chalets, often available in campsites and caravan parks, are common in tourist areas such as the coast and around parks and reserves. Many are located in scenic but remote locations, more suited to travellers with a car.

Parks and reserves
South Africa National (SAN) Parks (☏012-465 000; www.sanparks.org) has good-value, fully equipped

bungalows, cottages and luxury tents. These suit family groups and start at around R400 per person. Some parks and reserves also have simpler huts, with shared bathrooms, from about R150 per person.

Reservations Booking ahead is essential. You normally have to pay 50% or 100% in advance. In a small community, there's a chance you'll get a ride to the cottage if you don't have a car.

Activities

Thanks to South Africa's diverse terrain and favourable climate, almost anything is possible – from ostrich riding to zip lining. Good facilities and instruction mean that most activities are accessible to anyone, whatever their experience level.

There are dozens of operators. In addition to the companies below, ask other travellers and at hostels. Also see the listings and advice on p596 and p605.

Aerial Pursuits

Favourable weather conditions year-round and an abundance of high points to launch yourself from make South Africa a fine destination for aerial pursuits. Taking to the South African skies is fairly inexpensive; a helpful contact for getting started is the **Aero Club of South Africa** (☏011-082 1100; www.aeroclub.org.za).

Paragliding South Africa is one of the world's top paragliding destinations, particularly Table Mountain. The strongest thermals are from November to April. For experienced pilots, airspace restrictions are minimal and there's great potential for long-distance, cross-country flying. **South African Hang Gliding & Paragliding Association** (☏074-152 2505; www.sahpa.co.za) can provide information on flying sites, schools and clubs.

Microlighting A useful resource with forums and a list of airfields is http://microlighters.co.za.

Birdwatching

With its enormous diversity of habitats, South Africa is a paradise for birdwatchers. There are birdwatching clubs nationwide, and most parks and reserves can provide birding lists. Many parks and reserves also have field guides, but it's still worth bringing your own. Useful resources:

BirdLife South Africa (www.birdlife.org.za) Useful links and articles.

BirdLife South Africa Avitourism (www.birdingroutes.co.za) Promotes avitourism (birding ecotourism).

Bird-Watch Cape (www.birdwatch.co.za) Small, Cape Town–based outfit for twitchers, with tours including a 17-day, nationwide package.

Cape Birding Route (www.capebirdingroute.org) Covers western South Africa.

Greater Limpopo Birding Routes (www.limpopobirding.com) Lists guides and four routes including the Kruger to Canyons trail, which takes in the national park and the Blyde River Canyon.

Southern Africa Birding (www.sabirding.co.za) This outfit also covers Lesotho and Swaziland.

Zululand Birding Route (www.zbr.co.za) BirdLife South Africa avitourism project in northern KwaZulu-Natal.

Canoeing, Kayaking & Rafting

South Africa has few major rivers, but the ones that do flow year-round offer rewarding rafting and canoeing. Rafting is highly dependent on rain, with the best months in most areas from December/January to April.

Felix Unite (www.felixunite.com) Runs trips on the

SAFE DIVING

In popular diving areas such as Sodwana Bay, there is a range of diving companies – including slipshod operations. When choosing an operator, make quality, rather than cost, the priority. Factors to consider include an operator's experience and qualifications; knowledge and seriousness of staff; whether it's a fly-by-night operation or well established; and the type and condition of equipment and frequency of maintenance. Assess whether the overall attitude is professional, and ask about safety considerations, such as radios, oxygen, emergency-evacuation procedures, boat reliability and back-up engines, first-aid kits, safety flares and life jackets. On longer dives, do you get an energising meal, or just tea and biscuits?

Using operators offering courses certified by **PADI** (www.padi.com) gives you the flexibility to go elsewhere in the world and have your certification recognised at other PADI dive centres.

Breede, Cunene and Senqu (Orange) Rivers.

Hardy Ventures (www.iafrica.com) Runs trips on the Blyde, Olifants and Sabie Rivers.

Induna Adventures (www.indunaadventures.com) Runs trips on the Sabie and Blyde Rivers.

Intrapid (www.raftsa.co.za) Runs trips on rivers including the Senqu (Orange) and Doring.

Sea Kayaking Association of South Africa (www.doorway.co.za/kayak/recskasa) Has news and contacts.

Swazi Trails (www.swazitrails.co.sz) Runs trips on Swaziland's Great Usutu River.

Diving

Take the plunge off the southernmost end of Africa into the Atlantic and Indian Oceans. Strong currents and often windy conditions mean advanced divers can find challenges all along the coast. Sodwana Bay on KwaZulu Natal's Elephant Coast is good for beginners.

Conditions These vary widely. The best time to dive the KwaZulu-Natal shoreline is from May to September,

when visibility tends to be highest. In the west, along the Atlantic seaboard, the water is cold year-round, but is at its most diveable, with many days of high visibility, between November and January/February.

Costs Prices are generally lower in South Africa than elsewhere in the region. Expect to pay over R3000 for a three- or four-day open-water certification course, and over R300 per day for equipment rental.

Equipment Coastal towns where diving is possible have dive outfitters. With the exception of Sodwana Bay during the warmer months (when a 3mm wetsuit will suffice), you'll need at least a 5mm wetsuit for many sites, and a dry suit for sites to the south and west.

Fishing

Sea fishing is popular, with a wide range of species in the warm and cold currents that flow past the east and west coasts, respectively.

River fishing, especially for introduced trout, is popular in parks and reserves, with some good highland streams in the Drakensberg.

Licences are available for a few rand at the park offices, and some places also rent equipment.

Bass Fishing South Africa (www.bassfishing.co.za)

South African Fishing (www.south-african-fishing.co.za)

Southern African Trout and Flyfishing Directory (www.flyfisher.co.za)

Wild Trout Association (www.wildtrout.co.za)

Lesotho is an insider's tip among trout anglers. As in South Africa, the season runs from September to May.

There is a small licence fee, a size limit and a bag limit of 12 fish. Only rod and line and artificial nonspinning flies may be used.

The nearest fishing area to Maseru is the Makhaleng River, 2km downstream from Molimo-Nthuse Lodge (a two-hour drive from Maseru).

Hiking
SOUTH AFRICA

South Africa is a wonderful destination for hiking, with an excellent system of well-marked trails varied enough to suit every ability.

Accommodation Some trails offer accommodation, from camping to simple huts with electricity and running water; book well in advance.

Guided walks These are possible in many national parks, accompanied by armed rangers. You won't cover much distance, but they offer the chance to experience the wild with nothing between you and nature. Parks, including Kruger, offer hikes ranging from two- to three-hour bush walks to multinight wilderness trails.

Off-trail hiking Some designated wilderness areas offer this. Little information is available on suggested routes; it's up to you to survive on your own.

Regulations Many trails have limits as to how many hikers can be on them at any one time. Most longer routes and wilderness areas require hikers to be in a group of at least three or four.

Resources Most trails are administered by **SAN Parks** (www.sanparks.org) along with the various forestry authorities.

Best Walks of the Drakensberg by David Bristow.

Ezemvelo KZN Wildlife (www.kznwildlife.com) Controls most trails in KwaZulu-Natal.

Hiking South Africa (www.hiking-south-africa.info) Suggests hikes.

Hiking Trails of Southern Africa by Willie and Sandra Olivier.

Lonely Planet (http://tinyurl.com/6m9u5x2) Suggests multiday hikes.

Safety This is not a major issue on most trails, although longer trails and Table Mountain have seen muggings and burglaries in accommodation. Check with the local hiking club when booking your walk. On longer and quieter trails, hike in a group, and limit the valuables you carry.

Seasons Hiking is possible year-round, although you'll need to be prepared in summer for extremes of heat and wet. The best time is March to October.

LESOTHO

» The entire country is ideal for hiking, away from major towns.

» The eastern highlands and the Drakensberg crown attract serious hikers.

» There are few organised hiking trails – just footpaths.

» You can walk almost everywhere, accompanied by a compass and the relevant topographical maps.

» In all areas, especially the remote eastern highlands, rugged conditions can make walking dangerous if you aren't experienced and prepared. Temperatures can plummet to near zero even in summer, and thunderstorms and thick fog are common.

» Waterproof gear and warm clothes are essential.

» In summer, rivers flood and fords can become dangerous; be prepared to change your route or wait until the river subsides.

» By the end of the dry season, good water can be scarce, especially in higher areas.

SWAZILAND

» Some of the nature reserves are particularly good for hiking.

» In most rural areas, you can follow the generations-old tracks that criss-cross the countryside.

» Weather conditions aren't as extreme as in Lesotho, but if you're hiking during the summer, be prepared for torrential downpours and hailstorms.

Horse Riding & Pony Trekking

» In South Africa, Lesotho and Swaziland it's easy to find rides ranging from several hours to several days, and for all experience levels.

» Riding is offered in several South African national parks.

» Pony trekking on tough Basotho ponies is a popular way of seeing the Lesotho highlands.

Equus Horse Safaris (www.equus.co.za) In the Waterberg, Limpopo.

Fynbos Trails (www.fynbostrails.com) In the Western Cape.

Haven Horse Safaris (www.havenhotel.co.za) In the Wild Coast region, Eastern Cape.

Horizon Horseback Adventures (www.ridinginafrica.com) In the Waterberg, Limpopo.

Khotso Horse Trails (www.khotsotrails.co.za) In the Drakensberg, including Lesotho.

Nyanza Horse Trails (www.btinternet.com/~duplessis/nyanza_stable) In Swaziland.

Kloofing (Canyoning)

Kloofing (called canyoning elsewhere) is a mixture of climbing, hiking, swimming and some serious jumping. It has a small following that is rapidly growing in South Africa.

There's an element of risk in the sport, so when hunting for operators, check their credentials carefully before signing up.

Mountain Biking

There are trails almost everywhere in South Africa, from the Garden Route to Sani Pass, the tough ride up (and down) the pass on the border between South Africa and Lesotho. Cape Town is an unofficial national hub for mountain biking. Some resources:

Linx Africa (www.linx.co.za/trails/lists/bikelist.html)

Mountain Bike South Africa (www.mtbsa.co.za)

Mountain Bike South Africa e-zine (www.mtb.org.za)

Ride (www.ride.co.za) Monthly South African mountain-biking magazine.

Rock Climbing

Mountain Club of South Africa (www.mcsa.org.za) Information and links to regional clubs.

Roc'n Rope (www.rocrope.com) Runs climbing and abseiling trips and courses, and offers information in French.

SA Climbing Info Network (www.saclimb.co.za) This network has listings and photos of climbing and bouldering routes.

Surfing

The best time of the year for surfing the southern and eastern coasts is autumn and early winter (from about

April to July). Boards and gear can be bought in most of the big coastal cities. New boards typically cost about R3000. Resources:

Wavescape (www.wavescape.co.za)

Zig Zag (www.zigzag.co.za) South Africa's main surf magazine.

Whale Watching

» South Africa is considered one of the world's best spots to sight whales without needing to go out in a boat.

» Southern right and humpback whales are regularly seen offshore between June/July and November, with occasional spottings of Bryde's and killer whales.

» Whale-watching spots dot the southern and eastern coastlines, from False Bay to iSimangaliso Wetland Park.

» Hermanus, where southern right whales come to calve, is the unofficial whale-watching capital.

Wildlife Watching

South Africa's populations of large animals are one of the country's biggest attractions. In comparison with other countries in the region (Botswana and Zambia, for example), wildlife-watching in South Africa tends to be very accessible, with good roads and accommodation for all categories of traveller. It is also comparatively inexpensive, although there are plenty of pricier choices for those seeking a luxury experience in the bush.

Swaziland also offers excellent wildlife-watching.

Business Hours

Usual business hours are as follows. Exceptions are noted in listings.

Banks 9am–3.30pm Monday to Friday, 9am–11am Saturday; many foreign-exchange bureaus have longer hours.

Bars 4pm–2am

Businesses and shopping 8.30am–5pm Monday to Friday, 8.30am–1pm Saturday; many supermarkets also open 9am–noon Sunday; shopping centres to 9pm.

Cafes breakfast 7am–noon, lunch noon–5pm.

Government offices 8am–4.30pm Monday to Friday (Lesotho 8am–12.45pm & 2pm–4.30pm; Swaziland 8am–4pm).

Post offices 8.30am–4.30pm Monday to Friday, 8.30am–noon Saturday.

Restaurants lunch 11.30am–3pm, dinner 7pm–10pm (last orders); many open 3pm–7pm.

Customs Regulations

» You're permitted to bring 1L of spirits, 2L of wine, 200 cigarettes and up to R3000 worth of goods into South Africa without paying duties.

» The import and export of protected animal products such as ivory is not permitted.

» Visit www.southafrica.info/travel/advice/redtape.htm for more information

Discount Cards

» A **Hostelling International** (HI; www.hihostels.com) membership card entitles you to discounts with its 25 affiliated South African hostels, as well as on various trips and activities.

» A valid student ID will get you discounts on bus tickets, museum admission and so on.

» Inquire at backpackers about the discount card **Moola Magic** (www.backpackingsouthafrica.co.za), which covers accommodation, transport, tours and even overland trips.

» If you're planning to spend lots of time in national parks, consider buying a **Wild Card** (www.sanparks.org/wild).

Electricity

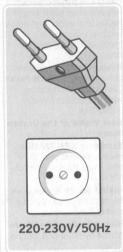

220-230V/50Hz

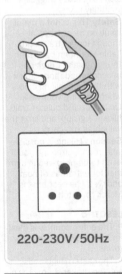

220-230V/50Hz

Embassies & Consulates

Embassies & Consulates in South Africa

Most countries have their main embassy in Pretoria, with an office or consulate in Cape Town (which may become the embassy during Cape Town's parliamentary sessions).

Most open for visa services and consular matters on weekday mornings, between about 9am and noon.

For more listings, see www.dfa.gov.za/consular/index.html.

Australia (☎012-423 6000; www.australia.co.za; 292 Orient St, Arcadia) High commission in Pretoria.

Botswana (www.mofaic.gov. bw) High commission, Pretoria (☎012-430 9640; 24 Amos St, Colbyn); Cape Town (☎021-421 1045; 13th fl, Metropolitan Life Bldg, 7 Coen Steyler Ave, City Bowl) Also has a consulate in Jo'burg.

Canada (www.dfait-maeci. gc.ca/southafrica); High commission, Pretoria (☎012-422 3000; 1103 Arcadia St, Hatfield); Cape Town (☎021-423 5240; 5 De Lorentz St, Gardens) Also has missions in Durban and Jo'burg.

France (www.ambafrance -rsa.org) Embassy, Pretoria (☎012-425 1600; 250 Melk St, New Muckleneuk); Cape Town (☎021-423 1575; www.con sulfrance-lecap.org; 78 Queen Victoria St, Gardens) Also has a consulate in Jo'burg.

Germany (www.southafrica. diplo.de) Embassy, Pretoria (☎012-427 8900; 180 Blackwood St, Arcadia; consular section 1267 Pretorius St, Hatfield); Cape Town (☎021-405 3000; 19th fl, Triangle House, 22 Riebeeck St, City Bowl) Also has missions in Durban and Port Elizabeth.

Ireland Embassy, Pretoria (☎012-452 1000; www. embassyofireland.org.za; 2nd fl, Parkdev Bldg, Brooklyn Bridge Office Park, 570 Fehrsen St, Brooklyn); Cape Town (☎021-419 0636; LG Bldg, 1 Thibault Sq, Long St, City Bowl)

Lesotho High commission, Pretoria ☎012-460 7648; www. foreign.gov.ls; 391 Anderson St, Menlo Park)

Mozambique (www.minec. gov.mz) High commission, Pretoria (☎012-401 0300; 529 Edmond St, Arcadia); Cape Town (☎021-426 2944; 11th fl, Pinnacle Bldg, 8 Burg St, City Bowl); Nelspruit (☎013-752 7396; 32 Bell St) Also has missions in Durban and Jo'burg.

Namibia (☎012-481 9100; www.namibia.org.za; 197 Blackwood St, Arcadia) High commission in Pretoria.

Netherlands (www.dutch embassy.co.za) Embassy, Pretoria (☎012-425 4500; 210 Queen Wilhelmina Ave, New Muckleneuk); Cape Town (☎021-421 5660; 100 Strand St, City Bowl) Also has a mission in Durban.

New Zealand (www.nz embassy.com/south-africa) Embassy, Pretoria (☎012-435 9000; 125 Middel St, New Muckleneuk); Cape Town (☎021-683 5762; 5 Eastry Road, Claremont)

Swaziland (www.swazihigh com.co.za) High commission, Pretoria (☎012-344 1910; 715 Government Ave, Arcadia) Also has an office in Jo'burg.

UK (http://ukinsouthafrica.fco. gov.uk) High commission, Pretoria (☎012-421 7500; 255 Hill St, Arcadia; consular section 256 Glyn St, Hatfield); Cape Town (☎021-405 2400; 15th fl, Norton Rose House, 8 Riebeeck St, City Bowl) Also has missions in Durban, Jo'burg and Port Elizabeth.

USA (http://southafrica. usembassy.gov) Embassy, Pretoria (☎012-431 4000; 877 Pretorius St, Arcadia); Cape Town (☎021-702 7300; 2 Reddam Ave, Westlake) Also has missions in Durban and Jo'burg.

Zimbabwe (www.zimfa.gov. zw) Embassy, Pretoria (☎012-342 5125; 798 Merton St, Arcadia) Also has a consulate in Jo'burg.

Embassies & Consulates in Lesotho

The following are in Maseru. Missions in South Africa often have responsibility for Lesotho. For more listings, visit www.foreign.gov.ls.

Canada (☎2231 5365; www. dfait-maeci.gc.ca/southafrica; 2nd fl, Quadrant Sales Bldg, Orpen Rd, Old Europa)

France (☎2232 5722; www. alliance.org.za/consular-services.html; Alliance Française, cnr Kingsway & Pioneer Rd)

Germany (☎2233 2292/ 2233 2983; www.southafrica. diplo.de; Alliance Française, cnr Kingsway & Pioneer Rd)

Ireland (☎2231 4068; www. embassyofireland.org.ls; Tonakholo Rd)

Netherlands (☎2231 2114; www.dutchembassy.co.za; c/o Lancer's Inn)

South Africa (☎2231 5758; www.dfa.gov.za; cnr Kingsway & Old School Rd)

UK (☎2231 3929; http://ukin southafrica.fco.gov.uk)

USA (☎2231 2666; http:// maseru.usembassy.gov; 254 Kingsway Rd)

Embassies & Consulates in Swaziland

The following are in Mbabane. Missions in South Africa often have responsibility for Swaziland. For more listings, visit www.gov.sz.

Germany (☎404 3174; www. southafrica.diplo.de; 3rd fl, Lilunga House, Samhlolo St)

Mozambique (☎404 1296; www.minec.gov.mz; Highlands View, Princess Drive Rd)

South Africa (☎404 4651; www.dfa.gov.za; 2nd fl, the New Mall, Dr Sishayi Rd)

UK (☎551 6247; http://ukin southafrica.fco.gov.uk)

USA (☎404 6441; swaziland. http://usembassy.gov; 7th fl, Central Bank Bldg, Mahlokohla St)

Food

Dining in South Africa is pleasurable and good value. Sit-down meals in restaurants (not haute cuisine) average between R70 and R90 per person (less in pubs), and fresh produce everywhere is good value.

For more on eating well in South Africa, Lesotho and Swaziland, see p533.

The following price ranges refer to the average cost of a main course.

$ less than R60

$$ R60 to R150

$$$ more than R150

Gay & Lesbian Travellers

South Africa's constitution is one of the few in the world that explicitly prohibits discrimination on the grounds of sexual orientation. There are active gay and lesbian communities and scenes in Cape Town and Jo'burg, and to a lesser degree in Pretoria and Durban. Cape Town is the focal point, and is the most openly gay city on the continent.

Attitudes Despite the liberality of the new constitution, it will be a while before the more-conservative sections of society begin to accept it. Particularly in rural areas, and in both black and white communities, homosexuality remains frowned upon, if not taboo.

Lesotho There is no official prohibition of homosexual activity, though gay sexual relationships are taboo, and open displays of affection, whatever your orientation, are frowned upon.

Swaziland More conservative than South Africa. Both male homosexual and lesbian activities are officially illegal, and gay sexual relationships are culturally taboo.

Resources

See Cape Town, Jo'burg and Durban for further listings. Check chain bookstores such as CNA and gay venues for newspapers and magazines.

Behind the Mask (www.mask.org.za) Johannesburg-based organisation catering to Africa's lesbian, gay, bisexual, transgender and intersex (LGBTI) community, with a range of news, listings and links on its website.

Exit (www.exit.co.za) LGBT monthly newspaper.

Gay Johannesburg (gay-johannesburg.blogspot.com) News and links.

Gay Pages (www.gaypagessa.co.za) Bimonthly glossy magazine, available nationwide.

OUTright Glossy monthly for gay males.

South African Tourism (www.southafrica.net) Lists gay and lesbian events.

Triangle Project (www.triangle.org.za) The Cape Town–based organisation campaigns for LGBTI rights and supports the community through various programs.

Events

See Cape Town, Jo'burg and Durban for further listings.

Jo'burg Pride (joburgpride.org) Dating to 1990, Africa's first ever gay and lesbian Pride parade takes place every September/October.

Mother City Queer Project (www.mcqp.co.za) Cape Town's gay and lesbian extravaganza features dozens of dance floors and performers every December.

Out in Africa (www.oia.co.za) Gay and lesbian film festival, held in Jo'burg and Cape Town in October.

Insurance

» Travel insurance covering theft, loss and medical problems is highly recommended.

» Before choosing a policy, shop around; policies designed for short European package tours may not be suitable for the South African veld.

» Read the fine print – some policies specifically exclude 'dangerous activities', which can mean scuba diving, motorcycling, bungee jumping and more.

» Some policies ask you to call (reverse charge) a centre in your home country, where an immediate assessment of your problem is made.

» See also p608 and, for information on vehicle insurance, p601.

» Worldwide travel insurance is available at www.lonelyplanet.com/travel_services. You can buy, extend and claim online anytime – even if you're already on the road.

Internet Access

» Internet access is widely available in South Africa.

» Connections are often slower than in other First World countries.

» Accommodation options usually offer wi-fi or, less commonly, a computer with internet access for guest use.

» We have used the (🛜) icon where an establishment has a wi-fi network.

» The (@) icon is used in sleeping reviews where an accommodation option offers a computer with internet access for guest use.

» Many malls, cafes, restaurants and bars (including chains such as Café Sofia) have wi-fi, often for free. Alternatively, it may be through a provider such as **Skyrove** (www.skyrove.com) or **Red Button** (www.redbutton.co.za), for which you will need to buy credit online using a credit card, or from the hot-spot owner.

» Using a SIM card from a mobile-phone company such as **MTN** (www.mtn.co.za), you can access the internet by plugging a USB dongle into your laptop.

» There are internet cafes in major towns and, sometimes, smaller locations. Charges average at about R30 per hour.

» In Lesotho, web access is available in Maseru.

» In Swaziland, you can log on in spots including Mbabane, Manzini and Malkerns Valley.

Language Courses

There are numerous language schools for learning Xhosa, Zulu, Sotho, Afrikaans and English, including the following:

Inlingua (www.inlingua.co.za; Green Point, Cape Town) Afrikaans, English.

Interlink (www.interlink.co.za; Sea Point, Cape Town) English.

Language Teaching Centre (www.languageteachingcentre.co.za; City Bowl, Cape Town) Xhosa, Zulu, Afrikaans, English.

Phaphama Initiatives (www.phaphama.org; Soweto, Gauteng) Organises immersive tours and homestays in Cape Town, Jo'burg, Gauteng townships including Soweto, and rural KwaZulu-Natal – offering opportunities to learn languages outside a classroom.

UBuntu Bridge (www.learnxhosa.co.za; Claremont and Newlands, Cape Town) Xhosa.

University of the Witwatersrand (www.witslanguageschool.com/aae.aspx; Braamfontein, Jo'burg) Zulu, Sotho, Afrikaans.

Legal Matters

» Key areas to watch out for are traffic offences such as speeding and drunk driving, and drug use and possession.

» Despite a relatively open drug culture, use and possession are illegal: arrests happen and penalties are stiff.

» South Africans may complain about police corruption and claim to have bribed police officers, but offering bribes is not recommended, as it could easily backfire.

» If you get arrested in South Africa, you have the following rights: to remain silent; to be released on bail or warning, unless there's a good reason to keep you in jail; to a lawyer; and to food and decent conditions.

Maps

Maps are widely available at bookshops and tourist offices. **Map Studio** (www.mapstudio.co.za) sells maps from road atlases to pocket maps, with branches in Cape Town and Jo'burg.

Money

Visit www.southafrica.info/travel/advice/currency.htm for more information on money in South Africa.

Foreign currencies The best currencies to bring are US dollars, euros or British pounds in a mixture of cash and travellers cheques, plus a debit or credit card for withdrawing money from ATMs.

Major banks South Africa's major banks are Absa, FNB (First National Bank), Nedbank and Standard Bank.

South Africa South Africa's currency is the rand (R), which is divided into 100 cents. The coins are one, two, five, 10, 20 and 50 cents, and R1, R2 and R5. The notes are R10, R20, R50, R100 and R200. The rand remains weak against Western currencies, making travelling in South Africa less expensive than in Europe and North America.

Swaziland and Lesotho Swaziland's currency is the lilangeni (plural emalangeni, E). Lesotho's is the loti (plural maloti, M), divided into 100 lisente. Both are fixed at a value equal to the rand. Rand are accepted everywhere in both Lesotho and Swaziland, though you will invariably be given maloti or emalangeni in change.

ATMs

» ATMs are widespread in South Africa, both in the cities and beyond.

» For safety precautions, see the boxed text, p590.

» Stash some cash if visiting rural areas such as Kruger National Park.

» In Lesotho there is an ATM in Maseru that accepts international cards. All other ATMs in Lesotho only work if you have a local bank account.

» In Swaziland, there are ATMs that accept international cards in Mbabane, the Ezulwini Valley and a few other locations around the country.

Cards

Because South Africa has a reputation for scams, many banks abroad automatically prevent transactions in the country. Particularly if you plan to use a credit card in South Africa, contact your bank before leaving home and inform it of your travel plans.

TIPPING

Wages are low, and tipping is expected. The main exceptions are in rural parts of Lesotho and Swaziland, where it's generally the custom to simply round up the bill.

SERVICE	TIP
Cafe	10%
Car guard	R2 (R5 for longer periods)
Hotel porter	R10
Petrol-station attendant	R5
Restaurant	10% to 15%
Taxi	Round up fare

» MasterCard and Visa are widely accepted in South Africa; Diners Club and American Express are less commonly accepted.

» Credit and debit cards can be used at many ATMs to withdraw cash.

» In both Lesotho and Swaziland, credit cards are only accepted at major tourist establishments.

» If you get a failed transaction or anything irregular happens while making a payment with a credit or debit card, retrieve your card as quickly as possible and do not try the procedure again.

Moneychangers
SOUTH AFRICA

» Cash is readily exchanged at banks and foreign-exchange bureaus in the major cities.

» Most banks change travellers cheques in major currencies with varying commissions.

» Thomas Cook has travellers cheques in rand, though it may work out better to buy cheques in a stronger currency such as US dollars.

» If you buy rand cheques, do so just before departure to minimise the effects of devaluation.

» The Thomas Cook agent in South Africa is the **Rennies Travel** (www.renniestravel. com) chain of travel agencies, which has branches in the major cities.

» There are American Express foreign-exchange offices in major cities.

» Rennies Travel and American Express do not charge a commission for changing travellers cheques, but banks often offer better exchange rates.

» Keep at least some of your exchange receipts, as you'll need them to reconvert leftover rand when you leave.

LESOTHO

» Maseru is the only place where you can reliably exchange foreign cash and travellers cheques.

» Commissions average 2.5% on travellers cheques (minimum M25) and 1.25% on cash (minimum M40).

» Rand notes are usually available on request.

SWAZILAND

» FNB and Nedbank change cash and travellers cheques; their rates are similar, but commissions vary.

» Most banks ask to see the purchase receipt when cashing travellers cheques.

» Standard Bank has branches in Mbabane, Manzini, Nhlangano, Piggs Peak, Simunye, Tshaneni, Matsapha and Big Bend.

» FNB has branches around the country.

» Nedbank is in Mbabane, Manzini and Matsapha.

Taxes & Refunds
SOUTH AFRICA

» South Africa has a value-added tax (VAT) of 14%, but departing foreign visitors can reclaim about 11% on goods being taken out of the country.

» To make a claim, the goods must have been bought at a VAT-registered vendor, their total value must exceed R250, and you need a tax invoice for each item.

» Your receipt usually covers the requirements for a tax invoice; it must include the following: the words 'tax invoice'; the seller's 10-digit VAT registration number; the seller's name and address; a description of the goods purchased; the cost of the goods in rand; the amount of VAT charged, or a statement that VAT is included in the total cost; a tax-invoice number; the date of the transaction; and for purchases more than R3000, the buyer's name and address and the quantity or volume of the goods.

» All invoices must be originals – no photocopies.

» At your point of departure, you'll need to fill in a form or two and show the goods to a customs inspector.

» At airports, make sure you have goods checked by the inspector before you check in your luggage.

» After going through immigration, make the claim and pick up your refund, issued in the form of a cheque (which, at Cape Town and Jo'burg international airports, can then be cashed at a bank); a Visa electron card, which will be loaded with foreign currency after your departure from South Africa; or a foreign draft (in major currencies including US dollars or pound stirling).

» If your claim comes to more than R3000, the refund will not be given on the spot and will arrive up to six weeks later.

» To process the paperwork beforehand, take your invoices and passport to the preprocessing office at the Clock Tower, Waterfront, Cape Town or Sandton City, Jo'burg.

» You can claim at the international airports in Jo'burg, Cape Town and Durban, and at the smaller airports in Bloemfontein, Gateway, Lanseria, Mpumalanga Kruger (Nelspruit), Pilanesberg, Port Elizabeth and Upington.

» It's also possible to claim at major harbours, and at some posts on the borders with Botswana, Mozambique, Namibia, Swaziland and Zimbabwe.

» Visit www.tax refunds. co.za for more information.

LESOTHO & SWAZILAND

» Both Lesotho and Swaziland have a VAT of 14%, applied similarly to that in South Africa, although there are not yet any systems for refunds in place.

» In both countries, many hotels omit the tax when quoting rates, although we've included it in the listings in this book.

Photography

» In South Africa, film (slide and print), cameras, memory cards and accessories are readily available in large towns.

» Camera and film selection is more limited in Lesotho and Swaziland, with a modest selection of equipment available in major towns.

» In all three countries, don't photograph or film soldiers, police, airports, defence installations and government buildings.

» You should always ask permission before taking a photo of anyone, but particularly so if you're in a tribal village.

» Lonely Planet's *Travel Photography: A Guide to Taking Better Pictures* by Richard l'Anson will help you do exactly what the title says.

Post

» In South Africa and Swaziland, both domestic and international deliveries are generally reliable, but can be slow.

» In Lesotho, delivery is slow and unreliable.

» For mailing anything of value, consider using one of the private mail services, such as **PostNet** (www. postnet.co.za).

Public Holidays

South Africa

Visit www.info.gov.za/aboutsa/holidays.htm for background on the following. In addition 17 June 2013 is a public holiday.

New Year's Day 1 January
Human Rights Day 21 March
Good Friday March/April
Family Day April
Freedom Day 27 April
Workers' Day 1 May
Youth Day 16 June

National Women's Day 9 August
Heritage Day 24 September
Day of Reconciliation 16 December
Christmas Day 25 December
Day of Goodwill 26 December

Lesotho

New Year's Day 1 January
Moshoeshoe Day 11 March
Good Friday March/April
Easter Monday March/April
Workers' Day 1 May
Ascension Day May
Africa or Heroes' Day April/May
King's Birthday 17 July
Independence Day 4 October
Christmas Day 25 December
Boxing Day 26 December

Swaziland

New Year's Day 1 January
Good Friday March/April
Easter Monday March/April
King Mswati III's Birthday 19 April
National Flag Day 25 April
King Sobhuza II's Birthday 22 July
Umhlanga (Reed) Dance August/September
Somhlolo (Independence) Day 6 September
Christmas Day 25 December
Boxing Day 26 December
Incwala Ceremony December/January

School Holidays

» School holiday periods are approximately from: late March to mid-April (varying, depending when Easter is); late June to mid-July; late September to early October; and early December to mid-January.

» The inland provinces (Free State, Gauteng, Mpumalanga, North-West Province and Limpopo) and coastal provinces (Eastern Cape, KwaZulu-Natal, Northern Cape and Western Cape) stagger their school holidays.

» For exact dates, see the calendars at www.saschools.co.za.

» The main school-holiday periods in Lesotho and Swaziland parallel those in South Africa.

Telephone

South Africa

» South Africa has good telephone facilities.

» **Telkom** (www.telkom.co.za) phonecards and, for international calls, Worldcall cards are widely available.

» Local phone calls cost R0.47 per minute.

» Domestic long-distance calls cost about R0.90 per minute.

» Rates drop between 7pm and 7am Monday to Friday, and over the weekend.

» Calls to South African mobiles cost R1.89 per minute; R1.17 between 8pm and 7pm Monday to Friday, and over the weekend.

» Coin-operated public phones are blue; card-operated phones are green.

» There are private phone centres where you can pay cash for your call, but at high rates. These are recommended if you want to make a quick local call, as are the phones you see on tables in the street.

» International calls are cheaper between 8pm and 8am Monday to Friday, and over the weekend.

» Off-peak calls to an Australian landline cost R1.40 per minute; to Canada, R1.10; to Germany, R2.03; to the UK, R0.90. See www.telkom.co.za/common/AugFiling/international_list.html for all international rates.

» A good way to avoid high charges when calling home, or to make reverse-charge

IMPORTANT NUMBERS

See also p19.

South Africa

Ambulance (☎10177)

Cape Town emergencies (☎107)

Cape Town emergencies from mobiles (☎021-480 7700)

Cape Town Rape Crisis (☎021-447 9762)

Collect/reverse-charge calls (☎0900)

Directory services (☎1023)

International call centre (☎10903)

Lifeline Johannesburg rape counselling (☎011-728 1347)

Mobile Yellow Pages via SMS (☎34310)

Netcare private medical assistance (☎082 911)

Police (☎10111)

Talking Yellow Pages (☎10118)

Lesotho

Ambulance (☎2231 2501)

Fire (☎115)

Police (☎2231 9900)

Swaziland

Fire (☎2404 3333, 933)

Police (☎999)

calls, is to dial a 'Home Direct' number, which puts you through to an operator in your country. Call Telkom's 24-hour international call centre to find out the number for your country.

» For more information about making calls in South Africa, visit www.south africa.info/travel/advice/telecoms.htm.

PHONE CODES

Telephone numbers in South Africa are 10 digits, including the local area code, which must always be dialled.

In South Africa, there are several four-digit nationwide prefixes, followed by six-digit numbers. These include:

» ☎080 (usually 0800; toll free)

» ☎0860 (charged as a local call)

» ☎0861 (flat-rate calls)

MOBILE PHONES

» Mobile-phone networks cover most of South Africa, and mobile-phone ownership is widespread.

» There are GSM and 3G digital networks.

» GSM phones on roaming from everywhere apart from the USA, Canada, Mexico and most South American countries should work here.

» The major mobile networks, and their main phone codes: **Cell C** (www.cellc.co.za; 084), **MTN** (www.mtn.co.za; 083), **Virgin Mobile** (www.virginmobile.co.za; 0741) and **Vodacom** (www.vodacom.co.za; 082).

» 07 numbers are increasingly in use as more customers join the networks.

» You can hire a mobile phone through your car-rental provider.

» A cheaper alternative is to use a local prepaid SIM card in your own phone, provided it's unlocked and on roaming.

» SIM cards and credit are available almost everywhere in shops and malls throughout the cities and larger towns.

» SIM cards tend to be more expensive in airport shops.

» You need some form of ID and proof of South African address to buy and 'RICA' (register) a SIM card.

» The proof of address can be an accommodation receipt, or a signed statement from your host or accommodation that you are residing with them.

» MTN calls to landlines and other networks typically cost between R1.30 and R2.19 per minute.

» Sending text messages with MTN typically costs R0.80; international messages cost R1.60.

Lesotho

» Lesotho's telephone system works reasonably well, but coverage is limited in the highlands.

» There are no area codes.

» International calls are expensive.

» For international reverse charge calls dial ☎109.

» Mobile-phone signals are rare in the highlands, and can only be picked up on a few mountain passes.

» The main mobile-phone service provider is **Vodacom Lesotho** (www.vodacom.co.ls).

» Vodacom's coverage area extends northeast from Maseru to 'Muela, south to Quthing (Moyeni) and east to Mohale Dam.

Swaziland

» Swaziland has a reasonably good telephone network.

» There are no area codes.

» Dial ☎94 to make a reverse-charge call.

» International calls are most easily made using MTN phonecards.

» Outside of the major towns, dial ☎94 to book international calls.

» MTN and Vodacom provide mobile-phone networks.

» These do not generally reach mountainous regions.

» In April 2010, all Swazi mobile-phone numbers acquired a prefix of 7; a number that began with the digits 602, now begins with 7602.

» Since then, all landlines have been prefixed with 2, so a number that began 416, now begins 2416.

Time

» SAST (South Africa Standard Time) is two hours ahead of GMT/UTC.

» There is no daylight-saving period.

» Lesotho and Swaziland are in the same time zone as South Africa.

» This is a wide region to be covered by one time zone; the sun can rise and set an hour earlier in Durban than in Cape Town.

» Most timetables and businesses use the 24-hour clock.

Toilets

» Finding a clean, sit-down toilet in South Africa is usually not a problem.

» There are few public toilets, but malls generally have them.

» Tourist offices and restaurants are normally happy to let you use their facilities.

Tourist Information

South Africa

Almost every town in the country has a tourist office.

These are often private entities, which will only recommend member organisations and may add commissions to bookings they make on your behalf. They are worth visiting, but you may have to push to find out about all the possible options.

In state-run offices, staff are often badly informed and lethargic; asking for assistance at your accommodation may prove more useful.

South African Tourism (www.southafrica.net) has a helpful website, with practical information and inspirational features.

PROVINCIAL TOURIST BOARDS

Eastern Cape Tourism Board (www.ectourism. co.za)

Free State Tourism Authority (www.freestatetourism.org)

Gauteng Tourism Authority (www.gauteng.net)

KwaZulu-Natal Tourism Authority (www.kzn.org.za)

Limpopo Tourism & Parks Board (www.golimpopo.com)

Mpumalanga Tourism & Parks Agency (www.mpumalanga.com)

Northern Cape Tourism Authority (www.northerncape.org.za)

North-West Province Parks & Tourism Board (www.tourismnorthwest.co.za)

Western Cape Tourism (www.thewesterncape.co.za)

TOURIST OFFICES ABROAD

Visit www.southafrica.net for details of South African Tourism's offices and call centres in: Amsterdam, Netherlands; Beijing, China; Frankfurt, Germany; London, UK; Los Angeles, USA; Milan, Italy; Mumbai, India; New York, USA; Paris, France; Tokyo, Japan; Sydney, Australia.

Lesotho & Swaziland

Lesotho Tourism Development Corporation (visitlesotho.travel) The website has tips including suggested routes and information on culture and history.

See Lesotho (www.seelesotho.com) Private website with suggestions and links.

Swaziland Tourism Authority (www.welcometoswaziland.com) The website lists sights and activities, and has useful practical information.

DIFFERENCES FROM STANDARD SOUTH AFRICA TIME

COUNTRY	CAPITAL CITY	DIFFERENCE FROM SOUTH AFRICA (HOURS)
Australia	Canberra	+8
Canada	Ottawa	-7
France	Paris	-1
Germany	Berlin	-1
Japan	Tokyo	+7
Netherlands	Amsterdam	-1
New Zealand	Wellington	+10
Spain	Madrid	-1
UK	London	-2
USA	Washington, DC	-7

The Government of the Kingdom of Swaziland (www.gov.sz) Has section on tourist attractions.

Travellers with Disabilities

» South Africa is one of the best destinations on the continent for disabled travellers, with an ever-expanding network of facilities catering to those who are mobility impaired or blind.

» Establishments and destinations with facilities and access for the disabled have been noted throughout the book.

» Wheelchairs are sometimes available at sights such as botanical gardens, though you should call in advance to confirm.

» Several gardens and nature reserves have Braille or guided trails for the visually impaired.

» Boardwalks for wheelchair access are found at many parks and attractions, and some offer activities geared towards travellers with disabilities.

» Hand-controlled vehicles can be hired at major car-rental agencies.

» See also p392.

Resources

Access-Able Travel Source (www.access-able. com) Lists operators offering tours for travellers with disabilities.

Disabled Travel (www. disabledtravel.co.za) Countrywide recommendations of accommodation, restaurants and services from an occupational therapist.

Eco-Access (www.eco -access.org) A South African charity championing the rights of people with disabilities, and promoting better access to nature.

Epic-Enabled (www.epic-enabled.com) Offers accommodation, transport and tours, including Kruger safaris.

Flamingo Tours (www. flamingotours.co.za) Tours around Cape Town, along the Garden Route and elsewhere.

Linx Africa (www.linx.co.za/ trails/lists/disalist.html) List of disabled-friendly trails.

National Council for Persons with Physical Disabilities in South Africa (www.ncppdsa.org.za) A useful initial contact.

QuadPara Association of South Africa (www.qasa. co.za) Has wheelchairs for beach use in Durban and the KwaZulu-Natal south coast.

Rolling SA (www.rollingsa. co.za) Tours including a nine-day safari covering Kruger.

SAN Parks (www.sanparks. org) Has a detailed and inspirational overview of accommodation and accessibility for blind, deaf and mobility-impaired travellers at its parks, including Kruger.

South African Tourism (www.southafrica.net) Has a page of information and suggestions, accessed by clicking on 'Travel tips'.

The Sponge Project (http://thespongeproject.yola site.com) SMS information service for disabled people.

Visas

If you have recently travelled in a yellow-fever area, you need to show a vaccination certificate to get into South Africa, Lesotho and Swaziland.

South Africa

» Travellers from most Commonwealth countries (including Australia, New Zealand and the UK), most Western European countries, Japan and the USA are issued with a free 90-day visitor's permit on arrival.

» Your passport should be valid for at least 30 days after the end of your intended visit.

» Immigration officers rarely ask to see it, but you should be able to present evidence of a return flight, or onward travel plans, from South Africa.

» If you have an onward flight, print a copy of your e-ticket, or ask your airline's help desk at the departing airport to print a copy of your itinerary.

» If you aren't entitled to a visitor's permit, you'll need to obtain a visa (R425 or equivalent) at a South African diplomatic mission in your home country, or one nearby.

» Visas are not issued at the borders.

» If you do need a visa, get a multiple-entry visa if you plan to visit Lesotho, Swaziland or any other neighbouring country. This avoids the hassle of applying for another South African visa.

» For more information, visit the **Department of Home Affairs website** (www.home -affairs.gov.za) and **South African Tourism** (www. southafrica.net).

VISA EXTENSIONS

» Applications for extensions to visas and visitor's permits should be made at the Department of Home Affairs, with branches in Cape Town, Durban, Jo'burg and Pretoria.

» Extensions normally allow another 30 days in South Africa.

» Anecdotal evidence suggests it is possible to do one 'visa run' to get a new visitor's permit, particularly if you leave for a few weeks or you re-enter by plane.

Lesotho

» Citizens of most Western European countries, the USA and most Commonwealth countries are granted a free entry permit at the border or airport.

» The standard permitted stay is two weeks.

» If you ask for longer, it's often granted, although some countries need a visa for stays over 14 days.

» Travellers who require a visa can get one at diplomatic missions in countries including South Africa.

» If you arrive at the Maseru Bridge border crossing without a visa, with some luck you'll be issued a temporary entry permit to allow you to get to Maseru, where you can apply for a visa at the **Ministry of Home Affairs** (www.gov.ls; Maseru). However, don't count on this, as it depends on the whim of the border officials.

» To extend your stay, apply at the Ministry of Home Affairs, or cross the border to South Africa and re-enter Lesotho.

Swaziland

» Visitors from most Western countries don't need a visa to enter Swaziland for up to 30 days.

» People who need visas can get them at Swazi diplomatic missions in Jo'burg, Pretoria and elsewhere.

» Visa applications must be accompanied by documents that also include a letter of invitation.

» Visas cost R80 for single entry; from R300 for multiple entry.

» To stay for longer than 30 days, apply at the **Ministry of Home Affairs immigration department** (www.gov. sz; Mbabane).

Volunteering

Volunteer work is possible, especially if you're interested in teaching or wildlife conservation.

To work on an unpaid, voluntary basis, a visitor's permit or visa suffices. If you want to take a lengthy placement (in South Africa for example, longer than the 60 days afforded by a visitor's permit and extension), the

organisation facilitating your placement should help you apply for the correct visa.

Voluntourism is a growing area. There are some rip-off operators, often around animal-related projects. Book through local rather than foreign organisations, and check most of your money goes to the schemes involved rather than middlemen.

Shorter experiences of a few hours, days or weeks are available through accommodation options and tourist businesses, which often give ongoing support to one or two local schemes. Short visits are interesting for the visitor, but of limited use to the project, beyond any fee paid for the trip.

African Conservation Experience (www.conservationafrica.net) The UK-based organisation offers places on conservation projects in Southern Africa.

African Impact (www.africanimpact.com) The recommended organisation specialises in volunteering, internships and responsible travel across South Africa, Lesotho, Swaziland and beyond.

All Out Africa (www.alloutafrica.com) Offers two-week to one-year places on projects in South Africa, Swaziland and beyond; and expeditions combining volunteering with tours.

Backpacking South Africa (www.backpackingsouthafrica.co.za) Province by province listings of opportunities.

Fair Trade in Tourism South Africa (www.fairtourismsa.org.za) Links to South African organisations.

i-to-i (www.i-to-i.com) The UK-based organisation offers a range of opportunities in South Africa, Swaziland and beyond, such as working with children in a township near Cape Town.

Kick 4 Life (www.kick4life.org) Opportunities in Lesotho including the annual football tour, which mixes

HIV/AIDS education and soccer matches.

OneWorld365 (www.oneworld365.org) UK-based organisation offering volunteering, teaching and other work opportunities.

Pride of Table Mountain (www.wildernessfoundation.org) Volunteer on an educational day walk for deprived children through Cape Town's Kirstenbosch Botanical Gardens to the Table Mountain contour path.

Streetfootballworld (www.streetfootballworld.org) A good starting point for football-related volunteering opportunities.

Volunteer Abroad (www.volunteerabroad.com) A good starting point, with listings of opportunities in South Africa, Lesotho and Swaziland.

Volunteer Africa 32° South (www.volunteerafrica.co.za) Fair Trade-accredited schools project teaching basic computer literacy in the Wild Coast area; also preschool, horse rehabilitation and wildlife conservation projects (see p204 and p207).

Voluntours (www.voluntours.co.za) Recommended Jo'burg-based organisation, offering hands-on involvement in bona fide projects at reasonable prices.

World Wide Opportunities on Organic Farms (www.wwoof.org) Opportunities to stay and work on organic farms across South Africa; Fynbos Estate (host SAF080) is recommended.

Women Travellers

Attitudes Towards Women

Old-fashioned attitudes to women are still common among South African men, regardless of colour. However, you should not tolerate sexist behaviour.

There's a high level of sexual assault and other violence against women in South

Africa, the majority of which occurs in townships and rural areas. Given the extremely high levels of HIV/AIDS, the problem is compounded by the transfer of infection. Rape victims have escaped infection by persuading the attacker to wear a condom.

There have been incidents of travellers being raped, but cases are isolated, and cause outrage in local communities.

For most female visitors, paternalistic attitudes and mildly sleazy behaviour are the main issues.

Safety Precautions

» Single female travellers have a curiosity value that makes them conspicuous, but it may also bring forth generous offers of assistance and hospitality. There is a risk of assault, but many women travel alone safely in South Africa.

» The risk depends on where you go and what you do. Hiking alone is foolhardy, as are hitching and picking up hitchers.

» Risks are reduced if two women travel together or, better, if a woman travels as part of a mixed-sex couple or group.

» Inland and in the more traditional black communities, it's best to behave conservatively. On the coast, casual dress is the norm, but elsewhere dress modestly (full-length clothes that aren't too tight) if you do not wish to draw attention to yourself.

» Always keep common sense and caution at the front of your mind, particularly at night.

» Don't go out alone in the evenings on foot; always take a taxi, preferably with others.

» Even during the day, avoid isolated areas, roadsides and quiet beaches.

» Carry a mobile phone if you'll be driving by yourself.

» If you are spending a long period in a more-dangerous place such as Jo'burg, consider buying a can of pepper spray or similar to keep in your handbag.

Safe Travel

Crime

South Africa

Crime is the national obsession. Apart from car accidents, it's the major risk that you'll face in South Africa. However, despite the statistics and newspaper headlines, the majority of travellers visit the country without incident.

The risks are highest in Jo'burg, followed by some townships and other urban centres. See destination chapters for safety tips in hot spots, and p602 for advice on carjackings.

You can minimise risks by following basic safety precautions, including the following:

» If arriving or changing planes at OR Tambo International Airport (Jo'burg), keep your valuables in your hand luggage and consider vacuum-wrapping your baggage. Items are sometimes pilfered from bags before they reach the carousel.

» Store your travel documents and valuables in your room, if it's secure, or in a safe, if one is available.

» Don't flash around valuables such as cameras, watches and jewellery.

» Don't look like you might be carrying valuables; avoid wearing expensive-looking clothes.

» Completely avoid external money pouches.

» Divide your cash into several stashes, and always have some 'decoy' money or a 'decoy' wallet readily accessible to hand over if you are mugged.

» Keep a small amount of cash handy and separate from your other money, so that you don't need to pull out a large wad of bills for making purchases.

» Don't keep money in your back pocket.

» Avoid groups of young men; trust older mixed-sex groups.

» One of the greatest dangers during muggings or carjackings (most common in Jo'burg) is that your assailants will assume that you are armed, and that you will kill them if you get a chance. Stay calm, and don't resist or give them any reason to think you will fight back.

» Listen to local advice on unsafe areas.

» Avoid deserted areas day and night, including beaches in some urban areas.

» Avoid the downtown and CBD areas of larger towns and cities at night and weekends.

» To travel around towns and cities after dark, take a taxi or, if your destination is close, walk with others.

» If you're visiting a township, join a tour or hire a trusted guide.

» Try not to look apprehensive or lost.

» Avoid driving at night.

» Keep your car doors locked and windows up.

GOVERNMENT TRAVEL ADVICE

For the latest information, check the following websites:

German Federal Foreign Office (www.auswaertiges -amt.de)

UK Foreign & Commonwealth Office (www.fco.gov. uk/travel)

Dutch Ministry of Foreign Affairs (www.minbuza.nl)

Japanese Ministry of Foreign Affairs (www.mofa.go.jp)

New Zealand Ministry of Foreign Affairs and Trade (www.safetravel.govt.nz)

Australian Ministry of Foreign Affairs and Trade (www.smartraveller.gov.au)

US Department of State's Bureau of Consular Affairs (www.travel.state.gov)

Canadian Ministry of Foreign Affairs and International Trade (www.voyage.gc.ca)

BEATING THE ATM SCAMS

There are dozens of ATM scams that involve stealing your cash, your card or your personal identification number (PIN) – usually all three. Thieves are just as likely to operate in Stellenbosch as in downtown Jo'burg, and they are almost always well-dressed and well-mannered men.

In the most common scam, the thief tampers with the ATM so your card becomes jammed. By the time you realise this you've entered your PIN. The thief will have seen this, and when you go inside to report that your card has been swallowed, he will take the card – along with several thousand rand. Always bearing the following rules in mind will help you avoid scams.

» Avoid ATMs at night and in secluded places. Rows of machines in shopping malls are usually the safest.

» Most ATMs have security guards. If there's no guard around when you're withdrawing cash, watch your back, or get someone else to watch it for you.

» Watch the people using the ATM ahead of you carefully. If they look suspicious, go to another machine.

» Use ATMs during banking hours, and if possible, take a friend. If your card jams in a machine, one person can stay at the ATM while the other seeks assistance from the bank.

» When you put your card into the ATM, press cancel immediately. If the card is returned, you know there is no blockage in the machine and it should be safe to proceed.

» Don't hesitate to refuse any offers of help to complete your transaction.

» If someone does offer, end your transaction immediately and find another machine.

» Carry your bank's emergency phone number, and report card loss immediately.

» Avoid using ATMs that inform you at the beginning of the transaction that they will not issue a receipt.

» If there are complications or the withdrawal fails, don't try again; retrieve your card.

» Especially if you'll be driving alone, hire a mobile phone, put your home mobile on roaming or buy a local SIM card.

» Leave your car in secure parking at night and avoid parking in secluded areas during the day.

» Don't leave anything valuable in your car, or give the impression that you are on a road trip with bags in the boot.

Lesotho & Swaziland

Crime rates are nowhere near as high as they are in South Africa. As long as you follow the basic precautions, you should be fine.

» Maseru, Lesotho has seen an increase in armed robberies, break-ins and carjackings targeting expats (though it's small-scale compared with South Africa).

» Street crime is rising in Mbabane and Manzini, Swaziland.

» Elsewhere in Lesotho and Swaziland, crime is negligible.

Drugs

» The legal system does not distinguish between soft and hard drugs.

» *Dagga* or *zol* (marijuana) is illegal but widely used.

» People often use marijuana openly, as you may discover in some backpacker hostels and bars. This is not recommended; there are heavy penalties for use and possession.

» Ecstasy is as much a part of club culture and the rave scene in South Africa as it is elsewhere.

» South Africa is a major market for the barbiturate Mandrax, which is banned there and in many other countries, because of its devastating effects.

» Drugs such as cocaine and heroin are becoming widely available and their use accounts for much crime.

Solo Travel

» Solo travel in South Africa, Lesotho and Swaziland is straightforward.

» While you may be a minor curiosity in rural areas, especially solo women travellers, it's likely that in most places nobody will even bat an eyelid.

» Times when you'll likely want to join a group include at night and on hiking trails.

» Particularly for women, going it alone on hiking trails is not recommended. There is normally a three-person minimum on trails for safety reasons – incidents have occurred.

» Especially in urban areas and at night, lone women travelling should use caution, and avoid isolating situations. See also p587.

Transport

GETTING THERE & AWAY

Flights, tours and rail tickets can be booked online at lonelyplanet.com/bookings.

Entering South Africa, Lesotho & Swaziland

Passport

As long as you have complied with visa and entry-permit requirements (see p586), there are no restrictions on any nationalities for entering South Africa, Lesotho or Swaziland.

If you have recently travelled in a yellow-fever area, you need to show a vaccination certificate to get into South Africa, Lesotho and Swaziland.

South Africa

» Once you have an entry permit or visa, South Africa is straightforward and hassle-free to enter.

» Immigration officials rarely ask to see it, but travellers should technically be able to show an onward ticket; preferably an air ticket, although an overland ticket is also acceptable.

» The same applies to proof that you have sufficient funds for your stay; it pays to be neat, clean and polite.

» For more information and links, visit www.southafrica.info.

Lesotho

» Entry permits are easy to get at Lesotho's land borders and Maseru's Moshoeshoe 1 International Airport.

» If you are a citizen of a country for which a visa is required, it's best to arrange this in advance.

Swaziland

» Entry via Swaziland's land borders and Manzini's Matsapha International Airport is usually hassle-free.

» People who need visas can get them at Swazi diplomatic missions in Jo'burg, Pretoria and elsewhere.

Air

Airports & Airlines

South African Airways (SA; www.flysaa.com; hub JIA) is South Africa's national airline, with an excellent route network and safety record. In addition to its long-haul flights, it operates regional and domestic and routes together with its partners **SA Airlink** (SAA; www.flyairlink.com) and **South African Express** (XZ; www.flyexpress.aero).

OR Tambo International Airport (JIA, JNB, ORTIA; www.airports.co.za), east of Jo'burg, is the major hub for South Africa and the surrounding region.

The other principal international airports:

Cape Town International Airport (CPT, CTIA; www.acsa.co.za, www.capetown-airport.com)

CLIMATE CHANGE & TRAVEL

Every form of transport that relies on carbon-based fuel generates CO_2, the main cause of human-induced climate change. Modern travel is dependent on aeroplanes, which might use less fuel per kilometre per person than most cars but travel much greater distances. The altitude at which aircraft emit gases (including CO_2) and particles also contributes to their climate change impact. Many websites offer 'carbon calculators' that allow people to estimate the carbon emissions generated by their journey and, for those who wish to do so, to offset the impact of the greenhouse gases emitted with contributions to portfolios of climate-friendly initiatives throughout the world. Lonely Planet offsets the carbon footprint of all staff and author travel.

DEPARTURE TAX

South Africa Airport departure tax is included in ticket prices.

Lesotho Departure tax is M50.

Swaziland Departure tax is E50.

King Shaka International Airport (DUR; www.acsa.co.za, http://kingshakainternational.co.za) Durban.

Matsapha International Airport (MTS) Manzini, Swaziland.

Moshoeshoe 1 International Airport (MSU) Maseru, Lesotho.

INTERNATIONAL AIRLINES

South Africa Numerous airlines fly to South Africa, mostly Jo'burg, from all over the world.

Lesotho SA Airlink connects Moshoeshoe 1 and OR Tambo (roughly R2000 to R3000 return).

Swaziland SA Airlink–affiliated **Swaziland Airlink** (www.flyswaziland.com) connects Matsapha and OR Tambo.

Tickets

South Africa is served by numerous airlines that are from Europe, as well as several direct flights going to and from Australasia and North America.

Fares from Europe, North America and Australia are usually at their highest during December and January, and between July and September. They are at their lowest in April and May (except for during the Easter holiday period) and in November. The rest of the year falls into the shoulder-season category.

London is a major hub for airlines offering discounted fares.

It's normally cheaper to fly via Jo'burg than directly to Cape Town.

INTERCONTINENTAL (ROUND-THE-WORLD) TICKETS

Many standard RTW itineraries include South Africa.

It's possible to include both Jo'burg and Cape Town; this usually means flying into one city and out of the other, and making your own way between the two.

The easiest and cheapest option may be to fly in and out of Jo'burg on a RTW ticket, and make separate arrangements from there for Southern African travel.

From Africa

There are good connections between Jo'burg and most major African cities.

South African Airways, SA Airlink, South African Express, the other countries' national carriers and **British Airways** (www.britishairways.com) are good starting points.

Most transcontinental flights have set pricing, with little of the competition-driven discounting that you'll find in other parts of the world.

SOUTHERN AFRICA

Jo'burg is also connected to secondary Southern African airports. For example, **Air Botswana** (www.airbotswana.co.bw) offers direct flights to Francistown, Kasane and Maun as well as Gaborone.

Two budget South African airlines serve other countries in the region:

1Time (www.1time.aero) Jo'burg to Livingstone, Mombasa (Kenya), Zanzibar.

Kulula.com (www.kulula.com) Jo'burg to Harare (Zimbabwe), Livingstone (Zambia), Mauritius, Vilanculous (Mozambique) and Windhoek (Namibia).

From Asia

Singapore, Hong Kong, Bangkok, Shanghai, Tokyo and the major Indian cities are the best places to shop for tickets.

Direct flights to Jo'burg:

Cathay Pacific (www.cathaypacific.com) From Hong Kong.

Singapore Airlines (www.singaporeair.com) From Singapore, with connections to Cape Town, Durban, Port Elizabeth and East London.

South African Airways From Bangkok, Beijing, Hong Kong, Mumbai and Singapore.

Indirect flights:

Air Mauritius (www.airmauritius.com) Singapore, Hong Kong, Shanghai, Kuala Lumpur, Delhi and Mumbai via Mauritius to Jo'burg, Cape Town and Durban.

From Australia & New Zealand

It often works out cheaper to travel via Asia, the Middle East or London.

Services:

Air Mauritius From Perth, Melbourne and Sydney via Mauritius to Jo'burg, Cape Town and Durban.

Emirates (www.emirates.com) From Perth, Melbourne, Sydney and Brisbane via Dubai to Jo'burg, Cape Town and Durban. Also from Auckland via Australia and Dubai, and Christchurch via Sydney, Bangkok and Dubai.

Qantas (www.qantas.com.au) From Sydney and Perth to Jo'burg. Flying with Qantas and/or South African Airways is the quickest route by far, but costs about AU$1000 more than with other carriers.

South African Airways Sydney and Perth to Jo'burg.

Singapore Airlines From Perth, Adelaide, Melbourne, Sydney, Brisbane, Auckland

and Christchurch via Singapore to Jo'burg.

From Canada & the USA

The cheapest route is often via London or Continental Europe. A discounted trans-Atlantic ticket and separate onward ticket to Jo'burg or Cape Town may work out cheaper than a through-fare.

Some airlines fly via West African airports such as Accra (Ghana) and Dakar (Senegal).

From the US west coast, you can sometimes get good deals via Asia.

South African Airways flies New York direct to Jo'burg, and from Washington, DC via Dakar.

From Continental Europe

» You can fly to South Africa from most European capitals.

» Paris, Amsterdam, Frankfurt, Munich and Zurich are hubs; all are within about nine hours of Jo'burg.

» Several airlines fly direct to both Jo'burg and Cape Town, including **KLM** (www.klm.com) from Amsterdam and South African Airways from Frankfurt.

» South African Airways also flies direct from Munich and Zurich to Jo'burg.

» An 'open jaw' ticket, allowing you to fly into one city and out of another, may be available for no extra charge.

» **Turkish Airlines** (www.thy.com) offers competitive fares to Jo'burg and Cape Town via Istanbul (Turkey).

From the Middle East

Good routes:

Egyptair (www.egyptair.com) Cairo to Jo'burg, with connections to Cape Town and Durban.

Emirates Dubai to Jo'burg, Cape Town and Durban.

Qatar Airways (www.qatarairways.com) Doha to Jo'burg and Cape Town.

South African Airways Cairo to Jo'burg; Dubai to Jo'burg, Cape Town and Durban.

Turkish Airlines Istanbul to Jo'burg and Cape Town.

From South America

Travelling via Continental Europe, for example through Madrid with **Iberia** (www.iberia.com), opens up more choice.

South African Airways Buenos Aires and Saõ Paulo to Jo'burg.

From the UK & Ireland

Virgin Atlantic (www.virgin-atlantic.com), British Airways and South African Airways fly direct from London to Jo'burg and Cape Town. Fares are competitive.

Cheap fares are also available via the Middle East, with airlines such as Emirates, Qatar Airways and Turkish Airlines, and Continental Europe.

From Ireland, you'll need to fly via London or Continental Europe.

As well as travel agents, such as those registered with the **Association of British Travel Agents** (ABTA; www.abta.com), check ads in the travel sections of weekend newspapers; in *Time Out*, the *Evening Standard*, and the free publications *TNT* (www.tntmagazine.com) and the *South African* (www.thesouthafrican.com).

Land

Bicycle

There are no restrictions on bringing your own bicycle into South Africa, Lesotho or Swaziland. Sources of information:

Cycling South Africa (www.cyclingsa.com)

International Bicycle Fund (www.ibike.org)

Border Crossings

See p586 for info on visas for South Africa, Lesotho and Swaziland.

The times given are subject to change.

BOTSWANA

There are 18 official South Africa–Botswana border posts, open between at least 8am and 4pm.

Some of the more remote crossings are impassable to 2WD vehicles, and may be closed during periods of high water. Otherwise, the crossings are hassle-free.

Grobler's Bridge/Martin's Drift (⊗8am-10pm) Northwest of Polokwane (Pietersburg).

Kopfontein Gate/Tlokweng Gate (⊗6am-10pm) Next to Madikwe Game Reserve; a main border post.

Pont Drif (⊗8am-4pm) Convenient for Mapungubwe National Park (Limpopo) and Tuli Block (Botswana).

Ramatlabama (⊗6am-8pm) North of Mafikeng; a main border post.

Skilpadshek/Pioneer Gate (⊗6am-10pm) Northwest of Zeerust; a main border post.

Swartkopfontein Gate/Ramotswa (⊗7am-7pm) Northwest of Zeerust.

Twee Rivieren (⊗7.30am-4pm) At the South African entrance to Kgalagadi Transfrontier Park.

LESOTHO

All of Lesotho's borders are with South Africa and are straightforward to cross.

The main crossing is at Maseru Bridge, east of Bloemfontein. Queues here are often very long exiting and, on some weekend evenings, entering Lesotho; use other posts if possible.

MOZAMBIQUE

The following are the Mozambique–South Africa border posts. See p594 for crossings to/from Swaziland.

Giriyondo (⊗8am-4pm Oct-Mar, to 3pm Apr-Sep) Between Kruger National Park's Phalaborwa Gate and Massingir (Mozambique).

Kosi Bay/Ponta d'Ouro
(☺8am-4pm) On the coast, well north of Durban.

Lebombo/Ressano Garcia (☺6am-midnight) The main crossing, east of Nelspruit.

Pafuri (☺8am-4pm) In Kruger National Park's northeastern corner.

NAMIBIA
South Africa–Namibia border posts include the following.

Alexander Bay/Oranjemund (☺6am-10pm) On the Atlantic coast; public access sometimes not permitted.

Nakop/Ariamsvlei (☺24hr) West of Upington.

Rietfontein/Aroab (☺8am-4.30pm) Just south of Kgalagadi Transfrontier Park.

Vioolsdrif/Noordoewer (☺24hr) North of Springbok, en route to/from Cape Town.

SWAZILAND
There are 11 South Africa–Swaziland border posts, all of which are hassle-free, including the following. Note that small posts close at 4pm.

Goba/Mhlumeni (☺24hr) To/from Mozambique.

Golela/Lavumisa (☺7am-10pm) En route between Durban and Swaziland's Ezulwini Valley.

Josefdal/Bulembu (☺8am-4pm) Between Piggs Peak and Barberton (Mpumalanga); can be tricky in wet weather.

Lomahasha/Namaacha (☺7am-8pm) The busy post in extreme northeast Swaziland is the main crossing to/from Mozambique.

Mahamba (☺7am-10pm) The best crossing to use from Piet Retief in Mpumalanga. Casinos nearby attract traffic, especially on weekends.

Mananga (☺7am-6pm) Southwest of Komatipoort.

Matsamo/Jeppe's Reef (☺7am-8pm) Southwest of Malelane and a possible route to Kruger National Park. Casinos nearby attract traffic, especially on weekends.

Onverwacht/Salitje (☺7am-6pm) North of Pongola in KwaZulu-Natal.

Oshoek/Ngwenya (☺7am-10pm) This is the busiest crossing, located about 360km southeast of Pretoria.

ZIMBABWE

Beitbridge (☺24hr) Situated on the Limpopo River, this is the only border post between Zimbabwe and South Africa. There is lots of smuggling, so searches are very thorough and the queues are often quite long. The closest South African town to the border is Musina (15km south), where you can change money. Ignore touts on the Zimbabwe side trying to 'help' you through Zimbabwe immigration and customs; there is no charge for the government forms needed for immigration.

Bus

» Numerous bus lines cross between South Africa and its neighbours, including those listed on p598.

» It's the most efficient way to travel overland, unless you have your own vehicle.

» Sometimes-lengthy queues usually the only major hassle.

» You'll have to disembark to take care of visa formalities, then reboard and carry on.

» Visa prices not included in ticket prices.

» Some bus lines offer student and backpacker discounts, upon presentation of student ID.

MINIBUS TAXI

» You can travel to/from South Africa's neighbours by local minibus taxi.

LESOTHO BORDERS

BORDER	OPENING HOURS	NEAREST LESOTHO CROSSING/SOUTH AFRICA TOWN
Caledonspoort	6am-10pm	Butha-Buthe/Fouriesburg
Makhaleng Bridge	8am-4pm	Mohale's Hoek/Zastron
Maputsoe Bridge	24hr	Maputsoe/Ficksburg
Maseru Bridge	24hr	Maseru/Ladybrand
Nkonkoana	8am-4pm	Sehlabathebe/Bushman's Nek
Ongeluksnek	8am-4pm	Mphaki/Matatiele
Peka Bridge	8am-4pm	Peka/Clocolan
Qacha's Nek	8am-8pm	Qacha's Nek/Matatiele
Ramatseliso's Gate	8am-4pm	Tsoelike/Matatiele
Sani Pass	8am-4pm (summer 6pm)	Mokhotlong/Himeville
Sephapo's Gate	8am-4pm	Mafeteng/Boesmanskop
Tele Bridge	8am-10pm	Quthing/Sterkspruit
Van Rooyensnek Gate	6am-10pm	Mafeteng/Wepener

» A few routes go direct.

» It's normally necessary to walk across the border and pick up a new taxi on the other side.

» Long-distance services generally leave early in the morning.

BOTSWANA

Intercape (www.intercape. co.za) runs daily between Gaborone (Botswana) and Pretoria (R260 to R380, eight hours) via Jo'burg.

Minibuses (less safe and comfortable than buses) run between Jo'burg and Gaborone via Mafikeng (North-West Province).

You can also pick up minibuses over the border from Mafikeng to Lobatse (1½ hours) and Gaborone (2½ hours).

Another route from Jo'burg is to/from Palapye (Botswana) via Grobler's Bridge/Martin's Drift (eight hours).

LESOTHO

Minibus taxis connect Jo'burg and Maseru.

It's quicker and easier to catch a bus to Bloemfontein, then continue by minibus taxi to Maseru (three hours), changing in Botshabelo (Mtabelo) or Ladybrand.

Bus services also run to Ladybrand.

Leaving Maseru, long-distance minibus taxis leave from the rank at the Maseru Bridge crossing.

Other routes:

» Mokhotlong (Lesotho) to/from Underberg (KwaZulu-Natal) via Sani Pass.

» Qacha's Nek (Lesotho) to/from Matatiele (Eastern Cape).

» Maputsoe Bridge crossing, 6km southeast of Ficksburg (Free State), to/from Butha-Buthe and northern Lesotho.

» Jo'burg to/from Butha-Buthe via Fouriesburg (Free State) and the Caledonspoort crossing.

MOZAMBIQUE

Bus companies including **Greyhound** (www.greyhound.

co.za), **Intercape** (www. intercape.co.za) and **Translux** (www.translux.co.za) run daily 'luxury' coaches between Jo'burg/Pretoria and Maputo (Mozambique) via Nelspruit and Komatipoort (R300, nine hours).

The above route can be tackled in minibus taxis.

Calanga Beach Resort (www.mozambiquecalanga. co.za) and **Cheetah Express** (http://tinyurl.com/6oh2x4l), both based in Mozambique, run shuttles between Nelspruit and Maputo.

Taxis run between Maputo and the Namaacha/Lomahasha post on the Swazi border (1¾ hours); some continue to Manzini (3¼ hours).

NAMIBIA

Intercape (www.intercape. co.za) buses go from Windhoek (Namibia) to Cape Town (R640 to R920, 21 hours) on Monday, Wednesday, Friday and Sunday, returning Tuesday, Thursday, Friday and Sunday.

SWAZILAND

A daily shuttle runs between Jo'burg and Mbabane (see p489).

Minibus taxis routes:

» Jo'burg to/from Manzini (four hours) via Mbabane.

» Durban to/from Manzini (eight hours).

» Manzini to/from Maputo (3¼ hours).

ZIMBABWE

Greyhound (www.greyhound. co.za) and **Intercape** (www. intercape.co.za) services operate daily buses between Jo'burg and Harare (16½ hours, R420), and between Jo'burg and Bulawayo (14 hours, R400), via Pretoria and Limpopo.

Minibus taxis run south from Beitbridge to Musina and beyond.

Car & Motorcycle

» If you hire a car in South Africa and plan to take it across an international border, you'll need a permission letter from the hire company.

» Most companies permit entry to most neighbouring countries, including Lesotho and Swaziland but some may be reluctant regarding Mozambique.

» Check that the right information is on the permission letter; companies often get it wrong.

» South African car hire companies typically charge the following for a permission letter to take a car to the following countries: Botswana R1000, Lesotho R400, Mozambique R1500, Namibia R1000, Swaziland R200, Zimbabwe R1000.

BRINGING YOUR OWN VEHICLE

» You'll need the vehicle's registration papers, liability insurance and your driving licence.

» You'll also need a *carnet de passage en douane*, the international customs document, which allows the temporary admission of motor vehicles.

» Obtain a carnet through your local automobile association.

» Cars registered in South Africa, Lesotho, Swaziland, Botswana and Namibia don't need a carnet to visit the other countries in this group.

» Drivers of vehicles from outside Southern Africa must pay a security deposit of between 10% and 100% of the vehicle's value.

BOTSWANA

See also p593. The following crossings are passable in 2WD cars:

» Grobler's Bridge/Martin's Drift

» Kopfontein Gate/Tlokweng Gate

» Ramatlabama

» Skilpadshek/Pioneer Gate

LESOTHO

The easiest entry points for cars and motorcycles are on the northern and western sides of the country.

Most of the entry points to the south and east are unpaved, though most are passable in a 2WD, depending on weather conditions.

A sealed road runs westwards from Qacha's Nek.

You'll need a 4WD to enter or exit via Sani Pass.

It's more economical to hire a car in South Africa than in Lesotho (you'll need a permission letter from the hire company to cross the border; this costs about R400).

There's a small road tax of about M5 payable on entering Lesotho.

MOZAMBIQUE

You must have two red hazard triangles in your car in case of a breakdown.

Kosi Bay/Ponta d'Ouro
Travelling to/from Mozambique via this border post, you'll need your own vehicle (4WD on the Mozambique side). Accommodation options in Ponta d'Ouro (Mozambique) offer transfers.

Lebombo The N4 and EN4 freeways connect Jo'burg/Pretoria with Maputo via this border post, with six tolls on the South African side (two via the N12 from Jo'burg) and one on the Mozambique side.

Namaacha/Lomahasha
The roads leading to this border post with Swaziland are sealed, and negotiable with 2WD.

NAMIBIA

2WD Freeways lead to the Vioolsdrif/Noordoewer and Nakop/Ariamsvlei crossings.

4WD A 4WD opens up more options for crossing the border, including through the Kgalagadi and |Ai-|Ais/Richtersveld Transfrontier Parks.

SWAZILAND

Swaziland's borders can be crossed in a 2WD. There's a road tax of about E50 payable on entering Swaziland.

ZIMBABWE

Entering or leaving South Africa, vehicles pay a toll at the border to use the Limpopo Bridge.

Train

See p606 for details of cross-border train cruises to/from South Africa.

The Man in Seat Sixty-One (www.seat61.com) has ideas for train travel throughout Southern Africa, including the following journey.

MOZAMBIQUE

You can travel from Jo'burg/Pretoria on a domestic **Shosholoza Meyl** (www.shosholozameyl.co.za) train to Komatipoort, then cross the border on foot and continue to Maputo on a Caminhos de Ferro do Moçambique (CFM) train.

Sea

South Africa is an important stop on world shipping routes. Cape Town is a major port of call for cruise ships, and many also stop at Durban. Both are good places to look for a crew berth on private yachts sailing up the East African coast.

It's possible to find cruise and freighter lines linking South Africa with Mozambique, Madagascar and Mauritius. Many freighters have comfortable passenger cabins.

Even on freighter lines, the thrill of approaching the tip of the continent by sea certainly doesn't come cheap. Fares from South Africa tend to be lower than those to the country.

Contacts

Cruise People (UK; www.cruisepeople.co.uk)

Cruiser Log (South Africa; www.cruiser.co.za/crewfinder.asp)

LBH Group (South Africa and Mozambique; www.tallships.co.za)

Maris Freighter Cruises (USA; www.freightercruises.com)

Perpetual Travel (Australia; http://perpetualtravel.com/rtw/rtwfreighters.html) Suggests reference books and further links.

Royal Mail Ship St Helena (UK; www.rms-st-helena.com)

Safmarine (USA; www.safmarine.com)

Starlight Lines (South Africa; www.starlight.co.za)

Strand Voyages (UK; www.strandtravelltd.co.uk)

Tours

Dozens of tour and safari companies organise package tours to South Africa, Lesotho, Swaziland and their neighbouring countries.

If you prefer a more independent approach, you can prebook flights and accommodation for the first few nights, then join tours locally (see p605).

Itineraries typically include Kruger National Park and Cape Town and the Cape Peninsula.

For special interests such as birdwatching and botany, check the advertisements in specialist magazines.

Australia

Adventure World (www.adventureworld.com.au) A range of tours and safaris in South Africa and the region.

African Wildlife Safaris (www.africanwildlifesafaris.com.au) Customised wildlife safaris in South Africa and neighbouring countries.

Peregrine Travel (www.peregrine.net.au) Itineraries range from transcontinental missions to two-week safaris.

France

Makila Voyages (www.makila.fr) Upper-end tailored tours and safaris in South Africa and its neighbours.

UK

Dragoman (www.dragoman.co.uk) Overland tours.

Exodus Travels (www.exodustravels.co.uk) A variety of tours, including overland trips and walking, cycling and wildlife itineraries, covering South Africa and surrounds.

Face Africa (www.faceafrica.com) Tailor-made ethical tours around South Africa and beyond, incorporating interaction with locals.

In the Saddle (www.inthesaddle.com) Strictly for horse aficionados, with various rides in South Africa and its northern neighbours, including the Wild Coast and the Waterberg.

Intrepid Travel (www.intrepidtravel.com) Tours espousing the philosophy of independent travel; numerous itineraries cover South Africa and the region.

Naturetrek (www.naturetrek.co.uk) Specialist nature tours, visiting parts of South Africa and its northern neighbours including Namakwa and the Drakensberg.

Temple World (www.templeworld.co.uk) Upper-end 'educational' tours in South Africa, Swaziland and elsewhere in the region, focusing on themes such as history, culture and wildlife.

USA

Adventure Center (www.adventurecenter.com) Adventure tours and activity-focused trips, covering South Africa, Lesotho and Swaziland.

Africa Adventure Company (www.africa-adventure.com) Upper-end wildlife safaris, including the private reserves around Kruger National Park, plus itineraries in and around Cape Town.

Born Free Safaris (www.safaris2africa.com) Itineraries covering areas from the Cape to Swaziland.

Bushtracks (www.bushtracks.com) Luxury safaris and private air charters.

GETTING AROUND

Air

Airlines in South Africa, Lesotho & Swaziland

Domestic fares aren't cheap. Jo'burg to Cape Town, a popular route served by numerous airlines, typically costs about R750.

Keep costs down by booking online months before travelling.

It can save money, or offer convenience at no extra cost, to tie domestic flights into an international ticket; eg fly from London to Jo'burg and on to Cape Town with South African Airways.

See destination chapters for more-detailed information about routes, fares and local travel agents.

Comair (☑0860 435 922; www.comair.co.za) Operates British Airways flights in Southern Africa, and has flights linking Jo'burg, Cape Town, Durban and Port Elizabeth.

SA Airlink (☑0861 606 606; www.flyairlink.com) South African Airways' partner has a good network, including smaller destinations such as Upington, Mthatha and Maseru/Moshoeshoe 1.

South African Airways (☑0861 359 722; www.flysaa.com) The national airline, with an extensive and efficient domestic network.

South African Express (☑0861 729 227; www.flyexpress.aero) This South African Airways partner also has a good network, including three direct weekly flights between Cape Town and Hoedspruit (for Kruger National Park).

Swaziland Airlink (☑518 6155; www.flyswaziland.com) Flies between Jo'burg and Manzini/Matsapha.

BUDGET AIRLINES

The following also offer hotel bookings, car hire and holiday packages.

1time (☑011-086 8000; www.1time.aero) Links Jo'burg, Cape Town, Durban, East London, George and Port Elizabeth.

Kulula.com (☑0861 585 852; www.kulula.com) Links Jo'burg, Cape Town, Durban, George, Nelspruit and Port Elizabeth.

Mango (☑0861 001 234; www.flymango.com) Links Jo'burg, Cape Town, Durban and Bloemfontein.

Bicycle

South Africa

As long as you are fit enough to handle the hills, South Africa offers some rewarding cycling opportunities. It has scenic and diverse terrain, abundant campsites, and numerous quiet secondary roads.

See p593 for cycling websites.

Good areas The Cape Peninsula and Winelands are excellent; the Wild Coast is beautiful and challenging; the northern lowveld offers wide plains.

Public transport Trains can carry bicycles, but most bus lines don't want bicycles in their luggage holds, and minibuses don't carry luggage on the roof.

Purchase Larger South African cities, especially Cape Town, have a good selection of mountain bikes for sale. Jo'burg and Cape Town are the best places to look for touring bikes. To resell your bicycle at the end of your trip, try hostel bulletin boards, bike shops and clubs, and www.gumtree.co.za.

Hire For day rides, some hostels offers short-term mountain bike hire. Mountain-bike hire can also sometimes be arranged through bike shops in the cities, though you'll usually be required to leave a credit-card deposit.

Safety Distances between major towns are often long, although, except in isolated areas such as the Karoo, you're rarely far from a village or farmhouse. Many roads don't have a hard shoulder; on those that do, motorists use the shoulder as an unofficial slow lane. It's illegal to cycle on highways, and roads near urban areas are too busy and hazardous. Before heading off anywhere, contact other cyclists, through local cycling clubs or bicycle shops, to get recent information on the routes you're considering. Bring a good lock to counter the ever-present risk of theft, store the bike inside your accommodation (preferably inside your room) and chain it to something solid.

Spare parts Mountain bikes and parts are widely available. It's often difficult to find specialised parts for touring bikes, especially outside Cape Town and Jo'burg. Establish a relationship with a good bike shop in a city before you head off into the veld, in case you need something couriered to you.

Weather Much of the country (except for Western Cape and the west coast) gets most of its rain in summer (late November to March), often in the form of violent thunderstorms. When it isn't raining, summer days can be unpleasantly hot, especially in the steamy lowveld.

Lesotho & Swaziland

Both are excellent cycling destinations, for which you need a mountain bike. Stock up on spares in South Africa. Summer thunderstorms and flooding are an issue. Trans-porting bicycles on public transport is uncommon, but you can often arrange something with the driver.

Lesotho The mountainous terrain means Lesotho is only for the physically fit. There are countless routes, but for experienced cyclists, the Sani Pass is Lesotho's classic mountain-bike route. It's sometimes possible to hire bicycles through lodges on the South Africa side of the pass. Beware of icy roads in winter.

Swaziland Avoid the main towns and the heavily travelled Ezulwini Valley. Options include the shorter mountain-bike trails in Hlane Royal National Park and in Mlilwane Wildlife Sanctuary, both of which hire bicycles.

Boat

There are few opportunities to travel by boat. The most likely possibilities are between Cape Town, Port Elizabeth and Durban.

Local yacht clubs are good starting points.

For more information and resources, see p596.

Bus
South Africa

A good network of buses, of varying reliability and comfort, links the major cities.

Classes There are no class tiers on the bus lines, although major companies generally offer a 'luxury' service, with features such as air-con, a toilet and films.

Discounts The major bus lines offer student, backpacker and senior-citizen discounts, as well as specials; check their websites for details. Inquire about travel passes if you'll be taking several bus journeys.

Fares Roughly calculated by distance, although short runs are disproportionately expensive. Prices also rise during school holidays.

Safety Apart from where noted, the lines listed in this chapter are generally safe. Note, however, that many long-distance services run through the night. On overnight journeys, travellers should take care of their valuables and women might feel more comfortable sitting near the front of the bus.

Ticket purchase For the main lines, purchase tickets at least 24 hours in advance, and as far in advance as possible for travel during peak periods. Tickets can be bought through bus offices, **Computicket** (www.compu ticket.co.za) and Shoprite/Checkers supermarkets.

BUS LINES

Greyhound and Translux are considered the premium lines.

City to City (☏0861 589 282; www.citytocity.co.za) In partnership with Translux, it operates the routes that once carried people between the homelands and the cities under apartheid. The no-frills service is less expensive than the other lines, and serves many off-the-beaten-track places, including townships and mining towns. Destinations include Mthatha, Nelspruit, Hazyview, Beitbridge (for Zimbabwe), Piet Retief and various towns in KwaZulu-Natal.

Greyhound (☏083 915 9000; www.greyhound.co.za, www.citiliner.co.za) An extensive network of comfortable buses, including Jo'burg to Durban via Richards Bay. Also operates other lines including the cheaper Citiliner buses.

Intercape (☏0861 287 287; www.intercape.co.za) An extensive network stretching from Cape Town to Limpopo and beyond. For longer hauls (including Cape Town to Windhoek, Namibia and Mossel Bay to Jo'burg), it's worth paying extra for a reclining seat on an overnight Sleepliner bus.

SA Roadlink (☎011-333 2223; www.saroadlink.co.za) Links Jo'burg/Pretoria with Bloemfontein, Port Elizabeth, East London, Mthatha, Durban, Cape Town, Polokwane and points in between. A smaller network than the others, but prices are reasonable – generally just above City to City fares.

Translux (☎0861 589 282; www.translux.co.za) The main long-distance operator, serving destinations including Cape Town, Durban, Bloemfontein, Port Elizabeth, East London, Mthatha, Nelspruit and the Garden Route.

Lesotho

Buses and minibus taxis A good network of buses and minibus taxis (known locally as just 'taxis') covers most of the country. Minibus taxis serve the major towns, and many smaller towns. Buses, slightly cheaper and somewhat slower, serve the major towns. There are no classes, and service is decidedly no-frills.

Departures Most departures are in the morning (generally, the longer the journey, the earlier the departure).

Northern Lesotho Heading northeast from Maseru, you usually have to change at Maputsoe. The transfer sometimes happens en route into Maputsoe if your bus meets another bus.

Tickets On larger buses, although you'll be quoted long-distance fares, it's best to just buy a ticket to the next major town. Most passengers will likely get off there, leaving you stuck waiting for the bus to fill up again while others leave. Buying tickets in stages is only slightly more expensive than buying a direct ticket. It's not necessary (or pos-

sible) to reserve a seat in advance.

Swaziland

» Minibuses are the main form of public transport.
» Run almost everywhere; frequent stops en route.
» Leave when full; no reservations necessary.
» Only a few domestic buses.
» Most start and terminate at the main stop in central Mbabane.
» Slightly cheaper than minibuses.

Car & Motorcycle

South Africa is one of the world's great countries for a road trip.

Away from the main bus and train routes, having your own wheels is the best way to get around.

If you're in a group, hiring a car is often the most economical option.

For information about bringing your own vehicle, see p595.

Road maps, a worthwhile investment, are readily available in all three countries.

BAZ BUS

A convenient alternative to standard bus lines, **Baz Bus** (☎0861 229 287; www.bazbus.com) caters almost exclusively to backpackers and travellers. It offers hop-on, hop-off fares and door-to-door service between Cape Town and Jo'burg via the Garden Route, Port Elizabeth, Durban and Northern Drakensberg.

Baz Bus drops off and picks up at hostels, and has transfer arrangements with those off its route in areas such as the Wild Coast. You can book directly with Baz Bus or at most hostels.

Point-to-point fares are more expensive than on the major bus lines, but it can work out economically if you take advantage of the hop-on/hop-off feature.

Sample one-way hop-on, hop-off fares to Cape Town: from Jo'burg/Pretoria R2900; from Durban R2430; from Port Elizabeth R1250.

One-/two-/three-week travel passes cost R1400/R2100/2600.

Automobile Associations

Automobile Association of South Africa (AASA; ☎011-799 1000, emergencies 083 843 22; www.aasa.co.za) offers a vehicle breakdown service, which can be useful if you'll be driving in the areas it covers.

Its fleet of emergency response vehicles operates out of Gauteng, Cape Town, Durban, Port Elizabeth, East London, Bloemfontein, Nelspruit and Pietermaritzburg.

Membership costs from R35 per month.

Members of foreign clubs in the **Fédération Internationale de l'Automobile** (FIA; www.fia.com) group have free access to AASA services for three months, including roadside repairs in Jo'burg, Pretoria, Cape Town, Durban and Port Elizabeth.

In Lesotho and Swaziland, you'll need to rely on local repair facilities in the major towns.

Driving Licence

» You can use your driving licence from your home country, provided it is in

English (or you have a certified translation).

» In South Africa, it should also carry your photo.

» Otherwise you'll need an international driving permit.

» Police generally ask to see foreign drivers' passports, so keep a photocopy in your car.

Fuel & Spare Parts

» Unleaded petrol costs R11 per litre in all three countries.

» An attendant will fill your tank and clean your windows.

» Tip R2.

» If they check your oil, water or tyres, tip R5.

» Along the main roads in South Africa and Swaziland, there are plenty of petrol stations.

» Many stay open 24 hours.

» There are petrol stations in all major South African towns.

» In Swaziland, Mbabane and Manzini have the best facilities.

» Manzini is the best place in Swaziland for spare parts.

» In rural areas, and throughout Lesotho, fill up whenever you can.

» In Lesotho, the main petrol stations are in Maseru.

» Other major towns have limited facilities.

» Carry a jerry can in Lesotho, where fuel is not readily available in remote areas.

Hire
SOUTH AFRICA

» Car hire is inexpensive in South Africa compared with Europe and North America, starting below R200 per day.

» Most companies have a minimum age requirement of 21 years (23 in Swaziland).

» Most companies ask for a credit card. Most will not accept a debit card. Most use a chip-and-pin machine, so you need to know your credit card's pin number.

» For low rates, book online months in advance.

» Most companies stipulate a daily mileage limit, with an extra fee payable for any mileage over this limit. This can be a drawback if you're planning a long road trip. Four hundred kilometres a day is generally sufficient. If you plan one- or two-day stops along the way, 200km a day might be sufficient. If you hire through an international company, and book through an overseas branch, you may get unlimited kilometres for no extra cost, except at peak times such as December to January.

» Make sure that quoted prices include the 14% value-added tax (VAT).

» One-way hire is charged according to the distance of the relocation.

» If loaded up with people or luggage, small cars may struggle on hills. Even on major highways, hills can be steep in areas such as the Wild Coast.

» Steep hills may also make automatics unpleasant to drive.

» South Africa has hire operations in major cities and airports.

» It's generally cheapest to hire in a hub like Jo'burg or Cape Town.

LESOTHO & SWAZILAND

» Lesotho has hire operations in Maseru and Moshoeshoe 1 International Airport.

» It usually works out cheaper to hire a vehicle in South Africa and drive it over the Lesotho border (you'll need a permission letter from the hire company to cross the border; this costs about R400).

» Swaziland has hire operations in Mbabane and at Matsapha International Airport.

» Swazi rates are similar to those in South Africa.

HIRE COMPANIES
The budget airlines listed on p597 offer competitive hire rates.

Also check with backpacker hostels and travel agents, as many offer good deals.

Local companies are usually less expensive, though they tend to come and go, and their vehicles are often older.

Abba (www.abbacarrental. co.za) South Africa.

Argus (www.arguscarhire. co.za) South Africa, Lesotho and Swaziland. Online consolidator.

Around About Cars (www. aroundaboutcars.com) South Africa and Lesotho. This recommended budget agent

---

PARKING & CAR GUARDS

Parking is readily available at sights, eateries and accommodation throughout South Africa, Lesotho and Swaziland. Particularly in Jo'burg and other locations where crime is a problem, secure parking is often offered. We have indicated parking availability in Sleeping and Sights listings with the (P) icon.

If you are parking in the street or even a car park in larger South African towns and cities, you will often be approached by a 'car guard'. They will keep an eye on your motor in exchange for a tip; R2 for a short period, R5 to R10 for longer stays. They may also offer to wash your car for an extra R20. Do not pay them until you are leaving, or if they did not approach you when you arrived. Ensure you give the money to the right person; in Cape Town, for example, approved car guards often wear high-visibility vests.

gets low rates with other operators, including Budget, Tempest and First. One of the few companies offering unlimited mileage.

Avis (www.avis.co.za) South Africa, Lesotho and Swaziland.

Budget (www.budget.co.za) South Africa and Lesotho.

Europcar (www.europcar.co.za) South Africa, Lesotho and Swaziland.

First (www.firstcarrental.co.za) South Africa.

Hertz (www.hertz.co.za) South Africa.

Sixt (www.sixt.com) South Africa.

Tempest (www.tempest carhire.co.za) South Africa.

Thrifty (www.thrifty.co.za) South Africa.

CAMPERVANS, 4WD & MOTORCYCLES

» Some campervan/motorhome hire includes camping gear.

» One-way hire is not always possible.

» 'Bakkie' campers, sleeping two in the back of a canopied pick-up, are cheaper.

» Mopeds and scooters are available for hire in Cape Town and other tourist areas.

» For Lesotho and provinces such as the Northern Cape with many national parks, consider a 4WD.

» In addition to the above, check: **African Leisure Travel** (www.africanleisure.co.za) Jo'burg, 4WD and campervans; **Britz 4x4 Rentals** (www.britz.co.za) Cape Town and Jo'burg, 4WD; **LDV Biking** (www.ldvbiking.co.za) Cape Town, motorcycles; **Maui** (www.maui.co.za) Cape Town and Jo'burg, motorhomes; and **Motozulu** (www.motozu.lu.ms) Port Shepstone (KwaZulu-Natal), motorcycles.

Insurance

Insurance for third-party damage and damage to or loss of your vehicle is highly recommended, though not legally required.

Generally it is only available on an annual basis.

When hiring a vehicle, insurance with an excess should be included, with an excess waiver or reduction available for extra.

Check the car insurance or hire agreement covers hail damage; a distinct and costly possibility during summer.

Insurers:

Automobile Association of South Africa (www.aasa.co.za)

Outsurance (www.outsurance.co.za)

Sansure (www.sansure.com)

Purchase

South Africa is the best place in the region to buy a vehicle for a Southern African, or larger sub-Saharan, journey. It's worth buying a vehicle if you plan to stay longer than about three months.

Jo'burg is the best place to buy; prices are often lower and cars build up rust in Cape Town and coastal towns. Cape Town is the best place to resell; the market is smaller and prices higher.

In Jo'burg, you'll find a good congregation of used-car dealers on Great North Rd, Benoni; in Cape Town, on Voortrekker Rd between Maitland and Bellville metro train stations.

It's best to buy from a dealer rather than a private seller, as the vendor will have to help you with the arduous process of registering the car. Dealers should have some of the forms you need, and you may find one willing to agree to a buy-back deal. Buying privately, you won't have any dealer warranties, but prices will be cheaper.

In 2011, one reader reported paying R124,000, at a Benoni dealership, for a four-year-old Nissan 2.4 4WD *bakkie* (pick-up truck) with a canopy and 135,000km on the clock. Canopies typically cost R10,000.

PAPERWORK

Make sure that the car details correspond with the ownership (registration) papers, that there is a current licence disc on the windscreen, and that the vehicle has been checked by the police clearance department.

Check the owner's name against their identity document, and check the car's engine and chassis numbers.

Consider getting the car tested by a garage.

Cheap cars will often be sold without a roadworthy certificate – required when you register the change-of-ownership form and pay tax for a licence disc. Some private garages are allowed to issue certificates for a few hundred rand, and some will overlook minor faults.

REGISTRATION

Registering your car is a bureaucratic headache, and will likely take a couple of weeks. Officials have told travellers they cannot register a car without South African citizenship, but this is untrue.

The forms you need to complete should be available at vehicle-registration offices, dealers or through the websites listed on p602. They include:

» RLV/NCO5 (notification of change of ownership/sale of motor vehicle)

» ANR8 (application and notice in respect of traffic register number)

Present yourself at a vehicle-registration office along with:

» your passport and a photocopy

» a copy of the seller's ID

» the registration certificate (in the seller's name)

» a roadworthy certificate

» proof of purchase

» proof of address (a letter from your accommodation should suffice)

» a valid licence

» your money.

It will help if the seller comes with you and brings their ID.

Call ahead to check how much cash you'll need. Charges rise annually, and are currently about R400 for a small car and R800 for a 4WD.

If the licence has expired, you will also have to pay a penalty.

CONTACTS & RESOURCES

Auto Trader (www. autotrader.co.za) Car ads nationwide.

Cape Ads (www.capeads. com) Car ads around Cape Town.

Capetown.gov.za (http:// tinyurl.com/72c42nw) Details of vehicle registration offices in and around the city.

Enatis.com (http://tinyurl. com/6nm5ugc) Information on registering a used vehicle.

Graham Duncan Smith (☑021-797 3048) Land Rover expert offering consultation, repairs and sales.

Mahindra Benoni (http:// mahindrabenoni.co.za) Jo'burg dealer offering car and *bakkie* sales and trade-ins; has experience of selling to foreigners and helping them register vehicles.

Services.gov.za (http://tiny url.com/6o3674x) Information on changing ownership or a titleholder's particulars.

South African Forum (http://southafricanforum. co.za) Vehicle purchase is among the topics on this forum.

Suedafrika Forum (http:// suedafrika-forum.net) Another forum, mostly in German.

Westerncape.gov.za (http://tinyurl.com/aox358) Forms and advice on registering a vehicle in the Western Cape.

Road Conditions
SOUTH AFRICA

» A good network of freeways covers the country.

» Major roads are generally in good condition.

» Outside large cities and towns, you may encounter dirt roads, most of which are graded and reasonably smooth.

» Check locally on secondary roads' condition, which can deteriorate when it rains.

» In the former homeland areas, beware of hazards such as dangerous potholes, washed-out roads and unannounced hairpin bends.

» The N2 through the Wild Coast region is in bad condition.

LESOTHO

» Driving in Lesotho can be challenging, with steep terrain, hairpin turns and inclement weather.

» New roads are built in conjunction with the Highlands Water Project.

» The sealed roads in the highlands are good, but very steep in places.

» Rain will slow you down and ice and snow in winter can make driving dangerous.

» If you're driving an automatic, you'll rely heavily on your brakes to negotiate steep downhill corners.

» Away from main roads, there are many places where even a 4WD will struggle.

» Rough roads and river floodings after summer storms are the biggest problems.

» People and animals on the road can also be a hazard.

» There are sometimes army roadblocks.

» If you're driving a car hired in South Africa and get stopped, you'll need to present the letter from the hire agency giving you permission to take the car into Lesotho.

SWAZILAND

» Swaziland's road network is good.

» Most major routes are tarred.

» The MR3, which crosses Swaziland roughly from west to east, is a major highway as far east as Manzini.

» Good tarmac roads connect other major towns.

» Elsewhere are mostly unpaved roads, most in reasonably good condition, except after heavy rains.

» There are some rough back roads through the bush.

» Malagwane Hill, from Mbabane into the Ezulwini Valley, was once listed in the *Guinness Book of Records* as the world's most dangerous road.

» Driving down the Ezulwini Valley in heavy traffic and bad conditions can be dangerous.

» Away from the population centres and border-crossing areas there is little traffic.

Road Hazards

» South Africa has a horrific road-accident record, with

CARJACKING

In Jo'burg, and to a lesser extent in the other big cities and elsewhere in the northeastern provinces, carjacking is a danger. It's more likely if you're driving something flash rather than a standard hire car. Stay alert, keep your taste in cars modest, and avoid driving in urban areas at night; if you have to do so, keep windows wound up and doors locked. If you're waiting at a red light and notice anything suspicious, it's standard practice to check that the junction is clear, and jump the light. If you do get carjacked, don't resist; just hand over the keys immediately. The carjackers are almost always armed, and people have been killed for their cars.

ROAD DISTANCES (KM)

	Bloemfontein	Cape Town	Durban	East London	George	Graaff-Reinet	Johannesburg	Kimberley	Maseru	Mbabane	Nelspruit	Polokwane (Pietersburg)	Port Elizabeth	Pretoria	Springbok	Upington
Bloemfontein	---															
Cape Town	998	---														
Durban	628	1660	---													
East London	546	1042	667	---												
George	764	436	1240	630	---											
Graaff-Reinet	422	672	945	388	342	---										
Johannesburg	396	1405	598	992	1168	826	---									
Kimberley	175	960	842	722	734	501	467	---								
Maseru	157	1160	590	630	913	519	438	334	---							
Mbabane	677	1680	562	1238	1450	1097	361	833	633	---						
Nelspruit	754	1779	689	1214	1509	1167	358	832	713	173	---					
Polokwane (Pietersburg)	727	1736	929	1323	1499	1595	331	798	769	488	315	---				
Port Elizabeth	676	756	927	300	330	251	1062	763	822	1548	1373	1398	---			
Pretoria	454	1463	656	1050	1226	859	58	525	488	372	328	273	1119	---		
Springbok	975	554	1642	1365	846	911	1274	800	1252	1678	1543	1474	1289	1200	---	
Upington	576	821	1243	958	857	667	875	401	731	1157	1144	1075	902	813	387	---

an annual death toll of about 14,000.

» Notably dangerous stretches of road: N1 between Cape Town and Beaufort West; N2 between Cape Town and Somerset West; N2 between East London and Kokstad; N1 between Mokopane (Potgietersrus) and Polokwane; and N2 between Durban and Tongaat.

» The main hazards are your fellow drivers. Motorists from all sections of society drive sloppily and aggressively. Be particularly wary of minibus taxi drivers, who operate under pressure on little sleep in shoddy vehicles.

» Overtaking blind and with insufficient passing room are common.

» On freeways, drivers coming up behind you will expect you to move into the hard shoulder to let them pass, even if you are approaching a corner and regardless of what is happening in the hard shoulder. Motorists often remain hard on your tail until you move over.

» Drivers on little-used rural roads often speed and assume that there is no other traffic.

» Watch out especially for oncoming cars at blind corners on secondary roads.

» Despite road blocks and alcohol breath-testing in South Africa and Swaziland, particularly in urban areas, drink driving is widespread.

» Farm animals, wildlife (particularly baboons) and pedestrians stray onto the roads, especially in rural areas. If you hit an animal in an area where you're uncertain of your safety, continue to the nearest police station and report it there.

» During the rainy season, thick fog can slow you to a crawl. Especially in higher areas of KwaZulu-Natal.

» In the lowveld, summer hailstorms can damage your car.

» Lesotho's mountainous terrain and road conditions are its principal dangers.

» In Swaziland, look out for drunk drivers, wandering cattle and speeding minibuses, especially on gravel roads.

Road Rules

» In South Africa, Lesotho and Swaziland, driving is on the left-hand side of the road.

» Seatbelts are mandatory for the driver and front-seat passenger.

» The main local idiosyncrasy is the 'four-way stop' (crossroad), found even on major roads. All vehicles are required to stop, with those arriving first the first to go (even if they're on a minor cross street).

MINIBUS TAXI ETIQUETTE

» Passengers with lots of luggage should sit in the first row behind the driver.

» Pay the fare with coins, not notes.

» Pass the money forward (your fare and those of the people around you) when the taxi is full. Hand the money to a front-seat passenger, rather than the driver. If you're sitting in the front seat, you might have to collect fares and dole out change from the driver's stash.

» If you sit on the folding seat by the door, it's your job to open and close the door when passengers get out. You'll have to get out of the taxi each time.

» Say 'Thank you, driver!' when you want to get out, rather than just 'Stop!'

» In Swaziland, if an official or royal motorcade approaches, you're required to pull over and stop.

SPEED LIMITS
South Africa 100km/h on open roads and 120km/h on most major highways, though limits are widely ignored; in towns, usually 60km/h.

Lesotho 80km/h on main roads; 50km/h in villages.

Swaziland 80km/h on open roads; 60km/h in towns.

Signage

On alternative routes, signposting is sparse, generally only giving route numbers or directing you to nearby towns, rather than the next large town or city.

Smaller roads are numbered (eg R44, shown in this book as Rte 44). When you ask directions, most people will refer to these numbers.

In Lesotho, main routes are numbered, beginning with A1 (Main North Rd). Side roads branching off from these have 'B' route numbers.

Tolls

On some freeways a toll is payable, based on distance.

There's always plenty of warning that you're about to enter a toll section (marked by a black 'T' in a yellow circle).

There's always an alternative route (marked by a black 'A' in a yellow circle).

Hitching

Hitchhiking and picking up hitchers are inadvisable in all three countries, especially South Africa.

If you're strapped for cash, you could look into share-drives. Hostel noticeboards often have details of free or shared-cost lifts. Also check out **Junk Mail** (http://junk mail.co.za).

Local Transport

See p607 for information on metro commuter trains.

Bus

» Several urban areas, including Cape Town, Durban, Pretoria and Jo'burg, have city bus networks.

» Fares are cheap.

» Routes, which are signboarded, are extensive.

» Services usually stop running early in the evening, and there aren't many on weekends.

» In terms of safety and convenience, only Cape Town's MyCiTi buses and Durban People Mover are recommended.

Minibus Taxi

Minibus taxis run almost everywhere – around cities, to the suburbs and to neighbouring towns.

» They leave when full.

» 'Full' in South Africa isn't as packed as in many African countries.

» Most accommodate 14 to 16 people.

» Slightly larger 'Sprinters' accommodate about 20.

» Away from train and bus routes, minibus taxis may be the only choice of public transport.

» They offer an insight into local life.

» At weekends they generally have reduced services or no departures.

SECURITY
Money saved by taking minibus taxis is far outweighed by safety considerations.

» Overall, taking minibus taxis is not recommended.

» Driving standards and vehicle conditions are poor.

» There are frequent accidents.

» There are occasional gangster-style clashes between rival companies.

» Minibus taxi stations and their immediate surroundings are often unsafe.

» Muggings, pickpocketing, sexual harassment and other incidents are common.

» If you want to try riding in a minibus taxi, don't travel at night; read the newspapers and seek local advice on lines and areas to avoid.

» In a few areas, minibus taxis are relatively safe during daylight hours. Notably central Cape Town, where locals from different social and racial backgrounds use minibus taxis.

» Do not travel with luggage; partly because most minibus taxis don't carry bags on the roof, and stowing backpacks can be a hassle.

LESOTHO & SWAZILAND

Minibus taxis don't have stellar road safety records, but have none of the violence associated with their South African counterparts. They are widely used for short and long routes.

Private Taxi

» Larger cities in all three countries have private taxi services.

» There are taxi stands in popular areas.

» Phoning for a cab is often safer; you will have to wait for the taxi to arrive, but the vehicle will likely be better quality than those at the stands.

» Rates vary between cities; in Cape Town, they average R10 per kilometre, often with a R20 minimum charge.

» In Lesotho, only Maseru has taxis, but they can be chartered for long-distance journeys to other parts of the country.

» Places such as Cape Town and Durban have local variations on private and shared taxis, such as *Rikkis*, rickshaws and *tuk-tuk* (motorised tricycle).

Shared Taxi

» A smaller version of the minibus taxi.

» In some towns, and on some longer routes, it may be the only transport option.

» Slightly more expensive than minibus taxis, and comparable in safety.

Tours

There are dozens of tours by local companies, ranging from budget overland truck journeys to exclusive luxury safaris, 4WD adventures to half-day overviews.

Backpacker hostels around the country are good sources of information on tours geared towards budget travellers. Many are affiliated with budget tour operators, and have bulletin boards.

Try to book day or overnight trips as close to the destination as possible. For example, if you're in Durban and want to visit a reserve in northern KwaZulu-Natal, it's usually cheaper to travel to a hostel near the reserve and take a day trip from there, rather than booking a longer excursion from Durban. You usually also get to spend more time at the reserve.

See also the activities listings on p575, train cruises on p606 and voluntourism information on p587.

Bok Bus (www.bokbus. com) Budget-oriented tours along the Garden Route and around.

Cape Gourmet Adventure Tours (http://gourmet.cape -tour.info) Mouth-watering tours of Cape Town and the Western Cape, ranging from catching your own seafood to a gourmet treasure hunt.

Go 2 Africa (www.go2africa. com) African Safari specialist, covering South Africa, Lesotho and Swaziland.

Malealea Lodge (www. malealea.co.ls) Lesotho tours from pony trekking and 4WD excursions to voluntourism.

Oasis Overland (www. oasisoverland.co.uk) UK-based overland specialist covering South Africa and the region.

Signature Tours (www. signaturetours.co.za) Tours focused on topics including botany, birding and the environment, including a four-day West Coast spring-flower tour.

Springbok-Atlas (www. springbokatlas.com) Coach tours nationwide and around the region.

Swazi Trails (www.swazi trails.co.sz) Specialises in day and half-day tours around Swaziland, including white-water rafting, cultural tours and hiking.

Thaba Tours (www.thaba tours.co.za) Mountain-bike, 4WD, quad-bike, horseback and hiking tours of Lesotho and the Drakensberg.

Thompsons Africa (www. thompsonsafrica.com) Mid-range and top-end package tours and safaris, with itineraries focused on themes from elephants to wine.

Ukholo (www.ukholotrave landtours.co.za/) Western Cape itineraries, from Cape Town city tours to four days on the Garden Route.

Wilderness Safaris (www. wilderness-safaris.com) Upscale, conservation-focused operator offering high-end safaris and special-interest trips; also operates several luxury bush camps.

Wilderness Travel (www. wildernesstravel.com) Various Southern Africa packages, covering locations from Cape Town to the Drakensberg and focused mainly on wildlife and walking.

Wildlife Safaris (www.wild lifesaf.co.za) Midrange safaris from Jo'burg to Kruger and Pilanesberg National Parks, Madikwe Game Reserve and Blyde River Canyon for individuals and small groups.

Train

South Africa's **Shosholoza Meyl** (☑0860 008 888, www. shosholozameyl.co.za, www. premierclasse.co.za) offers regular services connecting major cities.

For an overview and valuable advice, visit **The Man in Seat Sixty-One** (www.seat61. com/SouthAfrica.htm).

Classes

Tourist and economy classes are affordable options. Unlike on long-distance buses, fares on short sectors are not inflated.

Premier class A luxurious experience, offering an affordable alternative to the *Blue Train*. Fares include meals in the deluxe air-conditioned dining car; single travellers occupy two-berth coupés, couples occupy four-berth compartments.

RIDING THE RAILS

In addition to the Shosholoza Meyl services mentioned in this section, there are numerous special lines.

Blue Train

(www.bluetrain.co.za) South Africa's famous train travels between Pretoria and Cape Town, stopping en route in Matjiesfontein or Kimberley. For 27 hours of luxury, one-way fares (per person sharing) are R13,485/14,685 for deluxe/luxury during high season (September to mid-November), including all meals and drinks. Fares drop by about R3000 during low season. Travel agents, both in South Africa and overseas, take bookings; including **New Fusion** (www.newfusion.co.za). Inquire about packages including accommodation and one-way flights between Pretoria/Jo'burg and Cape Town.

Rovos Rail

(www.rovos.co.za) Rivalling the *Blue Train* as Africa's luxurious and expensive service. Regular cruises include Pretoria–Cape Town over two nights/three days, with stops at Kimberley and Matjiesfontein; Pretoria–Durban; Pretoria–Swakopmund (Namibia) over nine days, via Etosha National Park and other Namibian highlights; Pretoria–Victoria Falls (Zimbabwe) over three days.

Shongololo Express

(www.shongololo.com) Not as sumptuous as the other special lines, Shongolo offers four train tours, including between Jo'burg/Pretoria and Victoria Falls, and a 12-night, 13-day cruise between Jo'burg/Pretoria and Cape Town via Swaziland and Durban. You travel by night and disembark during the days.

JB Train Tours

(www.jbtours.co.za) Train tours, mostly from Jo'burg, to locations including Cape Town, Kruger National Park and neighbouring countries.

Umgeni Steam Railway

(www.umgenisteamrailway.co.za) Steam-train excursions in KwaZulu-Natal and the Western Cape.

Atlantic Rail

(www.atlanticrail.co.za) Steam-train excursions between Cape Town and Simon's Town.

There's a lounge car and vehicles can be transported. **Tourist class** Recommended: scenic, authentic but safe, and more comfortable than taking the bus, albeit sometimes slower. The overnight journey from Jo'burg to Cape Town is a wonderful way to get a sense of the country's enormity; entering the Karoo as night falls and breakfasting as the train swishes through the Winelands (read an account at http://tinyurl.com/6v2rs93). There's a dining car and the fare includes accommodation in a two-berth coupé or four-berth compartment. Depending on what's available, couples are given coupés and single travellers and groups are put in compartments. If you are travelling alone and you want a coupé to yourself, you could buy two tickets. There's an additional R40 charge for bedding hire.

Economy class Does not have sleeping carriages and is not a comfortable or secure option for overnight travel.

Tickets & Fares

» At the time of writing, Jo'burg to Cape Town in tourist/economy class cost R430/260.

» Tickets can be purchased up to three months in advance, and should be bought at least 24 hours before travel.

» Popular routes such as Jo'burg–Cape Town fill up, so book well in advance.

» Purchases can be made at train stations, through the website or over the phone.

» You can buy tickets online using a credit card, but the site is temperamental.

» For tourist and economy classes, Shosholoza Meyl does not accept credit-card payments over the phone.

» If booking telephonically, within two days (at least 24 hours before departure) you must: pay in person at a station;

or deposit the money in Shosholoza Meyl's bank account and send the company proof of payment.

» Tickets must be collected from the ticket office before you can board the train.

» You can also buy tickets for premier and tourist classes through **Africa Sun Travel** (http://africansuntravel.com) and **New Fusion** (www.new fusion.co.za).

Routes

Jo'burg–Cape Town Via Kimberly and Beaufort West; 27 hours; premier (twice weekly), tourist (Wednesday, Friday and Sunday) and economy (daily).

Jo'burg–Durban Via Ladysmith and Pietermaritzburg; 13 hours; premier (weekly), tourist and economy (Wednesday, Friday and Sunday).

Jo'burg–East London Via Bloemfontein; 20 hours; economy (three times weekly).

Jo'burg–Port Elizabeth Via Kroonstad, Bloemfontein and Cradock; 21 hours; tourist and economy (Wednesday, Friday and Sunday).

Jo'burg–Musina Via Pretoria and Louis Trichardt (Makhado); 17 hours; economy (twice weekly).

Jo'burg–Komatipoort Via Pretoria and Nelspruit; 13 hours; economy (three times weekly).

Metro Trains

Cape Metro Rail (www.cape metrorail.co.za) Services from Cape Town to either Simon's Town or the Winelands are quite safe during the day.

Gautrain (www.gautrain. co.za) Connects Jo'burg with Pretoria and OR Tambo International Airport. Other metro trains in Jo'burg and Pretoria aren't recommended for security reasons.

Health

As long as you stay up to date with vaccinations and take basic preventive measures, you're unlikely to succumb to most of the hazards covered in this chapter.

While South Africa, Lesotho and Swaziland have an impressive selection of tropical diseases, suffering from diarrhoea or a cold is more likely than contracting a more-exotic malady.

The main exception to this is malaria, which is a real risk in lower-lying areas of Swaziland, and in northeastern South Africa.

BEFORE YOU GO

» Get a check-up from your doctor if you have any regular medication or chronic illness, eg high blood pressure or asthma.

» Organise spare contact lenses and glasses (and take your optical prescription with you).

» Assemble a medical and first-aid kit.

» Arrange vaccinations; some don't ensure immunity for two weeks, so visit a doctor four to eight weeks before departure.

» Become a member of the International Association for Medical Advice to Travellers, which lists trusted English-speaking doctors.

» If you'll be spending much time in more-remote areas, such as parts of Lesotho, consider doing a first-aid course, for example one offered by the **American Red Cross** (www.redcross.org) or **St John's Ambulance** (www.sja.org.uk; UK).

» Particularly if you're going trekking, you could take a wilderness medical-training course, such as those offered in the UK by **Wilderness Medical Training** (WMT; wildernessmedicaltraining.co.uk) and the **Royal Geographical Society** (www.rgs.org).

» Bring medications in their original, clearly labelled containers.

» A signed and dated letter from your physician describing your medical conditions and medications, including generic names, is helpful.

» If carrying syringes or needles, ensure you have a physician's letter documenting their medical necessity.

» See your dentist before a long trip.

Insurance

» Find out in advance whether your insurer will make payments directly to providers or reimburse you later for overseas health expenditures.

» If your policy requires you to pay first and claim later for medical treatment, be sure to keep all documentation.

» It's vital to ensure that your travel insurance will cover any emergency transport required to get you to a hospital in a major city, or all the way home, by air and with a medical attendant if necessary.

» If you'll be in Lesotho and Swaziland, check whether the evacuation plan extends to these countries.

» Also see p580.

Recommended Vaccinations

America's Centers for Disease Control and Prevention (CDC) suggests immunisations including the following as routine for adults. See www.immunize.org/catg.d/p4030.pdf for the complete list.

» Diphtheria
» Tetanus
» Measles
» Mumps
» Pertussis (whooping cough)
» Rubella
» Polio

The CDC also suggests the following for South Africa, Lesotho and Swaziland:

» Hepatitis A and B
» Rabies
» Typhoid

Ask your doctor for an international certificate of vaccination, listing all the vaccinations you've received.

Medical Checklist

Consider packing:

» antibacterial ointment (eg Bactroban) for cuts and abrasions

» antibiotics (if travelling off the beaten track)

» antidiarrhoeal drugs (eg loperamide)

» antihistamines (for hay fever and allergic reactions)

» anti-inflammatory drugs (eg ibuprofen)

» antimalaria pills (if you'll be in malarial areas)

» bandages, gauze

» DEET-containing insect repellent

» insect spray for clothing, tents and bed nets

» iodine or other water-purification tablets

» oral rehydration salts (eg Dioralyte)

» paracetamol or aspirin

» scissors, safety pins, tweezers, pocket knife

» sterile needles and syringes (if travelling to remote areas)

Websites

Useful to consult prior to departure:

Centers for Disease Control and Prevention (www.cdc.gov/travel) American site.

Health Canada (http://tinyurl.com/4tj653u)

International Association for Medical Advice to Travellers (www.iamat.org)

Lonely Planet (www.lonelyplanet.com)

MD Travel Health (www.mdtravelhealth.com) American site.

Netdoctor (www.netdoctor.co.uk/travel) British site.

National Health Service (www.fitfortravel.nhs.uk) British site.

Smarttraveller (www.smarttraveller.gov.au) Australian site.

World Health Organisation (WHO; www.who.int/ith)

Further Reading

In addition to the following, the WHO and CDC publish annual handbooks.

» *Comprehensive Guide to Wilderness and Travel Medicine* by Eric A Weiss

» *Healthy Travel: Africa* by Isabelle Young

» *International Travel Health Guide* by Stuart Rose

» *The Essential Guide to Travel Health* by Jane Wilson-Howarth

» *Travel in Health* by Graham Fry

» *Travel with Children* by Brigitte Barta et al

» *Traveller's Good Health Guide* by Ted Lankester

» *Traveller's Health* by Dr Richard Dawood

IN SOUTH AFRICA, LESOTHO & SWAZILAND

Availability & Cost of Health Care

» Good-quality health care is available in all of South Africa's major urban areas.

» Private hospitals are generally of excellent standard.

» Public hospitals are often underfunded and overcrowded.

» In off-the-beaten-track areas, such as the former homelands and in Lesotho and Swaziland, reliable medical facilities are rare.

» Your accommodation should be able to recommend the nearest source of medical help.

» Embassy websites (see p578) sometimes list doctors and clinics and your travel insurer might also be able to help.

» In an emergency, contact your embassy or consulate.

» Most doctors expect payment immediately after the consultation.

» Bring drugs for chronic diseases from home.

» There is a risk of contracting HIV from infected blood transfusions.

» **The Blood Care Foundation** (www.bloodcare.org.uk) is a useful source of safe, screened blood, which can be transported to any part of the world; join before you need its services.

Infectious Diseases

Cholera

Spread through Contaminated drinking water. The risk is low, and mostly confined to rural parts of Limpopo, Mpumalanga and KwaZulu-Natal.

Symptoms and effects Profuse watery diarrhoea, which causes debilitation if fluids are not replaced quickly.

Prevention and treatment In rural eastern parts of South Africa, pay close attention to drinking water (don't drink tap water) and avoid potentially contaminated food such as unpeeled or uncooked fruits and vegetables. Treatment is by fluid replacement (orally or via a drip); sometimes antibiotics are needed. Self-treatment is not advised.

Dengue Fever

Spread through Mosquito bites; in the north of KwaZulu-Natal's Elephant Coast and eastern Swaziland, and from there up South Africa's northeastern border to the top of Kruger National Park.

Symptoms and effects Feverish illness with headache and muscle pains, similar to those experienced during severe, prolonged influenza attacks. There might be a rash.

Prevention and treatment Avoid mosquito bites. Self-treatment: paracetamol (not asprin or non-steroidal anti-inflammatory drugs such as ibuprofen), hydration and rest. Dengue haemorrhagic fever, which mostly affects children, is more serious and requires medical attention.

Hepatitis A

Spread through Contaminated food (particularly shellfish) and water.

Symptoms and effects Jaundice, dark urine, a yellowing of the whites of the eyes, fever and abdominal pain. Although rarely fatal, it can cause prolonged lethargy – recovery can be slow.

Prevention and treatment Vaccine (Avaxim, Vaqta, Havrix) is given as an injection, with a booster extending the protection offered. Hepatitis A and typhoid vaccines can also be given as a combined single-dose vaccine (Hepatyrix or Viatim). If you've had hepatitis A, you shouldn't drink alcohol for up to six months afterwards.

Hepatitis B

Spread through Infected blood, contaminated needles and sexual intercourse.

Symptoms and effects Jaundice and liver problems (occasionally failure).

Prevention Those visiting high-risk areas for long periods or those with increased social or occupational risk should be immunised. Regular travellers should consider having hepatitis B as a routine vaccination.

HIV/AIDS

Spread through Infected blood and blood products; sexual intercourse with an infected partner; 'blood to blood' contacts, such as through contaminated instruments during medical, dental, acupuncture and other body-piercing procedures, or sharing used intravenous needles. HIV and AIDS are widespread in South Africa, Lesotho and Swaziland.

Symptoms and effects Progressive failure of the immune system, leading to death.

Prevention and treatment Be cautious about relationships with locals, regardless of their colour, and don't have one-night stands. Travellers and aid workers have been infected by locals.

If you think you might have been infected, a blood test is necessary; a three-month gap after exposure is required to allow antibodies to appear in the blood. There is no cure, but medication to keep the disease under control is available.

Lymphatic Filariasis (Elephantiasis)

Spread through The bite of an infected mosquito. Larvae are deposited on the skin and migrate to the lymphatic vessels, where they turn into worms.

Symptoms and effects Localised itching and abnormal enlargement of body parts, commonly the legs and/or genitalia, causing pain and disability. In severe cases, the kidneys and lymphatic and immune systems are damaged.

Prevention and treatment Avoid mosquito bites. If infected, seek treatment, preferably by a specialist in infectious diseases or tropical medicine. Diethylcarbamazine (DEC) is the drug of choice to treat travellers.

Malaria

Spread through A parasite in the bloodstream, spread via the bite of the female Anopheles mosquito. Malaria is mainly confined to northeastern South Africa (northern KwaZulu-Natal, Mpumalanga, Limpopo and Kruger National Park) and Swaziland.

Symtoms and effects Falciparum malaria, the most dangerous type of malaria, is the predominant form in South Africa. The early, flulike symptoms of malaria include headaches, fevers, aches and pains, and malaise. Abdominal pain, diarrhoea and a cough can also occur. If not treated, the next stage can develop within 24 hours (particularly if falciparum malaria is the parasite): jaundice, then reduced consciousness and coma (also known as cer-

---

ANTIMALARIAL A TO D

A Awareness of the risk. No medication is totally effective, but protection of up to 95% is achievable with most drugs, as long as other measures are taken.

B Bites, to be avoided at all costs. Sleep in a screened room, use a mosquito spray or coils, and sleep under a permethrin-impregnated net. Cover up at night with long trousers and long sleeves – preferably permethrin-treated clothing. Apply repellent to all areas of exposed skin in the evenings.

C Chemical prevention (ie antimalarial drugs) is usually needed in malarial areas. Get medical advice, as resistance patterns can change, and new drugs are in development. Not all antimalarial drugs are suitable for everyone. Most antimalarial drugs need to be started at least a week before and continued for four weeks after the last possible exposure to malaria.

D Diagnosis. If you have a fever or flulike illness within a year of travel to a malarial area, malaria is a possibility, and immediate medical attention is necessary.

ebral malaria) followed by death. Malaria in pregnancy frequently results in miscarriage or premature labour; the risks to both mother and foetus are considerable.

Prevention Infection rates vary with the season and climate, so check out the situation before departure. During the summer months, prophylaxis is essential. Several drugs are available and up-to-date advice from a travel health clinic or similar is essential; some medication is more suitable than others (eg people with epilepsy should avoid mefloquine, and doxycycline should not be taken by pregnant women or children aged under 12). There is no conclusive evidence that antimalarial homeopathic preparations are effective, and many homeopaths do not recommend their use. It's a dangerous misconception that malaria is a mild illness, and that taking antimalarial drugs causes more illness through side effects than actually getting malaria. Immunity, developed by surviving a bout of malaria, wanes after 18 months of nonexposure; even if you have had malaria or lived in a malaria-prone area, you may no longer be immune. If you decide against taking antimalarial prophylaxis, you must understand the risks and be obsessive about avoiding mosquito bites.

Treatment If you develop a fever in a malarial area, assume malarial infection until a blood test proves negative, even if you have been taking antimalarial medication. Report any fever or flulike symptoms to a doctor as soon as possible. Treatment in hospital is essential; even in the best intensive-care facilities, there is still a chance of fatality in the worst cases.

Rabies

Spread through Bites or licks on broken skin from an infected animal. Few human cases are reported in South Africa, with the risks highest in rural areas.

Symptoms and effects Initial symptoms are pain or tingling at the site of the bite, with fever, loss of appetite and headache. If untreated, both 'furious' and less-common 'dumb' rabies are fatal.

Prevention and treatment People travelling to remote areas, where a reliable source of postbite vaccine is not available within 24 hours, should be vaccinated. Any bite, scratch or lick from a warm-blooded, furry animal should immediately be thoroughly cleaned. If you have not been vaccinated and you get bitten, you will need a course of injections starting as soon as possible after the injury. Vaccination does not provide immunity, it merely buys you more time to seek medical help.

Schistosomiasis (Bilharzia)

Spread through Flukes (minute worms) are carried by a species of freshwater snail, which sheds them into slow-moving or still water. The parasites penetrate human skin during swimming and migrate to the bladder or bowel. They are excreted via stool or urine and could contaminate fresh water, beginning the cycle again. Bilharzia is found in northeast South Africa and Swaziland, reaching as far south as the Wild Coast and as far west as the Northern Cape section of the Senqu (Orange) River.

Symptoms and effects Early symptoms may include fever, loss of appetite, weight loss, abdominal pain, weakness, headaches, joint and muscle pains, diarrhea, nausea, and cough, but most infections are asymptomatic at first. Untreated, bilharzia can cause problems including kidney failure and permanent bowel damage.

Prevention and treatment Avoid swimming in suspect freshwater lakes and slow-running rivers. Heat baths and showers and vigorously towel yourself after swimming. A blood test can detect the parasite, and treatment is available – usually taking the drug praziquantel.

Tuberculosis

Spread through Close respiratory contact and, occasionally, infected milk or milk products. Tuberculosis is highly endemic in South Africa, Lesotho and Swaziland. People mixing closely with the local population, for example working as a teacher or health-care worker, or planning a long stay are most at risk.

Symptoms and effects Can be asymptomatic, although symptoms can include a cough, loss of appetite or weight, fatigue, fever or night sweats months or even years after exposure. An X-ray is the best way to confirm if you have TB.

Prevention and treatment Avoid crowded environments where TB carriers might be found, such as hospitals and homeless shelters. Travellers at risk should have a predeparture skin test and be retested after leaving the country. Treatment is a multiple-drug regimen for six to nine months.

Typhoid

Spread through Food or water that has been contaminated by infected human faeces.

Symptoms and effects Initially, fever, a pink rash on the abdomen, appetite loss and listlessness. Septicaemia (blood poisoning) may also occur.

Prevention Typhim Vi or typherix vaccine. In some countries, the oral vaccine Vivotif is also available. Antibiotics are usually given as treatment.

Environmental Hazards

Heat Exhaustion

Causes Occurs following heavy sweating and excessive fluid loss with inadequate replacement of fluids and salt. This is common in hot climates when taking unaccustomed exercise before full acclimatisation.

Symptoms and effects Headache, dizziness and tiredness.

Prevention Dehydration is already happening by the time you feel thirsty – drink sufficient water such that you produce pale, diluted urine. The Southern African sun can be fierce, so bring a hat.

Treatment Fluid replacement with water and/or fruit juice, and cooling by cold water and fans. Treat the salt loss by consuming salty fluids such as soup or broth, and adding a little more table salt to foods than usual.

Heatstroke

Causes Extreme heat, high humidity, physical exertion or use of drugs or alcohol in the sun and dehydration. Occurs when the body's heat-regulating mechanism breaks down.

Symptoms and effects An excessive rise in body temperature, accompanied by sweating ceasing, irrational and hyperactive behaviour,

and eventually loss of consciousness and death.

Treatment Rapid cooling by spraying the body with water and fanning. Emergency fluid and electrolyte replacement by intravenous drip is usually also required.

Insect Bites & Stings

Causes Mosquitoes, scorpions (found in arid areas), ticks (a risk outside urban areas), bees and wasps.

Symptoms and effects Bites can cause irritation and get infected. The scorpion's painful bite can be life-threatening. If you're stung, take a painkiller and seek medical treatment if your condition worsens.

Prevention and treatment Take the same precautions as for avoiding malaria. If you pick up a tick, press down around its head with tweezers, grab the head and gently pull upwards. Avoid pulling the rear of the body, as this may squeeze the tick's gut contents through its mouth into your body, or leave its head inside you; both outcomes increase the risk of infection and disease. Smearing chemicals on the tick will not make it let go and is not recommended.

Snake Bites

Causes Venomous snakes found in South Africa include various types of cobra and mamba. Snakes like to bask on rocks and sand, retreating during the heat of the day.

Prevention Do not walk barefoot or stick your hand into holes or cracks.

Treatment If bitten, do not panic. Half of those bitten by venomous snakes are not actually injected with poison (envenomed). Immobilise the bitten limb with a splint (eg a stick) and apply a bandage over the site with firm pressure, similar to bandaging a sprain. Do not apply a tourniquet, or cut or suck the bite. Get medical help as soon as possible.

Water

High-quality water is widely available in South Africa and drinking from taps is fine, except in rural areas.

In Lesotho and Swaziland, stick to bottled water, and purify stream water before drinking it.

Traditional Medicine

If you are ill, some locals may recommend you see a *sangoma* (traditional healer, usually a woman) or *inyanga* (traditional healer and herbalist, usually a man). These practitioners hold revered positions in many communities and are often interesting characters to meet on a tour. However, if you are ill, recourse to tried-and-tested Western medicine is a wiser option. Likewise, treat the traditional medicinal products found in local markets with circumspection.

Language

WANT MORE?

For in-depth language information and handy phrases, check out Lonely Planet's *Africa Phrasebook*. You'll find it at **shop.lonelyplanet.com**, or you can buy Lonely Planet's iPhone phrasebooks at the Apple App Store.

South Africa has 11 official languages – English, Afrikaans and nine indigenous languages (Ndebele, Northern Sotho, Southern Sotho, Swati, Tsonga, Tswana, Venda, Xhosa and Zulu). Forms, brochures and timetables are usually in English and Afrikaans, but road signs alternate. Most Afrikaans speakers also speak English, but this is not always the case in small rural towns and among older people. In and around Cape Town three languages are prominent: Afrikaans, English and Xhosa.

The official languages of Lesotho are Southern Sotho and English. In Swaziland, Swati and English are both official.

AFRIKAANS

Afrikaans developed from the dialect spoken by the Dutch settlers in South Africa from the 17th century. Until the late 19th century it was considered a Dutch dialect (known as 'Cape Dutch'), and in 1925 it became one of the official languages of South Africa. Today, it has about six million speakers.

If you read our coloured pronunciation guides as if they were English, you should be understood. The stressed syllables are in italics. Note that aw is pronounced as in 'law', eu as the 'u' in 'nurse', ew as the 'ee' in 'see' with rounded lips, oh as the 'o' in 'cold', uh as the 'a' in 'ago', kh as the 'ch' in the Scottish *loch*, zh as the 's' in 'pleasure', and r is trilled.

Basics

Hello.	Hallo.	ha·*loh*
Goodbye.	Totsiens.	tot·*seens*
Yes.	Ja.	yaa
No.	Nee.	ney
Please.	Asseblief.	a·si·*bleef*
Thank you.	Dankie.	*dang*·kee
Sorry.	Jammer.	*ya*·min

How are you?
Hoe gaan dit? — hu khaan dit

Fine, and you?
Goed dankie, en jy? — khut *dang*·kee en yay

What's your name?
Wat's jou naam? — vats yoh naam

My name is ...
My naam is ... — may naam is ...

Do you speak English?
Praat jy Engels? — praat yay *eng*·ils

I don't understand.
Ek verstaan nie. — ek vir·*staan* nee

Accommodation

Where's a ...?	Waar's 'n ...?	vaars i ...
campsite	kampeerplek	kam·*peyr*·plek
guesthouse	gastehuis	*khas*·ti·hays
hotel	hotel	hu·*tel*

Do you have a single/double room?
Het jy 'n enkel/dubbel kamer? — het yay i *eng*·kil/*di*·bil *kaa*·mir

How much is it per night/person?
Hoeveel kos dit per nag/persoon? — hu·*fil* kos dit pir nakh/pir·*soon*

Eating & Drinking

Can you recommend a ...?	Kan jy 'n ... aanbeveel?	kan yay i ... aan·bi·feyl
bar	kroeg	krukh
dish	gereg	khi·rekh
place to eat	eetplek	eyt·plek

SOUTH AFRICAN ENGLISH

English has undergone some changes during its use in South Africa. Quite a few words have changed meaning, new words have been appropriated and, thanks to the influence of Afrikaans, a distinctive accent has developed. Vocabulary tends to lean more towards British rather than US English (eg 'lift', not 'elevator'; 'petrol', not 'gas'), as do grammar and spelling, and there are influences from other indigenous languages such as Zulu and Xhosa as well. Repetition for emphasis is common: something that burns you is 'hot hot', fields after the rains are 'green green', a crowded minibus with no more room is 'full full' and so on. Here's just a smattering of the local lingo you're likely to hear:

babalaas (from Zulu) – a monster hangover

bakkie – pick-up truck (US); ute/utility (Aus)

bonnet – car hood (US)

boot – car trunk (US)

cool drink – soda (US)

Howzit? – Hello/Greetings; How are you?

Izzit? – Is that so? Really?

just now – soon

lekker – nice, delicious

naartjie – tangerine

petrol – gasoline (US)

robot – traffic light

rubbish – garbage (US)

(Og) Shame! – Ohh, how cute! (in response to something like a new baby or a little puppy); Really! Oh no! (with a sympathetic tone)

soda – soda water; club soda (US)

sweeties – lollies; candy

tekkies – runners; joggers

I'd like ..., please.	Ek wil asseblief ... hê.	ek vil a·si·bleef ... he
a table for two	'n tafel vir twee	i taa·fil fir twey
that dish	daardie gereg	daar·dee khi·rekh
the bill	die rekening	dee rey·ki·ning
the menu	die spyskaart	dee spays·kaart

Emergencies

Help!	Help!	help
Call a doctor!	Kry 'n dokter!	kray i dok·tir
Call the police!	Kry die polisie!	kray dee pu·lee·see

I'm lost.
Ek is verdwaal.   ek is fir·dwaal

Where are the toilets?
Waar is die toilette?   vaar is dee toy·le·ti

I need a doctor.
Ek het 'n dokter nodig.   ek het i dok·tir noo·dikh

Numbers

1	een	eyn
2	twee	twey
3	drie	dree
4	vier	feer
5	vyf	fayf
6	ses	ses
7	sewe	see·vi
8	agt	akht
9	nege	ney·khi
10	tien	teen

Shopping & Services

I'm looking for ...
Ek soek na ...   ek suk naa ...

How much is it?
Hoeveel kos dit?   hu·fil kos dit

What's your lowest price?
Wat is jou laagste prys? vat is yoh laakh·sti prays

I want to buy a phonecard.
Ek wil asseblief   ek vil a·si·bleef
'n foonkaart koop.   i foon·kaart koop

I'd like to change money.
Ek wil asseblief geld ruil. ek vil a·si·bleef khelt rayl

I want to use the internet.
Ek wil asseblief die   ek vil a·si·bleef dee
Internet gebruik.   in·tir·net khi·brayk

Transport & Directions

A ... ticket, please.	Een ... kaartjie, asseblief.	eyn ... *kaar*·kee a·si·*bleef*
one-way	*eenrigting*	eyn·*rikh*·ting
return	*retoer*	ri·*tur*

How much is it to ...?
Hoeveel kos dit na ...?   hu·fil kos dit naa ...

Please take me to (this address).
Neem my asseblief na   neym may a·si·*bleef* naa
(hierdie adres).   (*heer*·dee a·*dres*)

Where's the (nearest) ...?
Waar's die (naaste) ...?   vaars dee (*naas*·ti) ...

Can you show me (on the map)?
Kan jy my   kan yay may
(op die kaart) wys?   (op dee kaart) vays

What's the address?
Wat is die adres?   vat is dee a·*dres*

NDEBELE

Ndebele is spoken as a first language in relatively small numbers in South Africa's northern provinces.

Hello.	Lotsha.
Goodbye.	*Khamaba kuhle./ Sala kuhle.*
Yes.	*I-ye.*
No.	*Awa.*
Please.	*Ngibawa.*
Thank you.	*Ngiyathokaza.*
What's your name?	*Ungubani ibizo lakho?*
My name is ...	*Ibizo lami ngu ...*
I come from ...	*Ngibuya e ...*

NORTHERN SOTO

Most mother-tongue speakers of Northern Soto (also known as Sepedi) inhabit South Africa's northeastern provinces, with the vast majority to be found in Limpopo.

Hello.	Thobela.
Goodbye.	*Sala gabotse.*
Yes.	*Ee.*
No.	*Aowa.*
Please.	*Ke kgopela.*
Thank you.	*Ke ya leboga.*
What's your name?	*Ke mang lebitso la gago?*
My name is ...	*Lebitso laka ke ...*
I come from ...	*Ke bowa kwa ...*

SOUTHERN SOTO

Southern Sotho is the official language of Lesotho, alongside English. It is also spoken by the Basotho people in the Free State, North-West Province and Gauteng in South Africa. It's useful to learn some phrases if you're planning to visit Lesotho, especially if you want to trek in remote areas.

Hello.	Dumela.
Greetings father.	*Lumela ntate.*
Peace father.	*Khotso ntate.*
Greetings mother.	*Lumela 'me.*
Peace mother.	*Khotso 'me.*
Greetings brother.	*Lumela abuti.*
Peace brother.	*Khotso abuti.*
Greetings sister.	*Lumela ausi.*
Peace sister.	*Khotso ausi.*

There are three common ways of saying 'How are you?', each one with a standard response. Note, however, that these questions and answers are interchangeable.

How are you?	O kae? (sg)
	Le kae? (pl)
I'm here.	*Ke teng.*
We're here.	*Re teng.*
How do you live?	*O phela joang?* (sg)
	Le phela joang? (pl)
I live well.	*Ke phela hantle.*
We live well.	*Re phela hantle.*
How did you get up?	*O tsohela joang?* (sg)
	Le tsohele joang? (pl)
I got up well.	*Ke tsohile hantle.*
We got up well.	*Re tsohile hantle.*

When trekking, people always ask *Lea kae?* (Where are you going?) and *O tsoa kae?* or the plural *Le tsoa kae?* (Where have you come from?). When parting, use the following expressions:

Stay well.	Sala hantle. (sg)
	Salang hantle. (pl)
Go well.	*Tsamaea hantle.* (sg)
	Tsamaeang hantle. (pl)

'Thank you' is *kea leboha* (pronounced 'ke·ya le·bo·wa'). The herd boys may ask for *chelete* (money) or *lipompong* (sweets), pronounced 'dee·pom·pong'. If you want to reply 'I don't have any', just say *ha dio* (pronounced 'ha dee·o').

SWATI

Swati is the official language of Swaziland, along with English. It's also widely spoken as a first language in South Africa's Mpumalanga province. It's very similar to Zulu, and the two languages are mutually intelligible.

Hello. (to one person)	Sawubona.
Hello. (to a group)	Sanibonani.
How are you?	Kunjani?
I'm fine.	Kulungile.
We're very well.	Natsi sikhona.
Goodbye. (if leaving)	Salakahle.
Goodbye. (if staying)	Hambakahle.
Yes.	Yebo. (also a common all-purpose greeting)
No.	Cha. (pronounced as a click)
Please.	Ngicela.
I thank you.	Ngiyabonga.
We thank you.	Siyabonga.
Sorry.	Lucolo.
What's your name?	Ngubani libito lakho?
My name is ...	Libitolami ngingu ...
I'm from ...	Ngingewekubuya e ...
Do you have ...?	Une yini ...?
How much?	Malini?
Is there a bus to ...?	Kukhona ibhasi yini leya ...?
When does it leave?	Isuka nini?
Where is the tourist office?	Likuphi lihovisi leti vakashi?
morning	ekuseni
afternoon	entsambaba
evening	kusihlwa
night	ebusuku
yesterday	itolo
today	lamuhla
tomorrow	kusasa

TSONGA

Tsonga is spoken as a first language in South Africa's north, predominantly in the provinces of Limpopo and Gauteng, and to a lesser extent in Mpumalanga and North-West Province.

Hello. (morning)	Avusheni.
Hello. (afternoon)	Inhelekani.
Hello. (evening)	Riperile.
Goodbye.	Salani kahle.
Yes.	Hi swona.
No.	A hi swona.
Please.	Nakombela.
Thank you.	I nkomu.
What's your name?	U mani vito ra wena?
My name is ...	Vito ra mina i ...
I come from ...	Ndzihuma e ...

TSWANA

Tswana is spoken in South Africa as a first language mainly in Gauteng and North-West Province, with lesser numbers of first-language speakers in the eastern areas of Northern Cape and the western parts of the Free State.

Hello.	Dumela.
Goodbye.	Sala sentle.
Yes.	Ee.
No.	Nnya.
Please.	Ke a kopa.
Thank you.	Ke a leboga.
What's your name?	Leina la gago ke mang?
My name is ...	Leina la me ke ...
I come from ...	Ke tswa ...

VENDA

Venda is spoken mainly in the northeastern border region of South Africa's Limpopo province.

Hello. (morning)	Ndi matseloni.
Hello. (afternoon)	Ndi masiari.
Hello. (evening)	Ndi madekwana.
Goodbye.	Kha vha sale zwavhudi.
Yes.	Ndi zwone.
No.	A si zwone.
Please.	Ndikho u humbela.
Thank you.	Ndo livhuwa.
What's your name?	Zina lavho ndi nnyi?
My name is ...	Zina langa ndi ...
I come from ...	Ndi bva ...

XHOSA

Xhosa belongs to the Bantu language family, along with Zulu, Swati and Ndebele. It is the most widely distributed indigenous language in South Africa, and is also spoken in the Cape Town area. About six and a half million people speak Xhosa.

In our pronunciation guides, the symbols b', ch', k', p', t' and ts' represent sounds that are 'spat out' (only in case of b' the air is

Numbers – Xhosa
English numbers are commonly used.

1	*wani*	waa·nee
2	*thu*	tu
3	*thri*	tree
4	*fo*	faw
5	*fayifu*	faa·yee·fu
6	*siksi*	seek'·see
7	*seveni*	se·ve·nee
8	*eyithi*	e·yee·tee
9	*nayini*	naa·yee·nee
10	*teni*	t'e·nee

sucked in), a bit like combining them with the sound in the middle of 'uh-oh'. Note also that hl is pronounced as in the Welsh *llewellyn* and dl is like hl but with the vocal cords vibrating. Xhosa has a series of 'click' sounds as well; they are not distinguished in this chapter.

Hello.	*Molo.*	maw·law
Goodbye.	*Usale ngoxolo.*	u·saa·le ngaw·kaw·law
Yes.	*Ewe.*	e·we
No.	*Hayi.*	haa·yee
Please.	*Cela.*	ke·laa
Thank you.	*Enkosi.*	e·nk'aw·see
Sorry.	*Uxolo.*	u·aw·law
How are you?	*Kunjani?*	k'u·njaa·nee

Fine, and you?
Ndiyaphila, unjani wena? — ndee·yaa·pee·laa u·njaa·nee we·naa

What's your name?
Ngubani igama lakho? — ngu·b'aa·nee ee·gaa·maa laa·kaw

My name is ...
Igama lam ngu ... — ee·gaa·maa laam ngu ...

Do you speak English?
Uyasithetha isingesi? — u·yaa·see·te·taa ee·see·nge·see

I don't understand.
Andiqondi. — aa·ndee·kaw·ndee

ZULU

Zulu is a language from the Bantu group, and it's closely related to the other Bantu languages in southern Africa, particularly Xhosa. About 10 million Africans speak Zulu as a first language, with the vast majority (more than 95 per cent) in South Africa. It is also spoken in Lesotho and Swaziland.

In our pronunciation guides, the symbols b', ch', k', p', t' and ts' represent sounds that are 'spat out' (only in case of b' the air is sucked in), a bit like combining them with the sound in the middle of 'uh-oh'. Note also that hl is pronounced as in the Welsh *llewellyn* and dl is like hl but with the vocal cords vibrating. Xhosa has a series of 'click' sounds as well; they are not distinguished in this chapter.

Hello.
Sawubona. (sg) — saa·wu·b'aw·naa
Sanibonani. (pl) — saa·nee·b'aw·naa·nee

Goodbye. (if leaving)
Sala kahle. (sg) — saa·laa gaa·hle
Salani kahle. (pl) — saa·laa·nee gaa·hle

Goodbye. (if staying)
Hamba kahle. (sg) — haa·mbaa gaa·hle
Hambani kahle. (pl) — haa·mbaa·nee gaa·hle

Yes.
Yebo. — ye·b'aw

No.
Cha. — kaa

Thank you.
Ngiyabonga. — ngee·yaa·b'aw·ngaa

Sorry.
Uxolo. — u·kaw·law

How are you?
Unjani?/Ninjani? (sg/pl) — u·njaa·nee/nee·njaa·nee

Fine. And you?
Sikhona. — see·kaw·naa
Nawe?/Nani? (sg/pl) — naa·we/naa·nee

What's your name?
Ngubani igama lakho? — ngu·b'aa·nee ee·gaa·maa laa·kaw

My name is ...
Igama lami ngu-... — ee·gaa·maa laa·mee ngu·...

Do you speak English?
Uyasikhuluma isiNgisi? — u·yaa·see·ku·lu·maa ee·see·ngee·see

I don't understand.
Angizwa. — aa·ngee·zwaa

Numbers – Zulu
English numbers are commonly used.

1	*uwani*	u·waa·nee
2	*uthu*	u·tu
3	*uthri*	u·three
4	*ufo*	u·faw
5	*ufayifi*	u·faa·yee·fee
6	*usiksi*	u·seek·see
7	*usevene*	u·se·ve·nee
8	*u-eyithi*	u·e·yeet
9	*unayini*	u·naa·yee·nee
10	*utheni*	u·the·nee

GLOSSARY

For more food and drink terms, see the Menu Decoder (p536).

Afrikaans – the language spoken by Afrikaners, derived from Cape Dutch

Afrikaner – Afrikaans-speaking white person

amahiya – traditional Swazi robe

ANC – African National Congress; national democratic organisation formed in 1912 to represent blacks

AWB – Afrikaner Weerstandsbeweging, Afrikaner Resistance Movement; an Afrikaner extremist right-wing group

bakkie – pick-up truck

balimo – ancestors (Sotho)

Bantu – literally 'people'; during the apartheid era, used derogatorily to refer to blacks; today, used only in reference to ethnolinguistics ie Bantu languages, Bantu-speaking peoples

Bantustans – see homelands

BCP – Basotholand Congress Party

Big Five (the) – lion, leopard, elephant, buffalo and black rhino

bilharzia – another name for schistosomiasis, a disease caused by blood flukes, passed on by freshwater snails

biltong – dried meat

bittereinders – 'bitter enders' in Afrikaans; Boer resistors in the 1899–1902 South African War who fought until the 'bitter end'

BNP – Basotholand National Party

bobotie – curried mince with a topping of savoury egg custard

Boers – see *Trekboers*

braai – short for *braaivleis*, a barbecue at which meat is cooked over an open fire

Broederbond – secret society open only to Protestant Afrikaner men; was highly influential under National Party rule

bubblegum – a form of township music influenced by Western pop

byala – traditional beer

coloureds – apartheid-era term used to refer to those of mixed-race descent

dagga – marijuana, also known as *zol*

Democratic Alliance – the official opposition party to the ANC

diamantveld – diamond fields

difaqane – 'forced migration' of many of Southern Africa's Nguni peoples; known as *mfecane* in Zulu

dorp – small village or rural settlement

drostdy – residence of a Landdrost

free-camp – camping where you want, away from a formal campsite; permission should be sought and money offered

fynbos – literally 'fine-leafed bush', primarily proteas, heaths and ericas

gogo – grandmother

highveld – high-altitude grassland region

homelands – areas established for blacks under apartheid and considered independent countries by South Africa (never accepted by the UN); reabsorbed into South Africa after 1994

IFP – Inkatha Freedom Party; black political movement, founded around 1975 and lead by Chief Mangosouthu Buthelezi

igogogo – musical instrument made from an oil can

igqirha – Xhosa spiritual healer

impi – Zulu warriors; also any group of soldiers

indunas – tribal headmen

inyanga – traditional medicine man and herbalist who also studies patterns of thrown bones

isicathamiya – a soft-shoe-shuffle style of vocal music from KwaZulu-Natal

ixhwele – Xhosa herbalist

jol – party, good time

karamat – tomb of a Muslim saint

Khoekhoen – pastoralist San

Khoe-San – collective term referring to the closely related San and Khoekhoen peoples

kloof – ravine

kloofing – canyoning

knobkerry – traditional African weapon; a stick with a round knob at the end, used as a club or missile

kommando – Boer militia unit

kopje – small hill

kraal – a hut village, often with an enclosure for livestock; also a Zulu fortified village

kroeg – bar

kwaito – form of township music; a mix of *mbaqanga*, jive, hip hop, house, ragga and other dance styles

kwela – township interpretation of American swing music

landdrost – an official acting as local administrator, tax collector and magistrate

lapa – a circular building with low walls and a thatched roof, used for cooking, partying etc

LCD – Lesotho Congress for Democracy

lekgotla – place of gathering

lekker – very good, enjoyable or tasty

lekolulo – a flutelike instrument played by herd boys

lesokoana – wooden stick or spoon, traditionally used for stirring mealie pap

liqhaga – 'bottles' that are so tightly woven that they are used for carrying water

lowveld – low-altitude area, having scrub vegetation

maskanda – Zulu form of guitar playing

matjieshuis – Afrikaans term for traditional woven Nama 'mat' huts

mbaqanga – form of township music; literally 'dumpling' in Zulu, combining church choirs, doo-wop and sax-jive

mdube – vocal style mixing European and African church choirs

mfeqane – see *difaqane*

minwane – dinosaur footprints

Mkhulumnchanti – Swazi deity

mokorotlo – conical hat worn by the Basotho

molianyeoe – see *mokorotlo*

moraba-raba – popular board game played with wooden beads and four rows of hollows; known elsewhere in Africa as *mancala* and *bao*

moroka-pula – rainmaker

mqashiyo – similar vocal style to mbaqanga

muti – traditional medicine

Ncwala – Swazi first-fruits ceremony

ndlovukazi – she-elephant, and traditional title of the Swazi royal mother

ngaca – (also *ngaka*) learned man

ngwenyama – lion, and traditional title of the Swazi king

PAC – Pan African Congress; political organisation of blacks founded in 1959 to work for majority rule and equal rights

peri peri – hot pepper

pinotage – a type of wine, a cross between Pinot noir and Hermitage or shiraz

pont – river ferry

Poqo – armed wing of the PAC

Rikki – an open, small van used as public transport in Cape Town

robot – traffic light

rondavel – a round hut with a conical roof

San – nomadic hunter-gatherers who were South Africa's earliest inhabitants

sangoma – traditional healer

sandveld – dry, sandy belt

setolo-tolo – stringed instrument played with the mouth by men

shebeen – drinking establishment in black township; once illegal, now merely unlicensed

slaghuis – butchery

slenter – fake diamond

snoek – firm-fleshed migratory fish that appears off the Cape in June and July; served smoked, salted or curried

sourveld – a type of grassland

swart gevaar – 'black threat'; term coined by Afrikaner nationalists during the 1920s

Telkom – government telecommunications company

thkolosi – small, maliciously playful beings

thomo – stringed instrument played by women

thornveld – a vegetation belt dominated by acacia thorn trees and related species

tokoloshe – malevolent spirit or short manlike animal, similar to the Sotho *thkolosi*

township – planned urban settlement of blacks and coloureds, legacy of the apartheid era

Trekboers – the first Dutch who trekked off into the interior of what is now largely Western Cape; later shortened to Boers

trokkie – truck stop

tronk – jail

tuk-tuk – motorised tricycle

uitlanders – 'foreigners'; originally the name given by Afrikaners to the immigrants who poured into the Transvaal after the discovery of gold

Umkhonto we Sizwe – the ANC's armed wing during the years of the struggle; now defunct

veld – elevated open grassland (pronounced 'felt')

velskoene – handmade leather shoes

VOC – Vereenigde Oost-Indische Compagnie (Dutch East India Company)

volk – collective Afrikaans term for Afrikaners

volkstaal – people's language

volkstaat – an independent, racially pure Boer state

Voortrekkers – original Afrikaner settlers of Orange Free State and Transvaal who migrated from the Cape Colony in the 1830s in search of greater independence

behind the scenes

SEND US YOUR FEEDBACK

We love to hear from travellers – your comments keep us on our toes and help make our books better. Our well-travelled team reads every word on what you loved or loathed about this book. Although we cannot reply individually to postal submissions, we always guarantee that your feedback goes straight to the appropriate authors, in time for the next edition. Each person who sends us information is thanked in the next edition – the most useful submissions are rewarded with a selection of digital PDF chapters.

Visit **lonelyplanet.com/contact** to submit your updates and suggestions or to ask for help. Our award-winning website also features inspirational travel stories, news and discussions.

Note: We may edit, reproduce and incorporate your comments in Lonely Planet products such as guidebooks, websites and digital products, so let us know if you don't want your comments reproduced or your name acknowledged. For a copy of our privacy policy visit lonelyplanet.com/privacy.

OUR READERS

Many thanks to the travellers who used the last edition and wrote to us with helpful hints, useful advice and interesting anecdotes:

Yvette Aalders-Daniels, David Almassian, Jan-Jaap Altink, Cristina Amato, Marion Ancker, Lesley Baddeley, Peggy Baier, Andres Bautista, Patrick Beauquesne, Trevor Beckett, Bert Berger & Ellen Geeraerts, Pera Bergman, Matt Binks, Jens Bjerkvig, Jerry Blackman, Adam Blanar-oviatt, Crystal Bolton, Jorgen Borg, Philippe Bourdin, Marcel Broennimann, Werner Bruyninx, Kim Burgers, Andrea Burton, Jeffrey Cammack, Nicola Carpanoni, Yo-han Cha, Erik Cherlet, David Chidell, Lynda Chidell, Scott Cochrane, Elizabeth Coll, David Cook, Sarah Cooper, Heleen Cousijn, James Cowen, Gerald Czamanske, Kate Davenport, Agnes De Vries, Frieda De Meij, Kaj De Vries, Roelof De Boer, Marc Defila, Cherie Devesh, Frederike Diersen, Thomas Ditlhoiso, Rudolf Douqué, Suzanne Dowse, Craig Dreves, Roy Drew, Christine Duxbury, Jasmine Ehsanullah, Melina Ekholm, Ellen Elmore, Bob Erickson, Monika Faber, Amy Fallon, Doreen Ferguson, Aya Feurst, Dennis Foldager, Gabi Ford, Flavia Frangini, Nicolas Gandin, Vassos Georgiadis, Dang Gessner, Veronique Gindrey, Christopher Godden-miller, Cathalia Goodall, Esther Gorlee, Giada Gorno, Amir Gur, Bob Guy, Patrick Heck, Alex Herbst, Bas Heres, Anjuli Hesse, Wendy Hicks, Geoff Hill, Julie Hindley, Rob Hoekstra, Mark Hopson, Marijke Hornstra, Julie Hughes & Melanie Wilkinson, Greg Ingham, Daisy Jackson, Pascal Jalanjalan, Guinevere Jandrell, Kareen Jetz, Dr. Jim Pulfer, Dorothée Jobert, Martin Jones, Jennie Joslin, Schultz Jürgen, Markus Kaim, Ajay Kamalakaran, Thomas Keiz, David Kevey, Roel Klaassen, Saul Kornik, Jim Lambert, Paul Lambert, Rene Lambrechts, Mark Langford, Christopher Lautemann, Heather Lilley, Stefan Logosz, Anna Longland, Sylvie Lorente, Basani Maluleke, Meryl Marr, Julie May, Rhonda Mccarthy, Tommy Mcseveney, Steven Mobron, James & Philippa Moir, Francis Moore, Jacky Morgan, Steven Neufeld, Ema O'connor, Mikkel Ottosen, Nicholas Pace, Leigh Payton, Seymour Pearman, Felipe Perez, Monique Philipse, Rochelle Pincini, Frank Plata, M Platt, Pavel Pokora, Charlie Radclyffe, Carla Raffinetti, Marion Ransome, Petra Roberts, Gonzalo Rubio Sologuren, Tommy Rudolph, Brenda Ryan, Hector Sanchez, David Sanger, Gabriele Savarino, Klaus Schmied, André Schoeman, Kate Scott, Wanda Serkowska, Ganesh Sethuraman, Scott Skinner, Victoria Smith, Vidar Steenmeijer, Mrs Stephanie Goenka, Therese Svensson, Seda Toksoy, Valérie Tremblay, Peter Ulz, Jean Uncles, Anita Van Gastel, Anne-marie Van, Arie Van

Oosterwijk, Danny Van Houtum, Doortje Van De Wouw, Michiel Van Agtmael, Pauline Van Wijk, Wim Vandenbussche, Bart Verbauwh-ede, Anna Veronika Bjarkadóttir, Laurence Verriest, Jørund Vier Skriubakken, Astrid Vol-mer, Brenda Walters, David Watson, Maria Weems, Bruyninx Werner, James Wesson, Roger Whetton, Holly Wickham, Marlies Wil-lemen, Francien Wilms, Jackie Wong, Laura Woollard, Joshua Wrinkle, Donna Ziegler

AUTHOR THANKS

James Bainbridge

Thanks to everyone who aided and abetted, entertained and enlightened me on the road, including Kgomotso in Madikwe for your insights into bush guiding. Numerous folk on the Northern Cape's long, empty freeways generously offered assistance and hospital-ity, among them Steve Lunderstedt, Jurg Wagener and Richard and family at Witsand. Thanks also to my coauthors for your diligent research and helpful input, and to everyone at home in Cape Town, especially my wife Leigh-Robin.

Kate Armstrong

In Swaziland, a special thanks to the Raw family and Katie McCarthy for their kind-ness; in KZN, thank you Rose, Camilla and Carlos; Peter Bendheim and Jenny Govender of Durban Tourism; Alex Miles of Ezemvelo KZN Wildlife. A special *ngiyabonga* to Elmar Neethling and Edmund Salomons for their knowledge, laughs and friendship, and 'SB' who helped me (re)tap into my inner spring-bok. Finally, to the generous strangers who extricated my car and numerous travellers. Of course, to David Carroll, James Bain-bridge, Brigitte Ellemor, Adrian Persoglia and the LP team.

Lucy Corne

Huge thanks to staff at tourist information offices around the Western Cape, especially those in Knysna, Tulbagh, Swellendam, Lam-bert's Bay and Robertson. Thanks to fellow authors James and Simon for their support, to Denis and Debbie for their hospitality, to my dad for his help and to my husband, Shawn, for coping alone in our first month of marriage!

Michael Grosberg

Many thanks to the following for taking the time to share their insights and experience: Sean Price, Lloyd Staples, Liza Weschta, Lisa Ker, Chantelle Marais, Richard and Joan Worsfold, Giles and Jennifer Gush, Loren Sampson, Daryn Sinclair, Helena and Brad Haines, Anita Lennox, Monica, Samantha and Justin Hewitson, Ang and Adie Badenhorst, Candy in Hogsback, Tanya and Jay Accone

and to Carly Neidorf back home in NYC for her support.

Alan Murphy

I'd like to thank my wife, Alison Fogarty, for her support, research assistance and com-panionship (not to mention her clear thinking in treating paper-wasp bites). Thanks to the many people I met on the road who contrib-uted so much to the research for this edition. A special mention to the guides around Pre-toriuskop with whom an early morning con-versation in the middle of the bush in Kruger enlightened me as to the plight of local South African communities.

Helen Ranger

Thanks specially to David Carroll, Bronwyn Hicks and Naomi Jennings for their sup-port. James Bainbridge was an excellent coordinating author, as always. Lucy Corne saved the day by stepping in to research the Western Cape chapter while I was in hospital in Casablanca. In South Africa, thanks to all those chefs and winemakers who made my job so enjoyable, to the Sher family for their hospitality, and to Patrick, Kristy and Tamsin for their insights into local culture, sport and music.

Simon Richmond

Cheers to the following amazing people who made my time in Cape Town such a pleasure and constant education: Lucy, James, Lee, Toni, Brent, Belinda, Sheryl, Nicole Biondi, Alison Foat, Sally Grierson, Iain Harris, Cam-eron and Justin, Madelen Johansen, Tamsin Turbull, Lauren, Misha and Jeremy, Tim James, Hannah Deall, Patrick Craig, Sam Walker, Oliver Hermanus, Rashiq Fataar, Lau-ren Beukes, Zayd Minty, Lameen Abdul-Malik, Tony Osborne and Neil Turner – the Mother City will always be extra special to me now.

Tom Spurling

Massive thanks to Mike the Czech, a gener-ous driver and friend, for keeping me sharp around Gauteng. In Jo'burg thanks also to Heidi for her kind conversation. To Amu and Bronson, next time, eh? In Lesotho, thanks to the crew at Malealea and Ramabanta for filling in my blanks. In Maseru, to the Harvard trio for all that jazz. Thanks to James for his keen coordination and to David for the chance. And to my family – Lucy, Ollie and Poppy – so much love.

ACKNOWLEDGMENTS

Climate map data adapted from Peel MC, Finlayson BL & McMahon TA (2007) 'Updated World Map of the Köppen-Geiger Climate Classification', *Hydrology and Earth System Sciences*, 11, 163344.

BEHIND THE SCENES

BEHIND THE SCENES

Quote p518, Nelson Mandela, 20 April 1964,
Rivonia Trial. Used by permission of the
Nelson Mandela Centre of Memory.
Quote p521, Nelson Mandela, 1994, Inaugura-
tion Speech. Used by permission of the
Nelson Mandela Centre of Memory.

Cover photograph: African elephant calf,
Science Photo Library, Getty Images.

THIS BOOK

This 9th edition of Lonely Planet's *South Africa, Lesotho & Swaziland* guidebook was researched and written by James Bainbridge, Kate Armstrong, Lucy Corne, Michael Grosberg, Alan Murphy, Helen Ranger, Simon Richmond and Tom Spurling.

This guidebook was commissioned in Lonely Planet's Melbourne office, and produced by the following:

Commissioning Editor
David Carroll

Coordinating Editors
Justin Flynn, Alison Ridgway

Coordinating Cartographer Andy Rojas
Coordinating Layout Designer Wendy Wright
Managing Editors Brigitte Ellemor, Anna Metcalfe
Managing Cartographer Alison Lyall, Adrian Persoglia
Managing Layout Designer Jane Hart
Assisting Editors Elizabeth Anglin, Kate Evans, Cathryn Game, Kate Kiely, Bella Li, Joanne Newell, Charlotte Orr
Assisting Cartographers Enes Basic, Valeska Canas, Joelene Kowalski

Assisting Layout Designer Clara Monitto
Cover Research Naomi Parker
Internal Image Research Aude Vauconsant
Language Content Branislava Vladisavljevic

Thanks to Barbara Delissen, Ryan Evans, Larissa Frost, Errol Hunt, Anna Lorincz, Annelies Mertens, Ryan Miller, Trent Paton, Martine Power, Sam Trafford, Gerard Walker

NOTES

index

how to use this book

These symbols will help you find the listings you want:

- 👁 Sights
- 🏄 Beaches
- 🏃 Activities
- 🎓 Courses
- 👉 Tours
- 🎊 Festivals & Events
- 🛏 Sleeping
- 🍴 Eating
- 🍷 Drinking
- ☆ Entertainment
- 🛍 Shopping
- ℹ Information/Transport

These symbols give you the vital information for each listing:

- ☎ Telephone Numbers
- ⊙ Opening Hours
- Ⓟ Parking
- ⊖ Nonsmoking
- ❄ Air-Conditioning
- @ Internet Access
- 📶 Wi-Fi Access
- 🏊 Swimming Pool
- 🥗 Vegetarian Selection
- 📖 English-Language Menu
- 👪 Family-Friendly
- 🐾 Pet-Friendly
- 🚌 Bus
- ⛴ Ferry
- Ⓜ Metro
- Ⓢ Subway
- 🚊 Tram
- 🚆 Train

Reviews are organised by author preference.

Look out for these icons:

TOP CHOICE — Our author's recommendation

FREE — No payment required

🌿 — A green or sustainable option

Our authors have nominated these places as demonstrating a strong commitment to sustainability – for example by supporting local communities and producers, operating in an environmentally friendly way, or supporting conservation projects.

Map Legend

Sights
- 🟠 Beach
- 🔵 Buddhist
- 🟠 Castle
- 🟢 Christian
- 🟣 Hindu
- ⚫ Islamic
- 🟤 Jewish
- 🟠 Monument
- 🟤 Museum/Gallery
- 🟢 Ruin
- 🟢 Winery/Vineyard
- 🟢 Zoo
- 🔵 Other Sight

Activities, Courses & Tours
- 🔵 Diving/Snorkelling
- 🟢 Canoeing/Kayaking
- 🔵 Skiing
- 🟠 Surfing
- 🔵 Swimming/Pool
- 🟠 Walking
- 🔵 Windsurfing
- 🟢 Other Activity/Course/Tour

Sleeping
- 🟢 Sleeping
- 🔵 Camping

Eating
- 🔴 Eating

Drinking
- 🟢 Drinking
- 🟢 Cafe

Entertainment
- 🟢 Entertainment

Shopping
- 🟢 Shopping

Information
- ✉ Post Office
- ℹ Tourist Information

Transport
- ✈ Airport
- ⊗ Border Crossing
- 🚌 Bus
- 🚠 Cable Car/Funicular
- 🚲 Cycling
- ⛴ Ferry
- 🚝 Monorail
- Ⓟ Parking
- Ⓢ S-Bahn
- 🚕 Taxi
- 🚉 Train/Railway
- 🚊 Tram
- ⊖ Tube Station
- Ⓤ U-Bahn
- Ⓜ Underground Train Station
- • Other Transport

Routes
- Tollway
- Freeway
- Primary
- Secondary
- Tertiary
- Lane
- Unsealed Road
- Plaza/Mall
- Steps
- Tunnel
- Pedestrian Overpass
- Walking Tour
- Walking Tour Detour
- Path

Boundaries
- International
- State/Province
- Disputed
- Regional/Suburb
- Marine Park
- Cliff
- Wall

Population
- ⭐ Capital (National)
- ◉ Capital (State/Province)
- ● City/Large Town
- ○ Town/Village

Geographic
- 🏠 Hut/Shelter
- 🔵 Lighthouse
- 🔭 Lookout
- ▲ Mountain/Volcano
- 🟠 Oasis
- 🟢 Park
-)(Pass
- 🟢 Picnic Area
- ⚫ Waterfall

Hydrography
- River/Creek
- Intermittent River
- Swamp/Mangrove
- Reef
- Canal
- Water
- Dry/Salt/Intermittent Lake
- Glacier

Areas
- Beach/Desert
- Cemetery (Christian)
- Cemetery (Other)
- Park/Forest
- Sportsground
- Sight (Building)
- Top Sight (Building)